your Bovée/Thill?

Balanced Presentation of Fundamentals

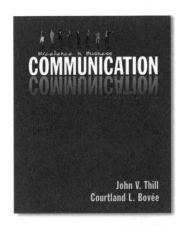

ISBN: 0-13-187076-9

Business Communication Today Custom One-Color Option

The Core

Optional Chapters

Contact your local PH Rep for more information on the custom/core option.

BUSINESS COMMUNICATION TODAY

BUSINESS COMMUNICATION TODAY

Ninth Edition

COURTLAND L. BOVÉE

Professor of Business Communication
C. Allen Paul Distinguished Chair
Grossmont College

JOHN V. THILL

Chairman and Chief Executive Officer
Global Communication Strategies

PEARSON

Prentice
Hall

Upper Saddle River, New Jersey 07458

Library of Congress Cataloging-in-Publication Data

Bovée, Courtland L.
   Business communication today / Courtland L. Bovée, John V. Thill.—9th ed.
      p. cm.
   Includes bibliographical references and index.
   ISBN 978-0-13-199535-2
  1. Business communication—United States—Case studies. 2. Communication in organizations—United States—Case studies.   I. Thill, John V.   II. Title.
   HF5718.B66 2008
   658.4'5—dc22

                           2007007595

Editor-in-Chief: David Parker
Product Development Manager: Ashley Santora
Editorial Assistant: Kristen Varina
Media Project Manager: Ashley Lulling
Marketing Manager: Jodi Bassett
Marketing Assistant: Ian Gold
Associate Managing Editor: Renata Butera
Project Manager, Production: Renata Butera
Permissions Project Manager: Charles Morris
Senior Operations Supervisor: Arnold Vila
Senior Art Director: Janet Slowik
Cover Design: Judy Allen
Interior Design: Liz Harasymczuk/Jill Little
Cover Photo: Purestock/Getty Images, Inc.
Director, Image Resource Center: Melinda Patelli
Manager, Rights and Permissions: Zina Arabia
Manager, Visual Research: Beth Brenzel
Image Permission Coordinator: Nancy Seise
Photo Researcher: Teri Stratford
Composition: Carlisle Publishing Services
Full-Service Project Management: Lynn Steines, Carlisle Publishing Services
Printer/Binder: Courier/Kendallville
Typeface: 10.5/12 Minion

Credits and acknowledgments borrowed from other sources and reproduced, with permission, in this textbook appear on page AC-1.

Pearson Prentice Hall™ is a trademark of Pearson Education, Inc.
Pearson® is a registered trademark of Pearson plc
Prentice Hall® is a registered trademark of Pearson Education, Inc.

Pearson Education Ltd.
Pearson Education Singapore, Pte. Ltd.
Pearson Education Canada, Ltd.
Pearson Education—Japan

Pearson Education Australia PTY, Limited
Pearson Education North Asia Ltd.
Pearson Educación de Mexico, S.A. de C.V.
Pearson Education Malaysia, Pte. Ltd.

10 9 8 7 6 5 4 3
ISBN-13: 978-0-13-199535-2
ISBN-10:   0-13-199535-9

Contents in Brief

Contents

The first text that can prepare students for today's electronic communication challenges, and the only text with model documents in every important medium

The leading text in the field for more than two decades, *Business Communication Today* is now more current and vital than ever. The thoroughly revised ninth edition offers dozens of updated model documents, encompassing every medium that students will be expected to use on the job—from conventional printed documents to e-mail and instant messages to blogs, podcasts, and wikis. While competitive texts continue to emphasize paper-based messages, only *Business Communication Today* prepares students for the many electronic media choices they will encounter on the job.

The marginal annotations that accompany every document help students understand how to apply the principles discussed in the chapter, and for this edition, both the documents and the annotations have been extensively revised and improved in response to reviewer input.

The headline and tagline combine to clearly indicate the source and the nature of this blog

Postings can be either complete articles or introductions that have links to the complete pieces

Postings are accompanied by a line that indicates who posted the material and when; most blogs also allow visitors to comment on posts

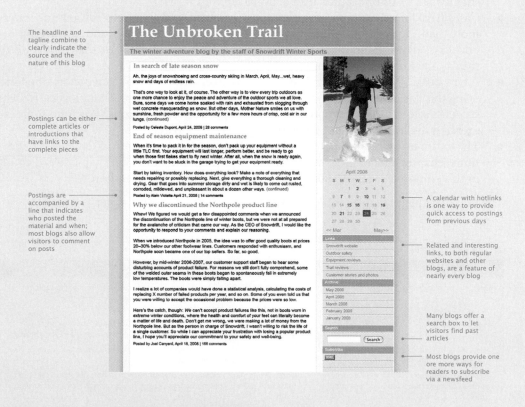

Annotations show students the specific elements that make messages successful.

A calendar with hotlinks is one way to provide quick access to postings from previous days

Related and interesting links, to both regular websites and other blogs, are a feature of nearly every blog

Many blogs offer a search box to let visitors find past articles

Most blogs provide one ore more ways for readers to subscribe via a newsfeed

WHAT'S NEW IN THIS EDITION

With business communication evolving so rapidly, textbooks and learning packages need to evolve just as quickly. Here are the highlights of the extensive revisions in this edition:

Complex topics are clearly explained in both text and visuals.

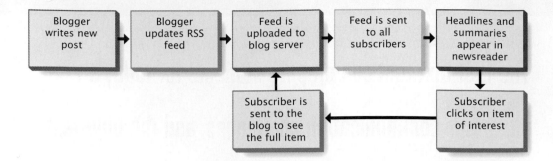

- In this edition, students will learn from dozens of practical examples in a variety of media, including blogs, wikis, and podcasts, that show both effective and ineffective communication efforts.
- A unique new chapter (Chapter 7) on crafting messages for electronic media covers e-mail, instant messaging, blogging, and podcasting. Coverage of wikis was added to the teamwork chapter, and writing website content was added to the report writing section.
- New coverage of audience psychology (in Chapter 1) gives students important insights into how audiences receive, process, and respond to messages.
- Expanded coverage of visual communication (in Chapter 12) helps students understand the growing importance of visual media in business today. Key topics include the power of images, the evolution of visual communication, visual design principles, and the ethics of visual design.
- More than half of the chapter-opening vignettes and accompanying end-of-chapter exercises are new.
- The text now has more emphasis on strategic and managerial communication with slightly less focus on tactical, transactional communication.
- Cases have long been a popular pedagogical feature, and the ninth edition now offers more than 140 cases, including more than 100 short-message cases, short- and long-report cases, PowerPoint cases, and employment-message cases. More than one-third of the cases are new in this edition.
- A new career planning Prologue features advice on creating employment portfolios and using this course as a way to create work samples to show potential employers. To help students select appropriate projects for their portfolios, numerous "Portfolio Builder" exercises and cases are highlighted throughout the book.
- The entire text was thoroughly revised for clarity and conciseness. Even with an additional chapter and all these major additions and updates, the total chapter word count in this edition is nearly 10,000 words less than in the previous edition.

The following pages itemize the extensive improvements in every chapter.

Numerous quick reference tables and checklists offer practical advice for successful communication.

TABLE 7.2 Tips for Effective Business Blogging

TIP	WHY IT'S IMPORTANT
Have a clear plan before you start blogging.	Without a clear plan, your blog is likely to wander from topic to topic without providing compelling information or building a sense of community with your audience.
Post frequently.	The whole point of a blog is fresh material; if you don't have a constant supply of new information or new links, create a traditional website instead.
Make it about your customers and the issues that are important to them.	Readers want to know how your blog will help them, entertain them, or give them a chance to communicate with others who have similar interests.
Write in an authentic voice; never create an artificial character who supposedly writes a blog.	*Flogs*, or fake blogs, violate the spirit of blogging, show disrespect for your audience, and will turn audiences against you as soon as they uncover the truth.
Link generously—but carefully.	Providing interesting links to other blogs and websites is a fundamental aspect of blogging, but think twice before putting these links in your blog. Make sure the links will be of value to your readers, and make sure they don't point to material that could damage your reputation.
Keep it brief.	Most online readers don't have the patience to read lengthy reports.

Chapter-by-Chapter Changes and Improvements

FEATURE	CHAPTER 1	CHAPTER 2	CHAPTER 3	CHAPTER 4	CHAPTER 5
Learning objectives	More emphasis on understanding the communication process and how audiences receive and process messages	More emphasis on collaborative writing and wikis for team communication	More emphasis on improving intercultural communication skills	Comparable to BCT8	More emphasis on building credibility
Chapter-opening vignette	**New:** Six Apart, one of the leaders in blogging technology	The Container Store, a growing retail chain with a reputation for excellent teamwork	**New:** IBM, highly regarded for its successful diversity initiatives	The Complete Idiot's Guides, a publishing phenomenon built around audience needs	**New:** Creative Commons, a new approach to copyrights for digital publishing
Chapter content (subject areas that were added, clarified, expanded, streamlined, or updated for this edition)	• *Inside the Mind of Your Audience*, new section that explains how audiences receive, process, and respond to messages • New section on legal aspects of communication, including intellectual property concerns • Stealth marketing as an example of ethical dilemma • Virtual communities • Technology highlight box on Web 2.0	• Collaborative writing technologies, including content management systems and wikis • Instant messaging now covered in new Chapter 7	• Appreciating diversity in religion and in ability differences • Use of assistive technologies for communicating with people with disabilities	• Streamlined coverage of media types • New coverage of visual media • Revised coverage of electronic media	• Revised coverage of plain English • Clarified coverage of denotation and connotation
Model documents and other exhibits	• **Revised:** Communication process (Fig. 1.5) • New: Audience-centered communication (Fig 1.7) • **New:** Becoming an Effective Business Communicator (Fig 1.8)	• **New:** Using a wiki for collaborative communication (Fig. 2.1) • **Updated:** Typical meeting agenda (Fig 2.2) • **Updated:** Typical minutes of a meeting (Fig 2.3) • **Updated:** Shared workspaces (Fig 2.4) • **New:** Assembling a business wardrobe (Table 2.2) • **New:** Quick tips for improving phone skills (Table 2.3)	• **New:** Languages of the world (language map) (Fig. 3.1)	• **New:** Audience-focused report (Fig. 4.4) • **New:** Visual media (Fig. 4.5) • **New:** E-mail message with improved organization (Fig. 4.7) • **New:** Media advantages and disadvantages (Table 4.1)	• **New:** Step two in the three-step writing process (Fig 5.1) • **New:** Fostering a positive relationship with an audience (Fig 5.2) • **New:** Choosing strong words (Fig 5.3) • **New:** Unified para-graphs (Fig 5.4)
End-of-chapter exercises	• New exercises on audience psychology and blogging policies	• New exercises on wikis, blogging, and voice-mail	• New exercise on podcasting for non-native English speakers	• New exercise on ethical choices • New end-of-chapter exercises for Complete Idiot's vignette	• New exercises on the "you" attitude, topic sentences, transitions, and ethics
End-of-chapter cases	N/A	N/A	N/A	N/A	N/A

(continued)

Chapter-by-Chapter Changes and Improvements

FEATURE	CHAPTER 6	CHAPTER 7	CHAPTER 8	CHAPTER 9	CHAPTER 10
Learning objectives	Comparable to BCT8	New chapter	Comparable to BCT8	More emphasis on importance of ethics and etiquette in negative messages	More emphasis on identifying objections before writing persuasive messages
Chapter-opening vignette	**New:** Mercedes-AMG's multimedia website	**New:** Boeing executive blog	Cone, Inc., which specializes in crafting positive messages for corporate and nonprofit clients	**New:** KMPG, which recently had to make a strategic decision about apologizing for illegal accounting practices	**New:** ClubMom, the first online social network for mothers
Chapter content (subject areas that were added, clarified, expanded, streamlined, or updated for this edition)	• Communication miscues highlight box on medication instructions • Coverage of RSS newsfeeds now in Chapter 7	New content: • Choosing electronic media for brief messages • Creating effective e-mail messages • Creating effective instant messages and text messages • Creating effective business blogs • Creating effective podcasts • Distributing blog and podcast content	• Communication miscues highlight box on lawsuits stemming from recommendation letters	• Revised coverage of internal versus external audiences • Revised coverage of ethics and etiquette	• Revised coverage of balancing emotional and logical appeals • Revised coverage of anticipating objections
Model documents and other exhibits	• **New:** Step three in the three-step writing process (Fig. 6.1) • **New:** Comments attached to a PDF file (Fig. 6.5) • **New:** Ineffective and effective document design (Fig. 6.6)	New exhibits & tables: • E-mail for business communication • IM for business communication • Video blogging • Elements of an effective business blog • The podcasting process • The syndication process for blogs • Viewing blog headlines in newsreader software • Tagging on a social bookmarking site • Tips for effective e-mail messages • Tips for effective business blogging	• **New:** Routine messages (Fig. 8.1) • **New:** Effective message requesting action (Fig. 8.2) • **New:** Effective IM response to information request (Fig. 8.2) • **New:** News release announcing positive news (Fig 8.9) • **New:** Congratulating a business partner (Fig 8.10)	Comparable to BCT8	• **Updated:** Persuasive letter using the AIDA model (Fig. 10.3) • **New:** Explaining the benefits of product features (Fig 10.5) • **New:** The spectrum of emotional and logical appeals (Fig 10.6) • **Updated:** Opt-in e-mail newsletter (Fig 10.8)
End-of-chapter exercises	• New exercises on revising, readability, document design, and ethics	• 25 new exercises	• New exercises on ethics and revising for clarity and conciseness	• New exercises on buffers, crisis communication, and de-emphasizing bad news	• New exercises on avoiding hard sells, anticipating objections, podcasting, subject lines, and product benefits
End-of-chapter cases	N/A	**25 new cases,** utilizing e-mail, IM, blogging, and podcasting	**9 new cases,** utilizing e-mail, text messaging, blogging, and podcasting	**13 new cases,** utilizing telephone skills, e-mail, blogging, and podcasting	**9 new cases,** utilizing e-mail, blogging, and podcasting

(continued)

Chapter-by-Chapter Changes and Improvements

FEATURE	CHAPTER 11	CHAPTER 12	CHAPTER 13	CHAPTER 14	CHAPTER 15
Learning objectives	More emphasis on the latest online research tools	More emphasis on visual ethics, visual quality, and the use of photographs	More emphasis on business plans and organizing online reports and other website content	More emphasis on effective writing for the web	Comparable to BCT8
Chapter-opening vignette	**New:** Tesco, the leading grocery retailer in the UK, and its extensive audience research program	Stone Yamashita Partners, an unconventional management consulting firm that relies on visuals to help clients develop new business strategies	Kenwood USA, which relies on reports to convey U.S. market trends to product designers in Japan	**New:** Tellabs, a major producer of Internet equipment, and its highly regarded annual reports	Bill and Melinda Gates Foundation, and the role reports and proposals play in the operation of one of the world's premiere charitable organizations
Chapter content (subject areas that were added, clarified, expanded, streamlined, or updated for this edition)	• The challenge of finding information in the hidden Internet • New section: *Taking Advantage of Innovative Research Technologies*, covers desktop and enterprise search, research and content managers, social bookmarking, and research newsfeeds • Making computer-based surveys adaptive in order to improve results	• Comprehensive new section, *Understanding Visual Communication*, covers the power of images, the evolution of business communication, visuals design principles, and the ethics of visual design • Updated coverage of using digital photos	• Creating successful business plans • Organizing website content	• Drafting online content • Revised coverage of helping readers find their way	• Revising web content
Model documents and other exhibits	• **New:** Survey software (Fig. 11.3) • **Updated:** Important resources for business research (Table 11.2) • **Updated:** Best of Internet searching (Table 11.3)	• **New:** Visual symbolism (Fig. 12.1) • **New:** Influencing perception through visual design (Fig 12.3) • **New:** Mapping using geographic information system (Fig 12.13b) • **New:** Diagram (Fig 12.14)	• **Revised:** Direct approach versus indirect approach in an introduction (Fig. 13.2) • **New:** Information architecture (Fig. 13.5)	• **New:** Step two in the three-step writing process for reports (Fig. 14.1) • **New:** Choosing the right tone for business reports (Fig. 14.2) • **New:** Effective report expressing action plan in the close (Fig. 14.5)	• **New:** Step three in the three-step writing process for reports (Fig. 15.1) • **New:** Report synopsis (Fig. 15.3)
End-of-chapter exercises	• New exercises on planning research projects	• New exercises on improving visual design and using digital photographs	• New exercises on organizing reports, business plans, and website organization • New end-of-chapter exercises for Kenwood USA vignette	• New exercises on maintaining the "you" attitude, writing strategies, online composition, and effective hyperlinks	• New exercise on revising for clarity and conciseness
End-of-chapter cases	N/A	N/A	N/A	**1 new case** involving a proposal to sell a GPS fleet tracking system	Comparable to BCT8

(continued)

Chapter-by-Chapter Changes and Improvements

FEATURE	CHAPTER 16	CHAPTER 17	CHAPTER 18	CHAPTER 19
Learning objectives	Comparable to BCT8	More emphasis on the effective use of transitions and builds in electronic slide shows	More emphasis on the importance of networking, résumé fraud, and résumé formats	Comparable to BCT8
Chapter-opening vignette	Fitch, a global leader in design, uses unconventional presentation strategies to attract new clients	Hewlett-Packard using oral presentations to win a $3 billion order	New: Hersha Hospitality Management's use of an applicant tracking system	Revised: Google's continuing search for the best technical and business talent in the online industry
Chapter content (subject areas that were added, clarified, expanded, streamlined, or updated for this edition)	• Clarified discussions of getting the audience's attention in the introduction, then holding it throughout the presentation	• Clarified coverage of writing readable slide content • Revised coverage of creating navigation and support slides, title, agenda, program detail, and blueprint slides • New checklist for enhancing presentations with visuals • Expanded coverage of online presentations	• Updated advice on staying abreast of business and financial news, including subscribing to blogs and podcasts • Expanded coverage of networking • Creating PDF versions of résumés • Material on pp. 518-522 in BCT8 is now in the new Prologue	• Updated coverage of situation, behavioral, and working interview formats • New section on interview media, describing telephone, e-mail, IM, virtual, and video interviews • Updated coverage on substance abuse testing
Model documents and other exhibits	Comparable to BCT8	• New: Presentation style (Fig. 17.1) • New: Modifying graphs for slides (Fig 17.3) • New: Distractions from decorative artwork (Fig 17.4) • New: Presentation slide master (Fig 17.5) • New: Navigation and support slides (Fig 17.9) • New: Moving blueprint slides (Fig 17.9)	• New: Combination résumé (Fig 18.6)	• New: Interview simulators (Fig 19.3) • New: Finding out about an organization and a job opportunity (Table 19.2)
End-of-chapter exercises	• New exercises involving effective language in a podcast (students can download this recording) and possible presentation topics	• New exercises on converting reports to presentations and using animation (students can download a presentation file to analyze)	• New exercises on planning the job search, networking, HTML résumés, and creating a vidcast to accompany a résumé	• New exercises on working interviews, handling qualification weaknesses in an interview, and matching personality to company culture
End-of-chapter cases	N/A	4 new cases for practice in creating effective PowerPoint presentations	Comparable to BCT8	1 new case involving applying outside one's field of education

A COMPLETE TEACHING AND LEARNING SOLUTION

Business Communication Today has helped millions of students master essential skills for succeeding in the workplace. The ninth edition extends that tradition by offering an unmatched set of tools that simplify teaching, promote active learning, and stimulate critical thinking. These components work together at four levels to provide seamless coverage of vital knowledge and skills:

- **Previewing:** Each chapter prepares students with clear learning objectives and a brief compelling vignette featuring a successful professional role model.
- **Developing:** Chapter content develops, explains, and elaborates on concepts with a concise, carefully organized presentation of textual and visual material. The three-step process of planning, writing, and completing is clearly explained and reinforced throughout the text in examples ranging from e-mail messages to blogs to formal reports.
- **Enhancing:** Contemporary examples, many accompanied by the three-step diagram adapted to each message, show students the specific elements that contribute to—or detract from—successful messages.
- **Reinforcing:** Hundreds of realistic business English exercises and activities let student practice vital skills and put newfound knowledge to immediate use. Interactive Document Makeovers let students experience firsthand the elements that make a document successful, giving them the insights they need to analyze and improve their own business messages. Communication cases, most featuring real companies, encourage students to think about contemporary business issues as they put their skills to use in a variety of media, including blogging and podcasting.

At every stage of the learning experience, *Business Communication Today* provides the tools that instructors and students need to succeed.

Features that help students build essential knowledge and skills	Previewing	Developing	Enhancing	Reinforcing
Learning objectives (beginning of chapter)	•			
Communication Close-Up (beginning of chapter)	•			
Concise presentations of fundamentals (within chapter)		•		
Managerial perspectives on key topics (within chapter)		•		
Three-step writing process diagrams (within chapter)		•		
Real-life examples (within chapter)			•	
Annotated model documents (within chapter)			•	
Highlight boxes (within chapter)			•	
Handbook of Grammar, Mechanics, and Usage (end of book)			•	
Marginal notes (within chapter)				•
Checklists (within chapter)				•
Communication Challenges (end of chapter)				•
Summary of Learning Objectives (end of chapter)				•
Test Your Knowledge questions (end of chapter)				•
Apply Your Knowledge questions (end of chapter)				•
Practice Your Knowledge activities and exercise (end of chapter)				•
Expand Your Knowledge web resources (end of chapter/online)				•
Cases (following Chapters 7, 8, 9, 10, 14, 15, 17, 18, and 19)				•
Document Makeovers (online)				•
Interactive Study Guide (online)				•
Peak Performance Grammar and Mechanics (online)				•

UP-TO-DATE COVERAGE OF IMPORTANT TOPICS

From teamwork, listening, ethics, and etiquette to the latest communication technologies, *Business Communication Today* has always helped instructors and students stay on the leading edge of contemporary practice. That emphasis continues in the ninth edition, with innovative coverage of audience psychology, electronic media, and visual communication.

Audience Psychology (Chapter 1)

Too many business professionals, particularly early in their careers, make avoidable mistakes caused by poor understanding of how audiences receive, process, and respond to incoming messages. The ninth edition addresses this challenge with unique new coverage of audience psychology. These concepts are tightly integrated with the discussion of the communication process and concludes with a graphic (Figure 1.8) that clearly identifies the skills communicators need to succeed at every stage of the process.

Electronic Media (Chapter 7)

Businesses continue to adapt virtually any technology that promises faster and more effective communication, and the past couple of years have seen astounding changes in business media habits. Practically overnight, blogs, wikis, and podcasts have moved from the high-tech fringe into the business mainstream. *Business Communication Today* further extends its lead in technology coverage with a unique new chapter, *Crafting Messages for Electronic Media*, that helps students adapt the skills they're learning to these new media.

Visual Media and Visual Communication Design (Chapters 4 and 12)

Technology isn't the only fundamental change occurring in the world of business communication. In recent years, more communicators have discovered the power of visual media, both to convey complex ideas quickly and to connect with audiences whose verbal skills might be insufficient for traditional, text-heavy messages.

Chapter 4 introduces students to visual media, and Chapter 12 adds significant new coverage of effective visual communication, including the power of images, visual literacy, the visual evolution of business communication, principles of effective visual design, and the ethics of visual communication.

Compelling real-life examples show students how principles such as visual design are put to use.

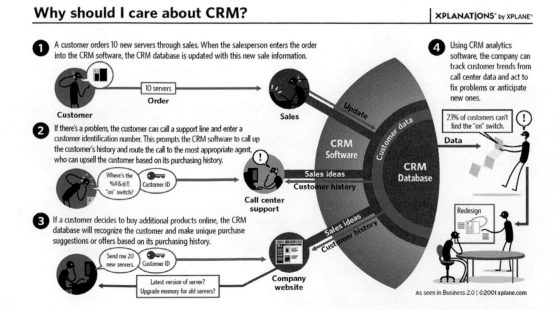

Communication Technology

Vital topics in communication technology are interwoven throughout the text, reflecting the expectations and opportunities in today's workplace:

- aggregators
- assistive technologies
- autocompletion and autocorrection
- blogging
- commenting tools
- computer animation
- content management systems
- desktop publishing
- desktop search engines
- digital photography
- electronic forms
- electronic presentations
- e-mail
- e-mail hygiene
- enterprise IM
- enterprise search engines
- enterprise wikis
- e-portfolios
- extranets
- geographic information systems
- global position system (GPS)
- graphic design software
- groupware
- hidden Internet
- HTML résumé production
- hyperlinks
- instant messaging
- intellectual property rights
- interactive media
- Internet telephony (VoIP)
- interview simulators
- intranets
- knowledge management systems
- linked and embedded documents
- machine translation
- mobile blogs
- multimedia documents
- multimedia presentations
- newsfeeds
- natural language search
- online brainstorming systems
- online chat systems
- online research techniques
- online survey tools
- opt-in e-mail
- peer-to-peer networking
- PDF documents
- podcasting
- podcatchers
- proposal writing software
- research and content managers
- résumé scanning systems
- RSS
- screencasting
- search and metasearch engines
- security and privacy concerns in electronic media
- shared online workspaces
- short messaging service (SMS)
- social bookmarking
- social networking
- streaming media
- survey software
- syndication
- tagging
- text messaging
- templates and stylesheets
- translation software
- video blogging
- video podcasts
- videoconferencing and telepresence
- virtual agents and bots
- voice synthesis and recognition
- Web 2.0
- web content management systems
- web directories
- web-based virtual meetings
- webcasting
- website accessibility
- wikis
- wireless networks (Wi-Fi and Wi-MAX)
- wizards

VERSATILE RESOURCES FOR INSTRUCTORS AND STUDENTS

The multimedia *Business Communication Today* package helps instructors and students take full advantage of the latest advances in instructional technology.

New Instructor Website: www.businesscommunicationblog.com

Stay on top of hot topics, important trends, and new technologies with **Business Communication Headline News**, which uses the newest Internet technologies to deliver late-breaking news in headlines with concise summaries. You can scan incoming items in a matter of seconds, then simply click through to read the full articles that interest you.

This free service offers numerous ways to enhance lectures and student activities:

- Keep current with the latest information and trends in the field
- Easily update your lecture notes with fresh material
- Create visuals for your classroom presentations
- Supplement your lectures with cutting-edge handouts
- Gather podcasts, online video, and other new media examples to use in the classroom
- Enhance your research projects with the newest data
- Compare best practices from other instructors
- Improve the quality and effectiveness of your teaching by reading about new teaching tips and techniques

While visiting the website, you can also get free access to these powerful instructional resources:

- The **Business Communication Web Directory**, available only on this site, where you'll find over 240 topics and more than 5,000 links, with a search engine for the site to help you find exactly what you want.
- Thirty-six **Business Communication Newsletters** updated every 15 minutes, each devoted to a specific topic, such as business correspondence, blogging, e-mail, podcasting, and instant messaging.
- **Business Communication News Links**, with links to dozens of business communication topics from sources including Google News, Live Search, Ask.com, Clipmarks, and Yahoo! News.
- **The Business Communication Library**, available only on this site, where you'll find dozens of articles on a wide variety of topics with a newsfeed available to alert you to new articles.
- **Business Communication Search**, featuring a better way to search for business communication materials, developed by Bovée & Thill.
- **Business Communication Multimedia Resources**, with thousands of PowerPoint presentations, online videos, podcasts, and photographs from Google Video, Dailymotion, Yahoo! Images, Podscope, Podzinger, and many more. Download these resources today and use them in your classes tomorrow.

You can subscribe to Business Communication Headline News and get delivery by e-mail, MyYahoo or Google homepage, RSS newsreader, cell phone, instant messenger, hear the headlines on your MP3 player, or a host or other options. Learn more today by visiting www.businesscommunicationblog.com.

New Student Website:

www.buscommresources.com

The new Bovée/Thill student website, **www.buscommresources. com**, offers a subset of the instructor site features: Business Communication Headline News (headlines oriented toward students), Business Communication Web Directory, Business Communication Newsletters, Business Communication News Links, Business Communication Search, Business Communication Library, Business Communication Multimedia Resources, and Textbook Resources. Students can use the site for a variety of assignments, special projects, and independent research.

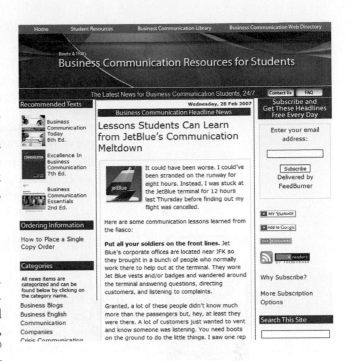

Authors' E-Mail Hotline for Faculty

Integrity, excellence, and responsiveness are the authors' hallmarks. That means providing you with textbooks that are academically sound, creative, timely, and sensitive to instructor and student needs. As an adopter of *Business Communication Today*, you are invited to use the authors' E-mail Hotline (hotline@ businesscommunicationblog.com) if you ever have a question or concern related to the text or its supplements.

Instructor's Resource Center

At **www.prenhall.com/irc**, instructors can access a variety of print, digital, and presentation resources available with this text in downloadable format. Registration is simple and gives you immediate access to new titles and new editions. As a registered faculty member, you can download resource files and receive immediate access and instructions for installing course management content on your campus server.

If you ever need assistance, our dedicated technical support team is ready to help with the media supplements that accompany this text. Visit **www.247.prenhall.com** for answers to frequently asked questions and toll-free user support phone numbers.

The following supplements are available to adopting instructors (for detailed descriptions, please visit **www.prenhall.com/irc**):

- Instructor's Resource Center (IRC) on CD-ROM—ISBN: 0-13-238017-X
- Printed Instructor's Manual—ISBN: 0-13-223933-7
- Printed Test Item File—ISBN: 0-13-243529-2
- TestGen Test Generating Software—Available at the IRC (online or on CD-ROM)
- PowerPoint Slides—Both basic and enhanced versions are available at the IRC
- Classroom Response Systems (CRS)—Available at the IRC (both online and on CD-ROM); learn more at www.prenhall.com/crs
- Image Bank—Visit the IRC on CD-ROM for this resource
- Custom Videos on DVD—ISBN: 0-13-175692-3
- Transparency Package—ISBN: 0-13-223929-9

OneKey Online Courses: Convenience, Simplicity, and Success

OneKey offers complete teaching and learning online resources all in one place. OneKey is all that instructors need to plan and administer courses, and OneKey is all that students need for anytime, anywhere access to online course material. Conveniently organized by textbook chapter, these resources save time and help students reinforce and apply what they have learned. OneKey is available in three course management platforms: Blackboard, CourseCompass, and WebCT.

OneKey resources include

- **Learning modules** (Each chapter offers a 5-question pretest, a summary for review, an online learning activity, and a 10-question posttest.)
- **Peak Performance Grammar and Mechanics***
- **Two versions of Document Makeovers*** (One version feeds your gradebook, and one provides student practice.)
- **Access to Mydropbox.com**
- **Peer review software**

OneKey requires an access code, which can be shrink-wrapped with new copies of this text. Please contact your local sales representative for the correct ISBN. Codes may also be purchased separately at www.prenhall.com/management.

Companion Website

This text's Companion Website at www.prenhall.com/bovée contains valuable resources for both students and professors, including access to a student version of the PowerPoint package, an online Study Guide, the "English-Spanish Audio Glossary of Business Terms," the "Handbook of Grammar, Mechanics, and Usage," and the "Business Communication Study Hall," which allows students to brush up on several aspects of business communication—grammar, writing skills, critical thinking, report writing, résumés, and PowerPoint development.

Student Study Guide

This study guide includes a variety of review questions and study quizzes. Page references to the review questions and quizzes are included.

Vango Notes

Study on the go with VangoNotes (www.VangoNotes.com), detailed chapter reviews in downloadable MP3 format. Now wherever you are and whatever you're doing, you can study on the go by listening to the following for each chapter of your textbook:

- Big Ideas: Your "need to know" for each chapter
- Practice Test: Gut check for the Big Ideas—tells you if you need to keep studying
- Key Terms: Audio "flashcards"—help you review key concepts and terms
- Rapid Review: Quick-drill session—use it right before your test

VangoNotes are *flexible:* Download all the material (or only the chapters you need) directly to your player. And *VangoNotes* are *efficient:* Use them in your car, at the gym, walking to class, wherever you go. So get yours today, and get studying.

SafariX eTextbooks Online

Developed for students looking to save money on required or recommended textbooks, SafariX eTextbooks Online saves students money compared to the suggested list price of the print text. Students simply select their eText by title or author and purchase immediate access to the content for the duration of the course using any major credit card. With a SafariX eText, students can search for specific keywords or page numbers, make notes online, print out reading assignments that incorporate lecture notes, and bookmark important passages for later review. For more information, or to purchase a SafariX eTextbook, visit www.safarix.com.

---

*Instructors who wish to use "Peak Performance Grammar and Mechanics" and "Document Makeovers" but not the rest of the OneKey content can access these features in a special section of the Companion Website. This section requires an access code, which you can ask to have shrink-wrapped with new copies of this text. Please contact your local sales representative for the correct ISBN. Codes may also be purchased separately at www.prenhall.com/management.

FEEDBACK

The authors and the product team would appreciate hearing from you! Let us know what you think about this textbook by writing to college_marketing@prenhall.com. Please include "Feedback about Bovée/Thill 9e" in the subject line.

For any questions related to this product, please contact our customer service department online at www.247.prenhall.com.

ACKNOWLEDGMENTS

The ninth edition of *Business Communication Today* reflects the professional experience of a large team of contributors and advisors. We express our thanks to the many individuals whose valuable suggestions and constructive comments influenced the success of this book.

Reviewers

We especially want to thank the reviewers. Their detailed and perceptive comments resulted in excellent refinements. These reviewers include:

Timothy Alder, Pennsylvania State University—University Park
Heather Allman, University of West Florida
Janice Cooke, University of New Orleans
Terry Engebrertsen, Idaho State University
Joyce Hicks, Valaparaiso University
Lynda Hodge, Guilford Technical Community College
Mary Humphrys, University of Toledo
Iris Johnson, Virginia Commonwealth University
Marsha Kruger, University of Nebraska—Omaha
Marianna Larsen, Utah State University
Anita Leffel, University of Texas—San Antonio
Richard Malamud, California State University—Dominguez Hills
Thomas Marshall, Robert Morris University
Leanne Maunu, Palomar College
Michael Mclane, University of Texas—San Antonio
Bronna McNeely, Midwestern State University
Holly Payne, University of Southern Indiana
Kathy Peacock, Utah State University
Folke Person, Idaho State University
Diza Sauers, University of Arizona
Lucinda Sinclair, Longwood University
Rodney Smith, University of Dubuque
Bruce Strom, University of Indianapolis
Dana Swesen, Utah State University
Dennielle True, Florida Gulf Coast University
Robyn Walker, University of Arizona
Judy Walton, Howard University

Reviewers of Document Makeovers

We sincerely thank the following reviewers for their assistance with the Document Makeover feature: Lisa Barley, Eastern Michigan University; Marcia Bordman, Gallaudet University; Jean Bush-Bacelis, Eastern Michigan University; Bobbye Davis, Southern Louisiana University; Cynthia Drexel, Western State College; Kenneth Gibbs, Worcester State College; Ellen Leathers, Bradley University; Diana McKowen, Indiana University; Bobbie Nicholson, Mars Hill College; Andrew Smith, Holyoke Community College; Jay Stubblefield, North Carolina Wesleyan College; Dawn Wallace, South Eastern Louisiana University.

Reviewers of Model Documents

The many model documents in the text and their accompanying annotations received invaluable review from Dacia Charlesworth, Robert Morris University; Diane Todd Bucci, Robert Morris University; Estelle Kochis, Suffolk County Community College; Sherry Robertson, Arizona State University; Nancy Goehring, Monterey Peninsula College; James Hatfield, Florida Community College at Jacksonville; Avon Crismore, Indiana University.

Personal Acknowledgments

We wish to extend a heartfelt thanks to our many friends, acquaintances, and business associates who provided materials or agreed to be interviewed so that we could bring the real world into the classroom.

A very special acknowledgment goes to George Dovel, whose superb editorial skills, distinguished background, and wealth of business experience assured this project of clarity and completeness. Also, recognition and thanks to Jackie Estrada for her outstanding skills and excellent attention to details. Her creation of the "Peak Performance Grammar and Mechanics" material is especially noteworthy.

We also feel it is important to acknowledge and thank the Association for Business Communication, an organization whose meetings and publications provide a valuable forum for the exchange of ideas and for professional growth.

Additionally, we would like to thank the supplement authors who prepared material for this new edition. They include: Dacia Charlesworth, Robert Morris University; Jay Stubblefield, North Carolina Wesleyan College; William Peirce, Prince George's Community College; Martha Laham, Diablo Valley College; and Myles Hassell, University of New Orleans.

We want to extend our warmest appreciation to the devoted professionals at Prentice Hall. They include Jerome Grant, president; David Parker, editor-in-chief; Jodi Bassett, senior marketing manager; Ashley Santora, product development manager, Kristen Varina, editorial assistant; all of Prentice Hall Business Publishing; and the outstanding Prentice Hall sales representatives. Finally, we thank Judy Leale, senior managing editor of production, and Marcela Boos, production editor, for their dedication; and we are grateful to Lynn Steines, senior production editor at Carlisle Communications, and Janet Slowik, senior art director, for their superb work.

Courtland L. Bovée
John V. Thill

Dedication

To the millions of students throughout the world who have learned about business communication from *Business Communication Today*

and

to the Text and Academic Authors Association, which awarded *Business Communication Today* its prestigious Award for Excellence

and

to the Association for Business Communication, whose meetings and publications provide a valuable forum for the exchange of ideas and professional growth

Building a Career with Your Communication Skills

USING THIS COURSE TO HELP LAUNCH YOUR CAREER

Few courses offer the two-for-the-price-of-one value you get from a business communication class. Not only will the skills you develop in this course be vital to your business career, but they'll also play a key role in launching your career. As you'll see in Chapters 18 and 19, every activity in the job search process relies on communication, and the better you can communicate, the more successful you'll be in landing interesting and rewarding work.

This brief prologue sets the stage by helping you understand today's dynamic workplace, the steps you can take to adapt to the job market, and the importance of creating an employment portfolio. Take a few minutes to read these sections while you think about the career you hope to create for yourself.

UNDERSTANDING TODAY'S DYNAMIC WORKPLACE

Social, political, and financial events continue to change workplace conditions from year to year, so the job market you read about this year might not be the same market you try to enter a year or two from now. However, you can count on a few forces that are likely to affect your entry into the job market and your career success in years to come:[1]

- **Stability.** Your career probably won't be as stable as careers were in your parents' generation. In today's business world, your career will be affected by globalization, mergers and acquisitions, short-term mentality driven by the demands of stockholders, ethical upheavals, and the relentless quest for lower costs. On the plus side, new opportunities, new companies, and even entire industries can appear almost overnight, so while your career might not be as predictable as careers used to be, it could well be more of an adventure.

- **Lifetime employment.** The idea of *lifetime employment,* in which employees spend their entire working lives with a single firm that takes care of them throughout their careers, is all but gone in many industries. Boeing, the Chicago-based aerospace giant, speaks of lifetime *employability,* rather than lifetime employment, putting the responsibility on employees to track market needs and keep their skills up to date—even changing careers if necessary. In fact, most U.S. employees will not only change employers multiple times but will even change careers anywhere from three to five times over their working lives.

Would you like to pursue a career in business but have the flexibility to work from home? Many professionals now do so, as either independent contractors or corporate employees who telecommute.

- **Growth of small business.** Small business continues to be the primary engine of job creation in the United States, so chances are good that you'll work for a small firm at some point. One expert predicts that before long, 80 percent of the U.S. labor force will be working for firms employing fewer than 200 people.
- **Increase in independent contractors.** The nature of employment itself is changing for many people. As companies try to become more flexible, more employees are going solo and setting up shop as independent contractors, sometimes selling their services back to the very companies they just left.
- **Changing view of job-hopping.** Given all these changes, job-hopping doesn't have quite the negative connotation it once had. Even so, you still need to be careful about jumping at every new opportunity that promises more money or prestige. Recruiting and integrating new employees takes time and costs money, and most employers are reluctant to invest in someone who has a history of switching jobs numerous times without good reason.

What do all these forces mean to you? First, take charge of your career—and stay in charge of it. Understand your options, have a plan, and don't count on others to watch out for your future. Second, as you will learn throughout this course, understanding your audience is key to successful communication, starting with understanding how employers view today's job market.

How Employers View Today's Job Market

From the employer's perspective, the employment process is always a question of balance. Maintaining a stable workforce can improve practically every aspect of business performance, yet many employers feel they need the flexibility to shrink and expand payrolls as business conditions change. Employers obviously want to attract the best talent, but the best talent is more expensive and more vulnerable to offers from competitors, so there are always financial trade-offs to consider.

Employers also struggle with the ups and downs of the economy, just as employees do. When unemployment is low, the balance of power shifts to employees, and employers have to compete in order to attract and keep top talent. In the Internet boom of the late 1990s, companies were practically throwing money at hot, young talent, sometimes even paying new hires more than seasoned professionals. Unfortunately, many of those high-flying jobs evaporated almost overnight, so the party didn't last long.[2] When unemployment is high, the power shifts back to employers, who can afford to be more selective and less accommodating. In other words, pay attention to the economy whenever you're job hunting; at times, you can be more aggressive, but at other times, you should be more accommodating.

Rather than looking for lifelong employees for every position, many employers now fill some needs by hiring temporary workers or engaging contractors on a project-by-project basis. Many U.S. employers are now also more willing to move jobs to cheaper labor markets outside the country and to recruit globally to fill positions in the United States. Both trends have stirred controversy, especially in the technology sector, as U.S. firms recruit top engineers and scientists from other countries while shifting mid- and low-range jobs to India, China, Russia, and other countries with lower wage structures.[3]

What Employers Look for in Job Applicants

Given the forces in the contemporary workplace, employers are looking for people who can adapt to the new dynamics of the business world, can survive and thrive in fluid and uncertain situations, and can continue to learn throughout their careers. Companies want team players with strong work records, leaders who are versatile, and employees with diversified skills and varied job experience.[4] In addition, most employers expect college graduates to be sensitive to cultural differences and to have a sound understanding of international affairs.[5] In fact, in some cases, your chances of being hired are better if you have studied abroad or learned another language or can otherwise demonstrate an appreciation of other cultures.

ADAPTING TO TODAY'S JOB MARKET

Adapting to the workplace is a lifelong process of seeking the best fit between what you want to do and what employers are willing to pay you to do. For instance, if money is more important to you than anything else, you can certainly pursue jobs that promise high pay; just be aware that most of these jobs require years of experience, and many produce a lot of stress, require frequent travel, or have other drawbacks you'll want to consider. In contrast, if location, lifestyle, intriguing work, or other factors are more important to you, you may well have to sacrifice some level of pay to achieve them. The important question is to know what you want to do, what you have to offer, and how to make yourself more attractive to employers.

What Do You Want to Do?

Economic necessities and the vagaries of the marketplace will influence much of what happens in your career, of course; nevertheless, it's wise to start your employment search by examining your own values and interests. Identify what you want to do first, then see whether you can find a position that satisfies you at a personal level while also meeting your financial needs.

- **What would you like to do every day?** Research occupations that interest you. Find out what people really do every day. Ask friends, relatives, or alumni from your school. Visit Career One Stop, www.careeronestop.com, to see short videos of real people doing real work in hundreds of different professions.
- **How would you like to work?** Consider how much independence you want on the job, how much variety you like, and whether you prefer to work with products, machines, people, ideas, figures, or some combination thereof. Constant change or a predictable role?
- **What specific compensation do you expect?** What do you hope to earn in your first year? What's your ultimate earnings goal? Are you willing to settle for less money in order to do something you really love?
- **Can you establish some general career goals?** Consider where you'd like to start, where you'd like to go from there, and the ultimate position you'd like to attain.
- **What size company would you prefer?** Do you like the idea of working for a small, entrepreneurial operation or a large corporation?
- **What sort of corporate culture are you most comfortable with?** Would you be happy in a formal hierarchy with clear reporting relationships? Or do you prefer less structure? Teamwork or individualism? Do you like a competitive environment?
- **What location would you like?** Would you like to work in a city, a suburb, a small town, an industrial area, or an uptown setting? Do you favor a particular part of the country? Another country?

Filling out the assessment in Table 1 might help you get a clearer picture of the nature of work you would like to pursue in your career.

What Do You Have to Offer?

Knowing what you *want* to do is one thing. Knowing what you *can* do is another. You may already have a good idea of what you can offer employers. If not, some brainstorming can help you identify your skills, interests, and characteristics. Start by jotting down 10 achievements you're proud of, such as learning to ski, taking a prize-winning photo, tutoring a child, or editing your school paper. Think carefully about what specific skills these achievements demanded of you. For example, leadership skills, speaking ability, and artistic talent may have helped you coordinate a winning presentation to your school's administration. As you analyze your achievements, you'll begin to recognize a pattern of skills. Which of them might be valuable to potential employers?

Next, look at your educational preparation, work experience, and extracurricular activities. What do your knowledge and experience qualify you to do? What have you learned

TABLE P.1 **Career Self-Assessment**
What work-related activities and situations do you prefer? Evaluate your preferences in each of these following areas and use the results to help guide your job search.

ACTIVITY OR SITUATION	STRONGLY AGREE	AGREE	DISAGREE	NO PREFERENCE
1. I want to work independently.				
2. I want variety in my work.				
3. I want to work with people.				
4. I want to work with technology.				
5. I want physical work.				
6. I want mental work.				
7. I want to work for a large organization.				
8. I want to work for a nonprofit organization.				
9. I want to work for a small family business.				
10. I want to work for a service business.				
11. I want to start or buy a business someday.				
12. I want regular, predictable work hours.				
13. I want to work in a city location.				
14. I want to work in a small town or suburb.				
15. I want to work in another country.				
16. I want to work outdoors.				
17. I want to work in a structured environment.				
18. I want to avoid risk as much as possible.				
19. I want to enjoy my work, even if that means making less money.				
20. I want to become a high-level corporate manager.				

from volunteer work or class projects that could benefit you on the job? Have you held any offices? Won any awards or scholarships? Mastered a second language?

Take stock of your personal characteristics. Are you aggressive? A born leader? Or would you rather follow? Are you outgoing? Articulate? Great with people? Or do you prefer working alone? Make a list of what you believe are your four or five most important qualities. Ask a relative or friend to rate your traits as well.

If you're having difficulty figuring out your interests, characteristics, or capabilities, consult your college placement office. Many campuses administer a variety of tests to help you identify interests, aptitudes, and personality traits. These tests won't reveal your "perfect" job, but they'll help you focus on the types of work best suited to your personality.

How Can You Make Yourself More Valuable?

While you're figuring out what you want from a job and what you can offer an employer, you can take positive steps now toward building your career. First, look for volunteer projects, temporary jobs, freelance work, or internships that will help expand your experience base and skill set. These temporary assignments not only help you gain valuable experience and relevant contacts but also provide you with important references and with items for your employment portfolio (see the following section).[6]

Second, learn more about the industry or industries in which you want to work, and stay on top of new developments. Join networks of professional colleagues and friends who can help you keep up with trends and events. Many professional societies have student chapters or offer students discounted memberships. Take courses and pursue other educational or life experiences that would be hard to get while working full time.

Even after an employer hires you, it's a good idea to continue improving your skills, in order to distinguish yourself from your peers and to make yourself more valuable to current and potential employers. Acquire as much technical knowledge as you can, build broad-based life experience, and develop your social skills. Learn to respond to change in positive, constructive ways; doing so will help you adapt if your "perfect" career path eludes your grasp. Learn to see each job, even so-called entry-level jobs, as an opportunity to learn more and to expand your knowledge, experience, and social skills. Share what you know with others instead of hoarding knowledge in the hope of becoming indispensable; helping others excel is a skill, too.[7]

BUILDING AN EMPLOYMENT PORTFOLIO

Employers want proof that you have the skills to succeed on the job. Fortunately, if you don't have much relevant work experience, you can use your college classes to assemble that proof. Simply create and maintain an **employment portfolio**, which is a collection of projects that demonstrate your skills and knowledge. You can create both a *print portfolio* and an *e-portfolio*; both can help with your career effort. A print portfolio gives you something tangible to bring to interviews, and it lets you collect project results that might not be easy to show online, such as a handsomely bound report.

An e-portfolio is a multimedia presentation of your skills and experiences.[8] Think of it as a website that contains your résumé, work samples, letters of recommendation, articles you have written, and other information about you and your skills. Be creative. For example, a student who was pursuing a degree in meteorology added a video clip of himself delivering a weather forecast.[9] The portfolio can be burned on a CD-ROM for physical distribution or, more commonly, posted online—whether it's a personal website, your college's site (if student pages are available), or a networking site such as www.collegegrad.com or www.portfolios.com. To see a selection of student e-portfolios from colleges around the United States, go to www.businesscommunicationheadlinenews.com and click on Textbook Resources. Locate *Business Communication Today 9*, click on Prologue, then click on Student E-Portfolios.

Throughout the course, pay close attention to the activities and cases marked "Portfolio Builder" (they start in Chapter 7). These items will make particularly good samples of not only your communication skills but your ability to understand and solve business-related challenges. By combining these projects with samples from your other courses, you can create a compelling portfolio by the time you're ready to start interviewing. Your portfolio is also a great resource for writing your résumé because it reminds you of all the great work you've done over the years. Moreover, you can continue to refine and expand your portfolio throughout your career; many professionals use e-portfolios to advertise their services, for instance (see Figure 1).

As you assemble your portfolio, collect anything that shows your ability to perform, whether it's in school, on the job, or in other venues. However, you *must* check with an employer before including any items that you created while you were an employee. Many business documents contain confidential information that companies don't want distributed to outside audiences.

For each item you add to your portfolio, write a brief description that helps other people understand the meaning and significance of the project. Include such items as these:

- **Background.** Why did you undertake this project? Was it a school project? An article you wrote on your own initiative? and so on.
- **Project objectives.** Explain the project's goals, if relevant.
- **Collaborators.** If you worked with others, be sure to mention that and discuss team dynamics if appropriate. For instance, if you led the team or worked with others long-distance as a *virtual team*, point that out.

FIGURE 1 Professional Portfolio
Claudia Volpi, a creative director and writer based in Santa Monica, California, uses Portfolios.com to host her professional portfolio. From the thumbnail images on the front page, viewers can click to see samples of her work, such as this television commercial. They can also click to learn more about her background and qualifications.

- **Constraints.** Sometimes the most impressive thing about a project is the time or budget constraints under which it was created. If these apply to a project, consider mentioning them in a way that doesn't sound like an excuse for poor quality. If you had only one week to create a website, for example, you might say that "One of the intriguing challenges of this project was the deadline; I had only one week to design, compose, test, and publish this material."
- **Outcomes.** If the project's goals were measurable, what was the result? For example, if you wrote a letter soliciting donations for a charitable cause, how much money did you raise?
- **Learning experience.** If appropriate, describe what you learned during the course of the project.

Keep in mind that the portfolio itself is a communication project, too, so be sure to apply everything you'll learn in this course about effective communication and good design. Also, assume that every potential employer will find your e-portfolio site (even if you don't tell them about it), so don't include anything that could come back to haunt you.

To get started, first check with the career center at your college; many schools now offer e-portfolio systems for their students. (Some schools now require e-portfolios, so you may already be building one.) You can also find plenty of advice online; search for "e-portfolio" or "student portfolio." Finally, consider a book such as *Portfolios for Technical and Professional Communicators* by Herb J. Smith and Kim Haimes-Korn. This book is intended for communication specialists, but it offers great advice for anyone who wants to create a compelling employment portfolio.

Best wishes for success in this course and in your career!

PART *1*

Understanding the Foundations of Business Communication

CHAPTER 1

Achieving Success Through Effective Business Communication

LEARNING OBJECTIVES

After studying this chapter, you will be able to

1 Explain why effective communication is important to your success in today's business environment

2 Describe the five characteristics of effective business communication

3 Identify seven communication skills that successful employers expect from their employees

4 List five ways in which business communication differs from social communication

5 Describe six strategies for communicating more effectively on the job

6 Explain what must occur for an audience to successfully receive, decode, and respond to messages

7 Explain four strategies for using communication technology successfully

8 Discuss the importance of ethics in business communication and differentiate between ethical dilemmas and ethical lapses

COMMUNICATION CLOSE-UP AT SIX APART

www.sixapart.com

Many people transform personal interests into successful business enterprises, using their hobbies to start a wide variety of businesses. Mena Trott used her hobby to help start a revolution. She was among the first wave of web users to keep a *web log*, or *blog*, an online journal that can cover any topic from politics to pets. As the popularity of her blog grew, the rudimentary blogging tools available at the time couldn't keep up. Trott and her husband, Ben, decided to create their own software that would handle high-volume blogging—and make it easy for anyone to blog.

The Trotts' first product, Movable Type, caught on quickly as web users around the world welcomed the opportunity to become instant online publishers. Before long, Ben and Mena become first-name celebrities in the "blogosphere," and an

Through both the company she co-founded with her husband, Ben, and her own widely read blog, Six Apart's Mena Trott is an influential figure in the world of blogging.

effort that had started as an extension of a hobby soon grew into a multinational business. (The Trotts named their new company Six Apart in honor of the fact that the two of them were born just six days apart.)

With help from companies such as Six Apart, bloggers began to influence the worlds of politics and journalism—and business. The best of these business blogs tear down the barriers that can make companies seem impersonal or unresponsive. Companies ranging from Boeing to General Motors to Microsoft now use blogs to put a human face on commercial organizations, and millions of people read these blogs to keep up on the latest news about the products and companies that interest them.

Blogging is changing so rapidly that it's hard to predict what the future holds for Six Apart, but Trott summed up the impact of blogging when she said, "I can't imagine where we'll be in a year, let alone five years, but I'm certain web logging is here to stay."[1]

ACHIEVING SUCCESS IN TODAY'S COMPETITIVE ENVIRONMENT

1 LEARNING OBJECTIVE

Explain why effective communication is important to your success in today's business environment

Your career success depends on effective communication.

Successful professionals such as Mena Trott (profiled in the chapter-opening Communication Close-Up) will tell you that to succeed in business today, you need the ability to communicate with people both inside and outside your organization. Whether you are competing to get the job you want or to win the customers your company needs, your success or failure depends to a large degree on your ability to communicate. In fact, if you're looking for a surefire way to stand out from your competition in the job market, improving your communication skills may be the single most important step you can take. Employers often express frustration at the poor communication skills of many employees—particularly recent college graduates who haven't yet learned how to adapt their casual communication style to the professional business environment. If you learn to write well, speak well, listen well, and recognize the appropriate way to communicate in various business situations, you'll gain a major advantage that will serve you throughout your career.[2]

Whether you are posting entries on a blog, giving a formal presentation, or chatting with co-workers at lunch, you are engaging in **communication**, the process of sending and receiving messages. The essence of communication is sharing—providing data, information, and insights in an exchange that benefits both you and the people with whom you are communicating.[3] Effective communication helps businesses in numerous ways. These benefits include[4]

- Stronger decision making and faster problem solving
- Earlier warning of potential problems
- Increased productivity and steadier workflow
- Stronger business relationships
- Clearer and more persuasive marketing messages
- Enhanced professional images for both employers and companies
- Lower employee turnover and higher employee satisfaction
- Better financial results and higher return for investors

Communication is vital to every company's success.

Effective communication strengthens the connection between a company and all of its **stakeholders**, those groups affected in some way by the company's actions: customers, employees, shareholders, suppliers, neighbors, the community, and the nation.[5] Conversely, when communication breaks down, the results can be anything from time-wasting to tragic. At every stage of your career, communication is the way you'll succeed, and the higher you rise in your organization, the more important it becomes. In fact, top managers spend as much as 85 percent of their time communicating with others.[6]

Communicating in Organizational Settings

Messages flow into, through, and out of business organizations in a variety of ways. **Internal communication** takes place between people inside the company, whereas **external communication** takes place between the company and outside parties. In addition, messages travel over both *formal* and *informal* channels (see Figure 1.1).

	Internal	**External**
Formal	Planned communication among insiders (such as memos, reports, e-mail, instant messages, executive blogs, conference calls, and presentations) that follows the company's chain of command	Planned communication with outsiders (such as letters, reports, speeches, websites, instant messages, and news releases, advertising, and executive blogs)
Informal	Casual communication among employees (such as e-mail, instant messages, face-to-face conversations, phone calls, team blogs, and wikis) that do not follow the company's chain of command	Casual communication with suppliers, customers, investors, and other outsiders (such as face-to-face conversations, e-mail, instant messages, phone calls, and customer-support blogs)

FIGURE 1.1 Forms of Communication

Business communication can be both formal or informal and internal or external. As you can see from this chart, many of the same tools can be used in any of these four situations.

Every organization has a **formal communication network**, in which ideas and information flow along the lines of command (the hierarchical levels) in the company's organization structure (see Figure 1.2). Throughout the internal formal network, information flows in three directions. *Downward communication* flows from executives to employees, conveying executive decisions and providing information that helps employees do their jobs. *Upward communication* flows from employees to executives, providing insight into problems, trends, opportunities, grievances, and performance—thus allowing executives to solve problems and make intelligent decisions. *Horizontal communication* flows between departments to help employees share information, coordinate tasks, and solve complex problems.[7]

Formal communications flows in three directions.

Every organization also has an **informal communication network**—a *grapevine*—that operates anywhere two or more employees are in contact, from the lunchroom to the golf course to the company's e-mail and instant messaging (IM) systems. Some executives are wary of the informal network, but savvy managers tap into it to spread and receive informal messages.[8] Smart managers also know that a particularly active grapevine is a sign the formal communication network is not providing the information employees believe they need.

Grapevines flourish when employees don't receive information they want or need.

FIGURE 1.2 Formal Communication Network

In the formal communication network—defined by the relationships between the various job positions in the organization—messages flow upward, downward, and horizontally.

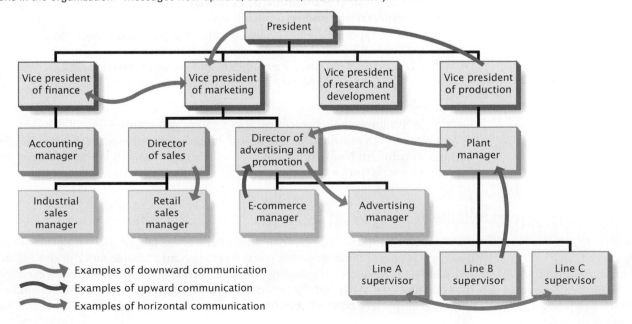

Examples of downward communication
Examples of upward communication
Examples of horizontal communication

External communication flows into and out of the organization by both formal (carefully prepared letters, announcements, and so on) and informal (meeting potential sales contacts at industry gatherings or networking at social events) means. In fact, informal exchanges are now considered so important that a new class of technology has sprung up to enable them. Just as Facebook, MySpace, and similar **social networking technologies** help students and other individuals connect, software and websites such as Spoke Connect, LinkedIn.com, and Ryze.com help businesspeople connect. These business-oriented solutions typically work by indexing e-mail and IM address books, calendars, and message archives, then looking for connections between names. For instance, you may find that the sales lead you've been struggling to contact at a large customer is a golf buddy of someone who works just down the hall from you.[9]

The concept of social networking is also evolving in some companies into the form of *virtual communities* or *communities of practice* that link employees with similar professional interests throughout the company and, occasionally, with customers and suppliers as well. For example, the heavy-equipment manufacturer Caterpillar has more than 2,700 such communities that discuss problems and share insights into improving quality and productivity. In some companies, these communities are informal and "organic," springing up and growing as employees connect with one another. In other companies, such as Caterpillar, the communities are planned and managed in a more formal fashion.[10]

Recognizing Effective Communication

2 LEARNING OBJECTIVE

Describe the five characteristics of effective business communication

You can have the greatest ideas in the world, but they're no good to your company or your career if you can't express them clearly and persuasively. To make your messages effective, make them practical, factual, concise, clear, and persuasive:[11]

- **Provide practical information.** Give recipients useful information, whether it's to help them perform a desired action or understand a new company policy. For instance, if you review Mena Trott's blog (**www.sixapart.com/corner**), you'll see that every posting helps advance the cause of blogging in some way—and as blogging continues to grow, so do the business opportunities for Six Apart.
- **Give facts rather than vague impressions.** Use concrete language, specific detail, and information that is clear, convincing, accurate, and ethical. Even when an opinion is called for, present compelling evidence to support your conclusion.
- **Present information in a concise, efficient manner.** Highlight the most important information, rather than dumping everything on the reader. Audiences respond better to messages that clarify and summarize effectively.
- **Clarify expectations and responsibilities.** Write messages to generate a specific response from a specific audience. Clearly state what you expect from audience members or what you can do for them.
- **Offer compelling, persuasive arguments and recommendations.** Show your readers precisely how they will benefit from responding to your message the way you want them to.

Keep these five important characteristics in mind as you review Figure 1.3 and Figure 1.4. At first glance, both e-mails appear to be well constructed, but Figure 1.3 is far less effective, as the comments (in blue) explain. In contrast, Figure 1.4 shows how an effective message can help everyone work more efficiently.

Understanding What Employers Expect from You

3 LEARNING OBJECTIVE

Identify seven communication skills that successful employers expect from their employees

No matter how good you are at accounting, engineering, law, or whatever professional specialty you pursue, employers expect you to be competent at a wide range of communication tasks. In fact, employers start judging your ability to communicate before you even show up for your first interview, and the process of evaluation never really stops. Fortunately, the skills that employers expect from you are the same skills that will help you advance in your career:

FIGURE 1.3 Ineffective Business Communication

At first glance, this e-mail message looks like a reasonable attempt at communicating with the members of a project team. However, review the blue annotations to see just how many problems the message really has.

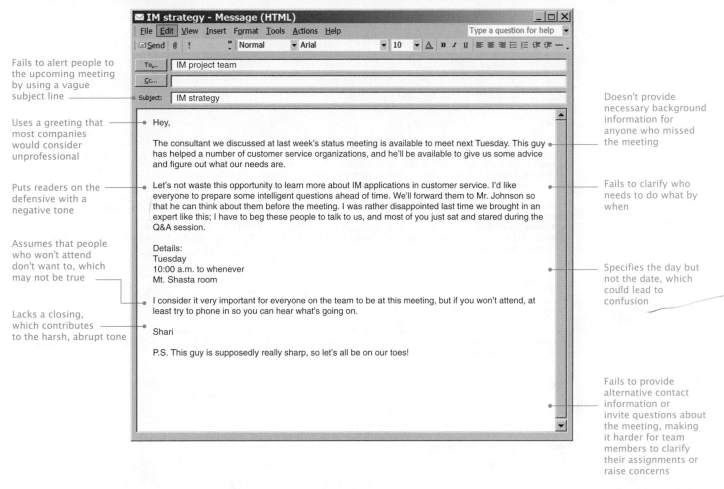

Fails to alert people to the upcoming meeting by using a vague subject line

Uses a greeting that most companies would consider unprofessional

Puts readers on the defensive with a negative tone

Assumes that people who won't attend don't want to, which may not be true

Lacks a closing, which contributes to the harsh, abrupt tone

Doesn't provide necessary background information for anyone who missed the meeting

Fails to clarify who needs to do what by when

Specifies the day but not the date, which could lead to confusion

Fails to provide alternative contact information or invite questions about the meeting, making it harder for team members to clarify their assignments or raise concerns

- Organizing ideas and information logically and completely
- Expressing ideas and information coherently and persuasively
- Listening to others effectively
- Communicating effectively with people from diverse backgrounds and experiences
- Using communication technologies effectively and efficiently
- Following accepted standards of grammar, spelling, and other aspects of high-quality writing and speaking
- Communicating in a civilized manner that reflects contemporary expectations of business etiquette
- Communicating ethically, even when choices aren't crystal clear

You'll have the opportunity to practice all these skills throughout this course—but don't stop there. Successful professionals continue to hone communication skills throughout their careers.

Employers are constantly evaluating your communication skills.

Understanding Why Business Communication Is Unique

If you have some experience in the business world, you already know that business communication is often more complicated and demanding than the social communication you typically engage in with family, friends, and school associates. Expectations are higher on the job, and the business environment is so complex that your messages can fail for reasons you've never even heard of before. Business communication is affected by factors such as the

4 LEARNING OBJECTIVE

List five ways in which business communication differs from social communication

FIGURE 1.4 Effective Business Communication
This improved version of the e-mail message from Figure 1.1 does a much better job of communicating the information people need in order to effectively prepare for the meeting.

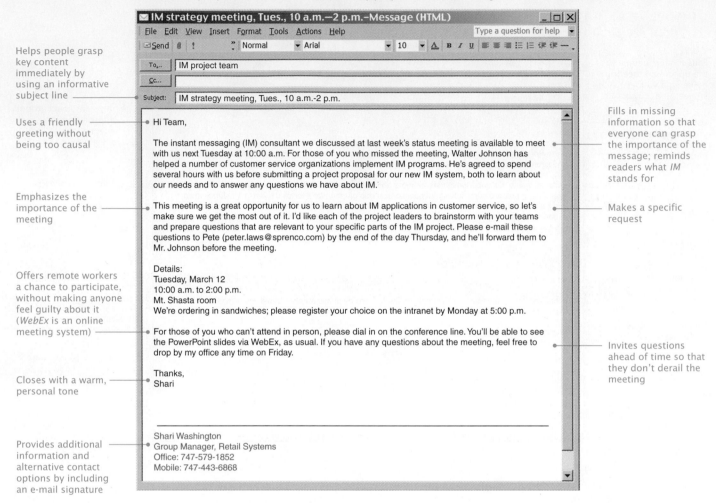

Helps people grasp key content immediately by using an informative subject line

Uses a friendly greeting without being too causal

Emphasizes the importance of the meeting

Offers remote workers a chance to participate, without making anyone feel guilty about it (*WebEx* is an online meeting system)

Closes with a warm, personal tone

Provides additional information and alternative contact options by including an e-mail signature

Fills in missing information so that everyone can grasp the importance of the message; reminds readers what *IM* stands for

Makes a specific request

Invites questions ahead of time so that they don't derail the meeting

globalization of business and the increase in workforce diversity, the increasing value of information, the pervasiveness of technology, the evolution of organizational structures, and the growing reliance on teamwork.

The Increasing Value of Business Information

Information has become one of the most important resources in business today.

As competition for jobs, customers, and resources continues to grow, the importance of information continues to escalate as well. Even companies not usually associated with the so-called Information Age often rely on **knowledge workers**, those employees at all levels of the organization who specialize in acquiring, processing, and communicating information. Three examples help to illustrate the value of information in today's economy:

- **Competitive insights.** The more a company knows about its competitors and their plans, the better able it will be to adjust its own business plans.
- **Customer needs.** Most companies invest significant time and money in the effort to understand the needs of their customers, and this information needs to be analyzed and summarized in order to develop goods and services that better satisfy customer needs.
- **Regulations and guidelines.** Today's businesses must understand and follow a wide range of government regulations and guidelines covering such areas as employment, environment, taxes, and accounting. In the field of accounting and finance, for instance, executives say that communication skills are more important than ever, not only for the increasing requirements of government reporting but also for the increase in interdepartmental collaboration.[12]

No matter what the specific type of information, the better you are able to understand it, use it, and communicate it to others, the more competitive you and your company will be.

The Globalization of Business and the Increase in Workforce Diversity

Today's businesses increasingly reach across international borders to market their products, partner with other businesses, and employ workers and executives—an effort known as **globalization**. Many U.S. companies rely on exports for a significant portion of their sales, sometimes up to 50 percent or more, so managers and employees in these firms need to communicate with many other cultures. Moreover, thousands of companies from all around the world vie for a share of the massive U.S. market, so chances are you'll do business with or even work for a company based in another country at some point in your career.

As people and products cross borders, businesses of all shapes and sizes are paying more attention to **workforce diversity**—all those differences among the people who work together, including differences in age, gender, sexual orientation, education, cultural background, religion, life experience, and so on. As Chapter 3 discusses, successful companies realize two important facts: (1) the more diverse their workforce, the more attention they need to pay to communication; and (2) a diverse workforce can yield a significant competitive advantage by bringing new ideas and new communication skills.

Successful companies know that diverse workforces can create powerful competitive advantages, but such workforces require closer attention to communication in order to eliminate barriers between groups with different communication styles.

The Pervasiveness of Technology

The blogging innovations from Mena Trott and her colleagues at Six Apart represent another important theme in contemporary business communication: the influence of technology in virtually every aspect of the field (see "Connecting Through Technology: Is Web 2.0 the Future or the Past Revisited?" on the following page). However, taking advantage of technology requires time, energy, and frequent improvement of skills. If your level of technical expertise doesn't keep up with that of your colleagues and co-workers, the imbalance can put you at a disadvantage and complicate the communication process. Throughout this course, you'll learn how to use numerous technological tools and systems more effectively.

Technology can help or hinder communication, depending on how it's designed and used.

The Evolution of Organizational Structures

Every business has a particular structure that defines the relationships between the various people and departments within the organization. These relationships in turn affect the nature and quality of communication throughout the organization. *Tall structures* have many layers of management between the lowest and highest positions, so they can suffer communication breakdowns and delays as messages are passed up and down through multiple layers.[13]

Organizations with tall structures may unintentionally restrict the flow of information.

To overcome such problems, many businesses are adopting *flat structures* that reduce the number of layers. With fewer layers, communication generally flows faster and with fewer disruptions and distortions. On the other hand, with fewer formal lines of control and communication in these organizations, individual employees are expected to assume more responsibility for communication—particularly in the horizontal direction, from department to department across the company.

Flatter organizational structures usually make it easier to communicate effectively.

In the pursuit of speed and agility, some businesses have adopted flexible organizations that pool the talents of employees and external partners. For instance, when launching a new product, a company might supplement the efforts of internal departments with help from a public relations firm, an advertising agency, a marketing consultant, a web developer, and a product distributor. With so many individuals and organizations involved

Connecting with Technology

Is Web 2.0 the Future or the Past Revisited?

Take your pick: (a) It unleashes the power of the individual while harnessing the collective wisdom of crowds; it shifts the web from consumption to contribution; and far into the future it "will be recognized as the largest, most complex, and most surprising event on the planet." (b) It is a load of baloney that at best is meaningless marketing nonsense and at worst is an attempt to repackage failed business models from the dot-com boom of the late 1990s.

"It" is Web 2.0. Defining Web 2.0 is difficult, and estimating its eventual impact on business is even harder. Web 2.0 could be described as a shift in both the philosophy and the technology of the World Wide Web, from static, isolated, and tightly controlled websites to connected, interactive, user-driven services. However, the term is used so widely and so loosely that no accepted definition has yet emerged.

Companies frequently cited as examples of the Web 2.0 approach include the news website Digg.com (www.digg.com), which allows users to select the most important news stories from around the world; the social bookmarking site del.icio.us (http://del.icio.us), which helps web surfers find interesting and useful websites; and Technorati (www.technorati.com), a search engine that specializes in blogs, podcasts, and online video. Communication technologies often included under the Web 2.0 umbrella include blogging, podcasting, wikis, and newsfeeds; you'll learn more about all of these in Chapter 7.

Web 2.0 detractors generally don't dispute the value of these sites and tools; rather, they question whether Web 2.0 is really the profound philosophical shift in human behavior that some of its proponents seem to claim—and whether a whole class of profitable businesses can be built around the concept. While that debate rages on, here's some pragmatic advice: Take advantage of these powerful new communication tools without getting too caught up in what exactly Web 2.0 means or where it might be going.

CAREER APPLICATIONS

1. Read several online opinions that promote or downplay the importance of Web 2.0 (you can find a number of links in the Web 2.0 article on Wikipedia, www.wikipedia.org).
2. After reading those opinions, write your own one- or two-sentence description of Web 2.0. (Good luck! This could prove to be an extremely challenging assignment.)

Corporate cultures with an open climate benefit from free-flowing information and employee input.

in the project, everyone must share the responsibility for giving and getting necessary information, or communication will break down.

Regardless of the particular structure a company uses, your communication efforts will also be influenced by the organization's **corporate culture**, the mixture of values, traditions, and habits that give a company its atmosphere and personality. Successful companies encourage employee contributions by ensuring that communication flows freely down, up, and across the organization chart. Open climates encourage candor and honesty, helping employees feel free enough to admit their mistakes, disagree with the boss, and share negative or unwelcome information.

The Growing Reliance on Teamwork

Working in a team makes you even more responsible for communicating effectively.

You'll probably find yourself on a number of teams throughout your career, either as a full-time assignment or as part of a temporary project. Teams are commonly used in business today, but they're not always successful—and a key reason that teams fail to meet their objectives is poor communication. Chapter 2 offers insights into the complex dynamics of team communication and identifies skills you'll need to be an effective communicator in group settings.

COMMUNICATING MORE EFFECTIVELY ON THE JOB

Communication in today's business environment is clearly a challenge, but a careful combination of strategies can improve your ability to communicate effectively. The most important of these strategies include learning to connect with your audiences, minimizing distractions, adopting an audience-centered approach, improving your basic communication skills, using constructive feedback, and being sensitive to business etiquette.

Connecting with Your Audience

No matter what the circumstances, successful communication is all about making connections with your audience. You have no doubt had experiences in which a single word or even just a glance successfully communicated what you wanted to say—as well as experiences in which you talked for hours or sent what seemed like a million text messages but just couldn't get your audience to understand your message. Why do some efforts succeed while others fail?

Human communication is a complex process with many opportunities for messages to get lost, ignored, or misinterpreted. Fortunately, by understanding this process, you can improve the odds that your messages will reach their intended audiences and produce their intended effects.

The Communication Process

By viewing communication as a process (Figure 1.5), you can identify and improve the skills you need to be more successful. The original version of this process model was created to describe electronic communication,[14] but it provides helpful insights into any form of communication:

1. **The sender has an idea.** You conceive an idea and want to share it.

2. **The sender encodes the idea as a message.** When you put your idea into a message (words, images, or a combination of both) that your receiver will understand, you are **encoding** it.

3. **The sender produces the message in a transmittable medium.** With the appropriate message to express your idea, you now need some way to present that message to your intended audience. As you'll read in Chapter 4, media for transmitting messages can be divided into *oral, written, visual,* and various *electronic* forms of the other three.

4. **The sender transmits the message through a channel.** Just as technology continues to multiply the number of media options at your disposal, it continues to provide new **communication channels** you can use to transmit your messages. The distinction between medium and channel can get a bit murky, but think of medium as the *form* a message takes and channel as the system used to *deliver* the message. The channel can be anything from a face-to-face conversation to the Internet to another person or even another company. Getting your message through the channel can be a challenge, because you often have to contend with a variety of environmental barriers (see the following section) that can block or distort your message.

5. **The audience receives the message.** If all goes well, your message survives the trip through the channel and arrives at your intended audience. However, arrival is no guarantee that the message will be noticed or understood correctly.

5 LEARNING OBJECTIVE

Describe six strategies for communicating more effectively on the job

Viewing communication as a process helps you identify steps you can take to improve your success as a communicator.

FIGURE 1.5 The Communication Process

These eight steps illustrate how ideas travel from sender to receiver. The process is presented in more detail in the following pages, and Figure 1.8 on page 19 offers advice on improving your skills at each step.

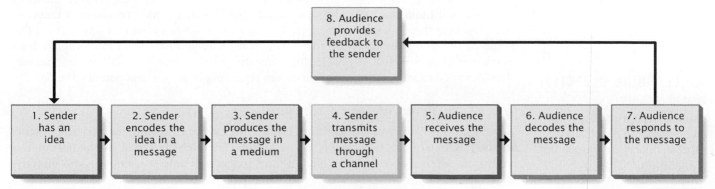

6. **The audience decodes the message.** If your audience actually does receive the message, he or she then needs to extract your idea from the message, a step known as **decoding**.

7. **The audience responds to the message.** By crafting your messages in ways that show the benefits of responding, you can increase the chances that your audiences will respond as you'd like them to.

8. **The audience sends feedback.** Aside from responding (or not responding) to the message, audience members may also give **feedback** that helps you evaluate the effectiveness of your communication effort. For instance, a quizzical look suggests that a person to whom you are speaking either didn't hear or didn't understand the words you spoke. As you'll see in Chapter 4, feedback is an important consideration when choosing media, because some media accommodate feedback much more easily than others.

These eight steps offer a useful summary of the overall process. The following sections take a closer look at two important aspects of the process: environmental barriers that can block or distort messages and the steps audiences take to receive, decode, and respond to messages.

Barriers in the Communication Environment

Communication barriers include
- *Noise and distractions*
- *Competing messages*
- *Filters*
- *Channel breakdowns*

Within any communication environment, messages can be disrupted by a variety of **communication barriers**. These include noise and distractions, competing messages, filters, and channel breakdowns:

- **Noise and distractions.** External distractions range from poor acoustics to uncomfortable meeting rooms to crowded computer screens with instant messages and reminders popping up all over the place. The common habit of *multitasking*, attempting more than one task at a time, is a recipe for distractions. Internal distractions are thoughts and emotions that prevent audiences from focusing on incoming messages. For instance, a person worried about losing his job might ignore any message that doesn't apply to his immediate concerns.

- **Competing messages.** Having your audience's undivided attention is a rare luxury. In many cases, you must compete with other messages that are trying to reach your audience at the same time. Too many messages can result in **information overload**, which not only makes it difficult to discriminate between useful and useless information but also amplifies workplace stress.[15]

- **Filters.** Messages can be blocked or distorted by *filters,* which are any human or technology intervention between the sender and the receiver. Filtering can be both intentional (such as automatically filing e-mail messages based on sender or content) or unintentional (such as an overly aggressive spam filter that deletes legitimate e-mail). As you read earlier, the structure and culture of an organization can also inhibit the flow of vital messages. And, in some cases, the people or companies you rely on to deliver your message can distort it, either accidentally or to meet their own needs.

- **Channel breakdowns.** Sometimes the channel simply breaks down and fails to deliver your message at all. A colleague you were counting on to deliver a message to your boss might have forgotten to do so, a brochure you sent to a customer might have gotten lost in the mail, or a computer server might have crashed and prevented your blog from displaying.

As a communicator, try to be aware of any barriers that could prevent your messages from reaching their intended audiences. As a manager, keep an eye out for any barriers that could be inhibiting the flow of information. Make sure you haven't unintentionally built barriers around yourself. If people don't feel that you are approachable for any reason, they'll avoid communicating with you—even regarding messages that you need to hear.[16]

6 LEARNING OBJECTIVE

Explain what must occur for an audience to successfully receive, decode, and respond to messages

Inside the Mind of Your Audience

After a message survives the journey through the communication channel and reaches its intended audience, it encounters a whole new set of challenges. Understanding how audiences receive, decode, and respond to messages will help you create more-effective messages.

How Audiences Receive Messages   Messages often reach the intended audience but have no effect whatsoever. For an audience member to actually receive a message, three events need to occur: the receiver has to *sense* the presence of a message, *select* it from all the other messages clamoring for attention, then *perceive* it as an actual message (as opposed to random, pointless noise).[17] You can appreciate the magnitude of this challenge by driving down any busy street in a commercial section of town. You'll encounter literally hundreds of messages—billboards, posters, store window displays, other people's thumping car stereos, pedestrians waving or talking on cell phones, car horns honking, street signs, traffic lights, and so on. However, you sense, select, and perceive only a small fraction of these messages. In fact, if you *didn't* ignore most of these messages, you would be one very dangerous driver!

To actually receive a message, audience members need to sense it, select it, then perceive it as a message.

Today's business audiences are much like drivers on busy streets. They are inundated with so many messages and so much noise that they miss or ignore many of the messages intended for them. The good news is that through this course, you will learn a variety of techniques to craft messages that do get noticed. In general, follow these five principles to increase your chances of success:

Trying to send and receive multiple messages simultaneously is so distracting that it can actually reduce a worker's functioning intelligence level.

- **Consider audience expectations.** Deliver messages using the media and channels that the audience expects. Of course, sometimes going *against* expectations can stimulate audience attention, which is why advertisers sometimes do wacky and creative things to get your attention. However, for most business communication efforts, following the expectations of your audience is the most efficient way to get your message across.

- **Ensure ease of use.** Even if audiences are actively looking for your messages, they probably won't see your messages if you make them hard to find. Poorly designed websites with confusing navigation are common culprits in this respect.

To improve the odds that your messages will be successfully perceived by your audience, pay close attention to expectations, ease of use, familiarity, empathy, and technical compatibility.

- **Emphasize familiarity.** Use words, images, and designs that are familiar to your audience. For example, most visitors to business websites now expect to see information about the company on a page called "About Us."

- **Practice empathy.** Make sure your messages "speak to the audience" by clearly addressing *their* wants and needs—not yours. People are much more inclined to notice messages that relate to their individual concerns.[18]

- **Design for compatibility.** With so many messages delivered electronically these days, be sure to verify technical compatibility with your audience. For instance, if your website requires visitors to have the Adobe Flash capability on their computers, you won't reach those audience members who don't have that software.

How Audiences Decode Messages   Even though a message may have been received by the audience, it still doesn't "mean" anything until the recipient decodes it and assigns meaning to it. Unfortunately, there is no guarantee that your audience will assign the same meaning that you intended. Even well-crafted, well-intentioned communication efforts can fail at this stage, because assigning meaning through decoding is a highly personal process that is affected by culture, individual experience, learning and thinking styles, hopes, fears, and even temporary moods. Moreover, audiences tend to extract the meaning they *expect* to get from a message, even if it's the opposite of what the sender intended.[19] In fact, rather than extracting your meaning, it's more accurate to state that your audience re-creates their own meaning—or meanings—from the message.

Decoding a message to assign meaning to it is a complicated and often highly personal process.

As you'll discover in Chapter 3, culture shapes people's views of the world in profound ways, from determinations of right and wrong to details such as the symbolic meanings attached to specific colors. For instance, because U.S. culture celebrates youth and individual accomplishment, it is "natural" for people raised in this country to admire young, independent-minded leaders who rebel against older, established ways of doing business. Compare this approach to that in places such as Japan, which generally places a higher value on respect for older colleagues, consensus decision making, and group accomplishment. Given these differences, a younger colleague's bold proposal to radically reshape business strategy could be interpreted more positively in one culture than in the other—quite independent of the proposal's merits alone.

At an individual level, beliefs and biases also influence the meaning that audiences extract from messages. For instance, our minds organize incoming sensations into a mental map that represents our individual **perception** of reality. If a detail doesn't quite fit for any reason, people are inclined to distort the information rather than rearrange their pattern—a process known as **selective perception**.[20] For example, a manager who believes wholeheartedly in a particular business strategy might distort or ignore evidence that suggests the strategy is failing.

Selective perception occurs when people ignore or distort incoming information to fit their preconceived notions of reality.

Language differences also influence received meaning. If you ask an employee to send you a report on sales figures "as soon as possible," does that mean within 10 seconds, 10 minutes, or 10 days? By clarifying expectations and resolving any potential ambiguities in your messages, you can reduce the odds of such interpretation uncertainties. The more experiences you share with another person, the more likely you are to share perception and thus share meaning (see Figure 1.6).

Individual thinking styles are another important factor in message decoding. For example, even though business decisions are supposedly made on the basis of objective analysis and clear logic, emotion and intuition (reaching conclusions without using rational processes) can influence the interpretation of messages. Let's say you return from a sales trip with a hunch that several major customers may start buying more products from your firm, and you share that optimistic assessment with your colleagues. Someone who tends to respond to the emotional element in messages and to put a lot of faith in "gut feel" may conclude that sales are about to increase. Someone else with a more cautious, analytical approach may view your input as an interesting data point but hardly proof of an imminent increase.

How Audiences Respond to Messages

You are almost there. Your message has been delivered, received, and correctly decoded. Now what? Will audience members respond in the way you'd like them to? Probably—if three events occur.

Audiences will likely respond to a message if they remember it, if they're able to respond, and if they're properly motivated to respond.

First, the recipient has to *remember* the message long enough to act on it. Simplifying greatly, memory works in several stages: *sensory memory* momentarily captures incoming data from the senses; then, whatever the recipient pays attention to is transferred to *short-term memory*. Information in short-term memory will quickly disappear if it isn't transferred to *long-term memory,* which can be done either actively (such as by memorizing a list of items) or passively (such as when a new piece of information connects with something else the recipient already has stored in long-term memory). Finally, the information needs to be *retrieved* when the recipient needs to act on it.[21] In general, people find it easier to remember and retrieve information that is important to them personally or professionally. Consequently, by communicating in ways that are sensitive to your audience's wants and needs, you greatly increase the chance that your messages will be remembered and retrieved.

FIGURE 1.6 How Shared Experience Affects Understanding

The more your audience shares your experiences—personal, professional, and cultural—the more likely they will be to extract the same meanings that you encode in your messages.

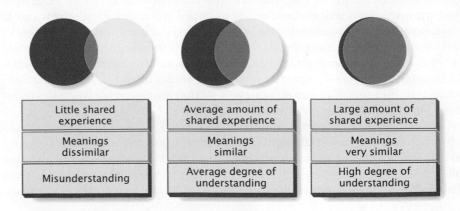

Little shared experience	Average amount of shared experience	Large amount of shared experience
Meanings dissimilar	Meanings similar	Meanings very similar
Misunderstanding	Average degree of understanding	High degree of understanding

Second, the recipient has to be *able* to respond as you wish. Obviously, if recipients simply cannot do what you want them to do, such as paying for a product you are promoting, they will not respond according to your plan. By understanding your audience (see Chapter 4), you can work to minimize these scenarios.

Third, the recipient has to be *motivated* to respond. You'll encounter many situations in which your audience has the option of responding but isn't required to—the record company may or may not offer your band a contract, the boss may or may not respond to your request for a raise, and so on. The good news is that you often have a fair amount of influence over whether the recipient will respond as you'd like. Throughout this course, you'll learn the techniques for crafting messages that motivate readers to respond.

By explaining why audiences will benefit by responding to your messages, you'll increase their motivation to respond.

Minimizing Distractions

Although distractions are a major problem in business communication, everyone in the organization can help overcome them. A small dose of common sense and courtesy goes a long way. Turn off that cell phone before you step into a meeting. Don't talk across the tops of cubicles when people inside them are trying to work. Be sensitive to personal differences, too; for instance, some people enjoy working with music on, but music is an enormous distraction for others.[22]

Overcome distraction by
- *Using common sense and courtesy*
- *Not sending unnecessary messages*
- *Not isolating yourself*
- *Informing receivers of message priority*

Take steps to insulate yourself from distractions, too. Don't let e-mail, IM, or telephones interrupt you every minute of the day. Set aside time to attend to messages all at once so that you can think and focus the rest of the time.

Perhaps above all else, don't send unnecessary messages. You never want to undercommunicate, but sending unnecessary messages or sending the right message to the wrong people is almost as bad. E-mail has compounded this problem, making it too easy to send and forward messages to dozens or hundreds of people at once. In fact, one of the reasons that blogging is taking off so quickly in business is that it can significantly reduce internal e-mail traffic.[23]

In addition, if you must send a message that isn't urgent or crucial, let people know so that they can prioritize. If a long report requires no action from recipients, tell them upfront so that they don't have to search through it looking for action items. Also, most systems let you mark messages as urgent; however, use this feature only when it's truly needed. Too many so-called urgent messages that aren't particularly urgent will lead to annoyance and anxiety, not action.

Try to overcome emotional distractions by recognizing your own feelings and by anticipating emotional reactions from others.[24] When a situation may cause tempers to flare, choose your words carefully. As a receiver, avoid placing blame and reacting subjectively.

Emotionally charged situations require extra care when communicating.

Adopting an Audience-Centered Approach

An **audience-centered approach** means focusing on and caring about the members of your audience, making every effort to get your message across in a way that is meaningful to them (see Figure 1.7). This approach is also known as adopting the **"you" attitude**, in contrast to messages that are about "me." Learn as much as possible about the biases, education, age, status, style, and personal and professional concerns of your receivers. If you're addressing strangers and unable to find out more about them, try to project yourself into their position by using your common sense and imagination. This ability to relate to the needs of others is a key part of *emotional intelligence*, widely considered to be a vital characteristic of successful managers and leaders.[25] The more you know about the people you're communicating with, the easier it will be to concentrate on their needs—which, in turn, will make it easier for them to hear your message, understand it, and respond positively.

Keeping your audience's needs in mind helps you ensure successful messages.

If you haven't had the opportunity to communicate with a diverse range of people in your academic career so far, you might be surprised by the different communication styles you will encounter on the job. Recognizing and adapting to your audience's style will improve not only the effectiveness of your communication but also the quality of your working relationship.[26] The audience-centered approach is emphasized throughout this book, so you'll have plenty of opportunity to practice this approach to communicating more effectively.

FIGURE 1.7 Audience-Centered Communication
After an upgrade to its TypePad blog-hosting system resulted in a period of poor performance for customers, Six Apart's Mena Trott and her staff communicated openly and honestly with customers. They explained what happened, acknowledged customer frustrations, apologized for the inconvenience, offered compensation, and kept their audience up to date. Trott and her colleagues even shared what the experience had taught them as managers and communicators—insights that can help customers handle their own business communication challenges.

TYPEPAD | MOVABLE TYPE | LIVEJOURNAL | **ABOUT US** | SUPPORT

ABOUT SIX APART
News & Events
Management
History
Offices
Jobs
Press Center
Our Blogs

MENA'S CORNER

Mena Trott is president and a co-founder of Six Apart.

Mena's Corner is my chance to show the inner workings of a start-up and give the outside world a glimpse into our challenges, our achievements, and our professional passions.

ARCHIVES BY MONTH:
December 2005
November 2005
October 2005
September 2005
August 2005
July 2005
June 2005
May 2005
April 2005
February 2005
January 2005
December 2004
October 2004
August 2004
July 2004
May 2004
April 2004
March 2004

XML Feed

BLOG NOW!
Fully-featured.

TypePad Update & Lessons Learned

Mena | November 17, 2005

During the last month, we've been very open about TypePad's performance problems and the solutions we're implementing to bring the service up to a high standard. We're happy to say that, since things have stabilized, we've been able to offer compensation to our customers for the inconvenience caused by slow service and downtime.

As Barak said in his email and post, we offer our sincere apologies for any inconvenience and hope that customers of TypePad view the compensation as fair.

Not only did the people here at Six Apart feel the pain of poor performance (as employees and users), but we also spent a great deal of time reading customer emails, comments and posts which helped us understand that every customer is different. Some customers didn't want any compensation, they just wanted us to spend resources fixing the problems; others felt that the performance of TypePad hindered their businesses and personal communications; and some didn't notice any service degradation at all.

So, what are the lessons?

- **Read what your customers have to say**
  This is the most obvious piece of advice, but the most important. Customers who are invested in a service usually want the company that's supporting them to succeed. The best advice comes from your customers, and they aren't afraid to tell it like it is. That said...

- **Ignore the tone of nasty complaints, but pay attention to the underlying messages**
  When people are disappointed, their frustrations are often expressed in the form of anger. But at the same time, the fact that they took the time to write what they feel rather than shrugging it off indicates a deep desire for a solution, not just blame. We're all human and the nasty stuff hurts, but we love passionate users, so that involves taking the good and the bad comments in stride.

- **Understand that the people giving feedback represent many who remain silent**
  For every person who complains, realize that there are probably ten people conscious of the problem but not interested in speaking out

Offers links to related discussions so that anyone landing on this page can get the full story

Assures customers that their concerns and feedback were taken seriously

Helps everyone benefit from the experience (the list continues down the screen)

Fine-Tuning Your Business Communication Skills

Work on your communication skills before you start or restart your business career.

Your skills as a communicator will be as much a factor in your business success as anything else you'll do. No matter what your skill level, opportunities to improve are numerous and usually easy to find. Many employers provide communication training in both general skills and specific scenarios, but don't wait. Use this course to begin mastering your skills now.

Lack of experience may be the only obstacle between you and effective communication. Perhaps you're worried about having a limited vocabulary or uncertain about questions of grammar, punctuation, and style. If you're intimidated by the idea of writing an important document or appearing before a group, you're not alone. Everyone gets nervous about communicating from time to time, even people you may think of as "naturals." People aren't born writing and speaking well; they master these skills through study and practice. Even simple techniques, such as keeping a reading log and writing practice essays, will improve not only your writing skills but also your overall performance in school.[27]

This course lets you practice in an environment that provides honest and constructive feedback. You'll have ample opportunity to plan and produce documents, collaborate in teams, listen effectively, improve nonverbal communication, and communicate across cultures—all skills that will serve your career well.

Giving—and Responding to—Constructive Feedback

You will encounter numerous situations in which you are expected to give and receive feedback regarding communication efforts. Whether giving or receiving criticism, be sure you do so in a constructive way. **Constructive feedback**, sometimes called *constructive criticism*, focuses on the process and outcomes of communication, not on the people involved (see Table 1.1). In contrast, **destructive feedback** delivers criticism with no effort to stimulate improvement.[28] For example, "This proposal is a confusing mess, and you failed to convince me of anything" is destructive feedback. Your goal is to be more constructive: "Your proposal could be more effective with a clearer description of the construction process and a well-organized explanation of why the positives outweigh the negatives." When giving feedback, avoid personal attacks and give the person clear guidelines for improvement.

Constructive feedback focuses on improvement, not personal criticism.

When you receive constructive feedback, resist the immediate urge to defend your work or deny the validity of the feedback. Remaining open to criticism isn't easy when you've poured your heart and soul into a project, but feedback is a valuable opportunity to learn and improve. Try to disconnect your emotions from the work and view it simply as something you can make better. Many writers also find it helpful to step back, think about the feedback for a while, and let their emotions settle down before diving in to make corrections. Of course, don't automatically assume that even well-intentioned feedback is necessarily correct. You have the responsibility for the final quality of the message, so make sure that any suggested changes are valid ones.

Try to react unemotionally when you receive constructive feedback.

TABLE 1.1 Giving Constructive Feedback

HOW TO BE CONSTRUCTIVE	EXPLANATION
Think through your suggested changes carefully.	Because many business documents must illustrate complex relationships between ideas and other information, isolated and superficial edits can do more harm than good.
Discuss improvements rather than flaws.	Instead of saying "this is confusing," explain how the writing can be improved to make it clearer.
Focus on controllable behavior.	Because the writer may not have control over every variable that affected the quality of the message, focus on those aspects the writer can control.
Be specific.	Comments such as "I don't get this" or "Make this clearer" don't identify what the writer needs to fix.
Keep feedback impersonal.	Focus comments on the message, not the person who created it.
Verify understanding.	Ask for confirmation from the recipient to make sure that the person understood your feedback.
Time your feedback carefully.	Make sure the writer will have sufficient time to implement the changes you suggest.
Highlight any limitations your feedback may have.	If you didn't have time to give the document a thorough edit, or if you're not an expert in some aspect of the content, let the writer know so that he or she can handle your comments appropriately.

Being Sensitive to Business Etiquette

Understanding communication etiquette can help you avoid needless blunders.

In today's hectic, competitive world, the notion of **etiquette** (the expected norms of behavior in a particular situation) can seem outdated and unimportant. However, the way you conduct yourself can have a profound influence on your company's success and your career. When executives hire and promote you, they expect your behavior to protect the company's reputation. The more you understand such expectations, the better chance you have of avoiding career-damaging mistakes.

Throughout this book, you'll encounter advice for a variety of business situations, but even if you don't know the specific expectations in a given situation, some general guidelines will get you through any rough spots. Start by being sensitive to the fact that people can have different expectations about the same situation. Something you find appalling or embarrassing might be business as usual for a colleague, and vice versa. Moreover, etiquette expectations don't always make sense, nor are they always fair in the eyes of everyone concerned. For example, some high-ranking women executives say some male colleagues who aren't bothered when men use coarse language (particularly, words and phrases with sexual undertones) often view such language as unacceptable from women. These executives acknowledge that the situation isn't fair, but they've learned to work within the prevailing behavior norms in order to avoid hindering their careers.[29]

Respect, courtesy, and common sense will get you through most etiquette challenges on the job.

Long lists of etiquette "rules" can be overwhelming, and you'll never be able to memorize all of them. Fortunately, you can count on three principles to get you through just about any situation: respect, courtesy, and common sense. Moreover, these principles will encourage forgiveness if you do happen to make a mistake. As you encounter new situations, take a few minutes to learn the expectations of the other people involved. Travel guidebooks are a great source of information about norms and customs in other countries. Check to see if your library has online access to the CultureGram database, or review the country profiles at www.kwintessential.co.uk. Don't be afraid to ask questions, either. People will respect your concern and curiosity. You'll gradually accumulate considerable knowledge, which will help you feel comfortable and be effective in a wide range of business situations.

Applying What You've Learned to the Communication Process

With these additional insights into what makes communication succeed, take another look at the communication process model. Figure 1.8 identifies the key challenges in the process and summarizes the steps you can take along the way to become a more effective communicator.

USING TECHNOLOGY TO IMPROVE BUSINESS COMMUNICATION

7 LEARNING OBJECTIVE

Explain four strategies for using communication technology successfully

Communicating in today's business environment requires some level of technical competence as well.

Today's businesses rely heavily on technology to improve the communication process. Companies and employees who use technology wisely can communicate more effectively and therefore compete more successfully.

You will find technology discussed extensively throughout this book, with specific advice on using both common and emerging tools to meet communication challenges. The four-page photo essay "Powerful Tools for Communicating Efficiently" (pages 20–23) offers an overview of the technologies that connect people in offices, factories, and other business settings.

Anyone who has used a computer knows that the benefits of technology are not automatic. Poorly designed or inappropriately used technology can hinder communication more than it helps. To communicate effectively, learn to keep technology in perspective, use technological tools productively, spend time and money on technology wisely, and disengage from the computer frequently to communicate in person.

Keeping Technology in Perspective

Don't rely too much on technology or let it overwhelm the communication process.

Technology is an aid to interpersonal communication, not a replacement for it. Technology can't think for you or communicate for you; and if you lack some essential skills, technology probably can't fill in the gaps. Your spell checker is happy to run all your words through

FIGURE 1.8 Becoming an Effective Business Communicator

The communication process presents many opportunities for messages to get lost, distorted, or misinterpreted as they travel from sender to receiver. Fortunately, you can take action at every step in the process to increase your chances of success.

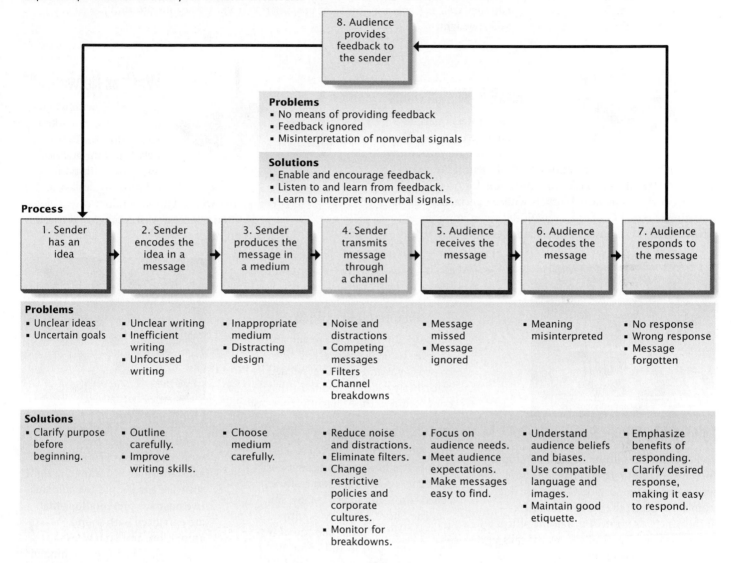

the dictionary, but it doesn't know whether you're using the correct words or crafting powerful sentences.

The sheer number of possibilities in many technological tools can get in the way of successful communication. For instance, the content of a message may be obscured if an electronic presentation is overloaded with visual effects. Moreover, if technological systems aren't adapted to user or organizational needs, people won't adapt to the technology—they won't use it effectively, or worse, they won't use it at all. Perhaps even more ominously, some workers are beginning to show signs of information technology addiction—possibly to the point of craving the stimulation of being connected practically around the clock, even while on vacation.[30]

Using Technological Tools Productively

Communication technologies can save time and money, but they can also waste time and money if not used efficiently. You don't have to become an expert to use most communication technologies efficiently, but you will need to be familiar with the basic features and functions of the tools you are expected to use on the job. As a manager, you'll also need to ensure that your employees have sufficient training to productively use the tools you expect them to use.

Employees who are comfortable using communication technologies have a competitive advantage in today's marketplace.

Powerful Tools for Communicating Effectively

The tools of business communication evolve with every new generation of digital technology. Selecting the right tool for each situation can enhance your business communication in many ways. In today's flexible office settings, communication technology helps people keep in touch and stay productive. When co-workers in different cities need to collaborate, they can meet and share ideas without costly travel. Manufacturers use communication technology to keep track of parts, orders, and shipments—and to keep customers well-informed. Those same customers can also communicate with companies in many ways at any time of day or night.

Flexible Workstations

Many professionals have abandoned desktop PCs for laptops they can carry home, on travel, and to meetings. Back at their desks, a docking station transforms the laptop into a full-featured PC with network connection. Workers without permanent desks sometimes share PCs that automatically reconfigure themselves to access each user's e-mail and files.

Wireless Networks

Laptop PCs with wireless access cards let workers stay connected to the network from practically anywhere within the office—any desk, any conference room. This technology offers high-speed Internet access within range of a wireless access point.

Follow-Me Phone Service

To be reachable without juggling multiple forwarding numbers, some people have follow-me phone service. Callers use one number to reach the person anywhere—at the office, a remote site, a home office. The system automatically forwards calls to a list of preprogrammed numbers and transfers unanswered calls to voice mail.

Redefining the Office

Technology makes it easier for people to stay connected with co-workers and retrieve needed information. Some maintain that connection without having a permanent office, a desktop PC, or even a big filing cabinet. For example, Sun Microsystems lets staff members choose to work either at the main office or at remote offices called "drop-in centers." Many Sun facilities have specially equipped "iWork" areas that can quickly reconfigure phone and computer connections to meet individual requirements.

Electronic Presentations

Combining a color projector with a laptop or personal digital assistant (PDA) running the right software lets people give informative business presentations that are enhanced with sound, animation, and even website hyperlinks. Having everything in electronic form also makes it easy to customize a presentation or to make last-minute changes.

Intranets

Businesses use Internet technologies to create an intranet, a private computer network that simplifies information sharing within the company. Intranets can handle company e-mail, instant messaging (IM), websites, and even Internet phone connections. To ensure the security of company communication and information, intranets are shielded from the public Internet.

Communicating in the Office

Wall Displays

Teams commonly solve problems by brainstorming at a whiteboard. Wall displays take this concept one step further, letting participants transmit words and diagrams to distant colleagues via the corporate intranet. Users can even share the virtual pen to make changes and additions from more than one location.

Web-Based Meetings

Workers can actively participate in web-based meetings by logging on from a desktop PC, laptop, or cell phone. Websites such as WebEx help users integrate voice, text, and video and let them share applications such as Microsoft PowerPoint and Microsoft Word in a single browser window.

Internet Videophone

Person-to-person video calling has long been possible through popular instant messaging programs. Internet videophone services do even more, letting multiple users participate in a videoconference without the expense and complexity of a full-fledged videoconferencing system. Some services are flexible enough to include telecommuters who have broadband Internet connections.

Collaborating

Working in teams is essential in almost every business. Teamwork can become complicated, however, when team members work in different parts of the company, in different time zones, or even for different companies. Technology helps bridge the distance by making it possible to brainstorm, attend virtual meetings, and share files from widely separated locations. Communication technology also helps companies save money on costly business travel without losing most of the benefits of face-to-face collaboration.

Shared Workspaces

Online workspaces such as eRoom and Groove make it easy for far-flung team members to access shared files anywhere, anytime. Accessible through a browser, the workspace contains a collection of folders and has built-in intelligence to control which team members can read, edit, and save specific files.

Communicating Remotely

Videoconferencing and Telepresence

Less costly than travel, videoconferencing provides many of the same benefits as an in-person meeting. Advanced systems include telepresence and robot surrogates, which use computers to "place" participants in the room virtually, letting them see and hear everyone while being seen and heard themselves. Such realistic interaction makes meetings more productive.

RFID

Throughout the distribution chain, from factories to ships to warehouses to retail shelves, companies can replace manual tracking and reporting with automated systems that monitor small radio-frequency identification (RFID) tags attached to goods and containers.

Extranets

Extranets are secure, private computer networks that use Internet technology to share business information with suppliers, vendors, partners, and customers. Think of an extranet as an extension of the company intranet that is available to people outside the organization by invitation only.

Wireless Warehouses

Communication technology is a key source of competitive advantage for shipping companies such as FedEx and UPS. Hand-worn scanners use wireless links to help warehouse personnel access instant information that lets them process more packages in less time at transit hubs.

Sharing the Latest Information

Companies use a variety of communication technologies to create products and services and deliver them to customers. The ability to easily access and share the latest information improves the flow and timing of supplies, lowers operating costs, and boosts financial performance. Easy information access also helps companies respond to customer needs by providing them timely, accurate information and service and by delivering the right products to them at the right time.

Package Tracking

Senders and receivers often want frequent updates when packages are in transit. Handheld devices such as the FedEx PowerPad enhance customer service by letting delivery personnel instantly upload package data to the FedEx network. The wireless PowerPad also aids drivers by automatically receiving weather advisories.

Communicating About Products and Services

Supply Chain Management

Advanced software applications let suppliers, manufacturers, and retailers share information—even when they have incompatible computer systems. Improved information flow increases report accuracy and helps each company in the supply chain manage stock levels.

Over-the-Shoulder Support

For online shoppers who need instant help, many retail websites make it easy to connect with a live sales rep via phone or instant messaging. The rep can provide quick answers to questions and, with permission, can even control a shopper's browser to help locate particular items.

Help Lines

Some people prefer the personal touch of contact by phone. Moreover, some companies assign preferred customers special ID numbers that let them jump to the front of the calling queue. Many companies are addressing the needs of foreign-language speakers by connecting them with external service providers who offer multilingual support.

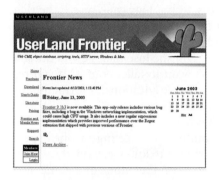

Corporate Blogs

Web-based journals let companies offer advice, answer questions, and promote the benefits of their products and services. Elements of a successful blog include frequent updates and the participation of knowledgeable contributors. Adding a subtle mix of useful commentary and marketing messages helps get customers to read or listen to them.

Interacting

Maintaining an open dialog with customers is a great way to gain a better understanding of their likes and dislikes. Today's communication technologies make it easier for customers to interact with a company whenever, wherever, and however they wish. A well-coordinated approach to phone, web, and in-store communication helps a company build stronger relationships with its existing customers, which increases the chances of doing more business with each one.

Podcasting

With the portability and convenience of downloadable audio and video recordings, podcasts have quickly become a popular means of delivering everything from college lectures to marketing messages. Podcasts are also used for internal communication, replacing conference calls, newsletters, and other traditional communication vehicles.

Communicating with Customers

In-Store Kiosks

Staples is among the retailers that let shoppers buy from the web while they're still in the store. Web-connected kiosks were originally used to let shoppers custom-configure their PCs, but the kiosks also give customers access to roughly 8,000 in-store items as well as to the 50,000 products available online.

Another major productivity consideration is personal use of music players, IM, blogging, and other technological tools (and toys) on the job. Few companies go to the extreme of banning all personal use of such technologies while on the job or of trying to restrict employees' personal blogs, but every company needs to address this issue—and address it again every time a new technology shows up. For instance, inappropriate web surfing not only distracts employees from work responsibilities but also can leave employers open to lawsuits for sexual harassment if inappropriate images are displayed in or transmitted around the company.[31] In addition, e-mail and instant messages are considered legal documents, and both can be used as evidence in lawsuits or criminal trials.[32] Blogging has created another set of managerial challenges, given the risk that employee blogs can expose confidential information or damage a firm's reputation in the marketplace. With all of these technologies, the best solution lies in clear policies that are enforced evenly for all employees.[33]

Reconnecting with People Frequently

In spite of their efficiency and speed, technological tools may not be the best choice for every communication situation. Even in the best circumstances, technology can't match the rich experience of person-to-person contact. Let's say you IM a colleague asking how she did with her sales presentation to an important client, and her answer comes back simply as "Fine." What does *fine* mean? Is an order expected soon? Did she lose the sale and doesn't want to talk about it? Was the client rude and she doesn't want to talk about it? If you reconnect with her, perhaps visit her in person, she might provide additional information or you might be able to offer advice or support during a difficult time.

No matter how much technology is involved, communication is still about people connecting with people.

Moreover, most human beings need to connect with other people. You can create amazing documents and presentations without ever leaving your desk or meeting anyone in person. But if you stay hidden behind technology, people won't get to know you nearly as well. You may be funny, bright, and helpful, but you're just a voice on the phone or a name on a document until people can interact with you in person. As technological options increase, people seem to need the human touch even more.

8 LEARNING OBJECTIVE

Discuss the importance of ethics in business communication and differentiate between ethical dilemmas and ethical lapses

MAKING ETHICAL COMMUNICATION CHOICES

Ethics are the accepted principles of conduct that govern behavior within a society. Put another way, ethical principles define the boundary between right and wrong. Former Supreme Court Justice Potter Stewart defined ethics as "knowing the difference between what you have a right to do and what is the right thing to do."[34] To make the right choices as a business communicator, you have a responsibility to think through not only what you say but also the consequences of saying it.

Of course, people in a society don't always agree on what constitutes ethical behavior. For instance, the emergence of **stealth marketing**, in which customers don't know they're being marketed to, has raised a new set of concerns about ethics. One common stealth-marketing technique is sending people into public places to use particular products in a conspicuous manner and then discuss them with strangers—as though they were just regular people on the street, when in fact they are employed by a marketing firm. Another is paying consumers or rewarding them with insider information and other benefits to promote products to their friends without telling the friends it's a form of advertising. Critics complain that such techniques are deceptive because they don't give their targets the opportunity to raise their instinctive defenses against the persuasive powers of marketing messages.[35]

Ethical behavior is a companywide concern, of course; but because communication efforts are the public face of a company, they are subjected to particularly rigorous scrutiny from regulators, legislators, investors, consumer groups, environmental groups, labor organizations, and anyone else affected by business activities. **Ethical communication** includes all relevant information, is true in every sense, and is not deceptive in any way. In contrast, unethical communication can include falsehoods and misleading information (or can withhold important information). Some examples of unethical communication include:[36]

- **Plagiarism.** Plagiarism is presenting someone else's words or other creative product as your own. Note that plagiarism can also be illegal if it violates a copyright, which is a form of legal protection for the expression of creative ideas.[37]
- **Selective misquoting.** Deliberately omitting damaging or unflattering comments to paint a better (but untruthful) picture of you or your company.
- **Misrepresenting numbers.** Increasing or decreasing numbers, exaggerating, altering statistics, or omitting numerical data.
- **Distorting visuals.** Making a product look bigger or changing the scale of graphs and charts to exaggerate or conceal differences.

Any time you try to mislead your audience, the result is unethical communication.

In contrast, an ethical message is accurate and sincere. It avoids language and images that manipulate, discriminate, or exaggerate. On the surface, such ethical practices appear fairly easy to recognize, but deciding what is ethical can be a considerable challenge in complex business situations.

Distinguishing Ethical Dilemmas from Ethical Lapses

Every company has responsibilities to its stakeholders, and those various groups often have competing interests. An **ethical dilemma** involves choosing among alternatives that aren't clear-cut. Perhaps two conflicting alternatives are both ethical and valid, or perhaps the alternatives lie somewhere in the gray area between clearly right and clearly wrong. Suppose you are the chief executive of a company whose sales are declining and you might be forced to reduce costs by laying off 100 employees. You've decided to wait two months before making this tough decision. Here's your dilemma: Do you tell the workforce now that several hundred jobs could disappear in the near future? Telling them now would give people more time to look for new jobs and adjust their finances—clearly a good thing. However, if you tell them now, vital employees nervous about their future could jump ship, which could drive sales down even more—clearly not a good thing. And what if you tell them now and many people leave but then sales improve enough in the next two months that you can avoid the layoffs? You will have unnecessarily disrupted many careers and families. Situations such as these often have no clear answer.

An ethical dilemma is a choice between alternatives that may all be ethical and valid.

In contrast, an **ethical lapse** is a clearly unethical (and frequently illegal) choice. In 2004, several insurance companies were accused of misleading military personnel at Fort Benning in Georgia, Camp Pendleton in California, and other bases around the country. Many of these young men and women thought they were signing up for savings programs when in fact they were buying extremely expensive and frequently unnecessary life insurance policies. The policies were often sold during mandatory financial training sessions for the soldiers, who were given no time to read the documents they signed. After the situation was brought to national attention by the *New York Times* and other news media, at least two of the companies involved, Madison National Life Insurance Company and American Amicable Life Insurance, began issuing full refunds.[38]

An ethical lapse is knowing that something is wrong and doing it anyway.

With both internal and external communication efforts, the pressure to produce results or justify decisions can make unethical communication a tempting choice. Compare the messages in Figure 1.9 and Figure 1.10 on the following pages, in which the results of a marketing research project are presented to company executives.

Ensuring Ethical Communication

Ensuring ethical business communication requires three elements: ethical individuals, ethical company leadership, and the appropriate policies and structures to support employees' efforts to make ethical choices.[39] Moreover, these three

DOCUMENT MAKEOVER

IMPROVE THIS MEMO

To practice correcting drafts of actual documents, visit your online course or the access-code-protected portion of the Companion Website. Click "Document Makeovers," then click Chapter 1. You will find a memo that contains problems and errors relating to what you've learned in this chapter about improving business communication. Use the Final Draft decision tool to create an improved version of this memo. Check the message for ethical communication and an audience-centered approach.

FIGURE 1.9 Unethical Communication
The writers of this memo clearly wanted the company to continue funding their pet project, even though the marketing research didn't support such a decision. By comparing this memo with the version shown in Figure 1.10, you can see how the writers twisted the truth and omitted evidence in order to put a positive "spin" on the research.

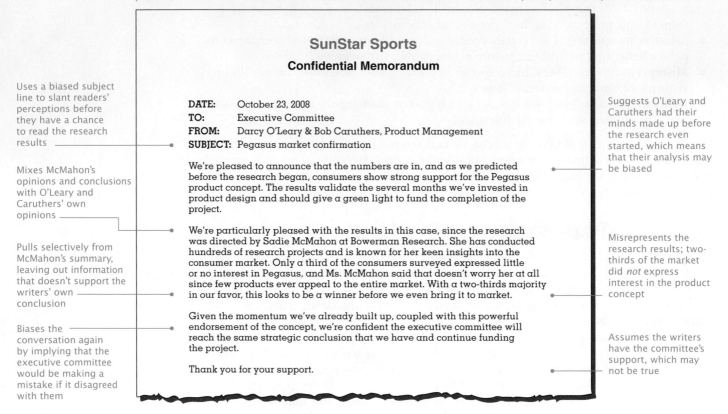

Uses a biased subject line to slant readers' perceptions before they have a chance to read the research results

Mixes McMahon's opinions and conclusions with O'Leary and Caruthers' own opinions

Pulls selectively from McMahon's summary, leaving out information that doesn't support the writers' own conclusion

Biases the conversation again by implying that the executive committee would be making a mistake if it disagreed with them

Suggests O'Leary and Caruthers had their minds made up before the research even started, which means that their analysis may be biased

Misrepresents the research results; two-thirds of the market did *not* express interest in the product concept

Assumes the writers have the committee's support, which may not be true

SunStar Sports

Confidential Memorandum

DATE: October 23, 2008
TO: Executive Committee
FROM: Darcy O'Leary & Bob Caruthers, Product Management
SUBJECT: Pegasus market confirmation

We're pleased to announce that the numbers are in, and as we predicted before the research began, consumers show strong support for the Pegasus product concept. The results validate the several months we've invested in product design and should give a green light to fund the completion of the project.

We're particularly pleased with the results in this case, since the research was directed by Sadie McMahon at Bowerman Research. She has conducted hundreds of research projects and is known for her keen insights into the consumer market. Only a third of the consumers surveyed expressed little or no interest in Pegasus, and Ms. McMahon said that doesn't worry her at all since few products ever appeal to the entire market. With a two-thirds majority in our favor, this looks to be a winner before we even bring it to market.

Given the momentum we've already built up, coupled with this powerful endorsement of the concept, we're confident the executive committee will reach the same strategic conclusion that we have and continue funding the project.

Thank you for your support.

Responsible employers establish clear ethical guidelines for their employees to follow.

elements need to work in harmony. If employees see company executives making unethical decisions and flouting company guidelines, they might conclude that the guidelines are meaningless and emulate their bosses' unethical behavior.

Employers have a responsibility to establish clear guidelines for ethical behavior, including business communication. In a recent global survey by the International Association of Business Communicators, 70 percent of communication professionals said their companies clearly define what is considered ethical and unethical behavior. On a somewhat less positive note, slightly fewer than half said their companies encourage open discussion of ethical issues and dilemmas.[40]

Many companies establish an explicit ethics policy by using a written **code of ethics** to help employees determine what is acceptable. A code is often part of a larger program of employee training and communication channels that allow employees to ask questions and report instances of questionable ethics. For example, United Technologies, a large aerospace and defense company based in Hartford, Connecticut, offers employees, customers, and suppliers a confidential way to report suspected fraud and other ethical concerns. The people who share their concerns through the program then receive a written response that explains how the situation was resolved.[41] To ensure ongoing compliance with their codes of ethics, many companies also conduct **ethics audits** to monitor ethical progress and to point out any weaknesses that need to be addressed.

However, whether or not formal guidelines are in place, every employee has the responsibility to communicate in an ethical manner. In the absence of clear guidelines, ask yourself the following questions about your business communications:[42]

- Have you defined the situation fairly and accurately?
- What is your intention in communicating this message?

FIGURE 1.10 Ethical Communication
This version of the memo shown in Figure 1.9 presents the evidence in a more honest and ethical manner.

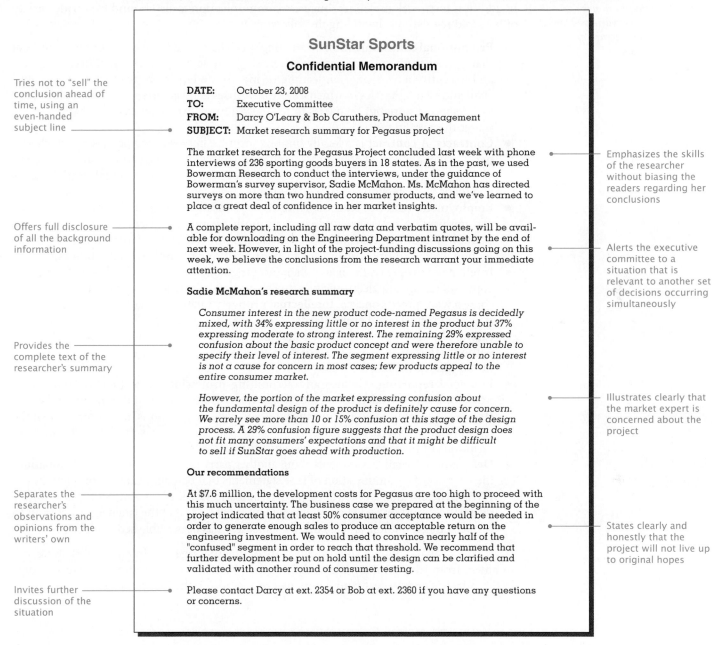

Tries not to "sell" the conclusion ahead of time, using an even-handed subject line

Offers full disclosure of all the background information

Provides the complete text of the researcher's summary

Separates the researcher's observations and opinions from the writers' own

Invites further discussion of the situation

Emphasizes the skills of the researcher without biasing the readers regarding her conclusions

Alerts the executive committee to a situation that is relevant to another set of decisions occurring simultaneously

Illustrates clearly that the market expert is concerned about the project

States clearly and honestly that the project will not live up to original hopes

SunStar Sports

Confidential Memorandum

DATE: October 23, 2008
TO: Executive Committee
FROM: Darcy O'Leary & Bob Caruthers, Product Management
SUBJECT: Market research summary for Pegasus project

The market research for the Pegasus Project concluded last week with phone interviews of 236 sporting goods buyers in 18 states. As in the past, we used Bowerman Research to conduct the interviews, under the guidance of Bowerman's survey supervisor, Sadie McMahon. Ms. McMahon has directed surveys on more than two hundred consumer products, and we've learned to place a great deal of confidence in her market insights.

A complete report, including all raw data and verbatim quotes, will be available for downloading on the Engineering Department intranet by the end of next week. However, in light of the project-funding discussions going on this week, we believe the conclusions from the research warrant your immediate attention.

Sadie McMahon's research summary

Consumer interest in the new product code-named Pegasus is decidedly mixed, with 34% expressing little or no interest in the product but 37% expressing moderate to strong interest. The remaining 29% expressed confusion about the basic product concept and were therefore unable to specify their level of interest. The segment expressing little or no interest is not a cause for concern in most cases; few products appeal to the entire consumer market.

However, the portion of the market expressing confusion about the fundamental design of the product is definitely cause for concern. We rarely see more than 10 or 15% confusion at this stage of the design process. A 29% confusion figure suggests that the product design does not fit many consumers' expectations and that it might be difficult to sell if SunStar goes ahead with production.

Our recommendations

At $7.6 million, the development costs for Pegasus are too high to proceed with this much uncertainty. The business case we prepared at the beginning of the project indicated that at least 50% consumer acceptance would be needed in order to generate enough sales to produce an acceptable return on the engineering investment. We would need to convince nearly half of the "confused" segment in order to reach that threshold. We recommend that further development be put on hold until the design can be clarified and validated with another round of consumer testing.

Please contact Darcy at ext. 2354 or Bob at ext. 2360 if you have any questions or concerns.

- What impact will this message have on the people who receive it, or who might be affected by it?
- Will the message achieve the greatest possible good while doing the least possible harm?
- Will the assumptions you've made change over time? That is, will a decision that seems ethical now seem unethical in the future?
- Are you comfortable with your decision? Would you be embarrassed if it were printed in tomorrow's newspaper or spread across the Internet?

If all else fails, think about a person whom you admire and ask yourself what he or she would think of your decision. If you wouldn't be proud to describe your choice to someone you admire and respect, you might be making a poor ethical choice.

If you can't decide whether a choice is ethical, picture yourself explaining it someone whose opinion you value.

Ensuring Legal Communication

In addition to ethical guidelines, business communication is also bound by a wide variety of laws and regulations, including the following areas:

- **Promotional communication.** Marketing specialists need to be aware of the many laws that govern truth and accuracy in advertising. These laws address such issues as false and deceptive advertising, misleading or inaccurate labels on product packages, and "bait and switch" tactics in which a store advertises a lower-priced product to lure consumers into a store but then tries to sell them a more expensive item.[43] Chapter 10 explores this area in more detail.

- **Contracts.** A **contract** is a legally binding promise between two parties, in which one party makes a specified offer and the other party accepts. Contracts are fundamental to virtually every aspect of business, from product sales to property rental to credit cards and loans to professional service agreements.[44]

- **Employment communication.** A variety of local, state, and federal laws govern communication between employers and both potential and current employees. For example, job descriptions must be written in a way that doesn't intentionally or unintentionally discriminate against women, minorities, or people with disabilities.[45]

- **Intellectual property.** In an age when instant global connectivity makes it effortless to copy and retransmit electronic files, the protection of intellectual property (IP) has become a widespread concern. **Intellectual property** includes patents, copyrighted materials, trade secrets, and even Internet domain names.[46] Bloggers need to be particularly careful about IP protection, given the carefree way that some post the work of others without offering proper credit. For guidelines on this hot topic, get the free *Legal Guide for Bloggers* at **www.eff.org/bloggers/lg**.

- **Financial reporting.** Finance and accounting professionals, particularly those who work for publicly traded companies (those that sell stock to the public), must adhere to stringent reporting laws. For instance, a number of corporations have recently been the target of both government investigations and shareholder lawsuits for misleading descriptions of financial results and revenue forecasts.

- **Defamation.** Negative comments about another party raise the possibility of **defamation**, the intentional communication of false statements that damage character or reputation.[47] (Written defamation is called *libel*; spoken defamation is called *slander*.) Someone suing for defamation must prove (1) that the statement is false, (2) that the language is injurious to the person's reputation, and (3) that the statement has been published.

If you have any doubts about the legality of any message you intend to distribute, ask for advice from your company's legal department. A small dose of caution can prevent huge legal headaches and protect your company's reputation in the marketplace.

COMMUNICATION CHALLENGES AT SIX APART

As president of Six Apart, Mena Trott plays a vital role in keeping communication flowing within the company and between the company and external audiences. To assist her with a growing workload of communication tasks, she has recently hired you as assistant with special responsibilities for communication. Use your knowledge of communication to choose the best response for each of the following situations. Be prepared to explain why your choice is best.

Individual Challenge: One of the reasons for Six Apart's success is its friendly, open style of communication with its customers, even those occasional customers who make unrealistic demands or expect special treatment. Unfortunately, you've learned that some of the customer service representatives have been letting their emotions get in the way when dealing with these difficult people. Several customers have complained about rude treatment. You're sensitive to the situation because you know that customer service can be a difficult job. However, a reputation for hostile customer service could spell doom for the company, so you need to communicate your concerns immediately. Draft the first sentence of an internal blog posting that you will write for the customer service staff to initiate a discussion on this subject.

Team Challenge: Six Apart has developed a corporate culture that reflects both the engaging personalities of Ben and Mena Trott and the informal "vibe" of the blogosphere. However, as the company continues to grow, new employees bring a variety of communication styles and expectations. In particular, the new accounting manager tends to communicate in a formal, distant style that some company old-timers find off-putting and impersonal. Several of these people have expressed concerns that the new manager "doesn't fit in," even though she's doing a great job otherwise. Draft a short e-mail message to Trott advising her on handling this situation.

SUMMARY OF LEARNING OBJECTIVES

1 **Explain why effective communication is important to your success in today's business environment.** Your ability to communicate will influence people's perceptions of you as a business professional. Moreover, because your communication plays a key role in efforts to improve efficiency, quality, responsiveness, and innovation, your communication affects your company's success. As your career advances and you achieve positions of greater responsibility and leadership with an organization, communication will become an increasingly visible and important part of your job.

2 **Describe the five characteristics of effective business communication.** To be effective, business messages must be practical, providing the information that receivers need. Effective messages either leave out personal impressions or support such opinions with objective facts. Effective business communication is also concise—it clarifies and condenses information in a way that helps the receiver see and understand the most important issues. Effective messages are also clear about expectations. They state precise responsibilities to eliminate confusion over who needs to do what next. Finally, effective messages are persuasive, when necessary, convincing others to accept the sender's ideas or recommendations.

3 **Identify seven communication skills that successful employers expect from their employees.** Employers expect employees to have skills such as organizing ideas and information coherently and completely, expressing and presenting ideas and information coherently and persuasively, listening to others effectively, communicating effectively with people from diverse backgrounds and experiences, using communication technologies effectively and efficiently, communicating in a civilized manner that reflects contemporary expectations of business etiquette, and communicating ethically—even when choices aren't crystal clear.

4 **List five ways in which business communication differs from social communication.** Business communication differs from social communication because it is affected by the ongoing globalization of business and the increasing recognition of the value of workforce diversity, the growing importance that many businesses place on information, the pervasiveness of technology throughout both internal and external communication, the growing reliance on teamwork, and the evolution of organizational structures into flatter and more flexible arrangements.

5 **Describe six strategies for communicating more effectively on the job.** To communicate more effectively on the job, use six strategies. First, work to understand the communication process so that you can craft more effective messages. Second, reduce distractions in the work environment, including not sending unnecessary messages. Third, adopt an audience-centered approach, focusing on the needs of your audience and working to ensure successful transmission and reception of your messages. Fourth, fine-tune your business communication skills. Fifth, give and receive feedback that is constructive rather than destructive so that you can focus on improvement rather than criticism. And sixth, be sensitive to business etiquette, thereby reducing the chance of interpersonal blunders that might negatively affect communication.

6 **Explain what must occur for an audience to successfully receive, decode, and respond to messages.** For audience members to successfully receive messages, they must first sense the presence of the message, then select it from other sensory input, then perceive it as a message. To de-code messages successfully, they need to extract the same meaning that the sender encoded into the message. And to respond in a manner that the sender would consider successful, audiences need to remember the message, have the ability to respond to it, and have the motivation to respond.

7 **Explain four strategies for using communication technology successfully.** First, be sure to keep technology in perspective. Make sure that it supports the communication effort rather than overwhelming or disrupting it. Second, learn how to use technological tools productively. Doing so allows you to focus on communicating rather than on the tool being used. Third, try to spend time and money wisely, at a level that reflects the importance of the communication effort. Fourth, by reconnecting with people frequently, you ensure that communication is successful and that technology doesn't come between you and the people you need to reach.

8 **Discuss the importance of ethics in business communication and differentiate between ethical dilemmas and ethical lapses.** Ethical communication is particularly important in business because communication is the public face of a company, which is why communication efforts are intensely scrutinized by company stakeholders. The difference between an ethical dilemma and an ethical lapse is a question of clarity. An ethical dilemma occurs when the choice is unclear because two or more alternatives seem equally right or equally wrong. In contrast, an ethical lapse occurs when a person makes a conscious choice that is clearly unethical.

Test Your Knowledge

1. What role will your communication skills play in your company's success?
2. What three principles will help you minimize missteps in business etiquette?
3. How does formal communication differ from informal communication?
4. In what directions can information travel within an organization's formal hierarchy?
5. What is the grapevine, and why should managers be aware of it?
6. What steps have to occur before an audience member perceives the presence of an incoming message?
7. Why should communicators take an audience-centered approach to communication?
8. How is communication affected by information overload?
9. How can you make sure your feedback is constructive?
10. Why is ethical communication important?

Apply Your Knowledge

1. Why do you think good communication in an organization improves employee attitudes and performance? Explain briefly.
2. Is it possible for companies to be too dependent on communication technology? Explain briefly.
3. How can a lack of shared experience between sender and receiver result in communication failures?
4. As a manager, how can you impress on your employees the importance of strong business ethics when dealing with colleagues, customers, and the general public?
5. **Ethical Choices** Because of your excellent communication skills, your boss always asks you to write his reports for him. When you overhear the CEO complimenting him on his logical organization and clear writing style, he responds as if he'd written all those reports himself. What kind of ethical choice does this response represent? What can you do in this situation? Briefly explain your solution and your reasoning.

Practice Your Knowledge

Message for Analysis

Read the following blog posting, then (1) analyze whether the message is effective or ineffective communication (be sure to explain why), and (2) revise the message so that it follows this chapter's guidelines.

> It has come to my attention that many of you are lying on your time cards. If you come in late, you should not put 8:00 on your card. If you take a long lunch, you should not put 1:00 on your time card. I will not stand for this type of cheating. I simply have no choice but to institute an employee monitoring system. Beginning next Monday, video cameras will be installed at all entrances to the building, and your entry and exit times will be logged each time you use electronic key cards to enter or leave.
>
> Anyone who is late for work or late coming back from lunch more than three times will have to answer to me. I don't care if you had to take a nap or if you girls had to shop. This is a place of business, and we do not want to be taken advantage of by slackers who are cheaters to boot.
>
> It is too bad that a few bad apples always have to spoil things for everyone.

Exercises

For active links to all websites discussed in this chapter, visit this text's website at **www.prenhall.com/bovee**. Locate your book and click on its Companion Website link. Then select Chapter 1, and click on "Featured Websites." Locate the name of the page or the URL related to the material in the text. Please note that links to sites that become inactive after publication of the book will be removed from the Featured Websites section.

1.1   **Effective Business Communication: Understanding the Difference** Bring to class a sales letter that you received in the mail or via e-mail. Comment on how well the communication
  a. provides practical information
  b. gives facts rather than impressions
  c. clarifies and condenses information
  d. states precise responsibilities
  e. persuades others and offers recommendations

1.2   **Internal Communication: Planning the Flow** For the following tasks, identify the necessary direction of communication (downward, upward, horizontal), suggest an appropriate type or types of communication (casual conversation, formal interview, meeting, workshop, web conference, instant messaging, memo, blog, bulletin board notice, and so on), and briefly explain your suggestions.
  a. As human resources manager, you want to announce details about this year's company picnic.
  b. As director of internal communication, you want to convince top management of the need for an internal executive blog.

  c. As production manager, you want to make sure that both the sales manager and the finance manager receive your scheduling estimates.
  d. As marketing manager, you want to help employees throughout the company understand the marketplace and customer needs.

1.3   **Communication Networks: Formal or Informal?** An old college friend phoned you out of the blue to say, "Truth is, I had to call you. You'd better keep this under your hat, but when I heard my company was buying you guys out, I was dumbfounded. I had no idea that a company as large as yours could sink so fast. Your group must be in pretty bad shape over there!" Your stomach suddenly turned queasy, and you felt a chill go up your spine. You'd heard nothing about any buyout, and before you could even get your college friend off the phone, you were wondering what you should do. Of the following, choose one course of action and briefly explain your choice.
  a. Contact your CEO directly and relate what you've heard.
  b. Ask co-workers whether they've heard anything about a buyout.
  c. Discuss the phone call confidentially with your immediate supervisor.
  d. Keep quiet about the whole thing (there's nothing you can do about the situation anyway).

1.4   **Ethical Choices** In less than a page, explain why you think each of the following is or is not ethical.
  a. Keeping quiet about a possible environmental hazard you've just discovered in your company's processing plant
  b. Overselling the benefits of instant messaging to your company's management; they never seem to understand the benefits of technology, so you believe it's the only way to convince them to make the right choice
  c. Telling an associate and close friend that she'd better pay more attention to her work responsibilities or management will fire her
  d. Recommending the purchase of excess equipment to use up your allocated funds before the end of the fiscal year so that your budget won't be cut next year

1.5   **The Changing Workplace: Personal Expression at Work** Blogging has become a popular way for employees to communicate with customers and other parties outside the company. In some cases, employee blogs have been quite beneficial for both companies and their customers by providing helpful information and "putting a human face" on other formal and imposing corporations. However, in some other cases, employees have been fired for posting information that their employers said was inappropriate. One particular area of concern is criticism of the company or individual managers. Should employees be allowed to criticize their employers in a public forum such as a blog? In a brief e-mail message, argue for or against company policies that prohibit any critical information in employee blogs.

1.6 **Internet** Cisco is a leading manufacturer of equipment for the Internet and corporate networks and has developed a code of ethics that it expects employees to abide by. Visit the company's website at www.cisco.com and find the *Code of Conduct.* In a brief paragraph, describe three specific examples of things you could do that would violate these provisions; then list at least three opportunities that Cisco provides its employees to report ethics violations or ask questions regarding ethical dilemmas.

1.7 **Communication Etiquette** Potential customers frequently visit your production facility before making purchase decisions. You and the people who report to you in the sales department have received extensive training in etiquette issues because you deal with high-profile clients so frequently. However, the rest of the workforce has not received such training, and you worry that someone might inadvertently say or do something that would offend one of these potential customers. In a two-paragraph e-mail, explain to the general manager why you think anyone who might come in contact with customers should receive basic etiquette training.

1.8 **Ethical Choices** Knowing that you have numerous friends throughout the company, your boss relies on you for feedback concerning employee morale and other issues affecting the staff. She recently approached you and asked you to start reporting any behavior that might violate company polices, from taking office supplies home to making personal long-distance calls. List the issues you'd like to discuss with her before you respond to her request.

1.9 **Formal Communication: Self-Introduction** Write an e-mail message or prepare an oral presentation introducing yourself to your instructor and your class. Include such things as your background, interests, achievements, and goals. If you write an e-mail message, keep it under one normal screen in length, and use Figure 1.4 as a model for the format. If you prepare an oral presentation, plan to speak for no more than two minutes.

1.10 **Teamwork** Your boss has asked your work group to research and report on corporate child-care facilities. Of course, you'll want to know who (besides your boss) will be reading your report. Working with two team members, list four or five other things you'll want to know about the situation and about your audience before starting your research. Briefly explain why each of the items on your list is important.

1.11 **Communication Process: Analyzing Miscommunication** Use the eight phases of the communication process to analyze a miscommunication you've recently had with a co-worker, supervisor, classmate, teacher, friend, or family member. What idea were you trying to share? How did you encode and transmit it? Did the receiver get the message? Did the receiver correctly decode the message? How do you know? Based on your analysis, identify and explain the barriers that prevented your successful communication in this instance.

1.12 **Ethical Choices** You've been given the critical assignment of selecting the site for your company's new plant. After months of negotiations with landowners, numerous cost calculations, and investments in ecological, social, and community impact studies, you are about to recommend building the new plant on the Lansing River site. Now, just 15 minutes before your big presentation to top management, you discover a possible mistake in your calculations: Site-purchase costs appear to be $500,000 more than you calculated, nearly 10 percent over budget. You don't have time to recheck all your figures, so you're tempted to just go ahead with your recommendation and ignore any discrepancies. You're worried that management won't approve this purchase if you can't present a clean, unqualified solution. You also know that many projects run over their original estimates, so you can probably work the extra cost into the budget later. On your way to the meeting room, you make your final decision. In a few paragraphs, explain the decision you made.

1.13 **Communication Etiquette** In group meetings, some of your colleagues have a habit of interrupting and arguing with the speaker, taking credit for ideas that aren't theirs, and shooting down ideas they don't agree with. You're the newest person in the group and not sure if this is accepted behavior in this company, but it concerns you both personally and professionally. Should you go with the flow and adopt their behavior or stick with your own communication style, even though you might get lost in the noise? In two paragraphs, explain the pros and cons of both approaches.

Expand Your Knowledge
Exploring the Best of the Web

Check Out These Resources at the Business Writer's Free Library
www.mapnp.org/library/commskls/cmm_writ.htm
The Business Writer's Free Library is a terrific resource for business communication material. Categories of information include basic composition skills, basic writing skills, correspondence, reference material, and general resources and advice. Log on and read about the most common errors in English, become a word detective, ask Miss Grammar, review samples of common forms of correspondence, fine-tune your interpersonal skills, join a newsgroup, and more. Follow the links and improve your effectiveness as a business communicator.

1. What are some strategies for communicating with an uncooperative audience?
2. What is the value of diversity in the workplace?
3. Why is bad etiquette bad for business?

Surfing Your Way to Career Success

Bovée and Thill's Business Communication Resources offers links to hundreds of online resources that can help you with this course, your other college courses, and your career. Visit www.buscommresources.com, then click on "Business Communication Web Directory." The "Communication" section connects you to a variety of websites and articles on basic communication skills, communication challenges on the job, and intriguing topics such as communication ethics and disinformation. Identify three websites from this section that could be useful in your business career. For each site, write a two-sentence summary of what the site offers and how it could help you launch and build your career.

Learn Interactively

Interactive Study Guide

Visit **www.prenhall.com/bovee**, then locate your book and click on its "Companion Website" link. Select Chapter 1 to take advantage of the interactive "Chapter Quiz" to test your knowledge of chapter concepts. Receive instant feedback on whether you need additional studying. Also, visit the "Study Hall," where you'll find an abundance of valuable resources that will help you succeed in this course.

Peak Performance Grammar and Mechanics

If your instructor has required the use of "Peak Performance Grammar and Mechanics," either in your online course or on CD, you can improve your skill with nouns and pronouns by using the "Peak Performance Grammar and Mechanics" module. (Mechanics are basic style issues such as capitalization, spelling, and numbers.) Click on "Grammar Basics," and then click "Nouns and Pronouns." Take the Pretest to determine whether you have any weak areas. Then review those areas in the Refresher Course. Take the Follow-Up Test to check your grasp of nouns and pronouns. For an extra challenge or advanced practice, take the Advanced Test. Finally, for additional reinforcement in nouns, visit the Companion Website, click on any chapter, then click on "Improve Your Grammar, Mechanics, and Usage."

CHAPTER 2

Communicating in Teams and Mastering Listening and Nonverbal Communication Skills

LEARNING OBJECTIVES

After studying this chapter, you will be able to

1 Highlight the advantages and disadvantages of working in teams

2 Identify eight guidelines for successful collaborative writing

3 Explain how wiki technology can help teams collaborate

4 Explain how group dynamics can affect team effectiveness

5 Discuss the role of etiquette in team settings, both in the workplace and in social settings

6 Describe how meeting technologies can help participants communicate more successfully

7 Describe the listening process and explain how good listeners overcome barriers at each stage of the process

8 Clarify the importance of nonverbal communication and briefly describe six categories of nonverbal expression

COMMUNICATION CLOSE-UP AT THE CONTAINER STORE

www.containerstore.com

Let's face it: frontline jobs in retail don't have the greatest reputation. For employees, these positions often combine low pay with high stress, leading to rapid burnout and frequent turnover. From a customer's perspective, retail employees seem to fall into two categories: unmotivated rookies or aggressive sellers who seem more intent on getting their commissions than helping customers.

When they founded The Container Store, Garrett Boone and Kip Tindell set out to shatter these expectations by creating a pleasant, welcome working and shopping experience. As millions of frustrated consumers know all too well, though, delivering great customer service isn't easy. The Container Store manages to do so through respect for employees, open communication, and a structure that promotes teamwork over individual competition.

When selecting new employees, for instance, the company engages in a comprehensive interviewing and

Daily "huddles" at The Container Store, informal meetings among team members, reinforce company values and let people exchange important information.

selection process to find the perfect person for each position, driven by the belief that one great employee equals three good ones. At The Container Store, a great employee is self-motivated, team-oriented, and passionate about customer service.

That emphasis on teamwork is reinforced twice a day, before opening and after closing, through a meeting called "the huddle." Similar to a huddle in football, it helps to give everyone a common purpose: set goals, share information, boost morale, and bond as a team. Team-building efforts are further encouraged by participation in community outreach activities, such as school supply drives, and through purely recreational activities dreamed up by the employees on the Fun Committee.

Through a commitment to teamwork and effective communication, The Container Store paves the way for its employees to deliver great customer service. Tindell believes that full, open communication with employees takes courage but says, "The only way that people feel really, really a part of something is if they know everything."[1]

IMPROVING YOUR PERFORMANCE IN TEAMS

You may never work in a retail operation such as The Container Store (profiled in the chapter-opening Communication Close-Up), but chances are quite good that your career will involve working in teams and other group situations that will test your communication skills. A **team** is a unit of two or more people who share a mission and the responsibility for working to achieve a common goal.[2] Companies can create *formal teams* that become part of the organization's structure, or they can establish *informal teams* that aren't part of the formal organization but are created to solve a problem, work on a specific activity, or encourage employee participation.

Team members have a shared mission and are collectively responsible for their work.

Problem-solving teams and **task forces** are informal teams that assemble to resolve specific issues and then disband once their goal has been accomplished. Such teams are often *cross-functional*, pulling together people from a variety of departments with different areas of expertise and responsibility. The resulting diversity of opinions and interests can lead to tensions that highlight the need for effective communication. For instance, consider a cross-functional team charged with making a product more competitive in the marketplace. A representative from the sales department might complain that the product's price is too high because manufacturing hasn't done enough to lower production costs. Someone from manufacturing might counter that costs are already as low as possible but perhaps the sales department doesn't know how to sell the product effectively. Balancing these competing interests and opinions without letting them boil over into personal animosity requires skill at listening, speaking, and writing.

Two popular types of informal teams are problem-solving teams and task forces.

Committees are formal teams that usually have a long life span and can become a permanent part of the organizational structure. Committees typically deal with regularly recurring tasks, such as an executive committee that meets monthly to plan strategy and review results.

Whatever the purpose and function of the team, you and your fellow team members must be able to communicate effectively with each other and with people outside your team. As Chapter 1 points out, this ability often requires taking on additional responsibility for communication: sharing information with team members, listening carefully to their inputs, and crafting messages that reflect the team's collective ideas and opinions.

Effective communication is essential to every aspect of team performance.

Advantages and Disadvantages of Teams

1 LEARNING OBJECTIVE

Highlight the advantages and disadvantages of working in teams

When teams are successful, they improve productivity, creativity, employee involvement, and even job security.[3] Teams are frequently at the core of **participative management**, the effort to involve employees in the company's decision making. Getting employees involved in the daily operation of their own stores is one of the central principles of participative management at The Container Store, as managers and employees share vital business information every day.

Teams can play a vital role in helping an organization reach its goals, but they are not appropriate for every situation—and even when they are appropriate, companies need to weigh both the advantages and disadvantages of a team-based approach. A successful team can provide a number of advantages:[4]

- **Increased information and knowledge.** By pooling the resources of several individuals, teams have access to more information in the decision-making process.
- **Increased diversity of views.** Team members can bring a variety of perspectives to the decision-making process. Keep in mind, however, that unless these diverse viewpoints are guided by a shared goal, the multiple perspectives can actually hamper a team's efforts.[5]
- **Increased acceptance of a solution.** Those who participate in making a decision are more likely to support the decision enthusiastically and encourage others to accept it.
- **Higher performance levels.** Working in teams can unleash new amounts of creativity and energy in workers who share a sense of purpose and mutual accountability. Effective teams can be better than top-performing individuals at solving complex problems.[6] Furthermore, teams fill the individual worker's need to belong to a group, reduce employee boredom, increase feelings of dignity and self-worth, and reduce stress and tension between workers.

Companies in fast-moving industries rely on teams to work closely and quickly to solve problems and capitalize on market opportunities.

Although teamwork has many advantages, it also has a number of potential disadvantages. At their worst, teams are unproductive and frustrating and they waste everyone's time. Teams need to be aware of and work to counter the following disadvantages:

- **Groupthink.** Like all social structures, business teams can generate tremendous pressures to conform with accepted norms of behavior. **Groupthink** occurs when these peer pressures cause individual team members to withhold contrary or unpopular opinions. The result can be decisions that are worse than ones the team members might have made individually.
- **Hidden agendas.** Some team members may have a **hidden agenda**—private, counterproductive motives, such as a desire to take control of the group or to undermine someone else on the team.
- **Free riders.** Some team members may be **free riders**—those who don't contribute their fair share to the group's activities. Perhaps these members aren't being held individually accountable for their work. Or perhaps they don't believe they'll receive adequate recognition for their individual efforts.
- **Cost.** Still another drawback to teamwork is the high cost of coordinating group activities. Aligning schedules, arranging meetings, and coordinating individual parts of a project can eat up a lot of time and money.

Teams need to avoid the negative impact of groupthink, hidden agendas, free riders, and excessive costs.

Characteristics of Effective Teams

To be an effective collaborator in a team setting, you and your colleagues should recognize that each individual brings valuable assets, knowledge, and skills to the team. Strong collaborators are willing to exchange information, examine issues, and work through conflicts that arise. They trust each other, working toward the greater good of the team and organization rather than focusing on personal agendas.[7]

The most effective teams have a clear objective and a shared sense of purpose, communicate openly and honestly, reach decisions by consensus, think creatively, and know how to resolve conflict.[8] Learning these team skills takes time and practice, so U.S. companies now teach teamwork more frequently than any other aspect of business.[9]

In contrast, unsuccessful teamwork can waste time and money, generate lower-quality work, and frustrate both managers and employees. A lack of trust is cited as the most common reason for the failure of teams. This lack of trust can result from team members who are suspicious of one another's motives or ability to contribute.[10] Another common reason for failure is poor communication, particularly when teams operate across cultures, countries, and time zones.[11] Poor communication can also result from basic differences in conversational styles. Some people expect conversation to follow an orderly pattern in which team members wait their turns to speak. Others view conversation as more spontaneous and are comfortable with an overlapping, interactive style.[12]

Team Communication

Collaborating on reports, websites, presentations, and other communication projects gives teams the opportunity to capitalize on each person's unique presentation and communication skills. In other words, the collective energy and expertise of the team can be used to create something that transcends what each individual could do otherwise.[13] However, collaborating on team messages requires special effort; the following section offers a number of guidelines to help you write well as a team.

Collaborative Writing Guidelines

In any collaborative effort, remember that team members coming from different backgrounds may have different work habits or concerns: A technical expert may focus on accuracy and scientific standards, whereas an editor may be more concerned about organization and coherence, and a manager may focus on schedules, cost, and corporate goals. In addition, team members will differ in writing styles and personality traits—two factors that can complicate the creative nature of communication.

To collaborate effectively, everyone involved must be flexible and open to other opinions, focusing on team objectives rather than on individual priorities.[14] Successful writers know that most ideas can be expressed in many ways, so they avoid the "my way is best" attitude. The following guidelines will help you collaborate more successfully:[15]

- **Select collaborators carefully.** Choose a combination of people who have the experience, information, and talent needed for each project.
- **Agree on project goals before you start.** Starting without a clear idea of what you hope to accomplish inevitably leads to frustration and wasted time.
- **Give your team time to bond before diving in.** If people haven't had the opportunity to work together before, make sure they can get to know each other before being asked to collaborate.
- **Clarify individual responsibilities.** Because members will be depending on each other, make sure individual responsibilities are clear, including who is supposed to do what and by when.
- **Establish clear processes.** Make sure everyone knows how the work will be done, including checkpoints and decisions to be made along the way.
- **Avoid writing as a group.** The actual composition is the only part of developing team messages that does not usually benefit from group participation. Group writing is often a slow, painful process that delivers bland results. In most cases, the best approach is to plan, research, and outline together but assign the actual writing to one person or divide larger projects among multiple writers. If you divide the writing, try to have one person do a final revision pass to ensure a consistent style.
- **Make sure tools and techniques are ready and compatible across the team.** Even minor details such as different versions of software can delay projects. If you plan to use technology for sharing or presenting materials, test the system before work begins. (See the following section for more on collaboration technologies.)
- **Check to see how things are going along the way.** Don't assume everything is working just because you don't hear anything negative.

Collaborative Writing Technologies

A variety of collaboration tools now exist to help writing teams, including group review and commenting features in word processors, multiauthor blogs, and **content management**

---

2 LEARNING OBJECTIVE

Identify eight guidelines for successful collaborative writing

Successful collaboration requires a number of steps, from selecting the right partners and agreeing on project goals to establishing clear processes and avoiding writing as a group.

Collaboration tools include multiauthor blogs, content management systems, and wikis.

systems that organize and control the content for websites. Each of these tools addresses specific needs, but none offers quite the level of direct collaboration as the wiki. A **wiki**, from the Hawaiian word for *quick*, is a website that allows anyone with access to add new material and edit existing material (see Figure 2.1). Public wikis allow anyone to edit pages; private wikis are accessible only by permission. For instance, Yahoo! uses private wikis to facilitate communication among hundreds of team members around the world involved in creating and documenting new services.[16]

Key wiki benefits include simple operation—writers don't need to know any of the techniques normally required to create web content—and the freedom to post new or revised material without prior approval. This approach is quite different from the content management system, in which both the organization of the website and the *workflow* (the rules for creating, editing, reviewing, and approving content) are tightly controlled.[17] But with a wiki, if you see a way to improve a particular page or want to add a new page, you simply edit or write using your web browser and it's done. A content management system is a great way to maintain consistent presentation on a company's primary public website, whereas wikis allow teams to collaborate with speed and flexibility.

Enterprise wiki systems extend the wiki concept with additional features for business use that ensure information quality and confidentiality without losing the speed and

3 LEARNING OBJECTIVE

Explain how wiki technology can help teams collaborate

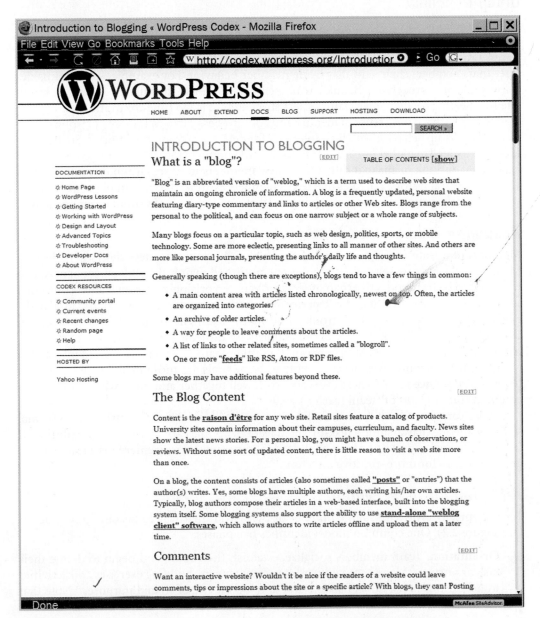

FIGURE 2.1 Using a Wiki for Collaborative Communication
The "[EDIT]" links on this webpage are telltale signs of a wiki—in this case, the online user's manual for the WordPress blogging system. Anyone who wants to contribute can expand and improve the instructions and advice that benefit the entire community of WordPress users.

flexibility of a wiki. For instance, *access control* lets a team leader identify who is allowed to read and modify the wiki. *Change monitoring* alerts team members when significant changes or additions are made. And *rollback* allows the team to "travel back in time" to see all previous versions of pages.[18]

To use a wiki productively, keep these points in mind:[19]

- Contributors need to let go of traditional expectations of authorship, including individual recognition, because they can be edited by anyone with access to the wiki.
- Team members sometimes need to be encouraged to edit and improve each other's work; doing so provides one of the key benefits of the wiki.
- The focus of wikis is on text content; formatting and design options are usually quite limited.
- Many wikis provide both editing and commenting capabilities, and participants should use the appropriate tool for each. For instance, if you want to comment on a page, use the commenting feature rather than using editing tools to insert comments into the text.
- New users should take advantage of the *sandbox,* if available; this is a "safe," nonpublished section of the wiki where team members can practice editing and writing.

Group Dynamics

4 LEARNING OBJECTIVE

Explain how group dynamics can affect team effectiveness

The interactions and processes that take place among the members of a team are called **group dynamics**. Productive teams tend to develop rules of interaction that are conducive to business. Often unstated, these rules become group **norms**—informal standards of conduct that members share and that guide member behavior. For example, some teams develop a casual approach to schedules, with members routinely showing up 10 or 15 minutes late for meetings, while other teams expect strict adherence to time commitments.

Teams with a strong sense of identity and cohesiveness can develop overly strong expectations for group behavior with little tolerance for deviations from those norms. Such strong identity can lead to higher levels of commitment and performance. Unfortunately, it can also lead to groupthink or make it difficult for new members to fit in. Group dynamics are affected by several factors: the roles that team members assume, the current phase of team development, the team's success in resolving conflict, and its success in overcoming resistance.

Assuming Team Roles

Each member of a group plays a role that affects the outcome of the group's activities.

Members of a team can play various roles, which fall into three categories (see Table 2.1). Members who assume **self-oriented roles** are motivated mainly to fulfill personal needs, so they tend to be less productive than other members. Surprisingly, "dream teams" composed of multiple superstars often don't perform as well as one might expect because high-performing individuals can have trouble putting the team's needs ahead of their own.[20] In addition, highly skilled and experienced people with difficult personalities might not contribute as they could for the simple reason that other team members may avoid interacting with them.[21] Far more likely to contribute to team goals are those members who assume **team-maintenance roles** to help everyone work well together and those who assume **task-oriented roles** to help the team reach its goals.[22]

Roles can also change over time. For instance, in a self-directed team with no formal leader, someone may assume a task-oriented leadership role early in the team's evolution. If this person doesn't prove to be a capable leader, someone else may emerge as a leader as the group searches for more-effective direction.[23]

Allowing for Team Evolution

Teams typically evolve through five phases: orientation, conflict, brainstorming, emergence, and reinforcement.

Teams typically evolve through a number of phases on their way to becoming productive (see Figure 2.2). One common model identifies five phases:[24]

1. **Orientation.** Team members socialize, establish their roles, and begin to define their task or purpose. Many companies use a variety of team-building exercises and activities to help teams break down barriers and develop a sense of shared purpose.[25] Note that

TABLE 2.1 Team Roles People Play

DYSFUNCTIONAL		FUNCTIONAL
SELF-ORIENTED ROLES	**TEAM-MAINTENANCE ROLES**	**TASK-FACILITATING ROLES**
Controlling: Dominating others by exhibiting superiority or authority	**Encouraging:** Drawing out other members by showing verbal and nonverbal support, praise, or agreement	**Initiating:** Getting the team started on a line of inquiry
Withdrawing: Retiring from the team either by becoming silent or by refusing to deal with a particular aspect of the team's work	**Harmonizing:** Reconciling differences among team members through mediation or by using humor to relieve tension	**Information giving or seeking:** Offering (or seeking) information relevant to questions facing the team
Attention seeking: Calling attention to oneself and demanding recognition from others	**Compromising:** Offering to yield on a point in the interest of reaching a mutually acceptable decision	**Coordinating:** Showing relationships among ideas, clarifying issues, summarizing what the team has done
Diverting: Focusing the team's discussion on topics of interest to the individual rather than on those relevant to the task		**Procedure setting:** Suggesting decision-making procedures that will move the team toward a goal

team building can be a particular challenge with geographically dispersed *virtual teams* (see page 48), because the members may never meet in person. Agreeing to a "team operating agreement" that sets expectations for online meetings, communication processes, and decision making can help teams overcome the disadvantages of distance.[26]

2. **Conflict.** Team members begin to discuss their positions and become more assertive in establishing their roles. Disagreements and uncertainties are natural in this phase.

3. **Brainstorming.** Team members air all the options and discuss the pros and cons fully. At the end of this phase, members begin to settle on a single solution to the problem. Note that while group brainstorming remains a highly popular activity in today's companies, it may not always be the most productive way to generate new ideas. Some research indicates that having people brainstorm individually then bring their ideas to a group meeting is more successful.[27]

4. **Emergence.** Consensus is reached when the team finds a solution that is acceptable enough for all members to support (even if they have reservations).

5. **Reinforcement.** The team clarifies and summarizes the agreed-upon solution. Members receive their assignments for carrying out the group's decision, and they make arrangements for following up on those assignments.

You may also hear the process defined as *forming, storming, norming, performing,* and *adjourning,* the phases identified by researcher Bruce Tuckman when he proposed one of the earliest models of group development.[28] View these stages as a general framework for team development. Some teams may move forward and backward through several stages before they become productive, and other teams may be productive right away even while some or all members are in a state of conflict.[29]

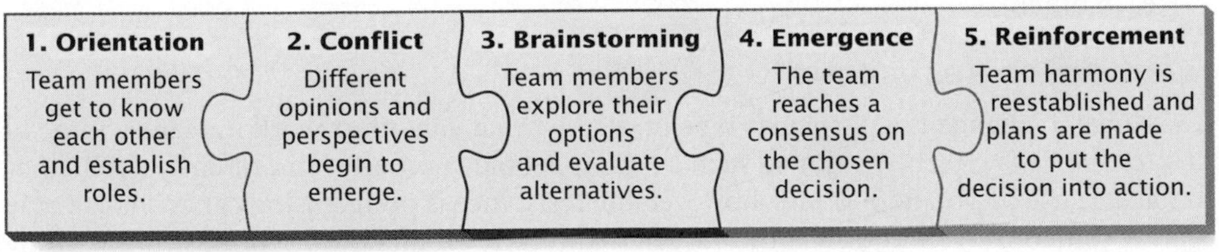

1. Orientation	2. Conflict	3. Brainstorming	4. Emergence	5. Reinforcement
Team members get to know each other and establish roles.	Different opinions and perspectives begin to emerge.	Team members explore their options and evaluate alternatives.	The team reaches a consensus on the chosen decision.	Team harmony is reestablished and plans are made to put the decision into action.

FIGURE 2.2 Phases of Group Development
Groups generally progress through several stages on their way to becoming productive and reaching their objectives.

Resolving Conflict

Conflict is a natural part of any team experience, but conflict isn't necessarily bad. When handled poorly, conflict can lead to complete failure of a group's efforts. However, the right approach to conflict can push a team to better performance.

Conflict can arise for any number of reasons. Team members may believe that they need to compete for money, information, or other resources. Or members may disagree about who is responsible for specific tasks (usually the result of poorly defined responsibilities and job boundaries). Various members can also bring ideas that are equally good but incompatible. Poor communication can lead to misunderstanding, and intentionally withholding information can undermine trust. Basic differences in values, attitudes, and personalities may lead to arguments. Power struggles may result when one member questions the authority of another or when people with limited authority attempt to increase their power or exert more influence. Conflict can also arise because individuals or teams are pursuing different goals.[30]

Conflict in teams can be either constructive or destructive.

Conflict can be either constructive or destructive. Conflict is constructive if it forces important issues into the open, increases the involvement of team members, and generates creative ideas for the solution to a problem. Teamwork isn't necessarily about happiness and harmony—even teams that have some interpersonal friction can excel with effective leadership and team players committed to strong results. As teamwork experts Andy Boynton and Bill Fischer put it, "Virtuoso teams are not about getting polite results."[31]

In contrast, conflict is destructive if it diverts energy from more important issues, destroys the morale of teams or individual team members, or polarizes or divides the team.[32] Destructive conflict can lead to win-lose or lose-lose outcomes, in which one or both sides lose, to the detriment of the entire team. If you approach conflict with the idea that both sides can satisfy their goals to at least some extent (*win-win strategy*), you can minimize losses for everyone. For the win-win strategy to work, everybody must believe that (1) it's possible to find a solution that both parties can accept, (2) cooperation is better for the organization than competition, (3) the other party can be trusted, and (4) greater power or status doesn't entitle one party to impose a solution.

To craft a win-win solution, start by considering the other party's needs. Find out what the other party considers acceptable. Search for mutually satisfactory solutions or compromises, the results of which are better for the team overall.[33] In many cases, the resolution process is chiefly an exchange of opinions and information that gradually leads to a mutually acceptable solution.[34]

Conflict is an inevitable part of working in teams, but effective teams know how to keep destructive conflict from distracting the team from its objectives.

Here are seven measures that can help team members successfully resolve conflict:

- **Proaction.** Deal with minor conflict before it becomes major conflict.
- **Communication.** Get those directly involved in the conflict to participate in resolving it.
- **Openness.** Get feelings out in the open before dealing with the main issues.
- **Research.** Seek factual reasons for the problem before seeking solutions.
- **Flexibility.** Don't let anyone lock into a position before considering other solutions.
- **Fair play.** Don't let anyone avoid a fair solution by hiding behind the rules.
- **Alliance.** Get opponents to fight together against an "outside force" instead of against each other.

Overcoming Resistance

When you encounter resistance or hostility, try to maintain your composure and address the other person's emotional needs.

Resistance to change is a particular type of conflict that can affect work in teams. Some of this resistance is clearly irrational, such as when people resist any kind of change, whether it makes sense or not. Sometimes, however, the resistance is perfectly logical. A change may require someone to relinquish authority or give up comfortable ways of doing things. In any event, you can help overcome resistance with calm, reasonable communication:

- **Express understanding.** You might say, "I can understand that this change might be difficult, and if I were in your position, I might be reluctant myself." Help the other person relax and talk about his or her anxiety so that you have a chance to offer reassurance.[35]

- **Bring resistance out into the open.** When people are noncommittal and silent, they may be tuning you out without even knowing why. Continuing with your argument is futile. Deal directly with the resistance, without accusing. You might say, "You seem cool to this idea. Have I made some faulty assumptions?" Such questions force people to face and define their resistance.[36]

- **Evaluate others' objections fairly.** Don't simply repeat yourself. Focus on what the other person is expressing, both the words and the feelings. Get the person to open up so that you can understand the basis for the resistance. Others' objections may raise legitimate points that you'll need to discuss, or they may reveal problems that you'll need to minimize.[37]

- **Hold your arguments until the other person is ready for them.** Getting your point across depends as much on the other person's frame of mind as it does on your arguments. You can't assume that a strong argument will speak for itself. By becoming more audience-centered, you will learn to address the other person's emotional needs first.

Etiquette in Team Settings

Etiquette is particularly important in team settings because the ability to get along with teammates is vital to everyone's success. Nobody wants to spend weeks or months working with someone who is rude to colleagues or an embarrassment to the company. Here are some key etiquette points to remember when you're in the workplace and out in public. None of the following material is unique to team settings, of course; it's good advice for all your business efforts.

In the Workplace

Knowing how to behave and how to interact with people in business will help you appear polished, professional, and confident.[38] Understanding business etiquette also helps you put

5 LEARNING OBJECTIVE

Discuss the role of etiquette in team settings, both in the workplace and in social settings

---

Ethics Detective

How Did "We" Turn into "I"?

Your entire team has been looking forward to this meeting for weeks. When the company president assembled this team to find creative solutions to the company's cash flow problems, few people thought the team would succeed. However, through plenty of hard work, you and your colleagues found new sources of investment capital that should save the company. Now it's time to present your accomplishments to the board of directors. Because exposure in front of the board can be a major career boost, the team planned to present the results together, giving each person a few minutes in the limelight.

However, Jackson Mueller, the chief financial officer and the leader of your team, had a surprise for you this morning. He said he'd received word at the last minute that the board wants a short, concise presentation, and he said the only way to do so was with a single presenter. No one was happy about the change, but Jackson was the highest-ranking employee on the team and the only one with experience presenting to the board.

Disappointment turned to dismay as you and your teammates watched from the back of the conference room. Jackson deftly compressed your 60-minute presentation down to 20 minutes, and the board showered him with praise. However, he never introduced anyone else on the team, so your moment in the sun passed without recognition.

ANALYSIS

Did Jackson behave unethically by not introducing you and your colleagues to the board? Explain your answer. Later on, you complain to a colleague that by stressing "my team" so often, Jackson actually made the presentation all about him, not the team. But one of your colleagues argues that the team's assignment was to solve the problem, not score career points with the board, so that goal shouldn't have been such a top priority. Explain why you agree or disagree.

Personal appearance can have considerable impact on your success in business.

others at ease so that they are comfortable enough to do business with you.[39] Both of these factors will be major contributors to your career success.

For instance, rightly or wrongly, your personal appearance often has considerable impact on your career success. Pay attention to the style of dress where you work and adjust your style to match. Expectations for specific jobs, companies, and industries can vary widely. The financial industries tend to be more formal than high technology, for instance, and sales and executive positions usually come with more formal expectations than staff positions in engineering or manufacturing. Observe others carefully, and don't be afraid to ask for advice if you're not sure. If you're not sure, dress moderately and simply—earn a reputation for what you can do, not for what you can wear. Table 2.2 offers some general guidelines on assembling a business wardrobe that's both cost-effective and flexible.

In addition to your clothing, grooming affects the impression you give others in the workplace. Pay close attention to cleanliness and avoid using products with powerful scents, such as perfumed soaps, colognes, shampoos, and after-shave lotions (many people are bothered by these products, and some are allergic to them). Shampoo frequently, keep hands and nails neatly manicured, use mouthwash and deodorant, and make regular trips to a hair stylist.[40] Some companies have specific policies regarding hairstyles, which you may be expected to follow.[41]

Something as simple as your smile also affects the way people do business with you. When you smile, do so genuinely. A fake smile is obvious because the timing is frequently off and the expression fails to involve all the facial muscles that a genuine smile would.[42] Repeated false smiling may earn you the reputation of being a phony. However, certain occasions require smiling, such as when you're introduced to someone, when you give or receive a compliment, and when you applaud someone's efforts.[43]

Plan phone calls as carefully as you plan meetings.

Phone skills have a definite impact on your success. Phone calls lack the visual richness of face-to-face conversations, so you have to rely on your attitude and tone of voice to convey confidence and professionalism. Schedule calls for times that are convenient for the other party and be ready with relevant questions or information. Table 2.3 summarizes helpful tips for placing and receiving phone calls in a confident, professional manner.

TABLE 2.2 Assembling a Business Wardrobe

1 SMOOTH AND FINISHED (START WITH THIS)	2 ELEGANT AND REFINED (TO COLUMN 1, ADD THIS)	3 CRISP AND STARCHY (TO COLUMN 2, ADD THIS)	4 UP-TO-THE-MINUTE TRENDY (TO COLUMN 3, ADD THIS)
1. Wear well-tailored clothing that fits well.	1. Choose form-fitting (but not skin-tight) clothing—not swinging or flowing fabrics, frills, or fussy trimmings.	1. Wear blouses or shirts that are or appear starched.	1. Add trendy clothing items to your wardrobe often.
2. Keep buttons, zippers, and hemlines in good repair.	2. Choose muted tones and soft colors or classics, such as the dark blue suit or the basic black dress.	2. Choose closed top-button shirts or button-down shirt collars, higher-neckline blouses, long sleeves with French cuffs and cuff links.	2. Choose bold colors (but sparingly so that you won't appear garish).
3. Keep shoes shined and in good condition.	3. If possible, select a few classic pieces of jewelry (such as a string of pearls or diamond cuff links) for formal occasions.	3. Wear creased trousers or longer skirt hemline.	3. Embellish your look with trendy jewelry and hairstyles.
4. Make sure the fabrics you wear are clean, are carefully pressed, and do not wrinkle easily.		4. Wear jackets that complement an outfit and lend an air of formality to your appearance. Avoid jackets with more than two tones—one color should dominate.	
5. Choose colors that flatter your height, weight, skin tone, and style.			

TABLE 2.3 Quick Tips for Improving Your Phone Skills

GENERAL TIPS	PLACING CALLS	RECEIVING CALLS	USING VOICE MAIL
Use frequent verbal responses that show you're listening ("Oh yes," "I see," "That's right").	Be ready before you call so that you don't waste the other person's time.	Answer promptly and with a smile so that you sound friendly and positive.	When recording your own outgoing message, make it brief and professional.
Increase your volume just slightly to convey your confidence.	Minimize distractions and avoid making noise that could annoy the other party.	Identify yourself and your company (some companies have specific instructions for what to say when you answer).	If you can, record temporary greetings on days when you are unavailable all day so that callers will know you're gone for the day.
Don't speak in a monotone; vary your pitch and inflections so people know you're interested.	Identify yourself and your organization, briefly describe why you're calling, and verify that you've called at a good time.	Establish the needs of your caller by asking, "How may I help you?" If you know the caller's name, use it.	Check your voice-mail messages regularly and return all necessary calls within 24 hours.
Slow down when conversing with people whose native language isn't the same as yours.	Don't take up too much time. Speak quickly and clearly, and get right to the point of the call.	If you can, answer questions promptly and efficiently; if you can't help, tell them what you can do for them.	Leave simple, clear messages with your name, number, purpose for calling, and times when you can be reached.
Stay focused on the call throughout; others can easily tell when you're not paying attention.	Close in a friendly, positive manner and double-check all vital information such as meeting times and dates.	If you must forward a call or put someone on hold, explain what you are doing first.	State your name and telephone number slowly so that the other person can easily write them down; repeat both if the other person doesn't know you.
		If you forward a call to someone else, try to speak with that person first to verify that he or she is available and to introduce the caller.	Be careful what you say; most voice-mail systems allow users to forward messages to anyone else in the system.
		If you take a message for someone else, be complete and accurate, including the caller's name, number, and organization.	Replay your message before leaving the system to make sure it is clear and complete.

If you're accustomed to using your cell phone anywhere and everywhere, get ready to change your habits. Cell phones are causing so much disruption in the workplace that some senior executives now ban their use in meetings.[44] Even if cell phones aren't banned in your office, don't let yours become a source of annoyance to your colleagues.

In Social Settings

From business lunches to industry conferences, you represent your company when you're out in public, so make sure your appearance and actions are appropriate to the situation. Get to know the customs of the culture when you meet new people. In North America, a firm handshake is expected when two people meet, whereas a respectful bow of the head is more appropriate in Japan. If you are expected to shake hands, be aware that the passive "dead fish" handshake creates an extremely negative impression. Also, women and men should shake hands on equal terms; the days of a woman offering just her fingertips are long gone in the business world. If you are physically able, always stand when shaking someone's hand.

You represent your company when you're out in public, so etiquette continues to be important.

When introducing yourself, include a brief description of your role in the company. When introducing two other people, speak both their first and last names clearly, then try to offer some information (perhaps a shared professional interest) to help these two people ease into a conversation.[45] Generally speaking, the lower-ranking person is introduced to the senior-ranking person, without regard to gender.[46] When you're introduced to someone, repeat the person's name as soon as possible. Doing so is both a compliment and a good way to remember it.[47]

DOCUMENT MAKEOVER

Business is often conducted over meals, and knowing the basics of dining etiquette will make you more effective in these situations.[48] Choose foods that are easy to eat; you don't want to wrestle with a lobster while trying to carry on a conversation. If a drink is appropriate, save it for the end of the meal. Leave business papers under your chair until entrée plates have been removed; the business aspect of the meal doesn't usually begin until then.

Just as in the office, when you use your cell phone in public, you send the message that people around you aren't as important as your call and that you don't respect your caller's privacy.[49] If it's not a matter of life and death—literally—wait until you're back in the office.

Finally, always remember that business meals are a forum for business, period. Don't get on your soapbox about politics, religion, or any other topic likely to stir up emotions. Don't complain about work, don't ask deeply personal questions, avoid profanity, and be careful with humor—a joke that entertains some people could easily offend others.

MAKING YOUR MEETINGS MORE PRODUCTIVE

Much of the communication you'll participate in will take place in meetings.

Meetings are a primary communication venue for today's businesses, whether held in formal conference rooms, in informal settings such as The Container Store's daily huddles, or on the Internet as *virtual meetings*. Well-run meetings can help you solve problems, develop ideas, and identify opportunities. Much of your workplace communication will occur in small-group meetings; therefore, your ability to contribute to the company and to be recognized for those contributions will depend on your meeting skills.

Unfortunately, many meetings are unproductive. In one study, senior and middle managers reported that only 56 percent of their meetings were actually productive and that 25 percent of them could have been replaced by a phone call or a memo.[50] The three most frequently reported problems with meetings are getting off the subject, not having an agenda, and running too long.[51] You can help ensure productive meetings by preparing carefully, conducting meetings efficiently, and using meeting technologies wisely.

Preparing for Meetings

Careful preparation helps you avoid the two biggest meeting mistakes: (1) holding a meeting when a blog posting or other message would do the job or (2) holding a meeting without a specific goal in mind. Before you even begin preparing for a meeting, make sure it's truly necessary. Once you're sure, proceed with four preparation tasks:

To ensure a successful meeting, decide on your purpose ahead of time, select the right participants, choose the time and facility carefully, and set a clear agenda.

- **Identify your purpose.** Although many meetings combine purposes, most focus on one of two types: *Informational meetings* involve sharing information and perhaps coordinating action. *Decision-making meetings* involve persuasion, analysis, and problem solving. Whatever your purpose, make sure it is clear and clearly communicated to all participants.
- **Select participants for the meeting.** If the session is purely informational and one person will do most of the talking, you can invite a large group. For problem-solving and decision-making meetings, invite only those people who are in a direct position to help the meeting reach its objective. The more participants, the more comments and confusion you're likely to get and the longer the meeting will take. However, make sure you invite all the key decision makers, or your meeting will fail to satisfy its purpose.
- **Choose the time and the facility.** For working sessions, morning meetings are usually more productive than afternoon sessions. Also, consider the seating arrangements: Are rows of chairs suitable, or do you need a conference table or some other setting? Plus, give some attention to details such as room temperature, lighting, ventilation, acoustics, and refreshments; any of these seemingly minor details can make or break a meeting.

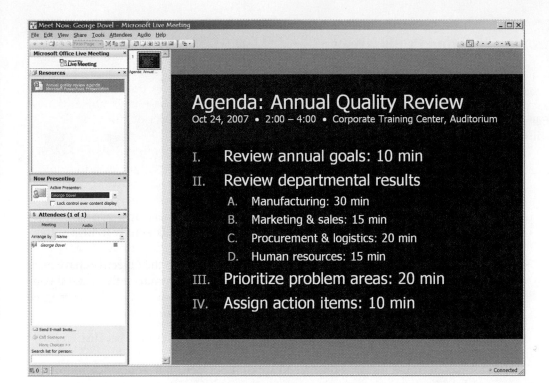

FIGURE 2.3 Typical
Meeting Agenda
Agenda formats vary widely,
depending on the complexity
of the meeting and the
presentation technologies that
are used.

- **Set the agenda.** The success of any meeting depends on the preparation of the participants. Distribute a carefully written agenda to participants, giving them enough time to prepare as needed (see Figure 2.3). A productive agenda answers three key questions: (1) What do we need to do in this meeting to accomplish our goals? (2) What issues will be of greatest importance to all participants? (3) What information must be available in order to discuss these issues?[52]

Leading and Participating in Meetings

Everyone in a meeting shares the responsibility for keeping the meeting productive and making it successful. If you're the designated leader of a meeting, however, you have an extra degree of responsibility and accountability. To ensure productive meetings, be sure to do the following:

Everyone shares the responsibility for successful meetings.

- **Keep the discussion on track.** A good meeting draws out the best ideas and information the group has to offer. Good leaders guide, mediate, probe, stimulate, and summarize as the situation demands. Experience will help you recognize when to push the group forward and when to step back and let people talk.
- **Follow agreed-upon rules.** Business meetings run the gamut from informal to extremely formal, complete with detailed rules for speaking, proposing new items to discuss, voting on proposals, and so on. The larger the meeting, the more formal you'll need to be to maintain order. Formal meetings use **parliamentary procedure**, a time-tested method for planning and running effective meetings. The best-known guide to this procedure is *Roberts Rules of Order.*
- **Encourage participation.** As the meeting gets under way, you'll discover that some participants are too quiet and others are too talkative. The quiet participants may be shy, they may be expressing disagreement or resistance, or they may be answering e-mail or instant messaging on their laptop computers. Draw them out by asking for their input on issues that pertain to them. For the overly talkative, simply say that time is limited and others need to be heard from.
- **Participate actively.** If you're a meeting participant, try to contribute to both the subject of the meeting and the smooth interaction of the participants. Use your listening skills and powers of observation to size up the interpersonal dynamics of the people,

CHECKLIST: Improving Meeting Productivity

A. Prepare carefully.
- Make sure the meeting is necessary.
- Decide on your purpose.
- Select participants carefully.
- Choose the time and facility.
- Set the agenda.

B. Lead effectively and participate fully.
- Keep the meeting on track.
- Follow agreed-upon rules.
- Encourage participation.
- Participate actively.
- Close effectively.

then adapt your behavior to help the group achieve its goals. Speak up if you have something useful to say, but don't monopolize the discussion or talk simply to bring attention to yourself.

- **Close effectively.** At the conclusion of the meeting, verify that the objectives have been met; if not, arrange for follow-up work as needed. Either summarize the general conclusion of the discussion or list the actions to be taken. Make sure all participants agree on the outcome and give people a chance to clear up any misunderstandings.

To review the tasks that contribute to productive meetings, refer to "Checklist: Improving Meeting Productivity."

For formal meetings, it's good practice to appoint one person to record the minutes, a summary of the important information presented and the decisions made during a meeting. In smaller or informal meetings, attendees often make their own notes on their copies of the agenda. In either case, a clear record of the decisions made and the people responsible for follow-up action is essential.

If your company doesn't have a specific format for minutes, follow the generic format shown in Figure 2.4. Key elements include a list of those present and a list of those who were invited but didn't attend, followed by the times the meeting started and ended, all major decisions reached at the meeting, all assignments of tasks to meeting participants, and all subjects that were deferred to a later meeting. In addition, the minutes objectively summarize important discussions, noting the names of those who contributed major points. Outlines, subheadings, and lists help organize the minutes; additional documentation (such as tables or charts submitted by meeting participants) is noted in the minutes and attached. Many companies now post meeting minutes on an intranet site for easy reference. Whichever method you use, make sure that responsibilities are clear so that all issues raised at the meeting will be addressed.

Using Meeting Technologies

6 LEARNING OBJECTIVE

Describe how meeting technologies can help participants communicate more successfully

Virtual meeting technologies connect people spread around the country or around the world.

You can expect to use a variety of meeting-related technologies throughout your career. These technologies have spurred the emergence of **virtual teams**, whose members work in different locations and interact electronically through **virtual meetings**. At times, technology replaces meetings entirely, such as when team members use e-mail or instant messaging to interact over the course of several hours or days, rather than meeting online or over the phone at a specific time. One of the newest virtual tools is *online brainstorming,* in which companies conduct "idea campaigns" to generate new ideas from people across the organization. These range from small team meetings to huge events such as IBM's giant InnovationJam, in which 100,000 IBM employees, family members, and customers from 160 countries were invited to brainstorm online for three days.[53]

As with most new technologies, electronic meeting tools are evolving rapidly, and the lines separating these tools have become blurred. For example, instant messaging and video-conferencing are both stand-alone capabilities; both are also common features in **groupware**, an umbrella term for systems that let people communicate, share files, present materials, and work on documents simultaneously.

FIGURE 2.4 Typical Minutes of a Meeting

The use of intranet and blog postings is a common way to distribute meeting minutes. The specific format of the minutes is less important than making sure you record all the key information, particularly regarding responsibilities that were assigned during the meeting.

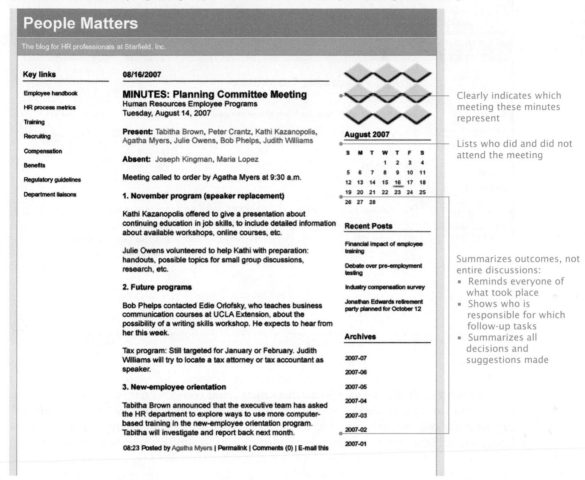

Shared workspaces are "virtual offices" that give everyone on a team access to the same set of resources and information: databases, calendars, project plans, pertinent instant messaging and e-mail exchanges, shared reference materials, and team-created documents (see Figure 2.5). Workspaces such as Documentum eRoom, Microsoft SharePoint, and IBM Lotus Team Workspace create a seamless environment for collaboration. Such workspaces make it easy for geographically dispersed team members to access shared files anytime, anywhere.

Shared workspaces give team members instant access to shared resources and information.

Most systems also have built-in intelligence to control which team members can read, edit, and save specific files. *Revision control* goes one step farther: It allows only one person at a time to check out a given file or document and records all the changes that person makes. This feature prevents two people from independently editing the same report at the same time, thus avoiding the messy situation in which a team would end up with two versions of the same document.[54]

Virtual meeting technologies encompass a wide range of tools that let team members in different locations interact at the same time without the hassle, risk, and cost of travel.[55] Instant messaging chat sessions and telephone conference calls are the simplest forms of virtual meetings. **Videoconferencing** combines audio communication with live video, letting team members see each other, demonstrate products, and transmit other visual information. Videoconferencing is available in both *room systems*—specialized conference room facilities with large-screen displays—and *desktop systems,* which typically use a webcam attached to each participant's computer.

Virtual meetings range from videoconferencing to web-based systems.

FIGURE 2.5 Shared Workspaces

Shared workspaces, such as this example from Microsoft's SharePoint system, give virtual teams instant access to the documents, calendars, and other files and information needed for successful collaboration.

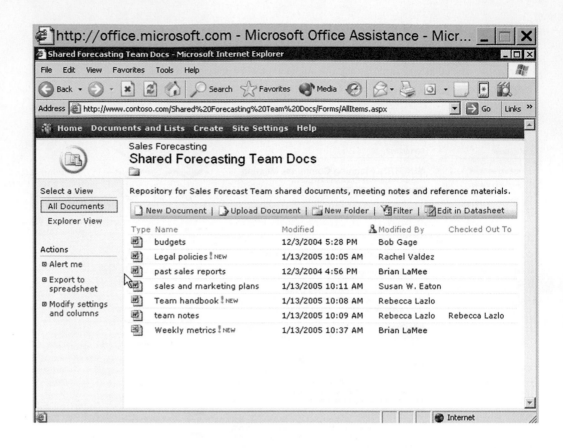

The most sophisticated **web-based meeting systems** combine the best of instant messaging, shared workspaces, and videoconferencing with other tools such as *virtual whiteboards* that let teams collaborate in real time (see Figure 2.6). Attendees can log on from a desktop or laptop PC, a PDA, or even a web-enabled cell phone from almost anywhere in the world.

FIGURE 2.6 Web-Based Meetings

Online meetings offer powerful tools for communication, but you'll need to be proficient at using these tools if you are to be effective during online meetings.

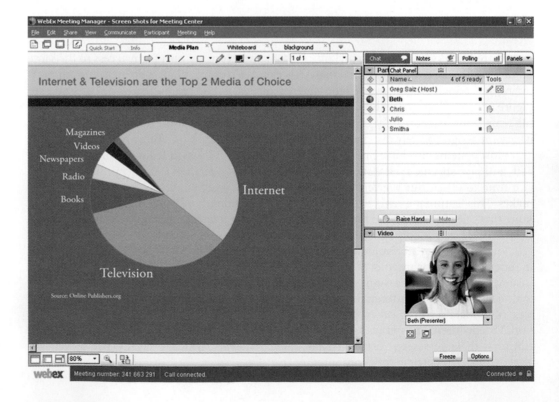

IMPROVING YOUR LISTENING SKILLS

The importance of listening, whether in meetings and other business contexts or in your personal life, is self-evident: If a receiver won't or can't listen, the speaker's message simply won't get through. Some 80 percent of top executives say that listening is the most important skill needed to get things done in the workplace.[56]

Listening is one of the most important skills in the workplace.

Effective listening strengthens organizational relationships, enhances product delivery, alerts the organization to opportunities for innovation, and allows the organization to manage growing diversity both in the workforce and in the customers it serves.[57] Companies whose employees and managers listen effectively stay informed, up to date, and out of trouble. Conversely, poor listening skills can cost companies millions of dollars a year as a result of lost opportunities, legal mistakes, and other errors. Effective listening is vital to the process of building trust not only between organizations but also between individuals.[58] Throughout your career, effective listening will give you a competitive edge, enhancing your performance and thus the influence you have within your company. Learn from the example of Carol Kobuke Nelson, whose "quietly effective" leadership skills helped her become president and CEO of Seattle-based Cascade Bank. Says one of her peers, "She's a good listener. A lot of times people just want someone to listen to them. By understanding what that person's real concern is and doing something about it—that's how you win people over."[59]

Recognizing Various Types of Listening

Understanding the nature of listening is the first step toward improving your listening skills. People listen in a variety of ways, which influences both what they hear and the meaning they extract. In fact, relying on a single approach to listening limits your effectiveness. A people-oriented listener might miss important information about an upcoming deadline, whereas an action-oriented listener might miss an important clue that there's a personal problem brewing between two team members.[60] As you read about the major types of listening, reflect on your own inclination as a listener, and consider how learning to use several methods could make your listening more effective.

The primary goal of **content listening** is to understand and retain the speaker's message. For example, Henry Nordhoff, CEO of the San Diego–based pharmaceutical company Gen-Probe, has a business background and relies on content listening to gather technical information from the scientists whose work he oversees.[61] When you're listening for content, the emphasis is on information and understanding. Ask questions to clarify the material, and probe for details. Because you're not evaluating at this point, it doesn't matter whether you agree or disagree, approve or disapprove—only that you understand. Try to overlook the speaker's style and any limitations in the presentation; just focus on the information.[62]

To be a good listener, adapt the way you listen to suit the situation.

The goal of **critical listening** is to understand and evaluate the meaning of the speaker's message on several levels: the logic of the argument, the strength of the evidence, the validity of the conclusions, the implications of the message for you and your organization, the speaker's intentions and motives, and the omission of any important or relevant points. If you're skeptical, ask questions to explore the speaker's point of view and credibility. Be on the lookout for bias that could color the way the information is presented, and be careful to separate opinions from facts.[63]

The goal of **empathic listening** is to understand the speaker's feelings, needs, and wants so that you can appreciate his or her point of view, regardless of whether you share that perspective. By listening in an empathic way, you help the individual

When you engage in empathic listening, you pay attention to feelings, needs, and wants—not just the spoken words.

vent the emotions that prevent a calm, clear-headed approach to the subject. Sometimes the only thing an upset colleague is looking for is somebody to listen, so avoid the temptation to jump in with advice unless the person specifically asks for it. Also, don't judge the speaker's feelings and don't try to tell people they shouldn't feel this or that emotion. Instead, let the speaker know that you appreciate his or her feelings and understand the situation. Once you establish that connection, you can then help the speaker move on to search for a solution.[64]

No matter what mode they are using at any given time, effective listeners try to engage in **active listening**, making a conscious effort to turn off their own filters and biases to truly hear and understand what the other party is saying. They ask questions to verify key points and encourage the speaker through positive body language.[65]

Understanding the Listening Process

7 LEARNING OBJECTIVE

Describe the listening process and explain how good listeners overcome barriers at each stage of the process

Listening is a far more complex process than most people think. As a consequence, most of us aren't very good at it. Given such complexity, it's no wonder most of us listen at or below a 25 percent efficiency rate, remember only about half of what's said during a 10-minute conversation, and forget half of that within 48 hours.[66] Furthermore, when questioned about material we've just heard, we are likely to get the facts mixed up.[67]

Why is such a seemingly simple activity so difficult? The answer lies in the complexity of the process. Listening follows the same sequence as the general communication process model you explored in Chapter 1 (page 11), with the added burden that it happens in real time. To listen effectively, you need to successfully complete five separate steps:[68]

Listening involves five steps: receiving, decoding, remembering, evaluating, and responding.

- **Receiving.** You start by physically hearing the message and acknowledging it. Physical reception can be blocked by noise, impaired hearing, or inattention. Some experts also include nonverbal messages as part of this stage, because these factors influence the listening process as well.
- **Decoding.** Your next step is to assign meaning to sounds, which you do according to your own values, beliefs, ideas, expectations, roles, needs, and personal history.
- **Remembering.** Before you can act on the information, you need to store it for future processing. As you learned in Chapter 1, incoming messages must first be captured in short-term memory, then transferred to long-term memory for more permanent storage.
- **Evaluating.** With the speaker's message captured, your next step is to evaluate it by applying critical thinking skills. Separate fact from opinion and evaluate the quality of the evidence.
- **Responding.** After you've evaluated the speaker's message, you now react. If you're communicating one-on-one or in a small group, the initial response generally takes the form of verbal feedback. If you're one of many in an audience, your initial response may take the form of applause, laughter, or silence. Later on, you may act on what you have heard.

If any one of these steps breaks down, the listening process becomes less effective or even fails entirely. As both a sender and a receiver, you can reduce the failure rate by recognizing and overcoming a variety of physical and mental barriers to effective listening.

Overcoming Barriers to Effective Listening

Good listeners actively try to overcome the barriers to successful listening.

Good listeners look for ways to overcome potential barriers throughout the listening process (see Table 2.4). You are unlikely to have control over some barriers to physical reception, such as conference room acoustics or poor cell phone reception. However, you can certainly take steps to control other barriers. If you have questions for a speaker, wait until he or she has finished speaking. And don't think that you're not interrupting just because you're not talking. Rustling papers, tapping on your PDA, checking your watch—these are just a few of the many nonverbal behaviors that can interrupt a speaker and hamper listening for everyone.

Selective listening is one of the most common barriers to effective listening. If your mind wanders, you often stay tuned out until you hear a word or phrase that gets your attention once more. But by that time, you're unable to recall what the speaker *actually* said; instead, you remember what you *think* the speaker probably said.[69]

TABLE 2.4 Distinguishing Effective Listeners from Ineffective Listeners

EFFECTIVE LISTENERS	INEFFECTIVE LISTENERS
• Listen actively.	• Listen passively.
• Take careful and complete notes.	• Take no notes or ineffective notes.
• Make frequent eye contact with the speaker (depends on culture to some extent).	• Make little or no eye contact.
• Stay focused on the speaker and the content.	• Allow their minds to wander; are easily distracted.
• Mentally paraphrase key points to maintain attention level and ensure comprehension.	• Fail to paraphrase.
• Adjust listening style to the situation.	• Listen with the same style, regardless of the situation.
• Give the speaker nonverbal cues (such as nodding to show agreement or raising eyebrows to show surprise or skepticism).	• Fail to give the speaker nonverbal feedback.
• Save questions or points of disagreement until an appropriate time.	• Interrupt whenever they disagree or don't understand.
• Overlook stylistic differences and focus on the speaker's message.	• Are distracted by or unduly influenced by stylistic differences; are judgmental.
• Make distinctions between main points and supporting details.	• Are unable to distinguish main points from details.
• Look for opportunities to learn.	• Assume they already know everything that's important to know.

One reason listeners' minds tend to wander is that people think faster than they speak. Most people speak at about 120 to 150 words per minute, but listeners can process audio information at up to 500 words per minute.[70] In other words, your brain has a lot of free time whenever you're listening and, if left unsupervised, it will find a thousand other things to think about. Make a conscious effort to focus on the speaker, and use the extra time to analyze what you hear or prepare questions you want to ask.

Your mind can process information much faster than most speakers talk.

Overcoming such interpretation barriers can be difficult because you may not even be aware of them. As Chapter 1 noted, selective perception leads listeners to mold messages to fit their own conceptual frameworks. Listeners sometimes make up their minds before fully hearing the speaker's message, or they engage in defensive listening—protecting their self-esteem by tuning out anything that doesn't confirm their view of themselves.

Even when your intentions are the best, recall that you can still misinterpret incoming messages if you and the speaker don't share enough language or experience. Lack of common ground is why misinterpretation is so frequent between speakers of different native languages, even when they're trying to speak the same language. When listening to a speaker whose native language or life experience is different from yours, try to paraphrase that person's ideas. Give the speaker a chance to confirm what you think you heard or to correct any misinterpretation.

Overcoming memory barriers is a slightly easier problem to solve, but it takes some work. One simple rule: Don't count on your memory. If the information is crucial, try to record it in some fashion. If you do need to memorize something, you can hold information in short-term memory by repeating it silently or organizing a long list of items into several shorter lists. To store information in long-term memory—particularly information that you might not be immediately interested in—four techniques can help: (1) associate new information with something closely related (such as the restaurant in which you met a new client), (2) categorize the new information into logical groups (such as alphabetizing the names of products you're trying to remember), (3) visualize words and ideas as pictures, and (4) create mnemonics such as acronyms or rhymes. Note that all four techniques have an important factor in common: You have to *do* something to make the information stick.

When information is crucial, don't count on your memory.

For a reminder of the steps you can take to overcome listening barriers, see "Checklist: Overcoming Barriers to Effective Listening."

CHECKLIST: Overcoming Barriers to Effective Listening

- Control whatever barriers to physical reception you can (such as avoiding interrupting speakers by asking questions or by exhibiting disruptive nonverbal behaviors).
- Avoid selective listening by trying to focus on the speaker and analyzing what you hear.
- Keep an open mind by avoiding any prejudgment and by not listening defensively.

- Try to paraphrase the speaker's ideas, giving that person a chance to confirm or correct your interpretation.
- Don't count on your memory; write down or record important information.
- Improve your short-term memory by repeating information or breaking it into shorter lists.
- Improve your long-term memory by association, categorization, visualization, and mnemonics.

IMPROVING YOUR NONVERBAL COMMUNICATION SKILLS

8 LEARNING OBJECTIVE

Clarify the importance of nonverbal communication and briefly describe six categories of nonverbal expression

The boss walks out of the conference room after explaining that your department needs to double its sales next year. You're skeptical, though. You turn to a colleague on your right and raise your eyebrows. She smiles and nods, sitting upright on the edge of her seat—she seems to relish the challenge. You turn to the left, but that colleague seems to dread what lies ahead, rolling his eyes and sighing. He is slumped so far down in his chair you wonder how he keeps from sliding off.

A complex conversation has just taken place without a single word being spoken. **Nonverbal communication** is the interpersonal process of sending and receiving information, both intentionally and unintentionally, without using written or spoken language. Nonverbal signals play three important roles in communication. The first is complementing verbal language. Nonverbal signals can strengthen a verbal message (when nonverbal signals match words), weaken a verbal message (when nonverbal signals don't match words), or replace words entirely.

Nonverbal cues help you ascertain the truth of spoken information.

The second role for nonverbal signals is revealing truth. People find it much harder to deceive with nonverbal signals. You might tell a client that the project is coming along nicely, but your forced smile and nervous glances send a different message. In fact, nonverbal communication often conveys more to listeners than the words you speak—particularly when they're trying to decide how you really feel about a situation or when they're trying to judge your credibility and aptitude for leadership.[71] However, even the power of nonverbal cues is not infallible when it comes to detecting truth. In one recent study, most people failed to detect dishonest speech roughly half the time; only a tiny fraction of the population are able to consistently detect when people are lying to them.[72]

The third role for nonverbal signals is conveying information efficiently. Nonverbal signals can convey both nuance and rich amounts of information in a single instant, as the previous conference room example suggests.

Recognizing Nonverbal Communication

Paying special attention to nonverbal signals in the workplace will enhance your ability to communicate successfully. Moreover, as you interact with business associates from other backgrounds, you'll discover that some nonverbal signals don't necessarily translate across cultures. You'll learn more about cultural influences on nonverbal communication in Chapter 3. The range and variety of nonverbal signals are almost endless, but you can grasp the basics by studying six general categories:

Nonverbal signals include facial expression, gesture and posture, vocal characteristics, personal appearance, touch, and time and space.

- **Facial expression.** Your face is the primary site for expressing your emotions; it reveals both the type and the intensity of your feelings.[73] Your eyes are especially effective for indicating attention and interest, influencing others, regulating interaction, and establishing dominance.[74]
- **Gesture and posture.** By moving or not moving your body, you express both specific and general messages, some voluntary and some involuntary. Many gestures—a wave

Communicating Across Cultures

Actions Speak Louder Than Words All Around the World

The weeklong meeting with your new business partner in Hong Kong went extremely well. Over the long dinners during which you hashed out various details of the contract, you also sensed a friendship beginning to form. He was even kind enough to drive you to the airport when you left on Friday afternoon. As you said good-bye, you impulsively reached out to give him a quick hug around the shoulder, with one arm only, just to express that new sense of friendship. You were quite surprised when he stood as stiff as a statue and didn't return the gesture. What happened to the friendship? Had you misread the signals all week?

No, you probably just missed a key point of nonverbal behavior in Hong Kong culture, where businesspeople are unaccustomed to colleagues making any kind of physical contact. Nonverbal cues vary widely between cultures, as you can see by comparing just a few:

- Canadian listeners nod to signal agreement.
- Japanese listeners nod to indicate only that they have understood.
- British listeners stare at the speaker, blinking their eyes to indicate understanding.

- People in the United States are taught that it's impolite to stare.

To adjust your nonverbal communication to other cultures, learn as much as you can. Consult books, seminars, and motion pictures on cultural differences. Try renting movies and television shows from other countries. Examine illustrations in news and business magazines to get an idea of expected business dress and personal space. Above all, remain flexible as you interact with people from other cultures.

CAREER APPLICATIONS

1. Explain how watching a movie from another country could help you prepare to interpret nonverbal behavior from that culture correctly—or incorrectly.
2. One of your co-workers is originally from Saudi Arabia. You like him, and the two of you work well together. However, he stands so close when you speak with him that it makes you uncomfortable. Do you tell him of your discomfort or try to cover it up?

---

of the hand, for example—have a specific and intentional meaning. Other types of body movement are unintentional and express a more general message. Slouching, leaning forward, fidgeting, and walking briskly are all unconscious signals that reveal whether you feel confident or nervous, friendly or hostile, assertive or passive, powerful or powerless.

- **Vocal characteristics.** Your voice also carries both intentional and unintentional messages. Consider the sentence, "What have you been up to?" If you repeat that question, changing your tone of voice and stressing various words, you can consciously convey quite different messages. However, your voice can also reveal things of which you are unaware. Your tone and volume, your accent and speaking pace, and all the little *ums* and *ahs* that creep into your speech say a lot about who you are, your relationship with the audience, and the emotions underlying your words.
- **Personal appearance.** People respond to others on the basis of their physical appearance, sometimes fairly and other times unfairly. Although an individual's body type and facial features impose limitations, most people are able to control their appearance to some degree. Grooming, clothing, accessories, style—you can control all of these. If your goal is to make a good impression, adopt the style of the people you want to impress.
- **Touch.** Touch is an important way to convey warmth, comfort, reassurance—or control. Touch is so powerful, in fact, that it is governed by cultural customs that establish who can touch whom and how in various circumstances. In the United States and Great Britain, for instance, people usually touch less frequently than people in France or Costa Rica. Even within each culture's norms, however, individual attitudes toward touch can vary widely. A manager might be comfortable using hugs to express support or congratulations, but his or her subordinates could interpret those hugs as either a show of dominance or sexual interest.[75] Touch is a complex subject. The best advice: When in doubt, don't touch.

Dressing too casually or too formally for a given business setting can send a signal that you don't understand or don't respect the situation.

Work to make sure your nonverbal signals match the tone and content of your spoken communication.

- **Time and space.** Like touch, time and space can be used to assert authority, imply intimacy, and send other nonverbal messages. For instance, some people try to demonstrate their own importance or disregard for others by making other people wait; others show respect by being on time. The manipulation of space works in a similar way. When top executives gather for lunch in a private dining room, they send a strong signal to all the employees crowding into the cafeteria downstairs. The decision to respect or violate someone's "private space" is another powerful nonverbal signal. Again, attitudes toward time and space vary from culture to culture (see Chapter 3).

Using Nonverbal Communication Effectively

Paying attention to nonverbal cues will make you both a better speaker and a better listener. When you're talking, be more conscious of the nonverbal cues you could be sending. Are they effective without being manipulative? Consider a situation in which an employee has come to you to talk about a raise. This situation is a stressful one for the employee, so don't say you're interested in what she has to tell you and then spend your time glancing at your computer or checking your watch. Conversely, if you already know you won't be able to give her the raise, be honest in expressing your emotions. Don't overcompensate for your own stress by smiling too broadly or shaking her hand too vigorously. Both nonverbal signals would raise her hopes without justification. In either case, match your nonverbal cues to the tone of the situation.

Also consider the nonverbal signals you send when you're not talking—the clothes you wear, the way you sit, the way you walk. Are you talking like a serious business professional but dressing like you belong in a dance club or a frat house?

When you listen, be sure to pay attention to the speaker's nonverbal cues. Do they amplify the spoken words or contradict them? Is the speaker intentionally using nonverbal signals to send you a message that he or she can't put into words? Be observant, but don't assume that you can "read someone like a book." Nonverbal signals are powerful, but they aren't infallible. Contrary to popular belief, just because someone doesn't look you squarely in the eye doesn't mean he or she is lying.[76] If something doesn't feel right, ask the speaker an honest and respectful question—doing so may clear everything up, or it may uncover issues you need to explore further. See "Checklist: Improving Nonverbal Communication Skills" for a summary of key ideas regarding nonverbal skills.

 CHECKLIST: Improving Nonverbal Communication Skills

A. **Understand the roles that nonverbal signals play in communication.**
- Nonverbal signals complement verbal language by strengthening, weakening, or replacing words.
- Nonverbal signals often reveal the truth, sometimes conveying more to listeners than spoken words.

B. **Recognize nonverbal communication signals.**
- Note that facial expressions (especially eye contact) reveal the type and intensity of a speaker's feelings.
- Watch for cues from gesture and posture.

- Listen for vocal characteristics that signal who the speaker is, the speaker's relationship with the audience, and the emotions underlying the speaker's words.
- Recognize that listeners are influenced by physical appearance.
- Be careful with physical contact; touch can convey positive attributes but can also be interpreted as dominance or sexual interest.
- Pay attention to the use of time and space.

COMMUNICATION CHALLENGES AT THE CONTAINER STORE

During one of your frequent visits to the local Container Store, the manager asks if you'd like to interview for a job (the company often hires its best customers). Three weeks later you report for work and attend your first huddle. Surprisingly, it isn't as energizing or informative as described in your communication textbook; the shift manager, Tamara, lets two people do most of the talking and does little to encourage input from others. Still, the huddle ends on time and everyone spreads out for another busy day.

Individual Challenge: A month later, co-founder Kip Tindell drops in for a visit—early enough to attend the morning huddle. Tamara leads another lackluster session, even with a co-founder attending. Tindell spends the morning wandering the store, talking to employees and customers. During his chat with you, Tindell describes what he observed during the huddle and asks what you would do to improve the situation. What will you suggest? Compile your suggestions in a two- or three-paragraph e-mail message.

Team Challenge: Information meetings such as the huddle seem to be an effective communication tool in a retail operation such as The Container Store. In a small group, discuss the value of a huddle in (a) an electronics manufacturing company and (b) an advertising agency. In either company, how would you ensure the effectiveness of a huddle held via teleconference or online meeting? List your conclusions in writing.

SUMMARY OF LEARNING OBJECTIVES

1 Highlight the advantages and disadvantages of working in teams. Teams can achieve a higher level of performance than individuals because of the combined intelligence and energy of the group. Motivation and creativity can flourish in team settings. Moreover, individuals tend to perform better because they achieve a sense of purpose by belonging to a group. Teams also bring more input and a greater diversity of views, which tends to result in better decisions. And because team members participate in the decision process, they are committed to seeing the results succeed. Teams are not without disadvantages, however. Poorly managed teams can be a waste of everyone's time. For example, if members are pressured to conform, they may develop groupthink, which can lead to poor-quality decisions and ill-advised actions. Some members may let their private motives get in the way. Others may not contribute their fair share, so certain tasks may not be completed.

2 Identify eight guidelines for successful collaborative writing. Collaborative communication is a great opportunity for teams to pool their diverse talents and knowledge to produce messages that are of higher quality than any single team member could produce on his or her own. However, collaborative writing requires close attention. Select team members carefully to balance talents and viewpoints, and be sure to agree on project goals at the outset to avoid confusion and wasted time. If the team hasn't worked together before, make sure team members have time to get to know one another. Next, make sure that everyone clearly understands individual responsibilities, processes, and tools. Also, resist the temptation to write as a group; research and plan as a group, but assign the actual writing to one person or at least assign separate sections to individual writers and have one person edit them all. Finally, make sure tools and techniques are compatible across the team.

3 Explain how wiki technology can help teams collaborate. Wikis can help teams collaborate by providing a fast, easy, and flexible way to work together on documents, particularly when the team is geographically dispersed. Wikis provide a much greater degree of organization and centralization than trying to pass around individual word-processing documents, for instance, while avoiding the rigid rules and structure of a content management system.

4 Explain how group dynamics can affect team effectiveness. When group dynamics encourage full participation and constructive resolution of conflict, teams communicate more effectively, both internally and externally. In contrast, when group dynamics are negative, communication breaks down within the team—whether from groupthink, too many members assuming dysfunctional self-oriented roles, or excessive levels of conflict. As a result, the team is also less able to communicate externally in a clear and coherent manner.

5 Discuss the role of etiquette in team settings, both in the workplace and in social settings. The ability of all members of the team to get along, day in and day out, is vital to every team's success. Etiquette plays an important part in this process. If team members get on each other's nerves through inconsiderate behavior, communication gradually breaks down and vital energy gets diverted away from the team's real mission. In the workplace, team members need to pay attention to factors such as personal appearance, grooming, and phone skills as they affect not only other team members but also the people with whom the team interacts. Team communication often extends into social settings, and each team member needs to keep in mind that he or she represents the company when out in public. Proper etiquette in these situations helps foster good communication, particularly when new people are introduced to the group.

6 Describe how meeting technologies can help participants communicate more successfully. Communication and groupware technologies such as shared workspaces and virtual meetings enhance communication by helping teams break down the barriers of time and distance. Shared workspaces give teams instant access to a common set of project resources, including documents, databases, schedules, and other materials. Virtual meetings combine several of these technologies with others (such as virtual whiteboards) to emulate in-person meetings over long distances.

7 Describe the listening process, and explain how good listeners overcome barriers at each stage of the process. The listening process involves five activities: (1) receiving (physically hearing the message), (2) decoding (assigning meaning to what you hear), (3) remembering (storing the message for future reference), (4) evaluating (thinking about the message), and (5) responding (reacting to the message, taking action, or giving feedback). Several barriers can interfere with the listening process. To improve reception, minimize certain distractions by holding questions until the speaker finishes and avoiding distracting nonverbal behaviors, such as rustling papers, tapping on your PDA, or not looking at the speaker. To improve decoding and interpretation, avoid prejudgment and defensive listening by taking a patient, open-minded approach. To improve remembering, capture information in some physical way, recording it or writing it down. Store information for the short term by repeating it to yourself or breaking a long list into several shorter lists. Also, transfer information from short-term to long-term memory through association, categorization, visualization, and mnemonics. To improve evaluating, overcome selective listening by focusing on the speaker, taking careful notes, mentally paraphrasing what's being said, and analyzing the speaker's argument. To improve responding, react naturally when appropriate and plan out any response to a more complex message.

8 Clarify the importance of nonverbal communication, and briefly describe six categories of nonverbal expression. Nonverbal communication is important because actions speak louder than words. Body language is more difficult to control than words and may reveal a person's true feelings, motivation, or character. Therefore, people believe nonverbal signals over words. In addition, nonverbal communication is more efficient; with a wave of your hand or a wink, you can streamline your thoughts and do so without much thought. Types of nonverbal expression include facial expression, gesture and posture, vocal characteristics, personal appearance, touching behavior, and use of time and space.

Test Your Knowledge

1. How can organizations and employees benefit from successful teamwork?
2. What steps should teams take to ensure successful communication results?
3. How do self-oriented team roles differ from team-maintenance roles and task-facilitating roles?
4. What is groupthink, and how can it affect an organization?
5. How can organizations help team members successfully resolve conflict?
6. Why is etiquette so important in team settings?
7. Why would a company choose a wiki to support team collaboration rather than a content management system?
8. What are the main activities that make up the listening process?
9. How does content listening differ from critical listening and empathic listening?
10. In what six ways can an individual communicate nonverbally?

Apply Your Knowledge

1. How can nonverbal communication help you run a meeting? How can it help you call a meeting to order, emphasize important topics, show approval, express reservations, regulate the flow of conversation, and invite a colleague to continue with a comment?

2. Whenever your boss asks for feedback during department meetings, she blasts anyone offering criticism, which causes people to agree with everything she says. You want to talk to her about it, but what should you say? List some of the points you want to make when you discuss this issue with your boss.

3. Is conflict in a team good or bad? Explain your answer.

4. At your last department meeting, three people monopolized the entire discussion. What can you do at the next meeting to encourage other department members to voluntarily participate?

5. **Ethical Choices** Strange instant messages occasionally pop up on your computer screen during your team's virtual meetings, followed quickly by embarrassed apologies from one of your colleagues in another city. You eventually figure out that this person is working from home, even though he says he's in the office; moreover, the messages suggest that he's running a sideline business from his home. You're concerned about the frequent disruptions, not to mention your colleague's potential ethical violations. What should you do? Explain your choice.

Practice Your Knowledge

Message for Analysis

A project leader has made notes about covering the following items at the quarterly budget meeting. Prepare a formal agenda by putting these items into a logical order and rewriting, where necessary, to give phrases a more consistent sound.

- Budget Committee Meeting to be held on December 12, 2008, at 9:30 a.m.
- I will call the meeting to order.
- Real estate director's report: A closer look at cost overruns on Greentree site.
- The group will review and approve the minutes from last quarter's meeting.
- I will ask the finance director to report on actual versus projected quarterly revenues and expenses.
- I will distribute copies of the overall divisional budget and announce the date of the next budget meeting.
- Discussion: How can we do a better job of anticipating and preventing cost overruns?
- Meeting will take place in Conference Room 3, with WebEx active for remote employees.
- What additional budget issues must be considered during this quarter?

Exercises

For active links to all websites discussed in this chapter, visit this text's website at www.prenhall.com/bovee. Locate your book and click on its Companion Website link. Then select Chapter 2, and click on "Featured Websites." Locate the name of the page or the URL related to the material in the text. Please note that links to sites that become inactive after publication of the book will be removed from the Featured Websites section.

2.1 **Teamwork** With a classmate, attend a local community or campus meeting where you can observe a group discussion, vote, or other group action. During the meeting, take notes individually and, afterward, work together to answer the following questions.

a. What is your evaluation of this meeting? In your answer, consider (1) the leader's ability to articulate the meeting's goals clearly, (2) the leader's ability to engage members in a meaningful discussion, (3) the group's dynamics, and (4) the group's listening skills.

b. How did group members make decisions? Did they vote? Did they reach decisions by consensus? Did those with dissenting opinions get an opportunity to voice their objections?

c. How well did the individual participants listen? How could you tell?

d. Did any participants change their expressed views or their votes during the meeting? Why might that have happened?

e. Did you observe any of the communication barriers discussed in Chapter 1? Identify them.

f. Compare the notes you took during the meeting with those of your classmate. What differences do you notice? How do you account for these differences?

2.2 **Team Communication: Overcoming Barriers** Every month, each employee in your department is expected to give a brief oral presentation on the status of his or her project. However, your department has recently hired an employee with a severe speech impediment that prevents people from understanding most of what he has to say. As department manager, how will you resolve this dilemma? Please explain.

2.3 **Team Development: Resolving Conflict** Describe a recent conflict you had with a team member at work or at school, and explain how you resolved it. Did you find a solution that was acceptable to both of you and to the team?

2.4 **Ethical Choices** During team meetings, one member constantly calls for votes before all the members have voiced their views. As the leader, you asked this member privately about his behavior. He replied that he was trying to move the team toward its goals, but you are concerned that he is really trying to take control. How can you deal with this situation without removing the member from the group?

2.5 **Online Communication: Staying on Track with Blog Replies** As the leader of a product development team, you write a daily blog to inform team members of questions, concerns, and other developments related to your project. Team members are always encouraged to reply to your online posts, but lately a number of people have been wandering off track with their replies, raising new issues in the middle of a discussion thread or posting on matters unrelated to the item to which they're replying. As a result, the blog is becoming less useful for everyone because individual message threads no longer stick to a single topic. Write a brief blog posting, three or four sentences at most, courteously reminding everyone why it's important to stick to the subject at hand when replying to blog items.

2.6   Internet Visit the PolyVision website at www.websterboards.com and read about electronic whiteboards. What advantages do you see in using this kind of whiteboard during a meeting? Draft a short e-mail to your boss outlining the product's advantages.

2.7   Telephones and Voice Mail Late on a Friday afternoon, you learn that the facilities department is going to move you—and your computer, your desk, and all your files—to another office first thing Monday morning. However, you have an important client meeting scheduled in your office for Monday afternoon, and you need to finalize some contract details on Monday morning. You simply can't lose access to your office at this point, and you're more than a little annoyed that your boss didn't ask you before approving the move. He has already left for the day, but you know he usually checks his voice mail over the weekend so you decide to leave a message asking him to cancel the move or at least call you at home as soon as possible. Using the voice mail guidelines listed in Table 2.3, plan your message (use an imaginary phone number as your contact number and make up any other details

you need for the call). As directed by your instructor, submit either a written script of the message or a podcast recording of the actual message.

2.8   Nonverbal Communication: Analyzing Written Messages Select a business letter and envelope that you have received at work or home. Analyze their appearance. What nonverbal messages do they send? Are these messages consistent with the content of the letter? If not, what could the sender have done to make the nonverbal communication consistent with the verbal communication?

2.9   Nonverbal Communication: Analyzing Body Language Describe what the following body movements suggest when someone exhibits them during a conversation. How do such movements influence your interpretation of spoken words?
  a. Shifting one's body continuously while seated
  b. Twirling and playing with one's hair
  c. Sitting in a sprawled position
  d. Rolling one's eyes
  e. Extending a weak handshake

2.10   Listening Skills: Self-Assessment How good are your listening skills? Use the following chart to rate yourself on each element of listening. Then examine your ratings to identify where you are strongest and where you can improve, using the tips in this chapter.

ELEMENT OF LISTENING	ALWAYS	FREQUENTLY	OCCASIONALLY	NEVER
1. I look for areas of interest when people speak.	____	____	____	____
2. I focus on content rather than delivery.	____	____	____	____
3. I wait to respond until I understand the content.	____	____	____	____
4. I listen for ideas and themes, not isolated facts.	____	____	____	____
5. I take notes only when needed.	____	____	____	____
6. I really concentrate on what speakers are saying.	____	____	____	____
7. I stay focused even when the ideas are complex.	____	____	____	____
8. I keep an open mind despite emotionally charged language.	____	____	____	____

Expand Your Knowledge
Exploring the Best of the Web

Making Meetings Work with the 3M Meeting Network
www.3m.com/meetingnetwork
The 3M Meeting Network contains a wide selection of articles on planning meetings, designing activities to build teamwork, and making better presentations. Click on "Articles and Advice," find the appropriate articles, and then answer the following questions.
  1. How can you know if a meeting should be held or not?
  2. How can good leaders show they trust the group's ability to perform successfully?

  3. What are the advantages and disadvantages of "open space" meetings, which take place without formal agendas or facilitation?

Surfing Your Way to Career Success

Bovée and Thill's Business Communication Resources offers links to hundreds of online resources that can help you with this course, your other college courses, and your career. Visit www.buscommresources.com, then click on "Business Communication Web Directory." The "Business Communication" section connects you to a variety of websites and articles on business English and business writing, as well as such important topics as information overload, company culture, company image, and business etiquette. Identify three websites from this section that could be useful in your business career. For each site, write a two-sentence summary of what the site offers and how it could help you launch and build your career.

Learn Interactively

Interactive Study Guide

Go to the Companion Website at www.prenhall.com/bovee and locate your book, then click "Companion Website." Select Chapter 2 to take advantage of the interactive "Chapter Quiz" to test your knowledge of chapter concepts. Receive instant feedback on whether you need additional studying. Also, visit the "Study Hall," where you'll find an abundance of valuable resources that will help you succeed in this course.

Peak Performance Grammar and Mechanics

If your instructor has required the use of "Peak Performance Grammar and Mechanics," either in your online course or on CD, you can continue to improve your skill with nouns and pronouns by using the "Peak Performance Grammar and Mechanics" module. Click on "Grammar Basics," and then click "Nouns and Pronouns." Take the Pretest to determine whether you have any weak areas. Then review those areas in the Refresher Course. Take the Follow-Up Test to check your grasp of nouns and pronouns. For an extra challenge or advanced practice, take the Advanced Test. Finally, for additional reinforcement in nouns, visit the Companion Website, click on any chapter, then click on "Improve Your Grammar, Mechanics, and Usage."

CHAPTER 3

Communicating in a World of Diversity

LEARNING OBJECTIVES

After studying this chapter, you will be able to

1 Discuss the opportunities and challenges of intercultural communication

2 Define culture and explain how culture is learned

3 Define ethnocentrism and stereotyping, then give three suggestions for overcoming these limiting mindsets

4 Explain the importance of recognizing cultural variations and list eight categories of cultural differences

5 Identify the steps you can take to improve your intercultural communication skills

6 Outline strategies for studying other cultures

7 List seven recommendations for writing clearly in multilanguage business environments

COMMUNICATION CLOSE-UP AT IBM

www.ibm.com

The "I" in IBM stands for "International," but it could just as easily stand for "Intercultural" as a testament to the computer giant's long-standing commitment to embracing diversity. Ted Childs, IBM's vice president of global workforce diversity, knows from years of experience that communicating successfully across cultures is no simple task, however—particularly in a company that employs more than 325,000 people and sells to customers in roughly 175 countries around the world.

Language alone presents a formidable barrier to communication when you consider that IBM's workforce speaks more than 165 languages, but language is just one of many elements that play a role in communication between cultures. Differences in age, ethnic background, gender, sexual orientation, physical ability, and economic status can all affect the communication process. Childs recognizes that these differences represent both a challenge and an opportunity, and a key part of his job is helping IBM executives and employees work together in a way that transforms their cultural differences into a critical business strength. As he

Ted Childs oversees IBM's efforts to build competitive advantage by capitalizing on the benefits of a diverse workforce.

puts it, workforce diversity has "moved from being a moral imperative to being a strategic imperative."

Throughout its long history of employing and working with people from different cultures, IBM has learned some powerful lessons. Perhaps the most significant is its conclusion that successfully managing a diverse workforce and competing in a diverse marketplace start with em-bracing those differences, not trying to ignore them or pretending they don't affect interpersonal communication. And it's a lesson that every aspiring business professional can take to heart. As Ted Childs puts it, "No matter who you are, you're going to have to work with people who are different from you . . . and manage people who are different from you."[1]

UNDERSTANDING THE OPPORTUNITIES AND CHALLENGES OF COMMUNICATION IN A DIVERSE WORLD

1 LEARNING OBJECTIVE

Discuss the opportunities and challenges of intercultural communication

Effective intercultural communication
- *Opens up business opportunities around the world.*
- *Improves the contributions of employees in a diverse workforce.*

IBM's experience (profiled in the chapter-opening Communication Close-Up) illustrates both the challenges and the opportunities for business professionals who know how to communicate with diverse audiences. Although the concept is often framed in terms of ethnic background, a broader and more useful definition of **diversity** "includes all the characteristics and experiences that define each of us as individuals."[2] As you'll learn in this chapter, these characteristics and experiences can have a profound effect on the way businesspeople communicate.

To a large degree, these effects on communication are the result of fundamental differences between cultures. **Intercultural communication** is the process of sending and receiving messages between people whose cultural background could lead them to interpret verbal and nonverbal signs differently. Every attempt to send and receive messages is influenced by culture, so to communicate successfully, you'll need a basic grasp of the cultural differences you may encounter and how you should handle them. Your efforts to recognize and surmount cultural differences will open up business opportunities throughout the world and maximize the contribution of all the employees in a diverse workforce.

The Opportunities in a Global Marketplace

You will communicate with people from other cultures throughout your career.

You might be a business manager looking for new customers or new sources of labor. Or you might be an employee looking for new work opportunities. Either way, chances are good that you'll be looking across international borders sometime in your career.

Thousands of U.S. businesses depend on exports for significant portions of their revenues. Every year, these companies export roughly $700 billion in materials and merchandise, along with billions more in personal and professional services. If you work in one of these companies, you may well be called on to visit or at least communicate with a wide variety of people who speak languages other than English and who live in cultures quite different from what you're used to (see Figure 3.1). Of the top ten export markets for U.S. products, only three (Canada, Great Britain, and Singapore) speak English as an official language, and two of those three (Canada and Singapore) have more than one official language.[3]

In the global marketplace, most natural boundaries and national borders are no longer the impassable barriers they once were. Domestic markets are opening to worldwide competition as businesses of all sizes look for new growth opportunities outside their own countries. For example, automotive giant Ford markets to customers in some 130 countries, providing websites that offer local information, usually in the local language.[4]

The Advantages of a Diverse Workforce

The diversity of today's workforce brings distinct advantages to businesses:
- *A broader range of views and ideas*
- *A better understanding of diverse, fragmented markets*
- *A broader pool of talent from which to recruit*

Even if you never visit another country or transact business on a global scale, you will interact with colleagues from a variety of cultures with a wide range of characteristics and life experiences. Over the past few decades, many innovative companies have changed the way they approach diversity, from seeing it as a legal requirement to provide equal opportunities to seeing it as a strategic opportunity to connect with customers and take advantage of the broadest possible pool of talent.[5] Smart business leaders such as IBM's Ted

FIGURE 3.1 Languages of the World

This map illustrates the incredible array of languages used around the world. Each dot represents the geographic center of the more than 6,900 languages tracked by the linguistic research firm SIL International. Even if all of your business communication takes place in English, you will interact with audiences who speak a variety of other native languages.

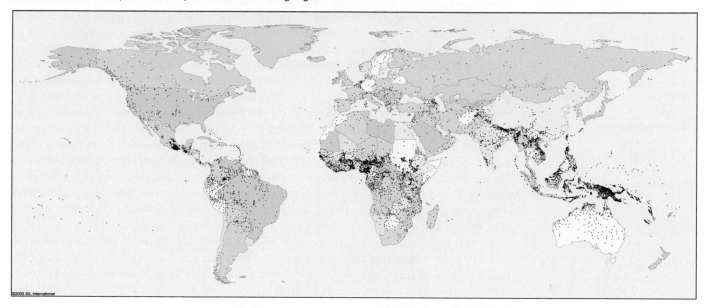

©2005 SIL International

Childs recognize the competitive advantages of a diverse workforce that offers a broader spectrum of viewpoints and ideas, helps companies understand and identify with diverse markets, and enables companies to benefit from a wider range of employee talents. As Renee Wingo of Virgin Mobile USA, a cell phone operator based in Warren, New Jersey, puts it, "You're not going to create any magic as a manager unless you bring together people with diverse perspectives who aren't miniversions of you."[6]

Diversity is simply a fact of life for all companies. The United States has been a nation of immigrants from the beginning, and that trend continues today. The Western and Northern Europeans who made up the bulk of immigrants during the nation's early years now share space with people from across Asia, Africa, Eastern Europe, and other parts of the world. By 2010 recent immigrants will account for half of all new U.S. workers.[7] Even the term *minority*, as it applies to non-white residents, makes less and less sense every year: In two states (California and New Mexico) and several dozen large cities, Caucasian Americans no longer constitute a clear majority.[8] Nor is this pattern of immigration unique to the United States: Workers from Africa, Asia, and the Middle East are moving to Europe in search of new opportunities, while workers from India, the Philippines, and Southeast Asia contribute to the employment base of the Middle East.[9]

Communication among people of diverse cultural backgrounds and life experiences is not always easy, but doing it successfully can create tremendous strategic advantages.

However, you and your colleagues don't need to be recent immigrants to constitute a diverse workforce. Differences in everything from age and gender to religion and ethnic heritage to geography and military experience enrich the workplace. Both immigration and workforce diversity create advantages—and challenges—for business communicators throughout the world.

The Challenges of Intercultural Communication

Diversity affects how business messages are conceived, planned, sent, received, and interpreted in the workplace. Today's increasingly diverse workforce encompasses a wide range of skills, traditions, backgrounds, experiences, outlooks, and attitudes toward work—all of which can affect employee behavior on the job. Supervisors face the challenge of communicating with these diverse employees, motivating them, and fostering cooperation and harmony among them. Teams face the challenge of working together closely, and companies are challenged to coexist peacefully with business partners and with the community as a whole.

The interaction of culture and communication is so pervasive that separating the two is virtually impossible. The way you communicate—from the language you speak and the nonverbal signals you send to the way you perceive other people—is influenced by the culture in which you were raised. The meaning of words, the significance of gestures, the importance of time and space, the rules of human relationships—these and many other aspects of communication are defined by culture. To a large degree, your culture influences the way you think, which naturally affects the way you communicate as both a sender and a receiver.[10] So you can see how intercultural communication is much more complicated than simply matching language between sender and receiver. It goes beyond mere words to beliefs, values, and emotions.

Throughout this chapter, you'll see numerous examples of how communication styles and habits vary from one culture to another. These examples are intended to illustrate the major themes of intercultural communication, not to give an exhaustive list of styles and habits of any particular culture. With an understanding of these major themes, you'll then be prepared to explore the specifics of any culture.

ENHANCING YOUR SENSITIVITY TO CULTURE AND DIVERSITY

The good news is that you're already an expert in culture, at least in the culture you grew up with. You understand how your society works, how people are expected to communicate, what common gestures and facial expressions mean, and so on. The bad news is that because you're such an expert in your own culture, your communication is largely automatic; that is, you rarely stop to think about the communication rules you're following. An important step toward successful intercultural communication is becoming more aware of these rules and of the way they influence your communication. A good place to start is to understand what culture is.

Understanding the Concept of Culture

2 LEARNING OBJECTIVE

Define culture and explain how culture is learned

Culture is a shared system of symbols, beliefs, attitudes, values, expectations, and norms for behavior. Your cultural background influences the way you prioritize what is important in life, helps define your attitude toward what is appropriate in any given situation, and establishes rules of behavior.[11] One study suggests that people from different cultures even look at the world—literally—in different ways. Shown a variety of pictures, Chinese subjects focused more on the whole picture and the harmony of elements within it whereas North Americans of European descent focused more on the dominant, individual objects in the scene.[12]

Actually, you belong to several cultures. In addition to the culture you share with all the people who live in your own country, you belong to other cultural groups, including an ethnic group, possibly a religious group, and perhaps a profession that has its own special language and customs. With its large population and long history of immigration, the United States is home to a vast array of cultures. As one indication of this diversity, the inhabitants of this country now speak more than 160 languages.[13] In contrast, Japan is much more homogeneous, having only a few separate cultural groups.[14]

Members of a given culture tend to have similar assumptions about how people should think, behave, and communicate, and they all tend to act on those assumptions in much the same way. Cultures can differ widely and vary in their rate of change, their degree of complexity, and their tolerance toward outsiders. These differences affect the level of trust and openness that you can achieve when communicating with people of other cultures.

People learn culture directly and indirectly from other members of their group. As you grow up in a culture, you are taught who you are and how best to function in that culture by the group's members. Sometimes you are explicitly told which behaviors are acceptable; at other times you learn by observing which values work best in a particular group. In these ways, culture is passed on from person to person and from generation to generation.[15]

In addition to being automatic, cultures tend to be *coherent*; that is, they appear to be fairly logical and consistent when viewed from the inside. For instance, the notion of progress is deeply embedded in the culture of the United States. Those who achieve are admired and rewarded, and those who don't are sometimes viewed negatively, even if they live perfectly happy and contented lives. Such coherence generally helps a culture function more smoothly internally, although it can create disharmony between cultures that don't view the world in the same way.

Finally, cultures also tend to be complete; that is, they provide most of their members with most of the answers to life's big questions. This idea of completeness dulls or even suppresses curiosity about life in other cultures. Therefore, such completeness can complicate communication with other cultures.[16]

Overcoming Ethnocentrism and Stereotyping

Ethnocentrism is the tendency to judge all other groups according to the standards, behaviors, and customs of one's own group. Given the automatic influence of one's own culture, when people compare their culture to others, they often conclude that their own group is superior.[17] An even more extreme reaction is **xenophobia**, a fear of strangers and foreigners. Clearly, businesspeople who take these views are not likely to communicate successfully across cultures.

Distorted views of other cultures or groups also result from **stereotyping**, assigning a wide range of generalized attributes to an individual on the basis of membership in a particular culture or social group. Whereas ethnocentrism and xenophobia represent negative views of everyone in a particular group, stereotyping is more a matter of oversimplifying and of failing to acknowledge individuality. For instance, assuming that an older colleague will be out of touch with the youth market or that a younger colleague can't be an inspiring leader is an example of stereotyping age groups.

Those who want to show respect for other people and to communicate effectively in business need to adopt a more positive viewpoint, in the form of **cultural pluralism**—the practice of accepting multiple cultures on their own terms. When crossing cultural boundaries, you'll be even more effective if you move beyond simple acceptance and adapt your own communication style to that of the new cultures you encounter—even integrating aspects of those cultures into your own.[18] A few simple habits can help you avoid both the negativity of ethnocentrism and the oversimplification of stereotyping:

- **Avoid assumptions.** Don't assume that others will act the same way you do, use language and symbols the same way you do, or even operate from the same values and beliefs. For instance, in a comparison of the 10 most important values in three cultures, people from the United States had no values in common with people from Japanese or Arab cultures.[19]
- **Avoid judgments.** When people act differently, don't conclude that they are in error or that their way is invalid or inferior.
- **Acknowledge distinctions.** Don't ignore the differences between another person's culture and your own.

Unfortunately, overcoming ethnocentrism and stereotyping is no simple task, even for people who are highly motivated to do so. You may need to change lifelong beliefs about yourself and your culture. Moreover, recent research suggests that people often have beliefs

Participation in group activities is an important method of learning about a culture's rules and expectations.

3 LEARNING OBJECTIVE

Define ethnocentrism and stereotyping, then give three suggestions for overcoming these limiting mindsets

Ethnocentrism is the tendency to judge all other groups according to the standards, behaviors, and customs of one's own group.

Stereotyping is assigning generalized attributes to an individual on the basis of membership in a particular group.

Cultural pluralism is the acceptance of multiple cultures on their own terms.

and biases that they're not even consciously aware of—and that may even conflict with the beliefs they *think* they have. (To see if you have some of these *implicit beliefs*, visit the Project Implicit website at **https://implicit.harvard.edu/implicit** and take some of the simple online tests.)[20]

Recognizing Variations in a Diverse World

4 LEARNING OBJECTIVE

Explain the importance of recognizing cultural variations and list eight categories of cultural differences

Cultural differences can lead to miscommunication in the workplace.

Whenever you communicate, your instinct is to encode your message using the assumptions of *your* culture. However, members of your audience decode your message according to the assumptions of *their* culture. Consequently, the greater the difference between cultures, the greater the chance for misunderstanding.[21] From having brand names that are obscene slang in another language to misunderstanding attitudes about worker-manager relationships, companies around the world have made numerous mistakes that have damaged relationships and lost sales. In one classic example, exhibitors at a trade show could not understand why Chinese visitors were not stopping by their booth. The exhibitors were wearing green hats and giving them away as promotional items. They soon discovered that for many Chinese people, green hats are associated with infidelity: the Chinese expression "He wears a green hat" indicates that a man's wife has been cheating on him. As soon as the exhibitors discarded the green hats and started giving out T-shirts instead, the Chinese attendees began visiting the booth.[22]

Treat people the way they expect to *be treated, not the way you* expect *to be treated.*

Intercultural communication breakdowns occur for a variety of reasons, from simple carelessness to assuming that other people's attitudes and lives are like ours. Part of the problem stems from treating others the way *you* want to be treated. The best approach when communicating with people from other cultures is to treat them the way *they* want to be treated.

Communicating Across Cultures

Test Your Intercultural Knowledge

Even well-intentioned businesspeople can make mistakes if they aren't aware of simple but important cultural differences. Can you spot the erroneous assumptions in these scenarios?

1. You're tired of the discussion and you want to move on to a new topic. You ask your Australian business associate, "Can we table this for a while?" To your dismay, your colleague ignores the request and keeps right on discussing the topic.
2. You finally made the long trip overseas to meet the new German director of your division. Despite slow traffic, you arrive only four minutes late. His door is shut, so you knock on it and walk in. The chair is too far away from the desk, so you pick it up and move it closer. Then you lean over the desk, stick out your hand and say, "Good morning, Hans, it's nice to meet you." Why is his reaction so chilly?
3. Your meeting went better than you'd ever expected. In fact, you found the Japanese representative for your new advertising agency to be very agreeable; she said yes to just about everything. When you share your enthusiasm with your boss, he doesn't appear very excited. Why?

Here's what went wrong in each situation:

1. To "table" something in Australia means to bring it forward for discussion, the opposite of the usual U.S. mean-

ing. The English that's spoken in Australia is closer to British than to U.S. English.
2. You've just broken four rules of German polite behavior: punctuality, privacy, personal space, and proper greetings. In time-conscious Germany, you should never arrive even a few minutes late. Also, Germans like their privacy and space, and many adhere to formal greetings of "Frau" and "Herr," even if the business association has lasted for years.
3. The word *yes* may not always mean "yes" in the Western sense. Japanese people may say *yes* to confirm they have heard or understood something but not necessarily to indicate that they agree with it. You'll seldom get a direct no. Some of the ways that Japanese people say no indirectly include "It will be difficult," "I will ask my supervisor," "I'm not sure," "We will think about it," and "I see."

CAREER APPLICATIONS

1. Have you ever been on the receiving end of an intercultural communication error, such as when someone inadvertently used an inappropriate gesture or figure of speech? How did you respond?
2. If you had arrived late at the office of the German colleague, what would have been a better way to handle the situation?

You can begin to learn how people in other cultures want to be treated by recognizing and accommodating eight main types of cultural differences: contextual, legal and ethical, social, nonverbal signals, age, gender, religion, and ability.

Contextual Differences

Every attempt at communication occurs within a **cultural context**, the pattern of physical cues, environmental stimuli, and implicit understanding that convey meaning between two members of the same culture. However, cultures around the world vary widely in the role that context plays in communication (see Figure 3.2).

In a **high-context culture** such as that of South Korea or Taiwan, people rely less on verbal communication and more on the context of nonverbal actions and environmental setting to convey meaning. For instance, a Chinese speaker expects the receiver to discover the essence of a message and uses indirectness and metaphor to provide a web of meaning.[23] In high-context cultures, the rules of everyday life are rarely explicit; instead, as individuals grow up, they learn how to recognize situational cues (such as gestures and tone of voice) and how to respond as expected.[24] The primary role of communication is building relationships, not exchanging information.[25]

In a **low-context culture** such as the United States or Germany, people rely more on verbal communication and less on circumstances and cues to convey meaning. A British speaker feels responsible for transmitting the meaning of the message and often places sentences in chronological sequence to establish a cause-and-effect pattern.[26] In a low-context culture, rules and expectations are usually spelled out through explicit statements such as "Please wait until I'm finished" or "You're welcome to browse."[27] The primary task of communication in low-context cultures is exchanging information.[28]

Contextual differences are apparent in the way cultures approach situations such as decision making, problem solving, and negotiating. For instance, in lower-context cultures, businesspeople tend to focus on the results of the decisions they face, a reflection of the cultural emphasis on logic and progress. Will this be good for our company? For my career? In comparison, higher-context cultures emphasize the means or the method by which the decision will be made. Building or protecting relationships can be as important as the facts and

Cultural context is the pattern of physical cues, environmental stimuli, and implicit understanding that conveys meaning between members of the same culture.

High-context cultures rely heavily on nonverbal actions and environmental setting to convey meaning; low-context cultures rely more on explicit verbal communication.

FIGURE 3.2 How Cultural Context Affects Business
Cultural context influences the nature of business communication in many ways. Note that these are generalized assessments of each culture; contextual variations can be found within each culture and from one individual to another.

IN LOW-CONTEXT CULTURES	IN HIGH-CONTEXT CULTURES
Executive offices are separate with controlled access.	Executive offices are shared and open to all.
Workers rely on detailed background information.	Workers do not expect or want detailed information.
Information is highly centralized and controlled.	Information is shared with everyone.
Objective data are valued over subjective relationships.	Subjective relationships are valued over objective data.
Business and social relationships are discrete.	Business and social relationships overlap.
Competence is valued as much as position and status.	Position and status are valued much more than competence.
Meetings have fixed agendas and plenty of advance notice.	Meetings are often called on short notice, and key people always accept.

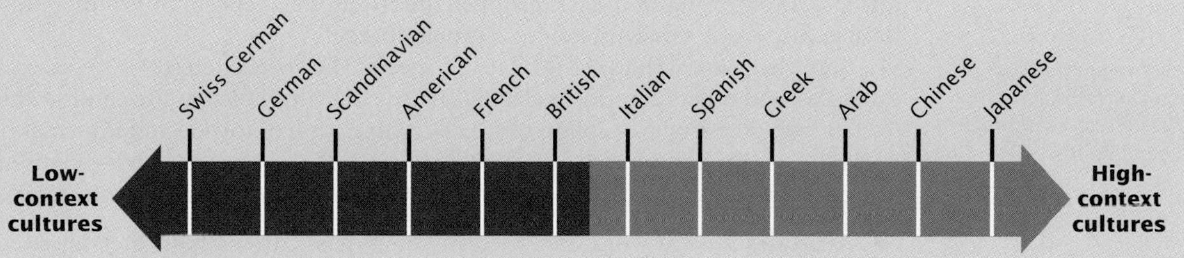

Low-context cultures ← Swiss German · German · Scandinavian · American · French · British · Italian · Spanish · Greek · Arab · Chinese · Japanese → High-context cultures

information used in making the decisions.[29] Consequently, negotiators working on business deals in such cultures may spend most of their time together building relationships rather than hammering out contractual details.

Whether you're making a decision, solving a problem, or negotiating a business deal, the communication tactics that work well in a high-context culture may backfire in a low-context culture, and vice versa. The key to success is understanding why the other party is saying and doing particular things and then adapting your approach accordingly.

Legal and Ethical Differences

Low-context cultures tend to value written agreements and interpret laws strictly, whereas high-context cultures view adherence to laws as being more flexible.

Cultural context also influences legal and ethical behavior. For example, because low-context cultures value the written word, they consider written agreements binding. But high-context cultures put less emphasis on the written word and consider personal pledges more important than contracts. They also tend to take a more flexible approach regarding adherence to the law, whereas low-context cultures would adhere to the law strictly.[30]

As you conduct business around the world, you'll find that both legal systems and ethical standards differ from culture to culture. In the United Kingdom and the United States, for instance, someone is presumed innocent until proved guilty, a principle rooted in English common law. However, in Mexico and Turkey, someone is presumed guilty until proved innocent, a principle rooted in the *Napoleonic Code.*[31]

Cultural differences can complicate ethical choices.

Similarly, bribing government officials appears to be a fairly common practice in countries such as Kenya, where businesspeople and consumers alike find themselves forced to pay *kitu kidogo* ("something small") to government officials in order to gain admittance to a hospital, receive a driver's license, or accomplish myriad other objectives of daily life.[32] Similar traditions exist in other countries, such as *huilu* in China, *vzyatka* in Russia, *baksheesh* in the Middle East, and *una mordida* ("a small bite") in Mexico.[33] In contrast, U.S. law prohibits U.S. companies from paying bribes, even in countries where the practice is accepted (or expected).[34]

Making ethical choices across cultures can seem complicated, but you can keep your messages ethical by applying four basic principles:[35]

Honesty and respect are cornerstones of ethical communication, regardless of culture.

- **Actively seek mutual ground.** To allow the clearest possible exchange of information, both parties must be flexible and avoid insisting that an interaction take place strictly in terms of one culture or another.
- **Send and receive messages without judgment.** To allow information to flow freely, both parties must recognize that values vary from culture to culture, and they must trust each other.
- **Send messages that are honest.** To ensure that the information is true, both parties must see things as they are—not as they would like them to be. Both parties must be fully aware of their personal and cultural biases.
- **Show respect for cultural differences.** To protect the basic human rights of both parties, each must understand and acknowledge the other's needs and preserve each other's dignity by communicating without deception.

Social Differences

The nature of social behavior varies among cultures, sometimes dramatically. Wal-Mart learned this when the giant retailer tried to expand into Germany. Store clerks resisted the company requirement of always smiling at customers because doing so was sometimes misinterpreted as flirting. Wal-Mart dropped the requirement and, after a number of other cultural and strategic missteps, left the German market.[36]

Formal rules of etiquette are explicit and well defined, but informal rules are learned through observation and imitation.

Some behavioral rules are formal and specifically articulated (table manners are a good example), and others are informal and learned over time (such as the comfortable distance to stand when talking to a colleague). The combination of formal and informal rules influences the overall behavior of most people in a society most of the time. In addition to the factors already discussed, social rules can vary from culture to culture in the following areas:

- **Attitudes toward work and success.** Many U.S. citizens hold the view that material comfort earned by individual effort is a sign of superiority and that people who work

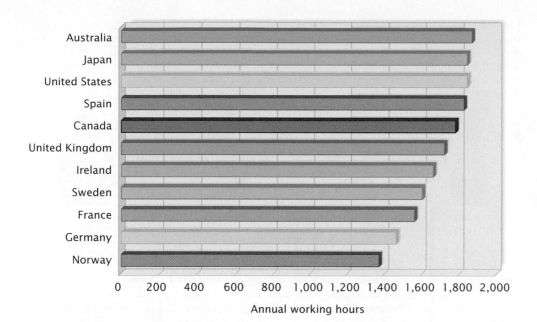

FIGURE 3.3 Working Hours Vary from Culture to Culture

Workers in Australia, Japan, Spain, and the United States average at least 1,800 hours of work per year, significantly more than workers in France, Germany, and Norway.

hard are better than those who don't. This view is reflected in the number of hours that U.S. employees work every year (see Figure 3.3).

- **Roles and status.** Culture dictates, or at least tries to dictate, the roles that people play, including who communicates with whom, what they communicate, and in what way. For example, in some countries women still don't play a prominent role in business, so women executives who visit these countries may find that they're not taken seriously as businesspeople.[37] Culture also dictates how people show respect and signify rank. For example, people in the United States show respect by addressing top managers as "Mr. Roberts" or "Ms. Gutierrez." However, people in China are addressed according to their official titles, such as "President" or "Manager."[38]

  Respect and rank are reflected differently from culture to culture in the way people are addressed in their working environment.

- **Use of manners.** What is polite in one culture may be considered rude in another. For instance, asking a colleague "How was your weekend?" is a common way of making small talk in the United States but the question sounds intrusive to people in cultures in which business and private lives are seen as totally separate. In Arab countries, it's impolite to take gifts to a man's wife but it's acceptable to take gifts to his children. In India, if you're invited to visit someone's home "any time," you should make an unexpected visit without waiting for a definite invitation. Failure to take the "any time" invitation literally would be an insult, a sign that you don't care to develop the friendship. Research a country's expectations before you visit, then watch carefully and learn after you arrive.

  The rules of polite behavior vary from country to country.

- **Concepts of time.** Business runs on schedules, deadlines, and appointments, but these matters are regarded differently from culture to culture. People in high-context cultures see time as a way to plan the business day efficiently, often focusing on only one task during each scheduled period and viewing time as a limited resource. However, executives from low-context cultures often see time as more flexible. Meeting a deadline is less important than building a business relationship. So the workday isn't expected to follow a rigid, preset schedule.[39] Trying to coax a team into staying on a strict schedule would be an attractive attribute in U.S. companies but could be viewed as pushy and overbearing in other cultures.

  Attitudes toward time, such as strict adherence to meeting schedules, can vary throughout the world.

Nonverbal Differences

As discussed in Chapter 2, nonverbal communication can be a reliable guide to determining the meaning of a message. However, this notion of reliability is valid only when the communicators belong to the same culture. For instance, the simplest hand gestures change meaning from culture to culture. A gesture that communicates good luck in Brazil is the equivalent of giving someone "the finger" in Colombia.[40] In fact, the area of gestures is so complicated that entire books have been written about it. Don't assume that the gestures you grew up with will translate to another culture; doing so could lead to embarrassing mistakes (see Figure 3.4).

FIGURE 3.4 Avoiding Nonverbal Mishaps

These examples illustrate some of the many nuances of nonverbal communication across cultures. Even smiling isn't quite as simple as it might seem. Americans tend to smile at strangers more often than people in many other cultures, so they are sometimes put off by what they consider unfriendly responses from strangers. Conversely, people from other cultures can be put off by the American habit of frequent smiling, which some view as insincere.

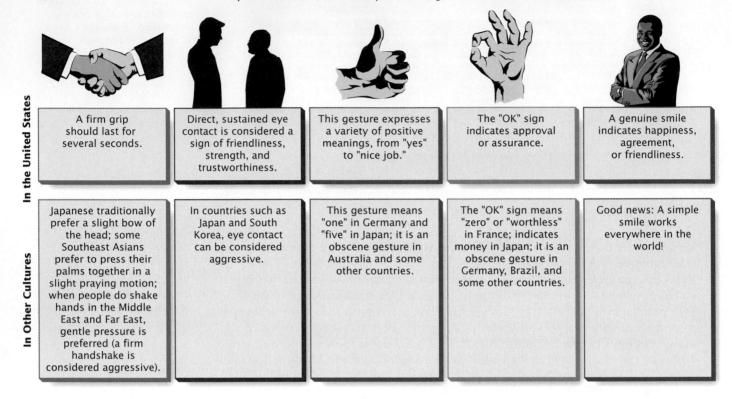

	In the United States			
A firm grip should last for several seconds.	Direct, sustained eye contact is considered a sign of friendliness, strength, and trustworthiness.	This gesture expresses a variety of positive meanings, from "yes" to "nice job."	The "OK" sign indicates approval or assurance.	A genuine smile indicates happiness, agreement, or friendliness.

	In Other Cultures			
Japanese traditionally prefer a slight bow of the head; some Southeast Asians prefer to press their palms together in a slight praying motion; when people do shake hands in the Middle East and Far East, gentle pressure is preferred (a firm handshake is considered aggressive).	In countries such as Japan and South Korea, eye contact can be considered aggressive.	This gesture means "one" in Germany and "five" in Japan; it is an obscene gesture in Australia and some other countries.	The "OK" sign means "zero" or "worthless" in France; indicates money in Japan; it is an obscene gesture in Germany, Brazil, and some other countries.	Good news: A simple smile works everywhere in the world!

Nonverbal differences can vary widely from culture to culture.

From colors to facial expression, nonverbal elements add yet another layer of richness and complexity to intercultural communication. When you have the opportunity to interact with people in another culture, the best advice is to study the culture in advance, then observe the way people behave in the following areas:

- **Greetings.** Do people shake hands, bow, or kiss lightly (on one side of the face or both)?
- **Personal space.** When people are conversing, do they stand closer together or farther away than you are accustomed to?
- **Touching.** Do people touch each other on the arm to emphasize a point or slap each other on the back to show congratulation? Or do they refrain from touching altogether?
- **Facial expressions.** Do people shake their heads to indicate "no" and nod them to indicate "yes"? This is what people are accustomed to in the United States, but it is not universal.
- **Eye contact.** Do people make frequent eye contact or avoid it? Frequent eye contact is often taken as a sign of honesty and openness in the United States, but in other cultures it can be a sign of aggressiveness or lack of respect.
- **Posture.** Do people slouch and relax in the office and in public, or do they sit up straight?
- **Formality.** In general, does the culture seem more or less formal than yours?

Following the lead of people who grew up in the culture is not only a great way to learn but a good way to show respect as well.

Age Differences

A culture's views on youth and aging affect how people communicate with one another.

In U.S. culture, the emphasis on youth is so strong that millions of older people spend millions of dollars every year trying to look or feel younger. Youth is associated with strength, energy, possibilities, and freedom. In contrast, age is too often associated with declining powers and a loss of respect and authority—even though older workers can offer broader experience, the benefits of important business relationships nurtured over many years, and high degrees of "practical intelligence"—the ability to solve complex, poorly defined problems.[41]

In contrast, in cultures that value age and seniority, longevity earns respect and increasing power and freedom. For instance, in many Asian societies, the oldest employees hold the most powerful jobs, the most impressive titles, and the greatest degree of freedom and decision-making authority. If a younger employee disagrees with one of these senior executives, the discussion is never conducted in public. The notion of "saving face," of avoiding public embarrassment, is too strong. Instead, if a senior person seems to be in error about something, other employees will find a quiet, private way to communicate whatever information they feel is necessary.[42]

As with all diversity issues, the solution to age-related conflicts can be found in respecting one another and working toward common goals. As Virginia Byrd, a veteran career counselor from Encinitas, California, put it, "It's a real blessing to have different generations in our workplaces. There is so much we can share, if we make the effort."[43]

Communication styles and expectations can vary widely between age groups, putting extra demands on teams that include workers of varying ages.

Gender Differences

The perception of men and women in business also varies from culture to culture. In the United States today, women find a much wider range of business opportunities than existed just a few decades ago. For instance, women now hold top positions or are in line for the top job at a number of leading corporations, including Archer Daniels Midland, eBay, Avon, MTV, Lucent Technologies, and Xerox.[44] However, such opportunity is not the case in more tradition-oriented societies, where men tend to hold most or all of the positions of authority and women are expected to play a more subservient role. Female executives who visit other cultures may not be taken seriously until they successfully handle challenges to their knowledge, capabilities, and patience.[45]

As more women enter the workforce and take on positions of increasing responsibility, it's important for company leaders to revisit assumptions and practices.[46] For instance, company cultures that have been dominated by men for years may have adopted communication habits that some women have difficulty relating to—such as the frequent use of sports metaphors or the acceptance of coarse language.

Whatever the culture, evidence suggests that men and women tend to have slightly different communication styles. Broadly speaking, men tend to emphasize content in their communication efforts whereas women place a higher premium on relationship maintenance.[47] This difference can create friction when two parties in a conversation have different needs and expectations from the interchange. Again, these are broad generalizations that do not apply to every person in every situation, but keeping them in mind can help men and women overcome communication hurdles in the workplace.

Men tend to emphasize content in their messages, and women tend to emphasize relationship maintenance.

Religious Differences

Religion is a dominant force in many cultures and the source of many differences between cultures.[48] The effort to accommodate employees' life interests on a broader scale has led a number of companies to address the issue of religion in the workplace. As one of the most personal and influential aspects of life, religion does bring potential for controversy in a work setting. On the one hand, some employees feel they should be able to express their beliefs in the workplace and not be forced to "check their faith at the door" when they come to work. On the other hand, companies want to avoid situations in which openly expressed religious differences may cause friction between employees or distract employees from their responsibilities. To help address such concerns, firms such as Ford, Intel, Texas Instruments, and American Airlines allow employees to form faith-based employee-support groups as part of their diversity strategies. In contrast, Proctor & Gamble is among those companies that don't allow organized religious activities at their facilities.[49] As more companies work to establish inclusive workplaces, and as more employees seek to integrate religious convictions into their daily work, you can expect to see this issue being discussed at many companies in the coming years.

Ability Differences

Colleagues and customers with disabilities that affect communication represent another important aspect of the diversity picture. People whose hearing, vision, or physical ability to operate computers is impaired can be at a significant disadvantage in today's workplace. As with other elements of diversity, success starts with respect for individuals and sensitivity to differences. Employers can also invest in a variety of *assistive technologies* that help people with disabilities perform activities that might otherwise be difficult or impossible. These technologies include devices and systems that help people communicate orally and visually, interact with computers and other equipment, and enjoy greater mobility in the workplace. For example, web designers can take steps to make websites more accessible to people with limited vision. Assistive technologies create a vital link for thousands of employees with disabilities, giving them the opportunity to pursue a greater range of career paths and giving employers access to a broader base of talent. With the United States heading for a potentially serious shortage of workers in a few years, the economy will benefit from everyone who can make a contribution and assistive technologies will be an important part of the solution.[50]

Adapting to U.S. Business Culture

If you are a recent immigrant to the United States or, otherwise, grew up in a culture outside the U.S. mainstream, you can apply all of the concepts and skills in this chapter to help you adapt to U.S. business culture. Here are some key points to remember as you become accustomed to business communication in this country:[51]

- **Individualism.** In contrast to cultures that value group harmony and group success, U.S. culture expects individuals to succeed by their own efforts and it rewards individual success. Even though teamwork is emphasized in many companies, competition between individuals is expected and even encouraged in many cases.
- **Equality.** Although the country's historical record on equality has not always been positive and inequalities still exist, equality is considered a core American value. This applies to race, gender, social background, and even age. To a greater degree than people in many other cultures, Americans believe that every person should be given the opportunity to pursue whatever dreams and goals he or she may have in life.
- **Privacy and personal space.** People in this country are accustomed to a fair amount of privacy, and this includes their "personal space" at work. For example, they expect you to knock before entering a closed office and to avoid asking questions about personal beliefs or activities until they get to know you well.
- **Time and schedules.** U.S. businesses value punctuality and the efficient use of time. For instance, meetings are expected to start and end at designated times.
- **Religion.** The United States does not have an official state religion. Many religions are practiced throughout the country, and people are expected to respect each other's beliefs.
- **Communication style.** Communication tends to be direct and focused on content and transactions, not relationships or group harmony.

These are generalizations, of course. Any nation of 300 million people will exhibit a wide variety of behaviors. However, following these guidelines will help you succeed in most business communication situations.

5 LEARNING OBJECTIVE

Identify the steps you can take to improve your intercultural communication skills

Improving intercultural skills is a career-long effort.

IMPROVING INTERCULTURAL COMMUNICATION SKILLS

Communicating successfully from one culture to another requires a variety of skills (see Figure 3.5). You can improve your intercultural skills throughout your entire career by studying other cultures and languages, respecting preferences for communication styles, learning to write and speak clearly, listening carefully, knowing when to use interpreters and translators, and helping others adapt to your culture.

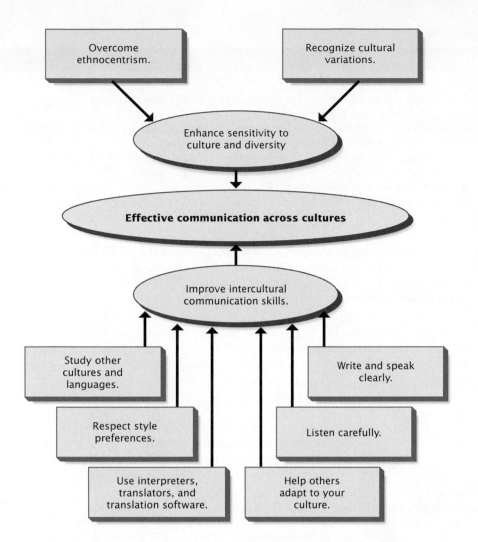

FIGURE 3.5
Components of Successful Intercultural Communication
Communicating in a diverse business environment is not always an easy task, but you can continue to improve your sensitivity and build your skills as you progress in your career.

Studying Other Cultures

Effectively adapting your communication efforts to another culture requires not only knowledge about the culture but also both the ability and the motivation to change your personal habits as needed.[52] In other words, it's not a simple task. Unfortunately, a thorough knowledge of another culture and its communication patterns (both verbal and nonverbal) can take years to acquire. Fortunately, you don't need to learn about the whole world all at once. Many companies appoint specialists for specific countries or regions, giving you a chance to focus on fewer cultures at a time. Some firms also provide resources to help employees prepare for interaction with other cultures. On IBM's global workforce diversity intranet site, for instance, employees can click on the GoingGlobal link to learn about customs in specific cultures.[53]

Even a small amount of research and practice will help you get through many business situations. In addition, most people respond positively to honest effort and good intentions and many business associates will help you along if you show an interest in learning more about their cultures.

Try to approach situations with an open mind and a healthy sense of humor. When you make a mistake, simply apologize if appropriate, ask the other person to explain the accepted way, and then move on. As business becomes ever more global, even the most tradition-bound cultures are learning to deal with outsiders more patiently and overlook the occasional cultural blunder.[54]

Numerous websites and books offer advice on traveling to and working in specific cultures. Also try to sample newspapers, magazines, and even the music and movies of another

6 LEARNING OBJECTIVE

Outline strategies for studying other cultures

Mistakes will happen, and when they do, apologize (if appropriate), ask about the accepted way, and move on.

TABLE 3.1 Doing Business in Other Cultures

ACTION	DETAILS TO CONSIDER
Understand social customs	• Is the society homogeneous or heterogeneous? • How do people react to strangers? Are they friendly? Hostile? Reserved? • How do people greet each other? Should you bow? Nod? Shake hands? • How do you express appreciation for an invitation to lunch, dinner, or someone's home? Should you bring a gift? Send flowers? Write a thank-you note? • Are any phrases, facial expressions, or hand gestures considered rude? • How do you attract the attention of a waiter? Do you tip the waiter? • When is it rude to refuse an invitation? How do you refuse politely? • What topics may or may not be discussed in a social setting? In a business setting?
Learn about clothing and food preferences	• What occasions require special clothing? • What colors are associated with mourning? Love? Joy? • Are some types of clothing considered taboo for one gender or the other? • How many times a day do people eat? • How are hands or utensils used when eating? • Where is the seat of honor at a table?
Assess political patterns	• How stable is the political situation? • Does the political situation affect businesses in and out of the country? • What are the traditional government institutions? • Is it appropriate to talk politics in social or business situations?
Understand religious and folk beliefs	• To which religious groups do people belong? • Which places, objects, actions, and events are sacred? • Is there a tolerance for minority religions? • How do religious holidays affect business and government activities? • Does religion require or prohibit eating specific foods? At specific times?
Learn about economic and business institutions	• Is the society homogeneous or heterogeneous? • What languages are spoken? • What are the primary resources and principal products? • Are businesses generally large? Family controlled? Government controlled? • Is it appropriate to do business by telephone? By fax? By e-mail? • What are the generally accepted working hours? • How do people view scheduled appointments? • Are people expected to socialize before conducting business?
Appraise the nature of ethics, values, and laws	• Is money or a gift expected in exchange for arranging business transactions? • Do people value competitiveness or cooperation? • What are the attitudes toward work? Toward money? • Is politeness more important than factual honesty?

country. For instance, a movie can demonstrate nonverbal customs even if you don't grasp the language. (However, be careful not to rely solely on entertainment products. If people in other countries based their opinions of American culture only on the silly teen flicks and violent action movies that the United States exports around the globe, what sort of impression do you imagine they'd get?) For some of the key issues to research before doing business in another country, refer to Table 3.1.

Studying Other Languages

English is the most prevalent language in international business, but don't assume that everyone understands it or speaks it the same way.

Consider what it must be like to work at IBM, where the global workforce speaks more than 165 languages. Without the ability to communicate in more than one language, how could this diverse group of people ever conduct business? As commerce continues to become more globalized, the demand for multilingual communicators continues to grow as well. Some countries have emphasized language diversity more than others over the years. For instance, in the Netherlands, with its long history of international trade, fluency in multiple languages is considered an essential business skill.[55] Shifts in business patterns can dramatically affect language learning, too. As U.S. companies continue to outsource a variety of business functions to facilities in India, many Indians now view English skills as an important career asset. Conversely, the growing international status of China as a manufacturing powerhouse is prompting many professionals in the United Sates and other countries to learn Mandarin, the official language in China.[56]

To simplify matters, some multinational companies ask all their employees to use English when communicating with employees in other countries, wherever they're located. Employees of Nissan, Japan's third-largest automaker, use English for communicating with colleagues around the world. When the company formed a strategic relationship with Renault, a French carmaker, the situation at Nissan headquarters became even more interesting because English is not the native language of either Japanese or French employees.[57]

Similarly, a number of U.S. companies are teaching their English-speaking employees a second language to facilitate communication with their co-workers. The Target retail chain is among those sponsoring basic Spanish classes for English-speaking supervisors of immigrant employees. Elsewhere around the country, enrollment is growing in specialized classes such as health-care Spanish and Spanish for professionals.[58]

Even if your colleagues or customers in another country do speak your language, it's worth the time and energy to learn common phrases in theirs. Learning the basics not only helps you get through everyday business and social situations but also demonstrates your commitment to the business relationship. After all, the other person probably spent years learning your language.

Finally, don't assume that two countries speaking the same language speak it the same way. The French spoken in Quebec and other parts of Canada is often noticeably different from the French spoken in France. Similarly, it's often said that the United States and the United Kingdom are two countries divided by a common language. For instance, *period* (punctuation), *elevator*, and *gasoline* in the United States are *full stop*, *lift*, and *petrol* in the United Kingdom.

Many companies find that they must be able to conduct business in languages other than English.

If you have a long-term business relationship with people of another culture, it is helpful to learn at least some basic words and phrases of their language.

Respecting Preferences for Communication Style

Communication style—including the level of directness, the degree of formality, preferences for written versus spoken communication, and other factors—varies widely from culture to culture. Knowing what your communication partners expect can help you adapt to their particular style. Once again, watching and learning are the best ways to improve your skills. However, you can infer some generalities from what you already know about a culture. For instance, U.S. workers typically prefer an open and direct communication style; they find other styles frustrating or suspect. Directness is also valued in Sweden as a sign of efficiency; but, unlike discussions in the United States, heated debates and confrontations are unusual. Italian, German, and French executives don't soften up colleagues with praise before they criticize—doing so seems manipulative to them. However, professionals from high-context cultures, such as Japan or China, tend to be less direct.[59]

Business correspondence in other countries is often more formal than the style used by U.S. businesspeople (see Figure 3.6). Of course, if you carry formality to extremes, you'll sound unnatural.

Business correspondence is often more formal in other countries than it is in the United States.

Writing and Speaking Clearly

When sending written communication to businesspeople from another culture, familiarize yourself with their written communication preferences and adapt your approach, style, and tone to meet their expectations. Follow these recommendations:[60]

- **Use simple, clear language.** Use precise words that don't have the potential to confuse with multiple meanings. For instance, the word *rich* has at least half a dozen different meanings, whereas *wealthy h*as exactly one, leaving no room for ambiguity.
- **Be brief.** Use simple sentences and short paragraphs, breaking information into smaller chunks that are easier for your reader to capture and translate. Remember that your messages need to be translated one word at a time.[61]

7 LEARNING OBJECTIVE

List seven recommendations for writing clearly in multilanguage business environments

FIGURE 3.6 Effective German Business Letter (Translated)
In Germany, business letters usually open with a reference to the business relationship and close with a compliment to the recipient. In this letter written by a supplier to a nearby retailer, you can see how the tone is more formal than would typically be used in the United States.

- **Use transitional elements.** Help readers follow your train of thought by using plenty of transitional words and phrases. Precede related points with expressions such as *in addition* and *first, second,* and *third.*
- **Address international correspondence properly.** Refer to Table A.1 through Table A.5 in Appendix A for an explanation of different address elements and salutations commonly used in certain foreign countries.
- **Cite numbers and dates carefully.** In the United States, 12-05-07 means December 5, 2007, but in many other countries, it means May 12, 2007. Dates in Japan and China are usually expressed with the year first, followed by the month and then the day; therefore, to write December 5, 2007 in Japan, write it as 2007-12-05. Similarly, 1.000 means one with three decimal places in the United States and Great Britain, but it means one thousand in many European countries.
- **Avoid slang, idiomatic phrases, and business jargon.** Everyday speech and writing are full of slang and **idiomatic phrases,** phrases that mean more than the sum of their lit-

FIGURE 3.7 Ineffective Intercultural Letter

This letter from a U.S. sales representative to a manager in France exhibits several intercultural mistakes, including the informal tone and use of American slang. Compare this with the improved version in Figure 3.8.

Fails to follow French preferences for title and address format

Uses reader's first name, which is much too informal for most French business correspondence

Uses slang and idioms throughout the message, creating the potential for confusion (e.g., hammered, bottlenecks, shut-eye, crunch, struck out, jam)

Fails to provide a total of the extra expenses

Fails to alert the reader that other documents are enclosed

Uses the U.S. format for the date, rather than the international format typically used by French writers

Wastes reader's time with unnecessarily dramatic and long description of weather problems

Buries specific information in awkward phrasing

Closes with a self-centered tone rather than trying to help the reader

---

La Cristallerie

Troy Halford, U.S. Sales Representative
163 Pico Boulevard
Los Angeles, CA 90032
Voice: (213) 975-8924
Fax: (213) 860-3489
halford@home.com

April 7, 2008

Mr. Pierre Coll
Director of Accounting
La Cristallerie
22 Marne Blvd.
Beaune, France 21200

Dear Pierre:

I know you've had gorgeous spring weather, with sunny skies and balmy days. But here in the States, it's been a spring of another color. We've been hammered with storms, flooding, and even late snow. Travel over here has been a nightmare, which is why you'll find my expenses a bit elevated this month.

I realize that you've asked all the reps to reduce rather than increase our expenses, but there were extenuating circumstances this last month. All the bad weather we've been having has caused major bottlenecks, with flights canceled and people forced to sleep in the terminals wherever they could find a spot.

After being stuck in the Chicago airport for 18 hours straight, I was desperate for a hot shower and some shut-eye, so I decided to wait out the crunch in a hotel. I know that hotels near airports are expensive, but I struck out trying to book a cheaper room in town. The bottom line is I had to spend extra funds for a hotel at $877; meals, which came to some $175; $72 just in transportation from the terminal to the hotel, and extra phone calls totaling $38.

I appreciate your understanding these unique circumstances. I was really in a jam.

Sincerely,

Troy Halford

Troy Halford
U.S. Sales Rep

---

eral parts. Many of these informal usages are so deeply ingrained, in fact, that you may not even be aware that you're using them. Examples from U.S. English include phrases like "Off the top of my head" and "More bang for the buck." Your audience may have no idea what you're talking about when you use such phrases.

- **Avoid humor and other references to popular culture.** Jokes and references to popular entertainment usually rely on subtle cultural issues that might be completely unknown to your audience.

Although some of these differences may seem trivial, meeting the expectations of an international audience illustrates both knowledge of and respect for the other cultures (see Figure 3.7 and Figure 3.8).

When talking with people whose native language is different from yours, remember that the processing of even everyday conversations can be difficult. For instance, speakers from the United States are notorious for stringing together multiple words into a single, mystifying pseudoword. "Did you eat yet?" becomes "Jeetyet?" and "Can I help you?" becomes

FIGURE 3.8 Effective Intercultural Letter
This version of the letter to a manager in France follows French standards for correspondence and is also easier to read and to scan.

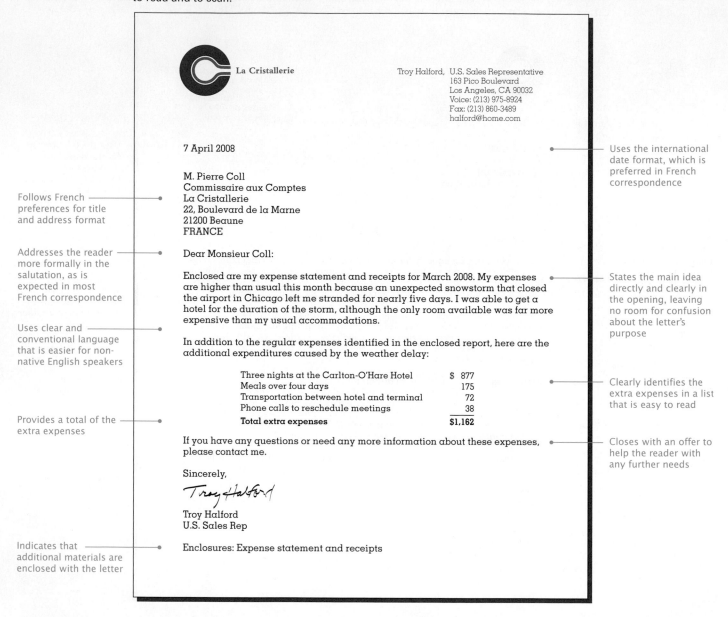

Follows French preferences for title and address format

Addresses the reader more formally in the salutation, as is expected in most French correspondence

Uses clear and conventional language that is easier for non-native English speakers

Provides a total of the extra expenses

Indicates that additional materials are enclosed with the letter

Uses the international date format, which is preferred in French correspondence

States the main idea directly and clearly in the opening, leaving no room for confusion about the letter's purpose

Clearly identifies the extra expenses in a list that is easy to read

Closes with an offer to help the reader with any further needs

DOCUMENT MAKEOVER

IMPROVE THIS LETTER

To practice correcting drafts of actual documents, visit your online course or the access-code-protected portion of the Companion Website. Click "Document Makeovers," then click Chapter 3. You will find a letter that contains problems and errors relating to what you've learned in this chapter about developing effective intercultural communication skills. Use the Final Draft decision tool to create an improved version of this letter. Check the message for a communication style that keeps the message brief; does not become too familiar or informal; uses transitional elements appropriately; and avoids slang, idioms, jargon, and technical language.

"Cannahepya?" Similarly, the French language frequently uses a concept known as *liaison*, in which one word is intentionally joined with the next. Without a lot of practice, new French speakers have a hard time telling when one word ends and the next one begins.

To be more effective in intercultural conversations, remember to (1) speak slowly and clearly; (2) don't rephrase until it's obviously necessary (immediately rephrasing something you've just said doubles the translation workload for the listener); (3) look for and ask for feedback to make sure your message is getting through; (4) don't talk down to the other person by overenunciating words or oversimplifying sentences; and (5) at the end of the conversation, double-check to make sure you and the listener agree on what has been said and decided.

Listening Carefully

Languages vary considerably in the significance of tone, pitch, speed, and volume. The English word *progress* can be a noun or a verb, depending on which syllable you accent. In Chinese, the meaning of the word *mà* changes depending on the speaker's tone; it can mean *mother, pileup, horse,* or *scold*. Regular Arabic speech can sound excited or angry to an English-speaking U.S. listener.[62] Conversely, businesspeople from Japan tend to speak more softly than Westerners.

With some practice, you can start to get a sense of vocal patterns. The key is simply to accept what you hear first, without jumping to conclusions about meaning or motivation. Let other people finish what they have to say. If you interrupt, you may miss something important. You'll also show a lack of respect. If you do not understand a comment, ask the person to repeat it. Any momentary awkwardness you might feel in asking for extra help is less important than the risk of unsuccessful communication.

Speaking clearly and getting plenty of feedback are two of the keys to successful intercultural conversations.

To listen more effectively in intercultural situations, accept what you hear without judgment and let people finish what they have to say.

Using Interpreters, Translators, and Translation Software

You may encounter business situations that require using an *interpreter* (for spoken communication) or a *translator* (for written communications). In addition, most customers expect to be addressed in their native language, particularly concerning advertising, warranties, repair and maintenance manuals, and product labels. These documents certainly require the services of a translator. Microsoft spends several hundred million dollars a year to make virtually all of its software products, websites, and help documents available in dozens of languages.[63]

Interpreters and translators can be expensive, but skilled professionals provide invaluable assistance for communicating in other cultural contexts.[64] Keeping up with current language usage in a given country or culture is also critical in order to avoid embarrassing blunders. Landor Associates, a leading marketing agency, usually engages three native-language speakers to review translated materials to make sure the sense of the message is compatible with current usage and slang in a given country.[65] Some companies use *back-translation* to ensure accuracy. Once a translator encodes a message into another language, a different translator retranslates the same message into the original language. This back-translation is then compared with the original message to discover any errors or discrepancies.

The time and cost required for professional translation has encouraged the development of **machine translation**, any form of computerized intelligence used to translate one language to another. Dedicated software tools and online services such as WorldLingo (www.worldlingo.com) offer some form of automated translation. Major search engines such as Alta Vista and Google let you request a translated version of the websites you find. Although none of these tools promises translation quality on a par with human translators, they can be quite useful with individual words and short phrases, and they can give you the overall gist of a message (see "Connecting with Technology: The Gist of Machine Translation").[66]

Helping Others Adapt to Your Culture

Now that you have a good appreciation for the complexity of getting your message across to someone in another culture, you can also appreciate the challenge faced by people from other cultures when they try to communicate with you. Whether a younger person is unaccustomed to the formalities of a large corporation or a colleague from another country is working on a team with you, look for opportunities to help people fit in and adapt their communication style. For more

Experienced international speakers such as Dr. Eric Schmidt, Google's Chairman and CEO, are careful to incorporate culture and language variations into their communication efforts.

Connecting with Technology

The Gist of Machine Translation

What is the writer trying to say in the following sentence?

> We have the need to balance for the barriers on this one or the market could draw well after us.

Here's the original sentence, which uses a tone that is overly casual and colloquial—a common problem in U.S. business documents:

> We need to swing for the fences on this one or the market could shoot right past us.

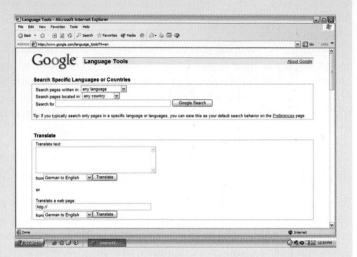

When this sentence was run through a simple computerized translation service, from English to French and back to English, the software clearly had trouble with the "swing for the fences" and "shoot right past us" figures of speech. Without hands-on intervention from experienced human translators, machine translation systems can produce results that are anywhere from amusing to nonsensical to dangerous.

However, you won't always have the luxury of waiting for, or paying for, a human translator. For example, your sales department might receive an unexpected e-mail message from somebody who appears to be a potential customer in another country. You don't want the expense of hiring a translator this early in the relationship, but you don't want to let a big deal slip away either. By running the message through a basic machine translator, chances are you can get a basic idea of the message almost instantly. At the very least, you'll probably be able to tell whether the message is important enough to warrant the time and expense of a translator. If you get results that make you scratch your head or laugh out loud, do call in a translator to

make sure that you and the sender understand one another correctly.

CAREER APPLICATIONS

1. Why do you think a computer might have trouble translating "swing for the fences" (a baseball phrase for trying as hard as one can to hit the ball out of the park)?
2. What are some examples of business documents that would probably be safe to read via machine translation? What are some that would be dangerous to trust to software?

ideas on how to improve communication in the workplace, see "Checklist: Improving Intercultural Communication Skills."

Remember that speaking and listening are usually much harder in a second language than writing and reading are. Oral communication requires participants to create and process sound in addition to decoding meaning, and it doesn't provide any time to go back and reread

 CHECKLIST: Improving Intercultural Communication Skills

- Study other cultures so that you can appreciate cultural variations.
- Study the languages of people with whom you communicate, even if you can learn only a few basic words and phrases.
- Help nonnative speakers learn your language.
- Respect cultural preferences for communication style.
- Write clearly, using brief messages, simple language, generous transitions, and appropriate international conventions.

- Avoid slang, humor, and references to popular culture.
- Speak clearly and slowly, giving listeners time to translate your words.
- Ask for feedback to ensure successful communication.
- Listen carefully and ask speakers to repeat anything you don't understand.
- Use interpreters and translators for important messages.

or rewrite. So instead of asking a foreign colleague to provide information in a conference call, you could set up an intranet site where the person can file a written report. Similarly, using instant messaging, e-mail, or blogging is often easier for colleagues with different native languages than participating in live conversations. An added plus with many of these technologies is overcoming the barrier of time zones. You can simply carry on a written conversation online, rather than participating in phone calls early in the morning or late at night.

Whatever assistance you can provide will be greatly appreciated. Smart businesspeople recognize the value of intercultural communication skills. Moreover, chances are that while you're helping others, you'll learn something about other cultures, too.

COMMUNICATION CHALLENGES AT IBM

Ted Childs is responsible for overall diversity planning and strategy at IBM, but every manager throughout the company is expected to foster a climate of inclusion and support for employees of every cultural background. As a team leader in one of IBM's software development labs, you're learning to exercise sound business judgment and use good listening skills to help resolve situations that arise within your diverse group of employees. How would you address these challenges?

Individual Challenge: Vasily Pevsner, a Russian immigrant, has worked in the department for five years. He works well alone, but he resists working with other employees, even in team settings where collaboration is expected. Given the importance that you place on teamwork, how should you handle the situation? List several alternatives for addressing this dilemma, identify which one you would choose, then explain why.

Team Challenge: Your employees are breaking into ethnically based cliques. Members of ethnic groups eat together, socialize together, and often chat in their native languages while they work. You appreciate how these groups give their members a sense of community, but you worry that these informal communication channels are alienating nonmembers and fragmenting the flow of information. How can you encourage a stronger sense of community and teamwork across your department? Brainstorm at least three steps you can take to encourage better cross-cultural communication in your group.

SUMMARY OF LEARNING OBJECTIVES

1 **Discuss the opportunities and challenges of intercultural communication.** The global marketplace spans natural boundaries and national borders, allowing worldwide competition between businesses of all sizes. Therefore, today's businesspeople are likely to communicate across international borders with people who live in different cultures. Moreover, even domestic workforces are becoming more and more diverse, with employees having different national, religious, and ethnic backgrounds. In this environment, companies can benefit from a broader range of viewpoints and ideas, have a better understanding of diverse markets, and recruit workers from the broadest possible pool of talent. However, intercultural communication presents challenges as well, including motivating diverse employees to cooperate and to work together in teams, as well as understanding enough about how culture affects language to prevent miscommunication.

2 **Define culture and explain how culture is learned.** Culture is a shared system of symbols, beliefs, attitudes, values, expectations, and norms for behavior. Culture is learned by listening to advice from other members of a society and by observing their behaviors. This double-edged method uses direct and indirect learning to ensure that culture is passed from person to person and from generation to generation.

3 **Define *ethnocentrism* and *stereotyping*, then give three suggestions for overcoming these limiting mindsets.** Ethnocentrism is the tendency to judge all other groups according to the standards, behaviors, and customs of one's own group. Stereotyping is assigning a wide range of generalized attributes to individuals on the basis of their membership in a particular culture or social group, without considering an individual's unique characteristics. To overcome ethnocentrism and stereotyping, follow three suggestions: (1) avoid assumptions, (2) avoid judgments, and (3) acknowledge distinctions.

4 **Explain the importance of recognizing cultural variations, and list eight categories of cultural differences.** People from different cultures encode and decode messages differently, increasing the chances of misunderstanding. By recognizing and accommodating cultural differences, we avoid automatically assuming that everyone's thoughts and actions are just like ours. Begin by focusing on eight categories of differences: contextual differences (the degree to which a culture relies on verbal or nonverbal actions to convey meaning), legal and ethical differences (the degree to which laws and ethics are regarded and obeyed), social differences (how members value work and success, recognize status, define manners, and think about time), nonverbal differences (differing attitudes toward greetings, personal space, touching, facial expression, eye contact, posture, and formality), age differences (how members think about youth, seniority, and longevity), gender differences (how men and women communicate), religious differences (how beliefs affect workplace relationships), and ability differences (inclusive strategies that enable people with disabilities to more fully communicate with the rest of the workforce).

5 **Identify the steps you can take to improve your intercultural communication skills.** Communicating successfully from one culture to another requires a variety of skills, all of which you can continue to improve throughout your career. Make your intercultural communication effective by studying other cultures; studying other languages; respecting your audience's preferences for communication style; writing as clearly as possible; speaking as clearly as you can; listening carefully; using interpreters, translators, and translation software when necessary; and helping others adapt to your own culture.

6 **Outline strategies for studying other cultures.** Although a thorough knowledge of another culture and its language(s) can take years to acquire, conducting research will help you grasp the big picture and recognize enough basics to get through most business situations. Find websites and books that offer advice on traveling to and working in specific cultures. Also sample newspapers, magazines, music, and movies of the culture you're interested in to get an idea of dress, nonverbal customs, manners, and so on—always being careful not to read too much into entertainment products.

7 **List seven recommendations for writing clearly in multilanguage business environments.** Take extra care with your writing, adapting your approach, style, and tone to meet audience expectations. To write effectively to multicultural audiences, follow these recommendations: (1) use simple, clear language; (2) be brief; (3) use transitional elements; (4) address international correspondence properly; (5) cite numbers and dates carefully; (6) avoid slang, idiomatic phrases, and unfamiliar jargon; and (7) avoid humor and other references to popular culture.

Test Your Knowledge

1. How have market globalization and cultural diversity contributed to the increased importance of intercultural communication?
2. What are the potential advantages of a diverse workforce?
3. How do high-context cultures differ from low-context cultures?
4. In addition to contextual differences, what other categories of cultural differences exist?
5. What is ethnocentrism, and how can it be overcome in communication?
6. What four principles apply to ethical intercultural communication?
7. Why should you avoid slang and idioms when addressing a culturally diverse audience?

8. What are some ways to improve speaking and listening skills when communicating with people of other cultures?
9. What are the risks of using computerized translation when you need to read a document written in another language?
10. What steps can you take to help someone from another culture adapt to your culture?

Apply Your Knowledge

1. What are some of the intercultural differences that managers of a U.S.-based firm might encounter during a series of business meetings with a China-based company whose managers speak English fairly well?
2. What are some of the intercultural communication issues to consider when deciding whether to accept a job in an overseas

branch of a U.S. company? How about a job in the United States with a local branch of a foreign-owned firm? Explain.

3. How do you think company managers from a country that has a relatively homogeneous culture might react when they do business with the culturally diverse staff of a company based in a less homogeneous country? Explain your answer.

4. Your company has relocated to a U.S. city where Vietnamese culture is strongly established. Many of your employees will be from this culture. What can you do to improve communication between your management and the Vietnamese Americans you are currently hiring?

5. **Ethical Choices** Your office in Turkey desperately needs the supplies that have been sitting in Turkish customs for a month. Should you bribe a customs official to speed up delivery? Explain your decision.

Practice Your Knowledge

Message for Analysis

Your boss wants to send a brief e-mail message welcoming employees recently transferred to your department from the company's Hong Kong branch. They all speak English, but your boss asks you to review his message for clarity. What would you suggest your boss change in the following e-mail message—and why? Would you consider this message to be audience centered? Why or why not?

> I wanted to welcome you ASAP to our little family here in the States. It's high time we shook hands in person and not just across the sea. I'm pleased as punch about getting to know you all, and I for one will do my level best to sell you on America.

Exercises

For active links to all websites discussed in this chapter, visit this text's website at **www.prenhall.com/bovee**. Locate your book and click on its Companion Website link. Then select Chapter 3, and click on "Featured Websites." Locate the name of the page or the URL related to the material in the text. Please note that links to sites that become inactive after publication of the book will be removed from the Featured Websites section.

3.1 **Intercultural Sensitivity: Recognizing Variations** You represent a Canadian toy company that's negotiating to buy miniature truck wheels from a manufacturer in Osaka, Japan. In your first meeting, you explain that your company expects to control the design of the wheels as well as the materials that are used to make them. The manufacturer's representative looks down and says softly, "Perhaps that will be difficult." You press for agreement, and to emphasize your willingness to buy, you show the prepared contract you've brought with you. However, the manufacturer seems increasingly vague and uninterested. What cultural differences may be interfering with effective communication in this situation? Explain.

3.2 **Ethical Choices** A U.S. manager wants to ship machine parts to a West African country, but a government official there expects a special payment before allowing the shipment into the country. How can the two sides resolve their different approaches without violating U.S. rules against bribing foreign officials? On the basis of the information presented in Chapter 1, would you consider this situation an ethical dilemma or an ethical lapse? Please explain.

3.3 **Teamwork** Working with two other students, prepare a list of 10 examples of slang (in your own language) that might be misinterpreted or misunderstood during a business conversation with someone from another culture. Next to each example, suggest other words you might use to convey the same message. Do the alternatives mean *exactly* the same as the original slang or idiom?

3.4 **Intercultural Communication: Studying Cultures** Choose a specific country, such as India, Portugal, Bolivia, Thailand, or Nigeria, with which you are not familiar. Research the culture and write a brief summary of what a U.S. manager would need to know about concepts of personal space and rules of social behavior in order to conduct business successfully in that country.

3.5 **Multicultural Workforce: Bridging Differences** Differences in gender, age, and physical abilities contribute to the diversity of today's workforce. Working with a classmate, role-play a conversation in which
a. A woman is being interviewed for a job by a male personnel manager.
b. An older person is being interviewed for a job by a younger personnel manager.
c. An employee who is a native speaker of English is being interviewed for a job by a hiring manager who is a recent immigrant with relatively poor English skills.
How did differences between the applicant and the interviewer shape the communication? What can you do to improve communication in such situations?

3.6 **Intercultural Sensitivity: Understanding Attitudes** As the director of marketing for a telecommunications firm based in Germany, you're negotiating with an official in Guangzhou, China, who's in charge of selecting a new telephone system for the city. You insist that the specifications be spelled out in the contract. However, your Chinese counterpart seems to have little interest in technical and financial details. What can you do or say to break this intercultural deadlock and obtain the contract so that both parties are comfortable?

3.7 **Cultural Variations: Ability Differences** You are a new manager at K & J Brick, a masonry products company that is now run by the two sons of the man who founded it 50 years ago. For years, the co-owners have invited the management team to a wilderness lodge for a combination of outdoor sports and annual business planning meetings. You don't want to miss the event, but you know that the outdoor activities weren't designed for someone with your physical impairments. Draft a short memo to the rest of the management team, suggesting changes to the annual event that will allow all managers to participate.

3.8 Culture and Time: Dealing with Variations When a company knows that a scheduled delivery time given by an overseas firm is likely to be flexible, managers may buy in larger quantities or may order more often to avoid running out of product before the next delivery. Identify three other management decisions that may be influenced by differing cultural concepts of time, and make notes for a short (two-minute) presentation to your class.

3.9 Intercultural Communication: Using Interpreters Imagine that you're the lead negotiator for a company that's trying to buy a factory in Prague, capital of the Czech Republic. Although you haven't spent much time in the country in the past decade, your parents grew up near Prague, so you understand and speak the language fairly well. However, you wonder about the advantages and disadvantages of using an interpreter anyway. For example, you may have more time to think if you wait for an intermediary to translate the other side's position. Decide whether to hire an interpreter, and then write a brief (two- or three-paragraph) explanation of your decision.

3.10 Internet: Translation Software Explore the powers and limitations of computer translation at AltaVista, www.altavista.com. Click on "translate" and enter a sentence such as "We are enclosing a purchase order for four dozen computer monitors." Select "English to Spanish" and click to complete the translation. Once you've read the Spanish version, cut and paste it into the "text for translation" box, select "Spanish to English," and click to translate. Try translating the same English sentence into German, French, or Italian and then back into English. How do the results of each translation differ? What are the implications for the use of automated translation services and back-translation? How could you use this website to sharpen your intercultural communication skills?

3.11 Intercultural Communication: Improving Skills You've been assigned to host a group of Swedish college students who are visiting your college for the next two weeks. They've all studied English, but this is their first trip to your area. Make a list of at least eight slang terms and idioms they are likely to hear on campus. How will you explain each phrase? When speaking with the Swedish students, what word or words might you substitute for each slang term or idiom?

3.12 Intercultural Communication: Podcasting Your company was one of the first to use the Apple iPod and other digital music players as business communication tools. Executives often record messages (such as monthly sales reports) as digital audio files and post them on the company's intranet site, a technique known as *podcasting*. Employees from the 14 offices in Europe, Asia, and North America then download the files to their music players and listen to the messages while riding the train to work, eating lunch at their desks, and so on. Your boss asks you to draft the opening statement for a podcast that will announce a revenue drop caused by intensive competitive pressure. She reviews your script, then hands it back with a gentle explanation that it needs to be revised for international listeners. Improve the following statement in as many ways as you can:

Howdy, comrades. Shouldn't surprise anyone that we took a beating this year, given the insane pricing moves our knucklehead competitors have been making. I mean, how those clowns can keep turning a profit is beyond me, what with steel costs still going through the roof and labor costs heating up— even in countries where everybody goes to find cheap labor—and hazardous waste disposal regs adding to operating costs, too.

Expand Your Knowledge

Exploring the Best of the Web

Cultural Savvy for Competitive Advantage
www.executiveplanet.com
Want to be more competitive when doing business across borders? Executive Planet offers quick introductions to expected business practices in a number of countries, from setting up appointments to giving gifts to negotiating deals. Visit www.executiveplanet.com and browse the country reports to answer the following questions.

1. What sort of clothes should you pack for a business trip to Mexico that will include both meetings and social events?
2. You've been trying to sell your products to a Saudi Arabian company whose executives treat you to an extravagant evening of dining and entertainment. Can you take this as a positive sign that they're likely to buy from you?
3. You collect antique clocks as a hobby, and you plan to give one of your favorites to the president of a Chinese company you plan to visit. Would such a gift likely help or hurt your relationship with this person?

Surfing Your Way to Career Success

Bovée and Thill's Business Communication Resources offers links to hundreds of online resources that can help you with this course, your other college courses, and your career. Visit www.buscommresources.com, then click on "Business Communication Web Directory." The "Intercultural Communication" section connects you to a variety of websites and articles on intercultural communication, international business etiquette, English as a second language, and language barriers. Identify three websites from this section that could be useful in your business career. For each site, write a two-sentence summary of what the site offers and how it could help you launch and build your career.

Learn Interactively

Interactive Study Guide

Visit www.prenhall.com/bovee, then locate your book and click on its "Companion Website" link. Select Chapter 3 to take advantage of the interactive "Chapter Quiz" to test your knowledge of chapter concepts. Receive instant feedback on whether you need additional studying. Also, visit the "Study Hall," where you'll find an abundance of valuable resources that will help you succeed in this course.

Peak Performance Grammar and Mechanics

If your instructor has required the use of "Peak Performance Grammar and Mechanics," either in your online course or on CD, you can improve your skill with verbs by using the "Peak Performance Grammar and Mechanics" module. Click on "Grammar Basics," and then click "Verbs." Take the Pretest to determine whether you have any weak areas. Then review those areas in the Refresher Course. Take the Follow-Up Test to check your grasp of verbs. For an extra challenge or advanced practice, take the Advanced Test. Finally, for additional reinforcement in verbs, visit the Companion Website, click on any chapter, then click on "Improve Your Grammar, Mechanics, and Usage."

PART 2

Applying the Three-Step Writing Process

CHAPTER 4
Planning Business Messages

CHAPTER 5
Writing Business Messages

CHAPTER 6
Completing Business Messages

Planning Business Messages

LEARNING OBJECTIVES

After studying this chapter, you will be able to

1 Describe the three-step writing process

2 Explain why it's important to define your purpose carefully and list four questions that can help you test that purpose

3 Describe the importance of analyzing your audience and identify the six factors you should consider when developing an audience profile

4 Discuss gathering information for simple messages and identify three attributes of quality information

5 List factors to consider when choosing the most appropriate medium for your message

6 Explain why good organization is important to both you and your audience

7 Summarize the process for organizing business messages effectively

COMMUNICATION CLOSE-UP AT THE COMPLETE IDIOT'S GUIDES

www.idiotsguides.com

How many times have you gotten frustrated with some new electronic device, turned to the user manual for help—and gotten even more frustrated? Joe Kraynak, the successful writer of such helpful books as *The Complete Idiot's Guide to PCs* and *The Complete Idiot's Guide to Microsoft Office 2000*, is on your side. He thinks people are right to criticize the manuals that come with personal computers, cell phones, and other complex products. Many high-tech products make intelligent people feel, well, like idiots. That frustration with ineffective attempts at explaining complex topics has fueled the rapid growth of the cheekily titled *Complete Idiot's* series, which now covers hundreds of subjects.

In Kraynak's mind, the problem is that too many product manuals are written without enough attention to the reader's real needs. The engineers or technicians who often do the writing are intimately familiar with their products and technologies, and they sometimes mistakenly assume that readers are too. This disregard for what readers need can

Its tongue-in-cheek name aside, the Idiot's Guide series has grown to hundreds of volumes on the strength of its clear, audience-focused writing.

lead not only to inadequate explanations of new topics but also to overuse of befuddling jargon and acronyms. Moreover, too many manuals focus on descriptions of products when what readers really want are explanations of how to use them.

I try to put myself in the shoes of a new user, to think like somebody I know," says Kraynak. He advises all writers to do the same. What essential information do your readers need first? Which less-important details can wait until later? What style of writing will be most effective? You may not write books on the latest high-tech gadgets, but all business messages can suffer from the same flaws that plague so many user manuals. Follow Kraynak's example, and your readers will grow to count on you for clear messages too.[1]

UNDERSTANDING THE THREE-STEP WRITING PROCESS

1 LEARNING OBJECTIVE

Describe the three-step writing process

The three-step writing process consists of planning, writing, and completing your messages.

The problems that Joe Kraynak describes (profiled in the chapter-opening Communication Close-Up) aren't limited to high-tech product manuals. All too often, people writing about finances, government regulations, business processes, and other important topics fail to understand and accommodate their readers' needs. The result is confusing, frustrating messages that don't help the reader—or the writer, for that matter. Fortunately, by following a proven process, you can learn to create effective messages that will not only satisfy audience needs but also highlight your skills as a perceptive, quality-conscious business leader.

The three-step writing process (see Figure 4.1) helps ensure that your messages are both *effective* (meeting your audience's needs and getting your points across) and *efficient* (making the best use of your time and your audience's time).

- **Step 1: Planning business messages.** To plan any message, first *analyze the situation* by defining your purpose and developing a profile of your audience. Once you're sure what you need to accomplish with your message, *gather information* that will meet your audience's needs. Next, *select the right medium* (oral, written, visual, or electronic) to deliver your message. With those three factors in place, you're ready to *organize the information* by defining your main idea, limiting your scope, selecting a direct or an indirect approach, and outlining your content. Planning messages is the focus of this chapter.

FIGURE 4.1 The Three-Step Writing Process
This three-step process will help you create more effective messages in any medium. As you get more practice with the process, it will become easier and more automatic.

Plan

Analyze the Situation
Define your purpose and develop an audience profile.

Gather Information
Determine audience needs and obtain the information necessary to satisfy those needs.

Select the Right Medium
Select the best medium for delivering your message.

Organize the Information
Define your main idea, limit your scope, select a direct or an indirect approach, and outline your content.

Write

Adapt to Your Audience
Be sensitive to audience needs with a "you" attitude, politeness, positive emphasis, and bias-free language. Build a strong relationship with your audience by establishing your credibility and projecting your company's image. Control your style with a conversational tone, plain English, and appropriate voice.

Compose the Message
Choose strong words that will help you create effective sentences and coherent paragraphs.

Complete

Revise the Message
Evaluate content and review readability, then edit and rewrite for conciseness and clarity.

Produce the Message
Use effective design elements and suitable layout for a clean, professional appearance.

Proofread the Message
Review for errors in layout, spelling, and mechanics.

Distribute the Message
Deliver your message using the chosen medium; make sure all documents and all relevant files are distributed successfully.

1   **2**   **3**

- **Step 2: Writing business messages.** Once you've planned your message, *adapt to your audience*. Be sensitive to your audience's needs by adopting the "you" attitude, being polite, emphasizing the positive, and using bias-free language. Build strong relationships with your audience by establishing your credibility and projecting your company's image. Be sure to control your style by using a conversational tone, plain English, and the correct voice. Then you're ready to *compose your message* by choosing strong words, creating effective sentences, and developing coherent paragraphs. Writing business messages is discussed in Chapter 5.

- **Step 3: Completing business messages.** After writing your first draft, *revise your message* by evaluating the content, reviewing readability, and then editing and rewriting until your message comes across concisely and clearly, with correct grammar, proper punctuation, and effective format. Next, *produce your message*. Put it into the form that your audience will receive, and review all design and layout decisions for an attractive, professional appearance. *Proofread* the final draft for typos, spelling errors, and other mechanical problems. Finally, *distribute your message*, using the best combination of personal and technological tools. Completing business messages is discussed in Chapter 6.

Home Depot, the world's largest home improvement retailer, keeps its operations running smoothly by carefully planning communication efforts and designing messages that meet the needs of its customers, suppliers, and employees.

Throughout this book, you'll learn how to apply these steps to a wide variety of business messages: short messages such as e-mails and blog postings (Chapter 7 through Chapter 10), longer messages such as reports (Chapter 13 through Chapter 15), oral presentations (Chapter 16 and Chapter 17), and the employment messages you can use to build a great career (Chapter 18 and Chapter 19).

Optimizing Your Writing Time

The more you use the three-step writing process, the more intuitive and automatic it will become. You'll also get better at allotting your time for each task during a writing project. As a general rule, try using roughly half your time for planning and about a quarter of your time for writing. Reserve the remaining quarter of your time for completing the project, so that you don't shortchange important completion steps such as revising, producing, proofreading, and distributing.[2]

As a starting point, try to use half your time for planning, one quarter for writing, and one quarter for completing your messages.

Of course, these time allotments will change significantly, depending on the project. For example, if you already know your material intimately, the planning step may take less than half your time. Then again, if you're delivering your message via multimedia such as CD-ROM or interactive website, the completion step could take far longer than a quarter of your time. Simpler efforts such as instant messages take far less time and energy than long reports, websites, and other sophisticated projects.

Seasoned professionals understand that there is no right or best way to write all business messages. As you work through the writing process presented in this chapter and in Chapter 5 and Chapter 6, try not to view it as a list of how-to directives but as a way to understand the various tasks involved in effective business writing.[3]

Planning Effectively

As soon as the need to create a message appears, inexperienced communicators are often tempted to dive directly into writing. However, even a few minutes of planning can sometimes save hours of rework and frustration later on. Even if you have only 20 or 30 minutes to prepare and send a message, work through all three steps quickly to ensure that your time is well used. Analyzing your audience helps you to find and assemble the facts they're looking for and to deliver that information in a concise and compelling way. Planning your message also reduces indecision as you write and helps eliminate work as you review and revise.

Trying to save time by skimping on planning usually costs you more time in the long run.

ANALYZING YOUR SITUATION

A successful message starts with a clear purpose that connects the sender's needs with the audience's needs. Identifying your purpose and your audience is usually a straightforward task for simple, routine messages; however, this task can be more demanding in more intricate situations. For instance, if you need to communicate about a shipping problem between your Beijing and Los Angeles factories, your purpose might be simply to alert upper management to the situation, or it might involve asking the two factory managers to explore and solve the problem. These two scenarios have different purposes and different audiences, so they naturally yield dramatically different messages. If you launch directly into writing without clarifying both your purpose and your audience, you'll waste time and energy and you'll probably generate a less-effective message.

Defining Your Purpose

All business messages have a **general purpose:** to inform, to persuade, or to collaborate with your audience. This purpose helps define the overall approach you'll need to take, including the information you need to gather, your choice of medium (or media), and even the way you organize your message. For instance, a clear purpose is key to the success of Joe Kraynak's work on *The Complete Idiot's Guide to Computer Basics*; he knows he isn't trying to turn readers into computer experts but, rather, is helping them understand how to use their computer more successfully.

The general purpose also determines both the appropriate degree of audience participation and the amount of control you have over your message. Informing your audience requires little interaction (see Figure 4.2). Audience members absorb the information and accept or reject it, but they don't contribute to message content; you control the message. To persuade your audience, you require a moderate amount of participation, such as giving people the chance to ask questions so that you can answer any doubts; nevertheless, you need to retain a moderate amount of message control. Finally, to collaborate with audience members, you need maximum participation. Your control of the message is reduced because you must adjust to new, unexpected input and reactions.

To determine the specific purpose, think of how the audience's ideas or behavior should be affected by the message.

Within the scope of its general purpose, each message also has a **specific purpose**, which identifies what you hope to accomplish with your message and what your audience should do or think after receiving your message. For instance, is your goal simply to update your audience on an event, or do you want audience members to take immediate action? State your specific purpose as precisely as possible, even identifying which audience members should respond, how they should respond, and when.

Once you have defined your specific purpose, you can decide whether that purpose merits the time and effort required for you to prepare and send the message. Test your purpose by asking four questions:

- **Will anything change as a result of your message?** Make sure you don't contribute to information overload by sending messages that won't change anything. For instance, if

FIGURE 4.2 The Relationship Between General Purpose and Communicator Control

Your control over the message is inversely related to the degree of audience participation. The more participation from the audience, the less control you'll have, and vice versa.

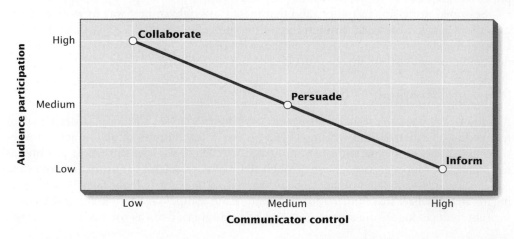

you don't like your company's latest advertising campaign but you're not in a position to influence it, sending a critical message to your colleagues won't change anything and won't benefit anyone.

- **Is your purpose realistic?** If your purpose involves a radical shift in action or attitude, go slowly. Consider proposing a first step so that your message acts as the beginning of a learning process.
- **Is the time right?** Think through the potential impact of your message—both intentional and unintentional—to see whether this is a good time to send it. Many professions and departments have recurring cycles in their workloads, so messages sent during peak times may be ignored. Similarly, employees in departments that are in the midst of a reorganization, series of layoffs, or other changes won't be able to give your message their full attention.
- **Is your purpose acceptable to your organization?** Your company's business objectives may dictate whether a purpose is acceptable. For instance, you may be tempted to fire off a stern reply to a particularly unpleasant customer suggesting that the person take his or her business elsewhere, but this may go against your company's priorities of retaining all current customers.

Once you are satisfied that you have a clear and meaningful purpose and this is a smart time to proceed, your next step is to understand the members of your audience and their needs.

Developing an Audience Profile

Before your audiences will take the time to read or hear your messages, they need to be interested in what you're saying. They need to see what's in it for them: How will listening to your advice or doing what you ask help them, personally or professionally? The more you know about your audience, their needs, and their expectations, the more effectively you'll be able to communicate with them.

If you're communicating with someone you know well, audience analysis is relatively easy. You can identify the person's needs and predict his or her reaction to any given message without a lot of research. On the other hand, your audience could be made up of strangers—potential customers or suppliers you've never met, a new boss, or new employees. In these situations, you'll need to learn more in order to adjust your message appropriately. For an example of the kind of information you need to compile in an audience analysis, see Figure 4.3. To conduct an audience analysis:

- **Identify your primary audience.** For some messages, certain audience members may be more important than others. Don't ignore the needs of less influential members, but make sure you address the concerns of the key decision makers.
- **Determine audience size and geographic distribution.** A message aimed at 10,000 people spread around the globe will probably require a different approach than one aimed at a dozen people down the hall.
- **Determine audience composition.** Look for both similarities and differences in culture, language, age, education, organizational rank and status, attitudes, experience, motivations, and any other factors that could affect the successful reception and decoding of your message.
- **Gauge audience members' level of understanding.** If audience members share your general background, they'll probably understand your material without difficulty. If not, your message will need an element of education, and deciding how much information to include can be a challenge. Include only enough information to accomplish the specific purpose of your message; and if the members of your audience have various levels of understanding, gear your coverage to your primary audience.
- **Understand audience expectations and preferences.** Will members of your audience expect complete details or just a summary of the main points? Do they want an e-mail message or will they expect a formal report? In general, the higher up the organization your message goes, the fewer details people want to see, simply because they have less time to read them.

Defer a message, or do not send it at all, if
- *Nothing will change as a result of sending*
- *The purpose is not realistic*
- *The timing is not right*
- *The purpose is not acceptable to your organization*

3 LEARNING OBJECTIVE

Describe the importance of analyzing your audience and identify the six factors you should consider when developing an audience profile

Ask yourself some key questions about your audience members:
- *Who are they?*
- *How many people do you need to reach?*
- *How much do they already know about the subject?*
- *What are their expectations and preferences?*
- *What is their probable reaction to your message?*

If audience members have different levels of understanding of the topic, aim your message at the most influential decision makers.

FIGURE 4.3 Audience Analysis Helps You Plan Your Message

For simple, routine messages, you usually don't need to analyze your audience in depth. However, for complex messages or messages for indifferent or hostile audiences, take the time to study their information needs and potential reactions to your message.

Audience analysis notes

Project: A report recommending that we close down the on-site exercise facility and subsidize private memberships at local health clubs.

- **Primary audience:** Nicole Perazzo, vice president of operations, and her supervisory team.

- **Size and geographic distribution:** Nine managers total; Nicole and five of her staff are here on site; three other supervisors are based in Hong Kong.

- **Composition:** All have experience in operations management, but several are new to the company.

- **Level of understanding:** All will no doubt understand the financial considerations, but the newer managers may not understand the importance of the on-site exercise facility to many of our employees.

- **Expectations and preferences.** They're expecting a firm recommendation, backed up with well-thought-out financial rationale and suggestions for communicating the bad news to employees. For a decision of this magnitude, a formal report is appropriate; e-mail distribution is expected.

- **Probable reaction.** From one-on-one discussions, I know that several of the managers receiving this report are active users of the on-site facility and won't welcome the suggestion that we should shut it down. However, some nonexercisers generally think it's a luxury the company can't afford. Audience reactions will range from highly positive to highly negative; the report should focus on overcoming the highly negative reactions since they're the ones I need to convince.

A gradual approach and plenty of evidence are required to win over a skeptical audience.

- **Forecast probable audience reaction.** As you'll read later in the chapter, audience reaction affects message organization. If you expect a favorable response, you can state conclusions and recommendations up-front and offer minimal supporting evidence. If you expect skepticism, you can introduce conclusions gradually with more proof.

GATHERING INFORMATION

Discuss gathering information for simple messages and identify three attributes of quality information

With a clear picture of who your audience is, your next step is to assemble the information that you will include in your message. For simple messages, you may already have all the information at hand, but more complex messages can require considerable research and analysis before you're ready to begin writing. Chapter 11 explores formal techniques for finding, evaluating, and processing information. You can often use a variety of informal techniques to gather insights and focus your research efforts:

- **Consider other viewpoints.** Putting yourself in someone else's position helps you consider what that person may be thinking, feeling, or planning.
- **Read reports and other company documents.** Consider annual reports, financial statements, news releases, blogs, marketing reports, and customer surveys for helpful information. Find out whether your company has a *knowledge-management system,* a centralized database that collects the experiences and insights of employees throughout the organization.
- **Talk with supervisors, colleagues, or customers.** Fellow workers and customers may have information you need, or they may know what your audience will be interested in.
- **Ask your audience for input.** If you're unsure of what audience members need from your message, ask them. Admitting you don't know but want to meet their needs will impress an audience more than guessing and getting it wrong.

Uncovering Audience Needs

Joe Kraynak organizes his writing to overcome a common flaw in manuals for technical products: providing too little of the right information (how to use the equipment) and too much of the wrong information (how the equipment works). In many situations, your audience's information needs are readily apparent, such as when a consumer sends an e-mail asking a specific question. In other cases, your audience may be unable to articulate exactly what is needed. If someone makes a vague or broad request, ask questions to narrow the focus. If your boss says, "Find out everything you can about Interscope Records," ask which aspect of the company and its business is most important. Asking a question or two often forces the person to think through the request and define more precisely what is required.

If you're given a vague request, ask questions to clarify it before you plan a response.

Also, try to think of information needs that your audience may not have expressed. Suppose you've been asked to compare two health insurance plans for your firm's employees, but your research uncovered a third alternative that might be even better. You could then expand your report to include a brief explanation of why the third plan should be considered, then compare it to the two original plans.

Include any additional information that may be helpful, even though the requester didn't specifically ask for it.

Providing Required Information

Once you've defined your audience's information needs, be sure you satisfy those needs completely. One good way to test the thoroughness of your message is to use the **journalistic approach:** Check to see whether your message answers *who, what, when, where, why,* and *how.* Using this test, you can quickly tell whether a message fails to deliver—such as this message requesting information from employees:

Test the completeness of your document by making sure it answers all the important questions: who, what, when, where, why, and how.

> We are exploring ways to reduce our office space leasing costs and would like your input on a proposed plan in which employees who telecommute on alternate days could share offices. Please let me know what you think of this proposal.

The message fails to tell employees everything they need to know in order to provide meaningful responses. The *what* could be improved by identifying the specific information points the writer needs from employees (such as whether individual telecommuting patterns are predictable enough to allow scheduling of shared offices). The writer also doesn't specify *when* the responses are needed or *how* the employees should respond. By failing to address such points, the request is likely to generate a variety of responses, some possibly helpful but some probably not.

To gauge the quality of the information you provide in your messages, check to ensure that the information is accurate, ethical, and pertinent.

Be Sure the Information Is Accurate

Inaccurate information in business messages can cause a host of problems, from embarrassment and lost productivity to serious safety and legal issues. Inaccurate information may persist for months or years after you distribute it, or you may commit the organization to promises it isn't able to keep—and the error could harm your reputation as a reliable businessperson.

Be certain that the information you provide is accurate and that the commitments you make can be kept.

You can minimize mistakes by double-checking every piece of information you collect. If you are consulting sources outside the organization, ask yourself whether they are current and reliable. Be particularly careful when using sources you find on the Internet. As you'll see in Chapter 11, the simplicity of online publishing and common lack of editorial oversight call for extra care in using online information. Be sure to review any mathematical or financial calculations. Check all dates and schedules, and examine your own assumptions and conclusions to be certain they are valid.

Ethics Detective

Am I Getting the Whole Story?

Your company, Furniture Formations, creates a variety of home furniture products with extensive use of fine woods. To preserve the look and feel of the wood, your craftspeople use an oil-based finish that you purchase from a local building products wholesaler. The workers apply the finish with rags, which are thrown away after each project. After a news report about spontaneous combustion of waste rags in other furniture shops, you grow concerned enough to contact the wholesaler and ask for verification of the product's safety. The wholesaler knows that you've been considering a nonflammable, water-based alternative from another source but assures you that as long as you dispose of the rags and other waste in a safe manner, you have no need to worry:

> Seal the rags in an approved container and dispose of it according to local regulations. As you probably already know, county regulations require all commercial users of solvent-based materials to dispose of leftover finishes at the county's hazardous waste facility.

You're still not satisfied. After some further research, you visit the website of the manufacturer, Minwax, **www.minwax. com/shoptalk/resources/faq.cfm**, and find the following cautionary statement about the product you're currently using:

> For some products, when oil-soaked rags and other porous waste are improperly discarded, heat can build up which may result in flames that immediately feed on the oil-soaked material. This phenomenon is known as spontaneous combustion and can be avoided simply by immersing all wood-finishing materials, including rags, steel wool and other waste, in a water-filled, metal container. Seal the container and dispose of in accordance with local regulations.

ANALYSIS

Was the wholesaler guilty of an ethical lapse in this case? If yes, explain what you think the lapse is and why you believe it is unethical. If no, explain why you think the statement qualifies as ethical.

Be Sure the Information Is Ethical

Ethics should guide your decisions when determining how much detail to include in your message.

By working hard to ensure the accuracy of the information you gather, you'll also avoid many ethical problems in your messages. If you do make an honest mistake, such as delivering information you initially thought to be true but later found to be false, contact the recipients of the message immediately and correct the error. No one can reasonably fault you in such circumstances, and most people will respect your honesty.

Messages can also be unethical if important information is omitted (see "Ethics Detective: Am I Getting the Whole Story?"). Of course, as a business professional, you may have legal or other sound business reasons for not including every detail about every matter. So just how much detail should you include? Make sure you include enough detail to avoid misleading your audience. If you're unsure how much information your audience needs, offer as much as you believe best fits your definition of complete, then offer to provide more upon request.

Be Sure the Information Is Pertinent

Try to figure out what points will especially interest your audience, then give those points the most attention.

When gathering information for your message, remember that some points will be more important to your audience than others. They will appreciate your efforts to prioritize the information they need and filter out the information they don't. Moreover, by focusing on the information that concerns your audience the most, you increase your chances of accomplishing your own communication goals.

Rely on common sense if you don't know enough about your audience members to know exactly what will interest them.

If you don't know your audience or if you're communicating with a large group of people with diverse interests, use common sense to identify points of interest. Audience factors such as age, job, location, income, and education can give you a clue. If you're trying to sell memberships in a health club, you might adjust your message for athletes, busy professionals, families, and people in different locations or in different income brackets. The comprehensive facilities and professional trainers would appeal to athletes, whereas the low monthly rates would appeal to college students on tight budgets.

Some messages necessarily reach audiences with a diverse mix of educational levels, subject awareness, and other variables. In these cases, your only choice is to try to accommodate the likely range of audience members (see Figure 4.4).

FIGURE 4.4 An Audience-Focused Report (Selected Pages)

These two pages from a local water district's annual water quality report do a good job of presenting a technical subject to the general public (all of the households in this particular city). Notice how the report presents scientific information accurately but supplements that with clear explanations of what the information means and how it pertains to water users.

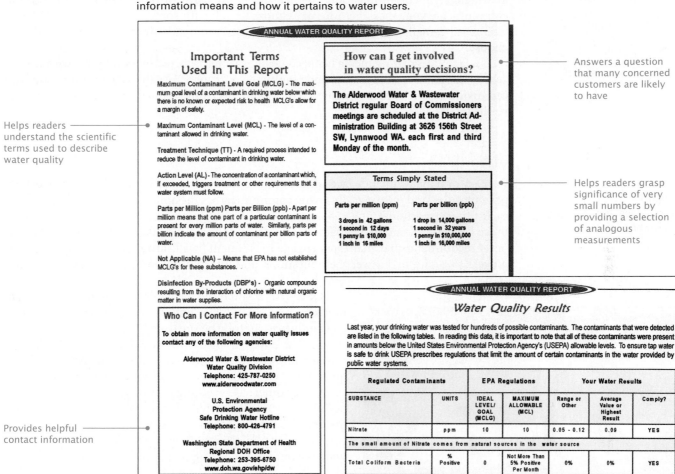

Helps readers understand the scientific terms used to describe water quality

Provides helpful contact information

Answers a question that many concerned customers are likely to have

Helps readers grasp significance of very small numbers by providing a selection of analogous measurements

Shows test results in appropriate scientific format but helps nontechnical readers by explaining what the various substances are and whether the water complies with government standards

SELECTING THE RIGHT MEDIUM

Selecting the best medium for your message can make the difference between effective and ineffective communication.[4] A **medium** is the form through which you choose to communicate your message. You may choose to talk with someone face to face, post to a blog, send e-mail, or create a webcast—and there are many other media from which to choose.

In fact, categorizing media has become increasingly blurred in recent years with the advent of so many options that include multimedia formats. For the sake of discussion, you can divide media into oral, written, visual, and electronic (which often combines several media types).

Oral Media

Oral communication is best when you need to encourage interaction, express emotions, or monitor emotional responses.

Primary oral media include face-to-face conversations, interviews, speeches, and in-person presentations and meetings. By giving communicators the ability to see, hear, and react to each other, traditional oral media are useful for encouraging people to ask questions, make comments, and work together to reach a consensus or decision. In particular, experts recommend that managers engage in frequent "walk-arounds," chatting with employees to get input, answer their questions, and interpret important business events and trends.[5]

The higher you rise in an organization, the more time you'll spend talking and listening. Your ability to communicate with people from virtually any background will be key to your success.

Of course, if you don't want a lot of questions or interaction, oral media can be an unwise choice. However, consider your audience carefully before deciding to limit interaction by choosing a different medium. As a manager, you will encounter unpleasant situations (declining an employee's request for a raise, for example) in which sending an e-mail message or otherwise avoiding personal contact will seem appealing. However, in many such cases, you owe the other party the opportunity to ask questions or express concerns. Moreover, facing the tough situations in person will earn you a reputation as an honest, caring manager.

Written Media

Written messages take many forms, from traditional memos to glossy reports that rival magazines in production quality. Most letters and memos are relatively brief documents, generally one or two pages, although some run much longer. **Memos** are used for the routine, day-to-day exchange of information within an organization. Because of their open construction and informal method of delivery (such as being placed in baskets), memos are less private than letters. In many organizations, e-mail messages, blogs, and other electronic media have largely replaced paper memos.

Letters are brief written messages sent to recipients outside the organization. In addition to conveying a particular message, they perform an important public relations function in fostering good working relationships with customers, suppliers, and others. Many organizations rely on form letters to save time and money on routine communication. Form letters are particularly handy for such one-time mass mailings as sales messages about products, information about organizational activities, and goodwill messages such as seasonal greetings.

Reports and proposals are usually longer than memos and letters, although both can be created in memo or letter format. These documents come in a variety of lengths, ranging from a few pages to several hundred, and are usually fairly formal in tone. Chapter 13 through Chapter 15 discuss reports and proposals in detail.

FIGURE 4.5 Visual Media

In traditional business messages, visual elements usually support the text. However, in some instances, the message can be presented more effectively by reversing that relationship—basing the message on a dominant visual and using text to support that image. (*CRM* stands for *customer relationship management*, a category of software that helps companies manage their interactions with customers.)

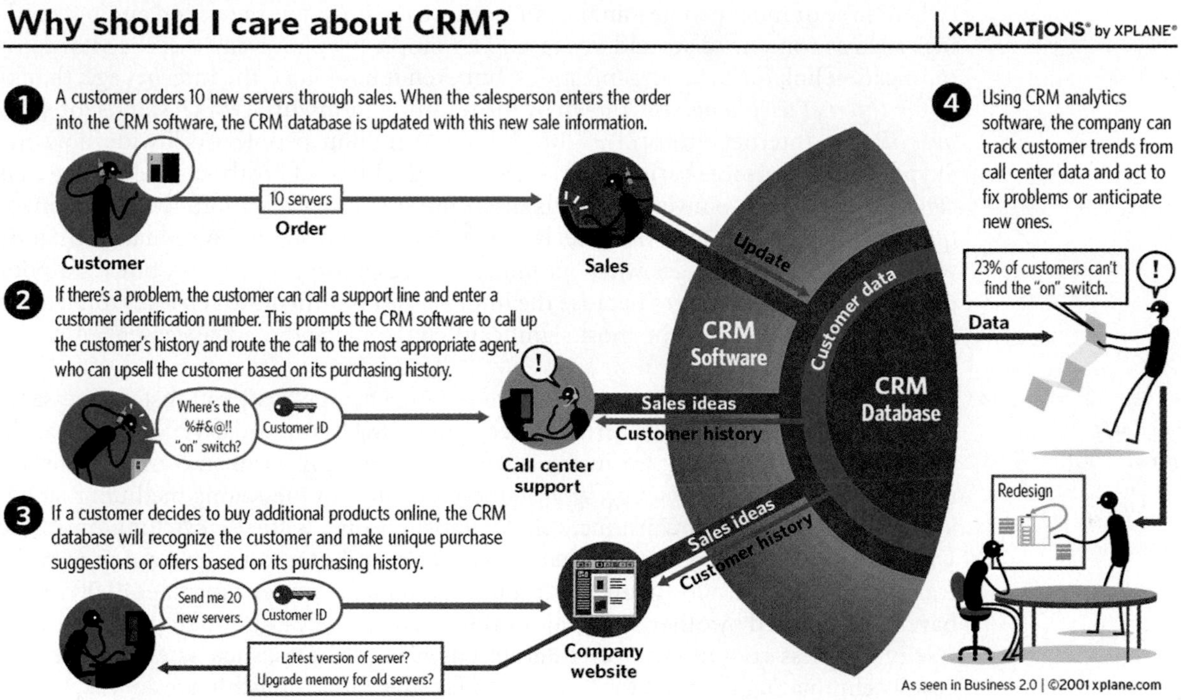

Visual Media

Although you probably won't work with many messages that are purely visual (with no text), the importance of visual elements in business communication continues to grow. Traditional business messages rely primarily on text, with occasional support from graphical elements such as charts, graphs, or diagrams to help illustrate points discussed in the text. However, many business communicators are discovering the power of messages in which the visual element is dominant and supported by small amounts of text. For the purposes of this discussion, you can think of *visual media* as any formats in which one or more visual elements play a central role in conveying the message content (see Figure 4.5).

Messages that combine powerful visuals with supporting text can be effective for a number of reasons. Today's audiences are pressed for time and bombarded with messages, so anything that communicates quickly is welcome. Visuals are also effective at describing complex ideas and processes because they can reduce the work required for an audience to identify the parts and relationships that make up the whole. Also, in a multilingual business world, diagrams, symbols, and other images can lower communication barriers by requiring less language processing. Finally, visual images can be easier to remember than purely textual descriptions or explanations.

In some situations, a message that is predominantly visual with text used to support the illustration can be more effective than a message that relies primarily on text.

Electronic Media

The range of electronic media is broad and continues to grow even broader, from telephones and podcasts to blogs and wikis to e-mail and text messaging. When you want to make a powerful impression, using electronic media can increase the excitement and visual appeal with computer animation, video, and even music.

The growth of electronic communication options is both a blessing and a curse for business communicators. On the one hand, you have more tools than ever to choose from, with more ways to deliver rational and emotional content. On the other hand, the sheer

In general, use electronic media to deliver messages quickly, to reach widely dispersed audiences, and to take advantage of rich multimedia formats.

range of choices can complicate your job because you often need to choose among multiple media and you need to know how to use each medium successfully. You'll learn more about using electronic media throughout this book (and in Chapter 7, in particular); but for now, here is a quick overview of the major electronic media now used in business:

Electronic written media have largely replaced traditional written media in many companies.

- **Electronic versions of oral media.** These include telephone calls, teleconferencing (when three or more people join the same call), voice-mail messages, and audio recordings such as compact discs and podcasts. The simple telephone call is still a vital communication link for many organizations, but even it has joined the Internet age, thanks to the *Internet telephony*, also known by the technical term VoIP (which stands for *Voice over IP*, the Internet Protocol). More than 100 million people worldwide now use Skype, which offers free basic phone service over the Internet.[6] Although telephone calls can't convey all the nonverbal signals of an in-person conversation, they can convey quite a few, including tone of voice, laughter, pauses, and so on. Voice mail is a handy way to send brief messages when an immediate response isn't crucial, but it's a poor choice for lengthy messages because the information is difficult to retrieve. You'll learn about podcasts, perhaps the most significant electronic audio advancement of recent years, in Chapter 7.

- **Electronic versions of written media.** These range from e-mail and instant messages to blogs, websites, and wikis. Instant messaging (IM) is rapidly overtaking e-mail in some companies. At IBM, for instance, employees send more than 5 million instant messages a month.[7] *Text messaging*, a phone-based instant messaging medium that has long been popular with consumers in Asia and Europe, is finally catching on in the United States.[8] Even documents that were once distributed on paper are now easily transferred electronically, thanks to Adobe's portable document format (PDF). Faxes have been replaced by other electronic options in many cases, although they still have a role in business communication. Internet-based fax services, such as eFax, lower the cost by eliminating the need for a dedicated fax line and fax machine.

- **Electronic versions of visual media.** These can include electronic presentations (using Microsoft PowerPoint and other software), computer animation (using software such as Adobe Flash to create many of the animated sequences you see on websites), and video. Businesses have made extensive use of video (particularly for training, new product promotions, and executive announcements) for years, first on tape, then on DVD, and now online. Video is also incorporated in podcasting, creating vidcasts, and in blogging, creating *video blogs* (*vlogs*) and *mobile blogs* (*moblogs*).[9] **Multimedia** refers to use of two or more media to craft a single message, typically some combination of audio, video, text, and visual graphics.

Factors to Consider When Choosing Media

5 LEARNING OBJECTIVE

List factors to consider when choosing the most appropriate medium for your message

Complicated messages often require richer media.

Choosing the right medium for each message is a question of balancing your needs with your audience's needs. You certainly want to select the medium whose advantages offer you the best fit with the situation and your audience (see Table 4.1). Just as critical, however, is considering how your message is affected by important factors such as the following:

- **Media richness.** Richness is a medium's ability to (1) convey a message through more than one *informational cue* (visual, verbal, vocal), (2) facilitate feedback, and (3) establish personal focus. The richest medium is face-to-face communication; it's personal, it provides immediate feedback (verbal and nonverbal), and it conveys the emotion behind a message.[10] Multimedia presentations and multimedia webpages are also quite rich, with the ability to present images, animation, text, music, sound effects, and other elements. Many can be personalized to a degree. At the other end of the richness continuum are the leanest media—those that communicate in the simplest ways, provide no opportunity for audience feedback, and aren't personalized (see Figure 4.6). Use the richest media to send nonroutine or complex messages, to humanize your presence throughout the organization, to communicate caring to employees, and to gain employee commitment to company goals. Use leaner media to send simple, routine messages.

TABLE 4.1 Media Advantages and Disadvantages

MEDIA	ADVANTAGES	DISADVANTAGES
Oral	• Provide opportunity for immediate feedback • Allow a certain ease of interaction • Involve rich nonverbal cues (both physical gesture and vocal inflection) • Allow you to express the emotion behind your message	• Restrict participation to those physically present • Unless recorded, provide no permanent, verifiable record of the communication • Reduce communicator's control over the message • Other than for messages that are prewritten and rehearsed, offer no opportunity to revise or edit your spoken words
Written	• Allow you to plan and control your message • Reach geographically dispersed audiences • Offer a permanent, verifiable record • Minimize the distortion that can accompany oral messages • Can be used to avoid immediate interactions • De-emphasize any inappropriate emotional components	• Usually not conducive to speedy feedback • Lack the rich nonverbal cues provided by oral media • Often take more time and more resources to create and distribute • Elaborate printed documents can require special skills in preparation and production
Visual	• Can convey complex ideas and relationships quickly • Often less intimidating than long blocks of text • Can reduce the burden on the audience to figure out how the pieces fit	• Can require artistic skills to design • Require some technical skills to create • Can require more time to create than equivalent amount of text • More difficult to transmit and store than simple textual messages
Electronic	• Deliver messages quickly • Reach geographically dispersed audiences • Offer the persuasive power of multimedia formats • Can increase accessibility and openness in an organization	• Are easy to overuse (sending too many messages to too many recipients) • Privacy risks and concerns (exposing confidential data; employer monitoring of e-mail and IM; accidental forwarding) • Security risks (viruses; spyware) • Productivity concerns (frequent interruptions; nonbusiness web surfing)

FIGURE 4.6 Media Richness

Business media vary widely in terms of *richness*, which encompasses the number of informational cues available, their ability to incorporate feedback, and the degree to which they can be personalized.

Leaner:
fewer cues,
no interactivity,
no personal focus

Standard reports	Custom reports	Telephone calls	Face-to-face
Static webpages	Letters & memos	Teleconferencing	conversations
Mass media	E-mail & IM	Video (including	Multimedia
Posters & signs	Wikis	vodcasts,	presentations
	Blogs	voblogs,	Multimedia
	Podcasts	video IM)	webpages
			Virtual reality

Richer:
multiple cues,
interactive,
personalized

- **Message formality.** Your media choice governs the style and tone of your message. If your purpose is to share simple information with employees, such as changes in the cafeteria hours, you would probably send an e-mail message or post an announcement on a blog rather than write a formal printed memo or make a face-to-face presentation.
- **Media limitations.** Every medium has limitations. Although face-to-face communication is one of the richest media, it's also one of the most restrictive because you and your audience must be in the same place at the same time.[11] Similarly, instant messaging is perfect for communicating simple, straightforward messages, but it is ineffective for sending complex ones.

Your intentions heavily influence your choice of medium.

- **Sender intentions.** Your choice of medium influences your audience's perception of your intentions. If you want to emphasize the formality of your message, use a more formal medium such as a memo or a letter. To convey emotion, consider a visual medium such as a personal speech or a videoconference. For immediate feedback, meet face-to-face, make a phone call, or use IM.[12] However, if you need a written record, use one of the written media or an electronic equivalent such as an intranet posting.

Time and cost also affect medium selection.

- **Urgency and cost.** If your message is urgent, you'll probably use the in-person conversation, a phone call, or perhaps IM. But don't forget to weigh cost against speed. For instance, you wouldn't think twice about telephoning an important customer in Australia if you just discovered that your company had erroneously sent the wrong shipment, but you'd probably choose to e-mail a routine order acknowledgment to that same customer.

When choosing the appropriate medium, don't forget to consider your audience's expectations.

- **Audience preferences.** Make sure to consider which medium or media your audience expects or prefers.[13] What would you think if your college tried to deliver your diploma by fax? You'd expect the college to hand the diploma to you at graduation or mail it to you. In addition, some cultures tend to favor one channel over another. For example, the United States, Canada, and Germany emphasize written messages, whereas Japan emphasizes oral messages—perhaps because its high-context culture carries so much of the message in nonverbal cues and "between-the-lines" interpretation.[14]

Once you select the best medium for your purpose, situation, and audience, you are ready to start thinking about the organization of your message.

ORGANIZING YOUR INFORMATION

For anything beyond the simplest messages, organization can make the difference between success and failure. Compare the two versions of the message in Figure 4.7. The ineffective version exhibits several common organization mistakes: taking too long to get to the point, including irrelevant material, getting ideas mixed up, and leaving out necessary information.

To organize a message
- *Define your main idea*
- *Limit the scope*
- *Choose the direct or indirect approach*
- *Group your points*

As you'll see in the following chapters, various types of messages may require different organizational schemes. Nevertheless, in every case, you can organize your message in a logical and compelling way by recognizing the importance of good organization, defining your main idea, limiting your scope, choosing either a direct or an indirect approach, and outlining your content.

Recognizing the Importance of Good Organization

6 LEARNING OBJECTIVE

Explain why good organization is important to both you and your audience

At best, poor organization creates unnecessary work for your readers, forcing them to piece your message together in a sensible way. At worst, poor organization leads readers to form inaccurate conclusions or tempts them to stop reading or listening. If you gain a reputation as a disorganized communicator, people will begin to ignore your messages and question your thinking skills. In other words, poorly organized messages are bad for business and bad for your career.

Effective organization also saves you time and consumes less of your creative energy. Your draft goes more quickly because you don't waste time putting ideas in the wrong places or composing material that you don't need. You may also use your organizational plan to get advance input from your audience. That way, you can be sure you're on the right track *before*

FIGURE 4.7 E-Mail Message with Improved Organization

The improved version of this e-mail is clear and efficient, presenting only the necessary information in a logical sequence.

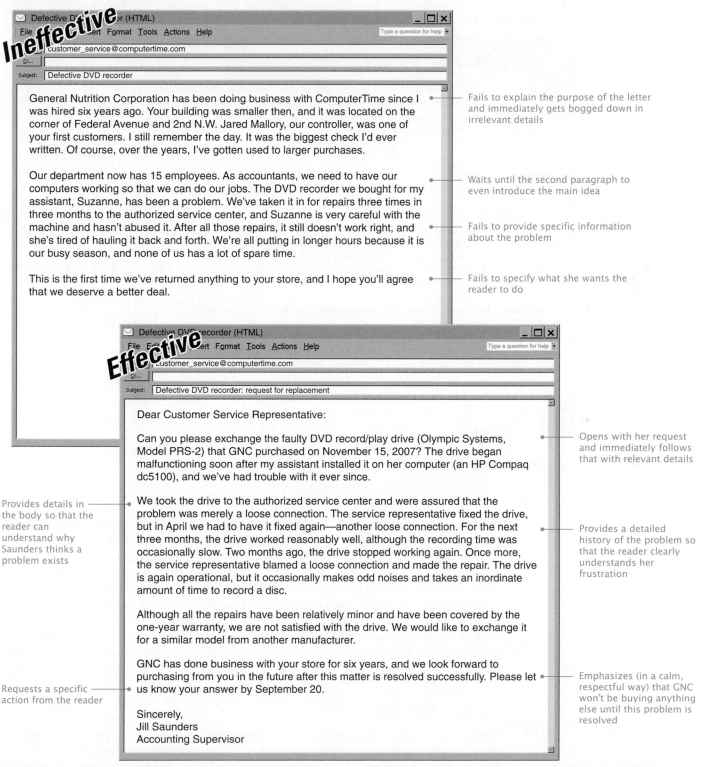

Ineffective

Fails to explain the purpose of the letter and immediately gets bogged down in irrelevant details

Waits until the second paragraph to even introduce the main idea

Fails to provide specific information about the problem

Fails to specify what she wants the reader to do

Effective

Opens with her request and immediately follows that with relevant details

Provides details in the body so that the reader can understand why Saunders thinks a problem exists

Provides a detailed history of the problem so that the reader clearly understands her frustration

Requests a specific action from the reader

Emphasizes (in a calm, respectful way) that GNC won't be buying anything else until this problem is resolved

you spend hours working on your draft. Furthermore, if you're working on a large, complex project, you can use your organization plan to divide the writing job among co-workers.

In addition to helping you, good organization helps the members of your audience in three key ways. First, it helps your audience understand your message. By making your main point clear at the outset and by presenting information logically, a well-organized message satisfies your audience's need for information.

Good organization helps audience members understand your message, accept your message, and save time.

FIGURE 4.8 Message Demonstrating a Diplomatic Organization Plan

In the case of ComputerTime's response to Jill Saunders's request for a replacement product from a different manufacturer, ComputerTime isn't able to do exactly what Saunders requested (the firm arranged a replacement from the same manufacturer instead). Consequently, the response letter from Linda Davis has a negative aspect to it, but the style of the letter is tactful and positive.

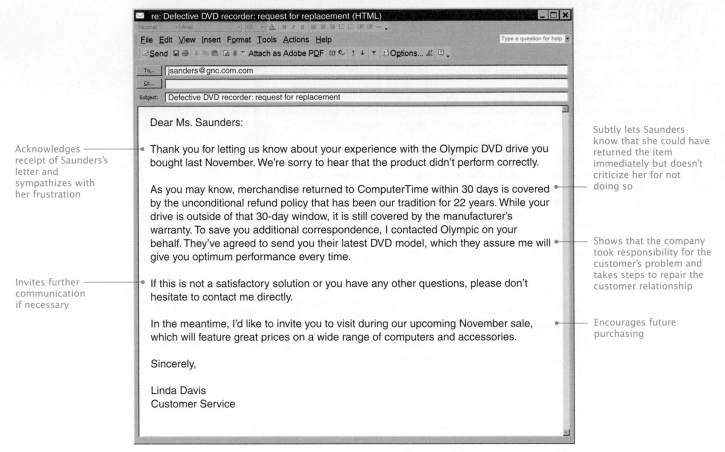

Acknowledges receipt of Saunders's letter and sympathizes with her frustration

Invites further communication if necessary

Subtly lets Saunders know that she could have returned the item immediately but doesn't criticize her for not doing so

Shows that the company took responsibility for the customer's problem and takes steps to repair the customer relationship

Encourages future purchasing

Second, it helps your audience accept your message. Effective messages often require a bit more than simple, clear logic. A diplomatic approach helps receivers accept your message, even if it's not exactly what they want to hear (see Figure 4.8).

Third, good organization saves your audience time. Well-organized messages are efficient. They contain only relevant ideas, and they are brief. Moreover, all the information in a well-organized message is in a logical place. Audience members receive only the information they need, and because that information is presented as accessibly and succinctly as possible, audience members can follow the thought pattern without a struggle. Before you can even begin arranging the information in your message, take a moment to define your main idea.

Defining Your Main Idea

7 LEARNING OBJECTIVE

Summarize the process for organizing business messages effectively

The topic is the broad subject; the main idea makes a statement about the topic.

The broad subject, or **topic**, of every well-organized business message can be condensed to one idea, whether it's soliciting the executive committee for a larger budget or apologizing to a client for an incident of poor customer service. Your entire message supports, explains, or demonstrates your **main idea**—a specific statement about the topic of your message (see Table 4.2).

Your main idea may be obvious when you're preparing a brief message with simple facts that have little emotional impact on your audience. If you're responding to a request for information, your main idea may be simply, "Here is what you wanted." However, defining your main idea is more complicated when you're trying to persuade someone or when you

TABLE 4.2 Defining Topic and Main Idea

GENERAL PURPOSE	SPECIFIC PURPOSE	TOPIC	MAIN IDEA
To inform	Teach customer service representatives how to file insurance claims	Insurance claims	Proper filing saves the company time and money.
To persuade	Convince top managers to increase spending on research and development	Funding for research and development	Competitors spend more than we do on research and development.
To collaborate	Solicit ideas for a companywide incentive system that ties wages to profits	Incentive pay	Tying wages to profits motivates employees and reduces compensation costs in tough years.

have disappointing information to convey. In these situations, try to define a main idea that will establish a good relationship with your audience. For example, you may choose a main idea that highlights an interest you share with your audience or one that emphasizes a point you can both agree on.

Defining your main idea is more difficult when you're trying to persuade someone or convey disappointing information.

In longer documents and presentations, you often need to unify a mass of material, so you'll need to define a main idea that encompasses all the individual points you want to make. Finding a common thread through all these points can be a challenge. Sometimes you won't even be sure what your main idea is until you sort through the information. For tough assignments like these, consider a variety of techniques to generate creative ideas:

- **Brainstorming.** Working alone or with others, generate as many ideas and questions as you can without stopping to criticize or organize. After you capture all these pieces, look for patterns and connections to help identify the main idea and the groups of supporting ideas. For example, if your main idea concerns whether or not to open a new restaurant in Denver, you'll probably find a group of ideas related to financial return, another related to competition, and so on. Identifying such groups helps you see the major issues that will lead you to a conclusion you can feel confident about.
- **Journalistic approach.** Introduced earlier in the chapter, the journalistic approach asks *who*, *what*, *when*, *where*, *why*, and *how* questions to distill major ideas from piles of unorganized information.
- **Question-and-answer chain.** Start with a key question, from the audience's perspective, and work back toward your message. In most cases, you'll find that each answer generates new questions until you identify the information that needs to be in your message.
- **Storyteller's tour.** Some writers find it easier to talk through a communication challenge before they try to write. Pretend you're giving a colleague a guided tour of your message and capture it on a tape recorder. Then listen to your talk, identify ways to tighten and clarify the message, and repeat the process. Working through this recording several times will help you distill the main idea down to a single, concise message.
- **Mind mapping.** You can also generate and organize ideas using a graphic method called mind mapping. Start with a main idea, and then branch out to connect every other related idea that comes to mind. For instance, the map in Figure 4.9 outlines the writer's own concerns about a report, her insights into the audience's concerns, and several issues related to writing and distributing the report.

Limiting Your Scope

The **scope** of your message is the range of information you present, the overall length, and the level of detail—all of which need to correspond to your main idea. For a report outlining your advice on whether to open a new restaurant in Denver, your message, including all supporting evidence, needs to focus on that question alone. Your plan for new menu selections and your idea for a new source of financing both would be outside the scope of your message. In Joe Kraynak's case, because computers are complicated devices that could fill an entire encyclopedia with descriptive detail, he limits his scope carefully—providing only

FIGURE 4.9 Using the Mind-Mapping Technique to Plan a Writing Project
Mind mapping is a helpful technique for identifying and organizing the many ideas and pieces of information that a complex writing task usually entails. Software (MindJet's MindManager in this case) makes it easy to create graphical output such as this diagram.

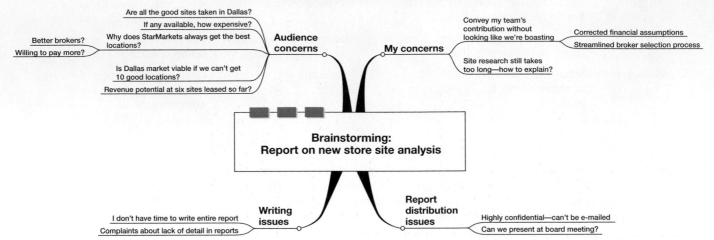

enough information to fulfill his specific purpose of helping people use computers more successfully.

Whether your audience expects a one-page memo or a one-hour speech, work within that framework to develop your main idea with major points and supporting evidence. Once you have a tentative statement of your main idea, test it against the length limitations that have been imposed on your message. If you don't have enough time or space to develop your main idea fully or if your main idea won't fill up the time and space allotted, you'll need to redefine it accordingly. If you don't have a fixed limit to work against, plan to make the document or presentation only as long as it needs to be to convey your main idea and critical support points.

Whatever the length of your message, limit the number of major support points to half a dozen or so—and if you can get your idea across with fewer points, all the better. Listing 20 or 30 support points may feel as if you're being thorough, but your audience will view such detail as disorganized and rambling. Instead, look for ways to group supporting points under major headings, such as finance, customers, competitors, employees, or whatever is appropriate for your subject. Just as you may need to refine your main idea, you may also need to refine your major support points so that you have a smaller number with greater impact.

If your message is brief, such as a one-page letter, plan on only one paragraph each for the introduction, conclusion, and major points. Because the amount of evidence you can present is limited, your main idea will have to be both easy to understand and easy to accept. However, if your message is long, you can develop the major points in considerable detail.

How much you can communicate in a given number of words depends on the nature of your subject, your audience members' familiarity with the topic, their receptivity to your conclusions, and your credibility. You'll need fewer words to present routine information to a knowledgeable audience that already knows and respects you. You'll need more words to build a consensus about a complex and controversial subject, especially if the members of your audience are skeptical or hostile strangers.

Limit the number of support points; having fewer, stronger points is a better approach than using many, weaker points.

Choosing Between Direct and Indirect Approaches

After you've defined your ideas, you're ready to decide on the sequence you will use to present your points. You have two basic options for identifying the sequence in which you present those points:

Use a direct approach if the audience's reaction is likely to be positive and an indirect approach if it is likely to be negative.

- **Direct approach (deductive).** When you know your audience will be receptive to your message, use a **direct approach:** Start with the main idea (such as a recommendation, a conclusion, or a request) and follow that with your supporting evidence.

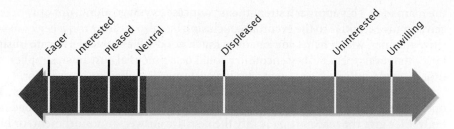

FIGURE 4.10 Choosing Between the Direct and Indirect Approaches
Think about the way your audience is likely to respond before choosing your approach.

	Direct approach	Indirect approach	
Audience Reaction	Eager/interested/ pleased/neutral	Displeased	Uninterested/unwilling
Message Opening	Start with the main idea, the request, or the good news.	Start with a neutral statement that acts as a transition to the reasons for the bad news.	Start with a statement or question that captures attention.
Message Body	Provide necessary details.	Give reasons to justify a negative answer. State or imply the bad news, and make a positive suggestion.	Arouse the audience's interest in the subject. Build the audience's desire to comply.
Message Close	Close with a cordial comment, a reference to the good news, or a statement about the specific action desired.	Close cordially.	Request action.

- **Indirect approach (inductive).** When your audience will be skeptical about or even resistant to your message, use an **indirect approach:** Start with the evidence first and build your case before presenting the main idea.

To choose between these two alternatives, analyze your audience's likely reaction to your purpose and message (see Figure 4.10). Bear in mind, however, that Figure 4.10 presents only general guidelines; always consider the unique circumstances of each message and audience situation. For example, although an indirect approach may be best when you're sending bad news to outsiders, if you're writing a message to a close associate you may want to get directly to the point, even if your message is unpleasant. The following sections offer more insight on choosing the best approach for routing and positive messages, negative messages, and persuasive messages.

Audience reaction can range from eager to unwilling.

Routine and Positive Messages

The most straightforward business messages are *routine* and *positive* messages. Routine messages involve the daily matters of operating a business, from placing orders to updating employees about process changes. Positive messages convey some sort of good news, whether you're announcing a price cut, accepting an invitation, or congratulating a colleague. In most instances, your audience will be pleased to hear from you. When you're providing routine information as part of your regular business, your audience will probably be neutral, neither pleased nor displeased.

Aside from being easy to understand, routine messages are easy to prepare. In most cases, you use a direct approach. In the opening, state your main idea directly. If you have good news to share, conveying that right away puts your audience members in a positive frame of mind and encourages them to be receptive to whatever else you have to say. The body of your message can then provide all necessary details. The close is cordial and emphasizes your good news or makes a statement about the specific action desired. Routine and positive messages are discussed in greater detail in Chapter 8.

Negative Messages

Unfortunately, being a business communicator also means you'll face situations in which you need to deliver bad news. Because your audience will be disappointed, these messages usually benefit from the indirect approach—putting the evidence first and building up to

In many situations, you can cushion the blow of negative news by introducing it with other, more positive information.

the main idea. This approach strengthens your case as you go along, not only making the receiver more receptive to the eventual conclusion but also treating the receiver in a more sensitive manner, which helps you retain as much goodwill as possible. Astute businesspeople know that every person they encounter could be a potential customer, supplier, or contributor or could influence someone who is a customer, supplier, or contributor.

Successful communicators take extra care with their negative messages. They often open with a neutral statement that acts as a transition to the reasons for the bad news. In the body, they give the reasons that justify the negative answer, announcement, or information before they state or imply the bad news. And they are always careful to close cordially.

The challenge of negative messages lies in being honest but kind. You don't want to sacrifice ethics and mislead your audience, nor do you want to be overly blunt. To achieve a good mix of candor and kindness, focus on some aspect of the situation that makes the negative news a little easier to take.

Keep in mind that the indirect approach is neither manipulative nor unethical. As long as you can be honest and reasonably brief, you're often better off opening a bad-news message with a neutral point and putting the negative information after the explanation. Then, if you can close with something fairly positive, you're likely to leave the audience feeling at least neutral—not great but not hostile either (which is often about all you can hope for when you must deliver bad news). Negative messages are discussed further in Chapter 9.

Persuasive Messages

Persuasive messages can be a challenge because you're generally asking your audience to give up something, such as time, money, power, and so on.

Persuasive messages present a special communication challenge because you're asking your audience to give, do, or change something, whether it's buying a product or agreeing to fund a new project. Before you try to persuade people to do something, you try to capture their attention and get them to consider your message with an open mind. Make an interesting point, and provide supporting facts that encourage your audience to continue paying attention. In most persuasive messages, the opening mentions a reader benefit, refers to a problem that the recipient may have, poses a question, or mentions an interesting statistic. Then the body builds interest in the subject and arouses audience members' desire to comply. Once you have them thinking, you can introduce your main idea. The close is cordial and requests the desired action. Persuasive messages are discussed at greater length in Chapter 10.

DOCUMENT MAKEOVER

IMPROVE THIS LETTER

To practice correcting drafts of actual documents, visit your online course or the access-code-protected portion of the Companion Website. Click "Document Makeovers," then click Chapter 4. You will find a letter that contains problems and errors relating to what you've learned in this chapter about planning and organizing business messages. Use the Final Draft decision tool to create an improved version of this letter. Check the document for audience focus, the right choice of medium, and the proper choice of direct or indirect approach.

Outlining Your Content

Once you have chosen the right approach, it's time to figure out the most logical and effective way to present your major points and supporting details. Even if you've resisted creating outlines in your school assignments over the years, try to get into the habit of creating outlines when you're preparing business messages. You'll save time, get better results, and do a better job of navigating through complicated business situations. Even if you're just jotting down three or four points on a notepad, making a plan and sticking to it will help you cover the important details. For a look at some of the most powerful outlining tools available today, see "Using the Power of Technology: Create and Collaborate with Powerful Outlining Tools."

A good way to visualize how all the points will fit together is to construct an outline.

When you're preparing a longer, more complex message, an outline is indispensable because it helps you visualize the relationships among the various parts. Without an outline, you may be inclined to ramble. As you're describing one point, another point may occur to you so you describe it as well. One detour leads to another, and before you know it you've forgotten the original point and wasted precious time and energy. With an outline to guide you, however, you can communicate in a more systematic way. Following an outline also helps you insert transitions so that your message is coherent and your audience can understand the relationships among your ideas.

Connecting with Technology

Create and Collaborate with Powerful Outlining Tools

Experienced business communicators recognize the power of a well-planned outline. However, outlining doesn't have to be the dull exercise you may remember from book reports and other school projects. Today's outlining tools, such as Microsoft Word's outline mode, make it easy to organize and reorganize ideas quickly. Some can even help ignite your creativity and generate new ideas.

For example, by following a consistent scheme of headings and subheadings, you can quickly add, delete, and rearrange sections to make sure your overall structure is logical and coherent. Also, if you ever feel like you've gotten lost in a long document after you've started writing, you can find your way again by shifting to outline mode. Collapse the outline down to just the first-level headings, then expand one level at a time—it's a great way to rediscover the shape of the forest when you're lost in the trees. Outline software is also a powerful way to study the layout of a website because you can see the entire structure underneath the homepage and make sure that your visitors won't get lost in or frustrated by confusing navigation.

For complex reports, you'll often need to collaborate on the outline with one or more colleagues who may be in different locations around the world. Groupware collaboration tools let multiple people work on an outline at the same time, often with integrated IM so that you can brainstorm and evaluate ideas on the fly. Rather than sending the outline around via e-mail and letting each person modify it individually—which can create endless rounds of revision and compromise—using a groupware outliner lets everyone contribute, argue, and collaborate all at once.

CAREER APPLICATIONS

1. Assume your boss has asked you to deliver a presentation on a report you've just completed. She says you don't need to start from scratch, though. Figure out the steps needed to transfer your report structure from Microsoft Word to Microsoft PowerPoint.

2. Product designers use a process called *reverse engineering* to find out how a finished product is put together. You can do the same thing with finished articles and reports to see how they're organized. Cut and paste the text of a substantial online news article into your word processor, then distill it down to an outline. Do you see any ways to improve the organization of the article?

You're no doubt familiar with the basic outline formats that identify each point with a number or letter and that indent certain points to show which ones are of equal status. A good outline divides a topic into at least two parts, restricts each subdivision to one category, and ensures that each subdivision is separate and distinct (see Figure 4.11).

Another way to visualize the outline of your message is to create an "organization chart" similar to the charts used to show a company's management structure (see Figure 4.12). The main idea is shown in the highest-level box and, like a top executive, establishes the big

You may want to experiment with other organizational schemes in addition to traditional outlines.

Alphanumeric Outline

I. First major point
   A. First subpoint
   B. Second subpoint
      1. Evidence
      2. Evidence
         a. Detail
         b. Detail
      3. Evidence
   C. Third subpoint
II. Second major point
   A. First subpoint
      1. Evidence
      2. Evidence
   B. Second subpoint

Decimal Outline

1.0 First major point
   1.1 First subpoint
   1.2 Second subpoint
      1.2.1 Evidence
      1.2.2 Evidence
         1.2.2.1 Detail
         1.2.2.2 Detail
      1.2.3 Evidence
   1.3 Third subpoint
2.0 Second major point
   2.1 First subpoint
      2.1.1 Evidence
      2.1.2 Evidence
   2.2 Second subpoint

FIGURE 4.11 Two Common Outline Forms

Your company may have a tradition of using a particular outline form for formal reports and other documents. If not, either of these two approaches will work for most any writing project.

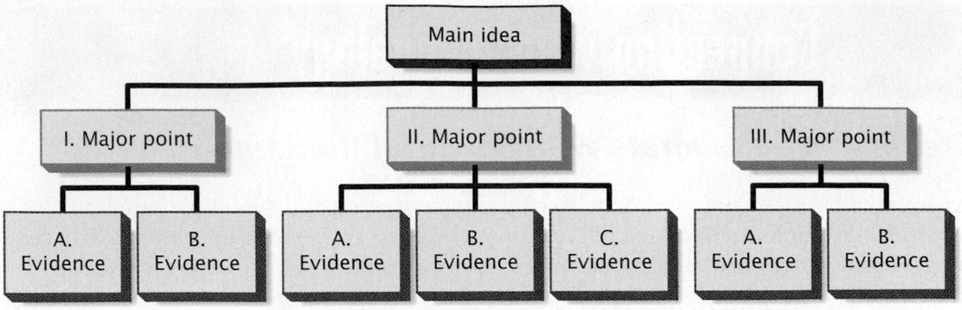

FIGURE 4.12
Organization Chart Method for Outlining
Consider the organization chart approach when you're faced with a large variety of facts, figures, and other bits of information and aren't quite sure how they all may relate to one another. Gathering pieces of evidence together under major points allows a clearer picture of the main idea to emerge.

picture. The lower-level ideas, like lower-level employees, provide the details. All the ideas are logically organized into divisions of thought, just as a company is organized into divisions and departments.[15] Using a visual chart instead of a traditional outline has many benefits. Charts help you (1) see the various levels of ideas and how the parts fit together, (2) develop new ideas, and (3) restructure your information flow. The mind-mapping technique used to generate ideas works in a similar way.

Whichever outlining or organizing scheme you use, start your message with the main idea, follow that with major supporting points, and then illustrate these points with evidence.

Start with the Main Idea

The main idea helps you establish the goals and general strategy of the message, and it summarizes two vital things: (1) what you want your audience members to do or think and (2) why they should do so. Everything in your message either supports the main idea or explains its implications. As discussed earlier in this chapter, some messages state the main idea quickly and directly, whereas other messages delay the main idea until after the evidence is presented.

State the Major Points

Major supporting points clarify your main idea.

You can divide major points according to physical relationships, the description of a process, the components of an object, or a historical chronology.

Now it's time to support your main idea with the major points that clarify and explain your ideas in more concrete terms. If your purpose is to inform and the material is factual, your major points may be based on something physical or financial—something you can visualize or measure, such as activities to be performed, functional units, spatial or chronological relationships, or parts of a whole. When you're describing a process, the major points are almost inevitably steps in the process. When you're describing an object, the major points often correspond to the parts of the object. When you're giving a historical account, major points represent events in the chronological chain. If your purpose is to persuade or to collaborate, select major points that develop a line of reasoning or a logical argument that proves your central message and motivates your audience to act.

Illustrate with Evidence

After you've defined the main idea and identified supporting points, you're ready to illustrate each point with specific evidence that helps audience members understand and remember the more abstract concepts you're presenting. For example, if you're advocating that your company increase its advertising budget, you can support your major point by providing evidence that your most successful competitors spend more on advertising than you do. You can also describe a case in which a particular competitor increased its advertising budget and achieved an impressive sales gain. Then you can show that over the past five years, your firm's sales have gone up and down in response to the amount spent on advertising.

If you're developing a long, complex message, you may need to carry the outline down several levels. Remember that every level is a step along the chain from the abstract to the

TABLE 4.3 Six Types of Detail

TYPE OF DETAIL	EXAMPLE	COMMENT
Facts and figures	Sales are strong this month. We have two new contracts worth $5 million and a good chance of winning another worth $2.5 million.	Adds more credibility than any other type. Can become boring if used excessively. Most common type used in business.
Example or illustration	We've spent four months trying to hire recent accounting graduates, but so far, only one person has joined our firm. One candidate told me that she would love to work for us, but she can get $5,000 more a year elsewhere.	Adds life to a message, but one example does not prove a point. Idea must be supported by other evidence as well.
Description	Upscale hamburger restaurants target burger lovers who want more than the convenience and low prices of a McDonald's. These places feature wine and beer, half-pound burgers, and generous side dishes (nachos, potato skins). "Atmosphere" is key.	Helps audience visualize the subject by creating a sensory impression. Does not prove a point, but clarifies it and makes it memorable. Begins with overview of function; defines its purpose, lists major parts, and explains how it operates.
Narration	Under former management, executives worked in blue jeans, meetings rarely started on time, and lunches ran long. When Jim Wilson became CEO, he completely overhauled the operation. A Harvard MBA who favors Brooks Brothers suits, Wilson has cut the product line in half and chopped $12 million off expenses.	Works well for attracting attention and explaining ideas, but lacks statistical validity.
Reference to authority	I discussed this idea with Jackie Loman in the Chicago plant, and she was very supportive. As you know, Jackie has been in charge of that plant for the past six years. She is confident that we can speed up the number 2 line by 150 units an hour if we add another worker.	Bolsters a case while adding variety and credibility. Works only if "authority" is recognized and respected by audience.
Visual aids	Graphs, charts, tables	Helps audience grasp specific data. Used more in memos and reports than in letters.

concrete, from the general to the specific. The lowest level contains the evidence, the individual facts and figures that tie the generalizations to the observable, measurable world. The higher levels are the concepts that reveal why those facts are significant.

To a certain extent, the more evidence you provide, the more conclusive your case will be. If your subject is complex and unfamiliar or if your audience is skeptical, you may need a lot of facts and figures to demonstrate your points. On the other hand, if your subject is routine and your audience is positively inclined, you can be more sparing with the evidence. You want to provide enough support to be convincing but not so much that your message becomes boring or inefficient.

Another way to keep your audience interested is to vary the type of detail you include. As you draft your message, try to incorporate the methods described in Table 4.3. Switch from facts and figures to narration, add a dash of description, throw in some examples or a reference to authority. If it makes sense, you can reinforce all these details with visual aids. Think of your message as a stew: a mixture of ingredients seasoned with a blend of spices. Each separate flavor adds to the richness of the whole.

If your schedule permits, try to put aside your outline for a day or two before you begin composing your first draft. Then review it with a fresh eye, looking for opportunities to improve the flow of ideas. For a reminder of the planning tasks involved in preparing your messages, see "Checklist: Planning Business Messages."

Each major point must be supported with enough specific evidence to be convincing, but not so much that your message becomes long and boring.

✔ CHECKLIST: Planning Business Messages

A. Analyze your situation.
- Determine whether the purpose of your message is to inform, persuade, or collaborate.
- Identify what you want your audience to think or do.
- Make sure your purpose is worthwhile and realistic.
- Make sure the time is right for your message.
- Make sure your purpose is acceptable to your organization.
- Identify the primary audience.
- Determine audience size and composition.
- Estimate your audience's level of understanding and probable reaction to your message.

B. Gather information.
- Decide whether to use formal or informal techniques for gathering information.

- Find out what your audience wants to know.
- Provide all required information and make sure it's accurate, ethical, and pertinent.

C. Select the best medium for your message.
- Understand the advantages and disadvantages of oral, written, visual, and electronic media.
- Consider media richness, formality, media limitations, sender intentions, urgency, cost, and audience preference.

D. Organize your information.
- Define your main idea.
- Limit your scope.
- Choose a direct or indirect approach.
- Outline content by starting with the main idea, adding major points, and illustrating with evidence.

COMMUNICATION CHALLENGES AT THE COMPLETE IDIOT'S GUIDES

 Alpha Books has commissioned Joe Kraynak to write a new book entitled *The Complete Idiot's Guide to the Motorola Razr*. This enormously popular phone features everything from video playback to Bluetooth wireless capability for adding wireless headsets and other accessories. The challenge in writing the book will be balancing the needs of several types of users, including people who have never used a cell phone before, people who have used phones before but don't care about advanced features, and "power users" who want to use every feature possible in every way imaginable. You're working as Kraynak's assistant and are responsible for researching key topics and writing some sections of the book.

Individual Challenge: Alpha Books has provided a brief project summary that focuses on the audience's expectations and preferences, including clear, concise text that's humorous and easy to read; lists of key points; and lots of illustrations. Kraynak wants more detail about the readers—so your first assignment is to develop a detailed audience profile. What kinds of questions will you ask Megan Aires, Kraynak's contact at Alpha, about the target audience for the book? Draft an e-mail message with six to eight questions. (Aires knows Kraynak but hasn't met you yet, so you'll need to introduce yourself as well.)

Team Challenge: Based on the need to provide information for everyone from "newbies" to power users and for people who want to know only the basics to people who want to know everything, what's the best way to organize this book? With your team, analyze these three options: Option 1: Organizing the entire book like an encyclopedia, describing the phone's individual features and functions in detail and in alphabetical order; Option 2: Organizing the book as three books in one, including an introductory guide that explains the basic concepts of using a cell phone and offers instructions on basic operation, an experienced user's guide that covers just the instructions on basic operation, and a power user's guide that covers the basic operation as well as all the advanced features; and Option 3: Organizing the book in five sections, including an introduction to cell phones, a quick graphical overview of the phone that identifies all the buttons and features, a guide to basic operation of the phone, a guide to advanced capabilities, and a brief glossary/index that defines the various features and functions. Draft a short e-mail to Kraynak identifying which of the three options is best and why.

SUMMARY OF LEARNING OBJECTIVES

1 **Describe the three-step writing process.** (1) Planning consists of four tasks: analyzing the situation (defining your purpose and profiling your audience), gathering the information to meet your audience's needs, selecting the best medium for the message and the situation, and organizing the information (defining your main idea, limiting your scope, selecting an approach, and outlining your content). (2) The writing step consists of two tasks: adapting to your audience and composing the message. Adapt your message to your audience by being sensitive to audience needs, building a strong relationship with your audience, and controlling your style. Compose your message by drafting your thoughts with strong words, effective sentences, and coherent paragraphs. (3) Completing your message consists of four tasks: revising your message by evaluating content and then rewriting and editing for clarity and conciseness, producing your message by using effective design elements and suitable delivery methods, proofreading your message for mistakes in spelling and mechanics, and distributing it in a way that meets both your needs and your audience's needs.

2 **Explain why it's important to define your purpose carefully, and list four questions that can help you test that purpose.** You must know enough about your purpose to shape your message in a way that will achieve your goal. To decide whether you should proceed with your message, ask four questions: (1) Will anything change as a result of this message? (2) Is this message realistic? (3) Is it acceptable to my organization? (4) Is it being delivered at the right time?

3 **Describe the importance of analyzing your audience, and identify the six factors you should consider when developing an audience profile.** Analyzing your audience helps you discover who the members of your audience are, what their attitudes are, what they need to know, and why they should care about your purpose in communicating. An effective profile helps you predict how your audience will react to your message. It also helps you know what to include in your message and how to include it. To develop an audience profile, you need to determine your primary audience (key decision makers), the size of your audience, the makeup of your audience, the level of your audience's understanding, your audience's expectations, and audience members' probable reactions.

4 **Discuss gathering information for simple messages, and identify three attributes of quality information.** Gathering the information that will fulfill your audience's needs is a vital step before attempting to organize your content. For more complex documents, you may need to plan a research project to acquire all the necessary information. However, for simple messages, if you don't already have all the information you need, you can gather it using other methods such as considering other viewpoints, reading existing reports and other company documents, talking with supervisors and others who have information and insight, and asking your audience members directly for their input. To determine whether the information you've gathered is good enough, verify that it is accurate, ethical, and pertinent to the audience's needs.

5 **List factors to consider when choosing the most appropriate medium for your message.** The first factor to consider is media richness. Richness is determined by the medium's ability to (1) convey a message using more than one informational cue such as sound, motion, nonverbal cues, and so on; (2) facilitate feedback; and (3) establish personal focus. Other factors to consider when selecting media include the level of formality, the specific limitations of each medium, your intentions in sending the message, the level of urgency balanced with the cost of using a particular channel, and your audience's preferences.

6 **Explain why good organization is important to both you and your audience.** When you organize messages carefully, you save time and conserve creative energy because the writing process is quicker. You can also use your organization plan to get advance input from your audience members and to make sure you're on the right track. Finally, good organization can help you divide portions of the writing assignment among co-workers. Audiences also benefit from good organization in several ways. When audience members receive a message that is well organized, they don't have to read and reread a message to make sense of it, so they save time. They are also better able to understand the content, so they can accept the message more easily and make better decisions based on the information conveyed.

7 **Summarize the process for organizing business messages effectively.** To organize messages effectively, begin with recognizing the importance of good organization. Then define the main idea by making a specific statement about the topic. Limit the scope of the message by adjusting the space and detail you allocate to major points (which should number no more than half a dozen, and fewer if possible). To choose either a direct or an indirect approach, anticipate the audience's reaction to the message (positive, neutral, or negative) and match the approach to both message length (short or long) and message type (routine, positive, negative, or persuasive). Finally, group the points by constructing an outline to visualize the relationship between the ideas and the supporting material.

Test Your Knowledge

1. What are the three steps in the writing process?
2. What two types of purposes do all business messages have?
3. What do you need to know in order to develop an audience profile?
4. How can you test the thoroughness of the information you include in a message?
5. What three factors determine media richness?
6. What are the main advantages of oral media? Of written media?
7. What are the advantages and disadvantages of electronic media?
8. What is the process for organizing messages?
9. Why is it important to limit the scope of your message?
10. What three elements do you consider when choosing between a direct and an indirect approach?

Apply Your Knowledge

1. Some writers argue that planning messages wastes time because they inevitably change their plans as they go along. How would you respond to this argument? Briefly explain.
2. As a member of the public relations department, what medium would you recommend using to inform the local community that your toxic-waste cleanup program has been successful? Why?
3. Would you use a direct or an indirect approach to ask employees to work overtime to meet an important deadline? Please explain.
4. Which approach would you use to let your boss know that you'll be out half a day this week to attend your father's funeral—direct or indirect? Why?
5. **Ethical Choices** A day after sending an e-mail to all 1,800 employees in your company regarding income tax implications of the company's retirement plan, you discover that one of the sources you relied on for your information plagiarized from other sources. Your quickly double-check all the information in your message and confirm that it is accurate. However, you are concerned about using plagiarized information, even though you did nothing wrong. Write a brief e-mail message to your instructor explaining how you would handle the situation.

Practice Your Knowledge

Message for Analysis

A writer is working on an insurance information brochure and is having trouble grouping the ideas logically into an outline. Prepare the outline, paying attention to appropriate subordination of ideas. If necessary, rewrite phrases to make them all consistent.

Accident Protection Insurance Plan

- Coverage is only pennies a day
- Benefit is $100,000 for accidental death on common carrier
- Benefit is $100 a day for hospitalization as result of motor vehicle or common carrier accident
- Benefit is $20,000 for accidental death in motor vehicle accident
- Individual coverage is only $17.85 per quarter; family coverage is just $26.85 per quarter
- No physical exam or health questions
- Convenient payment—billed quarterly
- Guaranteed acceptance for all applicants
- No individual rate increases
- Free, no-obligation examination period
- Cash paid in addition to any other insurance carried
- Covers accidental death when riding as fare-paying passenger on public transportation, including buses, trains, jets, ships, trolleys, subways, or any other common carrier
- Covers accidental death in motor vehicle accidents occurring while driving or riding in or on automobile, truck, camper, motor home, or nonmotorized bicycle

Exercises

For active links to all websites discussed in this chapter, visit this text's website at www.prenhall.com/bovee. Locate your book and click on its Companion Website link. Then select Chapter 4, and click on "Featured Websites." Locate the name of the page or the URL related to the material in the text. Please note that links to sites that become inactive after publication of the book will be removed from the Featured Websites section.

4.1 **Message Planning Skills: Self-Assessment** How good are you at planning business messages? Use the following chart to rate yourself on each element of planning an audience-centered business message. Then examine your ratings to identify where you are strongest and where you can improve using the tips in this chapter.

Element of Planning	Always	Frequently	Occasionally	Never
1. I start by defining my purpose.	_____	_____	_____	_____
2. I analyze my audience before writing a message.	_____	_____	_____	_____
3. I investigate what my audience wants to know.	_____	_____	_____	_____
4. I check that my information is accurate, ethical, and pertinent.	_____	_____	_____	_____
5. I consider my audience and purpose when selecting media.	_____	_____	_____	_____

4.2 **Planning Messages: General and Specific Purpose** Make a list of communication tasks you'll need to accomplish in the next week or so (for example, a job application, a letter of complaint, a speech to a class, an order for some merchandise). For each, determine a general and a specific purpose.

4.3 **Planning Messages: Specific Purpose** For each of the following communication tasks, state a specific purpose (if you have trouble, try beginning with "I want to . . ."").
  a. A report to your boss, the store manager, about the outdated items in the warehouse
  b. A memo to clients about your booth at the upcoming trade show
  c. A letter to a customer who hasn't made a payment for three months
  d. A memo to employees about the department's high cell phone bills
  e. A phone call to a supplier checking on an overdue parts shipment
  f. A report to future users of the computer program you have chosen to handle the company's mailing list

4.4 **Planning Messages: Audience Profile** For each communication task that follows, write brief answers to three questions: Who is my audience? What is my audience's general attitude toward my subject? What does my audience need to know?
  a. A final-notice collection letter from an appliance manufacturer to an appliance dealer that is 3 months behind on payments, sent 10 days before initiating legal collection procedures
  b. An unsolicited e-mail message asking readers to purchase computer disks at near-wholesale prices
  c. An advertisement for peanut butter
  d. Fliers to be attached to doorknobs in the neighborhood announcing reduced rates for chimney cleaning or repairs
  e. A cover letter sent along with your résumé to a potential employer
  f. A website that describes the services offered by a consulting firm that helps accounting managers comply with government regulations

4.5 **Meeting Audience Needs: Necessary Information** Choose an electronic device (such as a digital music player or digital camera) that you know how to operate well. Write two sets of instructions for operating the device: one set for a reader who has never used that type of device and one set for someone who is generally familiar with that type of machine but has never operated the specific model. Briefly explain how your two audiences affect your instructions.

4.6 **Selecting Media: Defining the Purpose** List five messages you have received lately, such as direct-mail promotions, letters, e-mail messages, phone solicitations, and lectures. For each, determine the general and the specific purpose; then answer the following questions: (a) Was the message well timed? (b) Did the sender choose an appropriate medium for the message? (c) Was the sender's purpose realistic?

4.7 **Selecting Media: Identifying an Audience** Barbara Marquardt is in charge of public relations for a cruise line that operates out of Miami. She is shocked to read a letter in a local newspaper from a disgruntled passenger complaining about the service and entertainment on a recent cruise. Marquardt will have to respond to these publicized criticisms in some way. What audiences will she need to consider in her response? What medium should she choose? If the letter had been published in a travel publication widely read by travel agents and cruise travelers, how might her course of action have differed?

4.8 **Teamwork: Audience Analysis** Your team has been studying a new method for testing the durability of your company's power tools. Now the team needs to prepare three separate reports on the findings: first, a report for the administrator who will decide whether to purchase the equipment needed for this new testing method; second, a report for the company's engineers who design and develop the hand tools; and third, a report for the trainers who will be showing workers how to use the new equipment. To determine the audience's needs for each of these reports, the team has listed the following questions: (1) Who are the readers? (2) Why will they read my report? (3) Do they need introductory or background material? (4) Do they need definitions of terms? (5) What level or type of language is needed? (6) What level of detail is needed? (7) What result does my report aim for? Working with two other students, answer the questions for each of these audiences:

a. The administrator

b. The engineers

c. The trainers

4.9   Internet: Planning Your Message Go to the PepsiCo website at www.pepsico.com and follow the link to the latest annual report. Then locate and read the chairman's letter. Who is the audience for this message? What is the general purpose of the message? What do you think this audience wants to know from the chairman of PepsiCo? Summarize your answers in a brief (one-page) memo or oral presentation.

4.10   Message Organization: Outlining Your Content Using the improved version of the GNC e-mail message in Figure 4.7, draw an organizational chart similar to the one shown in Figure 4.12. Fill in the main idea, the major points, and the evidence provided in this letter. (Note: Your diagram may be smaller than the one provided in Figure 4.12).

4.11   Message Organization: Limiting Scope Suppose you are preparing to recommend that top management install a new heating system that uses the cogeneration process. The following information is in your files. Eliminate topics that aren't essential; then arrange the other topics so that your report will give top managers a clear understanding of the heating system and a balanced, concise justification for installing it.

- History of the development of the cogeneration heating process
- Scientific credentials of the developers of the process
- Risks assumed in using this process
- Your plan for installing the equipment in your building
- Stories about its successful use in comparable facilities
- Specifications of the equipment that would be installed
- Plans for disposing of the old heating equipment
- Costs of installing and running the new equipment
- Advantages and disadvantages of using the new process
- Detailed 10-year cost projections
- Estimates of the time needed to phase in the new system
- Alternative systems that management may wish to consider

4.12   Message Organization: Choosing an Approach Indicate whether a direct or an indirect approach would be best in each of the following situations, then briefly explain why. Would any of these messages be inappropriate for e-mail? Explain.

a. A letter asking when next year's automobiles will be put on sale locally

b. A letter from a recent college graduate requesting a letter of recommendation from a former instructor

c. A letter turning down a job applicant

d. An announcement that because of high air-conditioning costs, the plant temperature will be held at 78ºF during the summer

e. A final request to settle a delinquent debt

4.13   Message Organization: Audience Focus If you were trying to persuade people to take the following actions, how would you organize your argument?

a. You want your boss to approve your plan for hiring two new people.

b. You want to be hired for a job.

c. You want to be granted a business loan.

d. You want to collect a small amount from a regular customer whose account is slightly past due.

e. You want to collect a large amount from a customer whose account is seriously past due.

4.14   Ethical Choices: Providing Information Your supervisor, whom you respect, has asked you to withhold important information that you think should be included in a report you are preparing. Disobeying him could be disastrous for your relationship and your career. Obeying him could violate your personal code of ethics. What should you do? On the basis of the discussion in Chapter 1, would you consider this situation to be an ethical dilemma or an ethical lapse? Please explain.

4.15   Three-Step Process: Other Applications How can the material discussed in this chapter also apply to meetings as discussed in Chapter 2? (Hint: Review the section headings in Chapter 4 and think about making your meetings more productive.)

Expand Your Knowledge

Exploring the Best of the Web

Corporate Blogging with a European Flavor

www.corporateblogging.info/basics

See how blogging is changing the business of business communication and learn the basic steps needed to set up your own company blog. Plus, you can explore a variety of blogs hosted by European companies to get a feel for the international nature of blogging. Browse the Business Blogging Basics section and sample a few of the European blogs (the blogs from the United Kingdom are in English, as are selected blogs from other countries), then answer the following questions:

1. What are the key advantages of creating a company blog?
2. What are the various methods of reading content from other blogs?
3. Do the European blogs differ in style from one another or from blogs you've seen from U.S. companies?

Surfing Your Way to Career Success

Bovée and Thill's Business Communication Resources offers links to hundreds of online resources that can help you with this course, your other college courses, and your career. Visit www.buscommresources.com, then click on "Business Communication Web Directory." The "Writing Process" section connects you to a variety of websites and articles on planning, writing, revision, audience analysis, and brainstorming. Identify three websites from this section that could be useful in your business career. For each site, write a two-sentence summary of what the site offers and how it could help you launch and build your career.

Learn Interactively

Interactive Study Guide

Visit www.prenhall.com/bovee, then locate your book and click on its "Companion Website" link. Select Chapter 4 to take advantage of the interactive "Chapter Quiz" to test your knowledge of chapter concepts. Receive instant feedback on whether you need additional studying. Also, visit the "Study Hall," where you'll find an abundance of valuable resources that will help you succeed in this course.

Peak Performance Grammar and Mechanics

If your instructor has required the use of "Peak Performance Grammar and Mechanics," either in your online course or on CD, you can improve your skill with adjectives and adverbs by using the "Peak Performance Grammar and Mechanics" module. Click on "Grammar Basics," and then click "Adjectives and Adverbs." Take the Pretest to determine whether you have any weak areas. Then review those areas in the Refresher Course. Take the Follow-Up Test to check your grasp of adjectives and adverbs. For an extra challenge or advanced practice, take the Advanced Test. Finally, for additional reinforcement in adjectives and adverbs, visit the Companion Website, click on any chapter, then click on "Improve Your Grammar, Mechanics, and Usage."

CHAPTER 5

Writing Business Messages

LEARNING OBJECTIVES

After studying this chapter, you will be able to

1 Explain the importance of adapting your messages to the needs and expectations of your audience

2 Explain why establishing credibility is vital to the success of your communication efforts

3 Discuss four ways of achieving a businesslike tone with a style that is clear and concise

4 Briefly describe how to select words that are not only correct but also effective

5 Explain how sentence style affects emphasis within your message

6 List five ways to develop coherent paragraphs

COMMUNICATION CLOSE-UP AT CREATIVE COMMONS

www.creativecommons.org

Have you ever noticed that tiny © symbol on books, DVDs, music CDs, and other media products? It means that the person or organization who created the item is granted *copyright* protection, the exclusive legal right to produce, distribute, and sell that creation. Anyone who wants to resell, redistribute, or adapt such works usually needs to secure permission from the current copyright holder.

However, what if you *want* people to remix the song you just recorded? Or suppose you need a few photos for a website? Other than for limited personal and educational use, a conventional copyright requires every person to negotiate a contract for every application or adaptation of every piece of work he or she wants to use.

The search for some middle ground between "all rights reserved" and simply giving your work away led Stanford University law professor Lawrence Lessig to co-found Creative Commons. This nonprofit organization's goal is to provide a simple, free, and legal way for musicians, artists, writers, teachers, scientists, and others to collaborate and benefit through the sharing of art and ideas. Instead of the everything-or-nothing approach of traditional copyright, Creative Commons offers a more flexible range of "some rights reserved" options.

Through books, articles, and speeches, Lessig has been a tireless promoter of the Creative Commons concept, work-ing to convince people that society benefits from the free exchange of art and ideas and that overuse of the copyright law is endangering not only creative expression but also important scientific research. The message is clearly getting through: Within the first year, more than a million of these innovative license agreements were initiated for musical works, short films, educational materials, novels, and more. This approach can't solve the entire dilemma of copyrights in the digital age, but it has already created a better way for creative people to communicate and collaborate.[1]

Lawrence Lessig, co-founder of Creative Commons, uses a variety of communication vehicles to convince copyright owners to explore new ways of sharing and protecting their creative works.

BRINGING YOUR IDEAS TO LIFE

As they work to persuade their audiences to consider new forms of copyright protection, Lawrence Lessig and his colleagues at Creative Commons (profiled in the chapter-opening Communication Close-Up) realize it takes more than just a great idea to change the way people think. Expressing ideas clearly and persuasively will be key to your success as well.

With a solid plan in place (see Chapter 4), you're ready to choose the words and craft the sentences and paragraphs that will carry your ideas to their intended audiences. Figure 5.1 lists the tasks involved in adapting to your audience and composing your message.

ADAPTING TO YOUR AUDIENCE

1 LEARNING OBJECTIVE

Explain the importance of adapting your messages to the needs and expectations of your audience

A good relationship with your audience is essential to effective communication.

Whether consciously or not, audiences greet most incoming messages with a question: "What's in this for me?" If your intended audience members think a message does not apply to them or doesn't meet their needs, they'll be far less inclined to pay attention to it. Follow the example set by the Creative Commons website, which addresses an extremely diverse audience of artists, lawyers, and business professionals but fine-tunes specific messages for each group of people. By adapting your communication to the needs and expectations of your audiences, you'll provide a more compelling answer to the "What's in this for me?" question and improve the chances of your message being successful.

Note that adapting your message is not always a simple task. Some situations will require you to balance competing or conflicting needs—for example, when you're trying to convince people to change their minds or when you're delivering bad news. To successfully adapt your message to your audience, try to be sensitive to your audience's needs, build a strong relationship with your audience, and control your style to maintain a professional tone.

Being Sensitive to Your Audience's Needs

Even in simple messages intended merely to share information, it's possible to use all the right words and still not be sensitive to your audience members and their needs. You can improve your audience sensitivity by adopting the "you" attitude, maintaining good standards of etiquette, emphasizing the positive, and using bias-free language.

FIGURE 5.1 Step Two in the Three-Step Writing Process: Write Your Messages
The second step in the three-step writing process includes two vital tasks: adapting to your audience and composing your message.

Plan → **Write** → **Complete**

Adapt to Your Audience
Be sensitive to audience needs with a you " attitude, politeness, positive emphasis, and bias-free language. Build a strong relationship with your audience by establishing your credibility and projecting your company's image. Control your style with a conversational tone, plain English, and appropriate voice.

Compose the Message
Choose strong words that will help you create effective sentences and coherent paragraphs.

1   **2**   **3**

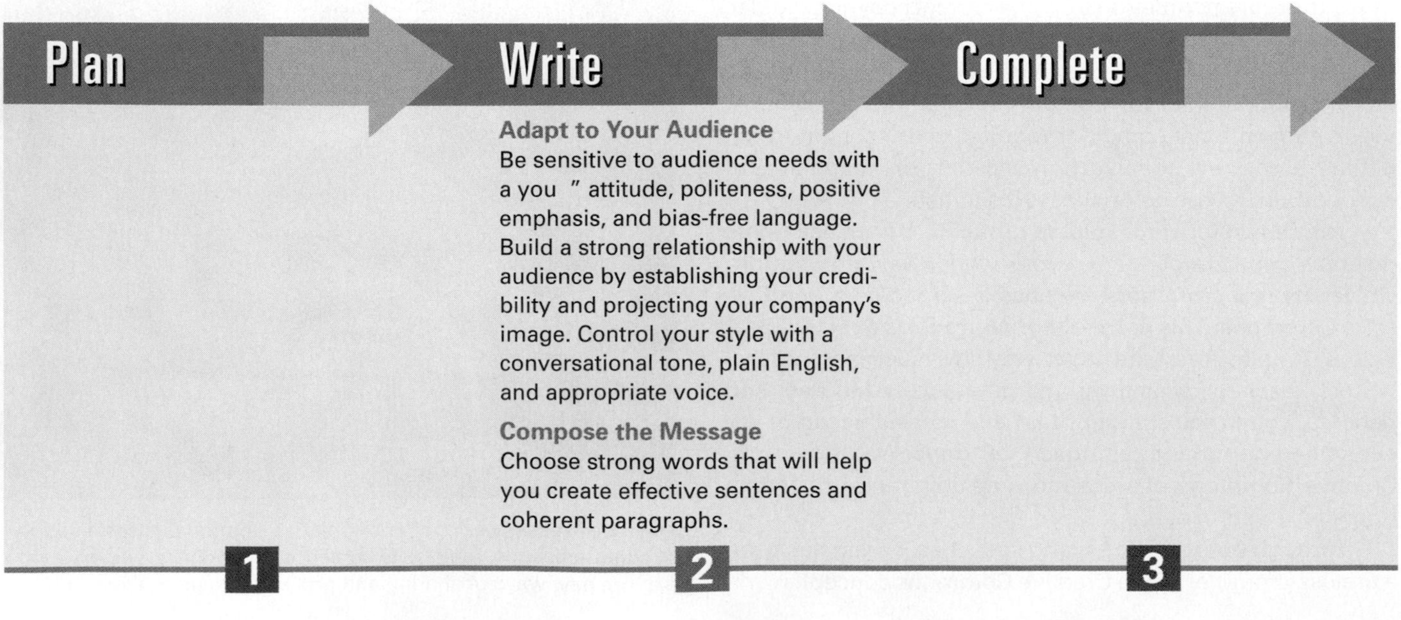

Using the "You" Attitude

Chapter 1 introduced the notion of audience-centered communication and the "you" attitude—that is, by speaking and writing in terms of your audience's wishes, interests, hopes, and preferences. On the simplest level, you can adopt the "you" attitude by replacing terms that refer to yourself and your company with terms that refer to your audience. In other words, use *you* and *yours* instead of *I, me, mine, we, us,* and *ours*:

The "you" attitude is best implemented by expressing your message in terms of the audience's interests and needs.

INSTEAD OF THIS	WRITE THIS
To help us process this order, we must ask for another copy of the requisition.	So that your order can be filled promptly, please send another copy of the requisition.
We are pleased to announce our new flight schedule from Atlanta to New York, which is any hour on the hour.	Now you can take a plane from Atlanta to New York any hour on the hour.
We offer MP3 players with 50, 75, or 100 gigabytes of storage capacity.	Select your MP3 player from three models with 50, 75, or 100 gigabytes of storage capacity.

When business messages use an "I" or "we" attitude, they risk sounding selfish and uninterested in the audience. The message is all about the sender, and the audience is just expected to go along with it. Even so, using *you* and *yours* requires finesse. If you overdo it, you're likely to create some rather awkward sentences, and you run the risk of sounding overly enthusiastic and artificial.[2]

The "you" attitude is not intended to be manipulative or insincere. It's an extension of the audience-centered approach. In fact, the best way to implement the "you" attitude is to sincerely think about your audience when composing your message.

Nor is the "you" attitude simply a matter of using one pronoun rather than another; it's a matter of genuine empathy. You can use *you* 25 times in a single page and still ignore your audience's true concerns. In other words, it's the thought and sincerity that count, not the pronoun *you*. If you're talking to a retailer, try to think like a retailer; if you're dealing with a production supervisor, put yourself in that position; if you're writing to a dissatisfied customer, imagine how you would feel at the other end of the transaction.

Be aware that on some occasions it's better to avoid using *you*, particularly if doing so will sound overly authoritative or accusing. For instance, instead of saying, "You failed to deliver the customer's order on time," you could minimize ill will by saying, "The customer didn't receive the order on time," or "Let's figure out a system that will ensure on-time deliveries."

Avoid using you *and* yours *when doing so*
- *Makes you sound dictatorial*
- *Makes someone else feel guilty*
- *Goes against your organization's style*

INSTEAD OF THIS	WRITE THIS
You should never use that type of paper in the copy machine.	That type of paper doesn't work very well in the copy machine.
You must correct all five copies by noon.	All five copies must be corrected by noon.

As you practice using the "you" attitude, be sure to consider the attitudes of other cultures and the policies of your organization. In some cultures, it is improper to single out one person's achievements because the whole team is responsible for the outcome; in that case, using the pronoun *we* or *our* (when you and your audience are part of the same team) would be more appropriate. Similarly, some companies have a tradition of avoiding references to *you* and *I* in most messages and reports.

Maintaining Standards of Etiquette

Another good way to demonstrate interest in your audience members and to earn their respect is to demonstrate etiquette in your messages. You know how it feels to be treated inconsiderately; when that happens, you probably react emotionally and then pay less attention to the offending message. By being courteous to members of your audience, you show consideration for them and foster a more successful environment for communication.

Although you may be tempted now and then to be brutally frank, try to express the facts in a kind and thoughtful manner.

On those occasions when you experience frustration with co-workers, customers, or others you deal with, you may be tempted to say what you think in blunt terms. But venting your emotions rarely improves the situation and can jeopardize your audience's goodwill. Demonstrate your diplomatic skills by controlling your emotions and communicating calmly and politely:

INSTEAD OF THIS	**WRITE THIS**
Once again, you've managed to bring down the entire website through your incompetent programming.	Let's review the last website update so that we can find out how to improve the process.
You've been sitting on our order for two weeks, and we need it now!	Our production schedules depend on timely delivery of parts and supplies, but we have not yet received the order you promised to deliver two weeks ago. Please respond today with a firm delivery commitment.

Use extra tact when communicating with people higher up the organization chart or outside the company.

Of course, some situations require more diplomacy than others. If you know your audience well, a less formal approach may be more appropriate. However, when you are communicating with people who outrank you or with people outside your organization, an added measure of courtesy is usually needed.

Written communication and most forms of electronic media generally require more tact than oral communication (Figure 5.2). When you're speaking, your words are softened by your tone of voice and facial expression. Plus, you can adjust your approach according to the feedback you get. If you inadvertently offend someone in writing or in a podcast, for example, you usually won't get the immediate feedback you would need to resolve the situation. In fact, you may never know that you offended your audience.

Emphasizing the Positive

You can communicate negative news without being negative.

During your career, you will have many occasions to communicate bad news—maybe dozens or hundreds of times. As you rise through the ranks of management, you will encounter situations in which unpleasant news can significantly affect the personal and financial well-being of employees, customers, and investors. However, there is a big difference between delivering negative news and being negative. When the tone of your message is negative, you put unnecessary strain on business relationships, which can cause people to distance themselves from you and your ideas.

If you're facing a potentially negative situation, look for ways to soften the blow or emphasize positive aspects of a situation. For example, when Alaska Airlines instituted surcharges for heavy luggage in an attempt to reduce injuries to baggage handlers, the company presented the change to passengers with posters that said, "Pack Light & Save."[3] By presenting the situation as an opportunity to save money rather than as an added cost of travel, Alaska worked to maintain a positive relationship with its customers. Never try to hide the negative news, but always be on the lookout for positive points that will foster a good relationship with your audience:[4]

INSTEAD OF THIS	**WRITE THIS**
It is impossible to repair your laptop today.	Your computer can be ready by Tuesday. Would you like a loaner until then?
We apologize for inconveniencing you during our remodeling.	The renovations now under way will help us serve you better.
We wasted $300,000 advertising in that magazine.	Our $300,000 advertising investment did not pay off; let's analyze the experience and apply the insights to future campaigns.

FIGURE 5.2 Fostering a Positive Relationship with an Audience

In the "ineffective" example, notice how the customer service agent's unfortunate word choices immediately derail this instant messaging exchange. In the "effective" example, a more sensitive approach allows both people to focus on solving the problem.

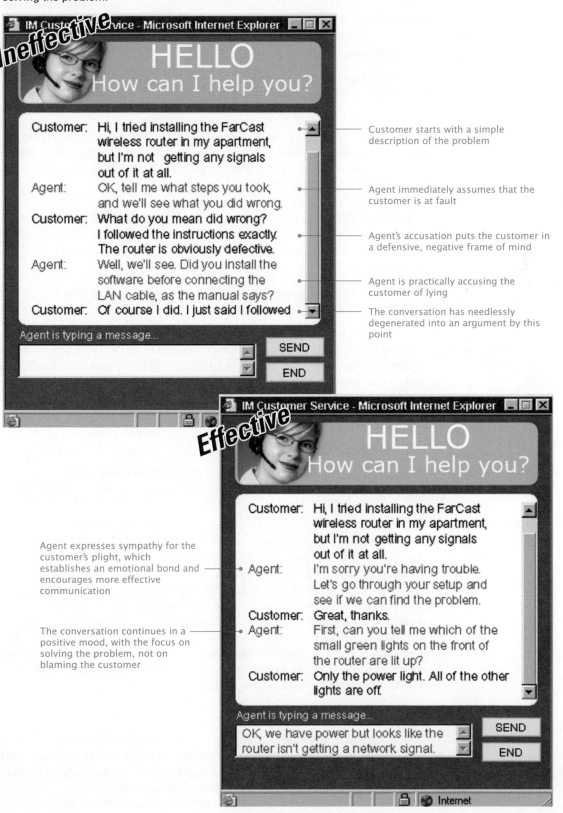

When you are offering criticism or advice, focus on what the person can do to improve.

When you find it necessary to criticize or correct, don't dwell on the other person's mistakes. Avoid referring to failures, problems, or shortcomings. Focus instead on what the person can do to improve:

INSTEAD OF THIS	WRITE THIS
The problem with this department is a failure to control costs.	The performance of this department can be improved by tightening cost controls.
You failed to provide all the necessary information on the previous screen.	Please review the items marked in red on the previous screen so that we can process your order as quickly as possible.

Show your audience members how they will benefit from complying with your message.

If you're trying to persuade audience members to buy a product, pay a bill, or perform a service for you, emphasize what's in it for them. Don't focus on why *you* want them to do something. An individual who sees the possibility for personal benefit is more likely to respond positively to your appeal:

INSTEAD OF THIS	WRITE THIS
We will notify all three credit reporting agencies if you do not pay your overdue bill within 10 days.	Paying your overdue bill within 10 days will prevent a negative entry on your credit record.
I am tired of seeing so many errors in the customer-service blog.	Proofreading your blog postings will help you avoid embarrassing mistakes that generate more customer-service complaints.

Try to avoid words with negative connotations; use meaningful euphemisms instead.

In general, try to state your message without using words that may hurt or offend your audience. Substitute *euphemisms* (mild terms) for those that have unpleasant associations. You can be honest without being harsh. Gentle language won't change the facts, but it will make them more acceptable:

INSTEAD OF THIS	WRITE THIS
Cheap merchandise	Economy merchandise
Failing	Underperforming
Fake	Imitation or faux

On the other hand, don't carry euphemisms to extremes or your audience will view your efforts as insincere. And if you're too subtle, people won't know what you're talking about. If employees need to become 10 percent more productive to save the company from bankruptcy, don't tell them they need to "make positive performance adjustments"—tell them they need to become 10 percent more productive. Also, when using euphemisms, you walk a fine line between softening the blow and hiding the facts. It would be unethical to speak to your local community about "manufacturing by-products" when you're really talking about your plans for disposing of toxic waste. Such an attempt to hide the facts would likely backfire, damaging your business image and reputation. Even if it is unpleasant, people respond better to an honest message delivered with integrity than they do to a sugar-coated message that obscures the truth.

Using Bias-Free Language

Avoid biased language that may offend your audience.

Chapter 3 points out that you are often unaware of the influence of your own culture on your behavior, and this circumstance extends to the language you use. Any bias present in your culture is likely to show up in your language, often in subtle ways that you may not even recognize. However, chances are that your audience will.

Bias-free language avoids words and phrases that unfairly and even unethically categorize or stigmatize people in ways related to gender, race, ethnicity, age, or disability. Contrary to what some may think, biased language is not simply about "labels." To a significant degree, language reflects the way we think and what we believe, and biased language may

TABLE 5.1 Overcoming Bias in Language

EXAMPLES	UNACCEPTABLE	PREFERABLE
Gender Bias		
Using words containing "man"	Man-made	Artificial, synthetic, manufactured, constructed
	Mankind	Humanity, human beings, human race, people
	Manpower	Workers, workforce
	Businessman	Executive, manager, businessperson
	Salesman	Sales representative, salesperson, clerk
	Foreman	Supervisor
Using female-gender words	Actress, stewardess	Actor, flight attendant
Using special designations	Woman doctor, male nurse	Doctor, nurse
Using "he" to refer to "everyone"	The average worker . . . he	The average worker . . . he or she
Identifying roles with gender	The typical executive spends four hours of his day in meetings.	Most executives spend four hours a day in meetings.
	the consumer . . . she	consumers . . . they
	the nurse/teacher . . . she	nurses/teachers . . . they
Identifying women by marital status	Mr. and Mrs. Norm Lindstrom	Norm and Ellie Lindstrom
	Norm Lindstrom and Ms. Drake	Mr. Lindstrom and Ms. Drake
Racial/Ethnic Bias		
Assigning stereotypes	My African-American assistant speaks more articulately than I do.	My assistant speaks more articulately than I do.
	Jim Wong is an unusually tall Asian.	Jim Wong is tall.
Identifying people by race or ethnicity	Mario M. Cuomo, Italian American politician and ex-governor of New York	Mario M. Cuomo, politician and ex-governor of New York
Age Bias		
Including age when irrelevant	Mary Kirazy, 58, has just joined our trust department.	Mary Kirazy has just joined our trust department.
Disability Bias		
Putting the disability before the person	Crippled workers face many barriers on the job.	Workers with physical disabilities face many barriers on the job.
	An epileptic, Tracy has no trouble doing her job.	Tracy's epilepsy has no effect on her job performance.

well perpetuate the underlying stereotypes and prejudices that it represents.[5] Moreover, because communication is all about perception, being fair and objective isn't enough; to establish a good relationship with your audience, you must also *appear* to be fair.[6] Good communicators make every effort to change biased language (see Table 5.1). Bias can come in a variety of forms:

- **Gender bias.** Avoid sexist language by using the same label for everyone (don't call a woman *chairperson* and then call a man *chairman*). Reword sentences to use *they* or to use no pronoun at all rather than referring to all individuals as *he*. Vary traditional patterns by sometimes putting women first (*women and men, she and he, her and his*). Note that the preferred title for women in business is *Ms.*, unless the individual asks to be addressed as *Miss* or *Mrs.* or has some other title, such as *Dr.*

- **Racial and ethnic bias.** Avoid language suggesting that members of a racial or an ethnic group have stereotypical characteristics. The best solution is to avoid identifying people by race or ethnic origin unless such a label is relevant to the matter at hand—and it rarely is.
- **Age bias.** As with gender, race, and ethnic background, mention the age of a person only when it is relevant. Moreover, be careful of the context in which you use words that refer to age. Such words carry a variety of positive and negative connotations—and not only when referring to people beyond a certain age. For example, *young* can imply youthfulness, inexperience, or even immaturity, depending on how it's used.
- **Disability bias.** No painless label exists for people with a physical, mental, sensory, or emotional impairment. Avoid mentioning a disability unless it is pertinent. However, if you must refer to someone's disability, avoid terms such as *handicapped, crippled,* or *retarded.* Put the person first and the disability second.[7] Present the whole person, not just the disability, by showing the limitation in an unobtrusive manner.

Building Strong Relationships with Your Audience

Focusing on your audience's needs is vital to effective communication, but you also have your own priorities as a communicator. Sometimes these needs are obvious and direct, such as when you're appealing for a budget increase for your department. At other times, the need may be more subtle. For instance, you might want to demonstrate your understanding of the marketplace or your company's concern for the natural environment. Two key efforts help you address your own needs while building positive relationships with your audience: establishing your credibility and projecting your company's image.

Establishing Your Credibility

Your audience's response to every message you send depends heavily on its perception of your **credibility**, a measure of your believability based on how reliable you are and how much trust you evoke in others. With colleagues and long-term customers, you've already established some degree of credibility based on past communication efforts, and these people automatically lean toward accepting each new message from you because you haven't let them down in the past. With audiences who don't know you, however, you need to establish credibility before they'll listen fully to your message. Whether you're working to build credibility with a new audience, to maintain credibility with an existing audience, or even to restore credibility after a mistake, consider emphasizing the following characteristics:

- **Honesty.** Demonstrating honesty and integrity will earn you the respect of your audiences, even if they don't always agree with or welcome your messages.
- **Objectivity.** Show that you can distance yourself from emotional situations and look at all sides of an issue.
- **Awareness of audience needs.** Let your audiences know that you understand what's important to them.
- **Credentials, knowledge, and expertise.** Audiences need to know that you have whatever it takes to back up your message, whether it's education, professional certification, special training, past successes, or simply the fact that you've done your research.
- **Endorsements.** If your audiences don't know anything about you, try to get assistance from someone they do know and trust.
- **Performance.** Demonstrating impressive communication skills is not enough; people need to know they can count on you to get the job done.
- **Confidence.** Audiences also need to know that you believe in yourself and your message. If you are convinced that your message is sound, you can state your case confidently, without sounding boastful or arrogant.
- **Communication style.** Support your points with evidence, not empty terms such as *amazing, incredible,* or *extraordinary.*

---

2 LEARNING OBJECTIVE

Explain why establishing credibility is vital to the success of your communication efforts

People are more likely to react positively to your message when they have confidence in you.

- **Sincerity.** When you offer praise, don't use hyperbole, such as "you are the most fantastic employee I could ever imagine." Instead, point out specific qualities that warrant praise.

Even though arrogance turns listeners off, displaying too much modesty or too little confidence can hurt your credibility. If you lack faith in yourself, you're likely to communicate an uncertain attitude that undermines your credibility. The key to being believable is to believe in yourself. If you are convinced that your message is sound, you can state your case with authority so that your audience has no doubts. Avoid vague sentiments and confidence-draining words such as *if,* *hope,* and *trust:*

INSTEAD OF THIS	**WRITE THIS**
We hope this recommendation will be helpful.	We're glad to make this recommendation.
If you'd like to order, mail us the reply card.	To order, mail the reply card.
We trust that you'll want to extend your service contract.	By extending your service contract, you can continue to enjoy top-notch performance from your equipment.

Finally, keep in mind that credibility can take days, months, or even years to establish—and it can be wiped out in an instant. An occasional mistake or letdown is usually forgiven, but major lapses in honesty or integrity can destroy your reputation. On the other hand, when you do establish credibility, communication becomes much easier because you no longer have to spend time and energy convincing people that you are a trustworthy source of information and ideas.

Projecting Your Company's Image

When you communicate with outsiders, on even the most routine matter, you serve as the spokesperson for your organization. The impression you make can enhance or damage the reputation of the entire company. Consequently, the interests and preferred communication style of your company must take precedence over your own views and personal communication style.

Many organizations have specific communication guidelines that show everything from the correct use of the company name to preferred abbreviations and other grammatical details. Specifying a desired style of communication is more difficult, however. Observe more experienced colleagues to see how they communicate, and never hesitate to ask for editorial help to make sure you're conveying the appropriate tone. For instance, with clients entrusting thousands or millions of dollars to it, an investment firm communicates in a style quite different from that of a clothing retailer. And a clothing retailer specializing in high-quality business attire communicates in a different style than a store catering to the latest trends in casual wear.

Controlling Your Style and Tone

Style is the way you use words to achieve a certain **tone,** or overall impression. You can vary your style—your sentence structure and vocabulary—to sound forceful or objective, personal or formal, colorful or dry. The right choice depends on the nature of your message and your relationship with the reader. Although style can be refined during the revision phase (see Chapter 6), you'll save time and a lot of rewriting if you use a style that allows you to achieve the desired tone from the start.

Whether you're blogging, updating a website, or even just exchanging IM with a customer, you are responsible for projecting your company's preferred image to the outside world.

3 LEARNING OBJECTIVE

Discuss four ways of achieving a businesslike tone with a style that is clear and concise

Most business messages aim for a conversational style that is warm but still businesslike.

Using a Conversational Tone

The tone of your business messages can range from informal to conversational to formal. If you're in a large organization and you're communicating with your superiors or with customers, your tone would tend to be more formal and respectful.[8] However, that formal tone might sound distant and cold if used with close colleagues.

Compare the three versions of the letter in Table 5.2. The first is too formal and stuffy for today's audiences, whereas the third is too casual for any audience other than close associates or friends. The second message demonstrates the conversational tone used in most business communication—using plain language that sounds businesslike without being stuffy or full of jargon. You can achieve a conversational tone in your messages by following these guidelines:

- **Avoid obsolete and pompous language.** Business language used to be much more formal than it is today, but some out-of-date phrases still find their way into communication efforts. You can avoid using such language if you ask yourself, "Would I say this if I were talking with someone face-to-face?" Similarly, avoid using big words, trite expressions, and overly complicated sentences to impress others. Such pompous language sounds self-important (see Table 5.3).
- **Avoid preaching and bragging.** Few things are more irritating than people who think that they know everything and that others know nothing. If you do need to remind your audience of something obvious, try to work in the information casually, perhaps in the middle of a paragraph, where it will sound like a secondary comment rather than a major revelation. Also, avoid bragging about your accomplishments or those of your organization (unless your audience is a part of your organization).

TABLE 5.2 Three Levels of Tone: Formal, Conversational, and Informal Tones

FORMAL TONE	CONVERSATIONAL TONE	INFORMAL TONE
Reserved for the most formal occasions	**Preferred for most business communication**	**Reserved for communication with friends and close associates**
Dear Ms. Navarro:	Dear Ms. Navarro:	Hi Gabriella:
Enclosed please find the information that was requested during our telephone communication of May 14. As was mentioned at that time, Midville Hospital has significantly more doctors of exceptional quality than any other health facility in the state.	Here's the information you requested during our phone conversation on Friday. As I mentioned, Midville Hospital has the best doctors and more of them than any other hospital in the state.	Hope all is well. Just sending along the information you asked for. As I said on Friday, Midville Hospital has more and better doctors than any other hospital in the state.
As you were also informed, our organization has quite an impressive network of doctors and other health-care professionals with offices located throughout the state. In the event that you should need a specialist, our professionals will be able to make an appropriate recommendation.	In addition, we have a vast network of doctors and other health professionals with offices throughout the state. If you need a specialist, they can refer you to the right one.	We also have a large group of doctors and other health professionals with offices close to you at work or at home. Need a specialist? They'll refer you to the right one.
In the event that you have questions or would like additional information, you may certainly contact me during regular business hours.	If you would like more information, please call any time between 9:00 and 5:00, Monday through Friday.	Just give me a ring if you want to know more. Any time from 9:00 to 5:00 should be fine.
Most sincerely yours,	Sincerely,	Take care,
Samuel G. Berenz	Samuel G. Berenz	Sam

TABLE 5.3   Weeding Out Obsolete Phrases

OBSOLETE PHRASE	UP-TO-DATE REPLACEMENT
We are in receipt of	*We received*
Kindly advise	*Please let me/us know*
Attached please find	*Enclosed is* or *I/We have enclosed*
It has come to my attention	*I have just learned* or *[Someone] has just informed me*
The undersigned	*I/We*
In due course	(Specify a specific time or date.)
Permit me to say that	(Omit; just say whatever you need to say.)
Pursuant to	(Omit; just say whatever you need to say.)
In closing, I'd like to say	(Omit; just say whatever you need to say.)
We wish to inform you that	(Omit; just say whatever you need to say.)
Please be advised that	(Omit; just say whatever you need to say.)

- **Be careful with intimacy.** Most business messages should avoid intimacy, such as sharing personal details or adopting a casual, unprofessional tone. However, when you do have a close relationship with your audience, such as among the members of a close-knit team, a more intimate tone is sometimes appropriate and even expected.
- **Be careful with humor.** Humor can be an effective tool to inject interest into dry subjects or take the sting out of negative news. However, use it with great care: Humor can easily backfire and divert attention from your message. The humor must be connected to the point you're trying to make; business messages are not a forum for sharing jokes. Never use humor in formal messages or when you're communicating across cultural boundaries. If you don't know your audience well or you're not skilled at using humor in a business setting, don't use it at all. When in doubt, leave it out.

Using Plain English

What do you think this sentence is trying to say?

> We continually exist to synergistically supply value-added deliverables such that we may continue to proactively maintain enterprise-wide data to stay competitive in tomorrow's world.[9]

If you don't have any idea what it means, you're not alone. However, this is a real sentence from a real company, written in an attempt to explain what the company does and why. This sort of incomprehensible, buzzword-filled writing is driving a widespread call to use *plain English*.

Plain English is a way of presenting information in a simple, unadorned style so that your audience can easily grasp your meaning, without struggling through specialized, technical, or convoluted language. Because it's close to the way people normally speak, plain English is easily understood by anyone with a basic education. The Plain English Campaign (a nonprofit group in England campaigning for clear language) defines plain English as language "that the intended audience can read, understand and act upon the first time they read it."[10] You can see how this definition supports using the "you" attitude and shows respect for your audience.

Audiences can understand and act on plain English without reading it over and over.

On the Creative Commons website, for instance, licensing terms are available in two versions: a complete document that spells out contractual details in specific legal terms that meet the needs of legal professionals, and a second version labeled "human-readable," which explains the licensing terms in nontechnical language that anyone can understand.[11]

Even though readers overwhelmingly appreciate plain English and its merits have been demonstrated in a variety of audience tests,[12] murky, pompous, and unnecessarily complex writing is still more common than it should be. One reason is that writers are sometimes unsure about their own writing skills and about the impact their messages will have. They mistakenly believe that packaging simple ideas in complex writing makes their messages seem more impressive. Another reason is inadequate planning, which results in messages that meander in search of a conclusion. A third reason is that some writers intentionally try to create distance between themselves and their audiences. Whatever the cause, the result of unnecessarily complex writing is always the same: ineffective communication that wastes time, wastes money, and annoys everyone who comes in contact with it.

Even though plain English is intended for audiences who speak English as their primary language, plain English can also help you simplify the messages you prepare for audiences who speak English only as a second or even third language. For example, by choosing words that have only one interpretation, you will communicate more clearly with your intercultural audience (see "Communicating Across Cultures: Communicating with a Global Audience on the Web").[13]

Bear in mind that plain English doesn't have to be simplistic, dull, or imprecise. The point is to be clear, not lifeless. Also, be sure to consider the needs and expectations of your audience. For instance, scientific, technical, legal, and other specialized messages often require specialized terminology. Use these specific terms whenever you need to; just be sure to use them in clearly constructed sentences and well-organized paragraphs.

Selecting Active or Passive Voice

Your choice of active or passive voice also affects the tone of your message. You are using **active voice** when the subject performs the action and the object receives the action: "John rented the office." You're using **passive voice** when the subject receives the action: "The of-

Communicating Across Cultures

Communicating with a Global Audience on the Web

Reaching an international audience on the web involves more than simply offering translations of the English language. Successful global sites address the needs of international customers in five ways:

1. **Consider the reader's perspective.** Many communication elements that you may take for granted may be interpreted differently by audiences in different countries. Should you use the metric system, different notations for times or dates, or even different names for countries? For example, German citizens don't refer to their country as *Germany*; it's *Deutschland* to them. Review the entire online experience and look for ways to improve communication, including such helpful tools as interactive currency converters and translation dictionaries.

2. **Take cultural differences into account.** For instance, because humor is rooted in cultural norms, U.S. humor may not be so funny to Asian or European readers. Avoid idioms and references that aren't universally recognized, such as "putting all your eggs in one basket" or "jumping out of the frying pan into the fire."

3. **Keep the message clear.** Use simple words and sentences and write in the active voice. Define abbreviations, acronyms, and words an international audience may not be familiar with.

4. **Complement language with visuals.** Use drawings, photos, and other visuals to help communicate when words can't.

5. **Consult local experts.** Seek the advice of local experts about phrases and references that may be expected. Even terms as simple as *homepage* differ from country to country. Spanish readers refer to the "first page," or *pagina inicial*, whereas the French term is "welcome page," or *page d'accuei*.

CAREER APPLICATIONS

1. Visit Sony's Global Headquarters website at www.sony.net and examine Sony's music-oriented websites for Argentina, France, and Germany. How does Sony "localize" each country's site?

2. Compare Sony Music's international sites to IBM's global webpages at www.ibm.com. How does Sony's approach differ from IBM's? Do both corporations successfully address the needs of a global audience? Write a two-paragraph summary that compares the international sites of both companies.

TABLE 5.4 Choosing Active or Passive Voice

IN GENERAL, AVOID PASSIVE VOICE IN ORDER TO MAKE YOUR WRITING LIVELY AND DIRECT	
Dull and Indirect in Passive Voice	**Lively and Direct in Active Voice**
The new procedure was developed by the operations team.	The operations team developed the new procedure.
Legal problems are created by this contract.	This contract creates legal problems.
Reception preparations have been undertaken by our PR people for the new CEO's arrival.	Our PR people have begun planning a reception for the new CEO.
HOWEVER, PASSIVE VOICE IS HELPFUL WHEN YOU NEED TO BE DIPLOMATIC OR WANT TO FOCUS ATTENTION ON PROBLEMS OR SOLUTIONS RATHER THAN ON PEOPLE	
Accusatory or Self-congratulatory in Active Voice	**More Diplomatic in Passive Voice**
You lost the shipment.	The shipment was lost.
I recruited seven engineers last month.	Seven engineers were recruited last month.
We are investigating the high rate of failures on the final assembly line.	The high rate of failures on the final assembly line is being investigated.

fice was rented by John." As you can see, the passive voice combines the helping verb *to be* with a form of the verb that is usually similar to the past tense. When you use active sentences, your messages generally sound less formal and make it easier for readers to figure out who performed the action (see Table 5.4). In contrast, using passive voice de-emphasizes the subject and implies that the action was done by something or someone.

Using the active voice help makes your writing more direct, livelier, and easier to read. In contrast, the passive voice is not wrong grammatically, but it is often cumbersome, can be unnecessarily vague, and can make sentences longer. In most cases, the active voice is your best choice.[14] Nevertheless, using the passive voice can help you demonstrate the "you" attitude in some situations:

Active sentences are usually stronger than passive ones.

- When you want to be diplomatic about pointing out a problem or error of some kind (the passive version seems less like an accusation)
- When you want to point out what's being done without taking or attributing either the credit or the blame (the passive version shifts the spotlight away from the person or persons involved)
- When you want to avoid personal pronouns in order to create an objective tone (the passive version may be used in a formal report, for example)

Use passive sentences to soften bad news, to put yourself in the background, or to create an impersonal tone.

For example, to explain its 90-day limit on product returns, Gap says the following on its website: "Merchandise returned more than 90 days after the purchase date will not be eligible for a return,"[15] instead of saying something like "You cannot return products more than 90 days after the purchase date." The second half of Table 5.4 illustrates several other situations in which the passive voice helps you focus your message on your audience.

COMPOSING YOUR MESSAGE

With these insights into how you can adapt to your audience, you're ready to begin composing your message. Composition is much easier if you've already figured out what to say and in what order (refer to the outlining advice in Chapter 4). However, you may also discover as you move along that you can improve on your outline. Feel free to rearrange, delete, and add ideas, as long as you don't lose sight of your purpose.

As you compose your first draft, try to let your creativity flow. Don't try to draft and edit at the same time or worry about getting everything perfect. Make up words if you can't think of the right word, draw pictures, talk out loud—do whatever it takes to get the ideas out of your head and onto your computer screen or a piece of paper. You'll have time to revise and refine the material later before showing it to anyone. In fact, many writers find it helpful to establish a personal rule of *never* showing a first draft to anyone. By working in this "safe zone," away from the critical eyes of others, your mind will stay free to think clearly and creatively.

If you get stuck and feel unable to write, try to overcome writer's block by jogging your brain in creative ways. The introduction is often the hardest part to write, so put it aside and work on whichever parts of the document you're most comfortable with at any given moment. In most cases, you don't need to write the sections in any particular order.[16] Work on nontext elements such as graphics or your cover page. Revisit your purpose and confirm your intent in writing the message. Give yourself a mental break by switching to a different project. Sometimes all you need to do is start writing without worrying about the words you're using or how they will sound to the audience. Words will start flowing, your mind will engage, and the writing will come easier.

As you create and refine your messages, learn to view your writing at three levels: strong words, effective sentences, and coherent paragraphs.

Choosing Strong Words

4 LEARNING OBJECTIVE

Briefly describe how to select words that are not only correct but also effective

Using correct grammar enhances your image.

Effectiveness is the second consideration when choosing words.

Functional words (conjunctions, prepositions, articles, and pronouns) express the relationships among content words (nouns, verbs, adjectives, and adverbs).

Effective messages depend on carefully chosen words, whether you select them during your first draft or edit them in later.[17] First, pay close attention to correctness. The "rules" of grammar and usage can be a source of worry for all writers, because many of these rules are complex and can evolve over time. Even professional editors and grammarians occasionally have questions about correct usage, and they sometimes disagree about the answers. For example, the word *data* is the plural form of *datum,* yet some experts now prefer to treat *data* as a singular noun when it's used in nonscientific material to refer to a body of information.

Although debating the finer points of usage may seem like nitpicking, using words correctly is important. If you make grammatical or usage errors, you lose credibility with your audience—even if your message is otherwise correct. Poor grammar implies that you're uninformed, and audiences put less faith in an uninformed source. Worse still, poor grammar can imply that you don't respect your audience enough to get things right. Even if an audience is broad-minded enough to withhold such a judgment, grammatical errors are distracting.

If you have doubts about what is correct, look up the answer and use the proper form of expression. Check the "Handbook of Grammar, Mechanics, and Usage" at the end of this book, or consult the many special reference books and resources available in libraries, in bookstores, and on the Internet. Most authorities agree on the basic conventions.

Just as important as selecting the correct word is selecting the most suitable word for the job at hand. Naturally, using the right words is important in life-and-death situations. But even when you're dealing with less perilous circumstances, the right words can make all the difference in the success of your communication efforts. Word effectiveness is generally more difficult to achieve than correctness, particularly in written communication. Even professional writers with decades of experience continue to work at their craft to use functional and content words correctly and to find the words that communicate well (see Figure 5.3).

Using Functional and Content Words Correctly

Words can be divided into two main categories. **Functional words** express relationships and have only one unchanging meaning in any given context. They include conjunctions, prepositions, articles, and pronouns. Your main concern with functional words is to use them correctly. **Content words** are multidimensional and, therefore, frequently subject to various interpretations. They include nouns, verbs, adjectives, and adverbs. These words carry the meaning of a sentence. In your sentences, content words are the building blocks, and functional words are the mortar that holds them together. In the following sentence, all the content words are underlined:

FIGURE 5.3 Choosing Effective Words

Through the use of such words and phrases as *paradise, at their own pace, smooth,* and *trouble-free,* The Moorings conveys a sense of relaxed adventure on its website.

Carlo Firenze noted that custom ringtones have generated several billion dollars in sales so far, but he isn't sure if this momentum will transfer to other mobile data services.

Both functional words and content words are necessary, but your effectiveness as a communicator depends largely on your ability to choose the right content words for your message.

Denotation and Connotation   Content words have both a denotative and a connotative meaning. The **denotative meaning** is the literal, or dictionary, meaning. The **connotative meaning** includes all the associations and feelings evoked by the word.

The denotative meaning of *desk* is "a piece of furniture with a flat work surface and various drawers for storage." The connotative meaning of *desk* may include thoughts associated with work or study, but the word *desk* has fairly neutral connotations—neither strong nor emotional. However, some words have much stronger connotations than others. For example, the connotations of the word *fail* are negative and can carry strong emotional meaning. If you say that the sales department *failed* to meet its annual quota, the connotative meaning suggests that the group is inferior, incompetent, or below some standard of performance. However, the reason for not achieving 100 percent might be an inferior product, incorrect pricing, or some other factor outside the control of the sales department. In contrast, by saying that the sales department achieved 85 percent of its

Content words have both a denotative (explicit, specific) meaning and a connotative (implicit, associative) meaning.

quota, you clearly communicate that the results were less than expected—without triggering all the negative emotions associated with *failure*.

The more abstract a word is, the more it is removed from the tangible, objective world of things that can be perceived with the senses.

Abstraction and Concreteness   Words also vary dramatically in the degree of abstraction or concreteness they convey. An **abstract word** expresses a concept, quality, or characteristic. Abstractions are usually broad, encompassing a category of ideas, and they are often intellectual, academic, or philosophical. *Love, honor, progress, tradition,* and *beauty* are abstractions, as are such important business concepts as *productivity, profits, quality, and motivation.* In contrast, a **concrete word** stands for something you can touch, see, or visualize. Most concrete terms are anchored in the tangible, material world. *Chair, table, horse, rose, kick, kiss, red, green,* and *two* are concrete words; they are direct, clear, and exact. Incidentally, technology continues to generate new words and new meanings that describe things that don't have a physical presence but are nonetheless concrete: *software, database, signal,* and *code* are all concrete terms as well.

In business communication, use concrete, specific terms whenever possible; use abstractions only when necessary.

You might assume that concrete words are better than abstract words because they are more precise, but that isn't always the case. For example, try to rewrite this sentence without using the underlined abstract words:

> We hold these <u>truths</u> to be <u>self-evident</u>, that all men are <u>created equal</u>, that they are <u>endowed</u> by their <u>Creator</u> with certain <u>unalienable Rights</u>, that among these are <u>Life, Liberty</u>, and the <u>Pursuit of Happiness</u>.

As you can see, the Declaration of Independence needs abstractions, and so do most business messages. Abstractions let you rise above the common and tangible.

Even though they're indispensable, abstractions can be troublesome. They tend to be fuzzy and subject to multiple interpretations. Moreover, it isn't always easy to get excited about ideas, especially if they're unrelated to concrete experience. The best way to minimize such problems is to blend abstract terms with concrete ones, the general with the specific. State the concept, then pin it down with details expressed in more concrete terms. Save the abstractions for ideas that cannot be expressed any other way.

Because words such as *small, numerous, sizable, near, soon, good,* and *fine* are imprecise, try to replace them with terms that are more accurate. Instead of referring to a *sizable loss*, talk about a *loss of $32 million*.

Finding Words That Communicate Well

By practicing your writing, learning from experienced writers and editors, and reading extensively, you'll find it easier to choose words that communicate exactly what you want to say. When you compose your business messages, think carefully to find the most powerful words for each situation (see Table 5.5).

Try to use words that are powerful and familiar.

- **Choose powerful words.** Choose words that express your thoughts most clearly, specifically, and dynamically. Nouns and verbs are the most concrete and should do most of the communication work in your messages. Verbs are especially powerful because they tell what's happening in the sentence, so make them dynamic and specific. For instance, you could replace *fall* with *plummet, drop,* or *decline* to suggest the magnitude of the decrease. Here's another helpful clue: If you find yourself using a lot of adjectives and adverbs, you're probably trying to compensate for weak nouns and verbs. Saying that *sales plummeted* is stronger and more efficient than saying *sales dropped dramatically* or *sales experienced a dramatic drop*.

- **Choose familiar words.** You'll communicate best with words that are familiar to both you and your readers. Efforts to improve a situation can be *ameliorative*, to be sure, but saying they are *helpful* is a lot more effective. Moreover, trying to use an unfamiliar word for the first time in an important document can lead to embarrassing mistakes.

Avoid clichés and trendy buzzwords in your writing and use jargon only when your audience is completely familiar with it.

- **Avoid clichés and buzzwords.** Although familiar words are generally the best choice, beware of terms and phrases so common or so trendy that they have lost some of their power to communicate. Because clichés are used so often, readers tend to slide right by

TABLE 5.5 Finding the Words That Communicate with Power

AVOID WEAK PHRASES	USE STRONG TERMS
Wealthy businessperson	Tycoon
Business prosperity	Economic boom
Hard times	Slump

AVOID UNFAMILIAR WORDS	USE FAMILIAR WORDS
Ascertain	Find out, learn
Consummate	Close, bring about
Peruse	Read, study
Circumvent	Avoid
Increment	Growth, increase
Unequivocal	Certain

AVOID CLICHÉS AND BUZZWORDS	USE PLAIN LANGUAGE
An uphill battle	A challenge
Writing on the wall	Prediction
Call the shots	Be in charge
Take by storm	Attack
Cost an arm and a leg	Expensive
A new ball game	Fresh start
Fall through the cracks	Be overlooked
Think outside the box	Be creative
Run it up the flagpole	Offer for consideration
Eat our own dog food	Use our own products
Mission critical	Vital
Disintermediate	Get rid of

them to whatever is coming next. Most people use these phrases not because they think it makes their message more vivid and inviting but because they don't know how to express themselves otherwise, they don't invest the energy required for original writing, or they worry too much about keeping up with the latest trendy language.[18]

- **Use jargon carefully.** Handle technical or professional terms with care. Although jargon has a bad reputation in general, it's usually an efficient way to communicate within specific groups that understand their own special terms. After all, that's how jargon develops in the first place, as people with similar interests develop ways to communicate complex ideas quickly. For instance, when a recording engineer wants to communicate that a particular piece of music is devoid of reverberation and other sound effects, it's a lot easier to simply describe the track as "dry." Of course, to people who aren't familiar with such insider terms, jargon is meaningless and intimidating—one more reason it's so important to understand your audience before you start writing.

Remember, you improve your business writing skills through imitation and practice. As you read business journals, newspapers, and even novels, make a note of the words you think are effective and keep them in a file. Look through your file before drafting your next message, and try using some of these words in your document. You may be surprised how they can strengthen your writing.

Creating Effective Sentences

Arranging your words in effective sentences is the next step in creating powerful messages. Start by selecting the optimum type of sentence, then arrange words to emphasize the most important point in each sentence.

Choosing from the Four Types of Sentences

Sentences come in four basic varieties: simple, compound, complex, and compound-complex. A **simple sentence** has one main *clause* (a single subject and a single predicate), although it may be expanded by nouns and pronouns serving as objects of the action and by modifying phrases. Here's a typical example (with the subject underlined once and the predicate verb underlined twice):

> <u>Profits</u> <u>increased</u> in the past year.

A **compound sentence** has two main clauses that express two or more independent but related thoughts of equal importance, usually joined by *and, but,* or *or.* In effect, a compound sentence is a merger of two or more simple sentences (independent clauses) that are related. For example:

> Wage <u>rates</u> <u>have declined</u> by 5 percent, and employee <u>turnover</u> <u>has been</u> high.

The independent clauses in a compound sentence are always separated by a comma or by a semicolon (in which case the conjunction—*and, but,* or—is dropped).

A **complex sentence** expresses one main thought (the independent clause) and one or more subordinate thoughts (dependent clauses) related to it, often separated by a comma. The subordinate thought, which comes first in the following sentence, could not stand alone as a valid sentence:

> Although you may question Gerald's conclusions, <u>you</u> <u>must admit</u> that his research is thorough.

A **compound-complex sentence** has two main clauses, at least one of which contains a subordinate clause:

> <u>Profits</u> <u>have increased</u> in the past year, and although you may question Gerald's conclusions, <u>you</u> <u>must admit</u> that his research is thorough.

When constructing a sentence, choose the form that matches the relationship of the ideas you want to express. If you have two ideas of equal importance, express them as two simple sentences or as one compound sentence. However, if one of the ideas is less important than the other, place it in a dependent clause to form a complex sentence. For example, although the following compound sentence uses a conjunction to join two ideas, they aren't truly equal:

> The chemical products division is the strongest in the company, and its management techniques should be adopted by the other divisions.

By making the first thought subordinate to the second, you establish a cause-and-effect relationship. So, the following complex sentence is much more effective:

> Because the chemical products division is the strongest in the company, its management techniques should be adopted by the other divisions.

To make your writing as effective as possible, strive for variety and balance using all four sentence types. If you use too many simple sentences, you won't be able to properly

---

5 LEARNING OBJECTIVE

Explain how sentence style affects emphasis within your message

A simple sentence has one main clause.

A compound sentence has two main clauses.

A complex sentence has one main clause and one subordinate clause.

A compound-complex sentence has two main clauses and at least one dependent clause.

express the relationships among your ideas, and your writing will sound choppy and abrupt. If you use too many long, compound sentences, your writing will sound monotonous. On the other hand, an uninterrupted series of complex or compound-complex sentences is hard to follow.

Writing is more effective if it balances all four sentence types.

Using Sentence Style to Emphasize Key Thoughts

In every message, some ideas are more important than others. You can emphasize these key ideas through your sentence style. One obvious technique is to give important points the most space. When you want to call attention to a thought, use extra words to describe it. Consider this sentence:

Emphasize parts of a sentence by
- *Devoting more words to them*
- *Putting them at the beginning or at the end of the sentence*
- *Making them the subject of the sentence*

> The chairperson called for a vote of the shareholders.

To emphasize the importance of the chairperson, you might describe her more fully:

> Having considerable experience in corporate takeover battles, the chairperson called for a vote of the shareholders.

You can increase the emphasis even more by adding a separate, short sentence to augment the first:

> The chairperson called for a vote of the shareholders. She has considerable experience in corporate takeover battles.

You can also call attention to a thought by making it the subject of the sentence. In the following example, the emphasis is on the person:

> I can write letters much more quickly using a computer.

However, by changing the subject, the computer takes center stage:

> The computer enables me to write letters much more quickly.

Another way to emphasize an idea is to place it either at the beginning or at the end of a sentence:

> **Less emphatic.** We are cutting the price to stimulate demand.
> **More emphatic.** To stimulate demand, we are cutting the price.

In complex sentences, the placement of the dependent clause hinges on the relationship between the ideas expressed. If you want to emphasize the idea, put the dependent clause at the end of the sentence (the most emphatic position) or at the beginning (the second most emphatic position). If you want to downplay the idea, bury the dependent clause within the sentence.

Dependent clauses can determine emphasis.

> **Most emphatic.** The electronic parts are manufactured in Mexico, which has lower wage rates than the United States.
> **Emphatic.** Because wage rates are lower there, the electronic parts are manufactured in Mexico.
> **Least emphatic.** Mexico, which has lower wage rates, was selected as the production site for the electronic parts.

Techniques such as these give you a great deal of control over the way your audience interprets what you have to say.

Crafting Unified, Coherent Paragraphs

6 LEARNING OBJECTIVE

List five ways to develop coherent paragraphs

After arranging powerful words in effective sentences, your next step is to arrange those sentences into coherent paragraphs. Paragraphs organize sentences related to the same general topic. Readers expect each paragraph to focus on a single unit of thought and to be a logical link in an organized sequence of the thoughts that make up a complete message. By carefully arranging the elements of each paragraph, you help your readers grasp the main idea of your document and understand how the specific pieces of support material back up that idea (see Figure 5.4).

Elements of the Paragraph

Most paragraphs consist of
- *A topic sentence that reveals the subject of the paragraph*
- *Related sentences that support and expand the topic*
- *Transitional elements that help readers move between sentences and paragraphs*

Paragraphs vary widely in length and form, but the typical paragraph contains three basic elements: a topic sentence, support sentences that develop the topic, and transitional words and phrases.

Topic Sentence   An effective paragraph is *unified*; it deals with a single topic. The sentence that introduces that topic is called the **topic sentence.** In informal and creative writing, the topic sentence may be implied rather than stated. In business writing, the topic sentence is generally explicit and is often the first sentence in the paragraph. The topic sentence gives readers a summary of the general idea that will be covered in the rest of the paragraph. The following examples show how a topic sentence can introduce the subject and suggest the way that subject will be developed:

FIGURE 5.4 Unified Paragraphs
In two brief paragraphs, Whirlpool assured its trade partners (retailers and commercial laundries) that business would continue as usual after its acquisition of rival Maytag.

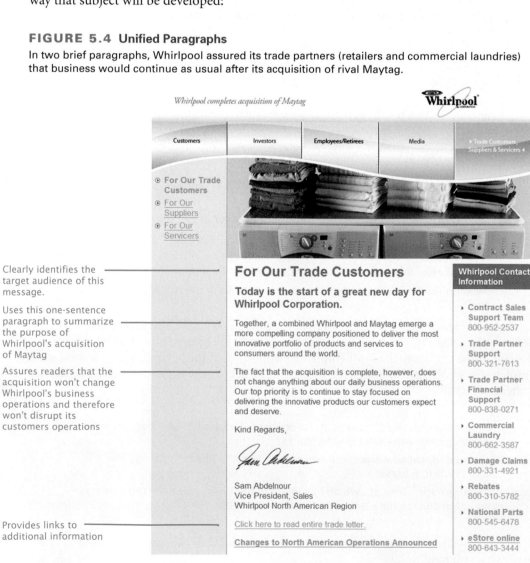

Clearly identifies the target audience of this message.

Uses this one-sentence paragraph to summarize the purpose of Whirlpool's acquisition of Maytag

Assures readers that the acquisition won't change Whirlpool's business operations and therefore won't disrupt its customers operations

Provides links to additional information

> The medical products division has been troubled for many years by public relations problems. [In the rest of the paragraph, readers will learn the details of the problems.]
>
> Relocating the plant in New York has two main disadvantages. [The disadvantages will be explained in subsequent sentences.]
>
> To get a refund, please supply us with the following information. [The details of the necessary information will be described in the rest of the paragraph.]

In addition to helping your readers, topic sentences help you as a writer because they remind you of the purpose of each paragraph and thereby help you stay focused. In fact, a good way to test the effectiveness of your writing is to prepare a summary version that consists of only the first sentences of all your paragraphs. If this summary communicates the essence of your message in a sensible, compelling way, you've probably done a good job of presenting your information.[19]

Support Sentences   In most paragraphs, the topic sentence needs to be explained, justified, or extended with one or more support sentences. These related sentences must all have a bearing on the general subject and must provide enough specific details to make the topic clear:

> The medical products division has been troubled for many years by public relations problems. Since 2002 the local newspaper has published 15 articles that portray the division in a negative light. We have been accused of everything from mistreating laboratory animals to polluting the local groundwater. Our facility has been described as a health hazard. Our scientists are referred to as "Frankensteins," and our profits are considered "obscene."

The support sentences are all more specific than the topic sentence. Each one provides another piece of evidence to demonstrate the general truth of the main thought. Also, each sentence is clearly related to the general idea being developed, which gives the paragraph its unity. A paragraph is well developed when (1) it contains enough information to make the topic sentence convincing and interesting and (2) it contains no extraneous, unrelated sentences.

Transitional Elements   In addition to being unified and well supported, effective paragraphs are *coherent*; that is, they are arranged in a logical order so that the audience can understand the train of thought. You achieve coherence by using transitions that show the relationship between paragraphs and among sentences within paragraphs. Notice how this paragraph began; the transitional phrase "In addition to . . ." helped move you from the previous discussion to this new topic.

Transitions are words or phrases that tie ideas together by showing how one thought is related to another. They not only help readers understand the connections you're trying to make but also smooth your writing. In fact, effective transitions are one of the hallmarks of polished, effective writing.

Ideally, you begin planning these transitions while you're outlining, as you decide how the various ideas and blocks of information will be arranged and connected.[20] You can establish transitions in a variety of ways:

Transitional elements include
- *Connecting words (conjunctions)*
- *Repeated words or phrases*
- *Pronouns*
- *Words that are frequently paired*

- **Use connecting words.** Use words such as *and, but, or, nevertheless, however, in addition,* and so on.
- **Echo a word or phrase from a previous paragraph or sentence.** "A system should be established for monitoring inventory levels. *This system* will provide . . ."
- **Use a pronoun that refers to a noun used previously.** "Ms. Arthur is the leading candidate for the president's position. *She* has excellent qualifications."
- **Use words that are frequently paired.** "The machine has a *minimum* output of . . . Its *maximum* output is. . . ."

Some transitional elements serve as mood changers, alerting the reader to a change in mood from the previous material. Some announce a total contrast with what's gone on before, some announce a causal relationship, and some signal a change in time. Transitional elements prepare your reader for what is coming. Here is a list of transitions frequently used to move readers smoothly between sentences and paragraphs:

Additional detail	moreover, furthermore, in addition, besides, first, second, third, finally
Causal relationship	therefore, because, accordingly, thus, consequently, hence, as a result, so
Comparison	similarly, here again, likewise, in comparison, *still*
Contrast	yet, conversely, whereas, nevertheless, on the other hand, however, but, nonetheless
Condition	although, if
Illustration	for example, in particular, in this case, for instance
Time sequence	formerly, after, when, meanwhile, sometimes
Intensification	indeed, in fact, in any event
Summary	in brief, in short, to sum up
Repetition	that is, in other words, as I mentioned earlier

Keep in mind that although transitional words and phrases are necessary, they're not sufficient in themselves to overcome poor organization. Put your ideas into a strong framework first, and then use transitions to link them together even more strongly.

Consider using a transition whenever it could help the reader understand your ideas and follow you from point to point. You can use transitions inside paragraphs to tie related points together and between paragraphs to ease the shift from one distinct thought to another. In longer reports, transitions that link major sections or chapters are often complete paragraphs that serve as mini-introductions to the next section or as summaries of the ideas presented in the section just ending. Here's an example:

> Given the nature of this product, our alternatives are limited. As the previous section indicates, we can stop making it altogether, improve it, or continue with the current model. Each of these alternatives has advantages and disadvantages, which are discussed in the following section.

This paragraph makes it clear to the reader that the analysis of the problem (offered in the previous section) is now over and that the document is making a transition to an analysis of alternatives (to be offered in the next section).

Five Ways to Develop a Paragraph

Unification and coherence strongly depend on how you develop your paragraphs. Use a structure that is familiar to your readers, appropriate to the idea you're trying to portray, and suited to your purpose. Five of the most common development techniques are illustration, comparison or contrast, cause and effect, classification, and problem and solution (see Table 5.6).

In practice, you'll occasionally combine two or more methods of development in a single paragraph. For instance, you could begin by using illustration, shift to comparison or contrast, and then shift to problem and solution. However, when combining approaches, do so carefully so that you don't lose readers partway through the paragraph. In addition, before settling for the first approach that comes to mind, consider the alternatives. Think through various methods before committing yourself, or even write several test paragraphs to see which method works best. By avoiding the easy habit of repeating the same old paragraph pattern time after time, you can keep your writing fresh and interesting.

TABLE 5.6   Five Techniques for Developing Paragraphs

TECHNIQUE	DESCRIPTION	EXAMPLE
Illustration	Giving examples that demonstrate the general idea	Some of our most popular products are available through local distributors. For example, Everett & Lemmings carries our frozen soups and entrees. The J. B. Green Company carries our complete line of seasonings, as well as the frozen soups. Wilmont Foods, also a major distributor, now carries our new line of frozen desserts.
Comparison or contrast	Using similarities or differences to develop the topic	When the company was small, the recruiting function could be handled informally. The need for new employees was limited, and each manager could comfortably screen and hire her or his own staff. However, our successful bid on the Owens contract means that we will be doubling our labor force over the next six months. To hire that many people without disrupting our ongoing activities, we will create a separate recruiting group within the human resources department.
Cause and effect	Focusing on the reasons for something	The heavy-duty fabric of your Wanderer tent probably broke down for one of two reasons: (1) a sharp object punctured the fabric, and without reinforcement, the hole was enlarged by the stress of pitching the tent daily for a week or (2) the fibers gradually rotted because the tent was folded and stored while still wet.
Classification	Showing how a general idea is broken into specific categories	Successful candidates for our supervisor trainee program generally come from one of several groups. The largest group, by far, consists of recent graduates of accredited business management programs. The next largest group comes from within our own company, as we try to promote promising staff workers to positions of greater responsibility. Finally, we do occasionally accept candidates with outstanding supervisory experience in related industries.
Problem and solution	Presenting a problem and then discussing the solution	Selling handmade toys online is a challenge because consumers are accustomed to buying heavily advertised toys from major chain stores or well-known websites such as Amazon.com. However, if we develop an appealing website, we can compete on the basis of product novelty and quality. In addition, we can provide unusual crafts at a competitive price: a rocking horse of birch, with a hand-knit tail and mane; a music box with the child's name painted on the top; a real teepee, made by Native American artisans.

USING TECHNOLOGY TO COMPOSE AND SHAPE YOUR MESSAGES

As with every phase of business communication, careful use of technology can help you compose and shape better messages in less time. You're likely to use a variety of electronic tools to compose messages, from word-processing programs to software for creating web content, blogs, and instant messages (IM).

Careful and informed use of technology can help you compose and shape better messages in less time. As you probably know, today's software (including both word processors and online publishing systems for websites and blogs) provides a wide range of tools to help writers compose documents:

Take full advantage of your software's formatting capabilities to help you produce effective, professional messages in less time.

- **Style sheets and templates.** *Style sheets* are master lists of predefined styles (typeface, type size, and so on) for headlines, paragraph text, and so on (here, the word *style* should not be confused with *writing style*, discussed earlier in the chapter). Many organizations provide employees with approved style sheets to ensure a consistent look for all company documents. Moreover, style sheets can eliminate hours of design time by making many of your choices for you. *Templates* can go beyond style sheets by defining such factors as page design, available fonts, and other features. A template can include *boilerplate*, a section of text that is reused from document to document. Like style sheets, templates save time by making choices for you in advance. (Depending on the version of Microsoft Word you're using, style sheets may have been replaced by templates.)

- **Autocompletion.** A software feature called *autocompletion* (or something similar) inserts a ready-made block of text when you type the first few characters. For example, instead of typing your company's name, address, phone number, fax number, e-mail address, and website URL, you can set the software to enter all this information as soon as you type the first three letters of the company name.

- **Autocorrection.** Another automatic feature in some programs instantly corrects spelling and typing errors and converts text to symbols, such as converting (c) to the © copyright symbol. However, autocorrection may make changes that you *don't* want made, such as converting "nd," "st," or "th" to superscript characters when paired with numbers, as in "21st century." (Although the use of such superscripts is common in word processing, many design professionals consider it poor typesetting.)

- **File merge and mail merge.** Today's software makes it easy to combine files—an especially handy feature when several members of a team write different sections of a report. For particularly complex reports, you can set up a master document that merges a number of subdocuments automatically when it's time to print. *Mail merge* lets you personalize form letters by inserting names and addresses from a database.

- **Endnotes, footnotes, indexes, and tables of contents.** Your computer can also help you track footnotes and endnotes, renumbering them every time you add or delete references. For a report's indexes and table of contents, you can simply flag the items you want to include, and the software assembles the lists for you.

- **Wizards.** Many programs offer *wizards* that guide you through the process of creating letters, résumés, webpages, and other common documents.

As with other forms of communication technology, using these tools efficiently and effectively requires some balance. You need to learn enough about the features to be handy with them, without spending so much time that the tools distract the writing process. For a reminder of the tasks involved in writing your messages, see "Checklist: Writing Business Messages."

 CHECKLIST: Writing Business Messages

A. Adapt to your audience.
- Use the "you" attitude.
- Maintain good etiquette through polite communication.
- Emphasize the positive whenever possible.
- Use bias-free language.
- Establish your credibility in the eyes of your audience.
- Project your company's preferred image.
- Use a conversational but still professional and respectful tone.
- Use plain English for clarity.

B. Compose your message.
- Choose strong words that communicate efficiently.
- Make sure you use functional and content words correctly.

- Pay attention to the connotative meaning of your words.
- Balance abstract and concrete terms to convey your meaning accurately.
- Avoid clichés and trendy buzzwords.
- Use jargon only when your audience understands it and prefers it.
- Vary your sentence structure for impact and interest.
- Develop coherent, unified paragraphs.
- Use transitional elements generously to help your audience follow your message.

COMMUNICATION CHALLENGES AT CREATIVE COMMONS

To achieve their mission of popularizing a new approach to copyrighting songs, artwork, literature, and other creative works, Lawrence Lessig and his staff at Creative Commons need to convince people that the traditional approach to copyright doesn't meet the needs of today's digital society. This is no small challenge: Not only do they need to convince people to reconsider more than 200 years of legal precedent and habit, they also need to communicate with an extremely diverse audience—everyone from lawyers and business managers to artists, writers, musicians, and scientists. After graduating with a business degree, you've joined Creative Commons as a communication intern for a year before entering law school. Apply your knowledge of effective writing to these scenarios.

Individual Challenge: Visit the licensing of the Creative Commons website at www.creativecommons.org/license and find the information on the Sampling licenses. Write a one- or two-sentence description that explains how the Sampling, Sampling Plus, and Noncommercial Sampling Plus variations of this license differ. Imagine that your audience is a group of music and art majors.

Team Challenge: A key aspect of the communication challenge for Creative Commons is translating legal documents into language that musicians, artists, and others with no legal training can easily understand. In a small group, brainstorm ways to rewrite the following legal phrase (which is part of the licensing contracts) into language for a general audience:

The above rights may be exercised in all media and formats whether now known or hereafter devised. The above rights include the right to make such modifications as are technically necessary to exercise the rights in other media and formats.

SUMMARY OF LEARNING OBJECTIVES

1 **Explain the importance of adapting your messages to the needs and expectations of your audience.** By adapting your communication to the needs and expectations of your audience members, you provide more compelling answers to their questions and improve the chances that your messages will be received successfully. If your intended audience members think a message does not apply to them or does not offer them anything useful or interesting, they'll be far less inclined to pay attention to it.

2 **Explain why establishing credibility is vital to the success of your communication efforts.** Your audience members' response to every message you send depends heavily on their perception of your believability, based on how reliable they think you are and how much trust you evoke in them. Even if you're trying to convey information that is correct in every way, audiences will be reluctant to accept your message if they don't think you are a trustworthy source. Conversely, if audiences already accept you as a trustworthy source, they are inclined to accept and believe all of your messages.

3 **Discuss four ways of achieving a businesslike tone with a style that is clear and concise.** To ensure that messages are businesslike, clear, and concise, start by using a

conversational tone: avoid obsolete and pompous language, avoid preaching and bragging, avoid intimacy unless you have a close relationship with the audience, and use humor with great care. Support this conversational tone by using plain English, which is easily understood by anyone with an eighth- or ninth-grade education. Then select the best voice for your message. Use the active voice to emphasize the subject of the message and to produce shorter, stronger sentences; use the passive voice to be diplomatic, to avoid taking credit or placing blame, and to create an objective tone.

4 **Briefly describe how to select words that are not only correct but also effective.** To select the best words, first make sure they are correct by checking grammar and usage guides. Next, make sure they are effective by knowing how to use functional and content words. Choose words that have fewer connotations (to reduce the chance of misinterpretation) and no negative connotations (to reduce the chance of offending your audience). Blend abstract words with concrete ones, narrowing from the general to the specific, and select words that communicate clearly, specifically, and dynamically. Choose words that are strong, choose words that are familiar, avoid clichés and buzzwords, and use jargon only when your audience will understand it.

5 **Explain how sentence style affects emphasis within your message.** The order and placement of words within each sentence affect the emphasis your audience perceives. You can employ the following techniques to focus emphasis on specific parts of the sentence: give the most important idea the most emphasis by dedicating more words to it, add an additional sentence to clarify the key idea from the first sentence, or put the key idea at either the beginning or the end of the sentence.

6 **List five ways to develop coherent paragraphs.** Paragraphs can be developed by illustration (giving examples), by comparison and contrast (pointing out similarities or differences), by focusing on cause and effect (giving reasons), by classification (discussing categories), and by focusing on the solution to a problem (stating a problem and showing how to solve it).

Test Your Knowledge

1. Do you have to use the word "you" in order to demonstrate the "you" attitude? Why or why not?
2. Why is it important to establish your credibility when communicating with an audience of strangers?
3. How does using bias-free language help communicators establish a good relationship with their audiences?
4. How does the denotative meaning of a word differ from its connotative meaning?
5. What is style, and how do you decide on the appropriate style for a message?
6. How does an abstract word differ from a concrete word?
7. In what three situations is passive voice appropriate?
8. How can topic sentences help readers?
9. How can topic sentences help writers?
10. What functions do transitions serve?

Apply Your Knowledge

1. How can you apply the "you" approach when you don't know your audience personally?
2. When composing business messages, how can you be yourself and project your company's image at the same time?
3. What steps can you take to make abstract concepts such as *opportunity* feel more concrete in your messages?
4. Should you bother using transitional elements if the logical sequence of your message is already obvious? Why or why not?
5. **Ethical Choices** Eleven million people in the United States are allergic to one or more food ingredients. Every year, 30,000 of these people end up in the emergency room after suffering an allergic reaction, and hundreds of them die. Many of these tragic events are tied to poorly written food labels that either fail to identify dangerous allergens or use scientific terms that most consumers don't recognize.[21] Do food manufacturers have a responsibility to ensure that consumers read, understand, and follow warnings on food products? Explain your answer.

Practice Your Knowledge

Message for Analysis

Read the following e-mail draft, then (1) analyze the strengths and weaknesses of each sentence and (2) revise the document so that it follows this chapter's guidelines. The message was written by the marketing manager of an online retailer of baby-related products in the hope of becoming a retail outlet for Inglesina strollers and high chairs. As a manufacturer of stylish, top-quality products, Inglesina (based in Italy) is extremely selective about the retail outlets through which it allows its products to be sold.

Our e-tailing site, www.BestBabyGear.com, specializes in only the very best products for parents of newborns, infants, and toddlers. We constantly scour the world looking for products that are good enough and well-built enough and classy enough—good enough that is to take their place alongside the hundreds of other carefully selected products that adorn the pages of our award-winning website, www.bestbabygear.com. We aim for the fences every time we select a product to join this portfolio; we don't want to waste our time with onesey-twosey products that might sell a half dozen units per annum—no, we want every product to be a top-drawer success, selling at least one hundred units per specific model per year in order to justify our expense and hassle factor in adding it to the abovementioned portfolio. After careful consideration, we thusly concluded that your Inglesina lines meet our needs and would therefore like to add it.

Exercises

For active links to all websites discussed in this chapter, visit this text's website at www.prenhall.com/bovee. Locate your book and click on its Companion Website link. Then select Chapter 5, and click on "Featured Websites." Locate the name of the page or the URL related to the material in the text. Please note that links to sites that become inactive after publication of the book will be removed from the Featured Websites section.

5.1 **Audience Relationship: Courteous Communication**
Substitute a better phrase for each of the following:
a. You claim that
b. It is not our policy to
c. You neglected to
d. In which you assert
e. We are sorry you are dissatisfied
f. You failed to enclose
g. We request that you send us
h. Apparently you overlooked our terms
i. We have been very patient
j. We are at a loss to understand

5.2 **Audience Relationship: The "You" Attitude** Rewrite these sentences to reflect your audience's viewpoint.

a. Your e-mail order cannot be processed; we request that you use the order form on our website instead.

b. We insist that you always bring your credit card to the store.

c. We want to get rid of all our 15-inch LCD screens to make room in our warehouse for the new 19-, 23-, and 35-inch monitors. Thus, we are offering a 25 percent discount on all sales of 15-inch models this week.

d. I am applying for the position of bookkeeper in your office. I feel my grades prove that I am bright and capable, and I think I can do a good job for you.

e. As requested, we are sending the refund for $25.

5.3 **Audience Relationship: Emphasize the Positive** Revise these sentences to be positive rather than negative.

a. To avoid the loss of your credit rating, please remit payment within 10 days.

b. We don't make refunds on returned merchandise that is soiled.

c. Because we are temporarily out of Baby Cry dolls, we won't be able to ship your order for 10 days.

d. You failed to specify the color of the blouse that you ordered.

e. You should have realized that waterbeds will freeze in unheated houses during winter. Therefore, our guarantee does not cover the valve damage, and you must pay the $9.50 valve-replacement fee (plus postage).

5.4 **Audience Relationship: Emphasize the Positive** Provide euphemisms for the following words and phrases:

a. Stubborn

b. Wrong

c. Stupid

d. Incompetent

e. Loudmouth

5.5 **Audience Relationship: Bias-Free Language** Rewrite each of the following to eliminate bias:

a. For an Indian, Maggie certainly is outgoing.

b. He needs a wheelchair, but he doesn't let his handicap affect his job performance.

c. A pilot must have the ability to stay calm under pressure, and then he must be trained to cope with any problem that arises.

d. Candidate Renata Parsons, married and the mother of a teenager, will attend the debate.

e. Senior citizen Sam Nugent is still an active salesman.

5.6 **Ethical Choices** Your company has been a major employer in the local community for years, but shifts in the global marketplace have forced some changes in the company's long-term direction. In fact, the company plans to reduce local staffing by as much as 50 percent over the next 5 to 10 years, starting with a small layoff next month. The size and timing of future layoffs have not been decided, although there is little doubt more layoffs will happen at some point. In the first draft of a letter aimed at community leaders, you write that "this first layoff is part of a continuing series of staff reductions anticipated over the next several years."

However, your boss is concerned about the vagueness and negative tone of the language and asks you to rewrite that sentence to read "this layoff is part of the company's ongoing efforts to continually align its resources with global market conditions." Do you think this suggested wording is ethical, given the company's economic influence in the community? Please explain your answer.

5.7 **Message Composition: Controlling Style** Rewrite the following e-mail to customer Betty Crandall so that it conveys a helpful, personal, and interested tone:

We received your order complaint via our website response system. Owing to the fact that you neglected to include the size of the dress you ordered, please be advised that no shipment of your order was made, but the aforementioned shipment will occur at such time as we are in receipt of the aforementioned information.

5.8 **Message Composition: Selecting Words** Write a concrete phrase for each of these vague phrases:

a. Sometime this spring

b. A substantial saving

c. A large number attended

d. Increased efficiency

e. Expanded the work area

f. Flatten the website structure

5.9 **Message Composition: Selecting Words** List terms that are stronger than the following:

a. Ran after

b. Seasonal ups and downs

c. Bright

d. Suddenly rises

e. Moves forward

5.10 **Message Composition: Selecting Words** As you rewrite these sentences, replace the clichés with fresh, personal expressions:

a. Being a jack-of-all-trades, Dave worked well in his new general manager job.

b. Moving Leslie into the accounting department, where she was literally a fish out of water, was like putting a square peg into a round hole, if you get my drift.

c. I knew she was at death's door, but I thought the doctor would pull her through.

d. Movies aren't really my cup of tea; as far as I am concerned, they can't hold a candle to a good book.

e. It's a dog-eat-dog world out there in the rat race of the asphalt jungle.

5.11 **Message Composition: Selecting Words** Suggest short, simple words to replace each of the following:

a. Inaugurate	i. Consummate
b. Terminate	j. Advise
c. Utilize	k. Alteration
d. Anticipate	l. Forwarded
e. Assistance	m. Fabricate
f. Endeavor	n. Nevertheless
g. Ascertain	o. Substantial
h. Procure	

5.12   Message Composition: Selecting Words Write up-to-date, less-stuffy versions of these phrases; write *none* if you think there is no appropriate substitute:

a. As per your instructions

b. Attached herewith

c. In lieu of

d. In reply I wish to state

e. Please be advised that

5.13   Message Composition: Creating Sentences. Suppose that end-of-term frustrations have produced this e-mail message to Professor Anne Brewer from a student who believes he should have received a B in his accounting class. If this message were recast into three or four clear sentences, the teacher might be more receptive to the student's argument. Rewrite the message to show how you would improve it:

I think that I was unfairly awarded a C in your accounting class this term, and I am asking you to change the grade to a B. It was a difficult term. I don't get any money from home, and I have to work mornings at the Pancake House (as a cook), so I had to rush to make your class, and those two times that I missed class were because they wouldn't let me off work because of special events at the Pancake House (unlike some other students who just take off when they choose). On the midterm examination, I originally got a 75 percent, but you said in class that there were two different ways to answer the third question and that you would change the grades of students who used the "optimal cost" method and had been counted off 6 points for doing this. I don't think that you took this into account, because I got 80 percent on the final, which is clearly a B. Anyway, whatever you decide, I just want to tell you that I really enjoyed this class, and I thank you for making accounting so interesting.

5.14   Message Composition: Creating Sentences Rewrite each sentence so that it is active rather than passive:

a. The raw data are entered into the customer relationship management system by the sales representative each Friday.

b. High profits are publicized by management.

c. The policies announced in the directive were implemented by the staff.

d. Our computers are serviced by the Santee Company.

e. The employees were represented by Janet Hogan.

5.15   Message Composition: Writing Paragraphs In the following paragraph, identify the topic sentence and the related sentences (those that support the idea of the topic sentence):

Sync is a snap with Auto-Sync. By default, iTunes automatically copies your entire music library to iPod and deletes songs on iPod that are not listed in iTunes. Or you can use Playlist Sync and select the playlists you want to sync with your iPod. If you have more songs in your iTunes library than you can fit on your iPod, let iTunes create a playlist to fill your iPod, or just update your iPod by dragging over individual songs.[22]

Now add a topic sentence to this paragraph:

Our analysis of the customer experience should start before golfers even drive through the front gate here at Glencoe Meadows; it should start when they phone in or log onto our website to reserve tee times. When they do arrive, the first few stages in the process are also vital: the condition of the grounds leading up to the club house, the reception they receive when they drop off their clubs, and the ease of parking. From that point, how well are we doing with check-in at the pro shop, openings at the driving range, and timely scheduling at the first tee? Then there's everything associated with playing the course itself and returning to the club house at the end of the round.

5.16   Teamwork Working with four other students, divide the following five topics among yourselves and each write one paragraph on his or her selected topic. Be sure each student uses a different technique when writing his or her paragraph: One student should use the illustration technique, one the comparison or contrast technique, one a discussion of cause and effect, one the classification technique, and one a discussion of problem and solution. Then exchange paragraphs within the team and pick out the main idea and general purpose of the paragraph one of your teammates wrote. Was everyone able to correctly identify the main idea and purpose? If not, suggest how the paragraph could be rewritten for clarity.

a. Types of digital cameras (or dogs or automobiles) available for sale

b. Advantages and disadvantages of eating at fast-food restaurants

c. Finding that first full-time job

d. Good qualities of my car (or house, or apartment, or neighborhood)

e. How to make a dessert recipe (or barbecue a steak or make coffee)

5.17   Internet Visit the Security and Exchange Commission's (SEC) plain-English website at **www.sec.gov**, click on "Online Publications," and review the online handbook. In one or two sentences, summarize what the SEC means by the phrase "plain English." Now read the SEC's online advice about how to invest in mutual funds. Does this document follow the SEC's plain-English guidelines? Can you suggest any improvements to organization, words, sentences, or paragraphs?

5.18   Message Organization: Transitional Elements Add transitional elements to the following sentences to improve the flow of ideas. (Note: You may need to eliminate or add some words to smooth out your sentences.)

a. Steve Case saw infinite possibilities in online business. Steve Case was determined to turn his vision into reality. The techies scoffed at his strategy of building a simple Internet service for ordinary people. Case doggedly pursued his dream. He analyzed other online services. He assessed the needs of his customers. He responded to their desires for an easier way to access information over the Internet. In 1992, Steve Case named his company America Online (AOL). Critics predicted the company's demise. By the end of the century, AOL was a profitable powerhouse. An ill-fated merger with Time Warner was a financial disaster and led to Case's ouster from the company.

b. Facing some of the toughest competitors in the world, Harley-Davidson had to make some changes. The company introduced new products. Harley's management team set out to rebuild the company's production process. New products were coming to market and the company was turning a profit. Harley's quality standards were not on par with those of its foreign competitors. Harley's costs were still among the highest in the industry. Harley made a U-turn and restructured the company's organizational structure. Harley's efforts have paid off.

c. Whether you're indulging in a doughnut in New York or California, Krispy Kreme wants you to enjoy the same delicious taste with every bite. The company maintains consistent product quality by carefully controlling every step of the production process. Krispy Kreme tests all raw ingredients against established quality standards. Every delivery of wheat flour is sampled and measured for its moisture content and protein levels. Krispy Kreme blends the ingredients. Krispy Kreme tests the doughnut mix for quality. Krispy Kreme delivers the mix to its stores. Financial critics are not as kind to the company as food critics have been. Allegations of improper financial reporting have left the company's future in doubt.

5.19 Ethical Choices Under what circumstances would you consider the use of terms that are high in connotative meaning to be ethical? When would you consider it to be unethical? Explain your reasoning.

Expand Your Knowledge

Exploring the Best of the Web

Compose a Better Business Message
owl.english.purdue.edu
At Purdue University's Online Writing Lab (OWL), you'll find tools to help you improve your business messages. For advice on composing written messages, for help with grammar, and for referrals to other information sources, you'd be wise to visit this site.

Purdue's OWL offers online services and an introduction to Internet search tools. You can also download a variety of handouts on writing skills. Check out the resources at the OWL homepage, then answer the following questions:

1. Explain why positive wording in a message is more effective than negative wording. Why should you be concerned about the position of good news or bad news in your written message?
2. What six factors of tone should you consider when conveying your message to your audience?
3. What points should you include in the close of your business message? Why?

Surfing Your Way to Career Success

Bovée and Thill's Business Communication Resources offers links to hundreds of online resources that can help you with this course, your other college courses, and your career. Visit www. buscomm-resources.com, then click on "Business Communication Web Directory." The "Working with Words" section connects you to a variety of websites and articles on abstract versus concrete words, abusive words, bias-free writing, euphemisms, obsolete language, plain English, and profane words. Identify three websites from this section that could be useful in your business career. For each site, write a two-sentence summary of what the site offers and how it could help you launch and build your career.

Learn Interactively

Interactive Study Guide

Visit www.prenhall.com/bovee, then locate your book and click on its "Companion Website" link. Select Chapter 5 to take advantage of the interactive "Chapter Quiz" to test your knowledge of chapter concepts. Receive instant feedback on whether you need additional studying. Also, visit the "Study Hall," where you'll find an abundance of valuable resources that will help you succeed in this course.

Peak Performance Grammar and Mechanics

If your instructor has required the use of "Peak Performance Grammar and Mechanics," either in your online course or on CD, you can continue to improve your skill with adjectives and adverbs by using the "Peak Performance Grammar and Mechanics" module. Click on "Grammar Basics," and then click "Adjectives and Adverbs." Take the Pretest to determine whether you have any weak areas. Then review those areas in the Refresher Course. Take the Follow-Up Test to check your grasp of adjectives and adverbs. For an extra challenge or advanced practice, take the Advanced Test. Finally, for additional reinforcement in adjectives and adverbs, visit the Companion Website, click on any chapter, then click on "Improve Your Grammar, Mechanics, and Usage."

CHAPTER **6**

Completing Business Messages

LEARNING OBJECTIVES

After studying this chapter, you will be able to

1 Discuss the value of careful revision and list the main tasks involved in completing a business message

2 List four writing techniques you can use to improve the readability of your messages

3 Describe the steps you can take to improve the clarity of your writing

4 Discuss why it's important to make your message more concise and give four tips on how to do so

5 Explain how design elements help determine the effectiveness of your documents

6 Highlight the types of errors to look for when proofreading

7 Discuss the most important issues to consider when distributing your messages

COMMUNICATION CLOSE-UP AT MERCEDES-AMG

www.mercedes-amg.com

Every business message tries to create a particular impression in the minds of the audience, but what if the impression you want to create is how it feels to drive one of the world's most luxurious cars that has been customized with one of the world's most powerful engines? Merely saying the words "power" and "luxury" isn't likely to be very convincing in today's advertising-saturated world.

The German firm AMG is revered among automotive connoisseurs for its high-performance engines, which are available in special Mercedes-Benz models. To promote the newest models, the marketing communication specialists at the Mercedes-AMG partnership knew they needed to go beyond mere words and photos to use every media option and design technique possible to reach their target audience. "Our goal was to create immersive experiences that build an emotional connection between the Mercedes-AMG brand and automotive enthusiasts," said Scott Preacher, vice president of Mercedes-AMG's interactive

Elegant design and attention to every detail of text, graphics, audio, and video convey a message of sophisticated quality on the Mercedes-AMG website.

advertising agency, Avenue A|Razorfish. The result was an innovative multimedia website that won the Webby award from the International Academy of Digital Arts and Sciences, considered by many to be the online media equivalent of an Oscar or Emmy.

When visitors "start" the virtual engine to begin a virtual tour of the AMG factory in Affalterbach, Germany, their web browsers even shake slightly to suggest the physical sensation of firing up the mighty AMG engine they can hear

growling through their computer speakers. Visitors "drive" to the factory via online video, then enter various buildings to learn more about Mercedes-AMG products.

The message of powerful luxury is delivered in ways that business communicators could only dream about even a few years ago, but with ageless attention to quality. In every respect—word choices, color palette, photography, audio, video, and interactive features—the website reflects the renowned "fit and finish" of the cars it represents.[1]

MOVING BEYOND YOUR FIRST DRAFT

First drafts are rarely effective as they could be.

Your business messages may not require the sophisticated design or technology of the Mercedes-AMG website (profiled in the chapter-opening Communication Close-Up), but they can benefit from the same rigorous attention to detail in the third step of the three-step writing process: completing your messages.

Once you've completed the first draft of your message, you may be tempted to breathe a sigh of relief, send the message on its way, and move on to the next project. Resist the temptation. Successful communicators recognize that the first draft is rarely as tight, clear, and compelling as it needs to be. Careful revision can mean the difference between a rambling, unfocused message and a lively, direct message that gets results. Figure 6.1 lists the tasks in the third step of the three-step writing process: revising your message to achieve optimum quality, then producing, proofreading, and distributing it.

FIGURE 6.1 Step Three in the Three-Step Writing Process: Complete Your Messages
Resist the temptation to cut corners when performing the tasks in the third step of the three-step writing process. You've spent a lot of time and energy planning and writing a strong message, so make sure it is produced and delivered with professional quality.

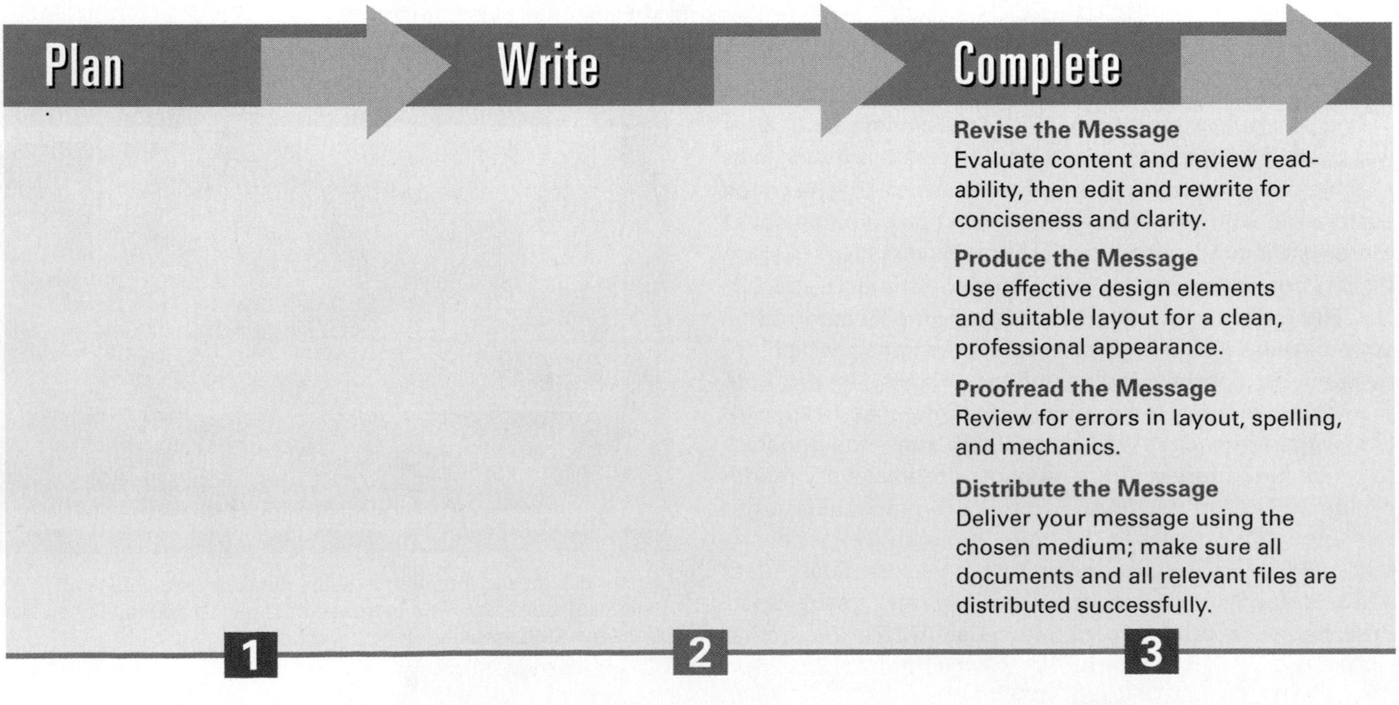

Plan	Write	Complete
		Revise the Message Evaluate content and review readability, then edit and rewrite for conciseness and clarity.
		Produce the Message Use effective design elements and suitable layout for a clean, professional appearance.
		Proofread the Message Review for errors in layout, spelling, and mechanics.
		Distribute the Message Deliver your message using the chosen medium; make sure all documents and all relevant files are distributed successfully.

1   2   3

REVISING YOUR MESSAGE

The nature of the revision task varies somewhat according to the medium you're using and the nature of your message. For informal messages to internal audiences, particularly when using instant messaging, text messaging, e-mail, or blogging, the revision process is often as simple as quickly looking over your message to correct any mistakes before sending or posting the message. However, don't fall into the common trap of thinking that these electronic media are so new and different and informal that you don't need to worry about grammar, spelling, clarity, and other fundamentals of good writing. These qualities can be even *more* important in electronic media, not less, particularly if these electronic messages are the only contact your audience has with you. Audiences are likely to equate the quality of your writing with the quality of your thinking, decision making, and other business skills. Moreover, even minor errors can cause confusion, frustration, and costly delays.

Fortunately, revising simple messages doesn't take much time or effort. With instant messaging, for example, you need only a second or two to scan each message to make sure you haven't said something clumsy or incorrect.

With more complex messages, try to put your draft aside for a day or two before you begin the revision process so that you can approach the material with a fresh eye. Then start with the "big picture," making sure that the document accomplishes your overall goals before moving to finer points such as readability, clarity, and conciseness. Compare the letters in Figures 6.2 and 6.3 for an example of how careful revision improves a customer letter.

1 LEARNING OBJECTIVE

Discuss the value of careful revision and list the main tasks involved in completing a business message

If you have time, put your draft aside for a day or two before you begin the revision process.

Evaluating Your Content, Organization, Style, and Tone

When you begin the revision process, focus your attention on content, organization, style, and tone. To evaluate the content of your message, ask yourself these questions:

- Is the information accurate?
- Is the information relevant to your audience?
- Is there enough information to satisfy your readers' needs?
- Is there a good balance between the general and the specific?

Once you are satisfied with the content of your message, you can review its organization. Ask yourself another set of questions:

- Are all your points covered in the most logical order?
- Do the most important ideas receive the most space, and are they placed in the most prominent positions?
- Would the message be more convincing if it were arranged in another sequence?
- Are any points repeated unnecessarily?
- Are details grouped together logically, or are some still scattered through the document?

With the content in place and effectively organized, next consider whether you have achieved the right style and tone for your audience. Is your writing formal enough to meet the audience's expectations without being too formal or academic? Is it too casual for a serious subject? Does your message emphasize the audience's needs over your own?

Spend a few extra moments on the beginning and ending of your message; these sections have the greatest impact on the audience. Be sure that the opening is relevant, interesting, and geared to the reader's probable reaction. In longer messages, check to see that the first few paragraphs establish the subject, purpose, and organization of the material. Review the conclusion to be sure that it summarizes the main idea and leaves the audience with a positive impression.

The beginning and end of a message have the greatest impact on your readers, so spend a few extra minutes on them.

Reviewing for Readability

Once you're satisfied with the content, organization, style, and tone of your message, make a second pass to look at its readability. Most professionals are inundated with more reading material than they can ever hope to consume, and they'll appreciate your efforts to make your documents easier to read. You'll benefit from this effort, too: If you earn a reputation

FIGURE 6.2 Improving a Customer Letter Through Careful Revision

Careful revision makes this draft shorter, clearer, and more focused. These *proofreading symbols* (see Appendix C) are still widely used whenever printed documents are edited and revised. However, in many instances, you'll use the electronic markup features in your word processor or other software, as shown later in this chapter on page 162.

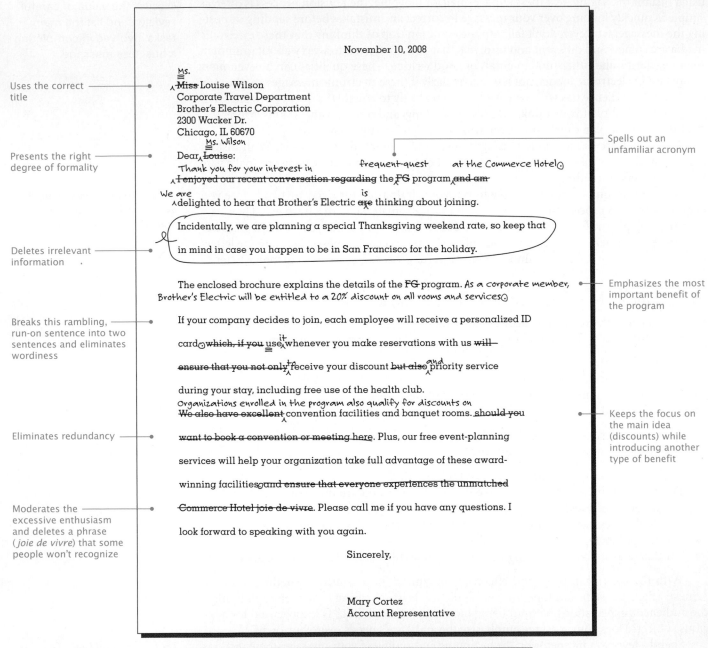

Uses the correct title

Presents the right degree of formality

Deletes irrelevant information

Breaks this rambling, run-on sentence into two sentences and eliminates wordiness

Eliminates redundancy

Moderates the excessive enthusiasm and deletes a phrase (*joie de vivre*) that some people won't recognize

Spells out an unfamiliar acronym

Emphasizes the most important benefit of the program

Keeps the focus on the main idea (discounts) while introducing another type of benefit

Common Proofreading Symbols (see page A-29 for more)

~~strikethrough~~	Delete text
ℓ	Delete individual character or a circled block of text
∧	Insert text (text to insert is written above)
⊙	Insert period
⅄	Insert comma
⌐	Start new line
¶	Start new paragraph
≡	Capitalize

FIGURE 6.3 Revised Customer Letter
This revised letter provides the requested information more clearly, in a more organized fashion, with a friendlier style, and with precise mechanics.

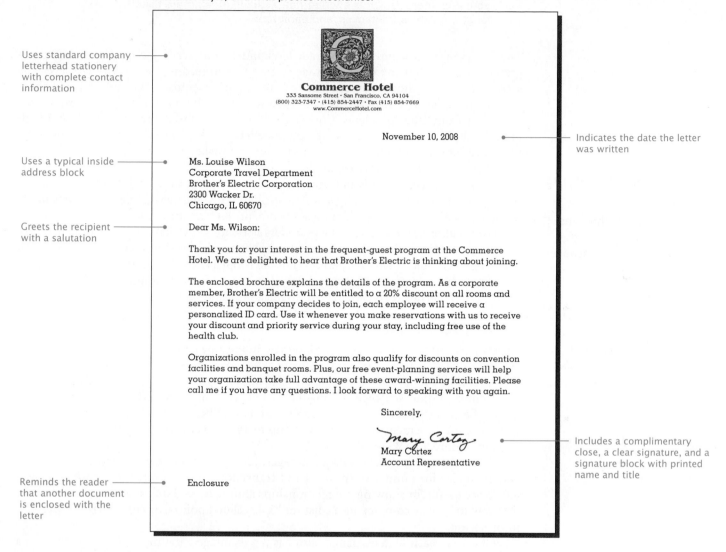

Uses standard company letterhead stationery with complete contact information

Commerce Hotel
333 Sansome Street · San Francisco, CA 94104
(800) 323-7347 · (415) 854-2447 · Fax (415) 854-7669
www.CommerceHotel.com

November 10, 2008 — Indicates the date the letter was written

Uses a typical inside address block

Ms. Louise Wilson
Corporate Travel Department
Brother's Electric Corporation
2300 Wacker Dr.
Chicago, IL 60670

Greets the recipient with a salutation

Dear Ms. Wilson:

Thank you for your interest in the frequent-guest program at the Commerce Hotel. We are delighted to hear that Brother's Electric is thinking about joining.

The enclosed brochure explains the details of the program. As a corporate member, Brother's Electric will be entitled to a 20% discount on all rooms and services. If your company decides to join, each employee will receive a personalized ID card. Use it whenever you make reservations with us to receive your discount and priority service during your stay, including free use of the health club.

Organizations enrolled in the program also qualify for discounts on convention facilities and banquet rooms. Plus, our free event-planning services will help your organization take full advantage of these award-winning facilities. Please call me if you have any questions. I look forward to speaking with you again.

Sincerely,

Mary Cortez
Mary Cortez
Account Representative

Includes a complimentary close, a clear signature, and a signature block with printed name and title

Reminds the reader that another document is enclosed with the letter

Enclosure

for well-crafted documents that respect the audience's time, people will pay more attention to your work.

You may be familiar with one of the many indexes that have been developed over the years in an attempt to measure readability. For example, the Flesch-Kincaid Grade Level score computes reading difficulty relative to grade-level achievement. Thus, a score of 10 suggests that a document can be read and understood by the average 10th grader. Most business documents score in the 8–11 range. Technical documents often score in the 12–14 range. A similar scoring system, the Flesch Reading Ease score, ranks documents on a 100-point scale; the higher the score, the easier the document is to read. Both of these measurements are built into Microsoft Word, making them easy to use for most business communicators.

Readability indexes offer a useful reference point, but they are all limited by what they are able to measure: word length, number of syllables, sentence length, and paragraph length. They can't measure any of the other factors that affect readability, such as audience analysis, writing clarity, and document design. Compare these two paragraphs:

Readability formulas can give you a helpful indication, but they can't measure everything that affects readability.

> Readability indexes offer a useful reference point, but they are all limited by what they are able to measure: word length, number of syllables, sentence length, and paragraph length. They can't measure any of the other factors that affect readability, from "you" orientation to writing clarity to document design.

> Readability indexes can help. But they don't measure everything. They don't measure whether your writing clarity is good. They don't measure whether your document design is good or not. Reading indexes are based on word length, syllables, sentences, and paragraphs.

The first paragraph scores 12.0 on grade level and 27.4 on reading ease. The second paragraph scores much better on both grade level (8.9) and reading ease (45.8). However, the second example is choppy, unsophisticated, and poorly organized. As a general rule, then, don't assume that a piece of text is readable if it scores well on a readability index—it may still suffer from other problems. Conversely, if a piece of text scores poorly (with a high grade level or a low reading ease score), examine it carefully to see whether you can use simpler words or shorter sentences. Chances are you can make the piece easier to read without making it sound choppy or amateurish.

Beyond shortening words and sentences, you can improve the readability of a message by making the document interesting and easy to skim. Most business audiences—particularly influential senior managers—skim most documents looking for key ideas, conclusions, and recommendations. Skimming also helps readers assess the worthiness of the document. If they determine that the document contains valuable information or requires a response, they will read it more carefully when time permits. You can adopt a number of techniques to make your message easier to skim: varying sentence length, using shorter paragraphs, using lists and bullets instead of narrative, and adding effective headings and subheadings.

Varying Your Sentence Length

Variety is a creative way to make your messages interesting and readable. By choosing words and sentence structure with care, you can create a rhythm that emphasizes important points, enlivens your writing style, and makes your information appealing to your reader. For example, a short sentence that highlights a conclusion at the end of a substantial paragraph of evidence makes your key message stand out. Effective messages, therefore, usually use a mixture of sentences that are short (up to 15 words or so), medium (15–25 words), and long (more than 25 words).

Each sentence length has its advantages. Short sentences can be processed quickly and are easier for nonnative speakers and translators to interpret. Medium-length sentences are useful for showing the relationships among ideas. Long sentences are often the best way to convey complex ideas, list multiple related points, or summarize or preview information.

Of course, each sentence length also has disadvantages. Too many short sentences in a row can make your writing choppy. Medium sentences lack the punch of short sentences and the informative power of longer sentences. Meanwhile, long sentences are usually harder to understand than short sentences because they are packed with information and ideas. Because readers can absorb only a few words per glance, longer sentences are also more difficult to skim. Thus, the longer your sentence, the greater the possibility that the reader who skims it will not read enough words to process its full meaning. By choosing the best sentence length for each communication need and remembering to mix sentence lengths for variety, you'll get your points across while keeping your messages lively and interesting.

Keeping Your Paragraphs Short

Large blocks of text can be visually daunting, so the optimum paragraph length is short to medium in most cases. Unless you break up your thoughts somehow, you'll end up with lengthy paragraphs that are guaranteed to intimidate even the most dedicated reader. Short paragraphs, generally 100 words or fewer (this paragraph has 88 words), are easier to read than long ones, and they make your writing look inviting. They help audiences read more carefully, too. You can also emphasize ideas by isolating them in short, forceful paragraphs.

However, don't go overboard with short paragraphs. Be careful to use one-sentence paragraphs only occasionally and only for emphasis. Also, if you need to divide a subject into several pieces in order to keep paragraphs short, be sure to help your readers keep the ideas connected by guiding them with plenty of transitional elements.

---

2 LEARNING OBJECTIVE

List four writing techniques you can use to improve the readability of your messages

To keep readers' interest, use a variety of long, medium, and short sentences.

Short paragraphs are easier to read than long ones.

Using Lists and Bullets to Clarify and Emphasize

An effective alternative to using conventional sentences is to set off important ideas in a **list**—a series of words, names, or other items. Lists can show the sequence of your ideas, heighten their impact visually, and increase the likelihood that a reader will find your key points. In addition, lists help simplify complex subjects, highlight main points, break up a page or screen visually, ease the skimming process for busy readers, and give the reader a breather. Consider the difference between the following two approaches to the same information:

Lists are effective tools for highlighting and simplifying material.

NARRATIVE

Owning your own business has many advantages. One is the ease of establishment. Another advantage is the satisfaction of working for yourself. As a sole proprietor, you also have the advantage of privacy because you do not have to reveal your information or plans to anyone.

LIST

Owning your own business has three advantages:
- Ease of establishment
- Satisfaction of working for yourself
- Privacy of information

When creating a list, you can separate items with numbers, letters, or bullets (a general term for any kind of graphical element that precedes each item). Bullets are generally preferred over numbers, unless the list is in some logical sequence or ranking or you need to refer to specific items in the list elsewhere. The following three steps need to be performed in the order indicated, and the numbers make that clear:

1. Find out how many employees would like on-site day-care facilities.
2. Determine how much space the day-care center would require.
3. Estimate the cost of converting a conference room for the on-site facility.

Lists are easier to locate and read if the entire numbered or bulleted section is set off by a blank line before and after, as the preceding examples demonstrate. Furthermore, when using lists, make sure to introduce them clearly so that people know what they're about to read. Of course, you can also add further discussion after the list. One way to introduce lists is to make them a part of the introductory sentence:

The board of directors met to discuss the revised annual budget. To keep expenses in line with declining sales, the directors voted to
- Cut everyone's salary by 10 percent
- Close the employee cafeteria
- Reduce travel expenses

Another way to introduce a list is to precede it with a complete introductory sentence, followed by a colon:

The decline in company profit is attributable to four factors:
- Slower holiday sales
- Increased transportation and fuel costs
- Higher employee wages
- Slower inventory turnover

Regardless of the format you choose, the items in a list should be parallel; that is, they should all use the same grammatical pattern. For example, if one list item begins with a verb, all list items should begin with a verb. If one item is a noun phrase, all should be noun phrases.

NONPARALLEL LIST ITEMS
- Improve our bottom line
- Identification of new foreign markets for our products
- Global market strategies
- Issues regarding pricing and packaging size

PARALLEL LIST ITEMS
- Improving our bottom line
- Identifying new foreign markets for our products
- Developing our global market strategies
- Resolving pricing and packaging issues

Parallel forms are easier to read and skim. You can create parallelism by repeating the pattern in words, phrases, clauses, or entire sentences (see Table 6.1).

TABLE 6.1 Achieving Parallelism

METHOD	EXAMPLE
Parallel words	The letter was approved by Clausen, Whittaker, Merlin, and Carlucci.
Parallel phrases	We are gaining market share in supermarkets, in department stores, and in specialty stores.
Parallel clauses	I'd like to discuss the issue after Vicki gives her presentation but before Marvin shows his slides.
Parallel sentences	In 2006, we exported 30 percent of our production. In 2007, we exported 50 percent.

Adding Headings and Subheadings

Use headings to grab the reader's attention and organize material into short sections.

A **heading** is a brief title that tells readers about the content of the section that follows. **Subheadings** are subordinate to headings, indicating subsections with a major section. Headings and subheadings serve these important functions:

- **Organization.** Headings show your reader at a glance how the document is organized. They act as labels to group related paragraphs together and effectively organize your material into short sections.
- **Attention.** Informative, inviting, and in some cases intriguing headings grab the reader's attention, make the text easier to read, and help the reader find the parts he or she needs to read—or skip.
- **Connection.** Using headings and subheadings together helps readers see the relationship between main ideas and subordinate ones so that they can understand your message more easily. Moreover, headings and subheadings visually indicate shifts from one idea to the next.

Informative headings are generally more helpful than descriptive ones.

Headings fall into two categories. **Descriptive headings**, such as "Cost Considerations," identify a topic but do little more. **Informative headings**, such as "A New Way to Cut Costs," put your reader right into the context of your message.

Informative headings guide readers to think in a certain way about the topic. They are also helpful in guiding your work as a writer, especially if written in terms of questions you plan to address in your document. Well-written informative headings are self-contained, which means that readers can read just the headings and subheadings and understand them without reading the rest of the document. For example, "Introduction" conveys little information, whereas the heading "Staffing Shortages Cost the Company $150,000 Last Year" provides a key piece of information and captures the reader's attention. Whatever types of headings you choose, keep them brief and use parallel construction as you would for an outline, lists, or a series of words.

Use the same grammatical form for each heading.

Editing for Clarity and Conciseness

Clarity is essential to getting your message across accurately and efficiently.

Once you've reviewed and revised your message for readability, your next step is to make sure your message is as clear and as concise as possible. To ensure clarity, look closely at your paragraph organization, sentence structure, and word choices. Perhaps a sentence is so complicated that readers can't unravel it. You might have chosen a word that is so vague that readers can interpret it in several ways. Perhaps pronouns or tenses switch midsentence so that readers lose track of who is talking or when an event took place. Sentence B may not be a logical sequel to sentence A, or an important word may be used incorrectly.[2]

3 LEARNING OBJECTIVE

Describe the steps you can take to improve the clarity of your writing

Ask yourself whether your sentences are easy to decipher. Do your paragraphs have clear topic sentences? Are the transitions between ideas obvious? Are your statements simple and direct? A clear sentence is no accident. Few sentences come out exactly right the first time. See Table 6.2 for examples of the following tips:

Communication Miscues

Missing the Message with Prescription Medications

Few messages in life are as important as the instructions for prescription medications. Yet, according to the American Academy of Pediatrics, nearly half of all parents fail to correctly follow the information contained on the labels of medications prescribed for their children. Errors abound among elderly patients as well, who often need to take multiple medications every day. Blaming the parents and patients for these errors may be tempting, but evidence suggests that the labels themselves are responsible for many mistakes.

Experts cite such communication problems as confusing terminology, information overload, and poor prioritization—highlighting nonessential information such as the name of the pharmacy at the expense of truly critical information such as the correct dosage, drug interaction warnings, or even the name of the medication itself. The situation can get even worse in households where two or more people have prescriptions, creating the possibility of patients accidentally taking the wrong medication. Moreover, the information now included with many medications is split between the label on the bottle, the box the bottle comes in, and a government-mandated printed insert. Ironically, those inserts are meant to clarify important information for the patient, but many patients toss them aside rather than reading what can be several pages of dense, tiny type and unfamiliar terminology.

Fortunately, some improvements are taking place. After her grandmother accidentally took some of her grandfather's pills, graphic designer Deborah Adler decided that a major change was needed. Overhauling the round pill bottle that has been in use and unchanged for 60 years, Adler and industrial designer Klaus Rosburg crafted a new design that features a large, flat labeling surface that wraps over the top of the bottle. The label prioritizes vital information, particularly the name of the drug, the patient's name, and dosage instructions. Color-coded bands can be attached as well to help various members of a household identify the right bottles. Adler's design, named ClearRx, is now in use at Target pharmacies nationwide.

CAREER APPLICATIONS

1. Why is information prioritization so important with medicine labels?
2. Aside from medications, what other situations have you encountered in your life in which confusing labels, signs, instructions, or other messages created a health or safety hazard? Choose one of these situations and write a brief description of the poor communication and your advice on how it could have been improved.

- **Break up overly long sentences.** Don't connect too many clauses with *and* or *or*. If you find yourself stuck in a long sentence, you're probably trying to make the sentence do more than it can reasonably do, such as expressing two dissimilar thoughts or peppering the reader with too many pieces of supporting evidence at once (did you notice how difficult this long sentence was to read?). You can often clarify your writing style by separating a string of items into individual sentences.

- **Rewrite hedging sentences.** Sometimes you have to write *may* or *seems* to avoid stating a judgment as a fact. However, when you have too many such hedges, you come across as being unsure of what you're saying.

  Don't be afraid to present your opinions without qualification.

- **Impose parallelism.** When you have two or more similar ideas to express, make them parallel. Repeating the same grammatical construction shows that the ideas are related, of similar importance, and on the same level of generality. Parallelism is discussed earlier in this chapter in the section on lists.

  When you use the same grammatical pattern to express two or more ideas, you show that they are comparable thoughts.

- **Correct dangling modifiers.** Sometimes a modifier is not just an adjective or an adverb but an entire phrase modifying a noun or a verb. Be careful not to leave this type of modifier *dangling*, with no connection to the subject of the sentence. The first unacceptable example under "Dangling Modifiers" in Table 6.1 implies that the red sports car has both an office and the legs to walk there. The second example shows one frequent cause of dangling modifiers: passive construction.

- **Reword long noun sequences.** When multiple nouns are strung together as modifiers, the resulting sentence can be hard to read. You may be trying too hard to create the desired effect; first, see if a single well-chosen word will do the job. If the nouns are all necessary, consider moving one or more to a modifying phrase as shown in Table 6.1. Although you add a few more words, your audience won't have to work as hard to understand the sentence.

TABLE 6.2 Revising for Clarity

ISSUES TO REVIEW	INEFFECTIVE	EFFECTIVE
OVERLY LONG SENTENCES		
Taking compound sentences too far	The magazine will be published January 1, and I'd better meet the deadline if I want my article included.	The magazine will be published January 1. I'd better meet the deadline if I want my article included.
HEDGING SENTENCES		
Overqualifying sentences	I believe that Mr. Johnson's employment record seems to show that he may be capable of handling the position.	Mr. Johnson's employment record shows that he is capable of handling the position.
UNPARALLEL SENTENCES		
Using dissimilar construction for similar ideas	Mr. Sims had been drenched with rain, bombarded with telephone calls, and his boss shouted at him.	Mr. Sims had been drenched with rain, bombarded with telephone calls, and shouted at by his boss.
	Ms. Reynolds printed the letter, and next she signed it and left the office.	Ms. Reynolds printed the letter, signed it, and left the office.
	To waste time and missing deadlines are bad habits.	Wasting time and missing deadlines are bad habits.
	Interviews are a matter of acting confident and to stay relaxed.	Interviews are a matter of acting confident and staying relaxed.
DANGLING MODIFIERS		
Placing modifiers close to the wrong nouns and verbs	Walking to the office, a red sports car passed her.	A red sports car passed her while she was walking to the office.
	After a three-week slump, we increased sales.	After a three-week slump, sales increased.
LONG NOUN SEQUENCES		
Stringing too many nouns together	The window sash installation company will give us an estimate on Friday.	The company that installs window sashes will give us an estimate on Friday.
CAMOUFLAGED VERBS		
Changing verbs and nouns into adjectives	The manager undertook implementation of the rules.	The manager implemented the rules.
	Verification of the shipments occurs weekly.	Shipments are verified weekly. *or* We verify shipments weekly.
Changing verbs into nouns	reach a conclusion about make a discovery of give consideration to	conclude discover consider
SENTENCE STRUCTURE		
Separating subject and predicate	A 10 percent decline in market share, which resulted from quality problems and an aggressive sales campaign by Armitage, the market leader in the Northeast, was the major problem in 2007.	The major problem in 2007 was a 10 percent loss of market share, which resulted from both quality problems and an aggressive sales campaign by Armitage, the market leader in the Northeast.
Separating adjectives, adverbs, or prepositional phrases from the words they modify	Our antique desk lends an air of strength and substance with thick legs and large drawers.	With its thick legs and large drawers, our antique desk lends an air of strength and substance.

TABLE 6.2 *Continued*

AWKWARD REFERENCES	The Law Office and the Accounting Office distribute computer supplies for legal secretaries and beginning accountants, respectively.	The Law Office distributes computer supplies for legal secretaries; the Accounting Office distributes those for beginning accountants.
TOO MUCH ENTHUSIASM	We are extremely pleased to offer you a position on our staff of exceptionally skilled and highly educated employees. The work offers extraordinary challenges and a very large salary.	We are pleased to offer you a position on our staff of skilled and well-educated employees. The work offers challenges and an attractive salary.

- **Replace camouflaged verbs.** Watch for words that end in *-ion*, *-tion*, *-ing*, *-ment*, *-ant*, *-ent*, *-ence*, *-ance*, and *-ency*. These endings often change verbs into nouns and adjectives, requiring you to add a verb just to get your point across. To prune and enliven your messages, use verbs instead of noun phrases.
- **Clarify sentence structure.** Keep the subject and predicate of a sentence as close together as possible. When the subject and predicate are far apart, readers may need to read the sentence twice to figure out who did what. Similarly, adjectives, adverbs, and prepositional phrases usually make the most sense when they're placed as close as possible to the words they modify.
- **Clarify awkward references.** In an effort to save words, business writers sometimes use expressions such as *the above-mentioned*, *as mentioned above*, *the aforementioned*, *the former*, *the latter*, and *respectively*. These words cause readers to jump from point to point, which hinders effective communication. You'll often be more successful using specific references (such as "as described in the second paragraph on page 22"), even if that means adding a few more words.
- **Moderate your enthusiasm.** An occasional adjective or adverb to intensify and emphasize your meaning is fine, but too many can degrade your writing and damage your credibility.

Subject and predicate should be placed as close together as possible, as should modifiers and the words they modify.

In addition to clarity, readers appreciate conciseness in business messages. The good news is that most first drafts can be cut by as much as 50 percent.[3] By reorganizing your content, improving the readability of your document, and correcting your sentence structure for clarity, you will have already eliminated most of the excess. Now it is time to examine every word you've written. As you begin your editing task, simplify, prune, and strive for order. See Table 6.3 for examples of the following tips:

Showing enthusiasm for ideas is fine, but be careful not to go so far that you sound unprofessional or unbelievable.

4 LEARNING OBJECTIVE

Discuss why it's important to make your message more concise and give four tips on how to do so

- **Delete unnecessary words and phrases.** To test whether a word or phrase is essential, try the sentence without it. If the meaning doesn't change, leave it out. For instance, *very* is often simply clutter. There's no need to call someone "very methodical." The person is either methodical or not. In addition, avoid the clutter of too many or poorly placed relative pronouns (*who*, *that*, *which*). Even articles can be excessive (such as repeating *the* in a list of items). However, well-placed relative pronouns and articles prevent confusion, so make sure you don't obscure the meaning of the sentence by removing these.
- **Shorten long words and phrases.** Short words are generally more vivid and easier to read than long ones. The idea is to use short, simple words, *not* simple concepts.[4] Plus, by using infinitives in place of some phrases, you not only shorten your sentences but also make them clearer.
- **Eliminate redundancies.** In some word combinations, the words tend to say the same thing. For instance, "visible to the eye" is redundant because *visible* is enough without further clarification; "to the eye" adds nothing.
- **Recast "It is/There are" starters.** If you start a sentence with an indefinite pronoun such as *it* or *there*, odds are the sentence could be shorter and more active. For instance, "We believe . . ." is a stronger opening than "It is believed that . . ."

TABLE 6.3 Revising for Conciseness

ISSUES TO REVIEW	INEFFECTIVE	EFFECTIVE
UNNECESSARY WORDS AND PHRASES		
Using wordy phrases	for the sum of	for
	in the event that	if
	prior to the start of	before
	in the near future	soon
	at this point in time	now
	due to the fact that	because
	in view of the fact that	because
	until such time as	when
	with reference to	about
Using too many relative pronouns	Cars that are sold after January will not have a six-month warranty.	Cars sold after January will not have a six-month warranty.
	Employees who are driving to work should park in the underground garage.	Employees driving to work should park in the underground garage.
Using too few relative pronouns	The project manager told the engineers last week the specifications were changed.	The project manager told the engineers last week that the specifications were changed.
		The project manager told the engineers that last week the specifications were changed.
LONG WORDS AND PHRASES		
Using overly long words	During the preceding year, the company accelerated productive operations.	Last year, the company sped up operations.
	The action was predicated on the assumption that the company was operating at a financial deficit.	The action was based on the belief that the company was losing money.
Using wordy phrases rather than infinitives	If you want success as a writer, you must work hard.	To succeed as a writer, you must work hard.
	He went to the library for the purpose of studying.	He went to the library to study.
	The employer increased salaries so that she could improve morale.	The employer increased salaries to improve morale.
REDUNDANCIES		
Repeating meanings	absolutely complete	complete
	basic fundamentals	fundamentals
	follows after	follows
	free and clear	free
	refer back	refer
	repeat again	repeat
	collect together	collect
	future plans	plans
	return back	return
	important essentials	essentials
	end result	result
	actual truth	truth
	final outcome	outcome
	uniquely unusual	unique
	surrounded on all sides	surrounded
Using double modifiers	modern, up-to-date equipment	modern equipment

TABLE 6.3 *Continued*

IT IS/THERE ARE STARTERS		
Starting sentences with *it* or *there*	It would be appreciated if you would sign the lease today.	Please sign the lease today.
	There are five employees in this division who were late to work today.	Five employees in this division were late to work today.

As you rewrite, concentrate on how each word contributes to an effective sentence and on how each sentence builds to a coherent paragraph. Be sure to consider the effect your words will have on readers. Look for opportunities to make the material more interesting through the use of strong, lively words and phrases (as discussed in Chapter 5). For a reminder of the tasks involved in revision, see "Checklist: Revising Business Messages."

Sometimes you'll find that the most difficult problem in a sentence can be solved by simply removing the problem itself. When you come upon a troublesome element, ask yourself, "Do I need it at all?" Possibly not. In fact, you may find that it was giving you so much grief precisely because it was trying to do an unnecessary job.[5] Once you remove the troublesome element, the afflicted sentence will spring to life and breathe normally. Take advantage of the "undo" and "redo" functions in your software to experiment with adding and removing various elements.

DOCUMENT MAKEOVER

IMPROVE THIS LETTER

To practice correcting drafts of actual documents, visit your online course or the access-code-protected portion of the Companion Website. Click "Document Makeovers," then click Chapter 6. You will find a letter that contains problems and errors relating to what you've learned in this chapter about revising messages. Use the Final Draft decision tool to create an improved version of this letter. Check the message for organization, readability, clarity, and conciseness.

Using Technology to Revise Your Message

When it's time to revise and polish your message, your word processor can help you add, delete, and move text with functions such as *cut and paste* (taking a block of text out of one section of a document and pasting it in somewhere else) and *search and replace* (tracking down words or phrases and changing them if you need to). Be careful using this feature, though; choosing the "replace all" option can result in some unintended errors. For example,

---

 CHECKLIST: Revising Business Messages

A. Evaluate content, organization, style, and tone.
- Make sure the information is accurate, relevant, and sufficient.
- Check that all necessary points appear in logical order.
- Verify that you present enough support to make the main idea convincing and interesting.
- Be sure the beginning and ending are effective.
- Make sure you've achieved the right tone.

B. Review for readability.
- Consider using a readability index, being sure to interpret the answer carefully.
- Use a mix of short and long sentences.
- Keep paragraphs short.
- Use bulleted and numbered lists to emphasize key points.
- Make the document easy to scan with headings and subheadings.

C. Edit for clarity.
- Break up overly long sentences and rewrite hedging sentences.
- Impose parallelism to simplify reading.
- Correct dangling modifiers.
- Reword long noun sequences and replace camouflaged verbs.
- Clarify sentence structure and awkward references.
- Moderate your enthusiasm to maintain a professional tone.

D. Edit for conciseness.
- Delete unnecessary words and phrases.
- Shorten long words and phrases.
- Eliminate redundancies.
- Rewrite sentences that start with "It is" or "There are."

finding *power* and replacing all occurrences with *strength* will also change the word *powerful* to *strengthful*. Software tools such as *revision marks* and *commenting* keep track of proposed editing changes electronically and provide a history of a document's revisions. In Microsoft Word, the revisions appear in a different font color than the original text (see Figure 6.4), giving you a chance to review changes before accepting or rejecting them. Adobe Acrobat lets you attach notes to PDF files (see Figure 6.5). Revision marks and commenting features are also a great way to keep track of editing changes made by team members. Both Word and Acrobat let you choose different colors for different reviewers as well, so you can keep everyone's comments separate.

Spell checkers, grammar checkers, and computerized thesauruses can all help with the revision process, but they can't take the place of good writing and editing skills.

In addition to the many revision tools, four software functions can help bring out the best in your documents. First, a *spell checker* compares your document with an electronic dictionary, highlights unrecognized words, and suggests correct spellings. Spell checkers are a wonderful way to weed major typos out of your documents, but they are no substitute for good spelling skills. For example, if you use *their* when you mean to use *there*, your spell checker won't notice, because *their* is spelled correctly. If you're in a hurry and accidentally omit the *p* at the end of *top*, your spell checker will read *to* as correct. Plus, some of the "errors" that the spell checker indicates may actually be proper names, technical words, words that you misspelled on purpose, web addresses, or simply words that weren't included in the spell checker's dictionary. It's up to you to decide whether each flagged word should be corrected or left alone, and it's up to you to find the errors that your spell checker has overlooked.

Second, a computer *thesaurus* gives you alternative words, just as a printed thesaurus does. A computer thesaurus is much faster and lets you try multiple alternatives in just a few seconds to see which works best. The best uses of any thesaurus, printed or computerized, are to find fresh, interesting words when you've been using the same word too many times and to find words that most accurately convey your intended meaning. Don't fall into the temptation of using your thesaurus to find impressive words to spice up your writing; if you're not comfortable using the word, it won't sound natural in your documents.

FIGURE 6.4 Revision Marks in Microsoft Word
Microsoft Word, the most commonly used word processor in business offices, offers handy tools for reviewing draft documents. In this example, text to be added is shown in blue and text to be deleted is shown in red. The writer can then choose to accept or reject each suggested change.

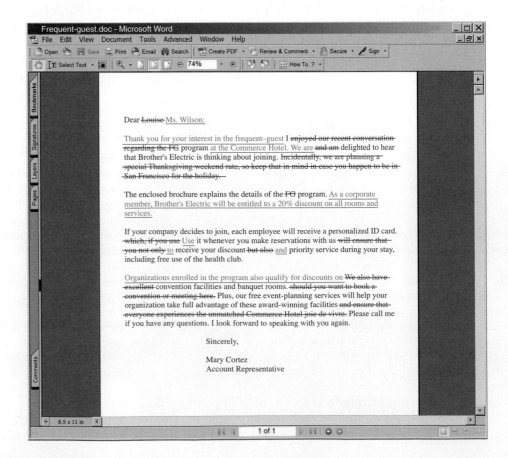

FIGURE 6.5 Comments Attached to a PDF File
Adobe Acrobat lets reviewers attach comments to any PDF document.

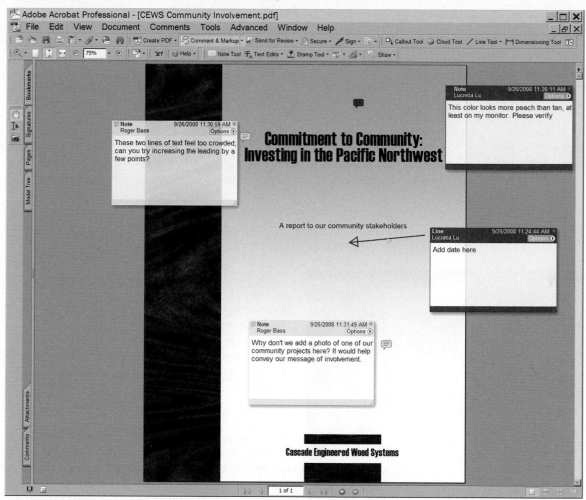

Third, the *grammar checker* tries to do for your grammar what a spell checker does for your spelling. Because the program doesn't have a clue about what you're trying to say, it can't tell whether you've said it correctly. Moreover, even if you've used all the rules correctly, a grammar checker still can't tell whether your document communicates clearly. However, grammar checkers can highlight items you should consider changing, such as passive voice, long sentences, and words that tend to be misused.

Fourth, a *style checker* can also monitor your word and sentence choices and suggest alternatives that might produce more effective writing. For instance, the style-checking options in Microsoft Word range from basic issues, such as spelling out numbers and using contractions, to more subjective matters, such as sentence structure and the use of technical terminology.

By all means, use any software that you find helpful when revising your documents. Just remember that it's unwise to rely on them to do all your revision work, and you're responsible for the final product.

PRODUCING YOUR MESSAGE

Now it's time to put your hard work on display. The *production quality* of your message—the total effect of page or screen design, graphical elements, typography, and so on—plays an important role in the effectiveness of your message. A polished, inviting design not only makes your material easier to read but also conveys a sense of professionalism and importance.[6]

The quality of your document or screen design affects both readability and audience perceptions of you and your message.

Naturally, the production task varies widely, depending on both the medium you've chosen and the degree of formality you need to achieve. In the simplest media, such as text messaging, you have virtually nothing to do. Moving up to instant messaging and e-mail, you can control a variety of aspects, such as type size and color. With documents prepared with a word processor, your options multiply considerably—particularly if you plan to deliver the documents electronically.

Adding Graphics, Sound, Video, and Hypertext

Take advantage of your word processor's ability to incorporate other communication elements.

Today's word processors and other software tools make it easy to produce impressive documents and online materials that enliven your messages with full-color pictures, sound and video recordings, and hypertext links. The software for creating business visuals falls into two basic groups: *presentation software*, which helps you create electronic slide shows for in-person or online meetings (see Chapter 16), and *graphics software*, which ranges from basic tools that help you create simple business diagrams to the comprehensive tools preferred by artists and graphic designers. You can create graphics yourself, use *clip art* (collections of uncopyrighted images), or scan in drawings or photographs.

Adding sound bites or video clips to electronic documents can be an effective way to help get your message across. Several systems let you record brief messages and attach them to particular places in a document. The reader then clicks on a speaker icon to play each comment.

You can also use hypertext markup language (HTML) to insert hyperlinks into your documents. Readers can easily jump from one document to another by clicking on such a link. They can go directly to a website, jump to another section of your document, or go to a different document or program altogether. Suppose you're preparing a report on this year's budget. Rather than include pages and pages of budget details from prior years, you can connect to them using hyperlinks. If readers need to access details from prior years, they simply click on the appropriate links. By using hyperlinks, you can customize your documents to meet the individual information needs of your readers—just as you can on a webpage. Of course, you'll have to make sure that the file (or the software program used to open that file) is included with your electronic document, installed on the recipient's computer, or accessible via a network connection.

By embedding multimedia elements in reports and other documents, you can enhance your messages with audio and video.

Designing for Readability

5 LEARNING OBJECTIVE

Explain how design elements help determine the effectiveness of your documents

Design affects readability in two important ways. First, if done carefully, design elements can improve the effectiveness of your message. If done poorly, design elements can act as barriers, blocking your communication. For example, people age 65 and over are the fastest-growing segment of online consumers in the United States, but many websites don't take into account the natural changes that occur in eyesight as people age. Older people often find it difficult to read the small type that is common on websites—and many websites make the even greater mistake of preventing viewers from enlarging type size in their browsers.[7]

Second, the visual design itself sends a nonverbal message to the audience, influencing their perceptions of the communication before they read a single word (see Figure 6.6). For example, the elegant style of the Mercedes-AMG website conveys a message that matches the nature of the products themselves. The black, silver, gray, and white color palette sends a distinctly different message than a website with wild, clashing colors would send.

FIGURE 6.6 Ineffective and Effective Document Design

Compare these two e-mail screens. They contain virtually the same information but send dramatically different messages to the reader. The unprofessional appearance of the "ineffective" version makes it uninviting and difficult to read. The amateurish use of color is distracting. In contrast, the "effective" version is clear, inviting, and easy to either read entirely or scan quickly.

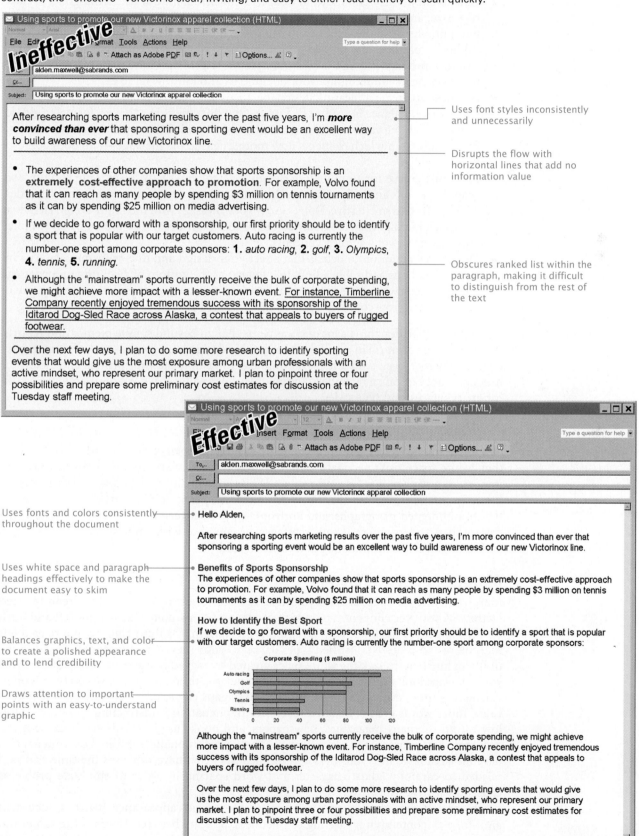

Effective design helps you establish the tone of your document and helps guide your readers through your message. To achieve an effective design, pay careful attention to the following design elements:

For effective design, pay attention to
- *Consistency*
- *Balance*
- *Restraint*
- *Detail*

- **Consistency.** Throughout each message, be consistent in your use of margins, typeface, type size, and spacing (such as in paragraph indents, between columns, and around photographs). Also be consistent when using recurring design elements, such as vertical lines, columns, and borders. In many cases, you'll want to be consistent not only within a message but also across multiple messages; that way, audiences who receive messages from you recognize your documents and know what to expect.
- **Balance.** To create a pleasing design, balance the space devoted to text, artwork, and white space. Balance is a subjective issue. One document may have a formal, rigid design in which the various elements are placed in a grid pattern, while another has a less formal design in which elements flow more freely across the page—and both could be in balance.
- **Restraint.** Strive for simplicity in design. Elegant simplicity, using only enough text, graphics, audio, and video to get each point across, is one of the reasons the Mercedes-AMG website is so effective. Don't clutter your message with too many design elements, too much highlighting, too many colors, or too many decorative touches. Let "simpler" and "fewer" be your guiding concepts.
- **Detail.** Pay attention to details that affect your design and thus your message. For instance, headings and subheadings that appear at the bottom of a column or a page can annoy readers when the promised information doesn't appear until the next column or page. Also, narrow columns with too much space between words can be distracting.

If you will be designing a lot of documents that go beyond simple memos and reports, consider taking a course in page layout or graphic design to make the most of your creative efforts. However, even without special training, you can make your printed and electronic messages more effective by understanding the use of white space, margins and line justification, typefaces, and type styles.

White Space

White space separates elements in a document and helps guide the reader's eye.

Any space free of text or artwork, both in print and online, is considered **white space** (note that "white space" isn't necessarily white). These unused areas provide visual contrast and important resting points for your readers. White space includes the open area surrounding headings, margins, vertical space between columns, paragraph indents or extra space between unindented paragraphs, and horizontal space between lines of text. To increase the chance that readers will read your messages, be generous with white space; it makes pages and screens feel less intimidating and easier to read.[8]

Margins and Justification

Margins define the space around your text and between text columns. They're influenced by the way you place lines of type, which can be set (1) justified (flush on the left and flush on the right), (2) flush left with a ragged right margin, (3) flush right with a ragged left margin, or (4) centered. Justified type "darkens" your message's appearance, because the uniform line lengths lack the white space created by ragged margins. It also tends to make your message look more formal and less like a personalized message. Justified type is often considered more difficult to read, because large gaps can appear between words and because more words are hyphenated (excessive hyphenation is distracting and hard to follow). Even so, many magazines, newspapers, and books use justified type because it can accommodate more text in a given space. These professionally published documents also have an advantage most business communicators don't have, which is the time and skill needed to carefully adjust character and word spacing in order to eliminate problems caused by justification.

Most business documents use a flush-left margin and a ragged-right margin.

Flush-left, ragged-right type "lightens" your message's appearance. It gives a document an informal, contemporary feeling of openness. Spacing between words is the same, and only long words that fall at the ends of lines are hyphenated.

TABLE 6.4 Typeface Personalities: Serious to Casual to Playful

SERIF TYPEFACES (BEST FOR TEXT)	SANS SERIF TYPEFACES (BEST FOR HEADLINES; SOME WORK WELL FOR TEXT)	SPECIALTY TYPEFACES (FOR DECORATIVE PURPOSES ONLY)
Bookman Old Style	Arial	ANNA
Century Schoolbook	**Eras Bold**	Bauhaus
Courier	Franklin Gothic Book	*Edwardian*
Garamond	Frutiger	*Lucida Handwriting*
Rockwell	Gill Sans	Old English
Times Roman	Verdana	**STENCIL**

Centered type is rarely used for text paragraphs but is commonly used for headings and subheadings. Flush-right, ragged-left type is rarely used in business documents.

Typefaces

Typeface or **font** refers to the physical design of letters, numbers, and other text characters. Typeface style influences the tone of your message, making it look authoritative or friendly, businesslike or casual, classic or modern, and so on (see Table 6.4). Be sure to choose fonts that are appropriate for your message. Most computers offer dozens of font choices, but most of these are inappropriate for general business usage.

Serif typefaces have small crosslines (called serifs) at the ends of each letter stroke. Serif typefaces such as Times Roman are commonly used for text; they can look busy and cluttered when set in large sizes for headings or other display treatments. Typefaces with rounded serifs can look friendly; those with squared serifs can look official.

Serif typefaces are commonly used for text; sans serif typefaces are commonly used for headings.

Sans serif typefaces have no serifs. Typefaces such as Helvetica and Arial are ideal for display treatments that use larger type. Sans serif typefaces can be difficult to read in long blocks of text. They look best when surrounded by plenty of white space—as in headings or in widely spaced lines of text.

For most documents, you shouldn't need to use more than two typefaces, although if you want to make captions or other text elements stand out, you can use another font.[9] You can't go too far wrong with a sans serif typeface (such as Arial) for heads and subheads, and a serif typeface (such as Times New Roman) for text and captions. Using too many typefaces clutters the document and can produce an amateurish look (as seen in Figure 6.6).

Type Styles

Type style refers to any modification that lends contrast or emphasis to type, including boldface, italic, underlining, and other highlighting and decorative styles. Using boldface type for subheads breaks up long expanses of text. You can also boldface isolated words in the middle of a text block to draw more attention to them. However, if you set too many words in boldface, you may create a "checkerboard" appearance within a paragraph and darken the overall appearance of your message, making it look heavy and uninviting.

Use italic type for emphasis. Although italics are sometimes used when irony or humor is intended, quotation marks are usually best for that purpose. Italics can also be used to set off a quote and are often used in captions. Boldfaced type and italics are most effective when reserved for key words—those that help readers understand the main point of the text. A good example of using boldface type effectively is found in the revision tips listed under the heading "Editing for Clarity and Conciseness" on pages 156–161 of this chapter. Here the boldfaced type draws attention to the key tips, followed by a short, regular-typeface explanation of each tip.

As a general rule, avoid using any style in a way that slows your audience's progress through the message. For instance, underlining or using all-uppercase letters can interfere with your

Avoid using any type style that inhibits your audience's ability to read your messages.

reader's ability to recognize the shapes of words, improperly placed boldface or italicized type can slow down your reader, and shadowed or outlined type can seriously hinder legibility.

Make sure the size of your type is proportionate to the importance of your message and the space allotted. For most business messages, use a type size of 10 to 12 points for regular text, and 12 to 18 points for headings and subheadings (a point is approximately 1/72 of an inch). Resist the temptation to reduce your type size to squeeze in text or to enlarge it to fill up space. Type that is too small is hard to read, whereas extra-large type looks unprofessional. Be particularly careful with small type online; high-resolution computer screens can reduce this type even further, making it extremely difficult to read.

Using Technology to Produce Your Message

Learning to use the basic features of your communication tools will help you produce better messages in less time.

The production tools you'll have at your disposal vary widely, depending on the software and systems you're using. Some IM and e-mail systems offer limited formatting and production capabilities, whereas most word processors now offer some capabilities that rival professional publishing software for many day-to-day business needs. *Desktop publishing* software such as Quark XPress and Adobe InDesign goes beyond word processing with more advanced layout capabilities that are designed to accommodate photos, technical drawings, and other elements. (These programs are used mainly by design professionals.) For online content, web publishing systems make it easy to produce great-looking webpages quickly. Similarly, most blogging systems now simplify the production of blog content, making it easy to rapidly post new material. Multimedia production tools such as Microsoft Producer let you combine slides, audio commentary, video clips, and other features into computer-based presentations that once cost thousands of dollars to create.

No matter what system you're using, become familiar with the basic formatting capabilities. A few hours of exploration on your own or an introductory training course can dramatically improve the production quality of your documents. Depending on the types of messages you're creating, you'll benefit from being proficient with the following features:

- **Templates and stylesheets.** As Chapter 5 noted, you can save a tremendous amount of time by using templates and stylesheets. Many companies provide these to their employees to ensure a consistent look and feel for all print and online documents.
- **Page setup.** Use page setup to control margins, orientation (*portrait* is vertical; *landscape* is horizontal), and the location of *headers* (text and graphics that repeat at the top of every page) and *footers* (similar to headers but at the bottom of the page).
- **Column formatting.** Most business documents use a single column of text per page, but multiple columns can be an attractive format for documents such as newsletters. Columns are also a handy way to format long lists.
- **Paragraph formatting.** Take advantage of the various paragraph formatting controls to enhance the look of your documents. For instance, you can offset quotations by increasing margin width around a single paragraph, subtly compress line spacing to fit a document on a single page, or use hanging indents to offset the first line of a paragraph.
- **Numbered and bulleted lists.** Let your word processor or online publishing system do the busywork of formatting numbered and bulleted lists, too. It can also automatically renumber lists when you add or remove items, saving you the embarrassment of misnumbered lists.
- **Tables.** Tables are a great way to display any information that lends itself to rows and columns: calendars, numerical data, comparisons, and so on. Use paragraph and font formatting thoughtfully within tables for the best look.
- **Pictures, text boxes, and objects.** Word processors let you insert a wide variety of *pictures* (using one of the industry-standard formats such as JPEG or GIF). *Text boxes* are small blocks of text that stand apart from the main text (great for captions, callouts, margin notes, and so on). *Objects* can be anything from a spreadsheet to a sound clip to an engineering drawing. Similarly, blogging systems, wikis, and other web development tools let you insert a variety of pictures, audio and video clips, and other multimedia elements.

Paragraph formatting gives you greater control over the look of your documents.

By improving the appearance of your documents with these tools, you'll improve your readers' impressions of you and your messages, too.

Formatting Formal Letters and Memos

Formal business letters usually follow certain design conventions, as the letter in Figure 6.3 (see page 153) illustrates. Most business letters are printed on *letterhead stationery*, which includes the company's name, address, and other contact information. The first thing to appear after the letterhead is the date, followed by the inside address, which identifies the person receiving the letter. Next is the salutation, usually in the form of *Dear Mr.* or *Ms. Last Name*. The message comes next, followed by the complimentary close, usually *Sincerely* or *Cordially*. And last comes the signature block: space for the signature, followed by the sender's printed name and title. Your company will probably have a standard format to follow for letters, possibly along with a template in Microsoft Word or whatever word processor is standard in the organization. For in-depth format information on letter formats, see Appendix A: "Format and Layout of Business Documents."

Like letters, business memos usually follow a preset design (see Figure 6.7), and your employer will probably have a standard format or template for you to use. Most memos begin with a title such as *Memo, Memorandum,* or *Interoffice Correspondence*. Following that

Letters typically have the following elements:
- *Preprinted letterhead stationery*
- *Date*
- *Inside address*
- *Salutation*
- *Complimentary close*
- *Signature block*

Memos are usually identified by a title such as Memo or Memorandum.

FIGURE 6.7 A Typical Business Memo

This document shows the elements usually included in a formal business memo. Note that in many instances today, this information would be transmitted via e-mail instead of a printed memo.

Uses standard company memo stationery with title indicating that this is a memo

Uses four standard headings for memos

Does not begin with a salutation

Carnival

INTERNAL MEMORANDUM

DATE: June 11, 2008
TO: Lauren Eastman
FROM: Brad Lymans
SUBJECT: Capacity for Carnival Corporation Cruise Ships

Here is the capacity data you requested along with a brief explanation of the figures:

Cruise Brand	Number of Ships	Passenger Capacity	Primary Market
Carnival	15	30,020	North America
Holland America	10	13,348	North America
Costa	7	9,200	Europe
Cunard	2	2,458	Worldwide
Seabourn	6	1,614	North America
Windstar	4	756	North America
Airtours-Sun	4	4,352	Europe
Total	48	61,748	

All passenger capacities are calculated based on two passengers per cabin, even though some cabins can accommodate three or four passengers.

Cruising capacity has grown in recent years, and management expects it to continue because all the major cruise companies are planning to introduce new ships into service. Carnival Corporation will build 16 additional cruise ships over the next five years, increasing the company's passenger capacity by 36,830, which will bring the total to 98,578.

To utilize this new capacity, we must increase our share of the overall vacation market. Keep in mind that demand for cruises may be affected by (1) the strength of the countries where the ships operate; (2) political instability in areas where the ships travel; and (3) adverse incidents involving cruise ships in general.

Please let me know if you have any further questions or need any additional data.

Does not include a complimentary close or a signature block

are usually four headings: *Date, To, From,* and *Subject* (*Re:,* short for *Regarding,* is sometimes used instead of *Subject*). Memos usually don't use a salutation, complimentary close, or signature, although signing your initials next to your name on the *From* line is standard practice in most companies. Bear in mind that memos are often distributed without sealed envelopes, so they are less private than most other message formats.

PROOFREADING YOUR MESSAGE

Your credibility is affected by your attention to the details of mechanics and form.

Imagine that you're a quality inspector for a car company. As each car rolls off the assembly line, you make sure the engine runs properly, the doors close tightly, the paint shines to glossy perfection, and so on. All the work is supposedly final, but you look closely just in case. Your company's reputation is at stake, and you don't want to let a faulty product out the door.

Think of proofreading as the quality inspection stage for your documents, as your last chance to make sure that your document is ready to carry your message—and your reputation—to the intended audience. (Strictly speaking, *proofreading* is the process of inspecting a printed piece to make sure that all necessary corrections have been made, but you can benefit by approaching proofreading as an overall quality-assurance review.)

6 LEARNING OBJECTIVE

Highlight the types of errors to look for when proofreading

Look for two types of problems: (1) undetected mistakes from the writing, design, and layout stages; and (2) mistakes that crept in during production. For the first category, you can review format and layout guidelines in Appendix A on page A-1 and brush up on writing basics with "Handbook of Grammar, Mechanics, and Usage" on page H-1. The second category can include anything from computer glitches such as missing fonts or misaligned page elements to problems with the ink used in printing. Be particularly vigilant with complex documents and complex production processes that involve teams of people and multiple computers. Strange things can happen as files move from computer to computer, especially when lots of graphics and different fonts are involved.

A methodical approach to proofreading will help you find the problems that need fixing.

Far from being a casual scan up and down the page or screen, proofreading should be a methodical procedure in which you look for specific problems that may occur. Use these techniques from professional proofreaders to help ensure high-quality output:

- **Make multiple passes.** Go through the document several times, focusing on a different aspect each time. The first pass may be to look for omissions and errors in content; the second pass may be to check for typographical, grammatical, and spelling errors; and a final pass could be for layout, spacing, alignment, colors, page numbers, margins, and other design features.
- **Use perceptual tricks.** You've probably experienced the frustration of reading over something a dozen times and still missing an obvious error that was staring you right in the face. This happens because your brain has developed a wonderful skill of subconsciously supplying missing pieces and correcting mistakes when it "knows" what is supposed to be on the page. To keep your brain from tricking you, you need to trick it by changing the way you process the visual information. Try (1) reading each page backward, from the bottom to the top; (2) placing your finger under each word and reading it silently; (3) making a slit in a sheet of paper that reveals only one line of type at a time; and (4) reading the document aloud and pronouncing each word carefully.
- **Double-check high-priority items.** Double-check the spelling of names and the accuracy of dates, addresses, and any number that could cause grief if incorrect (such as telling a potential employer that you'd be happy to work for $5,000 a year when you meant to say $50,000).
- **Give yourself some distance.** If possible, don't proofread immediately after finishing the document; let your brain wander off to new topics, then come back fresh later on.
- **Be vigilant.** Avoid reading large amounts of material in one sitting, and try not to proofread when you're tired.
- **Stay focused.** Concentrate on what you're doing. Try to block out distractions, and focus as completely as possible on your proofreading task.

- **Review complex electronic documents on paper.** Some people have trouble proof-reading webpages, online reports, and other electronic documents on screen. If you have trouble, try to print the materials to review them on paper.
- **Take your time.** Quick proofreading is not careful proofreading.

The amount of time you need to spend on proofing depends on the length and complexity of the document and the situation. A typo in an e-mail message to your team may not be a big deal; but a typo in a financial report, a contract, or a medical file certainly could be serious. As with every task in the writing process, practice helps—you become not only more familiar with what errors to look for but also more skilled in identifying those errors. See "Checklist: Proofing Business Messages" for a handy list of items to review during proofing.

Plan to spend more time proofing documents that are long, complex, and important.

DISTRIBUTING YOUR MESSAGE

With the production finished, you're ready to distribute the message. As with every other aspect of business communication, your options for distribution multiply with every advance in technology. In some cases, the choice is obvious: just hit the Send button in your e-mail program, and your message is on its way. In other cases, such as when you have a 100-page report with full-color graphics or a multimedia presentation that is too big to e-mail, you'll need to plan the distribution carefully so that your message is received by everyone who needs it and only those who need it. When planning your distribution, consider the following factors:

7 LEARNING OBJECTIVE

Discuss the most important issues to consider when distributing your messages

- **Cost.** Cost won't be a concern for most messages, but for lengthy reports or multimedia production it may well be. Printing, binding, and delivering reports can be an expensive proposition, so weigh the cost versus the benefits before you decide. If you're trying to land a million-dollar client, spending $1,000 on presentation materials could be a wise investment.
- **Convenience.** How much work is involved for you and your audience? Although it's easy to attach a document to an e-mail message, things might not be so simple for the people on the other end. They may not have access to a printer, might be accessing your message from a slow wireless connection or on a handheld device with a tiny screen, or might not have the software needed to open your file. If you're sending large files as IM or e-mail attachments, consider a file-compression utility such as WinZip or StuffIt to shrink the file first. For extremely large files, see whether your audience would prefer a CD-ROM instead.
- **Time.** How soon does the message need to reach the audience? Don't waste money on overnight delivery if the recipient won't read the report for a week.

 CHECKLIST: Proofing Business Messages

A. Look for writing errors.
- Typographical mistakes
- Misspelled words
- Grammatical errors
- Punctuation mistakes

B. Look for missing elements.
- Missing text sections
- Missing exhibits (drawings, tables, photographs, charts, graphs, online images, and so on)
- Missing source notes, copyright notices, or other reference items

C. Look for design, formatting, and programming mistakes.
- Incorrect or inconsistent font selections
- Column sizing, spacing, and alignment
- Margins
- Special characters
- Clumsy line and page breaks
- Page numbers
- Page headers and footers
- Adherence to company standards
- Links (make sure they're active and link to the correct pages)
- Downloadable files (make sure they're stored in the appropriate folder)

- **Security and privacy.** The convenience offered by IM, e-mail, blogs, and other technologies needs to be weighed against security and privacy concerns. For the most sensitive documents, your company will probably restrict both the people who can receive the documents and the means you can use to distribute them. In addition, most computer users are wary of opening attachments these days. Instead of sending Word files (which are vulnerable to macro viruses and other risks), consider using Adobe Acrobat to convert your documents to PDF files.

Chapter 7 offers more advice on distributing podcasts, blogs, and other messages in electronic formats.

COMMUNICATION CHALLENGES AT MERCEDES-AMG

 You've just joined the Mercedes-AMG marketing team as a communication specialist. Your duties include creating new material for the Mercedes-AMG website and, occasionally, reviewing materials created by your colleagues. Using what you've learned in this chapter about revising for readability, clarity, and conciseness, address these challenges.[10]

Individual Challenge: You've been asked to review the following statement that concerns the protection of personal data collected from website visitors (DaimlerChrysler is the parent company of Mercedes-Benz, so its name appears in all legal documentation):

> As a worldwide leader in the automotive industry, DaimlerChrysler uses a wide variety of technical and organizational security measures in order to protect the data we have under our control. We employ these measures in order to protect against accidental or intentional manipulation, loss, or destruction. We also use these measures in order to protect said collected data against access by persons unauthorized to access such information. Of course, we constantly strive to maintain the latest and most sophisticated data protection possible, so our security procedures are continually enhanced as new technology becomes available.

Without losing any essential information, revise this statement to make it more concise (it is currently 94 words; you should be able to reduce it to no more than 50 or 60 words).

Team Challenge: In a section that discusses the history of AMG from its founding as a manufacturer of race car engines, the Mercedes-AMG website includes the following sentence: "The technology transfer from the race circuit to the road is still an integral part of the company's philosophy, which is to the benefit of every Mercedes-AMG customer." In a team with two or three other students, first study this sentence to decide what it means. Then, individually, rewrite the sentence without using the term "technology transfer." Reconvene as a team, share your individual rewrites, then decide which revision is most effective.

SUMMARY OF LEARNING OBJECTIVES

1 **Discuss the value of careful revision, and list the main tasks involved in completing a business message.** Revision is a vital step in producing effective business messages; even if the first draft conveys the necessary information, chances are it can be made tighter, clearer, and more compelling—making it more successful for you. Revision occurs throughout the writing process, again after you complete the first draft of your business message, and again after you produce the final version. Revision consists of three main tasks: (1) evaluating content, organization, style, and tone; (2) reviewing for readability and scannability; and (3) editing for clarity and conciseness. After you revise your message, you complete it by using design elements to give your message a professional look, proofreading the final version after it has been produced, and distributing it to your audience.

2 List four writing techniques you can use to improve the readability of your messages. The four techniques that improve readability are varying sentence length, keeping paragraphs short, using lists and bullets, and adding headings and subheadings. Varying sentence length helps keep your writing fresh and dynamic while giving you a chance to emphasize the most important points. Paragraphs, on the other hand, are usually best kept short to make it easier for readers to consume your information in manageable chunks. Lists and bullets are effective devices for delineating sets of items, steps in a procedure, or other collections of related information. Headings and subheadings organize your message, call attention to important information, and help readers make connections between related pieces of information.

3 Describe the steps you can take to improve the clarity of your writing. Clear writing doesn't happen the first time, so you need to revise your work. As you try to clarify your message, (1) break up overly long sentences, (2) rewrite hedging sentences, (3) impose parallelism, (4) correct dangling modifiers, (5) reword long noun sequences, (6) replace camouflaged verbs, (7) clarify sentence structure, (8) clarify awkward references, and (9) moderate your enthusiasm.

4 Discuss why it's important to make your message more concise, and give four tips on how to do so. Businesspeople are more likely to read documents that give information efficiently. So to make business messages more concise, try to include only necessary material and write clean sentences by (1) deleting unnecessary words and phrases, (2) shortening overly long words and phrases, (3) eliminating redundancies, and (4) recasting sentences that begin with "It is" and "There are."

5 Explain how design elements help determine the effectiveness of your documents. White space provides contrast and gives readers a resting point. Margins define the space around the text and contribute to the amount of white space. Typefaces influence the tone of the message. Type styles provide contrast or emphasis. When selecting and applying design elements, you can ensure their effectiveness by being consistent throughout your document; balancing your space between text, art, and white space; showing restraint in the number of elements you use; and paying attention to every detail.

6 Highlight the types of errors to look for when proofreading. When proofreading the final version of your document, always keep an eye out for errors in grammar, usage, and punctuation. In addition, watch for spelling errors and typos. Make sure that nothing is missing (whether a source note, an exhibit, or text). Correct design errors such as elements that appear in the wrong typeface, elements that appear in the wrong type style, misaligned elements (columns in a table, exhibits on a page, etc.), and graphic characters (such as ampersands and percent signs) that appear in both symbol and spelled-out form. Look for typographical errors such as uneven spacing between lines and words, a short line of type at the top of a page, a heading at the bottom of a page, or incorrect hyphenation. In addition, make sure your layout conforms to company guidelines.

7 Discuss the most important issues to consider when distributing your messages. Consider cost, convenience, time, security, and privacy when choosing the method to distribute your messages. Cost isn't a major issue for most messages, although production, printing, and distribution of lengthy or complex reports can be a concern. In general, balance the cost with the importance and urgency of the message. Make sure the distribution method is convenient for your audience; it might be easy for you to simply attach a document to an e-mail message, but that might not be the best approach for a given audience. As with cost, balance the time factor with your needs and the needs of your audience. Lastly, consider security and privacy issues before distributing documents that contain sensitive or confidential information.

Test Your Knowledge

1. What are the three main tasks involved in revising a business message?
2. How can you increase the readability of your paragraphs?
3. What functions do headings serve?
4. What are some ways you can make a document more concise?
5. What computer tools can you use when revising messages?
6. What is parallel construction, and why is it important?
7. Why is it a good idea to use verbs instead of noun phrases?
8. How do readers benefit from white space?
9. Why is proofreading an important part of the writing process?
10. What factors should you consider when choosing a distribution method for your messages?

Apply Your Knowledge

1. Why is it helpful to put your first draft aside for a while before you begin the editing process?
2. Given the choice of only one, would you prefer to use a grammar checker or a spell checker? Why?
3. Why is it important to spend extra time reviewing and polishing the beginning and ending of a message?
4. Which distribution method would you choose for a highly confidential strategic planning report that needs to be sent to top executives at six locations in North America, Asia, and Europe? Explain your choice.
5. **Ethical Choices** What are the ethical implications of murky, complex writing in a document explaining how customers can appeal the result of a decision made in the company's favor during a dispute?

Practice Your Knowledge

Message for Analysis

Read the following messages, then (1) analyze the strengths and weaknesses of each sentence and (2) revise each document so that it follows the guidelines in Chapters 4 through 6.

Message 6.A

As an organization, the North American Personal Motorsports Marketing Association has committed ourselves to helping our members—a diverse group comprising of dealers of motorcycles, all-terrain vehicles, Snowmobiles, and personal watercraft—achieve their business objectives. Consequently, our organization, which usually goes under the initials NAPMMA, has the following aims, goals, and objectives. Firstly, we endeavor to aid or assist our members in reaching their business objectives. Second, NAPMMA communicates ("lobbying" in slang terms) with local, state, and national governmental agencies and leaders on issues of importance to our members. And lastly, we educate the motorsports public, that being current motorsports vehicle owners, and prospective owners of said vehicles, on the safe and enjoyable operation of they're vehicles.

Message 6.B

Dear Ms. Giraud:

Enclosed herewith please find the manuscript for your book, *Careers in Woolgathering*. After perusing the first two chapters of your 1,500-page manuscript, I was forced to conclude that the subject matter, handicrafts and artwork using wool fibers, is not coincident with the publishing program of Framingham Press, which to this date has issued only works on business endeavors, avoiding all other topics completely.

Although our firm is unable to consider your impressive work at the present time, I have taken the liberty of recording some comments on some of the pages. I am of the opinion that any feedback that a writer can obtain from those well versed in the publishing realm can only serve to improve the writer's authorial skills.

In view of the fact that your residence is in the Boston area, might I suggest that you secure an appointment with someone of high editorial stature at the Cambridge Heritage Press, which I believe might have something of an interest in works of the nature you have produced.

Wishing you the best of luck in your literary endeavors, I remain

Arthur J. Cogswell

Editor

Exercises

For active links to all websites discussed in this chapter, visit this text's website at **www.prenhall.com/bovee**. Locate your book and click on its Companion Website link. Then select Chapter 6, and click on "Featured Websites." Locate the name of the page or the URL related to the material in the text. Please note that links to sites that become inactive after publication of the book will be removed from the Featured Websites section.

6.1   Message Readability: Writing Paragraphs Rewrite the following paragraph to vary the length of the sentences and to shorten the paragraph so it looks more inviting to readers.

> Although major league baseball remains popular, more people are attending minor league baseball games because they can spend less on admission, snacks, and parking and still enjoy the excitement of America's pastime. Connecticut, for example, has three AA minor league teams, including the New Haven Ravens, who are affiliated with the St. Louis Cardinals; the Norwich Navigators, who are affiliated with the New York Yankees; and the New Britain Rock Cats, who are affiliated with the Minnesota Twins. These teams play in relatively small stadiums, so fans are close enough to see and hear everything, from the swing of the bat connecting with the ball to the thud of the ball landing in the outfielder's glove. Best of all, the cost of a family outing to see rising stars play in a local minor league game is just a fraction of what the family would spend to attend a major league game in a much larger, more crowded stadium.

6.2   Message Readability: Using Bullets Rewrite the following paragraph using a parallel bulleted list and one introductory sentence:

> Our forensic accounting services provide the insights needed to resolve disputes, recover losses, and manage risk intelligently. One of our areas of practice is insurance claims accounting and preparation services, designed to help you maximize recovery of insured value. Another practice area is dispute advisory, in which we can assist with discovery, expert witness testimony, and economic analysis. A third practice: construction consulting. This service helps our clients understand why large-scale construction projects fail to meet schedule or budget requirements. Fourth, we offer general investigative and forensic accounting services, including fraud detection and proof of loss analysis.[11]

6.3   Revising Messages: Clarity Break these sentences into shorter ones by adding more periods:

  a. The next time you write something, check your average sentence length in a 100-word passage, and if your sentences average more than 16 to 20 words, see whether you can break up some of the sentences.

  b. Don't do what the village blacksmith did when he instructed his apprentice as follows: "When I take the shoe out of the fire, I'll lay it on the anvil, and when I nod my head, you hit it with the hammer." The apprentice did just as he was told, and now he's the village blacksmith.

  c. Unfortunately, no gadget will produce excellent writing, but using a yardstick like the Fog Index gives us some guideposts to follow for making writing easier to read because its two factors remind us to use short sentences and simple words.

d. Know the flexibility of the written word and its power to convey an idea, and know how to make your words behave so that your readers will understand.

e. Words mean different things to different people, and a word such as *block* may mean city block, butcher block, engine block, auction block, or several other things.

6.4 Revising Messages: Conciseness Cross out unnecessary words in the following phrases:

a. Consensus of opinion
b. New innovations
c. Long period of time
d. At a price of $50
e. Still remains

6.5 Revising Messages: Conciseness Revise the following sentences, using shorter, simpler words:

a. The antiquated calculator is ineffectual for solving sophisticated problems.
b. It is imperative that the pay increments be terminated before an inordinate deficit is accumulated.
c. There was unanimity among the executives that Ms. Jackson's idiosyncrasies were cause for a mandatory meeting with the company's personnel director.
d. The impending liquidation of the company's assets was cause for jubilation among the company's competitors.
e. The expectations of the president for a stock dividend were accentuated by the preponderance of evidence that the company was in good financial condition.

6.6 Revising Messages: Conciseness Use infinitives as substitutes for the overly long phrases in these sentences:

a. For living, I require money.
b. They did not find sufficient evidence for believing in the future.
c. Bringing about the destruction of a dream is tragic.

6.7 Revising Messages: Conciseness Rephrase the following in fewer words:

a. In the near future
b. In the event that
c. In order that
d. For the purpose of
e. With regard to
f. It may be that
g. In very few cases
h. With reference to
i. At the present time
j. There is no doubt that

6.8 Revising Messages: Conciseness Condense these sentences to as few words as possible:

a. We are of the conviction that writing is important.
b. In all probability, we're likely to have a price increase.
c. Our goals include making a determination about that in the near future.
d. When all is said and done at the conclusion of this experiment, I'd like to summarize the final windup.
e. After a trial period of three weeks, during which time she worked for a total of 15 full working days, we found her work was sufficiently satisfactory so that we offered her full-time work.

6.9 Revising Messages: Modifiers Remove all the unnecessary modifiers from these sentences:

a. Tremendously high pay increases were given to the extraordinarily skilled and extremely conscientious employees.
b. The union's proposals were highly inflationary, extremely demanding, and exceptionally bold.

6.10 Revising Messages: Hedging Rewrite these sentences so that they no longer contain any hedging:

a. It would appear that someone apparently entered illegally.
b. It may be possible that sometime in the near future the situation is likely to improve.
c. Your report seems to suggest that we might be losing money.
d. I believe Nancy apparently has somewhat greater influence over employees in the e-marketing department.
e. It seems as if this letter of resignation means you might be leaving us.

6.11 Revising Messages: Indefinite Starters Rewrite these sentences to eliminate the indefinite starters:

a. There are several examples here to show that Elaine can't hold a position very long.
b. It would be greatly appreciated if every employee would make a generous contribution to Mildred Cook's retirement party.
c. It has been learned in Washington today from generally reliable sources that an important announcement will be made shortly by the White House.
d. There is a rule that states that we cannot work overtime without permission.
e. It would be great if you could work late for the next three Saturdays.

6.12 Revising Messages: Parallelism Present the ideas in these sentences in parallel form:

a. Mr. Hill is expected to lecture three days a week, to counsel two days a week, and must write for publication in his spare time.
b. She knows not only accounting, but she also reads Latin.
c. Both applicants had families, college degrees, and were in their thirties, with considerable accounting experience but few social connections.
d. This book was exciting, well written, and held my interest.
e. Don is both a hard worker and he knows bookkeeping.

6.13 Revising Messages: Awkward References Revise the following sentences to delete the awkward references:

a. The vice president in charge of sales and the production manager are responsible for the keys to 34A and 35A, respectively.
b. The keys to 34A and 35A are in executive hands, with the former belonging to the vice president in charge of sales and the latter belonging to the production manager.
c. The keys to 34A and 35A have been given to the production manager, with the aforementioned keys being gold embossed.

d. A laser printer and an inkjet printer were delivered to John and Megan, respectively.

e. The walnut desk is more expensive than the oak desk, the former costing $300 more than the latter.

6.14 Revising Messages: Dangling Modifiers Rewrite these sentences to clarify the dangling modifiers:

a. Running down the railroad tracks in a cloud of smoke, we watched the countryside glide by.

b. Lying on the shelf, Ruby saw the seashell.

c. Based on the information, I think we should buy the property.

d. Being cluttered and filthy, Sandy took the whole afternoon to clean up her desk.

e. After proofreading every word, the memo was ready to be signed.

6.15 Revising Messages: Noun Sequences Rewrite the following sentences to eliminate the long strings of nouns:

a. The focus of the meeting was a discussion of the bank interest rate deregulation issue.

b. Following the government task force report recommendations, we are revising our job applicant evaluation procedures.

c. The production department quality assurance program components include employee training, supplier cooperation, and computerized detection equipment.

d. The supermarket warehouse inventory reduction plan will be implemented next month.

e. The State University business school graduate placement program is one of the best in the country.

6.16 Revising Messages: Sentence Structure Rearrange the following sentences to bring the subjects closer to their verbs:

a. Trudy, when she first saw the bull pawing the ground, ran.

b. It was Terri who, according to Ted, who is probably the worst gossip in the office (Tom excepted), mailed the wrong order.

c. William Oberstreet, in his book *Investment Capital Reconsidered*, writes of the mistakes that bankers through the decades have made.

d. Judy Schimmel, after passing up several sensible investment opportunities, despite the warnings of her friends and family, invested her inheritance in a jojoba plantation.

e. The president of U-Stor-It, which was on the brink of bankruptcy after the warehouse fire, the worst tragedy in the history of the company, prepared a press announcement.

6.17 Revising Messages: Camouflaged Verbs Rewrite each sentence so that the verbs are no longer camouflaged:

a. Adaptation to the new rules was performed easily by the employees.

b. The assessor will make a determination of the tax due.

c. Verification of the identity of the employees must be made daily.

d. The board of directors made a recommendation that Mr. Ronson be assigned to a new division.

e. The auditing procedure on the books was performed by the vice president.

6.18 Producing Messages: Design Elements Review a copy of the syllabus your instructor provided for this course. Which design elements were used to improve readability? Can you identify ways to make the document easier to read or more user friendly in general? Create your own version, experimenting with different design elements and design choices. How do your changes affect readability? Exchange documents with another student and critique each other's work.

6.19 Web Design Visit the stock market page of Bloomberg's website at **www.bloomberg.com** and evaluate the use of design in presenting the latest news. What design improvements can you suggest to enhance readability of the information posted on this page?

6.20 Teamwork Team up with another student and exchange your revised versions of Message 6.A or Message 6.B (see exercises under "Messages for Analysis"). Review the assignment to be sure the instructions are clear. Then read and critique your teammate's revision to see whether it can be improved. After you have critiqued each other's work, take a moment to examine the way you expressed your comments and the way you felt listening to the other student's comments. Can you identify ways to improve the critiquing process in situations such as this?

6.21 Proofreading Messages: E-Mail Proofread the following e-mail message and revise it to correct any problems you find:

Our final company orrientation of the year will be held on Dec. 20. In preparation for this sesssion, please order 20 copies of the Policy handbook, the confidentiality agreenemt, the employee benefits Manual, please let me know if you anticipate any delays in obtaining these materials.

6.22 Ethical Choices The time and energy required for careful revision can often benefit you or your company directly, such as by increasing the probability that website visitors will buy your products. But what about situations in which the quality of your writing and revision work really doesn't stand to benefit you directly? For instance, assume you are putting a notice on your website informing the local community about some upcoming construction to your manufacturing plant. The work will disrupt traffic for nearly a year and generate a significant amount of noise and air pollution, but knowing the specific dates and times of various construction activities will allow people to adjust their commutes and other activities to minimize the negative impact on their daily lives. However, your company does not sell products in the local area, so the people affected by all this are not potential customers. Moreover, providing accurate information to the surrounding community and updating it as the project progresses will take time away from your other job responsibilities. Do you have an ethical obligation to keep the local community informed with accurate, up-to-date information? Why or why not?

Expand Your Knowledge

Exploring the Best of the Web

Write It Right: Tips to Help You Rethink and Revise
www.powa.org
Are you sure that readers perceive your written message as you intended? If you want help revising a message that you're completing, use the Paradigm Online Writing Assistant (POWA). With this interactive writer's guide, you can select topics to get tips on how to edit your work, reshape your thoughts, and rewrite for clarity. Read discussions about perfecting your writing skills, complete one of the many online activities provided to reinforce what you've learned, or join the Forum to talk about writing. At POWA's website, you'll learn how to improve the final draft of your message. Explore POWA's advice, then answer the following questions:

1. Why is it better to write out ideas in a rough format and later reread your message to revise its content? When revising your message, what questions can you ask about your writing?
2. Name the four elements of the "writing context." Imagine that you're the reader of your message. What questions might you ask?
3. When you revise a written message, what is the purpose of "tightening"? What is one way to tighten your writing as you complete a message?

Surfing Your Way to Career Success

Bovée and Thill's Business Communication Resources offers links to hundreds of online resources that can help you with this course, your other college courses, and your career. Visit **www. buscommresources.com**, then click on "Business Communication Web Directory." The "Interpersonal" section connects you to a variety of websites and articles on effective questions, interpersonal dialogs, listening, and feedback. Identify three websites from this section that could be useful in your business career. For each site, write a two-sentence summary of what the site offers and how it could help you launch and build your career.

Learn Interactively

Interactive Study Guide

Visit **www.prenhall.com/bovee**, then locate your book and click on its "Companion Website" link. Select Chapter 6 to take advantage of the interactive "Chapter Quiz" to test your knowledge of chapter concepts. Receive instant feedback on whether you need additional studying. Also, visit the "Study Hall," where you'll find an abundance of valuable resources that will help you succeed in this course.

Peak Performance Grammar and Mechanics

If your instructor has required the use of "Peak Performance Grammar and Mechanics," either in your online course or on CD, you can improve your skill with prepositions, conjunctions, and articles by using the "Peak Performance Grammar and Mechanics" module. Click on "Grammar Basics," then click "Prepositions, Conjunctions, and Articles." Take the Pretest to determine whether you have any weak areas. Then review those areas in the Refresher Course. Take the Follow-Up Test to check your grasp of prepositions, conjunctions, and articles. For an extra challenge or advanced practice, take the Advanced Test. Finally, for additional reinforcement in prepositions, conjunctions, and articles, visit the Companion Website, click on any chapter, then click on "Improve Your Grammar, Mechanics, and Usage."

PART 3

Crafting Brief Messages

Crafting Messages for Electronic Media

LEARNING OBJECTIVES

After studying this chapter, you will be able to

1 Compare the strengths and weaknesses of the print and electronic media available for short messages

2 Explain how overuse of e-mail can reduce productivity

3 Identify the qualities of an effective e-mail subject line

4 Identify guidelines for successful instant messaging (IM) in the workplace

5 Describe the role of blogging in business communication today

6 Explain why identifying your audience, purpose, and scope is vital to successful blogging

7 Explain how to adapt the three-step writing process for podcasts

8 Describe the syndication process and explain how it helps you distribute blog and podcast content

COMMUNICATION CLOSE-UP AT BOEING COMMERCIAL AIRPLANES

www.boeing.com/randy

"Take down your blog. You embarrass us, everyone who reads it, and you make the world a dumber place." Ouch.

Probably not the reaction Randy Baseler anticipated when he joined the ranks of executive bloggers. As vice president of marketing for Boeing Commercial Airplanes, Baseler is one of the company's primary communicators with external audiences, and he figured a blog would be a good way to share his thoughts on the commercial airline industry.

The reaction from blog readers was less than complimentary, to put it mildly. Some criticized the fact that *Randy's Journal* had no features to let visitors sign up for automated delivery of new material, search the archives, or leave comments. Others criticized the style and tone of his writing, dismissing it as nothing more than "marketing spin." Some objected to the fact that it looked too "slick." In Baseler's own words, he got "hammered" by criticism of all kinds, and not all of it constructive.

Boeing's Randy Baseler listened and responded to criticism about his initial blogging efforts; his blog is now one of the most widely read in the aerospace industry.

Baseler listened, learned—and changed. Within a few months, he relaunched the blog with a new design that included the missing features. To his credit, his first post on the new-look blog addressed the criticism directly, and he even displayed some of the most stinging attacks (including the aforementioned quotation) in his post. Some observers noted that he also began to develop a voice that was more "real," more personal and conversational.

However, he didn't respond as every critic might have liked. For instance, he doesn't display every comment read-ers leave on the blog but instead offers a selection of both positive and negative reactions. He also didn't start sharing industry gossip or bashing his employer, which seemed to have been expectations expressed by some critics. As Baseler puts it, "I happen to like the fact that I work for Boeing." By listening to his audience and responding thoughtfully, Baseler and his team developed what is now a widely read and widely respected information source in the aviation industry.[1]

CHOOSING ELECTRONIC MEDIA FOR BRIEF MESSAGES

You now have multiple options for sending short messages:
* *Printed memos and letters*
* *E-mail messages*
* *Instant messages*
* *Text messages*
* *Blog postings*
* *Podcasts*

In recent years, the options for sending short business messages have expanded considerably, from traditional printed memos and letters to a variety of electronic formats, including blogs like Randy Baseler's (profiled in the chapter-opening Communication Close-Up). Don't be surprised if you continue to encounter new media options on the job, too. Whenever a new communication technology appears, creative businesspeople usually find a way to apply it to business challenges.

Here are the short-message media you are likely to encounter on the job in the next few years:

* **Memos and letters.** Printed memos (for internal communication) and letters (for external communication) have been primary communication vehicles for hundreds of years. In many companies, however, e-mail and other electronic media have largely replaced traditional printed memos. Letters are still used often for external communication with customers, but electronic media are replacing many letters as well. Both memos and letters can be distributed via fax machines, in addition to hand delivery and postal services. For more on formatting printed letters and memos, see Chapter 6 and Appendix A.
* **E-mail.** The high speed and low cost of e-mail make it an attractive alternative to printed messages, and in fact e-mail is now a primary medium for most companies. However, as technologies continue to evolve and users tire of fighting the flood of spam, viruses, and other problems related to e-mail, this medium is in turn being replaced in many instances by instant messaging, blogging, wikis (see Chapter 2), and other tools that provide better support for instant communication and real-time collaboration.
* **Instant messaging (IM).** After consumers around the world began to adopt IM as a faster and simpler alternative to e-mail, businesses weren't far behind; computer-based IM usage now rivals e-mail in many companies. IM offers even greater speed than e-mail as well as simple operation and—so far at least—fewer problems with unwanted messages or security and privacy problems.
* **Text messaging.** Phone-based text messaging offers the near-instantaneous communication of IM, with the added advantage of almost universal portability. Of course, small screen sizes and the lack of a regular keyboard on most phone devices do make text messaging somewhat less convenient than computer-based IM. Text messaging is just beginning to make inroads into business communication, with marketing messages as one of the first applications.[2]
* **Blogs.** Blogs are another great example of how businesses quickly adopt technologies that promise more efficient and effective communication. From internal communica-

Text messaging is beginning to take off as an advertising and customer communication medium, although it is still not nearly as widespread in business as computer-based instant messaging.

tion among small teams to executive blogs such as Randy Baseler's with thousands of regular readers, blogs are now a common feature in business communication. The ability to update content quickly and easily makes blogs a natural whenever communicators need to get messages out in a hurry; bloggers can also publish information to vast audiences with relatively little effort. Perhaps the biggest downside of blogs is the sheer number of them—millions, in fact, with more created virtually every minute—making it a challenge for individual bloggers to stand out from the crowd.

- **Podcasts.** You may be familiar with podcasts as the online equivalent of recorded radio or video broadcasts (video podcasts are often called *vidcasts* or *vodcasts*). Businesses are now using podcasts to replace or supplement conference calls, training courses, and other communication activities. (Note that although the term *podcast* was derived from *iPod*, podcasts are in no way restricted to Apple's digital music players. Any device capable of playing the audio or video file, including computers, PDAs, many phones, and who-knows-what new devices in the future, can play podcasts.) Podcasts offer a simple way for anyone to publish audio or video messages. They do require more work to create than blogs, and high-quality podcasts require both a modest set of specialized equipment and plenty of network bandwidth.

Carleton University in Ottawa, Ontario, Canada, reaches students all over the world with its lecture vodcasts.

While most of your communication is likely to be via electronic means, don't automatically dismiss the benefits of printed messages. Here are several good reasons for using a printed message over electronic alternatives:

- **When you want to make a formal impression.** For special messages, such as sending congratulations or condolences, the formality of printed documents usually makes them a much better choice than electronic messages.
- **When you need to accompany products or other items that you are physically sending to someone.** If you're mailing brochures or shipping products, for example, a printed letter is a great way to accompany the delivery with a short message to the recipient.
- **When you want to stand out from the flood of electronic messages.** Ironically, the rapid growth of electronic messages creates an opportunity for printed memos and letters. If your audience's computers are overflowing with e-mail, IM, and newsfeeds, a printed message could stand out enough to get noticed.
- **When you are legally required to provide information in printed form.** Business contracts and government regulations sometimes require information to be provided on paper. The laws that cover such disclosures continue to evolve, so make sure you consult with your firm's legal staff if you're not sure.

Consider printed messages when you want to create a more formal impression, to accompany other physical material, to stand out from electronic messages, or when you are legally or contractually required to do so.

Obviously, if your audience doesn't have access to electronic media or you don't have the necessary e-mail or IM addresses, you'll need to use a printed message.

The following sections offer advice on using e-mail, IM, blogging, and podcasting for business communication. And for a brief look at some of the other interesting communication technologies you may encounter on the job, see "Connecting with Technology: More Ways to Spread the Message."

CREATING EFFECTIVE E-MAIL MESSAGES

Chances are you already have quite a bit of experience using e-mail, but e-mail in the workplace is a more formal medium than you are probably accustomed to for personal communication (see Figure 7.1). Consequently, it's important to approach e-mail as a professional communication medium that uses an important company resource, as explained in the following section.

Treating E-Mail as a Professional Communication Medium

Perhaps the most important single point to recognize about e-mail in the workplace is that the nature of business e-mail is dramatically different from that of personal e-mail. The expectations of writing quality are higher, and the consequences of bad writing or

Business e-mail messages are more formal than the e-mail messages you send to family and friends.

FIGURE 7.1 E-Mail for Business Communication

In this response to an e-mail query from a colleague, Elaine Burgman takes advantage of her e-mail system's features to create an efficient and effective message.

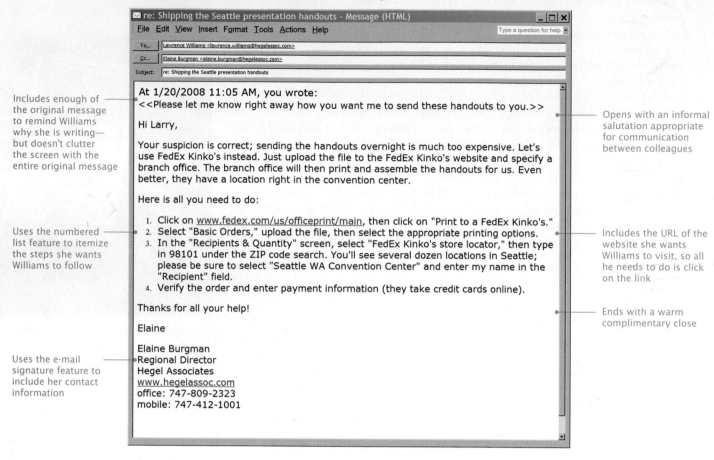

Includes enough of the original message to remind Williams why she is writing—but doesn't clutter the screen with the entire original message

Uses the numbered list feature to itemize the steps she wants Williams to follow

Uses the e-mail signature feature to include her contact information

Opens with an informal salutation appropriate for communication between colleagues

Includes the URL of the website she wants Williams to visit, so all he needs to do is click on the link

Ends with a warm complimentary close

E-mail presents considerable legal hazards, and many companies now have formal e-mail policies.

poor judgment in the use of e-mail can be much more serious. For example, e-mail and other electronic documents have the same legal weight as printed documents. In numerous instances in recent years, e-mail and other electronic message forms have been used as evidence in lawsuits and criminal investigations involving everything from sexual harassment to financial fraud.[3]

The legal hazards of inappropriate e-mail are only one of the serious risks that e-mail presents. Other concerns include the possibility of disclosing confidential information and exposing company networks to security problems. To minimize the potential for trouble, many companies now have formal e-mail policies that specify how employees can use e-mail, including restrictions against personal use of company e-mail service and sending material that might be deemed objectionable. More than a quarter of U.S. employers have terminated employees for misuse of company e-mail systems, according to one recent survey.[4] In addition, roughly the same percentage of employers now monitor internal e-mail, and half of them monitor incoming and outgoing e-mail. This monitoring can involve both automated scans using software programmed to look for sensitive content and manual scans in which selected e-mail messages are actually read by security staff.[5]

Of course, company e-mail policies are effective only if employees are diligent about following them. Every e-mail user has a responsibility to avoid actions that could cause trouble, from downloading virus-injected software to sending objectionable photographs. *E-mail hygiene* refers to all the efforts that companies are making to keep e-mail clean and safe—from spam blocking and virus protection to content filtering.[6] Make sure you understand what your employer expects from you, and follow those guidelines.

Connecting with Technology

More Ways to Spread the Message

Businesses invest significant amounts of money in technologies designed to improve both internal and external communication. In some instances, technologies such as *electronic data interchange* and its newer web-based equivalents replace the human element in the communication process. In others, technology attempts to enhance human communication by increasing mobility, lowering cost, improving responsiveness, or creating new capabilities. Here are some of the more intriguing communication-enhancement technologies:

- **Voice synthesis and recognition.** The human voice will always be central to business communication, but that doesn't mean two human beings are required for every conversation. *Voice synthesis* regenerates a human speaking voice from computer files that represent words or parts of words. *Voice recognition* converts human speech to computer-compatible data. Both technologies continue to improve every year, with richer vocabularies and more human-sounding voices.

- **Virtual agents.** *Virtual agents*, also known as *bots* (derived from *robot*), are a class of automated tools that perform a variety of communication tasks, such as answering customer service questions and responding to requests for electronic documents. They can function in either voice-based (over the telephone) or text-based environments (via IM or text messaging).

- **Mobile communication.** If you're accustomed to studying on the go, you'll fit right into today's untethered work environment. In some cases, mobile workers don't even have traditional offices, using temporary cubicles at work, home offices, cars, airports, and even new Internet-equipped airplanes for office space. Geographic data from the **global positioning system (GPS)** are also creating new forms of mobile communication, such as location-based advertising (getting an advertisement on your cell phone from a store you're walking past, for instance) and remote monitoring of medical patients and trucking fleets.

- **Networking advances.** You might already be using some of the new networking technologies that help businesspeople communicate and collaborate. **Peer-to-peer (P2P) computing** lets multiple PCs communicate directly so that they can share files or work on large problems simultaneously. **Wireless networking** extends the reach of the Internet through the commonly used *Wi-Fi* technology for local area networks and the emerging *Wi-MAX* standard, which can cover entire metropolitan areas.

CAREER APPLICATIONS

1. Have you ever encountered a bot or a voice-recognition system when you expected to reach a fellow human being (such as reaching a voice-response system when you telephoned a business)? Describe the situation and purpose of your "conversation." Were you satisfied with the outcome of the conversation? Why or why not?

2. What are the ethical implications of using GPS to track the movement of employees such as truck drivers?

Adapting the Three-Step Process for Successful E-Mail

E-mail messages can range from simple one-paragraph memos to multipage reports, but the three-step writing process can help you in every instance. With practice, you'll be able to complete the various planning, writing, and completing tasks in a manner of minutes for most messages—which will be a significant benefit to your career. In addition to the skills you've practiced in Chapter 4 through Chapter 6, apply the guidelines in the following sections.

Planning E-Mail Messages

The ease of e-mail communication is its greatest strength—and its greatest weakness. Because sending e-mail is so easy, it is often overused and misused. Consequently, attention to e-mail etiquette is essential, and that starts in the planning stage. Most important, make sure every e-mail you send is necessary so that you don't contribute to the deluge of messages of dubious importance. Many busy professionals now struggle to keep up with the flow of e-mail messages—some report receiving as many as 50 messages an hour from colleagues and clients.[7] The flood of messages from an expanding array of electronic sources can significantly impact employees' ability to focus on their work. In one recent study, in fact, workers exposed to a constant barrage of e-mail, IM, and phone calls experienced an average

2 LEARNING OBJECTIVE

Explain how overuse of e-mail can reduce productivity

Attention to etiquette is vital with e-mail communication.

TABLE 7.1 Tips for Effective E-Mail Messages

TIP	WHY IT'S IMPORTANT
When you request information or action, make it clear what you're asking for, why it's important, and how soon you need it; don't make your reader write back for details.	People will be tempted to ignore your messages if they're not clear about what you want or how soon you want it.
When responding to a request, either paraphrase the request or include enough of the original message to remind the reader what you're replying to.	Some businesspeople get hundreds of e-mail messages a day and may need reminding what your specific response is about.
If possible, avoid sending long, complex messages via e-mail.	Long messages are easier to read as printed reports or web content.
Adjust the level of formality to the message and the audience.	Overly formal messages to colleagues are perceived as stuffy and distant; overly informal messages to customers or top executives are perceived as disrespectful.
Activate a signature file, which automatically pastes your contact information into every message you create.	Saves you the trouble of retyping vital information and ensures that recipients know how to reach you through other means.
Don't let unread messages pile up in your in-basket.	You'll miss important information and create the impression that you're ignoring other people.
Never type in all caps.	ALL CAPS ARE INTERPRETED AS SCREAMING.
Don't overformat your messages with background colors, colored type, unusual fonts, and so on.	Such messages can be difficult and annoying to read on screen.
Remember that messages can be forwarded anywhere and saved forever.	Don't let a moment of anger or poor judgment haunt you for the rest of your career.
Use the "return receipt requested" feature only for the most critical messages.	This feature triggers a message back to you whenever someone receives or opens your message; many consider this an invasion of privacy.
Make sure your computer has up-to-date virus protection.	One of the worst breaches of "netiquette" is unknowingly infecting other computers because you haven't bothered to protect your own system.
Pay attention to grammar, spelling, and capitalization.	Some people don't think e-mail needs formal rules, but careless messages make you look unprofessional and can annoy readers.
Use acronyms sparingly.	Shorthand such as IMHO (in my humble opinion) and LOL (laughing out loud) can be useful in informal correspondence with colleagues, but don't use them in other messages.

10-point drop in their functioning IQ.[8] You can help keep electronic messages from causing problems in your organization by following the tips in Table 7.1.

When analyzing your audience, think twice before sending copies to multiple recipients with the "cc" (courtesy copy) function. Let's say you send a message to your boss and cc five colleagues, simply because you want them to see that you're giving the boss some good information. Those five people now not only have to read your message but might also feel compelled to reply so that the boss doesn't think they're being negligent. Then everyone will start replying to *those* replies, and on and on. What should have been a single message exchange between you and your boss quickly turns into a flurry of messages that wastes everybody's time.

Conversely, as a manager, make sure that your e-mail habits don't cause productivity problems for your staff. For example, assume you hear about a new competitor and send a message to your entire team that includes "Let's look into this" without specifying who should do the investigation or what you want to know. Chances are, several people will drop

As a manager, make sure your e-mail habits don't inadvertently cause productivity problems for your employees.

what they're doing and start looking into the situation. As a result, they won't get their other work done, they'll overlap efforts, and they may not even find what you want to know, because you haven't been specific.

Finally, be sure to respect the chain of command. In many companies, any employee can e-mail anyone else, including the president and CEO. However, take care that you don't abuse this freedom. For instance, when corresponding with superiors, don't send an e-mail complaint straight to the top just because it's easy to do so. Your e-mail will usually be more effective if you follow the organizational hierarchy and give each person a chance to address the situation in turn.

Writing E-Mail Messages

Too many people, particularly younger professionals accustomed to using e-mail (and IM, text messaging, and blogging) for personal communication, assume that the usual standards and expectations of business communication don't apply to e-mail. Some seasoned businesspeople even advocate a general disregard for punctuation, grammar, spelling, and other conventions in e-mail writing because paying attention to such details takes too much time.

Granted, you don't need to compose perfect works of literature to inform people that lunch will be served in the conference room, but as a general rule, the time you might save with careless e-mail writing won't make up for the damage it can do to your career.[9] First, haphazard planning and sloppy writing may require less time for writers, but they usually demand *more* time from readers who are forced to dig the meaning out of misspelled words, confusing sentences, and disjointed paragraphs. Second, people who care about effective communication—a group that includes most senior executives, the people who often decide whether you'll get promoted and how much you'll get paid—often judge the quality of your *work* by the quality of your *writing*. Third, at the click of somebody else's mouse, e-mail messages can travel to places you never imagined, including the CEO's computer screen, a newspaper, a lawyer's office, or any number of websites and blogs. Always assume that whatever you write in an e-mail message could end up in places you might never have imagined.

Writing Effective Subject Lines The subject line in an e-mail might seem like a minor detail, but it's actually one of the most important parts of every e-mail message because it helps recipients decide which messages to read and when to read them. Missing or poorly written subject lines often result in messages being deleted without even being opened. To capture your audience's attention, make sure your subject line is both informative and compelling. Describing or classifying your message content is important, but you can go beyond that as well. Use the opportunity to build interest with keywords, quotations, directions, or questions:[10]

INEFFECTIVE SUBJECT LINE	EFFECTIVE SUBJECT LINE
July sales results	July sales results: good news and bad news
Tomorrow's meeting	Bring consultant's report to Friday's meeting
Marketing reports	Marketing reports are due Monday morning
Employee parking	Revised resurfacing schedule for parking lot
Status report	Website redesign falling behind schedule

Consider the first of these examples. "July sales results" accurately describes the content of the message, but "July sales results: good news and bad news" is more intriguing. Readers will want to know why some news is good and some is bad. "Status report" doesn't even specify which project the report is about, whereas "Website redesign falling behind schedule" both identifies the project and alerts people to a problem.

If you and someone else are replying back and forth based on the same original message, periodically modify the subject line of your message to reflect the revised message content. Most e-mail programs will copy the subject line when you click on Reply, so you need only revise it. When numerous messages have identical subject lines, trying to find a particular one can be confusing and frustrating. For instance, if you come up with a solution to the scheduling problem on the website redesign project, modify the subject line to read something like "Website redesign: staffing solution" so that people can find that specific message when they need to.

3 LEARNING OBJECTIVE

Identify the qualities of an effective e-mail subject line

A poorly written subject line could mean that a message will be deleted or ignored.

Keep your emotions in check when you compose e-mail messages; flaming can damage relationships—and your reputation.

Keeping Your Emotions Under Control Never let your emotions get the best of you when you're composing e-mail. A message that contains insensitive, insulting, or critical comments is called a *flame*. If you're upset about something or angry with someone, compose yourself before composing your e-mail. If you're fuming, cool off before writing your e-mail message. If you do write an emotionally charged message, let it sit for at least a day. Ask yourself two questions: First, "Would I say this to my audience face to face?" And second, "Am I comfortable with this message becoming a permanent part of the company's communication history?" Remember that a living, breathing human being is on the receiving end of your communication—and that your message can be forwarded easily and stored forever.

Completing E-Mail Messages

The revision, production, and proofing you've studied earlier all apply to e-mail messages. Again, don't let the speed and simplicity of e-mail lull you into thinking that careless writing is acceptable. Particularly for important messages, a few moments of revising and proofing might save you hours of headaches and damage control. Also, lean in favor of simplicity when it comes to producing your e-mail messages. A clean, easily readable font, in black on a white background, is sufficient for nearly all e-mail messages.

Take advantage of your e-mail system's ability to include a *signature* (most corporate systems support this). This is a small text file that is automatically appended to your outgoing messages. Use it to include your full name, job title, company, and contact information. The signature gives your messages a more professional appearance and makes it easy for others to communicate with you through other channels.

When you're ready to distribute your message, pause to verify what you're doing before you click "Send." Double-check your addressees to make sure you've included everyone necessary—and no one else. Did you click on "Reply All" when you meant to hit "Reply"? The difference could be embarrassing or even career-threatening. Don't include people in the cc (courtesy copy) or bcc (blind courtesy copy) fields unless you know how these features work (everyone who receives the message can see who is on the cc line, but not who is on the bcc line). Also, don't set the message priority to "High" or "Urgent" unless your message is truly urgent.

To review the tips and techniques for successful e-mail, see "Checklist: Creating Effective E-Mail Messages."

 CHECKLIST: Creating Effective E-Mail Messages

A. Treat e-mail as a professional communication medium.
- Remember that it is more formal than personal e-mail.
- Recognize that e-mail messages carry the same legal weight as other business documents.
- Follow company e-mail policy; understand the restrictions that your company places on e-mail usage.
- Practice good e-mail hygiene by not opening suspicious messages, keeping virus protection up to date, and following other guidelines.

B. Adapt the three-step process for effective e-mail.
- Make sure every e-mail you send is necessary.
- Don't cc or bcc anyone who doesn't really need to see the message.

- As a manager, make sure you understand the productivity implications of your messages.
- Follow the chain of command.
- Pay attention to the quality of your writing and use correct grammar, spelling, and punctuation.
- Make your subject lines informative by clearly identifying the purpose of your message.
- Make your subject lines compelling by wording them in a way that intrigues your audiences.
- Update the subject line if you reply to the same message back and forth multiple times.
- Keep your emotions under control.
- Don't mark messages as "urgent" unless they truly are urgent.

CREATING EFFECTIVE INSTANT MESSAGES AND TEXT MESSAGES

While e-mail is here to stay as a business medium, its disadvantages—including viruses, spam, and rampant overuse—are driving many people to explore alternatives.[11] One of the most important of those alternatives is instant messaging (IM). For both routine communication and exchanges during online meetings, IM is now widely used throughout the business world and is beginning to replace e-mail for internal communication in many companies.[12] Business-grade IM systems offer a range of capabilities, including basic chat, *presence awareness* (the ability to quickly see which people are at their desks and available to IM), remote display of documents, video capabilities, remote control of other computers, automated newsfeeds from blogs and websites, and the automated bot capabilities (see page 183).[13]

IM is taking the place of e-mail for routine communication in many cases.

Text messaging is beginning to find applications in business as well. Although they perform the similar function of nearly instantaneous communication between devices, IM is primarily a computer-based technology, whereas text messaging is primarily a phone-based technology. (Of course, as often happens, continuing innovation blurs the lines between technologies, and now you can send a text message to a phone from your computer and so on.) Text messaging has long been popular in other parts of the world, where it is often referred to as *short messaging service* (*SMS*) and where phones have had texting capability for years. With text messaging now well entrenched among young consumers in North America, expanded business applications are likely to follow. In addition to person-to-person communication between colleagues, text messaging is taking off in such areas as marketing (alerting customers about new sale prices, for example) and entertainment (such as letting viewers predict the outcome of sporting events or place votes on reality television programs).[14] Because IM is currently more versatile and more widely used in business than text messaging, the following sections focus on IM. However, as text messaging evolves along with wireless devices and networking, you can expect that many of the benefits, risks, and guidelines that pertain to IM will eventually pertain to text messaging as well.

Phone-based text messaging is fast and portable but not as versatile as computer-based IM.

Understanding the Benefits and Risks of Instant Messaging

The benefits of IM include its rapid response to urgent messages, lower cost than both phone calls and e-mail, ability to mimic conversation more closely than e-mail, and availability on a wide range of devices from PCs to mobile phones to PDAs.[15] In addition, because it more closely mimics real conversation, IM doesn't get misused as a broadcast mechanism as often as e-mail does.[16]

IM offers many benefits:
- *Rapid response*
- *Lower cost*
- *Ability to mimic conversation*
- *Wide availability*

Of course, wherever technology goes, trouble seems to follow. The potential drawbacks of IM include security problems (both the risks of computer viruses and the worry that sensitive messages might be intercepted by outsiders), the need for *user authentication* (making sure that online correspondents are really who they appear to be), the challenge of logging messages for later review and archiving, and incompatibility between competing IM systems. Fortunately, with the growth of *enterprise instant messaging* (*EIM*), IM systems designed for large-scale corporate use, many of these problems are being overcome. Security remains an ongoing concern, however, with attacks on IM systems, both public and corporate, continuing to rise.[17] A new breed of virus spread by bots is a particular concern. IM users who fall prey to these bots believe they are chatting with a trusted correspondent when in fact they are exchanging information with an automated bot that imitates human IM chat. The bot encourages the user to download a file or otherwise expose his or her computer to malicious software, then spreads the virus through the user's IM address book.[18]

Adapting the Three-Step Process for Successful IM

Although instant messages are often conceived, written, and sent within a matter of seconds, the principles of the three-step process still apply:

- **Planning instant messages.** View every IM exchange as a conversation; while you may not deliberately plan every individual statement you make or question you pose, take a moment to plan the overall exchange. If you're requesting something, think through exactly what you need and the most effective way to ask for it. If someone is asking you for something, consider his or her needs and your ability to meet them before you respond. And although you rarely organize instant messages in the sense of creating an outline, try to deliver information in a coherent, complete way that minimizes the number of individual messages required.

- **Writing instant messages.** As with e-mail, the appropriate writing style for business IM is more formal than the style you may be accustomed to with personal IM or text messaging. In particular, you should generally avoid IM acronyms (such as "FWIW" for "for what it's worth" or "HTH" for "hope that helps") except when communicating with close colleagues. In the IM exchange in Figure 7.2, notice how the participants communicate quickly and rather informally but still maintain good etiquette and a professional tone. This style is even more important if you or your staff use IM to communicate with customers and other outside audiences. In the coming years, business IM writing may become less formal, but for now, the best approach is to maintain a businesslike style and tone.
- **Completing instant messages.** One of the biggest attractions of IM is that the completing step is so easy. Once you've selected some basic font settings that apply to all your messages, you generally don't need to do anything in terms of producing each message, and distributing is as simple as clicking the Send button. However, don't skip over the revising and proofreading tasks. Take a second to scan each message before you send it to make sure you don't have any missing or misspelled words and that your message is clear and complete.

When using IM, be aware of the potential for constant interruptions and wasted time.

To use IM effectively, all users need to pay attention to some important behavioral issues: the potential for constant interruptions, the ease of accidentally mixing personal and business messages, the risk of being out of the loop (if a hot discussion or impromptu meeting flares up when you're away from your PC or other IM device), and the "vast potential for wasted time" (in the words of MIT labor economist David Autor). On top of all that, users are at the mercy of other people's typing abilities, which can make IM agonizingly slow.[19]

FIGURE 7.2 Instant Messaging for Business Communication
Instant messaging is widely used in business, but it does not use the same informal style of communication you probably use to IM your friends and family.

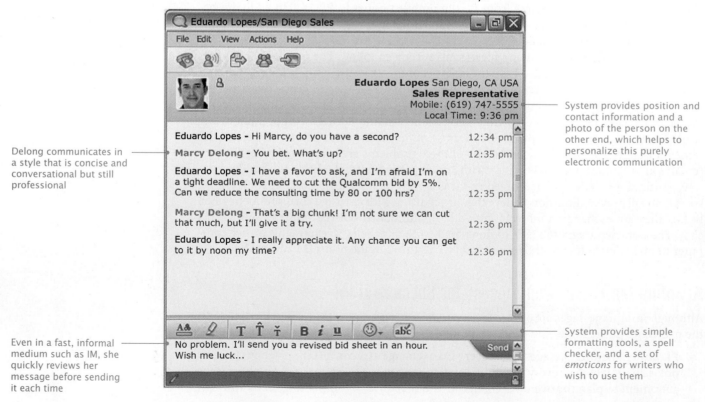

Delong communicates in a style that is concise and conversational but still professional

System provides position and contact information and a photo of the person on the other end, which helps to personalize this purely electronic communication

Even in a fast, informal medium such as IM, she quickly reviews her message before sending it each time

System provides simple formatting tools, a spell checker, and a set of *emoticons* for writers who wish to use them

CHECKLIST: Using IM Productively

- Pay attention to security and privacy issues, and be sure to follow all company guidelines.
- Treat IM as a professional communication medium, not an informal, personal tool; avoid using IM slang with all but close colleagues.
- Maintain good etiquette, even during simple exchanges.

- Protect your own productivity by making yourself unavailable when you need to focus.
- In most instances, don't use IM for confidential messages, complex messages, or personal messages.

Regardless of the system you're using, you can make IM more efficient and effective by following these tips:[20]

- Unless a meeting is scheduled, make yourself unavailable when you need to focus on other work.
- If you're not on a secure system, don't send confidential information.
- Be extremely careful about sending personal messages—they have a tendency to pop up on other people's computers at embarrassing moments.
- Don't use IM for important but impromptu meetings if you can't verify that everyone concerned will be available.
- Unless your system is set up for it, don't use IM for lengthy, complex messages; e-mail is better for those.
- Try to avoid carrying on multiple IM conversations at once, to minimize the chance of sending messages to the wrong people.
- If your IM system has filters for *spim*, the IM version of e-mail spam, make sure they're active and up to date.[21]

To review the advice for effective IM in the workplace, see "Checklist: Using IM Productively."

CREATING EFFECTIVE BUSINESS BLOGS

On the surface, blogs might seem like just another new medium, but at their best, blogs redefine the very nature of business communication. To an extent perhaps unmatched by any other medium, blogs can engage large, widely distributed audiences. In a sense, a blog combines the global reach and reference value of a conventional website with the conversational exchanges of e-mail or IM. Good business blogs pay close attention to several important elements:

- **Communicating with personal style and an authentic voice.** Most business messages designed for large audiences are carefully scripted and written in a "corporate voice" that is impersonal and objective. In contrast, successful business blogs are written by individuals and exhibit their personal style. Audiences relate to this fresh approach and often build closer emotional bonds with the blogger's organization as a result. For instance, Microsoft's Channel 9 video blog, or *vlog* (http://channel9.msdn.com) features online informal, personable video clips in which several of the company's technical experts answer questions and criticisms from software developers. Channel 9 and other employee blogs are credited with helping to repair Microsoft's reputation among software customers.[22]
- **Delivering new information quickly.** Today's blogging tools let you post new material within minutes of writing it or filming it (see Figure 7.3). Not only does this feature allow you to respond quickly when needed—such as during a corporate crisis—but it also lets your audiences know that an active conversation is taking place. Blogs that don't offer a continuous stream of new and interesting content are quickly ignored in today's online environment.

4 LEARNING OBJECTIVE

Identify guidelines for successful instant messaging (IM) in the workplace

Blogs have a unique ability to encourage interaction with a large, geographically dispersed audience.

5 LEARNING OBJECTIVE

Describe the role of blogging in business communication today

FIGURE 7.3 Video
Blogging
With the addition of video, blogging becomes a true multimedia experience that gives bloggers an easy way to share sights and sounds with their audiences. Here, Ford Motor Company integrates video blogging with elements of a conventional website.

- **Choosing topics of peak interest to audiences.** Successful blogs cover topics that readers care about. For instance, General Motors' popular FastLane blog (http://fastlane.gmblogs.com) features top executives writing about GM cars and responding to questions and criticisms from car enthusiasts. The people who read the blog and write comments obviously care about cars and want the latest information from GM.[23]

Most business blogs invite readers to leave comments.

- **Encouraging audiences to join the conversation.** Not all blogs invite comments, although most do. As Boeing's Randy Baseler learned, many blog readers expect to be able to leave comments. These comments can be a valuable source of news, information, and insights. In addition, the less-formal nature of blogging seems to make it easier for companies to "let their guards down" and converse with their audiences. For instance, when blogging consultant Paul Chaney wanted to devise a new strategy for his company, Radiant Marketing Group, he asked his blog audience for input. Readers responded with comments ranging from their impressions of his reputation in the industry to critiques of his proposed company slogans.[24] Of course, not all comments are helpful or appropriate, which is why some bloggers follow Randy Baseler's approach of reviewing all comments and selecting the most helpful or interesting ones to post.

Given the unique ability of blogs to convey topical information quickly in a conversational format, their rapid adop-

DOCUMENT MAKEOVER

IMPROVE THIS BLOG

To practice correcting drafts of actual documents, visit your online course or the access-code-protected portion of the Companion Website. Click "Document Makeovers," then click Chapter 7. You will find a blog posting that contains problems and errors relating to what you've learned in this chapter about writing for electronic media. Use the Final Draft decision tool to create an improved version of this posting.

TABLE 7.2   Tips for Effective Business Blogging

TIP	WHY IT'S IMPORTANT
Have a clear plan before you start blogging.	Without a clear plan, your blog is likely to wander from topic to topic without providing compelling information or building a sense of community with your audience.
Post frequently.	The whole point of a blog is fresh material; if you don't have a constant supply of new information or new links, create a traditional website instead.
Make it about your customers and the issues that are important to them.	Readers want to know how your blog will help them, entertain them, or give them a chance to communicate with others who have similar interests.
Write in an authentic voice; never create an artificial character who supposedly writes a blog.	*Flogs*, or fake blogs, violate the spirit of blogging, show disrespect for your audience, and will turn audiences against you as soon as they uncover the truth.
Link generously—but carefully.	Providing interesting links to other blogs and websites is a fundamental aspect of blogging, but think twice before putting these links in your blog. Make sure the links will be of value to your readers, and make sure they don't point to material that could damage your reputation.
Keep it brief.	Most online readers don't have the patience to read lengthy reports.
Don't post anything you wouldn't want the entire world to see.	Future employers, government regulators, competitors, journalists, and community critics are just a few of the people who might see what you've written. Assume that anything you write will be spread through the online world.
Don't engage in blatant product promotion.	Readers who think they're being advertised to will stop reading.
Take time to write compelling, specific headlines for your postings.	Readers usually decide within a couple of seconds whether to read your postings; boring or vague headlines will turn them away instantly.
Pay attention to spelling, grammar, and mechanics.	No matter how smart or experienced you are, poor-quality writing undermines your credibility with discriminating audiences.
Respond to criticism openly and honestly.	Hiding sends the message that you don't have a valid response to the criticism. If your critics are wrong, patiently explain why you think they're wrong. If they are right, explain how you'll fix the situation.
Listen and learn.	If you don't take the time to analyze the comments people leave on your blog or the comments other bloggers make about you, you're missing out on one of the most valuable aspects of blogging.
Respect intellectual property.	Presenting the work of others as your own is not only unethical but can violate copyright laws.
Be scrupulously honest and careful with facts.	Honesty is an absolute requirement for every ethical business communicator, of course, but you need to be extra careful online because inaccuracies (both intentional and unintentional) are likely to be discovered quickly and shared widely.

tion by businesses in virtually every industry should come as no surprise. The following sections offer an overview of the business applications of blogging, and Table 7.2 offers a number of suggestions for successful blogging.

Understanding the Business Applications of Blogging

Blogs are a potential solution whenever you have a continuing stream of information to share with virtually any online audience—and particularly when you want the audience to have the opportunity to respond. Blogs designed for internal audiences can spread the corporate culture, help teams collaborate, and give everyone access to the collective knowledge of the organization. Blogs for external audiences can help sell products and services, build

The business applications of blogs include a wide range of internal and external communication tasks.

Moblogs are blogs adapted for display on mobile devices such as phones.

relationships with stakeholder groups, and strengthen the awareness and image of your company and its brands.[25] Here are some of the many ways businesses are using blogs:[26]

- **Project management and team communication.** Blogs are a good way to keep project teams up to date, particularly when team members are geographically dispersed. For instance, the time-honored trip reports that employees file after visiting customers or other external parties can be enhanced vividly with *mobile blogs*, or *moblogs*. Thanks to the convenience of camera phones and other multimedia wireless devices, employees on the go can send text, audio, images, and video to their colleagues. Conversely, mobile employees can also stay in touch with their team blogs using handheld devices. As Chapter 2 pointed out, many teams also use wikis now to collaborate on projects.
- **Company news.** On a broader scope, companies can use blogs to keep employees informed about general business matters, from facility news to benefit updates. Blogs also serve as online community forums, giving everyone in the company a chance to raise questions and voice concerns.
- **Customer support.** Building on the tradition of online customer support forums that have been around since the earliest days of the Internet, customer support blogs answer questions, offer tips and advice, and inform customers about new products.
- **Public relations and media relations.** Like Boeing's Randy Baseler, many corporate executives now share company news with both the general public and journalists via their blogs.
- **Recruiting.** Blogs are a great way to let potential employees know more about your company, the people who work there, and the nature of the company culture.
- **Policy and issue discussions.** Executive blogs in particular provide a public forum for discussing legislation, regulations, and other broad issues of interest to an organization.
- **Crisis communication.** Blogs are a convenient way to provide up-to-the-minute information during emergencies, correct misinformation, or respond to rumors.
- **Market research.** Blogs can be a clever way to solicit feedback from customers and experts in the marketplace. In addition to using their own blogs for research, today's companies need to monitor blogs that are likely to discuss them, their executives, and their products. Negative product reviews, rumors, and other information can spread across the globe in a matter of hours, and managers need to know what the online community is saying—whether it's positive or negative. *Reputation analysts* such as Evolve24 (**www.evolve24.com**) have developed ways to automatically monitor blogs and other online sources to see what people are saying about their corporate clients.[27]
- **Brainstorming.** Online brainstorming via blogs offers a way for people to toss ideas around and build on each others' contributions.
- **Viral marketing.** The interconnected nature of the blogosphere makes it a natural vehicle for spreading the word about your company and your products. Bloggers often make a point to provide links to other blogs and websites that interest them, giving marketers a great opportunity to spread their messages. *Viral marketing* refers to the transmission of messages in much the same way that biological viruses are transmitted from person to person.
- **E-mail replacement.** As spam filters and message overload make it more difficult to reach people via e-mail, many companies have turned to blogs as a way to distribute information to customers and other audiences. Using *newsfeeds* from a company's blog (see page 194), audiences can subscribe to categories of information that interest them. These messages are then delivered via an *aggregator*, bypassing the increasingly clogged e-mail channel.
- **News syndication.** Blogging also allows both individuals and companies to become publishers of news and other information. For example, by subscribing to the update service at **www.buscommresources.com**, the student resource site for this textbook, you can get the latest news about business communication skills and tools. Syndication is explained on page 197.

Blogs are an ideal medium for viral marketing, the organic spread of messages from one audience member to another.

The uses of blogs are limited only by your creativity, so be on the lookout for new ways you can foster positive relationships with colleagues, customers, and other important audiences. For a good example of business blogging, see Figure 7.4.

FIGURE 7.4 Elements of an Effective Business Blog
Blogs exist in many forms and formats, but visitors expect a few basic elements, such as access to archives, links to related information, and a convenient way to subscribe to an automatic newsfeed. Note the style and tone of the writing in this blog; it is far more engaging and conversational than the traditional "corporate voice." Moreover, it is about the *customers*, not the *company*.

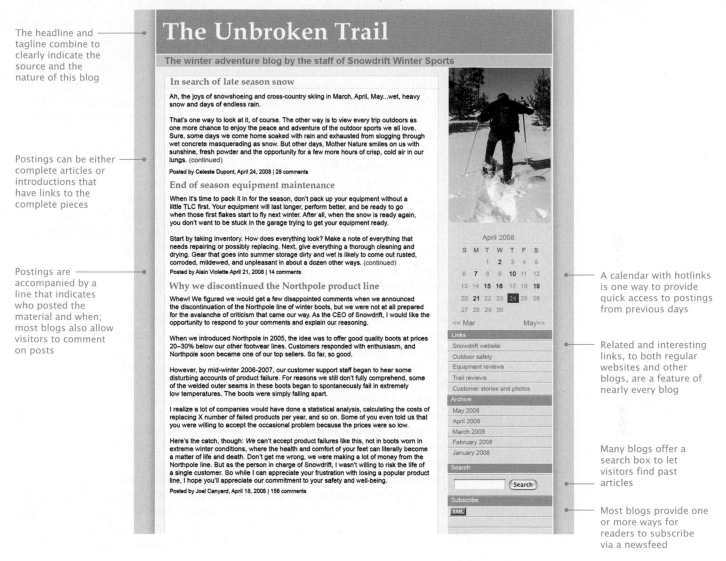

The headline and tagline combine to clearly indicate the source and the nature of this blog

Postings can be either complete articles or introductions that have links to the complete pieces

Postings are accompanied by a line that indicates who posted the material and when; most blogs also allow visitors to comment on posts

A calendar with hotlinks is one way to provide quick access to postings from previous days

Related and interesting links, to both regular websites and other blogs, are a feature of nearly every blog

Many blogs offer a search box to let visitors find past articles

Most blogs provide one or more ways for readers to subscribe via a newsfeed

Adapting the Three-Step Process for Successful Blogging

Although blogs deliver business messages in a unique way, the three-step writing process you've already learned is easy to adapt to blogging tasks. The planning step is particularly important if you're considering starting a blog, because you're planning an entire communication channel, not just a single message. Pay close attention to your audience, your purpose, and your scope:

- **Audience.** Except for team blogs and other efforts with an obvious and well-defined audience, defining your target audience can be a challenge. You want an audience large enough to justify the time you'll be investing, but narrow enough that you can provide an identifiable focus for the blog. For instance, if you work for a firm that develops computer games, would you focus your blog on "hardcore" players, the type who spend thousands of dollars on super-fast PCs optimized for video games, or would you broaden the reach to include all video gamers? The decision often comes down to business strategy.

6 LEARNING OBJECTIVE

Explain why identifying your audience, purpose, and scope is vital to successful blogging

- **Purpose.** Unlike a personal blog, in which you typically write about whatever interests you, a business blog needs to have a business-related purpose that is important to both your company and your chosen audience. Moreover, the purpose has to "have legs," meaning that it is something that can drive the blog's content for months or years, rather than focusing on a single event or issue of only temporary interest. For instance, if you're a technical expert, you might create a blog to give the audience tips and techniques for using your company's products more effectively—a business-oriented and audience-focused purpose that will always be of interest. This would be the *general purpose* of your blog, then each posting would have a *specific purpose* within the context of that general purpose. Finally, if you are not writing an official company blog but rather blogging as an individual employee, make sure you understand your employer's blogging guidelines. As with e-mail and IM, more and more companies are putting policies in place to prevent employee mistakes with blogging.[28]

- **Scope.** As with your audience, defining the scope of your blog can be a bit tricky. You want to cover a subject area that is broad enough to offer discussion possibilities for months or years, but narrow enough to have an identifiable focus. For instance, GM's FastLane blog is about GM cars only—not GM's stock price, labor negotiations, and so on. Moreover, the scope of your blog needs to remain fairly stable so that you can build an audience over time. If you start out discussing product support but then shift to talking about your company's advertising programs, you'll probably lose readers along the way.

After you begin writing your blog (or posting messages to a multiauthor blog that someone else has created), the careful planning needs to continue with each message. Unless you're posting to a restricted-access blog, such as an internal blog on a company intranet, you can never be sure who might see your posts. Other bloggers might link to them months or years later. Consider the situation before you post to make sure the information you'll be putting online is appropriate for a public audience.

Write blog postings in a comfortable—but not careless—style.

Write in a comfortable, personal style. Blog audiences don't want to hear from your company; they want to hear from *you*. Bear in mind, though, that *comfortable* does not mean *careless*. Sloppy writing damages your credibility. In addition, while audiences expect you to be knowledgeable in the subject area your blog covers, you don't need to know everything about a topic. If you don't have all the information yourself, simply provide links to other blogs and websites that supply relevant information. In fact, many blog audiences consider carefully screened links to be an essential part of blogging.

Completing messages for your blog is usually quite easy. Evaluate the content and readability of your message, proofread to correct any errors, then post using your blogging system's tools for doing so. If your blog doesn't already have one, be sure to include one or more *newsfeed* options so that your audience can automatically receive headlines (and summaries, if you choose) of new blog posts (see "Distributing Blog and Podcast Content" on page 196).

"Checklist: Blogging for Business" summarizes some of the key points to remember when creating and writing a business blog, and you can always get updated advice from some of the many blogs and websites dedicated to blogging.

 CHECKLIST: Blogging for Business

- Consider a blog whenever you have a continuing stream of information to share with an online audience.
- Identify an audience that is broad enough to justify the effort but narrow enough to have common interests.
- Identify a purpose that is comprehensive enough to provide fuel for a continuing stream of posts.
- Consider the scope of your blog carefully; make it broad enough to attract an audience but narrow enough to keep you focused.

- Communicate with a personal style and an authentic voice, but don't write carelessly.
- Deliver new information quickly.
- Choose topics of peak interest to your audience.
- Encourage audiences to join the conversation.
- Offer a newsfeed option so that subscribers can get automatic updates.

CREATING EFFECTIVE PODCASTS

Podcasting offers a number of interesting possibilities for business communication. Its most obvious use is to replace existing audio and video messages, such as large teleconferences in which a speaker provides information without expecting to engage in conversation with the listeners. Training is another good use of podcasting. One of the first podcasts recorded by technical experts at IBM gave other employees advice on setting up blogs, for example.[29] Sales representatives who travel to meet with potential customers can listen to podcasts or view video podcasts to get the latest information on their companies' products. Podcasts are also an increasingly common feature on blogs, letting audiences listen to or watch recordings of their favorite bloggers. New services can even transcribe blogs into podcasts, and vice versa.[30]

Podcasting can be used to deliver a wide range of audio and video messages.

As more businesspeople become comfortable with podcasting, it should find applications in a variety of new areas, wherever audio or video content can convey business messages effectively. For instance, real estate agents can record audio podcasts that potential homebuyers can listen to while walking through houses. Marketing departments can replace expensive printed brochures with video podcasts that demonstrate new products in action. Human resource departments can offer video tours of their companies to entice new recruits.

Adapting the Three-Step Process for Successful Podcasting

Although it might not seem obvious at first, the three-step writing process adapts quite nicely to podcasting. You've already chosen the medium, so focus the planning step on analyzing the situation, gathering the information you'll need, and organizing your material. One vital planning step depends on whether you intend to create podcasts for limited use and distribution (such as a weekly audio update to your virtual team) or you plan to create a *podcasting channel* with regular recordings on a consistent theme, designed for a wider public audience. As with planning a blog, if you intend to create a podcasting channel, be sure you think through the range of topics you want to address over time to verify you have a sustainable purpose. If you plan to comment on the stock market or breaking news in your industry, for instance, you'll have a recurring source of topics to discuss. In contrast, if you plan to share marketing ideas for small business owners, make sure you have or can find plenty of ideas over time so that your podcasting efforts don't run out of steam. If you bounce from one theme to another over time, you risk losing your audience.[31]

7 LEARNING OBJECTIVE

Explain how to adapt the three-step writing process for podcasts

As you organize and begin to think about the words or images you'll use as content, pay close attention to previews, transitions, and reviews. These steering devices are especially vital in audio and video recordings because these formats lack the "street signs" that audiences rely on in print media. For instance, if readers get lost or confused while reading a printed document, they can easily scan backward to find key phrases or subheadings. With audio and video, scanning back and forth to find specific parts of the message is much harder, so you need to do everything possible to make sure your audience successfully receives and interprets your message on the first try.

Generous use of previews, transitions, and reviews helps podcast audiences follow the thread of your recording.

As you'll see in Chapter 16 in the discussion of oral presentations, you'll need to decide whether to script your podcast completely then read it word for word or improvise from a speaking outline and notes. One of the attractions of podcasting is the conversational, person-to-person feel of the recordings, so unless you need to capture exact wording, speaking from an outline and notes is usually the best choice. However, no one wants to listen to rambling podcasts that struggle to make a point, so don't try to make up your content "on the fly." Effective podcasts, like effective stories, have a clear beginning, middle, and end.

In the completing step, keep in mind that making edits is much more difficult in an audio or video medium such as podcasting. Therefore, take extra care to revise your script or think through your speaking notes before you begin to record. You don't want to get halfway through the recording process and realize that you should have said something else in the introduction.

Plan your podcast content carefully; edits are much more difficult to make than in textual messages.

FIGURE 7.5 The Podcasting Process
Creating a podcast requires a few easy steps, and basic podcasts can be created using free or low-cost hardware and software.

| 1. Install recording software | 2. Connect and verify microphone | 3. Click the record button and start talking | 4. Review your file and edit if needed | 5. Convert file to MP3 format and save | 6. Create and validate your feed | 7. Upload your file and let RSS alert your subscribers |

Finally, consider integrating your podcasting efforts with a related blog. Not only can you provide additional information, but you can use the commenting feature of the blog to encourage feedback from your audience.[32]

Assembling a Podcasting System

For basic podcasts, your computer probably has most of the hardware you already need, and you can download recording software.

The equipment needed to record podcasts depends on the degree of production quality you want to achieve. For the most basic podcasts, such as those you might record for internal audiences, most contemporary personal computers probably have the equipment you need: a low-cost microphone (most laptop computers now have built-in microphones), a sound card to convert the microphone signal to digital format (most computers have them now), and some recording software (free versions are available online). However, a basic system might not deliver the audio quality or production flexibility you need for a public podcast. For instance, the microphone built into your laptop can't reproduce sound nearly as well as a professional-quality microphone can, and because it's physically located on the computer, the built-in microphone will pick up the noise from the computer's fan. Similarly, the low-cost sound cards built into many computers can also add a significant amount of noise to your signal.[33]

If you need higher production quality or greater flexibility, you'll need additional pieces of hardware and software, such as an audio processor (to filter out extraneous noise and otherwise improve the audio signal), a mixer (to combine multiple audio or video signals), a better microphone, and more sophisticated recording and editing software (see Figure 7.5). You may also need to improve the acoustics of the room in which you are recording, to minimize echoes, noise, and other problems. To learn more about the technical requirements of podcasting, pick up one of the many new books on the subject. Some of them even come with free recording software.[34]

With a few upgrades beyond a basic computer, you can assemble a studio capable of producing professional-quality podcasts.

For a quick review of the key points of business podcasting, see "Checklist: Planning and Producing Business Podcasts."

DISTRIBUTING BLOG AND PODCAST CONTENT

With today's blog and podcast technologies, you can easily reach a vast audience—an audience that can continue to grow if your "fans" spread the word for you. To distribute effectively, get into the mind-set of *publishing*, rather than sending, your content.

CHECKLIST: Planning and Producing Business Podcasts

- Consider podcasting whenever you have the opportunity to replace existing audio or video messages.
- If you plan a podcast channel with a regular stream of new content, make sure you've identified a theme or purpose that is rich enough to sustain your effort.
- Pay close attention to previews, transitions, and reviews to help keep your audience from getting lost.
- Decide whether you want to improvise your podcast or speak or film from a written script.

- If you improvise, do enough planning and organization to avoid floundering and rambling in search of a point.
- Remember that editing is much harder to do with audio or video, and plan your content and recording carefully.
- Consider linking your podcast to a blog in order to provide additional information and a forum for audience feedback.
- Syndicate your podcast, if appropriate, via RSS enclosures.

Publishing Your Content

As with newspapers and magazines, blog and podcast publishing requires some action from both the publisher and the subscriber. The publisher creates the content and submits it to a distribution channel, which delivers it to anyone who has chosen to subscribe. This process of publication for blogs and podcasts is often referred to as **syndication** (see Figure 7.6).[35] As a publisher, you initiate syndication by creating a **feed** or *newsfeed*, a file that contains information about the items you have written or recorded. In the case of podcasts, the audio or video file is enclosed within the feed file as well. Several formats now exist for these feeds, but the most common is known as **RSS**, which is short for *really simple syndication*. (Although this process sounds fairly technical, popular blogging and podcasting systems take care of most of the details for you.) As a communicator, the benefit of syndication via an RSS feed is that you have the potential to build up a vast audience over time, provided you offer compelling content and make that content easy to find.

On the receiving end, audiences subscribe to your content through a piece of software called an **aggregator** or *newsreader*. (*Aggregating* is simply another word for *collecting*.) A wide variety of aggregators now exist, including some that specialized in certain types of media. Aggregators specifically for podcasts are usually called **podcatchers.** Whenever you create a feed for a new blog post or podcast, your subscribers are automatically alerted via the feed. In the case of blogs, aggregators usually display a headline and brief summary of your post. Anyone who then wants to read the full item can click on the headline and be directed back to your blog to see the entire post (see Figure 7.7). In the case of podcasts, subscribers can choose to have new podcasts downloaded to their computer or other device automatically, or they can download them manually. For audiences, the key benefit of syndication is automatically collecting interesting content from many different sources in a variety of formats. In a sense, it's like creating personal versions of the Internet.

8 LEARNING OBJECTIVE

Describe the syndication process and explain how it helps you distribute blog and podcast content

Syndication is the process of distributing blog and podcast content via feeds.

Aggregators automatically collect information about new blog postings and podcasts.

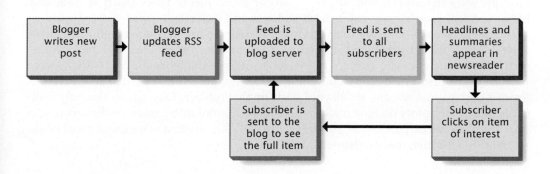

FIGURE 7.6 The Syndication Process for Blogs
The publish/subscribe model lets bloggers reach a potentially vast audience and lets audiences automatically acquire fresh content from an unlimited number of sources.

FIGURE 7.7 Viewing Blog Headlines in Newsreader Software
Aggregators or *newreaders* offer a simple means of automatically collecting and viewing the latest material from any number of blogs (as well as podcasts and regular web content). To view a full post, the viewer simply clicks on any item of interest and then is sent to the associated blog or website to see the full item.

Connecting with Audiences

Adding feed capability is the most important step in staying connected with your blog or podcast audiences.

This publish/subscribe process generally works nicely once publishers and subscribers take the necessary steps to send and receive content. Of course, both parties need to find each other in the first place. This connection can happen in a variety of ways. The most fundamental step for blog publishers is to add the feed capability to their blogs so that interested audiences can easily subscribe through their aggregators. Bloggers and podcasters can also take advantage of services such as FeedBurner, www.feedburner.com, which make sure files are properly formatted and help publicize content.[36]

Beyond that, publishers can get themselves listed in a variety of directories, some of which specialize in blogs (such as Technorati, www.technorati.com), others in podcasts (such as Juice, http://juicereceiver.sourceforge.net), some in only video feeds (such as FireAnt, www.fireant.tv), and others in two or more media types (such as Mefeedia, http://mefeedia.com, which covers both podcasts and vodcasts).

Tagging involves assigning descriptive words to each post of a podcast.

Content creators can also make their material easier to find through **tagging**, which involves assigning descriptive words to each post or podcast. For instance, for a blog posting on the clever techniques for attracting new employees, you might tag the post with the word *recruiting*. Visitors to your blog who want to read everything you've written about recruiting just click on that word to see all your posts on that subject. Tagging can also help audiences locate your posts on blog trackers such as Technorati or on *social bookmarking* sites such as del.icio.us, http://del.icio.us/ (see Figure 7.8). You can read more about social bookmarking as a research tool in Chapter 11.

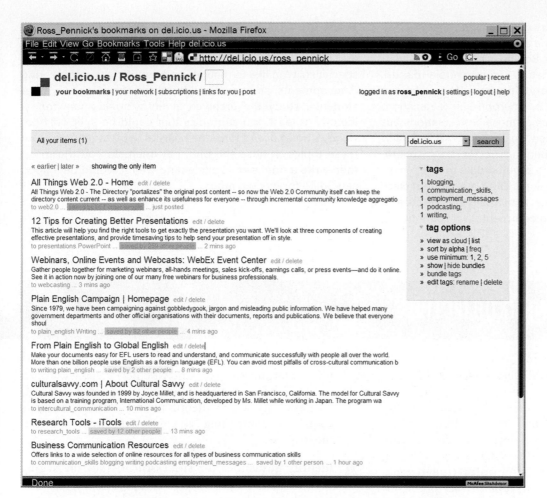

Bloggers can also help each other by identifying blogs they themselves read. This list, called a *blogroll*, can be found on many blogs. In addition, when bloggers comment on individual posts on other blogs, they can also use a feature called *trackback* to let readers of the original post know that other bloggers have commented on it. Both blogrolls and trackbacks help "spread the word" for bloggers by showing audiences other blogs they might like as well.

New capabilities and services emerge constantly in the world of online media, and this chapter has provided just a broad overview. To learn the latest on blogging, podcasting, and other new media choices, visit **www.buscommresources.com**, click on "Business Communication Web Directory," then click on the subject of interest.

Bloggers can help each other find audiences by listing favorite blogs in their blogrolls.

COMMUNICATION CHALLENGES AT BOEING COMMERCIAL AIRPLANES

Randy Baseler recently brought you on board as a market development manager, with responsibilities ranging from market research to customer communications. Study the two scenarios that follow and apply what you learned about blogging in this chapter to offer the requested information or advice.

Individual Challenge: Pressure is building to stop the practice of reviewing blog visitor comments and selecting which ones will appear on the website. You've received a number of adamant messages saying that *Randy's Journal* won't be a "real" blog until anyone is allowed to write any sort of comment. However, Baseler has made it quite clear that he doesn't want the blog to become a "free for all." In addition, like all large international firms, Boeing is always involved in a variety of complex and sometimes controversial discussions. These could include everything from labor relations and global outsourcing to the environment to taxation. Baseler respects the importance of these conversations but wants the blog to stay focused on the aviation industry. Moreover, from your own experience in the blogosphere, you know that virtually any blog is vulnerable to rude, inappropriate, and irrelevant comments. Draft a polite but clear message to be posted on the site, explaining that the current policy of reviewing and filtering comments will continue.

Team Challenge: *Randy's Journal* is now read by thousands of people with widely varying interests—frequent flyers who want to know about new planes, technical specialists who like to read about scientific and engineering developments, and so on. With a team of one or two other students, study the archives at www.boeing.com/randy. Identify at least two subtopics that could be split off from *Randy's Journal* and form the basis of separate blogs. From these topics, choose the one that interests you the most, then write a brief e-mail explaining why it would be a good candidate for its own blog.

SUMMARY OF LEARNING OBJECTIVES

1 **Compare the strengths and weaknesses of the print and electronic media available for short messages.** Printed memos and letters offer a degree of formality that is sometimes hard to achieve with electronic media, but they lack the speed, richness, and convenience of electronic media. E-mail offers high speed, low cost, and widespread availability, but it suffers from overuse and a variety of spam, security, and privacy problems. Computer-based instant messaging is even faster than e-mail, is simple to use, and hasn't yet accumulated problems with spam, security, and privacy to the same degree that e-mail has. Phone-based text messaging offers high speed as well, with the added benefit of portability. Its primary disadvantage relates to convenience and flexibility; it can't yet perform the wide array of functions now available in business-grade IM. Blogging offers a fast, simple way to publish information online and to reach wide audiences. Blogging's biggest downside is competition from the millions of other blogs on the Internet. Podcasts offer a simple way for anyone to broadcast audio or video messages. They do require more work to create than blogs, and high-quality podcasts require both a modest set of specialized equipment and plenty of network bandwidth.

2 **Explain how overuse of e-mail can reduce productivity.** Overuse of e-mail, including sending unimportant e-mail messages, sending too many messages to too many people, and copying people who don't need to see particular messages, reduces productivity by increasing the number of messages that people read and respond to and by creating interruptions that cause people to lose focus on their work.

3 **Identify the qualities of an effective e-mail subject line.** The wording of an e-mail message's subject line

often determines when—and whether—recipients open and read the message. Effective subject lines are both informative (concisely identifying what the message is about) and compelling (giving readers a reason to read the message).

4 **Identify guidelines for successful instant messaging (IM) in the workplace.** Use IM productively and effectively by making yourself unavailable when you need to focus on other work, refraining from sending confidential information if you're not on a secure system, refraining from sending personal messages at work, not using IM for impromptu meetings if you can't verify that everyone concerned will be available, not using IM for lengthy and complex messages, avoiding carrying on multiple IM conversations at once, avoiding IM slang with anyone other than close colleagues, and keeping spim filters and other security and privacy measures current.

5 **Describe the role of blogging in business communication today.** Blogs are used in numerous ways in business today, including project management and team communication, company news, customer support, public relations and media relations, employee recruiting, policy and issue discussions, crisis communication, market research, brainstorming, and viral marketing.

6 **Explain why identifying your audience, purpose, and scope is vital to successful blogging.** First, identifying your target audience is a vital step because you want an audience large enough to justify the time you'll be investing but narrow enough that you can provide an identifiable focus for the blog. Second, identifying your purpose is important as well because you want a purpose that will last beyond your initial posts. You don't want to start a blog only to run out of things to write about within a few weeks or months. Third, identifying your scope is important so that audiences can identify what your blog is about. A scope that is too narrow will limit both your available topic possibilities and your target audience. A scope that is too broad makes your blog seem vague and hard to pin down.

7 **Explain how to adapt the three-step writing process for podcasts.**   Although you'll be recording audio or video when creating podcasts, rather than writing messages, the three-step process is an effective way to develop podcasts as well. Focus the planning step on analyzing the situation, gathering the information you'll need, and organizing your material. If you plan to create a series of podcasts on a given theme (the equivalent of starting a radio or television show), make sure you've identified a range of topics extensive enough to keep you going over time. As you organize and begin to think about the words or images you'll use as content, pay close attention to

previews, transitions, and reviews so that audiences don't get lost while listening or watching. Before you record, think through what you plan to say or shoot so that you don't ramble on while trying to make your key points. Finally, consider the necessary level of production quality; good-quality podcasts usually require some specialized hardware and software.

8 **Describe the syndication process, and explain how it helps you distribute blog and podcast content.** Syndication involves creating a feed, usually an RSS feed, that identifies the content of your podcast episode or your blog post, and in the case of podcasts, also encloses the audio or video file itself. This feed is then distributed to your subscribers, who receive it via software programs known as aggregators. In the case of blogs, audiences usually then click on a headline and summary to return to your blog site to read the entire post. For podcasts, they can choose to have the audio or video file downloaded automatically or do so manually themselves.

Test Your Knowledge

1. What four electronic media choices are replacing traditional memos and letters in many instances?
2. Why are subject lines important in e-mail messages?
3. How does the overuse of e-mail (sending too many messages to too many people) lower productivity?
4. What are the benefits of IM in business communication?
5. Should you use common IM slang terms and abbreviations such as IMHO (in my humble opinion) or TY (thank you) in business IM? Why or why not?
6. Why does a personal style of writing help blogs build stronger relationships with audiences?
7. Why is it important to have a long-term, sustainable purpose in mind before you begin creating and syndicating your blog or podcast?
8. How can blogs help with viral marketing efforts?
9. Could a podcast replace an employee newsletter that is currently printed and mailed to employees' homes? Why or why not?
10. How does syndication help blog and podcast creators reach a wider audience?

Apply Your Knowledge

1. Is instant messaging replacing many instances of e-mail for the same reasons that e-mail replaced many instances of printed memos and letters? Explain your answer.
2. If one of the benefits of blogging is the personal, intimate style of writing, is it a good idea to limit your creativity by adhering to conventional rules of grammar, spelling, and mechanics? Why or why not?
3. In your work as a video game designer, you know how eager players search the web for any scrap of information they can find about upcoming releases. In fact, to build interest, your

company's public relations department carefully doles out small bits of information in the months before a new title hits the market. However, you and others in the company are also concerned about competitors getting their hands on all this "prerelease" information. If they learn too much too soon, they can use that information to improve their own products more quickly. You and several other designers and programmers maintain blogs that give players insights into game design techniques and that occasionally share tips and tricks. You have thousands of readers, and you know your blog helps build customer loyalty. The company president wants to ban blogging entirely so that bloggers don't accidentally share too much prerelease information about upcoming games. Would this be a wise move? Why or why not?
4. Should podcasting be considered as a potential replacement for your company's employee newsletter, which is currently sent by e-mail? Why or why not?
5. **Ethical Choices** Your boss wants you to send a message to the production staff, thanking all six members for their hard work and overtime to get the new manufacturing line set up and running on schedule. Your boss has been working a lot of overtime herself, and she's been under a lot of pressure. She wants to send the thank-you message by e-mail and asks you to work on the wording. You think each member of the production staff should receive a formal letter to keep for future promotions or other jobs. You know your boss won't like being interrupted about an issue that she thinks is off her desk, and you know how valuable her time is.
   a. Should you draft the letter and produce six copies so that you don't have to bother your boss?
   b. Should you simply draft the e-mail message as requested to save everyone time?
   c. Should you discuss the issue with your boss, regardless of taking her away from the tasks she so desperately needs to get done?

Practice Your Knowledge

Messages for Analysis

Review the following messages, then (1) analyze the strengths and weaknesses of each message and (2) revise as indicated.

Message 7.A: Improving IM Skills

Review this IM exchange and explain how the customer service agent could have handled the situation more effectively.

Agent:	Thanks for contacting Home Exercise Equipment. What's up?
Customer:	I'm having trouble assembling my home gym.
Agent:	I hear that a lot! LOL
Customer:	So is it me or the gym?
Agent:	Well, let's see <grin> Where are you stuck?
Customer:	The cross bar that connects the vertical pillars doesn't fit.
Agent:	What do you mean doesn't fit?
Customer:	It doesn't fit. It's not long enough to reach across the pillars.
Agent:	Maybe you assembled the pillars in the wrong place. Or maybe we sent the wrong cross bar.
Customer:	How do I tell?
Agent:	The parts aren't labeled so could be tough. Do you have a measuring tape? Tell me how long your cross bar is.

Message 7.B: Drafting Effective Blog Posts

Revise this blog post based on what you've learned in this chapter.

We're DOOMED!!!!!

[post]

I was at the Sikorsky plant in Stratford yesterday, just checking to see how things were going with the assembly line retrofit we did for them last year. I think I saw the future, and it ain't pretty. They were demo'ing a prototype robot from Motoman that absolutely blows our stuff out of the water. They wouldn't let me really see it, but based on the 10-second glimpse I got, it's smaller, faster, and more maneuverable than any of our units. And when I asked about the price, the guy just grinned. And it wasn't the sort of grin designed to make me feel good.

I've been saying for years that we need to pay more attention to size, speed, and maneuverability instead of just relying on our historical strengths of accuracy and payload capacity, and you'd have to be blind not to agree that this experience proves me right. If we can't at least show a design for a better unit within two or three months, Motoman is going to lock up the market and leave us utterly in the dust.

Believe me, being able to say "I told you so" right now is not nearly as satisfying as you might think!!

Message 7.C: Plan A Better Podcast

To access this message, visit www.businesscommunication-headlinenews.com and click on Textbook Resources. Locate *Business Communication Today*, 9th ed., click on Chapter 7, then select page 202, Message 7.C. Download and listen to this podcast.

Identify at least three ways in which the podcast could be improved, then draft a brief e-mail message that you could send to the podcaster with your suggestions for improvement.

Exercises

For active links to all websites discussed in this chapter, visit this text's website at www.prenhall.com/bovee. Locate your book and click on its Companion Website link. Then select Chapter 7, and click on "Featured Websites." Locate the name of the page or the URL related to the material in the text. Please note that links to sites that become inactive after publication of the book will be removed from the Featured Websites section.

7.1 Choose Your Medium: Selecting the Best Technology for a Message For each of these message needs, choose a medium that you think would work effectively and explain your choice (more than one medium could work in some cases; just be able to support your particular choice):

    a. A technical support service for people trying to use their digital music players

    b. A message of condolence to the family of an employee who passed away recently

    c. A message from the CEO of a small company explaining that she is leaving the company to join a competitor

    d. For a series of observations on the state of the industry

    e. For a series of messages, questions, and answers surrounding the work of a project team

7.2 E-Mail: Making Subject Lines Informative Using your imagination to make up whatever details you need, revise the following e-mail subject lines to make them more informative:

    a. New budget figures

    b. Marketing brochure—your opinion

    c. Production schedule

7.3 E-Mail: Message Outlining a New Employee Procedure The following e-mail message contains numerous errors related to what you've learned about planning and writing business messages. Using the information it contains, write a more effective version:

TO: Felicia August <fb_august@evertrust.com>

SUBJECT: Those are the breaks, folks

Some of you may not like the rules about break times; however, we determined that keeping track of employees while they took breaks at times they determined rather than regular breaks at prescribed times was not working as well as we would have liked it to work. The new rules are not going to be an option. If you do not follow the new rules, you could be docked from your pay for hours when you turned up missing, since your direct supervisor will not be able to tell whether you were on a "break" or not and will assume that you have walked away from your job. We cannot be responsible for any errors that result from your inattentiveness to the new rules. I have already heard complaints from some of you and I hope this memo will end this issue once and for all. The decision has already been made.

Starting Monday, January 1, you will all be required to take a regular 15-minute break in the morning and again in the afternoon, and a regular thirty-minute lunch at the times specified by your supervisor, NOT when you think you need a break or when you "get around to it."

There will be no exceptions to this new rule!

Felicia August
Manager
Billing and accounting

7.4 **Instant Messaging: Let's Get Professional** Your firm, which makes professional paint sprayers, uses IM extensively for internal communication and frequently for external communication with customers and suppliers as well. Several customers recently forwarded copies of messages they've received from your staff, asking if you knew how casual some employees were treating this important medium. You decide to revise parts of several messages to show your staff a more appropriate writing style. Rewrite these sentences, making up any information you need, to convey a more businesslike style and tone. (Look up the acronyms online if you need to.)

a. IMHO, our quad turbo sprayer is best model 4U.
b. No prob; happy2help!
c. FWIW, I use the L400 myself & it rocks
d. Most cust see 20–30% reduct in fumes w/this sprayer --- of course, YMMV.

7.5 **Blogging: Keeping Emotions Under Control** The members of the project team of which you are the leader have enthusiastically embraced blogging as a communication medium. Unfortunately, as emotions heat up during the project, some of the blog postings are getting too casual, too personal, and even sloppy. Because your boss and other managers around the company also read this project blog, you don't want the team to look unprofessional in anyone's eyes. Revise the following blog posting so that it communicates in a more businesslike manner while retaining the informal, conversational tone of a blog (be sure to correct any spelling and punctuation mistakes you find as well).

Well, to the profound surprise of absolutely nobody, we are not going to be able meet the June 1 commitment to ship 100 operating tables to Southeast Surgical Supply. (For those of you who have been living in a cave the past six month, we have been fighting to get our hands on enough high-grade chromium steel to meet our production schedule.) Sure enough, we got news, this morning that we will only get enough for 30 tables. Yes, we look lik fools for not being able to follow through on promises we made to the customer, but no, this didn't have to happpen. Six month's ago, purchasing warned us about shrinking supplies and suggested we advance-buy as much as we would need for the next 12 months, or so. We naturally tried to follow their advice, but just as naturally were shot down by the bean counters at corporate who trotted out the policy about never buying more than three months worth of materials in advance. Of course, it'll be us—not the bean counters—who'll take the flak when everybody starts asking why revenues are down next quarter and why Southeast is talking to our friends at Crighton Manuf!!! Maybe, some day this company will get its head out of the sand and realize that we need to have some financial flexibility in order to compete.

 7.6 **Blogging: Blog Post Informing Employees About an Office Relocation** From what you've learned about effective blogging as well as planning and writing business messages in general, you should be able to identify numerous errors made by the writer of the following blog posting. First identify the flaws, then draft a version that fixes them.

Get Ready!
We are hoping to be back at work soon, with everything running smoothly, same production schedule and no late projects or missed deadlines. So you need to clean out your desk, put your stuff in boxes, and clean off the walls. You can put the items you had up on your walls in boxes, also.

We have provided boxes. The move will happen this weekend. We'll be in our new offices when you arrive on Monday.

We will not be responsible for personal belongings during the move.

Posted by David Burke at 10:42 AM 09-27-08

7.7 **Podcasting: Where Are We Going with This, Boss?** You've recently begun recording a weekly podcast to share information with your large and far-flung staff. After a month, you ask for feedback from several of your subordinates, and you're disappointed to learn that some people stopped listening to the podcast after the first couple of weeks. Someone eventually admits that many staffers feel the recordings are too long and rambling, and the information they contain isn't valuable enough to justify the time it takes to listen. You aren't pleased, but you want to improve. An assistant transcribes the introduction to last week's podcast so you can review it. You immediately see two problems. Revise the introduction based on what you've learned in this chapter.

So there I am, having lunch with Selma Gill, who just joined and took over the Northeast sales region from Jackson Stroud. In walks our beloved CEO with Selma's old boss at Uni-Plex; turns out they were finalizing a deal to co-brand our products and theirs and to set up a joint distribution program in all four domestic regions. Pretty funny, huh? Selma left Uni-Plex because she wanted to sell our products instead, and now she's back selling her old stuff, too. Anyway, try to chat with her when you can; she knows the biz inside and out and probably can offer insight into just about any sales challenge you might be running up against. We'll post more info on the co-brand deal next week; should be a boost for all of us. Other than those two news items, the other big news this week is the change in commission reporting. I'll go into the details in minute, but when you log onto the intranet, you'll now see your sales results split out by product line and industry sector. Hope this helps you see where you're doing well and where you might beef things up a bit. Oh yeah, I almost forgot the most important bit. Speaking of our beloved CEO, Thomas is going to be our guest of honor, so to speak, at quarterly sales meeting next week and wants an update on how petroleum prices are affecting customer behavior. Each district manager should be ready with a brief reports. After I go through the commission reporting scheme, I'll outline what you need to prepare.

Expand Your Knowledge

Exploring the Best of the Web

Ready to Start Blogging?

Blogging is easy to do if you have the right information. Start with the helpful tutorials at www.website101.com/RSS-Blogs-Blogging. More than 30 brief articles cover everything from creating a blog to attracting more readers to setting up RSS newsfeeds. Learn the techniques for adding audio and photo files to your blog. Review how search engines treat blogs and how you can use search engines to help more people find your blog, then answer the following questions.

1. What are five ways to attract more readers to your blog?
2. Why are blogs good for marketing?
3. What is a newsfeed and why is it a vital part of blogging?

Surfing Your Way to Career Success

Bovée and Thill's Business Communication Resources offers links to hundreds of online resources that can help you with this course, your other college courses, and your career. Visit www.buscommresources.com, then click on "Business Communication Web Directory." The "Letters, Memos, E-Mail, Instant Messages, Blogs, and Web Content" section connects you to a variety of websites and articles on routine, positive, and negative messages; persuasive messages; letters and memos; e-mail; IM; blogging; and web writing. Identify three websites from this section that could be useful in your business career. For each site, write a two-sentence summary of what the site offers and how it could help you launch and build your career.

Learn Interactively

Interactive Study Guide

Visit www.prenhall.com/bovee, then locate your book and click on its "Companion Website" link. Select Chapter 7 to take advantage of the interactive "Chapter Quiz" to test your knowledge of chapter concepts. Receive instant feedback on whether you need additional studying. Also, visit the "Study Hall," where you'll find an abundance of valuable resources that will help you succeed in this course.

Peak Performance Grammar and Mechanics

If your instructor has required the use of "Peak Performance Grammar and Mechanics," either in your online course or on CD, you can continue to improve your skill with prepositions, conjunctions, and articles by using the "Peak Performance Grammar and Mechanics" module. Click "Grammar Basics," and then click "Prepositions, Conjunctions, and Articles." Take the Pretest to determine whether you have any weak areas. Then review those areas in the Refresher Course. Take the Follow-Up Test to check your grasp of prepositions, conjunctions, and articles. For an extra challenge or advanced practice, take the Advanced Test. Finally, for additional reinforcement in prepositions, conjunctions, and articles, visit the Companion Website, click on any chapter, then click on "Improve Your Grammar, Mechanics, and Usage."

CASES

Applying the Three-Step Writing Process to Cases
Apply each step to the following cases, as assigned by your instructor.

Plan ➤

Analyze the Situation
Identify both your general purpose and your specific purpose. Clarify exactly what you want your audience to think, feel, or believe after receiving your message. Profile your primary audience, including their backgrounds, differences, similarities, and likely reactions to your message.

Gather Information
Identify the information your audience will need to receive, as well as other information you may need in order to craft an effective message.

Select the Right Medium
The medium is identified for each case here, but when on the job, make sure your medium is both acceptable to the audience and appropriate for the message.

Organize the Information
Define your main idea, limit your scope, choose a direct or indirect approach, and outline necessary support points and other evidence.

1

Write ➤

Adapt to Your Audience
Show sensitivity to audience needs with a "you" attitude, politeness, positive emphasis, and bias-free language. Understand how much credibility you already have—and how much you may need to establish. Project your company's image by maintaining an appropriate style and tone. Consider cultural variations and the differing needs of internal and external audiences.

Compose the Message
For written messages, draft your message using clear but sensitive words, effective sentences, and coherent paragraphs. For podcasts, outline your message and draft speaking notes to ensure smooth recording; use plenty of previews, transitions, and review to help audiences follow along.

2

Complete ➤

Revise the Message
Evaluate content and review readability, then edit and rewrite for conciseness and clarity.

Produce the Message
For written messages, use effective design elements and suitable layout for a clean, professional appearance. For podcasts, record your messages using whatever equipment you have available (professional podcasts may require upgraded equipment).

Proofread the Message
Review for errors in layout, spelling, and mechanics. Listen to podcasts to check for recording problems.

Distribute the Message
Deliver your message using the chosen medium; make sure all documents and all relevant files are distributed successfully.

3

Blogging SKILLS

1. Selling without selling: Blog posting about a GPS rescue Promoting products through customer success stories can be a great marketing tactic, as long as you keep the customer as the "star" of the story and don't promote the product too blatantly. You've recently joined Garmin, a leading manufacturer of electronic navigation equipment, including a popular line of handheld global positioning system (GPS) devices used by hikers, kayakers, and others who venture off the beaten path.

Your task: As a communication specialist, your responsibilities include writing blog postings that highlight dramatic stories in which people used Garmin GPS units to rescue themselves or others from potentially dangerous situations. Visit Garmin's website at www.garmin.com, click on What's New, then GPS Adventures (or access the page directly at www.garmin.com/whatsNew/adventures.html). Select a customer story that involves a wilderness

rescue in which a Garmin product played an important role. Using the information provided by the customer, rewrite the story in the third person (changing "I" or "we" references to "he," "she," or "they") for an audience that isn't familiar with the product in question. Subtly work in references to the product and the benefits it provided in this scenario, but keep the focus on the customer. Limit yourself to 400 words.

Blogging SKILLS

2. Come on to Comic-Con: Explaining the benefits of attending Comic-Con International is an annual convention that highlights a wide variety of pop culture and entertainment media, from comic books and collectibles to video games and movies. From its early start as a comic book convention that attracted several hundred fans and publishing industry insiders, Comic-Con has become a major international event with over 100,000 attendees.

Your task: Several readers of your pop culture blog have been asking for your recommendation about visiting Comic-Con in San Diego next summer. Write a two- or three-paragraph posting for your blog that explains what Comic-Con is and what visitors can expect to experience at the convention. Be sure to address your posting to fans, not industry insiders. You can learn more at www.comic-con.org.[37]

E-Mail SKILLS

3. Keeping the fans happy: Analyzing advertising on Espn.com ESPN leads the pack both online and off. Its well-known cable television sports channels are staple fare for sports enthusiasts, and ESPN.com (http://espn.go.com) is the leader in sports websites, too. Advertisers flock to ESPN.com because it delivers millions of visitors in the prime 18- to 34-year-old demographic group. With a continually refreshed offering of sporting news, columnists, video replays, and fantasy leagues (online competitions in which participants choose players for their teams, and the outcome is based on how well the real players do in actual live competition), ESPN.com has become one of the major advertising venues on the web.

As an up-and-coming web producer for ESPN.com, you're concerned about the rumblings of discontent you've heard from friends and read in various blogs and other sources. ESPN.com remains popular with millions of sports fans, but some say they are getting tired of all the ads on the site (both ads on the site itself as well as pop-up ads). A few say they are switching to other websites with fewer advertising intrusions. Your site traffic numbers are holding fairly steady for now, but you're worried that the few visitors leaving ESPN.com might be the start of a significant exodus in the future.

Your task: Write an e-mail message to your manager expressing your concern about the amount of advertising content on ESPN.com. Acknowledge that advertising is a vital source of revenue, but share what you're learned about site visitors who claim to be migrating to other sites. Offer to lead a comprehensive review effort that will compare the advertising presence on ESPN.com with that of other sports websites and explore ways to maintain strong advertising sales without alienating readers.[38]

4. That's not the way things really are: Correcting economic misinformation As the CEO of a small manufacturing company, your interests and responsibilities range far beyond the four walls of the factory. You have to be in tune with the global economy, politics, taxation policies, and other external forces that affect your company and your employees. Along with your peers in other companies, you've learned to speak out on issues—particularly when you believe that misguided government policies or misinformed public opinions threaten the viability of your company, your industry, and the economy as a whole.

An item in this morning's newspaper certainly got your attention. A prominent national political leader claimed that jobgrowth figures in recent years prove that the government's economic policies are working. The economy is in reasonably good shape considering the battering it has taken in recent years, but you believe the situation would improve considerably if the government would address a variety of issues, from health-care costs to economic incentives for investing in manufacturing upgrades. Moreover, you know that the politician's claim about job growth is only partly true. Yes, the U.S. economy added nearly 2 million new jobs in the past five years, but a recent *BusinessWeek* article pointed out that virtually all of those jobs were in health care. Not only did all other industries not add jobs as a whole, but the dramatic rise in health-care employment suggests no end to the rise in health-care costs.

Your task: Write a brief letter (no more than 300 words) to the editor of the newspaper. Correct the impression that job growth is occurring throughout the economy and encourage political leaders to address problems that you believe continue to limit growth in other industries, including health-care costs, taxation policies in the manufacturing sector, and unfair competitive practices from companies in certain other countries. Make up whatever information you need to back up your claims.[39]

E-Mail SKILLS

5. Must be an opportunity in here somewhere: The growing market of women living without husbands For the first time in history (aside from special situations such as major wars), more than half—51 percent—of all U.S. adult women now live without a spouse. (In other words, they live alone, with roommates, or as part of an unmarried couple.) Twenty-five percent have never married, and 26 percent are divorced, widowed, or married but living apart from their spouses. In the 1950s and into the 1960s, only 40 percent of women lived without a spouse, but every decade since, the percentage has increased. In your work as a consumer trend specialist for Seymour Powell (www.seymourpowell.com), a product design firm based in London that specializes in the home, personal, leisure, and transportation sectors, it's your business to recognize and respond to demographic shifts such as this.

Your task: With a small team of classmates, brainstorm possible product opportunities that respond to this trend. In an e-mail to be sent to the management team at Seymour Powell, list your ideas for new or modified products that might sell well in a society in which more than half of all adult women live without a spouse. For each idea, list a one-sentence explanation of why you think the product has potential.[40]

E-Mail SKILLS

6. Help is on the way: Encouraging Ford dealers The "Big Three" U.S. automakers—General Motors, Chrysler, and Ford—haven't had much good news to share lately. Ford in particular has been going through a rough time, losing billions of dollars and being overtaken in sales volume by Toyota.

Your task: Write an e-mail to be sent to all Ford dealers in North America, describing an exciting new model about to be introduced to the public. For this exercise, you can use either an upcoming Ford model that you have researched in the automotive media or a fictitious car of your own imagination (make sure it's something that could conceivably be introduced by Ford).[41]

Blogging SKILLS

7. Legitimate and legal: Defending technology sales to Chinese police agencies Cisco, a leading manufacturer of computer networking equipment, is one of several technology companies that have been criticized recently for selling high-tech equipment to police agencies in China. After the Chinese government killed hundreds of protestors in Tiananmen Square in 1989, U.S. officials began restricting the export of products that could be used by Chinese security forces. The restrictions cover a range of low-tech devices, from helmets and handcuffs to fingerprint powder and teargas, but not certain high-tech products such as the networking equipment that Cisco sells, which can conceivably be used by security forces in ways that violate human rights. Critics contend that by not restricting products such as Cisco's, the U.S. government is not enforcing the full intent of the restrictions. Moreover, they suggest that Cisco could be enabling abuse. For example, its Chinese marketing brochure promotes the equipment's ability to "strengthen police control."

Your task: Write a brief post for the Cisco executive blog that explains the following points: The company rigorously follows all U.S. export regulations; the company's marketing efforts in China are consistent with the way it markets products to other police organizations throughout the world; the products are simply tools, and like all tools, they can be applied in good or bad ways and responsible application is the customer's responsibility, not Cisco's; if Cisco didn't sell this equipment to the Chinese government, another company from another country would.[42]

IM SKILLS

8. The very definition of confusion: Helping consumers sort out high-definition television High-definition television can be a joy to watch—but oh what a pain to buy. The field is littered with competing technologies and arcane terminology that is meaningless to most consumers. Moreover, it's nearly impossible to define one technical term without invoking two or three others, leaving consumers swimming in an alphanumeric soup of confusion. The manufacturers themselves can't even agree on which of the *18* different digital TV formats truly qualify as "high definition." As a sales support manager for Crutchfield (www.crutchfield.com), a leading online re-

tailer of audio and video systems, you understand the frustration buyers feel—your staff is deluged daily by their questions.

Your task: To help your staff respond quickly to consumers who ask questions via Crutchfield's online IM chat service, you are developing a set of "canned" responses to common questions. When a consumer asks one of these questions, a sales advisor can simply click on the ready-made answer. Start by writing concise, consumer-friendly definitions of the following terms: *resolution, HDTV, 1080p,* and *HDMI.* (Visit Crutchfield's educational site, www.crutchfieldadvisor.com, and click on the "Learning Center for Home Theater and A/V," where you can learn more about these terms. Answers.com and Cnet.com are two other handy sources.)[43]

Podcasting SKILLS

9. Based on my experience: Recommending your college or university With any purchase decision, from a restaurant meal to a college education, recommendations from satisfied customers are often the strongest promotional messages.

Your task: Write a script for a one- to two-minute podcast (roughly 150 to 250 words) explaining why your college or university is a good place to get an education. Your audience is high school juniors and seniors. You can choose to craft a general message, something that would be useful to all prospective students, or you can focus on a specific academic discipline, the athletic program, or some other important aspect of your college experience. Either way, make sure your introductory comments make it clear whether you are offering a general recommendation or a specific recommendation. If your instructor indicates, record the podcast and submit the file electronically.

Podcasting SKILLS

10. Based on my experience: Suggestions for improving your college or university Every organization, no matter how successfully it operates, can find ways to improve customer service.

Your task: Write a script for a one- to two-minute podcast (roughly 150 to 250 words) identifying at least one way in which your college experience could have been or still could be improved through specific changes in policies, programs, facilities, or other elements. Your audience is the school's administration. Offer constructive criticism and specific arguments why your suggestions would help you—and possibly other students as well. Be sure to focus on meaningful and practical opportunities for improvement. If your instructor indicates, record the podcast and submit the file electronically.

Blogging SKILLS

11. Look sharp: Travel safety tips for new employees As the travel director for a global management consulting firm, your responsibilities range from finding the best travel deals to helping new employees learn the ins and outs of low-risk, low-stress travels. One of the ways in which you dispense helpful advice is through an internal blog.

Your task: Research advice for safe travel and identify at least six tips that every employee in your company should know. Write a brief blog posting that introduces and identifies the six tips.

E-Mail SKILLS

12. Your work does matter: Encouraging an unhappy colleague You certainly appreciate your company's "virtual team" policy of letting employees live wherever they want while using technology to communicate and collaborate. The company is headquartered in a large urban area, but you get to live in the mountains, only a step or two away from some of the best fly fishing in the world. Most of the time, this approach to work couldn't get any better.

However, the lack of face-to-face contact with your colleagues definitely has its disadvantages. For example, when a teammate seems to be upset about something, you wish you could go for a walk with the person and talk it out, rather than relying on phone calls, e-mail, or IM. In the past couple of weeks, Chris Grogan, the graphic designer working with you on a new e-commerce website project, seems to be complaining about everything. His negative attitude is starting to wear down the team's enthusiasm at a critical point in the project. In particular, he has complained several times that no one on the team seems to care about his design work. It is rarely mentioned in team teleconferences, and no one asks him about it. That part is true, actually, but the reason is that there is nothing wrong with his work—some critical technical issues unrelated to the graphic design are consuming everyone's attention.

Your task: After a couple of unsuccessful attempts at encouraging Grogan over the phone, you decide to write a brief e-mail message to assure him of the importance of his work on this project and the quality of his efforts. Let him know that graphic design is a critical part of the project's success and that as soon as those technical issues are resolved and the project is completed, everyone will have a chance to appreciate his contribution to the project. Make up whatever details you need to craft your message.

E-Mail SKILLS

13. She's one of us: Promoting a new lifestyle magazine Consumers looking for beauty, health, and lifestyle magazines have an almost endless array of choices, but even in this crowded field, Logan Olson found her own niche. Olson, who was born with congenital heart disease, suffered a heart attack at age 16 that left her in a coma and caused serious brain damage. The active and outgoing teen had to relearn everything from sitting up to feeding herself. As she recovered, she looked for help and advice in conquering such daily challenges as finding fashionable clothes that were easier to put on and makeup that was easier to apply. Mainstream beauty magazines didn't seem to offer any information for young women with disabilities, so she started her own magazine. Oprah Winfrey has *Oprah*, and now Logan Olson has *Logan*. The magazine not only gives young women tips on buying and using a variety of products but lets women with disabilities know there are others out there like them, facing and meeting the same challenges.

Your task: Write a promotional e-mail message to be sent to young women with disabilities as well as families and friends who might like to give gift subscriptions, promoting the benefits of subscribing to *Logan*. You can learn more about *Logan* at www.loganmagazine.com.[44]

E-Mail SKILLS

14. We're the one: Explaining why a company should hire your firm You work for Brainbench (www.brainbench.com), one of many companies that offer employee screening services. Brainbench's offerings include a variety of online products and consulting services, all designed to help employers find and develop the best possible employees. For example, Brainbench's Pre-Hire Testing products help employers test for job skills, communication skills, personality, and employment history red flags (such as chronic absenteeism or performance problems). Employers use these test results to either screen out candidates entirely or ask focused interview questions about areas of concern.

Sonja Williamson, the human resources director of a large retail company, has just e-mailed your sales team. She would like an overview of the Pre-Hire Testing products and some background on your company.

Your task: Write an e-mail response to Williamson's query. Be sure to thank her for her interest, briefly describe the Pre-Hire Testing products, and summarize Brainbench's qualifications. Include at least one hyperlink back to the Brainbench website, and consider attaching one or more PDF files from the website as well.

E-Mail SKILLS

15. Firing the customer: When a particular customer is always wrong Many companies operate on the principle that the customer is always right, even when the customer isn't right. They take whatever steps are necessary to ensure happy customers, lots of repeat sales, and a positive reputation among potential buyers. Overall, this is a smart and successful approach to business. However, most companies eventually encounter that one nightmare customer who drains so much time, energy, and profits that the only sensible option is to refuse the customer's business. For example, the nightmare customer might be someone who constantly berates you and your employees, repeatedly makes outlandish demands for refunds and discounts, or who simply requires so much help that you not only lose money on this person but you also no longer have enough time to help your other customers. "Firing" a customer is an unpleasant step that should be taken only in the most extreme cases and only after other remedies have been attempted (such as talking with the customer about the problem), but it is sometimes necessary for the well-being of your employees and your company.

Your task: If you are currently working or have held a job in the recent past, imagine that you've encountered just such a customer. If you don't have job experience to call on, imagine that you work in a retail location somewhere around campus or in your neighborhood. Identify the type of behavior this imaginary customer exhibits and the reasons that the behavior can no longer be accepted. Now write a brief e-mail message to the customer to explain that you will no longer be able to accommodate him or her as a customer. Calmly explain why you have had to reach this difficult decision. Maintain a professional tone by keeping your emotions in check.

Podcasting
SKILLS

16. Podcasting pitch: Training people to sell your favorite product What product do you own (or use regularly) that you can't live without? It could be something as seemingly minor as a favorite pen or something as significant as a medical device that you literally can't live without. Now imagine you're a salesperson for this product; think about how you would sell it to potential buyers. How would you describe it, and how would you explain the benefits of owning it? After you've thought about how you would present the product to others, now imagine you've just been promoted to sales manager, and it is your job to train other people to sell the product.

Your task: Write the script for a brief podcast (200 to 300 words) that summarizes for your sales staff the most important points to convey about the product. Imagine that they'll listen to your podcast while driving to a customer's location or preparing for the day's activity in a retail store (depending on the nature of the product). Be sure to give your staffers a concise overview message about the product and several key support points.

E-Mail
SKILLS

17. Time to think: E-mail requesting a change in your workload The description of your job as a global marketing manager for New Balance is full of responsibilities that require creative thinking, from predicting consumer and retailing trends to establishing seasonal priorities for the global merchandising effort. You love these challenges—in fact, they're the main reason you took the job at this respected maker of athletic shoes and apparel. Unfortunately, between department meetings, status reports, budgets, and an endless array of other required chores, you hardly have time to think at all, much less engage in the sort of unstructured, "blue sky" thinking that is crucial to creative strategizing. You have virtually no time at work for such thinking, and after 50 or 60 hours a week at the office or on the road, you're too exhausted to brainstorm on your own time.

Your task: Write an e-mail to your boss, Paul Heffernan, the executive vice president of global marketing, persuading him that you need to reshuffle your assignments to free up more time to think. This is a tricky request because you know that Heffernan faces the same challenge. However, you're convinced that by spending less time on tasks that could be done by someone else (or perhaps shouldn't be done at all), you'll be able to do a better job of creating marketing strategies—and maybe even set a good example for other New Balance executives. You have a preliminary list of changes you'd like to make, but you know you need to discuss the entire scope of your job with Heffernan before finalizing the list. Your purpose: Invite him to lunch to begin a discussion of reshaping your responsibilities.[45]

E-Mail
SKILLS

18. Mercedes merchandise: Message announcing exclusive online gift shop Mercedes-Benz owners take their accessories seriously, which is why you get angry letters and e-mails when they buy Mercedes-branded merchandise that turns out to be fake. Even though your company has nothing to do with these low-quality, unauthorized knock-offs, customers sometimes blame you anyway. To battle the problem, Mercedes has opened an online store where every item comes with a certificate of authenticity that it was manufactured by a Mercedes-approved partner and meets Mercedes quality standards. At **www.mbusi.com**, the website for the Mercedes-Benz manufacturing plant in Tuscaloosa, Alabama, shoppers can follow the "Store" link to the online gift shop. But first they need to know it exists.

Your task: As assistant for Steve Beaty, vice president of accessories marketing, draft an e-mail message to registered Mercedes owners telling them about the online gift shop. Visit the website to learn more about it, then write the message using a style you think suits the car manufacturer's image.

Team
SKILLS

19. Measuring suppliers: E-mail requesting reviews at Microsoft Microsoft evaluates employees regularly to determine their performance—so why not do the same with the independent contractors the company hires to perform key functions? Nearly every department uses outside providers these days—a practice called *outsourcing*. So if there's a gap between what Microsoft expects from contractors and what the contractors actually deliver, shouldn't Microsoft tell them how they can improve their performance?

You've been discussing these questions all morning in a meeting with other members of the Employee Services Group. Your boss is convinced that regular reviews of independent contractors are essential.

"It's all about improving clarity in terms of goals and expectations," he says, adding that if contractors receive constructive feedback, Microsoft can develop good relationships with them instead of having to look for new service suppliers all the time.

Your boss assigns your team the task of informing all Microsoft departments that they'll be required to evaluate subcontractors every six months, beginning immediately. The goal of the review is to determine the performance of independent contractors so that Microsoft can (1) give them constructive feedback and continue a strong relationship or (2) end the relationship if service is substandard. Departments will need to rate each contractor on a scale of 1 (poor) to 5 (excellent) for each of several factors that your group is going to determine. Departments will be sending their reports to Roxanna Frost, group program manager for Microsoft's Executive Management and Development Group.

Your task: Working as a team with your classmates, develop a list of factors that will help you rate the overall service of independent contractors. You'll need to consider "cost," "quality of work," "innovation," "delivery," and other factors similar to those you'd encounter in a job performance review. Then compose an e-mail to all Microsoft department managers: Explain the new review requirements and include your list of factors to be rated on the 1-to-5 scale.[46]

IM SKILLS

20. Yes, we do purple: Instant message from Lands' End When clothing retailer Lands' End offered its 2,500 telephone service representatives the chance to train on its new instant messaging system, "Lands' End Live," you jumped at the opportunity. As it turned out, so many volunteered for the new training that the company had to give preference to a few hundred who'd been on the job longest. You were one of the lucky ones.

Now you've had months of practice answering messages like the one you just received from a customer named Alicia. She wants to know if she can have a red Polartec Aircore-200 Scarf custom monogrammed—not in the standard, contrasting, wheat-colored thread, but in radiant purple as a gift for her husband, whose favorite colors are red and purple.

On its website, Lands' End promises to fulfill nonstandard monogram requests "if technical limitations allow." You've done a quick check and yes, her husband can have his initials in bright purple on the red background.

Your task: Write the instant message reply to Alicia, telling her the good news.[47]

E-Mail SKILLS

21. No exaggeration: Short e-mail describing internship duties You've been laboring all summer at an internship, learning how business is conducted. You've done work nobody else wanted to do, but that's okay. Even the smallest tasks can make a good impression on your future résumé.

This morning, your supervisor asks you to write a description of the job you've been doing. "Include everything, even the filing," she suggests, "and address it to me in an e-mail message." She says a future boss might assign such a task prior to a performance review. "You can practice describing your work without exaggeration—or too much modesty," she says, smiling.

Your task: Using good techniques for short messages and relying on your real-life work experience, write an e-mail that will impress your supervisor. Make up any details you need.

Blogging SKILLS

22. Meet the parents: Blog posting announcing the acquisition of Golden West As the human resources director for Golden West Financial, you know how proud your fellow employees are to work for one of the most admired banking companies in the United States. Golden West, which serves retail customers through its World Savings Bank branches across the West, was founded in Oakland, California, in the 1960s by the husband-and-wife team of Herbert and Marion Sandler. For decades, Golden West flourished as an independent company, but in 2006, the Sandlers decided to sell Golden West to Wachovia, a financial giant based in Charlotte, North Carolina.

Over the coming weeks, you'll provide Golden West employees with more information about the impact of the huge deal, but for now you want them to be aware of four key points:

- The deal allows Golden West to expand beyond its core offering of home mortgages to provide other financial services that its customers have requested for some time.
- The Sandlers carefully selected Wachovia because of its compatible values of integrity, customer-first business practices, and teamwork.
- World Savings Bank operations will continue from existing locations under the existing World Savings Bank brand name. New financial services from Wachovia will be added over time.
- The company's commitment to providing excellent career opportunities for women and minorities will not change.[48]

Your task: Write a short posting for Golden West's internal blog, announcing the deal and communicating the four aforementioned key points listed (in your own words). Close by telling your colleagues how excited you are by the deal and that you'll be providing more information in the days and weeks ahead.

E-Mail SKILLS

23. Environmental planning: E-mail announcing a committee meeting You've probably worked as a volunteer on a committee or with team members for class assignments. You know how hard it is to get a diverse group of individuals together for a productive meeting. Maybe you've tried different locations—one member's home or a table at the library. This time you're going to suggest a local restaurant.

The committee you're leading is a volunteer group planning a trash-clearing project at an area park. Your meeting goal is to brainstorm ways to encourage public participation in this environmental event, to be held next Earth Day.

Your task: Develop a short e-mail message telling committee members about the meeting. Include time, date, duration, and location (choose a place you know). Mention the meeting goal to encourage attendance.

Podcasting SKILLS

24. Why me? Introducing yourself to a potential employer While writing the many letters and e-mail messages that are part of the job search process, you find yourself wishing that you could just talk to some of these companies so your personality could shine through. Well, you've just gotten that opportunity. One of the companies that you've applied to has e-mailed you back, asking you to submit a two-minute podcast introducing yourself and explaining why you would be a good person to hire.

Your task: Identify a company that you'd like to work for after graduation and select a job that would be a good match for your skills and interests. Write a script for a two-minute podcast (two minutes represents roughly 250 words for most speakers). Introduce yourself and the position you're applying for, describe your background, and explain why you think you're a good candidate for the job. Make up any details you need. If your instructor indicates, record the podcast and submit the file.

25. Hi, my name is: Introducing yourself on a business network Business networking websites such as www.linkedin.com, www.ryze.com, and www.spoke.com have become popular ways for professionals to make connections that would be difficult or impossible to make without the Internet. (You might be familiar with MySpace.com or Friendster.com, sites that help individuals meet through networks of people they already know and trust.) These business-oriented sites follow the same principle, but instead of using them to find new friends or dates, you use them to find new customers, new suppliers, or other important business connections. For instance, you might find that the ideal contact person in a company you'd like to do business with is the aunt of your boss's tennis partner.

An important aspect of business networking is being able to provide a clear description of your professional background and interests. For example, a manufacturing consultant can list the industries in which she has experience, the types of projects she has worked on, and the nature of work she'd like to pursue in the future (such as a full-time position for a company or additional independent projects).

Your task: Write a brief statement introducing yourself, including your educational background, your job history, and the types of connections you'd like to make. Feel free to "fast forward" to your graduation and list your degree, the business specialty you plan to pursue, and any relevant experience. If you have business experience already, feel free to use that information instead. Make sure your statement is clear, concise (no more than two sentences), and compelling, so that anyone looking for someone like you would want to get in touch with you after reading your introduction.

CHAPTER 8

Writing Routine and Positive Messages

LEARNING OBJECTIVES

After studying this chapter, you will be able to

1 Apply the three-step writing process to routine and positive messages

2 Outline an effective strategy for writing routine requests

3 Explain how to ask for specific action in a courteous manner

4 Describe a strategy for writing routine replies and positive messages

5 Discuss the importance of knowing who is responsible when granting claims and requests for adjustment

6 Explain how creating informative messages differs from responding to information requests

7 Describe the importance of goodwill messages and explain how to make them effective

COMMUNICATION CLOSE-UP AT CONE, INC.

www.coneinc.com

Considering the number of corporate scandals in recent years, it's easy to forget that thousands of companies continue to conduct business ethically and work to make significant contributions in their communities. Ready to help them in their efforts to help others is Carol Cone of Cone, Inc., a Boston-based agency that specializes in *cause branding*, linking corporate brands to socially beneficial programs.

One of Cone's biggest success stories has been publicizing the efforts of ConAgra Foods, which took up the cause of child hunger in the United States through its Feeding Children Better program. A centerpiece of those efforts is the Kids Cafés, an after-school program that serves free, hot, nutritious meals to kids in need. Since it became the national sponsor of Kids Cafés, ConAgra has funded 150 new Kids Cafés, each one providing more than 10,000 meals a year. ConAgra also helps in the battle against childhood hunger by helping to improve the distribution of food nationwide.

Cone focuses news releases, web content, and other messages on the three main goals of the program: (1) getting food to children who need it, (2) repairing the breakdowns in food distribution, and (3) raising national awareness about child hunger. ConAgra and Cone have received numerous

ConAgra's Feeding Children Better program supports thousands of children every year, and the company's public relations agency uses these successes to focus nationwide attention on the problems of childhood hunger.

awards for their good work and effective communication, such as the Corporate Citizenship Award from the U.S. Chamber of Commerce and the Cause Marketing Halo Award.

What makes Cone's messages so effective? Simply calling attention to ConAgra's good deeds would be a positive business result, but doing so would primarily benefit ConAgra, not the various hunger relief programs. Instead, Cone puts her news releases to work by highlighting ConAgra's progress toward the goal of eradicating childhood hunger, thereby helping her client accomplish even more positive outcomes through the use of positive messages.[1]

USING THE THREE-STEP WRITING PROCESS FOR ROUTINE AND POSITIVE MESSAGES

1 LEARNING OBJECTIVE

Apply the three-step writing process to routine and positive messages

Regardless of the subject matter of your business messages, you can make them more effective by following Carol Cone's advice (profiled in the chapter-opening Communication Close-Up) to stay focused on your overall business goals and to emphasize the audience's concerns whenever you write. Like Cone, you'll be composing numerous routine and positive messages during the typical business day. In fact, most business communication is about routine matters: customer orders, company policies, employees, products, operations, and so on. Such messages are rarely long or complex, but the three-step writing process still gives you a great way to produce effective messages efficiently.

Step 1: Plan Your Message

Even simple messages can benefit from thoughtful planning.

Even though planning routine and positive messages may take only a few minutes, the four tasks of planning still apply. First, analyze the situation, making sure that your purpose is clear and that you know enough about your audience to craft a successful message. Second, gather whatever information your audience needs to know. Even something as simple as a team meeting can involve dozens of details, from presentation setups to lunch arrangements to parking. Including all necessary information the first time saves you and your audience the time and trouble of additional messages to fill in the gaps. Third, select the right medium for the message and the audience. Both routine and positive messages are often sent via e-mail or instant messaging today, but printed memos, letters, and other media are used in some instances. Fourth, organize your information effectively. This task includes defining your main idea, limiting your scope, selecting a direct or an indirect approach, and outlining your content. Throughout this chapter, you'll learn more about performing all four of these tasks for a variety of routine and positive message types.

Step 2: Write Your Message

Start by adapting your approach to your audience. Be sensitive to your audience's needs by maintaining a "you" attitude, being polite, emphasizing the positive, and using bias-free language. To strengthen your relationship with your audience, establish your credibility and project your company's image. Also, even though your tone is usually conversational, some messages may need to be more formal than others. You'll want to use plain English and make your writing as active as possible.

With some practice, you'll be able to compose most routine messages quickly. In fact, the ability to generate such messages quickly is a key skill for most business executives because you won't have a lot of time to spend on most messages. Your main idea is probably well defined already; just be sure you stick to it by limiting the scope of your message (see Figure 8.1).

For routine requests and positive messages,
- *State the request or main idea*
- *Give necessary details*
- *Close with a cordial request for specific action*

Also, your readers in most cases will be interested or at least neutral, so you can usually adopt the direct approach for routine and positive messages: Open with a clear statement of the main idea, include all necessary details in the body, and then close cordially. Keep in mind that even though these messages are the least complicated to write, communicating across cultural boundaries can be a challenge, especially if you're not familiar with the cultural differences involved.

FIGURE 8.1 Routine Messages
Routine and positive messages are best conveyed using a direct approach. Google uses this blog to keep users of its AdWords search engine advertising system up to date on maintenance interruptions and other important news.

Step 3: Complete Your Message

No matter how brief or straightforward your message, maximize its impact by giving yourself plenty of time to revise, produce, proofread, and distribute it. First, revise your message by evaluating content and organization to make sure you've said what you want to in the order you want to say it. Review your message's readability. Edit and rewrite to make it concise and clear. Second, design your document to suit your purpose and your audience. Even simple e-mails and instant messages can benefit from careful font selection, the wise use of white space, and other design choices. Next, proofread the final version of your message, looking for typos, errors in spelling and mechanics, alignment problems, poor print quality, and so on. Finally, choose a distribution method that balances cost, convenience, time, security, and privacy. Refer to Chapter 7 for the most common media formats for brief messages.

MAKING ROUTINE REQUESTS

Making requests—for information, action, products, adjustments, or other matters—is a routine part of business. In most cases, your audience will be prepared to comply, as long as you're not being unreasonable or asking people to do something they would expect you to do yourself. By applying a clear strategy and tailoring your approach to each situation, you'll be able to generate effective requests quickly.

Strategy for Routine Requests

2 LEARNING OBJECTIVE

Outline an effective strategy for writing routine requests

Like all business messages, routine requests have three parts: an opening, a body, and a close. Using the direct approach, open with your main idea, which is a clear statement of your request. Use the body to give details and justify your request. Then close by requesting specific action.

State Your Request Up Front

Take care that your direct approach doesn't come across as abrupt or tactless.

Begin routine requests by placing your request first—up front is where it stands out and gets the most attention. Of course, getting right to the point should not be interpreted as a license to be abrupt or tactless:

- **Pay attention to tone.** Even though you expect a favorable response, the tone of your initial request is important. Instead of demanding action ("Send me the latest personnel cost data"), soften your request with words such as *please* and *I would appreciate.*
- **Assume your audience will comply.** An impatient demand for rapid service isn't necessary. You can generally make the assumption that your audience will comply with your request once the reason for it is clearly understood.
- **Be specific.** State precisely what you want. For example, if you request the latest market data from your research department, be sure to say whether you want a one-page summary or a hundred pages of raw data.

Explain and Justify Your Request

Use the body of your message to explain your initial request. Make the explanation a smooth and logical outgrowth of your opening remarks. If possible, point out how complying with the request could benefit the reader. For instance, if you would like some assistance interpreting complex quality-control data, you might point out how a better understanding of quality-control issues would improve customer satisfaction and ultimately lead to higher profits for the entire company.

Using a list format helps readers sort through multiple questions or requests.

Whether you're writing a formal letter or a simple instant message, you can use the body of your request to list a series of questions. This list of questions helps organize your message and helps your audience identify the information you need. Just keep in mind a few basics:

- **Ask the most important questions first.** If cost is your main concern, you might begin with a question such as "What is the cost for shipping the merchandise by air versus truck?" Then you may want to ask more specific but related questions about, say, discounts for paying early.
- **Ask only relevant questions.** To help expedite the response to your request, ask only those questions that are central to your main request. Doing so will generate an answer sooner and make better use of the other person's time.
- **Deal with only one topic per question.** If you have an unusual or complex request, break it down into specific, individual questions so that the reader can address each one separately. Don't put the burden of untangling a complicated request on your reader. This consideration not only shows respect for your audience's time but also gets you a more accurate answer in less time.

Request Specific Action in a Courteous Close

3 LEARNING OBJECTIVE

Explain how to ask for specific action in a courteous manner

Close your message with three important elements: (1) a specific request, (2) information about how you can be reached (if it isn't obvious), and (3) an expression of appreciation or goodwill. When you ask readers to perform a specific action, ask that they respond by a specific time, if appropriate ("Please send the figures by April 5 so that I can return first-quarter results to you before the May 20 conference"). Plus, by including your phone number, e-mail address, office hours, and other contact information, you help your readers respond easily.

Close request messages with
- *A request for some specific action*
- *Information about how you can be reached*
- *An expression of appreciation*

Conclude your message by sincerely expressing your goodwill and appreciation. However, don't thank the reader "in advance" for cooperating. If the reader's reply warrants a

CHECKLIST: Writing Routine Requests

A. State your request up front.
- Write in a polite, undemanding, personal tone.
- Use the direct approach, because your audience will probably respond favorably to your request.
- Be specific and precise in your request.

B. Explain and justify your request.
- Justify the request or explain its importance.
- Explain any potential benefits of responding.

- Ask the most important questions first.
- Break complex requests into individual questions that are limited to only one topic each.

C. Request specific action in a courteous close.
- Make it easy to comply by including appropriate contact information.
- Express your gratitude.
- Clearly state any important deadlines for the request.

word of thanks, send it after you've received the reply. To review, see "Checklist: Writing Routine Requests."

Common Examples of Routine Requests

The various types of routine requests are innumerable, from asking favors to requesting credit. However, many of the routine messages that you'll be writing will likely fall into a few main categories: asking for information and action, asking for recommendations, and making claims and requesting adjustments.

Asking for Information and Action

When you need to know about something, elicit an opinion from someone, or request a simple action, you usually need only ask. In essence, simple requests say

- What you want to know or what you want readers to do
- Why you're making the request
- Why it may be in your readers' interest to help you

If your reader is able to do what you want, such a straightforward request gets the job done quickly. Follow the direct approach by opening with a clear statement of your reason for writing. In the body, provide whatever explanation is needed to justify your request. Then close with a specific description of what you expect, and include a deadline if appropriate (see Figure 8.2). In more complex situations, readers might be unwilling to respond unless they understand how the request benefits them so be sure to include this information in your explanation. The proper tone is usually matter-of-fact, and you can assume some shared background when communicating about a routine matter to someone in the same company.

In contrast to requests sent internally, those sent to people outside the organization usually adopt a more formal tone. You'll most likely be in a position to ask businesses, customers, or others outside your organization to provide information or to take some simple action (attend a meeting, join a professional organization, provide or confirm information, and so on). Such requests are often in letter form, although some are sent via e-mail. These messages are usually short and simple but still formal and professional, like the following request for information:

Dear Bioverse:

Please provide additional information on distribution opportunities for your Healthy Ponds product line, as mentioned on your website. Enviro Domestic is a 20-year old firm with a well-established design, retail, and service presence in the Oklahoma City area, and we believe your bioremediation products would make a compelling addition to our offerings.

Makes overall request in polite question form (no question mark)

Identifies the writer's affiliation and reason for writing

FIGURE 8.2 Effective Message Requesting Action
In this e-mail request to district managers across the country, Helene Clausen asks them to fill out an attached information collection form. While the request is not unusual and responding to it is part of the managers' responsibility, Clausen asks for their help in a courteous manner and points out the benefits of responding.

Plan

Analyze the Situation
Verify that purpose is to request information from company managers.

Gather Information
Gather accurate, complete information about local competitive threats.

Select the Right Medium
Choose e-mail for this internal message, which also allows the attachment of a Word document to collect the information.

Organize the Information
Clarify that the main idea is collecting information that will lead to a better competitive strategy, which will in turn help the various district managers.

Write

Adapt to Your Audience
Show sensitivity to audience needs with a "you" attitude, politeness, positive emphasis, and bias-free language. Writer already has credibility as manager of the department.

Compose the Message
Maintain a style that is conversational but still businesslike, using plain English and appropriate voice.

Complete

Revise the Message
Evaluate content and review readability; avoid unnecessary details.

Produce the Message
Simple e-mail format is all the design this message needs.

Proofread the Message
Review for errors in layout, spelling, and mechanics.

Distribute the Message
Deliver the message via the company's e-mail system.

1 **2** **3**

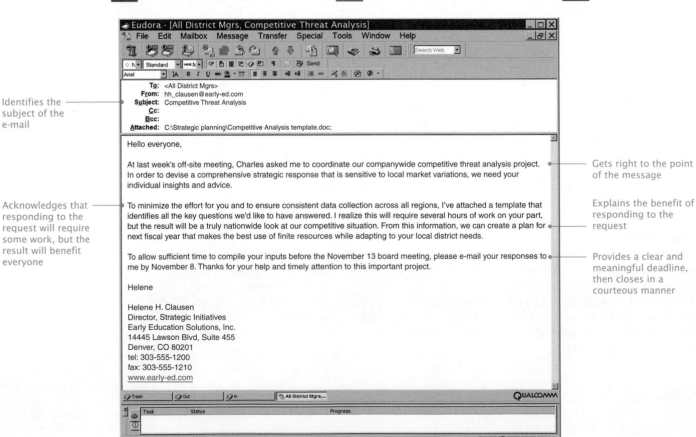

Identifies the subject of the e-mail

Acknowledges that responding to the request will require some work, but the result will benefit everyone

Gets right to the point of the message

Explains the benefit of responding to the request

Provides a clear and meaningful deadline, then closes in a courteous manner

In particular, we would appreciate answers to the following questions:

1. Do you offer exclusive regional distribution contracts?

2. Do you offer factory training for sales and service specialists?

3. Do you plan to expand beyond water bioremediation solutions into other landscaping products?

Please let us hear from you by February 15.

Specifies exactly what the writer wishes to know to assist the recipient in responding

Closes with a polite request and a specific answer deadline

A more complex request might require not only greater detail but also information on how responding will benefit the reader.

Sometimes you may need to reestablish a relationship with former customers or suppliers. In many cases, when customers are unhappy about some purchase or about the way they were treated, they don't complain; they simply stay away from the offending business. Thus, a letter of inquiry might encourage customers to use idle credit accounts, offering them an opportunity to register their displeasure and then move on to a good relationship. In addition, a customer's response to such an inquiry may give you insights into ways to improve your products and customer service. Even if they have no complaint, customers still welcome the personal attention.

The purpose of some routine requests to customers is simply to reestablish communication.

Asking for Recommendations

The need to inquire about people arises often in business. For example, before awarding credit, contracts, jobs, promotions, scholarships, and so on, companies often ask applicants to supply references. If you're applying for a job and your potential employer asks for references, you may want to ask a close personal or professional associate to write a letter of recommendation. Or, if you're an employer considering whether to hire an applicant, you may want to write directly to the person the applicant named as a reference.

Companies ask applicants to supply references who can vouch for their ability, skills, integrity, character, and fitness for the job. Before you volunteer someone's name as a reference, ask permission do to so. Some people won't let you use their names, perhaps because they don't know enough about you to feel comfortable writing a letter or because they have a policy of not providing recommendations. In any event, you are likely to receive the best recommendation from people who agree to write about you, so check first.

Always ask for permission before using someone as a reference.

Because requests for recommendations and references are routine, you can assume your reader will honor your request, and you can organize your inquiry using the direct approach. Open your message by clearly stating that you're applying for a position and that you would like your reader to write a letter of recommendation. If you haven't had contact with the person for some time, use the opening to recall the nature of the relationship you had, the dates of association, and any special events that might bring a clear and favorable picture of you to mind. Consider including an updated résumé if you've had significant career advancement since your last contact.

Refresh the memory of any potential reference you haven't been in touch with for a while.

Close your message with an expression of appreciation and the full name and address of the person to whom the letter should be sent. When asking for an immediate recommendation, you should also mention the deadline. Always be sure to enclose a stamped, preaddressed envelope as a convenience to the other party. See Figure 8.3 for a request that follows these guidelines.

Making Claims and Requesting Adjustments

If you're dissatisfied with a company's product or service, you can opt to make a **claim** (a formal complaint) or request an **adjustment** (a claim settlement). In either case, it's important to maintain a professional tone in all your communication, no matter how angry or frustrated you might be. Keeping your cool will help you get the situation resolved sooner. In addition, be sure to document your initial complaint and every correspondence after that.

In most cases, and especially in your first letter, assume that a fair adjustment will be made and follow the plan for direct requests. Open with a straightforward statement of the problem. In the body, give a complete, specific explanation of the details. Provide any

In your claim letter,
• Explain the problem and give details
• Provide backup information
• Request specific action

FIGURE 8.3 Effective Letter Requesting a Recommendation

This writer uses a direct approach when asking for a recommendation from a former professor. Note how she takes care to refresh the professor's memory because the class was taken a year and a half ago. She also indicates the date by which the letter is needed and points to the enclosure of a stamped, preaddressed envelope.

Plan

Analyze the Situation
Verify that the purpose is to request a recommendation letter from a college professor.

Gather Information
Gather information on classes and dates to help the reader recall you and to clarify the position you seek.

Select the Right Medium
The letter format gives this message an appropriate level of formality, although many professors prefer to be contacted by e-mail.

Organize the Information
Messages like this are common and expected, so a direct approach is fine.

Write

Adapt to Your Audience
Show sensitivity to audience needs with a "you" attitude, politeness, positive emphasis, and bias-free language.

Compose the Message
Style is respectful and businesslike, while still using plain English and appropriate voice.

Complete

Revise the Message
Evaluate content and review readability; avoid unnecessary details.

Produce the Message
Simple memo format is all the design this message needs.

Proofread the Message
Review for errors in layout, spelling, and mechanics.

Distribute the Message
Deliver the message via postal mail or e-mail if you have the professor's e-mail address.

1   **2**   **3**

1181 Ashport Drive
Tate Springs, TN 38101
March 14, 2008

Professor Lyndon Kenton
School of Business
University of Tennessee, Knoxville
Knoxville, TN 37916

Dear Professor Kenton:

I recently interviewed with Strategic Investments and have been called for a second interview for their Analyst Training Program (ATP). They have requested at least one recommendation from a professor, and I immediately thought of you. May I have a letter of recommendation from you?

As you may recall, I took BUS 485, Financial Analysis, from you in the fall of 2006. I enjoyed the class and finished the term with an "A." Professor Kenton, your comments on assertiveness and cold-calling impressed me beyond the scope of the actual course material. In fact, taking your course helped me decide on a future as a financial analyst.

My enclosed résumé includes all my relevant work experience and volunteer activities. I would also like to add that I've handled the financial planning for our family since my father passed away several years ago. Although I initially learned by trial and error, I have increasingly applied my business training in deciding what stocks or bonds to trade. This, I believe, has given me a practical edge over others who may be applying for the same job.

If possible, Ms. Blackmon in Human Resources needs to receive your letter by March 30. For your convenience, I've enclosed a preaddressed, stamped envelope.

I appreciate your time and effort in writing this letter of recommendation for me. It will be great to put my education to work, and I'll keep you informed of my progress. Thank you for your consideration in this matter.

Sincerely,

Joanne Tucker

Joanne Tucker

Enclosure

Includes information near the opening to refresh the reader's memory about this former student

Gives a deadline for response and includes information about the person expecting the recommendation

Opens by stating the purpose of the letter and making the request, assuming the reader will want to comply with the request

Refers to résumé in the body and mentions experience that could set applicant apart from other candidates

Mentions the preaddressed, stamped envelope to encourage a timely response

CHECKLIST: Making Claims and Requesting Adjustments

- Maintain a professional tone, even if you're extremely frustrated.
- Open with a straightforward statement of the problem.
- Provide specific details in the body.
- Present facts honestly and clearly.

- Politely summarize desired action in the closing.
- Clearly state what you expect as a fair settlement, or ask the reader to propose a fair adjustment.
- Explain the benefits of complying with the request, such as your continued patronage.

information an adjuster would need to verify your complaint. In your close, politely request specific action or convey a sincere desire to find a solution. And, if appropriate, suggest that the business relationship will continue if the problem is solved satisfactorily.

Companies usually accept the customer's explanation of what's wrong, so it is important to be entirely honest when filing claims. Also, be prepared to back up your claim with invoices, sales receipts, canceled checks, dated correspondence, and any other relevant documents. Send copies and keep the originals for your files.

Be prepared to document your claim. Send copies and keep the original documents.

If the remedy is obvious, tell your reader exactly what you expect from the company, such as exchanging incorrectly shipped merchandise for the right item or issuing a refund if the item is out of stock. In some cases, you might ask the reader to resolve a problem. However, if you're uncertain about the precise nature of the trouble, you could ask the company to make an assessment then advise you on how the situation could be fixed. Supply your contact information so that the company can discuss the situation with you if necessary. Compare the ineffective and effective versions in Figure 8.4 for an example of making a claim.

A rational, clear, and courteous approach is best for any routine request. To review the tasks involved in making claims and requesting adjustments, see "Checklist: Making Claims and Requesting Adjustments."

SENDING ROUTINE REPLIES AND POSITIVE MESSAGES

Just as you'll make numerous requests for information and action throughout your career, you'll also respond to similar requests from other people. When responding positively to a request, sending routine announcements, or sending a positive or goodwill message, you have several goals: to communicate the information or the good news, answer all questions, provide all required details, and leave your reader with a good impression of you and your firm.

4 LEARNING OBJECTIVE

Describe a strategy for writing routine replies and positive messages

Strategy for Routine Replies and Positive Messages

Like requests, routine replies and positive messages have an opening, a body, and a close. Because readers receiving these messages will generally be interested in what you have to say, you'll usually use the direct approach. Place your main idea (the positive reply or the good news) in the opening. Use the body to explain all the relevant details, and close cordially—perhaps highlighting a benefit to your reader.

Use the direct organizational plan for positive messages.

Start with the Main Idea

By opening your routine and positive messages with the main idea or good news, you're preparing your audience for the detail that follows. Try to make your opening clear and concise. Although the following introductory statements make the same point, one is cluttered with unnecessary information that buries the purpose, whereas the other is brief and to the point:

Prepare your audience for the detail that follows by beginning your positive message with the main idea or good news.

INSTEAD OF THIS

I am pleased to inform you that after careful consideration of a delightfully talented pool of applicants, our human resources committee has recommended you for appointment as a financial analyst.

WRITE THIS

Congratulations. You've been selected to join our Cleveland office as a financial analyst, beginning March 20.

FIGURE 8.4 Ineffective and Effective Versions of Claim

Note the difference in both tone and information content in these two versions. The ineffective version is emotional and unprofessional, whereas the effective version communicates calmly and clearly.

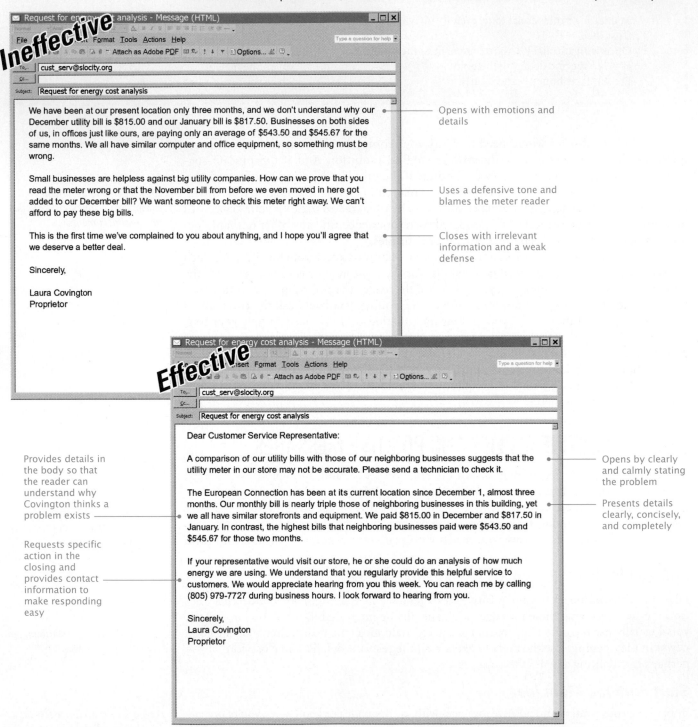

Ineffective

To...: cust_serv@slocity.org
Subject: Request for energy cost analysis

We have been at our present location only three months, and we don't understand why our December utility bill is $815.00 and our January bill is $817.50. Businesses on both sides of us, in offices just like ours, are paying only an average of $543.50 and $545.67 for the same months. We all have similar computer and office equipment, so something must be wrong.

Small businesses are helpless against big utility companies. How can we prove that you read the meter wrong or that the November bill from before we even moved in here got added to our December bill? We want someone to check this meter right away. We can't afford to pay these big bills.

This is the first time we've complained to you about anything, and I hope you'll agree that we deserve a better deal.

Sincerely,

Laura Covington
Proprietor

- Opens with emotions and details
- Uses a defensive tone and blames the meter reader
- Closes with irrelevant information and a weak defense

Effective

To...: cust_serv@slocity.org
Subject: Request for energy cost analysis

Dear Customer Service Representative:

A comparison of our utility bills with those of our neighboring businesses suggests that the utility meter in our store may not be accurate. Please send a technician to check it.

The European Connection has been at its current location since December 1, almost three months. Our monthly bill is nearly triple those of neighboring businesses in this building, yet we all have similar storefronts and equipment. We paid $815.00 in December and $817.50 in January. In contrast, the highest bills that neighboring businesses paid were $543.50 and $545.67 for those two months.

If your representative would visit our store, he or she could do an analysis of how much energy we are using. We understand that you regularly provide this helpful service to customers. We would appreciate hearing from you this week. You can reach me by calling (805) 979-7727 during business hours. I look forward to hearing from you.

Sincerely,
Laura Covington
Proprietor

Provides details in the body so that the reader can understand why Covington thinks a problem exists

Requests specific action in the closing and provides contact information to make responding easy

- Opens by clearly and calmly stating the problem
- Presents details clearly, concisely, and completely

The best way to write a clear opening is to have a clear idea of what you want to say. Before you put one word on paper, ask yourself, "What is the single most important message I have for the audience?"

Provide Necessary Details and Explanation

The body of routine and positive messages is typically the longest. You need the space to explain your point completely so that your audience will experience no confusion or lingering doubt. In addition to providing details in the body, maintain the supportive tone established in the opening. This tone is easy to continue when your message is entirely positive, as in this example:

> Your educational background and internship have impressed us, and we believe you would be a valuable addition to Green Valley Properties. As discussed during your interview, your salary will be $4,300 per month, plus benefits. Please plan to meet with our benefits manager, Paula Sanchez, at 8 a.m. on Monday, March 21. She will assist you with all the paperwork necessary to tailor our benefit package to your family situation. She will also arrange various orientation activities to help you acclimate to our company.

However, if your routine message is mixed and must convey mildly disappointing information, put the negative portion of your message into as favorable a context as possible:

Try to embed any negative information in a positive context.

INSTEAD OF THIS

No, we no longer carry the Sportsgirl line of sweaters.

WRITE THIS

The new Olympic line has replaced the Sportsgirl sweaters that you asked about. Olympic features a wider range of colors and sizes and more contemporary styling.

The more complete description is less negative and emphasizes how the audience can benefit from the change. Be careful, though: You can use negative information in this type of message *only* if you're reasonably sure the audience will respond positively. Otherwise, use the indirect approach (discussed in Chapter 9).

If you are communicating to customers, you might also want to use the body of your message to assure the customer of the wisdom of his or her purchase selection (without being condescending or self-congratulatory). Using such favorable comments, often known as *resale*, is a good way to build customer relationships. These comments are commonly included in acknowledgments of orders and other routine announcements to customers, and they are most effective when they are relatively short and specific:

> The zipper on the laptop carrying case you purchased is double-stitched and guaranteed for the life of the product.
>
> The KitchenAid mixer you ordered is our best-selling model. It should meet your cooking needs for many years.

End with a Courteous Close

Your message is most likely to succeed if your readers are left feeling that you have their best interests in mind. You can accomplish this task either by highlighting a benefit to the audience or by expressing appreciation or goodwill. If follow-up action is required, clearly state who will do what next. See "Checklist: Writing Routine Replies and Positive Messages" to review the primary tasks involved in this type of business message.

Make sure audience members understand what to do next and how that action will benefit them.

Common Examples of Routine Replies and Positive Messages

As with routine requests, you'll encounter the need for a wide variety of routine replies and positive messages. You can expect to write letters or e-mail messages for most routine messages directed to people outside the company, although e-mail and instant messaging (with live operators or automated bots) are gaining in popularity in customer-service applications. Most routine and positive messages fall into six main categories: answers to requests for information and action, grants of claims and requests for adjustment, recommendations, informative messages, good-news announcements, and goodwill messages.

DOCUMENT MAKEOVER

IMPROVE THIS E-MAIL MESSAGE

To practice correcting drafts of actual documents, visit your online course or the access-code-protected portion of the Companion Website. Click "Document Makeovers," then click Chapter 8. You will find an e-mail message that contains problems and errors relating to what you've learned in this chapter about routine, good news, and goodwill messages. Use the "Final Draft" decision tool to create an improved version of this routine e-mail. Check the message for skilled presentation of the main idea, clarity of detail, appropriate use of resale, and the inclusion of a courteous close.

CHECKLIST: Writing Routine Replies and Positive Messages

A. Start with the main idea.
- Be clear and concise.
- Identify the single most important message before you start writing.

B. Provide necessary details and explanation.
- Explain your point completely to eliminate any confusion or lingering doubts.
- Maintain a supportive tone throughout.

- Embed negative statements in positive contexts or balance them with positive alternatives.
- Talk favorably about the choices the customer has made.

C. End with a courteous close.
- Let your readers know that you have their personal well-being in mind.
- If further action is required, tell readers how to proceed and encourage them to act promptly.

Answering Requests for Information and Action

Every professional answers requests for information and action from time to time, and some business functions answer such requests many times a day. If the response to a request is a simple yes or some other straightforward information, the direct plan is appropriate. A prompt, gracious, and thorough response will positively influence how people think about you and the organization you represent. Depending on the resources your company offers, you might use letters, memos, e-mail, or instant messaging to answer these requests (see Figure 8.5).

Many requests can be similar. For example, a human resources department gets numerous routine inquiries about job openings, and sales departments get requests for information about products. To handle repetitive queries like these quickly and

FIGURE 8.5 Effective IM Response to Information Request
This quick and courteous exchange is typical of IM communication in such areas as customer service and technical support. The agent (Janice) solves the problem quickly and leaves the customer with a positive impression of the company.

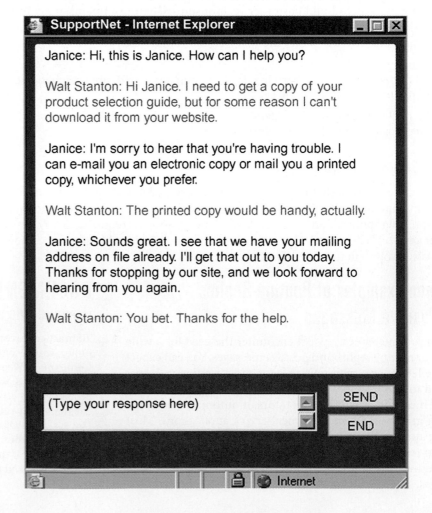

FIGURE 8.6 Personalized Reply to Request for Information
This e-mail message personalizes a standardized response by including the recipient's name in the greeting.

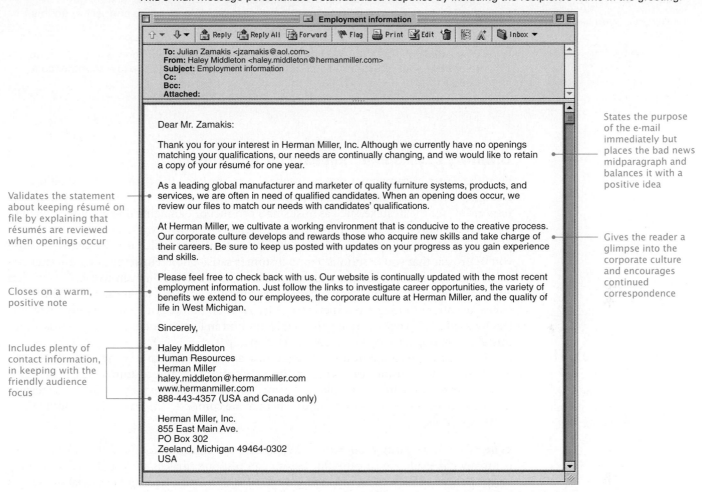

States the purpose of the e-mail immediately but places the bad news midparagraph and balances it with a positive idea

Validates the statement about keeping résumé on file by explaining that résumés are reviewed when openings occur

Gives the reader a glimpse into the corporate culture and encourages continued correspondence

Closes on a warm, positive note

Includes plenty of contact information, in keeping with the friendly audience focus

---

consistently, companies usually develop form responses that can be customized as needed (see Figure 8.6). These ready-made message templates can be printed forms, word processor documents, e-mail templates, or blocks of instant messaging text that can be dropped into a messaging window with the click of a mouse.

When you're answering requests and a potential sale is involved, you have three main goals: (1) to respond to the inquiry and answer all questions, (2) to leave your reader with a good impression of you and your firm, and (3) to encourage the future sale. The following message meets all three objectives:

Here is the brochure "Entertainment Unlimited" that you requested. This booklet describes the vast array of entertainment options available to you with an Ocean Satellite Device (OSD).

Starts with a clear, statement of the main point

On page 12 of "Entertainment Unlimited" you'll find a list of the 338 channels that the OSD brings into your home. You'll have access to movie, sport, and music channels; 24-hour news channels; local channels; and all the major television networks. OSD gives you a clearer picture and more precise sound than those old-fashioned dishes that took up most of your yard—and OSD uses only a small dish that mounts easily on your roof.

Presents key information immediately, along with resale and sales promotion

More music, more cartoons, more experts, more news, and more sports are available to you with OSD than with any other cable or satellite connection in this region. Yes, it's all there, right at your fingertips.

Just call us at 1-800-786-4331, and an OSD representative will come to your home to answer your questions. You'll love the programming and the low monthly cost. Call us today!

Granting Claims and Requests for Adjustment

Even the best-run companies make mistakes, from shipping the wrong order to billing the customer's credit card inaccurately. In other cases, the customer or a third party might be responsible for the mistake, such as misusing a product or damaging it in shipment. Each of these events represents a turning point in your relationship with your customer. If you handle the situation well, your customer will likely be even more loyal than before because you've proven that you're serious about customer satisfaction. However, if a customer believes that you mishandled a complaint, you'll make the situation even worse. Dissatisfied customers often take their business elsewhere without notice and tell numerous friends and colleagues about the negative experience. A transaction that might be worth only a few dollars by itself could cost you many times that amount in lost business. In other words, every mistake is an opportunity to improve a relationship.

Few people go to the trouble of requesting an adjustment unless they actually have a problem, so most businesses start from the assumption that the customer is correct. From there, your response to the complaint depends on both your company's policies for resolving such issues and your assessment of whether the company, the customer, or some third party is at fault.

When Your Company Is at Fault   Whenever you communicate about a mistake your company has made, do so carefully. Before you respond, make sure you know your company's policies in such cases, which might even dictate specific legal and financial steps to be taken. For serious problems that go beyond routine errors, your company should have a *crisis management plan* that outlines communication steps both inside and outside the organization (see Chapter 9).

Most routine responses should take your company's specific policies into account and address the following points:

- **Acknowledge receipt of the customer's claim or complaint.** Even if you can't solve the problem immediately, at least let the other party know that somebody is listening.
- **Take (or assign) personal responsibility for setting matters straight.** Customers don't want their complaints to fall into a bureaucratic black hole.
- **Sympathize with the customer's inconvenience or frustration.** Letting the customer see that you're on his or her side helps defuse the emotional element of the situation.
- **Explain precisely how you have resolved or plan to resolve the situation.** If you can respond exactly as the customer requested, be sure to communicate that. If you can't, explain why.
- **Take steps to repair the relationship.** Keeping your existing customers is almost always less expensive than acquiring new customers, so look for ways to go beyond simply granting the claim or fixing the problem, such as offering coupons to encourage future business.
- **Follow up to verify your response was correct.** Follow-up not only helps improve customer service but also gives you another opportunity to show how much you care about your customer.

In addition to these positive steps, maintain professional demeanor by avoiding some key negative steps as well: Don't blame anyone in your organization by name, don't make

---

5 LEARNING OBJECTIVE

Discuss the importance of knowing who is responsible when granting claims and requests for adjustment

exaggerated apologies that sound insincere, don't imply that the customer is at fault, and don't promise more than you can deliver.

As with requests for information or action, some claims are likely to occur again and again, such as claims made against insurance policies or requests to correct orders. A form letter is an efficient way to begin the communication process. In the following example, a large mail-order clothing company created a form letter to respond to customers who complain that they haven't received exactly what was ordered. The form letter can easily be customized through word processing (perhaps to state the good news in the opening) and then individually signed:

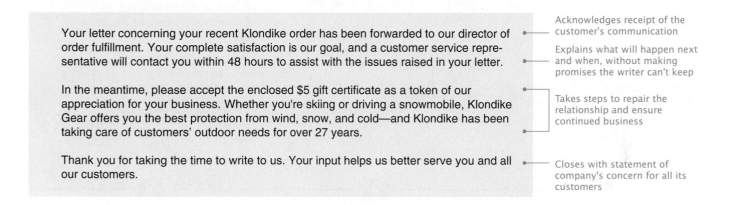

Your letter concerning your recent Klondike order has been forwarded to our director of order fulfillment. Your complete satisfaction is our goal, and a customer service representative will contact you within 48 hours to assist with the issues raised in your letter.

In the meantime, please accept the enclosed $5 gift certificate as a token of our appreciation for your business. Whether you're skiing or driving a snowmobile, Klondike Gear offers you the best protection from wind, snow, and cold—and Klondike has been taking care of customers' outdoor needs for over 27 years.

Thank you for taking the time to write to us. Your input helps us better serve you and all our customers.

Acknowledges receipt of the customer's communication

Explains what will happen next and when, without making promises the writer can't keep

Takes steps to repair the relationship and ensure continued business

Closes with statement of company's concern for all its customers

In contrast, a response letter written as a personal answer to a unique claim would open with a clear statement of the good news: the settling of the claim according to the customer's request. The following is a more personal response from Klondike Gear:

Here is your heather-blue wool-and-mohair sweater (size large) to replace the one returned to us with a defect in the knitting. Thanks for giving us the opportunity to correct this situation. Customers' needs have come first at Klondike Gear for 27 years.

I've enclosed our newest catalog and a $5 gift certificate that's good toward any purchase from it. Whether you are skiing or driving a snowmobile, Klondike Gear offers you the best protection available from wind, snow, and cold. Please let us know how we may continue to serve you and your sporting needs.

When granting an unjustified claim, maintain a respectful and positive tone while informing the customer that the claim was a result of misuse or mistreatment of the product.

When the Customer Is at Fault   Communication about a claim is a delicate matter when the customer is clearly at fault. You can (1) refuse the claim and attempt to justify your refusal or (2) simply do what the customer asks. If you refuse the claim, you may lose your customer—as well as many of the customer's friends and colleagues, who will hear only one side of the dispute. You must weigh the cost of making the adjustment against the cost of losing future business from one or more customers.

If you choose to grant the claim, you can open with the good news: You're replacing the merchandise or refunding the purchase price. However, the body needs more attention. Your job is to make the customer realize that the merchandise was mistreated, but you want to avoid being condescending ("Perhaps you failed to read the instructions carefully") or preachy ("You should know that wool shrinks in hot water"). The dilemma is this: If the customer fails to realize what went wrong, you may commit your firm to an endless procession of returned merchandise; but if you insult the customer, your cash refund will have been wasted because you'll lose your customer anyway. Close in a courteous manner that expresses your appreciation for the customer's business (see Figure 8.7).

FIGURE 8.7 Responding to a Claim When the Buyer Is at Fault
In the interest of positive customer relationships, this company agreed to provide replacement parts for a customer's in-line skates, even though the product is outside its warranty period. (For the sake of clarity, the content of the customer's original e-mail message is not reproduced here.)

Plan

Analyze the Situation
Verify that the purpose is to grant the customer's claim, tactfully educate him, and encourage further business.

Gather Information
Gather information on product care, warranties, and resale information.

Select the Right Medium
An e-mail message is appropriate in this case because the customer contacted the company via e-mail.

Organize the Information
You're responding with a positive answer, so a direct approach is fine.

Write

Adapt to Your Audience
Show sensitivity to audience needs with a "you" attitude, politeness, positive emphasis, and bias-free language.

Compose the Message
Maintain a style that is respectful while still managing to educate the customer on product usage and maintenance.

Complete

Revise the Message
Evaluate content and review readability; avoid unnecessary details.

Produce the Message
Emphasize a clean, professional appearance.

Proofread the Message
Review for errors in layout, spelling, and mechanics.

Distribute the Message
E-mail the reply.

1   2   3

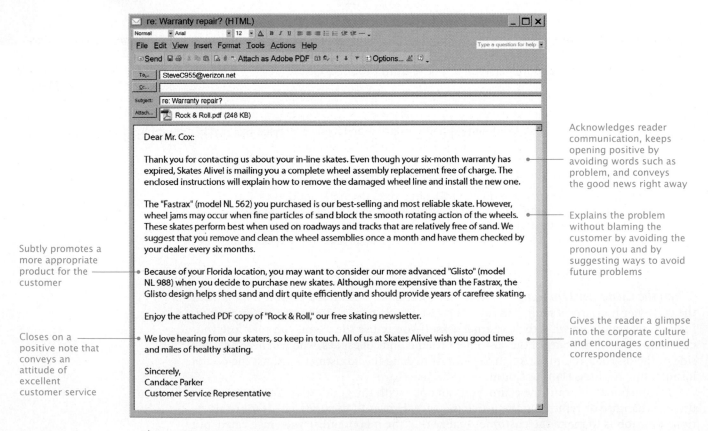

Acknowledges reader communication, keeps opening positive by avoiding words such as problem, and conveys the good news right away

Explains the problem without blaming the customer by avoiding the pronoun you and by suggesting ways to avoid future problems

Subtly promotes a more appropriate product for the customer

Closes on a positive note that conveys an attitude of excellent customer service

Gives the reader a glimpse into the corporate culture and encourages continued correspondence

When a Third Party Is at Fault   Sometimes neither your company nor your customer is at fault. For example, ordering a book from Amazon.com involves not only Amazon.com but also a delivery service such as Federal Express or the U.S. Postal Service, the publisher and possibly a distributor of the book, a credit card issuer, and a company that processes credit card transactions. Any one of these other partners might be at fault, but the customer is likely to blame Amazon.com because that is the entity that receives the customer's pay-

CHECKLIST: Granting Claims and Adjustment Requests

A. Responding when your company is at fault
- Be aware of your company's policies in such cases before you respond.
- For serious situations, refer to the company's crisis management plan.
- Start by acknowledging receipt of the claim or complaint.
- Take or assign personal responsibility for resolving the situation.
- Sympathize with the customer's frustration.
- Explain how you have resolved the situation (or plan to).
- Take steps to repair the customer relationship.
- Verify your response with the customer and keep the lines of communication open.

B. Responding when the customer is at fault
- Weigh the cost of complying with or refusing the request.
- If you choose to comply, open with the good news.
- Use the body of the message to respectfully educate the customer about steps needed to avoid a similar outcome in the future.
- Close with an appreciation for the customer's business.

C. Responding when a third party is at fault
- Evaluate the situation and review your company's policies before responding.
- Avoid placing blame; focus on the solution.
- Regardless of who is responsible for resolving the situation, let the customer know what will happen to resolve the problem.

ment. In some transactions, the customer might not even be aware that third parties were involved.

No general scheme applies to every case involving a third party, so evaluate the situation carefully and know your company's policies before responding. For instance, an online retailer and the companies that manufacture its merchandise might have an agreement specifying that the manufacturers automatically handle all complaints about product quality. However, regardless of who eventually resolves the problem, if customers contact you, you need to respond with messages that explain how the problem will be solved. Pointing fingers is both unproductive and unprofessional; resolving the situation is the only issue customers care about. See "Checklist: Granting Claims and Adjustment Requests" to review the tasks involved in these kinds of business messages.

When a third party is at fault, your response depends on your company's agreements with that organization.

Providing Recommendations

When writing a letter of recommendation, your goal is to convince readers that the person being recommended has the characteristics necessary for the job, project assignment, scholarship, or other objective the person is seeking. A successful recommendation letter contains a number of relevant details:

- The candidate's full name
- The position or other objective the candidate is seeking
- The nature of your relationship with the candidate
- An indication of whether you're answering a request from the person or taking the initiative to write
- Facts and evidence relevant to the candidate and the opportunity
- A comparison of this candidate's potential with that of peers, if available (for example, "Ms. Jonasson consistently ranked in the top 10 percent of her class")
- Your overall evaluation of the candidate's suitability for the opportunity

As surprising as this might sound, the most difficult recommendation letters to write are often those for truly outstanding candidates. Your audience will have trouble believing uninterrupted praise for someone's talents and accomplishments. To enhance your credibility—and the candidate's—illustrate your general points with specific examples that point out the candidate's abilities and fitness for the job opening.

Most candidates aren't perfect, however, and you'll need to decide how to handle each situation that comes your way. Omitting a reference to someone's shortcomings may be tempting, especially if the shortcomings are irrelevant to the demands of the job in question. Even so, you have an obligation to refer to any serious shortcoming that

Handling routine communication in a friendly, audience-focused way is one of the many reasons that the Alexandria, Virginia–based bank Burke & Hebert enjoys almost fanatical customer loyalty. President Hunt Burke helps ensure that customer inquiries are handled promptly and courteously.

Communication Miscues

When Recommendation Letters Lead to Lawsuits

Recommendation letters are classified as routine messages, but with all the legal troubles they can get employers into these days they've become anything but routine. Over the years, employees have won thousands of lawsuits that charged former employers with defamation related to job recommendations. In addition to charges of defamation—which can be successfully defended if the "defamatory" statements are proven to be true—employers have been sued for retaliation by ex-employees who believed that negative letters were written expressly for purposes of revenge. And as if that weren't enough, employers have even sued each other over recommendation letters when the recipient of a letter believed the writer failed to disclose important negative information.

No wonder many companies now refuse to divulge anything more than job titles and dates of employment. But even that doesn't always solve the problem: Ex-employees have been known to sue for retaliation when their employers refused to write on their behalf. (This refusal to write recommendations also causes problems for hiring companies. If they can't get any real background information on job candidates, they risk hiring employees who lack the necessary skills or who are disruptive or even dangerous in the workplace.)

For companies that do let managers write recommendations, what sort of information should or should not be included? Even though the majority of states now have laws protecting companies against recommendation-related law-suits when the employer acts in good faith, individual cases vary so much that no specific guidelines can ever apply to all cases. However, asking yourself the following questions before drafting a recommendation letter will help you avoid trouble:

- Does the party receiving this personal information have a legitimate right to it?
- Does all the information I've presented relate directly to the job or benefit being sought?
- Have I put the candidate's case as strongly and as honestly as I can?
- Have I avoided overstating the candidate's abilities or otherwise misleading the reader?
- Have I based all my statements on firsthand knowledge and provable facts?

No matter what the circumstances, experts also advise that you always consult your human resources or legal department for advice.

CAREER APPLICATIONS

1. A former employee was often late for work but was an excellent and fast worker who got along well with everyone. Do you think it's important to mention the tardiness to potential employers? If so, how will you handle it?
2. Step outside yourself for a moment and write a letter of recommendation about you from a former employer's perspective. Practice honesty, integrity, and prudence.

A serious shortcoming cannot be ignored, but beware of being libelous:
- *Include only relevant, factual information*
- *Avoid value judgments*
- *Balance criticisms with favorable points*

could be related to job performance. You owe it to your audience, to your own conscience, and even to better-qualified candidates. You don't have to present the shortcomings as simple criticisms, however. A good option is to list them as areas for improvement, even as areas the person might be working on now.

The danger in writing a critical letter is that you might inadvertently engage in *libel*, publishing a false and malicious written statement that injures the candidate's reputation. On the other hand, if that negative information is truthful and relevant, it may be unethical and even illegal to omit it from your recommendation (see "Communication Miscues: When Recommendation Letters Lead to Lawsuits").

If you must refer to a shortcoming, you can best protect yourself by sticking to the facts, avoiding value judgments, and placing your criticism in the context of a generally favorable recommendation, as in Figure 8.8. In this letter, the writer supports all statements and judgments with evidence.

Before you dash off any recommendation letter, even for someone you know closely and respect without reservation, keep in mind that every time you write a recommendation, you're putting your own reputation on the line. If the person's shortcomings are so pronounced that you don't think he or she is a good fit for the job, the only choice is to not write the letter at all. Unless your relationship with the person warrants an explanation, simply suggest that someone else might be in a better position to provide a recommendation.

6 LEARNING OBJECTIVE

Explain how creating informative messages differs from responding to information requests

Creating Informative Messages

All companies send routine informative messages such as reminder notices and policy statements. For instance, you may need to inform employees of organizational changes or tell

FIGURE 8.8 Effective Recommendation Letter
This letter clearly states the nature of the writer's relationship to the candidate and provides specific examples to support the writer's endorsements.

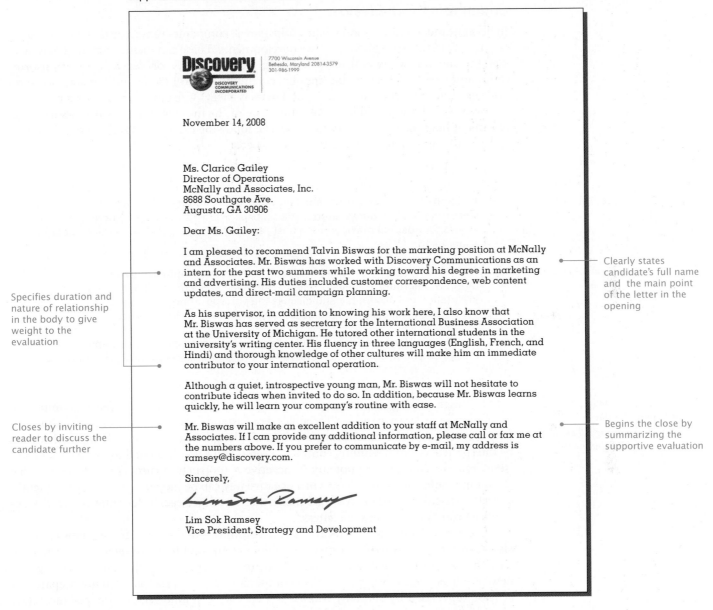

Specifies duration and nature of relationship in the body to give weight to the evaluation

Closes by inviting reader to discuss the candidate further

Clearly states candidate's full name and the main point of the letter in the opening

Begins the close by summarizing the supportive evaluation

---

customers about new shipping and return policies. Use the opening of informative messages to state the purpose (to inform) and briefly mention the nature of the information you are providing. Unlike the replies discussed earlier, informative messages are not solicited by your reader, so make it clear up front why the reader is receiving this particular message. In the body, provide the necessary details and end your message with a courteous close.

Most informative communications are neutral. That is, they stimulate neither a positive nor a negative response from readers. For example, when you send departmental meeting announcements and reminder notices, you'll generally receive a neutral response from your readers (unless the purpose of the meeting is unwelcome). Simply present the factual information in the body of the message and don't worry too much about the reader's attitude toward the information.

Some informative messages may require additional care. For instance, policy statements or procedural changes may be good news for a company (perhaps by saving money). However, it may not be obvious to employees that such savings may make available additional employee resources or even pay raises. In instances in which the reader may not initially

When writing informative messages,
- *State the purpose at the beginning and briefly mention the nature of the information you are providing*
- *Provide the necessary details*
- *End with a courteous close*

view the information positively, use the body of the message to highlight the potential benefits from the reader's perspective.

Announcing Good News

To develop and maintain good relationships, smart companies recognize that it's good business to spread the word about positive developments. These can include opening new facilities, hiring a new executive, introducing new products or services, or sponsoring community events—such as the announcements that Carol Cone and her staff write for ConAgra and other clients. Because good news is always welcome, use the direct approach.

Writing to a successful job applicant is one of the most pleasant good-news messages you might have the opportunity to write. The following example uses the direct approach and provides information that the recipient needs:

Announces news in a friendly, welcoming tone

Explains all necessary details

Explains first day's routine to ease new employee's uncertainty

> Welcome to Lake Valley Rehabilitation Center. A number of excellent candidates were interviewed, but your educational background and recent experience at Memorial Hospital make you the best person for the position of medical records supervisor.
>
> As we discussed, your salary is $39,200 a year. We would like you to begin on Monday, February 1. Please come to my office at 9 a.m. I will give you an in-depth orientation to Lake Valley and discuss the various company benefits available to you. You can also sign all the necessary employment documents.
>
> After lunch, Vanessa Jackson will take you to the medical records department and introduce you to your staff. I look forward to seeing you first thing on February 1.

Job-offer letters should be reviewed by legal experts familiar with employment law because they can be viewed as legally binding contracts.

Although messages like these are pleasant to write, they require careful planning and evaluation in order to avoid legal troubles. For instance, messages that imply lifetime employment or otherwise make promises about the length or conditions of employment can be interpreted as legally binding contracts, even if you never intended to make such promises. Similarly, downplaying potentially negative news (such as rumors of a takeover) that turns out to affect the hired person in a negative way can be judged as fraud. Consequently, experts advise that a company's legal staff either scrutinize each offer letter or create standardized content to use in such letters.[2]

Good-news announcements are usually communicated via a letter or a **news release**, also known as a *press release*, a specialized document used to share relevant information with the local or national news media. (News releases are also used to announce negative news, such as plant closings.) In most companies, news releases are usually prepared or at least supervised by specially trained writers in the public relations department (see Figure 8.9). The content follows the customary pattern for a positive message: good news, followed by details and a positive close. However, news releases have a critical difference: You're not writing directly to the ultimate audience (such as the readers of a newspaper); you're trying to interest an editor or reporter in a story, and that person will then write the material that is eventually read by the larger audience. To write a successful news release, keep the following points in mind:[3]

- Above all else, make sure your information is both newsworthy and relevant to the specific publications or websites to which you are sending it. Editors are overwhelmed with news releases, so those without real news content are disposed of quickly—and can damage the writer's credibility, too.
- Focus on one subject; don't try to pack a single news release with multiple, unrelated news items.
- Put your most important idea first. Don't force editors to hunt for the news.
- Be brief: Break up long sentences and keep paragraphs short.

FIGURE 8.9 News Release Announcing Positive News

In this news release, the U.S. Patent and Trademark Office announces a significant milestone for its online trademark application system. Notice how the news is conveyed through three levels of detail: the headline, the first paragraph, and successive paragraphs.

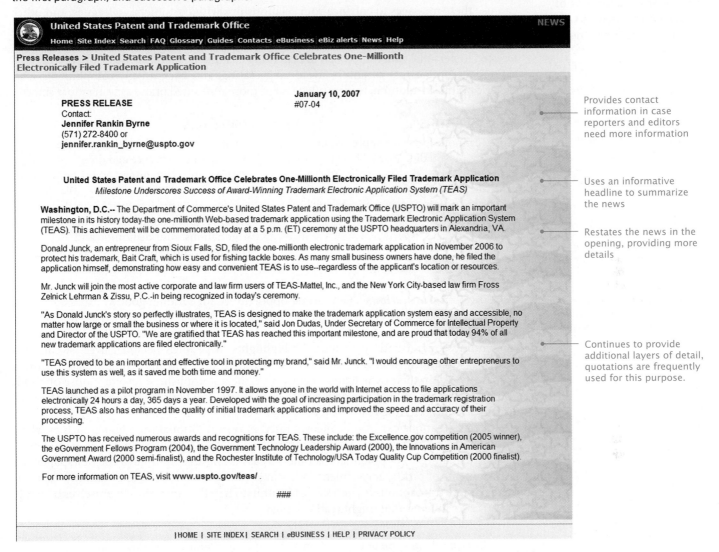

Provides contact information in case reporters and editors need more information

Uses an informative headline to summarize the news

Restates the news in the opening, providing more details

Continues to provide additional layers of detail, quotations are frequently used for this purpose.

- Eliminate clutter such as redundancy and extraneous facts.
- Be as specific as possible.
- Minimize self-congratulatory adjectives and adverbs; if the content of your message is newsworthy, the media professionals will be interested in the news on its own merits.
- Follow established industry conventions for style, punctuation, and format.

As with many aspects of business communication, the process of creating and distributing news releases and other media materials is continually improved by technological advances. Online distribution systems such as PR Newswire and BusinessWire make it easy for even the smallest companies to reach editors and reporters at the most prominent publications around the world. Many companies also create special media pages on their websites that contain their latest news releases, background information on the company, and archives of past news releases.

7 LEARNING OBJECTIVE

Describe the importance of goodwill messages and explain how to make them effective

Goodwill is the positive feeling that encourages people to maintain a business relationship.

Make sure your compliments are both sincere and honest.

Fostering Goodwill

All business messages should be written with an eye toward fostering goodwill among business contacts, but some messages are written primarily and specifically to build goodwill. You can use these messages to enhance your relationships with customers, colleagues, and other businesspeople by sending friendly, even unexpected notes with no direct business purpose.

Effective goodwill messages must be sincere and honest. Otherwise, you'll appear to be interested in personal gain rather than in benefiting customers, fellow workers, or your organization. To come across as sincere, avoid exaggerating, and back up any compliments with specific points. In addition, readers often regard more restrained praise as being more sincere:

INSTEAD OF THIS	WRITE THIS
Words cannot express my appreciation for the great job you did. Thanks. No one could have done it better. You're terrific! You've made the whole firm sit up and take notice, and we are ecstatic to have you working here.	Thanks again for taking charge of the meeting in my absence and doing such an excellent job. With just an hour's notice, you managed to pull the legal and public relations departments together so that we could present a united front in the negotiations. Your dedication and communication abilities have been noted and are truly appreciated.

Taking note of significant events in someone's personal life helps cement the business relationship.

Sending Congratulations   One prime opportunity for sending goodwill messages is to congratulate individuals or companies for significant business achievements—perhaps for being promoted or for attaining product sales milestones (see Figure 8.10). Other reasons for sending congratulations include the highlights in people's personal lives—weddings, births, graduations, success in nonbusiness competitions. You may congratulate business acquaintances on their own achievements or on the accomplishments of a spouse or child. You may also take note of personal events, even if you don't know the reader well. If you're already friendly with the reader, a more personal tone is appropriate.

Congratulations can also be incorporated into promotional campaigns, such as when companies send messages to new parents or to recent home buyers. Some companies even develop a mailing list of potential customers by assigning an employee to clip newspaper announcements of births, engagements, weddings, and graduations or to obtain information on real estate transactions in the local community. Then they introduce themselves by sending out a form letter that might read like this:

> Congratulations on your new home! All of us at Klemper Security Solutions hope it brings you and your family many years of security and happiness.
>
> Please accept the enclosed *Homeowner's Guide to Home Security* with our compliments. It lists a number of simple steps you can take to keep your home, your family, and your possessions safe.

This simple message has a natural, friendly tone, even though the sender has never met the recipient.

An effective message of appreciation documents a person's contributions.

Sending Messages of Appreciation   An important managerial quality is the ability to recognize the contributions of employees, colleagues, suppliers, and other associates. Your praise does more than just make the person feel good; it encourages further excellence. Moreover, a message of appreciation may become an important part of someone's personnel file. So when you write a message of appreciation, try to specifically mention the person or people you want to praise. The brief message that follows expresses gratitude and reveals the happy result:

> Thank you and everyone on your team for the heroic efforts you took to bring our servers back up after last Friday's flood. We were able to begin serving clients first thing Monday morning. You went far beyond the level of contractual service in restoring our data center within 16 hours. I would especially like to

FIGURE 8.10 Congratulating Business Partners
Goodwill messages serve a variety of business functions. In this announcement, Business
Objects congratulates several of its customers for achieving a level of excellence in *business
intelligence* (the process of acquiring and applying information to business decisions).

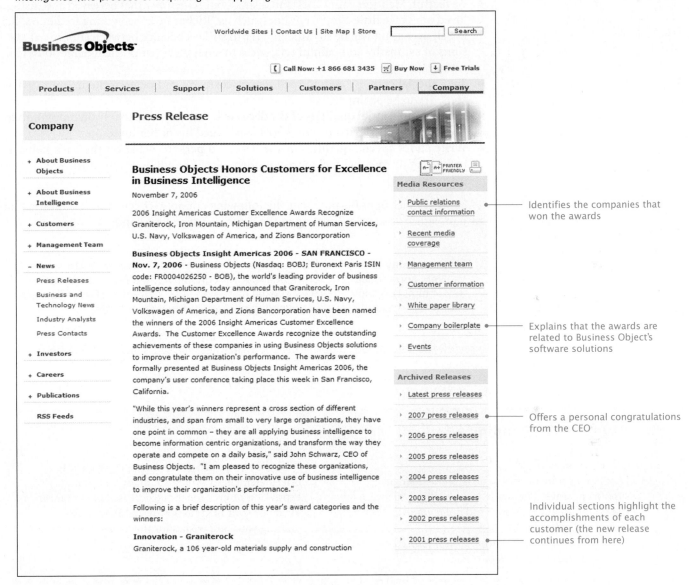

highlight the contribution of networking specialist Julienne Marks, who worked
for 12 straight hours to reconnect our Internet service. If I can serve as a
reference in your future sales activities, please do not hesitate to ask.

Offering Condolences   In times of serious trouble and deep sadness, well-written condolences and expressions of sympathy can mean a great deal to people who've experienced
loss. Granted, this type of message is difficult to write, but don't let the difficulty of the task
keep you from responding promptly. Those who have experienced a health problem, the
death of a loved one, or a business misfortune appreciate knowing that others care.

Open a condolence message with a brief statement of sympathy, such as "I was deeply
sorry to hear of your loss," in the event of a death, for example. In the body, mention the
good qualities or the positive contributions made by the deceased. State what the person
meant to you or your colleagues. In closing, you can offer your condolences and your best
wishes. Here are a few general suggestions for writing condolence messages:

- **Keep reminiscences brief.** Recount a memory or an anecdote (even a humorous one),
  but don't dwell on the details of the loss lest you add to the reader's anguish.

*The primary purpose of condolence
messages is to let the audience
know that you and the
organization you represent care
about the person's loss.*

- **Write in your own words.** Write as if you were speaking privately to the person. Don't quote "poetic" passages or use stilted or formal phrases. If the loss is a death, refer to it as such rather than as "passing away" or "departing."
- **Be tactful.** Mention your shock and dismay, but remember that bereaved and distressed loved ones take little comfort in lines such as "Richard was too young to die" or "Starting all over again will be so difficult." Try to strike a balance between superficial expressions of sympathy and painful references to a happier past or the likelihood of a bleak future.
- **Take special care.** Be sure to spell names correctly and be accurate in your review of facts. Try to be prompt.
- **Write about special qualities of the deceased.** You may have to rely on reputation to do this, but let the grieving person know you valued his or her loved one.
- **Write about special qualities of the bereaved person.** A pat on the back helps a bereaved family member feel more confident about handling things during such a traumatic time.[4]

Supervisor George Bigalow sent the following condolence letter to his administrative assistant, Janice Case, after learning of the death of Janice's husband:

> My sympathy to you and your children. All your friends at Carter Electric were so very sorry to learn of John's death. Although I never had the opportunity to meet him, I do know how very special he was to you. Your tales of your family's camping trips and his rafting expeditions were always memorable.

To review the tasks involved in writing goodwill messages, see "Checklist: Sending Goodwill Messages."

 CHECKLIST: Sending Goodwill Messages

- Be sincere and honest.
- Don't exaggerate or use vague, grandiose language; support positive statements with specific evidence.
- Use congratulatory messages to build goodwill with clients and colleagues.
- Send messages of appreciation to emphasize how much you value the work of others.

- When sending condolence messages, open with a brief statement of sympathy, followed by an expression of how much the deceased person meant to you or your firm (as appropriate), then close by offering your best wishes for the future.

COMMUNICATION CHALLENGES AT CONE, INC.

 In addition to serving hot meals, the Kids Café program provides a safe, nurturing environment that keeps kids out of trouble during the risky afternoon hours from 3:00 to 6:00. To make that time more valuable, many Kids Cafés have started offering sports, crafts, mentoring, and tutoring. These activities require qualified volunteers who are willing to spend a few hours each week working with the kids.

Individual Challenge: To staff the tutoring program, ConAgra has asked Cone to create a recruiting campaign that will attract volunteers qualified to help with math, English, and science homework. One of the most important recruiting tools will be a letter addressed to current monetary donors, asking them to give as little as three hours a month. Carol has asked you, her executive assistant, to draft the request letter. What key points should you include in the introduction, body, and close of the letter? Make a brief outline for your instructor.

Team Challenge: It's nine months later and the recruiting program has been a success: most Kids Cafés are now offering more tutoring sessions. Carol now asks you to draft a letter of appreciation, which is reviewed by executives at ConAgra. During this review process, ConAgra executives have suggested using the letter to ask volunteers to increase the amount of time they spend tutoring each month. With a small group, discuss the pros and cons of adding this request to your letter. In a brief paragraph, explain your team's conclusions.

SUMMARY OF LEARNING OBJECTIVES

1 Apply the three-step writing process to routine and positive messages. Even though routine messages are usually short and simple, they benefit from the three-step writing process. Planning routine messages may take only a few moments to (1) analyze your purpose and audience, (2) investigate your readers' needs and make sure that you have all the facts to satisfy them, and (3) adapt your message to your audience through your choice of medium and your use of the "you" attitude. When writing routine messages, use the direct approach, as long as your readers will be positive (or neutral) and have minimal cultural differences. Completing routine messages means making them as professional as possible by (1) revising for clarity and conciseness, (2) selecting appropriate design elements and delivery methods, and (3) careful proofreading.

2 Outline an effective strategy for writing routine requests. When writing a routine request, open by stating your specific request. At the same time, avoid being abrupt or tactless: pay attention to tone, assume your audience will comply, avoid personal introductions, end polite requests with a period, and be specific. Use the middle of a routine request to justify your request and explain its importance. Close routine requests by asking for specific action (including a deadline as often as possible) and expressing goodwill. Be sure to include all contact information so that your reader can respond easily.

3 Explain how to ask for specific action in a courteous manner. A courteous close contains three important elements: (1) a specific request, (2) information about how you can be reached (if it isn't obvious), and (3) an expression of appreciation or goodwill.

4 Describe a strategy for writing routine replies and positive messages. First, open your message with a clear and concise statement of the main idea or your good news. Second, in the body of your message, provide the details and explanations necessary to meet the audience's information needs. If your message has a mix of positive and negative information, try to put the negative news in a positive context. If you are communicating with customers, you can also use the body of the message to share marketing and customer relationship information. Third, end your message with a courteous close that indicates to your audience members that you have their best interests at heart.

5 Discuss the importance of knowing who is responsible when granting claims and requests for adjustment. Your response to a claim or a request for an adjustment can vary significantly depending on which party you determine to be at fault. If your company is at fault, your message should acknowledge receipt of the customer's claim or complaint, take responsibility, sympathize with the customer, explain how you will resolve the situation, take steps to repair the relationship, and keep the lines of communication open. If the customer is at fault, you have to decide whether to grant the claim in the interest of keeping the customer's business. If a third party is at fault, your response will be determined by whatever arrangements are in place between your company and the third party.

6 Explain how creating informative messages differs from responding to information requests. The key difference between creating informative messages and responding to information requests is a matter of who initiates the communication. When you create an informative message, your audience members may or may not be expecting it and may or may not be motivated to read it, so you need to gauge their potential reaction and plan your message accordingly. In contrast, when someone else initiates the request, that person will obviously be anticipating your response. The person may or may not like what you have to say, of course, but at least your message will be expected.

7 Describe the importance of goodwill messages, and explain how to make them effective. Goodwill messages are important for building relationships with customers, colleagues, and other businesspeople. These friendly, unexpected notes have no direct business purpose, but they make people feel good about doing business with the sender. To make goodwill messages effective, make them honest and sincere. Avoid exaggerating, back up compliments with specific points, and give restrained praise.

Test Your Knowledge

1. When is a request routine?
2. What are some of the guidelines for asking a series of questions in a routine request?
3. What information should be included in an order request?
4. Should you use the direct or indirect approach for most routine messages? Why?
5. Where in a routine message should you state your actual request?
6. How does a claim differ from an adjustment?
7. How does the question of fault affect what you say in a message granting a claim?
8. What is the appropriate strategy for responding to a request for a recommendation about a job candidate whose performance was poor?
9. How can you avoid sounding insincere when writing a goodwill message?
10. What are some of the guidelines for writing condolence messages?

Apply Your Knowledge

1. Why is it good practice to explain why replying to a request could benefit the reader?
2. Your company's error cost an important business customer a new client; you know it, and your customer knows it. Do you apologize, or do you refer to the incident in a positive light without admitting any responsibility? Briefly explain.
3. You've been asked to write a letter of recommendation for an employee who worked for you some years ago. You recall that the employee did an admirable job, but you can't remember any specific information at this point. Should you write the letter anyway? Explain.
4. Every time you send a direct-request e-mail message to Ted Jackson, who works in another department in your company, he delays or refuses to comply. You're beginning to get impatient. Should you send Jackson a memo to ask what's wrong? Complain to your supervisor about Jackson's uncooperative attitude? Arrange a face-to-face meeting with Jackson? Bring up the problem at the next staff meeting? Explain your answer.
5. **Ethical Choices.** You have a complaint against one of your suppliers, but you have no documentation to back it up. Should you request an adjustment anyway? Why or why not?

Practice Your Knowledge

Messages for Analysis

Read the following documents, then (1) analyze the strengths and weaknesses of each sentence and (2) revise each document so that it follows this chapter's guidelines.

Message 8.A: Requesting Routine Information from a Business

Our college is closing its dining hall for financial reasons, so we want to do something to help the students prepare their own food in their dorm rooms if they so choose. Your colorful ad in *Collegiate Magazine* caught our eye. We need the following information before we make our decision.

- Would you be able to ship the microwaves by August 15th? I realize this is short notice, but our board of trustees just made the decision to close the dining hall last week and we're scrambling around trying to figure out what to do.
- Do they have any kind of a warranty? College students can be pretty hard on things, as you know, so we will need a good warranty.
- How much does it cost? Do you give a discount for a big order?
- Do we have to provide a special outlet?
- Will students know how to use them, or will we need to provide instructions?

As I said before, we're on a tight time frame and need good information from you as soon as possible to help us make our decision about ordering. You never know what the board might come up with next. I'm looking at several other companies, also, so please let us know ASAP.

Message 8.B: Making Claims and Requests for Adjustment

At a local business-supply store, I recently purchased your *Negotiator Pro* for my computer. I bought the CD because I saw your ad for it in *Macworld* magazine, and it looked as if it might be an effective tool for use in my corporate seminar on negotiation.

Unfortunately, when I inserted it in my office computer, it wouldn't work. I returned it to the store, but since I had already opened it, they refused to exchange it for a CD that would work or give me a refund. They told me to contact you and that you might be able to send me a version that would work with my computer.

You can send the information to me at the letterhead address. If you cannot send me the correct disk, please refund my $79.95. Thanks in advance for any help you can give me in this matter.

Message 8.C: Responding to Claims and Adjustment Requests When the Customer Is at Fault

We read your letter requesting your deposit refund. We couldn't figure out why you hadn't received it, so we talked to our maintenance engineer as you suggested. He said you had left one of the doors off the hinges in your apartment in order to get a large sofa through the door. He also confirmed that you had paid him $5.00 to replace the door since you had to turn in the U-Haul trailer and were in a big hurry.

This entire situation really was caused by a lack of communication between our housekeeping inspector and the maintenance engineer. All we knew was that the door was off the hinges when it was inspected by Sally Tarnley. You know that our policy states that if anything is wrong with the apartment, we keep the deposit. We had no way of knowing that George just hadn't gotten around to replacing the door.

But we have good news. We approved the deposit refund, which will be mailed to you from our home office in Teaneck, New Jersey. I'm not sure how long that will take, however. If you don't receive the check by the end of next month, give me a call.

Next time, it's really a good idea to stay with your apartment until it's inspected as stipulated in your lease agreement. That way, you'll be sure to receive your refund when you expect it. Hope you have a good summer.

Message 8.D: Letter of Recommendation

Your letter to Kunitake Ando, President of Sony, was forwarded to me because I am the human resources director. In my job as head of HR, I have access to performance reviews for all of the Sony employees in the United States. This means, of course, that I would be the person best qualified to answer your request for information on Nick Oshinski.

In your letter of the 15th, you asked about Nick Oshinski's employment record with us because he has applied to work for your company. Mr. Oshinski was employed with us from January 5, 1998, until March 1, 2008. During that time, Mr. Oshinski received ratings ranging from 2.5 up to 9.6, with 10 being the top score. As you can see, he must have done better reporting to some managers than to others. In addition, he took all vacation days, which is a bit unusual. Although I did not know Mr. Oshinski personally, I know that our best workers seldom use all the vacation time they earn. I do not know if that applies in this case.

In summary, Nick Oshinski performed his tasks well depending on who managed him.

Exercises

For active links to all websites discussed in this chapter, visit this text's website at www.prenhall.com/bovee. Locate your book and click on its Companion Website link. Then select Chapter 8, and click on "Featured Websites." Locate the name of the page or the URL related to the material in the text. Please note that links to sites that become inactive after publication of the book will be removed from the Featured Websites section.

8.1 **Revising Messages: Directness and Conciseness** Revise the following short e-mail messages so that they are more direct and concise; develop a subject line for each revised message.

a. I'm contacting you about your recent e-mail request for technical support on your cable Internet service. Part of the problem we have in tech support is trying to figure out exactly what each customer's specific problem is so that we can troubleshoot quickly and get you back in business as quickly as possible. You may have noticed in an online support request form there are a number of fields to enter your type of computer, operating system, memory, and so on. While you did tell us you were experiencing slow download speeds during certain times of the day, you didn't tell us which times specifically, nor did you complete all the fields telling us about your computer. Please return to our support website and resubmit your request, being sure to provide all the necessary information, then we'll be able to help you.

b. Thank you for contacting us about the difficulty you had collecting your luggage at Denver International Airport. We are very sorry for the inconvenience this has caused you. As you know, traveling can create problems of this sort regardless of how careful the airline personnel might be. To receive compensation, please send us a detailed list of the items that you lost

and complete the following questionnaire. You can e-mail it back to us.

c. Sorry it took us so long to get back to you. We were flooded with résumés. Anyway, your résumé made the final ten, and after meeting three hours yesterday, we've decided we'd like to meet with you. What is your schedule like for next week? Can you come in for an interview on June 15 at 3:00 p.m.? Please get back to us by the end of this work week and let us know if you will be able to attend. As you can imagine, this is our busy season.

d. We're letting you know that because we use over a ton of paper a year and because so much of that paper goes into the wastebasket to become so much more environmental waste, starting Monday, we're placing white plastic bins outside the elevators on every floor to recycle that paper and in the process, minimize pollution.

8.2 **Revising Messages: Directness and Conciseness** Rewrite the following sentences so that they are direct and concise. If necessary, break your answer into two sentences.

a. We wanted to invite you to our special 40% off by-invitation-only sale; the sale is taking place on November 9.

b. We wanted to let you know that we are giving a tote bag and a voucher for five iTunes downloads with every $50 donation you make to our radio station.

c. The director planned to go to the meeting that will be held on Monday at a little before 11 a.m.

d. In today's meeting, we were happy to have the opportunity to welcome Paul Eccelson, who reviewed the shopping cart function on our website and offered some great advice; if you have any questions about these new forms, feel free to call him at his office.

8.3 **Internet** Visit the Workplace eCards section of the Blue Mountain site at www.bluemountain.com and analyze one of the electronic greeting cards bearing a goodwill message of appreciation for good performance. Under what circumstances would you send this electronic message? How could you personalize it for the recipient and the occasion? What would be an appropriate close for this message?

8.4 **Teamwork** With another student, identify the purpose and select the most appropriate medium for communicating these written messages. Next, consider how the audience is likely to respond to each message. Based on this audience analysis, determine whether the direct or indirect approach would be effective for each message, and explain your reasoning.

a. A notice to all employees about the placement of recycling bins by the elevator doors

b. The first late-payment notice to a good customer who usually pays his bills on time

8.5 **Revising Messages: Conciseness, Courteousness, and Specificity** Critique the following closing paragraphs.

How would you rewrite each to be concise, courteous, and specific?

a. I need your response sometime soon so I can order the parts in time for your service appointment. Otherwise your air-conditioning system may not be in tip-top condition for the start of the summer season.

b. Thank you in advance for sending me as much information as you can about your products. I look forward to receiving your package in the very near future.

c. To schedule an appointment with one of our knowledgeable mortgage specialists in your area, you can always call our hotline at 1-800-555-8765. This is also the number to call if you have more questions about mortgage rates, closing procedures, or any other aspect of the mortgage process. Remember, we're here to make the home-buying experience as painless as possible.

8.6 **Ethical Choices** Your company markets a line of automotive accessories for people who like to "tune" their cars for maximum performance. A customer has just written a furious e-mail, claiming that a supercharger he purchased from your website didn't deliver the extra engine power he expected. Your company has a standard refund process to handle situations such as this, and you have the information you need to inform the customer about that. You also have information that could help the customer find a more compatible supercharger from one of your competitors, but the customer's e-mail message is so abusive that you don't feel obligated to help. Is this an appropriate response? Why or why not?

Expand Your Knowledge

Exploring the Best of the Web

Recommended Advice for Recommendation Letters
http://businessmajors.about.com
Whether you're continuing on to graduate school or entering the workforce with your undergraduate degree, recommendation letters could play an important role in the next few steps of your career. From selecting the people to ask for recommendation letters to knowing what makes an effective letter, About.com extends the advice offered in this chapter with real-life examples and suggestions. Visit About.com's Business Majors website and click on "Recommendation letters." Read the advice you find, then answer the following questions:

1. What's a good process for identifying the best people to ask for recommendation letters?
2. What information should you provide to letter writers to help them produce a credible and compelling letter on your behalf?
3. What are the most common mistakes you need to avoid with recommendation letters?

Surfing Your Way to Career Success

Bovée and Thill's Business Communication Resources offers links to hundreds of online resources that can help you with this course, your other college courses, and your career. Visit www.buscommresources.com, then click on "Business Communication Web Directory." The "Communication on the Job" section connects you to a variety of websites and articles on committees and teams, group communication, team conflict, negation, office politics, and the grapevine. Identify three websites from this section that could be useful in your business career. For each site, write a two-sentence summary of what the site offers and how it could help you launch and build your career.

Learn Interactively

Interactive Study Guide

Visit www.prenhall.com/bovee, then locate your book and click on its "Companion Website" link. Select Chapter 8 to take advantage of the interactive "Chapter Quiz" to test your knowledge of chapter concepts. Receive instant feedback on whether you need additional studying. Also, visit the "Study Hall," where you'll find an abundance of valuable resources that will help you succeed in this course.

Peak Performance Grammar and Mechanics

If your instructor has required the use of "Peak Performance Grammar and Mechanics," either in your online course or on CD, you can improve your skill with sentences by using the "Peak Performance Grammar and Mechanics" module. Click "Sentences." Take the Pretest to determine whether you have any weak areas. Then review those areas in the Refresher Course. Take the Follow-Up Test to check your grasp of sentences. For an extra challenge or advanced practice, take the Advanced Test. Finally, for additional reinforcement in sentences, visit the Companion Website, click on any chapter, then click on "Improve Your Grammar, Mechanics, and Usage."

CASES

Applying the Three-Step Writing Process to Cases
Apply each step to the following cases, as assigned by your instructor.

Plan

Analyze the Situation
Identify both your general purpose and your specific purpose. Clarify exactly what you want your audience to think, feel, or believe after receiving your message. Profile your primary audience, including their backgrounds, differences, similarities, and likely reactions to your message.

Gather Information
Identify the information your audience will need to receive, as well as other information you may need in order to craft an effective message.

Select the Right Medium
Make sure the medium is both acceptable to the audience and appropriate for the message.

Organize the Information
Choose a direct or indirect approach based on the audience and the message; most routine requests and routine and positive messages should employ a direct approach. Identify your main idea, limit your scope, then outline necessary support points and other evidence.

1

Write

Adapt to Your Audience
Show sensitivity to audience needs with a "you" attitude, politeness, positive emphasis, and bias-free language. Understand how much credibility you already have—and how much you may need to establish. Project your companys image by maintaining an appropriate style and tone.

Compose the Message
Draft your message using powerful words, effective sentences, and coherent paragraphs.

2

Complete

Revise the Message
Evaluate content and review readability, then edit and rewrite for conciseness and clarity.

Produce the Message
Use effective design elements and suitable layout for a clean, professional appearance.

Proofread the Message
Review for errors in layout, spelling, and mechanics; verify overall document quality.

Distribute the Message
Deliver your message using the chosen medium; make sure all documents and all relevant files are distributed successfully.

3

ROUTINE REQUESTS

E-Mail SKILLS

1. Breathing life back into your biotech career: E-mail requesting a recommendation. After five years of work in the human resources department at Cell Genesys (a company that is developing cancer treatment drugs), you were laid off in a round of cost-cutting moves that rippled through the biotech industry in recent years. The good news is that you found stable employment in the grocery distribution industry. The bad news is that in the three years since you left Cell Genesys, you have truly missed working in the exciting biotechnology field and having the opportunity to be a part of something as important as helping people recover from life-threatening diseases. You know that careers in biotech are uncertain, but you have a few dollars in the bank now and you're willing to ride that rollercoaster again.

Your task: Draft an e-mail to Calvin Morris, your old boss at Cell Genesys, reminding him of the time you worked together and asking him to write a letter of recommendation for you.[5]

IM SKILLS

2. Trans-global exchange: Instant message request for information from a Chinese manufacturer. Thank goodness your company, Diagonal Imports, chose the enterprise instant messaging software produced by IBM Lotus, called Sametime. Other products also allow you to carry on real-time exchanges with colleagues on the other side of the planet, but Sametime supports bidirectional machine translation, and you're going to need it.

The problem is that production on a popular line of decorative lighting appliances produced at your Chinese manufacturing plant inexplicably came to a halt last month. As the

product manager in the United States, you have many resources you could call on to help, such as new sources for faulty parts. But you can't do anything if you don't know the details. You've tried telephoning top managers in China, but they're evasive, telling you only what they think you want to hear.

Finally, your friend Kuei-chen Tsao has returned from a business trip. You met her during your trip to China last year. She doesn't speak English, but she's the line engineer responsible for this particular product: a fiber-optic lighting display, featuring a plastic base with a rotating color wheel. As the wheel turns, light emitted from the spray of fiber-optic threads changes color in soothing patterns. Product #3347XM is one of Diagonal's most popular items and you've got orders from novelty stores around the United States waiting to be filled. Kuei-chen should be able to explain the problem, determine whether you can help, and tell you how long before regular shipping resumes.

Your task: Write the first of what you hope will be a productive instant message exchange with Kuei-Chen. Remember that your words will be machine-translated.[6]

▌Text-Messaging ▌SKILLS

3. Tracking the new product buzz: Text message to colleagues at a trade show. The vast Consumer Electronics Show (CES) is the premier promotional event in the industry. More than 130,000 industry insiders from all over the world come to see the exciting new products on display from nearly 1,500 companies—everything from video game gadgets to Internet-enabled refrigerators with built-in computer screens. You've just stumbled on a video game controller that has a built-in webcam to allow networked gamers to see and hear each other while they play. Your company also makes

game controllers, and you're worried that your customers will flock to this new controller-cam. You need to know how much "buzz" is circulating around the show: Have people seen it? What are they saying about it? Are they excited about it?

Your task: Compose a text message to your colleagues at the show, alerting them to the new controller-cam and asking them to listen for any "buzz" that it might be generating among the attendees at the Las Vegas Convention Center and the several surrounding hotels where the show takes place. Here's the catch: Your text-messaging service limits messages to 160 characters, including spaces and punctuation, so your message can't be any longer than this.[7]

4. Step on it: Letter to Floorgraphics requesting information about underfoot advertising. You work for Alberta Greenwood, owner of Better Bike and Ski Shop. Yesterday, Alberta met with the Schwinn sales representative, Tom Beeker, who urged her to sign a contract with Floorgraphics. That company leases floor space from retail stores, then creates and sells floor ads to manufacturers such as Schwinn. Floorgraphics will pay Alberta a fee for leasing the floor space, as well as a percentage for every ad it sells. Alberta was definitely interested, and turned to you after Beeker left.

"Tom says that advertising decals on the floor in front of the product reach consumers right where they're standing when making a decision," explained Alberta. "He says the ads increase sales from 25 to 75 percent."

You both look down at the dusty floor, and Alberta laughs. "It seems funny that manufacturers will pay hard cash to put their names where customers are going to track dirt all over them! But if Tom's telling the truth, we could profit three ways: from the leasing fee, the increased sales of products being advertised, and the share in ad revenues. That's not so funny."

Your task: Alberta Greenwood asks you to write a letter for her signature to CEO Richard Rebh at Floorgraphics, Inc. (5 Vaughn Dr., Princeton, NJ 08540) asking for financial details and practical information about the ads. For example, how will you clean your floors? Who installs and removes the ads? Can you terminate the lease if you don't like the ads?[8]

5. Air rage fiasco: Letter requesting refund from British Airways. "There we were, cruising over the Atlantic, and the guy just went berserk! I couldn't believe it!" Samantha Alberts, vice president of sales at Richter Office Solutions, is standing over your desk, describing the scene for you. You notice that your boss is still pale and shaky, even though it's Monday and the "incident" happened last Friday.

She was flying back from a conference in London to make a presentation at your New York branch, before heading back home to San Francisco on Saturday. She admits it was a crushing schedule and probably foolish to plan to prepare her notes on the plane, but she never expected this.

"So how did it start?" you ask mildly, hoping your calm will help steady her nerves. She's got another meeting in two hours.

"Well, I didn't notice anything until this guy leaped up and lunged for the flight attendant with both fists flailing. But later I heard that he'd been viewing offensive images on his laptop and that other passengers complained that they could see the screen. When the steward politely asked him to stop, the guy went nuts!

He was a stocky, red-faced, bull-necked guy, and it took six crew members to handcuff him and strap him into a back-row seat. Maybe he was drunk or on drugs, I don't know, but he just kept screaming, 'I'm going to kill you!' and hitting people with his head, which was bleeding everywhere."

"Finally a passenger who was a pediatrician came forward and offered to inject the guy with a sedative for the rest of the flight. Thank goodness. Otherwise we would've been listening to his profanity for the next 10 hours. . . ." she trails off. "You know, I thought he was a hijacker and I was going to die on that plane."

"So did they arrest him?"

"As soon as we got on the ground. Police cars were everywhere. He just kept mumbling, 'I thought they were going to kill me.'" She shudders. "But the flight attendants and airline officials were wonderful. They told us to write to the airline, explain the details, and ask for a refund. Of course, I was late and unprepared for my meeting. Thank goodness it wasn't a client! When they heard about my 'air rage' encounter, the folks in our home office just handed me a cup of strong coffee and sat me down on a couch with a blanket."

Your task: You always handle Samantha's travel arrangements, and she's left you with her ticket stubs and other documents. Write the letter requesting a refund to British Airways Ticket Refunds USA, 75-20 Astoria Blvd., Jackson Heights, NY 11370. (Make up any necessary times, dates, or flight numbers.)[9]

6. Unhappy customer: Claim letter requesting an adjustment. As a consumer, you've probably bought something that didn't work right or paid for a service that did not turn out the way you expected. Maybe it was a pair of jeans with a rip in a seam that you didn't find until you got home or a watch that broke a week after you bought it. Or maybe your family hired a lawn service to do some yard work—and no one from the company showed up on the day promised; and when the gardeners finally appeared, they did not do what they'd been hired for but did other things that wound up damaging valuable plants.

Your task: Choose such an incident from your own experience, and write a claim letter asking for a refund, repair, replacement, or other adjustment. You'll need to include all the details of the transaction, plus your contact address and phone number. If you can't think of such an experience, make up details for an imaginary situation. If your experience is real, you might want to mail the letter. The reply you receive will provide a good test of your claim-writing skills.

**E-Mail
SKILLS**

7. A juicy position: E-mail requesting information about careers at Jamba Juice. You did not expect to find a job while working out at 24-Hour Fitness, but you're willing to explore an opportunity when it appears. As you were buying a smoothie at the Jamba Juice bar inside the gym, you overheard the manager talking about the company's incentives for employees, especially those interested in becoming managers. You ask her about it and she suggests you log on to the company's website (www.jambajuice.com) for more information.

You're still in business school, and you need a part-time job. Finding one at a company that offers a good future after graduation would be even better than simply earning some money to keep you going now. You check the Jamba Juice website.

You discover that the juice-bar chain has created a good reputation in the health, fitness, and nutrition industry. Also, you can submit your résumé online for an entry-level job. That sounds promising. If you could start now while finishing your degree, you'd be in a prime spot for promotion once you graduate. You start to wonder if Jamba Juice could be a long-term career opportunity.

Your task: Write an e-mail message requesting additional information about careers and advancement at Jamba Juice. First, visit www.jambajuice.com to learn all that you can about the company, then compose your message. Specifically, ask for information about career long-term advancement, beyond the store level, to corporate management. You might want to mention that you're still in school, studying business (make up any details you need).[10]

**E-Mail
SKILLS**

8. Blockbuster shake-up: Message requesting information from retail managers. Everyone knew there was trouble at Blockbuster's new headquarters in Dallas when CEO Bill Fields, a former Wal-Mart whiz, suddenly resigned. Then Sumner Redstone and Tom Dooley (chairman and deputy chairman of Blockbuster's parent company, Viacom) flew in to assess the damage wrought by Fields's departure. They started by giving orders—particularly to you, Fields's former executive assistant.

Before Fields resigned to take a position with Hudson's Bay Company in Canada, his strategy had been to boost Blockbuster's sagging movie and game rentals by establishing a new niche as a "neighborhood entertainment center." Using strategies he'd learned at Wal-Mart, he ordered the reconfiguration of more than 1,000 Blockbuster outlets, surrounding the cash registers with flashy displays of candy, potato chips, magazines, tie-in toys, and new and used DVDs for sale. His stated goal was to add $1 in retail purchases to every rental transaction. Meanwhile, he also relocated Blockbuster's headquarters from Florida to Dallas, losing 75 percent of the company's top staff when they declined to make the move. Then Fields initiated the construction of an 818,000-square-foot warehouse 25 miles outside Dallas to centralize a new, highly sophisticated distribution operation (Fields's special expertise) for Blockbuster's 3,600 North American outlets. But revenues were still falling.

Redstone and Dooley's new plan is to get Blockbuster back into its core business of movie and game rentals. "This is still a healthy, growing business," Dooley insists. He believes that consumers coming in to rent movies and games were confused by the array of retail products that greeted them.

Dooley and Redstone have been hiring new headquarters staff at the rate of about 50 people per week, they've been to the warehouse construction site, they've ordered outlets to rearrange merchandise to emphasize rentals, and now they've turned to you. "We've got a job you'll love," Dooley smiles. "We want to know what our store managers know, and we want you to ask them."

Your task: Briefly state the purpose of your message. Then draft an e-mail request asking retail managers if customers walk out when current hits aren't available, whether the emphasis on retail products affected cash flow, and whether sales and rental figures have changed now that the clutter has been removed. Ask them: Where's the cash coming from—movie and game rentals, movie and game sales, or candy bars? Dooley says, "I want a full report from every manager by the end of next week!" To get that kind of cooperation, you'd better organize your questions effectively.[11]

ROUTINE MESSAGES

▌ Blogging
▌ SKILLS

9. Here's how it will work: Explaining the brainstorming process. Austin, Texas, advertising agency GSD&M Advertising brainstorms new advertising ideas using a process it calls *dynamic collaboration*. A hand-picked team of insiders and outsiders is briefed on the project and given a key question or two to answer. The team members then sit down at computers and anonymously submit as many responses as they can within five minutes. The project moderators then pore over these responses, looking for any sparks that can ignite new ways of understanding and reaching out to consumers.

Your task: For these brainstorming sessions, GSD&M recruits an eclectic mix of participants from both inside and outside the agency—figures as diverse as economists and professional video gamers. To make sure everyone understands the brainstorming guidelines, prepare a message to be posted on the project blog. In your own words, convey the following four points as clearly and succinctly as you can:

- *Be yourself.* We want input from as many perspectives as possible, which is why we recruit such a diverse array of participants. Don't try to get into what you believe is the mindset of an advertising specialist—we want you to ap-

proach the given challenge using whatever analytical and creative skills you normally employ in your daily work.
- *Create, don't edit.* Don't edit, refine, or self-censor while you're typing during the initial five-minute session. We don't care if your ideas are formatted beautifully, phrased poetically, or even spelled correctly. Just crank 'em out as quickly as you can.
- *It's about the ideas, not the participants.* Just so you know up front, all ideas are collected anonymously. We can't tell who submitted the brilliant ideas, the boring ideas, or the already-tried-that ideas. So while you won't get personal credit, you can also be crazy and fearless. Go for it!
- *The winning ideas will be subjected to the toughest of tests.* Just in case you're worried about submitting ideas that could be risky, expensive, or difficult to implement—don't fret. As we narrow down the possibilities, the few that remain will be judged, poked, prodded, and assessed from every angle. In other words, let us worry about containing the fire; you come up with the sparks.[12]

▌ Podcasting   ▌ Portfolio
▌ SKILLS   ▌ BUILDER

10. Listening to business: Using the iPod to train employees. As a training specialist in Winnebago Industry's human resources department, you're always on the lookout for new ways to help employees learn vital job skills. While watching a production worker page through a training manual while learning how to assemble a new recreational vehicle, you get what seems to be a great idea: record the assembly instructions as audio files that workers can listen to while performing the necessary steps. With audio instructions, they wouldn't need to keep shifting their eyes between the product and the manual—and constantly losing their place. They could focus on the product and listen for each instruction. Plus, the new system wouldn't cost much at all; any computer can record the audio files, and you'd simply make them available on an intranet site for download into iPods or other digital music players.

Your task: You immediately run your new idea past your boss, who has heard about podcasting but doesn't think it has any place in business. He asks you to prove the viability of the idea by recording a demonstration. Choose a process that you engage in yourself—anything from replacing the strings on a guitar to sewing a quilt to changing the oil in a car—and write a brief (one page or less) description of the process that could be recorded as an audio file. Think carefully about the limitations of the audio format as a replacement for printed text (for instance, do you need to tell people to pause the audio while they perform a time-consuming task?). If directed by your instructor, record your instructions as podcast.

▌ Portfolio
▌ BUILDER

11. Got it covered? Letter from American Express about SUV rentals. You can always tell when fall arrives at American Express—you are deluged with complaints from customers who have just received their summer vacation bills. Often these angry calls are about a shock-inducing damage repair bill from a car rental agency. Vacation car rentals can be a lot more complicated than most people think. Here's what happens.

Your credit card customers are standing at the Hertz or Avis counter, ready to drive away, when the agent suggests an upgrade to, say, a Ford Expedition or another large SUV. Feeling happy-go-lucky on vacation, your customers say, "Why not?" and hand over their American Express card.

As they drive off in large vehicles that many are unaccustomed to handling, 9 out of 10 are unaware that the most common accidents among rental cars take place at low speeds in parking lots. Plus, the upgraded vehicle they're driving is no longer fully covered either by their regular auto insurance or by the secondary car rental insurance they expect from American Express. If they've agreed to pay the additional $10 to $25 a day for the car rental agency's "collision and liability damage wavier fee," they will be able to walk away from any accident with no liability. Otherwise, they're running a costly risk.

Soon they pull into a shopping mall with the kids to pick up the forgotten sunscreen and sodas, where they discover that luxury road-warrior mobile is not so easy to park in stalls designed in the 1970s and 1980s when compact cars were all the rage. *Thwack*—there goes the door panel. *Crunch*—a rear bumper into a light post. *Wham!* There goes the family bank account, but they don't realize it yet—not until they receive the bill from the rental agency, the one that comes *after* their auto insurance and credit card companies have already paid as much as they're going to pay for damages.

Auto insurers typically provide the same coverage for rentals as you carry on your own car. When customers use their credit card to pay for car rentals, American Express offers secondary protection that generally covers any remaining, unpaid damages. But there are important exceptions.

Neither insurance nor credit card companies will pay the "loss of vehicle use fees" that car rental agencies always tack on. These fees can run into thousands of dollars, based on the agency's revenue losses while the car is in the repair shop. When your customers are billed for this fee, they invariably call you, an-

grily demanding to know why American Express won't pay it. And if they've rented an SUV, they're even angrier.

American Express Green and Gold cards provide secondary coverage up to $55,000, and the Platinum card extends that to $75,000. But large SUVs such as the Ford Expedition, the GMC Yukon, and the Chevrolet Suburban are not covered at all. Such exclusions are common. For instance, Diners Club specifically excludes "high-value, special interest or exotic cars"—such as the Ferraris, Maseratis, and even Rolls-Royces that are urged on customers by rental agencies.

Your task: As assistant vice president of customer service, you'd like to keep the phone lines cooler this summer and fall. It's April, so there's still time. Write a form letter to be sent to all American Express customers, urging them to check their rental car coverages, advising them against renting vehicles that are larger than they really require, and encouraging them to consider paying the rental agency's daily loss waiver fees.[13]

12. Mind your own e-mail: Message outlining electronic privacy policy at the *Los Angeles Times*. When you stepped into your office at the *Los Angeles Times* this morning, the place was buzzing with gossip about a reporter in the paper's Moscow bureau. Apparently, he'd been snooping into his fellow reporters' e-mail. To catch him, supervisors there set up a sting operation, planting an exchange of phony e-mail messages with the Jerusalem bureau, which cooperated in catching the snoop. The bogus e-mail referred to "shrinking travel allowances."

The suspect took the bait, apparently using a co-worker's password to view the e-mail. When he later mentioned the new travel rules, he was slapped with a reassignment back to Los Angeles, to an as-yet-undesignated job—probably writing obituaries, or so the rumormongers in your office have decided.

The *Los Angeles Times* has always observed strict discipline with regard to journalistic ethics. But because journalists traditionally hold confidentiality in high regard, management assumed that e-mail privacy needed no special rules or enforcement policies. Clearly, that assumption was wrong. In the past, the company casually conveyed a list of commonsense e-mail guidelines such as not using the system for personal business; being aware that employee e-mail is not invisible to computer system administrators or even managers; not using derogatory language, obscenity, or copyrighted material; and so on. Now, a strict privacy policy will be added to the list, which will be sent out to bureau managers in an official memo.

As an employee of the newspaper's legal department, you've been handed the task of writing the memo to managers. Outline the company's policy for handling e-mail privacy violations. Management has already decided the penalties: reassignment, suspension without pay, or termination of employment. What you'll be communicating is how the new penalties are to be implemented. You will also suggest that managers immediately introduce these new rules to employees in a special meeting and that they routinely explain all the rules and guidelines to new hires.

For a first offense, the penalty will be a verbal warning in a personal meeting with a direct supervisor, which will also be entered in writing in the employee's human resources file. For a second offense, the penalty will be reassignment or suspension without pay, for a period to be determined by the employee's supervisor (who will know best the most appropriate length of time). A third offense will result in immediate termination without severance pay.

Your task: Address your memo to news bureau managers (who oversee editorial offices around the globe). Outline the company's policy for handling employees who violate e-mail privacy rules. Explain that a more detailed company-issued policy memo covering all issues will be in their hands in a few weeks and must be posted at each bureau in an area visible to employees. For managerial reference in the meantime, list the penalties for privacy violations and the appropriate sequence for applying them.[14]

E-Mail SKILLS **Portfolio BUILDER**

13. Temper, temper: E-mail to Metro Power employees about technology failures. This is the third time in two months that your company, Metro Power, has had to escort an employee from the building after a violent episode. Frankly, everyone is a little frightened by this development. As a human resources administrator, you have the unhappy task of trying to quell the storm.

Metro Power rarely fires employees, preferring to transfer them to new responsibilities, which may either draw out their finer points (and prove better for everyone in the long run) or help them decide to seek greener pastures. But in three cases, you had no choice. In one incident, a man punched out his computer screen after the system failed. In another, a man threw his keyboard across the room when he couldn't get access to the company's intranet. And in a third incident, a woman kicked a printer while screaming obscenities.

In all three cases, co-workers were terrified by these sudden outbursts. Too many disgruntled workers have committed too many violent acts against others in recent years; and whenever workers lose their temper on the job these days, it causes great fear—not to mention financial losses from the destruction of property and the disruption of work flow.

People are on edge at Metro Power right now. Rising energy costs, public and government scrutiny, and cries of price gouging are causing additional work and stress for all your employees. Plus, too much overtime, unrealistic expectations for overworked departments, and high demands on sensitive equipment are contributing to the problem. Tempers are frayed and nerves strained. You're concerned that these three incidents are just the tip of the iceberg.

Your department head suggests that you write a reminder to all employees about controlling tempers in the workplace. "Tell them that technology glitches are commonplace and not some unholy disaster. And remind them to report routine computer failures to Bart Stone. He'll get to them in due course."

You say nothing to contradict her idea, but you wonder how to do what she asks without sounding trite or condescending. You don't want to sound like some nagging parent—no one will pay attention to your message. You sigh deeply as your boss strolls calmly back to her office. You're fairly certain that every employee already knows about reporting computer failures to Bart Stone, assistant director of information services.

Even so, you can think of a few suggestions that might be helpful, such as taking a walk to cool down, or recognizing that machines, like humans, are not infallible. You want cooler heads to prevail, and that's just the sort of cliché you'd like to avoid in your message.

Your task: Write the e-mail message to all employees. Instead of uttering platitudes or wagging your finger, include preventive maintenance tips for office equipment, such as turning systems off at night, keeping food and liquids away from keyboards, making use of dusting sprays and special cloths, and so on. Your boss also asked you to make it clear that abusive behavior will be reprimanded, so include that point in a tactful way.[15]

ROUTINE REPLIES

E-Mail SKILLS **Portfolio BUILDER**

14. Window shopping at Wal-Mart: Offering advice to the webmaster. Wal-Mart has grown to international success because it rarely fails to capitalize on a marketing scheme, and its website is no exception. To make sure the website remains effective and relevant, the webmaster asks various people to check out the site and give their feedback. As administrative assistant to Wal-Mart's director of marketing, you have just received a request from the webmaster to visit Wal-Mart's website and give your feedback.

Your task: Visit www.wal-mart.com and do some online "window shopping." As you browse through the site, consider the language, layout, graphics, and overall ease of use. In particular, look for aspects of the site that might be confusing or frustrating—

annoyances that could prompt shoppers to abandon their quests and head to a competitor such as Target. Summarize your findings and recommendations in an e-mail message to the webmaster.

15. The special courier: Letter of recommendation for an old friend. In today's mail, you get a letter from Non-Stop Messenger Service, 899 Sparks St., Ottawa, Ontario K1A 0G9, Canada. It concerns a friend of yours who has applied for a job. Here is the letter:

Kathryn Norquist has applied for the position of special courier with our firm, and she has given us your name as a reference. Our special couriers convey materials of considerable value or confidentiality to their recipients. It is not an easy job. Special couriers must sometimes remain alert for periods of up to 20 hours, and they cannot expect to follow the usual "three square meals and a full night's sleep" routine because they often travel long distances on short notice. On occasion, a special courier must react quickly and decisively to threatening situations.

For this type of work, we hire only people of unquestioned integrity, as demonstrated both by their public records and by references from people, like you, who have known them personally or professionally.

We would appreciate a letter from you, supplying detailed answers to the following questions: (1) How long and in what circumstances have you known the applicant? (2) What qualities does she possess that would qualify her for the position of special courier? (3) What qualities might need to be improved before she is put on permanent assignment in this job?

As vice president of human resources at DHL, you know how much weight a strong personal reference can carry, and you don't really mind that Kathryn never contacted you for permission to list your name—that's Kathryn. You met her during your sophomore year at San Diego State University—that would have been 1994—and you two were roommates for several years after. Her undergraduate degree was in journalism, and her investigative reporting was relentless. You have never known anyone who could match Kathryn's stamina when she was on a story. Of course, when she was between stories, she could sleep longer and do less than anyone else you have ever known.

After a few years of reporting, Kathryn went back to school and earned her MBA from the University of San Diego. After that, you lost track of her for a while. Somebody said that she had joined the FBI—or was it the CIA?—you never really knew. You received a couple of postcards from Paris and one from Madrid.

Two years ago, you met Kathryn for dinner. Only in town for the evening, she was on her way to Borneo to "do the text" for a photographer friend of hers who worked for *National Geographic*. You read the article last year on the shrinking habitat for orangutans. It was powerful.

Although you're in no position to say much about Kathryn's career accomplishments, you can certainly recommend her energy and enthusiasm, her ability to focus on a task or assignment, her devotion to ethics, and her style. She always seems unshakable—organized, thorough, and honorable, whether digging into political corruption or trudging the jungles of Borneo. You're not sure that her free spirit would flourish in a courier's position, and you wonder if she is a bit overqualified for the job. But knowing Kathryn, you're confident she wouldn't apply for a position unless she truly wanted it.

Your task: Supplying any details you can think of, write as supportive a letter as possible about your friend Kathryn to Roscoe de la Penda, Human Resources Specialist, Non-Stop Messenger.

E-Mail SKILLS

16. Red dirt to go: Positive e-mail reply from Paradise Sportswear. As the owner of Paradise Sportswear in Hawaii, Robert Hedin was nearly done in by Hurricane Iniki in 1992, which wiped out his first silk-screened and airbrushed T-shirt business. He tried again, but then Hawaii's red dirt started seeping into his warehouse and ruining his inventory. Finally, a friend suggested that he stop trying to fight Mother Nature. Hedin took the hint: He mortgaged his condo and began producing Red Dirt Shirts, all made with dye created from the troublesome local dirt.

Bingo. Hedin's Red Dirt Sportswear designs are so popular, they're being snapped up by locals and tourists in Hedin's eight Paradise Sportswear retail outlets and in every Kmart on the islands. Hedin even added a new line: Lava Blues, made with real Hawaiian lava rock.

"You can make 500 shirts with a bucket of dirt," grins Hedin as he shows you around the operation on your first day. He's just a few years away from the usual retirement age, but he looks like a kid who's finally found the right playground.

Recently, Hedin decided to capitulate to all the requests he's received from retail outlets on the mainland. Buyers kept coming to the islands on vacation, discovering Hedin's "natural" sportswear, and begging him to set up a deal. For a long time, his answer was no; he simply couldn't handle the extra work. But now he's hired you.

As special sales representative, you'll help Hedin expand slowly into this new territory, starting with one store. Wholesaling to the local Kmarts is easy enough, but handling all the arrangements for shipping to the mainland would be too much for the current staff. So you'll start with the company Hedin has chosen to become the first mainland retailer to sell Red Dirt and Lava Blues sportswear: Surf's Up in Chicago, Illinois—of all places. The boss figures that with less competition than he'd find on either coast, his island-influenced sportswear will be a big hit in Chicago, especially in the dead of winter.

Your task: Write a positive response to the e-mail received from Surf's Up buyer Ronald Draeger, who says he fell in love with the Paradise clothing concept while on a surfing trip to Maui. Let him know he'll have a temporary exclusive and that you'll be sending a credit application and other materials by snail mail. His e-mail address is surfsup@insnet.com.[16]

E-Mail SKILLS

17. Auto-talk: E-mail messages for Highway Bytes computers to send automatically. You are director of customer services at Highway Bytes, which markets a series of small, handlebar-mounted computers for bicyclists. These Cycle Computers do everything, from computing speed and distance traveled to displaying street maps. Serious cyclists love them, but your company is growing so fast that you can't keep up with all the customer service requests you receive every day. Your boss wants not only to speed up response time but also to reduce staffing costs and allow your technical experts the time they need to focus on the most difficult and important questions.

You've just been reading about automated response systems, and you quickly review a few articles before discussing the options with your boss. Artificial intelligence researchers have been working for decades to design systems that can actually converse with customers, ask questions, and respond to requests. Some of today's systems have vocabularies of thousands of words and the ability to understand simple sentences. For example, *chatterbots* are automated bots that can actually mimic human conversation. (You can see what it's like to carry on a conversation with some of these bots by visiting www.botspot.com, clicking on Artificial Life Bots, and then selecting Chatterbots.)

Unfortunately, even though chatterbots hold a lot of promise, human communication is so complex that a truly automated customer service agent could take years to perfect (and may even prove to be impossible). However, the simplest automated systems are called *autoresponders* or *on-demand e-mail*. They are fast and extremely inexpensive. They have no built-in intelligence, so they do nothing more than send back the same reply to every message they receive.

You explain to your boss that although some of the messages you receive require the attention of your product specialists, many are simply requests for straightforward information. In fact, the customer service staff already answers some 70 percent of e-mail queries with three ready-made attachments:

- *Installing Your Cycle Computer.* Gives customers advice on installing the cycle computer the first time or reinstalling it on a new bike. In most cases, the computer and wheel sensor bolt directly to the bike without modification, but certain bikes do require extra work.
- *Troubleshooting Your Cycle Computer.* Provides a step-by-step guide to figuring out what might be wrong with a malfunctioning cycle computer. Most problems are simple, such as dead batteries or loose wires, but others are beyond the capabilities of your typical customer.
- *Upgrading the Software in Your Cycle Computer.* Tells customers how to attach the cycle computer to their home or office PC and download new software from Highway Bytes.

Your boss is enthusiastic when you explain that you can program your current e-mail system to look for specific words in incoming messages and then respond, based on what it finds. For example, if a customer message contains the word *installation*, you can program the system to reply with the *Installing Your Cycle Computer* attachment. This reconfigured system should be able to handle a sizable portion of the hundreds of e-mails your customer service group gets every week.

Your task: First, draft a list of keywords that you'll want your e-mail system to look for. You'll need to be creative and spend some time with a thesaurus. Identify all the words and word combinations that could identify a message as pertaining to one of the three subject areas. For instance, the word *attach* would

probably indicate a need for the installation material, whereas *new software* would most likely suggest a need for the upgrade attachment.

Second, draft three short e-mail messages to accompany each ready-made attachment, explaining that the attached document answers the most common questions on a particular subject (installation, troubleshooting, or upgrading). Your messages should invite recipients to write back if the attached document doesn't solve the problem—and don't forget to provide the e-mail address: support2@highwaybytes.com.

Third, draft a fourth message to be sent out whenever your new system is unable to figure out what the customer is asking for. Simply thank the customer for writing and explain that the query will be passed on to a customer service specialist who will respond shortly.

▌E-Mail
▌SKILLS

18. Lighten up: E-mail reply to a website designer at Organizers Unlimited. When Kendra Williams, owner of Organizers Unlimited, wanted to create a website to sell her Superclean Organizer, she asked you, her assistant, to find a designer. After some research, you found three promising individuals. Williams chose Pete Womack, whose résumé impressed both of you. Now he's e-mailed his first design proposal and Williams is not happy.

"I detest cluttered websites!" she explodes. "This homepage has too many graphics and animations, too much 'dancing baloney.' He must have included at least a megabyte of bouncing cotton balls and jogging soap bars! Clever, maybe, but we don't want it! If the homepage takes too long to load, our customers won't wait for it and we'll lose sales."

Williams's dislike of clutter is what inspired her to invent the Superclean Organizer in the first place, a neat device for organizing bathroom items.

Your task: "You found him," says Williams. "Now you can answer and tell him what's wrong with this design." Before you write the e-mail reply to Womack explaining the need for a simpler homepage, read some of the articles offering tips at **www.sitepoint.com**. On the homepage, under "Before You Code," select "Site Planning"; and under "Design and Layout" select "Design Principles." Use these ideas to support your message.[17]

E-Mail SKILLS

19. Shopping for talent: Memo at Clovine's recommending a promotion. You enjoy your duties as manager of the women's sportswear at Clovine's—a growing chain of moderate to upscale department stores in South Florida. You especially enjoy being able to recommend someone for a promotion. Today, you received an e-mail message from Rachel Cohen, head buyer for women's apparel. She is looking for a smart, aggressive employee to become assistant buyer for the women's sportswear division. Clovine's likes to promote from within, and Rachel is asking all managers and supervisors for likely candidates. You have just the person she's looking for.

Jennifer Ramirez is a salesclerk in the designer sportswear boutique of your main store in Miami, and she has caught your attention. She's quick, friendly, and good at sizing up a customer's preferences. Moreover, at recent department meetings, she has shared some insightful observations about fashion trends in South Florida.

Your task: Write an e-mail reply to Rachel Cohen, head buyer, women's sportswear, recommending Jennifer Ramirez and evaluating her qualifications for the promotion. Rachel can check with the human resources department about Jennifer's educational and employment history; you're mainly interested in conveying your positive impression of Jennifer's potential for advancement.

20. Impressive trainee: Letter of recommendation for a top-notch intern. As a project manager at Orbitz, one of the largest online travel services in the world, you've seen plenty of college interns in action. However, few have impressed you as much as Maxine "Max" Chenault. For one thing, she learned how to navigate the company's content management system virtually overnight and always used it properly, whereas other interns sometimes left things in a hopeless mess. She asked lots of intelligent questions about the business. You've been teaching her blogging and website design principles, and she's picked them up rapidly. Moreover, she is always on time, professional, and eager to assist. Also, she didn't mind doing mundane tasks.

On the downside, Chenault is a popular student. Early on, you often found her busy on the phone planning her many social activities when you needed her help. However, after you had a brief talk with her, this problem vanished.

You'll be sorry to see Chenault leave when she returns to school in the fall, but you're pleased to respond when she asks you for a letter of recommendation. She's not sure where she'll apply for work after graduation or what career path she'll choose, so she asks you to keep the letter fairly general.

Your task: Working with a team of your classmates, discuss what should and should not be in the letter. Prepare an outline based on your discussion, then draft the letter.

21. Satellite farming: Letter granting credit from Deere & Company. This is the best part of your job with Deere & Co. in Moline, Illinois: saying yes to a farmer. In this case, it's Arlen Ruestman in Toluca, Illinois. Ruestman wants to take advantage of new farming technology. Your company's GreenStar system uses GPS satellite technology to let farmers know exactly where they are as they drive equipment across their fields. For farmers like Reustman, that means a new ability to micromanage even as many as 10,000 acres of corn or soybeans.

For instance, using the GreenStar system, farmers can map and analyze characteristics such as acidity, soil type, or crop yields from a given area. Using this information, they know exactly how much herbicide or fertilizer to spread over precisely which spot—eliminating waste and achieving better results. With cross-referencing and accumulated data, farmers can analyze why crops are performing well in some areas and not so well in others. Then they can program farm equipment to treat only the problem area—for example, spraying a new insect infestation 2 yards wide, 300 yards down the row.

Some farms have already saved as much as $10 an acre on fertilizers alone. For 10,000 acres, that's $100,000 a year. Once Ruestman retrofits your GreenStar precision package on his old combine and learns all its applications, he should have no problem saving enough to pay off the $7,350 credit account you're about to grant him.

Your task: Write a letter to Ruestman (P.O. Box 4067, Toluca, IL 61369) informing him of the good news.[18]

POSITIVE MESSAGES

Blogging SKILLS   Portfolio BUILDER

22. Leveraging the good news: Blog announcement of a prestigious professional award. You and your staff in the public relations (PR) department at Epson of America were delighted when the communication campaign you created for the new PictureMate Personal Photo Lab (**www.epson.com/picturemate**) was awarded the prestigious Silver Anvil award by the Public Relations Society of America. Now you'd like to give your team a pat on the back by sharing the news with the rest of the company.

Your task: Write a one-paragraph message for the PR department blog (which is read by people throughout the company but is not accessible outside the company) announcing the award. Take care not to "toot your own horn" as the manager of the PR department, and use the opportunity to compliment the rest of the company for designing and producing such an innovative product.[19]

23. Intercultural condolences: Letter conveying sympathy at IBM. You've been working two years as administrative assistant to J. T. "Ted" Childs, Jr., vice president of global workforce diversity at IBM in Armonk, New York. Chana Panichpapiboon has been with Childs even longer than you have, and, sadly, her husband was killed (along with 19 others) in a bus accident yesterday. The bus skidded on icy pavement into a deep ravine, tipping over and crushing the occupants before rescue workers could get to them.

You met Surin last year at a company banquet. You can still picture his warm smile and the easy way he joked with you and others over chicken Florentine, even though you were complete strangers to him. He was only 32 years old, and he left Chana two children, a 12-year-old boy, Arsa, and a 10-year-old girl, Veera. His death is a terrible tragedy.

Normally, you'd write a condolence letter immediately. But Chana is a native of Thailand, and so was Surin. In the past two years, you've listened many times to Childs's rousing lectures to new managers on the benefits and demands of a multicultural workforce. You know you'd better do a little research first. Is Chana Buddhist or Catholic? Is there anything about the typical Western practice of expressing sympathy that might be inappropriate? Offensive?

After making some discreet inquiries among Chana's closest friends at work, you've learned that she is Theravada Buddhist, as are most people in Thailand. From a reference work in the company library about doing business around the world, you've gleaned only that, in the beliefs of many people in Thailand, "the person takes precedence over rule or law" and "people gain their social position as a result of karma, not personal achievement," which means Chana may believe in reincarnation. But the book also says that Theravada Buddhists are free to choose which precepts of their religion, if any, they will follow. So Chana's beliefs are still a mystery.

You do know that her husband was very important to her and much loved by all their family. That, at least, is universal. And you're toying with a phrase you once read, "The hand of time lightly lays, softly soothing sorrow's wound." Is it appropriate?

Your task: You've decided to handwrite the condolence note on a blank greeting card you've found that bears a peaceful, "Eastern-flavor" image. You know you're risking a cultural gaffe, but at least you won't commit the greater offense of not writing at all. Choose the most sincere wording you can, which should resonate through any differences in custom or tradition.[20]

▌Blogging ▌Portfolio
▌SKILLS ▌BUILDER

24. Green is the new green: Blog update on energy savings. Adobe Systems is well known as the maker of Acrobat, Photoshop, Flash, and other programs that are fundamental tools in the Internet Age. It is also becoming well known as one of the "greenest" companies in the country, adopting a variety of techniques and technologies that have not only reduced its energy usage considerably but also cut nearly a million dollars a year from its utility bills. In 2006, Adobe became the first company ever to receive the Platinum Certification from the U.S. Green Building Council.

Your task: Write a one- or two-paragraph post for an internal blog at Adobe letting employees know how well the company is doing in its efforts to reduce energy usage and thanking employees for

the energy-saving ideas they've submitted and the individual efforts they've made to reduce, reuse, and recycle. Learn more about the company's accomplishments by searching for the news release "Adobe Wins Platinum Certification Awarded by U.S. Green Building Council," available on the Adobe website at www.adobe.com/aboutadobe/pressroom. Select a few key details from this news release to include in your message.[21]

25. Congrats on that: Complimenting a former business acquaintance for national recognition. You pull the new issue of *Fortune* magazine out of the stack of mail and are quite pleased to see Indra Nooyi on the cover. Not only was Nooyi recently appointed CEO of PepsiCo, but *Fortune* has just named her the most powerful woman in American business. You got to know her briefly when PepsiCo acquired your previous employer, Quaker Oats, in 2001. You haven't spoken to her since then, but you have followed her accomplishments in the business media.

Your task: Write a brief letter (no more than one page) congratulating Nooyi on her promotion to CEO and on being recognized by *Fortune*. Make up any details you need to create a credible message. You can learn more about Nooyi's career and accomplishments in the news release, "PepsiCo's Board of Directors Appoints Indra K. Nooyi as Chief Executive Officer Effective October 1, 2006," on the PepsiCo website, www.pepsico.com (look under News, PepsiCo Releases, 2006). Address the letter to Indra Nooyi, CEO, PepsiCo, Inc., 700 Anderson Hill Road, Purchase, NY 10577.

26. Our sympathy: Condolence letter to an Aetna underwriter. As chief administrator for the underwriting department of Aetna Health Plans in Walnut Creek, California, you're facing a difficult task. One of your best underwriters, Hector Almeida, recently lost his wife in an automobile accident (he and his teenage daughter weren't with her at the time). Because you're the boss, everyone in the close-knit department is looking to you to communicate the group's sympathy and concern.

Someone suggested a simple greeting card that everyone could sign, but that seems so impersonal for someone you've worked with every day for nearly five years. So you decided to write a personal note on behalf of the whole department. You met Hector's wife, Rosalia, at a few company functions although you knew her mostly through Hector's frequent references to her. Although you didn't know her well, you do know important things about her life, which you can celebrate in the letter.

Right now he's devastated by the loss. But if anyone can overcome this tragedy, Hector can. He's always determined to get a job done no matter what obstacles present themselves, and he does it with an upbeat attitude. That's why everyone in the office likes him so much.

You also plan to suggest that when he returns to work, he might like to move his schedule up an hour so that he'll have more time to spend with his daughter, Lisa, after school. It's your way of helping make things a little easier for them during this period of adjustment.

Your task: Write the letter to Hector Almeida, who lives at 47 West Ave., #10, Walnut Creek, CA 94596. (Feel free to make up any details you need.)[22]

CHAPTER *9*

Writing Negative Messages

LEARNING OBJECTIVES

After studying this chapter, you will be able to

1 Apply the three-step writing process to negative messages

2 Explain the differences between the direct and the indirect approaches to negative messages, including when it's appropriate to use each one

3 Identify the risks of using the indirect approach, and explain how to avoid such problems

4 Adapt negative messages for internal and external audiences

5 Explain the importance of maintaining high standards of ethics and etiquette when delivering negative messages

6 Explain the role of communication in crisis management

7 List three guidelines for delivering negative news to job applicants and give a brief explanation of each one

COMMUNICATION CLOSE-UP AT KPMG

www.us.kpmg.com

When businesses make mistakes, should they apologize? Traditional thinking says they can't afford to, because doing so is an admission of guilt that can be used against them in lawsuits. However, an emerging school of thought says that apologizing isn't as risky as previously believed and that courts tend to show leniency toward companies that express remorse after making mistakes.

The large accounting firm KPMG recently faced this situation when the U.S. Internal Revenue Service ruled that certain *tax shelters* (investments created primarily to reduce tax burdens) the company had been recommending for some of its wealthy clients were illegal. Soon after, KPMG faced both a criminal investigation and multiple lawsuits from individual clients who accused the company of encouraging them to break the law. Just a few years earlier, KPMG competitor Arthur Andersen had been convicted in criminal matters of a different type and had collapsed as a result, putting 85,000 people out of work.

KPMG faced a classic dilemma. If it apologized in an effort to avoid criminal prosecution, that would be seen as an admission of guilt that could be used against it in all those civil suits.

When the accounting firm KPMG publicly apologized for the illegal actions of some of its partners (one of whom, Jeffrey Eischeid, is shown here leaving the courthouse), the admission of guilt helped save the firm from potentially devastating criminal charges but might well have worked against it in numerous client lawsuits.

Apparently deciding that a criminal charge would be more dangerous, KPMG issued the following statement: "KPMG takes full responsibility for the unlawful conduct by former KPMG partners . . . and we deeply regret that it occurred." The apology seemed to help, as the firm avoided a criminal indictment by agreeing to pay a fine of nearly a half-billion dollars and to get out of the tax shelter business. However, the admission of guilt was welcomed by lawyers representing KPMG clients. "It's stunning. Obviously, it's very helpful," said one. That optimism seemed warranted, as the firm was later forced to pay most of its tax shelter clients a total of more than $150 million and lawsuits from the remaining clients are likely to drag on for years.[1]

USING THE THREE-STEP WRITING PROCESS FOR NEGATIVE MESSAGES

1 LEARNING OBJECTIVE

Apply the three-step writing process to negative messages

Five goals of negative messages:
- *Give the bad news*
- *Ensure its acceptance*
- *Maintain reader's goodwill*
- *Maintain organization's good image*
- *Reduce future correspondence on the matter*

Chances are slim that you'll ever need to issue a message like KPMG's (profiled in the chapter-opening Communication Close-Up), but communicating other kinds of negative news is a fact of life for all business professionals, from rejecting job applicants to telling customers that shipments will be late to turning down speaking invitations.

When you need to deliver bad news, you have five goals: (1) to convey the bad news; (2) to gain acceptance for it; (3) to maintain as much goodwill as possible with your audience; (4) to maintain a good image for your organization; and (5) if appropriate, to reduce or eliminate the need for future correspondence on the matter (in a few cases, you want to encourage discussion). Five goals are clearly a lot to accomplish in one message. However, by learning some simple techniques and following the three-step process, you can develop negative messages that reduce the stress for everyone involved and improve the effectiveness of your communication efforts.

Step 1: Plan Your Message

When planning negative messages, you can't avoid the fact that your audience does not want to hear what you have to say. To minimize the damage to business relationships and to encourage the acceptance of your message, analyze the situation carefully to better understand the context in which the recipient will process your message.

Be sure to consider your purpose thoroughly—whether it's straightforward (such as rejecting a job application) or more complicated (such as drafting a negative performance review, in which you not only give the employee feedback on past performance but also help the person develop a plan to improve future performance). Similarly, your audience profile can be simple and obvious in some situations (such as rejecting a credit request) and far more complex in others (such as telling a business partner that you've decided to terminate the partnership).

With a clear purpose and your audience's needs in mind, identify and gather the information your audience will need in order to understand and accept your message. Negative messages can be intensely personal to the recipient, and in many cases recipients have a right to expect a thorough explanation of your answer (although this isn't always the case). For instance, if one of your hardest-working employees has asked for a raise but you don't think her performance warrants it, you can carefully explain the difference between hard work and productive results to help her accept your message.

Choose the medium with care when preparing negative messages.

Selecting the right medium is critical. For instance, experts advise that bad news for employees be delivered in person whenever possible, both to show respect for the employees and to give them an opportunity to ask questions. Of course, delivering bad news is never easy, and an increasing number of managers appear to be using e-mail and other electronic media to convey negative messages to employees.[2] However, employees are more likely to accept messages and maintain respect for the sender if bad news is delivered in person.

The appropriate organization helps readers accept your negative news.

Defining your main idea in a negative message is often more complicated than simply saying no. For instance, in the case of the hard-working employee who requested a raise, your message might go beyond saying no to explaining how she can improve her performance by working smarter, not just harder.

Step 2: Write Your Message

When you are adapting a negative message to your audience, pay close attention to both effectiveness and diplomacy. After all, your audience does not want to hear what you have to say and might disagree strongly with you, so messages perceived to be unclear or unkind will amplify the audience's stress. Be sure to maintain a "you" attitude, strive for polite language that emphasizes the positive whenever appropriate, and make sure your word choice is without bias. For more advice, see "Adapting to Your Audience" on page 262.

If your credibility hasn't already been established with an audience, lay out your qualifications for making the decision in question. Recipients of negative messages who don't think you are credible are more likely to challenge your decision or reject your message. And, as always, projecting and protecting your company's image are prime concerns; if you're not careful, a negative answer could spin out of control into negative feelings about your company.

When you use language that conveys respect and avoids an accusing tone, you protect your audience's pride. This kind of communication etiquette is always important, but it demands special care with negative messages. Moreover, you can ease the sense of disappointment by using positive words rather than negative, counterproductive ones (see Table 9.1).

Chances are you'll spend more time on word, sentence, and paragraph choices for negative messages than for any other type of business writing. People who receive negative messages often look for subtle shades of meaning, seeking flaws in your reasoning or other ways to challenge the decision. By writing clearly and sensitively, you can take some of the sting out of bad news and help your reader accept the decision and move on.

Audiences often expect significant negative messages to be delivered in person. Here, Ford Motor Company Executive Vice President and Chief Financial Officer Donat R. Leclair announces the close of up to 14 manufacturing plants and layoffs of up to 30,000 employees.

Step 3: Complete Your Message

Your need for careful attention to detail continues as you complete your message. Revise your content to make sure everything is clear, complete, and concise—bearing in mind that even small flaws are magnified as readers react to your negative news. Produce clean, professional documents; and proofread carefully to eliminate mistakes. Finally, be especially sure that your negative messages are delivered promptly and successfully; waiting for bad news is hard enough without wondering whether a message was lost.

DEVELOPING NEGATIVE MESSAGES

As you apply the three-step writing process to negative messages, keep three important aspects in mind. First, before you organize the main points of a message, determine whether it will be better to use a direct or an indirect approach. Second, before actually composing your message, be sensitive to variations across cultures or between internal and external

TABLE 9.1 Choosing Positive Words

EXAMPLES OF NEGATIVE PHRASINGS	POSITIVE ALTERNATIVES
Your request *doesn't make any sense.*	Please clarify your request.
The *damage* won't be fixed for a week.	The item will be repaired next week.
Although it wasn't our *fault,* there will be an *unavoidable delay* in your order.	We will process your order as soon as we receive an aluminum shipment from our supplier, which we expect to happen within 10 days.
You are clearly *dissatisfied.*	I recognize that the product did not live up to your expectations.
I was *shocked* to learn that you're unhappy.	Thank you for sharing your concerns about your shopping experience.
Unfortunately, we haven't received it.	The item hasn't arrived yet.
The enclosed statement is *wrong.*	Please verify the enclosed statement and provide a correct copy.

audiences. And third, to fulfill the spirit of audience focus, be sure you maintain high ethical standards.

Choosing the Best Approach

You need to consider a variety of factors when choosing between direct and indirect approaches.

You've been choosing between the direct and indirect approaches to deliver negative messages your entire life. When you come right out and tell somebody some bad news, you're using a direct approach. When you try to ease your way into the conversation before delivering the bad news, you're using an indirect approach. In your business writing, you'll need to make a similar choice whenever you deliver bad news; however, there are no clear guidelines to help you choose in every case. Some researchers even suggest that the way you organize the message is less important than achieving a personal tone.[3] Even so, you have to choose one approach or the other, so ask yourself the following questions:

- **Will the bad news come as a shock?** The direct approach is fine for business situations in which people readily acknowledge the possibility of receiving bad news. You know you won't get every job you apply for or close every sales opportunity, and consumers realize that orders are sometimes delayed or mishandled. However, if the bad news might come as a shock to readers, use the indirect approach to help them prepare for it.
- **Does the audience prefer short messages that get right to the point?** If you know that your boss always wants brief messages that get right to the point, even when they deliver bad news, the direct approach is your best choice.
- **How important is this news to the audience?** For minor or routine scenarios, the direct approach is nearly always best. When Amazon.com can't find an out-of-print book for a customer, the company sends a brief e-mail stating that fact directly. However, if the audience has an emotional investment in the situation or the consequences are considerable, the indirect approach is less jarring.
- **Do you need to maintain a close working relationship with the audience?** The indirect approach makes it easier to soften the blow of bad news and can therefore be the better choice when you need to preserve a good relationship.
- **Do you need to get the audience's attention?** If someone has ignored repeated messages from you or is buried under hundreds of e-mails, instant messages, and memos, the direct approach can help you get his or her attention. In fact, a poorly written indirect message that obscures the bad news might be the reason the person has been ignoring you in the first place.
- **What is your organization's preferred style?** Some companies have a distinct communication style, ranging from blunt and direct to gentle and indirect. However, going against expectations can be an effective way to get people's attention in a dramatic way. When Coca-Cola CEO E. Neville Isdell wanted to let both insiders and outsiders know that the company's continuing sales slump was due to more than just temporary market factors, he issued uncharacteristically blunt statements such as saying that the company suffers from "a people deficit and a skills deficit."[4]
- **How much follow-up communication do you want?** If you want to discourage a response from your reader, the direct approach signals the finality of your message more effectively. However, if you use the indirect approach to list your reasons before announcing a decision, you leave the door open for a follow-up response from the person—which might actually be the best strategy at times. For example, if you're rejecting a project team's request for funding, you might be wise to invite the team to provide any new information that could encourage you to reconsider your decision.

Using the Direct Approach Effectively

Use the direct approach when your negative answer or information will have minimal personal impact.

A negative message using the direct approach opens with the bad news, proceeds to the reasons for the situation or the decision, and ends with a positive statement aimed at maintaining a good relationship with the audience (see Figure 9.1). Depending on the circumstances, the message may also offer alternatives or a plan of action to fix the situation under discussion.

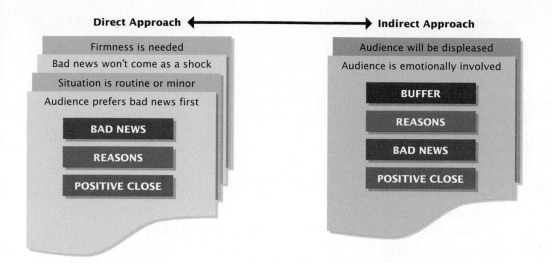

FIGURE 9.1 Choosing the Indirect or Direct Approach for Negative Messages
Analyze the situation carefully before choosing your approach to organizing negative messages.

Stating the bad news at the beginning can have two advantages: (1) It makes a shorter message possible, and (2) it requires less time for the audience to reach the main idea of the message.

Open with a Clear Statement of the Bad News   No matter what the news is, come right out and say it. However, even if the news is likely to be devastating, maintain a calm, professional tone that keeps the focus on the news and not on individual failures or other personal factors. Also, if necessary, remind the reader why you're writing:

Please modify our standing order for the FL-205 shipping cases from 3,000 per month to 2,500 per month.	Reminds the reader that your company has a standing order and announces the change immediately
Transnation Life is unable to grant your application for SafetyNet term life insurance.	Reminds the reader that he or she applied for life insurance with your firm, and announces your decision
In spite of everyone's best efforts to close more sales this past quarter, revenue fell 14 percent compared to the third quarter last year.	Introduces the topic of sales with a personal acknowledgment to the staff, then delivers the news directly and immediately

Notice how the third example still manages to ease into the bad news, even though it delivers the bad news directly and quickly. In all three instances, the recipient gets the news immediately without reading the reasons that the news is bad.

Provide Reasons and Additional Information   In most cases, you'll follow the direct opening with an explanation of why the news is negative:

Please modify our standing order for the FL-205 shipping cases from 3,000 per month to 2,500 per month. **The FL-205 continues to meet our needs for medical packaging, but our sales of that product line have leveled off.**	Reassures the reader that the product in question is still satisfactory but is no longer needed in the same quantity
Transnation Life is unable to grant your application for SafetyNet term life insurance. **The SafetyNet program has specific health history requirements that your application does not meet.**	Offers a general explanation as the reason the application was denied and discourages further communication on the matter
In spite of everyone's best efforts to close more sales this past quarter, revenue fell 14 percent compared to the third quarter last year. **Reports from the field offices indicate that the economic downturn in Asia has reduced demand for our products.**	Lets readers know why the news is negative and reassures them that job performance is not the reason

The amount of detail you should provide depends on your relationship with the audience.

During an investigation into charges that representatives of the company spied on journalists and company directors, HP CEO Mark Hurd, shown here testifying before a congressional committee investigating the affair, apologized to both the victims of the privacy invasions and to HP employees.[51]

The extent of your explanation depends on the nature of your news and your relationship with the reader. In the first example, for instance, a company wants to assure its longtime supplier that the product is still satisfactory. In the second example, the insurance company provides a general reason for the denial because listing a specific health issue might encourage additional communication from the reader and the company's decision is final. In the third example, the explanation points out why the news is bad and also reassures employees that no one in the firm is personally responsible for the failure.

However, you will encounter some situations in which explaining negative news is neither appropriate nor helpful, such as when the reasons are confidential, excessively complicated, or irrelevant to the reader. To maintain a cordial working relationship with the reader, you might want to explain why you can't provide the information.

Should you apologize when delivering bad news? As the KPMG vignette at the beginning of the chapter illustrated, the answer isn't quite as simple as one might think. The notion of *apology* is hard to pin down. To some people, it simply means an expression of sympathy that something negative has happened to another person. At the other extreme, it means admitting fault and taking responsibility for specific compensations or corrections to atone for the mistake.

Some experts have advised that a company should never apologize, even when it knows it has made a mistake, as the apology might be taken as a confession of guilt that could be used against the company in a lawsuit. This is the dilemma that KPMG faced when deciding how to respond to illegal actions taken by a few of its employees. However, several states have laws that specifically prevent expressions of sympathy from being used as evidence of legal liability. In fact, judges, juries, and plaintiffs tend to be more forgiving of companies that express sympathy for wronged parties; moreover, the apology can help repair the company's reputation. Recently, some prosecutors have begun pressing executives to publicly admit guilt and apologize as part of the settlement of criminal cases—unlike the common tactic of paying fines but refusing to admit any wrongdoing.[5]

The best general advice in the event of a serious mistake or accident is to immediately and sincerely express sympathy and offer help if appropriate, without admitting guilt; then seek the advice of your company's lawyers before elaborating. As one recent survey concluded, "The risks of making an apology are low, and the potential reward is high."[6]

Close on a Positive Note   After you've explained the negative news, close the message in a positive but still honest and respectful manner:

Reinforces the relationship you have with the reader and provides a positive view toward the future—without unduly promising a return to the old level of business

Ends on a respectful note, knowing that life insurance is an important subject for the reader, but also makes it clear that the company's decision is final

Helps readers respond to the news by letting them know that the company plans to fix the situation, even if the plan for doing so isn't clear yet

Please modify our standing order for the FL-205 shipping cases from 3,000 per month to 2,500 per month. The FL-205 continues to meet our needs for medical packaging, but our sales of that product line have leveled off. **We appreciate the great service you continue to provide and look forward to doing business with you.**

Transnation Life is unable to grant your application for SafetyNet term life insurance. The SafetyNet program has specific health history requirements that your application does not meet. **We wish you success in finding coverage through another provider.**

In spite of everyone's best efforts to close more sales this past quarter, revenue fell 14 percent compared to the third quarter last year. Reports from the field offices indicate that the economic downturn in Asia has reduced demand for our products. **However, I continue to believe that we have the best product for these customers, and we'll continue to explore ways to boost sales in these key markets.**

Notice how all three examples deliver bad news quickly and efficiently without being disrespectful or overly apologetic. Consider offering your readers an alternative solution if you can. Depending on the situation, you might also explain how you or your organization plan to respond to the negative news.

Using the Indirect Approach Effectively

The indirect approach helps readers prepare for the bad news by presenting the reasons for it first. However, don't assume that the indirect approach is meant to obscure bad news, delay it, or limit your responsibility. Rather, the purpose of this approach is to ease the blow and help readers accept the situation. When done poorly, the indirect approach can be disrespectful and even unethical. But when done well, it is a good example of audience-oriented communication crafted with attention to both ethics and etiquette.

Use the indirect approach when some preparation will help your audience accept your bad news.

Open with a Buffer   Messages using an indirect approach open with a **buffer:** a neutral, noncontroversial statement that is closely related to the point of the message (look back at Figure 9.1). A buffer establishes common ground with your reader; moreover, if you're responding to a request, a buffer validates that request. Some critics believe that using a buffer is manipulative and unethical, even dishonest. However, buffers are unethical only if they're insincere or deceptive. Showing consideration for the feelings of others is never dishonest.

A buffer establishes common ground with the reader.

A poorly written buffer might trivialize the reader's concerns, divert attention from the problem with insincere flattery or irrelevant material, or mislead the reader into thinking your message actually contains good news. A good buffer, on the other hand, can express your appreciation for being considered (if you're responding to a request), assure your reader of your attention to the request, or indicate your understanding of the reader's needs. A good buffer also needs to be relevant and sincere.

Consider these possible responses to a manager of the order-fulfillment department, who requested some temporary staffing help from your department (a request you won't be able to fulfill):

3 LEARNING OBJECTIVE

Identify the risks of using the indirect approach, and explain how to avoid such problems

Our department shares your goal of processing orders quickly and efficiently.	Establishes common ground with the reader and validates the concerns that prompted the original request—without promising a positive answer
As result of the last downsizing, every department in the company is running shorthanded.	Establishes common ground, but in a negative way that downplays the recipient's concerns
You folks are doing a great job over there, and I'd love to be able to help out.	Potentially misleads the reader into concluding that you will comply with the request
Those new state labor regulations are driving me crazy over here; how about in your department?	Trivializes the reader's concerns by opening with an irrelevant issue

Only the first of these buffers can be considered effective; the other three are likely to damage your relationship with the other manager—and lower his or her opinion of you. Table 9.2 shows several types of effective buffers you could use to tactfully open a negative message.

Given the damage that a poorly composed buffer can do, consider every buffer carefully before you send it. Is it respectful? Is it relevant? Is it neutral, implying neither yes nor no? Does it provide a smooth transition to the reasons that follow? If you can answer yes to every question, you can proceed confidently to the next section of your message. However, if that little voice inside your head tells you that your buffer sounds insincere or misleading, it probably is, in which case you'll need to rewrite it.

TABLE 9.2 Types of Buffers

BUFFER TYPE	STRATEGY	EXAMPLE
Agreement	Find a point on which you and the reader share similar views.	We both know how hard it is to make a profit in this industry.
Appreciation	Express sincere thanks for receiving something.	Your check for $127.17 arrived yesterday. Thank you.
Cooperation	Convey your willingness to help in any way you realistically can.	Employee Services is here to assist all associates with their health insurance, retirement planning, and continuing education needs.
Fairness	Assure the reader that you've closely examined and carefully considered the problem, or mention an appropriate action that has already been taken.	For the past week, we have carefully monitored those using the photocopying machine to see whether we can detect any pattern of use that might explain its frequent breakdowns.
Good news	Start with the part of your message that is favorable.	A replacement knob for your range is on its way, shipped February 10 via UPS.
Praise	Find an attribute or an achievement to compliment.	The Stratford Group clearly has an impressive record of accomplishment in helping clients resolve financial reporting problems.
Resale	Favorably discuss the product or company related to the subject of the letter.	With their heavy-duty, full-suspension hardware and fine veneers, the desks and file cabinets in our Montclair line have become a hit with value-conscious professionals.
Understanding	Demonstrate that you understand the reader's goals and needs.	So that you can more easily find the printer with the features you need, we are enclosing a brochure that describes all the Panasonic printers currently available.

Provide Reasons and Additional Information   An effective buffer serves as a stepping-stone to the next part of your message, in which you build up the explanations and information that will culminate in your negative news. The nature of the information you provide is similar to that of the direct approach—it depends on the audience and the situation—but the way you portray this information necessarily differs because your reader doesn't know your conclusion yet.

Phrase your reasons to signal the negative news ahead.

An ideal explanation section leads readers to your conclusion before you come right out and say it. In other words, before you actually say no, the reader has followed your line of reasoning and is ready for the answer. By giving your reasons effectively, you help maintain focus on the issues at hand and defuse the emotions that always accompany significantly bad news.

As you lay out your reasons, guide your reader's response by starting with the most positive points first and moving forward to increasingly negative ones. Provide enough detail for the audience to understand your reasons, but be concise; a long, roundabout explanation will just make your audience impatient. Your reasons need to convince your audience that your decision is justified, fair, and logical.

If appropriate, you can use the explanation section to suggest how the negative news might in fact benefit your reader in some way—but only if this is true, of course. And use this technique with care; it's easy to insult readers by implying that they shouldn't be asking for the benefits or opportunities they were seeking in the first place.

Don't hide behind "company policy" when you deliver bad news.

Avoid hiding behind company policy to cushion your bad news. If you say, "Company policy forbids our hiring anyone who does not have two years' supervisory experience," you imply that you won't consider anyone on his or her individual merits. Skilled and sympathetic communicators explain company policy (without referring to it as "policy") so that the audience can try to meet the requirements at a later time. Consider this response to an employee:

> Because these management positions are quite challenging, the human relations department has researched the qualifications needed to succeed in them. The findings show that the two most important qualifications are a bachelor's degree in business administration and two years' supervisory experience.

Shows the reader the decision is based on a methodical analysis of the company's needs and not on some arbitrary guideline

Establishes the criteria behind the decision and lets the reader know what to expect

The paragraph does a good job of stating reasons for the refusal:

- It provides enough detail to logically support the refusal.
- It implies that the applicant is better off avoiding a program in which he or she might fail.
- It explains the company's policy as logical rather than arbitrary.
- It doesn't offer an apology for the decision because no one is at fault.
- It avoids negative personal expressions (such as "You do not meet our requirements").

Well-written reasons are
- *Detailed*
- *Tactful*
- *Individualized*
- *Unapologetic if no one is at fault*
- *Positive*

Even valid, well-thought-out reasons won't convince every reader in every situation. However, if you've done a good job of laying out your reasoning, then you've done everything you can to prepare the reader for the main idea, which is the negative news itself.

Continue with a Clear Statement of the Bad News

Now that you've prepared the audience to receive the bad news, the next task is to present the news as clearly and as kindly as possible. Three techniques are especially useful for saying no. First, de-emphasize the bad news:

To handle bad news carefully
- *De-emphasize the bad news visually and grammatically*
- *Use a conditional statement if appropriate*
- *Tell what you did do, not what you didn't do*

- Minimize the space or time devoted to the bad news—without trivializing it or withholding any important information.
- Subordinate bad news in a complex or compound sentence ("My department is already shorthanded, so I'll need all my staff for at least the next two months"). This construction pushes the bad news into the middle of the sentence, the point of least emphasis.
- Embed bad news in the middle of a paragraph or use parenthetical expressions ("Our profits, which are down, are only part of the picture").

However, keep in mind that it's possible to abuse de-emphasis. For instance, if the primary point of your message is that profits are down, it would be inappropriate to marginalize that news by burying it in the middle of a sentence. State the negative news clearly, then make a smooth transition to any positive news that might balance the story.

Second, use a conditional (*if* or *when*) statement to imply that the audience could have received, or might someday receive, a favorable answer ("When you have more managerial experience, you are welcome to reapply"). Such a statement could motivate applicants to improve their qualifications.

Third, emphasize what you can do or have done rather than what you cannot do. Say "We sell exclusively through retailers, and the one nearest you that carries our merchandise is . . ." rather than "We are unable to serve you, so please call your nearest dealer." Also, by implying the bad news, you may not need to actually state it ("The five positions currently open have been filled with people whose qualifications match those uncovered in our research"). By focusing on the facts and implying the bad news, you make the impact less personal.

When implying bad news, be sure your audience understands the entire message—including the bad news. Withholding negative information or overemphasizing positive information is unethical and unfair to your reader. If an implied message might lead to

Don't disguise bad news when you emphasize the positive.

uncertainty, state your decision in direct terms. Just be sure to avoid overly blunt statements that are likely to cause pain and anger:

INSTEAD OF THIS	WRITE THIS
I *must refuse* your request.	I will be out of town on the day you need me.
We *must deny* your application.	The position has been filled.
I *am unable* to grant your request.	Contact us again when you have established . . .
We *cannot afford to* continue the program.	The program will conclude on May 1.
Much as I would like to attend . . .	Our budget meeting ends too late for me to attend.
We *must reject* your proposal.	We've accepted the proposal from AAA Builders.
We *must turn down* your extension request.	Please send in your payment by June 14.

A positive close
- *Builds goodwill*
- *Offers a suggestion for action*
- *Provides a look toward the future*

Close on a Positive Note As with the direct approach, the conclusion of the indirect approach is your opportunity to emphasize your respect for your audience, even though you've just delivered unpleasant news. Express best wishes without ending on a falsely upbeat note. If you can find a positive angle that's meaningful to your audience, by all means consider adding it to your conclusion. However, don't try to pretend that the negative news didn't happen or that it won't affect the reader. Suggest alternative solutions if such information is available. In a message to a customer or potential customer, an ending that includes resale information or sales promotion may also be appropriate. If you've asked readers to decide between alternatives or to take some action, make sure that they know what to do, when to do it, and how to do it. Whatever type of conclusion you use, follow these guidelines:

- **Avoid a negative or uncertain conclusion.** Don't refer to, repeat, or apologize for the bad news, and refrain from expressing any doubt that your reasons will be accepted (avoid statements such as "I trust our decision is satisfactory").
- **Limit future correspondence.** Encourage additional communication *only* if you're willing to discuss your decision further (if you're not, avoid wording such as "If you have further questions, please write").
- **Be optimistic about the future.** Don't anticipate problems that haven't occurred yet (avoid statements such as "Should you have further problems, please let us know").
- **Be sincere.** Steer clear of clichés that are insincere in view of the bad news (if you can't help, don't say, "If we can be of any help, please contact us").
- **Be confident.** Don't show any doubt about keeping the person as a customer (avoid phrases such as "We hope you will continue to do business with us").

Finally, keep in mind that the closing is the last thing audience members have to remember you by. Even though they're disappointed, leave them with the impression that they were treated with respect.

Adapting to Your Audience

Even more than other business messages, negative messages require that you maintain your audience focus and be as sensitive as possible to audience needs. Therefore, you may need to adapt your message to cultural differences or to the differences between internal and external audiences.

Cultural Variations

Expectations for the handling of bad news vary from culture to culture.

Bad news is unwelcome in any language, but the conventions for passing it on to business associates can vary considerably from country to country. For instance, French business letters are traditionally quite formal and writer-oriented, often without reference to audience needs or benefits. Moreover, when the news is bad, French writers take a direct approach. They open with a reference to the problem or previous correspondence and then state the bad news clearly. While they don't refer to the audience's needs, they often do apologize and express regret for the problem.[7]

In contrast, Japanese letters traditionally open with remarks about the season, business prosperity, or health. When the news is bad, these opening formalities serve as the buffer. Explanations and apologies follow, and then comes the bad news or refusal. Japanese writers protect their readers' feelings by wording the bad news ambiguously. Western readers may even misinterpret this vague language as a condition of acceptance rather than as the refusal it actually is.[8] In short, if you are communicating across cultures, you'll want to use the tone, organization, and other cultural conventions that your audience expects. Only then can you avoid the inappropriate or even offensive approaches that could jeopardize your business relationship.[9]

Internal Versus External Audiences

Internal audiences frequently have expectations for negative messages that differ from those of external audiences. In some cases, the two groups can interpret the news in different or even opposite ways. For example, employees will react negatively to news of an impending layoff, but company shareholders might welcome the news as evidence that management is trying to control costs. In addition, if a negative message such as a layoff is being sent to both internal and external audiences, employees will not only expect more detail but will also expect to be informed before the public is told.

As you move into positions of leadership, you should be aware that following years of seemingly endless upheavals and bad news, from market collapses to financial scandals, many employees are less inclined to believe what they hear from management. Cynicism and distrust are rampant today, and employees are tired of discussing change.[10] They want to know more than how changes will help the company; they want to know how changes are going to affect them personally. Managers can rebuild trust only by communicating openly, honestly, and quickly in both good times and bad.

Negative messages to outside audiences require attention to the diverse nature of your audience and the concern for confidentiality of internal information. A single message might have a half-dozen audiences, all with differing opinions and agendas. You may not be able to explain things to the level of detail that some of these people want if doing so would release proprietary information such as future product plans.

4 LEARNING OBJECTIVE

Adapt negative messages for internal and external audiences

You may need to adjust the content of negative messages for different groups within an external audience.

Maintaining High Standards of Ethics and Etiquette

All business messages demand attention to ethics and etiquette, of course, but these considerations take on special importance when you are delivering bad news, for several reasons. First, a variety of laws and regulations dictate the content and delivery of many business messages with potentially negative content, such as the release of financial information by a public company. Second, negative messages can have a significant negative impact on the lives of those receiving them. Even if the news is conveyed legally and conscientiously, good ethical practice demands that these situations be approached with care and sensitivity. Third, emotions often run high when negative messages are involved, for both the sender and the receiver. Senders need to not only manage their own emotions but also consider the emotional state of their audiences.

The challenge of sending—and receiving—negative messages fosters a tendency to delay, downplay, or distort the bad news (see "Ethics Detective: Did the CEO Soft-Sell the Bad News?").[11] However, doing so may be unethical, if not illegal. In recent years, numerous companies have been sued by shareholders, consumers, employees, and government regulators for allegedly withholding or delaying negative information in such areas as company finances, environmental hazards, and product safety.

In many of these incidences, the problem was slow, incomplete, or inaccurate communication between the company and external stakeholders. In others, problems stemmed from a reluctance to send or receive negative news within the organization. Effectively sharing bad news within an organization requires commitment from everyone involved. Employees must commit to sending negative messages when necessary, even when doing so is unpleasant or difficult. Conversely, managers must commit to maintaining open communication channels,

5 LEARNING OBJECTIVE

Explain the importance of maintaining high standards of ethics and etiquette when delivering negative messages

Sharing bad news effectively requires commitment from everyone in the organization.

Ethics Detective

Did the CEO Soft-Sell the Bad News?

You and your colleagues are nervous. Sales have been on the decline for months, and you see evidence of budget tightening all over the place—the fruit and pastries have disappeared from the coffee stations, accountants are going over expense reports with magnifying glasses, and managers are slow to replace people who leave the company. Instant messages fly around the office; everyone wants to know if anyone has heard anything about layoffs.

The job market in your area is weak, and you know you might have to sell your house and move your family out of state to find another position in your field. If your job is eliminated, you're ready to cope with the loss but you need as much time as possible. You breathe a sigh of relief when the following item from the CEO appears in the company's weekly e-mail newsletter:

> With news of workforce adjustments elsewhere in our industry, we realize many of you are concerned

about the possibility here. I'd like to reassure all of you that we remain confident in the company's fundamental business strategy and the executive team is examining all facets of company operations to ensure our continued financial strength.

The message calms your fears. Should it?

ANALYSIS

A month later, the CEO announces a layoff of 20 percent of the company's workforce—nearly 700 people. You're shocked by the news because you felt reassured by the newsletter item from last month. In light of what happened, you retrieve a copy of the newsletter and reread the CEO's message. Does it seem ethical now? Why or why not? If you had been in charge of writing this newsletter item and your hands were tied because you couldn't come out and announce the layoffs yet, how would you have rewritten the message?

---

to truly listening when employees have negative information to share, and to not punishing employees who deliver bad news.

The impulse to want to believe that everything is fine can be strong, and managers who are so inclined can fail to perceive or respond to negative messages from their employees. The energy company BP (formerly British Petroleum) recently experienced such breakdowns when managers didn't act on warnings from employees in the company's Alaska oil pipeline and Texas refining operations. After years of intense efforts by the company to reduce maintenance costs, corrosion and other problems led to a large oil spill along its Alaska pipeline and a tragic accident at its Texas refinery. Some employees said the emphasis on saving money was so strong that safety warnings sometimes went unheeded up the chain of command. Said one, "A scream at our level is, if anything, a whisper at their level."[12]

Although BP employees were not discouraged from reporting bad news, in corporate cultures that don't encourage open communication, employees who fear retribution may go to great lengths to avoid sending bad-news messages. In such dysfunctional environments, failure breeds still more failure, because decision makers don't get the honest, objective information they need to make wise choices.[13] In contrast, managers in open cultures expect or even demand that their employees bring them bad news whenever it happens so that corrective action can be taken. Whatever the case, if you do need to transmit bad news up the chain of command, don't try to pin the blame on anyone in particular. Simply emphasize the nature of the problem—and a solution, if possible. This tactic will help you earn a reputation as an alert problem solver rather than just a complainer.[14]

DOCUMENT MAKEOVER

IMPROVE THIS MEMO

To practice correcting drafts of actual documents, visit your online course or the access-code-protected portion of the Companion Website. Click "Document Makeovers," then click Chapter 9. You will find a memo that contains problems and errors relating to what you've learned in this chapter about handling negative messages. Use the "Final Draft" decision tool to create an improved version of this memo. Check the message for the use of buffers, apologies, explanations, subordination, embedding, positive action, conditional phrases, and upbeat perspectives.

Delaying the delivery of negative news can be unethical in many situations.

This ethical obligation to communicate the facts also brings with it the responsibility to do so promptly. Bad news often means that people need to make other plans. The longer you wait to deliver bad news, the harder you make it for recipients to react and respond.

CHECKLIST: Creating Negative Messages

A. Choose the best approach.
- Consider a direct approach when the audience is aware of the possibility of negative news, when the reader is not emotionally involved in the message, when you know that the reader would prefer the bad news first, when you know that firmness is necessary, and when you want to discourage a response.
- Consider an indirect approach when the news is likely to come as a shock or surprise, when your audience has a high emotional investment in the outcome, and when you want to maintain a good relationship with the audience.

B. For an indirect approach, open with an effective buffer.
- Establish common ground with the audience.
- Validate the request, if you are responding to a request.
- Don't trivialize the reader's concerns.
- Don't mislead the reader into thinking the coming news might be positive.

C. Provide reasons and additional information.
- Explain why the news is negative.
- Adjust the amount of detail to fit the situation and the audience.

- Avoid explanations when the reasons are confidential, excessively complicated, or irrelevant to the reader.
- If appropriate, state how you plan to correct or respond to the negative news.
- Seek the advice of company lawyers if you're unsure what to say.

D. Clearly state the bad news.
- State the bad news as positively as possible, using tactful wording.
- De-emphasize bad news by minimizing the space devoted to it, subordinating it, or embedding it.
- If your response might change in the future if circumstances change, explain the conditions to the reader.
- Emphasize what you can or have done rather than what you can't or won't do.

E. Close on a positive note.
- Express best wishes without being falsely positive.
- Suggest actions readers might take, if appropriate, and provide them with necessary information.
- Encourage further communication only if you're willing to discuss the situation further.
- Keep a positive outlook on the future.

Some negative news scenarios will also test your self-control and sense of etiquette. An employee lets you down, a supplier's faulty parts damage your company's reputation, a business partner violates the terms of your contract—such situations may tempt you to respond with a personal attack. Keep in mind that negative messages can have a lasting impact on both the people who receive them and the people who send them. As a communicator, you have a responsibility to minimize the negative impact of your negative messages through careful planning and sensitive, objective writing. As much as possible, focus on the actions or conditions that led to the negative news, not on personal shortcomings or character issues. Develop a reputation as a professional who can handle the toughest situations with dignity.

Negative news situations can put your sense of self-control and business etiquette to the test.

For a reminder of successful strategies for creating negative messages, see "Checklist: Creating Negative Messages."

EXPLORING COMMON EXAMPLES OF NEGATIVE MESSAGES

The following sections offer examples of the most common negative messages, dealing with topics such as routine business matters, organizational news, and employment messages.

Sending Negative Messages on Routine Business Matters

As you progress in your career and become more visible in your industry and community, you will receive a wide variety of personal invitations to speak at private or public functions or to volunteer your time for a variety of organizations. In addition, routine business matters such as credit applications and requests for adjustment will often require you to make negative responses. Neither you nor your company will be able to say yes to every request, so crafting negative responses quickly and graciously is an important skill for many professionals.

Refusing Routine Requests

When you are unable to meet a request, your primary communication challenge is to give a clear negative response without generating negative feelings or damaging either your personal reputation or the company's. As simple as these messages may appear to be, they can test your skills as a communicator because you often need to deliver negative information while maintaining a positive relationship with the other party.

Saying no is a routine part of business and shouldn't reflect negatively on you. If you said yes to every request that crossed your desk, you'd never get any work done. The direct approach will work best for most routine negative responses. It not only helps your audience get your answer quickly and move on to other possibilities but also helps you save time because the direct approach is often easier to write.

The indirect approach works best when the stakes are high for you or for the receiver, when you or your company has an established relationship with the person making the request, or when you're forced to decline a request that you might have said yes to in the past (see Figure 9.2).

Consider the following points as you develop your routine negative messages:

- **Manage your time carefully.** Focus your time on the most-important relationships and requests, then get in the habit of crafting quick standard responses for less-important situations.
- **If the matter is closed, don't imply that it's still open.** If your answer is truly no, don't use phrases such as "Let me think about it and get back to you" as a way to delay saying no.
- **Offer alternative ideas if you can.** If you can help, great. However, remember to use your time wisely in such matters. Unless the relationship is vital to your company, you probably shouldn't spend time researching alternatives for the other person.

- **Don't imply that other assistance or information might be available if it isn't.** Don't close your negative message with a cheery but insincere "Please contact us if we can offer any additional assistance." An empty attempt to mollify hostile feelings could simply lead to another request you'll have to refuse.

Handling Bad News About Transactions

Bad news about transactions, the sale and delivery of products and services, is always unwelcome and usually unexpected. Such messages have three goals: to modify the customer's expectations, to explain how you plan to resolve the situation, and to repair whatever damage might have been done to the business relationship.

The specific content and tone of each message can vary widely, depending on the nature of the transaction and your relationship with the customer. Telling an individual consumer that his new sweater will be arriving a week later than you promised is a much simpler task than telling General Motors that 30,000 transmission parts will be a week late, especially when you know the company will be forced to idle a multimillion-dollar production facility as a result.

If you haven't done anything specific to set the customer's expectations—such as promising delivery within 24 hours—the message simply needs to inform the customer, with little or no emphasis on apologies (see Figure 9.3). (Bear in mind, though, in this age of online ordering and overnight delivery, customers have been conditioned to expect instantaneous fulfillment of nearly every transaction, even if you haven't promised anything.)

If you did set the customer's expectations and now find you can't meet them, your task is more complicated. In addition to resetting the customer's expectations and explaining how you'll resolve the problem, you may need to include an element of apology. The scope of the apology depends on the magnitude of the mistake. For the customer who ordered the sweater, a simple apology followed by a clear statement of when the sweater will arrive would probably be sufficient. For larger business-to-business transactions, the customer may want an explanation of what went wrong in order to determine whether you'll be able to perform as you promise in the future.

To help repair the damage to the relationship and encourage repeat business, many companies offer discounts on future purchases, free merchandise, or other considerations.

FIGURE 9.2 Effective Letter Declining a Favor
May Yee Kwan's company has a long-standing relationship with the college Sandra Wofford represents and wants to maintain that positive relationship, but she can't meet this particular request. To communicate negative news, she therefore uses an indirect approach. If Kwan and Wofford shared a closer relationship (if they worked together in a volunteer organization, for instance), the direct approach might have been more appropriate.

Plan

Analyze the Situation
Verify that the purpose is to decline a request and offer alternatives; audience is likely to be surprised by the refusal.

Gather Information
Determine audience needs and obtain the necessary information.

Select the Right Medium
For formal messages, printed letters on company letterhead are best.

Organize the Information
Main idea is to refuse the request so limit your scope to that; select an indirect approach based on the audience and the situation.

1

Write

Adapt to Your Audience
Adjust the level of formality based on degree of familiarity with the audience; maintain a positive relationship by using the you "attitude, politeness, positive emphasis, and bias-free language.

Compose the Message
Use a conversational but professional style and keep the message brief, clear, and as helpful as possible.

2

Complete

Revise the Message
Evaluate content and review readability to make sure the negative information won't be misinterpreted; make sure your tone stays positive without being artificial.

Produce the Message
Emphasize a clean, professional appearance on company letterhead.

Proofread the Message
Review for errors in layout, spelling, and mechanics.

Distribute the Message
Deliver your message using the chosen medium.

3

InfoTech

927 Dawson Valley Road, Tulsa, Oklahoma 74151
Voice: (918) 669-4428   Fax: (918) 669-4429
www.infotech.com

March 6, 2008

Dr. Sandra Wofford, President
Whittier Community College
333 Whittier Avenue
Tulsa, OK 74150

Dear Dr. Wofford:

Infotech has been happy to support Whittier Community College in many ways over the years, and we appreciate the opportunities you and your organization provide to so many deserving students. Thank you for considering our grounds for your graduation ceremony on June 3.

We would certainly like to accommodate Whittier as we have in years past, but our companywide sales meetings will be held this year during the weeks of May 29 and June 5. With over 200 sales representatives and their families from around the world joining us, activities will be taking place throughout our facility.

My assistant, Robert Seagers, suggests you contact the Municipal Botanical Gardens as a possible graduation site. He recommends calling Jerry Kane, director of public relations.

We remain firm in our commitment to you, President Wofford, and to the fine students you represent. Through our internship program, academic research grants, and other initiatives, we will continue to be a strong corporate partner to Whittier College and will support your efforts as you move forward.

Sincerely,

May Yee Kwan

May Yee Kwan
Public Relations Director

lc

Buffers negative response by demonstrating respect and recapping the request

Suggests an alternative, showing that Kwan cares about the college and has given the matter some thought

States a meaningful reason for the negative response, without apologizing (because the company is not at fault)

Closes by emphasizing the importance of the relationship and the company's continuing commitment

FIGURE 9.3 Effective E-Mail Advising of a Back Order
This message, which is a combination of good and bad news, uses the indirect approach—with the good news serving as a buffer for the bad news. In this case, the customer wasn't promised delivery by a certain date, so the writer simply informed the customer when to expect the rest of the order. The writer also took steps to repair the relationship and encourage future business with her firm.

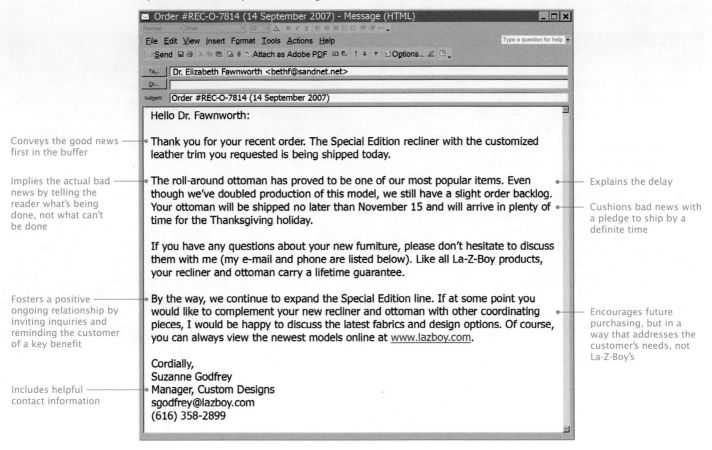

Conveys the good news first in the buffer

Implies the actual bad news by telling the reader what's being done, not what can't be done

Explains the delay

Cushions bad news with a pledge to ship by a definite time

Fosters a positive ongoing relationship by inviting inquiries and reminding the customer of a key benefit

Encourages future purchasing, but in a way that addresses the customer's needs, not La-Z-Boy's

Includes helpful contact information

Even modest efforts can go a long way to rebuilding the customer's confidence in your company. However, you don't always have a choice. Business-to-business purchasing contracts often include performance clauses that legally entitle the customer to discounts or other restitution in the event of late delivery. To review the concepts covered in this section, see "Checklist: Handling Bad News About Transactions."

Refusing Claims and Requests for Adjustment

Use the indirect approach in most cases of refusing a claim.

Almost every customer who makes a claim or requests an adjustment is emotionally involved; therefore, the indirect method is usually the best approach for a refusal. Your job as a writer is to avoid accepting responsibility for the unfortunate situation and yet avoid blaming or accusing the customer. To steer clear of these pitfalls, pay special attention to the tone of your letter. A tactful and courteous message can build goodwill even while denying the claim (see Figure 9.4).

 CHECKLIST: Handling Bad News About Transactions

- Reset the customer's expectations regarding the transaction.
- Explain what happened and why, if appropriate.
- Explain how you'll resolve the situation.

- Repair any damage done to the business relationship, perhaps offering future discounts, free merchandise, or other considerations.
- Offer a professional, businesslike expression of apology if your organization made a mistake.

FIGURE 9.4 Effective Letter Refusing a Claim

Daniel Lindmeier, who purchased a digital video camera from Village Electronics a year ago, wrote to say that the unit doesn't work properly and to inquire about the warranty. He incorrectly believed that the warranty covers one year, when it actually covers only three months. In this response, Walter Brodie uses an indirect approach to convey the bad news and to offer additional helpful information.

Plan — 1

Analyze the Situation
Verify that the purpose is to refuse a warranty claim and offer repairs; audience's likely reaction will be disappointment and surprise.

Gather Information
Gather information on warranty policies and procedures, repair services, and resale information.

Select the Right Medium
Choose the best medium for delivering your message; for formal messages, printed letters on company letterhead are best.

Organize the Information
Your main idea is to refuse the claim and promote an alternative solution; select an indirect approach based on the audience and the situation.

Write — 2

Adapt to Your Audience
Adjust the level of formality based on degree of familiarity with the audience; maintain a positive relationship by using the "you" attitude, politeness, positive emphasis, and bias-free language.

Compose the Message
Use a conversational but professional style and keep the message brief, clear, and as helpful as possible.

Complete — 3

Revise the Message
Evaluate content and review readability to make sure the negative information won't be misinterpreted; make sure your tone stays positive without being artificial.

Produce the Message
Emphasize a clean, professional appearance appropriate for a letter on company stationery.

Proofread the Message
Review for errors in layout, spelling, and mechanics.

Distribute the Message
Deliver your message using the chosen medium; make sure the reader receives any necessary support documents as well.

NUMBER ONE IN ENTERTAINMENT
Village Electronics
68 Lake Itasca Boulevard • Hannover, MN 55341
Voice: (612) 878-1312 • Fax: (612) 878-1316

May 2, 2008

Mr. Daniel Lindmeier
849 Cedar St.
Lake Elmo, MN 55042

Dear Mr. Lindmeier:

Thank you for your letter about the battery release switch on your JVC digital camera. Village Electronics believes, as you do, that electronic equipment should be built to last. That's why we stand behind our products with a 90-day warranty.

Even though your JVC camera is a year old and therefore out of warranty, we can still help. Please package your camera carefully and ship it to our store in Hannover. Include your complete name, address, phone number, and a brief description of the malfunction, along with a check for $35 for an initial examination. After assessing the unit, we will give you a written estimate of the needed parts and labor. Then just let us know whether you want us to make the repairs—either by phone or by filling out the prepaid card we'll send you with the estimate.

If you choose to repair the unit, the $35 will be applied toward your bill, the balance of which is payable by check or credit card. JVC also has service centers available in your area. If you would prefer to take the unit to one of them, please see the enclosed list.

Thanks again for inquiring about our service. I've also enclosed a catalog of our latest cameras and accessories, in which you'll find information about JVC's "Trade-Up Special." If you're ready to move up to one of the newest cameras, JVC will offer a generous trade-in allowance on your current model.

Sincerely,

Walter Brodie

Walter Brodie
Customer Service Manager

Enclosures: List of service centers
            Catalog

Annotations (left):
- Buffers the bad news by emphasizing a point the reader and writer both agree on
- States bad news indirectly, tactfully leaving the repair decision to the customer
- Closes by blending sales promotion with an acknowledgment of the customer's interests

Annotations (right):
- Puts company's policy in a favorable light
- Helps soothe the reader with a positive alternative

When refusing a claim
- *Demonstrate your understanding of the complaint*
- *Explain your refusal*
- *Suggest alternative action*

When refusing a claim, avoid language that might have a negative impact on the reader. Instead, demonstrate that you understand and have considered the complaint carefully. Then, even if the claim is unreasonable, rationally explain why you are refusing the request. Remember, don't apologize and don't hide behind "company policy." End the message on a respectful and action-oriented note.

If you deal with enough customers over a long enough period, chances are you'll get a request that is particularly outrageous. You might even be positive that the person is being dishonest. However, you need to control your emotions and approach the situation as calmly as possible to avoid saying or writing anything that the recipient might interpret as defamation. Someone suing for defamation must prove (1) that the statement is false, (2) that the language is injurious to the person's reputation, and (3) that the statement has been published. To avoid being accused of defamation, follow these guidelines:

You can help avoid defamation by not responding emotionally or abusively.

- Refrain from using any kind of abusive language or terms that could be considered defamatory.
- Provide accurate information and stick to the facts.
- Never let anger or malice motivate your messages.
- Consult your company's legal advisers whenever you think a message might have legal consequences.
- Communicate honestly, and make sure that what you're saying is what you believe to be true.
- Emphasize a desire for a good relationship in the future.

Most important, remember that nothing positive can come out of antagonizing a customer, even one who has verbally abused you or your colleagues. Reject the claim or request for adjustment and move on to the next challenge. For a brief review of the tasks involved when refusing claims, see "Checklist: Refusing Claims."

Sending Negative Organizational News

As a manager, you may need to issue negative announcements regarding some aspect of your products, services, or operations. Most of these scenarios have unique challenges that must be addressed on a case-by-case basis, but the general advice offered here applies to all of them. One key difference among all these messages is whether you have time to plan the announcement. The following section addresses those negative messages that you do have time to plan for, then "Communicating in a Crisis" offers advice on communication during emergencies.

Communicating Under Normal Circumstances

Negative organizational messages to external audiences can require extensive planning.

Businesses must convey a range of negative messages regarding their ongoing operations. Some of these messages are fairly simple, such as price increases or the decision to stop making a popular product. Others are more complicated and potentially traumatic, such as announcing that the company is being investigated by government regulators, that it is the subject of a lawsuit, or that it plans to reduce its workforce or close a facility.

 CHECKLIST: Refusing Claims

- Use an indirect approach because the reader is expecting or hoping for a positive response.
- Indicate your full understanding of the nature of the complaint.
- Explain why you are refusing the request, without hiding behind company policy.
- Provide an accurate, factual account of the transaction.

- Emphasize ways things should have been handled rather than dwelling on a reader's negligence.
- Avoid any appearance of defamation.
- Avoid expressing personal opinions.
- End with a positive, friendly, helpful close.
- Make any suggested action easy for readers to comply with.

As you plan the message, take extra care to consider all of your audiences and their unique needs. For simple messages, a direct approach is usually sufficient. For example, a significant negative event such as a plant closing can affect hundreds or thousands of people in many organizations. Employees need to find new jobs, get training in new skills, or perhaps get emergency financial help. For example, when Michael Gannaway, CEO of Pillowtex, informed employees that efforts to save the bedding company had failed and that it was shutting down, his letter included phone and web contacts where employees could go for assistance.[15] Outside the company, school districts may have to adjust budgets and staffing levels if many of your employees plan to move in search of new jobs. Your customers need to find new suppliers. Your suppliers may need to find other customers of their own. Government agencies may need to react to everything from a decrease in tax revenues to an influx of people seeking unemployment benefits.

When making negative announcements, follow these guidelines:

- **Match your approach to the situation.** A modest price increase won't shock most customers, so the direct approach is fine. However, canceling a product that people count on is another matter, so building up to the news via the indirect approach might be better.
- **Consider the unique needs of each group.** As the plant closing example illustrates, various people have different information needs.
- **Give each audience enough time to react as needed.** For instance, employees, particularly higher-level professionals and managers, may need three to six months or more to find new jobs.

Give people as much time as possible to react to negative news.

- **Give yourself enough time to plan and manage a response.** Chances are you're going to be hit with complaints, questions, or product returns after you make your announcement, so make sure you're ready with answers and additional follow-up information.
- **Look for positive angles but don't exude false optimism.** Laying off 10,000 people does not give them "an opportunity to explore new horizons." It's a traumatic event that can affect employees, their families, and their communities for years. Phony optimism would only make a bad situation worse. The best you may be able to do is to thank people for their past support and to wish them well in the future. On the other hand, if eliminating a seldom-used employee benefit means employees will save money, by all means promote that positive angle.
- **Minimize the element of surprise whenever possible.** This step can require considerable judgment on your part, as well as awareness of any applicable laws. In general, if you recognize that current trends are pointing toward negative results sometime in the near future, it's often better to let your audience know ahead of time.
- **Seek expert advice if you're not sure.** Many significant negative announcements have important technical, financial, or legal elements that require the expertise of lawyers, accountants, or other specialists.

Ask for legal help and other assistance if you're not sure how to handle a significant negative announcement.

Negative situations will test your skills as both a communicator and a leader. People may turn to you and ask, "OK, so things are bad; now what do we do?" Inspirational leaders try to seize such opportunities as a chance to reshape or reinvigorate the organization, and they offer encouragement to those around them (see Figure 9.5).

Communicating in a Crisis

6 LEARNING OBJECTIVE

Explain the role of communication in crisis management

Some of the most critical instances of business communication occur during crises, which can include anything from incidents of product tampering to industrial accidents, crimes or scandals involving company employees, on-site hostage situations, or terrorist attacks. During a crisis, employees, their families, the surrounding community, and others will demand information; plus, rumors can spread unpredictably and uncontrollably (see "Using the Power of Technology: Controlling Online Rumors"). You can also expect the news media to descend quickly, asking questions of anyone they can find.

Although you can't predict these events, you can prepare for them. Analysis of corporate crises over the past several decades reveals that companies that respond quickly with the information people need tend to fare much better in the long run than those that go into hiding or release inconsistent or incorrect information.[16] In contrast, poor communication

FIGURE 9.5 Effective E-Mail Providing Bad News About Company Operations
In this message to employees at Sybervantage, Frank Leslie shares the unpleasant news that a hoped-for licensing agreement with Warner Brothers has been rejected. Rather than dwell on the bad news, he focuses on options for the future. The upbeat close diminishes the effect of the bad news without hiding or downplaying the news itself.

Opens on a complimentary note and buffers the bad news with some good news about sales

Moves readers from good news to bad news with an effective transition

Involves readers in the challenge of finding a solution

Presents the bad news along with the possible explanations

Closes by being positive, looking toward the future, and encouraging the audience

Anticipation and planning are key to successful communication in a crisis.

can increase victims' trauma and damage company reputations. After an explosion at International Coal Group's Sago coal mine in West Virginia in 2006, one or more rescuers apparently began to spread the word that 12 trapped miners were still alive. Family and friends gathered in joyous anticipation to meet their loved ones when they returned to the surface. Tragically, the information was wrong; 11 of the 12 were in fact dead. Even though the company quickly realized the report from the mine was wrong, no one updated the family members for several more hours and they were understandably crushed when they finally learned the truth. Investigators criticized both the company and government officials for a disorganized communication effort and lack of control over outgoing messages.[17]

The key to successful communication efforts during a crisis is having a **crisis management plan.** In addition to defining operational procedures to deal with the crisis itself, the plan also outlines communication tasks and responsibilities, which can include everything from media contacts to news release templates (see Table 9.3). The plan should clearly specify which people are authorized to speak for the company, contact information for all key executives, and a list of the media outlets and technologies that will be used to disseminate information. Many companies now go one step further by regularly testing crisis communications in realistic practice drills lasting a full day or more.[18]

Sending Negative Employment Messages

Most managers must convey bad news about individual employees from time to time. Recipients usually have an emotional stake in your message, so an indirect approach is usually

Connecting with Technology

Controlling Online Rumors

Ah, the miracles of the Internet: spam, viruses, spyware, stolen bandwidth, hacked databases full of confidential information—all offering ruin and nuisance at the speed of light. If you work in corporate communications, you can add rapid-fire rumor mongering to that list.

Consumers can now share rumors and complaints through e-mail, instant messaging, blogs, chat rooms, newsgroups, complaint websites such as www.planetfeedback.com, and "corporate hate" sites such as www.paypalsucks.com and www.allstateinsurancesucks.com. On the positive side, consumers who feel they have been treated unfairly can use the public exposure as leverage. Many companies appreciate the feedback from these sites, too, and even buy complaint summaries so they can improve products and services.

Nevertheless, many of these venues don't verify rumors or complaints. E-mail is probably the worst offender in this respect, because messages are so easy to forward en masse. Among the classic and recent rumors spread online: products from Coca-Cola and PepsiCo are tainted, perfume samples arriving in the mail are poisonous, bananas from Costa Rica carry a flesh-eating bacteria, the small letter *k* on Snapple labels means the company supports the Ku Klux Klan, and Carmex lip balm has (take your pick) addictive ingredients or either an acid or ground glass fibers that damage your lips so you have to use more. Every one of these rumors is false.

Controlling false rumors is difficult, but you can help contain them by (1) responding quickly with clear information distributed in any way you can, (2) tracking down and responding to rumors wherever they appear, (3) enlisting the help of government agencies such as the Centers for Disease Control and Prevention (www.cdc.gov) and debunking sites such as www.snopes.com, and (4) even digging back through e-mail threads and responding personally to everyone who passed the message along. Moreover, don't wait for bad news to find you; monitor complaint sites and newsgroups so that you can jump on false information faster.

CAREER APPLICATIONS

1. A legitimate complaint about one of your products on PlanetFeedback.com also contains a statement that your company "doesn't care about its customers." How should you respond?
2. A few bloggers are circulating false information about your company, but the problem is not widespread—yet. Should you jump on the problem now and tell the world the rumor is false, even though most people haven't heard it yet? Explain your answer.

advised. In addition, the media you use for these messages should be chosen with care. For instance, e-mail and other written forms let you control the message and avoid personal confrontation, but one-on-one conversations are more sensitive and facilitate questions and answers.

Refusing Requests for Recommendation Letters

As Chapter 8 noted (page 230), many companies now refuse to write recommendation letters—especially for people whose job performance has been unsatisfactory. When sending refusals to prospective employers who have requested information about past employees, your message may be brief and direct:

> Our human resources department has authorized me to confirm that Yolanda Johnson worked for Tandy, Inc., for three years, from June 2005 to July 2007. Best of luck as you interview applicants.

— Uses direct approach

— Ends on a positive note

This message doesn't need to say, "We cannot comply with your request." It simply gets down to the business of giving readers the information that is allowable.

TABLE 9.3 How to Communicate in a Crisis

WHEN A CRISIS HITS: DO	DON'T
Prepare for trouble ahead of time by identifying potential problems, appointing and training a response team, and preparing and testing a crisis management plan.	Don't blame anyone for anything.
	Don't speculate in public.
Get top management involved as soon as the crisis hits.	Don't refuse to answer questions.
Set up a news center for company representatives and the media that is equipped with phones, computers, and other electronic tools for preparing news releases and online updates. At the news center, take the following steps:	Don't release information that will violate anyone's right to privacy.
	Don't use the crisis to pitch products or services.
• Issue frequent news updates, and have trained personnel available to respond to questions around the clock.	Don't play favorites with media representatives.
• Provide complete information packets to the media as soon as possible.	
• Prevent conflicting statements and provide continuity by appointing a single person trained in advance to speak for the company.	
• Tell receptionists and other employers to direct all media calls to the designated spokesperson in the news center.	
Tell the whole story—openly, completely, and honestly. If you are at fault, apologize.	
Demonstrate the company's concern by your statements and your actions.	

Refusing an applicant's direct request for a recommendation letter is another matter. Any refusal to cooperate may seem to be a personal slight and a threat to the applicant's future. Diplomacy and preparation help readers accept your refusal:

Uses the indirect approach since the other party is probably expecting a positive response	Thank you for letting me know about your job opportunity with Coca-Cola. Your internship there and the MBA you've worked so hard to earn should place you in an excellent position to land the marketing job.
Announces that the writer cannot comply with the request, without explicitly blaming it on "policy"	Although we do not send out formal recommendations here at PepsiCo, I can certainly send Coca-Cola a confirmation of your employment dates. And if you haven't considered this already, be sure to ask several of your professors to write evaluations of your marketing skills. Best of luck to you in your career.
Offers to fulfill as much of the request as possible, then offers an alternative	
Ends on a positive note	

This letter tactfully avoids hurting the reader's feelings, because it makes positive comments about the reader's recent activities, implies the refusal, suggests an alternative, and uses a polite close.

Rejecting Job Applications

Poorly written rejection letters tarnish your company's reputation and can even invite legal troubles.

Tactfully telling job applicants that you won't be offering them employment is another frequent communication challenge. Poorly written rejection letters can have negative consequences, ranging from the loss of qualified candidates for future openings to the loss of potential customers (not only the rejected applicants but also their friends and family).[19] Poorly phrased rejection letters can even invite legal troubles. When delivering bad news to job applicants, follow three guidelines:[20]

- **Choose your approach carefully.** Experts disagree on whether a direct or an indirect approach is best for rejection letters. On the one hand, job applicants know they won't get many of the positions they apply for so negative news during a job search is not generally a shock. On the other hand, people put their hopes and dreams on the line when they apply for work, so job applicants have a deep emotional investment in the process, which is one of the factors to consider in using an indirect approach. If you opt for a direct approach, try not to be brutally blunt in the opening. Tell your reader that the position has been filled rather than saying, "Your application has been rejected." If you opt for an indirect approach, be careful not to mislead the reader or delay the bad news for more than a sentence or two. A simple "Thank you for considering ABC as the place to start your career" is a quick, courteous buffer that shows your company is flattered to be considered. Don't mislead the reader in your buffer by praising his or her qualifications in a way that could suggest good news is soon to follow.

- **Clearly state why the applicant was not selected.** Make your rejection less personal by stating that you hired someone with more experience or whose qualifications match the position requirements more closely.

- **Close by suggesting alternatives.** If you believe the applicant is qualified, mention other openings within your company. You might suggest professional organizations that could help the applicant find employment, or you might simply mention that the applicant's résumé will be considered for future openings. Any of these positive suggestions may help the applicant be less disappointed and view your company more positively.

7 LEARNING OBJECTIVE

List three guidelines for delivering negative news to job applicants and give a brief explanation of each one

Compare the ineffective and effective versions of the message in Figure 9.6 to see how this writer followed these guidelines. Finally, resist the temptation to not respond to applicants. Some companies are now so swamped with e-mailed résumé and online applications that they no longer have time to respond to them all. However, a failure to respond to job applicants has traditionally been viewed as a fairly serious breach of business etiquette. Responding is not only good for your company's image but also initiates conversations that might lead to successful hiring when you have the right opportunities for the right people.[21]

Giving Negative Performance Reviews

A performance review is a manager's evaluation of an employee and may be formal or informal. Few other communication tasks require such a broad range of skills and strategy as those needed for performance reviews. The main purpose of these reviews is to improve employee performance by (1) emphasizing and clarifying job requirements; (2) giving employees feedback on their efforts toward fulfilling those requirements; and (3) guiding continued efforts by developing a plan of action, which includes rewards and opportunities. In addition to improving employee performance, performance reviews help companies set organizational standards and communicate organizational values.[22]

An important goal of any performance evaluation is giving the employee a plan of action for improving his or her performance.

Positive and negative performance reviews share several characteristics: The tone is objective and unbiased, the language is nonjudgmental, and the focus is problem resolution.[23] Also, to increase objectivity, more organizations are giving their employees feedback from multiple sources. In these "360-degree reviews," employees get feedback from all directions in the organization: above, below, and horizontally.[24]

Criticizing others is difficult for most people, but discussing shortcomings is a necessary first step to improvement. Moreover, if you eventually need to dismiss an employee for poor performance but his or her performance evaluations are all positive, the employee can sue your company, maintaining that you had no cause to terminate employment.[25] So, as difficult as it may be, make sure your performance evaluations are well balanced and honest.

When you need to give a negative performance review, follow these guidelines:[26]

- **Confront the problem right away.** Avoiding performance problems only makes them worse. Moreover, as already noted, if you don't document problems when they occur, you may make it more difficult to terminate employment later on if the situation comes to that.[27]

FIGURE 9.6 Ineffective and Effective E-Mails Rejecting a Job Application
This e-mail response was drafted by Marvin Fichter to communicate the bad news to Carol DeCicco following her interview with Bradley & Jackson. After reviewing the first draft, Fichter made several changes to improve the communication. The revised e-mail helps DeCicco understand that (1) she would have been hired if she'd had more tax experience and (2) she shouldn't be discouraged.

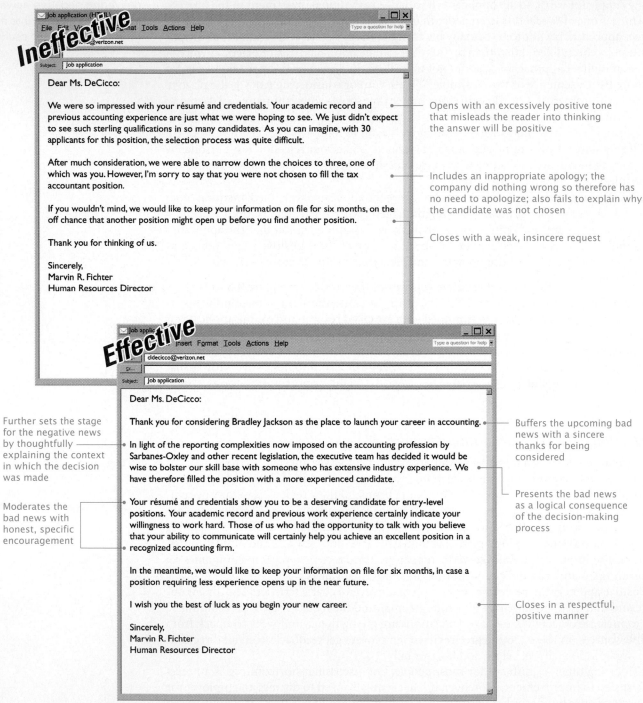

- **Plan your message.** Be clear about your concerns, and include examples of the employee's specific actions. Think about any possible biases you may have, and get feedback from others. Collect and verify all relevant facts (both strengths and weaknesses).

Address performance problems in private.

- **Deliver the message in private.** Whether in writing or in person, be sure to address the performance problem privately. Don't send performance reviews by e-mail or fax. If you're reviewing an employee's performance face-to-face, conduct that review in a meeting arranged expressly for that purpose and consider holding that meeting in a conference room or some other neutral area.

- **Focus on the problem.** Discuss the problems caused by the employee's performance (without attacking the employee). Compare the employee's performance with what's expected, with company goals, or with job requirements (not with the performance of other employees). Identify the consequences of continuing poor performance, and show that you're committed to helping solve the problem.

- **Ask for a commitment from the employee.** Help the employee understand that planning for and making improvements are the employee's responsibility. However, finalize decisions jointly so that you can be sure any action to be taken is achievable. Set a schedule for improvement and for following up with evaluations of that improvement.

Even if an employee's performance has been disappointing, you would do well to begin by mentioning some good points in your performance review. Then clearly and tactfully state how the employee can better meet the responsibilities of the job. If the performance review is to be effective, be sure to suggest ways that the employee can improve.[28] Remember that the ultimate goal is not to criticize but to help the employee succeed.

Terminating Employment

The decision to terminate employees is rarely easy or simple, but doing it effectively is an important managerial responsibility. When writing a termination message, you have three goals: (1) present the reasons for this difficult action, (2) avoid statements that might expose the company to a wrongful termination lawsuit, and (3) leave the relationship between the terminated employee and the firm as favorable as possible. For both legal and personal reasons, present specific justification for asking the employee to leave.[29] Your company's lawyers will be able to tell you whether the employee's performance is legal grounds for termination.

Make sure that all your reasons are accurate and verifiable. Avoid words that are open to interpretation, such as *untidy* and *difficult*. You can help protect personal feelings as you end the relationship by telling the truth about the termination and by helping as much as you can to make the employee's transition as smooth as possible.[30] To review the tasks involved in this type of message, see "Checklist: Writing Negative Employment Messages."

Carefully word a termination letter to avoid creating undue ill will and grounds for legal action.

 CHECKLIST: Writing Negative Employment Messages

A. Refusing requests for recommendation letters
- Don't feel obligated to write a recommendation letter if you don't feel comfortable doing so.
- Take a diplomatic approach to minimize hurt feelings.
- Compliment the reader's accomplishments.
- Suggest alternatives if available.

B. Rejecting job applications
- Always respond to applications.
- If you use a direct approach, take care to avoid being blunt or cold.
- If you use an indirect approach, don't mislead the reader in your buffer or delay the bad news for more than a sentence or two.
- Clearly state why the applicant was rejected.
- Suggest alternatives if possible.

C. Giving negative performance reviews
- Maintain an objective and unbiased tone.
- Use nonjudgmental language.
- Focus on problem resolution.
- Make sure negative feedback is documented and shared with the employee.
- Don't avoid confrontations by withholding negative feedback.
- Ask the employee for a commitment to improve.

D. Terminating employment
- State your reasons accurately and make sure they are objectively verifiable.
- Avoid statements that might expose your company to a wrongful termination lawsuit.
- Consult company lawyers to clarify all terms of the separation.
- End the relationship on terms as positive as possible.

COMMUNICATION CHALLENGES AT KPMG

With a good head for numbers and effective communication skills, you didn't take long to move up to a management position with KPMG. You're now an audit manager in the firm's Louisville, Kentucky, office (an *audit* is the process of reviewing a firm's accounting records for accuracy and legal compliance). Your responsibilities range from managing audits for KPMG's clients to helping members of your group develop their skills to coordinating with other managers in cross-functional team efforts. Not surprisingly, communication challenges are frequent and diverse.[31] Use the insights you gained in this chapter to address the following scenarios.

Individual Challenge: Another manager in the Louisville office stopped by this morning with a request to borrow two of your best auditors for a three-week emergency. Under normal conditions, you wouldn't hesitate to help, but your team has its own scheduling challenges to deal with. Plus, this isn't the first time this manager has run into trouble, and you are confident that poor project management is the reason. In one or two sentences, diplomatically state your refusal to help while suggesting that your colleague's management skills need improving.

Team Challenge: You've found it easy to say yes to recommendation letter requests from former employees who were top performers, and you've learned to say no to those people who didn't perform so well. The requests you struggle with are from employees in the middle, those people who didn't really excel but didn't really cause any trouble either. You've just received a request from a computer systems specialist who falls smack in the middle of the middle. Unfortunately, he's applying for a job at a firm that you know places high demands on its employees and generally hires the best of the best. He's a great person, and you'd love to help; but in your heart you know that if by some chance he does get the job, he probably won't last. Plus, you don't want to get a reputation in the industry for recommending weak candidates. With your team, brainstorm a sensitive but effective buffer that will help you set the stage for the negative news.

SUMMARY OF LEARNING OBJECTIVES

1 **Apply the three-step writing process to negative messages.** Because the way you say no can be far more damaging than the fact that you're saying it, planning your negative messages is crucial. Make sure your purpose is specific, necessary, and appropriate for written media. Find out how your audience prefers to receive bad news. Collect all the facts necessary to support your negative decision, and adapt your tone to the situation as well as to your audience. Negative messages may be organized according to the direct or the indirect approach, and your choice depends on audience preference as well as on the situation. In addition, carefully choose positive words to construct diplomatic sentences. Finally, revision, design, and proofreading are necessary to ensure that you are saying exactly what you want to say in the best possible way.

2 **Explain the differences between the direct and the indirect approaches to negative messages, including when it's appropriate to use each one.** The direct approach to negative messages puts the bad news up front, follows with the reasons (and perhaps offers an alternative), and closes with a positive statement. On the other hand, the indirect approach begins with a buffer (a neutral or positive statement), explains the reasons, clearly states the negative news (de-emphasizing it as much as possible), and closes with a positive statement. It's best to use the direct approach when you know your audience prefers receiving bad news up front or if the bad news will cause readers little pain or disappointment. Otherwise, the indirect approach is best.

3 **Identify the risks of using the indirect approach, and explain how to avoid such problems.** The indirect approach needs careful attention to avoid obscuring the bad news or misleading your audience into thinking you're actually delivering good news. The key to avoiding both problems is remembering that the purpose of the indirect approach is to cushion the blow, not to avoid delivering it. If you choose to start with a buffer, you must be sure it is neither deceptive nor insincere. To write an effective buffer, look for opportunities to express your appreciation for being considered, to assure your reader of your attention to the request, or to indicate your understanding of the reader's needs.

4 **Adapt your messages for internal and external audiences.** The key point to remember when considering internal versus external audiences is the issue of expectations. Internal audiences expect to get more detail in most cases, including information on how negative news affects their jobs. When messages will be sent to both internal and external audiences, internal audiences also expect to receive the message before it is sent to external audiences so they have time to prepare if necessary. Conversely, messages to external audiences may need a wider range of adaptation, given the diverse nature of many external audiences.

5 **Explain the importance of maintaining high standards of ethics and etiquette when delivering negative messages.** Ethics and etiquette are important in every message, of course, but they take on particular significance with negative messages for three reasons. First, in many cases, the communicator needs to adhere to a variety of laws and regulations when delivering negative messages. Second, good ethical practice demands care and sensitivity in the content and delivery of negative messages, as these messages can have a profoundly negative effect on the people who receive them. Third, communicators need to manage their own emotions when crafting and distributing negative messages while at the same time considering the emotional needs of their audiences.

6 **Explain the role of communication in crisis management.** Preparation is key for successful crisis management. Although you can't anticipate the nature and circumstance of every possible crisis, you can prepare by deciding such issues as who is in charge of communications, where the press and the public can get information, and what will be said in likely emergency scenarios. Rumor control is another important aspect; with the advent of instant messaging, text messaging on mobile phones, television, and other rapid communication vehicles, incorrect information can spread worldwide in seconds. A good crisis communication plan will also include such items as e-mail and phone lists for important media contacts, website templates for various emergency scenarios, and after-hours contact information for key personnel in the company.

7 **List three guidelines for delivering bad news to job applicants, and give a brief explanation of each one.** When rejecting job applicants, follow three guidelines: (1) Consider your approach carefully. Some managers advocate a direct approach on the grounds that job applicants realize they won't get every position they apply for, so bad news isn't necessarily a shock. Others assert that applicants have a significant emotional investment in the process, so while bad news may not be shocking, it is deeply disappointing. (2) State clearly why the applicant was not selected. This explanation can be specific without being personal if you explain that you hired someone with more experience or with qualifications that more closely match position requirements. (3) Suggest alternatives. Perhaps your company has other openings or you would be willing to consider the applicant for future openings.

Test Your Knowledge

1. What are the five main goals in delivering bad news?
2. Why is it particularly important to adapt your medium and tone to your audience's needs and preferences when writing a negative message?
3. What are the advantages of using the direct approach to deliver the negative news at the beginning of a message?
4. What is the sequence of elements in a negative message that is organized using the indirect approach?
5. What is a buffer, and what steps must you take to ensure that buffers you write are ethical?
6. When using an indirect approach to announce a negative decision, what is the purpose of presenting your reasons before explaining the decision itself?
7. What are three techniques for de-emphasizing negative news?
8. Why is it important to have one designated contact person during a crisis?
9. What are three guidelines for writing rejection letters to job applicants?
10. When giving a negative review to an employee, what five steps should you follow?

Apply Your Knowledge

1. Why is it important to end a negative message on a positive note?
2. If company policy changes, should you explain those changes to employees and customers at about the same time? Why or why not?
3. If your purpose is to convey bad news, such as refusing a request, should you take the time to suggest alternatives to your reader? Why or why not?
4. When a company suffers a setback, should you soften the impact by letting out the bad news a little at a time? Why or why not?
5. **Ethical Choices** Is intentionally de-emphasizing bad news the same as distorting graphs and charts to de-emphasize unfavorable data? Why or why not?

Practice Your Knowledge

Messages for Analysis

Read the following messages, then (1) analyze the strengths and weaknesses of each sentence and (2) revise each message so that it follows this chapter's guidelines.

Message 9.A: Providing Negative News About Transactions

Your spring fraternity party sounds like fun. We're glad you've again chosen us as your caterer. Unfortunately, we have changed a few of our policies, and I wanted you to know about these changes in advance so that we won't have any misunderstandings on the day of the party.

We will arrange the delivery of tables and chairs as usual the evening before the party. However, if you want us to set up, there is now a $100 charge for that service. Of course, you might want to get some of the brothers and pledges to do it, which would save you money. We've also added a small charge for cleanup. This is only $3 per person (you can estimate because I know a lot of people come and go later in the evening).

Other than that, all the arrangements will be the same. We'll provide the skirting for the band stage, tablecloths, bar setup, and, of course, the barbecue. Will you have the tubs of ice with soft drinks again? We can do that for you as well, but there will be a fee.

Please let me know if you have any problems with these changes and we'll try to work them out. I know it's going to be a great party.

Message 9.B: Refusing Requests for Claims and Adjustments

I am responding to your letter of about six weeks ago asking for an adjustment on your wireless hub, model WM39Z. We test all our products before they leave the factory; therefore, it could not have been our fault that your hub didn't work.

If you or someone in your office dropped the unit, it might have caused the damage. Or the damage could have been caused by the shipper if he dropped it. If so, you should file a claim with the shipper. At any rate, it wasn't our fault. The parts are already covered by warranty. However, we will provide labor for the repairs for $50, which is less than our cost, since you are a valued customer.

We will have a booth at the upcoming trade show there and hope to see you or someone from your office. We have many new models of hubs, routers, and other computer gear that we're sure you'll want to see. I've enclosed our latest catalog. Hope to see you there.

Message 9.C: Rejecting Job Applications

I regret to inform you that you were not selected for our summer intern program at Equifax. We had over a thousand résumés and cover letters to go through and simply could not get to them all. We have been asked to notify everyone that we have already selected students for the 25 positions based on those who applied early and were qualified.

We're sure you will be able to find a suitable position for summer work in your field and wish you the best of luck. We deeply regret any inconvenience associated with our reply.

Exercises

For active links to all websites discussed in this chapter, visit this text's website at www.prenhall.com/bovee. Locate your book and click on its Companion Website link. Then select Chapter 9, and click on "Featured Websites." Locate the name of the page or the URL related to the material in the text. Please note that links to sites that become inactive after publication of the book will be removed from the Featured Websites section.

9.1 **Selecting the Approach** Select which approach you would use (direct or indirect) for the following negative messages:

a. An e-mail message to your boss informing her that one of your key clients is taking its business to a different accounting firm

b. An e-mail message to a customer informing her that one of the books she ordered over the Internet is temporarily out of stock

c. An instant message to a customer explaining that the DVD recorder he ordered for his new computer is on back order and that, as a consequence, the shipping of the entire order will be delayed

d. A blog post to all employees notifying them that the company parking lot will be repaved during the first week of June and that the company will provide a shuttle service from a remote parking lot during that period

e. A letter from a travel agent to a customer stating that the airline will not refund her money for the flight she missed but that her tickets are valid for one year

f. A form letter from a U.S. airline to a customer explaining that the company cannot extend the expiration date of the customer's frequent-flyer miles even though the customer was living overseas for the past three years and unable to use the miles during that time

g. A letter from an insurance company to a policyholder denying a claim for reimbursement for a special medical procedure that is not covered under the terms of the customer's policy

h. A letter from an electronics store stating that the customer will not be reimbursed for a malfunctioning cell phone still under warranty (the terms of the warranty do not cover damages to phones that were accidentally dropped from a moving car)

i. An announcement to the repairs department listing parts that are on back order and will be three weeks late

9.2 **Teamwork** Working alone, revise the following statements to de-emphasize the bad news. (*Hint*: Minimize the space devoted to the bad news, subordinate it, embed it, or use the passive voice.) Then team up with a classmate and read each other's revisions. Did you both use the same approach in every case? Which approach seems to be most effective for each of the revised statements?

a. The airline can't refund your money. The "Conditions" segment on the back of your ticket states that there are no refunds for missed flights. Sometimes the airline makes exceptions but only when life and death are involved. Of course, your ticket is still valid and can be used on a flight to the same destination.

b. I'm sorry to tell you, we can't supply the custom decorations you requested. We called every supplier and none of them can do what you want on such short notice. You can, however, get a standard decorative package on the same theme in time. I found a supplier that stocks these. Of course, it won't have quite the flair you originally requested.

c. We can't refund your money for the malfunctioning MP3 player. You shouldn't have immersed the unit in water while swimming; the users manual clearly states the unit is not designed to be used in adverse environments.

9.3 Using Buffers As a customer service supervisor for a telephone company, you're in charge of responding to customers' requests for refunds. You've just received an e-mail from a customer who unwittingly ran up a $500 bill for long-distance calls after mistakenly configuring his laptop computer to dial an Internet access number that wasn't a local call. The customer says it wasn't his fault because he didn't realize he was dialing a long-distance number. However, you've dealt with this situation before; you know that the customer's Internet service provider warns its customers to choose a local access number, because customers are responsible for all long-distance charges. Draft a short buffer (one or two sentences) for your e-mail reply, sympathizing with the customer's plight but preparing him for the bad news (company policy specifically prohibits refunds in such cases).

9.4 Internet Public companies occasionally need to issue news releases announcing or explaining downturns in sales, profits, demand, or other business factors. Search the web to locate a company that has issued a press release that recently reported lower earnings or other bad news, and access the news release on that firm's website. Alternatively, find the type of press release you're seeking by reviewing press releases at www.prnewswire.com or www.businesswire.com. How does the headline relate to the main message of the release? Is the release organized according to the direct or the indirect approach? What does the company do to present the bad news in a favorable light—and does this effort seem sincere and ethical to you?

9.5 Ethical Choices The insurance company where you work is planning to raise all premiums for health-care coverage. Your boss has asked you to read a draft of her letter to customers announcing the new, higher rates. The first two paragraphs discuss some exciting medical advances and the expanded coverage offered by your company. Only in the final paragraph do customers learn that they will have to pay more for coverage starting next year. What are the ethical implications of this draft? What changes would you suggest?

Expand Your Knowledge

Exploring the Best of the Web

Protect Yourself When Sending Negative Employment Messages
www.toolkit.cch.com

A visit to CCH's Business Owner's Toolkit can help you reduce your legal liability, whether you are laying off an employee, firing an employee, or contemplating a companywide reduction in your workforce. Find out the safest way to fire someone from a legal standpoint before it's too late. Learn why it's important to document disciplinary actions. Discover why some bad news should be given face-to-face and never by a letter or over the phone. Read CCH's advice to find answers to these questions:

1. What should a manager communicate to an employee during a termination meeting?
2. Why is it important to document employee disciplinary actions?
3. What steps should you take before firing an employee for misconduct or poor work?

Surfing Your Way to Career Success

Bovée and Thill's Business Communication Resources offers links to hundreds of online resources that can help you with this course, your other college courses, and your career. Visit www.buscommresources.com, then click on "Business Communication Web Directory." The "Internet and the World Wide Web" section connects you to a variety of websites and articles on website design and development, HTML, web graphics, RSS, wikis, and related topics. Identify three websites from this section that could be useful in your business career. For each site, write a two-sentence summary of what the site offers and how it could help you launch and build your career.

Learn Interactively

Interactive Study Guide

Visit www.prenhall.com/bovee, then locate your book and click on its "Companion Website" link. Select Chapter 9 to take advantage of the interactive "Chapter Quiz" to test your knowledge of chapter concepts. Receive instant feedback on whether you need additional studying. Also, visit the "Study Hall," where you'll find an abundance of valuable resources that will help you succeed in this course.

Peak Performance Grammar and Mechanics

If your instructor has required the use of "Peak Performance Grammar and Mechanics," either in your online course or on CD, you can continue to improve your skill with sentences by using the "Peak Performance Grammar and Mechanics" module. Click "Sentences." Take the Pretest to determine whether you have any weak areas. Then review those areas in the Refresher Course. Take the Follow-Up Test to check your grasp of sentences. For an extra challenge or advanced practice, take the Advanced Test. Finally, for additional reinforcement in sentences, visit the Companion Website, click on any chapter, then click on "Improve Your Grammar, Mechanics, and Usage."

CASES

Applying the Three-Step Writing Process to Cases
Apply each step to the following cases, as assigned by your instructor.

Plan

Analyze the Situation
Identify both your general purpose and your specific purpose. Clarify exactly what you want your audience to think, feel, or believe after receiving your message. Profile your primary audience, including their backgrounds, differences, similarities, and likely reactions to your message.

Gather Information
Identify the information your audience will need to receive, as well as other information you may need in order to craft an effective message.

Select the Right Medium
Make sure your medium is both acceptable to the audience and appropriate for the message. Realize that written media are inappropriate for some negative messages.

Organize the Information
Choose a direct or indirect approach based on the audience and the message; many negative messages are best delivered with an indirect approach. If you use the indirect approach, carefully consider which type of buffer is best for the situation. Identify your main idea, limit your scope, and then outline necessary support points and other evidence.

Write

Adapt to Your Audience
Show sensitivity to audience needs with a "you" attitude, politeness, positive emphasis, and bias-free language. Understand how much credibility you already have—and how much you may need to establish. Project your company's image by maintaining an appropriate style and tone. Consider cultural variations and the differing needs of internal and external audiences.

Compose the Message
Draft your message using clear but sensitive words, effective sentences, and coherent paragraphs.

Complete

Revise the Message
Evaluate content and review readability, then edit and rewrite for conciseness and clarity.

Produce the Message
Use effective design elements and suitable layout for a clean, professional appearance.

Proofread the Message
Review for errors in layout, spelling, and mechanics.

Distribute the Message
Deliver your message using the chosen medium; make sure all documents and all relevant files are distributed successfully.

1   **2**   **3**

NEGATIVE MESSAGES ON ROUTINE BUSINESS MATTERS

Telephone
SKILLS

1. When a recall isn't really a recall: Voice recording informing customers that an unsafe product won't be replaced Vail Products of Toledo, Ohio, manufactured a line of beds for use in hospitals and other institutions where there is a need to protect patients who might otherwise fall out of bed and injure themselves (including patients with cognitive impairments or patterns of spasms or seizures). These "enclosed bed systems" use a netted canopy to keep patients in bed rather than the traditional method of using physical restraints such as straps or tranquilizing drugs. The intent is humane, but the design is flawed: At least 30 patients have become trapped in the various parts of the mattress and canopy structure, and 8 of them have suffocated.

Working with the U.S. Food and Drug Administration (FDA), Vail issued a recall on the beds, as manufacturers often do in the case of unsafe products. However, the recall is not really a recall. Vail will not be replacing or modifying the beds, nor will it accept returns. Instead, the company is urging institutions to move patients to other beds if possible. Vail has also sent out revised manuals and warning labels to be placed on the beds. The company also announced that it is ceasing production of enclosed beds.

Your task: A flurry of phone calls from concerned patients, family members, and institutional staff is overwhelming the support staff. As a writer in Vail's corporate communications office, you've been asked to draft a short script to be recorded on the company's phone system. When people call the main number, they'll hear "Press 1 for information regarding the recall of Model 500, Model 1000, and Model 2000 enclosed beds." After they press 1, they'll hear the message you're about to write, explaining that although the action is classified as a recall, Vail will not be accepting returned beds, nor will it replace any of the affected beds. The message should also assure customers that Vail company has already sent revised operating manuals and warning labels to every registered owner of the beds in question. The phone system has limited memory, and you've been directed to keep the message to 75 words or less.[32]

■ E-Mail ■ Portfolio
■ SKILLS ■ BUILDER

2. Message to the boss: Refusing a project on ethical grounds A not-so-secret secret is getting more attention than you'd really like after an article in *BusinessWeek* gave the world an inside look at how much money you and other electronics retailers make from extended warranties (sometimes called service contracts). The article explained that typically half of the warranty price goes to the salesperson as a commission and that only 20 percent of the total amount customers pay for warranties eventually goes to product repair.

You also know why extended warranties are such a profitable business. Many electronics products follow a predictable pattern of failure: a high failure rate early in their lives, then a "midlife" period during which failures go way down, and concluding with an "old age" period when failure rates ramp back up again (engineers refer to the phenomenon as the *bathtub curve* because it looks like a bathtub from the side—high at both ends and low in the middle). Those early failures are usually covered by manufacturers' warranties, and the extended warranties you sell are designed to cover that middle part of the life span. In other words, many extended warranties cover the period of time during which consumers are *least* likely to need them and offer no coverage when consumers need them *most*. (Consumers can actually benefit from extended warranties in a few product categories, including laptop computers and plasma televisions. Of course, the more sense the warranty makes for the consumer, the less financial sense it makes for your company.)[33]

Your task: Worried that consumers will start buying fewer extended warranties, your boss has directed you to put together a sales training program that will help cashiers sell the extended warranties even more aggressively. The more you ponder this challenge, though, the more you're convinced that your company should change its strategy so it doesn't rely on profits from these warranties so much. In addition to offering questionable value to the consumer, they risk creating a consumer backlash that could lead to lower sales of all your products. You would prefer to voice your concerns to your boss in person, but both of you are traveling on hectic schedules for the next week. You'll have to write an e-mail instead. Draft a brief message explaining why you think the sales training specifically and the warranties in general are both bad ideas.

3. Not this time: Letter denying debit adjustments to Union Bank of California customer You are an operations officer in the ATM Error Resolution Department at Union Bank of California. Your department often adjusts customer accounts for ATM debit errors. Mistakes are usually honest ones—such as a merchant swiping a customer's check debit card two or three times, thinking the first few swipes didn't "take," when they actually did.

Customers having problems on their statements are instructed to write a claim letter to your department that describes the situation and includes copies of receipts. Customers are notified of the outcome within 10 to 20 business days. Usually, you credit their account.

However, you've received a letter from Margaret Caldwell, who maintains several hefty joint accounts with her husband at your bank. Three debits to her checking account were processed on the same day and credited to the same market, Wilson's Gourmet. The debits carry the same transaction reference number, 1440022-22839837109, which is what caught Mrs. Caldwell's attention. But you know that number changes daily, not hourly, so multiple purchases made on the same day often carry the same number. Also, the debits are for different amounts ($23.02, $110.95, and $47.50), so these transactions were not a result of repeated card swipes. No receipts were enclosed.

Mrs. Caldwell writes that the store was trying to steal from her, but you doubt that and decide to contact Wilson's Gourmet. Manager Ronson Tibbits tells you that he's had no problems with his equipment. He also mentions that food shoppers commonly return at different times during the day to make additional purchases, particularly for beverages or merchandise they forgot the first time.

You decide that these charges did not the result from a bank or merchant error. It doesn't matter whether Mrs. Caldwell is merely confused or trying to commit an intentional fraud. Bank rules are clear for this situation: You must politely deny her request.

Your task: Write a letter to Margaret Caldwell, 2789 Aviara Parkway, Carlsbad, CA 92008, explaining your refusal of her claim #7899. Keep in mind that you don't want to lose this wealthy customer's business.[34]

■ IM
■ SKILLS

4. Midair letdown: Instant message about flight cancellations at United Airlines It used to be that airline passengers didn't learn about canceled connecting flights until after they'd landed. Sometimes a captain would announce cancellations just before touching down at a major hub, but how were passengers to notify waiting relatives or business associates on the ground?

As a customer service supervisor for United Airlines, you've just received information that all United flights from Chicago's

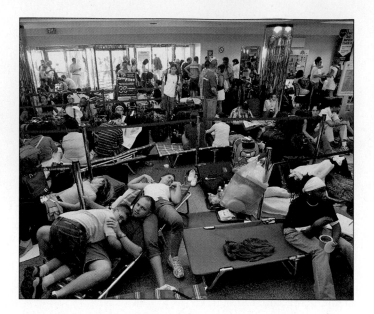

O'Hare International Airport to Boston's Logan International have been canceled until further notice. A late-winter storm has already blanketed Boston with snow, and freezing rain is expected overnight. The way the weather report looks, United will probably be lodging Boston-bound connecting passengers in Chicago-area hotels tonight. Meanwhile, you'll be using some of United's newest communication tools to notify travelers of the bad news.

United Airlines now partners with Verizon Airfone to provide JetConnect information services, giving travelers access to instant messaging and other resources while they're airborne. For a small fee, they can plug their laptop computers into the Airfone jack, activating their own instant messaging software to send and receive messages. If they've signed up for United's EasyUpdate flight status notification service, they'll also receive instant message alerts for flight cancellations, delays, seating upgrades, and so on.

Your task: Write the cancellation alert, staying within the 65-word limit of many instant messaging programs. You might want to mention the airline's policy of providing overnight lodging for passengers who planned to use the Boston route as a connecting flight to complete journeys in progress.[35]

▌IM ▌SKILLS

5. Quick answer: Instant message turning down employee request at Hewlett-Packard If she'd asked you a week ago, Lewinda Johnson might have been granted her request to attend a conference on the use of blogging for business, which is being held in New York City next month. Instead, Johnson waited until you were stuck in this meeting, and she needs your response within the hour. She'll have to take no for an answer: With travel budgets under tight restrictions, you would need at least three days to send her request up the chain of command. Furthermore, Johnson hasn't

given you sufficient justification for her attendance since she's already familiar with blogging.

Your task: Write a 60- to 75-word instant message to Lewinda Johnson, declining her request. Decide whether the direct or indirect approach is appropriate.[36]

▌Blogging ▌SKILLS ▌Portfolio ▌BUILDER

6. Coffee offer overflow: Undoing a marketing mistake at Starbucks Marketing specialists usually celebrate when target audiences forward their messages to friends and family—essentially acting as unpaid advertising and sales representatives. In fact, the practice of viral marketing (see page 192) is based on this hope. For one Starbucks regional office, however, viral marketing started to make the company just a bit sick. The office sent employees in the Southeast an e-mail coupon for a free iced drink and invited them to share the coupon with family and friends. To the surprise of virtually no one who understands the nature of online life, the e-mail coupon multiplied rapidly, to the point that Starbucks stores all around the country were quickly overwhelmed with requests for free drinks. The company decided to immediately terminate the free offer, a month ahead of the expiration date on the coupon.[37]

Your task: Write a one-paragraph message that can be posted on the Starbucks website and individual stores, apologizing for the mix-up and explaining that the offer is no longer valid.

7. No deal: Letter from Home Depot to faucet manufacturer As assistant to the vice president of sales for Atlanta-based Home Depot, you attended Home Depot's biannual product-line review held at Tropicana Field in St. Petersburg, Florida. Also attending were hundreds of vendor hopefuls, each eager to become one of the huge retail chain's 25,000 North American suppliers. During individual meetings with a panel of regional and national Home Depot merchandisers, these vendors did their best to win, keep, or expand their spot in the company's product lineup.

Vendors know that Home Depot holds all the cards; so, if they want to play, they have to follow Home Depot rules, offering low wholesale prices and swift delivery. Once chosen, they're constantly re-evaluated—and quickly dropped for infractions such as requesting a price increase or planning to sell directly to consumers via the Internet. They also receive sharp critiques of past performance, which are not to be taken lightly.

A decade ago, General Electric failed to keep Home Depot stores supplied with lightbulbs, causing shortages. Co-founder Bernard Marcus immediately stripped GE of its exclusive, 80-foot shelf space and flew off to negotiate with its Netherlands competitor, Phillips. Two years later, after high-level negotiations, GE lightbulbs were back on Home Depot shelves—but in a position inferior to Phillips's.

Such cautionary tales aren't lost on vendors. However, they know that despite tough negotiating, Home Depot is always looking for variety to please its customers' changing tastes and demands. The sales potential is so enormous that the compromises and concessions are worthwhile. If selected, vendors get immediate distribution in more than 1,700 stores (Home Depot, EXPO, and other subsidiary companies) across the United States, Canada, Mexico, and Puerto Rico.

Still, you've seen the stress on vendor reps' faces as they explain product enhancements and on-time delivery ideas in the review sessions. Their only consolation for this grueling process is that, although merchandisers won't say yes or no on the spot, they do let manufacturers know where they stand within a day or two. And the company is always willing to reconsider at the next product-line review—wherever it's held.

Your task: You're drafting some of the rejection letters, and the next one on your stack is to a faucet manufacturer, Roseway Manufacturing, 133 Industrial Ave., Gary, IN 46406. "Too expensive," "substandard plastic handles," and "a design not likely to appeal to Home Depot customers," say the panel's notes. (And knowing what its customers want has put Home Depot in the top 10 of the Fortune 500 list, with $40 billion in annual sales.) Find a way to soften the blow in your rejection letter to Roseway. After all, consumer tastes do change. Direct your letter to Pamela Wilson, operations manager.[38]

8. Suffering artists: Memo declining high-tech shoes at American Ballet Theatre Here at the American Ballet Theatre (ABT), where you're serving as assistant to Artistic Director Kevin McKenzie, the notion of suffering for the art form has been ingrained since the early 1800s, when the first ballerina rose up *en pointe*. Many entrepreneurs are viewing this painful situation with hopeful enthusiasm, especially when they discover that dancers worldwide spend about $150 million annually on their

shoes—those "tiny torture chambers" of cardboard and satin (with glued linen or burlap to stiffen the toes). The painful footwear (about $50 a pair) rarely last beyond a single hard performance.

A company the size of ABT spends about $500,000 a year on pointe shoes—plus the cost of a staff physical therapist and all those trips to chiropractors, podiatrists, and surgeons to relieve bad necks, backs, knees, and feet. Entrepreneurs believe there must be room for improvement, given the current advantages of orthopedics, space-age materials, and high-tech solutions for contemporary athletes. There's no denying that ballerinas are among the hardest-working athletes in the world.

The latest entrepreneur to approach ABT is Eliza Minden of Gaynor Minden, Inc. She wants to provide a solution to the shoe problem. She approached Michael Kaiser, executive director and a member of ABT's Board of Governing Trustees, with a proposal for providing new, high-performance pointe shoes in exchange for an endorsement.

Minden's alternative pointe shoes offer high-impact support and toe cushions. They're only $90 a pair and can be blow dried back into shape after a performance. When the cost-conscious board member urged the company to give them a try, you were assigned to collect feedback from dancers.

So far, not so good. For example, after a brief trial, one principal ballerina said she'd rather numb her feet in icy water, dance through "zingers" of toe pain, and make frequent visits to the physical therapist than wear Minden's shoes. The majority of others agree. Apparently, they *like* breaking in the traditional satin models with hammers and door slams and throwing them away after a single *Coppelia*. Too stiff, they say of the new shoes. Besides, they're simply not the shoes they grew up with and trained in. Only a few of the company's newest members, such as Gillian Murphy, liked Minden's high-tech shoes. That's not enough for a company endorsement.

You've seen all those feet bleeding backstage. You feel sorry for Minden; it *was* a good idea—just a hard sell among the tradition-oriented dancers.

Your task: McKenzie has asked you to write an internal memo in his name to Michael Kaiser, executive director of the American Ballet Theatre, explaining the dancers' refusal to use the new high-tech Gaynor Minden pointe shoes. In your memo, be sure to include the dancers' reasons as well as your own opinion regarding the matter. You'll need to decide whether to use the direct or the indirect approach; include a separate short note to your instructor justifying your selection of approach.[39]

9. Cyber-surveillance: Memo refusing claim from Silent Watch victim Your business is called Advertising Inflatables, and your specialty is designing and building the huge balloon replicas used for advertising atop retail stores, tire outlets, used-car lots, fast-food outlets, fitness clubs, and so on. You've built balloon recreations of everything from a 50-foot King Kong to a "small" 10-foot pizza.

Not long ago, you installed the "cyber-surveillance" software, Silent Watch, to track and record employees' computer usage. At the time, you sent out a memo informing all employees that they should limit their computer use and e-mail to work projects only. You also informed them that their work would be monitored. You did not mention that Silent Watch would record every keystroke of their work or that they could be monitored from a screen in your office.

As expected, Silent Watch caught two of the sales staff spending 50 to 70 percent of their time surfing Internet sites unrelated to their jobs. You withheld their pay accordingly, without warning. You sent them a memo notifying them that they were not fired but were on probation. You considered this wise, because when they work, both employees are very good at what they do, and talent is hard to find.

However, now sales representative Jarod Harkington has sent you a letter demanding reinstatement of his pay and claiming he was "spied on illegally." On the contrary, company attorneys have assured you that the courts almost always side with employers on this issue, particularly after employees receive a warning such as the one you wrote. The computer equipment belongs to Advertising Inflatables, and employees are paid a fair price for their time.

Your task: Write a letter refusing Mr. Harkington's claim.[40]

▌E-Mail
▌SKILLS

10. Cell phone violations: E-mail message to associates at Wilkes Artis Law Firm "Company policy states that personnel are not to conduct business using cell phones while driving," David Finch reminds you. He's a partner at the law firm of Wilkes Artis in Washington, D.C., where you work as his administrative assistant.

You nod, waiting for him to explain. He already issued a memo about this rule last year after that 15-year-old girl was hit and killed by an attorney from another firm. Driving back from a client meeting, the attorney was distracted while talking on her cell phone. The girl's family sued the firm and won $30 million, but that's not the point. The point is that cell phones can cause people to be hurt, even killed.

Finch explains, "Yesterday one of our associates called his secretary while driving his car. We can't allow this. According to the National Highway Transportation Safety Administration, 20 to 30 percent of all driving accidents are related to cell phone usage. From now on, any violation of our cell phone policy will result in suspension without pay, unless the call is a genuine health or traffic emergency."[41]

Your task: Finch asks you to write an e-mail message to all employees announcing the new penalty for violating company policy.

NEGATIVE ORGANIZATIONAL NEWS
▌Blogging
▌SKILLS

11. We're going to catch some flak for this: Alerting employees to the removal of a popular product XtremityPlus is known for its outlandish extreme sports products, and the Looney Launch is no exception. Fulfilling the dream of every childhood daredevil, the Looney Launch is an aluminum and fiberglass contraption that quickly unfolds to create the ultimate bicycle jump. The product

has been selling as fast as you can make it, even though it comes plastered with warning labels proclaiming that its use is inherently dangerous.

As XtremityPlus's CEO, you were nervous about introducing this product, and your fears were just confirmed: you've been notified of the first lawsuit by a parent whose child broke several bones after crash-landing off a Looney Launch.

Your task: Write a post for your internal blog explaining that the Looney Launch is being removed from the market immediately. Tell your employees to expect some negative reactions from enthusiastic customers and retailers, but explain that (a) the company can't afford the risk of additional lawsuits; and (b) even for XtremityPlus, the Looney Launch pushes the envelope a bit too far. The product is simply too dangerous to sell in good conscience.

▌E-Mail
▌SKILLS

12. Looney Launch coming back to Earth: Informing retailers about the demise of a popular product Now it's time to follow up the internal employee message about the Looney Launch (see Case 11) with a message to the retailers that carry the product.

Your task: Write an e-mail message to retailers explaining that the Looney Launch is being removed from the market and explaining why you've reached this decision. Apologize for the temporary disruption this will cause to their businesses, but emphasize that it's the right decision from both a legal and a social perspective. Thank them for their continuing efforts to sell XtremityPlus products, and assure them your company will continue to offer exciting and innovative products for extreme-sports enthusiasts.

▌Blogging ▌Portfolio
▌SKILLS ▌BUILDER

13. Communicating in a crisis: Informing the local community about a serious accident One of your company's worst nightmares has just come true. EQ Industrial Services (EQIS), based in Wayne, Michigan, operates a number of facilities around the country that dispose, recycle, and transport hazardous chemical wastes. Last night, explosions and fires broke out at the company's Apex, North Carolina, facility, forcing the evacuation of 17,000 local residents.

Your task: It's now Friday, the day after the fire. Write a brief post for the company's blog, covering the following points:

- A fire did break out at the Apex facility at approximately 10 P.M. Thursday.
- No one was in the facility at the time.
- Because of the diverse nature of the materials stored at the plant, the cause of the fire is not yet known.
- Rumors that the facility stores the extremely dangerous chlorine gas and that the fire was spreading to other nearby businesses are not true.

- Special industrial firefighters hired by EQIS have already brought the fire under control.
- Residents in the immediate area were evacuated as a precaution, and they should be able to return to their homes tomorrow pending permission by local authorities.
- Several dozen residents were admitted to local hospitals with complaints of breathing problems, but more have been released already; about a dozen emergency responders were treated as well.
- At this point (Friday afternoon), tests conducted by the North Carolina State Department of Environment and Natural Resources "had not detected anything out of the ordinary in the air."

Conclude by thanking the local police and fire departments for their assistance and directing readers to EQIS's toll-free hotline for more information.[42]

E-Mail SKILLS

14. Low-carb impact: E-mail announcing losses and new products at Monterey Pasta As marketing planning manager for Monterey Pasta Company, you know all about the impact that diet crazes can have on the food industry. When low-carb diets began to catch on, you knew it would be bad news for your firm. In fact, at Wal-Mart and Costco, Monterey Pasta's largest retail customers, sales plummeted nearly 30 percent in just a few months. Your company is not alone; many other traditional pasta makers are also showing losses because of the new diet preferences. In contrast, your major competitor, American Italian Pasta, introduced a line of low-carb pastas and continued to enjoy strong sales.

Now management has asked you to issue a revised forecast for fourth-quarter earnings. Previous predictions were for fourth-quarter sales to increase over last year's figures by 7 to 10 percent. Today's forecast from chief financial officer Scott S.

Wheeler is for a 3 to 5 percent *decrease* in revenue from last year's fourth-quarter earnings.

However, in the same message, management wants you to announce the release of Monterey Pasta's new CarbSmart line of fresh pastas, sauces, and prepared entrees. In a company meeting, Monterey Pasta President and CEO Jim Williams announced, "Americans love fresh pasta, but the current wave of low-carb diets has many consumers watching the amount of carbohydrates they consume. CarbSmart responds to that trend by delivering the flavor and convenience of traditional fresh pasta, but with half the carbs. So carb-counting pasta lovers can now have their ravioli . . . and eat it, too."

Your task: Write an e-mail to announce both the bad news (the declining financial projections) and the good news (the new CarbSmart line). Your message will go to shareholders, retail customers, distributors, and other interested parties. You can read more about the CarbSmart line at **www.montereygourmetfoods. com/kitchen/carbsmart**.[43]

15. Product recall: Letter from Perrigo Company about children's painkiller Your company is Perrigo, the leading manufacturer of more than 900 store-brand, over-the-counter (OTC) pharmaceuticals and nutritional products. These items are found beside brand-name products such as Tylenol, Motrin, Benadryl, NyQuil, Centrum, or Ex-Lax, but they're packaged under the name of the store that customers are shopping in. They're priced a bit lower but offer comparable quality and effectiveness. For retailers, selling Perrigo products yields a higher profit margin than name brands. For consumers, buying the store brands can mean significant savings.

However, your company has discovered that a batch of its cherry-flavored children's painkiller contains up to 29 percent more acetaminophen than the label indicates—enough to cause an overdose in the young children the product is designed for. Such overdoses can cause liver failure. As of this morning, your marketing department calculates that 6,500 4-ounce bottles of the "children's nonaspirin elixir" (a Tylenol look-alike) are already in the hands of consumers. That leaves some 1,288 bottles still on store shelves.

No one is telling you how this error happened, and it's only been found in lot number 1AD0228. However, finding a guilty party is not so important to your job. You're more concerned about getting the word out fast. Such errors do happen, and the best move is immediate and direct, being completely honest with retailers and the public. Full and prompt disclosure is especially crucial when consumers' health is involved, as it always is in your line of business.

The painkiller has been sold under the Kroger label at stores in Alabama, Arkansas, Georgia, Illinois, Indiana, Kentucky, Louisiana, Michigan, Mississippi, Missouri, North Carolina, Ohio, South Carolina, Tennessee, Texas, Virginia, and West Virginia. It was sold under the Hy-Vee label in Illinois, Iowa, Kansas, Minnesota, Missouri, Nebraska, and South Dakota and under the Good Sense label at independent retail chains throughout the United States. Perrigo must notify consumers throughout the United States that they should not give the product to children but, rather, should check the lot number and, if it's from the affected batch, return the bottle to the store they bought it from for a refund.

Your task: As Perrigo's customer service supervisor, you must notify retailers by letter. They've already been told verbally, but legal requirements mandate a written notification. That's good, because a form letter to your retail customers can also include follow-up instructions. Explain the circumstances behind the recall, and instruct stores to pull bottles from the shelves immediately for return to your company. Perrigo will, of course, reimburse the refunds provided to consumers. Questions should be directed to Perrigo at 1-800-321-0105—and it's okay if retailers give that number to consumers. Be sure to mention all that your company is doing, and use resale information.[44]

■ E-Mail ■ Portfolio
SKILLS   BUILDER

16. Sorry, but we don't have a choice: E-mail about monitoring employee blogs You can certainly sympathize with employees when they complain about having their e-mail and instant messages monitored, but you're only implementing a company policy that all employees agree to abide by when they join the company. Your firm, Webcor Builders of San Mateo, California, is one of the estimated 60 percent of U.S. companies with such monitoring systems in place. More and more companies use these systems (which typically operate by scanning messages for key words that suggest confidential, illegal, or otherwise inappropriate content) in an attempt to avoid instances of sexual harassment and other problems.

As the chief information officer, the manager in charge of computer systems in the company, you're often the target when employees complain about being monitored. Consequently, you know you're really going to hear it when employees learn that the monitoring program will be expanded to personal blogs as well.

Your task: Write an e-mail to be distributed to the entire workforce explaining that the automated monitoring program is about to be expanded to include employees' personal blogs. Explain that, while you sympathize with employee concerns regarding privacy and freedom of speech, it is the management team's responsibility to protect the company's intellectual property and the value of the company name. Therefore, employees' personal blogs will be added to the monitoring system to ensure that employees don't intentionally or accidentally expose company secrets or criticize management in a way that could harm the company.[45]

■ Blogging ■ Portfolio
SKILLS   BUILDER

17. Removing the obstacles on the on-ramp: Blog posting to Ernst & Young employees Like many companies these days, the accounting firm Ernst & Young is fighting a brain drain as experienced executives and professionals leave in midcareer to pursue charitable interests, devote more time to family matters, or pursue a variety of other dreams or obligations. The problem is particularly acute among women, because on average they step off the career track more often than men do. As general manager of the largest division in the company, you've been tapped to draft a set of guidelines to make it easier for employees who've taken some time off to move back into the company.

However, as soon as word gets out about what you're planning, several of your top performers, people who've never left the company for personal time off—or "taken the off-ramp," in current buzzword speak—march into your office to complain. They fear that encouraging the "off-rampers" to return isn't fair to the employees who've remained loyal to the firm, as they put it. One goes as far to say that anyone who leaves the company doesn't deserve to be asked back. Two others claim that the additional experience and skills they've gained as they continued to work should guarantee them higher pay and more responsibilities than employees who took time off for themselves.

Your task: As unhappy as these several employees are, the program needs to be implemented if Ernst & Young hopes to bring "off-rampers" back into the company—thereby making sure they don't go to work for competitors instead. However, you also can't afford to antagonize the existing workforce; if the people who've already complained are any indication, you have a sizable morale problem on your hands. You decide that your first step is to clearly explain why the program is necessary, including how it will benefit everyone in the company by making Ernst & Young more competitive. Write a short posting for the company's internal blog explaining that, in spite of the objections some employees have raised, the firm is going ahead with the program as planned. Balance this news (which some employees will obviously view as negative) with positive reassurances that all current employees will be treated fairly in terms of both compensation and promotion opportunities. Close with a call for continued communication on this issue inviting people to meet with you in person or to post their thoughts on the blog.[46]

■ Portfolio
BUILDER

18. Listen to the music, partner: Delivering an ultimatum to a business associate You're a marketing manager for Stanton, one of the premier suppliers of DJ equipment (turntables, amplifiers, speakers, mixers, and related accessories). Your company's latest creation, the FinalScratch system, has been flying off retailers' shelves. Both professional and amateur DJs love the way that FinalScratch gives them the feel of working with vinyl records by letting them control digital music files from any analog turntable or CD player while giving them access to the endless possibilities of digital music technology. (For more information about the product, go to **www.stantondj.com.**) Sales are strong everywhere except in Music99 stores, a retail chain in the Mid-Atlantic region. You suspect the cause: The owners of this chain refused to let their salespeople attend the free product training you offered when FinalScratch was introduced, claiming their people were smart enough to train themselves.

To explore the situation, you head out from Stanton headquarters in Hollywood, Florida, on an undercover shopping mission. After visiting a few Music99 locations, you're appalled by what you see. The salespeople in these stores clearly don't understand the FinalScratch concept, so they either give potential customers bad information about it or steer them to products from your competitors. No wonder sales are so bad at this chain.

Your task: You're tempted to pull your products out of this chain immediately, but you know how difficult and expensive it is to recruit new retailers in this market. However, this situation can't go on; you're losing thousands of dollars of potential business every week. Write a letter to Jackson Fletcher, the CEO of Music99 (14014 Preston Pike, Dover, DE 19901) expressing your disappointment in what you observed and explaining that the Music99 sales staff will need to agree to attend product training or else your company's management team will consider terminating the business relationship. You've met Mr. Fletcher in person once and talked on the phone several times, and you know him well enough to know that he will not be pleased by this ultimatum. Music99 does a good job selling other Stanton products—and he'll probably be furious to learn that you were "spying" on his sales staff.[47]

19. Refinancing rules: Letter explaining changes at People-First.com When you began as a customer service representative at PeopleFirst.com, you worked with only five employees to pioneer a web-based auto loan brokerage. Customers loved it.

From your website, they filled out a single application and faxed in any necessary verification documents. Then PeopleFirst matched them with the best loan for which they qualified, chosen from a variety of lenders. You mailed them a no-obligation "Blank Check®" to spend at any auto dealership up to the amount for which they qualified. The loan didn't begin until they spent the check. Later, if rates dropped, they could come back to PeopleFirst.com for refinancing.

All that changed when huge Capital One Financial Corporation bought out PeopleFirst.com. They changed your name to Capital One Auto Finance and converted all loans to Capital One loans. Under its new policies, Capital One will not refinance its own loans. However, your existing customers aren't charged a pre-

payment penalty if they want to pay off their loans early by finding (on their own) another lender for refinancing. You might lose some business this way, but Capital One would lose a lot more if it refinanced all its loans every time rates drop.

Your task: Explain the new policy in a letter to Faviola and Mary Franzone (7200 Poplar Ave., Memphis, TN 38197), who have inquired about refinancing their auto loan at today's lower rates.[48]

Podcasting SKILLS

20. Say good-bye to the concierge: Podcast announcing the end of a popular employee benefit An employee concierge seemed like a great idea when you added it as an employee benefit last year. The concierge handles a wide variety of personal chores for employees, everything from dropping off their dry cleaning to ordering event tickets to sending flowers. Employees love the service, and you know that the time they save can be devoted to work or family activities. Unfortunately, profits are way down and concierge usage is up—up so far that you'll need to add a second concierge to keep up with the demand. As painful as it will be for everyone, you decide that the company needs to stop offering the service.

Your task: Script a brief podcast announcing the decision and explaining why it was necessary. Make up any details you need. If your instructor directs, record your podcast and submit the file.

21. Safe selling: Memo about dangerous scooters at The Sports Authority You're not surprised that the Consumer Product Safety Commission (CPSC) has issued a consumer advisory on the dangers of motorized scooters. Unlike a motorcycle or bicycle, a scooter can be mastered by first-timers almost immediately. So both children and adults are hopping on, riding off—without helmets or other safety gear—and turning up with broken arms and legs, scraped faces, and bumped heads.

The popular electric or gas-powered scooters feature two wheels similar to in-line skates and travel 9 to 14 miles per hour. Over a six-month period, says the CPSC, emergency rooms around the country reported 2,250 motorized scooter injuries and three deaths. The riders who were killed (ages 6, 11, and 46) might all have lived if they'd been wearing helmets. As a result, some states have already enacted laws restricting scooter operations.

You are a merchandising assistant at The Sports Authority, which sells a wide selection of the foot-powered ($25 to $150) and motorized scooters ($350 to $1,000). Your company is as concerned about the rise in injuries as it is about the CPSC advisory's potential negative effect on sales and legality. Thus, you've been assigned to a team that will brainstorm ideas for improving the situation. For example, one team member has suggested developing a safety brochure to give to customers; another wants to train salespeople to discuss safety issues with customers before they buy.

"We'd like to see increased sales of reflective gear ($6 to $15), helmets ($24), and elbow and knee pads ($19)," a store executive tells your team, "not to improve on our $1.5 billion annual revenue, but to save lives."

Your task: Working with classmates, discuss how The Sports Authority can use positive actions (including those mentioned in the case) to soften the effect of the CPSC advisory. Choose the best ideas and decide how to use them in a negative-news memo notifying the chain's 198 store managers about the consumer advisory. Then write the memo your team has outlined.[49]

NEGATIVE EMPLOYMENT MESSAGES

Telephone SKILLS

22. Reacting to a lost contract: Phone call rescinding a job offer As the human resources manager at Alion Science and Technology, a military research firm in McLean, Virginia, you were thrilled when one of the nation's top computer visualization specialists accepted your job offer. Claus Gunnstein's skills would have made a major contribution to Alion's work in designing flight simulators and other systems. Unfortunately, the day after he accepted the offer, Alion received news that a major Pentagon contract had been canceled. In addition to letting several dozen current employees know that the company will be forced to lay them off, you need to tell Gunnstein that Alion has no choice but to rescind the job offer.

Your task: Outline the points you'll need to make in a telephone call to Gunnstein. Pay special attention to your opening and closing statements. (You'll review your plans for the phone call with Alion's legal staff to make sure everything you say follows employment law guidelines; for now, just focus on the way you'll present the negative news to Gunnstein. Feel free to make up any details you need.)[50]

23. Juggling diversity and performance: Memo giving a negative performance review at SBC Pacific Bell As billing adjustments department manager at SBC Pacific Bell, you've been trained to handle a culturally diverse workforce. One of your best recent hires is 22-year-old Jorge Gutierrez. In record time, he was entering and testing complex price changes, mastering the challenges of your monumental computerized billing software. He was a real find—except for one problem: his close family ties often distract him from work duties.

His parents immigrated from Central America when Jorge and his sisters were young children, and you understand and deeply respect the importance that family plays in the lives of many Hispanic Americans. However, every morning, Gutierrez's mother calls to be sure he got to work safely. Then his father calls. And three times this month, his younger sister has called him away from work with three separate emergencies. Friends and extended family members seem to call at all hours of the day.

Gutierrez says he's asked friends and family not to call his office number. Now they dial his cell phone instead. He's reluctant to shut off his cell phone during work hours in case someone in his family needs him.

At this point, you have given Gutierrez several verbal warnings. You really can't afford to lose him, so you're hoping that a written negative review will give him greater incentive to persuade friends and relatives. You'll deliver the letter in a meeting and help him find ways to resolve the issue within a mutually agreed-upon time frame.

Your task: Write the letter using suggestions in this chapter to help you put the bad news in a constructive light. Avoid culturally biased remarks or innuendo.

E-Mail SKILLS

24. Career moves: E-mail refusing to write a recommendation Tom Weiss worked in the office at Opal Pools and Patios for four months under your supervision (you're office manager). On the basis of what he told you he could do, you started him off as a file clerk. However, his organizational skills proved inadequate for the job, so you transferred him to logging in accounts receivable, where he performed almost adequately. Then he assured you that his "real strength" was customer relations, so you moved him to the complaint department. After he spent three weeks making angry customers even angrier, you were convinced that no place in your office was appropriate for his talents. Five weeks ago, you encouraged him to resign before being formally fired.

Today's e-mail brings a request from Weiss asking you to write a letter recommending him for a sales position with a florist shop. You can't assess Weiss's sales abilities, but you do know him to be an incompetent file clerk, a careless bookkeeper, and an insensitive customer service representative. Someone else is more likely to deserve the sales job, so you decide that you have done enough favors for Tom Weiss for one lifetime and plan to refuse his request.

Your task: Write an e-mail reply to Weiss (tomweiss@mailnet.com) indicating that you have chosen not to write a letter of recommendation for him.

25. Bad news for 80: Form letter to unsuccessful job candidates The Dean's Selection Committee screened 85 applications for the position of dean of arts and sciences at your campus. After two rounds of eliminations, the top five candidates were invited to "airport interviews," in which the committee managed to meet with each candidate for an hour. Then the top three candidates were invited to the campus to meet with students, faculty, and administrators.

The committee recommended to the university president that the job be given to Constance Pappas, who has a doctorate in American studies and has been chairperson of the history department at Minneapolis Metropolitan College for the past three years. The president agreed, and Dr. Pappas accepted the offer.

One final task remains before the work of the Dean's Selection Committee is finished: Letters must be sent to the 84 unsuccessful candidates. The four who reached the "airport interview" stage will receive personal letters from the chairperson of the committee. Your job, as secretary of the committee, is to draft the form letter that will be sent to the other 80 applicants.

Your task: Draft a letter of 100 to 200 words. All copies will be individually addressed to the recipients but will carry identical messages.

Portfolio BUILDER

26. What we have here is a failure to communicate: Writing a negative performance review Elaine Bridgewater, the former professional golfer you hired to oversee your golf equipment company's relationship with retailers, knows the business inside and out. As a former touring pro, she has unmatched credibility. She also has seemingly boundless energy, solid technical knowledge, and an engaging personal style. Unfortunately, she hasn't been quite as attentive as she needs to be when it comes to communicating with retailers. You've been getting complaints about voice-mail messages gone unanswered for days, confusing e-mails that require two or three rounds of clarification, and reports that are haphazardly thrown together. As valuable as Bridgewater's other skills are, she's going to cost the company sales if this goes on much longer. The retail channel is vital to your company's survival, and she's the employee most involved in the channel.

Your task: Draft a brief (one page maximum) informal performance appraisal and improvement plan for Bridgewater. Be sure to compliment her on the areas in which she excels, but don't shy away from highlighting the areas that need to improve, too: punctual response to customer messages; clear writing; and careful revision, production, and proofreading. Use what you've learned in this course so far to supply any additional advice about the importance of these skills.

CHAPTER 10

Writing Persuasive Messages

LEARNING OBJECTIVES

After studying this chapter, you will be able to

1 Apply the three-step writing process to persuasive messages

2 Identify seven ways to establish credibility in persuasive messages

3 Describe the AIDA model for persuasive messages

4 Distinguish between emotional and logical appeals and discuss how to balance them

5 Explain why it is important to identify potential objections before you start writing persuasive messages

6 Discuss an effective approach to identifying selling points and audience benefits

7 Identify steps you can take to avoid ethical lapses in marketing and sales messages

COMMUNICATION CLOSE-UP AT CLUBMOM

www.clubmom.com

Few roles in life require more information and insight than parenting. From prenatal care to early childhood development to education to socialization issues, parents are in continuous learning mode as their children grow. Parents also need to learn about themselves as they grow in their roles, from balancing work and home life to nurturing their own relationships. At the same time, parenting can be one of the most isolating experiences for adults, often making it difficult for people to acquire the information and support they need to succeed as parents.

Television personality Meredith Vieira, actor and activist Andrew Shue, and entrepreneur Michael Sanchez pondered this age-old challenge and saw the web as a solution. The three co-founded ClubMom, an online community and

ClubMom appeals to new members with a variety of attractive images and brief, upbeat statements that emphasize the benefits of joining.

information resource that helps mothers find answers, insights—and each other. In addition to providing a huge library of articles, several dozen blogs on various topics, question-and-answer forums, and an online shopping mall, ClubMom includes the MomNetwork, the first social networking site created specifically for mothers.

Information resources and social networks abound on the web, so like any web start-up, ClubMom faced the challenge of standing apart from the crowd and growing its membership audience large enough to create a viable business. One of the keys to its success is clear, audience-

focused messages that make a compelling case for joining ClubMom. Using straightforward statements such as "Join ClubMom and find answers, camaraderie, and support from other moms" and an upbeat but realistic writing style, the company communicates the features of its various online services and the benefits of joining.

The persuasive communication effort certainly seems to have been successful: ClubMom already has more than 2 million members and continues to expand as more mothers join in search of helpful insights and friendly support from their peers.[1]

1 LEARNING OBJECTIVE

Apply the three-step writing process to persuasive messages

USING THE THREE-STEP WRITING PROCESS FOR PERSUASIVE MESSAGES

Professionals such as ClubMom CEO Michael Sanchez (profiled in the chapter-opening Communication Close-Up) realize that successful businesses rely on persuasive messages in both internal and external communication. Whether you're convincing your boss to open a new office in Europe or encouraging potential customers to try your products, you'll use many of the same techniques of **persuasion**—the attempt to change an audience's attitudes, beliefs, or actions.[2] Persuasive techniques are a cornerstone of marketing and selling, but even if you never work in those fields you'll still need good persuasion skills to advance in your career. Successful professionals also understand that persuasion is not about trickery or getting people to make choices that aren't in their best interest; rather, it lets your audience members know they have a choice and helps them choose to agree with you.[3] As with every type of business message, the three-step writing process improves persuasive messages.

Persuasion is the attempt to change someone's attitudes, beliefs, or actions.

Step 1: Plan Your Message

In today's message-saturated environment, it's not enough to have a great idea or a great product.

In today's information-saturated business environment, having a great idea or a great product is no longer enough. Every day, untold numbers of good ideas go unnoticed and good products go unsold simply because the messages meant to promote them aren't compelling enough to rise above the competitive noise. Even if audiences agree that your idea or product is attractive, they usually have other options to consider as well, so you will need to convince them that your choice is the best of all the attractive alternatives. Creating successful persuasive messages in these challenging situations demands careful attention to all four tasks in the planning step, starting with an insightful analysis of your purpose and your audience.

Analyzing Your Situation

Failing to clarify your purpose is a common mistake with persuasive messages.

Your purpose might seem obvious—to persuade people to visit your website or buy your snowboards—but persuasive messages can suffer from three common mistakes related to purpose. The first mistake is failing to clarify your purpose before you continue with planning. Let's say you want to persuade members of top management to support a particular research project. But what does "support" mean? Do you want them to pat you on the back and wish you well? Or do you want them to pull five researchers off another project and assign them to your project? Having a specific goal is crucial to effective persuasion.

The second mistake is failing to clearly express your purpose to your audience. You may feel uncomfortable with the idea of asking others to give you time, money, promotions, or other considerations. However, if you don't ask or if you are vague about what you want, you're never going to get a positive response.

The third mistake is failing to realize that in some situations, the decision you want someone to make is too complicated or risky to make all in one leap. You can't sell a $10 million office building by writing someone a letter and asking him or her to buy it. You need to persuade in stages, with a message adapted to each stage. Your purpose in the first message might be to spark interest with a brief analysis of potential lease income. If that message is successful, you might then offer a tour of the site, and so on until you eventually ask for a decision. The idea is to generate a series of smaller positive answers on the way toward the final yes.

You can identify the right number and nature of messages by analyzing your audience. The best persuasive messages are closely connected to your audience's desires and interests.[4] Consider both the positives and the negatives—the wants, needs, and motivations of your audience members (the reasons they might respond favorably to your message), as well as their concerns and objections (the reasons they might *not* respond favorably). With these two insights as guides, you can then work to find common ground with your audience, while emphasizing positive points and minimizing negative ones.

To persuade successfully, you need to consider both the positive and negative aspects of your proposed solution.

If your message is aimed at a single large organization, you can direct it specifically toward a few top managers who make the kinds of decisions you're asking for. In contrast, for a message aimed at a million consumers, you'll never know each one individually. The best you can do is sample a small number who represent the entire audience, then from their expressed wants and needs craft messages that should appeal to everyone. For instance, Club-Mom does this by addressing questions and concerns that the vast majority of mothers are likely to have at some point in their lives.

Some theorists believe that certain needs have priority. Figure 10.1 represents psychologist Abraham Maslow's hierarchy of needs, with the most basic needs appearing at the bottom of the figure. Maslow suggests that only after lower-level needs have been met will a person seek to fulfill needs on higher levels.[5] Other theories of motivation exist as well, but the point here is that people have a variety of needs and that the most effective persuasive messages are aligned with the most important needs of every audience member.

Most persuasive communicators assume that their audiences have prioritized their own needs and desires.

To understand and categorize audience needs, you can refer to specific information such as **demographics** (the age, gender, occupation, income, education, and other quantifiable characteristics of the people you're trying to persuade) and **psychographics** (personality, attitudes, lifestyle, and other psychological characteristics). When analyzing your audience members, be sure to take into account their cultural expectations so that you don't undermine your persuasive message by using an inappropriate appeal or by organizing your message in a way that seems unfamiliar or uncomfortable to your audience.

Demographics include characteristics such as age, gender, occupation, income, and education.

Psychographics include characteristics such as personality, attitudes, and lifestyle.

Gathering Information

Once your situation analysis is complete, you need to gather the information necessary to close the gap between what your audience members know, believe, or feel right now and what you want them to know, believe, or feel as a result of receiving your message. Most persuasive messages are a combination of logical and emotional factors; see "Balancing Emotional and Logical Appeals" on page 302. Chapter 11 offers advice on using the latest research techniques to find the information you need.

FIGURE 10.1 Maslow's Hierarchy of Needs
Abraham Maslow theorized that human needs are arranged in a hierarchy and that people tend to fulfill lower-level needs before pursuing solutions to higher-level needs.

Self-actualization
Creativity—Self-realization—Wisdom—Vocation

Esteem and status
Self-worth—Uniqueness—Respect—Community

Social
Affection—Friendship—Group ties

Safety and security
Personal confidence—Stability—Protection from enemies

Survival (physiological)
Air—Food—Water—Sleep—Shelter

Businesses continue to find creative new ways to reach target audiences with persuasive messages. If you're a video gamer, you've probably noticed the brand name products that appear in many of today's games.

Limit your scope to include only the information needed to help your audience take the next step toward making a favorable decision.

Use the direct approach if your audience is ready to hear your proposal.

Selecting the Right Medium

Persuasive messages can be found in virtually every communication medium ever devised, from instant messages and podcasts to radio advertisements and skywriting. For persuasive messages intended for internal audiences, your choice of medium will closely follow the guidelines presented in Chapter 4. However, for marketing and sales messages, your options are far more numerous. In fact, advertising agencies employ media specialists whose only jobs are to analyze the media options available and select the most cost-effective combination for each client and each advertising campaign.

To further complicate matters, various members of your audience might prefer different media for the same message. Some consumers like to do all their car shopping in person, whereas others do most of their research online. Some people don't mind promotional e-mails for products they're interested in; others resent every piece of commercial e-mail they receive. If you can't be sure you can reach most or all of your audience with a single medium, you'll need to use two or more, such as following up an e-mail campaign with printed letters.

Organizing Your Information

Successful persuasion requires close attention to all four aspects of organizing your information: defining your main idea, limiting your scope, choosing a direct or indirect approach, and grouping your points in a meaningful way. The most effective main ideas for persuasive messages have one thing in common: they are about the receiver, not the sender. Take a cue from a successful advertiser such as Nike. The company's advertisements are never about the company and often aren't even about the products; they're about the customer's experience when using Nike products. You can benefit from this same approach for all persuasive messages. If you're trying to convince others to join you in a business venture, explain how it will help them, not how it will help you.

To limit the scope of each message effectively, include only the information needed to help your audience take the next step toward making the ultimate decision or taking the ultimate action you want. In simple scenarios such as persuading teammates to attend a special meeting, you might put everything you have to say into a single, short message. But if you want your company to invest several million dollars in your latest product idea, the scope of your first message might be limited to securing 10 minutes at the next executive committee meeting so that you can introduce your idea and get permission to explore it.

As with routine and negative messages, the best organizational approach is based on your audience's likely reaction to your message. However, because the nature of persuasion is to convince your audience members to change their attitudes, beliefs, or actions, most persuasive messages use an indirect approach. That means you'll want to explain your reasons and build interest before asking for a decision or action. Several examples of indirect approaches are presented throughout the chapter.

Consider the direct approach whenever you know your audience is ready to hear your proposal. If your boss wants to change shipping companies and asks for your recommendation, you'll probably want to open with your choice, then provide your reasons as backup. Similarly, if there's a good chance your audience members will agree with your message, don't force them to wade through pages of reasoning before seeing your main idea. If they happen not to agree with your pitch, they can move into your reasoning to see why you're promoting that particular idea. The direct approach is also called for if you've been building your case through several indirect messages and it's now time to make your request (see Figure 10.2).

If you use a direct approach, keep in mind that even though your audience may be easy to convince, you'll still want to include at least a brief justification or explanation. Don't expect your reader to accept your idea on blind faith. For example, consider the following two openers:

FIGURE 10.2 E-Mail Proposal Using a Direct Approach

Bette McGiboney, an administrative assistant to the athletic director of Auburn University, presented a solution to the problem of high phone bills during the month of August. She already has a close relationship with her boss, who is likely to welcome the money-saving idea, so the direct approach is a fast, efficient way to communicate her proposal.

Uses the subject line to announce the nature of the message (a proposal) and a compelling benefit to the reader (saving money)

Describes the solution in enough detail to help the reader imagine how it will work

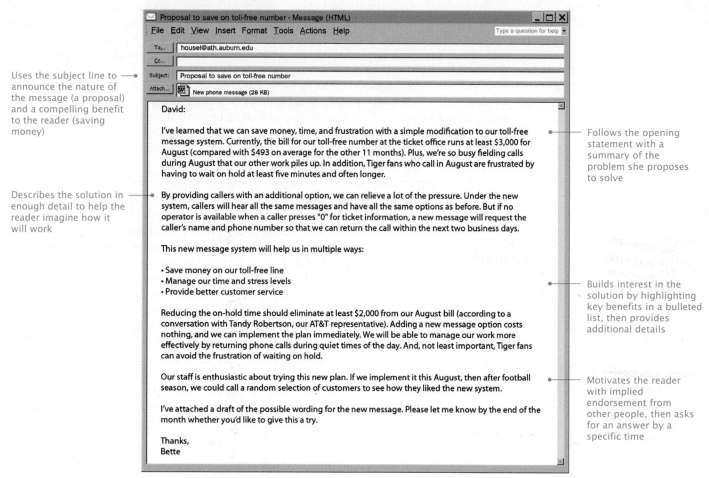

Follows the opening statement with a summary of the problem she proposes to solve

Builds interest in the solution by highlighting key benefits in a bulleted list, then provides additional details

Motivates the reader with implied endorsement from other people, then asks for an answer by a specific time

INSTEAD OF THIS

I recommend building our new retail outlet on the West Main Street site.

WRITE THIS

After comparing the four possible sites for our new retail outlet, I recommend West Main Street as the only site that fulfills our criteria for visibility, proximity to mass transportation, and square footage.

Your choice between the direct and indirect approaches is also influenced by the extent of your authority, expertise, or power in an organization. As a first-line manager writing a persuasive message to top management, you may try to be diplomatic and use an indirect approach. But your choice could backfire if some managers think your indirectness lacks confidence or even integrity. On the other hand, you may try to save your supervisors time by using a direct approach, which might be perceived as brash and presumptuous. Similarly, when writing a persuasive message to employees, you may use the indirect approach to ease into a major change, but your audience might see your message as weak, even wishy-washy. You need to think carefully about your corporate culture and what your audience expects before selecting your approach.

Choice of approach is also influenced by your position (or authority within the organization) relative to your audience's.

Step 2: Write Your Message

The generally uninvited and occasionally even unwelcome nature of persuasive messages means the "you" attitude is more critical than ever. Most people won't even pay attention to

Persuasive messages are often unexpected or even unwelcome, so the "you" attitude is crucial.

your message, much less respond to it, if it isn't about them. You can encourage a more welcome reception by (1) using positive and polite language, (2) understanding and respecting cultural differences, (3) being sensitive to organizational cultures, and (4) taking steps to establish your credibility.

Positive language usually happens naturally with persuasive messages, because you're promoting an idea or product you believe in. However, polite language isn't as automatic as you might think. Some writers inadvertently insult their readers by implying that they've been making poor choices in the past or need the writer's keen insights to make a good choice in the current situation.

Cultural differences influence your persuasion attempts.

Demonstrating an understanding of and respect for cultural differences is crucial to persuasion. For example, an aggressive, hard-sell technique is likely to antagonize a French audience. In Germany, where people tend to focus on technical matters, make sure you provide solid supporting evidence for all messages. In Sweden, audiences tend to focus on theoretical questions and strategic implications, whereas U.S. audiences are usually concerned with more practical matters.[6]

Just as culture within various social groups affects the success of persuasive messages, so too does the culture within various organizations. Over time, every company develops a particular internal culture that establishes numerous expectations regarding communication. For instance, some organizations handle disagreement and conflict in an indirect, behind-the-scenes way, whereas others accept and even encourage open discussion and sharing of differing viewpoints. Similarly, the degree of formality varies widely. When you accept and follow these traditions, even if they don't reflect your personal preferences, you show your audience members that you understand them and respect their values.

2 LEARNING OBJECTIVE

Identify seven ways to establish credibility in persuasive messages

Audiences often respond unfavorably to over-the-top language, so keep your writing simple and straightforward.

Finally, when trying to persuade a skeptical or hostile audience, you must convince people that you know what you're talking about and that you're not trying to mislead them. Without this credibility, your efforts to persuade will seem ineffective at best and manipulative at worst. Moreover, be aware that according to recent research, most managers overestimate their own credibility.[7] Establishing your credibility in persuasive messages takes time. Chapter 5 lists characteristics essential to building and maintaining your credibility, including honesty, objectivity, awareness of audience needs, knowledge and expertise, endorsements, performance, and communication style. To establish credibility in persuasive messages, try to go beyond these characteristics by:

- **Using simple language.** In most persuasive situations, your audience will be cautious, watching for fantastic claims, insupportable descriptions, and emotional manipulation.
- **Supporting your message with facts.** Specific and relevant support—documents, statistics, research results, and testimonials—can all provide objective evidence for what you have to say.
- **Identifying your sources.** Telling your audience where your information comes from and who agrees with you improves your credibility, especially if your audience already respects the source.
- **Being an expert (or finding one to support your message).** Your knowledge of your message's subject area helps you give your audience the quality information necessary to make a decision.
- **Establishing common ground.** Those beliefs, attitudes, and background experiences that you have in common with members of your audience will help them identify with you.
- **Being objective.** Your ability to understand and acknowledge all sides of an issue helps you present fair and logical arguments in your persuasive message.
- **Displaying your good intentions.** Your willingness to keep your audience's best interests at heart helps you create persuasive messages that are not only more effective but also more ethical (see "Ethics Detective: The Case of Incredible Credibility").

Step 3: Complete Your Message

The pros know from experience that the details can make or break a persuasive message, so they're careful not to shortchange this part of the writing process. For instance, advertisers may have a dozen or more people review a message before it's released to the public.

Ethics Detective

The Case of Incredible Credibility

As the director of human resources in your company, you're desperate for some help. You want to keep the costs of employee benefits under control while making sure you provide employees with a fair benefits package. However, you don't have time to research all the options for health insurance, wellness programs, retirement plans, family counseling, educational benefits, and everything else, so you decide to hire a consultant. You receive the following message from a consultant interested in working with you:

I am considered the country's foremost authority on employee health insurance programs. My clients offer universally positive feedback on the programs I've designed for them. They also love how much time I save them—hundreds and hundreds of hours.

I am absolutely confident that I can thoroughly analyze your needs and create a portfolio that realizes every degree of savings possible. I invite you to experience the same level of service that has generated such comments as "Best advice ever!" and "Saved us an unbelievable amount of money."

You'd love to get results like that, but the message almost sounds too good to be true. Is it?

ANALYSIS

The consultant's letter contains at least a dozen instances in which this writer's credibility might be questioned. Identify as many as you can and explain how you would bolster reader confidence by providing additional or different information.

When you evaluate your content, try to judge your argument objectively and try not to overestimate your credibility. When revising for clarity and conciseness, carefully match the purpose and organization to audience needs. If possible, ask an experienced colleague who knows your audience well to review your draft. Your design elements must complement, not detract from, your argument. In addition, meticulous proofreading will help identify any mechanical or spelling errors that would weaken your persuasive potential. Finally, make sure your distribution methods fit your audience's expectations as well as your purpose. Don't start your persuasive efforts on the wrong foot by annoying your audience with an unwelcome delivery method.

With the three-step model in mind, you're ready to begin composing persuasive messages, starting with *persuasive business messages* (those that try to convince audiences to approve new projects, enter into business partnerships, and so on), followed by *marketing and sales messages* (those that try to convince audiences to consider and then purchase products and services).

DEVELOPING PERSUASIVE BUSINESS MESSAGES

Persuasive business messages comprise a broad and diverse category, with audiences that range from a single person in your own department to government agencies, investors, business partners, community leaders, and other external groups. Your success as a businessperson is closely tied to your ability to convince others to accept new ideas, change old habits, or act on your recommendations. Even early in your career, you might have the opportunity to convince your manager to let you join an exciting project or to improve an important process. As you move into positions of greater responsibility, your persuasive messages could start to influence multimillion-dollar investments and the careers of hundreds or thousands of employees. Obviously, the increase in your persuasive skills needs to be matched by the care and thoroughness of your analysis and planning so that the ideas you convince others to adopt are sound.

Your success in business will depend on writing persuasive messages effectively.

Strategies for Persuasive Business Messages

The goals of persuasive business messages are to convince your audiences that your request or idea is reasonable and that it will benefit your readers in some way. Within the context of the three-step process, effective persuasion involves four essential strategies: structuring your message, balancing emotional and logical appeals, reinforcing your position, and anticipating objections. (Note that all of these concepts in this section apply as well to marketing and sales messages, covered later in the chapter.)

Structuring Your Message with the AIDA Model

Many persuasive messages follow a four-phase indirect approach. The first phase is to get your audience members' attention. The second phase then raises your audience members' interest, and the third attempts to change their attitude toward your offering or idea. The fourth phase then motivates readers to take specific action. The **AIDA model** organizes your message into these four phases: (1) **a**ttention, (2) **i**nterest, (3) **d**esire, and (4) **a**ction (see Table 10.1). Other models exist, but they all follow a pattern similar to this one:

- **Attention.** Your first objective is to encourage your audience to want to hear about your main idea. Write a brief and engaging opening sentence, with no extravagant claims or irrelevant points. Look for some common ground on which to build your case (see Figure 10.3). And while you want to be positive and confident, make sure you don't start out with a "hard sell," a pushy, aggressive opening. Doing so often puts audiences on guard and on the defensive.
- **Interest.** Explain the relevance of your message to your audience. Continuing the theme you started with, paint a more detailed picture of the problem you propose to solve with the solution you're offering (whether that's a new idea, a new process, a new product, or whatever).
- **Desire.** Help audience members embrace your idea by explaining how the change will benefit them, either personally or professionally. Reduce resistance by identifying and answering in advance any questions the audience might have. If your idea is complex, you might need to explain how you would implement it. Back up your claims in order to increase audience willingness to take the action that you suggest in the next section.
- **Action.** Suggest the action you want readers to take. Make it more than a statement such as "Please institute this program soon" or "Send me a refund." This is the opportunity to remind readers of the benefits of taking action. The secret of a successful action phase is making the action easy, so if possible, give your readers a couple of options for responding, such as a toll-free number to call and a website to visit. Include a deadline when applicable.

The AIDA plan is tailor-made for using the indirect approach, allowing you to save your main idea for the action phase. However, it can also be used for the direct approach, in which case you use your main idea as an attention-getter, build interest with your argument, create desire with your evidence, and re-emphasize your main idea in the action phase with the specific action you want your audience to take.

When your AIDA message uses an indirect approach and is delivered by memo or e-mail, keep in mind that your subject line usually catches your reader's eye first. Your challenge is to make it interesting and relevant enough to capture reader attention without

3 LEARNING OBJECTIVE

Describe the AIDA model for persuasive messages

Organize persuasive messages using the AIDA model:
- *Attention*
- *Interest*
- *Desire*
- *Action*

The AIDA model is ideal for the indirect approach.

TABLE 10.1 The AIDA Model

PHASE	OBJECTIVE
Attention	Get the reader's attention with a benefit that is of real interest or value.
Interest	Build the reader's interest by further explaining benefits and appealing to his or her logic or emotions.
Desire	Build desire by providing additional supporting details and answering potential questions.
Action	Motivate the reader to take the next step by closing with a compelling call to action and providing a convenient means for the reader to respond.

FIGURE 10.3 Persuasive Message Using the AIDA Model

Randy Thumwolt uses the AIDA model in a persuasive message about a program that would try to reduce Host Marriott's annual plastics costs and curtail consumer complaints about the company's recycling record. Note how Thumwolt "sells the problem" before attempting to sell the solution. Few people are interested in hearing about solutions to problems they don't know about or don't believe exist.

Plan

Analyze the Situation
Verify that the purpose is to solve an ongoing problem, so the audience will be receptive.

Gather Information
Determine audience needs and obtain the necessary information on recycling problem areas.

Select the Right Medium
Verify that an e-mail message is appropriate for this formal communication.

Organize the Information
Limit the scope to the main idea, which is to propose a recycling solution; use an indirect approach to lay out the extent of the problem.

Write

Adapt to Your Audience
Adjust the level of formality based on the degree of familiarity with the audience; maintain a positive relationship by using the you " attitude, politeness, positive emphasis, and bias-free language.

Compose the Message
Use a conversational but professional style and keep the message brief, clear, and as helpful as possible.

Complete

Revise the Message
Evaluate content and review readability to make sure the information is clear and complete without being overwhelming.

Produce the Message
Emphasize a clean, professional appearance.

Proofread the Message
Review for errors in layout, spelling, and mechanics.

Distribute the Message
Deliver your message using the chosen medium.

1   **2**   **3**

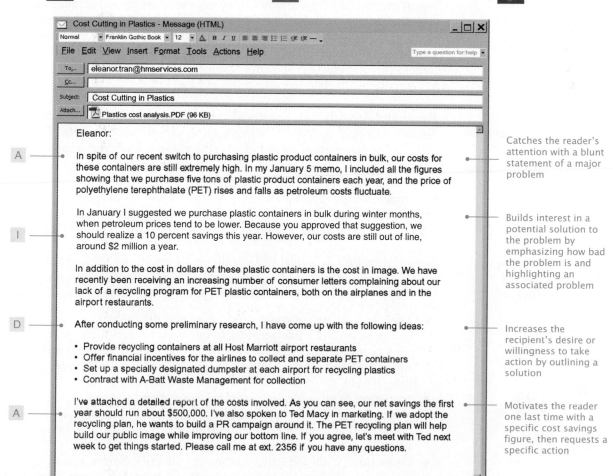

Cost Cutting in Plastics - Message (HTML)

To: eleanor.tran@hmservices.com
Cc:
Subject: Cost Cutting in Plastics
Attach: Plastics cost analysis.PDF (96 KB)

Eleanor:

A — In spite of our recent switch to purchasing plastic product containers in bulk, our costs for these containers are still extremely high. In my January 5 memo, I included all the figures showing that we purchase five tons of plastic product containers each year, and the price of polyethylene terephthalate (PET) rises and falls as petroleum costs fluctuate.

I — In January I suggested we purchase plastic containers in bulk during winter months, when petroleum prices tend to be lower. Because you approved that suggestion, we should realize a 10 percent savings this year. However, our costs are still out of line, around $2 million a year.

In addition to the cost in dollars of these plastic containers is the cost in image. We have recently been receiving an increasing number of consumer letters complaining about our lack of a recycling program for PET plastic containers, both on the airplanes and in the airport restaurants.

D — After conducting some preliminary research, I have come up with the following ideas:

- Provide recycling containers at all Host Marriott airport restaurants
- Offer financial incentives for the airlines to collect and separate PET containers
- Set up a specially designated dumpster at each airport for recycling plastics
- Contract with A-Batt Waste Management for collection

A — I've attached a detailed report of the costs involved. As you can see, our net savings the first year should run about $500,000. I've also spoken to Ted Macy in marketing. If we adopt the recycling plan, he wants to build a PR campaign around it. The PET recycling plan will help build our public image while improving our bottom line. If you agree, let's meet with Ted next week to get things started. Please call me at ext. 2356 if you have any questions.

Catches the reader's attention with a blunt statement of a major problem

Builds interest in a potential solution to the problem by emphasizing how bad the problem is and highlighting an associated problem

Increases the recipient's desire or willingness to take action by outlining a solution

Motivates the reader one last time with a specific cost savings figure, then requests a specific action

revealing your main idea. If you put your request in the subject line, you're likely to get a quick no before you've had a chance to present your arguments.

INSTEAD OF THIS	WRITE THIS
Proposal to install new phone message system	Reducing the cost of our toll-free number

You can also see from the AIDA model why it's so important to have a concise, focused purpose for your persuasive messages. Otherwise, you'll find it nearly impossible to guide your reader through each phase from attention to action. Focus on your primary goal when presenting your case, and concentrate your efforts on accomplishing that one goal. For example, if your main idea is to convince your company to install a new phone-messaging system, leave discussions about switching long-distance carriers until another day—unless it's relevant to your argument.

Balancing Emotional and Logical Appeals

Imagine you're sitting at a control panel with one knob labeled "logic" and another labeled "emotion." As you prepare your persuasive message, you carefully adjust each knob, tuning the message for maximum impact. Too little emotion and your audience might not care enough to respond. Too much emotion and your audience might think you haven't thought through the tough business questions.

Generally speaking, persuasive business messages rely more heavily on logical appeals than on emotional appeals, since the main idea is to save money, improve quality, and so on. While logic weighs heavily, don't assume that business decisions are purely logical and therefore ignore the emotional component. For example, you might be able to build a strong logical case for acquiring another company, based on projected financial return and other objective factors. However, the managers making the decision will experience a range of emotions, such as fear of making a wrong move that could be career-threatening. To find the optimum balance, consider four factors: (1) the actions you hope to motivate, (2) your reader's expectations, (3) the degree of resistance you need to overcome, and (4) how far you feel empowered to go to sell your point of view.[8]

Emotional appeals attempt to connect with the reader's feelings or sympathies.

Emotional Appeals   An **emotional appeal** calls on feelings, basing the argument on audience needs or sympathies; however, such an appeal must be subtle.[9] For instance, you can make use of the emotion surrounding certain words. The word *freedom* evokes strong feelings, as do words such as *success, prestige, compassion, free, value,* and *comfort.* Such words put your audience members in a certain frame of mind and help them accept your message. However, emotional appeals aren't necessarily effective by themselves. For most business situations, the best use of emotion is in tandem with logic. Even if your audience members reach a conclusion based on emotions, they'll look to you to provide logical support as well.

Logical appeals are based on the reader's notions of reason; these appeals can use analogy, induction, or deduction.

Logical Appeals   A **logical appeal** calls on reason. In any argument you might use to persuade an audience, you make a claim and then support your claim with reasons or evidence. When appealing to your audience's logic, you might use three types of reasoning:

- **Analogy.** With analogy, you reason from specific evidence to specific evidence. For instance, to convince management to buy a more robust firewall to protect your company's computer network, you might use the analogy of "circling the wagons," as when covered wagons crossing the continent gathered in a circle every night to form a safe space within.
- **Induction.** With inductive reasoning, you work from specific evidence to a general conclusion. To convince your team to change to a new manufacturing process, for example, you could point out that every company that has adopted it has increased profits, so it must be a smart idea.
- **Deduction.** With deductive reasoning, you work from a generalization to a specific conclusion. To persuade your boss to hire additional customer support staff, you might point to industry surveys that show how crucial customer satisfaction is to corporate profits.

Every method of reasoning is vulnerable to misuse, both intentional and unintentional, so verify your rational arguments carefully. For example, in the case of the manufacturing process, are there any other factors that affect the integrity of your reasoning? What if that process works well only for small companies with few products and your firm is a multinational behemoth with 10,000 products? To avoid faulty logic, follow these guidelines:[10]

- **Avoid hasty generalizations.** Make sure you have plenty of evidence before drawing conclusions.
- **Avoid circular reasoning.** *Circular reasoning* is a logical fallacy in which you try to support your claim by restating it in different words. The statement "We know temporary workers cannot handle this task because temps are unqualified for it" doesn't prove anything because the claim and the supporting evidence are essentially identical. It doesn't prove *why* the temps are unqualified.
- **Avoid attacking an opponent.** If your persuasive appeal involves countering a competitive appeal made by someone else, make sure you attack the argument your opponent is making, not his or her character.
- **Avoid oversimplifying a complex issue.** Make sure you present all the factors and don't reduce a wide range of choices to a simple "either/or" scenario if that isn't the case.
- **Avoid mistaken assumptions of cause and effect.** If you can't isolate the impact of a specific factor, you can't assume it's the cause of whatever effect you're discussing. The weather improves in spring, and people start playing baseball in spring. Does good weather cause baseball? No. There is a *correlation* between the two—meaning the data associated with them tend to rise and fall at the same time, but there is no *causation*—no proof that one causes the other. The complexity of many business situations makes cause and effect a particular challenge. You lowered prices and sales went up. Were lower prices the cause? Maybe, but it might have been caused by a competitor with delivery problems, a better advertising campaign, or any of a host of other factors.
- **Avoid faulty analogies.** Be sure that the two objects or situations being compared are similar enough for the analogy to hold. For instance, the analogy between circling the wagons and using a network firewall isn't entirely valid, because circling the wagons is a temporary move and computer networks need permanent protections.
- **Avoid illogical support.** Make sure the connection between your claim and your support is truly logical and not based on a leap of faith, a missing premise, or irrelevant evidence.

Logical flaws include hasty generalizations, circular reasoning, attacks on opponents, oversimplifications, false assumptions of cause and effect, faulty analogies, and illogical support.

Reinforcing Your Position

After you've worked out the basic elements of your argument, step back and look for ways to bolster the strength of your position. Can you find more powerful words to convey your message? For example, if your company is in serious financial trouble, talking about *survival* is more powerful than talking about *continued operations*. Using vivid abstractions such as this along with basic facts and figures can bring your argument to life. As with any powerful tool, though, use vivid language and abstractions carefully and honestly.

In addition to individual word choices, consider using *metaphors* and other figures of speech. If you want to describe a quality-control system as being designed to catch every possible product flaw, you might call it a *spider web* to imply that it catches everything that comes its way. Similarly, anecdotes and stories can help your audience grasp the meaning and importance of your arguments. Instead of just listing the average failure rates of older-model laptop computers, put a human face on the problem by describing what happened when your computer broke down during a critical presentation to your company's biggest customer.

Choose your words carefully and use abstractions to enhance emotional content.

Beyond the specific wording of your message, look for other forces and factors that can reinforce your position. When you're asking for something, your audience members will find it easier to grant your request if they stand to benefit from it as well. For instance, if you're asking for more money to increase your staff, you might offer to lend those new employees to other managers during peak workloads in other departments. The timing of your message can also help. Virtually all organizations operate in cycles of some sort—incoming payments from major customers, outgoing tax payments, seasonal demand for products,

Highlight the direct and indirect benefits of complying with your request.

and so on. Study these patterns to see whether they might work for or against you. For example, the best time to ask for additional staff might be right after a period of intense activity that prompted multiple customers to complain about poor service, when the experience is still fresh in everyone's mind. If you wait several months for the annual budgeting cycle, the emotional aspect of the experience will have faded and your request will look like just another cost increase.

Anticipating Objections

5 LEARNING OBJECTIVE

Explain why it is important to identify potential objections before you start writing persuasive messages

Even the most powerful persuasive messages can be expected to encounter some initial resistance. The best way to deal with audience resistance is to anticipate as many objections as you can and address them in your initial message before your audience can even bring them up. For instance, if you know that your proposal to switch to lower-cost materials will raise concerns about product quality and customer satisfaction, address these issues head-on in your message. If you wait until people raise the concern after reading your message, chances are they already will have gravitated toward a firm no before you have a chance to address their concerns. By addressing such issues right away, you also demonstrate a broad appreciation of the issue and imply confidence in your message.[11] This anticipation is particularly important in written messages, when you don't have the opportunity to detect and respond to objections on the spot.

Present both sides to an issue when you expect to encounter strong resistance.

If you expect a hostile audience, one biased against your plan from the beginning, present all sides of the story. As you cover each option, explain the pros and cons. You'll gain additional credibility if you present these options before presenting your recommendation or decision.[12]

To uncover audience objections, try some "What if?" scenarios. Poke holes in your own theories and ideas before your audience does. Then find solutions to the problems you've uncovered.

Also, recognize that people are more likely to support what they help create, so ask your audience members for their thoughts on the subject before you put your argument together. If appropriate, let your audience recommend some solutions. With enough thought and effort, you may even be able to turn problems into opportunities; for example, you may show how your proposal will be more economical in the long run, even though it may cost more now. Just be sure to be thorough, open, and objective about all the facts and alternatives.

Finally, keep in mind that compromise might be your best path to success. Rather than automatically countering audience objections or discounting alternative ideas, listen carefully, then engage your audience in discussion. Chances are you'll end up with a solution that is even better than your original.

To review the steps involved in developing persuasive messages, refer to "Checklist: Developing Persuasive Messages."

Common Examples of Persuasive Business Messages

Throughout your career, you'll have numerous opportunities to write persuasive messages within your organization: selling a supervisor on an idea for improving quality, suggesting more efficient operating procedures, eliciting cooperation from competing departments, winning employee support for a new benefits package, requesting money for new equipment or funding for a special project. Similarly, you may send a variety of persuasive messages to people outside the organization: soliciting investment funds, shaping public opinions, or requesting adjustments that go beyond a supplier's contractual obligations. In addition, many of the routine requests you studied in Chapter 8 can become persuasive messages if you want a nonroutine result or believe that you haven't received fair treatment. Most of these messages can be divided into persuasive requests for action, persuasive presentations of ideas, and persuasive claims and requests for adjustment.

Persuasive Requests for Action

When making a persuasive request for action, be sure to use the AIDA plan to frame your argument.

The bulk of your persuasive business messages will involve requests for action. In some cases, your request will be anticipated, so the direct approach is fine. In others, you'll need to intro-

CHECKLIST: Developing Persuasive Messages

A. Get your reader's attention.
- Open with an audience benefit, a stimulating question, a problem, or an unexpected statement.
- Discuss something your audience can agree with (establishing common ground).
- Show that you understand the audience's concerns.

B. Build your reader's interest.
- Expand and support your opening claim or promise.
- Emphasize the relevance of your message to your audience.

C. Increase your reader's desire.
- Make audience members want to change by explaining how the change will benefit them.
- Back up your claims with relevant evidence.

D. Motivate your reader to take action.
- Suggest the action you want readers to take.
- Stress the positive results of the action.
- Make the desired action clear and easy.

E. Balance emotional and logical appeals.
- Use emotional appeals to help the audience accept your message.
- Use logical appeals when presenting facts and evidence for complex ideas or recommendations.
- Avoid faulty logic.

F. Reinforce your position.
- Provide additional evidence of the benefits of your proposal and your own credibility in offering it.
- Use abstractions, metaphors, and other figures of speech to bring facts and figures to life.

G. Anticipate objections.
- Anticipate and answer potential objections.
- Present the pros and cons of all options if you anticipate a hostile reaction.

duce your intention indirectly, and the AIDA model is ideal for this purpose. Open with an attention-getting device and show readers that you know something about their concerns.

Use the interest and desire sections of your message to demonstrate that you have good reasons for making such a request and to cover what you know about the situation: the facts and figures, the benefits of helping, and any history or experience that will enhance your appeal. Your goals are (1) to gain credibility and (2) to make your readers believe that helping you will indeed help solve a significant problem. Once you've demonstrated that your message is relevant to your readers, you can close with a request for some specific action or decision (see Figure 10.4).

When requesting actions that are relatively minor (such as asking someone to attend a meeting in your absence), you can usually use a direct approach. However, when asking for a more significant action (such as asking upper management for a larger budget), use indirect persuasive techniques to convince your reader of the value of the action. Include all necessary information about the request and any facts and figures that will help convince your reader that the action or decision is in the company's best interest.

A direct approach is usually best for routine requests.

Persuasive Presentations of Ideas

Most internal persuasive messages focus on getting the audience to make a specific decision or take some specific action. However, you will encounter situations in which you simply want to change attitudes or beliefs about a particular topic, without asking the audience to decide or do anything—at least not yet. In complicated, multistep persuasive efforts, the goal of your first message might be nothing more than convincing your audience members to reexamine their opinions or assumption or to admit the possibility of new ways of thinking.

For instance, the Worldwide Web Consortium (a global association that defines many of the guidelines and technologies behind the World Wide Web) has launched a campaign called the Web Accessibility Initiative. Although the Consortium's ultimate goal is making websites more accessible to people with disabilities or age-related limitations, a key interim goal is simply making website developers more aware of the need. As part of this effort, the

Sometimes the objective of persuasive messages is simply to encourage people to consider a new idea.

DOCUMENT MAKEOVER

IMPROVE THIS E-MAIL MESSAGE

To practice correcting drafts of actual documents, visit your online course or the access-code-protected portion of the Companion Website. Click "Document Makeovers," then click Chapter 10. You will find an e-mail message that contains problems and errors relating to what you've learned in this chapter about writing persuasive messages. Use the "Final Draft" decision tool to create an improved version of this persuasive e-mail request for action. Check the message for its effectiveness at gaining attention, building interest, stimulating desire, motivating action, focusing on the primary goal, and dealing with resistance.

FIGURE 10.4 Persuasive Memo Using the AIDA Model to Request Action
Leslie Jorgensen believes the new Airbus A380 could help Qantas meet its growth needs while lowering its operating costs. Here she uses the AIDA model to solicit her boss's approval for a study of the plane's market potential. Note that because she also wants to provide some printed materials to support her argument, she opted for a printed memo rather than an e-mail message.

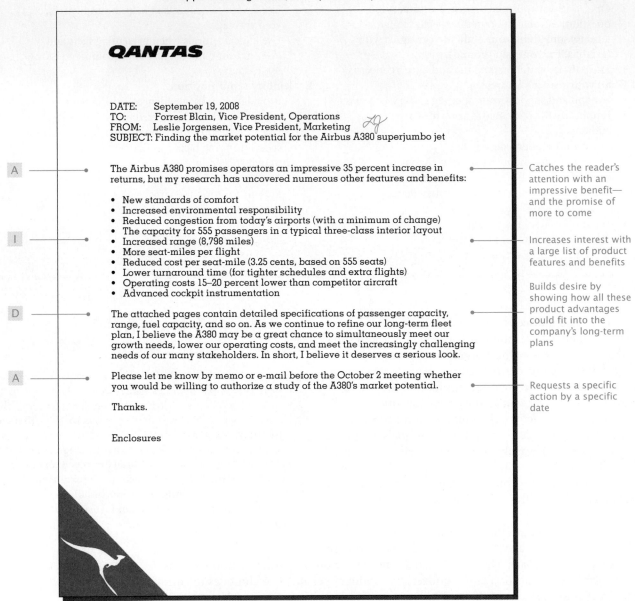

QANTAS

DATE: September 19, 2008
TO: Forrest Blain, Vice President, Operations
FROM: Leslie Jorgensen, Vice President, Marketing
SUBJECT: Finding the market potential for the Airbus A380 superjumbo jet

A

The Airbus A380 promises operators an impressive 35 percent increase in returns, but my research has uncovered numerous other features and benefits:

I

- New standards of comfort
- Increased environmental responsibility
- Reduced congestion from today's airports (with a minimum of change)
- The capacity for 555 passengers in a typical three-class interior layout
- Increased range (8,798 miles)
- More seat-miles per flight
- Reduced cost per seat-mile (3.25 cents, based on 555 seats)
- Lower turnaround time (for tighter schedules and extra flights)
- Operating costs 15–20 percent lower than competitor aircraft
- Advanced cockpit instrumentation

D

The attached pages contain detailed specifications of passenger capacity, range, fuel capacity, and so on. As we continue to refine our long-term fleet plan, I believe the A380 may be a great chance to simultaneously meet our growth needs, lower our operating costs, and meet the increasingly challenging needs of our many stakeholders. In short, I believe it deserves a serious look.

A

Please let me know by memo or e-mail before the October 2 meeting whether you would be willing to authorize a study of the A380's market potential.

Thanks.

Enclosures

Catches the reader's attention with an impressive benefit—and the promise of more to come

Increases interest with a large list of product features and benefits

Builds desire by showing how all these product advantages could fit into the company's long-term plans

Requests a specific action by a specific date

Consortium has developed a presentation that highlights the nature of the problems that many web visitors face.[13]

Persuasive Claims and Requests for Adjustments

Although persuasive claims and requests for adjustment are sometimes referred to as *complaint letters*, you don't write them merely to get a complaint off your chest. Your goal is to persuade someone to make an adjustment in your favor. You work toward this goal by demonstrating the difference between what you expected and what you actually received.

Most claim letters are routine messages and use the direct approach discussed in Chapter 8. However, both consumers and business professionals sometimes encounter situations in which they believe they haven't received a fair deal. For instance, you might have purchased a product but didn't use it immediately. When you finally do try to use it, you discover it is defective—but the warranty has already expired. You'll need to use persuasive communication to convince the seller that it should replace the product.

Because you've already paid for it, you obviously can't threaten to withhold payment. Instead, try to convey the essentially negative information in a way that will get positive results. Fortunately, most people in business are open to settling your claim fairly. It's to their advantage to maintain your goodwill and to resolve your problem quickly.

The key ingredients of a good persuasive claim are a complete and specific review of the facts and a confident and positive tone. Assume that the other person is not trying to cheat you and that you have the right to be satisfied with the transaction. Begin persuasive claims by stating the basic problem or reviewing what has been done about the problem so far. Include a statement that both you and your audience can agree with or that clarifies what you want to convince your audience about. Be as specific as possible about what you want to happen. Next, give your reader a good reason for granting your claim. Show how your audience is responsible for the problem, and appeal to your reader's sense of fair play, goodwill, or moral responsibility. Explain how you feel about the problem, but don't get carried away, don't complain too much, and don't make threats. People generally respond more favorably to requests that are both calm and reasonable.

DEVELOPING MARKETING AND SALES MESSAGES

Marketing and sales messages use the same basic techniques as other persuasive messages, with the added emphasis of encouraging someone to participate in a commercial transaction. Although the terms *marketing message* and *sales message* are often used interchangeably, they do represent separate but related efforts: Marketing messages usher potential buyers through the purchasing process without asking them to make an immediate decision; that's when sales messages take over. Marketing messages focus on such tasks as introducing new brands to the public, providing competitive comparison information, encouraging customers to visit websites for more information, and reminding buyers that a particular product or service is available. In contrast, a sales message makes a specific request for people to place an order for a particular product or service.

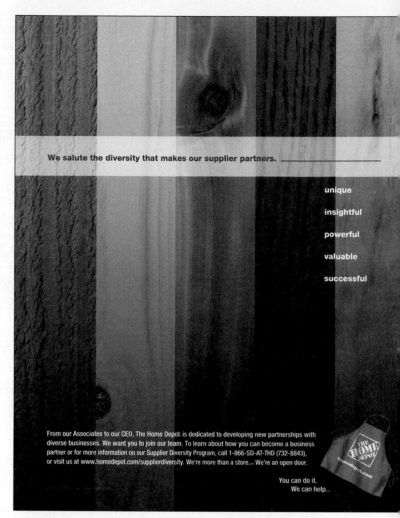

We salute the diversity that makes our supplier partners.

unique
insightful
powerful
valuable
successful

From our Associates to our CEO, The Home Depot is dedicated to developing new partnerships with diverse businesses. We want you to join our team. To learn about how you can become a business partner or for more information on our Supplier Diversity Program, call 1-866-SD-AT-THD (732-8843), or visit us at www.homedepot.com/supplierdiversity. We're more than a store.... We're an open door.

You can do it.
We can help....

In this magazine advertisement that promotes the idea of the company's commitment to an ethnically diverse supplier base, The Home Depot used the visual metaphor of diverse species of wood.

Strategies for Marketing and Sales Messages

Most marketing and sales messages, particularly in larger companies, are created and delivered by professionals with specific training in marketing, advertising, sales, or public relations. However, as a manager, you may be called on to review the work of these specialists or even to write such messages in smaller companies, so a good understanding of how these messages work will help you be a more effective manager. The basic strategies to consider include assessing customer needs; analyzing your competition; determining key selling points and benefits; anticipating purchase objections; applying the AIDA model; and maintaining high standards of ethics, legal compliance, and etiquette. Also, keep in mind that marketing and sales campaigns often include a series of messages in a coordinated effort that can last for weeks or months. In these campaigns, your message planning might encompass a website; syndicated blog posts; letters; brochures; personal sales presentations; and a mix of print, online, and broadcast media.

Assessing Audience Needs

Purchasing decisions often involve more than just the basic product or service.

As with every other business message, successful marketing and sales messages start with an understanding of audience needs. For some products and services, this assessment is a simple matter. For instance, customers compare only a few basic attributes when purchasing copy or printer paper, including weight, brightness, color, and finish. In contrast, they might consider dozens of features when shopping for real estate, cars, professional services, and other complex purchases.

In addition, customer needs often extend beyond the basic product or service. Clothes do far more than simply keep you warm. What you wear makes a statement about who you are, which social groups you want to be associated with (or not), and how you view your relationship with the people around you. In fact, a simple pair of shoes can meet multiple levels in Maslow's hierarchy of needs—every level except self-actualization, in fact.

Begin by assessing audience needs, interests, and emotional concerns—just as you would for any business message. Try to form a mental image of the typical buyer for the product you wish to sell. Ask yourself what audience members might want to know about this product. How can your product help them? Are they driven by bottom-line pricing, or is quality more important to them?

Note the advertisements you're exposed to every day. They often focus on just one or two attributes or issues, even if the product or service has many different facets to consider. The purpose of these narrow marketing messages is to grab your attention and then raise your interest level enough to encourage you to conduct further research.

Analyzing Your Competition

Most marketing and sales messages have to compete for the audience's attention.

Marketing and sales messages nearly always compete with messages from other companies trying to reach the same audience. When Chrysler plans a marketing campaign to introduce a new model to current customers, the company knows that its audience has also been exposed to messages from Ford, Honda, Volkswagen, and numerous other car companies. In crowded markets, writers sometimes have to search for words and phrases that other companies aren't already using. They might also want to avoid themes, writing styles, or creative approaches that are too similar to those of competitive messages.

6 LEARNING OBJECTIVE

Discuss an effective approach to identifying selling points and audience benefits

Determining Key Selling Points and Benefits

With some insight into audience needs and existing messages from the competition, you're ready to decide which benefits and features of your product or service to highlight. For all but the simplest products, you'll want to prioritize the items you plan to discuss. You'll also want to distinguish between the features of the product and the benefits that those features offer the customers. As Table 10.2 shows, **selling points** are the most attractive features of an idea or product, whereas **benefits** are the particular advantages that readers will realize from those features. Selling points focus on the product. Benefits focus on the user.

TABLE 10.2 Features Versus Benefits

PRODUCT FEATURE	CUSTOMER BENEFIT
Our easy financing plan includes no money down, no interest, and no payments for 24 months.	You can buy what you want right now, even if you have limited cash on hand.
Our marketing communication audit accurately measures the impact of your advertising and public relations efforts.	You can find out whether your message is reaching the target audience and whether you're spending your marketing budget in the best possible manner.
The spools in our fly fishing reels are machined from solid blocks of aircraft-grade aluminum.	Go fishing with confidence: These lightweight reels will stand up to the toughest conditions.

FIGURE 10.5 Explaining the Benefits of Product Features
On this webpage, Wachovia is careful to explain the customer benefits of its CAP Asset
Management Account.

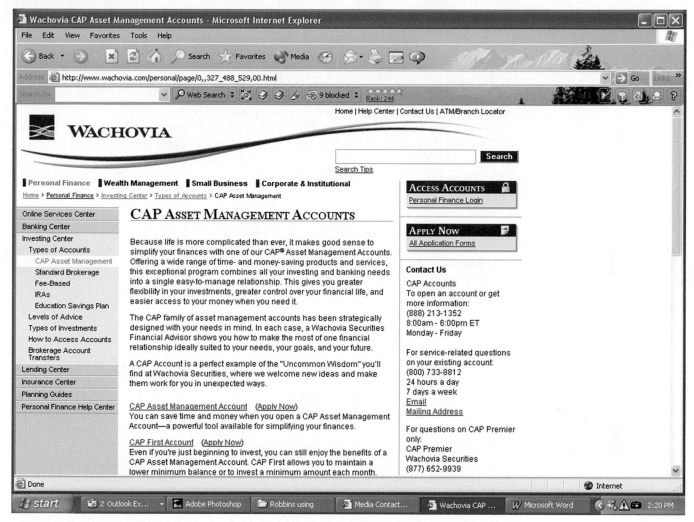

For example, ClubMom doesn't stress the online networking feature of its services; rather, it stresses the opportunity to connect with other moms who have similar concerns and interests—which is the benefit enabled by the networking feature. A common approach to communicating features and benefits is to show them in a list or a table, identifying each feature and then describing the benefits it offers (see Figure 10.5). Of course, for your message to be successful, your product's distinguishing benefit must correspond to your readers' primary needs or emotional concerns.

Anticipating Purchase Objections

As with persuasive business messages, marketing and sales messages often encounter objections; once again, the best way to handle them is to identify them up-front and try to address as many as you can in your message (or messages, as the case may be). However, with marketing and sales messages, you often don't get a second chance to explain yourself or to present your case. Your boss might feel an obligation to let you explain what you meant in the third paragraph of your persuasive proposal, but potential customers feel no such responsibility. If your website for fashion jewelry aimed at college-age consumers strikes visitors as too juvenile, for instance, they'll click to another site within seconds and probably never come back to yours.

Anticipating objections is crucial to effective marketing and sales messages.

Objections can range from high price to low quality to a lack of compatibility with existing products. Perceived risk is another common objection. Consumers might worry that a car won't be safe enough for a family, that a jacket will make them look unattractive, or that a hair salon will botch a haircut. Business buyers might worry about disrupting operations or failing to realize the financial returns on a purchase.

Price can be a particularly tricky issue in any message, whether audience members are consumers or business customers. Whether you highlight or downplay the price of your product, prepare your readers for it. Words such as *luxurious* and *economical* provide unmistakable clues about how your price compares with that of competitors. Such words help your readers accept your price when you finally state it.

If price is a major selling point, give it a position of prominence, such as in the headline or as the last item in a paragraph. If price is not a major selling point, you can handle it in several ways. You could leave the price out altogether or de-emphasize it by putting the figure in the middle of a paragraph that comes well after you've presented the benefits and selling points.

Emphasizes the rarity of the edition to signal value and thus prepare the reader for the big-ticket price that follows

Buries the actual price in the middle of a sentence and ties it in with another reminder of the exclusivity of the offer

> Only 100 prints of this exclusive, limited-edition lithograph will be created. On June 15, they will be made available to the general public, but you can reserve one now for only $350, the special advance reservation price. Simply rush the enclosed reservation card back today so that your order is in before the June 15 publication date.

The pros also use two other techniques for minimizing price. One is to break a quantity price into units. Instead of saying that a case of motor oil costs $24, you might say that each bottle costs $2. The other technique is to compare your product's price with the cost of some other product or activity: "The cost of owning your own exercise equipment is less than you'd pay for a health-club membership." Your aim is to make the cost seem as small and affordable as possible, thereby minimizing price as a possible objection.

If you've done your homework up front and assessed your audience thoroughly, you should be aware of most of these concerns. You might not be able to address every one of them in your message—if the product or service isn't ideal for the customer, your message can't fix that—but you will be prepared to do the best you can with the product or service you have to promote.

Applying the AIDA Model

Most marketing and sales messages are prepared according to the AIDA model or some variation of it. You begin with an attention-getting device, generate interest by describing some of the product or service's unique features, increase desire by highlighting the benefits that are most appealing to your audience, and close by suggesting the action you want the audience to take.

You can use a variety of attention-getting devices in marketing and sales messages.

Getting Attention You can use a wide range of techniques to attract your audience's attention:

- **Your product's strongest benefit.** "Carry a tune (or 2,000)" (for Apple iPod nano).[14]
- **A piece of genuine news.** "Take entertainment to a whole new place" (for Verizon's V Cast service, which lets people download a variety of entertainment services to their mobile phones).[15]
- **A point of common ground with the audience.** "An SUV adventurous enough to accommodate your spontaneity and the gear that comes with it."[16]
- **A personal appeal to the reader's emotions and values.** "The only thing worse than paying taxes is paying taxes when you don't have to."
- **The promise of insider information.** "You may be one of those people who dream of working and living in France and don't know how to go about simply doing it. This

guide tells how—from the inside out—others like yourself have managed to work within the French system."[17]

- **The promise of savings.** "Right now, you can get huge savings on a new camera phone."[18]
- **A sample or demonstration of the product.** "Here's your free sample of the new Romalite packing sheet."
- **A solution to a problem.** "This backpack's designed to endure all a kid's dropping and dragging."[19]

Of course, words aren't the only attention-getting device at your disposal. Strong, evocative images are a common attention-getter. With online messages, you have even more options, including audio, animation, and video.

Even more so than in persuasive business messages, it's important to carefully balance your emotional and logical appeals in marketing and sales messages. For example, when ClubMom promotes itself to mothers, it strikes a balance between emotional factors (such as "A few blogs a day keep the insanity away!") and logical factors (such as "Earn points by shopping with ClubMom partners and through the ClubMom Online Mall and Gift Card Store").[20] Figure 10.6 suggests the range of logical and emotional appeals that marketing messages can achieve, based on the product and the target audience.

Building Interest   Use the interest section of your message to build on the intrigue you created with your opening. This section should also offer support for whatever claims or promises you might have made in the opening. For instance, when Apple introduced a redesigned iPod nano, it started with the headline "Completely remastered," then continued with these support points:[21]

> A thinner design. Five stylish colors. A brighter display. Up to 24 hours of battery life. Just about the only thing that hasn't changed is the name. In 2GB, 4GB, and 8GB models starting at $149, iPod nano puts up to 2,000 songs in your pocket.

To build interest, expand on and support the promises in your attention-getting opening.

Itemizes the key improvements in the new iPod nano

Puts music capacity in a position of emphasis, since that—not price—is the major selling point the iPod nano

At this point in the message, Apple has substantiated the claim made in the headline and has whetted readers' appetites with some intriguing features and benefits.

Increasing Desire   To build desire for the product, continue to expand and explain what it offers, how it works, how customers can use it, and so on. On the iPod nano page, Apple continues with more details about the features summarized in the first paragraph of text, such as describing the size and appearance of the new design. Think carefully about the sequence of support points, and use plenty of subheadings and other devices to help people find the information they need quickly. Take advantage of whatever medium you are using to continue to offer additional information that will increase audience desire for the product and help you prepare for the action stage. For example, after reading this much about the iPod, some users might want to know more about the iTunes Music Store, whereas others will want to know about using iPods in their cars. Apple makes it easy to find the information each individual wants. This ability to provide flexible access to information is just one of the reasons the web is such a powerful medium for marketing and sales (see Figure 10.7)

Throughout the body of your message, remember to keep the focus on the audience, not on your company or your product. When you talk about product features, remember to stress the benefits and talk in terms that make sense to users. Listing the capacity of the iPod nano as 2,000 songs is a lot more meaningful for most readers than saying it has 8 gigabytes of memory. Action words give strength to any business message, but they are especially important in sales letters. Compare the following:

Add details and audience benefits to increase desire for the product or service.

INSTEAD OF THIS	WRITE THIS
The NuForm desk chair is designed to support your lower back and relieve pressure on your legs.	The NuForm desk chair supports your lower back and relieves pressure on your legs.

To keep readers interested, use strong, colorful language without overdoing it.

FIGURE 10.6 The Spectrum of Emotional and Logical Appeals

All marketing and sales messages strike a balance between logical and emotional appeals. Premier Building Systems, a maker of building materials, relies primarily on logical appeals. At the other extreme, ADiamondIsForever.com relies almost entirely on emotional appeals on its website. Gladiator GarageWork lies somewhere between these two, emphasizing both the logical and emotional advantages of its garage organizers.

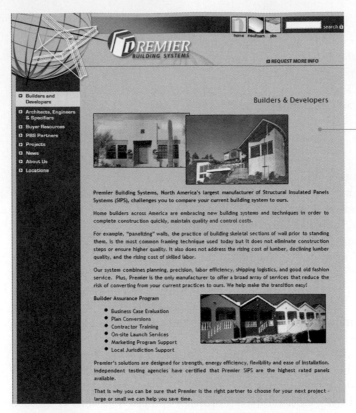

To help convince home builders to use its innovative panel system instead of traditional frame construction, Premier Building Systems focuses on logical factors such as cost, efficiency, and quality

Website photograph used with permission of Whirlpool Corporation

Gladiator Garage Works uses a combination of logical and emotional appeals by promising to make your garage" a place to work, entertain and show off to your friends and neighbors."

A Diamond Is Forever uses an appeal that is entirely emotional (for instance, it doesn't attempt to promote the investment value of a diamond)

FIGURE 10.7 Flexible Communication on the Web
Saturn's website offers a good example of the depth and breadth of information that interactive media can give customers to help them make informed decisions. By allowing the audience to interact via a variety of graphical presentations, Saturn lets shoppers explore at their own pace, finding answers to whatever questions they might have.

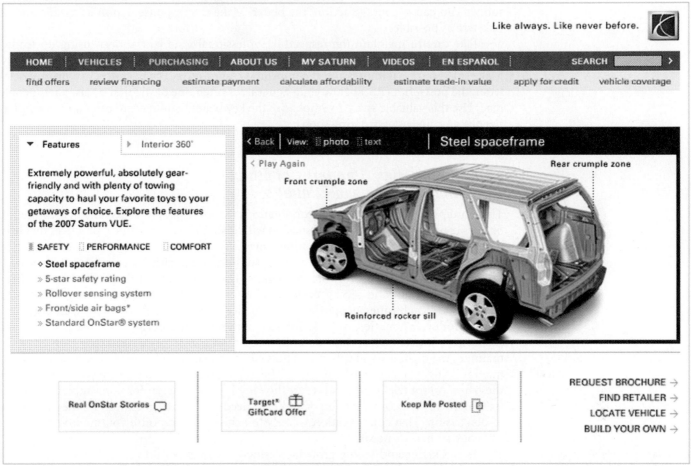

The second version says the same thing in fewer words and emphasizes what the chair does for the user ("supports") rather than the intentions of the design team ("is designed to support").

To keep readers interested, use colorful verbs and adjectives that convey a dynamic image. Be careful, however, not to overdo it: If you say "Your factory floors will sparkle like diamonds," your audience members will find it hard to believe, which may prevent them from believing the rest of your message.

To increase desire, as well as boost your credibility, provide support for your claims. You can't assume your audience members will believe what you say just because you've said it in writing. You'll have to give them proof. Support is especially important if your product is complicated, costs a lot, involves significant risk, or represents some unusual approach.

Creative marketers find many ways to provide support: testimonials from satisfied users, articles written by industry experts, competitive comparisons, product samples and free demonstrations, independent test results, and online movies that show a product in action. You can also highlight guarantees that demonstrate your faith in your product and your willingness to back it up.

Motivating Action After you have raised enough interest and built up the reader's desire for your offering, you're ready to ask your audience to take action. Whether you want

After you've generated sufficient interest and desire, you're ready to persuade readers to take the preferred action.

people to pick up the phone to place an order or visit your website to download a free demo version of your software, try to persuade them to do it right away. You might offer a discount for the first 1,000 people to order; put a deadline on the offer; or simply remind them that the sooner they order, the sooner they'll be able to enjoy the product's benefits. Even potential buyers who want the product can get distracted or forget to respond, so the sooner you can encourage action, the better. Make the response action as simple and as risk-free as possible.

Take care to maintain the respectful, professional tone you've been using up to this point. Don't resort to gimmicks and desperate-sounding pleas for the customer's business. Make sure your final impression is compelling and positive. For instance, in a printed sales letter, the postscript (P.S.) below your signature is often one of the first or last parts people read. Use this valuable space to emphasize the key benefit you have to offer and to emphasize the advantages of ordering soon.

Maintaining High Standards of Ethics, Legal Compliance, and Etiquette

The word *persuasion* has negative connotations for some people, especially in a marketing or sales context. They associate persuasion with dishonest and unethical practices that lead unsuspecting audiences into accepting unworthy ideas or buying unneeded products. However, effective businesspeople view persuasion as a positive force, aligning their own interests with what is best for their audiences. They influence audience members by providing information and aiding understanding, which allows audiences the freedom to choose.[22] Ethical businesspeople inform audiences of the benefits of an idea, an organization, a product, a donation, or an action so that these audiences can recognize just how well the idea, organization, product, donation, or action will satisfy a need they truly have. To maintain the highest standards of business ethics, make every attempt to persuade without manipulating. Choose words that won't be misinterpreted, and be sure you don't distort the truth. Adopt the "you" attitude by showing honest concern for your audience's needs and interests. Your consideration of audience needs is more than ethical; it's the proper use of persuasion. That consideration is likely to achieve the response you intend and to satisfy your audience's needs.

Marketing and sales messages are covered by a wide range of laws and regulations.

As marketing and selling grow increasingly complex, so do the legal ramifications of marketing and sales messages. In the United States, the Federal Trade Commission (FTC) has the authority to impose penalties (ranging from cease-and-desist orders to multimillion-dollar fines) against advertisers who violate federal standards for truthful advertising. Other federal agencies have authority over advertising in specific industries, such as transportation and financial services. Individual states have additional laws that apply. The legal aspects of promotional communication can be quite complex, from state to state and from country to country, and most companies require marketing and sales people to get clearance from company lawyers before sending messages. In any event, pay close attention to the following legal aspects of marketing and sales communication:[23]

7 LEARNING OBJECTIVE

Identify steps you can take to avoid ethical lapses in marketing and sales messages

- **Marketing and sales messages must be truthful and nondeceptive.** The FTC considers messages to be deceptive if they include statements that are likely to mislead reasonable customers and the statements are an important part of the purchasing decision. Failing to include important information is also considered deceptive. The FTC also looks at *implied claims*, those you don't explicitly make but that can be inferred from what you do or don't say.
- **You must back up your claims with evidence.** According to the FTC, offering a money-back guarantee or providing letters from satisfied customers is not enough; you must still be able to support your claims with objective evidence such as a survey or scientific study. If you claim that your food product lowers cholesterol, you must have scientific evidence to support that claim.
- **Marketing and sales messages are considered binding contracts in many states.** If you imply or make an offer and then can't fulfill your end of the bargain, you can be sued for breach of contract.

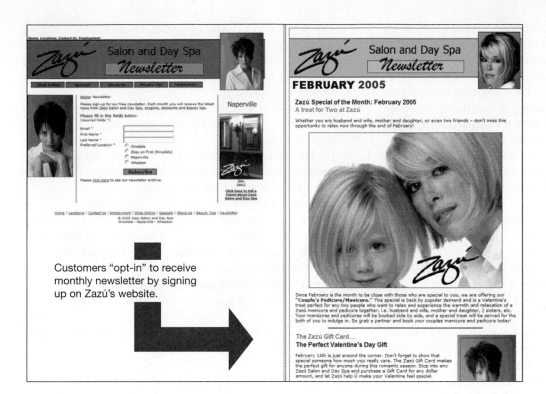

FIGURE 10.8 Opt-In E-Mail Newsletter
Zazú, a salon chain in Illinois, demonstrates the "you" attitude by sending its e-mail newsletter only to those clients who have specifically requested it.

Customers "opt-in" to receive monthly newsletter by signing up on Zazú's website.

- **In most cases, you can't use a person's name, photograph, or other identity without permission.** Doing so is considered an invasion of privacy. You can use images of people considered to be public figures as long as you don't unfairly imply that they endorse your message.

Maintaining high ethical standards is a key aspect of good communication etiquette.

Before you launch a marketing or sales campaign, make sure you're up to date on the latest regulations affecting spam (or *unsolicited bulk e-mail*, as it's officially known), customer privacy, and data security. New laws are likely to appear in all three areas in the next few years.

Meeting your ethical and legal obligations will go a long way toward maintaining good communication etiquette as well. However, you may still face etiquette decisions within ethical and legal boundaries. For instance, you can produce a marketing campaign that complies with all applicable laws and yet is still offensive or insulting to your audience. An audience-centered approach, involving respect for your readers and their values, should help you avoid any such etiquette missteps.

Communication technologies such as opt-in e-mail and blog syndication can help you be sensitive to audience needs.

Technology also gives communicators new ways to demonstrate sensitivity to user needs. One example is automated updates from blogs and websites, alerting customers to information in which they've expressed an interest. *Opt-in* e-mail newsletters are another technology that shows the "you" attitude at work. Unlike the unwelcome spam messages that litter e-mail inboxes these days, opt-in messages are sent only to those people who have specifically requested information (see Figure 10.8).

COMMUNICATION CHALLENGES AT CLUBMOM

You're the vice president of member services at ClubMom, reporting to CEO Michael Sanchez. In addition to developing new online services, a key

part of your job responsibility is crafting messages that describe the new services and persuade members to try them. Use what you've learned in this chapter and in your own experiences as a consumer (and as a parent, if applicable) to address these challenges.

Individual Challenge: You asked one of your staffers to write a benefit statement to communicate the advantages of the MomBlogs section of the ClubMom website, which offers more than three dozen blogs on a variety of parenting topics. She e-mails the following sentence: "We've worked hard to assemble a team of bloggers who share their knowledge, experience, and opinions on a wide variety of subjects, from pregnancy to schooling to religion." Write an e-mail in response, explaining why it's important to make marketing messages about the *customer*, not the *company*. Include a revised version that illustrates this vital aspect of the "you" attitude. You can learn more about the MomBlog feature at the ClubMom website, **www.clubmom.com**.

Team Challenge: A common challenge in marketing communication is distilling a long list of features to a single compelling message that can serve as the product's "headline." With your team, review this list of features and benefits of the MomNetwork service (extracted from various communications presented by ClubMom and its business partners). Brainstorm three one-sentence possibilities that could serve as the headline for a webpage promoting MomNetwork, then choose the most compelling of the three options. Don't assume that every feature or benefit in the list needs to be incorporated within your high-level message. You can learn more about the MomNetwork at the ClubMom website.

- The experiences of thousands of moms are now aggregated in a single place online.
- Connect with moms like you; search for moms by personal and family challenges, interests, age of kids, or location.
- Get and give support; find support and swap advice with other moms on a wide range of topics that matter most to you.
- Find the best of what moms have to say; discover thousands of helpful articles, know-how, and tips from ClubMom members and Mom Experts.
- Joining the MomNetwork is absolutely free.
- Setting up your own personal profile is fast and easy.
- Search for moms with similar interests, then send them private messages to establish online conversations.
- Use the My Network feature to collect the names of moms you've connected with online.
- Write as much or as little as you want to share in your personal profile.
- You have complete control over the privacy of your information.

SUMMARY OF LEARNING OBJECTIVES

1 **Apply the three-step writing process to persuasive messages.**   The three-step process is easily adapted to promotional messages. These messages require careful planning because such messages are often unexpected and at times unwelcome. To plan successfully, carefully clarify your purpose to make sure you focus on a single goal; clearly express your purpose to audience members so they are aware of what you would like them to feel, think, or do; and recognize that some audience decisions won't be made in a single step, and you'll need a series of persuasive messages to reach your ultimate objective. The information you need to gather involves a combination of emotional and logical elements, which you then blend together based on your knowledge of audience wants and needs. Most persuasive messages use an indirect approach to establish awareness and interest before asking the audience to take action, although the direct approach is often better for routine persuasive messages or when you're in a position of authority relative to the audience. The "you" attitude is critical in persuasive messages, and successful writers take care to adapt their appeals to the specific wants and needs of their audiences. They also work hard to establish credibility with their readers. The steps involved in completing persuasive

messages are essentially the same as for other message types, although even small errors can damage credibility, so persuasive communicators need to be doubly careful with presentation and proofreading.

2 **Identify seven ways to establish credibility in persuasive messages.**   The common ways to establish credibility include using simple language, supporting your message with factual evidence, naming your sources when you use information from others, demonstrating expertise (your own or others'), establishing common ground with the audience, being objective, and displaying good intentions.

3 **Describe the AIDA model for persuasive messages.** When using the AIDA model, you open your message by getting *attention* with a reader benefit, a problem, a stimulating question, a piece of news, or an unexpected statement. You build *interest* with facts, details, and additional reader benefits. You increase *desire* by providing more evidence and reader benefits and by anticipating and answering possible objections. You conclude by motivating a specific *action*, emphasizing the positive results of that action, and making it easy for the reader to respond.

4 **Distinguish between emotional and logical appeals and discuss how to balance them.** Emotional appeals call on human feelings, using arguments that are based on audience needs or sympathies. However, these appeals aren't effective by themselves. Logical appeals call on human reason (whether using analogy, induction, or deduction). If you're careful to avoid faulty logic, you can use logic together with emotion, thereby supplying rational support for an idea that readers have already embraced emotionally. In general, logic will be your strongest appeal, with only subtle emotion. However, when persuading someone to purchase a product, join a cause, or make a donation, you can heighten emotional appeals a bit.

5 **Explain why it is important to identify potential objections before you start writing persuasive messages.** If you don't identify objections and address them as you craft your messages, audiences who hold any objections are likely to gravitate toward a negative answer before you have the opportunity to ask them for a positive response. By addressing objections as you build your persuasive case, you can often resolve them before the audience has a chance to go on the defensive.

6 **Discuss an effective approach to identifying selling points and audience benefits.** Identifying selling points and audience benefits starts with deciding which benefits and features of your product or service to highlight, including prioritizing the items you want to discuss first. Also, be sure to distinguish between the features of the product, the *selling points*, and the benefits that those features offer the customers. If you focus too much on features, audiences may not grasp all the benefits that those features offer.

7 **Identify steps you can take to avoid ethical lapses in marketing and sales messages.** Effective and ethical persuasive communicators focus on aligning their interests with the interests of their audiences. They help audiences understand how their proposals will provide benefits to the audience, using language that is persuasive without being manipulative. They choose words that are less likely to be misinterpreted and take care not to distort the truth. Throughout, they maintain a "you" attitude with honest concern for the audience's needs and interests.

Test Your Knowledge

1. What are some questions to ask when gauging the audience's needs during the planning of a persuasive message?
2. What role do demographics and psychographics play in audience analysis during the planning of a persuasive message?
3. What are four of the ways you can build credibility with an audience when planning a persuasive message?
4. What is the AIDA plan, and how does it apply to persuasive messages?
5. How do emotional appeals differ from logical appeals?
6. What three types of reasoning can you use in logical appeals?
7. Why should you avoid a "hard sell" opening in persuasive messages?
8. What is likely to happen if you don't anticipate audience objections when crafting your messages?
9. How do benefits differ from features?
10. How does ethical behavior contribute to positive etiquette in persuasive messages?

Apply Your Knowledge

1. Why is it important to present both sides of an argument when writing a persuasive message to a potentially hostile audience?
2. How are persuasive messages different from routine messages?
3. When is it appropriate to use the direct organizational approach in persuasive messages?
4. What is likely to happen if your persuasive message starts immediately with a call to action? Why?

5. **Ethical Choices** Are emotional appeals ethical? Why or why not?

Practice Your Knowledge

Messages for Analysis

For Message 10.A and Message 10.B, read the following documents, then (1) analyze the strengths and weaknesses of each sentence and (2) revise each document so that it follows this chapter's guidelines.

Message 10.A: Writing Persuasive Claims and Requests for Adjustment

Dear TechStar Computing:

I'm writing to you because of my disappointment with my new multimedia PC display. The display part works all right, but the audio volume is also set too high and the volume knob doesn't turn it down. It's driving us crazy. The volume knob doesn't seem to be connected to anything but simply spins around. I can't believe you would put out a product like this without testing it first.

I depend on my computer to run my small business and want to know what you are going to do about it. This reminds me of every time I buy electronic equipment from what seems like any company. Something is always wrong. I thought quality was supposed to be important, but I guess not.

Anyway, I need this fixed right away. Please tell me what you want me to do.

Message 10.B: Writing Sales Letters

We know how awful dining hall food can be, and that's why we've developed the "Mealaweek Club." Once a week, we'll deliver food to your dormitory or apartment. Our meals taste great. We have pizza, buffalo wings, hamburgers and curly fries, veggie roll-ups, and more!

When you sign up for just six months, we will ask what day you want your delivery. We'll ask you to fill out your selection of meals. And the rest is up to us. At "Mealaweek," we deliver! And payment is easy. We accept MasterCard and Visa or a personal check. It will save money especially when compared with eating out.

Just fill out the enclosed card and indicate your method of payment. As soon as we approve your credit or check, we'll begin delivery. Tell all your friends about "Mealaweek." We're the best idea since sliced bread!

Message 10.C: Creating Podcasts

To access this message, visit www.businesscommunicationhea-dlinennews.com and click on Textbook Resources. Locate *Business Communication Today 9*, click on Chapter 10, then select page 318, Message 10.C. Download and listen to this podcast. Identify at least three ways in which the podcast could be more persuasive, then draft a brief e-mail message that you could send to the podcaster with your suggestions for improvement.

Exercises

For active links to all websites discussed in this chapter, visit this text's website at **www.prenhall.com/bovee**. Locate your book and click on its Companion Website link. Then select Chapter 10, and click on "Featured Websites." Locate the name of the page or the URL related to the material in the text. Please note that links to sites that become inactive after publication of the book will be removed from the Featured Websites section.

10.1 Teamwork With another student, analyze the persuasive e-mail message to Eleanor Tran at Host Marriott (Figure 10.3) by answering the following questions:
  a. What techniques are used to capture the reader's attention?
  b. Does the writer use a direct or indirect organizational approach? Why?
  c. Is the subject line effective? Why or why not?
  d. Does the writer use an emotional or a logical appeal? Why?
  e. What reader benefits are included?
  f. How does the writer establish credibility?
  g. What tools does the writer use to reinforce his position?

10.2 Composing Subject Lines Compose effective subject lines for the following persuasive messages:
  a. A recommendation sent by e-mail to your branch manager to install wireless networking throughout the facility. Your primary reason is that management has encouraged more teamwork, but teams often congregate in meeting rooms, the cafeteria, and other places that lack network access—without which they can't do much of the work they are expected to do.
  b. A letter to area residents soliciting customers for your new business, "Meals à la Car," a carryout dining service that delivers from most of the local restaurants. All local restaurant menus are on the Internet. Mom and Dad can dine on egg rolls and chow mein while the kids munch on pepperoni pizza.

  c. An e-mail message to the company president asking that employees be allowed to carry over their unused vacation days to the following year. Apparently, many employees canceled their fourth-quarter vacation plans to work on the installation of a new company computer system. Under their current contract, vacation days not used by December 31 can't be carried over to the following year.

10.3 Ethical Choices Your boss has asked you to post a message on the company's internal blog urging everyone in your department to donate money to the company's favorite charity, an organization that operates a special summer camp for physically challenged children. You wind up writing a lengthy posting packed with facts and heartwarming anecdotes about the camp and the children's experiences. When you must work that hard to persuade your audience to take an action such as donating money to a charity, aren't you being manipulative and unethical? Explain.

10.4 Focusing on Benefits Determine whether the following sentences focus on features or benefits; rewrite as necessary to focus all the sentences on benefits.
  a. All-Cook skillets are coated with a durable, patented nonstick surface.
  b. You can call anyone and talk as long as you like on Saturdays and Sundays with our new FamilyTalk wireless plan.
  c. With 8-millisecond response time, the Samsung LN-S4095D 40" LCD TV delivers fast video action that is both smooth and crisp.[24]

10.5 Internet Visit the Federal Trade Commission website and read the "Catch the Bandit in Your Mailbox" consumer warning at www.ftc.gov/bcp/conline/pubs/tmarkg/bandit.shtm. Select one or two marketing or sales letters you've recently received and see whether they contain any of the suspicious content mentioned in the FTC warning. What does the FTC suggest you do with any materials that don't sound legitimate?

Expand Your Knowledge

Exploring the Best of the Web

Influence an Official and Promote Your Cause
http://thomas.loc.gov
At the Thomas site compiled by the Library of Congress, you'll discover voluminous information about federal legislation, congressional members, and committee reports. You can also access committee homepages and numerous links to government agencies, current issues, and historical documents. You'll find all kinds of regulatory information, including laws and relevant issues that might affect you in the business world. Visit the site and stay informed. Maybe you'll want to convince a government official to

support a business-related issue that affects you. Explore the data at the Thomas site, and find an issue you can use to practice your skills at writing a persuasive message.

1. What key ideas would you include in an e-mail message to persuade your congressional representative to support an issue important to you?

2. In a letter to a senator or member of Congress, what information would you include to convince the reader to vote for an issue related to small business?

3. When sending a message to someone who daily receives hundreds of written appeals, what attention-getting techniques can you use? How can you get support for a cause that concerns you as a businessperson?

Surfing Your Way to Career Success

Bovée and Thill's Business Communication Resources offers links to hundreds of online resources that can help you with this course, your other college courses, and your career. Visit www.buscommresources.com, then click on "Business Communication Web Directory." The "Special Types" section offers links to websites covering crisis management, organizational communication, public and media relations, and advertising and promotion. Identify three websites from this section that could be useful in your business career. For each site, write a two-sentence summary of what the site offers and how it could help you launch and build your career.

Learn Interactively
Interactive Study Guide

Visit www.prenhall.com/bovee, then locate your book and click on its "Companion Website" link. Select Chapter 10 to take advantage of the interactive "Chapter Quiz" to test your knowledge of chapter concepts. Receive instant feedback on whether you need additional studying. Also, visit the "Study Hall," where you'll find an abundance of valuable resources that will help you succeed in this course.

Peak Performance Grammar and Mechanics

If your instructor has required the use of "Peak Performance Grammar and Mechanics," either in your online course or on CD, you can continue to improve your skill with commas, semicolons, and colons by using the "Peak Performance Grammar and Mechanics" module. Click "Punctuation," and then click "Punctuation I." Take the Pretest to determine whether you have any weak areas. Then review those areas in the Refresher Course. Take the Follow-Up Test to check your grasp of these elements. For an extra challenge or advanced practice, take the Advanced Test. Finally, for additional reinforcement in commas, visit the Companion Website, click on any chapter, then click on "Improve Your Grammar, Mechanics, and Usage."

CASES

Applying the Three-Step Writing Process to Cases
Apply each step to the following cases, as assigned by your instructor.

Plan

Analyze the Situation
Identify both your general purpose and your specific purpose. Clarify exactly what you want your audience to think, feel, or believe after receiving your message. Profile your primary audience, including their backgrounds, differences, similarities, and likely reactions to your message.

Gather Information
Identify the information your audience will need to receive, as well as other information you may need in order to craft an effective message.

Select the Right Medium
Make sure your medium is both acceptable to the audience and appropriate for the message.

Organize the Information
Choose a direct or indirect approach based on the audience and the message; most persuasive messages employ an indirect approach (often following the AIDA model). Identify your main idea, limit your scope, then outline necessary support points and other evidence.

1

Write

Adapt to Your Audience
Show sensitivity to audience needs with a "you" attitude, politeness, positive emphasis, and bias-free language. Understand how much credibility you already have—and how much you may need to establish with any particular audience. Project your company's image by maintaining an appropriate style and tone.

Compose the Message
Draft your message using clear but powerful words, effective sentences, and coherent paragraphs. Support your claims with objective evidence; balance emotional and logical arguments.

2

Complete

Revise the Message
Evaluate content and review readability, then edit and rewrite for conciseness and clarity.

Produce the Message
Use effective design elements and suitable layout for a clean, professional appearance.

Proofread the Message
Review for errors in layout, spelling, and mechanics.

Distribute the Message
Deliver your message using the chosen medium; make sure all documents and all relevant files are distributed successfully.

3

PERSUASIVE BUSINESS MESSAGES

Blogging SKILLS **Portfolio BUILDER**

1. That's the point: E-mail encouraging your boss to blog You've been trying for months to convince your boss, Will Florence, to start blogging. You've told him that top executives in many industries now use blogging as a way to connect with customers and other stakeholders without going through the filters and barriers of formal corporate communications. He was just about convinced—until he read the blog by Bob Lutz, the co-chair and design chief of General Motors.

"Look at this!" he calls from his office. "Bob Lutz is one of the most respected executives in the world, and all these people are criticizing him on his own blog. Sure, a lot of the responses are positive, but quite a few are openly hostile, disagreeing with GM strategy, criticizing the products, criticizing the subjects he chooses for his blog—you name it. If blogging is all about open-ing yourself up to criticism from every bystander with a keyboard, no way am I going to start a blog."

Your task: Write Florence an e-mail (w_florence@sprenco.com) persuading him that the freewheeling nature of blog communication is its key advantage, not a disadvantage at all. While they may not always agree with what he has to say, automotive enthusiasts and car buyers respect Lutz for communicating in his own words—and for giving them the opportunity to respond. For background information, read some of the postings from Lutz and other GM executives at http://fastlane.gmblogs.com.[25]

E-Mail SKILLS

2. Give a little to get a lot: Suggesting free wireless at Starbucks Like many students at the University of Wisconsin–Madison, you like to escape from your cramped apartment to work on school

projects at local coffee shops. With your wireless-equipped laptop, you hunt for places that offer free wireless so you can access course websites, do research, and occasionally see how Badger athletic teams are doing. But there's a problem: At the Starbucks right around the corner, you have to pay for wireless access through the service offered by T-Mobile. Several of the locally owned coffeehouses offer free wireless, but the closest one is a mile from your apartment. That's a long walk in a Wisconsin winter.

Your task: Write a persuasive message to Starbucks suggesting that the company drop its agreement with T-Mobile and offer free wireless instead. Try to convince the firm that free wireless will attract enough additional coffee-buying customers to offset the loss of revenue from wireless—and help Starbucks overcome the "big corporation" image that prompts some coffee drinkers to patronize locally owned establishments instead. While you don't have the data to prove that the cost of offering free wireless would be more than offset by increased coffee sales, at least make a convincing argument that Starbucks should consider making the change. You'll post your message to the Starbucks website, www.starbucks.com, which has a limit of 2,600 characters for such messages.[26]

E-Mail SKILLS

3. Travel turnaround: Memo convincing Travelfest boss to expand client services You are a successful agent with Travelfest, Inc., a full-service travel-management firm. Located in Austin, Texas, Travelfest has four offices and more than 50 employees. Headquarters are downtown, in the lobby of a 35-story office tower. The other three offices are located in major shopping centers in upscale suburbs. The company's business is made up of about 70 percent business travel and 30 percent leisure travel. However, much of the leisure sales also comes from corporate customers, so business travelers are clearly your key audiences.

Your boss, Gary Hoover, has been working night and day to make up for declining revenues brought about by the loss of airline commissions. He has tried everything, from direct-mail campaigns to discount coupons to drawings for cruises and weekend getaways. Still, revenues remain flat.

You've been doing some research and analysis of your office's existing customer profiles. You find that many of your customers are middle- to high-income sophisticated travelers, that business travel is bouncing back (with an eye to cheaper fares and less-costly accommodations), and that executives often make their own travel arrangements (now that many companies are cutting the cost of maintaining their own travel departments). Your research has triggered some ideas that you believe could substantially increase your revenue from existing customers.

You envision turning your headquarters office into a travel resource for corporate customers. First, you would like to provide as much information as you can on the most popular business destinations—both inside and outside the country. You could sell video and audio courses in Spanish, French, German, Japanese, and other languages. And you'd like to introduce a line of travel products, including luggage, maps, travel guides, and electronics—all aimed at the business traveler. You're even thinking about a special area with videos and other educational materials on various cultures and business practices around the world.

You realize your ideas won't generate a lot of direct profit. However, you believe they will get business customers in the door, where you and other agents can sell them travel-management services. If Hoover is willing to try your idea and it works, he may want to do something similar in the suburb offices, perhaps with an emphasis on leisure travel.

Your task: Write an e-mail proposal to Gary Hoover. Outline your ideas and suggest a meeting to discuss them further and determine what market research he'd like you to perform.[27]

E-Mail SKILLS

4. Life's little hassles: E-mail requesting satisfaction It's hard to go through life without becoming annoyed at the way some things work. You have undoubtedly been dissatisfied with a product you've bought, a service you've received, or an action of some elected official or government agency.

Your task: Write a three- to five-paragraph persuasive e-mail request expressing your dissatisfaction in a particular case. Specify the action you want the reader to take.

5. Nap time: Memo requesting space for power nappers at Phidias & Associates It's been one of those days. You were dragging by 10 A.M., ready to slump over into your computer monitor at Phidias & Associates architectural firm in San Francisco. How are you supposed to be creatively inspired when you can barely get your eyes to focus and your head feels as if it's full of cotton? No, you weren't out partying last night; you've just been working long, late hours on a rush job for one of the firm's biggest clients. If only you could stretch out for a little catnap, you'd be good as new in 15 minutes.

Groggily, you recall an item you tore out of the *Wall Street Journal* a year ago—a paragraph or two in the "Work Week" column, all about companies adding "nap rooms" to help employees recharge during the day. You know that on weekends, a quick nap helps you get a lot more done during the day; and didn't they teach you in school that Thomas Edison kept a cot in his office and got his best ideas when he was napping? And the article quotes an expert, William A. Anthony, author of *The Art of Napping* and professor of rehabilitation counseling at Boston University. He says most people aren't sleep deprived, they're "nap ready."

There are plenty of other precedents and pioneers out there in the business world. At *Macworld* magazine, the human resources director, Shelly Ginenthal, says their two-person nap room was installed all the way back in 1986 and usually has a waiting line. At Yarde Metals in Bristol, Connecticut, President Bruce Yarde says, "A quick little nap can rejuvenate you." He's fighting employee stress with a 25-person nap room. You do some quick research for more evidence and turn up a report from the prestigious National Institutes of Health, indicating that power napping not only helps prevent burnout but also enhances information processing and learning.

Your task: After you've had a good night's sleep, write a memo to Jonas T. Phidias, persuading the senior partner that the distinguished offices of Phidias & Associates could benefit from the addition of a corporate nap room and an organizational embrace of power napping as a way to be more competitive. On a separate page, include a short note to your instructor justifying your organizational approach (direct or indirect) and your selection of delivery medium (e-mail or interoffice mail).[28]

IM SKILLS

6. Helping children: Instant message holiday fund drive at IBM At IBM, you're one of the coordinators for the annual Employee Charitable Contributions Campaign. Since 1978, the company has helped employees contribute to more than 2,000 health and human service agencies. These groups may offer child care; treat substance abuse; provide health services; or fight illiteracy, homelessness, and hunger. Some offer disaster relief or care for the elderly. All deserve support. They're carefully screened by IBM, one of the largest corporate contributors of cash, equipment, and people to nonprofit organizations and educational institutions, both in the United States and around the world. As your literature states, the program "has engaged our employees more fully in the important mission of corporate citizenship."

During the winter holidays, you target agencies that cater to the needs of displaced families, women, and children. It's not difficult to raise enthusiasm. The prospect of helping children enjoy the holidays—children who otherwise might have nothing—usually awakens the spirit of your most distracted workers. But some of them wait until the last minute and then forget.

They have until December 16 to come forth with cash contributions. To make it in time for holiday deliveries, they can also bring in toys, food, and blankets through Tuesday, December 20. They shouldn't have any trouble finding the collection bins; they're everywhere, marked with bright red banners. But some will want to call you with questions or (hopefully) to make credit card contributions: 800-658-3899, ext. 3342.

Your task: It's December 14. Write a 75- to 100-word instant message encouraging last-minute gifts.[29]

E-Mail SKILLS

7. Tangled web: E-mail to PurelySoftware regarding an online order duplication Last week you ordered new design software for your boss, Martin Soderburgh, at ArtAlive, the small art consulting business where you work. As he requested, you used his Visa card to order Adobe InDesign and Adobe Photoshop from an Internet vendor, PurelySoftware.com.

When you didn't receive the usual e-mail order confirmation, you called the company's toll-free number. The operator said the company's website was having problems, and he took a second order over the phone: $649.00 for Adobe InDesign, $564.00 for Adobe Photoshop, including tax and shipping. Four days later, ArtAlive received two shipments of the software, and your boss's credit card was charged $1,213.00 twice, for a total of $2,426.00.

Your task: Technically, you authorized both orders. But you understood during the phone call that the first order was canceled, although you have no written proof. Send a persuasive e-mail to customerservice@purelysoftware.com, requesting (1) an immediate credit to your boss's Visa account and (2) a postage-paid return label for the duplicate order.[30]

E-Mail SKILLS

8. Helping out: Message to Whole Foods Market managers Whole Foods Market has grown into a nationwide chain by catering to consumer desires for healthier foods and environmentally sensitive household products. For instance, meats come from animals that were never fed antibiotics, and the cheese is from cows said to be raised on small farms and treated humanely.

Along with selling these products, the company makes a commitment "to the neighborhood and larger community that we serve and in which we live." Whole Foods not only donates 5 percent of after-tax profits to not-for-profit organizations but also financially supports employees who volunteer their time for community service projects. Many Whole Foods stores donate goods and supplies to soup kitchens in their local communities. Company executives want to encourage this type of activity, which reflects the "Whole Foods, Whole People, Whole Planet" corporate motto.

You are the manager of the Whole Foods Market on Ponce de Leon Avenue in Atlanta, Georgia. You've been very successful with a program you developed for donating surplus food to local food banks. You've been asked by top executives to help other Whole Foods stores coordinate this effort into a chainwide food donation program, "Whole Foods for Life." Ideally, by streamlining the process chainwide, the company would be able to increase the number of people it helps and get more of its employees involved.

You don't have a great deal of extra money for the program, so the emphasis has to be on using resources already available to the stores. One idea is to use trucks from suburban stores to make the program "mobile." Another idea is to join forces with a retailing chain to give food and clothing to individuals. You've decided that the key will be to solicit input from the other stores so that they'll feel more involved in the final outcome as the larger food-donation program takes shape.

Your task: Write a persuasive e-mail message to all managers at Whole Foods Market, explaining the new program and requesting that they help by pooling ideas they've gleaned from their local experience. Even if they don't have food-donation programs currently in place, you want to hear ideas from them and their employees for this charitable project. With their help, you'll choose the best ideas to develop the new "Whole Foods For Life" program.[31]

E-Mail SKILLS

9. No more driving: Telecommuting to Bachman, Trinity, and Smith Sitting in your Dallas office at the accounting firm of Bachman, Trinity, and Smith, clacking away on your computer, it seems as though you could be doing this work from your home. You haven't spoken to any co-workers in more than two hours. As long as you complete your work on time, does your location matter?

As an entry-level accountant, you've participated in on-location audits at major companies for nearly a year now. If your bosses trust you to work while staying at a hotel, why not let you work from home, where you already have an office with computer, phone, and fax machine? You'd love to regain those two hours you lose commuting to and from work every day.

Your task: To support this idea, visit the website of the International Telework Association and Council website at www. telcoa.org (be sure to check out the "Resources" page). You'll find statistics and other support for a memo persuading your boss, senior partner Marjorie Bachman, to grant you a six-month trial as a telecommuter.[32]

10. Always urgent: Memo pleading case for hosting a Red Cross blood drive This morning as you drove to your job as food services manager at the Pechanga Casino Entertainment Center in Temecula, California, you were concerned to hear on the radio that the local Red Cross chapter put out a call for blood because national supplies have fallen dangerously low. During highly publicized disasters, people are emotional and eager to help out by donating blood. But in calmer times, only 5 percent of eligible donors think of giving blood. You're one of those few.

Not many people realize that donated blood lasts for only 72 hours. Consequently, the mainstay of emergency blood supplies must be replenished in an ongoing effort. No one is more skilled, dedicated, or efficient in handling blood than the American Red Cross, which is responsible for half the nation's supply of blood and blood products.

Donated blood helps victims of accidents and disease, as well as surgery patients. Just yesterday you were reading about a girl named Melissa, who was diagnosed with multiple congenital heart defects and underwent her first open-heart surgery at one week old. Now five years old, she's used well over 50 units of donated blood, and she wouldn't be alive without them. In a thank-you letter, her mother lauded the many strangers who had "given a piece of themselves" to save her precious daughter—and countless others. You also learned that a donor's pint of blood can benefit up to four other people.

Today, you're going to do more than just roll up your own sleeve. You know the local Red Cross chapter takes its Blood Mobile to corporations, restaurants, beauty salons—anyplace willing to host public blood drives. What if you could convince the board of directors to support a blood drive at the casino? The slot machines and gaming tables are usually full, hundreds of employees are on hand, and people who've never visited before might come down to donate blood. The positive publicity certainly couldn't hurt Pechanga's community image. With materials from the Red Cross, you're confident you can organize Pechanga's hosting effort and handle the promotion. (Last year you headed the casino's successful Toys for Tots drive.)

To give blood, one must be healthy, be at least 17 years old (with no upper age limit), and weigh at least 110 pounds. Donors can give every 56 days. You'll be urging Pechanga donors to eat well, drink water, and be rested before the Blood Mobile arrives.

The local Red Cross chapter's mission statement says, in part, that the Red Cross is "a humanitarian organization led by volunteers and guided by the Fundamental Principles of the International Red Cross Movement" which will "prevent and alleviate human suffering wherever it may be found." All assistance is given free of charge, made possible by "contributions of people's time, money, and skills"—and in the case of you and your co-workers, a piece of yourselves.

Your task: Write a memo persuading the Pechanga board of directors to host a public Red Cross blood drive. You can learn more about what's involved in hosting a blood drive at www.givelife.org (click on "Sponsor a Drive"). Ask the board to provide bottled water, orange juice, and snacks for donors. You'll organize food service workers to handle the distribution, but you'll need the board's approval to let your team volunteer during work hours. Use a combination of logical and emotional appeals.[33]

E-Mail SKILLS   ## Portfolio BUILDER

11. Message to an angel: Introducing your company to an investor Your new company, WorldConnect Language Services, started well and is going strong. However, to expand beyond your Memphis, Tennessee, home market, you need a one-time infusion of cash to open branch offices in other cities around the Southeast. At the Entrepreneur's Lunch Forum you attended yesterday, you learned about several *angels*, as they are called in the investment community—private individuals who invest money in small companies in exchange for a share of ownership. One such angel, Melinda Sparks, told the audience that she is looking for investment opportunities outside of high technology, where angels often invest their money. She also indicated that she looks for entrepreneurs who know their industries and markets well, who are passionate about the value they bring to the marketplace, who are committed to growing their businesses, and who have a solid plan for how they will spend an investor's money. Fortunately, you meet all of her criteria.

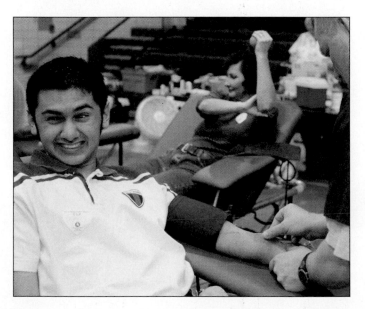

Your task: Draft an e-mail message to Sparks, introducing yourself and your business and asking for a meeting at which you would present your business plan in more detail. Explain that your Memphis office was booked to capacity within two months of opening, thanks to the growing number of international business professionals looking for translators and interpreters. You've researched the entire Southwest region and identified at least 10 other cities that could support a language services office such as yours. Making up whatever other information you need, draft a four-paragraph message following the AIDA plan, ending with a request for a meeting within the next four weeks.

Blogging SKILLS   Portfolio BUILDER

12. Web accessibility advocacy: It's not "World Wide" if it doesn't include everybody Like most companies today, your firm makes extensive use of the web for both internal and external communication. However, after reading about the Web Accessibility Initiative (WAI), you've become concerned that your company's various websites haven't been designed to accommodate people with disabilities or age-related limitations. Fortunately, as one of the company's top managers, you have a perfect forum for letting everyone in the company know how important accessible web design is—your internal blog is read by the vast majority of employees and managers throughout the company.

Your task: Visit the WAI website at www.w3.org/WAI and read the two articles "Introduction to Web Accessibility" (look in the "Introducing Accessibility" section) and "Developing a Web Accessibility Business Case for Your Organization: Overview" in the "Managing Accessibility" section. Using the information you learn in these articles, write a post for your blog that emphasizes how important it is for your company's websites to become more accessible. You don't have direct authority over the company's web developers, so it would be inappropriate for you to request them to take any specific action. Your goal is simply to raise awareness and encourage everyone to consider the needs of the company's online audiences. Don't worry about the technical aspects of web accessibility; focus instead on the benefits of improving accessibility.

E-Mail SKILLS

13. Too good to be true: E-mail to Paging South requesting adjustment Paging South offered its pager services for a mere $5 a month. You purchased an inexpensive pager and signed a contract for two years. After you thought your pager phone number was up and running for two weeks, you heard from co-workers and clients that they repeatedly get a busy signal when dialing your pager number. You call Paging South, and they resolve the problem—but doing so takes an additional week. You don't want to be charged for the time the pager wasn't in service. After discussing the situation with the local manager, she asks you to contact Judy Hinkley at the company's regional business office.

Your task: Send an e-mail message to Hinkley at Judy@pagingsouth.com and request an adjustment on your account. Request credit or partial credit for one month of service. Remember to write a summary of events in chronological order, supplying exact dates for maximum effectiveness.

14. Lock legends: Letter requesting refund and damages from Brookstone As a professional photographer, you travel the world for business, leaving from your home base in Williamstown, Massachusetts. Last month it was a trip to Australia, and you thought you'd finally found a way around the "no-locks-on-checked-baggage" rules.

After the World Trade Center attacks of September 11, 2001, the U.S. Travel Security Administration (TSA) forbade airline passengers to check locked luggage. TSA inspectors want easy access so that they can open and check bags for security purposes. But because you carry so much expensive equipment, including numerous camera bags, you've been nervous about the safety of your belongings—not to mention the loss of privacy.

So you were relieved when you read Joe Sharkey's "On the Road" column in the *New York Times* just before your trip. The columnist extolled a newly announced TSA program allowing airline travelers to lock their luggage *if they use special TSA-approved locks*, certified by a company called Travel Sentry. You immediately went to the Brookstone store in Albany after reading its web advertisement for "The luggage locks security won't cut off. Our Easycheck™ locks are certified by Travel Sentry™ and feature a secure system accepted and recognized by the Transportation Security Administration (TSA). Airport security personnel can now inspect and re-lock your bags quickly and easily." You bought eight locks, at $20 for each set of two.

When you left the Albany airport, TSA inspectors assured you that they had a master key for these locks, just as Sharkey's column had promised they would. But when you got to Melbourne after changing planes in Chicago and Los Angeles, you were stunned to discover the condition of your luggage. One bag was missing the new lock entirely; another was missing the lock and had a rip all along the seam—perhaps from an irritated inspector? Inside a third bag you found its broken Easycheck lock, with a terse TSA inspection notice reminding you that locked baggage is not allowed. On the return trip you tried again, using three of your remaining locks on camera bags. They arrived with no locks and no inspection notices.

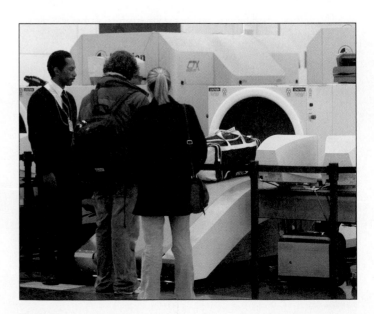

You've now called the airports in Chicago and Cleveland, where TSA inspectors told you they'd "never heard of the program." Brookstone will replace the broken lock, but the woman on the phone wasn't sure about the ones that went missing entirely, because you have nothing left to bring into the store except your receipt.

Your task: After 10 minutes of listening to music while on hold for the TSA, you've abandoned the idea of a phone complaint to the government agency. You're going to write a letter to Brookstone (120 Washington Ave., Albany, NY 12203) requesting damages for the ripped luggage (a 24-inch Expandable Ballistic Suitor, $320) and a refund for all eight locks ($80). Six of them were ruined or missing and your last two are essentially useless.[34]

MARKETING AND SALES MESSAGES

Portfolio BUILDER

15. Your new Kentucky home: Letter promoting the Bluegrass State Like all states, Kentucky works hard to attract businesses that are considering expanding into the state or relocating entirely from another state. The Kentucky Cabinet for Economic Development is responsible for reaching out to these companies and overseeing the many incentive programs the state offers to both new and established businesses.

Your task: As the communication director of the Kentucky Cabinet for Economic Development, you play the lead role in reaching out to companies that want to expand or relocate to Kentucky. Visit www.thinkkentucky.com and download the *Think Kentucky* brochure (look under the "Why Kentucky" link). Identify the eight benefits the state uses to promote Kentucky as a great place to locate a business. Summarize these eight reasons in a form letter that will be sent to business executives throughout the country. Be sure to introduce yourself and your purpose in the letter, and close with a compelling call to action (have them reach you by telephone at 800-626-2930 or by e-mail at econdev@ky.gov). As you plan your letter, try to imagine yourself as the CEO of a company and consider what a complex choice it would be to move to another state.

E-Mail SKILLS

16. Time to lose: Promoting the Six Week Solution at Curves The Curves franchise has grown quickly over the past several years by catering to women who may not feel at home in traditional gyms. As the owner of a successful Curves health club, you know that information and motivation are often the keys to healthy living in general and weight management in particular. You're excited about a new program the company offers called the Curves Six Week Solution, a series of classes that help women make better nutrition choices.

Your task: The corporate website offers a nice description of the Curves Six Week Solution, but it's over 600 words long, and you'd like a shorter version to e-mail to current and prospective clients. Visit that page on the Curves's website, www.curves.com/weight_loss, and summarize the description. Aim for no more than 300 words.

17. Give me liberty: Letter persuading customers to remain loyal to Colbar Art For many people in the United States, the Statue of Liberty is something of a tourist cliché, so much a part of New York City's tourist hype that it's taken for granted. But for many immigrants, the first sight of Liberty as they enter the city brings tears along with hopes for a new life. Ovidiu Colea knows the feeling. He immigrated to the United States in the early 1980s after a difficult past that included five long years in a Romanian hard-labor camp for trying to flee a Communist regime.

Colea worked two years as a cab driver to save enough money to start Colbar Art, a company that produces up to 80,000 hand-crafted replicas of the Liberty statue each year. He now helps other immigrants get a start in their new country by hiring them to design and produce Liberty models. Colea pays a royalty to the Liberty–Ellis Island Foundation for using Liberty's image. In fact, during the first year of operation, that royalty amounted to $250,000.

Painstaking labor produces the acrylic and bonded marble statues with a hand-painted patina, and most of that work is done by the very immigrants lady Liberty welcomes to New York. Colea insists on keeping production in the United States. Although labor costs are cheaper outside the country, he refuses to produce the statues in countries "where there is no liberty or no Statue of Liberty." By keeping jobs in the United States, he's doing his share to keep the American Dream alive.

But the meticulous labor also costs precious production time. With recent high demand for the replicas, the company has fallen behind on orders. To increase production to 120,000 statues per year, the company is leasing more space and training new employees. Meanwhile, the production deficits may continue for several months.

Your task: You work for Colbar Art as assistant manager, and Colea has asked you to write a persuasive form letter to all your customers, explaining the current delays and requesting patience. Be sure to explain the steps the company is taking to solve these delays, and describe the quality and creativity that go into the replicas. You can quote Bradford Hill (owner of the Liberty Island gift shop), who says Colbar Art's models represent 65 percent of his sales. Make a convincing argument for your customers to remain loyal to Colbar Art.[35]

Portfolio
BUILDER

18. Try it; you just might like it: Convincing consumers to sample beefalo You know enough about human nature to know that people tend to resist new ideas when it comes to food. In your job as public communications director for American Beefalo International, this knowledge presents a professional challenge as you try to convince people to give beefalo a try. The beefalo is a cross between bison (American buffalo) and beef cattle, and even though these animals are primarily cattle (genetically speaking), many consumers are reluctant to give up their familiar beef for something most have never tried.

But here's the good news: Many people are looking for healthier foods, and according to government tests, beefalo is lower in cholesterol, saturated fat, total fat, and calories. The comparison table below was published on your organization's website.

Your task: Write a small flier to be displayed in food stores that sell beefalo cuts. The page size will be 8-1/2 inches tall by 3-3/4 inches wide, so format your word processing page accordingly. Allow room for a photograph, and don't try to cram too much text on the page. Emphasize beefalo as a healthy alternative for people who want to continue enjoying meat in their diets.[36]

	PROTEIN (g)	CHOLESTEROL (mg)	SATURATED FATS (g)	TOTAL FAT (g)	CALORIES	PERCENTAGE OF CALORIES FROM FAT
Fish	22.9	47	0.104	0.81	105	6.9
Chicken	31.0	85	1.0	3.5	165	19.5
Pork	29.3	86	3.4	9.7	212	41
Beef	25.9	88	8.5	21.5	305	63.6
Beefalo	30.7	58	2.7	6.3	188	30.3

IM
SKILLS

19. Instant promotion: Text message from Hilton Hotels to frequent guests Hilton Hotels now uses a short messaging service (SMS) to send instant text promotions to customers who've signed up as "HHonors" members. But you work in marketing, and that means you're often struggling to condense elaborate travel packages into 65 enticing words (system maximum).

For example, today's promotion offers "A Golfer's Dream Come True: 'I just played a round of golf by the pyramids!'" For $575 per person per day (double room), valid through January 15, 2008, travelers can stay in the Hilton Pyramids Golf Resort in Cairo, Egypt, for seven nights/eight days, including breakfast, service charge, and tax. They'll be met at the airport, given transportation to the resort, plus two rounds of golf per person at Dreamland Golf course and two rounds of golf per person at Soleimaneia Pyramids Golf & Country Club course. That's 88 words so far.

But you also need to convey that the Dreamland course wraps like a serpent around the Hilton resort. Its lush greens and lakes, designed by Karl Litten, contrast sharply with the golden desert, culminating in a stunning view of the great Pyramids of Giza, one of the seven wonders of the world. The Soleimaneia course features the "biggest floodlit driving course in Egypt." The travel package provides free transportation to this nearby course.

Rates, of course, are subject to availability and other restrictions may apply. But interested travelers should mention code G7 Pyramids Golf Special when they call Hilton Reservations Worldwide. They can also e-mail RM_PYRAMIDS_GOLF@hilton.com,

or call the Cairo hotel directly at 20 2 8402402. That is, if you can entice them in 65 words.

Your task: Write the persuasive instant message.[37]

20. Selling your idea: Sales letter promoting a product of your own invention You never intended to become an inventor, but you saw a way to make something work more easily, so you set to work. You developed a model, found a way to mass-produce it, and set up a small manufacturing studio in your home. You know that other people are going to benefit from your invention. Now all you need is to reach that market.

Your task: Imagine a useful product that you have invented—perhaps something related to a hobby or sporting activity. List the benefits and features of your imaginary product. Then write a sales letter for it, using what you've learned in this chapter and making up details as you need them.

Podcasting
SKILLS

21. Listen up: Podcast promoting a podcast station Podcasting, the technique of recording individual sound files that people download from the Internet to listen to on their computers or music players, is quickly redefining the concept of radio. A growing crowd of musicians, essayists, journalists, and others with compelling content use podcasting to reach audiences they can't get to through traditional broadcast radio. The good news is that anyone with a microphone and a computer can record podcasts. That's also the bad news, at least from your perspective as a new podcaster: With so many podcasters now on the Internet, potential listeners have thousands and thousands of audio files to select from.

Your new podcast, School2Biz, offers advice to business students making the transition from college to career. You provide information on everything from preparing résumés to interviewing to finding one's place in the business world and building a successful career. As you expand your audience, you'd eventually like to turn School2Biz into a profitable operation (perhaps by selling advertising time during your podcasts). For now, you're simply offering free advice.

Your task: You've chosen The Podcast Bunker (www. podcastbunker. com) as the first website on which to promote School2Biz. The site also lets podcasters promote their feeds with brief text listings, such as this description of Pet Talk Radio: "A weekly lifestyle show for people with more than a passing interest in pets. Hosted by Brian Pickering & Kaye Browne with Australia's favourite vet Dr. Harry Cooper & animal trainer Steve Austin."

Option A: Write a 50-word description of your new podcast, making up any information you need to describe School2Biz. Be sure to mention who you are and why the information you present is worth listening to. Option B: If your instructor indicates, script and record a brief podcast (no more than three minutes long) that describes and promotes School2Biz.[38]

■ **Web Writing**   ■ **Portfolio**
■ **SKILLS**   ■ **BUILDER**

22. Don't forget print: Using the web to promote Time Inc.'s magazine advertising After a shaky start as the technology matured and advertisers tried to figure out this new medium, online advertising has finally become a significant force in both consumer and business marketing. Companies in a wide variety of industries are shifting some of the advertising budgets from traditional media such as television and magazines to the increasing selection of advertising possibilities online—and more than a few companies now advertise almost exclusively online. That's fine for companies that sell advertising time and space for websites and blogs, but your job involves selling advertising in those print magazines that are worried about losing market share to online publishers.

Online advertising has two major advantages that you can't really compete with: interactivity and the ability to precisely target individual audience members. On the other hand, you have several advantages going for you, including the ability to produce high-color photography, the physical presence of print (such as when a magazine sits on a table in a doctor's waiting room), portability, guaranteed circulation numbers, and close reader relationships that go back years or decades in many cases.

Your task: You work as an advertising sales specialist for the Time Inc. division of Time Warner, which publishes more than 150 magazines around the world. Write a brief persuasive message about the benefits of magazine advertising; the statement will be posted on the individual websites of Time Inc.'s numerous magazines, so you can't narrow in on any single publication. Also, Time

Inc. coordinates its print publications with an extensive online presence (including thousands of paid online advertisements), so you can't bash online advertising, either.[39]

■ **E-Mail**   ■ **Portfolio**
■ **SKILLS**   ■ **BUILDER**

23. Insure.com: E-mail promoting a better way to buy insurance The great thing about Insure.com is that no one is obligated to buy a thing, which makes your job in the company's marketing department easier. Free of charge, consumers can log on to your website, ask for dozens of insurance quotes, then go off and buy elsewhere. They can look at instant price-comparison quotes from more than 200 insurers, covering every kind of insurance from term life and medical to private passenger auto insurance. All rates are guaranteed up-to-the-day accurate against a $500 reward. And so far the online service has received positive press from *Nation's Business*, *Kiplinger's Personal Finance*, *Good Housekeeping*, *The Los Angeles Times*, *Money*, *U.S. News & World Report*, and *Forbes*.

Insure.com generates revenues primarily from the receipt of commissions and fees paid by insurers based on the volume of business produced. Customers can purchase insurance from the company of their choice via the Insure.com website or they can call a toll-free number to speak to one of the company's representatives. The reps are paid salaries versus commissions and do not directly benefit by promoting one insurance company's product over another.

And all of this is free. Too bad more people don't know about your services.

Your task: It's your job to lure more insurance customers to Insure.com. You've decided to use direct e-mail marketing (using a list of consumers who have inquired about rates in the past but never committed to purchase anything). Write an e-mail sales message promoting the benefits of Insure.com's services. Be sure your message is suited to an e-mail format, with an appropriate subject heading.[40]

■ **Portfolio**
■ **BUILDER**

24. Outsourcing: Letter from Kelly Services offering solutions In 1946, with his dynamic vision and pioneering spirit, William Russell Kelly started a new company to meet the office and clerical needs of Detroit-area businesses. Kelly temporary employees with skills in calculating, inventory, typing, and copying were soon in great demand. During the 1960s, the Kelly Girl became a nationwide icon, synonymous with high-quality temporary employees. The company changed its name to Kelly Services, Inc., in 1966, reflecting the increasing diversity of its services, customers, and employees.

Today, Kelly Services is a global Fortune 500 company that offers staffing solutions that include temporary services, staff leasing, outsourcing, vendor on-site and full-time placement. Kelly provides employees who have a wide range of skills across many disciplines including office services, accounting, engineering, information technology, law, science, marketing, light industrial, education, health care, and home care.

Workforce needs, in terms of quantity and skills mix, fluctuate greatly. At the same time, employees have adaptable skills and are far more mobile. The result is that more employers and employees alike want flexible staffing arrangements, and temporary staffing is often the best solution.

Companies use Kelly Services to strategically balance workload and workforce during peaks and valleys of demand, to handle special projects, and to evaluate employees prior to making a full-time hiring decision. This dramatic change in business has spurred the rapid growth of the contingent employment industry.

In turn, many individuals are choosing the flexibility of personal career management, increasing options of where, when, and how to work. It is now the desire of many employees to fit their work into their lifestyle, rather than fitting their lifestyle into their work. Therefore, more and more workers are becoming receptive to being a contract, temporary, or consulting employee.

This flexibility offers advantages to both the company and the employee. Both have the opportunity to evaluate one another prior to making a long-term commitment. Kelly Services earns a fee when its employees are hired permanently, but employers find that it's a small price to pay for such valuable preview time, which saves everyone the cost and pain of a bad hiring decision.

Kelly has received many supplier awards for providing outstanding and cost-efficient staffing services, including Daimler-Chrysler's Gold Award, Ford Motor Company's Q1 Preferred Quality Award, Intel Corporation's Supplier Continuous Quality Improvement (SCQI) Award, and DuPont Legal's Challenge Award.

A job as a marketing manager with Kelly holds challenge and promise. With 2,500 offices in 26 countries, Kelly provides its customers nearly 700,000 employees annually, generating revenue of $4.3 billion in 2003. The company provides staffing solutions to more than 90 percent of the Fortune 500 companies.

As companies increasingly face new competitive pressures to provide better service and quality at lower prices, many are turning to outsourcing suppliers to deliver complete operational management of specific functions or support departments, allowing the company the necessary time to focus on its core competencies. One solution is to choose a single supplier such as the Kelly Management Services (KMS) division to deliver "full service" outsourcing.

KMS combines management experience, people process improvements, technology enhancements, and industry expertise to optimize customer operations and reduce cost. KMS understands the unique challenges companies are facing in today's increasingly fast-paced business world and can provide customers with services across multiple functional offerings including call center operations, warehousing, distribution and light assembly, back office and administrative functions, and mail and reprographic services. The result is a department staffed by employees that can fluctuate as a company's needs change.

KMS customers who have implemented one service often add others when they see KMS-managed employees performing at high levels and producing substantial cost savings and operational efficiencies. By partnering with an outsourcing supplier such as KMS, companies will experience greater value and cost savings than with in-house operations.

Your task: Write a sales letter to companies similar to Daimler-Chrysler, Ford, Intel, and DuPont explaining what Kelly has to offer. For current information, visit the Kelly website at **www.kellyservices.com**.[41]

Portfolio BUILDER

25. Greener cleaners: Letter promoting environmentally sound Hangers franchise When you told everyone you aspired to work for an environmentally responsible business, you didn't imagine you'd end up in the dry-cleaning business. But now that you are director of franchise development for Hangers Cleaners, you go home every night with a "clean conscience" (your favorite new pun).

Micell Technologies first invented the revolutionary clean technology used by Hangers Cleaners and then in 2001 sold all licensing, all intellectual property, and all interest in Hangers Cleaners to Cool Clean Technologies, which now manufactures the "CO2OL Clean" dry-cleaning machine that your franchise relies on. This breakthrough in dry-cleaning technology is the first in nearly 50 years—made by Micell co-founders Joseph DeSimone, James McClain, and Timothy Romack. Their new cleaning process uses liquid carbon dioxide (CO_2) and specially developed detergents to clean clothes. The process requires no heat and no further need for the toxic perchloroethylene (perc) or petroleum traditionally used in dry cleaning.

Hangers franchise owners don't have to deal with regulatory paperwork, zoning restrictions, or expensive insurance and taxes for hazardous waste disposal. And unlike petroleum-based solvents, the CO_2 used in the "CO2OL Clean" machine is noncombustible. It's the same substance that carbonates beverages, and it's captured from the waste stream of industries that produce it as a by-product. Moreover, 98 percent of the CO_2 used in a Hangers outlet is recycled and used again, which helps keep prices competitive. The "CO2OL Clean" machine received accolades from the Environmental Protection Agency and was recently rated the best dry-cleaning alternative by a leading consumer products testing group.

You've already sold franchises in 60 locations, from Wilmington, North Carolina, to San Diego, California. Customers love the fact that their clothes don't carry toxic fumes after cleaning, and employees are happy to be working in a safe and cool environment. The process is actually gentler on clothes (no strong solvents or heat), reducing fading and shrinking and helping them last longer. You aren't dry cleaners; you are "garment care specialists."

And beyond the environmental boons, you simply love the design of Hangers stores. When Micell originally established the chain, it hired dry-cleaning experts and architects alike to come up with a sleek, modern, high-end retail "look" that features a cool, clean, light-filled interior and distinctive signage out front.

It's more akin to a Starbucks than the overheated, toxic-smelling storefront most customers associate with dry cleaning. This high-end look is making it easier to establish Hangers as a national brand, attracting investors and franchisees rapidly as word spreads about the new "greener cleaner."

Your task: Develop a sales letter that can be mailed in response to preliminary inquiries from potential franchise owners. You'll include brochures covering franchise agreements and "CO2OL Clean" specifics, so focus on introducing and promoting the unique benefits of Hangers Cleaners. Your contact information is Hangers Cleaners, 3505 County Road 42 West, Burnsville, MN 55306-3803; phone 952-882-5000; toll-free 866-262-9274.[42]

PART 4

Supporting Messages with Quality Information

CHAPTER 11

Finding, Evaluating, and Processing Information

LEARNING OBJECTIVES

After studying this chapter, you will be able to

1 Describe an effective process for conducting business research

2 Define primary and secondary research and explain when you use each method

3 Name nine criteria for evaluating the credibility of an information source

4 Explain the complementary nature of search engines, web directories, and databases

5 Provide five guidelines for conducting an effective online search

6 Identify four new tools that can make your research more effective and more efficient

7 Outline an effective process for planning and conducting information interviews

8 Explain the differences between drafting a summary, drawing a conclusion, and developing a recommendation

COMMUNICATION CLOSE-UP AT TESCO

www.tesco.com

Most consumers enjoy the benefits of stiff price competition among their local grocery stores, but the competition is anything but enjoyable for grocery retailers. In the United States, the average grocery store's after-tax profit margin hovers around 1 percent. With so little room for error, grocers need to constantly stay on top of consumer behavior to make sure they offer the right mix of products at the right prices.

Tesco, the leading grocery retailer in the United Kingdom, is not only surviving but thriving in this tough industry. Under the leadership of Richard Brasher, the company's top marketing executive in the United Kingdom, Tesco devotes considerable effort to acquiring and processing information about its customers, information that is used in a variety of documents to drive both strategic and tactical decisions.

For example, when demographic research indicated a growing number of immigrants from Poland, the store reached out to Polish-speaking consumers to learn more about their wants and needs. After a successful experiment on a small scale, Tesco decided to expand its Polish foods selection to as many as 100 other stores. In another in-

stance, the marketing team couldn't figure out why flowers and wine had become such hot sellers during a particular week at the beginning of summer that didn't coincide with any regular holidays. Analysis of sales data revealed that families were buying these items as gifts for their children's teachers at the end of the school year, so the company

British retail giant Tesco relies on extensive audience research to plan and craft its consumer messages.

responded by making sure both items were stocked in plentiful supply during that week.

Tesco is now busy applying its information-driven approach to the competitive U.S. market. After studying the market for two decades, the company decided 2007 was the time to move in. Research will continue to play a key role. As the company's website explains, "It's simple—we listen and respond, providing customers with what they tell us they want."[1]

SUPPORTING YOUR MESSAGES WITH SOLID RESEARCH

Make sure your business messages are supported with solid research.

Whether you're planning a simple blog posting or an entire business plan, follow Tesco's lead (profiled in the chapter-opening Communication Close-Up) and make sure your reporting, analysis, and recommendations are supported with solid research. Throughout your academic and business careers, you may be called upon to research everything from other companies and business trends to new technologies and tax laws. Research can be a challenge, but you can maximize your success if you follow productive research procedures:

1 LEARNING OBJECTIVE

Describe an effective process for conducting business research

1. **Plan your research.** A solid plan yields better results in less time.
2. **Locate the data and information you need.** The research plan tells you *what* to look for, so your next step is to figure out *where* these data and information are and *how* to access them.
3. **Process the data and information you located.** The data and information you locate probably won't be in a form you can use immediately and will require some analysis and processing.
4. **Apply your findings.** To apply your research findings, you can summarize information for someone else's benefit, draw conclusions based on what you've learned, or develop recommendations.
5. **Manage information efficiently.** Many companies today are trying to maximize the return on the time and money they invest in business research by collecting and sharing research results in a variety of computer-based systems.

Following a five-step research process will help you gather better information in less time.

Figure 11.1 lays out the steps and substeps in the research process; you'll learn about all of these tasks in the following sections. In most cases you'll perform tasks in order, but be aware that conducting research sometimes requires branching off or looping back as new discoveries lead you to additional questions that require further research, and so on.

PLANNING YOUR RESEARCH

You've learned to resist the temptation to dive into a new writing project without thoughtful planning; now apply that same level of discipline to research. With so much information online these days, it's tempting just to punch some keywords into a search engine and then dig through the results looking for something, anything, that looks promising. However,

FIGURE 11.1 The Research Process
By following a methodical research process, you can save time and money while uncovering better information.

1 Plan	2 Locate data and information	3 Process data and information	4 Apply your findings	5 Manage information
• Familiarize yourself with the subject; develop problem statement • Identify information gaps • Prioritize research needs • Maintain research ethics and etiquette	• Evaluate sources • Collect secondary information at the library, online, or elsewhere • Collect primary information through surveys and interviews	• Analyze numerical information • Quote, paraphrase, or summarize textual information	• Summarize findings • Draw conclusions • Make recommendations	• Make research results available to others via your company's knowledge management system

such a lack of planning can limit both your effectiveness and your efficiency, and you can't afford either mistake in today's competitive business environment.

Jumping online and researching without a plan can be ineffective for several reasons: Your favorite search engine might not index the websites that have the information you need, the engine might use different terms to identify the information you're looking for, the information might not be online, or the information might not even exist. Poor planning also limits your efficiency; and because you'll rarely have enough time to research as thoroughly as you'd like, you can't afford to waste any of it. If you don't frame the research challenge carefully before you start looking, chances are you'll discover something along the way that forces you to rethink the questions you're trying to answer or the approach you're taking. (Such discoveries can happen even when you are careful, but planning minimizes the chances.) Worse yet, you might move into the writing phase with inadequate information and waste additional time trying to construct a compelling message with insufficient support.

Researching without a plan wastes time and usually produces unsatisfactory results.

The good news is that you can minimize or avoid all these problems with a few well-considered planning steps: Familiarize yourself with the subject so that you can frame insightful questions, identify the most critical gaps in your information, and then prioritize your research needs. However, before launching any research project, take a moment or two to consider the ethics and etiquette of your approach.

Maintaining Ethics and Etiquette in Your Research

Your research tactics can affect both the people from whom you gather information and the people who use your results. To avoid ethical lapses, keep the following points in mind:

Take precautions to avoid ethical lapses in your research.

- **Don't force a specific outcome by skewing your research.** If you set out to prove or disprove a particular point, you're more likely to find information that supports your position and gloss over information that doesn't. Go in with an open mind and be willing to accept whatever you find.
- **Respect the privacy of your research participants.** Privacy is a contentious issue today. Businesses believe they have a right to protect their confidential information from competitors, and consumers believe they have a right to protect their personal information from businesses. For example, observing people without their consent, misleading them about the purposes of your research, or misleading them about the ways you plan to use the information they give you are all ethical lapses.[2]

  Privacy is one the hottest issues in the research field today.

- **Document sources and give appropriate credit.** Whether you are using published documents, personal interviews, or company records, citing your sources not only is fair to the people who created and provided the information but also helps your audience members confirm your information or explore it in more detail if they so choose.
- **Respect the intellectual property and digital rights of your sources.** *Intellectual property* refers to the ownership of unique ideas that have commercial value in the marketplace.[3] For example, your research might turn up a great new way to sell services online, but that doesn't mean you're free to implement that process. It might be protected by one of the many patents that have been granted in recent years for business process models.
- **Don't extract more from your sources than they actually provide.** In other words, don't succumb to the temptation to put words in a source's mouth. For instance, if an industry expert says that a sales increase is possible, don't quote him or her as saying that a sales increase is probable.
- **Don't misrepresent who you are or what you intend to do with the research results.** One prominent example of misrepresentation in recent years is known as *pretexting*, which is essentially lying about who you are in order to gain access to information that you couldn't get otherwise. Doing so is illegal for obtaining financial records but not for obtaining telephone records, at least not currently.[4]

In addition to ethics, research etiquette deserves careful attention, too. For example, respect the time of anyone who agrees to be interviewed or to be a research participant, and maintain courtesy throughout the interview or research process.

Familiarizing Yourself with the Subject

Familiarizing yourself with new subject areas before you start your research can save significant amounts of time.

Sometimes the toughest step in a research project is simply figuring out where to start, particularly if you've been handed a broad or vague task, such as "investigate ways we can grow this business" or "find out if Nintendo is a threat in this market." Careful planning will help you avoid missteps caused by starting out too broadly or too narrowly or simply looking in the wrong direction. Give yourself some unstructured time at the beginning of the project to explore the general subject area, perhaps by reading industry publications, visiting competitors' websites, and interviewing experts within your organization. A quick online search can also be helpful at this point to identify the terminology people use, key organizations and experts, and other potential sources of information. Scan the contents and indexes of books on the subject. As you explore, keep a bibliographical list of the helpful resources you find, as well as a list of potentially significant phrases, terms, and keywords that appear repeatedly. Some of new online search tools can be quite helpful in this regard; see "Taking Advantage of Innovative Research Technologies" on page 343.

The problem statement defines the purpose of your research and guides your investigation.

Now use what you have learned so far to clarify your project. Develop a **problem statement** that defines the problem or purpose of your research—the decision you need to make or the conclusion you need to reach at the end of the process, even if it's a simple one. Phrase the statement as a question if that helps, such as "How can we improve customer satisfaction?" or "Does Nintendo's new system pose a competitive threat to us?" If someone assigned you the research project, you can take this question back and ask whether answering this specific question will meet his or her expectations.

Identifying Information Gaps

Information gap analysis helps focus your research on the most critical questions.

Your problem statement frames the purpose of your research, but it usually doesn't tell you what specific information you need to find. **Information gap analysis** is an effective technique for focusing your research by identifying the information you need to acquire. It's a fairly simple process of identifying what you know already, determining what you need to know, and subtracting to identify the gap. Moreover, by focusing your effort, this type of analysis helps you make the best use of your limited research time (and money, if you're paying for research). The five columns in Table 11.1 represent the steps in gap analysis: (1) identify the decision or conclusion to be reached, (2) identify any subquestions that would help you address that ultimate decision or conclusion, (3) identify the information you need in order to answer those subquestions, (4) identify any information you already have, and (5) "subtract" column 4 from column 3 to assess your *information gap.*

Assume you work for the owner of Antique & Collectible Autos (www.acautos.com) in Buffalo, New York, a small company that sells replica parts for classic hot rods and sports cars as well as complete cars, built to order. Your boss wants to know which would be the easier way to increase revenues: (a) try to sell more parts to hobbyists who want to assemble their own cars, or (b) try to sell more complete cars. Following the example in Table 11.1, the conclusion you want to reach is in column 1. This is a complicated question with no immediately obvious answer, so you simplify the task by breaking it down to two subquestions (column 2): "How easy would it be to sell more parts?" and "How easy would it be to sell more cars?"

By comparing what you need to know with what you already know, you can quickly identify the most important research questions.

Next, identify the information that would help you answer each of these two subquestions. For instance, you would need several pieces of information to know how easy it would be to sell more parts; these are listed in column 3. Column 4 then lists the information you already have that relates to those answers. For example, regarding the total number of new customers who might want parts, you know how many people attend car shows and subscribe to car magazines, but this information doesn't give you a complete answer, so you list the information gap in column 5. This analysis takes some time, to be sure, but it can save time in the long run by making sure you focus on the most important research priorities.

Prioritizing Research Needs

In most cases, you need to prioritize your information needs because you won't have the time or money to answer every question you might have. Moreover, if you'll be interview-

TABLE 11.1 Information Gap Analysis

(1) TARGET CONCLUSION	(2) SUBQUESTIONS	(3) INFORMATION NEEDED	(4) INFORMATION AVAILABLE	(5) INFORMATION GAP
Would it be easier to sell more parts or more completed cars?	How easy would it be to sell more parts?	The number of existing customers who might want to buy more parts.	We know what each customer has purchased.	We don't know what other parts they might need.
		The total number of new customers who might want parts.	We know how many people attend the car builder shows every year. We've rented magazine mailing lists, so we know how many subscribe to enthusiast magazines.	We don't know how many people build cars but don't attend the shows or subscribe to magazines.
		The number of other companies trying to sell parts to this group.	We think we've identified all the major national suppliers.	What about local or regional companies?
	How easy would it be to sell more cars?	The number of existing customers who want to buy another car.	It doesn't seem likely that people will buy more than one.	We need to verify this assumption.

ing or surveying people to gather information, you'll need to limit the number of questions you ask so that you don't consume more time than people are willing to give. One simple way to prioritize is to divide your questions into "need to know" and "nice to know," then toss out all the "nice to know" questions. If you started with a technique such as information gap analysis, you will have a clear idea of the information you truly need to collect.

You usually won't have enough time or money to answer every question that comes to mind, so setting priorities is a must.

You may not have enough time even to answer all the "need to know" items. Scan your list of information gaps to decide which are (a) the most important to answer or (b) the least risky *not* to answer. In the example in Table 11.1, you might conclude that few people who have purchased a completed car would want another one. To save time, you remove this item from your list. You might also identify information gaps where your existing information, while incomplete, is safe enough to move ahead with. Naturally, experience and judgment are important when identifying these priorities, so call on experienced colleagues if necessary.

LOCATING DATA AND INFORMATION

A good plan and careful prioritization tell you *what* you need to know and *why* you need to know it; the next step is to identify *where* that information might exist and *how* to locate it. Start by seeing if anyone has already done the research for you. If you have a question about an industry, a company, a market, a new technology, or a financial topic, chances are fairly high that somebody else has already researched the topic. Research materials previously created for another purpose are considered **secondary research**. Secondary sources include magazines, newspapers, public websites, blogs, books, and other reports. Don't let the name fool you, though; you want to start with secondary research because it can save considerable time and money for many projects (although you may have to pay to see someone else's results). In contrast, **primary research** is new research

2 LEARNING OBJECTIVE

Define primary and secondary research and explain when you use each method

Primary research contains information that you gather specifically for a new research project; secondary research contains information that others have gathered for other purposes.

done specifically for your current project. Primary sources include surveys, interviews, observations, and experiments. Before you use any sources, though, you need to know whether you can trust them.

Evaluating Sources

3 LEARNING OBJECTIVE

Name nine criteria for evaluating the credibility of an information source

No matter where you're searching, it's your responsibility to separate quality information from unreliable junk so you don't taint your results or damage your reputation. The Internet—and, in particular, the rapid growth of blogging—has complicated this challenge by making so many new sources of information available. On the positive side, sources such as blogs, wikis, and podcasting channels can provide valuable and unique insights—often from experts whose voices might never be heard otherwise. On the negative side, you must remember that anyone can post virtually anything on a website or blog, and much of that information will be unverified by the editorial boards and fact checkers commonly used in traditional publishing. Ask yourself the following questions about each piece of material:

Evaluate your sources carefully to avoid embarrassing and potentially damaging mistakes.

- **Does the source have a reputation for honesty and reliability?** Naturally, you'll feel more comfortable using information from an established source that has a reputation for accuracy. (But don't let your guard down completely; even the finest reporters and editors can make mistakes.) For sources that are new or relatively unknown, your safest bet is to corroborate anything you learn with information from several other sources.
- **Is the source potentially biased?** Depending on what an organization stands for (and the source of its funding, in some cases), its messages may be written with a certain bias. This is neither inherently bad nor unethical, but you need to be aware of it so that you can interpret the information you find.
- **What is the purpose of the material?** Was the material designed to inform others of new research, advance a position, or stimulate discussion? Was it designed to promote or sell a product? Be sure to distinguish among advertising, advocating, and informing.
- **Is the author credible?** Find out whether the person or the publisher is well known in the field. Is the author an amateur? Merely someone with an opinion?
- **Where did the source get its information?** Many sources of secondary information get their material from other secondary sources, removing you even further from the original data.

- **Can you verify the material independently?** Verification can uncover biases or mistakes—particularly important when the information goes beyond simple facts to include projections, interpretations, and estimates.
- **Is the material current?** Make sure you are using the most current information available by checking the publication date of a source. Many business-related fields change quickly, and published information can become obsolete in a matter of months, weeks, or even days.
- **Is the material complete?** Have you accessed the entire document or only a selection from it? If it's a selection, which parts were excluded? Do you need more detail?
- **Do the source's claims stand up to scrutiny?** Step back and ask yourself whether the information makes sense. For example, if a researcher claims that the market for a particular product will triple in the next five years, what would have to happen for that prediction to come true? Will three times as many customers buy the product? Will existing customers buy three times more than they currently buy?

The U.S. Bureau of the Census is a credible source of information.

You probably won't have time to conduct a thorough background check on all your sources, so focus your efforts on the most important or most suspicious pieces of information. Always try to get independent verification of key pieces of information.

Conducting Secondary Research

Even if you intend to eventually conduct primary research, start with a review of any available secondary research. Inside the company, you might be able to find a variety of documents prepared for other projects that offer helpful information. Be sure to ask whether your company has a *knowledge management system* (see "Managing Information" on page 354 for more on this topic). Outside the company, business researchers can choose from a wide range of print and online resources, as you can see from the list in Table 11.2

You'll want to start most projects by conducting secondary research first.

TABLE 11.2 Important Resources for Business Research

COMPANY, INDUSTRY, AND PRODUCT RESOURCES (URLS ARE PROVIDED FOR ONLINE RESOURCES)

AnnualReports.com. www.reportgallery.com. Free access to annual reports from thousands of public companies.

Brands and Their Companies/Companies and Their Brands. Contains data on over 400,000 consumer products and 100,000 manufacturers, importers, marketers, and distributors.

CNN/Money. http://money.cnn.com. News, analysis, and financial resources covering companies, industries, and world markets.

Corporate and Industry Research Reports (CIRR). Collection of industry reports produced by industry analysts for investment purposes. Unique coverage includes industry profitability, comparative company sales, market share, profits, and forecasts.

D&B Directories. A variety of directories, including *America's Corporate Families* (ownership connections among companies), *Business Rankings* (25,000 leading companies), *Directory of Service Companies* (over 50,000 companies in the service sector), and *Industrial Guide* (over 120,000 manufacturing companies).

Forbes. Annual Report on American Industry published in first January issue of each year.

Hoover's Handbook of American Business. Profiles of over 500 public and private corporations.

Hoover's Online. www.hoovers.com. Database of 12 million companies worldwide, including in-depth coverage of 35,000 leading companies around the world. Basic information available free; in-depth information requires subscription.

Manufacturing and Distribution USA. Data on thousands of companies in the manufacturing, wholesaling, and retailing sectors.

NAICS Codes. www.census.gov/naics. North American Industry Classification System.

SEC filing. www.sec.gov/edgar.shtml. SEC filings including 10Ks, 10Qs, annual reports, and prospectuses for 35,000 U.S. public firms.

Standard & Poor's Industry Surveys. Concise investment profiles for a broad range of industries. Coverage is extensive, with a focus on current situation and outlook. Includes some summary data on major companies in each industry.

Standard & Poor's Register of Corporations, Directors, and Executives. Index of major U.S. and international corporations. Lists officers, products, sales volume, and number of employees.

Thomas's Register of American Manufacturers. Information on thousands of U.S. manufacturers indexed by company name and product. Also available online at www.thomasnet.com.

U.S. Industrial Outlook. Annual profiles of several hundred key U.S. industries. Each industry report covers several pages and includes tables, graphs, and charts that visually demonstrate how an industry compares with similar industries, including important component growth factors and other economic measures. Currently being transferred online; www.export.gov for latest information.

RESEARCH DIRECTORIES AND INDEXES

Books in Print. Index books in 62,000 subject categories currently available from U.S. publishers. Indexed by author and title. Professional online version indexes more than 5 million book, audio, and video titles.

Directories in Print. Information on over 15,000 business and industrial directories.

Encyclopedia of Associations. Index of thousands of associations listed by broad subject category, specific subject, association, and location.

(continued)

TABLE 11.2 *Continued*

RESEARCH DIRECTORIES AND INDEXES

Reader's Guide to Periodical Literature. Classis index of general-interest magazines, categorized by subject and author; also available in electronic format.

Ulrich's Periodicals Directory. Listings by title, publisher, editor, phone, and address of over 140,000 publications such as popular magazines, trade journals, government documents, and newspapers. Great for locating hard-to-find trade publications. Also available online by subscription.

PEOPLE

Dun & Bradstreet's Reference Book of Corporate Management. Professional histories of people serving as the principal officers and directors of more than 12,000 U.S. companies.

Who's Who in America. Biographies of living U.S. citizens who have gained prominence in their fields. Related book, *Who's Who in the World*, covers global achievers.

TRADEMARKS

Official Gazette of the United Patent and Trademark Office. Weekly publication (one for trademarks and one for patents) providing official record of newly assigned trademarks and patents, product descriptions, and product names. Also available online at www.uspto.gov.

United States Patent and Trademark Office. www.uspto.gov. Trademark and patent information records.

STATISTICS AND OTHER BUSINESS DATA

Bureau of Economic Analysis. www.bea.gov. Large collection of economic and government data.

Europa—The European Union Online. www.europa.eu.int. A portal that provides up-to-date coverage of current affairs, legislation, policies, and EU statistics.

FedStats. www.fedstats.gov. Access to full range of statistics and information from over 70 U.S. government agencies.

Industry Norms and Key Business Ratios (Dun & Bradstreet). Industry, financial, and performance ratios.

Information Please Almanac. Compilation of broad-range statistical data with strong focus on labor force.

Annual Statement Studies. Industry, financial, and performance ratios published by the Risk Management Association.

Statistical Abstract of the United States. Annual compendium of U.S. economic, social, political, and industrials statistics; also available online at www.census.gov.

STAT-USA. www.stat-usa.gov. Large collection of economic and government data.

The World Almanac and Book of Facts. Facts on economic, social, educational, and political events for major countries.

U.S. Bureau of Labor Statistics. www.bls.gov. Extensive national and regional information on labor and business, including employment, industry growth, productivity, Consumer Price Index (CPI), and overall U.S. economy.

U.S. Census Bureau. www.census.gov. Demographic data on both consumers and businesses based on census data.

COMMERCIAL DATABASES (REQUIRE SUBSCRIPTIONS)

Dialog. Hundreds of databases that include areas such as business and finance, news and media, medicine, pharmaceuticals, reference, social sciences, government and regulation, science and technology, and more.

Ebsco. Access to a variety of databases on a wide range of disciplines from leading information providers.

Highbeam. Thousands of full-text newspaper, magazine, and newswire sources, plus maps and photographs.

Gale Business & Company Resource Center. A comprehensive research tool designed for undergraduate and graduate students, job searchers, and investors; offers a wide variety of information on companies and industries.

LexisNexis. Several thousand databases covering legal, corporate, government, and academic subjects.

ProQuest. Thousands of periodicals and newspapers; archives continue to expand through its program to digitize over 5 billion pages of microfilm.

SRDS Media Solutions. A comprehensive database of magazine information and advertising rates, cataloging more than 100,000 U.S. and international media properties.

(of course, this list represents a tiny fraction of the secondary resources available).[5] For instance, if you want to know more about a specific company, one of the first things you'll need to find out is whether the company is public (sells shares of stock to the general public) or private. Public corporations, which are required to submit extensive financial reports to government agencies, generally have more information available than private companies. If your company doesn't have an in-house research librarian, consider beginning your search for secondary information at the nearest public or university library.

Finding Information at the Library

Libraries are where you'll find business books, electronic databases, newspapers, periodicals, directories, almanacs, and government publications. Many of these resources may be unavailable through a standard web search or may be available only with a subscription. Libraries are also where you'll find one of your most important resources: librarians. Reference librarians are trained in research techniques and spend their days managing information and helping people find materials. They can show you how to use the library's many databases, and they can help you find obscure information. Whether you're trying to locate information in printed materials or in databases, each type of resource serves a special function:

Libraries offer information and resources you can't find anywhere else—including specialized research librarians.

- **Newspapers and periodicals.** Libraries offer access to a wide variety of popular magazines, general business magazines, *trade journals* (which provide information about specific professions and industries), and *academic* journals (which provide research-oriented articles from researchers and educators). Check with a librarian to see which periodicals are available in print or electronic formats.
- **Business books.** Although less timely than newspapers and periodicals, business books provide in-depth coverage of a variety of business topics. Many libraries now offer online access to their card catalogs so you can see if they have specific titles in their collections.
- **Directories.** Thousands of directories are published in print and electronic formats in the United States, and many include membership information for all kinds of professions, industries, and special-interest groups.
- **Almanacs and statistical resources.** Almanacs are handy guides to factual and statistical information about countries, politics, the labor force, and so on. One of the most extensive, the *Statistical Abstract of the United States*, published annually by the U.S. Department of Commerce, contains statistics about occupations, government, population, health, business, crime, and the environment (also available online at www.census.gov).
- **Government publications.** Information on laws, court decisions, tax questions, regulatory issues, and other governmental concerns can often be found in collections of government documents. A librarian can direct you to the information you want.
- **Electronic databases.** Databases offer vast collections of computer-searchable information, often in specific areas such as business, law, science, technology, and education. Some libraries offer remote online access to some or all databases; for others you'll need to visit in person. The following section offers more information on using databases.

Local, state, and federal government agencies publish a huge array of information that is helpful to business researchers.

Finding Information Online

Experienced researchers know that the Internet can be a tremendous source of business information, much of it free and all of it available more or less instantly. They also know that the Internet can waste hours and hours of precious time and deliver inaccurate or biased information, exaggerated claims, and unsubstantiated rumors. If possible, try to learn something about an unfamiliar topic from a trusted source (such as an industry journal or an experienced colleague) before you start searching online. You'll be better able to detect skewed or erroneous information, and you can be more selective about which websites and documents to use.

Conduct online research with extreme care; much of the information online has not been subjected to the same quality controls common in traditional offline publishing.

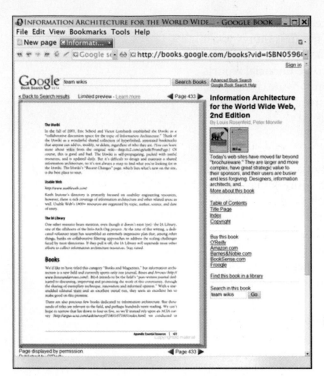

Specialized search capabilities such as Google Book can help you locate texts that might be of value in your research efforts.

4 LEARNING OBJECTIVE

Explain the complementary nature of search engines, web directories, and databases

Search engines are an important research tool, but they can't access a lot of the information that is stored online.

Web directories rely on human editors to evaluate and select websites.

Online databases give you access to the most important resources that search engines usually can't reach: millions of newspaper, magazine, and journal articles.

One good place to start on the web is the Internet Public Library at www.ipl.org. Modeled after a real library, this site provides you with a carefully selected collection of links to high-quality business resources that offer such information as company profiles, trade data, business news, corporate tax and legal advice, small-business information, prepared forms and documents, biographies of executives, financial reports, job postings, online publications, and so on.

If you're looking for specific company information, your best source may be the company's website. Company websites generally include detailed information about a firm's products, services, history, mission, strategy, financial performance, and employment needs. Many sites provide links to related company information, such as SEC filings, news releases, and more. Reputable companies are careful about the information they put online, but beware the possibility of biases and mistakes.

Understanding Search Engines, Web Directories, and Databases

You've probably used one or more search engines, web directories, or databases for school and personal projects already. All three provide online access to secondary source material (and in some cases via CD-ROM), but each operates in a unique way and therefore offers distinct advantages and disadvantages for business researchers.

Search engines identify individual webpages that contain a specific word or phrase you've asked for. Search engines have the advantage of scanning millions or billions of individual webpages, and the best engines use powerful ranking algorithms to present the pages that are probably the most relevant to your search request. For all their ease and power, search engines have three disadvantages you should be aware of: (1) no human editors are involved to evaluate the quality of the content you find on these pages; (2) various engines use different search techniques so one engine might miss a site or page that another one finds; and (3) search engines can't reach all of the content on many websites.

These out-of-reach pages are sometimes called the *hidden Internet* or the *deep web*, because conventional search techniques can't access them. Webpages can be hidden from search engines for a variety of reasons, including password protection, links that search engines typically can't follow (such as the links on websites that use Adobe Flash animation software), pages that webmasters specifically block from search engines, and *dynamic pages* that don't actually exist until a website visitor submits a query or request on a specific website. Why is it important to be aware of all this? The hidden Internet is estimated to be at least several times larger than the visible Internet, so depending on your research project, much of the material you might want to find could be unreachable through standard search engines.[6]

The good news is that you can take steps to get around all three search engine shortcomings when conducting research. **Web directories** address the first major shortcoming by using human editors to categorize and evaluate websites and other media. Directories such as those offered by Yahoo!, About, and the Open Directory Project at http://dmoz.org present lists of websites chosen by a team of editors. For instance, Open Directory lists more than 250,000 business-related websites by category, from individual companies to industry associations, all of which have been evaluated and selected by a team of volunteer editors.[7] And as Chapter 7 pointed out, a number of directories (and search engines) specialize in specific media types, such as Technorati's focus on blogs.

Metacrawlers or *metasearch engines* address the second shortcoming of search engines by formatting your search request for the specific requirements of multiple search engines and then telling you how many hits each engine was able to find for you. Table 11.3 lists some of the more popular search engines, directories, and metacrawlers available today.

Online databases address the third shortcoming of search engines by offering access to the newspapers, magazines, and journals that you're likely to need for many research projects. You can access such sources as *Fortune* and the *Wall Street Journal* either through the

TABLE 11.3 Best of Internet Searching

MAJOR SEARCH ENGINES

A9	www.a9.com	Google	www.google.com
AOL Search	http://search.aol.com	Lycos	www.lycos.com
AllTheWeb	www.alltheweb.com	Windows Live	www.live.com
Alta Vista	www.altavista.com	Yahoo search	http://search.yahoo.com
Ask.com	www.ask.com		

METACRAWLERS AND HYBRID SITES

Clusty	http://clusty.com	Search.com	www.search.com
DogPile	www.dogpile.com	Surfwax	www.surfwax.com
IXQuick	www.ixquick.com	Wakweb	www.wakweb.com
Kartoo	www.kartoo.com	Web Brain	www.webbrain.com
LookSmart	www.looksmart.com	WebCrawler	www.webcrawler.com
Mamma	www.mamma.com	Yahoo!	www.yahoo.com
MetaCrawler	www.metacrawler.com	Zapmeta	www.zapmeta.com
Fazzle	www.fazzle.com	Zworks	www.zworks.com
Infonetware RealTerm Search	www.infonetware.com		

WEB DIRECTORIES AND ONLINE LIBRARIES

About	www.about.com	Librarians' Index to the Internet	http://lii.org
Answers.com	www.answers.com		
Beaucoup	www.beaucoup.com	Library of Congress	www.loc.gov/rr/business
Digital Librarian	www.digital-librarian.com/business.html	Library Spot	www.libraryspot.com
		Open Directory	www.dmoz.com
Internet Public Library	www.ipl.org	Questia	www.questia.com

NEWS SEARCH ENGINES

AllTheWeb News	www.alltheweb.com/?cat=news	Memigo	www.memigo.com
		Newstrawler	www.newstrawler.com
AltaVista News	http://news.altavista.com	World News Network	www.wn.com
Digg.com	www.digg.com	Yahoo! News	http://news.yahoo.com
Google News	http://news.google.com		

BLOG AND PODCAST SEARCH ENGINES AND DIRECTORIES

Blinkx	www.blinkx.com	Podcast Pickle	www.podcastpickle.com
Blogdigger	www.blogdigger.com	Podcast Network	www.thepodcastnetwork.com
Bloglines	www.bloglines.com	PodRazor	www.podrazor.com
BlogStreet	http://blogstreet.com	Podscope	www.podscope.com
Bloogz	www.bloogz.com	PodSpider	www.podspider.com
Feedster	www.feedster.com	Podzinger	www.podzinger.com
GetAPodcast	www.getapodcast.com	Technorati	www.technorati.com
Google video search	http://video.google.com	Yahoo! video search	http://video.search.yahoo.com
Kinja	http://kinja.com		
Podcast Alley	www.podcastalley.com	Waypath	www.waypath.com
Podcast Bunker	www.podcastbunker.com		

MAGAZINE AND PERIODICAL SEARCH ENGINES

FindArticles.com	www.findarticles.com	Google Scholar	http://scholar.google.com
Full Free Text (scholarly articles)	www.freefulltext.com		

The Internet Public Library is one of the most important web directories for business researchers.

individual publishers' own sites or through a commercial database that offers access to multiple sources. Individual publisher sites often require a subscription to that publication for anything beyond the current issue, and commercial databases require subscriptions to access all content. Some commercial databases, such as High Beam (www.highbeam. com), are priced to attract individual users, whereas others, such as LexisNexis (www.lexisnexis.com/corporate) and ProQuest (www.proquest.com), are intended for use by companies, libraries, and other institutions. In addition to databases that primarily feature content from newspapers and periodicals, specialized databases such as Hoover's (www.hoovers.com) and OneSource's CorpTech (www.corptech.com) offer detailed information on thousands of individual companies. You can obtain company news releases from the free databases maintained by PRNewswire (www.prnewswire.com) and Business Wire (www.businesswire.com). News releases are good places to look for announcements of new products, management changes, earnings, dividends, mergers, acquisitions, and other company information.

Make sure you know how each search engine, directory, database, or metacrawler works.

Using Search Tools Effectively   Search engines, metacrawlers, and databases offer a variety of ways to find information. Unfortunately, no two of them work in exactly the same way, and many continue to refine and simplify their approaches, so you might have to modify your search techniques as you move from one tool to the next. The most basic form of searching is a *keyword search*, in which the engine or database attempts to find items that include all of the words you enter. A *Boolean search* expands on this capability by using search operators that let you define a query with greater precision. Common operators include AND (the search must include both words before and after the AND), OR (it can include either or both words), or NOT (the search ignores items with whatever word comes after NOT). For example:

- *corporate AND profits* finds webpages or database entries that contain both *corporate* and *profits*.
- *corporate OR profits* finds items that contain either *corporate* or *profit* but not necessarily both.
- *corporate NOT profit* finds items that contain *corporate* but excludes all those that contain the word *profit*.

Boolean searches can also include operators that let you find a particular word in close proximity to other words or use *wildcards* to find similar spellings (such as *profit*, *profits*, and *profitability*).

As a simpler alternative to Boolean searches, some search engines and databases offer *natural language searches*, which let you ask questions in normal, everyday English (natural language is what humans speak, as opposed to the languages computers speak). For example, "Which videogame companies are the most profitable?" is a natural language query. Be aware that some search tools let you select keyword, Boolean, or natural language searches, so make sure you know which method you're using.

Several search engines, including Google, Yahoo!, and AllTheWeb, have implemented *forms-based searches* that help you create powerful queries without the need to learn any special techniques.[8] As the name implies, you simply fill out an online form that typically lets you specify such parameters as date ranges, words to include or exclude, language, Internet domain name, and even file and media types. To access these forms, look for "advanced search" or a similar option.

To make the best use of any search engine or database, keep the following points in mind:

- **Read the instructions.** Unfortunately, there is no universal set of instructions that apply to every search tool. You can usually find a Help page that explains both basic and advanced functions, with advice on how to use a particular tool most effectively.
- **Pay attention to the details.** Details can make all the difference in a search. For instance, most search engines treat *AND* (uppercase) as a Boolean search operator and look only for pages or entries that contain both words. In contrast, *and* (lowercase) and similar basic words (called *stopwords*) are excluded from many searches because they are so common they'll show up in every webpage or database entry. Similarly, some engines and databases interpret the question mark as a wildcard to let you search for variations of a given word, but Google does not (Google searches for word variations automatically). Again, you need to know how to operate each search engine or database, and don't assume they all work in the same way.
- **Review the search and display options carefully.** Some sites and databases provide few options to control your queries, but others, such as Google's Advanced Search, let you make a variety of choices to include or exclude specific types of files and pages from specific sites. Also, pay attention to whether you are searching in the title, subject, or document field of the database. Each will return different results. Some databases default to searching only in the title field, meaning that you'll miss a lot of items unless you know the exact words used in the title. When the results are displayed, verify the presentation order. On HighBeam, for instance, you can choose to sort the results by either date or relevancy.
- **Try variations of your terms.** If you can't find what you're looking for, try abbreviations (*CEO*, *CPA*), synonyms (*man, male*), related terms (*child, adolescent, youth*), different spellings (*dialog, dialogue*), singular and plural forms (*woman, women*), nouns and adjectives (*manager, management, managerial*), and open and compound forms (*online, on line, on-line*). As mentioned earlier, Google searches for word variations automatically.[9]
- **Adjust the scope of your search if needed.** If a search yields little or no information, broaden your search by specifying fewer terms. Conversely, if you're inundated with too many hits, use more terms to narrow your search. For example, "Apple" yields many more hits than "Apple iPod," which yields many more than "Apple iPod nano."

Taking Advantage of Innovative Research Technologies As you conduct research throughout your career, keep an eye out for the latest technologies that can help you research more effectively and more efficiently. Four innovative tools now available are desktop and enterprise search engines, research and content managers, social bookmarking sites, and newsfeeds:

- **Desktop and enterprise search engines.** Unlike conventional search engines, which look for content on the web, **desktop search engines** look for content on a particular computer. These tools are designed to identify and organize the many information and message fragments that most people have stored in various forms on their computers—e-mail messages, IM, PowerPoint presentations, audio and video clips, word-processor files, and so on. Both leading search engines such as Google and Yahoo! and a variety of other software firms now offer desktop search tools.[10] **Enterprise search engines** perform a similar task, only across an entire network of computers.
- **Research and content managers.** A variety of tools known as *research managers* or *content managers* can be particularly helpful when your research involves numerous websites. These tools offer such features as letting you save and organize stored website links, providing permanent access to webpages you've visited even if the pages later change or disappear, and even automatically generating parts of reports such as tables of contents and bibliographies.[11]

5 LEARNING OBJECTIVE

Provide five guidelines for conducting an effective online search

6 LEARNING OBJECTIVE

Identify four new tools that can make your research more effective and more efficient

Software such as Net Snippets simplifies online research by helping you track, organize, and capture online sources and then quickly create reports complete with tables of contents, indexes, and bibliographies.

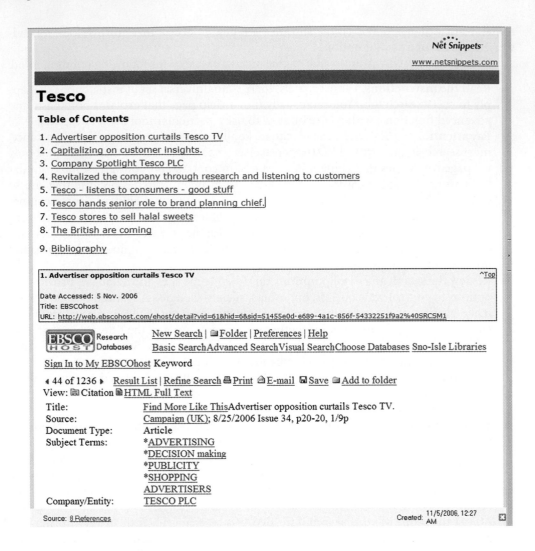

- **Social bookmarking sites.** The social bookmarking sites introduced in Chapter 7 can also assist with research. By highlighting websites, news articles, and other online items that other people find useful, bookmarking sites such as **www.digg.com** and **http://del.icio.us/** can alert you to helpful resources and offer some indication of what online audiences are interested in at a particular moment in time. When using bookmarking sites for research, however, be aware of two potential problems. First, the lack of uniformity in tagging can lead you to miss sites of interest (although this problem may be resolved as sites evolve). For instance, one person might tag a site with "MP3 players" while another tags the same site with "digital music players." Second, because the rankings aren't based on a carefully designed research sample, you can't assume that rankings truly represent any particular segment of the population.[12]
- **Newsfeeds.** Newsfeeds, also discussed in Chapter 7, are an ideal way to stay up to date on subjects that are likely to change or develop over time. For example, to stay on top of competitive moves in your industry, you can subscribe to newsfeeds from stock analysts who cover the industry, product user blogs, and blogs published by your competitors themselves.

Documenting Your Sources

Proper documentation of the sources you use is both ethical and an important resource for your readers.

Documenting the secondary sources you use in your writing serves three important functions: It properly and ethically credits the person who created the original material; it shows your audience that you have sufficient support for your message; and, as mentioned earlier, it helps your readers explore your topic in more detail if desired. Your results might be used by people long after you conducted the research, and these people won't always have the opportunity to query you in person for more information. Be sure to take advantage of the source documentation tools in your word processor rather than attempting to track source notes by hand. For instance, Microsoft Word automatically tracks and numbers endnotes for you, and you can use the "table of authorities" feature to create a bibliography of all the sources you've used. As computing technologies continue to advance, keep an eye out for other note-taking tools that can help you be a more efficient researcher. For example, software such as Microsoft's OneNote makes it easier to collect and organize notes wherever and however you find vital information, from meetings to websites to e-mail messages.[13]

You may document your sources through footnotes, endnotes, or some similar system (see Appendix B, "Documentation of Report Sources"). Whatever method you choose, documentation is necessary for books, articles, tables, charts, diagrams, song lyrics, scripted dialogue, letters, speeches—anything that you take from someone else, including ideas and information that you've re-expressed through paraphrasing or summarizing.

However, you do not have to cite a source for general knowledge or for specialized knowledge that's generally known among your readers. For example, most everyone knows that Nike is a large sporting goods company and that computers are pervasive in business today. You can say so on your own authority, even if you've read an article in which the author says the same thing.

Chapter 1 noted that copyright law covers the expression of creative ideas, and copyrights can cover a wide range of materials, including reports and other documents, web content, movies, musical compositions, lectures, computer programs, and even choreographed dance routines. Copyright protection is initiated the moment the expression is put into fixed form. Copyright law does not protect such elements as titles, names, short phrases, slogans, familiar symbols, or lists of ingredients or contents. It also doesn't protect ideas, procedures, methods, systems, processes, concepts, principles, discoveries, or devices, although it does cover their description, explanation, or illustration.[14] (Note that many of the entities that aren't covered under copyright law are covered under other legal protections, such as patents for devices and processes and trademarks for slogans.)

Merely crediting the source is not always enough. According to the *fair use doctrine*, you can use other people's work only as long as you don't unfairly prevent them from benefiting as a result. For example, if you reproduce someone else's copyrighted questionnaire in a report you're writing, even if you identify the source thoroughly, you may be preventing the author from selling a copy of that questionnaire to your readers.

In general, avoid relying to such a great extent on someone else's work. However, when you can't avoid it, contact the copyright holder (usually the author or publisher) for permission to reprint. You'll usually be asked to pay a fee.

For more information on copyrights, visit www.copyright.gov or www.creativecommons.org.

Conducting Primary Research

If secondary research can't provide the information and insights you need, your next choice is to gather the information yourself with primary research. The two most common primary research methods are surveys and interviews, the focus of this section. Other primary techniques include *observations* and *experiments* such as Tesco's test-marketing study with Polish foods (see page 331).

Surveys and interviews are the most common primary research techniques.

Conducting Surveys

Surveys can provide invaluable insights on a wide variety of business topics, but they are useful only when they're reliable and valid. A survey is *reliable* if it produces identical results when repeated. A survey is *valid* if it measures what it's intended to measure. To generate results that are both reliable and valid, you need to choose research participants carefully and develop an effective set of questions. (For surveys on high-risk topics, you're usually better off hiring a research specialist who knows how to avoid errors at each stage.)

For a survey to produce valid results, it must be based on a representative sample of the population of interest.

When selecting the people who'll participate in your survey, the most critical task is getting a representative sample of the population in question. For instance, if you want to know how U.S. consumers feel about a particular product or company, don't just randomly survey people in the local mall and assume their answers represent the opinions of everyone in the country. Different types of consumers shop at different times of the day and different days of the week, some consumers don't shop at malls regularly, and many who do won't stop to talk with researchers. The online surveys you see on many websites today potentially suffer from the same sampling bias; they capture the opinions of only those people who visit the sites and want to participate, which might not represent the population that the site owner really needs to know about. Even though millions of U.S. residents have responded to online surveys,[15] that's no guarantee that you'll get the right people for your specific survey. A good handbook on survey research will help you select the right people for your survey, including selecting enough people to have a statistically valid survey.[16]

To develop an effective survey questionnaire, start with the information gaps you identified earlier, then break these points into specific questions, choosing an appropriate type of question for each point (Figure 11.2 shows various types of survey questions). The following guidelines will help you produce results that are both valid and reliable:[17]

Provide clear instructions in questionnaires to prevent mistaken answers.

- **Provide clear instructions.** Respondents need to know exactly how to fill out your questionnaire.
- **Keep the questionnaire short and easy to answer.** Ask only questions that are relevant to your research. The longer the survey, the greater the chance that people will get frustrated and quit before finishing.
- **Whenever possible, formulate questions to provide answers that are easy to analyze.** Numbers and facts are easier to summarize than opinions, for instance. Of course, if you really want opinions, then ask questions to elicit them.
- **Avoid leading questions.** Questions that lead to a particular answer will bias your survey. If you ask, "Do you prefer that we stay open in the evenings for customer convenience?" you'll no doubt get a "yes." Instead, ask, "What time of day do you normally do your shopping?"
- **Avoid ambiguous questions.** If you ask "Do you shop online often?" some people might interpret *often* to mean "every day," whereas others might think it means "once a week" or "once a month."
- **Ask only one question at a time.** A compound question such as "Do you read books and magazines?" doesn't allow for the respondent who reads one but not the other.
- **Make the survey adaptive.** You can often obtain more useful results if you can adapt the question sequence based on audience responses. For instance, if you ask whether people buy your product, you would ideally like to present different follow-up questions to the group that answers yes and the group that answers no. With a paper-based survey, you can do so with instructions such as "If you answered no to this question, skip to Question 12." With an online survey, you can program the software to branch automatically based on audience inputs. Not only does this sort of real-time adaptation deliver better answers, but it reduces frustration for survey respondents as well.[18]

Be sure to test your survey before using it.

Before you conduct your survey, test it on a sample group first to identify questions that might be confusing or that might generate answers you don't expect (see "Communication Miscues: The Art of the Question").

The Internet is now a preferred survey mechanism for many researchers, and dozens of companies offer online survey services (see Figure 11.3).[19] Compared to traditional mail and in-person techniques, online surveys are usually faster to create, easier to administer, faster to analyze, and less expensive overall. The interactive capabilities of the web can enhance all kinds of surveys, from simple opinion polls to complex purchase simulations. Many groupware systems now have polling features that make it easy to ask your fellow team members to vote on specific issues. However, don't let the speed and convenience of online surveys lower the requirements for careful planning; online surveys require the same care as any other type of survey, including being on guard against sampling bias.[20]

QUESTION TYPE EXAMPLE

Open-ended How would you describe the flavor of this ice cream?

Either-or Do you think this ice cream is too rich?
_____ Yes
_____ No

Multiple choice Which description best fits the taste of this ice cream?
(Choose only one.)
a. Delicious
b. Too fruity
c. Too sweet
d. Too intensely flavored
e. Bland
f. Stale

Scale Please mark an X on the scale to indicate how you perceive the texture of this ice cream.

Too light   Light   Creamy   Too creamy

Checklist Which of the following ice cream brands do you recognize?
(Check all that apply.)
_____ Ben & Jerry's
_____ Breyers
_____ Carvel
_____ Dreyer's
_____ Häagen-Dazs

Ranking Rank these flavors in order of your preference, from 1 (most preferred) to 5 (least preferred):
_____ Vanilla
_____ Cherry
_____ Strawberry
_____ Chocolate
_____ Coconut

Short-answer In the past 2 weeks, how many times did you buy ice cream in a grocery store? _____

In the past 2 weeks, how many times did you buy ice cream in an ice cream shop? _____

FIGURE 11.2 Types of Survey Questions
For each question you have in your survey, choose the type of question that will elicit the most useful answers.

Conducting Interviews

Getting information straight from experts and other audiences can be a great method for collecting primary information. Although interviews are relatively easy to conduct, they require careful planning to get the best results and make the best use of the other person's time. Planning an interview is similar to planning any other form of communication. You begin by analyzing your purpose, learning about the other person, and formulating your main idea. Then you decide on the length, style, and organization of the interview. Interviews can take a variety of formats, from e-mail exchanges to group discussions. For example, Tesco invites thousands of customers to visit its stores every year for meetings known as Customer Question Time, when it asks customers how the company can serve them better.[21]

Interviews are easy to conduct but require careful planning to produce useful results.

FIGURE 11.3 Survey Software
Online survey systems such as the one offered by Object Planet make it easy to create, administer, and analyze surveys.

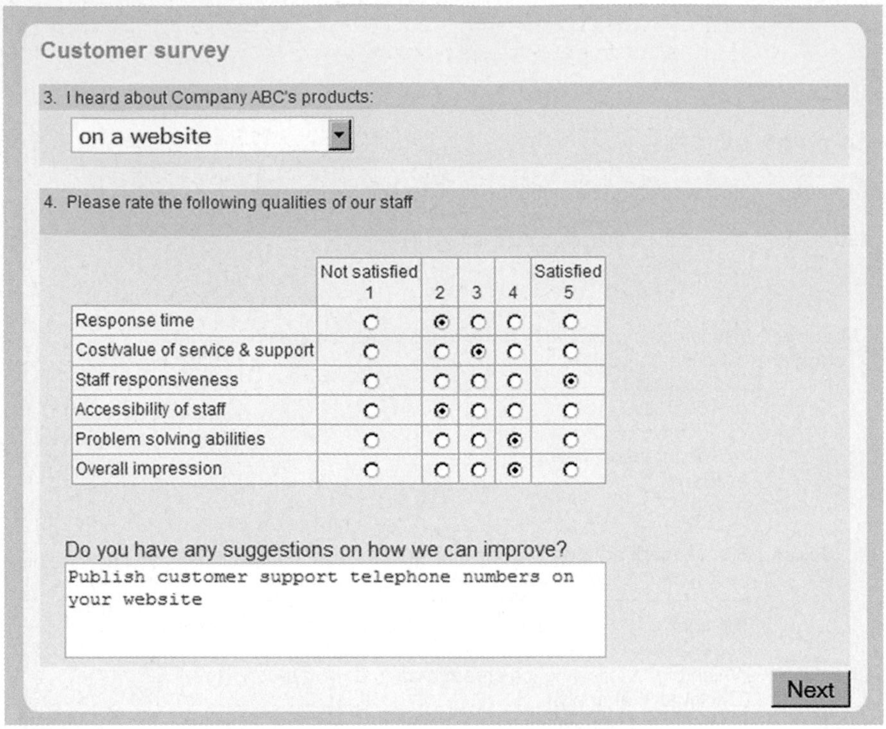

The answers you receive are influenced by the types of questions you ask, by the way you ask them, and by your subject's cultural and language background. Other influential factors include race, gender, age, educational level, and social status, so know your subject before you start writing questions.[22] In addition, be aware of ethical implications. For example, asking someone to divulge personal information about a co-worker may be asking that person to make an unethical choice. Always be careful about confidentiality, politics, and other sensitive issues.

Ask **open-ended questions** to invite the expert to offer opinions, insights, and information, such as "Why do you believe that South America represents a better opportunity than Europe for this product line?" Bear in mind that although open-ended questions can extract significant amounts of information, they do give you less control over the interview. Someone might take 10 seconds or 10 minutes to answer a question, so plan to be flexible.

Choose question types that will generate the specific type of information you need.

Ask **closed questions** to elicit a specific answer, such as yes or no. However, including too many closed questions in an interview will make the experience feel more like a simple survey and won't take full advantage of the interview setting. When you do ask a question that implies a straightforward answer, such as "Do you think we should expand distribution in South America?" explore the reasoning behind the expert's answer.

The following guidelines will help you come up with a great set of interview questions:[23]

7 LEARNING OBJECTIVE

Outline an effective process for planning and conducting information interviews

- **Think about sequence.** Arrange your questions in a way that helps uncover layers of information or that helps the subject tell you a complete story.
- **Rate your questions and highlight the ones you really need answers to.** If you start to run out of time during the interview, you may have to skip less-important questions.
- **Ask smart questions.** If you ask a question that your subject perceives to be less than intelligent, the interview could go downhill in a hurry.
- **Limit the number of questions.** For a half-hour interview, plan on 15 to 20 questions, bearing in mind that open-ended questions can take far longer to answer than closed questions.
- **Edit your questions.** Try to make your questions as neutral and as easy to understand as possible. Then practice them several times to make sure you're ready for the interview.

Consider providing the interviewee with a list of questions at least a day or two before the interview, especially if you'd like to quote your subject in writing or if your questions

Communication Miscues

The Art of the Question

Poorly worded questions can render a survey useless. Even worse, they can produce subtle differences in answers from one respondent to the next that you didn't anticipate and don't take into account in your analysis. Assume you receive regular surveys from the human resources department in your company, dealing with such issues as productivity, employee satisfaction, and employee benefits. This month's survey contains the following questions:

1. How would you rate the food in the company cafeteria? (Choose one.)
   _____ Fantastic
   _____ Nutritious
   _____ Delicious
   _____ Filling
   _____ A good value for the money
2. What is your opinion of the improved insurance sign-up process we instituted last month?
3. If the dental benefits plan were modified relative to the current plan, wherein employees are expected to pay a $20 co-payment at the time of each visit, with benefits subject to the normal companywide 80 percent co-insurance standard, provided the co-insurance ratio did not drop, would you continue to participate in the plan if co-payment

were increased to $50 but counterbalanced by a reduction in your monthly payroll deduction amount?
   _____ yes _____ no
4. Division supervisors continue to report problems with employees reporting for work late. Do the employees in your department tend to report for work
   _____ Always on time
   _____ Mostly on time
   _____ Usually on time
   _____ Occasionally late
   _____ Frequently late
5. How many times did you personally report for work late last year?
6. Do you ever feel poorly trained or insufficiently motivated in your job? _____ yes _____ no

CAREER APPLICATIONS

1. Which of these questions might result in unusable information? Why?
2. How would you help the human resources manager rewrite them to improve the quality of information they generate?

---

might require your subject to conduct research or think extensively about the answers. If you want to record the interview, ask the person ahead of time and respect his or her wishes.

As soon as possible after the interview, take a few moments to write down your thoughts, go over your notes, and organize your material. Look for important themes, helpful facts or statistics, and direct quotes. If you recorded the interview, *transcribe* it (take down word for word what the person said) or take notes from the recording just as you would while listening to someone in person.

Face-to-face interviews give you the opportunity to gauge the reaction to your questions and observe the nonverbal signals that accompany the answers, but interviews don't necessarily have to take place in person. E-mail interviews are becoming more common, partly because they give subjects a chance to think through their responses thoroughly rather than rushing to fit the time constraints of a face-to-face interview.[24] Also, e-mail interviews might be the only way you will be able to access some experts.

In addition to individual interviews, business researchers can use a form of group interview known as the **focus group**. In this format, a moderator guides the group through a series of discussion questions while the rest of the research team observes through a one-way mirror. The key advantage of focus groups is the opportunity to learn from group dynamics as the various participants bounce ideas and questions off each other. By allowing a group to discuss topics and problems in this manner, the focus group technique can uncover much richer information than a series of individual interviews.[25]

As a reminder of the tasks involved in interviews, see "Checklist: Conducting Effective Information Interviews."

Face-to-face interviews give you the opportunity to gauge nonverbal responses as well.

DOCUMENT MAKEOVER

IMPROVE THIS LIST OF INTERVIEW QUESTIONS

To practice correcting drafts of actual documents, visit your online course or the access-code-protected portion of the Companion Website. Click "Document Makeovers," then click Chapter 11. You will find a list of interview questions that contain problems and errors relating to what you've learned in this chapter about finding, evaluating, and processing information. Use the Final Draft decision tool to create an improved version of these questions. Check questions for sequencing; appropriateness; perceptiveness; and respect for ethical, confidential, political, or sensitive issues.

✓ CHECKLIST: Conducting Effective Information Interviews

- Learn about the person you're interviewing.
- Formulate your main idea to ensure effective focus.
- Choose the length, style, and organization of the interview.
- Select question types to elicit the specific information you want.
- Design each question carefully to collect useful answers.
- Limit the number of questions you ask.
- Consider recording the interview if the subject permits.
- Review your notes as soon as the interview ends.

PROCESSING DATA AND INFORMATION

After you collect your research, the next step is converting it into usable information.

Once you've collected all the necessary information, the next step is transforming it into the specific content you need. For simpler projects, you may be able to drop your material directly into your report, presentation, or other application. However, when you have a significant amount of information or raw data from surveys, you'll need to process the material before you can use it. This step can involve quoting, paraphrasing, and summarizing textual material or analyzing numerical data.

Quoting, Paraphrasing, and Summarizing

Quoting a source means reproducing the content exactly and indicating who created the information originally.

You can use information from secondary sources in three ways. *Quoting* a source means you reproduce it exactly as you found it, and you either set it off with quotation marks (for shorter passages) or extract it in an indented paragraph (for longer passages). Use direct quotations when the original language will enhance your argument or when rewording the passage would lessen its impact. However, try not to quote sources too frequently, because this creates a choppy patchwork of varying styles and gives the impression that all you've done is piece together the work of other people.

Paraphrasing is expressing someone else's ideas in your own words.

You can often maximize the impact of secondary material in your own writing by *paraphrasing* it, restating it in your own words and with your own sentence structures.[26] Paraphrasing helps you maintain consistent tone, present information using vocabulary more familiar to your audience, and avoid the choppy feel of too many quotations. Of course, you still need to credit the originator of the information but not with quotation marks or indented paragraphs.

To paraphrase effectively, follow these tips:[27]

- Reread the original passage until you fully understand its meaning.
- Record your paraphrase on a note card or in an electronic format.
- Use business language and jargon that your audience is familiar with.
- Check your version with the original source to verify that you have not altered the meaning.
- Use quotation marks to identify any unique terms or phrases you have borrowed exactly from the source.
- Record the source (including the page number) so that you can give proper credit if you use this material in your report.

Summarizing is similar to paraphrasing but distills the content into fewer words.

Summarizing is similar to paraphrasing but presents the gist of the material in fewer words than the original. An effective summary identifies the main ideas and major support points from your source material but leaves out minor details, examples, and other information that is less critical to your audience. Like quotations and paraphrases, summaries also require complete documentation of your sources.

Of course, all three approaches require careful attention to ethics. When quoting directly, take care not to distort the original intent of the material by quoting selectively or out of context. If an interview subject said "this market could grow dramatically next year if we

Ethics Detective

Did You Find the Real Answer or the Answer You Were Looking For?

To deal with a growing problem of employee turnover, your company recently hired a research firm to survey employees to find out why more employees are leaving than in past years. You and a colleague were assigned to work with the consultants and present their findings to upper management. Neither one of you welcomed the assignment because you suspect you'll have to present information that is critical of the management team.

As you feared, the researchers deliver a mixture of news that is mostly negative:

- Seventy-eight percent of employees believe management cares more about profits than people.
- Fifty-five percent aren't sure what's expected of them anymore.
- Forty percent believe wages at the company have not kept up with the industry average.
- Thirty-eight percent think management has done a good job of responding to competitive advances.
- Fifty-two percent expect to finish their careers at the company.
- Eighty percent believe the economy is too slow to support a productive job search.

While you're poring over the report, trying to figure out how you'll present the information tomorrow, an instant message from the CEO pops up on your partner's computer asking for a quick summary of the results. She types the following, then asks you to review it before she sends it:

> As you'd expect in a no-holds-barred investigation like this, the researchers did uncover some areas for improvements. The good news: only 20 percent of the workforce is even considering other options, and we could reasonably expect that only a fraction of that group will leave anytime soon.

ANALYSIS

You read your partner's summary twice, but something doesn't feel quite right. Does it present an accurate summary of the research? Why or why not? What's likely to happen when you present the complete research results to the CEO after first sending this IM?

---

invest heavily in new products," including just the phrase "this market could grow dramatically next year" in a report would be unethical.

When paraphrasing and summarizing, take care not to distort the original intent as you express the ideas in your own words and sentences. Remember that the goal is to help your audience relate to material that supports your message. Double-check your writing to make sure you didn't subconsciously skew the other writer's message to fit your own needs (see "Ethics Detective: Did You Find the Real Answer or the Answer You Were Looking For?").

Analyzing Your Data

Research often produces numerical data—everything from sales figures to population statistics to survey answers. By themselves, these numbers might not provide the insights you or your audience require. Are sales going up or going down? Are the age groups that represent our target markets growing or shrinking? What percentage of employees surveyed are so dissatisfied that they're ready to look for new jobs? These are the insights managers need in order to make good business decisions.

Gaining Insights

Even without advanced statistical techniques, you can use simple arithmetic to extract powerful insights from sets of research data. Table 11.4 shows some of the more common things you can learn about data you've collected. One useful way of looking at numerical data is to find measures that represent a group of numbers. Three useful measures are shown in Table 11.4. The **mean** (which is what most people refer to when they use the term *average*) is the sum of all the items in the group divided by the number of items in that group. The **median** is the "middle of the road," or the midpoint of a series (with an equal number of items above and below). The **mode** is the number that occurs more often than

Mean, median, and mode provide insight into sets of data.

TABLE 11.4 Three Types of Data Measures: Mean, Median, and Mode

SALESPERSON	SALES	
Wilson	$3,000	
Green	5,000	
Carrick	6,000	
Wimper	7,000	———— Mean
Keeble	7,500	———— Median
Kemble	8,500	
O'Toole	8,500	Mode
Mannix	8,500	
Caruso	9,000	
Total	$63,000	

any other in your sample. It's the best answer to a question such as "What is the usual amount?" Each of the three measures can give you different insights into a set of data.

Trends suggest patterns that repeat over time.

It's also helpful to look for **trends**, any repeatable patterns taking place over time, including growth, decline, and cyclical trends that vary between growth and decline. Trend analysis is common in business. By looking at data over a period of time, you can detect patterns and relationships that will help you answer important questions.

Causation shows cause-and-effect relationships; correlation indicates simultaneous changes in two variables that may not necessarily be causally related.

Statistical measures and trends identify *what* is happening. To help you understand *why* those things are happening, look at **causation** (the cause-and-effect linkage between two factors, where one of them causes the other to happen) and **correlation** (the simultaneous change in two variables that you're measuring, such as customer satisfaction dropping when product quality drops). Bear in mind that causation can be easy to assume but difficult to prove. The drop in customer satisfaction might have been caused by a new accounting system that fouled up customer invoices. In order to prove causation, you need to be able to isolate the suspected cause as the only potential source of the change in the measured effect. However, eliminating all but one possible cause isn't always feasible, so you often have to apply careful judgment to correlations. Researchers frequently explore the relationships between subsets of data using a technique called **cross-tabulation**. For instance, if you're trying to figure out why total sales rose or fell, you might look separately at sales data by age, gender, location, and product type.

Guarding Against Mistakes and Misinterpretations

Numbers are easy to manipulate with spreadsheets and other computer tools—sometimes too easy—so be sure to guard against both computational errors and misinterpretation of results. Make sure to double-check all of your calculations and document the operation of any spreadsheets you plan to share with colleagues. Common spreadsheet mistakes to watch for include errors in math formulas, references to unintended cells in the spreadsheet (resulting in the inclusion of data you don't want or the exclusion of data you do want), failures to refresh calculations after data changes, and failures to verify the specific operation of the spreadsheet's built-in math functions.

In addition to watching for computer errors, step back and look at your entire set of data before proceeding with any analysis. Do the numbers make sense based on what you know about the subject? Are any data points suspicious? If the production numbers you've been measuring have never varied more than 10 percent month to month and then suddenly jumped 50 percent last month, is that new number real or an erroneous measurement?

Even when your data points are accurate and your analysis is technically correct, it's still possible to misinterpret or misrepresent the results. Many analysis errors require statistical expertise to identify and fix, but even without advanced skills, you can take these precautions:

Watch out for errors that might have crept in during collection and processing of data.

- **Avoid faulty comparisons.** Many of the reports and presentations you'll make in your career—and the data you collect through research—will involve comparisons of some sort. In order for such analyses to be meaningful, they have to be constructed to ensure fair comparisons. Make sure you compare "apples to apples" and not "apples to oranges."
- **Don't push research results beyond their limits.** The temptation to extract insights and assurances that aren't really there can be quite strong, particularly in situations of great uncertainty. For instance, if you're about to recommend that your company invest millions of dollars in developing a new product based on your consumer research, you're likely to find every possible justification in the data. A common mistake in these situations is assuming that people who like a product will actually buy it. Millions of people like Ferraris, but very few buy one. Another mistake of this sort is assuming that a trend in the past will continue in the future.
- **Steer clear of misleading presentations.** As you'll see in Chapter 12, valid data can be presented in invalid ways, and it's your responsibility to make sure the visual presentation of data is accurate.

APPLYING YOUR FINDINGS

After all your planning, research, and processing, you're finally ready to apply your findings. Depending on the writing project, you may be summarizing your results, drawing conclusions based on your results, or making recommendations.

8 LEARNING OBJECTIVE

Explain the differences between drafting a summary, drawing a conclusion, and developing a recommendation

Summarizing Your Research

If your boss has asked you to summarize the competitive strengths and weaknesses of another company or the recent trends in a particular market, it's crucial that you provide an unbiased summary that is free of your own opinions, conclusions, or recommendations. If you do uncover something that sparks an idea or raises a concern, by all means communicate this, but do so separately; don't include such information in your summary report.

Summarizing is not always a simple task, and your boss will be judging your ability to separate significant issues from less-significant details. Identify the main idea and the key support points, and separate them from details, examples, and other supporting evidence (see Table 11.5). Focus your efforts on your audience, highlighting the information that is most important to the person who assigned the project or to those who will be reading the report.

However, focusing on the audience doesn't mean you're supposed to convey only the information your audience wants to hear. A good summary might contain nothing but bad news, if that's what your research uncovered. Even if the summary isn't pleasant, effective managers always appreciate and respect honest, complete, and perceptive information from their employees.

Drawing Conclusions

A conclusion is a logical interpretation of the facts and other information in your report. Reaching good conclusions based on the evidence at hand is one of the most important skills you can develop in your business career. For a conclusion to be sound, it must meet two criteria. First, it must be based strictly on the information included in your report. You can't ignore anything—even if it doesn't support your conclusion. Moreover, you shouldn't introduce any new information in your conclusion. (After all, if something is that important, it should be in the body of your report.) Second, the conclusion must be logical, meaning it must follow accepted patterns of inductive or deductive reasoning. Conclusions that

A conclusion is a logical interpretation of research results.

TABLE 11.5 Summarizing Effectively

ORIGINAL MATERIAL (110 WORDS)	45-WORD SUMMARY	22-WORD SUMMARY
Our facilities costs spiraled out of control last year. The 23 percent jump was far ahead of every other cost category in the company and many times higher than the 4 percent average rise for commercial real estate in the Portland metropolitan area. The rise can be attributed to many factors, but the major factors include repairs (mostly electrical and structural problems at the downtown office), energy (most of our offices are heated by electricity, the price of which has been increasing much faster than for oil or gas), and last but not least, the loss of two sublease tenants whose rent payments made a substantial dent in our cost profile for the past five years.	Our facilities costs jumped 23 percent last year, far ahead of every other cost category in the company and many times higher than the 4 percent local average. The major factors contributing to the increase are repairs, energy, and the loss of two sublease tenants.	Our facilities costs jumped 23 percent last year, due mainly to rising repair and energy costs and the loss of sublease income.

are based on unproven premises, appeal to emotion, make hasty generalizations, or contain any other logical fallacies are not valid.

Even though conclusions need to be logical, they may not automatically or obviously flow from the evidence. Most business decisions require assumptions and judgment; relatively few are based strictly on the available evidence. In fact, the ability to see patterns and possibilities that others can't see is one of the hallmarks of innovative business leaders. Your personal values or the organization's values may also influence your conclusions; just be sure that you're aware of how these biases affect your judgment. If a bias affects your conclusion, you should explain it to your audience. Also, don't expect all team members to examine the evidence and arrive at the same conclusion. One of the reasons for bringing additional people into a decision is to gain their unique perspective and experience.

Making Recommendations

A recommendation is a suggested course of action.

Whereas a conclusion interprets information, a **recommendation** suggests what to do about the information. The difference between a conclusion and a recommendation can be seen in the following example:

CONCLUSION

On the basis of its track record and current price, I conclude that this company is an attractive buy.

RECOMMENDATION

I recommend that we write a letter to the board of directors offering to buy the company at a 10 percent premium over the current market value of its stock.

To be credible, recommendations must be based on logical analysis and sound conclusions. They must also be practical and acceptable to your readers, the people who have to make your recommendations work. Finally, when making a recommendation, be certain that you have adequately described the steps that come next. Don't leave your readers wondering what they need to do in order to act on your recommendation.

MANAGING INFORMATION

Conducting your research well does more than provide strong support for your own writing projects. Your individual research projects are also an important contribution to your organization's collective knowledge base. According to Meg Murphy, president of Inquisite, an online survey company, "It's essential to take a big-picture approach to organizational knowledge and competencies."[28] That's why Inquisite is one of the many companies that have installed some form of **knowledge management (KM) system**, a set of technologies, policies, and procedures that let colleagues capture and share information throughout an organization. For instance, Roche Laboratories's Global Healthcare Intelligence Platform collects information from internal information systems, recommended websites, and other sources to give researchers access to materials that colleagues have already found.[29] Research results are one of the most important elements of value that these systems are designed to capture, so you can expect to see your work made available to colleagues all around the company. Even without a formal KM system, teams can use such tools as shared workspaces to make sure people get access to important information.

Knowledge management systems help organizations share research results and other valuable information and insights.

COMMUNICATION CHALLENGES AT TESCO

As a market development manager working for Richard Brasher, you are responsible for a variety of research, planning, and customer communication projects. Using what you've learned in this chapter about effective research methods, craft solutions to these two challenges.

Individual Challenge: Tesco has created several online stores (see **www.tesco.com**) and would like to expand the number of consumers who order goods and services online.

What information would you need in order to devise a plan to attract more online shoppers?

Team Challenge: Shoppers often make numerous purchase decisions in the store rather than arriving with a preset list of specific brands to purchase. Brasher would like more information on why consumers choose one brand over another while standing in front of an array of products on the shelf. Is it the brand name? Something about the packaging? The price? Other factors? With your team, brainstorm ways to collect this information from at least 500 shoppers. Be sure to consider the practical considerations of data collection as well as privacy concerns. Summarize your plan in a short report for your instructor.

SUMMARY OF LEARNING OBJECTIVES

1 **Describe an effective process for conducting business research.** Begin the research process with careful planning to make sure you focus on the most important questions and identify the best place to find answers. Then locate the data and information using primary and secondary research as needed. Process the results of your research, analyzing both textual and numerical information to extract averages, trends, and other insights. Apply your findings by summarizing information for someone else's benefit, drawing conclusions based on what you've learned, or developing recommendations. Lastly, manage information effectively so that you and others can retrieve it later and re-use it in other projects.

2 **Define primary and secondary research, and explain when you use each method.** Primary research is research that is being conducted for the first time, whereas secondary research involves information that was originally gathered for another research project or other effort. Secondary research is generally used first, both to

save time in case someone else has already gathered the information needed and to offer additional insights into your research questions.

3 **Name nine criteria for evaluating the credibility of an information source.** Information should come from a credible source that has a reputation for being honest and reliable; the source should also be unbiased. The purpose of the material should be known, and the author should be credible. The information should include references to sources (if obtained elsewhere), and it should be independently verifiable. The material should be current, and it should be complete. Finally, the information should seem logical.

4 **Explain the complementary nature of search engines, web directories, and databases.** Search engines offer quick access to millions of webpages but they have three limitations: (1) they don't offer any filtering by human editors, (2) various engines use different search techniques so you often need to use more than one, and (3) no search engine can access everything in the *hidden Internet*. Web directories overcome the first limitation, metasearch engines help overcome the second limitation, and online databases can partially overcome the third.

5 **Provide five guidelines for conducting an effective online search.** First and foremost, you need to read and understand the instructions for using each online research tool because they vary widely and may not search for or display results in the manner you expect. Second, pay attention to the details, because even minor aspects of searching can influence results dramatically. Third, review search and display options carefully to optimize results. Fourth, try variations on your search terms if you can't find what you're looking for. Fifth, try narrower or broader searches to adjust the scope of what you're looking for.

6 **Identify four new tools that can make your research more effective and more efficient.** Desktop and enterprise search engines apply website search engine techniques to files stored on individual computers and networks of computers, respectively. Research managers or content managers help you organize online resources and create reports, complete with tables of contents, indexes, and bibliographies. Social bookmarking sites help identify helpful online resources and can give an informal measure of what online users find interesting at any moment in time. Newsfeeds are a great way to stay informed about subjects that are likely to have a lot of new information available over time.

7 **Outline an effective process for planning and conducting information interviews.** Start by learning about the person(s) you plan to interview, then formulate your main idea to make sure your interview will stay focused. Choose the length, style, and organization of the interview, then select question types to elicit the sort of information you want, with each question designed to collect useful answers. Limit your questions to the most important queries. Record the interview if the person allows, and review your notes as soon as the interview ends.

8 **Explain the difference between drafting a summary, drawing a conclusion, and developing a recommendation.** A summary is a shortened version of one or more documents, research results, or other information; it filters out details and presents only the most important ideas. A conclusion is your analysis of what the findings mean (an interpretation of the facts). A recommendation is your opinion (based on reason and logic) about the course of action that should be taken.

Test Your Knowledge

1. What are the five steps in the research process?
2. How does primary information differ from secondary information?
3. What are the main advantages of electronic databases?
4. How does a search engine differ from a directory?
5. What is the purpose of information gap analysis?
6. How will you know when you are finished with the research process?
7. What is paraphrasing, and what is its purpose?
8. What is the difference between the mean, median, and mode?
9. What are the characteristics of a sound conclusion?
10. How does a conclusion differ from a recommendation?

Apply Your Knowledge

1. Why is it important to plan your research effort?
2. Why must you be careful when citing information from online sources?
3. One of your employees submitted a report comparing the market opportunities for two product ideas your company might develop. The report concludes that because the first idea yielded 340,000 hits in a Google search whereas the second idea yielded only 128,000 Google hits, the first idea clearly has more sales potential. Is this a valid conclusion? Why or why not?

4. After an exhaustive study of an important problem, you have reached a conclusion that you believe your company's management will reject. What will you do? Explain your answer.
5. **Ethical Choices** Companies occasionally make mistakes that expose confidential information, such as when employees lose laptop computers containing sensitive data files or webmasters forget to protect confidential webpages from search engine indexes. If you conducted a Google search that turned up competitive information on webpages that were clearly intended to be private, what would you do? Explain your answer.

Practice Your Knowledge

Message for Analysis

The following set of interview questions was prepared for a manager of Whirlpool Corporation. The goal of the interview was to learn some basic information about Whirlpool's meeting practices. Read the questions, then (1) critique them, as a whole, indicating what you like or dislike about this series of questions; and (2) select five questions and revise them to make them more effective.

1. What is your position in the company?
2. To whom do you report?
3. Do you attend or run many meetings?
4. Do your meetings start on time? Run late?

5. Do you distribute or receive a meeting agenda several days in advance of the meeting?
6. Do you like your job?
7. Do you travel a lot for your job?
8. Has your company cut back on travel expenditures? If so, how and why?
9. Does your company use videoconferencing or online meetings as an alternative to travel?
10. Does your company own its own videoconferencing equipment?
11. Are virtual meetings more or less effective than face-to-face meetings?
12. How long have you worked for Whirlpool?
13. Is Sears your largest retail customer?
14. How often does your management team meet with the managers of Sears?
15. Does your company produce only household appliances?
16. How do you keep your meetings on track?
17. Does someone prepare written minutes of meetings? Are the minutes distributed to meeting members?

Exercises

For active links to all websites discussed in this chapter, visit this text's website at www.prenhall.com/bovee. Locate your book and click on its Companion Website link. Then select Chapter 11, and click on "Featured Websites." Locate the name of the page or the URL related to the material in the text. Please note that links to sites that become inactive after publication of the book will be removed from the Featured Websites section.

11.1 **Understanding Your Topic: Subquestions** You and your business partners are considering buying several franchises in the fast-food business. You are all experienced managers or entrepreneurs, but none of you has experience in franchising. Visit www.amazon.com and search for books on this subject. Explore some of the books that you find by reading reviews and using the "search inside" feature.
   a. Use the information to develop a list of subquestions to help you narrow your focus.
   b. Write down the names of three books you might purchase to further aid your research.
   c. Summarize how a search like this can assist you with your research efforts and identify any risks of using this technique.

11.2 **Finding Secondary Information** Using online, database, or printed sources, find the following information. Be sure to properly cite your source using the formats discussed in Appendix B. (*Hint*: Start with Table 11.2, Major Business Resources.)
   a. Contact information for the American Management Association
   b. Median weekly earnings of men and women by occupation
   c. Current market share for Perrier water
   d. Performance ratios for office supply retailers
   e. Annual stock performance for Hewlett-Packard
   f. Number of franchise outlets in the United States
   g. Composition of the U.S. workforce by profession

11.3 **Finding Secondary Information** Businesspeople have to know where to look for secondary information when they conduct research. Identify five periodicals or online resources (websites, blogs, and so on) in each the following professions:
   a. Marketing and advertising
   b. Insurance
   c. Telecommunications
   d. Accounting

11.4 **Finding Information: Industry Information** Locate the NAICS codes for the following industries:
   a. Hotels and motels
   b. Breakfast cereals
   c. Bottled water
   d. Automatic vending machines

11.5 **Finding Information: Company Information** Select any public company and find the following information:
   a. Names of the company's current officers
   b. List of the company's products or services (summarize by product lines or divisions if the company offers many products and services)
   c. Current issues in the company's industry
   d. Outlook for the company's industry as a whole

11.6 **Finding Information: Secondary Information** You'd like to know if it's a good idea to buy banner advertisements on other websites to drive more traffic to your company's website. You're worried about the expense and difficulty of running an experiment to test banner effectiveness, so you decide to look for some secondary data. Identify three secondary sources that might offer helpful data on this question.

11.7 **Finding Information: Search Techniques** Analyze any recent school or work assignment that required you to conduct research. How did you approach your investigation? Did you rely mostly on sources of primary information or mostly on sources of secondary information? Now that you have studied this chapter, can you identify two ways to improve the research techniques you used during that assignment? Briefly explain.

11.8 **Finding Information: Primary Information** Deciding how to collect primary data is an important part of the research process. Which one or more of the five methods of data collection (examining documents, making observations, surveying people, conducting experiments, and performing interviews) would you use if you were researching these questions?
   a. Has the litter problem on campus been reduced since the cafeteria began offering fewer take-out choices this year than in past years?
   b. Has the school attracted more transfer students since it waived the formal application process and allowed students at other colleges simply to send their transcripts and a one-page letter of application?
   c. Have the number of traffic accidents at the school's main entrance been reduced since a traffic light was installed?

d. Has student satisfaction with the campus bookstore improved now that students can order their books over the Internet and pick them up at several campus locations?

11.9 Finding Information: Surveys You work for a movie studio that is producing a young director's first motion picture, the story of a group of unknown musicians finding work and making a reputation in a competitive industry. Unfortunately, some of your friends leave the first complete screening, saying that the 182-minute movie is simply too long. Others said they couldn't imagine any sequences to cut out. Your boss wants to test the movie on a regular audience and ask viewers to complete a questionnaire that will help the director decide whether edits are needed and, if so, where. Design a questionnaire that you can use to solicit valid answers for a report to the director about how to handle the audience's reaction to the movie.

11.10 Finding Information: Interviews Plan an informational interview with a professional working in your chosen field of study. Plan the structure of the interview and create a set of interview questions. Conduct the interview. Using the information you gathered, write a memo to another student describing the tasks, advantages, and disadvantages of jobs in this field of study. (Your reader is a person who also plans to pursue a career in this field of study.)

11.11 Finding Information: Interviews You're conducting an information interview with a manager in another division of your company. Partway through the interview, the manager shows clear signs of impatience. How should you respond? What might you do differently to prevent this from happening in the future? Explain your answers.

11.12 Teamwork: Evaluating Sources Break into small groups and surf the Internet to find websites that provide business information such as company or industry news, trends, analysis, facts, or performance data. Using the criteria discussed under "Evaluating Sources" on page 336, evaluate the credibility of the information presented at these websites.

11.13 Processing Information: Reading and Taking Notes Select an article from a business journal such as *BusinessWeek*, *Fortune*, or *Forbes*. Read the article and highlight the article's key points. Summarize the article in less than 100 words, paraphrasing the key points.

11.14 Processing Information: Documenting Sources Select five business articles from sources such as journals, books, newspapers, or websites. Develop a resource list using Appendix B as a guideline.

11.15 Analyzing Data: Calculating the Mean Your boss has asked you to analyze and report on your division's sales for the first nine months of this year. Using the following data from company invoices, calculate the mean for each

quarter and all averages for the year to date. Then identify and discuss the quarterly sales trends.

January	$24,600	June	26,800
February	25,900	July	$29,900
March	23,000	August	30,500
April	$21,200	September	26,600
May	24,600		

Expand Your Knowledge

Exploring the Best of the Web

Check Out This 24-Hour Library
www.ipl.org

Start your business research by visiting the Internet Public Library. Visit the reference center and explore the many online references available. These cover topics such as business, economics, law, government, science, technology, computers, education, and more. You can even submit questions for the IPL staff. Visit the reference center and explore the Business and Economics Reference section. Click on Business Directories, then perform these tasks:

1. Select five companies and use the links provided to find contact information (address, phone, website, officers' names, and so on) for each company. What kinds of contact information did you find at the company websites?
2. Gather information about the U.S. budget by using one of the site's directories: A Business Researcher's Interests. Why is using a directory such as this one an efficient way to obtain information?
3. Go back to the library's main reference center and click on Reference. Follow some of the reference links. How might these links help you when performing business research?

Surfing Your Way to Career Success

Bovée and Thill's Business Communication Resources offers links to hundreds of online resources that can help you with this course, your other college courses, and your career. Visit www.buscommresources.com, then click on "Business Communication Web Directory." The "Research" section connects you to a variety of websites and articles on such important topics as using research tools, analyzing and evaluating research materials, checking facts, interviewing and using online research tools. Identify three websites from this section that could be useful in your business career. For each site, write a two-sentence summary of what the site offers and how it could help you launch and build your career.

Learn Interactively

Interactive Study Guide

Visit www.prenhall.com/bovee, then locate your book and click on its "Companion Website" link. Select Chapter 11 to take advantage of the interactive "Chapter Quiz" to test your knowledge of chapter concepts. Receive instant feedback on whether you need additional studying. Also, visit the "Study Hall," where you'll find an abundance of valuable resources that will help you succeed in this course.

Peak Performance Grammar and Mechanics

If your instructor has required the use of "Peak Performance Grammar and Mechanics," either in your online course or on CD, you can continue to improve your skill with commas, semicolons, and colons by using the "Peak Performance Grammar and Mechanics" module. Click "Punctuation," and then click "Punctuation I." Take the Pretest to determine whether you have any weak areas. Then review those areas in the Refresher Course. Take the Follow-Up Test to check your grasp of these elements. For an extra challenge or advanced practice, take the Advanced Test. Finally, for additional reinforcement, visit the Companion Website, click on any chapter, then click on "Improve Your Grammar, Mechanics, and Usage."

CHAPTER 12

Designing Visual Communication

LEARNING OBJECTIVES

After studying this chapter, you will be able to

1 Describe the communication power of visuals

2 Discuss six principles of graphic design that can improve the quality of your visuals

3 Explain how to avoid ethical lapses when using visuals

4 Explain how to choose which points in your message to illustrate

5 Describe the most common options for presenting data in a visual format

6 Identify five guidelines for using photographs effectively

7 List three criteria to review in order to verify the quality of your visuals

COMMUNICATION CLOSE-UP AT STONE YAMASHITA PARTNERS

www.stoneyamashita.com

Keith Yamashita doesn't look or act like the stereotypical business consultant, but that hasn't stopped him from developing enthusiastic fans among top executives at IBM, Mercedes-Benz, Nike, General Electric, and other firms who have worked with his company, Stone Yamashita Partners (SYP).

Yamashita and designer Robert Stone started SYP in 1994, after working together at Apple Computer. Gradually, they assembled a diverse team that includes designers, writers, technologists, a poet, a sociologist, and a former lawyer—but very few MBAs. This eclectic group specializes in helping companies examine, revamp, and sometimes reinvent their vision and mission, business strategy, image, and company culture.

That kind of fundamental change affects everyone in a company, from the most senior executive to the newest hire. People tend to resist change, at least initially, but communication that is effective and compelling can help turn such resistance into commitment.

Communication is SYP's specialty, but Yamashita's team never relies on words alone. Instead, it uses strong visual elements to paint a picture—sometimes literally—of a company's new direction. Everything it produces is full of compelling visual cues, whether it's a short video, an interactive website, a pocket-size book, a giant story scroll, or a full-size store mockup. Highly visual content and offbeat

Compelling visual messages are critical to the success of consulting partners Keith Yamashita and Robert Stone.

presentation can make a message more tangible and thus more effective for employees, customers, and investors.

Both partners know that the right visuals can inspire people to move from resistance to commitment to action. "Strat-egy is not something that's done in a box with only a rational hat on," says Stone. "It needs to be visceral, human, and often emotional." Yamashita agrees, and adds, "We're trying to move people to a place where it makes sense to act."[1]

UNDERSTANDING VISUAL COMMUNICATION

Project teams from Stone Yamashita Partners (profiled in the chapter-opening "Communica-tion Close-Up) look for new ways to connect and explore business ideas through creative visuals, often helping clients see important concepts and relationships that weren't obvious using textual communication alone. Although the primary focus of this course is written mes-sages, visual communication has become an important skill for today's business profession-als and managers. This chapter helps you appreciate the power of images and the visual evolution of business communication. It then explains how to identify which points in your messages to illustrate; how to select the best visual for each of those points; and how to create effective visuals in any media, from memos to reports to webpages to electronic presentations.

The Power of Images

1 LEARNING OBJECTIVE

Describe the communication power of visuals

Well-designed visual elements can enhance the communication power of textual messages and, in some instances, even replace textual messages. Visuals can often convey some mes-sage points (such as spatial relationships, correlations, procedures, and emotions) more ef-fectively and more efficiently than words. Generally speaking, in a given amount of time, well-designed images can convey much more information than text.[2] In the numbers-oriented world of work, people rely heavily on trend lines, distribution curves, and visual presentations of numerical quantities. Visuals attract and hold people's attention, helping your audience understand and remember your message. Busy readers often jump to visuals to try to get the gist of a message, and attractive visuals can draw readers deeper into your reports and presentations. Pictures are also an effective way to communicate with the di-verse audiences that are common in today's business environment.

Like words, visuals often carry connotative or symbolic meanings.

In addition to their direct information value, visuals often convey connotative mean-ing as well. As you read in Chapter 5, many words and phrases carry connotative meanings, which are all the mental images, emotions, and other impressions that the word or phrase evokes in audience members. A significant part of the power—and risk—of visual elements derives from their connotative meanings as well. Even something as simple as a watermark symbol embedded in letterhead stationery can boost reader confidence in whatever mes-sage is printed on the paper.[3] Many colors, shapes, and other design elements have **visual symbolism**; and their symbolic, connotative meaning can evolve over time and mean dif-ferent things in different cultures (see Figure 12.1). Being aware of these symbolic mean-

FIGURE 12.1 Visual Symbolism
A red cross (with equal-length arms) on a white background is the well-known symbol of the Red Cross relief organization. It is also used to indicate the medical branches of many nations' military services. The red cross symbol is based on the flag of Switzerland (where the first Red Cross organization was formed), which over the course of hundreds of years developed from battle flags that originally used the Christian cross symbol. Although the Red Cross emblem is not based directly on the Christian symbol, the organization uses a red crescent in countries where Islam is the dominant religion and is known as the Red Crescent. To avoid association with religious symbols, the International Federation of Red Cross and Red Crescent Societies (the global umbrella organization for all national Red Cross and Red Crescent organizations), recently adopted the Red Crystal as its new symbol.

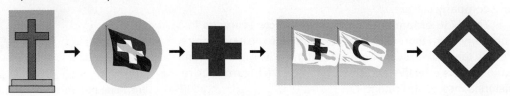

ings and using them to your advantage are important aspects of being an effective business communicator.

Because they have so much power to communicate, visuals must be carefully planned, created, and integrated with text. An awkward sentence or grammatical error deep within a report might not be noticed by the majority of readers, but a poorly chosen or clumsily implemented visual will be noticed by most—and can confuse or alienate audiences and damage your credibility. You don't need to be a professional designer to use visuals effectively, but you do need be aware of some basic design principles if you want to avoid making high-visibility mistakes. This chapter gives you enough background to begin creating your own business visuals, and with some practice you'll be able to craft effective visuals for nearly any communication project you might encounter.

The Visual Evolution in Business Communication

Several technological and social factors are contributing to the increasing use—and importance—of visuals in business communication. The process of creating and working with visual elements used to be the domain of experts with complex and expensive tools. However, digital technology has changed this situation dramatically. Digital cameras that can produce high-quality images and video are inexpensive and easy enough for anyone to use; the software needed to create diagrams, process photos, edit video, and prepare other visual elements continues to get both easier and more powerful all the time; the global reach of the Internet makes it easy to send images almost instantly; and more Internet users have high-speed connections that can handle the larger computer files that visuals tend to require. Design and production tasks that used to take days can now be completed in hours or even minutes. As technologies such as wireless networking continue to advance, business communicators will continue to reach wider audiences in less time, using equipment that costs less and requires fewer skills.[4]

Thanks to advances in technology and changing audience expectations, business communication is becoming more visual.

While technology has been putting visual design and production into the hands of everyday business communicators in recent years, audience skills and expectations have been evolving as well. Two changes in particular could affect your communication efforts in the coming years. First, U.S. government research indicates that only half of the adult population in the United States now have the literacy skills considered necessary for success in today's workplace.[5] In other words, depending on the nature of your work, you could find yourself communicating with audiences whose skills could keep them from successfully reading your documents. Visuals could play a vital role in communicating your messages to audiences with lower reading skills. Second, as technology has multiplied the ways in which communicators can create visuals and as people grow up and live in a more visual, media-saturated environment, audiences may well expect messages to be more visual.

Visual literacy is the ability to both create and interpret visuals.

As a result of these changes in both the tools and the communication environment, **visual literacy**, the ability (as a sender) to create effective images and (as a receiver) to correctly interpret visual messages, has become a key business skill.[6] Whether you need to use images to reach an audience with limited reading skills or want to use images to magnify the impact of your written messages, knowing how to help your audience see what you see will help you become a more effective communicator.

Visual Design Principles

Just as creating effective sentences, paragraphs, and documents requires working knowledge of the principles of good writing, creating effective visuals requires some knowledge of the principles of good design. Even though few businesspeople have the opportunity to formally study the "language" of line, mass, space, size, color, pattern, and texture, anyone can learn enough of the basic concepts to craft effective basic visuals.

When you encounter visuals that you find appealing or unappealing, or effective or ineffective, stop and ask yourself why you responded the way you did. Did a particular design grab you and practically force you to pay attention, or did you pass right by with hardly a notice? Did one graph reveal its information quickly and easily while another

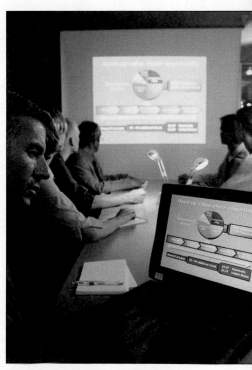

Creating effective visuals and correctly interpreting visuals that other people create are important business skills.

made you spend time decoding its confusing message? Did one photo appeal to you at an emotional level and therefore draw you into a document, whereas another repulsed you for some reason and caused you to lose interest in the document? By thinking about your own reactions to visual designs, you can become a more effective designer yourself.

As you consider your reactions to various designs and create designs of your own, you'll begin to see how six fundamental principles help distinguish ineffective and effective designs: consistency, contrast, balance, emphasis, convention, and simplicity (see Figure 12.2):

2 LEARNING OBJECTIVE

Discuss six principles of graphic design that can improve the quality of your visuals

- **Consistency.** Audiences view a series of visuals as a whole and assume that design elements will be consistent from one page to the next. For instance, if your first chart shows data for Division A in blue and for Division B in green, the audience will get confused if you later switch to green for Division A and red for Division B. Think of consistency as *visual parallelism*, in the same way that textual parallelism helps audiences understand and compare a series of ideas.[7] You can achieve visual parallelism in a variety of ways, through the consistent use of color, shape, size, texture, position, scale, or typeface.

- **Contrast.** Readers expect visual distinctions to match verbal ones. To emphasize differences, depict items in contrasting colors, such as red and blue, or black and white. But to emphasize similarities, make color differences more subtle. In a pie chart, you might show two similar items in two shades of blue and a dissimilar item in yellow. Keep in mind that accent colors draw attention to key elements, but they lose their effect if you overdo them.

- **Balance.** The human eye tends to compare visual images with physical structures, and images that appear to be out of balance can be as unsettling as a building that looks like it's about to tip over. Balance can be either *formal*, in which the elements in the images are arranged symmetrically around a central point or axis, or *informal*, in which elements are not distributed evenly but stronger and weaker elements are arranged in such a way that achieves an overall effect of balance. A common approach to informal balance is weighing one visually dominant element against several smaller or weaker elements.[8] Generally speaking, formal balance is more calming and serious, whereas informal balance tends to feel more dynamic and engaging (which is why most advertising uses this approach, for example).

- **Emphasis.** Audiences usually assume that the dominant element in a design is the most important, so make sure that the visually dominant element really does represent the most important information. You can do this through color, position, size, or placement, for instance. Conversely, be sure to visually downplay less important items. For instance, avoid using strong colors for minor support points, and de-emphasize background features such as the grid lines on a chart.

- **Convention.** Visual communication is guided by a variety of generally accepted rules or conventions, just as written communication is guided by an array of spelling, grammar, punctuation, and usage conventions. These conventions dictate virtually every aspect of design.[9] Moreover, many conventions are so ingrained that people don't even realize they are following conventions. For example, if English is your native language, you assume that ideas progress across the page from left to right, because that's the direction in which English text is written. Whether it's the sequence of steps in a process diagram or elapsed time along the bottom of a graph, you automatically expect this left-to-right flow. However, if you are a native Arabic or Hebrew speaker, you might automatically assume that flow on a page or screen is from right to left, because that is the direction in which these languages are written. Flouting conventions often causes breakdowns in communication, but in some cases, it can be done to great effect.[10] For instance, flipping an organization chart upside down to put the customers at the top, with front-line employees directly beneath them and on down to the chief executive at the bottom, can be an effective way to emphasize that customers come first and the responsibility of managers is supporting employees in their efforts to satisfy customers.

- **Simplicity.** As a general rule, simpler is better when it comes to visuals for business communication. When you're designing graphics for your documents, remember that you're conveying information, not decorating an apartment or creating artwork. Limit the number of colors and design elements you use, and take care to avoid *chartjunk*, a term coined by visual communication specialist Edward R. Tufte for dec-

Nearly every aspect of visual design is governed by conventions that set audience expectations.

FIGURE 12.2 Ineffective and Effective Design
The slide in Figure 12.2a violates numerous principles of effective design, as you can see in the annotations.
Figure 12.2b will never win any awards for exciting or innovative design, but it does its job efficiently and effectively.

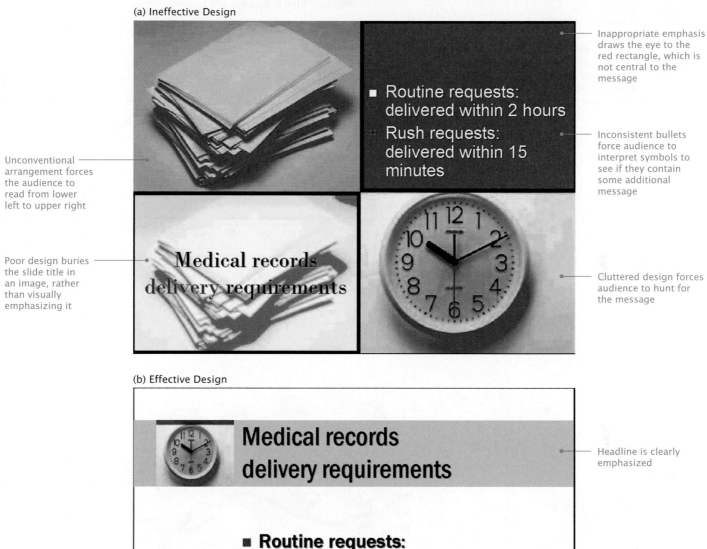

(a) Ineffective Design

Inappropriate emphasis draws the eye to the red rectangle, which is not central to the message

Unconventional arrangement forces the audience to read from lower left to upper right

Inconsistent bullets force audience to interpret symbols to see if they contain some additional message

Poor design buries the slide title in an image, rather than visually emphasizing it

Cluttered design forces audience to hunt for the message

(b) Effective Design

Headline is clearly emphasized

Consistent use of bullets lets audience focus on the message, not the mechanics

Conventional left-to-right, top-to-bottom arrangement makes it easy to find the message

orative elements that clutter documents and potentially confuse readers without adding any relevant information.[11] Computers make it far too easy to add chartjunk, from clip art illustrations to three-dimensional bar charts that display only two dimensions of data (see Figure 12.3). When you need to show distinctions between visual elements, follow Tufte's strategy of the *smallest effective difference*. In his words, "Make all visual distinctions as subtle as possible, but still clear and effective."[12] For example, the slices in a pie chart don't need to be distinguished by both color *and* texture; one or the other will do the job more efficiently.

FIGURE 12.3 The Power of Simplicity

These two graphs contain the same information, but Figure 12.3a is much easier to interpret. None of the additional elements in Figure 12.3b, including the extra colors, background design, and three-dimensional structure, add any information value—and they make the graph harder to interpret. Adding a false third dimension to two-dimensional information such as these sales figures is a common mistake.

(a)

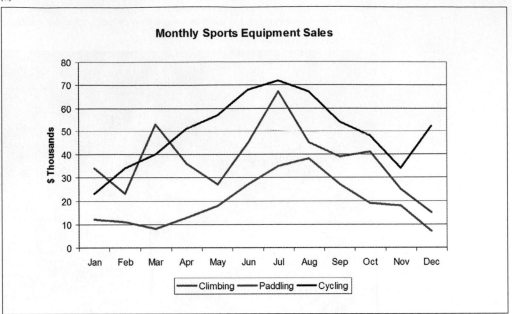

(b)

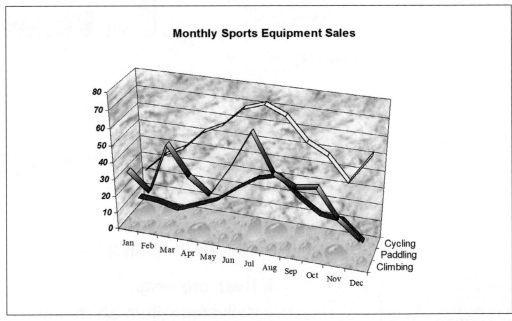

The Ethics of Visual Communication

Remember that the ability to communicate with visuals comes with the responsibility to communicate ethically.

Power always comes with responsibility—and the potential power of visuals places an ethical burden on every business communicator. This situation involves not only the obvious requirement of avoiding intentional ethical lapses but the more complicated and often more subtle requirement of avoiding unintentional lapses as well. Ethical problems can range from photos that play on racial or gender stereotypes to images that imply cause-and-effect relationships that may not exist to graphs that distort data (see Figure 12.4).

Just as subtle word choices shade the meaning of your writing, seemingly minor design variations can influence the message your readers take away from your business graphics. If all three graphs in Figure 12.4 show the same data, which—if any—would be more "hon-

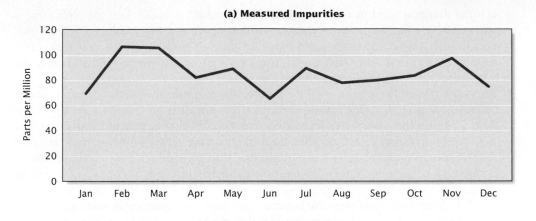

(a) Measured Impurities

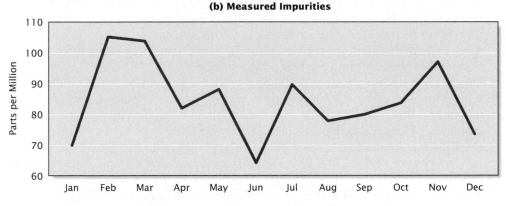

(b) Measured Impurities

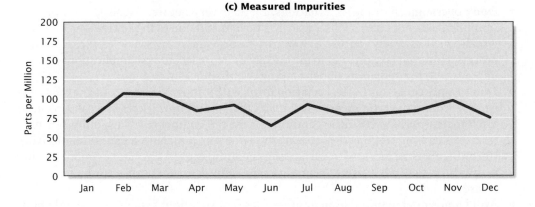

(c) Measured Impurities

FIGURE 12.4 Influencing Perception Through Visual Design
Figure 12.4a shows impurities measured over the course of a 12-month period; the vertical scale is set from 0 to 120, sufficient to cover the range of variations in the data. However, what if you wanted to make the variations from month to month look more severe? Less severe? Figure 12.4b, with the scale "zoomed in" to a narrow range of 60 to 110, makes the variations look much more dramatic. The result could be a stronger emotional impact on the reader, creating the impression that these impurities are out of control. In contrast, Figure 12.4c expands the scale, from 0 to 200, which appears to minimize the variations in the data. This graph is visually "calmer," potentially creating the opposite impression—that there's really nothing to worry about. The data shown in all three graphs are identical, but they send three different messages to the reader.

est" than the others? The answer to this question depends on your intent and your audience's information needs. For instance, if dramatic swings in the measurement from month to month suggest a problem with the quality of your product or the safety of a process that affects the public, then visually minimizing the swings might well be considered dishonest.

Altering the scale of data charts is just one of many ways that visuals can be designed to emphasize or de-emphasize certain aspects of information. For example, photographs can influence perceptions of physical size (and perhaps of quality, value, danger, or other associated variables), depending on the way the various elements are arranged in the picture. To increase the perceived size of a product, an advertiser might show a close-up of it being held by someone with smaller-than-average hands. Conversely, a large hand would make the product seem smaller.

You can work to avoid ethical lapses in your visuals by following these guidelines:[13]

- **Consider all possible interpretations—and misinterpretations.** Try to view your visuals from your audience members' perspective; will their biases, beliefs, or backgrounds lead them to different conclusions than you've intended? For instance,

You can take many steps to emphasize or de-emphasize specific elements in your visuals, but make sure you don't inadvertently commit an ethical lapse while doing so.

3 LEARNING OBJECTIVE

Explain how to avoid ethical lapses when using visuals

assume that you want to show how easy your product is to use, and the photograph you've chosen just happens to show a woman operating the product. Will anyone conclude that what you really mean to say is that your product is so simple that "even a woman can use it"? In other words, while trying to compliment your product, are you unintentionally insulting women?

Visuals can't always speak for themselves; make sure your audience has enough context to interpret your visuals correctly.

- **Provide context.** Even when they are completely accurate, all visuals can show only a partial view of reality. This limitation ranges from the obvious (photos can show only what is within the camera's view) to the subtle (graphs that appear to show variations in the quantity being measured when the differences are actually measurement errors). Part of your responsibility as a communicator is to provide not only accurate visuals but enough background information to help audiences interpret the visual information correctly.

- **Don't hide or minimize negative information that runs counter to your argument.** Let's say you're responsible for employee satisfaction in all 10 of your company's divisions, and you measure the results of your efforts every quarter through employee surveys. If satisfaction scores are up in four divisions, unchanged in three divisions, and down in three divisions, you can't legitimately "prove" that you're being successful with a graph that highlights only the four positive data points.

- **Don't exaggerate information that supports your argument.** Similarly, you have a responsibility not to oversell information in support of your argument. If employee satisfaction in those four divisions is improved but still lower than it should be, don't manipulate the graph to imply that all the problems have been solved. You should also resist the temptation to alter or enhance photographs and other images in ways that support your arguments. In skilled hands, image-processing software can alter photos in ways that most viewers cannot detect. The ethical burden rests on business communicators to ensure that all of their visuals are complete, honest, and truly representative of the underlying information.

- **Don't oversimplify complex situations.** By their very nature, visuals tend to present simplified views of reality. This is usually a benefit and one of the key reasons for using visuals, such as when you use a flowchart to provide an overview of a complicated process. However, take care not to mislead an audience by hiding complications that are important to the audience's understanding of the situation.

- **Don't imply cause-and-effect relationships without providing proof that they exist.** For example, if you create a line chart that shows how increasing sales seem to track increasing advertising expenditures, you can claim a correlation but not necessarily a causal relationship between the two. You can claim a causal relationship (meaning that the increase in advertising spending caused the increase in sales) only if you can isolate advertising spending as the *only* factor that can account for the increase in sales.

- **Avoid emotional manipulation or other forms of coercion.** Visuals, particularly photographs and video, can be persuasive elements to use in emotional appeals. However, you must take care not to overstep into unethical manipulation. For instance, a photograph of an unhappy child being treated as a social outcast because he or she doesn't wear the latest fashions or own the trendiest new toys could be considered an unethical way to persuade parents to buy those products for their children.

The ways in which you aggregate data for display can affect the messages and meanings that your audience extracts from your visuals.

- **Be careful with the way you aggregate data.** Preparing charts, graphs, and tables that present data often involves decisions about *aggregating*, or grouping, data. For example, you could summarize the output from one of your factories in a variety of ways. To show output over the course of one year, you could total the data by month, creating a graph with just 12 data points. This approach would emphasize monthly or seasonal variations, but it would hide weekly or daily variations that could be meaningful to your audience. You might find that production drops for the first few days of every quarter, for instance, perhaps because the staff has to work extra hard at the end of the quarter to meet quarterly production goals, then eases off for a few days to compensate. Or you could present the data from a different angle completely, such as showing average output per hour over the course

Ethics Detective

Is Something Hiding Behind These Numbers?

You've been assigned to present the results of an industrywide study of the effects of insecticide. Your audience consists of the department heads in your company, whose experience and education backgrounds vary widely, from chemical engineering to insurance to law. You're convinced you need to keep your report as simple and as jargon-free as possible. You'll then invite content-area specialists to contact you if they have technical questions.

You're not a scientific expert in insecticides, but your supervisor has introduced you to a scientist who works for a trade association that represents chemical producers, including your firm. The scientist is familiar with the study you'll be reporting on, and she has experience in communicating technical subjects to diverse audiences. You jumped at the chance to have such a knowledgeable person review your presentation for technical accuracy, but you're uncomfortable with some of her feedback. In particular, you question her advice to replace the following line chart, which shows the number of insecticide poisonings and deaths by age.

She suggests that this chart is too busy and too difficult for nonspecialists to read. As an alternative, she provides a bar chart that selects four specific ages from the entire range. She says this chart communicates the same basic idea as the line chart but is much easier to read.

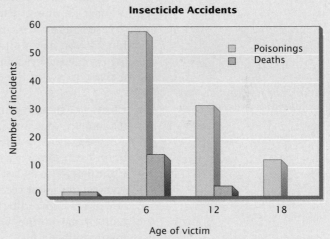

ANALYSIS

You agree with the scientist that the line chart is visually busy and takes more effort to process, but something bothers you about the bar chart. Does it present the insecticide situation accurately and honestly? Why or why not?

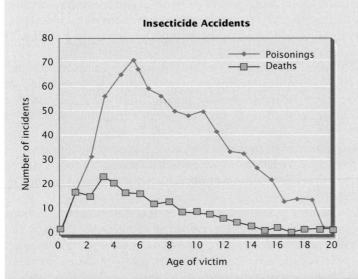

of the eight-hour workday, which might highlight completely different concerns. Low output in the first hour of the day could signal people frequently coming in late or problems getting the machinery up and running every morning. Whatever the situation, the decisions you make about aggregating the data can have a profound effect on the message your audience receives (see "Ethics Detective: Is Something Hiding Behind These Numbers?").

IDENTIFYING POINTS TO ILLUSTRATE

4 LEARNING OBJECTIVE

Explain how to choose which points in your message to illustrate

To help identify which parts of your message can benefit from visuals, either to support your textual message or perhaps to replace a section of text entirely, step back and consider the flow of your entire message from the audience's point of view. Which parts of the message are likely to seem complex, open to misinterpretation, or even just a little bit dull? Are there any connections between ideas or data sets that might not be obvious if they are addressed only in text? Is there a lot of numerical data or other discrete factual content that would be difficult to read if presented in paragraph form? Is there a chance that the main idea won't "jump off the page" if it's covered only in text? Will readers greet the message with skepticism and therefore look for plenty of supporting evidence?

If you answer yes to any of these questions, you probably need one or more visuals. For instance, detailed facts and figures may be confusing and tedious in paragraph form, but tables and charts can conveniently organize and display such detail with clarity. Some points may require a detailed description of physical relationships or procedures, in which case you might want to use flowcharts, drawings, or photographs to clarify the discussion. Or you may simply want to draw attention to a particular fact or detail by reinforcing the message visually. When you're deciding which points to present visually, think of the five Cs:

Effective visuals are clear, complete, concise, connected, and compelling.

- **Clear.** The human mind is extremely adept at processing visual information, whether it's something as simple as the shape of stop sign or as complicated as the floor plan for a new factory. If you're having difficultly conveying an idea in words, take a minute to brainstorm some visual possibilities.
- **Complete.** Visuals, particularly tables, often serve to provide the supporting details for your main idea or recommendation. Moreover, the process of summarizing, concluding, or recommending often requires you to narrow down your material or exclude details; a table or other visual can provide these details without getting in the way of your main message.
- **Concise.** You've probably heard the phrase "A picture is worth a thousand words." If a particular section of your message seems to require extensive description or explanation, see whether there's a way to convey this information visually. With a picture working in conjunction with text, you may be able to reduce your word count considerably.
- **Connected.** A key purpose of many business messages is showing connections of some sort—similarities or differences, correlations, cause-and-effect relationships, and so on. Whenever you want readers to see such a connection, see whether a chart, diagram, or other illustration can help.
- **Compelling.** Your readers live in a highly visual world. Will one or more illustrations make your message more persuasive, more interesting, more likely to get read? You never want to insert visuals simply for decorative purposes, of course, but even if a particular point can be expressed equally well via text or visuals, consider adding the visual in order to make your report or presentation more compelling.

As you identify which points in your document would benefit from a visual, make sure that each visual you decide on has a clear purpose (see Table 12.1).

SELECTING THE RIGHT TYPE OF VISUAL

Once you've identified which points would benefit most from visual presentation, your next decision is choosing which type of visual to use for each message point. As you can see in Figure 12.5, you have many choices for business graphics. For certain types of information,

TABLE 12.1 When to Use Visuals

PURPOSE	APPLICATION
To clarify	Support text descriptions of "graphic" topics: quantitative or numerical information, explanations of trends, descriptions.
To simplify	Break complicated descriptions into components that can be depicted with conceptual models, flowcharts, organization charts, or diagrams.
To emphasize	Call attention to particularly important points by illustrating them with line, bar, and pie charts.
To summarize	Review major points in the narrative by providing a chart or table that sums up the data.
To reinforce	Present information in visual and written form to increase reader's retention.
To attract	Make material seem more interesting by decorating the cover or title page and by breaking up the text with visual aids.
To impress	Build credibility by putting ideas into visual form to convey the impression of authenticity and precision.
To unify	Depict the relationship among points—for example, with a flowchart.

the decision is usually obvious. To present a large set of numerical values or detailed textual information, a table is the obvious choice in most cases. However, if you're presenting data broken down geographically, a color-coded map might be more effective to show overall patterns rather than individual data points. Also, certain visuals are used more commonly for certain applications, so your audience is likely to expect line charts and bar charts to show trends. Line charts usually show data variations relative to a time axis (such as sales month by month), whereas bar charts more often compare discrete groups (such as sales by demographic segment). Although a bar chart can show the percentages that make up a whole, this job is usually reserved for pie charts.

The following sections explore the most common types of visuals in more detail, starting with visuals designed to present data.

You have many types of visuals to choose from, and each is best suited to particular communication tasks.

Presenting Data

Business professionals have a tremendous number of choices for presenting data, from general purpose line, bar, and pie charts to specialized charts for product portfolios, financial analysis, and other professional functions. The visuals most commonly used to present data include tables; line and surface charts; bar charts, pictograms, and Gantt charts; scatter and bubble diagrams; and pie charts.

5 LEARNING OBJECTIVE

Describe the most common options for presenting data in a visual format

Tables

When you need to present detailed, specific information, choose a **table**, a systematic arrangement of data in columns and rows. Tables are ideal when your audience needs information that would be either difficult or tedious to handle in the main text.

Most tables contain the standard parts illustrated in Table 12.2. Every table includes vertical columns and horizontal rows, with useful headings along the top and side. The number of columns and rows you can comfortably fit in a table depends on the medium. For printed documents, you can adjust font size and column and row spacing to fit a considerable amount of information on the page and still maintain readability. For online documents, you'll need to reduce the number of columns and rows to make sure

Printed tables can display extensive amounts of data, but tables for online display and electronic presentations need to be simpler.

FIGURE 12.5 Selecting the Best Visual
For each point you want to illustrate, make sure you choose the most effective type of visual.

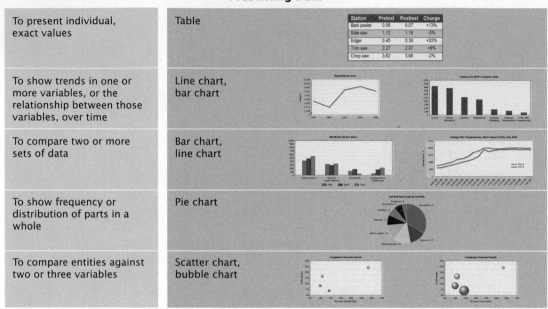

Presenting Data

Communication Challenge	Effective Visual Choice
To present individual, exact values	Table
To show trends in one or more variables, or the relationship between those variables, over time	Line chart, bar chart
To compare two or more sets of data	Bar chart, line chart
To show frequency or distribution of parts in a whole	Pie chart
To compare entities against two or three variables	Scatter chart, bubble chart

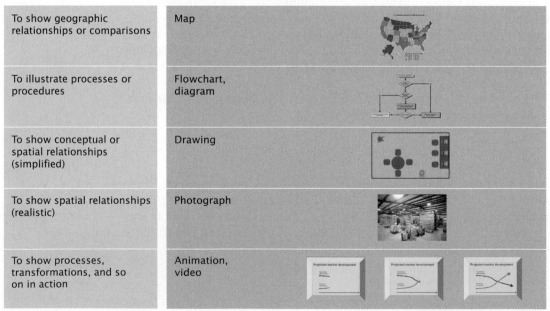

Presenting Information, Concepts, and Ideas

To show geographic relationships or comparisons	Map
To illustrate processes or procedures	Flowchart, diagram
To show conceptual or spatial relationships (simplified)	Drawing
To show spatial relationships (realistic)	Photograph
To show processes, transformations, and so on in action	Animation, video

your tables are easily readable online. Tables for oral presentations usually need to be the simplest of all, because you can't expect audiences to read detailed information from the screen.

Although complex information may require formal tables that are set apart from the text, you can present some data more simply within the text. You make the table, in essence, a part of the paragraph, typed in tabular format. Such text tables are usually introduced with a sentence that leads directly into the tabulated information. Here's an example:[14]

TABLE 12.2 Parts of a Table

	MULTICOLUMN HEAD*			
STUB HEAD	SUBHEAD	SUBHEAD	SINGLE-COLUMN HEAD	SINGLE-COLUMN HEAD
Row head	XXX	XXX	XX	XX
Row head				
Subhead	XX	XXX	XX	X
Subhead	XX	XXX	XX	XX
Total	XXX	XXX	XX	XX

Source: (In the same format as a text footnote; see Appendix B.)

*Footnote (For an explanation of elements in the table, a superscript number or small letter may be used instead of an asterisk or other symbol.)

Here is how the five leading full-service restaurant chains compare in terms of number of locations and annual revenue:

	OSI RESTAURANT PARTNERS	APPLEBEE'S	CARLSON	BRINKER	DARDEN
Major Chain(s)	Outback Steakhouse, Carrabba's	Applebee's	TGI Friday's, Pick Up Stix	Chili's, Romano's	Red Lobster, Olive Garden
Locations	1,300	1,800	900	1,600	1,400
Revenue ($ Million)	$3,602	$1,217	$2,400	$4,151	$5,721

Source: Hoover's Online [accessed 17 November 2006] www.hoovers.com.

When you prepare tables, follow these guidelines to make your tables easy to read:

- Use common, understandable units, and clearly identify the units you're using, whether it's dollars, percentages, price per ton, or whatever.
- Express all items in a column in the same unit and round off for simplicity.
- Label column headings clearly and use a subhead if necessary.
- Separate columns or rows with lines or extra space to make the table easy to follow; in complex tables, consider highlighting every other row or column in a pale, contrasting color.
- Provide totals or averages of columns or rows when relevant.
- Document the source of the data using the samze format as a test footnote (see Appendix II).

Although numerical tables are more common, tables can also contain words, symbols, or other facts and figures. Word tables are particularly appropriate for presenting survey findings or for comparing various items against a specific standard.

Line and Surface Charts

A **line chart** illustrates trends over time or plots the relationship of two or more variables. In line charts showing trends, the vertical, or *y*, axis shows the amount, and the horizontal, or *x*, axis shows the time or other quantity against which the amount is being measured. Both axes often start at zero in the lower left-hand corner, but you can exercise a fair amount of flexibility with both axes in order to present your data as clearly as possible. For instance, to show both positive and negative values (such as profit and loss), you can have the *y* axis span from a negative value up to a positive value, with zero somewhere in between. Of course, you should always avoid distorting the data in ways that could mislead your audience, as "The Ethics of Visual Communication" noted on page 366.

Line charts are commonly used to show trends over time or the relationship between two or more variables.

FIGURE 12.6 Line Chart
This two-line chart compares the temperatures measured inside two cement kilns from 8:00 A.M. to 5:00 P.M.

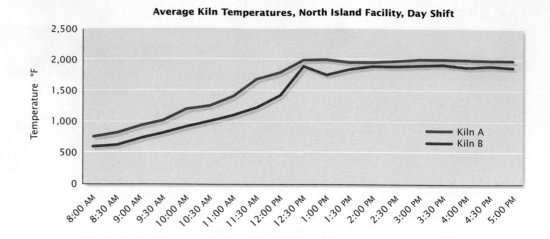

Average Kiln Temperatures, North Island Facility, Day Shift

FIGURE 12.7 Surface Chart
Surface or area charts can show a combination of trends over time and the individual contributions of the components of a whole.

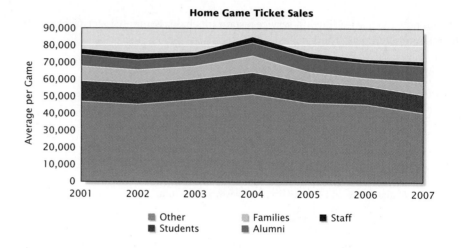

Home Game Ticket Sales

A spreadsheet offers ways to predict future values based on past values shown in a line chart.

If you need to compare two or more sets of data, you can plot them on the same chart for instant visual comparison (see Figure 12.6). Two or three lines on a single chart are usually easy to read, but beyond that, things can get confusing, particularly if the lines cross.

By their very nature, line charts often raise the question, "What happens next?" For instance, if you present sales data for the past 12 months, your audience may well ask what you think will happen in the next 12 months. Predicting the future is always a risky endeavor, but you can use your spreadsheet's forecasting tools to extend a line into the future using a statistical technique known as *regression analysis*. Check your spreadsheet's Help function for more information on using its *linear regression*, *trend line*, or *forecasting* functions. However, when using these tools, be aware that all they can do is extract patterns from past data and extend those patterns into the future. They don't have any awareness of the "real-life" factors that shaped that past data—and may or may not produce that same pattern in the future.

A **surface chart**, also called an **area chart**, is a form of line chart with a cumulative effect; all the lines add up to the top line, which represents the total (see Figure 12.7). This form of chart helps you illustrate changes in the composition of something over time. One common use is showing how sales of individual products contribute to the company's overall revenue.[15] When preparing a surface chart, put the most important segment on the bottom and build up from there.

Bar Charts, Pictograms, and Gantt Charts

A **bar chart** portrays numbers by the height or length of its rectangular bars, making a series of numbers easy to read or understand. Bar charts are particularly valuable when you want to

- Compare the size of several items at one time
- Show changes in one item over time

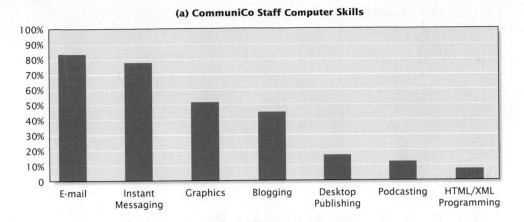

(a) CommuniCo Staff Computer Skills

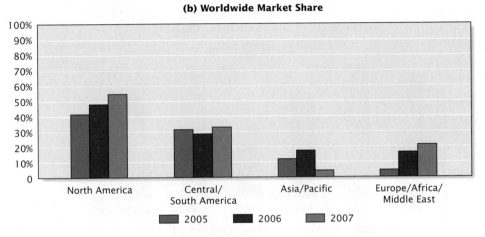

(b) Worldwide Market Share

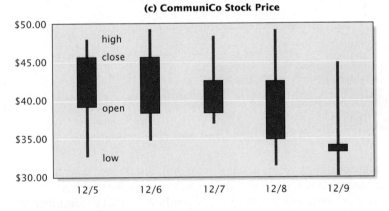

(c) CommuniCo Stock Price

FIGURE 12.8 The Versatile Bar Chart
Here are six of the dozens of variations possible with bar charts: *singular* (12.8a), *grouped* (12.8b), *deviation* (12.8c). (*continued*)

- Indicate the composition of several items over time
- Show the relative size of components of a whole

As the charts in Figure 12.8 show, bar charts can appear in various forms. *Grouped* bar charts compare more than one set of data, using a different color or pattern for each set. *Deviation* bar charts identify positive and negative values, or winners and losers. *Segmented* bar charts, also known as *stacked* bar charts, show how individual components contribute to a total number, using a different color or pattern for each component. *Combination* bar and line charts compare quantities that require different intervals. *Paired* bar charts show the correlations between two items.

Figure 12.8 also suggests how creative you can be with bar charts. You might align the bars either vertically or horizontally, or you might use bar charts to show both positive and negative quantities. Be careful, however, to keep all the bars in the chart the same width; different widths could suggest a relative importance to the viewer. In addition, space the bars evenly and place them in a logical order, such as chronological or alphabetical. Most of the software you'll

You can create bar charts in a wide variety of formats; choose the form that best illustrates the data and relationships in your message.

FIGURE 12.8 *Continued*
Segmented (12.8d), *combination* (12.8e), *and paired* (12.8f).

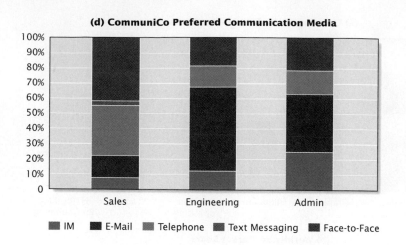

(d) CommuniCo Preferred Communication Media

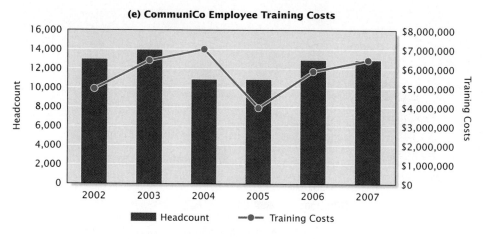

(e) CommuniCo Employee Training Costs

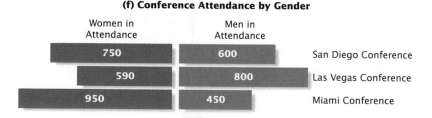

(f) Conference Attendance by Gender

be using to create charts makes these choices for you; just be sure to verify what the software has done and override any settings that don't seem to work well for a given chart.

You can also convert the bars into lines of symbols, so that the number or length of the symbols indicates the relative value of each item. A chart that portrays data as symbols instead of words or numbers is known as a **pictogram**. The chief value of pictograms is their novelty and ability to convey a more literal, visual message, but they tend to be more difficult to read and can present a less professional tone than a straightforward bar chart.

Closely related to the bar chart is the **time line chart**, which shows how much time is needed to complete each task in a given project. When you want to track progress toward completing a project, you can use a type of time line chart known as a **Gantt chart** (see Figure 12.9).

Scatter and Bubble Diagrams

Scatter diagrams compare entities against two variables; bubble diagrams compare them against three.

If you need to compare several entities (companies, markets, employees, and so on) by two variables, such as revenue and profit margin, use a **scatter diagram**, also known as an **XY diagram**. This diagram is similar to a line chart in the sense that one variable is plotted along the *x* (horizontal) axis and another along the *y* (vertical) axis. However, in a scatter diagram, individual points are plotted, not continuous lines. The **bubble diagram** expands to three variables, with the size of the bubble representing the third variable (see Figure 12.10).

FIGURE 12.9 Gantt Chart

This Gantt chart shows the activities involved in designing the prototype and conducting the marketing research for a new product. The maroon bars indicate completed tasks, the blue bars indicate activities not yet completed, and the black diamond is a milestone—in this case the prototype's due date.

ID	Project Time line	Start Date	End Date	Duration	Percentage Complete	2007			
						June	July	August	September
1	**Design Phase**	6/20/07	8/31/07	73d	90.00 %				
2	Design Project	6/20/07	7/31/07	42d	100.00				
3	Prototype Design	8/3/07	8/21/07	19d	100.00				
4	Test Prototype	8/24/07	8/28/07	5d	0.00				
5	Prototype Complete	8/31/07	8/31/07	0d	0.00				
6	**Marketing Research Phase**	8/3/07	9/25/07	54d	25.00				
7	Preliminary Research	8/3/07	8/7/07	5d	100.00				
8	Conduct Focus Groups	8/10/07	8/11/07	2d	100.00				
9	Interviews	8/12/07	8/14/07	3d	100.00				
10	Analyze Research Results	8/17/07	8/28/07	12d	0.00				
11	Create Marketing Plan	8/31/07	9/25/07	26d	0.00				

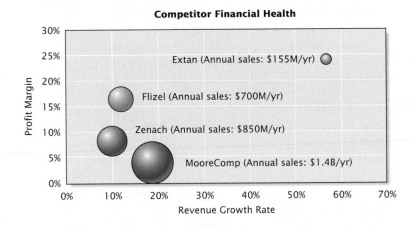

Competitor Financial Health

Profit Margin (y-axis): 0%, 5%, 10%, 15%, 20%, 25%, 30%

Extan (Annual sales: $155M/yr)
Flizel (Annual sales: $700M/yr)
Zenach (Annual sales: $850M/yr)
MooreComp (Annual sales: $1.4B/yr)

Revenue Growth Rate (x-axis): 0%, 10%, 20%, 30%, 40%, 50%, 60%, 70%

FIGURE 12.10 Bubble Diagram

The bubble diagram shows three variables: distance along the x and y axes, plus the diameter of each bubble. In this case, the rate of revenue growth is plotted on the x axis, profit margin is plotted on the y axis, and the size of the bubbles represents annual revenues. For instance, MooreComp has the greatest revenues but the lowest profit margin, although it is growing faster than two of its three competitors.

Pie Charts

Like segmented bar charts and area charts, a **pie chart** shows how the parts of a whole are distributed. However, pie charts have the advantage of familiarity; most people expect parts of a whole to be displayed via a pie chart. Each segment represents a slice of a complete circle, or *pie*. As you can see in Figure 12.11, pie charts are an effective way to show percentages or to compare one segment with another. You can also combine pie charts with tables to expand the usefulness of such visuals.

When creating pie charts, try to restrict the number of slices in the pie. Otherwise, the chart looks cluttered and is difficult to label. If necessary, lump the smallest pieces together in a "miscellaneous" category. Ideally, the largest or most important slice of the pie, the segment you want to emphasize, is placed at the 12 o'clock position; the rest are arranged clockwise either in order of size or in some other logical progression.

Most readers expect pie charts to show the distribution of parts within a whole.

FIGURE 12.11 Pie Chart
When creating pie charts, use different colors or patterns to distinguish the various pieces. Label all the segments and indicate their value in either percentages or units of measure so that your readers will be able to judge the value of the wedges.

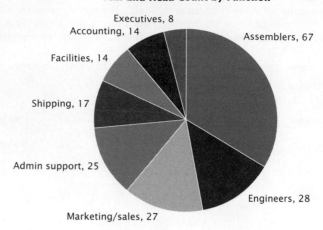

Year-End Head Count by Function

Executives, 8
Accounting, 14
Facilities, 14
Shipping, 17
Admin support, 25
Marketing/sales, 27
Engineers, 28
Assemblers, 67

Be sure to distinguish the slices in the pie chart with different colors or patterns.

Use different colors (or patterns, if you'll be printing or reproducing charts in black and white) to distinguish the various pieces. If you want to draw attention to the segment that is of the greatest interest to your readers, use a brighter color for that segment, draw an arrow to the segment, or *explode* it by pulling the segment away from the rest of the pie. In any case, label all the segments and indicate their value in either percentages or units of measure so that your readers will be able to judge the value of the wedges. Remember, the segments must add up to 100 percent if percentages are used or to the total number if numbers are used.

Presenting Information, Concepts, and Ideas

In addition to facts and figures, you'll need to present other types of information, from spatial relationships to abstract ideas. As Keith Yamashita and his colleagues at SYP demonstrate, words aren't always the best way to communicate information, concepts, or ideas, so these professionals often look for visual solutions to complement or even replace textual information. The most common types of visuals for these applications include flowcharts and organization charts; maps; drawings, diagrams, and photographs; and animation and video.

Flowcharts and Organization Charts

Use flowcharts to show a series of steps in a process or other sequential relationships.

If you need to show physical or conceptual relationships rather than numerical ones, you might want to use a flowchart or an organization chart. A **flowchart** (see Figure 12.12) illustrates a sequence of events from start to finish; it is indispensable when illustrating processes, procedures, and sequential relationships. For general business purposes, you don't need to be too concerned about the specific shapes, but keep them consistent. However, be aware that there is a formal flowchart "language" in which each shape has a specific meaning (diamonds are decision points, rectangles are process steps, and so on). If you're communicating with computer programmers and others who are accustomed to formal flowcharting, make sure you use the correct symbols in each case to avoid confusion. Graphics programs that have flowchart symbols usually label their functions, making it easy to use the right ones.

Use organization charts to depict the interrelationships among the parts of a whole.

As the name implies, an **organization chart** illustrates the positions, units, or functions of an organization and the way they interrelate (Figure 12.13). These charts aren't limited to organizational structures, of course; as you saw in Chapter 4, they can also be used to outline messages.

Maps

Use maps for such tasks as representing statistics by geographic area or showing spatial relationships.

Maps can be used in a variety of ways to show location, distance, points of interest (such as competitive retail outlets), and geographic distribution of data, such as sales by region or population by state. In addition to presenting facts and figures, maps are useful for showing market territories, distribution routes, and facilities locations. Maps are sometimes used in conjunction with aerial photographs to provide a richer view (see Figure 12.14).

Drawings, Diagra[...]

Although drawings, di[...]
communication special[...]
situations in which suc[...]
example, when Brian I[...]
about new competitive [...]
ucts are being displayed[...]
ages.[16] Simple drawings[...]
through a company, or [...]
agrams can convey tech[...]

Word processors a[...]
more precise and prof[...]
crosoft Visio or Adobe [...]
design (CAD) systems s[...]
tural and engineering d[...]

Photographs offer [...]
ited to specialized docu[...]
low-cost digital photog[...]
to add photographs to [...]
braries such as Getty Im[...]
one provided by AltaVi[...]
graphs. Some of these [...]
Getty Images, require ei[...]
or an annual payment [...]

However, as with a[...]
photographs successful[...]

- **Consider whethe**[...]
  Photographs are of[...]
  sizes, shapes, and [...]

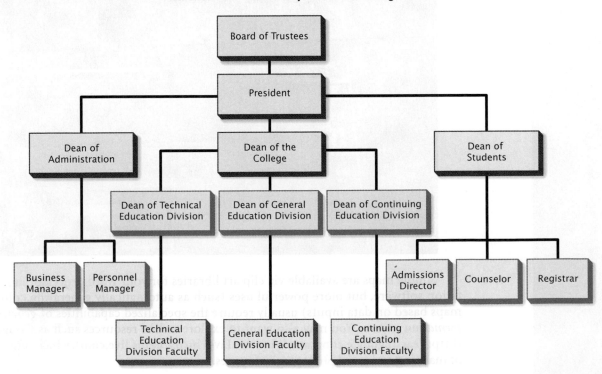

FIGURE 12.12
Flowchart
Flowcharts show sequences of
events and are most valuable
when the process or procedure
has a number of decision points
and variable paths.

FIGURE 12.13 Organization Chart
An organization chart is the expected way to illustrate the hierarchy of positions in an organization.

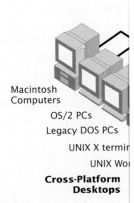

Remote
Computing

Telecomm[...]

Macintosh
Computers

OS/2 PCs

Legacy DOS PCs

UNIX X termi[...]

UNIX Wo[...]

Cross-Platform
Desktops

W[...]

FIGURE 12.14 M
Maps offer many oppor
for displaying data and
information. The map ir
12.14a shows populatio
projections for each stat
United States. Figure 12
simple version of a geo
information system, in t
showing hotels and mot
neighborhood near Nev
La Guardia Airport. A cc
looking for sites to builc
in this area could use su
map to identify potentia
competitors, traffic patte
other important variable

Match the resolution of your photo files to the application; use higher resolution for print and lower resolution for electronic display.

much information. For example, to show how to adjust a specific part of a complicated machine, a photo can be confusing because it shows all the parts within the camera's view. A simplified diagram is often more effective because it allows you to emphasize the specific parts that are relevant to the problem at hand.

- **Learn how to use basic image-processing tools.** For instance, you can drop photographs directly into your word processor or presentation files, then use that program to change the size of the file to fit the available space, but this isn't always the best approach. Rather than simply resizing, you might be better off *cropping*, or electronically cutting away part of the photo.

- **Match the file to the application.** Digital photos vary widely in *resolution*, which is the amount of detail in the image. Resolution can be expressed in one of two ways. Digital cameras are usually specified in *pixels*, the total number of *picture elements* in the file. For example, a 5-megapixel camera produces a photo with 5 million pixels in the image. Printers and scanners are usually specified in *dots per inch*, or *dpi*, which is the number of discrete points per linear inch. A 600 dpi office printer, therefore, outputs 360,000 (600×600) discrete dots per square inch. Up to the limits of the printer, greater resolution is usually better for printed documents, but it isn't always helpful for online use. High-resolution image files are significantly larger than low-resolution image files, so they consume more storage space and take longer to transmit or download. In addition, most computer monitors and other electronic displays have less than 100 dpi resolution and therefore can't display all the fine detail in high-resolution images anyway. (To be accurate, it is possible to show all the detail, but doing so requires scaling up the photo to large and unwieldy sizes.) If you plan to use photos on a website or online report, use the "save for web" feature in your image-processing software to reduce the resolution and therefore the file size.

- **Make sure the photographs have communication value.** Just because it's easy to drop photos into documents doesn't mean you should automatically do so, naturally. Judge photographs with the same discerning eye you use for every other element of your report or presentation.

- **Be aware of copyrights and model permissions.** Just as with the textual information that you find online, you can't simply insert online photographs into your documents. Unless they are specifically offered for free, you have to assume someone owns the photos and is entitled to payment or at least a photo credit. In addition, professional photographers are careful to have any person who poses in photos sign a model release form, which gives the photographer permission to use the person's image.

Altering or enhancing photographs can create ethical problems.

Technology makes it easy to use photographs in reports and presentations, but it also presents an important ethical concern. Software tools such as Photoshop and Paint Shop Pro allow you to easily make dramatic changes to photos—without leaving a clue that they've been altered. Altering photos in small ways has been possible for a long time (more than a few students have had blemishes airbrushed out of their yearbook photos), but computers make drastic changes easy and undetectable. You can remove people from photographs, put Person A's head on Person B's body, and make products look more attractive than they really are. Most people would agree that it's acceptable to make cosmetic improvements, such as brightening an underexposed photo to make it easier to view. But to avoid ethical lapses, don't make any alterations that mislead the viewer or substantially change the message conveyed by the photo.[17]

Animation and Video

Computer animation and video are among the most specialized forms of business visuals; when they are appropriate and done well, they offer unparalleled visual impact. At a simple level, you can animate shapes and text within electronic presentations (see Chapter 17). At a more sophisticated level, software such as Macromedia Flash enables the creation of multimedia files that include computer animation, digital video, and other elements. A wide variety of tools are also available for digital video production. Whether you use these tools yourself or employ a specialist to create animation or video for you, make sure the results follow all the guidelines for effective business messages.

PRODUCING AND INTEGRATING VISUALS

Now that you understand the communication power of visuals and have chosen the best visuals to illustrate key points in your report, website, or presentation, it's time to get creative. This section offers advice on creating visuals, integrating them with your text, and verifying the quality of your visual elements.

Creating Visuals

Technology has put powerful graphics tools in the hands of virtually every business computer user, so you no longer have to rely on professional designers as much as businesspeople had to only a few years ago. Unfortunately, computers can't provide the specialized training and hands-on experience of a professional designer. Computers make it easy to create visuals, but they also make it easy to create ineffective, distracting, and even downright ugly visuals. However, by following the basic design principles discussed on pages 363 to 365, you can create all the basic visuals you need—visuals that are both attractive and effective.

Whether you're using the charting functions offered in a spreadsheet or the design features of a specialized graphics program, take a few minutes to familiarize yourself with the software's quirks and capabilities. For instance, spreadsheets can create charts with just a few clicks of the mouse, but the default colors, fonts, or other design elements might not be the best for your particular needs. If possible, have a professional designer set up a *template* for the various types of visuals you and your colleagues need to create. In addition to helping ensure an effective design, using templates saves you the time of making numerous design decisions every time you create a chart or graphic.

However, be careful with the templates included with some commercial software programs. Some are "overdesigned" and inappropriate for serious business uses, and some clutter the image with fancy borders and backgrounds that can distract an audience from your real message.

No matter which tools you're using, take care to match the style and quality of your visuals with the subject matter and the situation at hand. The style of your visuals communicates a subtle message about your relationship with the audience. A simple sketch might be fine for a working meeting but inappropriate for a formal presentation or report. On the other hand, elaborate, full-color visuals may be viewed as extravagant for an informal report but may be entirely appropriate for a message to top management or influential outsiders.

To show investors what a new building would look like in its environment, an artist combined a photograph of a scale model of the building with a photograph of the actual street scene. Because the target audience clearly understands that the building doesn't exist, this sort of image manipulation is not unethical.

Integrating Visuals with Text

For maximum effectiveness and minimum disruption for the reader, visual elements need to be carefully integrated with the text of your message. In some instances, visual elements are somewhat independent from the text, as in the *sidebars* that occasionally accompany magazine articles. Such images are related to the content of the main story, but they aren't referred to by a specific title or figure number. This sort of treatment is used most often in promotional materials such as brochures and advertisements.

For reports and most other business documents, however, visuals are tightly integrated with the text so that readers can move back and forth between text and visuals with as little

The use of color in visuals accelerates learning, retention, and recall by 55 percent to 78 percent, and it increases motivation and audience participation up to 80 percent.

To tie visuals to the text, introduce them in the text and place them near the points they illustrate.

disruption as possible. Successful integration involves four decisions: maintaining a balance between visuals and text, referring to visuals in the text, placing the visuals in the document, and writing titles and other descriptions.

Maintaining a Balance Between Illustrations and Words

Strong visuals enhance the descriptive and persuasive power of your writing, but putting too many visuals into a report can distract your readers. If you're constantly referring to tables, drawings, and other visual elements, the effort to switch back and forth from words to visuals can make it difficult for readers to maintain focus on the thread of your message. The space occupied by visuals can also disrupt the flow of text on the page or screen.

The pacing of visuals throughout the text is also an important consideration. If most of your visuals are bunched in one section of the report, readers might spend more time there and less time in the text-heavy sections. Although it isn't always possible to have perfect distribution throughout the report, try to have a fairly even flow of text and visuals from page to page or screen to screen.

As always, take your readers' specific needs into account. If you're addressing an audience with multiple language backgrounds or widely varying reading skills, you can shift the balance toward more visual elements to help get around any language barriers. The professional experience, education, and training of your audience should influence your approach as well. For instance, detailed statistical plots and mathematical formulas are everyday reading material for quality-control engineers but not for most salespeople or top executives.

Referencing Visuals

Unless a visual element clearly stands on its own, as in the *sidebars* you often see in magazines, visuals should be clearly referred to by number in the text of your report. Some report writers refer to all visuals as "exhibits" and number them consecutively throughout the report; many others number tables and figures separately (everything that isn't a table is regarded as a figure). In a long report with numbered sections, illustrations may have a double number (separated by a period or a hyphen) representing the section number and the individual illustration number within that section. Whichever scheme you use, make sure it's clear and easy to follow.

Help your readers understand the significance of visuals by referring to them before readers encounter them in the document or on the screen. The following examples show how you can make this connection in the text:

Figure 1 summarizes the financial history of the motorcycle division over the past five years, with sales broken into four categories.

Total sales were steady over this period, but the mix of sales by category changed dramatically (see Figure 2).

The underlying reason for the remarkable growth in our sales of youth golf apparel is suggested by Table 4, which shows the growing interest in junior golf around the world.

When describing the data shown in your visuals, be sure to emphasize the main point you are trying to make. Don't make the mistake of simply repeating the data to be shown. Paragraphs that do are guaranteed to put the reader to sleep:

Among women who replied to the survey, 17.4 percent earn less than $5 per hour; 26.4 percent earn $5 to $7; 25.7 percent, $8 to $12; 18.0 percent, $13 to $24; 9.6 percent, $25 to $49; and 2.9 percent, $50 and over.

The visual will (or at least should) provide all these details; there is no need to repeat them in the text. Instead, use round numbers that sum up the message:

Over two-thirds of the women who replied earn less than $12 per hour.

Placing Visuals

Try to position your visuals so that your audience won't have to flip back and forth (in printed documents) or scroll (on screen) between the visuals and the text. Ideally, it's best to place each visual within, beside, or immediately after the paragraph it illustrates so that readers can consult the explanation and the visual at the same time. This scheme works well both in print and online. If at all possible, avoid bunching visuals at the end of a section or the end of a document; doing so asks a lot of the reader. (Bunching is unavoidable in some cases, such as when you have multiple visuals that accompany a single section of text.) Word-processing, desktop-publishing, and web-design programs let you place graphical elements virtually anywhere you wish, so take advantage of this flexibility.

Place each visual as close as possible to its in-text reference to help readers understand the illustration's relevance and to minimize the effort of reading.

Writing Titles, Captions, and Legends

Titles and legends provide two more opportunities to connect your visual and textual messages. A **title** is similar to a subheading, providing a short description that identifies the content and purpose of the visual, along with whatever label and number you're using to refer to the visual. A **caption** usually offers additional discussion of the visual's content and can be several sentences long if appropriate. Captions can also alert readers that additional discussion is available in the accompanying text. Titles usually appear above visuals and captions appear below, but effective designs can place these two elements in other positions. Sometimes titles and captions are combined in a single block of text as well. As with all design decisions, be consistent throughout your report or website. A **legend** helps readers "decode" the visual by explaining what various colors, symbols, or other design choices mean. Legends aren't necessary for simple graphs, such as a line chart or bar chart with only a series of data, but they are invaluable with more complex graphics.

By considering your word choices for all three of these textual elements, you can help readers link the visuals with the text and quickly grasp the most important points of each visual. Readers should be able to grasp the point of the visual without digging into the surrounding text. For instance, a title that says simply, "Refineries" doesn't say much at all. "Active Petroleum Refineries in the United States" provides a much better idea of what the chart is all about. You may also want to use informative titles, rather than basic descriptive titles. A **descriptive title** simply identifies the topic of the illustration, whereas an **informative title** calls attention to the conclusion that ought to be drawn from the data. Here's an example of the difference:

The title of a visual functions in the same way as a subheading, whereas the caption provides additional detail if needed.

> ### DOCUMENT MAKEOVER
> **IMPROVE THIS REPORT SUMMARY AND VISUALS**
>
> To practice correcting drafts of actual documents, visit your online course or the access-code-protected portion of the Companion Website. Click "Document Makeovers," then click Chapter 12. You will find a competitive analysis report summary that contains problems and errors relating to what you've learned in this chapter about communicating information through visuals. Use the Final Draft decision tool to create an improved version of this summary. Check the message for appropriate formatting of visuals and proper use of text with visuals.

DESCRIPTIVE TITLE	INFORMATIVE TITLE
Relationship Between Petroleum Demand and Refinery Capacity in the United States	Refinery Capacity Declines as Petroleum Demand Continues to Grow

Regardless of whether your titles and legends are informative or descriptive, phrase them consistently throughout the report.

Descriptive titles simply identify the topic of an illustration; informative titles help the reader understand the conclusion to be drawn from the illustration.

Verifying the Quality of Your Visuals

Visuals have a particularly strong impact on your readers and on their perceptions of you and your work, so verifying their quality is vital. Take a few extra minutes to make sure that your visuals are absolutely accurate, properly documented, and honest:

- **Is the visual accurate?** Be sure to check visuals for mistakes such as typographical errors, inconsistent color treatment, confusing or undocumented symbols, and misaligned elements. Also verify that information in visuals and text matches. For data presentations, particularly if you're producing charts with a spreadsheet, verify any

7 LEARNING OBJECTIVE

List three criteria to review in order to verify the quality of your visuals

CHECKLIST: Creating Effective Visuals

- Emphasize visual consistency to connect parts of a whole and minimize audience confusion.
- Avoid arbitrary changes of color, texture, typeface, position, or scale.
- Highlight contrasting points through color, position, and other design choices.
- Decide whether you want to achieve formal or informal balance.
- Emphasize dominant elements and de-emphasize less-important pieces in a design.
- Understand and follow (at least most of the time) the visual conventions your audience expects.
- Strive for simplicity and clarity; don't clutter your visuals with meaningless decoration.
- Follow the guidelines for avoiding ethical lapses.
- Carefully consider your message, the nature of your information, and your audience to choose which points to illustrate.

- Select the proper types of graphics for the information at hand and for the objective of the message.
- Be sure the visual contributes to overall understanding of the subject.
- Understand how to use your software tools to maximize effectiveness and efficiency.
- Integrate visuals and text by maintaining a balance between illustrations and words, clearly referring to visuals within the text, and placing visuals carefully.
- Use titles, captions, and legends to help readers understand the meaning and importance of your visuals.
- Verify the quality of your visuals by checking for accuracy, proper documentation, and honesty.

formulas used to generate the numbers, and make sure you've selected the right numbers for each chart. When you're in a hurry, it's easy to select the wrong column of numbers in a spreadsheet or the wrong set of numbers within a column. For flowcharts, organizational charts, diagrams, photos, and other visuals, compare the visuals you created with the visuals you had planned to create. Does each visual deliver your message accurately? Have you inserted the right photos, maps, or other files?

- **Is the visual properly documented?** As with the textual elements in your reports and presentations, visuals based on other people's research, information, and ideas require full citation. (Even if the graphical design is entirely yours, any underlying information taken from other sources needs to be documented.) Also, try to anticipate any questions or concerns your audience may have and address them with additional information as needed. For instance, if you're presenting the results of survey research, many readers will want to know who participated in the survey, how many people responded, and when the questions were asked. You could answer these questions with a note in the caption along the lines of "652 accountants, surveyed the week of January 17." Similarly, if you found a visual in a secondary source, list that source on or near the graphic to help readers assess the information. Alternatively, you can list sources in an appendix.

Review each visual to make sure it doesn't intentionally or unintentionally distort the meaning of the underlying information.

- **Is the visual honest?** As a final precaution, step back and make sure your visuals communicate truthful messages. Make sure they don't hide information the audience needs, imply conclusions that your information doesn't support, or play on audience emotions in manipulative or coercive ways.

For a review of the important points to remember when creating visuals, see "Checklist: Creating Effective Visuals."

COMMUNICATION CHALLENGES AT STONE YAMASHITA PARTNERS

In Canada, the Tim Horton's chain is famous for its coffee and donuts. However, with over 2,600 shops, Tim's has saturated the Canadian market and is looking to grow in the United States, where it has just over 300 shops. That growth won't be easy: Tim's faces Dunkin' Donuts, Krispy Kreme, and Starbucks in their home territory.

Individual Challenge: Tim's has hired SYP to help recruit franchise owners for its southward expansion, and Keith Yamashita is planning an event for the 100 most promising potential franchisees. To help illustrate the business opportunity, he has asked you to create compelling visuals for the following items:

- Compare the size of several items at one time
- Show changes in one item over time
- Indicate the composition of several items over time
- The planned growth in the number of Tim's outlets in four U.S. regions (North, West, South, and East) over the next 10 years

Decide what kind of visual to use for each item. Create example visuals by making up any data you need.

Team Challenge: SYP often uses life-size mockups to help people visualize new possibilities, such as the interior layout of a Tim's franchise. In a small group, brainstorm the layout of a coffeehouse that you think would appeal to customers on or near your college campus. Write a brief e-mail explaining how you could "stage" a life-size mockup of your store layout to help potential franchisors see what a Tim's store is like inside.

SUMMARY OF LEARNING OBJECTIVES

1 Describe the communication power of visuals. Visuals enhance the communication impact of your writing and in some cases even replace writing. First, visuals can convey some types of information better than text can. Second, visuals are an effective way to reach audiences of diverse professional and cultural backgrounds. Third, busy readers who may lack the time or inclination to read your entire message often look to visuals to quickly grasp the essence of what you're trying to communicate.

2 Discuss six principles of graphic design that can improve the quality of your visuals. When preparing visuals, (1) use elements of design consistently so you don't confuse your audience; (2) use color and other elements to show contrast effectively; (3) strive for a visual balance, either formal or informal, that creates a feel that is appropriate for your overall message; (4) use design choices to draw attention to key elements and to visually downplay less important items; (5) understand and follow design conventions that your audience expects (even if the expectation is subconscious), although you can consider unconventional design choices if they promise to convey your message more effectively; and (6) strive for simplicity in all your visuals, making design decisions that enhance the reception and understanding of information, rather than obscuring or confusing it.

3 Explain how to avoid ethical lapses when using visuals. Communicators have the responsibility to avoid both intentional and unintentional ethical lapses when using visual elements. They can work to avoid these lapses by (1) considering all possible interpretations—and misinterpretations—of their messages and avoiding design choices that could lead to unwanted interpretations; (2) providing sufficient context, whether visual or verbal, for audiences to understand the meaning and significance of visuals; (3) not hiding or minimizing negative information that runs counter to their arguments; (4) not exaggerating information that supports their arguments; (5) not oversimplifying complex situations by hiding complications that are relevant to the audience's understanding; (6) not implying cause-and-effect relationships without providing proof that they exist; (7) avoiding emotional manipulation or other forms of coercion; and (8) being careful with the way they aggregate data.

4 Explain how to choose which points in your message to illustrate. To decide which points to illustrate, first step back and consider the overall flow of your message from the audience's point of view. Identify elements of the message that might be complex, vulnerable to misinterpretation, or even dull. Look for connections between ideas that should be highlighted or extensive collections of data and other discrete factual content that might be difficult to read in textual format.

5 **Describe the most common options for presenting data in a visual format.** The visuals most commonly used to present data include tables, line and surface charts, bar charts, pictograms, Gantt charts, and pie charts. You will probably use line, bar, and pie charts most often in your business communication efforts.

6 **Identify five guidelines for using photographs effectively.** First, consider whether a diagram would communicate more effectively than a photograph. Second, learn how to use basic image-processing tools so that you can crop, size, and perform other necessary tasks with photos. Third, match the file to the application; high-resolution photos are usually desirable for printed documents but not for most online and electronic display applications. High-resolution images take up more storage space and take longer to transmit electronically, and the typical computer monitor can't display all the details in high-resolution photos. Fourth, make sure every photo has communication value and isn't just a decoration or distraction. Fifth, be aware of copyrights and model permissions.

7 **List three criteria to review in order to verify the quality of your visuals.** Make sure every visual you use is *accurate* (there are no mistakes or missing information), *properly documented* (the creator of any underlying data used in the visual has been given complete credit), and *honest* (the visual honestly reveals the real meaning of the underlying data or information).

Test Your Knowledge

1. What type of visual would you use to compare one part with a whole?
2. What type of visual would you use to present detailed, exact values?
3. What type of visual would you use to compare one item with another?
4. What type of visual would you use to illustrate trends over time?
5. When are combination bar and line charts used?
6. For what purposes are Gantt charts used?
7. How does a flowchart differ from an organization chart?
8. When would you use a bubble diagram instead of a scatter diagram?
9. What is the purpose of adding titles, captions, and legends to visuals in reports?
10. How do you check a visual for quality?

Apply Your Knowledge

1. What similarities do you see between visuals and nonverbal communication? Explain your answer.
2. You're writing a report to the director of human resources on implementing team-based management throughout your company. You want to emphasize that since the new approaches were implemented six months ago, absenteeism and turnovers have been sharply reduced in all but two departments. How do you visually present your data in the most favorable light while still maintaining honest communication? Explain.
3. Besides telling readers why an illustration is important, why refer to it in the text of your document?
4. When you read a graph, how can you be sure that the visual impression you are receiving is an accurate reflection of reality? Please explain.
5. **Ethical Choices** What ethical issue is raised by the use of technology to alter photographs in reports?

Practice Your Knowledge

Messages for Analysis

Message 12.A: Analyzing Pie Charts

Examine the pie charts in Figure 12.16 and point out any problems or errors you notice.

Message 12.B: Analyzing a Line Chart

Examine the line chart in Figure 12.17 and point out any problems or errors you notice.

Exercises

For active links to all websites discussed in this chapter, visit this text's website at www.prenhall.com/bovee. Locate your book and click on its Companion Website link. Then select Chapter 12, and click on "Featured Websites." Locate the name of the page or the URL related to the material in the text. Please note that links to sites that become inactive after publication of the book will be removed from the Featured Websites section.

12.1 **Improving Visual Design** Find a communication example that you believe could be improved by applying the visual design principles you learned in this chapter. It can be from any medium—a webpage, a magazine ad, a promotional e-mail message, an illustration from a report—anything that you can either copy or scan into a word-processing file. With the image in your word processor, annotate it with notes that identify visual weaknesses and describe ways to fix those weaknesses. (In Microsoft Word, for example, you can use the "AutoShapes Callouts" feature to place notes wherever you'd like on the page.) In a paragraph of accompanying text, explain why you believe the message isn't as effective as it could be and how your suggestions would make it more effective.

12.2 **Preparing Pie Charts** As a market researcher for a statewide chain of car dealerships, you're examining car

FIGURE 12.16 Pie Charts for Analysis

What Types of Life Insurance Policies Are in Effect?

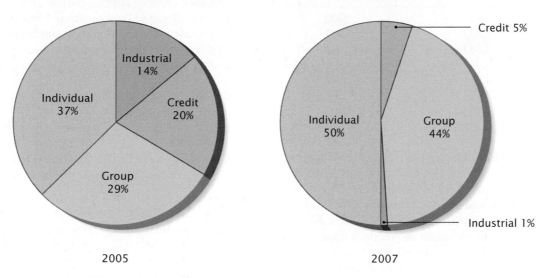

2005   2007

FIGURE 12.17 Line Chart for Analysis

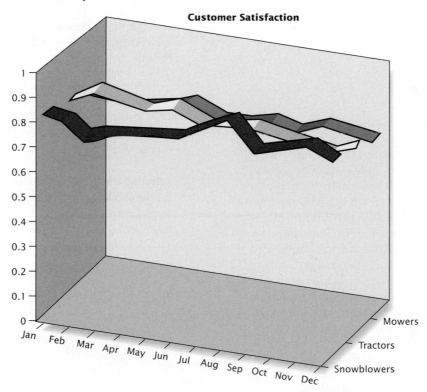

and truck ownership and lease patterns among single drivers in various age groups. By discovering which age groups have the highest percentages of owners, you will be better able to target advertising that promotes the leasing option. Using the information that follows, prepare a bar chart comparing the number of owners with the number of leasers in each age category. Be sure to label your chart, and include combined totals for owners and leasees ("total drivers"). Then prepare a pie chart showing the proportion of owners and leasers in the one age group that you think holds the most promise for leasing a new vehicle. Write a sentence that prepares your company's management for the information shown in the pie chart.

Age Group	Number of Owners (in Thousands)	Number of Leasees (in Thousands)
18–24	1,830	795
25–29	1,812	1,483
30–34	1,683	1,413
35–44	1,303	1,932
45–54	1,211	1,894
55–64	1,784	1,435
65–74	3,200	1,142
75+	3,431	854

12.3 **Preparing Line Charts** The pet food manufacturer you work for is interested in the results of a recent poll of U.S. pet-owning households. Look at the cat ownership statistics that follow and decide on the most appropriate scale for a chart; then create a line chart of the trends in cat ownership. What conclusions do you draw from the trend you've charted? Draft a paragraph or two discussing the results of this poll and the potential consequences for the pet food business. Support your conclusions by referring readers to your chart.

> In 1990, 22 million U.S. households owned a cat. In 1995, 24 million households owned a cat. In 2000, 28 million households owned a cat. In 2005, 32 million households owned a cat.

Portfolio BUILDER

12.4 **Creating Photographs** As directed by your instructor, team up with other students, making sure at least one of you has a digital camera or camera phone capable of downloading images to your word-processing software. Find a busy location on campus or in the surrounding neighborhood, someplace with lots of signs, storefronts, pedestrians, and traffic. Scout out two different photo opportunities, one that maximizes the visual impression of crowding and clutter, and one that minimizes this impression. For the first, assume that you are someone who advocates reducing the crowding and clutter, so you want to show how bad it is. For the second, assume you are a real estate agent or someone else motivated to show people that even though the location offers lots of shopping, entertainment, and other attractions, it's actually a rather calm and quiet neighborhood. Insert the two images in a word-processor document, and write a caption for each that emphasizes the two opposite messages just described. Finally, write a brief paragraph discussing the ethical implications of what you've just done. Have you distorted reality or just presented it in ways that work to your advantage? Have you prevented audiences for gaining the information they would need to make informed decisions?

12.5 **Selecting the Right Visual** You're preparing the annual report for FretCo Guitar Corporation. For each of the following types of information, select the right chart or visual to illustrate the text. Explain your choices.
  a. Data on annual sales for the past 20 years
  b. Comparison of FretCo sales, product by product (electric guitars, bass guitars, amplifiers, acoustic guitars), for this year and last year
  c. Explanation of how a FretCo acoustic guitar is manufactured
  d. Explanation of how the FretCo Guitar Corporation markets its guitars
  e. Data on sales of FretCo products in each of 12 countries
  f. Comparison of FretCo sales figures with sales figures for three competing guitar makers over the past 10 years

12.6 **Preparing Bar Charts** Team up with a classmate to design charts based on a comparison of the total tax burden of the U.S. taxpayer with that of people in other nations. One teammate should sketch a horizontal or vertical bar chart, and the other should sketch a pictogram from the estimates that follow. Then exchange charts and analyze how well each conveys the situation of the U.S. taxpayer. Would the bar chart look best with vertical or horizontal bars? Why? What scale is best? How does the symbol used in the pictogram enhance or obscure the meaning or impact of the data? What suggestions can each student make for improving the other's visual aid?

> Estimates show that Swedish taxpayers spend 51 percent of their incomes on taxes, British taxpayers spend 48 percent, French taxpayers spend 37 percent, Japanese taxpayers spend 28 percent, and U.S. taxpayers spend 27 percent.

12.7 **Selecting the Right Chart** Here are last year's sales figures for the appliance and electronics megastore where you work. Construct charts based on these figures that will help you explain to the store's general manager seasonal variations in each department.

Store Sales in 2007 (in $ Thousands)

Month	Home Electronics	Computers	Appliances
January	$68	$39	$36
February	72	34	34
March	75	41	30
April	54	41	28
May	56	42	44
June	49	33	48
July	54	31	43
August	66	58	39
September	62	58	36
October	66	44	33
November	83	48	29
December	91	62	24

Portfolio BUILDER

12.8 Creating Maps You work for C & S Holdings, a company that operates coin-activated, self-service car washes. Research shows that the farther customers live from a car wash, the less likely they are to visit. You know that 50 percent of customers at each of your car washes live within a 4-mile radius of the location, 65 percent live within 6 miles, 80 percent live within 8 miles, and 90 percent live within 10 miles. C & S's owner wants to open two new car washes in your city and has asked you to prepare a report recommending locations. Using a map of your city, choose two possible locations for car washes and create a visual depicting the customer base surrounding each location.

12.9 Creating Organization Charts Create an organization chart for your school. You will probably need to consult your school library or administration office for documents listing the various offices and departments. Figure 12.14 on page 380 can serve as a model for how to structure your chart.

12.10 Creating Line Charts Re-create the line chart in Figure 12.6 on page 374 as a bar chart and as a pie chart. Which of these three formats does the best job of conveying the information? Are any of the formats definitely inappropriate for this information? Explain your answers.

12.11 Selecting the Right Chart With a team of two or three other students, brainstorm and then sketch at least three types of charts you can use to compare the populations of all 50 states in the United States. You can use any of the graphic ideas presented in this chapter, as well as any ideas or examples you find from other sources.

12.12 Internet One of the best places to see how data can be presented visually is in government statistical publications, which are often available on the Internet. For example, the International Trade Administration (ITA), a branch of the U.S. Department of Commerce, publishes monthly reports about U.S. trade with other countries. Visit the report page of its website at http://trade.gov and follow the link to the latest monthly International Trade Update (you should find the link on the right side of the homepage). Download the complete issue as a PDF file. Using what you learned in this chapter, evaluate the charts in the report. Do they present the data clearly? Are they missing any elements? What would you do to improve the charts? Print out a copy of the report to turn in with your answers, and indicate which charts you are evaluating.

12.13 Ethical Choices Create a bar or line chart using data you find online or in a business publication. Make a copy of your chart and alter the chart's scale in several ways. How do the alterations distort the information? How might you detect whether a chart's scale has been altered?

Expand Your Knowledge

Exploring the Best of the Web

Brush Up on Your Computer-Graphics Skills
http://graphicssoft.about.com

Need some help using graphics software? Get started at the About.com graphics software website. Take the tutorials and learn how to manage fonts, images, and a variety of graphics-related tasks. View the illustrated demonstrations. Read the instructional articles. Learn how to use the most common file formats for graphics. Expand your knowledge of the basic principles of graphic design. And master some advanced color tips and theory. Don't leave without following the links to recommended books and magazines. Before you leave, answer these questions:

1. What are the most common file formats for online visuals?
2. What does *color depth* mean in computer visuals?
3. What is *dithering* and how can it affect your visuals?

Surfing Your Way to Career Success

Bovée and Thill's Business Communication Resources offers links to hundreds of online resources that can help you with this course, your other college courses, and your career. Visit www.buscommresources.com, then click on "Business Communication Web Directory." The "Online Videos" section provides links to a wide variety of free online videos on numerous business communication topics, from blogging and business plans to podcasting and résumé writing. Identify three websites from this section that could be useful in your business career. For each site, write a two-sentence summary of what the site offers and how it could help you launch and build your career.

Learn Interactively

Interactive Study Guide

Visit www.prenhall.com/bovee, then locate your book and click on its "Companion Website" link. Select Chapter 12 to take advantage of the interactive "Chapter Quiz" to test your knowledge of chapter concepts. Receive instant feedback on whether you need additional studying. Also, visit the "Study Hall," where you'll find an abundance of valuable resources that will help you succeed in this course.

Peak Performance Grammar and Mechanics

If your instructor has required the use of "Peak Performance Grammar and Mechanics," either in your online course or on CD, you can improve your skill with apostrophes, quotation marks, parentheses and brackets, question marks and exclamation points, dashes, hyphens, and ellipses by using the "Peak Performance Grammar and Mechanics" module. Click "Punctuation," and then click "Punctuation II." Take the Pretest to determine whether you have any weak areas. Then review those areas in the Refresher Course. Take the Follow-Up Test to check your grasp of these elements. For an extra challenge or advanced practice, take the Advanced Test. Finally, for additional reinforcement in commas, visit the Companion Website, click on any chapter, then click on "Improve Your Grammar, Mechanics, and Usage."

PART 5

Planning, Writing, and Completing Reports and Proposals

CHAPTER 13
Planning Reports and Proposals

CHAPTER 14
Writing Reports and Proposals

CHAPTER 15
Completing Reports and Proposals

CHAPTER *13*

Planning Reports and Proposals

LEARNING OBJECTIVES

After studying this chapter, you will be able to

1 Explain the differences between informational reports and analytical reports

2 Adapt the three-step writing process to reports and proposals

3 Explain the value of a work plan in the development of long reports

4 Describe the four major categories of informational reports and provide examples of each

5 List the key elements of a business plan

6 Identify three steps you can take to ensure effective organization of online reports and other website content

7 Describe the three major categories of analytical reports and provide examples of each

8 Discuss three major ways to organize analytical reports

9 Explain how your approach to writing proposals should differ when you are responding to a formal request for proposals (RFP)

COMMUNICATION CLOSE-UP AT KENWOOD USA

www.kenwoodusa.com

The last time you shopped for the latest audio or video product, probably the last thing on your mind was market research or communications. However, if a feature or design caught your attention, chances are it was the result of extensive research and effective reports and other business communication efforts. As Keith Lehmann, Senior Vice President at Kenwood USA, explains, "In rapidly changing markets such as consumer electronics, research gives us a road map for the products we need to build for the future, and communication with our customers helps us confirm the results of our research."

Recently, Lehmann's research team analyzed the mobile satellite radio market in the United States and determined that although fewer than 2 million drivers had either XM Radio or Sirius Satellite Radio, consumers were enthusiastic about satellite radio. The potential for market growth was tremendous, but despite the enthusiasm of Kenwood's marketing group, the product planning team was more cautious.

Kenwood relies heavily on reports to communicate market needs from managers and analysts in the United States to product designers in Japan.

Balancing risk and reward, they had detailed questions and needed more information about competitive offerings, projected prices, and other key issues before committing resources to a new product category.

Throughout its 50-plus years of worldwide operations, Kenwood has fostered close relationships with its base of dealers. This strategy has allowed the company to learn valuable information about specific customer wants and needs. Lehmann's team decided to conduct a comprehensive dealer survey that sought answers to the key questions from the product planners.

The survey ultimately validated Lehmann's convictions that satellite radio was indeed poised for rapid growth. His team was able to convince the product planners that the technology should be prominently featured in Kenwood's new mobile audio components, which enabled the company to capture the leading edge of a significant market trend. As Lehmann said later, "Solid market research and strong communications with both our dealers and customers provide the tools we need to seize emerging product trends in advance of our competitors."[1]

CREATING EFFECTIVE REPORTS AND PROPOSALS

As with all business professionals, reports and proposals play a significant role in Keith Lehmann's success at Kenwood (profiled in the chapter-opening Communication Close-Up). **Reports** are written accounts that objectively communicate information about some aspect of the business; **proposals** are a special category of reports that combine information delivery and persuasive communication. You'll encounter dozens of reports in all shapes and sizes throughout your career, but they all fall into three basic categories:

1 LEARNING OBJECTIVE

Explain the differences between informational reports and analytical reports

- **Informational reports** offer data, facts, feedback, and other types of information, without analysis or recommendations.
- **Analytical reports** offer both information and analysis, and they can also include recommendations.
- **Proposals** offer structured persuasion for internal or external audiences.

The nature of these reports can vary widely, depending on the circumstances surrounding them. Some of your reports will be voluntary, written at your own initiative and following the structure you find most effective. Other reports will be in response to a manager's or customer's request, and you may or may not receive guidance regarding the organization and content. You'll also write reports that follow strict, specific guidelines for content and layout, as with most reports that are required by government agencies. You may write some reports only once in your career; others you may write or update annually, monthly, weekly, or even daily.

The purpose and content of business reports vary widely; in some cases you'll follow strict guidelines, but in others the organization and format will be up to you.

Your audience will sometimes be internal, which gives you more freedom to discuss sensitive information with less regard for potential misinterpretation. At other times, your audience might include customers, investors, community members, or news media, any of which can create additional demands as you present company information to such external groups.

Finally, your reports will vary widely in length and complexity. You may write one-page, memo-format reports that are simple and straightforward. Or you may write reports that cover complicated subjects, that run into hundreds or even thousands of pages, and that involve multiple writers and an array of technological tools.

No matter what the circumstances, these longer messages require all the skills and knowledge that you've gained throughout this course and will continue to gain on the job. Memos, e-mails, and other short messages will constitute most of your daily communication on the job, but writing reports and proposals is your chance to really shine. Try to view every business report as an opportunity to demonstrate your understanding of your audience's challenges and your ability to contribute to your organization's success.

APPLYING THE THREE-STEP WRITING PROCESS TO REPORTS AND PROPOSALS

By carefully applying the three-step writing process (see Figure 13.1), you can reduce the time required to write effective reports and still produce documents that make a lasting and positive impression on your audience. The concepts are the same as those you explored in Chapters 4 through 6 and applied to shorter messages in Chapters 7 through 10; however, the emphasis on various substeps can vary considerably. For instance, the planning step alone can take days or weeks for a complex report or proposal.

Part 5 offers in-depth coverage of the three-step writing process for reports and proposals. This chapter discusses planning, Chapter 14 discusses writing, and Chapter 15 covers completing reports and proposals. Because much of the writing process is already covered in Chapters 4 through 6, Chapters 13 through 15 focus on those aspects that are unique to, or that require special attention for, longer messages.

2 LEARNING OBJECTIVE

Adapt the three-step writing process to reports and proposals

Analyzing the Situation

The complexity of most reports and the magnitude of the work involved heighten the need to analyze the situation carefully. With an e-mail or other short message, you can change direction halfway through the first draft and perhaps lose only a few minutes of work. In contrast, if you change direction halfway through a major report, you could lose days, weeks, or even months. To minimize that chance, pay special attention to your statement of purpose. In addition, for anything beyond the simplest reports, take the time to prepare a work plan before you start writing.

FIGURE 13.1 Three-Step Writing Process for Reports and Proposals
The three-step writing process becomes even more valuable with reports and proposals. By guiding your work at each step, the process helps you make the most of the time and energy you invest.

Plan

Analyze the Situation
Clarify the problem or opportunity at hand, define your purpose, develop an audience profile, and develop a work plan.

Gather Information
Determine audience needs and obtain the information necessary to satisfy those needs; conduct a research project if necessary.

Select the Right Medium
Choose the best medium for delivering your message; consider delivery through multiple media.

Organize the Information
Define your main idea, limit your scope, select a direct or an indirect approach, and outline your content using an appropriate structure for an informational report, analytical report, or proposal.

Write

Adapt to Your Audience
Be sensitive to audience needs with a you " attitude, politeness, positive emphasis, and bias-free language. Build a strong relationship with your audience by establishing your credibility and projecting your company's image. Control your style with a tone and voice appropriate to the situation.

Compose the Message
Choose strong words that will help you create effective sentences and coherent paragraphs throughout the introduction, body, and close of your report or proposal.

Complete

Revise the Message
Evaluate content and review readability, then edit and rewrite for conciseness and clarity.

Produce the Message
Use effective design elements and suitable layout for a clean, professional appearance; seamlessly combine text and graphical elements.

Proofread the Message
Review for errors in layout, spelling, and mechanics.

Distribute the Message
Deliver your report using the chosen medium; make sure all documents and all relevant files are distributed successfully.

1   2   3

Defining Your Purpose

Informational reports often address a predetermined need and must meet specific audience expectations. For example, you may be asked to write reports that verify your company's compliance with government regulations, that summarize sales, or that monitor a process—all of which have audiences who expect certain information in a certain format. You may also be asked to write other informational reports that require you to examine both audience needs and your own needs before you can define the optimum purpose.

Given the length and complexity of many reports, it's crucial to define your purpose clearly so you don't waste time having to rework material.

Analytical reports and proposals are almost always written in response to a perceived problem or a perceived opportunity. A clear statement of this problem or opportunity helps frame the communication challenge by identifying *what* you're going to write about, but it's insufficient to guide your writing efforts. To plan effectively, address the problem or opportunity with a clear **statement of purpose** that defines *why* you are preparing the report (see Table 13.1).

The most useful way to phrase your purpose statement is to begin with an infinitive phrase (*to* plus a verb). Using an infinitive phrase encourages you to take control and decide where you're going before you begin. When you choose an infinitive phrase (such as *to inform, to confirm, to analyze, to persuade,* or *to recommend*), you pin down your general goal in preparing the report. Consider these examples for informational reports:

To update clients on the progress of the research project (progress report)

To develop goals and objectives for the coming year (strategic plan)

To identify customers and explain how the company will serve them (marketing plan)

To submit monthly sales statistics to management (operating report)

To summarize what occurred at the annual sales conference (personal activity report)

To explain building access procedures (policy implementation report)

To submit required information to the Securities and Exchange Commission (compliance report)

Your statement of purpose for an analytical report often needs to be more comprehensive than one for an informational report. Linda Moreno, the cost accounting manager for Electrovision, a high-tech company based in Los Gatos, California, was recently asked to find ways of reducing employee travel and entertainment costs (her complete report appears in Chapter 15). Because Moreno was supposed to suggest specific ways to solve a problem, she phrased her statement of purpose accordingly:

... to analyze the T&E [travel and entertainment] budget, evaluate the impact of recent changes in airfares and hotel costs, and suggest ways to tighten management's control over T&E expenses.

TABLE 13.1 Problem Statements Versus Purpose Statements

PROBLEM STATEMENT	STATEMENT OF PURPOSE
Our company's market share is steadily declining.	To explore new ways of promoting and selling our products and to recommend the approaches most likely to stabilize our market share.
Our current computer network lacks sufficient bandwidth and cannot be upgraded to meet our future needs.	To analyze various networking options and to recommend the system that will best meet our company's current and future needs.
We need $2 million to launch our new product.	To convince investors that our new business would be a sound investment so that we can obtain desired financing.
Our current operations are too decentralized and expensive.	To justify the closing of the Newark plant and the transfer of East Coast operations to a single Midwest location in order to save the company money.

If Moreno had been assigned an informational report instead, she might have stated her purpose differently:

> To summarize Electrovision's spending on travel and entertainment

You can see from these two examples how much influence the purpose statement has on the scope of your report. If Moreno's manager had expected her to suggest ways to reduce costs but Moreno had collected only cost data, her report would have failed to meet expectations. Because she was assigned an analytical report rather than an informational report, Moreno had to go beyond merely collecting data; she had to draw conclusions and make recommendations.

Proposals must also be guided by a clear statement of purpose to help you focus on crafting a persuasive message. Here are several examples:

> To secure funding in next year's capital budget for a new conveyor system in the warehouse (funding proposal)
>
> To get management approval to reorganize the North American salesforce (general project proposal)
>
> To secure $2 million in venture capital funding to complete design and production of the new line of titanium mountain bikes (investment proposal as part of a business plan)
>
> To convince CommuniCo to purchase a trial subscription to our latest database offering (sales proposal)

Remember, the more specific your purpose statement, the more useful it will be as a guide to planning your report. Furthermore, always double-check your statement of purpose with the person who authorized the report. After seeing the purpose written down in black and white, the authorizer may decide that the report needs to go in a different direction. Once your statement of purpose is confirmed, you're ready to prepare your work plan.

Preparing Your Work Plan

You're already accustomed to some schedule pressure with school reports. This is good practice for your business career, when you'll be expected to produce quality reports quickly and efficiently. A carefully thought-out work plan is the best way to make sure you produce good work on schedule. By identifying all the tasks that must be performed, you ensure that nothing is overlooked.

If you are preparing the work plan for yourself, it can be relatively informal: a simple list of the steps you plan to take and an estimate of their sequence and timing. However, for more complicated projects, particularly those that involve multiple team members, you'll want to prepare a formal, detailed work plan that can guide the performance of many tasks over a span of time. For consultants and others whose work output is a formal report, the work plan can also become the basis for a contract if the proposal is accepted. A formal work plan might include the following elements (especially the first two):

- **Statement of the problem or opportunity.** The problem statement clarifies the challenge you face, helps you (and anyone working with you) stay focused on the core issues, and helps everyone avoid the distractions that are likely to arise along the way.
- **Statement of the purpose and scope of your investigation.** The purpose statement describes what you plan to accomplish and therefore also defines the boundaries of your work. Stating which subjects you will cover and which you won't is especially important for complex, lengthy investigations.
- **Discussion of tasks to be accomplished.** Be sure to indicate your sources of information; the research necessary; and any constraints on time, money, personnel, or data. For simple reports, the list of tasks to be accomplished will be short and probably obvious. However, longer reports and complex investigations require an exhaustive list so that you can reserve time with customers, with executives, or for outside services such as market researchers or print shops.
- **Description of any products that will result from your investigation.** In many cases, the only product of your efforts will be the report itself. In other cases, you'll need to produce something beyond a report, perhaps a new marketing plan or even a tangible

3 LEARNING OBJECTIVE

Explain the value of a work plan in the development of long reports product. Make these expectations clear at the outset, and be sure to schedule enough time and resources to get the job done.

- **Review of project assignments, schedules, and resource requirements.** Indicate who will be responsible for what, when tasks will be completed, and how much the investigation will cost. If more than one person will be involved, you may also want to include a brief section on coordinating report writing and production, such as whether you'll use a wiki to develop the report content. (Collaborative writing is discussed in detail in Chapter 2.)
- **Plans for following up after delivering the report.** Follow-up can be as simple as making sure people received the information they need or as complex as conducting additional research to evaluate the results of proposals included in your report. Even informal follow-up can help you improve your future reports and communicate that you care about your work's effectiveness and its impact on the organization.
- **Working outline.** Some work plans include a tentative outline of the report, as does the plan in Figure 13.2.

Gathering Information

Some reports require formal research projects to gather all the necessary information.

As you discovered in Chapter 11, you may need to use a variety of techniques to gather the information required to meet audience needs. For instance, the market researchers at Kenwood USA (see page 393) gather information in numerous ways, from conducting surveys and one-on-one interviews to getting anecdotal feedback from consumers and retailers, combing through industry publications, and checking competitors' marketing materials.[2]

The sheer volume of information in most reports and proposals requires careful planning—and may even require a separate research project just to acquire the data and information you need. To stay on schedule and on budget, be sure that you review both your statement of purpose and your audience's needs so that you collect all the information required—and only the information required. Prioritize your needs before you start, and focus on the most important questions. Experienced writers also try to avoid duplication of effort by using templates and boilerplate material whenever possible (not only for gathering information but also for writing).

Selecting the Right Medium

In some situations, you may be required to use a specific medium for your reports.

In addition to the general media selection criteria discussed in Chapter 4, consider several points for reports and proposals. Start with what you know about audience expectations. In some situations, audiences have specific media requirements, and you might not have a choice. For instance, executives in many corporations now expect to review reports via their in-house intranets, sometimes in conjunction with an *executive dashboard*, a customized online presentation of key operating variables such as revenue, profits, quality, customer satisfaction, and project progress.

Expect to deliver many or most of your reports in electronic format.

In other situations, your audience might be more flexible but still have preferences. If an audience of several managers is likely to make comments on your report, would the managers rather write on a paper copy or use the revision features in a word-processor file? Will you or someone else be revising or updating the report? Given the multiple benefits of electronic reports (including low distribution costs, searchability, and easy archiving), expect to deliver many or even most of your reports in electronic format in the future.

Consider delivering your report via multiple media, too. For instance, even the best-written reports can often benefit from in-person communication. To ensure effective communication, Kenwood employees in the United States and Japan discuss their reports frequently, via both teleconferences and meetings in both countries. Again, the decision comes down to a balance of what's best for both you and your audience.

Whatever you decide, bear in mind that your choice of media also sends a message. A proposal that requests a venture capital investment of $5 million would look unimpressive as just a plain, coarsely formatted word-processor document that could have been churned out on a manual typewriter. Conversely, a routine operating report dressed up in expensive multimedia will look like a waste of valuable company resources.

FIGURE 13.2 Work Plan for a Report
A formal work plan such as this is a vital tool for planning and managing complex writing projects. The preliminary outline here helps guide the research; the report writers may well modify the outline when they begin writing the report.

States the problem clearly enough for anyone to understand without additional research

STATEMENT OF THE PROBLEM
The rapid growth of our company over the past five years has reduced the sense of community among our staff. People no longer feel like part of an intimate organization that values teamwork.

PURPOSE AND SCOPE OF WORK
The purpose of this study is to determine whether a company newsletter would help rebuild a sense of community within the workforce. The study will evaluate the impact of newsletters in other companies and will attempt to identify features that may be desirable in our own newsletter. Such variables as length, frequency of distribution, types of articles, and graphic design will be considered. Costs will be estimated for several approaches, including print and electronic versions. In addition, the study will analyze the personnel and procedures required to produce a newsletter.

Explains exactly what will be covered by the research and included in the final report

Identifies the tasks to be accomplished and does so in clear, simple terms

SOURCES AND METHODS OF DATA COLLECTION
Sample newsletters will be collected from 10 to 20 companies similar to ours in size, growth rate, and types of employees. The editors will be asked to comment on the impact of their publications on employee morale. Our own employees will be surveyed to determine their interest in a newsletter and their preferences for specific features. Production procedures and costs will be analyzed through conversations with newsletter editors, printers, and our website development team.

Offers a preliminary outline to help readers understand the issues that will be addressed in the report

PRELIMINARY OUTLINE
The preliminary outline for this study is as follows:
  I. Do newsletters affect morale?
     A. Do people read them?
     B. How do employees benefit?
     C. How does the company benefit?
  II. What are the features of good newsletters?
     A. How long are they?
     B. What do they contain?
     C. How often are they published?
     D. How are they designed?
  III. How should a newsletter be produced?
     A. Should it be written and edited internally or externally?
     B. Should it be printed or produced electronically?
     C. If electronic, should it be formatted as e-mail, a blog, or regular web content?
  IV. What would a newsletter cost?
     A. What would the personnel cost be?
     B. What would the material cost be?
     C. What would outside services cost?
  V. Should we publish a company newsletter?
  VI. If so, what approach should we take?

Identifies who is responsible for each task and when it will be completed

TASK ASSIGNMENTS AND SCHEDULE
Each phase of this study will be completed by the following dates:

Collect/analyze newsletters	Hank Waters	September 15, 2008
Interview editors by phone	Hank Waters	September 22, 2008
Survey employees	Julienne Cho	September 29, 2008
Develop sample	Hank Waters	October 6, 2008
Develop cost estimates	Julienne Cho	October 13, 2008
Prepare report	Hank Waters	October 20, 2008
Submit final report	Hank Waters	October 24, 2008

Organizing Your Information

The length and complexity of most reports and proposals require extra emphasis on clear, reader-oriented organization. Your readers might have the patience to struggle through a disorganized e-mail message but not through a poorly organized 200-page report. As discussed in Chapter 4, when an audience is likely to be receptive or at least open-minded, use a direct approach: Lead off with a summary of your key findings, conclusions, recommendations, or proposal, as the case may be. This "up-front" arrangement is by far the most popular and convenient for business reports. It saves time and makes the rest of the report easier to follow. For those who have questions or want more information, later parts of the report provide complete findings and supporting details. A direct approach also produces a more

Most business reports use a direct approach.

forceful report. You sound sure of yourself when you state your conclusions confidently at the outset.

At times, however, confidence may be misconstrued as arrogance. If you're a junior member of a status-conscious organization or if your audience is skeptical or hostile, consider an indirect approach: Introduce your complete findings and discuss all supporting details before presenting your conclusions and recommendations. An indirect approach gives you a chance to prove your points and gradually overcome your audience's reservations. By deferring the conclusions and recommendations to the end of your report, you imply that you've weighed the evidence objectively. You also imply that you're subordinating your judgment to that of the audience, whose members are capable of drawing their own conclusions when they have access to all the facts.

Use the indirect approach when you need to build support for your main idea or you want to avoid coming across as arrogant.

Although the indirect approach has its advantages, some readers will always be in a hurry to get to the answer and will immediately flip to the recommendations anyway, thus defeating your purpose. Therefore, consider length before choosing the direct or indirect approach. In general, the longer the message, the less effective an indirect approach is likely to be.

Because both direct and indirect approaches have merit, businesspeople often combine them. They reveal their conclusions and recommendations as they go along rather than putting them either first or last. Figure 13.3 presents the introductions from two reports with

FIGURE 13.3 Direct Approach Versus Indirect Approach in an Introduction
In the direct version of this introduction, the writer quickly presents the report's recommendation, followed by the conclusions that led to that recommendation. In the indirect version, the same topics are introduced in the same order but no conclusions are drawn about them (the conclusions and the ultimate recommendation appear later, in the body of the report).

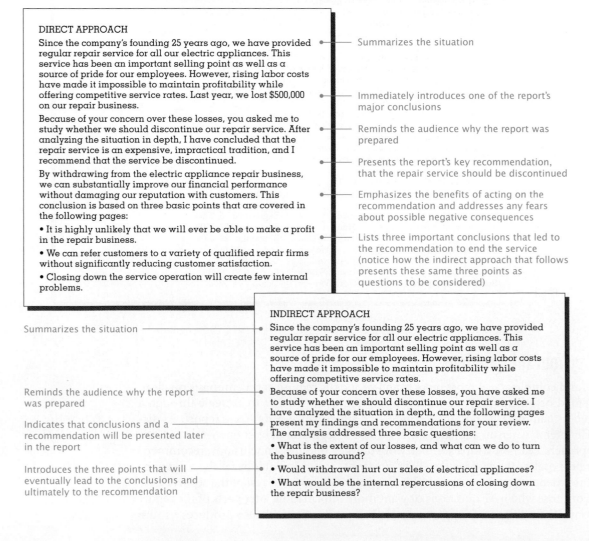

the same general outline. In the direct version, a series of statements summarizes the conclusion reached in relation to each main topic on the outline. In the indirect version, the same topics are introduced in the same order but without drawing any conclusions about them. Instead, the conclusions appear within the body of the report.

Regardless of the format, length, or order of your report, you must still decide how your ideas will be subdivided and developed. Suppose you're writing on a controversial topic and know that some of your readers will object to your ideas. You wisely decide to use indirect order, but how do you develop your argument? Your job is to choose the most logical argument structure—the one that suits your topic and goals and that makes the most sense to your audience.

Long reports sometimes combine direct and indirect approaches, building support for interim conclusions or recommendations along the way.

However you structure your argument, keep the following points in mind when organizing your report or proposal:

- **Understand and meet audience expectations.** Certain audiences expect or even require a specific organization, and your report might be rejected if it doesn't meet those requirements. Other audiences leave you room for some flexibility, as long as your report contains the right categories of information. Whenever possible, study an example of a successful report before writing a similar one. Such models will give you a feel not only for organization but also for content, emphasis, and tone.
- **Select a format that's appropriate to the task.** For reports of five pages or less, a memo or letter (or an electronic equivalent) is often sufficient. For longer reports, you'll want to include many of the elements of a formal report, which you'll read about in Chapter 15.
- **Keep it as short as possible.** Reports place enough burden on busy readers already; don't make the task harder by including unnecessary information or inconsequential details. Your readers will appreciate your brevity, and you'll stand a better chance of getting your message across.
- **"Talk" your way through your outline.** When you outline your content, use informative ("talking") headings rather than simple descriptive ("topical") headings (see Table 13.2). When in question or summary form, informative headings force you to really think through the content rather than simply identifying the general topic area. Using informative headings also facilitates collaborative writing. A heading such as "Industry characteristics" could mean five different things to the five people on your writing team, so use a heading that conveys a single, unambiguous meaning, such as "Flour milling is a mature industry."

Audience expectations are one of the most important considerations when deciding on the organization of your report.

For a quick review of adapting the three-step process to long reports, refer to "Checklist: Adapting the Three-Step Process to Informational and Analytical Reports." The following sections provide specific advice on how to plan informational reports, analytical reports, and proposals.

TABLE 13.2 Types of Outline Headings

| DESCRIPTIVE (TOPICAL) OUTLINE | INFORMATIVE (TALKING) OUTLINE | |
	QUESTION FORM	SUMMARY FORM
I. Industry Characteristics	I. What is the nature of the industry?	I. Flour milling is a mature industry.
A. Annual sales	A. What are the annual sales?	A. Market is large.
B. Profitability	B. Is the industry profitable?	B. Profit margins are narrow.
C. Growth rate	C. What is the pattern of growth?	C. Growth is modest.
1. Sales	1. Sales growth?	1. Sales growth averages less than 3 percent a year.
2. Profit	2. Profit growth?	2. Profits are flat.

CHECKLIST: Adapting the Three-Step Process to Informational and Analytical Reports

A. Analyze the situation.
- Clearly define your purpose before you start writing.
- If you need to accomplish several goals in the report, identify all of them in advance.
- Prepare a work plan to guide your efforts.

B. Gather information.
- Determine whether you need to launch a separate research project to collect the necessary information.
- Reuse or adapt existing material whenever possible.

C. Select the right medium.
- Base your decision on audience expectations (or requirements, as the case may be).

- Consider the need for commenting, revising, distributing, and storing.
- Remember that the medium you choose also sends a message.

D. Organize your information.
- Use a direct approach if your audience is receptive.
- Use an indirect approach if your audience is skeptical.
- Use an indirect approach when you don't want to risk coming across as arrogant.
- Combine approaches if that will help build support for your primary message.

PLANNING INFORMATIONAL REPORTS

4 LEARNING OBJECTIVE

Describe the four major categories of informational reports and provide examples of each

Informational reports are used to monitor and control operations, to implement policies and procedures, to demonstrate compliance, and to document progress.

Informational reports provide the information that employees, managers, and others need in order to make decisions and take action. Although dozens of particular formats exist, they can be grouped into four general categories:

- **Reports to monitor and control operations.** Just as doctors rely on medical reports to see how well the various systems in a patient's body are functioning, business managers rely on a wide range of reports to see how well the various systems inside their companies are functioning. *Plans* establish expectations and guidelines to direct future action. Plans can range from narrowly focused tactical plans covering short periods to high-level strategic plans that direct organizational activities over the course of several years (see "Creating Successful Business Plans" on page 404). *Operating reports* provide feedback on a wide variety of an organization's functions, including sales, inventories, expenses, shipments, and so on. *Personal activity reports* provide information regarding an individual's experiences during sales calls, industry conferences, market research trips, and so on.
- **Reports to implement policies and procedures.** Reports are the most common vehicle for conveying guidelines, approved procedures, and other organizational decisions. In some cases, you may write *policy reports* that are as short as a page or two, such as to share a new procedure with your colleagues. In other cases, the report might be a handbook or policy manual that run dozens or even hundreds of pages, either in print or online. *Position papers* are a special type of policy report that outlines an individual executive's (or the entire organization's) official position on issues that affect a company's success.
- **Reports to demonstrate compliance.** Even the smallest businesses are required to show that they are in compliance with government regulations of one sort or another. Some compliance reports, such as quarterly and annual tax reports, affect all businesses. Others concern particular industries, companies using hazardous materials, specific professional functions, or other special factors. Compliance reports are usually created in specific formats that must be followed precisely.
- **Reports to document progress.** Supervisors, investors, and customers frequently expect to be informed of the progress of projects and other activities. Progress reports range from simple updates in memo form to comprehensive reports that include such elements as measured progress toward goals, comparisons of budgeted versus actual expenses, and lists of ongoing concerns and risks.

Figure 13.4 shows the major subcategories within each of the major report categories, along with examples of the more common types. Specific titles may change depending on the company you're with, but chances are you'll be called upon to read nearly every one of these report types—and to write many of them, too.

FIGURE 13.4 Common Types of Business Reports and Proposals
You will have the opportunity to read and write many types of reports in your career; here are some of the most common.

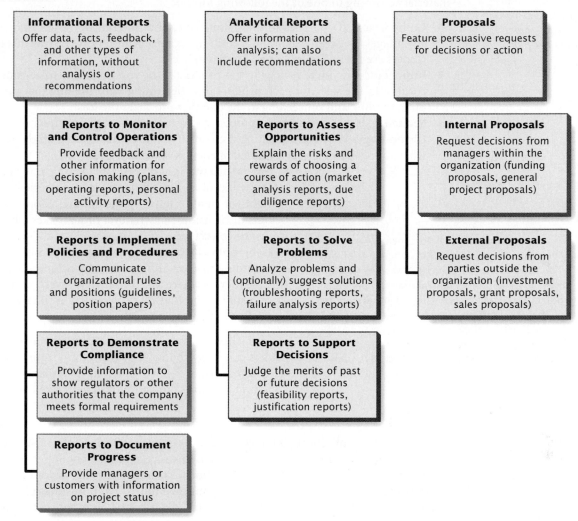

Organizational Strategies for Informational Reports

Informational reports can range from extremely positive (such as a report on great sales results) to neutral (a monitoring report that shows business as usual on the factory floor) to extremely negative (a report on customer satisfaction research that ranks the company poorly). Given the range of possibilities, the choice of direct or indirect approach warrants serious consideration before you start outlining in earnest. Because informational reports focus on the straightforward delivery of data and information, the direct approach is common. However, you will encounter situations in which an indirect approach is more effective, such as when you need to build up a series of facts to help your readers understand the main idea of your report.

In one sense, informational reports are the least complicated reports to write because they don't require analysis or persuasion. Your job is simply to deliver information in an effective and efficient manner. However, that simplicity doesn't mean that informational reports are necessarily easy to prepare. You still need to evaluate, process, and organize information—sometimes hundreds or thousands of individual facts and figures—in a way that appeals to your audience members and meets their needs. Moreover, because you're not expected to analyze or persuade in these reports, you must take care to remain objective throughout.

The messages conveyed by informational reports can range from extremely positive to extremely negative, so the approach you take warrants careful consideration.

A topical organization is built around the content itself, using such arrangements as comparison, importance, sequence, chronology, spatial orientation, geography, or category.

When writing an informational report, you can let the nature of whatever you're describing dictate your structure. Informational reports use a **topical organization,** arranging material according to one of the following topics:

- **Comparison.** If you need to show similarities and differences (or advantages and disadvantages) between two or more entities, organize your report in a way that helps your readers see those similarities and differences clearly.
- **Importance.** If you're reviewing five product lines, you might organize your study according to the sales for each product line, beginning with the line that produces the most revenue and proceeding to the one that produces the least.
- **Sequence.** If you're studying a process, discuss it step by step, in sequence.
- **Chronology.** When investigating a chain of events, organize the study according to what happened in January, what happened in February, and so on.
  - **Spatial orientation.** If you're explaining how a physical object works or a physical space looks, describe it from left to right (or right to left in some cultures), top to bottom, or outside to inside—in whatever order makes the most sense; just be consistent.
  - **Geography.** If location is important, organize your study according to geography, such as by country or by state.
  - **Category.** If you're asked to review several distinct aspects of a subject, look at one category at a time, such as sales, profit, cost, or investment.

Whichever pattern you choose, use it consistently so that readers can easily follow your discussion from start to finish. Of course, certain reports (such as compliance or monitor-and-control reports) must follow a prescribed flow.

DOCUMENT MAKEOVER

IMPROVE THIS REPORT

To practice correcting drafts of actual documents, visit your online course or the access-code-protected portion of the Companion Website. Click "Document Makeovers," then click Chapter 13. You will find an informational report that contains problems and errors relating to what you've learned in this chapter about planning business reports and proposals. Use the Final Draft decision tool to create an improved version of this report. Check the message for parallel construction, appropriate headings, suitable content, positive and bias-free language, and use of the "you" attitude.

---

5 LEARNING OBJECTIVE

List the key elements of a business plan

Creating Successful Business Plans

The most important report you may ever get the chance to write is the business plan for a new company. A comprehensive business plan forces you to think about personnel, marketing, facilities, suppliers, distribution, and a host of other issues vital to your success. If you are starting out on a small scale and using your own money, your business plan may be relatively informal. But at a minimum, you should describe the basic concept of the business and outline its specific goals, objectives, and resource requirements. A more formal plan, which is an absolute necessity when you want to persuade other people to invest in or join your organization, should cover these points:[3]

- **Summary.** In one or two pages, summarize your business concept. Describe your product or service and its market potential. Highlight some things about your company and its leaders that will distinguish your firm from the competition. Summarize your financial projections and the amount of money investors can expect to make on their investment. Be sure to indicate how much money you will need and where it will be spent.
- **Mission and objectives.** Explain the purpose of your business and what you hope to accomplish—and before you take another step, make sure this is a mission you can pursue with passion, through thick and thin, with every ounce of commitment and energy you can muster.
- **Company and industry.** Give full background information on the origins and structure of your venture and the characteristics of the industry in which you plan to compete.
- **Products or services.** Give a complete but concise description of your products or services, focusing on their unique attributes. Explain how customers will benefit from using your products or services instead of those of your competitors.
- **Market and competition.** Provide data that will persuade investors that you understand your target market and can achieve your sales goals. Be sure to identify the strengths and weaknesses of your competitors.
- **Management.** Summarize the background and qualifications of the key management personnel in your company. Include résumés in an appendix.

- **Marketing strategy.** Provide projections of sales volume and market share, and outline a strategy for identifying and contacting customers, setting prices, providing customer services, advertising, and so forth. Whenever possible, include evidence of customer acceptance, such as advance product orders.
- **Design and development plans.** If your product requires design or development, describe the nature and extent of what needs to be done, including costs and possible problems. For new or unusual products, you may want to explain how the product will be manufactured.
- **Operations plan.** Provide information on facilities, equipment, and personnel requirements.
- **Overall schedule.** Forecast important milestones in the company's growth and development, including when you need to be fully staffed and when your products will be ready for the market.
- **Critical risks and problems.** Identify all negative factors and discuss them honestly.
- **Financial projections and requirements.** Include a detailed budget of start-up and operating costs, as well as projections for income, expenses, and cash flow for the first few years of business. Identify the company's financing needs and potential sources, if appropriate.
- **Exit strategy.** Explain how investors will be able to cash out or sell their investment, such as through a public stock offering, sale of the company, or a buyback of the investors' interest.

A complete business plan obviously requires a considerable amount of work. However, by thinking your way through all these issues, you'll enjoy a smoother launch and a greater chance of success in your new adventure.

Organizing Website Content

Many websites, particularly company websites, function as informational reports, offering sections with information about the company, its history, its products and services, its executive team, and so on. While most of what you've already learned about informational reports applies to website writing, the online experience requires some special considerations and practices.

As you begin to plan a website, start by recognizing the unique nature of online communication:

- **Web readers are demanding.** If your site can't meet the audience's needs quickly, they'll find another site that can. Most visitors won't bother to dig for information. They scan navigation buttons, headings, images, and hyperlinks, looking for possibilities. If nothing looks promising, they're gone.[4]
- **Reading online can be difficult.** For most people, reading on a computer monitor is more difficult than reading from the printed page. In fact, studies show that reading speeds are about 25 percent slower on a monitor than on paper.[5] Reading from computer screens can also be tiring on the eyes, even to the point of causing headaches, double vision, blurred vision, and other physical problems.[6]
- **The web is a nonlinear, multidimensional medium.** Readers of online material move around in any order they please; there often is no beginning, middle, or end. As a web writer, you need to anticipate the various paths your readers will want to follow and make sure you provide the right hyperlinks in the right places to help readers explore successfully.

As you move on to define your purpose, bear in mind that most websites have to perform more than one communication function. Consequently, a single website could have a half-dozen purposes or more. Each of these individual purposes needs to be carefully defined and then integrated into a overall statement of purpose for the entire website. Then as you develop the site, you'll need to clearly identify the specific purpose of each section of the site so that readers always know where to find the information they need.[7]

Just as you probably will have a number of purposes for a single website, you're likely to have a number of different audiences as well. The global reach of the web further complicates

6 LEARNING OBJECTIVE

Identify three steps you can take to ensure effective organization of online reports and other website content

the audience analysis issue, because you may get visitors from all parts of the world. After you've identified your multiple audiences, you then need to analyze each group's unique information needs, then find a logical way to organize all that material. Professional website designers often use the term **information architecture** to describe the structure and navigational flow of all the parts of a website. In a sense, the information architecture is a three-dimensional outline of the site, showing (1) the vertical hierarchy of pages from the homepage down to the lower level; (2) the horizontal division of pages across the various sections of the site; and (3) the links that tie all these pages together, both internally (between various pages on the site) and externally (between your site and other websites).

As you develop the site architecture, you can begin to simulate how various audiences will use the site and refine the plan to meet everyone's needs (see Figure 13.5). For instance, can potential customers find new product information quickly? In contrast, can existing customers get support or warranty information quickly, without wading through pages of promotion for new products? You can also get a sense of how you'll need to assist visitors who enter the site at points other than the homepage, as often happens with search engine links. Accommodating these multiple entry points is one of the most difficult tasks in site design.[8]

FIGURE 13.5 Information Architecture
Anyone searching online for the "Green Goodness" brand of nutritional drink would likely land on this specific product page on the Bolthouse Farms website, rather than landing on the site's homepage. However, thanks to careful consideration of information architecture, virtually every site visitor can quickly link to the information in which he or she might be interested.

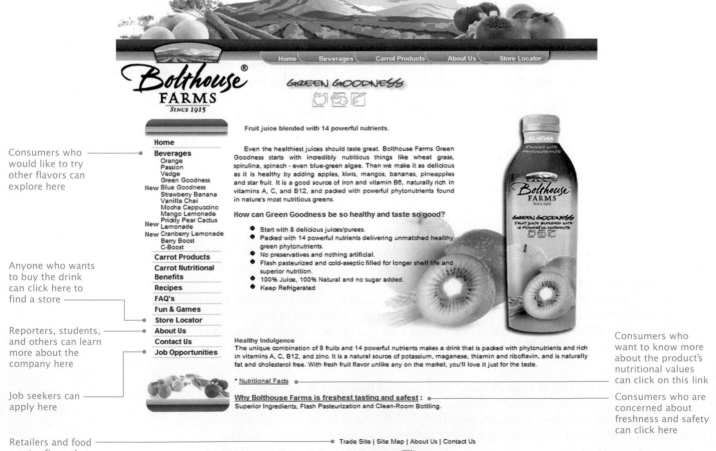

Consumers who would like to try other flavors can explore here

Anyone who wants to buy the drink can click here to find a store

Reporters, students, and others can learn more about the company here

Job seekers can apply here

Retailers and food service firms that want to carry the product can click on the "Trade Site" link

Consumers who want to know more about the product's nutritional values can click on this link

Consumers who are concerned about freshness and safety can click here

To organize your site effectively, keep the following advice in mind:

- **Plan your navigation first.** Some novice web writers make the mistake of writing a traditional report, then adding some links to make it a website. Websites don't work that way because readers don't read that way. They enter your site from an endless variety of other places on the web, with different needs and expectations. To ensure that readers will be able to navigate your document effectively and efficiently, plan your site structure and navigation before you write.[9]
- **Let your readers be in control.** Most readers want to navigate using paths they establish themselves, so create links and pathways that let them explore on their own. However, doing so doesn't mean abandoning them to figure out your site by themselves. Help your readers by starting with a homepage that clearly points the way to various sections of the site, then offer plenty of descriptive labels, subheads, and other devices that let readers figure out where to go next.
- **Break your information into chunks.** Help online readers scan and absorb information by breaking it into self-contained, easily readable "chunks" that are linked together logically. Doing so lets you provide comprehensive coverage in a way that is still easy to consume online. For longer sections, consider offering them as downloadable PDF files.

Effective Informational Reports: An Example

Effective informational reports are clearly and logically organized, with audience-centered content and generous use of previews and summaries. They are complete, without being unnecessarily long or detailed. One of the tasks your audience expects you to accomplish is to sort out the details and separate major points from minor points. In other words, readers expect you to put in all the thought and effort it takes to make the best use of their time. In addition, effective reports are honest and objective but not unduly harsh whenever negative information must be conveyed. Compare the differences between the report versions shown in Figures 13.6 and 13.7.

PLANNING ANALYTICAL REPORTS

The purpose of analytical reports is to analyze, to understand, to explain—to think through a problem or an opportunity and figure out how it affects the company and how the company should respond. In many cases, you'll also be expected to make a recommendation based on your analysis. As you saw in Figure 13.4, analytical reports fall into three basic categories:

- **Reports to assess opportunities.** Every business opportunity carries some degree of risk and also requires a variety of decisions and actions in order to capitalize on the opportunity. For instance, *market analysis reports* are used to judge the likelihood of success for new products or sales initiatives by suggesting potential opportunities in a given market and identifying competitive threats and other risks. *Due diligence reports* examine the financial aspects of a proposed decision, such as acquiring another company.
- **Reports to solve problems.** Managers often assign *troubleshooting reports* when they need to understand why something isn't working properly, from malfunctioning industrial processes to financial disappointments, and what needs to be done to fix it. A variation, the *failure analysis report*, studies events that happened in the past, with the hope of learning how to avoid similar failures in the future.
- **Reports to support decisions.** *Feasibility reports* are called for when managers need to explore the ramifications of a decision they're about to make (such as replacing an advertising agency or switching materials used in a manufacturing process). *Justification reports* justify a decision that has already been made.

Writing analytical reports presents a greater challenge than writing informational reports, for three reasons. First, you're doing more than simply delivering information; you're also thinking through a problem or opportunity and presenting your conclusions. The best

Analytical reports are used to assess opportunities, to solve problems, and to support decisions.

7 LEARNING OBJECTIVE

Describe the three major categories of analytical reports and provide examples of each

FIGURE 13.6 Ineffective Informational Report
While this report looks professional at first glance, it contains a number of weaknesses in tone, content, and formatting. Compare it with the version in Figure 13.7.

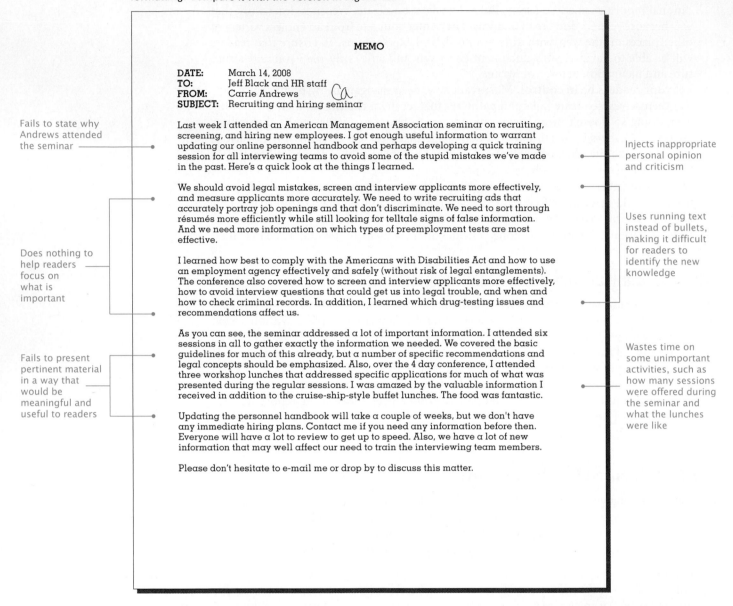

MEMO

DATE: March 14, 2008
TO: Jeff Black and HR staff
FROM: Carrie Andrews
SUBJECT: Recruiting and hiring seminar

Last week I attended an American Management Association seminar on recruiting, screening, and hiring new employees. I got enough useful information to warrant updating our online personnel handbook and perhaps developing a quick training session for all interviewing teams to avoid some of the stupid mistakes we've made in the past. Here's a quick look at the things I learned.

We should avoid legal mistakes, screen and interview applicants more effectively, and measure applicants more accurately. We need to write recruiting ads that accurately portray job openings and that don't discriminate. We need to sort through résumés more efficiently while still looking for telltale signs of false information. And we need more information on which types of preemployment tests are most effective.

I learned how best to comply with the Americans with Disabilities Act and how to use an employment agency effectively and safely (without risk of legal entanglements). The conference also covered how to screen and interview applicants more effectively, how to avoid interview questions that could get us into legal trouble, and when and how to check criminal records. In addition, I learned which drug-testing issues and recommendations affect us.

As you can see, the seminar addressed a lot of important information. I attended six sessions in all to gather exactly the information we needed. We covered the basic guidelines for much of this already, but a number of specific recommendations and legal concepts should be emphasized. Also, over the 4 day conference, I attended three workshop lunches that addressed specific applications for much of what was presented during the regular sessions. I was amazed by the valuable information I received in addition to the cruise-ship-style buffet lunches. The food was fantastic.

Updating the personnel handbook will take a couple of weeks, but we don't have any immediate hiring plans. Contact me if you need any information before then. Everyone will have a lot to review to get up to speed. Also, we have a lot of new information that may well affect our need to train the interviewing team members.

Please don't hesitate to e-mail me or drop by to discuss this matter.

Annotations (left):
- Fails to state why Andrews attended the seminar
- Does nothing to help readers focus on what is important
- Fails to present pertinent material in a way that would be meaningful and useful to readers

Annotations (right):
- Injects inappropriate personal opinion and criticism
- Uses running text instead of bullets, making it difficult for readers to identify the new knowledge
- Wastes time on some unimportant activities, such as how many sessions were offered during the seminar and what the lunches were like

writing in the world can't compensate for flawed analysis. Second, when your analysis is complete, you need to present your thinking in a compelling and persuasive manner. Third, analytical reports often convince other people to make significant financial and personnel decisions, so your reports carry the added responsibility of the consequences of these decisions.

In some situations, the problem or opportunity you address in an analytical report may be defined by the person who authorizes the report. In other cases, you will have to define it yourself. Be careful not to confuse a simple topic (quarterly profits) with a problem (the decline in profits over the past six quarters). Moreover, if you're the only person who thinks a particular issue is a problem, your readers won't be interested in your solution unless your report first convinces them that a problem does exist. Sometimes you need to "sell the problem" before you can sell the solution.

To help define the problem that your analytical report will address, answer these questions:

Clarify the problem in an analytical report by determining what you need to analyze, why the issue is important, who is involved, where the trouble is located, and how and when it started.

- What needs to be determined?
- Why is this issue important?

FIGURE 13.7 Effective Informational Report
This version of the report (see Figure 13.6) is much easier to read and presents pertinent information in a clear, concise way.

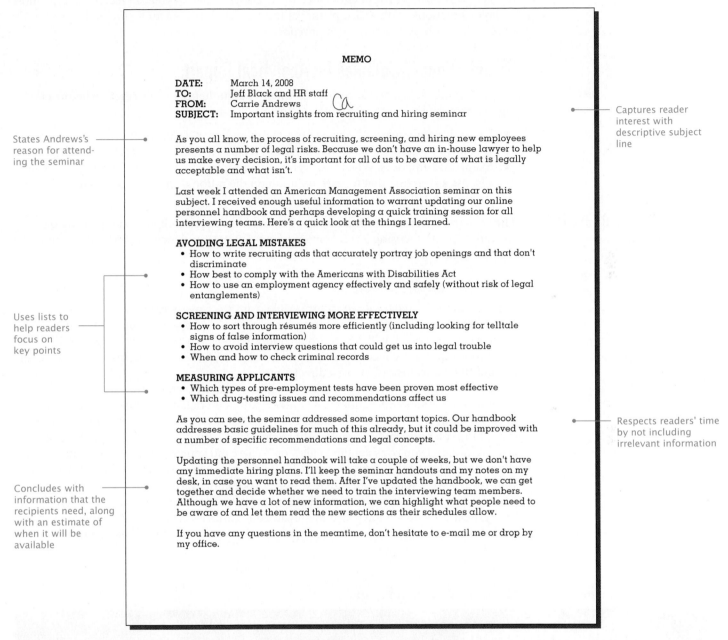

States Andrews's reason for attending the seminar

Uses lists to help readers focus on key points

Concludes with information that the recipients need, along with an estimate of when it will be available

Captures reader interest with descriptive subject line

Respects readers' time by not including irrelevant information

MEMO

DATE: March 14, 2008
TO: Jeff Black and HR staff
FROM: Carrie Andrews
SUBJECT: Important insights from recruiting and hiring seminar

As you all know, the process of recruiting, screening, and hiring new employees presents a number of legal risks. Because we don't have an in-house lawyer to help us make every decision, it's important for all of us to be aware of what is legally acceptable and what isn't.

Last week I attended an American Management Association seminar on this subject. I received enough useful information to warrant updating our online personnel handbook and perhaps developing a quick training session for all interviewing teams. Here's a quick look at the things I learned.

AVOIDING LEGAL MISTAKES
- How to write recruiting ads that accurately portray job openings and that don't discriminate
- How best to comply with the Americans with Disabilities Act
- How to use an employment agency effectively and safely (without risk of legal entanglements)

SCREENING AND INTERVIEWING MORE EFFECTIVELY
- How to sort through résumés more efficiently (including looking for telltale signs of false information)
- How to avoid interview questions that could get us into legal trouble
- When and how to check criminal records

MEASURING APPLICANTS
- Which types of pre-employment tests have been proven most effective
- Which drug-testing issues and recommendations affect us

As you can see, the seminar addressed some important topics. Our handbook addresses basic guidelines for much of this already, but it could be improved with a number of specific recommendations and legal concepts.

Updating the personnel handbook will take a couple of weeks, but we don't have any immediate hiring plans. I'll keep the seminar handouts and my notes on my desk, in case you want to read them. After I've updated the handbook, we can get together and decide whether we need to train the interviewing team members. Although we have a lot of new information, we can highlight what people need to be aware of and let them read the new sections as their schedules allow.

If you have any questions in the meantime, don't hesitate to e-mail me or drop by my office.

- Who is involved in the situation?
- Where is the trouble located?
- How did the situation originate?
- When did it start?

Not all these questions apply in every situation, but asking them helps you define the problem being addressed and limit the scope of your discussion.

Also try breaking down the perceived problem into a series of logical, connected questions that try to identify cause and effect. This process is sometimes called **problem factoring.** You probably subconsciously approach most problems this way. When your car won't start, what do you do? You use the available evidence to organize your investigation, to start a search for cause-and-effect relationships. For example, if the engine doesn't turn over at all, you might suspect a dead battery. If the engine does turn over but won't fire, you can conclude that the

Use problem factoring to divide a complex problem into more manageable pieces.

battery is OK but perhaps you're out of gas. When you speculate on the cause of a problem, you're forming a **hypothesis**, a potential explanation that needs to be tested. By subdividing a problem and forming hypotheses based on available evidence, you can tackle even the most complex situations. With a clear picture of the problem or opportunity in mind, you're ready to consider the best structure for your report.

Organizational Strategies for Analytical Reports

Before you choose an approach, determine whether your audience is receptive or skeptical.

To create powerful analytical reports, consider your audience's likely reaction before choosing the most effective organizational strategy:

- **Receptive audiences.** When you expect your audience to agree with you, use a structure that focuses attention on conclusions and recommendations (direct approach).
- **Skeptical audiences.** When you expect your audience to disagree with you or to be hostile, use a structure that focuses attention on the rationale behind your conclusions and recommendations (indirect approach).

8 LEARNING OBJECTIVE

Discuss three major ways to organize analytical reports

The three most common structural approaches for analytical reports are focusing on conclusions (direct), focusing on recommendations (direct), and focusing on logical arguments (indirect). See Table 13.3.

Focusing on Conclusions

Focusing on conclusions is often the best approach when you're addressing a receptive audience.

When writing an analytical report for people from your own organization who have asked you to study something, you're writing for your most receptive readers. They may know from experience that you'll do a thorough job, and they may trust your judgment. If they're likely to accept your conclusions—whatever they may be—you can structure your report around those conclusions, using a direct approach.

However, focusing directly on conclusions does have potential drawbacks. If your readers have reservations either about you or about your material, strong statements at the beginning may put an audience on the defensive. Also, focusing on conclusions may make everything you say seem too simple. Your readers could criticize your report as being superficial: "Why didn't you consider this angle?" or "Where did you get this number?" You're generally better off taking the direct approach in a report only when your credibility is high—when your readers trust you and are willing to accept your conclusions (see Figure 13.8).

You can use a similar structure whether you're asked to analyze a problem or an opportunity. Readers who are interested mainly in your conclusions can grasp them quickly, and readers who want to know more about your analysis can look at the data you provide.

TABLE 13.3 Common Ways to Structure Analytical Reports

ELEMENT	FOCUS ON CONCLUSIONS OR RECOMMENDATIONS	FOCUS ON LOGICAL ARGUMENT	
		USE 2 + 2 = 4 MODEL	USE YARDSTICK MODEL
Readers	Are likely to accept	Hostile or skeptical	Hostile or skeptical
Approach	Direct	Indirect	Indirect
Writer credibility	High	Low	Low
Advantages	Readers quickly grasp conclusions or recommendations	Works well when you need to show readers how you built toward an answer by following clear logical steps	Works well when you have a list of criteria (standards) that must be considered in a decision; alternatives are all measured against same criteria
Drawbacks	Structure can make topic seem too simple	Can make report longer	Readers must agree on criteria; can be lengthy because of the need to address each criteria for every alternative

FIGURE 13.8 Preliminary Outline of a Research Report Focusing on Conclusions
Cynthia Zolonka works on the human resources staff of a bank in Houston, Texas. Her company decided to have an outside firm handle its employee training, and a year after the outsourcing arrangement was established, Zolonka was asked to evaluate the results. Her analysis shows that the outsourcing experiment was a success, and she opens with that conclusion but supports it with clear evidence. Readers who accept the conclusion can stop reading, and those who desire more information can continue.

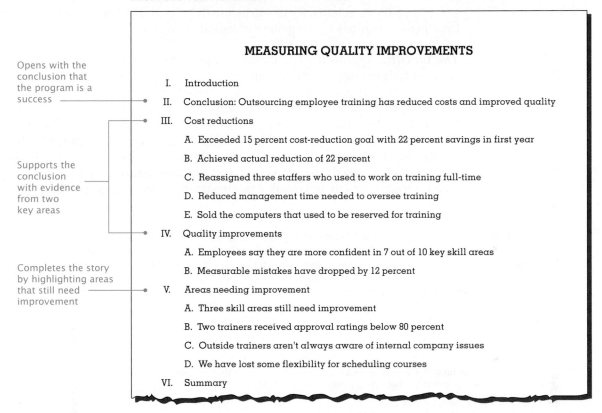

Opens with the conclusion that the program is a success

Supports the conclusion with evidence from two key areas

Completes the story by highlighting areas that still need improvement

MEASURING QUALITY IMPROVEMENTS

   I.   Introduction

  II.   Conclusion: Outsourcing employee training has reduced costs and improved quality

 III.   Cost reductions

         A. Exceeded 15 percent cost-reduction goal with 22 percent savings in first year

         B. Achieved actual reduction of 22 percent

         C. Reassigned three staffers who used to work on training full-time

         D. Reduced management time needed to oversee training

         E. Sold the computers that used to be reserved for training

  IV.   Quality improvements

         A. Employees say they are more confident in 7 out of 10 key skill areas

         B. Measurable mistakes have dropped by 12 percent

   V.   Areas needing improvement

         A. Three skill areas still need improvement

         B. Two trainers received approval ratings below 80 percent

         C. Outside trainers aren't always aware of internal company issues

         D. We have lost some flexibility for scheduling courses

  VI.   Summary

Focusing on Recommendations

In some situations, you'll be asked to provide advice on solving a problem or approaching an opportunity, rather than simply analyzing it. You can present your recommendations using a series of five steps:

When readers want to know what you think they should do, organize your report to focus on recommendations.

1. Establish or verify the need for action in the introduction, generally by briefly describing the problem or opportunity.
2. Introduce the benefit that can be achieved, without providing any details.
3. List the steps (recommendations) required to achieve the benefit, using action verbs for emphasis.
4. Explain each step more fully, giving details on procedures, costs, and benefits.
5. Summarize your recommendations.

If your recommendation carries any risks, be sure to clearly address those as well. Doing so not only makes your report more ethical but also offers you some protection in the event that your recommendation is implemented but doesn't work out as you had hoped. In short, make sure your readers know both the potential disadvantages and the potential benefits.

Whenever a recommendation carries some element of risk, you owe it to your audience to make this clear.

Focusing on Logical Arguments

When readers are skeptical or hostile to the conclusion or recommendation you plan to make, use an indirect approach that logically builds toward your conclusion or recommendation. If you guide audience members along a rational path toward the answer, they are more likely to accept it when they encounter it. The two most common logical approaches are known as the *2 + 2 = 4 approach* and the *yardstick approach.*

Two common logical patterns arguments are the 2 + 2 = 4 approach (adding everything up) and the yardstick approach (comparing solutions against criteria).

The 2 + 2 = 4 Approach   The **2 + 2 = 4 approach** is so named because it convinces readers of your point of view by demonstrating that everything adds up. The main points in your outline are the main reasons behind your conclusions and recommendations. You support each reason with the evidence you collected during your analysis.

Start by considering using the 2 + 2 = 4 approach; it's familiar and easy to develop.

Because of its natural feel and versatility, the 2 + 2 = 4 approach is generally the most persuasive and efficient way to develop an analytical report for skeptical readers. When organizing your own reports, try this structure first. You'll find that many business situations lend themselves nicely to this pattern of logical argumentation.

The Yardstick Approach   The **yardstick approach** is useful when you need to use a number of criteria to evaluate one or more possible solutions. These criteria become the "yardstick" by which you measure the various alternatives. With this approach, you begin by discussing the problem or opportunity, then list the criteria that will guide the decision. The body of the report then evaluates the alternatives against those criteria. The main points of the outline are either the criteria themselves or the alternatives (see Figure 13.9).

The yardstick approach compares a solution or several solutions to a set of predetermined standards.

The yardstick approach is particularly useful for proposals when the audience has provided a list of criteria the solution must meet. Say that your company has been asked to bid on a contract to design and install a factory-floor distribution system for a large corpora-

FIGURE 13.9 Outline of an Analytical Report Using the Yardstick Approach
This outline was prepared by J. C. Hartley, a market analyst for a large Sacramento company that makes irrigation equipment for farms and ranches. "We've been so successful in the agricultural market that we're starting to run out of customers to sell to," says Hartley. "To keep the company growing, we needed to find another market. Two obvious choices to consider were commercial buildings and residences," so she structured her report to compare these two opportunities.

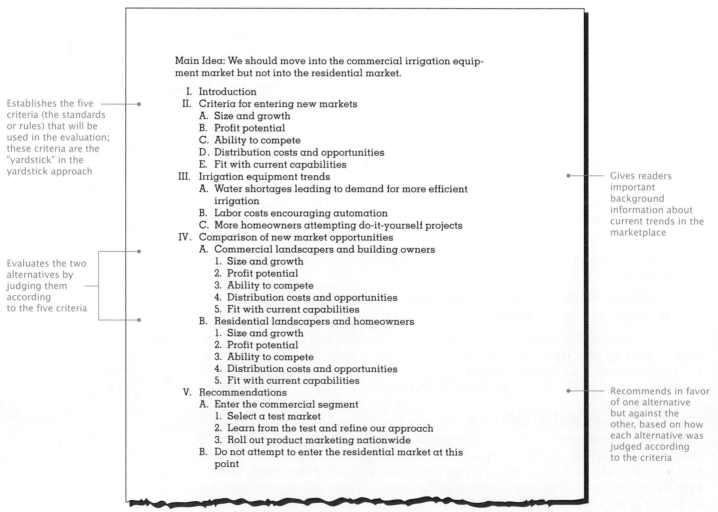

Establishes the five criteria (the standards or rules) that will be used in the evaluation; these criteria are the "yardstick" in the yardstick approach

Evaluates the two alternatives by judging them according to the five criteria

Gives readers important background information about current trends in the marketplace

Recommends in favor of one alternative but against the other, based on how each alternative was judged according to the criteria

Main Idea: We should move into the commercial irrigation equipment market but not into the residential market.

I. Introduction
II. Criteria for entering new markets
   A. Size and growth
   B. Profit potential
   C. Ability to compete
   D. Distribution costs and opportunities
   E. Fit with current capabilities
III. Irrigation equipment trends
   A. Water shortages leading to demand for more efficient irrigation
   B. Labor costs encouraging automation
   C. More homeowners attempting do-it-yourself projects
IV. Comparison of new market opportunities
   A. Commercial landscapers and building owners
      1. Size and growth
      2. Profit potential
      3. Ability to compete
      4. Distribution costs and opportunities
      5. Fit with current capabilities
   B. Residential landscapers and homeowners
      1. Size and growth
      2. Profit potential
      3. Ability to compete
      4. Distribution costs and opportunities
      5. Fit with current capabilities
V. Recommendations
   A. Enter the commercial segment
      1. Select a test market
      2. Learn from the test and refine our approach
      3. Roll out product marketing nationwide
   B. Do not attempt to enter the residential market at this point

tion. The client has listed the requirements (criteria) for the system, and you've developed a preliminary design to meet them. In the body of your proposal, you could use the client's list of requirements as the main headings and under each one explain how your preliminary design meets the requirement.

The yardstick approach has two potential drawbacks. First, your audience members need to agree with the criteria you're using in your analysis. If they don't, they won't agree with the results of the evaluation. If you have any doubt about their agreement, build consensus before you start your report, if possible, or take extra care to explain why the criteria you're using are the best ones in this particular case. Second, the yardstick approach can get a little boring when you have many options to consider or many criteria to compare them against. One way to minimize the repetition is to compare the options in tables and then highlight the more unusual or important aspects of each alternative in the text so that you get the best of both worlds. This approach allows you to compare all the alternatives against the same yardstick while calling attention to the most significant differences among them.

Effective Analytical Reports: An Example

As national sales manager of a New Hampshire sporting goods company, Binh Phan was concerned about his company's ability to sell to its largest customers. His boss, the vice president of marketing, shared these concerns and asked Phan to analyze the situation and recommend a solution. As Phan says, "We sell sporting goods to retail chains across the country. Large nationwide chains of superstores have been revolutionizing the industry, but we haven't had as much success with these big customers as we've had with smaller companies that operate strictly on a local or regional basis. With more and more of the industry in the hands of the large chains, we knew we had to fix the situation."

Phan's troubleshooting report appears in Figure 13.10. The main idea is that the company should establish separate sales teams for these major accounts, rather than continuing to service them through the company's four regional divisions. However, Phan knew his plan would be controversial because it required a big change in the company's organization and in the way sales reps are paid. His thinking had to be clear and easy to follow, so he used the $2 + 2 = 4$ approach to focus on his reasons.

PLANNING PROPOSALS

The specific formats for proposals are innumerable, but they can be grouped into two general categories. *Internal proposals* request decisions from managers within the organization, such as proposals to buy new equipment or launch new research projects. *External proposals* request decisions from parties outside the organization. Examples include *investment proposals*, which request funding from external investors; *grant proposals*, which request funds from government agencies and other sponsoring organizations; and *sales proposals*, which suggest individualized solutions for potential customers and request purchase decisions.

Regardless of the audience, the most significant factor in planning a proposal is whether the recipient has asked you to submit a proposal. *Solicited proposals* are generally prepared at the request of external parties that require a product or a service, but they may also be requested by such internal sources as management or the board of directors. When organizations require complex products, services, or systems, they often prepare a formal invitation to bid on the contract, called a **request for proposal (RFP)**, which includes instructions that specify the exact type of work to be performed or products to be delivered, along with budgets, deadlines, and other requirements. For example, when the National Aeronautics and Space Administration (NASA) wants to develop a new satellite, it prepares an RFP that specifies exactly what the satellite should accomplish and sends the RFP to several aerospace companies, inviting them to bid on the job. You respond to RFPs by preparing a proposal that shows how you would meet the potential customer's needs. Responding to RFPs can be a significant task; fortunately, new software products are available to lighten the load considerably (see "Connecting with Technology: Proposals Get a Software Assist").

Buyers often solicit proposals by publishing a request for proposals (RFP).

FIGURE 13.10 Analytical Report Using the 2 + 2 = 4 Approach
To make his logical argument both clear and compelling, Binh Phan used the 2 + 2 = 4 approach.

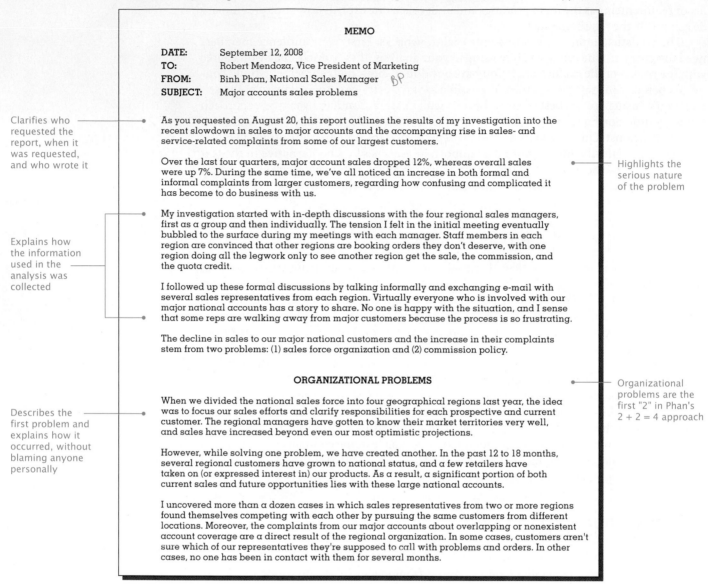

Clarifies who requested the report, when it was requested, and who wrote it

Explains how the information used in the analysis was collected

Describes the first problem and explains how it occurred, without blaming anyone personally

Highlights the serious nature of the problem

Organizational problems are the first "2" in Phan's 2 + 2 = 4 approach

MEMO

DATE: September 12, 2008
TO: Robert Mendoza, Vice President of Marketing
FROM: Binh Phan, National Sales Manager   *BP*
SUBJECT: Major accounts sales problems

As you requested on August 20, this report outlines the results of my investigation into the recent slowdown in sales to major accounts and the accompanying rise in sales- and service-related complaints from some of our largest customers.

Over the last four quarters, major account sales dropped 12%, whereas overall sales were up 7%. During the same time, we've all noticed an increase in both formal and informal complaints from larger customers, regarding how confusing and complicated it has become to do business with us.

My investigation started with in-depth discussions with the four regional sales managers, first as a group and then individually. The tension I felt in the initial meeting eventually bubbled to the surface during my meetings with each manager. Staff members in each region are convinced that other regions are booking orders they don't deserve, with one region doing all the legwork only to see another region get the sale, the commission, and the quota credit.

I followed up these formal discussions by talking informally and exchanging e-mail with several sales representatives from each region. Virtually everyone who is involved with our major national accounts has a story to share. No one is happy with the situation, and I sense that some reps are walking away from major customers because the process is so frustrating.

The decline in sales to our major national customers and the increase in their complaints stem from two problems: (1) sales force organization and (2) commission policy.

ORGANIZATIONAL PROBLEMS

When we divided the national sales force into four geographical regions last year, the idea was to focus our sales efforts and clarify responsibilities for each prospective and current customer. The regional managers have gotten to know their market territories very well, and sales have increased beyond even our most optimistic projections.

However, while solving one problem, we have created another. In the past 12 to 18 months, several regional customers have grown to national status, and a few retailers have taken on (or expressed interest in) our products. As a result, a significant portion of both current sales and future opportunities lies with these large national accounts.

I uncovered more than a dozen cases in which sales representatives from two or more regions found themselves competing with each other by pursuing the same customers from different locations. Moreover, the complaints from our major accounts about overlapping or nonexistent account coverage are a direct result of the regional organization. In some cases, customers aren't sure which of our representatives they're supposed to call with problems and orders. In other cases, no one has been in contact with them for several months.

(continued)

9 LEARNING OBJECTIVE

Explain how your approach to writing proposals should differ when you are responding to a formal request for proposals (RFP)

Unsolicited proposals require additional persuasive elements because the audience isn't expecting the proposal and might not even be conscious of the problem you propose to solve.

To attract a large pool of qualified bidders, organizations send RFPs to firms with good performance records in the field, print them in trade publications, or post them on the web. Federal government RFPs, for instance, can be found through Commerce Business Daily at **www.cbd-net.com**. Regardless of how you obtain an RFP, you and your company must decide whether you're interested in the contract and whether you have a reasonable chance of winning it (because responding to each RFP can take weeks or months of work). When the proposal effort actually begins, you review the requirements; define the scope of the deliverables; determine the methods and procedures to be used; and estimate time requirements, personnel requirements, and costs. Then you put it all in writing—exactly as specified in the RFP, following the exact format it requires and responding meticulously to every point it raises.[10] RFPs can seem surprisingly picky, even to the point of specifying the paper size to use and the number of copies to send, but you must follow every detail.

Unsolicited proposals are created by organizations attempting to obtain business or funding without a specific invitation from a potential client. Such proposals may also be initiated by employees or managers who want to convince company insiders to adopt a program, policy, or idea. In other words, with an unsolicited proposal, the writer makes the first

FIGURE 13.10 *Continued*

2

For example, having retail outlets across the lower tier of the country, AmeriSport received pitches from reps out of our West, South, and East regions. Because our regional offices have a lot of negotiating freedom, the three were offering different prices. But all AmeriSport buying decisions were made at the Tampa headquarters, so all we did was confuse the customer. The irony of the current organization is that we're often giving our weakest selling and support efforts to the largest customers in the country.

COMMISSION PROBLEMS

The regional organization problems are compounded by the way we assign commissions and quota credit. Salespeople in one region can invest a lot of time in pursuing a sale, only to have the customer place the order in another region. So some sales rep in the second region ends up with the commission on a sale that was partly or even entirely earned by someone in the first region. Therefore, sales reps sometimes don't pursue leads in their regions, thinking that a rep in another region will get the commission.

For example, Athletic Express, with outlets in 35 states spread across all four regions, finally got so frustrated with us that the company president called our headquarters. Athletic Express has been trying to place a large order for tennis and golf accessories, but none of our local reps seem interested in paying attention. I spoke with the rep responsible for Nashville, where the company is headquartered, and asked her why she wasn't working the account more actively. Her explanation was that last time she got involved with Athletic Express, the order was actually placed from their L.A. regional office, and she didn't get any commission after more than two weeks of selling time.

RECOMMENDATIONS

Our sales organization should reflect the nature of our customer base. To accomplish that goal, we need a group of reps who are free to pursue accounts across regional borders—and who are compensated fairly for their work. The most sensible answer is to establish a national account group. Any customers whose operations place them in more than one region would automatically be assigned to the national group.

In addition to solving the problem of competing sales efforts, the new structure will also largely eliminate the commission-splitting problem because regional reps will no longer invest time in prospects assigned to the national accounts team. However, we will need to find a fair way to compensate regional reps who are losing long-term customers to the national team. Some of these reps have invested years in developing customer relationships that will continue to yield sales well into the future, and everyone I talked to agrees that reps in these cases should receive some sort of compensation. Such a "transition commission" would also motivate the regional reps to help ensure a smooth transition from one sales group to the other. The exact nature of this compensation would need to be worked out with the various sales managers.

3

SUMMARY

The regional sales organization is effective at the regional and local levels but not at the national level. We should establish a national accounts group to handle sales that cross regional boundaries. Then we'll have one set of reps who are focused on the local and regional levels and another set who are pursuing national accounts.

To compensate regional reps who lose accounts to the national team, we will need to devise some sort of payment to reward them for the years of work invested in such accounts. This can be discussed with the sales managers once the new structure is in place.

Connecting with Technology

Proposals Get a Software Assist

Writing a new-business proposal should be an exciting time: a new opportunity is waiting for you, just out of reach. All you have to do is craft a document that explains how your company can meet customer needs better than anyone else, and the business is yours.

However, most businesspeople find proposal writing to be less than a wonderful opportunity and more of a chore. First of all, complicated proposals can involve dozens or even hundreds of detailed discussion points. In addition, the need to write a proposal is often unexpected, which means that you have to make room in your already-busy schedule. Also, deadlines are usually inflexible, which creates frequent last-minute rushes. To top it off, many proposals require similar information, so you end up writing the same thing, or nearly the same thing, over and over again.

Yet many companies live and die by proposals, so the chore of writing them is an ongoing part of doing business. Fortunately, a number of software companies have jumped in with promises to help beleaguered proposal writers. At the simplest level, you can use templates and cut-and-paste boiler-plate text in your word processor. This method reduces the typing, but doing all this insertion manually is still tedious. Also, the possibility of errors is quite high (such as when you reuse an existing proposal and forget to change the name of the customer). Moreover, every time you need a new piece of in-formation, you still need to track down the right expert in your company, draft the new material, then weave it into the pro-posal document.

Automated proposal solutions promise to solve all of these problems to one degree or another. Basic features include the ability to automatically personalize the proposal, ensure proper structure (making sure you don't forget any sections, for instance), and organize storage of all your boilerplate text. At a more advanced level, products such as Pragmatech's RFP Machine and Sant's RFPMaster can scan RFPs to identify questions and requirements, and then fill in potential answers from a centralized knowledge base that contains input from all the relevant experts in your company. Ideally, your job is then re-duced to verifying the answers, modifying or replacing any that aren't quite right, and adding any personalized touches that are beyond the system's abilities. With these tools at hand, you can spend a little more time profiting from that new business and less time struggling to get it.

CAREER APPLICATIONS

1. Research three commercially available software products that assist with proposal writing, then explain which one you think would be best for a small consulting firm.
2. Can you envision any disadvantages to using proposal-writing software? If so, how might you overcome them?

---

move. Even so, an unsolicited proposal should not come as a surprise to the recipient but, rather, should be the summation of a conversation that has been ongoing with the recipient.[11] Not only does this approach help ensure acceptance, but it gives you an oppor-tunity to explore the recipient's needs and therefore craft your proposal around them.

Unsolicited proposals also differ from solicited proposals in another important respect: Your audience may not be aware of the problem you are addressing, so your proposal must first convince readers that a problem or opportunity exists before convincing them that you can address it. Thus, unsolicited proposals generally spend considerable time explaining why readers should take action and convincing them of the benefits of doing so.

Unsolicited proposals vary widely in form, length, and purpose. For example, a univer-sity seeking funding for a specific research project might submit an unsolicited proposal to a large local corporation. To be convincing, the university's proposal would show how the research could benefit the corporation and would demonstrate that the university has the resources and expertise to conduct the research.[12]

Every proposal competes for something: money, time, attention, and so on.

With virtually any proposal, whether solicited or unsolicited, whether for internal au-diences or external, keep in mind that you are always competing for something—money, time, management attention, and so on. Even if yours is the only proposal on the table, you are still competing with all the other choices your audience members could make with their time, money, and attention.

Organizational Strategies for Proposals

Your choice of structure for proposals depends on whether your audience members ex-pect the proposal and, if they do, whether you expect them to be receptive. In general, your audience may be more receptive with solicited proposals, because the problem and the solution have already been identified. Submit your proposal for the solution specified in the RFP, and structure the proposal using a direct approach that focuses on your recommendation.

Depending on the circumstances and your relationship with the recipient, the indirect approach may be a better choice for unsolicited proposals. When writing unsolicited proposals, you must first convince the audience that a problem exists and establish your credibility if you are unknown to the reader. To convince the reader that your recommendations are solid and logical, you unfold your solution to the problem using the 2 + 2 = 4 approach or the yardstick approach. As you unfold your solution, you have two goals: to persuade readers to accept your idea and award you a contract, and to spell out the terms of your proposal.

An indirect approach is a good way to build your case in an unsolicited proposal.

Effective Proposals: An Example

A good proposal explains why a project or course of action is needed, what it will involve, how much it will cost, and how the recipient will benefit. You can see all of these elements in Shandel Cohen's internal proposal for an automatic mail-response system (see Figure 13.11, on pages 418–419).

Cohen manages the customer-response section of the marketing department at a Midwest personal computer manufacturer. Her section sends out product information requested by customers and the field salesforce. Cohen has observed that the demand for information increases when a new product is released and that it diminishes as a product matures. This fluctuating demand causes drastic changes in her section's workload.

"Either we have more work than we can possibly handle," says Cohen, "or we don't have enough to keep us busy. But I don't want to get into a hiring-and-firing cycle." Cohen is also concerned about the amount of printed material that's discarded when products are upgraded or replaced. Her report describes the problem, her proposed solutions, the benefits to the company, and the projected costs, giving her audience all the information needed to make a decision.

COMMUNICATION CHALLENGES AT KENWOOD USA

You've joined Keith Lehmann's team at Kenwood as a consumer electronics business and marketing analyst. Kenwood's product portfolio in mobile electronics now includes not only satellite radio but also conventional cassette and CD players, video players, and navigation systems.[13] Use your knowledge of business communication and report writing to address these challenges.

Individual Challenge: One of the latest mobile electronics innovations is onboard, high-speed Internet access for cars and trucks. KVH Industries (www.kvh.com) is an early leader in this segment. Its products provide Internet access on any television displays in the vehicle and even include a wireless hub that allows anyone in the vehicle to connect a laptop PC, PDA, or other wireless device to the Internet. In addition to commercial drivers (particularly long-distance truck drivers), families who like to take long road trips are an obvious target audience for such a system. You plan to ask the product design team in Japan to explore the feasibility of creating a system for Kenwood, but you want to make sure the designers have a clear picture of the U.S. consumer market. Draft a one- or two-page informational report that describes typical vacation scenarios involving families who might be interested in purchasing a mobile Internet system from Kenwood. Be sure to give the designers a clear and vivid picture of what family road trips are like in the United States, from the types of vehicles used to the wide variety of vacation destinations. You want them to accurately visualize what such a vacation would be like, even if they've never spent much time in the United States.

Team Challenge: You would also like the design team to have a solid assessment of strengths and potential weaknesses of the systems offered by KVH Industries. With your team, review the material on the KVH website and look for product reviews elsewhere online. Draft a short analytical report that summarizes what you've learned about the KVH product line, what its strengths and weaknesses appear to be, and what sort of product Kenwood might want to develop in order to compete with KVH. Feel free to use your imagination to create any information you might need to describe the future KVH product.

FIGURE 13.11 Internal Proposal
Shandel Cohen's internal proposal seeks management's approval to install an automatic mail-response system. Because the company manufactures computers, she knows that her boss won't object to a computer-based solution. Also, because profits are always a concern, her report emphasizes the financial benefits of her proposal.

Catches the reader's attention with a compelling promise in subject line

Explains the proposed solution in enough detail to make it convincing, without burdening the reader with excessive detail

Describes the current situation and explains why it should be fixed

Builds reader interest in the proposed solution by listing a number of compelling benefits

MEMO

DATE:	July 8, 2008
TO:	Jamie Engle
FROM:	Shandel Cohen _SC_
SUBJECT:	Saving $145k/year with an automated e-mail response system

THE PROBLEM:
Expensive and Slow Response to Customer Information Requests

Our new product line has been very well received, and orders have surpassed our projections. This very success, however, has created a shortage of printed brochures, as well as considerable overtime for people in the customer response center. As we introduce upgrades and new options, our printed materials quickly become outdated. If we continue to rely on printed materials for customer information, we have two choices: Distribute existing materials (even though they are incomplete or inaccurate) or discard existing materials and print new ones.

THE SOLUTION:
Automated E-Mail Response System

With minor additions and modifications to our current e-mail system, we can set up an automated system to respond to customer requests for information. This system can save us time and money and can keep our distributed information current.

Automated e-mail response systems have been tested and proven effective. Many companies already use this method to respond to customer information requests, so we won't have to worry about relying on untested technology. Using the system is easy, too: Customers simply send a blank e-mail message to a specific address, and the system responds by sending an electronic copy of the requested brochure.

Benefit #1: Always-Current Information

Rather than discard and print new materials, we would only need to keep the electronic files up to date on the server. We could be able to provide customers and our field sales organization with up-to-date, correct information as soon as the upgrades or options are available.

Benefit #2: Instantaneous Delivery

Almost immediately after requesting information, customers would have that information in hand. Electronic delivery would be especially advantageous for our international customers. Regular mail to remote locations sometimes takes weeks to arrive, by which time the information may already be out of date. Both customers and field salespeople will appreciate the automatic mail-response system.

Benefit #3: Minimized Waste

With our current method of printing every marketing piece in large quantities, we discard thousands of pages of obsolete catalogs, data sheets, and other materials every year. By maintaining and distributing the information electronically, we would eliminate this waste. We would also free up a considerable amount of expensive floor space and shelving that is required for storing printed materials.

(continued)

FIGURE 13.11 *Continued*

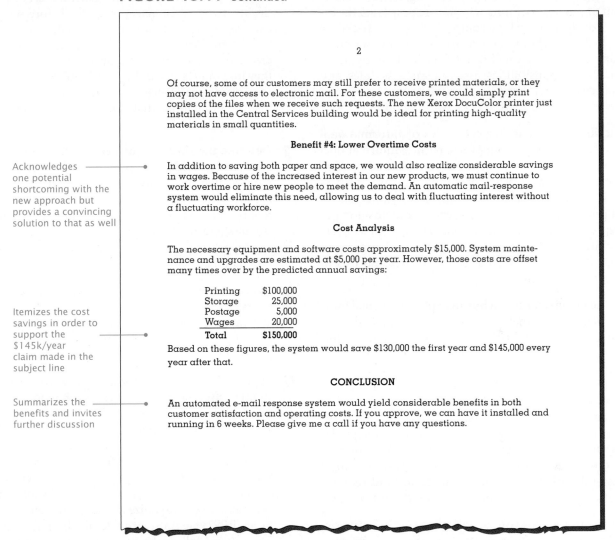

2

Of course, some of our customers may still prefer to receive printed materials, or they may not have access to electronic mail. For these customers, we could simply print copies of the files when we receive such requests. The new Xerox DocuColor printer just installed in the Central Services building would be ideal for printing high-quality materials in small quantities.

Benefit #4: Lower Overtime Costs

Acknowledges one potential shortcoming with the new approach but provides a convincing solution to that as well

In addition to saving both paper and space, we would also realize considerable savings in wages. Because of the increased interest in our new products, we must continue to work overtime or hire new people to meet the demand. An automatic mail-response system would eliminate this need, allowing us to deal with fluctuating interest without a fluctuating workforce.

Cost Analysis

The necessary equipment and software costs approximately $15,000. System maintenance and upgrades are estimated at $5,000 per year. However, those costs are offset many times over by the predicted annual savings:

Itemizes the cost savings in order to support the $145k/year claim made in the subject line

Printing	$100,000
Storage	25,000
Postage	5,000
Wages	20,000
Total	**$150,000**

Based on these figures, the system would save $130,000 the first year and $145,000 every year after that.

CONCLUSION

Summarizes the benefits and invites further discussion

An automated e-mail response system would yield considerable benefits in both customer satisfaction and operating costs. If you approve, we can have it installed and running in 6 weeks. Please give me a call if you have any questions.

SUMMARY OF LEARNING OBJECTIVES

1 **Explain the differences between informational reports and analytical reports.** Informational reports focus on the delivery of facts, figures, and other types of information, without making recommendations or proposing new ideas or solutions. In contrast, analytical reports assess a situation or problem and recommend a course of action in response.

2 **Adapt the three-step writing process to reports and proposals.** The comprehensive nature of the three-step process is ideal for the work involved in most reports and proposals. Use all of the advice you learned in Chapters 4 through 6, with added emphasis on a few specific points for longer documents: (1) identify your purpose clearly to avoid rework, (2) prepare a work plan to guide the research and writing tasks, (3) determine whether a separate research project might be needed to gather the necessary information, (4) choose the medium (or media, in some cases) that meets the needs of your audience, and (5) organize your information by selecting the best approach for an informational or analytical report.

3 **Explain the value of a work plan in the development of long reports.** A formal work plan makes the writing process more efficient and more effective by guiding you every step of the planning and writing process. Work plans usually include (1) a problem statement defining *what* you're going to investigate; (2) a statement of purpose defining *why* you are preparing the report; (3) the tasks to be accomplished and the sequence in which they should be performed; (4) a description of any product that will result from your study; (5) a review of responsibilities, assignments, schedules, and resource requirements; (6) plans for following up after delivering the report; and (7) a working outline.

4 **Describe the four major categories of informational reports and provide examples of each.**   Informational reports include reports for monitoring and controlling operations, such as plans, operating reports, and personal activity reports; reports for implementing policies and procedures, such as policy reports and position papers; reports to demonstrate compliance, such as quarterly and annual income tax reports; and reports to document progress, such as status reports and lists of project risks and concerns.

5 **List the key elements of a business plan.**   Formal business plans, those that are shown to outside audiences such as investors and bankers, typically contain the following elements: a summary of the business concept, the company's mission and objectives, background on the company and the industry in which it competes, descriptions of its products and services, an analysis of target markets and key competitors, a discussion of the management team, a summary of the marketing strategy, design and development plans, an operations plan, a schedule with major milestones, an analysis of critical risks and problems, financial projections and requirements, and a description of the proposed exit strategy.

6 **Identify three steps you can take to ensure effective organization of online reports and other website content.**   To help ensure effective organization of both online reports and websites in general, start by planning the structure and navigation paths before writing the content. Next, make sure you let readers be in control. Give them plenty of navigational flexibility so they can create their own paths according to the information they find interesting and useful. Don't force them to follow a rigid page-by-page scheme. Last, break your information into chunks that can be scanned and absorbed quickly.

7 **Describe the three major categories of analytical reports and provide examples of each.**   The most common analytical reports are those written to assess opportunities, such as market analysis and due diligence reports; reports written to solve problems, including troubleshooting and failure analysis reports; and reports to support decisions, including feasibility and justification reports.

8 **Discuss three major ways to organize analytical reports.**   The three most common ways to organize analytical reports are by focusing on conclusions, focusing on recommendations, and focusing on logical arguments.

9 **Explain how your approach to writing proposals should differ when you are responding to a formal request for proposals (RFP).**   The most important point to consider when responding to an RFP is to follow the RFP's instructions down to the tiniest detail, because any deviation could be grounds for rejecting your proposal. With unsolicited proposals, you can have a considerable degree of freedom in deciding what information to include and how to organize it. However, when responding to an RFP, you must provide all the information requested and follow the organizational scheme dictated by the RFP.

Test Your Knowledge

1. How can your written reports influence your professional success?
2. What is the major difference between informational and analytical reports?
3. What does a statement of purpose convey?
4. What should you include in the work plan for a complex report or proposal?
5. How can you determine the best medium to use for a report?
6. How are reports for monitoring and controlling operations used?
7. What are the seven major ways to organize an informational report?
8. How does a feasibility report differ from a justification report?
9. What is problem factoring?
10. What is an RFP and how does it relate to proposal writing?

Apply Your Knowledge

1. Why are unsolicited proposals more challenging to write than solicited proposals?
2. What are the advantages and disadvantages of asking your employees to "fill in the blanks" on standardized reporting forms? Briefly explain.
3. If you want to make a specific recommendation in your report, should you include information that might support a different recommendation? Explain your answer.
4. If your report includes only factual information, is it objective? Please explain.
5. **Ethical Choices** If you were writing a troubleshooting report to help management decide how to reduce quality problems at a manufacturing plant, what ethical issues might you face? How might these ethical issues conflict with your need to report all the relevant facts and to offer evidence for your conclusions? Explain briefly.

Practice Your Knowledge

Message for Analysis

The Securities and Exchange Commission (SEC) requires all public companies to file a comprehensive annual report (form 10-K) electronically. Many companies post links to these reports on their websites along with links to other company reports. Visit the website of Dell at and find the company's most recent annual reports: 10-K and Year in Review. Compare the style and format of the two reports. For which audience(s) is the Year in Review targeted? Who besides the SEC might be interested in the Annual Report 10-K? Which report do you find easier to read? More interesting? More detailed?

Exercises

For active links to all websites discussed in this chapter, visit this text's website at www.prenhall.com/bovee. Locate your book and click on its Companion Website link. Then select Chapter 13, and click on "Featured Websites." Locate the name of the page or the URL related to the material in the text. Please note that links to sites that become inactive after publication of the book will be removed from the Featured Websites section.

13.1 Understanding Business Reports and Proposals: How Companies Use Reports Interview several people working in a career you might like to enter, and ask them about the written reports they receive and prepare. How do these reports tie in to the decision-making process? Who reads the reports they prepare? Are the reports delivered on paper or online? Summarize your findings in writing, give them to your instructor, and be prepared to discuss them with the class.

13.2 Understanding Business Reports and Proposals: Report Classification Using the information presented in this chapter, identify the report type represented by each of the following examples. In addition, write a brief paragraph about each, explaining who the audience is likely to be, what type of data would be used, and whether conclusions and recommendations would be appropriate.
   a. A statistical study of the pattern of violent crime in a large city during the last five years
   b. A report prepared by a seed company demonstrating the benefits of its seed corn for farmers
   c. A report prepared by an independent testing agency evaluating various types of nonprescription cold remedies
   d. A trip report submitted at the end of a week by a traveling salesperson
   e. A report indicating how 45 acres of undeveloped land could be converted into an industrial park
   f. An annual report to be sent to the shareholders of a large corporation
   g. A report from a U.S. National Park wildlife officer to Washington, D.C., headquarters showing the status of the California condor (an endangered species)
   h. A report outlining the risks of closing a chain of retail stores and moving the entire business online

13.3 Internet Follow the step-by-step hints and examples for writing a funding proposal at www.learnerassociates.com/proposal. Review the writing hints and the entire sample proposal online. What details did the author decide to include in appendixes? Why was this material placed in the appendixes and not the main body of the report? According to the author's tips, when is the best time to prepare a project overview?

13.4 Informational Reports: Policy Report You're the vice president of operations for a Florida fast-food chain. In the aftermath of a major hurricane, you're drafting a report on the emergency procedures to be followed by personnel in each restaurant when storm warnings are in effect. Answer who, what, when, where, why, and how, and then prepare a one-page outline of your report. Make up any details you need.

13.5 Unsolicited Proposal You're getting ready to launch a new lawn-care business that offers mowing, fertilizing, weeding, and other services. The lawn surrounding a nearby shopping center looks as if it could use better care, so you target that business for your first unsolicited proposal. To help prepare this proposal, write your answers to these questions:
   a. What questions will you need to answer before you can write a proposal to solve the reader's problem? Be as specific as possible.
   b. What customer benefits will you include in your proposal?
   c. Will you use a letter or memo format for your proposal? Explain your answer.

13.6 Teamwork: Unsolicited Proposal Break into small groups and identify an operational problem occurring at your campus involving one of the following: registration, university housing, food services, parking, or library services. Then develop a workable solution to that problem. Finally, develop a list of pertinent facts that your team will need to gather to convince the reader that the problem exists and that your solution will work.

13.7 Analyzing the Situation: Statement of Purpose Sales at The Style Shop, a clothing store for men, have declined for the third month in a row. Your boss is not sure whether this decline is because of a weak economy or if it's because of another unknown reason. She has asked you to investigate the situation and to submit a report to her highlighting some possible reasons for the decline. Develop a statement of purpose for your report.

13.8 Preparing the Work Plan Using the situation described in Exercise 13.5, assume that you're the shopping center's facilities manager. You report to the general manager, who must approve any new contracts for lawn service. Before you contract for lawn care, you want to prepare a formal study of the current state of your lawn's health. The report will include conclusions and recommendations for your boss's consideration. Draft a work plan, including the problem statement, the statement of purpose and scope, a description of what will result from your investigation, the sources and methods of data collection, and a preliminary outline.

13.9 Organizing Reports: Choosing the Direct or Indirect Approach For each of the following scenarios, explain why a direct or indirect approach would be advisable.

a. The monthly financial report, prepared by the accounting department for upper management

b. An accountant fresh out of college who wants to propose a new way to present those monthly financial results to upper management

c. An unsolicited proposal to provide payroll processing services

d. An analytical report, requested by the CEO, explaining why the company has been losing money in the eastern sales region for the past two years

e. An unsolicited proposal to the board of directors, outlining why it makes strategic sense for your company to expand into international markets; the board rejected a similar—but poorly presented—idea last year

13.10 Choosing the Direct or Indirect Approach Look through recent issues (print or online) of *BusinessWeek*, *Fortune*, or other business publications for an article that describes how an executive's conclusions about his or her company's current situation or future opportunities led to changes in policy, plans, or products. Construct an outline of the material, first using a direct approach then using an indirect approach. Which approach do you think the executive would use when reporting these conclusions to stockholders? When reporting to other senior managers? Explain your answers.

13.11 Organizing Reports: Deciding on Format Go to the library or visit the Internet site www.annualreportservice.com and review the annual reports recently released by two corporations in the same industry. Analyze each report and be prepared to discuss the following questions in class:

a. What organizational differences, if any, do you see in the way each corporation discusses its annual performance? Are the data presented clearly so that shareholders can draw conclusions about how well the company performed?

b. What goals, challenges, and plans do top managers emphasize in their discussion of results?

c. How do the format and organization of each report enhance or detract from the information being presented?

13.12 Organizing Reports: Structuring Informational Reports Assume that your college president has received many student complaints about campus parking problems. You are appointed the chair of a student committee organized to investigate the problems and recommend solutions. The president gives you the file labeled "Parking: Complaints from Students," and you jot down the essence of the complaints as you inspect the contents. Your notes look like this:

- Inadequate student spaces at critical hours
- Poor night lighting near the computer center
- Inadequate attempts to keep resident neighbors from occupying spaces
- Dim marking lines
- Motorcycles taking up full spaces
- Discourteous security officers
- Spaces (often empty) reserved for college officials
- Relatively high parking fees
- Full fees charged to night students even though they use the lots only during low-demand periods
- Vandalism to cars and a sense of personal danger
- Inadequate total space
- Resident harassment of students parking on the street in front of neighboring houses

Prepare an outline for an informational report to be submitted to committee members. Use a topical organization that categorizes this information.

Portfolio BUILDER

13.13 Organizing Reports: Structuring Analytical Reports Three years ago, your company (a carpet manufacturer) modernized its Georgia plant in anticipation of increasing demand for carpets. Because of the depressed housing market, the increase in demand for new carpets has been slow to materialize. As a result, the company has excess capacity at both its Georgia and California plants. On the basis of your research, you have recommended that the company close the California plant. The company president, J. P. Lawrence, has asked you to prepare a justification report to support your recommendation. Here are the facts you gathered by interviewing the respective plant managers:

Operational Statistics

- Georgia plant: This plant has newer equipment, has higher productivity, employs 100 nonunion production workers, and ships $12 million in carpets a year. Hourly base wage is $16.
- California plant: California plant employs 80 union production workers and ships $8 million in carpets a year. Hourly base wage is $20.

Financial Implications

- Savings by closing California plant: (1) Increase productivity by 17 percent; (2) reduce labor costs by 20 percent (total labor savings would be $1 million per year; see assumptions); (3) annual local tax savings of $120,000 (Georgia has a more favorable tax climate).
- Sale of Pomona, California, land: Purchased in 1952 for $200,000. Current market value $2.5 million. Net profit (after capital gains tax) over $1 million.
- Sale of plant and equipment: Fully depreciated. Any proceeds a windfall.
- Costs of closing California plant: One-time deductible charge of $250,000 (relocation costs of $100,000 and severance payments totaling $150,000).

Assumptions

- Transfer five workers from California to Georgia.
- Hire 45 new workers in Georgia.
- Lay off 75 workers in California.
- Georgia plant would require a total of 150 workers to produce the combined volume of both plants.
  a. Which approach (focus on conclusions, recommendations, or logical arguments) will you use to structure your report to the president? Why?
  b. Suppose this report were to be circulated to plant managers and supervisors instead. What changes, if any, might you make in your approach?
  c. List some conclusions that you might draw from the preceding information to use in your report.
  d. Using the structure you selected for your report to the president, draft a final report outline with first- and second-level informative headings.

Expand Your Knowledge

Exploring the Best of the Web

Better Ideas for Better Business Plans
www.bizplanit.com/free.html
What's involved in a business plan? BizPlanIt.Com offers tips and advice, consulting services, a free e-mail newsletter, and a sample virtual business plan. You'll find suggestions on what details and how much information to include in each section of a business plan. You can explore the site's numerous links to business plan books and software, online magazines, educational programs, government resources, women and minority resources, and even answers to your business plan questions. Review the articles on the site and answer the following questions:

1. Why is the executive summary such an important section of a business plan? What kind of information is contained in the executive summary?
2. What is the product/services section? What information should it contain? List some of the common errors to avoid when planning this part.
3. What type of business planning should you describe in the exit strategy section? Why?

Surfing Your Way to Career Success

Bovée and Thill's Business Communication Resources offers links to hundreds of online resources that can help you with this course, your other college courses, and your career. Visit www.buscommresources.com, then click on "Business Communication Web Directory." The "Reports, Proposals, and Business Plans" section connects you to a variety of websites and articles on these important topics, as well as sites on designing and producing visual material to supplement your reports. Identify three websites from this section that could be useful in your business career. For each site, write a two-sentence summary of what the site offers and how it could help you launch and build your career.

Learn Interactively

Interactive Study Guide

Visit www.prenhall.com/bovee, then locate your book and click on its "Companion Website" link. Select Chapter 13 to take advantage of the interactive "Chapter Quiz" to test your knowledge of chapter concepts. Receive instant feedback on whether you need additional studying. Also, visit the "Study Hall," where you'll find an abundance of valuable resources that will help you succeed in this course.

Peak Performance Grammar and Mechanics

If your instructor has required the use of "Peak Performance Grammar and Mechanics," either in your online course or on CD, you can continue to improve your skill with apostrophes, quotation marks, parentheses and brackets, question marks and exclamation points, dashes, hyphens, and ellipses by using the "Peak Performance Grammar and Mechanics" module. Click "Punctuation," and then click "Punctuation II." Take the Pretest to determine whether you have any weak areas. Then review those areas in the Refresher Course. Take the Follow-Up Test to check your grasp of these elements. For an extra challenge or advanced practice, take the Advanced Test. Finally, for additional reinforcement in commas, visit the Companion Website, click on any chapter, then click on "Improve Your Grammar, Mechanics, and Usage."

CHAPTER 14

Writing Reports and Proposals

LEARNING OBJECTIVES

After studying this chapter, you will be able to

1 Explain how to adapt to your audiences when writing reports and proposals

2 List the topics commonly covered in the introduction, body, and close of informational and analytical reports

3 Name five characteristics of effective report content

4 Name six strategies to strengthen your proposal argument

5 List the topics commonly covered in a proposal's introduction, body, and close

6 Identify five characteristics of effective writing in online reports

7 Briefly describe three report elements that can help readers find their way in long documents

COMMUNICATION CLOSE-UP AT TELLABS

www.tellabs.com

Few reports get as much scrutiny as corporate annual reports, and the feedback from many readers is not particularly positive.

These compliance reports are required of every company listed on U.S. stock exchanges, and they are pored over by investors looking for clues about a company's financial health and prospects. However, investor surveys suggest that many readers don't believe they are getting the information they need in order to make intelligent decisions about investing in a company's stock. Some companies have even been sued in recent years over their annual reports, with investors accusing them of withholding or obscuring vital information.

In this environment of uncertainty and outright mistrust, writers who communicate clearly and openly tend to stand out from the crowd. One such writer is George Stenitzer, vice president of corporate communication for Tellabs, a major producer of equipment for Internet service providers based in Naperville, Illinois. According to one widely respected consultant who assesses the quality of annual reports, Stenitzer's work practically demands to be

The annual reports written by Tellabs's George Stenitzer go beyond regulatory compliance to helping investors understand the business and its financial performance.

read, thanks to its brevity, forthright style, full disclosure of important financial information, numerous features that enhance readability, and attractive design.

While annual report writers must comply with a complex array of legal compliance requirements, Stenitzer's view is that accuracy and compliance—while vital—are not enough. He recognizes that many companies still lean in the direction of minimal disclosure, saying just enough to satisfy government regulations, but Stenitzer's goal is to help investors truly understand the nature of Tellabs's business and its financial performance. As he puts it, "The test for investor communications is shifting from technical accuracy and legal compliance to clear communication and investor understanding."

The proof of his approach seems to bear out in investor surveys. In an environment in which many investors are extremely skeptical of, or even confused by, what they read in annual reports, one of Tellabs's recent annual reports was rated "good" or "very good" by an overwhelming 83 percent of readers.[1]

WRITING REPORTS AND PROPOSALS

George Stenitzer (profiled in the chapter-opening Communication Close-Up) and all other successful report writers will tell you how important the writing stage is in the development of effective reports and proposals. This chapter builds on the writing techniques and ideas you learned in Chapter 5 with issues that are particularly important when preparing longer message formats (see Figure 14.1). As with shorter messages, take a few moments before you start writing to make sure you're ready to adapt your approach to your audience.

1 LEARNING OBJECTIVE

Explain how to adapt to your audiences when writing reports and proposals

ADAPTING TO YOUR AUDIENCE

Effective reports and proposals are adapted to the intended audience as much as possible. To ensure your own success with reports, be sensitive to audience needs, build strong relationships with your audience, and control your style and tone.

FIGURE 14.1 Step Two in the Three-Step Writing Process for Reports
As you get ready to write your report or proposal, consider how you should adapt to your audience's needs and expectations.

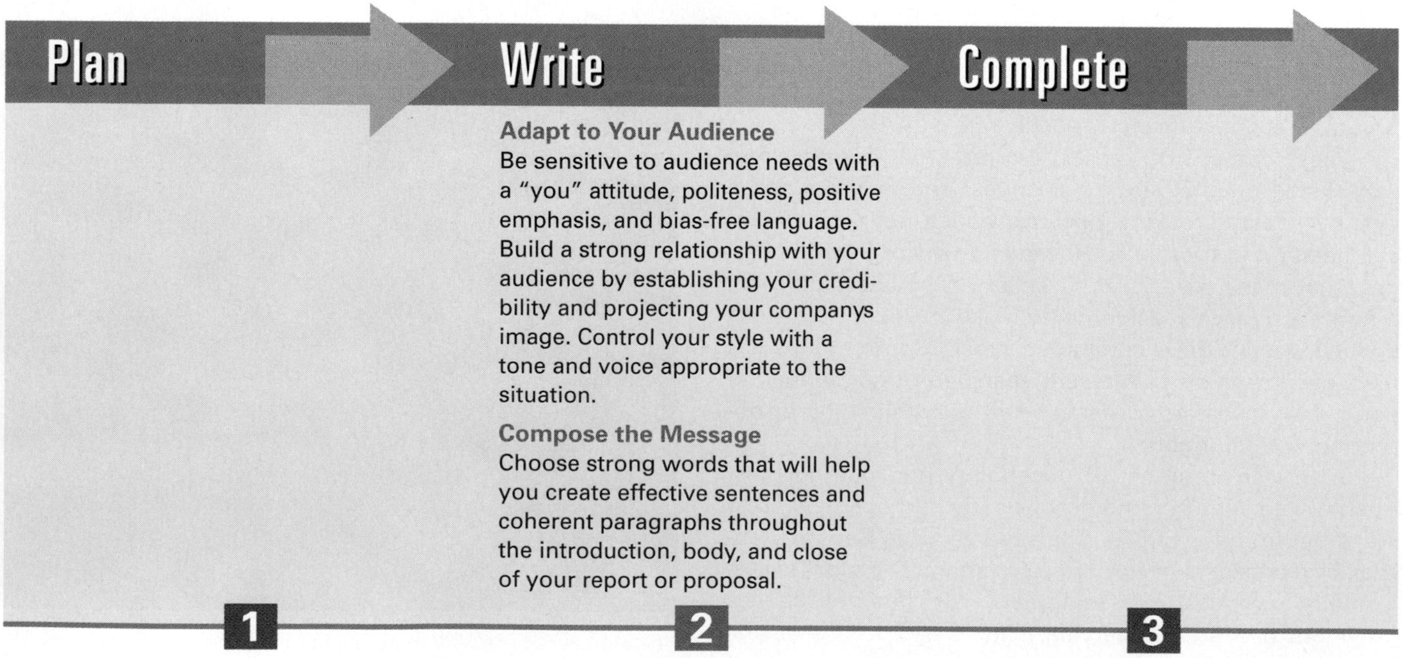

Plan → **Write** → **Complete**

1 **2** **3**

Adapt to Your Audience
Be sensitive to audience needs with a "you" attitude, politeness, positive emphasis, and bias-free language. Build a strong relationship with your audience by establishing your credibility and projecting your companys image. Control your style with a tone and voice appropriate to the situation.

Compose the Message
Choose strong words that will help you create effective sentences and coherent paragraphs throughout the introduction, body, and close of your report or proposal.

Being Sensitive to Your Audience's Needs

Chapter 5 discusses four aspects of audience sensitivity, and all four apply to reports and proposals: adopting the "you" attitude, maintaining a strong sense of etiquette, emphasizing the positive, and using bias-free language. Reports and proposals that are highly technical, complex, or lengthy can put heavy demands on your readers, so the "you" attitude takes on even greater importance with these long messages. As you'll see later in this chapter, part of that attitude includes helping your readers find their way through your material so that they can understand critical information.

In addition, various audience members can have widely different information needs. For instance, if you're reporting on the results of a customer satisfaction survey, the service manager might want every detail, whereas the president may want only a top-level summary. With previews, summaries, appendixes, and other elements, you can meet the needs of a diverse audience—provided you plan for these elements in advance.

Long or complex reports demand a lot from readers, making the "you" attitude more important than ever.

Building Strong Relationships with Your Audience

Whether your report is intended for people inside or outside the company, be sure to plan how you will adapt your style and your language to reflect the image of your organization. Bear in mind that some reports—particularly any reports that can be transmitted online—can take on lives of their own, reaching a wider audience than you ever imagined and being read years after you wrote them. Consequently, choose your content and language with care. Also, because many companies have specific guidelines for communicating with public audiences, make sure you're aware of these preferences before you start writing.

As discussed in Chapter 5, establishing your credibility is vital to successful communication. To gain your audience's trust, research all sides of your topic, and document your findings with credible sources. Also, be aware that setting audience expectations too high can lead to problems with your credibility if you can't deliver everything people expect you to.

Your reports may continue to be read for months or years after you write them—and reach audiences you never envisioned.

Controlling Your Style and Tone

If you know your readers reasonably well and your report is likely to meet with their approval, you can generally adopt a fairly informal tone—provided that doing so is acceptable in the situation and in your company's culture. To make your tone less formal, speak to readers in the first person, refer to them as *you*, and refer to yourself as *I* (or *we* if there are multiple report authors). Such style choices create the more personal tone that is often (but not always) used in brief memo or letter reports.

A more formal tone is usually appropriate for longer reports, especially those dealing with controversial or complex information. You'll also use a more formal tone when your report will be sent to other parts of the organization or to outsiders, such as customers, suppliers, or members of the community (see Figure 14.2).

If the situation calls for a more formal tone, use the impersonal journalism style, eliminating all references to *you* and *I* (including *we, us,* and *our*). When you use an impersonal style, you impose a controlled distance between you and your readers. Your tone is not only objective but also businesslike and unemotional. Be careful to avoid jokes, similes, and metaphors, and try to minimize the use of colorful adjectives or adverbs.

However, when crafting a more formal tone, take care not to overuse phrases such as *there are* and *it is*, which sound dull and can lead to wordy sentence constructions. In addition, don't inadvertently slip into the passive voice. You can avoid this potential weakness by making the report content itself the actor in a sentence. For example, to convert "I think we should buy TramCo" to a more formal tone, you could write "The financial analysis clearly shows that buying TramCo is the best alternative."

Adjust the level of formality to match the situation and your audience's expectations.

FIGURE 14.2 Choosing the Right Tone for Business Reports
Yahoo! is known for using a playful, informal tone in its advertising and in most communication with customers, but the company's tone is more formal when communicating with the public on more serious matters.

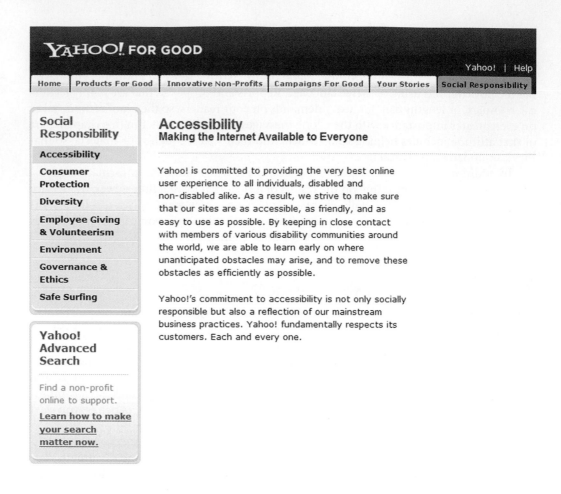

YAHOO! FOR GOOD

Yahoo! | Help

Home   Products For Good   Innovative Non-Profits   Campaigns For Good   Your Stories   Social Responsibility

Social Responsibility

Accessibility

Consumer Protection

Diversity

Employee Giving & Volunteerism

Environment

Governance & Ethics

Safe Surfing

Yahoo! Advanced Search

Find a non-profit online to support.

Learn how to make your search matter now.

Accessibility
Making the Internet Available to Everyone

Yahoo! is committed to providing the very best online user experience to all individuals, disabled and non-disabled alike. As a result, we strive to make sure that our sites are as accessible, as friendly, and as easy to use as possible. By keeping in close contact with members of various disability communities around the world, we are able to learn early on where unanticipated obstacles may arise, and to remove these obstacles as efficiently as possible.

Yahoo!'s commitment to accessibility is not only socially responsible but also a reflection of our mainstream business practices. Yahoo! fundamentally respects its customers. Each and every one.

COMPOSING REPORTS AND PROPOSALS

2 LEARNING OBJECTIVE

List the topics commonly covered in the introduction, body, and close of informational and analytical reports

With a clear picture of how you need to adapt to your audience, you're ready to begin composing your first draft. Before you put those first words down on paper, though, review your outline one last time. Verify that the organization you've chosen makes sense, given everything you've learned about your topic so far. Also, review the wording of the headings and subheadings to make sure they establish the right tone. For a hard-hitting, direct tone, use informative phrasing ("Quality Problems Result in Nearly 500 Customer Defections Every Year"). For an objective, indirect tone, use descriptive phrasing ("Effects of Product Quality on Customer Retention").

As with other business messages, the text of reports and proposals has three main sections: an introduction, a body, and a close. The content and length of each section vary with the type and purpose of the document, the document's organizational structure, the length and depth of the material, the document's degree of formality, and your relationship your audience.

The introduction needs to provide context for the reader, introduce the subject, preview main ideas, and establish the tone of the document.

The *introduction* (or *opening*) is the first section in the text of any report or proposal. An effective introduction accomplishes at least four things:

- Puts the report or proposal in a broader context by tying it to a problem or an assignment
- Introduces the subject or purpose of the report or proposal and indicates why the subject is important
- Previews the main ideas and the order in which they'll be covered
- Establishes the tone of the document and the writer's relationship with the audience

The body of a report presents, analyzes, and interprets the information you gathered during your investigation.

The *body*, the middle section in your report or proposal, presents, analyzes, and interprets the information gathered during your investigation. If appropriate, the body also con-

FIGURE 14.3 Effective Problem-Solving Report Focusing on Recommendations
In this report recommending that her firm expand its website to full e-commerce capability, Alycia Jenn uses the body of her report to provide enough information to support her argument, without burdening her high-level readership with a lot of tactical details.

MEMO

DATE: July 7, 2008
TO: Board of Directors, Executive Committee members
FROM: Alycia Jenn, Business Development Manager
SUBJECT: Website expansion

Reminds readers of the origin and purpose of the report ———

In response to your request, my staff and I investigated the potential for expanding our website from its current "brochureware" status (in which we promote our company and its products but don't provide any way to place orders online) to full e-commerce capability (including placing orders and checking on order delivery status). After analyzing the behavior of our customers and major competitors and studying the overall development of electronic retailing, we have three recommendations:

1. We should expand our online presence from "brochureware" to e-commerce capability within the next 6 months.

2. We should engage a firm that specializes in online retailing to design and develop the new e-commerce capabilities.

3. We must take care to integrate online retailing with our store-based and mail-order operations.

——— *Clarifies the recommendation by listing the necessary actions in clear, direct language*

1. WE SHOULD EXPAND THE WEBSITE TO FULL E-COMMERCE CAPABILITY

Presents logical reasons for recommending that the firm expand its website to include e-commerce ———

First, does e-commerce capability make sense today for a small company that sells luxury housewares? Even though books and many other products are now commonly sold online, in most cases, this enterprise involves simple, low-cost products that don't require a lot of hands-on inspection before purchasing. As we've observed in our stores, shoppers like to interact with our products before purchasing them. However, a small but growing number of websites do sell specialty products, using such tactics as "virtual product tours" (in which shoppers can interactively view a product in three dimensions, rather than simply looking at a static photograph) and generous return policies (to reduce the perceived risk of buying products online).

Second, do we need to establish a presence now in order to remain competitive in the future? The answer is an overwhelming "yes." The initial steps taken by our competitors are already placing us at a disadvantage among those shoppers who are already comfortable buying online, and every trend indicates our minor competitive weakness today will turn into a major weakness in the next few years:

• Several of our top competitors are beginning to implement full e-commerce, including virtual product tours. Our research suggests that these companies aren't yet generating significant financial returns from these online investments, but their online sales are growing.

• Younger consumers who grew up with the World Wide Web will soon be reaching their peak earning years (ages 35–54). This demographic segment expects e-commerce in nearly every product category, and we'll lose them to the competition if we don't offer it.

——— *Supports the reasoning with evidence*

• The web is erasing geographical shopping limits, presenting both a threat and an opportunity. Even though our customers can now shop websites anywhere in the world (so that we have thousands of competitors instead of a dozen), we can now target customers anywhere in the world.

(continued)

---

tains the detailed proof necessary to support your conclusions and recommendations (see Figure 14.3).

The *close*, the final section of your report or proposal, has three important functions:

• Emphasizes the main points of the message and briefly reiterates the logic behind any conclusions or recommendations you've made

• Summarizes the benefits to the reader if the document suggests a change or some other course of action

• Brings all the action items together in one place and gives the details about who should do what, when, where, and how

The close of your report should emphasize the main message, summarize audience benefits, gather together all the action items (if any), and indicate responsibilities for each one.

FIGURE 14.3 *Continued*

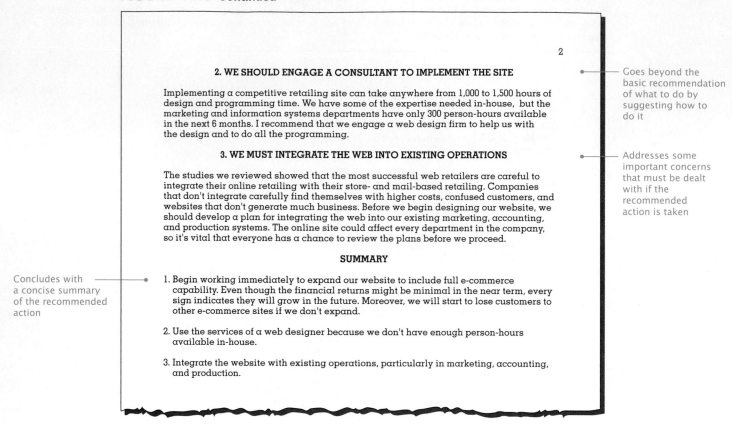

2

2. WE SHOULD ENGAGE A CONSULTANT TO IMPLEMENT THE SITE

Implementing a competitive retailing site can take anywhere from 1,000 to 1,500 hours of design and programming time. We have some of the expertise needed in-house, but the marketing and information systems departments have only 300 person-hours available in the next 6 months. I recommend that we engage a web design firm to help us with the design and to do all the programming.

Goes beyond the basic recommendation of what to do by suggesting how to do it

3. WE MUST INTEGRATE THE WEB INTO EXISTING OPERATIONS

The studies we reviewed showed that the most successful web retailers are careful to integrate their online retailing with their store- and mail-based retailing. Companies that don't integrate carefully find themselves with higher costs, confused customers, and websites that don't generate much business. Before we begin designing our website, we should develop a plan for integrating the web into our existing marketing, accounting, and production systems. The online site could affect every department in the company, so it's vital that everyone has a chance to review the plans before we proceed.

Addresses some important concerns that must be dealt with if the recommended action is taken

SUMMARY

Concludes with a concise summary of the recommended action

1. Begin working immediately to expand our website to include full e-commerce capability. Even though the financial returns might be minimal in the near term, every sign indicates they will grow in the future. Moreover, we will start to lose customers to other e-commerce sites if we don't expand.

2. Use the services of a web designer because we don't have enough person-hours available in-house.

3. Integrate the website with existing operations, particularly in marketing, accounting, and production.

The close might be the only part of your report some readers have time for, so make sure it conveys the full weight of your message.

Research shows that the final section of a report or proposal leaves a strong lasting impression. The close gives you one last chance to make sure that your report says what you intended.[2] In fact, readers who are in a hurry might skip the body of the report and read only the summary, so make sure it carries a strong, clear message.

Drafting Report Content

3 LEARNING OBJECTIVE

Name five characteristics of effective report content

The content and quality of your reports can have a direct impact on your professional success because they show how well you think, gather and analyze data, draw conclusions, and develop and support your recommendations. In other words, your credibility and prospects for the future are on the line with every business report you write. You'll create more successful reports if your content is:

- **Accurate.** Information presented in a report must be factually correct. When writing reports, be sure to double-check your facts and references in addition to checking for typos. If an audience ever gets the inkling that your information is shaky, they'll start to view all your work with a skeptical eye.
- **Complete.** To help audiences make informed decisions, include all the information necessary for readers to understand the situation, problem, or proposal. Support all key assertions using an appropriate combination of illustrations, explanations, and facts.[3] Tell your readers what they need to know—no more, no less—and present the information in a way that is geared to their needs. In a recent Tellabs annual report, for example, George Stenitzer and his team provided a concise and easily understandable overview of the company's complex and technical product line. Rather than burying the audience with technical details, the product overview clearly identified how the company's products deliver the benefits that Internet users want and how the products offer business advantages to Tellabs's customers. The subject matter is presented in a way that any investor interested in the company's stock can comprehend.[4]

- **Balanced.** Present all sides of the issue fairly and equitably, and include all the essential information, even if some of the information doesn't support your line of reasoning. Although you want to be as brief as possible, your readers need a minimum amount of information before they can grasp the issue being presented. Omitting relevant information or facts can bias your report.
- **Clear and logical.** Clear sentence structure and good transitions are essential.[5] Save your readers time by making sure your sentences are uncluttered, contain well-chosen words, and proceed logically. To help your readers move from one point to the next, make your transitions just as clear and logical. For a successful report, identify the ideas that belong together, and organize them in a way that's easy to understand.[6]
- **Documented properly.** If you use primary and secondary sources for your report or proposal, be sure to properly document and give credit to your sources, as Chapter 10 explains.

Keeping these points in mind will help you draft the most effective introduction, body, and close for your report (see Figure 14.4).

FIGURE 14.4 Effective Progress Report Offering Complete Content (Excerpt)
Note how Carlyce Johnson offers her client a complete, but efficient, update of her company's landscaping services. In addition to providing routine information, she also informs the client of progress on two problem areas, one that her firm has been able to resolve and one that they've just discovered. Johnson does the right thing by telling the client about the problems as early as possible, giving the client time to react and plan.

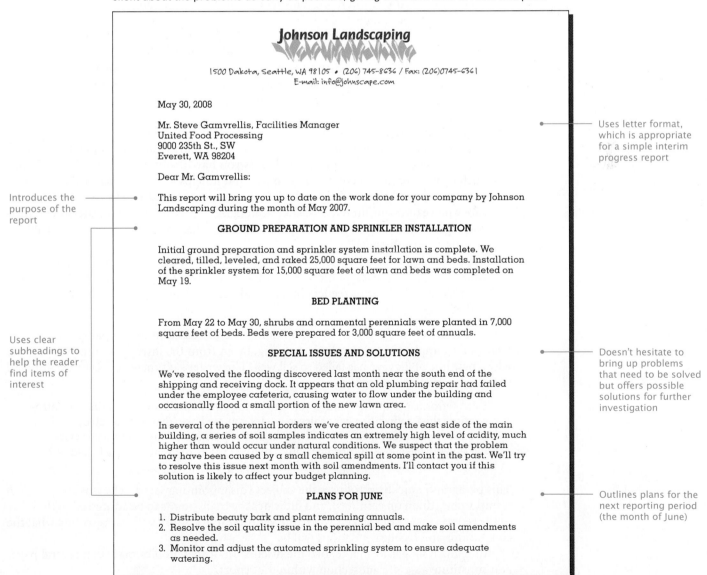

Uses letter format, which is appropriate for a simple interim progress report

Introduces the purpose of the report

Uses clear subheadings to help the reader find items of interest

Doesn't hesitate to bring up problems that need to be solved but offers possible solutions for further investigation

Outlines plans for the next reporting period (the month of June)

Report Introduction

The specific elements you should include in an introduction depend on the nature and length of the report, the circumstances in which you're writing it, and your relationship with the audience. An introduction could contain all of the following topics, although you'll want to pick and choose the best ones to include with each report you write:

- **Authorization.** When, how, and by whom the report was authorized; who wrote it; and when it was submitted. This material is especially important when no *letter of transmittal* is included.
- **Problem/opportunity/purpose.** The reason for the report's existence and what is to be accomplished as a result of your having written the report.
- **Scope.** What is and what isn't going to be covered in the report. The scope indicates the report's size and complexity; it also helps with the critical job of setting the audience's expectations.
- **Background.** The historical conditions or factors that led up to the report. This section enables readers to understand how the problem, situation, or opportunity developed and what has been done about it so far.
- **Sources and methods.** The primary and secondary sources of information used. As appropriate, this section explains how samples were selected, how questionnaires were constructed (which should be included in an appendix with any cover letters), what follow-up was done, and so on. This section builds reader confidence in the work and in the sources and methods used.
- **Definitions.** A list of terms that might be unfamiliar to your audience, along with brief definitions. This section is unnecessary if readers are familiar with the terms you've used in your report—and they all agree on what the terms mean, which isn't always the case. If you have any question about reader knowledge, define any terms that might be misinterpreted. Terms may also be defined where they appear in the body, in explanatory notes, or in a glossary.
- **Limitations.** Factors beyond your control that affect report quality, such as budget limitations, schedule constraints, or limited access to information or people. If appropriate, this section can also express any doubts you have about any aspect of your report. Such candor may be uncomfortable to you, but it helps your readers assess your information accurately, and it helps establish your report's integrity. However, always take care when expressing limitations. Don't apologize or try to explain away personal shortcomings (such as having put the report off until the last minute, so you weren't able to do a first-rate job on it).
- **Report organization.** The organization of the report (what topics are covered and in what order), along with a rationale for following this plan, if appropriate. This section is a road map that helps readers understand what's coming at each turn of the report and why.

In a relatively brief report, these topics may be discussed in only a paragraph or two. Here's an example of a brief indirect opening, taken from the introduction of a memo on why a new line of luggage has failed to sell well. The writer's ultimate goal is to recommend a shift in marketing strategy.

> Sales performance of the Venturer line can be improved. In the two years since its introduction, this product line has achieved a sales volume lower than we expected, resulting in a drain on the company's overall earnings. The purpose of this report is to review the luggage-buying habits of consumers in all markets where the Venturer line is sold, so that we can determine where to put our marketing emphasis.

This paragraph quickly introduces the subject (disappointing sales), tells why the problem is important (drain on earnings), and indicates the main points to be addressed in the body of the report (review of markets where the Venturer line is sold), without revealing what the conclusions and recommendations will be.

In a much longer formal report, the discussion of these topics may span several pages and constitute a significant section within the report.

Report Body

As with the introduction, the body of your report can require some tough decisions about which elements to include and how much detail to offer as supporting evidence. Some audiences and situations require detailed coverage; others can be handled with more concise treatment. Provide only enough detail in the body to support your conclusions and recommendations; you can put additional detail in tables, charts, and appendixes.

The report body should contain only enough information to convey your message convincingly; don't overload the body with excessive details.

The topics commonly covered in a report body include:

- Explanations of a problem or opportunity
- Facts, statistical evidence, and trends
- Results of studies or investigations
- Discussion and analyses of potential courses of action
- Advantages, disadvantages, costs, and benefits of a particular course of action
- Procedures or steps in a process
- Methods and approaches
- Criteria for evaluating alternatives and options
- Conclusions and recommendations (in direct reports)
- Supporting reasons for conclusions or recommendations

For analytical reports using a direct approach, you'll generally state your conclusions or recommendations in the introduction and use the body of your report to provide your evidence and support (as illustrated in Figures 14.3 and 14.4). If you're using an indirect approach, you'll likely use the body to discuss your logic and reserve your conclusions or recommendations until the very end.

Report Close

The content and length of your report close depend on your choice of direct or indirect order, among other variables. If your report is organized in a direct order, end with a summary of key points (although this is often not necessary in short reports), listed in the order they appear in the report body. If appropriate, briefly restate your conclusions or recommendations and the logical arguments you used to reach them. If your report is organized in an indirect order, your conclusions or recommendations might be presented for the first time at the end. Just remember that a conclusion or recommendation section isn't the place to introduce new facts; your audiences should have all the information they need by the time they reach this point in your report.

The nature of your close depends on the type of report (informational, analytical, or proposal) and the approach (direct or indirect).

If your report is intended to lead to action, use the ending to spell out exactly what should happen next. Readers may agree with everything you say in your report but still fail to take any action if you're vague about what should happen next. Providing a schedule and specific task assignments is helpful because concrete plans have a way of commanding action. If you'll be taking all the actions yourself, make sure your readers understand this fact so that they'll know what to expect from you (see Figure 14.5).

For long reports, you may need to divide your close into separate sections for conclusions, recommendations, and actions.

In a short report, the close may be only a paragraph or two. In contrast, the close of a long report might have separate sections for conclusions, recommendations, and actions. Separate sections help your reader locate this material and focus on each element. Such an arrangement also gives you a final opportunity to emphasize important content.

If you have multiple conclusions, recommendations, or actions, you may want to number and list them. An appropriate lead-in to such a list might be, "The findings of this study lead to the following conclusions." A statement that could be used for a list of recommendations might be, "Based on the conclusions of this study, we make the following recommendations." A statement that could be used for actions might be, "In order to accomplish our goals on time, we must complete the following actions before the end of the year."

DOCUMENT MAKEOVER

IMPROVE THIS POLICY REPORT

To practice correcting drafts of actual documents, visit your online course or the access-code-protected portion of the Companion Website. Click "Document Makeovers," then click Chapter 14. You will find a policy report that contains problems and errors relating to what you've learned in this chapter about writing business reports and proposals. Use the Final Draft decision tool to create an improved version of this report. Check the message for an effective opening; consistent levels of formality or informality; and the use of headings, lists, transitions, and previews and reviews to help orient readers.

FIGURE 14.5 Effective Report Expressing Action Plan in the Close
Roger Watson's personal activity report for July is a good example of efficiently conveying key information points, including a clear plan of action in the close. Note the use of hyperlinks to maps, photos, and a related report, all of which are stored on the same secure intranet site.

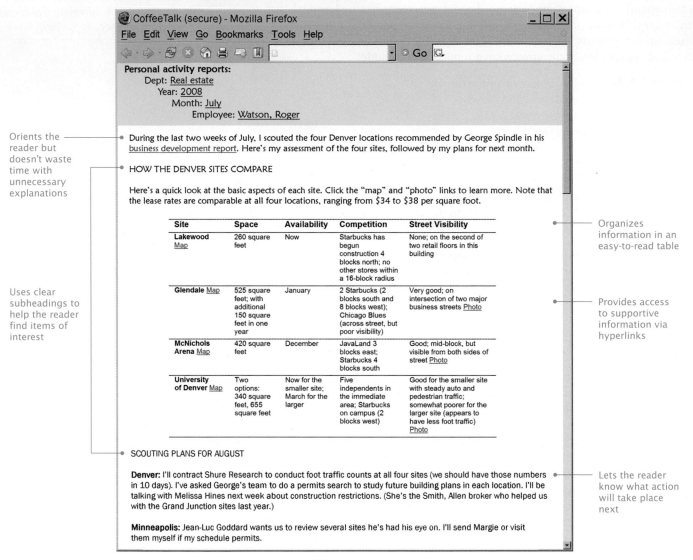

Drafting Proposal Content

Like reports, proposals have an introduction, a body, and a close. The content for each section is governed by many variables—the most important being the source of your proposal. If your proposal is unsolicited, you have some latitude in the scope and organization of content. However, the scope and organization of a solicited proposal are usually governed by the request for proposals. Most RFPs spell out precisely what you should cover and in what order. This uniformity lets the recipient evaluate competing proposals in a systematic way. In many organizations a team of evaluators splits up the proposals and looks at various sections. An engineer might review the technical portions of all the proposals submitted, and an accountant might review the cost estimates.

The general purpose of any proposal is to persuade readers to do something, such as purchase goods or services, fund a project, or implement a program. Thus, your writing approach for a proposal is similar to that used for persuasive sales messages (see Chapter 10). Your proposal must sell your audience on your ideas, product, service, methods, and company. Just as with any persuasive message, you can use the AIDA model to gain attention, build interest, create desire, and motivate action (of course, you may need to adapt if you're

The AIDA model you learned in Chapter 10 works well for proposals, although you may need to adapt it if you're responding to an RFP.

responding to an RFP or facing some other organizational constraints). Here are some additional strategies to strengthen your argument:[7]

- **Demonstrate your knowledge.** Everything you write should show the reader that you have the knowledge and experience to solve the problem or address the opportunity outlined in your proposal.
- **Provide concrete information and examples.** Enthusiasm and good intentions are no substitute for evidence. Avoid vague, unsupported generalizations such as "We are losing money on this program." Instead, provide quantifiable details such as the amount of money being lost, how, why, and so on. Explain how much money your proposed solution will save. Spell out your plan and give details on how the job will be done. Such concrete information persuades readers; unsupported generalizations do not.
- **Research the competition.** If you're competing against other companies for a potential customer's business, use trade publications and the Internet to become familiar with the products, services, and prices of these other companies. Even if you're not competing against other companies, find out what alternatives your audience might choose over your proposal so that you can emphasize why your solution is the optimum choice. In some cases, potential customers face a "buy or build" decision, in which they must choose between buying a solution from an external party or building it themselves. In these cases, you are effectively competing against your target customers.
- **Prove that your proposal is workable.** Your proposal must be appropriate and feasible for your audience. It should be consistent with your audience's capabilities. For instance, your proposal would be pointless if it recommended a plan of action that requires three times the number of employees or twice the available budget.
- **Adopt a "you" attitude.** Relate your product, service, or personnel to the reader's exact needs, either as stated in the RFP for a solicited proposal or as discovered through your own investigation for an unsolicited proposal.
- **Package your proposal attractively.** Make sure your proposal is letter perfect, inviting, and readable. Readers will prejudge the quality of your products or services by the proposal you submit. Errors, omissions, or inconsistencies will work against you—and may even cost you important career and business opportunities.

Proposals in various industries often have their own special challenges as well. For instance, management consultants have to convince every potential client that they have the skills and knowledge to solve the client's problem—without giving the answer away for free in the proposal. In other industries, such as transportation services, bidders may be asked to compute hundreds or thousands of individual pricing scenarios. Hands-on experience goes a long way in deciding what to include and exclude in a report; whenever possible, get advice from a senior colleague who's been through it before.

Proposal Introduction

The introduction presents and summarizes the problem you want to solve or the opportunity you want to pursue, along with your proposed solution. By doing so, the introduction orients readers to the remainder of the report. If your proposal is solicited, its introduction should refer to the RFP so that readers know which RFP you're responding to. If your proposal is unsolicited, your introduction should mention any factors that led you to submit your proposal, such as prior conversations with members of the recipient organization's staff. The following topics are commonly covered in a proposal introduction:

- **Background or statement of the problem or opportunity.** Briefly reviews the reader's situation and establishes a need for action. Readers may not perceive a problem or opportunity the same way you do. In unsolicited proposals, you need to convince them that a problem or opportunity exists before you can convince them to accept your solution. In a way that is meaningful to your reader, discuss the current situation and explain how things could be better. Emphasize how your goals align with your audience's goals.
- **Solution.** Briefly describes the change you propose and highlights your key selling points and their benefits, showing how your proposal will help readers meet their business objectives. In long proposals, the heading for this section might also be "Preliminary

4 LEARNING OBJECTIVE

Name six strategies to strengthen your proposal argument

Business proposals need to provide more than just attractive ideas—readers look for evidence of practical, achievable solutions.

5 LEARNING OBJECTIVE

List the topics commonly covered in a proposal's introduction, body, and close

In an unsolicited proposal, your introduction may need to convince readers that a problem or opportunity exists.

Analysis," "Overview of Approach," or some other wording that will identify this section as a preview of your solution.

- **Scope.** States the boundaries of the proposal, defining what you will and will not do. This section is sometimes called "Delimitations."
- **Organization.** Orients the reader to the remainder of the proposal and calls attention to the major divisions of information.

In short proposals, your discussion of these topics will be brief—perhaps only a sentence or two for each one. For long, formal proposals, each of these topics may warrant separate subheadings and several paragraphs of discussion.

Proposal Body

Readers understand that a proposal is a persuasive message, so they're willing to accommodate a promotional style—as long as it is professional and focused on their needs.

The proposal's body gives complete details on the proposed solution and specifies what the anticipated results will be. Because a proposal is by definition a persuasive message, your audience expects you to promote your offering in a confident but professional manner. Even when you're expressing an idea that you believe in passionately, maintain an objective tone so that you don't risk overselling your message (see "Ethics Detective: Am I Being Sold or Oversold?").

In addition to providing facts and evidence to support your conclusions, an effective body covers this information:

- **Proposed approach.** Describes what you have to offer: your concept, product, or service. This section may also be titled "Technical Proposal," "Research Design," "Issues for Analysis," or "Work Statement." To convince readers that your proposal has merit, focus on the strengths of your offer in relation to reader needs. Stress the benefits of your product, service, or investment opportunity that are relevant to your readers' needs, and point out any advantages that you have over your competitors.

Ethics Detective

Am I Being Sold or Oversold?

As the manager in charge of your company's New Ventures Group, you've read your share of proposals—hundreds, maybe thousands, of them. You've developed a sixth sense about these documents, an ability to separate cautious optimism from self-doubt and distinguish justified enthusiasm from insupportable hype.

Your company invests in promising smaller firms that could grow into beneficial business partners or even future acquisitions. In a typical scenario, a small company invents a new product but needs additional funding to manufacture and market it, so the owners approach you with funding proposals. Because you make the first major decision in this investment process, your choices and recommendations to the board of directors are crucial.

Moreover, the risks are considerable. If one of your recommendations doesn't pan out, the company could lose all the money it invested (often millions), and that's only the start. Failures consume your team's precious time and energy and can even put the company at risk for shareholder lawsuits and other serious headaches. In other words, mistakes in your line of work are costly.

The proposal in front of you today is intriguing. A small company in Oklahoma has designed a product called the Wireless Shopping List, and you think the idea might appeal to upscale homeowners. Small touchscreens are placed around the house, wherever occupants are likely to think of things they need to buy on the next shopping trip: on the refrigerator door, in the media room, in the nursery, in the garage, in the gardening shed. The system collects all these inputs, then on command prints out a shopping list or downloads it to a PDA. It's a clever idea, but one paragraph in the proposal bothers you:

> Everybody in our test market audience was absolutely stunned when we demonstrated the simulated system. They couldn't believe something like this was even possible. It was so handy and so convenient—everyone said it would change their lives forever. We haven't even specified the price yet, but every single person in the room wanted to place an order, on the spot.

ANALYSIS

This proposal potentially oversells the idea in at least three different ways. Identify them and explain how they could lead you to decline the investment opportunity.

- **Work plan.** Describes how you'll accomplish what must be done, unless you'll be providing a standard, off-the-shelf item. (Note that *work plan* in this context describes the work you'll perform if your proposal is accepted, rather than the work plan you may have written to help guide the writing of the proposal itself.) Explain the steps you'll take, their timing, the methods or resources you'll use, and the person(s) responsible. Specifically include when the work will begin, how it will be divided into stages, when you will finish, and whether any follow-up is involved. If appropriate, include a time line or Gantt chart highlighting any critical dates. For solicited proposals, make sure your dates match those specified in the RFP. Keep in mind that if your proposal is accepted, the work plan is contractually binding, so don't promise to deliver more than you can realistically achieve within the stated time period.

  The work plan indicates exactly how you will accomplish the solution presented in the proposal.

- **Statement of qualifications.** Describes your organization's experience, personnel, and facilities—all in relation to reader needs. If you work for a large company that frequently submits proposals, you might borrow much of this section intact from previous proposals. However, be sure to tailor any boilerplate material to suit the situation. The qualifications section can be an important selling point, and it deserves to be handled carefully. You can supplement your qualifications by including a list of client references, but get permission ahead of time to use these references.

- **Costs.** Covers pricing, reimbursable expenses, discounts, and so on. Coverage can vary widely, from a single price amount to detailed breakdowns by part number, service category, and so on. If you're responding to an RFP, follow its instructions. In other cases, your firm probably has a set policy for discussing costs. The amount of detail you provide depends on your relationship with your audience.

In an informal proposal, discussion of some or all of these elements may be grouped together and presented in a letter format, as the proposal in Figure 14.6 does. In a formal proposal, the discussion of these elements will be quite long and thorough. The format may resemble long reports with multiple parts, as Chapter 15 discusses.

Proposal Close

The final section of a proposal generally summarizes the key points, emphasizes the benefits that readers will realize from your solution, summarizes the merits of your approach, restates why you and your firm are the ones to perform the service or provide the products in question, and asks for a decision from the client. The close is your last opportunity to persuade readers to accept your proposal. In both formal and informal proposals, make this section relatively brief, assertive (but not brash or abrupt), and confident.

The close is your last chance to convince the reader of the merits of your proposal, so make doubly sure it's clear, compelling, and audience-oriented.

Drafting Online Content

In addition to the other advice in the chapter about report writing, here are five key aspects of web writing that will help make your web content more effective: First, take special care to build trust with your intended audiences, because careful readers can be skeptical of online content. Make sure your content is accurate, current, complete, and authoritative. Indicate the date material was originally posted and again when it is updated, so that readers can judge your content's currency.

6 LEARNING OBJECTIVE

Identify five characteristics of effective writing in online reports

Second, adapt your content for a global audience. This can be a complicated and expensive effort, however. Translating content is expensive, and *localizing* it so that it reflects not only the native language of your readers but their cultural norms, weights, measures, time, money, and so on is even more expensive. Some companies compromise by localizing the homepage and key secondary pages while keeping the deeper, more detailed content in its original language.

Localizing web content involves both translating the content and adapting it to local cultural norms and practices.

Third, compose web-friendly content. In an environment that can present as many reading challenges as the web, careful attention to composition is critical. Compelling, reader-oriented content is the key to success for any website.[8] Most readers won't return to websites that don't offer interesting, helpful content—it's too easy to find websites that serve them better. Wherever possible, use the *inverted pyramid* style, in which you cover the most important information briefly at first, then gradually reveal successive layers of detail—

FIGURE 14.6 Effective Solicited Proposal in Letter Format
This informal solicited proposal provides the information the customer needs to make a purchase. Note that by signing the proposal and returning it, the customer will enter into a legal contract to pay for the services described.

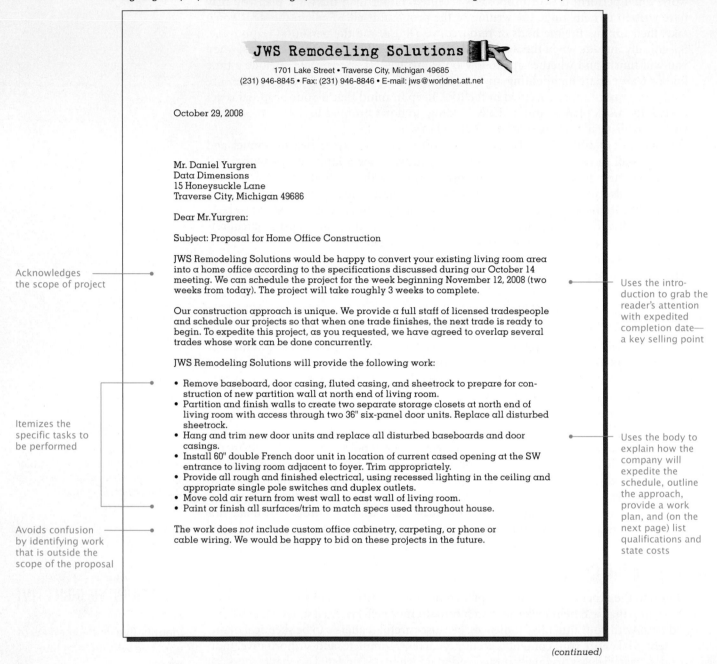

Acknowledges the scope of project

Itemizes the specific tasks to be performed

Avoids confusion by identifying work that is outside the scope of the proposal

Uses the introduction to grab the reader's attention with expedited completion date— a key selling point

Uses the body to explain how the company will expedite the schedule, outline the approach, provide a work plan, and (on the next page) list qualifications and state costs

> **JWS Remodeling Solutions**
> 1701 Lake Street • Traverse City, Michigan 49685
> (231) 946-8845 • Fax: (231) 946-8846 • E-mail: jws@worldnet.att.net
>
> October 29, 2008
>
> Mr. Daniel Yurgren
> Data Dimensions
> 15 Honeysuckle Lane
> Traverse City, Michigan 49686
>
> Dear Mr. Yurgren:
>
> Subject: Proposal for Home Office Construction
>
> JWS Remodeling Solutions would be happy to convert your existing living room area into a home office according to the specifications discussed during our October 14 meeting. We can schedule the project for the week beginning November 12, 2008 (two weeks from today). The project will take roughly 3 weeks to complete.
>
> Our construction approach is unique. We provide a full staff of licensed tradespeople and schedule our projects so that when one trade finishes, the next trade is ready to begin. To expedite this project, as you requested, we have agreed to overlap several trades whose work can be done concurrently.
>
> JWS Remodeling Solutions will provide the following work:
>
> - Remove baseboard, door casing, fluted casing, and sheetrock to prepare for construction of new partition wall at north end of living room.
> - Partition and finish walls to create two separate storage closets at north end of living room with access through two 36" six-panel door units. Replace all disturbed sheetrock.
> - Hang and trim new door units and replace all disturbed baseboards and door casings.
> - Install 60" double French door unit in location of current cased opening at the SW entrance to living room adjacent to foyer. Trim appropriately.
> - Provide all rough and finished electrical, using recessed lighting in the ceiling and appropriate single pole switches and duplex outlets.
> - Move cold air return from west wall to east wall of living room.
> - Paint or finish all surfaces/trim to match specs used throughout house.
>
> The work does *not* include custom office cabinetry, carpeting, or phone or cable wiring. We would be happy to bid on these projects in the future.

(continued)

letting readers choose to see those additional layers if they want to (links to subpages are ideal for this). Also, make sure your writing is compact and efficient; material on the web needs to be shorter because online readers tend to skip over long chunks of text.

Fourth, present your information in a concise, skimmable format. Effective websites use a variety of means to help readers skim pages quickly, including lists, careful use of color and boldface, informative headings (clever headings with lots of wordplay are usually more annoying than effective), and helpful summaries that give readers a choice of learning more if they want to.

Fifth, write effective links, because they serve for both site navigation and content skimming. Above all else, clearly identify where a link will take readers; don't force them to click through and try to figure out where they're going. If necessary, include a brief summary ex-

Effective links in online reports let readers know exactly what to expect before they click on them.

FIGURE 14.6 *Continued*

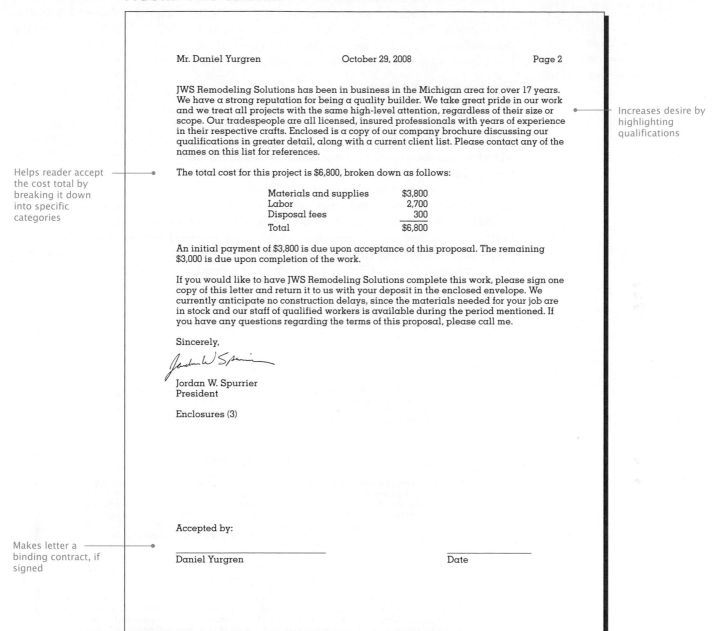

Mr. Daniel Yurgren   October 29, 2008   Page 2

JWS Remodeling Solutions has been in business in the Michigan area for over 17 years. We have a strong reputation for being a quality builder. We take great pride in our work and we treat all projects with the same high-level attention, regardless of their size or scope. Our tradespeople are all licensed, insured professionals with years of experience in their respective crafts. Enclosed is a copy of our company brochure discussing our qualifications in greater detail, along with a current client list. Please contact any of the names on this list for references.

Increases desire by highlighting qualifications

Helps reader accept the cost total by breaking it down into specific categories

The total cost for this project is $6,800, broken down as follows:

Materials and supplies	$3,800
Labor	2,700
Disposal fees	300
Total	$6,800

An initial payment of $3,800 is due upon acceptance of this proposal. The remaining $3,000 is due upon completion of the work.

If you would like to have JWS Remodeling Solutions complete this work, please sign one copy of this letter and return it to us with your deposit in the enclosed envelope. We currently anticipate no construction delays, since the materials needed for your job are in stock and our staff of qualified workers is available during the period mentioned. If you have any questions regarding the terms of this proposal, please call me.

Sincerely,

Jordan W. Spurrier
President

Enclosures (3)

Makes letter a binding contract, if signed

Accepted by:

_____   _____
Daniel Yurgren   Date

---

plaining what readers will experience if they click on the link—particularly if the link downloads or opens a PDF document or does anything else that might be unexpected. Also, try to avoid using directional words such as *back, forward, next, above, below, bottom,* or *top.* Such words are meaningful in a linear document, but not necessarily in a hypertext document, where visitors can enter your site at many places and from many directions. Instead, use absolute directions such as *Return to Tables, Next Learning Step,* or *Beginning of Tutorial.*[9]

Helping Readers Find Their Way

Just as travelers need maps to navigate through unfamiliar territory, your readers need directions to navigate through your reports, both in print and online. If you fail to provide this assistance, readers might miss important points or give up before they reach critical destinations. Providing directions is especially important for people from other cultures and countries, whose language skills and business expectations may differ from yours.

Help your audiences navigate through your reports by providing clear directions to key pieces of content.

7 LEARNING OBJECTIVE

Briefly describe three report elements that can help readers find their way in long documents

Moreover, readers often lack the time or the inclination to plow through long reports page by page or screen by screen. They typically want to browse quickly, find a section of interest, dive in for details, browse for another section, and so on. If you want readers to understand and accept your message, help them navigate your document using three helpful tools: headings and links, smooth transitions, and previews and reviews.

Headings and Links

As you learned in Chapter 6, headings are brief titles that cue readers about the content of sections that follow. They improve a document's readability and are especially useful markers for clarifying the framework of a report. Also, they visually indicate shifts from one idea to the next, and when you use a combination of headings and subheadings, you help readers see the relationship between subordinate and main ideas. In addition, busy readers can quickly understand the gist of a document simply by scanning the headings. In online reports, headings serve all these functions, plus they can be used to provide links to other sections and other websites.

Many companies specify a format for headings, either through style guide handbooks or document templates. If yours does, use the recommended format. Otherwise, create a simple arrangement that clearly distinguishes levels and is applied consistently throughout your document. Figure 14.7 shows an example of a simple scheme that's easy for readers to

FIGURE 14.7 Heading Format for Reports
If your company doesn't have a standard style guide or template for report headings, this simple design will work well for most reports.

TITLE

The title is centered at the top of the page in all capital letters, usually boldfaced (or underlined if typewritten), often in a large font (type size), and often using a sans serif typeface. When the title runs to more than one line, the lines are usually double-spaced and arranged as an inverted pyramid (the longer line on the top).

FIRST-LEVEL HEADING

A first-level heading indicates what the following section is about, perhaps by describing the subdivisions. All first-level headings are grammatically parallel, with the possible exception of such headings as "Introduction," "Conclusions," and "Recommendations." Some text appears between every two headings, regardless of their levels. Still boldfaced and sans serif, the font may be smaller than that used in the title but still larger than the typeface used in the text and still in all capital letters.

Second-Level Heading

Like first-level headings, second-level headings indicate what the following material is about. All second-level headings within a section are grammatically parallel. Still boldfaced and sans serif, the font may either remain the same or shrink to the size used in the text, and the style is now initial capitals followed with lowercase. Never use only one second-level heading under a first-level heading. (The same is true for every other level of heading.)

Third-Level Heading

A third-level heading is worded to reflect the content of the material that follows. All third-level headings beneath a second-level heading should be grammatically parallel.

Fourth-Level Heading. Like all the other levels of heading, fourth-level headings reflect the subject that will be developed. All fourth-level headings within a subsection are parallel.

Fifth-level headings are generally the lowest level of heading used. However, you can indicate further breakdowns in your ideas by using a list:

1. *The first item in a list.* You may indent the entire item in block format to set it off visually. Numbers are optional.
2. *The second item in a list.* All lists have at least two items. An introductory phrase or sentence may be italicized for emphasis, as shown here.

follow. In any event, resist the temptation to dress up headings and subheadings with overly bright colors, odd fonts, or gigantic font sizes. They may well call attention to themselves, but they'll also make your report feel less professional.

Transitions

Chapter 5 defines transitions as words or phrases that tie ideas together and show how one thought is related to another. Good report writers use transitions to help readers move from one section of a report to the next and from key point to key point within sections. Transitions can be words, sentences, or complete paragraphs. Here's an example:

Transitions connect ideas by helping readers move from one thought to the next.

> . . . As you can see, our profits have decreased by 12 percent over the past eight months.
>
> To counteract this decline in profits, we can explore alternatives. First, we can raise our selling prices. Second, we can work to reduce our manufacturing costs. Third, we can introduce new products that will support higher profit margins. However, each of these alternatives has both advantages and disadvantages.

The phrase *As you can see* alerts readers to the fact that they are reading a summary of the information just presented. The phrase *this decline in profits* refers back to the previous paragraph to let readers know that the text will be saying something else about that topic. The words *first*, *second*, and *third* help readers stay on track as the three alternatives are introduced, and the word *however* alerts readers to the fact that evaluating the three alternatives requires some additional discussion. Effective transitions such as these can help readers summarize and remember what they've learned so far while giving them a mental framework to process new information.

Previews and Reviews

Preview sections introduce important topics by helping readers get ready for new information; they are particularly helpful when the information is complex, unexpected, or unfamiliar (see Figure 14.8). Think of a preview as an opportunity for readers to arrange their mental file folders before you start giving them information to put in those folders.

Previews help readers prepare for upcoming information, and reviews help them verify and clarify what they've just read.

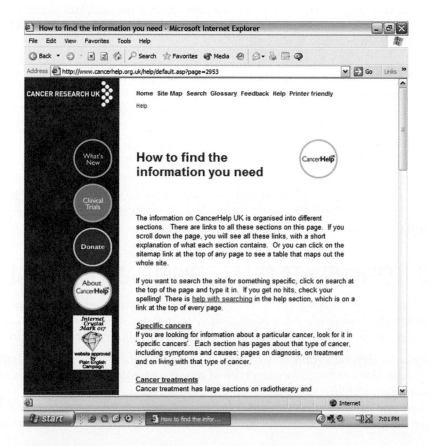

FIGURE 14.8 Helping Readers with Previews of Information
CancerHelp, the cancer information website of Cancer Research UK, helps visitors to its website find the information they need from a variety of online reports, even if they're new to the web.

CHECKLIST: Composing Business Reports and Proposals

A. Review and fine-tune your outline.
- Match your parallel headings to the tone of your report.
- Understand how the introduction, body, and close work together to convey your message.

B. Draft report content.
- Use the introduction to establish the purpose, scope, and organization of your report.
- Use the body to present and interpret the information you gathered.
- Use the close to summarize major points, discuss conclusions, or make recommendations.

C. Draft proposal content.
- Use the introduction to discuss the background or problem, your solution, the scope, and organization.
- Use the body to persuasively explain the benefits of your proposed approach.
- Use the close to emphasize reader benefits and summarize the merits of your approach.

D. Draft online content.
- Establish your credibility with information that is accurate, current, complete, and authoritative.
- Adapt your content to local audiences as much as possible.
- Compose compelling, web-friendly content in the inverted pyramid style.
- Present concise, scannable content.
- Create user-friendly links that clearly identify where the reader will be taken upon clicking.

E. Help readers find their way.
- Provide headings to improve readability and clarify the framework of your ideas.
- Create transitions that tie ideas together and show how one thought relates to another.
- Preview important topics to help readers get ready for new information.
- Review information to help readers absorb details and keep the big picture in mind.

Review sections come after a body of material and summarize the information just covered. They help readers absorb details while keeping track of the big picture. Long reports and those dealing with complex subjects can often benefit from multiple review sections, one at the end of every major subject block, as well as a more comprehensive review at the very end of a document.

Previews and reviews can be written in a sentence format, in bulleted lists, or a combination of the two. Both are effective, but bullets can increase your document's readability by adding white space to the document design. Consider the following preview, which is written using both formats:

SENTENCE FORMAT

The next section discusses the advantages of advertising on the Internet. Among them are currency, global reach, affordability, and interactivity

BULLETED LIST

As the next section shows, advertising on the Internet has four advantages:
- Currency
- Global reach
- Affordability
- Interactivity

For more on writing effective bullets and lists, see "Using Lists and Bullets to Clarify and Emphasize" on page 155 in Chapter 6. To review the tasks discussed in this section, see "Checklist: Composing Business Reports and Proposals."

USING TECHNOLOGY TO CRAFT REPORTS AND PROPOSALS

Look for ways to use technology to reduce the mechanical work involved in writing long reports.

Creating lengthy reports and proposals can be a huge task, so take advantage of technological tools to help throughout the process. You've read about some of these tools in earlier chapters; here are some of the most important ones for developing reports and proposals:

- **Templates.** Beyond simply formatting documents, report templates can identify the specific sections required for each type of report and even automatically insert headings for each section.
- **Linked and embedded documents.** In many reports and proposals, you'll include graphics, spreadsheets, databases, and other elements produced in other software pro-

grams. For instance, in Microsoft Office, you can choose to either *link* to another file (which ensures that changes in that file are reflected in your file) or *embed* another file (which doesn't include this automatic updating feature). Just make sure you know how your tools work.

- **Electronic forms.** For recurring forms such as sales reports and compliance reports, consider creating a word-processor file that combines boilerplate text for material that doesn't change from report to report. To accommodate information that does change (such as last week's sales results), use *form tools* such as text boxes (in which users can type new text) and check boxes (which can be used to select from a set of predetermined choices).

- **Electronic documents.** Portable document format (PDF) files have become a universal replacement for printed reports and proposals. With a copy of Adobe Acrobat (a separate product from the free Acrobat Reader), you can quickly convert reports and proposals to PDF files that are easy and safe to share electronically.

- **Multimedia documents.** When the written word isn't enough, combine your report with video clips, animation, presentation software slides, and other elements. As you'll see in Chapter 17, tools such as Microsoft Producer let you merge a variety of file types to create compelling multimedia presentations that supplement or replace traditional reports.

COMMUNICATION CHALLENGES AT TELLABS

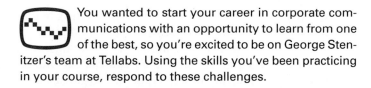 You wanted to start your career in corporate communications with an opportunity to learn from one of the best, so you're excited to be on George Stenitzer's team at Tellabs. Using the skills you've been practicing in your course, respond to these challenges.

Individual Challenge: Like many companies associated with the Internet, Tellabs's business declined when the dot-com boom of the late 1990s began to fizzle out by early 2001. The following excerpt from the company's 2005 annual report describes the effect this had on the company's operations (the *carriers* and *service providers* referred to are the companies that buy Tellabs's products; *material charges* are expenses that are significant enough to affect the company's stock price). As you review these two paragraphs (don't worry about all the technical and financial details), you can see that the first discusses the period from 2001 to 2003, when the company's financial results suffered. The second discusses the upturn that began in 2003 and continued through 2005. Write a transition sentence for the beginning of the second paragraph, signaling to readers that the story is about to change from the negative news of 2001–2003 to the more positive results that began in 2003.

> The markets for our products have undergone dynamic change over the last few years. Beginning in 2001, carrier overcapacity, a softening economy and other factors caused our customers to reduce their capital spending significantly. The impact on Tellabs was a dramatic decline in revenue for each of the years 2001 through 2003. In addition, we had manufacturing overcapacity, excess inventories and a cost structure that could not be supported by our smaller revenue base. We responded by closing manufacturing facilities, reducing global head count, consolidating office space, exiting certain product lines and instituting cost controls across the organization. We also reviewed our product portfolio and cut back or stopped development efforts on some products. In addition, at the end of 2003, we moved to outsource the majority of our remaining manufacturing operations to third-party electronics manufacturing services providers to take advantage of their greater purchasing power and other efficiencies. These actions caused us to record material charges in 2001 through 2005 for excess and obsolete inventory and excess purchase commitments, severance costs, facilities shutdown costs, including accelerated depreciation on certain manufacturing and office buildings and equipment due to shortened useful lives, and various contractual obligations. We also recorded charges for other impaired and surplus assets.

> Market stability began in 2003 and continued in 2004 and 2005 as service providers invested in their networks at levels at or above 2003. This stability enabled us to post year-over-year revenue growth in 2004 for the first time since fiscal 2000. Growing demand for wireless services, including third-generation (3G) services, drove capital investments by both wireless and wireline service providers and helped drive sales of our transport and managed access products.

Team Challenge: Stenitzer's audience-oriented approach to writing extends to the web, through such key elements as carefully worded hyperlinks that let website visitors know exactly what to expect before they click. He wants to make sure that the links on the Investor Relations page (www.tellabs.com/investors) are as good as they can possibly be. With your team, establish criteria that you believe make effective links, then review the investor pages on four other corporate websites (choose any four companies in any industries that interest you). Create a table that compares the four sites with Tellabs, using the criteria you established. Write a one-paragraph summary of the information in the table, along with a list of any improvements that you think could be made to the Tellabs investor section.

SUMMARY OF LEARNING OBJECTIVES

1 **Explain how to adapt to your audiences when writing reports and proposals.** Adapt to your audience by demonstrating sensitivity to their needs (adopting the "you" attitude, maintaining a strong sense of etiquette, emphasizing the positive, and using bias-free language), building a strong relationship with your audience (make sure your writing reflects the desired image of your organization and build your credibility), and controlling your style and tone to achieve the appropriate degree of formality, given the nature of the material and your relationship with the audience.

2 **List the topics commonly covered in the introduction, body, and close of informational or analytical reports.** The introduction highlights who authorized the report, the purpose and scope of a report, necessary background material, the sources or methods used to gather information, important definitions, any limitations, and the order in which the various topics are covered. The body can discuss such details as problems, opportunities, facts, evidence, trends, results of studies or investigations, analysis of potential courses of action, process procedures and steps, methods and approaches, evaluation criteria for options, conclusions, recommendations, and supporting reasons. The close summarizes key points, restates conclusions and recommendations if appropriate, and lists action items.

3 **Name five characteristics of effective report content.** Effective report content is accurate if it is factually correct and error-free. It is complete if it includes all necessary information and supports all key assertions. It is balanced if it presents all sides of an argument. It is clear and logical if it is well-written and organized logically. It is properly documented if credit is given to all primary and secondary sources of information used.

4 **Name six strategies to strengthen your proposal argument.** To strengthen your argument, you should demonstrate your knowledge, provide concrete examples, research the competition, prove that your proposal is workable, adopt a "you" attitude, and make your proposal attractive and error-free.

5 **List the topics commonly covered in a proposal's introduction, body, and close.** The introduction discusses the background or existing problem, the solution to the problem, the scope of the proposal, and the order in which information is presented in the document. For solicited proposals, the introduction should also reference the RFP. The body discusses the proposed approach and benefits to the reader, the work plan, the organization's qualifications, and the costs of the proposal. The close briefly summarizes the key points, the merits and benefits of the proposed approach, and the submitting firm's competencies.

6 **Identify five characteristics of effective writing in online reports.** First, effective web content builds trust with often-skeptical online audiences by being accurate, current, complete, and authoritative. Second, as much as possible, the content is adapted to global audiences, including localizing for specific languages and cultural norms. Third, effective content is web-friendly, meaning that it is compelling and interesting enough to hold the audience's attention, it communicates key points quickly while offering additional details in successive layers, and it is compact and efficient. Fourth, good web content is easy to scan quickly, because online readers often take a quick look at a webpage to see if anything promises to meet their information needs. Fifth, effective online reports make good use of links to enable both the scanning of content and navigation of the website.

7 **Briefly describe three report elements that can help readers find their way in long documents.** Effective reports help readers navigate the document by using these three elements: (1) Headings (and links for online reports) set off important ideas and provide the reader with clues as to the report's framework and shifts in discussion; (2) transitions tie ideas together and keep readers moving along; and (3) previews and reviews prepare readers for new information and summarize previously discussed information.

Test Your Knowledge

1. Why is the "you" attitude even more important with long, complex reports?
2. What writing choices can you make to adjust the formality of your reports?
3. Why is it helpful to review your outline one last time before you begin writing a report?
4. What is the function of a report introduction?
5. What information might you include in the close of a report?
6. What information might you include in the introduction of a proposal?
7. Why is the work plan a key component of a proposal?
8. How does giving dates for online content help your readers?
9. How does the inverted pyramid style help online readers?
10. What elements can you use to help readers follow the structure and flow of information in a long report?

Apply Your Knowledge

1. Should a report always explain the writer's method of gathering evidence or solving a problem? Why or why not?
2. What are the risks of not explaining the purpose of a proposal within the introduction?
3. Why do experts recommend that online content be shorter than printed content wherever possible?
4. If you want your audience to agree to a specific course of action, should you exclude any references to alternatives that you don't want the audience to consider? Why or why not?
5. **Ethical Choices** If a company receives a solicited proposal from a management consulting firm, is it ethical for the company to adopt the recommendations discussed in the proposal even though the company does not hire the submitting firm? Why or why not?

Practice Your Knowledge

Message for Analysis

Read the solicited proposal in Figure 14.9, then (1) analyze the strengths and weaknesses of this document and (2) revise the document so that it follows this chapter's guidelines.

Exercises

For active links to all websites discussed in this chapter, visit this text's website at **www.prenhall.com/bovee**. Locate your book and click on its Companion Website link. Then select Chapter 14, and click on "Featured Websites." Locate the name of the page or the URL related to the material in the text. Please note that links to sites that become inactive after publication of the book will be removed from the Featured Websites section.

14.1 Adapting Reports to the Audience Review the reports shown in Figures 14.2 to 14.5. Give specific examples of how each of these reports establishes a good relationship with the audience. Consider such things as using the "you" attitude, emphasizing the positive, establishing credibility, being polite, using bias-free language, and projecting a good company image.

14.2 Composing Reports: Report Content You are writing an analytical report on the U.S. sales of your newest product. Of the following topics, identify where in the report each element should be included—the introduction, body, or close. Briefly explain your decisions.
   a. Regional breakdowns of sales across the country
   b. Date the product was released in the marketplace
   c. Sales figures from competitors selling similar products worldwide
   d. Predictions of how the struggling U.S. economy will affect sales over the next six months
   e. Method used for obtaining the preceding predictions
   f. The impact of similar products being sold in the United States by Japanese competitors
   g. Your recommendation as to whether the company should sell this product internationally
   h. Actions that must be completed by year end if the company decides to sell this product internationally

14.3 Composing Reports Find an article in a business newspaper or journal (in print or online) that recommends a solution to a problem. Identify the problem, the recommended solution(s), and the supporting evidence provided by the author to justify his or her recommendation(s). Did the author cite any formal or informal studies as evidence? What facts or statistics did the author include? Did the author cite any criteria for evaluating possible options? If so, what were they?

14.4 Composing Web Content: Effective Links Write an effectively worded link for each of the following content sections on a website (make up any information you need):
   a. A page that summarizes the company's most recent quarterly financial results
   b. A page that lists the phone numbers and e-mail addresses for key contacts within the company
   c. A page containing a news release announcing that the company is being investigated by the Securities and Exchange Commission (SEC) for possible accounting irregularities
   d. A page that announces the launch of a major new product

14.5 Composing Reports: Navigational Clues Review a long business article in a journal or newspaper. Highlight examples of how the article uses headings, transitions, and previews and reviews to help the readers find their way.

14.6 Ethical Choices Your boss has asked you to prepare a feasibility report to determine whether the company should advertise its custom-crafted cabinetry in the weekly neighborhood newspaper. Based on your primary research, you think they should. As you draft the introduction to your report, however, you discover that the survey administered to the neighborhood newspaper subscribers was flawed. Several of the questions were poorly written and misleading. You used the survey results, among other findings, to justify your

FIGURE 14.9 Solicited Proposal

PROPOSAL

DATE: April 18, 2008
TO: Ken Estes, Northern Illinois Concrete   KB
FROM: Kris Beiersdorf, Memco Construction
PROJECT: IDOT Letting Item #83, Contract No. 79371, DuPage County

Memco Construction proposes to furnish all labor, material, equipment, and supervision to provide Engineered Fill—Class II and IV—for the following unit prices.

Engineered Fill—Class II and IV

Description	Unit	Quantity	Unit Price	Total
Mobilization*	Lump Sum	1	$4,500.00	$4,500.00
Engineered Fill Class II	Cubic Yards	1,267	$33.50	$42,444.50
Engineered Fill Class IV	Cubic Yards	1,394	$38.00	$52,972.00

* Mobilization includes one move-in. Additional move-ins to be billed at $1,100.00 each.

The following items clarify and qualify the scope of our subcontracting work:
1. All forms, earthwork, clearing, etc., to be provided and maintained by others at no cost to Memco Construction.
2. General Contractor shall provide location for staging, stockpiling material, equipment, and storage at the job site.
3. Memco Construction shall be paid strictly based upon the amount of material actually used on the job.
4. All prep work, including geotechnical fabrics, geomembrane liners, etc., to be done by others at no cost to Memco Construction.
5. Water is to be available at project site at no charge to Memco Construction.
6. Dewatering to be done by others at no cost to Memco Construction.
7. Traffic control setup, devices, maintenance, and flagmen are to be provided by others at no cost to Memco Construction.
8. Memco Construction LLC may withdraw this bid if we do not receive a written confirmation that we are the apparent low sub-bidder within 10 days of your receipt of this proposal.
9. Our F.E.I.N. is 36-4478095.
10. Bond is not included in above prices. Bond is available for an additional 1 percent.

If you have any questions, please contact me at the phone number listed below.

Kris Beiersdorf
Memco Construction
187 W. Euclid Avenue, Glenview, IL 60025
Office: (847) 352-9742, ext. 30
Fax: (847) 352-6595
E-mail: Kbeiersdorf@memco.com
www.memco.com

---

recommendation. The report is due in three days. What actions might you want to take, if any, before you complete your report?

14.7 **Composing Business Reports** Your boss, Len Chow (vice president of corporate planning), has asked you to research opportunities in the cosmetics industry and to prepare a report that presents your findings and your recommendation for where you think the company should focus its marketing efforts. Here's a copy of your note cards (data were created for this exercise):

Subject: Demand   ref: 1.1
Industrywide sales have grown consistently for several decades, fueled by both a growing population and increased per capita consumption

---

Subject: Competition   ref: 1.2
700 companies currently in cosmetics industry

Subject: Niches   ref: 1.3
Focusing on special niches avoids head-on competition with industry leaders

---

Subject: Competition   ref: 1.4
Industry dominated by market leaders: Revlon, Procter & Gamble, Avon, Gillette

---

Subject: Demand   ref: 1.5
Industry no longer recession-proof: Past year, sales sluggish; consumer spending is down; most affected were mid- to high-priced brands; consumers traded down to less expensive lines

Subject: Competition   ref: 1.6
Smaller companies (Neutrogena, Mary Kay, Softsoap, and Noxell) survive by: specializing in niches, differentiating product line, focusing on market segment

Subject: Demand   ref: 1.7
Consumption of cosmetics relatively flat for past five years

Subject: Competition   ref: 1.8
Prices are constant while promotion budgets are increasing

Subject: Niches   ref: 1.9
Men: 50 percent of adult population; account for one-fifth of cosmetic sales; market leaders have attempted this market but failed

Subject: Demand   ref: 1.10
Cosmetic industry is near maturity but some segments may vary. Total market currently produces annual retail sales of $14.5 billion: Cosmetics/lotions/fragrances—$5.635 billion; Personal hygiene products—$4.375 billion; Hair-care products—$3.435 billion; shaving products—$1.055 billion

Subject: Niches   ref: 1.11
Ethnic groups: Some firms specialize in products for African Americans; few firms oriented toward Hispanic, Asian, or Native Americans, which tend to be concentrated geographically

Subject: Demand   ref: 1.12
Average annual expenditure per person for cosmetics is $158

Subject: Competition   ref: 1.13
Competition is intensifying and dominant companies are putting pressure on smaller ones

Subject: Demand   ref: 1.14
First quarter of current year, demand is beginning to revive; trend expected to continue well into next year

Subject: Niches   ref: 1.15
Senior citizens: large growing segment of population; account for 6% of cosmetic sales; specialized needs for hair and skin not being met; interested in appearance

Subject: Demand   ref: 1.16
Demographic trends: (1) Gradual maturing of baby-boomer generation will fuel growth by consuming greater quantities of skincare products, hair replenishment and coloring products, and anti-aging products; (2) population is increasing in the South and Southwest, where some brands have strong distribution

List the main idea of your message (your recommendation), the major points (your conclusions), and supporting evidence. Then construct a final report outline with first- and second-level informative headings focusing on your conclusions. Because Chow requested this report, you can feel free to use the direct approach. Finish by writing a draft of your memo report to Chow.

Expand Your Knowledge
Exploring the Best of the Web
Research Before You Report
www.corporateinformation.com
Research your competition at Corporate Information, and find out what you need to know before you write your next report or proposal. This website has links to thousands of company profiles, data on many industries in dozens of countries, and current economic information for over 100 countries. You'll also find research reports analyzing sales, dividends, earnings, and profit ratios on some 15,000 companies, current foreign exchange rates, and the definitions of commonly used global company extensions such as GmbH, SA, de CV, and more. Scan the site and answer these questions:

1. Select an industry of your choice from one of the listed countries and follow the links to reports, analyses, and data on that industry. What specific types of information did you find on the industry? How might you use this information when writing a report or proposal?
2. Review one of the sample company research reports that are available for free. What types of specific information are available in these reports? How might you use this information when writing a report or proposal?
3. What do the company extensions GmbH, KK, LLC, OHG, SA, and SNC mean?

Surfing Your Way to Career Success
Bovée and Thill's Business Communication Resources offers links to hundreds of online resources that can help you with this course, your other college courses, and your career. Visit www.buscommresources.com, then click on "Business Communication Web Directory." The "Search Engines and Directories" section connects you to a variety of search and metasearch engines, online directories and libraries, specialized search engines for multimedia content, newsfeed aggregators, and other helpful tools. Identify three websites from this section that could be useful in your business career. For each site, write a two-sentence summary of what the site offers and how it could help you launch and build your career.

Learn Interactively
Interactive Study Guide
Visit www.prenhall.com/bovee, then locate your book and click on its "Companion Website" link. Select Chapter 14 to take advantage of the interactive "Chapter Quiz" to test your knowledge of chapter concepts. Receive instant feedback on whether you need additional studying. Also, visit the "Study Hall," where you'll find an abundance of valuable resources that will help you succeed in this course.

Peak Performance Grammar and Mechanics

If your instructor has required the use of "Peak Performance Grammar and Mechanics," either in your online course or on CD, you can improve your skill with document mechanics by using the "Peak Performance Grammar and Mechanics" module. Click "Mechanics of Style." Take the Pretest to determine whether you have any weak areas. Then review those areas in the Refresher Course. Take the Follow-Up Test to check your grasp of mechanics. For an extra challenge or advanced practice, take the Advanced Test. Finally, for additional reinforcement, visit the Companion Website, click on any chapter, then click on "Improve Your Grammar, Mechanics, and Usage."

CASES

Applying the Three-Step Writing Process to Cases

Apply each step to the following cases, as assigned by your instructor.

Plan

Analyze the Situation
Clarify the problem or opportunity at hand, develop an audience profile, and develop a work plan.

Gather Information
Determine audience needs and obtain the information necessary to satisfy those needs; conduct a research project if necessary.

Select the Right Medium
Choose the best medium for delivering your message; consider delivery through multiple media.

Organize the Information
Define your main idea, limit your scope, select a direct or an indirect approach, and outline your content using an appropriate structure for an informational report, analytical report, or proposal.

1

Write

Adapt to Your Audience
Be sensitive to audience needs with a "you" attitude, politeness, positive emphasis, and bias-free language. Build a strong relationship with your audience by establishing your credibility and projecting your company's image. Control your style with a tone and voice appropriate to the situation.

Compose the Message
Choose strong words that will help you create effective sentences and coherent paragraphs throughout the introduction, body, and close of your report or proposal.

2

Complete

Revise the Message
Evaluate content and review readability, edit and rewrite for conciseness and clarity.

Produce the Message
Use effective design elements and suitable layout for a clean, professional appearance; seamlessly combine text and graphical elements.

Proofread the Message
Review for errors in layout, spelling, and mechanics.

Distribute the Message
Deliver your report using the chosen medium; make sure all documents and all relevant files are distributed successfully.

3

INFORMAL INFORMATIONAL REPORTS

1. My progress to date: Interim progress report on your academic career As you know, the procedural requirements involved in getting a degree or certificate can be nearly as challenging as any course you could take.

Your task: Prepare an interim progress report detailing the steps you've taken toward completing your graduation or certification requirements. After examining the requirements listed in your college catalog, indicate a realistic schedule for completing those that remain. In addition to course requirements, include steps such as completing the residency requirement, filing necessary papers, and paying necessary fees. Use memo format for your report, and address it to anyone who is helping or encouraging you through school.

2. Gavel to gavel: Personal activity report of a meeting Meetings, conferences, and conventions abound in the academic world, and you have probably attended your share.

Your task: Prepare a personal activity report on a meeting, convention, or conference that you recently attended. Use memo format, and direct the report to other students in your field who were not able to attend.

Portfolio BUILDER

3. Check that price tag: Informational report on trends in college costs Are tuition costs going up, going down, or remaining the same? Your college's administration has asked you to compare your college's tuition costs with those of a nearby college and determine which has risen more quickly. Research the trend by

checking your college's annual tuition costs for each of the most recent four years. Then research the four-year tuition trends for a neighboring college. For both colleges, calculate the percentage change in tuition costs from year to year and between the first and fourth year.

Your task: Prepare an informal report (using the letter format) presenting your findings and conclusions to the president of your college. Include graphics to explain and support your conclusions.

4. Get a move on it: Lasting guidelines for moving into college dormitories Moving into a college dormitory is one experience you weren't quite prepared for. In addition to lugging all your earthly belongings up four flights of stairs in 90-degree heat, channeling electrical cords to the one outlet tucked in the corner of the room, lofting your beds, and negotiating with your roommate over who gets the bigger closet, you had to hug your parents good-bye in the parking lot in front of the entire freshman class— or so it seemed. Now that you are a seasoned pro, you've offered to write some lasting guidelines for future freshmen so they know what is expected of them on moving day.

Your task: Prepare an informational report for future freshmen classes outlining the rules and procedures to follow when moving into a college dorm. Lay out the rules such as starting time, handling trash and empty boxes, items permitted and not permitted in dorm rooms, common courtesies, and so on. Be sure to mention what the policy is for removing furniture from the room, lofting beds, and overloading electrical circuits. Of course, any recommendations on how to handle disputes with roommates would be helpful. So would some brief advice on how to cope with anxious parents. Direct your memo report to the college dean.

INFORMAL ANALYTICAL REPORTS

5. My next career move: Feasibility report organized around recommendations If you've ever given yourself a really good talking-to, you'll be quite comfortable with this project.

Your task: Write a memo report directed to yourself and signed with a fictitious name. Indicate a possible job that your college education will qualify you for, mention the advantages of the position in terms of your long-range goals, and then outline the actions you must take to get the job.

6. Staying the course: Unsolicited proposal using the 2 + 2 = 4 approach Think of a course you would love to see added to the core curriculum at your school. Conversely, if you would like to see a course offered as an elective rather than being required, write your e-mail report accordingly.

Your task: Write a short e-mail proposal using the 2 + 2 = 4 approach. Prepare your proposal to be submitted to the academic dean by e-mail. Be sure to include all the reasons supporting your idea.

7. Planning my program: Problem-solving report using the yardstick method Assume that you will have time for only one course next term.

Your task: List the pros and cons of four or five courses that interest you, and use the yardstick method to settle on the course that is best for you to take at this time. Write your report in memo format, addressing it to your academic adviser.

8. Restaurant review: Troubleshooting report on a restaurant's food and operations Visit any restaurant, possibly your school cafeteria. The workers and fellow customers will assume that you are an ordinary customer, but you are really a spy for the owner.

Your task: After your visit, write a short letter to the owner, explaining (a) what you did and what you observed, (b) any violations of policy that you observed, and (c) your recommendations for improvement. The first part of your report (what you did and what you observed) will be the longest. Include a description of the premises, inside and out. Tell how long it took for each step of ordering and receiving your meal. Describe the service and food thoroughly. You are interested in both the good and bad aspects of the establishment's décor, service, and food. For the second section (violations of policy), use some common sense. If all the servers but one have their hair covered, you may assume that policy requires hair to be covered; a dirty window or restroom obviously violates policy. The last section (recommendations for improvement) involves professional judgment. What management actions will improve the restaurant?

![Portfolio BUILDER]

9. On the books: Troubleshooting report on improving the campus bookstore Imagine that you are a consultant hired to improve the profits of your campus bookstore.

Your task: Visit the bookstore and look critically at its operations. Then draft a letter to the bookstore manager, offering recommendations that would make the store more profitable, perhaps suggesting products it should carry, hours that it should remain open, or added services that it should make available to students. Be sure to support your recommendations.

10. Day and night: Problem-solving report on stocking a 24-hour convenience store When a store is open all day, every day, when's the best time to restock the shelves? That's the challenge at Store 24, a retail chain that never closes. Imagine you're the assistant manager of a Store 24 branch that just opened near your campus. You want to set up a restocking schedule that won't conflict with prime shopping hours. Think about the number of customers you're likely to serve in the morning, afternoon, evening, and overnight hours. Consider, too, how many employees you might have during these four periods.

Your task: Write a problem-solving report in letter form to the store manager (Isabel Chu) and the regional manager (Eric Angstrom), who must agree on a solution to this problem. Discuss the pros and cons of each of the four periods, and include your recommendation for restocking the shelves.

PROPOSALS

![Portfolio BUILDER]

11. "Would you carry it?" Unsolicited sales proposal recommending a product to a retail outlet Select a product you are familiar with, and imagine that you are the manufacturer trying to get a local retail outlet to carry it. Use the Internet and other resources to gather information about the product.

Your task: Write an unsolicited sales proposal in letter format to the owner (or manager) of the store, proposing that the item be stocked. Use the information you gathered to describe some of the product's features and benefits to the store. Then make up some reasonable figures, highlighting what the item costs, what it can be sold for, and what services your company provides (return of unsold items, free replacement of unsatisfactory items, necessary repairs, and so on).

![Portfolio BUILDER]

12. Where is everybody? Proposal to sell GPS fleet tracking system As a sales manager for Air-Trak, one of your responsibilities is writing sales proposals for potential buyers of your company's Cloudberry tracking system. Cloudberry uses the Global Positioning System (GPS) to track the location of vehicles and other

assets. For example, the dispatcher for a trucking company can simply click a map display on a computer screen to find out where all the company's trucks are at that instant. Air-Trak lists the following as benefits of the system:

- Making sure vehicles follow prescribed routes with minimal loitering time
- "Geofencing," in which dispatchers are alerted if vehicles leave
- Route optimization, in which fleet managers can analyze routes and destinations to find the most time- and fuel-efficient path for each vehicle

- Comparisons between scheduled and actual travel
- Enhanced security, protecting both drivers and cargos

Your task: Write a brief proposal to Doneta Zachs, fleet manager for Midwest Express, 338 S.W. 6th, Des Moines, IA 50321. Introduce your company, explain the benefits of the Cloudberry system, and propose a trial deployment in which you would equip five Midwest Express trucks. For the purposes of this assignment, you don't need to worry about the technical details of the system; focus on promoting the benefits and asking for a decision regarding the test project. (You can learn more about the Air-Trak and the Cloudberry system at www.air-trak.com.)[10]

CHAPTER 15

Completing Reports and Proposals

LEARNING OBJECTIVES

After studying this chapter, you will be able to

1 Summarize the four tasks involved in completing business reports and proposals

2 Explain how computers have both simplified and complicated the report-production process

3 Identify the circumstances in which you should include letters of authorization and letters of acceptance in your reports

4 Explain the difference between a synopsis and an executive summary

5 Describe the three supplementary parts of a formal report

6 Identify the major components to include in a request for proposals (RFP)

COMMUNICATION CLOSE-UP AT THE BILL AND MELINDA GATES FOUNDATION

www.gatesfoundation.org

Microsoft co-founder Bill Gates is accustomed to creating change on a global scale, and he now applies the same energy and strategic thinking to charitable causes. Backed by billions of dollars in endowments, the Bill and Melinda Gates Foundation acts as a catalyst, bringing resources together in a way that "increases the momentum, scale, and sustainability of change." The strategy is applied to such important social challenges as containing the AIDS epidemic, eradicating malaria, improving high schools, and making sure people everywhere have access to the digital revolution made possible by the Internet.

Meeting challenges of such staggering complexity and coordinating the resources of organizations all over the world is obviously no small task, and communication plays a vital role in this effort. In particular, reports and proposals link the various groups involved in the foundation's activities and inform the public about ongoing challenges and progress.

The foundation is staffed with people who have demonstrated effective leadership and communication skills, including Patty Stonesifer, a former Microsoft executive, who

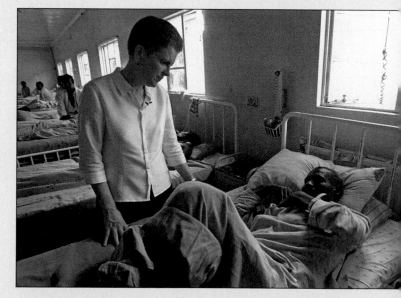

For Patty Stonesifer, co-chair and president of the Bill and Melinda Gates Foundation, much of her communication efforts involve one-on-one conversations with both the people the foundation helps and the researchers who create solutions to health and education challenges. However, written reports and proposals play an equally important role in her work.

serves as chief executive officer. Stonesifer is deeply involved in reports and proposals, both as a writer and a reader. In addition to co-authoring the foundation's annual report, she reads numerous proposals from organizations asking for part of the $1.5 billion the foundation provides every year. The foundation receives some 3,000 formal grant requests every month, and the review process is a thorough one.

Stonesifer examines proposals from various angles, listening to her colleagues' perspectives and asking all sorts of questions: Is this really the best approach? What's going to make the biggest difference? Could this proposal be a catalyst that attracts other organizations to participate?

Stonesifer and her colleagues recognize that they are tackling problems of almost unimaginable complexity, but with systematic thinking, unstoppable optimism, unmatched financial resources, and effective communication skills, they remain committed to improving life for people the world over.[1]

PUTTING THE FINAL TOUCHES ON REPORTS AND PROPOSALS

1 LEARNING OBJECTIVE

Summarize the four tasks involved in completing business reports and proposals

Experienced business communicators such as Patty Stonesifer (profiled in the chapter-opening Communication Close-Up) recognize that the process of writing a report or proposal doesn't end with a first draft. This chapter addresses all four tasks involved in completing longer messages: revising, producing, proofreading, and distributing (see Figure 15.1). Although the tasks covered in this chapter are similar in concept to those you studied for short messages in Chapter 6, the completion stage for reports and proposals can require considerably more work. And as you've probably experienced with school reports already, computers, copiers, and other resources have an uncanny knack for going haywire when you're frantic to finish and have no time to spare. When you're completing an important report on the job, try to leave yourself double or even triple the amount of time you think you'll need so that last-minute glitches don't compromise the quality of all your hard work.

Formal reports have a higher degree of polish and production quality, and they often contain elements not found in informal reports.

Most of the discussion in this chapter applies to *formal* reports and proposals, those documents that require an extra measure of polish and professionalism. Few reports and proposals require every component described in this chapter, but be sure to carefully select the elements you want to include in each of your documents.

FIGURE 15.1 Step Three in the Three-Step Writing Process for Reports
As you prepare to write your report or proposal, allow plenty of time for the four tasks needed to complete your project.

Plan	Write	Complete

1 · **2** · **3**

Revise the Message
Evaluate content and review readability, then edit and rewrite for conciseness and clarity.

Produce the Message
Use effective design elements and suitable layout for a clean, professional appearance; seamlessly combine text and graphical elements.

Proofread the Message
Review for errors in layout, spelling, and mechanics.

Distribute the Message
Deliver your report using the chosen medium; make sure all documents and all relevant files are distributed successfully.

REVISING YOUR REPORTS AND PROPOSALS

The revision process is essentially the same for reports as for any business message, although it may take considerably more time, depending on the length of your document. Evaluate your organization, style, and tone, making sure that you've said what you want to say and that you've said it in the most logical order and in a way that responds to your audience's needs. Then work to improve the report's readability by varying sentence length, keeping paragraphs short, using lists and bullets, and adding headings and subheadings. Keep revising the content until it is clear, concise, and compelling.

Tight, efficient writing that is easy to skim is always a plus, but it's even more important for impatient online audiences.[2] Review online report content carefully; strip out all information that doesn't meet audience needs, and condense everything else as much as possible. Audiences will gladly return to sites that deliver quality information quickly—and they'll avoid sites that don't.

The virtually unlimited graphical and technical possibilities of web design have had the unfortunate side effect of producing too many websites that are too hard to read. You've no doubt visited some of these hard-to-read sites yourself—webpages with backgrounds so busy that you can't make out the words, tiny type that has you reaching for a magnifying glass, quirky fonts that are difficult to read at any size, lines of text that are stretched and wrapped around images, unlabeled graphical hyperlinks that force you to click on them to see what each page is about, and so on. Even when these sites are visually attractive, which isn't often, they fail to meet the primary objective of providing information to the reader.

Web-design expert Dean Allen put it perfectly when he wrote that "the primary goal of communication design is to make vital, engaging work intended above all to be read."[3] As a business writer, you probably won't have the opportunity to do your own website design. Nonetheless, it's a good idea to familiarize yourself with the basics of good and bad design so that you can tell whether your writing is being presented in an effective, user-friendly manner.

Revising for clarity and conciseness is even more important for online reports, because reading online is more difficult.

PRODUCING YOUR REPORTS AND PROPOSALS

Once you are satisfied with your text, you're ready to produce your report by incorporating the design elements discussed in Chapter 6. At this point you should also start to add in charts, graphs, and other visuals, as well as any missing textual elements such as previews and reviews.

In some organizations, you'll be able to rely on the help of specialists in design and production, particularly when you are working on important, high-visibility reports or proposals. You may also have clerical help available to assist with the mechanical assembly and distribution. However, for most reports in many of today's lean-staffed companies, you should count on doing most or all of the production work yourself.

The good news is that computer tools are now generally easy enough for the average businessperson to use productively. A software suite such as Microsoft Office or Word Perfect Office lets you produce reports that incorporate graphics, spreadsheet data, and database records. Even features such as photography are relatively simple these days, with the advent of low-cost digital cameras, color desktop scanners, and photo-quality printers.

The bad news is that continually improving computer tools increase your audience's expectations. People are influenced by packaging, so a handsomely bound report with full-color graphics will impress your audience more than a plain report, even though the two documents may contain the same information. In other words, you may find yourself spending more time on production just to keep up with the competition.

2 LEARNING OBJECTIVE

Explain how computers have both simplified and complicated the report-production process

Components of a Formal Report

The parts you include in a report depend on the type of report you are writing, how long it is, what your audience expects and requires, and what your organization dictates. The components listed in Figure 15.2 fall into three categories, depending on where they are found in a report: prefatory parts, text of the report, and supplementary parts. For an illustration

Length, audience expectations, and organizational traditions all dictate what you should include in a formal report.

FIGURE 15.2 Parts of a Formal Report
Depending on the level of formality you need to achieve, you can select from these elements to complete your formal report.

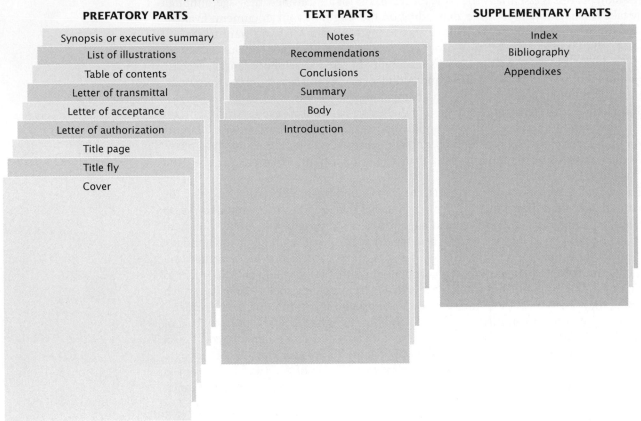

PREFATORY PARTS	TEXT PARTS	SUPPLEMENTARY PARTS
Synopsis or executive summary	Notes	Index
List of illustrations	Recommendations	Bibliography
Table of contents	Conclusions	Appendixes
Letter of transmittal	Summary	
Letter of acceptance	Body	
Letter of authorization	Introduction	
Title page		
Title fly		
Cover		

of how the various parts fit together, see Linda Moreno's Electrovision report in the "Report Writer's Notebook: Analyzing a Formal Report."

Many of the components in a formal report start on a new page, but not always. Inserting page breaks consumes more paper and adds to the bulk of your report. On the other hand, starting a section on a new page helps your readers navigate the report and recognize transitions between major sections or features.

If you want a section to stand out, start it on a new page.

When you want a particular section to stand apart, you'll generally start it on a new page (in the same way that each chapter in this book starts on a new page). Most prefatory parts, such as the table of contents, should also be placed on their own pages. However, the various parts in the report text are often run together. If your introduction is only a paragraph long, don't bother with a page break before moving into the body of your report. If the introduction runs longer than a page, however, a page break can signal the reader that a major shift is about to occur in the flow of the report.

Prefatory Parts

Formal reports can contain a variety of prefatory parts, from a cover page to a synopsis or executive summary.

Prefatory parts are front-end materials that provide key preliminary information so that readers can decide whether and how to read the report.[4] Note that many of these parts—such as the table of contents, list of illustrations, and executive summary—are easier to prepare after the text has been completed, because they directly reflect the contents. When your text is complete, you can also use your word processor to automatically compile the table of contents and the list of illustrations. Other parts can be prepared at almost any time.

Cover Many companies have standard covers for reports, made of heavy paper and imprinted with the company's name and logo. If your company doesn't have such covers, you can usually find something suitable in a good stationery store. Look for a cover that is attractive, convenient, and appropriate to the subject matter. Also, make sure it can be labeled with the report title, the writer's name (optional), and the submission date (also optional).

(Text continues on page 472)

Report Writer's Notebook

Analyzing a Formal Report

The report presented in the following pages was prepared by Linda Moreno, manager of the cost accounting department at Electrovision, a high-tech company based in Los Gatos, California. Electrovision's main product is optical character recognition equipment, which is used by the U.S. Postal Service for sorting mail. Moreno's job is to help analyze the company's costs. She has this to say about the background of the report:

> For the past three or four years, Electrovision has been on a roll. Our A-12 optical character reader was a real breakthrough, and the post office grabbed up as many as we could make. Our sales and profits kept climbing, and morale was fantastic. Everybody seemed to think that the good times would last forever. Unfortunately, everybody was wrong. When the Postal Service announced that it was postponing all new equipment purchases because of cuts in its budget, we woke up to the fact that we are essentially a one-product company with one customer. At that point, management started scrambling around looking for ways to cut costs until we could diversify our business a bit.
>
> The vice president of operations, Dennis McWilliams, asked me to help identify cost-cutting opportunities in travel and entertainment. On the basis of his personal observations, he felt that Electrovision was overly generous in its travel policies and that we might be able to save a significant amount by controlling these costs more carefully. My investigation confirmed his suspicion.
>
> I was reasonably confident that my report would be well received. I've worked with Dennis for several years and know what he likes: plenty of facts, clearly stated conclusions, and specific recommendations for what should be done next. I also knew that my report would be passed on to other Electrovision executives, so I wanted to create a good impression. I wanted the report to be accurate and thorough, visually appealing, readable, and appropriate in tone.

When writing the analytical report that follows, Moreno based the organization on conclusions and recommendations presented in direct order. The first two sections of the report correspond to Moreno's two main conclusions: that Electrovision's travel and entertainment costs are too high and that cuts are essential. The third section presents recommendations for achieving better control over travel and entertainment expenses. As you review the report, analyze both the mechanical aspects and the way Moreno presents her ideas. Be prepared to discuss the way the various components convey and reinforce the main message.

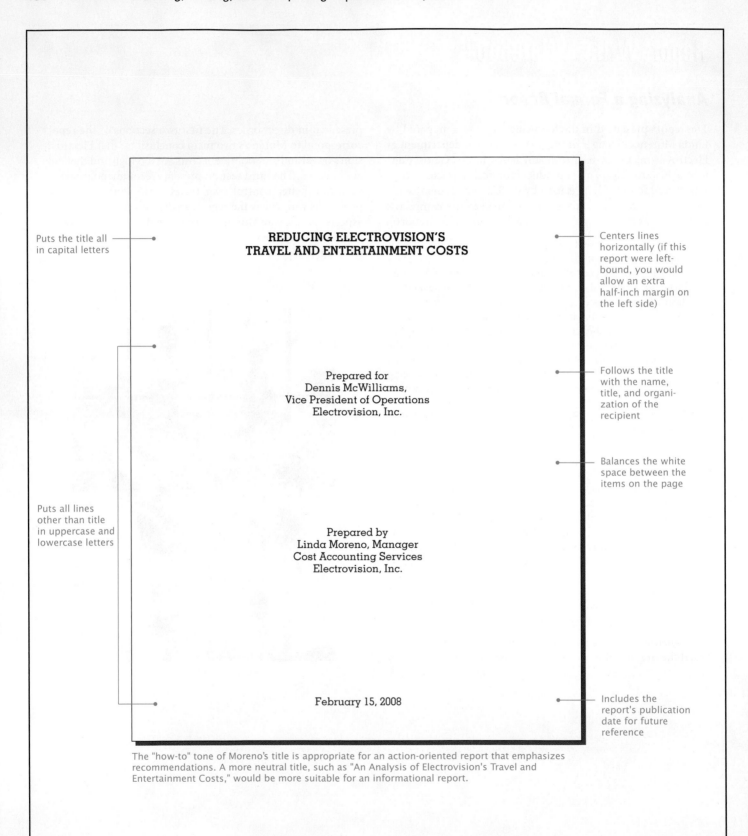

Puts the title all in capital letters

Puts all lines other than title in uppercase and lowercase letters

Centers lines horizontally (if this report were left-bound, you would allow an extra half-inch margin on the left side)

Follows the title with the name, title, and organization of the recipient

Balances the white space between the items on the page

Includes the report's publication date for future reference

**REDUCING ELECTROVISION'S
TRAVEL AND ENTERTAINMENT COSTS**

Prepared for
Dennis McWilliams,
Vice President of Operations
Electrovision, Inc.

Prepared by
Linda Moreno, Manager
Cost Accounting Services
Electrovision, Inc.

February 15, 2008

The "how-to" tone of Moreno's title is appropriate for an action-oriented report that emphasizes recommendations. A more neutral title, such as "An Analysis of Electrovision's Travel and Entertainment Costs," would be more suitable for an informational report.

Uses memo format for transmitting this internal report; otherwise, letter format would be used for transmitting external reports

Uses a conversational style

Acknowledges help that has been received

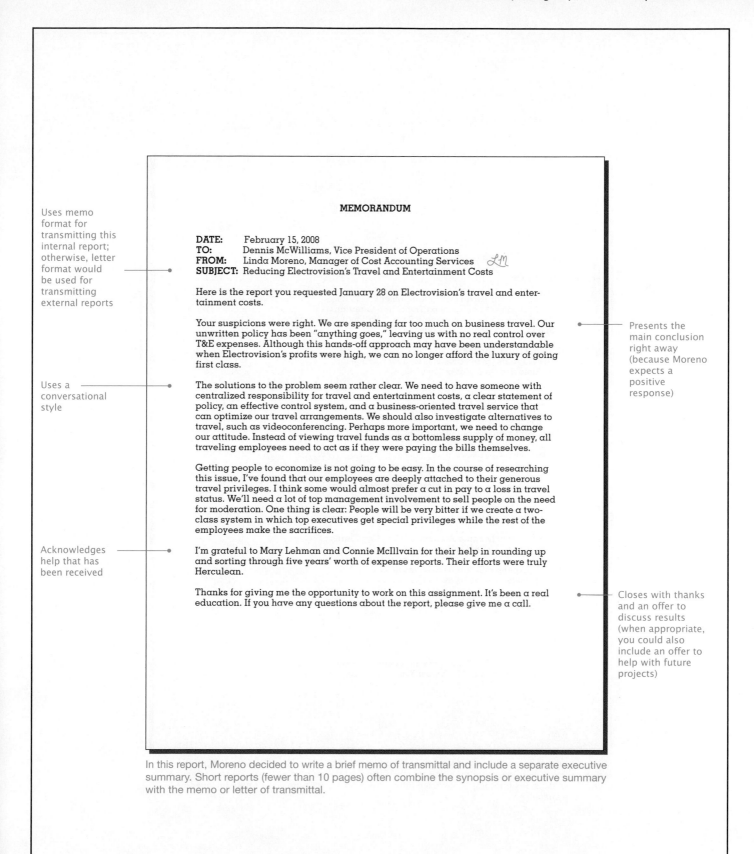

MEMORANDUM

DATE: February 15, 2008
TO: Dennis McWilliams, Vice President of Operations
FROM: Linda Moreno, Manager of Cost Accounting Services *LM*
SUBJECT: Reducing Electrovision's Travel and Entertainment Costs

Here is the report you requested January 28 on Electrovision's travel and entertainment costs.

Your suspicions were right. We are spending far too much on business travel. Our unwritten policy has been "anything goes," leaving us with no real control over T&E expenses. Although this hands-off approach may have been understandable when Electrovision's profits were high, we can no longer afford the luxury of going first class.

The solutions to the problem seem rather clear. We need to have someone with centralized responsibility for travel and entertainment costs, a clear statement of policy, an effective control system, and a business-oriented travel service that can optimize our travel arrangements. We should also investigate alternatives to travel, such as videoconferencing. Perhaps more important, we need to change our attitude. Instead of viewing travel funds as a bottomless supply of money, all traveling employees need to act as if they were paying the bills themselves.

Getting people to economize is not going to be easy. In the course of researching this issue, I've found that our employees are deeply attached to their generous travel privileges. I think some would almost prefer a cut in pay to a loss in travel status. We'll need a lot of top management involvement to sell people on the need for moderation. One thing is clear: People will be very bitter if we create a two-class system in which top executives get special privileges while the rest of the employees make the sacrifices.

I'm grateful to Mary Lehman and Connie McIllvain for their help in rounding up and sorting through five years' worth of expense reports. Their efforts were truly Herculean.

Thanks for giving me the opportunity to work on this assignment. It's been a real education. If you have any questions about the report, please give me a call.

Presents the main conclusion right away (because Moreno expects a positive response)

Closes with thanks and an offer to discuss results (when appropriate, you could also include an offer to help with future projects)

In this report, Moreno decided to write a brief memo of transmittal and include a separate executive summary. Short reports (fewer than 10 pages) often combine the synopsis or executive summary with the memo or letter of transmittal.

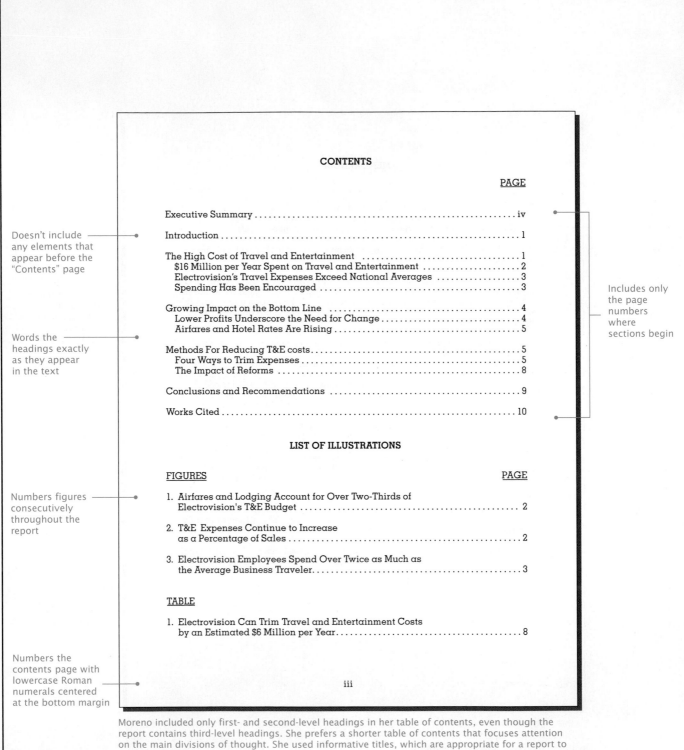

CONTENTS

LIST OF ILLUSTRATIONS

Moreno included only first- and second-level headings in her table of contents, even though the report contains third-level headings. She prefers a shorter table of contents that focuses attention on the main divisions of thought. She used informative titles, which are appropriate for a report to a receptive audience.

Doesn't include any elements that appear before the "Contents" page

Words the headings exactly as they appear in the text

Numbers figures consecutively throughout the report

Numbers the contents page with lowercase Roman numerals centered at the bottom margin

Includes only the page numbers where sections begin

Begins by stating
the purpose of
the report

Presents the points
in the executive
summary (see page
473) in the same
order as they
appear in the
report, using
subheadings
that summarize the
content of the
main sections of
the report

Continues
numbering the
executive
summary pages
with lowercase
Roman numerals

EXECUTIVE SUMMARY

This report analyzes Electrovision's travel and entertainment (T&E) costs and
presents recommendations for reducing those costs.

Travel and Entertainment Costs Are Too High

Travel and entertainment is a large and growing expense category for
Electrovision. The company spends over $16 million per year on business travel,
and these costs have been increasing by 12 percent annually. Company employees
make roughly 3,390 trips each year at an average cost per trip of $4,720. Airfares
are the biggest expense, followed by hotels, meals, and rental cars.

The nature of Electrovision's business does require extensive travel, but the
company's costs are excessive: Our employees spend more than twice the national
average on travel and entertainment. Although the location of the company's
facilities may partly explain this discrepancy, the main reason for our high costs
is a management style that gives employees little incentive to economize.

Cuts Are Essential

Electrovision management now recognizes the need to gain more control over this
element of costs. The company is currently entering a period of declining profits,
prompting management to look for every opportunity to reduce spending. At the
same time, rising airfares and hotel rates are making T&E expenses more significant.

Electrovision Can Save $6 Million per Year

Fortunately, Electrovision has a number of excellent opportunities for reducing
T&E costs. Savings of up to $6 million per year should be achievable, judging by
the experience of other companies. A sensible travel-management program can
save companies as much as 35 percent a year (Gilligan 39–40), and we should be
able to save even more, since we purchase many more business-class tickets than
the average. Four steps will help us cut costs:

1. Hire a director of travel and entertainment to assume overall responsibility for
   T&E spending, policies, and technologies, including the hiring and
   management of a national travel agency.
2. Educate employees on the need for cost containment, both in avoiding
   unnecessary travel and reducing costs when travel is necessary.
3. Negotiate preferential rates with travel providers.
4. Implement technological alternatives to travel, such as virtual meetings.

As necessary as these changes are, they will likely hurt morale, at least in the
short term. Management will need to make a determined effort to explain the
rationale for reduced spending. By exercising moderation in their own travel
arrangements, Electrovision executives can set a good example and help other
employees accept the changes. On the plus side, using travel alternatives such as
web conferencing will reduce the travel burden on many employees and help
them balance their business and personal lives.

iv

Targets a receptive
audience with a
hard-hitting tone in
the executive
summary (a more
neutral approach
would be better for
hostile or skeptical
readers)

Executive summary
uses the same font
and paragraph
treatment as the
text of the report

Moreno decided to include an executive summary because her report is aimed at a mixed
audience, some of whom are interested in the details of her report and others who just want the
"big picture." The executive summary is aimed at the second group, giving them enough information to make a decision without burdening them with the task of reading the entire report.

Her writing style matches the serious nature of the content without sounding distant or stiff.
Moreno chose the formal approach because several members of her audience are considerably
higher up in the organization, and she did not want to sound too familiar. In addition, her
company prefers the impersonal style for formal reports.

**REDUCING ELECTROVISION'S
TRAVEL AND ENTERTAINMENT COSTS**

INTRODUCTION

Electrovision has always encouraged a significant amount of business travel.
To compensate employees for the stress and inconvenience of frequent trips,
management has authorized generous travel and entertainment (T&E) allowances.
This philosophy has been good for morale, but last year Electrovision spent
$16 million on travel and entertainment—$7 million more than it spent on research
and development.

This year's T&E costs will affect profits even more, due to increases in airline fares
and hotel rates. Also, the company anticipates that profits will be relatively weak
for a variety of other reasons. Therefore, Dennis McWilliams, Vice President of
Operations, has asked the accounting department to explore ways to reduce the
T&E budget.

The purpose of this report is to analyze T&E expenses, evaluate the effect of recent
hotel and airfare increases, and suggest ways to tighten control over T&E costs.
The report outlines several steps that could reduce Electrovision's expenses, but
the precise financial impact of these measures is difficult to project. The estimates
presented here provide a "best guess" view of what Electrovision can expect
to save.

In preparing this report, the accounting department analyzed internal expense
reports for the past five years to determine how much Electrovision spends on
travel and entertainment. These figures were then compared with average
statistics compiled by Dow Jones (publisher of the *Wall Street Journal*) and
presented as the Dow Jones Travel Index. We also analyzed trends and
suggestions published in a variety of business journal articles to see how other
companies are coping with the high cost of business travel.

THE HIGH COST OF TRAVEL AND ENTERTAINMENT

Although many companies view travel and entertainment as an incidental cost of
doing business, the dollars add up. At Electrovision the bill for airfares, hotels,
rental cars, meals, and entertainment totaled $16 million last year. Our T&E budget
has increased by 12 percent per year for the past five years. Compared to the
average U.S. business traveler, Electrovision's expenditures are high, largely
because of management's generous policy on travel benefits.

In her brief introduction, Moreno counts on topic sentences and transitions to indicate that she is
discussing the purpose, scope, and limitations of the study.

2

Uses Arabic numerals to number the second and succeeding pages of the text in the upper right-hand corner where the top and right-hand margins meet

$16 Million per Year Spent on Travel and Entertainment

Electrovision's annual budget for travel and entertainment is only 8 percent of sales. Because this is a relatively small expense category compared with such things as salaries and commissions, it is tempting to dismiss T&E costs as insignificant. However, T&E is Electrovision's third-largest controllable expense, directly behind salaries and information systems.

Last year Electrovision personnel made about 3,390 trips at an average cost per trip of $4,720. The typical trip involved a round-trip flight of 3,000 miles, meals, and hotel accommodations for two or three days, and a rental car. Roughly 80 percent of trips were made by 20 percent of the staff—top management and sales personnel traveled most, averaging 18 trips per year.

Figure 1 illustrates how the T&E budget is spent. The largest categories are airfares and lodging, which together account for $7 out of $10 that employees spend on travel and entertainment. This spending breakdown has been relatively steady for the past five years and is consistent with the distribution of expenses experienced by other companies.

Places the visual as close as possible to the point it illustrates

Figure 1
Airfares and Lodging Account for Over
Two-Thirds of Electrovision's T&E Budget

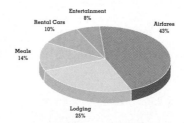

Although the composition of the T&E budget has been consistent, its size has not. As mentioned earlier, these expenditures have increased by about 12 percent per year for the past five years, roughly twice the rate of the company's sales growth (see Figure 2). This rate of growth makes T&E Electrovision's fastest-growing expense item.

Gives each visual a title that clearly indicates what it's about; titles are consistently placed to the left of each visual

Figure 2
T&E Expenses Continue to Increase as a
Percentage of Sales

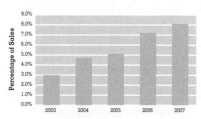

Moreno opens the first main section of the body with a topic sentence that introduces an important fact about the subject of the section. Then she orients the reader to the three major points developed in the section.

3

Electrovision's Travel Expenses Exceed National Averages

Much of our travel budget is justified. Two major factors contribute to Electrovision's high T&E budget:

- With our headquarters on the West Coast and our major customer on the East Coast, we naturally spend a lot of money on cross-country flights.

- A great deal of travel takes place between our headquarters here on the West Coast and the manufacturing operations in Detroit, Boston, and Dallas. Corporate managers and division personnel make frequent trips to coordinate these disparate operations.

However, even though a good portion of Electrovision's travel budget is justifiable, the company spends considerably more on T&E than the average business traveler (see Figure 3).

Figure 3
Electrovision Employees Spend Over Twice as Much as the Average Business Traveler

Source: *Wall Street Journal* and company records

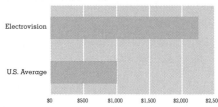

Dollars Spent per Day

The Dow Jones Travel Index calculates the average cost per day of business travel in the United States, based on average airfare, hotel rates, and rental car rates. The average fluctuates weekly as travel companies change their rates, but it has been running at about $1,000 per day for the last year or so. In contrast, Electrovision's average daily expense over the past year has been $2,250—a hefty 125 percent higher than average. This figure is based on the average trip cost of $4,720 listed earlier and an average trip length of 2.1 days.

Spending Has Been Encouraged

Although a variety of factors may contribute to this differential, Electrovision's relatively high T&E costs are at least partially attributable to the company's philosophy and management style. Since many employees do not enjoy business travel, management has tried to make the trips more pleasant by authorizing business-class airfare, luxury hotel accommodations, and full-size rental cars. The sales staff is encouraged to entertain clients at top restaurants and to invite them to cultural and sporting events.

Numbers the visuals consecutively and refers to them in the text by their numbers

Introduces visuals before they appear and indicates what readers should notice about the data

The chart in Figure 3 is simple but effective; Moreno includes just enough data to make her point. Notice how she is as careful about the appearance of her report as she is about the quality of its content.

4

Uses a bulleted list to make it easy for readers to identify and distinguish related points

Leaves an extra line of white space above headings to help readers associate each heading with the text it describes

Uses informative headings to focus reader attention on the main points (such headings are appropriate when a report uses direct order and is intended for a receptive audience; however, descriptive headings are more effective when a report is in indirect order and readers are less receptive)

The cost of these privileges is easy to overlook, given the weakness of Electrovision's system for keeping track of T&E expenses:

- The monthly financial records do not contain a separate category for travel and entertainment; the information is buried under Cost of Goods Sold and under Selling, General, and Administrative Expenses.

- Each department head is given authority to approve any expense report, regardless of how large it may be.

- Receipts are not required for expenditures of less than $100.

- Individuals are allowed to make their own travel arrangements.

- No one is charged with the responsibility for controlling the company's total spending on travel and entertainment.

GROWING IMPACT ON THE BOTTOM LINE

During the past three years, the company's healthy profits have resulted in relatively little pressure to push for tighter controls over all aspects of the business. However, as we all know, the situation is changing. We're projecting flat to declining profits for the next two years, a situation that has prompted all of us to search for ways to cut costs. At the same time, rising airfares and hotel rates have increased the impact of T&E expenses on the company's financial results.

Lower Profits Underscore the Need for Change

The next two years promise to be difficult for Electrovision. After several years of steady increases in spending, the Postal Service is tightening procurement policies for automated mail-handling equipment. Funding for the A-12 optical character reader has been canceled. As a consequence, the marketing department expects sales to drop by 15 percent. Although Electrovision is negotiating several other promising R&D contracts, the marketing department does not foresee any major procurements for the next two to three years.

At the same time, Electrovision is facing cost increases on several fronts. As we have known for several months, the new production facility now under construction in Salt Lake City, Utah, is behind schedule and over budget. Labor contracts in Boston and Dallas will expire within the next six months, and plant managers there anticipate that significant salary and benefits concessions may be necessary to avoid strikes.

Moreover, marketing and advertising costs are expected to increase as we attempt to strengthen these activities to better cope with competitive pressures. Given the expected decline in revenues and increase in costs, the Executive Committee's prediction that profits will fall by 12 percent in the coming fiscal year does not seem overly pessimistic.

Moreno designed her report to include plenty of white space so even those pages that lack visuals are still attractive and easy to read.

5

Airfares and Hotel Rates Are Rising

Business travelers have grown accustomed to frequent fare wars and discounting in the travel industry in recent years. Excess capacity and aggressive price competition, particularly in the airline business, made travel a relative bargain.

However, that situation has changed as weaker competitors have been forced out and the remaining players have grown stronger and smarter. Airlines and hotels are better at managing inventory and keeping occupancy rates high, which translates into higher costs for Electrovision. Last year saw some of the steepest rate hikes in years. Business airfares (tickets most likely to be purchased by business travelers) jumped more than 40 percent in many markets. The trend is expected to continue, with rates increasing another 5 to 10 percent overall (Phillips 331; "Travel Costs Under Pressure" 30; Dahl B6).

Given the fact that air and hotel costs account for 70 percent of our T&E budget, the trend toward higher prices in these two categories will have serious consequences, unless management takes action to control these costs.

METHODS FOR REDUCING T&E COSTS

By implementing a number of reforms, management can expect to reduce Electrovision's T&E budget by as much as 40 percent. This estimate is based on the general assessment made by American Express (Gilligan 39) and on the fact that we have an opportunity to significantly reduce air travel costs by eliminating business-class travel. However, these measures are likely to be unpopular with employees. To gain acceptance for such changes, management will need to sell employees on the need for moderation in T&E allowances.

Four Ways to Trim Expenses

By researching what other companies are doing to curb T&E expenses, the accounting department has identified four prominent opportunities that should enable Electrovision to save about $6 million annually in travel-related costs.

Institute Tighter Spending Controls

A single individual should be appointed director of travel and entertainment to spearhead the effort to gain control of the T&E budget. More than a third of all U.S. companies now employ travel managers ("Businesses Use Savvy Managers" 4). The director should be familiar with the travel industry and should be well versed in both accounting and information technology. The director should also report to the vice president of operations. The director's first priorities should be to establish a written T&E policy and a cost-control system.

Electrovision currently has no written policy on travel and entertainment, a step that is widely recommended by air travel experts (Smith D4). Creating a policy

---

Documents the facts to add weight to Moreno's argument

Gives recommendations an objective flavor by pointing out both the benefits and the risks of taking action

---

Moreno creates a forceful tone by using action verbs in the third-level subheadings of this section. This approach is appropriate to the nature of the study and the attitude of the audience. However, in a status-conscious organization, the imperative verbs might sound a bit too presumptuous coming from a junior member of the staff.

6

would clarify management's position and serve as a vehicle for communicating the need for moderation. At a minimum, the policy should include the following:

- All travel and entertainment should be strictly related to business and should be approved in advance.

- Except under special circumstances to be approved on a case-by-case basis, employees should travel by coach and stay in mid-range business hotels.

- The T&E policy should apply equally to employees at all levels.

To implement the new policy, Electrovision will need to create a system for controlling T&E expenses. Each department should prepare an annual T&E budget as part of its operating plan. These budgets should be presented in detail so that management can evaluate how T&E dollars will be spent and can recommend appropriate cuts. To help management monitor performance relative to these budgets, the director of travel should prepare monthly financial statements showing actual T&E expenditures by department.

The director of travel should also be responsible for retaining a business-oriented travel service that will schedule all employee business trips and look for the best travel deals, particularly in airfares. In addition to centralizing Electrovision's reservation and ticketing activities, the agency will negotiate reduced group rates with hotels and rental car firms. The agency selected should have offices nationwide so that all Electrovision facilities can channel their reservations through the same company. This is particularly important in light of the dizzying array of often wildly different airfares available between some cities. It's not uncommon to find dozens of fares along commonly traveled routes (Rowe 30). In addition, the director can help coordinate travel across the company to secure group discounts whenever possible (Barker 31; Miller B6).

Reduce Unnecessary Travel and Entertainment

One of the easiest ways to reduce expenses is to reduce the amount of traveling and entertaining that occurs. An analysis of last year's expenditures suggests that as much as 30 percent of Electrovision's travel and entertainment is discretionary. The professional staff spent $2.8 million attending seminars and conferences last year. Although these gatherings are undoubtedly beneficial, the company could save money by sending fewer representatives to each function and perhaps by eliminating some of the less valuable seminars.

Similarly, Electrovision could economize on trips between headquarters and divisions by reducing the frequency of such visits and by sending fewer people on each trip. Although there is often no substitute for face-to-face meetings, management could try to resolve more internal issues through telephone, electronic, and written communication.

Electrovision can also reduce spending by urging employees to economize. Instead of flying business class, employees can fly coach class or take advantage

---

Breaks up text with bulleted lists, which not only call attention to important points but also add visual interest

Specifies the steps required to implement recommendations

Moreno takes care not to overstep the boundaries of her analysis. For instance, she doesn't analyze the value of the seminars that employees attend every year, so she avoids any absolute statements about reducing travel to seminars.

7

of discount fares. Rather than ordering a $50 bottle of wine, employees can select a less expensive bottle or dispense with alcohol entirely. People can book rooms at moderately priced hotels and drive smaller rental cars.

Obtain Lowest Rates from Travel Providers

Apart from urging employees to economize, Electrovision can also save money by searching for the lowest available airfares, hotel rates, and rental car fees. Currently, few employees have the time or knowledge to seek out travel bargains. When they need to travel, they make the most convenient and comfortable arrangements. A professional travel service will be able to obtain lower rates from travel providers.

Judging by the experience of other companies, Electrovision may be able to trim as much as 30 to 40 percent from the travel budget simply by looking for bargains in airfares and negotiating group rates with hotels and rental car companies. Electrovision should be able to achieve these economies by analyzing its travel patterns, identifying frequently visited locations, and selecting a few hotels that are willing to reduce rates in exchange for guaranteed business. At the same time, the company should be able to save up to 40 percent on rental car charges by negotiating a corporate rate.

The possibilities for economizing are promising; however, making the best travel arrangements often requires trade-offs such as the following:

- The best fares might not always be the lowest. Indirect flights are usually cheaper, but they take longer and may end up costing more in lost work time.

- The cheapest tickets often require booking 14 or even 30 days in advance, which is often impossible for us.

- Discount tickets are usually nonrefundable, which is a serious drawback when a trip needs to be canceled at the last minute.

Replace Travel with Technological Alternatives

Less-expensive travel options promise significant savings, but the biggest cost reductions over the long term might come from replacing travel with virtual meeting technology. Both analysts and corporate users say that the early kinks that hampered online meetings have largely been worked out, and the latest systems are fast, easy to learn, and easy to use (Solheim 26). For example, Webex (a leading provider of webconferencing services) offers everything from simple, impromptu team meetings to major online events with up to 3,000 participants ("Online Meeting Solutions").

One of the first responsibilities of the new travel director should be an evaluation of these technologies and a recommendation for integrating them throughout Electrovision's operations.

Points out possible difficulties to show that all angles have been considered and to build confidence in her judgment

Note how Moreno makes the transition from section to section. The first sentence under the second heading on this page refers to the subject of the previous paragraph and signals a shift in thought.

8

The Impact of Reforms

By implementing tighter controls, reducing unnecessary expenses, negotiating more favorable rates, and exploring alternatives to travel, Electrovision should be able to reduce its T&E budget significantly. As Table 1 illustrates, the combined savings should be in the neighborhood of $6 million, although the precise figures are somewhat difficult to project.

Table 1
Electrovision Can Trim Travel and Entertainment Costs
by an Estimated $6 Million per Year

SOURCE OF SAVINGS	ESTIMATED SAVINGS
Switching from business-class to coach airfare	$2,300,000
Negotiating preferred hotel rates	940,000
Negotiating preferred rental car rates	460,000
Systematically searching for lower airfares	375,000
Reducing interdivisional travel	675,000
Reducing seminar and conference attendance	1,250,000
TOTAL POTENTIAL SAVINGS	**$6,000,000**

To achieve the economies outlined in the table, Electrovision will incur expenses for hiring a director of travel and for implementing a T&E cost-control system. These costs are projected at $115,000: $105,000 per year in salary and benefits for the new employee and a one-time expense of $10,000 for the cost-control system. The cost of retaining a full-service travel agency is negligible, even with the service fees that many are now passing along from airlines and other service providers.

The measures required to achieve these savings are likely to be unpopular with employees. Electrovision personnel are accustomed to generous T&E allowances, and they are likely to resent having these privileges curtailed. To alleviate their disappointment

- Management should make a determined effort to explain why the changes are necessary.

- The director of corporate communication should be asked to develop a multifaceted campaign that will communicate the importance of curtailing T&E costs.

- Management should set a positive example by adhering strictly to the new policies.

- The limitations should apply equally to employees at all levels in the organization.

Uses informative title in the table, which is consistent with the way headings are handled in this report and is appropriate for a report to a receptive audience

Uses complete sentence to help readers focus immediately on the point of the table

Includes financial estimates to help management envision the impact of the suggestions, even though estimated savings are difficult to project

Note how Moreno calls attention in the first paragraph to items in the following table, without repeating the information in the table.

9

Uses a descriptive heading for the last section of the text (in informational reports, this section is often called "Summary"; in analytical reports, it is called "Conclusions" or "Conclusions and Recommendations")

CONCLUSIONS AND RECOMMENDATIONS

Electrovision is currently spending $16 million per year on travel and entertainment. Although much of this spending is justified, the company's costs are high relative to competitors' costs, mainly because Electrovision has been generous with its travel benefits.

Electrovision's liberal approach to travel and entertainment was understandable during years of high profitability; however, the company is facing the prospect of declining profits for the next several years. Management is therefore motivated to cut costs in all areas of the business. Reducing T&E spending is particularly important because the bottom-line impact of these costs will increase as airline fares increase.

Summarizes conclusions in the first two paragraphs—a good approach because Moreno organized her report around conclusions and recommendations, so readers have already been introduced to them

Electrovision should be able to reduce T&E costs by as much as 40 percent by taking four important steps:

Emphasizes the recommendations by presenting them in list format

1. *Institute tighter spending controls.* Management should hire a director of travel and entertainment who will assume overall responsibility for T&E activities. Within the next six months, this director should develop a written travel policy, institute a T&E budget and a cost-control system, and retain a professional, business-oriented travel agency that will optimize arrangements with travel providers.

2. *Reduce unnecessary travel and entertainment.* Electrovision should encourage employees to economize on T&E spending. Management can accomplish this by authorizing fewer trips and by urging employees to be more conservative in their spending.

3. *Obtain lowest rates from travel providers.* Electrovision should also focus on obtaining the best rates on airline tickets, hotel rooms, and rental cars. By channeling all arrangements through a professional travel agency, the company can optimize its choices and gain clout in negotiating preferred rates.

4. *Replace travel with technological alternatives.* With the number of computers already installed in our facilities, it seems likely that we could take advantage of desktop videoconferencing and other distance-meeting tools. Technological alternatives won't be quite as feasible with customer sites, since these systems require compatible equipment at both ends of a connection, but such systems are certainly a possibility for communication with Electrovision's own sites.

Because these measures may be unpopular with employees, management should make a concerted effort to explain the importance of reducing travel costs. The director of corporate communication should be given responsibility for developing a plan to communicate the need for employee cooperation.

Moreno doesn't introduce any new facts in this section. In a longer report she might have divided this section into subsections, labeled "Conclusions" and "Recommendations," to distinguish between the two.

10

WORKS CITED

Barker, Julie. "How to Rein in Group Travel Costs." *Successful Meetings* Feb. 2004: 31.

"Businesses Use Savvy Managers to Keep Travel Costs Down." *Christian Science Monitor* 17 July 2004: 4.

Dahl, Jonathan. "2000: The Year Travel Costs Took Off." *Wall Street Journal* 29 Dec. 2004: B6.

Gilligan, Edward P. "Trimming Your T&E Is Easier Than You Think." *Managing Office Technology* Nov. 2004: 39–40.

Miller, Lisa. "Attention, Airline Ticket Shoppers." *Wall Street Journal* 7 July 2004: B6.

"Meet With Anyone, Anywhere, Anytime, "*Webex.com*. 2006. WebEx, 15 November 2006, <http://www.webex.com/solutions/online-meeting-suc.html>.

Phillips, Edward H. "Airlines Post Record Traffic." *Aviation Week & Space Technology* 8 Jan. 2005: 331.

Rowe, Irene Vlitos. "Global Solution for Cutting Travel Costs." *European* 12 Oct. 2004: 30.

Smith, Carol. "Rising, Erratic Airfares Make Company Policy Vital." *Los Angeles Times* 2 Nov. 2004: D4.

Solheim, Shelley. "Web Conferencing Made Easy." *eWeek* 22 Aug. 2005: 26.

"Travel Costs Under Pressure." *Purchasing* 15 Feb. 2004: 30.

Lists references alphabetically by the author's last name, and when the author is unknown, by the title of the reference (see Appendix B for additional details on preparing reference lists)

Moreno's list of references follows the style recommended in The MLA Style Manual. The box below shows how these sources would be cited following APA style.

10

REFERENCES

Barker, J. (2004, February). How to rein in group travel costs. *Successful Meetings*, 31.

Businesses use savvy managers to keep travel costs down. (2004, July 17). *Christian Science Monitor*, 4.

Dahl, J. (2004, December 29). 2000: The year travel costs took off. *Wall Street Journal*, B6.

Gilligan, E. (2004, November). Trimming your T&E is easier than you think. *Managing Office Technology*, 39–40.

Miller, L. (2004, July 7). Attention, airline ticket shoppers. *Wall Street Journal*, B6.

Phillips, E. (2005, January 8). Airlines post record traffic. *Aviation Week & Space Technology*, 331.

Rowe, I. (2004, October 12). Global solution for cutting travel costs. *European*, 30.

Smith, C. (2004, November 2). Rising, erratic airfares make company policy vital. *Los Angeles Times*, D4.

Solheim, S. (2005, August 22). Web conferencing made easy. *eWeek*, 26.

Travel costs under pressure. (2004, February 15). *Purchasing*, 30.

Webex.com. (2006). *Meet With Anyone, Anywhere, Anytime*. Retrieved 15 November 2006, from http://www.webex.com/solutions/online-meeting-suc.html.

Think carefully about the title you put on the cover. A business report is not a mystery novel, so give your readers all the information they need: the who, what, when, where, why, and how of the subject. At the same time, try to be concise. You can reduce the length of your title by eliminating phrases such as *A Report of*, *A Study of*, or *A Survey of*.

Title Fly and Title Page   The **title fly** is a single sheet of paper with only the title of the report on it. You don't really need one, but it adds a touch of formality. The **title page** includes four blocks of information: (1) the title of the report; (2) the name, title, and address of the person, group, or organization that authorized the report (if anyone); (3) the name, title, and address of the person, group, or organization that prepared the report; and (4) the date on which the report was submitted. On some title pages the second block of information is preceded by the words *Prepared for* or *Submitted to*, and the third block of information is preceded by *Prepared by* or *Submitted by*. In some cases the title page serves as the cover of the report, especially if the report is relatively short and is intended solely for internal use.

3 LEARNING OBJECTIVE

Identify the circumstances in which you should include letters of authorization and letters of acceptance in your reports

A letter of authorization is the document that instructed you to produce a report; a letter of acceptance is your written agreement to produce the report.

A letter or memo of transmittal introduces your report to your audience.

Letter of Authorization and Letter of Acceptance   If you received written authorization to prepare the report, you may want to include that letter or memo in your report. This **letter of authorization** (or *memo of authorization*) is a document you received, asking or directing you to prepare the report. If you wrote a **letter of acceptance** (or *memo of acceptance*) in response to that communication, accepting the assignment and clarifying any conditions or limitations, you might also include that letter here in the report's prefatory parts. If there is any chance that your report might not meet your audience's expectations, the letter of acceptance can remind your readers what you agreed to do and why.

In general, the letters of authorization and acceptance are included in only the most formal reports. However, in any case in which a significant amount of time has passed since you received the letter of authorization, or you do not have a close working relationship with the audience, consider including both letters to make sure everyone is clear about the report's intent and the approach you took to create it. You don't want your weeks or months of work to be diminished by any such misunderstandings.

Letter of Transmittal   The **letter of transmittal** (or *memo of transmittal*), a specialized form of a cover letter, introduces your report to your audience. The letter of transmittal says what you'd say if you were handing the report directly to the person who authorized it, so the style is often less formal than the rest of the report.

The transmittal letter usually appears right before the table of contents. If your report will be widely distributed, however, you may decide to include the letter of transmittal only in selected copies so that you can make certain comments to a specific audience. If your report discusses layoffs or other issues that affect people in the organization, you might want to discuss your recommendations privately in a letter of transmittal to top management. If your audience is likely to be skeptical of or even hostile to something in your report, the transmittal letter is a good opportunity to acknowledge their concerns and explain how the report addresses the issues they care about.

Depending on the nature of your report, your letter of transmittal can follow either the direct approach for routine or positive messages described in Chapter 8 or the indirect approach for negative messages described in Chapter 9. Open by officially conveying the report to your readers and summarizing its purpose. Such a letter typically begins with a statement such as "Here is the report you asked me to prepare on. . . ." The rest of the introduction includes information about the scope of the report, the methods used to complete the study, limitations, and any special messages you need to convey. For instance, in Patty Stonesifer's introduction to a recent Gates Foundation annual report, she began by explaining that while annual reports usually cover an organization's own accomplishments for the prior year, she wanted to focus on the good work that the foundation's partners had done instead.[5]

In the body of the transmittal letter, you may also highlight important points or sections of the report, make comments on side issues, give suggestions for follow-up studies, and offer any details that will help readers understand and use the report. You may also want to acknowledge help given by others. The conclusion of the transmittal letter often includes a note of thanks for having been given the report assignment, an expression of willingness to discuss the report, and an offer to assist with future projects.

If the report does not have a synopsis, the letter of transmittal may summarize the major findings, conclusions, and recommendations. This material would be placed after the opening of the letter.

If you don't include a synopsis, you can summarize the report's content in your letter of transmittal.

Table of Contents   The table of contents (usually titled simply "Contents") indicates in outline form the coverage, sequence, and relative importance of the information in the report. The headings used in the text of the report are the basis for the table of contents. Depending on the length and complexity of the report, you may need to decide how many levels of headings to show in the contents; it's a trade-off between simplicity and completeness. Contents that show only first-level heads are easy to scan but could frustrate people looking for specific subsections in the report. Conversely, contents that show every level of heading—down to fourth or fifth level in detailed reports—identify all the sections but can intimidate readers and blur the focus by detracting from your most important message points. Where the detailed table of contents could have dozens or even hundreds of entries, consider including two tables: a high-level table that shows only major headings, followed by a detailed table that includes everything (as this and many other textbooks do). No matter how many levels you include, make sure readers can easily distinguish between them.

Also, take extra care to verify that your table of contents is accurate, consistent, and complete. Even minor errors could damage your credibility if readers turn to a given page expecting to find something that isn't there, of if they find headings that seem similar to those in the table of contents but aren't worded quite the same. To ensure accuracy, construct the table of contents after your report is complete, thoroughly edited, and proofed. This way, the headings and subheadings aren't likely to change or move from page to page. And if at all possible, use the automatic features in your word processor to generate the table of contents. Doing so helps improve accuracy by eliminating typing mistakes, and it keeps your table current in the event you do have to repaginate or revise headings late in the process.

To save time and reduce errors, use the table of contents generator in your word processor.

List of Illustrations   If you have more than a handful of illustrations in your report, or if you want to call attention to your illustrations, include a list of illustrations after the table of contents. For simplicity's sake, some reports refer to all visuals as *illustrations* or *exhibits*. In other reports, as in Moreno's Electrovision report, tables are labeled separately from other types of visuals, which are called *figures*. Regardless of the system you use, be sure to include titles and page numbers.

If you have enough space on a single page, include the list of illustrations directly beneath the table of contents. Otherwise, put the list on the page after the contents page. When tables and figures are numbered separately, they should also be listed separately.

Synopsis or Executive Summary   A **synopsis** is a brief overview (one page or less) of a report's most important points, designed to give readers a quick preview of the contents (see Figure 15.3). It's often included in long informational reports dealing with technical, professional, or academic subjects and can also be called an **abstract**. Because it's a concise representation of the whole report, it may be distributed separately to a wide audience; then interested readers can request a copy of the entire report. Think carefully about the wording of your synopsis or abstract. Not only does it establish readers' expectations for the entire report, but this piece of text might also be indexed as a separate entry in databases.

A synopsis is a brief preview of the most important points in your report.

The phrasing of a synopsis can be either informative or descriptive. An informative synopsis presents the main points of the report in the order in which they appear in the text. A descriptive synopsis, on the other hand, simply tells what the report is about, using only moderately greater detail than the table of contents; the actual findings of the report are omitted. Here are examples of statements from each type:

INFORMATIVE SYNOPSIS	DESCRIPTIVE SYNOPSIS
Sales of super-premium ice cream make up 11 percent of the total ice cream market.	This report contains information about super-premium ice cream and its share of the market.

FIGURE 15.3 Report Synopsis
The introductory page of this online brochure serves as a synopsis, giving readers a brief overview of the main points covered. Those who want more information can click on the "Details" link to the left to get additional information.

The way you handle a synopsis reflects the approach you use in the text. If you're using an indirect approach in your report, you're better off with a descriptive synopsis, because an informative synopsis "gives away the ending" of your report. No matter which type of synopsis you use, be sure to present an accurate picture of the report's contents.[6]

Many business report writers prefer to include an **executive summary** instead of a synopsis or an abstract. Whereas a synopsis is a prose table of contents that outlines the main points of the report, an executive summary is a fully developed "mini" version of the report itself. Executive summaries are more comprehensive than a synopsis; many contain headings, well-developed transitions, and even visual elements. They are usually organized in the same way as the report, using a direct or an indirect approach, depending on the audience's receptivity.

Executive summaries are intended for readers who lack the time or motivation to study the complete text. As a general rule, keep the length of an executive summary proportionate to the length of the report. A brief business report may have only a one-page or shorter executive summary. Longer business reports may have a two- or three-page summary. Anything longer, however, might cease to be a summary.[7]

Many reports require neither a synopsis nor an executive summary. Length is usually the determining factor. Most reports of fewer than 10 pages either omit such a preview or combine it with the letter of transmittal. However, if your report is over 20 or 30 pages long, you'll probably want to include either a synopsis or an executive summary as a convenience for readers. Which one you'll provide depends on the traditions of your organization.

Text of the Report

Although reports may contain a variety of components, the heart of a report is always composed of three main parts: an introduction, a body, and a close (which may consist of a summary, conclusions, or recommendations, or some combination of the three). As Chapter 13 points out, the length and content of each of these parts vary with the length and type of re-

---

4 LEARNING OBJECTIVE

Explain the difference between a synopsis and an executive summary

---

No matter how many separate elements are in a formal report, the heart of the report is still the introduction, body, and close.

port, the organizational structure, and the reader's familiarity with the topic. Following is a brief review of the three major parts of the report text.

Introduction   A good introduction prepares your readers to follow and comprehend the information that follows. It invites audience members to continue reading by telling them what the report is about, why they should be concerned, and how the report is organized. If your report has a synopsis or an executive summary, minimize redundancy by balancing the introduction with the material in your summary—as Linda Moreno does in her Electrovision report. For example, Moreno's executive summary is fairly detailed, so she keeps her introduction brief. If you believe that your introduction needs to repeat information that has already been covered in one of the prefatory parts, try to vary the wording to minimize the feeling of repetition.

Body   This section contains the information that supports your conclusions and recommendations as well as your analysis, logic, and interpretation of the information. See the body of Linda Moreno's Electrovision report for an example of the types of supporting details commonly included in this section. Pay close attention to her effective use of visuals. Most inexperienced writers have a tendency to include too much data in their reports or place too much data in paragraph format instead of using tables and charts. Such treatment increases the chance of boring or losing an audience. If you find yourself with too much information, include only the essential supporting data in the body, use visuals, and place any additional information in an appendix.

Close   The close of your report should summarize your main ideas, highlight your conclusions or recommendations (if any), and list any courses of action that you expect readers to take or that you will be taking yourself. In a long report, this section may be labeled "Summary" or "Conclusions and Recommendations." If you have organized your report in a direct pattern, your close should be relatively brief, like Linda Moreno's. With an indirect organization, you may be using this section to present your conclusions and recommendations for the first time, in which case this section might be fairly extensive.

Supplementary Parts

Supplementary parts follow the text of the report and provide information for readers who seek more detailed discussion. For online reports, you can put supplements on separate webpages and allow readers to link to them from the main report pages. Supplements are more common in long reports than in short ones, and they typically include appendixes, a bibliography, and an index.

Appendixes   An **appendix** contains materials related to the report but not included in the text because they are too lengthy, too bulky, or perhaps not relevant to everyone in the audience. If your company has an intranet, shared workspaces, or other means of storing and accessing information online, consider putting your detailed supporting evidence there and referring readers to those sources for more detail.

The content of report appendixes varies widely, including any sample questionnaires and cover letters, sample forms, computer printouts, statistical formulas, financial statements and spreadsheets, copies of important documents, and multipage illustrations that would break up the flow of text. You might also include a glossary as an appendix or as a separate supplementary part.

If you have multiple categories of supporting material, give each type a separate appendix. Appendixes are usually identified with a letter and a short, descriptive title—for example, "Appendix A: Questionnaire," "Appendix B: Computer Printout of Raw Data," and so on. All appendixes should be mentioned in the text and listed in the table of contents.

Bibliography   To fulfill your ethical and legal obligation to credit other people for their work and to assist readers who may want to research your topic further, include a **bibliography,** a list of the secondary sources you consulted when preparing your report. In her Electrovision report, Linda Moreno labeled her bibliography "Works Cited" because she listed only the works that were mentioned in the report. You might call this section "Sources" or "References"

5 LEARNING OBJECTIVE

Describe the three supplementary parts of a formal report

Use an appendix for materials that are too lengthy for the body or not directly relevant to all audience members.

A bibliography fulfills your ethical obligation to credit your sources, and it allows readers to consult those sources for more information.

if it includes works consulted but not mentioned in your report. Moreno uses the author-date system to format her bibliographic sources. An alternative is to use numbered footnotes (bottom of the page) or endnotes (end of the report). For more information on citing sources, see Appendix B, "Documentation of Report Sources."

In addition to providing a bibliography, some authors prefer to cite references in the report text. Acknowledging your sources in the body of your report demonstrates that you have thoroughly researched your topic. Furthermore, mentioning the names of well-known or important authorities on the subject helps build credibility for your message. On the other hand, you don't want to make your report read like an academic treatise, dragging along from citation to citation. The source references should be handled as conveniently and inconspicuously as possible. One approach, especially for internal reports, is simply to mention a source in the text:

> According to Dr. Lewis Morgan of Northwestern Hospital, hip replacement operations account for 7 percent of all surgery performed on women age 65 and over.

However, if your report will be distributed to outsiders, include additional information on where you obtained the data. Most college students are familiar with citation methods suggested by the Modern Language Association (MLA) or the American Psychological Association (APA). *The Chicago Manual of Style* is a reference often used by typesetters and publishers. All of these sources encourage the use of in-text citations (inserting the author's last name and a year of publication or a page number directly into the text).

If your report is lengthy, an index can help readers locate specific topics quickly.

Index An **index** is an alphabetical list of names, places, and subjects mentioned in your report, along with the pages on which they occur (see the indexes in this book for examples). If you think your readers will need to access specific points of information in a lengthy report, consider including an index that lists all key topics, product names, markets, important persons—whatever is relevant to your subject matter. As with your table of contents, accuracy is critical. The good news is that you can also use your word processor to compile the index. Just be sure to update the index (and any automatically generated elements, for that matter) right before you produce and distribute the format.

Components of a Formal Proposal

Formal proposals must be produced with a high degree of polish and professionalism.

The goal of a proposal is to impress readers with your professionalism and to make your offering and your company stand out from the competition. Consequently, proposals addressed to external audiences, including potential customers and investors, are nearly always formal. For smaller projects and situations in which you already have a working relationship with the audience, the proposal can be less formal and skip some of the components described in this section.

Formal proposals contain many of the same components as other formal reports (see Figure 15.4). The difference lies mostly in the text, although a few of the prefatory parts are also different. With the exception of an occasional appendix, most proposals have few supplementary parts. As always, if you're responding to an RFP, follow its specifications to the letter, being sure to include everything it asks for and nothing it doesn't ask for.

Prefatory Parts

The cover, title fly, title page, table of contents, and list of illustrations are handled the same as in other formal reports. However, you'll want to handle other prefatory parts a bit differently, such as the copy of the RFP, the synopsis or executive summary, and the letter of transmittal.

An RFP may require you to include a copy of the RFP in your prefatory section; just be sure to follow instructions carefully.

Copy of the RFP RFPs usually have specific instructions for referring to the RFP itself in your proposal, because the organizations that issue RFPs need a methodical way to track all of their active RFPs and the incoming responses. Some organizations require that you include a copy of the entire RFP in your proposal; others simply want you to refer to the RFP by name or number or perhaps include just the introductory section of

FIGURE 15.4 Parts of a Formal Proposal
As with formal reports, you can select from a variety of components to complete a formal proposal.

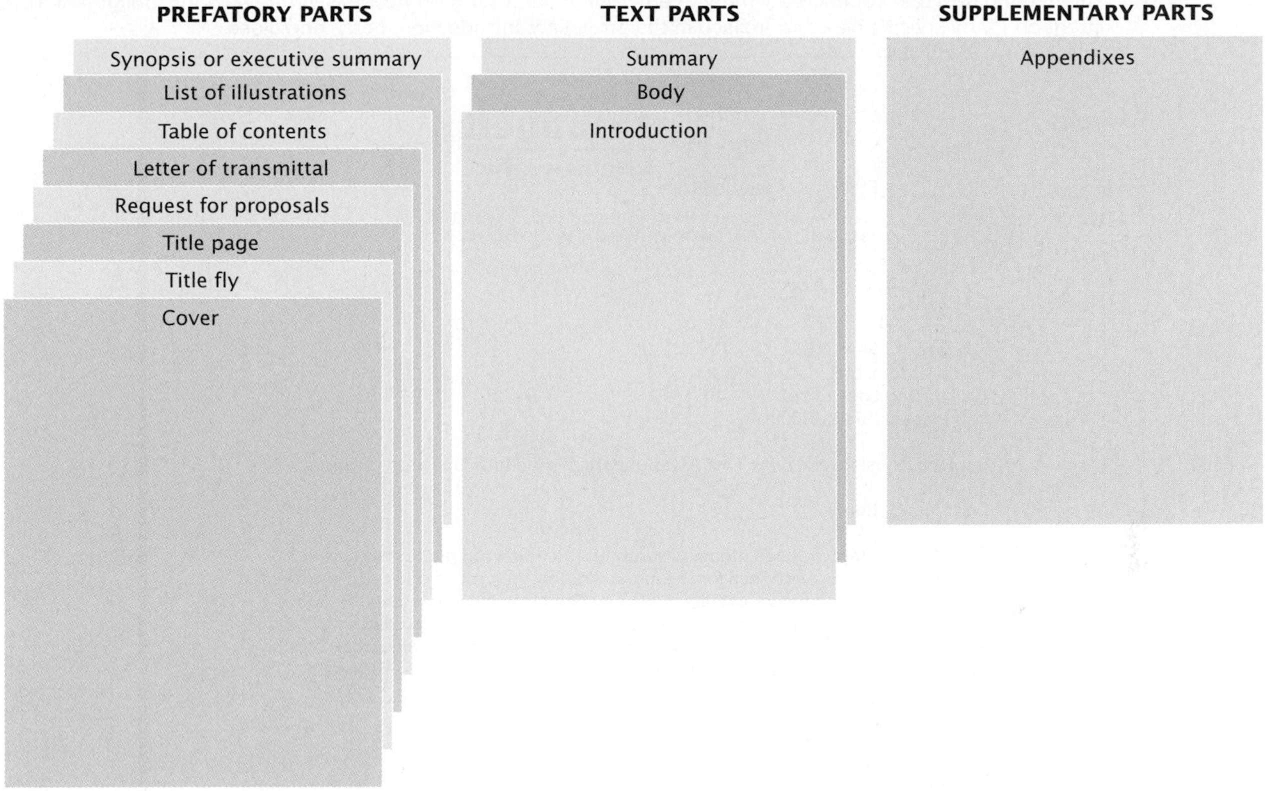

PREFATORY PARTS	TEXT PARTS	SUPPLEMENTARY PARTS
Synopsis or executive summary	Summary	Appendixes
List of illustrations	Body	
Table of contents	Introduction	
Letter of transmittal		
Request for proposals		
Title page		
Title fly		
Cover		

the RFP. Just make sure you follow the instructions in every detail. If there are no specific instructions, use your best judgment based on the length of the RFP and whether you received a printed copy or accessed it online. In any event, make sure your proposal refers to the RFP in some way so that the audience can associate your proposal with the correct RFP.

Synopsis or Executive Summary   Although you may include a synopsis or an executive summary for your reader's convenience when your proposal is quite long, these components are often less useful in a formal proposal than they are in a formal report. If your proposal is unsolicited, your transmittal letter will already have caught the reader's interest, making a synopsis or an executive summary redundant. It may also be less important if your proposal is solicited, because the reader is already committed to studying your proposal to find out how you intend to satisfy the terms of a contract. The introduction of a solicited proposal would provide an adequate preview of the contents.

Letter of Transmittal   The way you handle the letter of transmittal depends on whether the proposal is solicited or unsolicited. If the proposal is solicited, approach the transmittal letter as a positive message, highlighting those aspects of your proposal that may give you a competitive advantage. If the proposal is unsolicited, approach the transmittal letter as a persuasive message. The letter must persuade the reader that you have something worthwhile to offer, something that justifies the time required to read the entire proposal.

DOCUMENT MAKEOVER

IMPROVE THIS EXECUTIVE SUMMARY

To practice correcting drafts of actual documents, visit your online course or the access-code-protected portion of the Companion Website. Click "Document Makeovers," then click Chapter 15. You will find an excerpt from an executive summary that contains problems and errors relating to what you've learned in this chapter about completing formal reports and proposals. Use the "Final Draft" decision tool to create an improved version of this document. Check the executive summary for an appropriate degree of formality, parallel structures, and the skillful inclusion or exclusion of detail.

FIGURE 15.5 **Dixon O'Donnell's Informal Solicited Proposal**
This proposal was submitted by Dixon O'Donnell, vice president of O'Donnell & Associates, a geotechnical engineering firm that conducts a variety of environmental testing services. As you review this document, pay close attention to the specific items addressed in the proposal's introduction, body, and close.

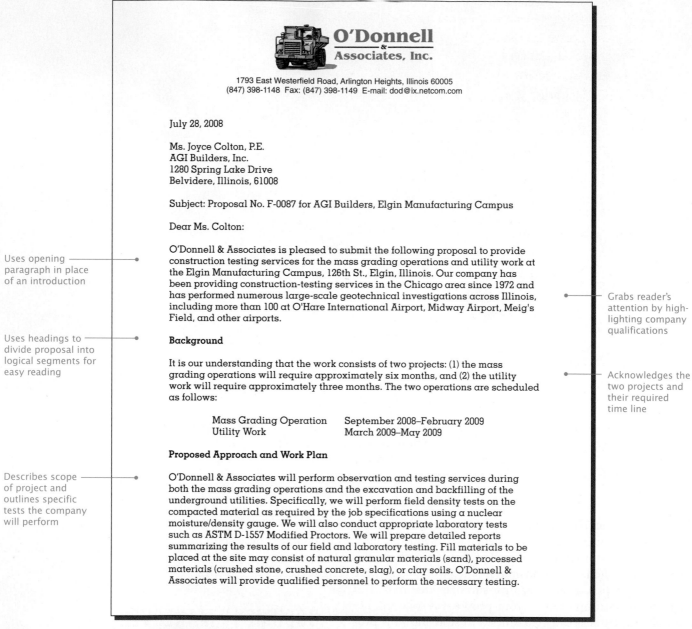

O'Donnell
&
Associates, Inc.

1793 East Westerfield Road, Arlington Heights, Illinois 60005
(847) 398-1148 Fax: (847) 398-1149 E-mail: dod@ix.netcom.com

July 28, 2008

Ms. Joyce Colton, P.E.
AGI Builders, Inc.
1280 Spring Lake Drive
Belvidere, Illinois, 61008

Subject: Proposal No. F-0087 for AGI Builders, Elgin Manufacturing Campus

Dear Ms. Colton:

Uses opening paragraph in place of an introduction

O'Donnell & Associates is pleased to submit the following proposal to provide construction testing services for the mass grading operations and utility work at the Elgin Manufacturing Campus, 126th St., Elgin, Illinois. Our company has been providing construction-testing services in the Chicago area since 1972 and has performed numerous large-scale geotechnical investigations across Illinois, including more than 100 at O'Hare International Airport, Midway Airport, Meig's Field, and other airports.

Grabs reader's attention by highlighting company qualifications

Uses headings to divide proposal into logical segments for easy reading

Background

It is our understanding that the work consists of two projects: (1) the mass grading operations will require approximately six months, and (2) the utility work will require approximately three months. The two operations are scheduled as follows:

Acknowledges the two projects and their required time line

| Mass Grading Operation | September 2008–February 2009 |
| Utility Work | March 2009–May 2009 |

Proposed Approach and Work Plan

Describes scope of project and outlines specific tests the company will perform

O'Donnell & Associates will perform observation and testing services during both the mass grading operations and the excavation and backfilling of the underground utilities. Specifically, we will perform field density tests on the compacted material as required by the job specifications using a nuclear moisture/density gauge. We will also conduct appropriate laboratory tests such as ASTM D-1557 Modified Proctors. We will prepare detailed reports summarizing the results of our field and laboratory testing. Fill materials to be placed at the site may consist of natural granular materials (sand), processed materials (crushed stone, crushed concrete, slag), or clay soils. O'Donnell & Associates will provide qualified personnel to perform the necessary testing.

(continued)

Text of the Proposal

Just as with reports, the text of a proposal is composed of three main parts: an introduction, body, and close. The content and depth of each part depend on whether the proposal is solicited or unsolicited, formal or informal. Here's a brief review:[8]

- **Introduction.** This section presents and summarizes the problem you intend to solve and your solution to that problem, including any benefits the reader will receive from your solution.

- **Body.** This section explains the complete details of the solution: how the job will be done, how it will be broken into tasks, what method will be used to do it (including the required equipment, material, and personnel), when the work will begin and end, how

FIGURE 15.5 *Continued*

Explains who will be responsible for the various tasks

O'Donnell & Associates, Inc.   July 28, 2008   Page 2

Kevin Patel will be the lead field technician responsible for the project. A copy of Mr. Patel's résumé is included with this proposal for your review. Kevin will coordinate field activities with your job site superintendent and make sure that appropriate personnel are assigned to the job site. Overall project management will be the responsibility of Joseph Proesel. Project engineering services will be performed under the direction of Dixon O'Donnell, P.E. All field personnel assigned to the site will be familiar with and abide by the Project Site Health and Safety Plan prepared by Carlson Environmental, Inc., dated April 2008.

Encloses résumé rather than listing qualifications in the document

Qualifications

O'Donnell & Associates has been providing quality professional services since 1972 in the areas of

Grabs attention by mentioning compelling qualifications

- Geotechnical engineering
- Materials testing and inspection
- Pavement evaluation
- Environmental services
- Engineering and technical support (CADD) services

The company provides Phase I and Phase II environmental site assessments, preparation of LUST site closure reports, installation of groundwater monitoring wells, and testing of soil/groundwater samples for environmental contaminants. Geotechnical services include all phases of soil mechanics and foundation engineering, including foundation and lateral load analysis, slope stability analysis, site preparation recommendations, see page analysis, pavement design, and settlement analysis.

O'Donnell & Associates materials testing laboratory is certified by AASHTO Accreditation Program for the testing of Soils, Aggregate, Hot Mix Asphalt and Portland Cement Concrete. A copy of our laboratory certification is included with this proposal. In addition to in-house training, field and laboratory technicians participate in a variety of certification programs, including those sponsored by the American Concrete Institute (ACI) and Illinois Department of Transportation (IDOT).

Gains credibility by describing certifications (approvals by recognized industry associations or government agencies)

Costs

On the basis of our understanding of the scope of the work, we estimate the total cost of the two projects to be $100,260.00, as follows:

(continued)

much the entire job will cost (including a detailed breakdown, if required or requested), and why your company is qualified.
- **Close.** This section emphasizes the benefits that readers will realize from your solution, and it urges readers to act.

Figure 15.5 provides an example of an informal proposal.

PROOFREADING YOUR REPORTS AND PROPOSALS

Once you have assembled all the components of your report or proposal, have revised the entire document's content for clarity and conciseness, and have designed the document to ensure readability and a positive impression on your readers, you have essentially produced your document in its final form. Now you need to review it thoroughly one last time, looking for inconsistencies, errors, and missing components. For instance, if you changed a heading in the report's text part, make sure that you also changed the corresponding heading in the table of contents and in all references to that heading in your report. Proofing can

FIGURE 15.5 *Continued*

O'Donnell & Associates, Inc.   July 28, 2008   Page 3

Cost Estimates

Cost Estimate: Mass Grading	Units	Rate ($)	Total Cost ($)
Field Inspection			
Labor	1,320 hours	$38.50	$ 50,820.00
Nuclear Moisture Density Meter	132 days	35.00	4,620.00
Vehicle Expense	132 days	45.00	5,940.00
Laboratory Testing			
Proctor Density Tests (ASTM D-1557)	4 tests	130.00	520.00
Engineering/Project Management			
Principal Engineer	16 hours	110.00	1,760.00
Project Manager	20 hours	80.00	1,600.00
Administrative Assistant	12 hours	50.00	600.00
Subtotal			$ 65,860.00

Itemizes costs by project and gives supporting details

Cost Estimate: Utility Work	Units	Rate ($)	Total Cost ($)
Field Inspection			
Labor	660 hours	$ 38.50	$ 25,410.00
Nuclear Moisture Density Meter	66 days	5.00	2,310.00
Vehicle Expense	66 days	45.00	2,970.00
Laboratory Testing			
Proctor Density Tests (ASTM D-1557)	2 tests	130.00	260.00
Engineering/Project Management			
Principal Engineer	10 hours	110.00	1,100.00
Project Manager	20 hours	80.00	1,600.00
Administrative Assistant	15 hours	50.00	750.00
Subtotal			$ 34,400.00
Total Project Costs			**$100,260.00**

This estimate assumes full-time inspection services. However, our services may also be performed on an as-requested basis, and actual charges will reflect time associated with the project. We have attached our standard fee schedule for your review. Overtime rates are for hours in excess of 8.0 hours per day, before 7:00 a.m., after 5:00 p.m., and on holidays and weekends.

Provides alternative option in case full-time service costs exceed client's budget

(continued)

catch minor flaws that might diminish your credibility—and major flaws that might damage your career.

Proofreading the textual part of your report is essentially the same as proofreading any business message—you check for typos, spelling errors, and mistakes in punctuation. However, reports often have elements that may not be included in other messages, so don't forget to proof your visuals thoroughly, as Chapter 12 points out, and make sure they are positioned correctly. If you need specific tips on proofreading documents, look back at Chapter 6 for some reminders on what to look for when proofreading text and how to proofread like a pro.

Ask for proofreading assistance from someone who hasn't been involved in the development of your proposal; he or she might see errors that you've been overlooking.

Whenever possible, arrange for someone with "fresh eyes" to proofread the report, somebody who hasn't been involved with the text so far. At this point in the process, you are so familiar with the content that your mind will fill in missing words, fix misspelled words, and subconsciously compensate for other flaws without you even being aware of it. Someone with fresh eyes might see mistakes that you've passed over a dozen times without noticing. An ideal approach is to have two people review it, one who is an expert in the subject

FIGURE 15.5 *Continued*

O'Donnell & Associates, Inc.   July 28, 2008   Page 4

Authorization

With a staff of over 30 personnel, including registered professional engineers, resident engineers, geologists, construction inspectors, laboratory technicians, and drillers, we are convinced that O'Donnell & Associates is capable of providing the services required for a project of this magnitude.

If you would like our firm to provide the services as outlined in this proposal, please sign this letter and return it to us along with a certified check in the amount of $10,000 (our retainer) by August 15, 2008. Please call me if you have any questions regarding the terms of this proposal or our approach.

Sincerely,

Dixon O'Donnell

Dixon O'Donnell
Vice President

Enclosures

Accepted for AGI BUILDERS, INC.

By_____   Date _____

Uses brief closing to emphasize qualifications and ask for client decision

Provides deadline and makes response easy

Makes letter a binding contract, if signed

matter and one who isn't. The first person can ensure its technical accuracy, and the second can ensure that a wide range of readers will understand it.[9]

DISTRIBUTING YOUR REPORTS AND PROPOSALS

All of the distribution issues you explored in Chapter 6 apply to reports and proposals, as long as you pay particular attention to the length and complexity of your documents. For physical distribution, consider spending the few extra dollars for a professional courier or package delivery service, if that will help your document stand apart from the crowd. The online tracking offered by FedEx, UPS, and other services can verify that your document arrived safely. On the other hand, if you've prepared the document for a single person or small group, delivering it in person can be a nice touch. Not only can you answer any immediate questions about it, but also you can promote the results in person—reminding the recipient of the benefits contained in your report or proposal.

CHECKLIST: **Producing Formal Reports and Proposals**

A. Prefatory parts
- Use your company's standard report covers, if available.
- Include a concise, descriptive title on the cover.
- Include a title fly only if you want an extra-formal touch.
- On the title page, list (1) report title; (2) name, title, and address of the group or person who authorized the report; (3) name, title, and address of the group or person who prepared the report; and (4) date of submission.
- Include a copy of the letter of authorization, if appropriate.
- Include a copy of the RFP (or its introduction only if the document is long), if appropriate.
- Include a letter of transmittal that introduces the report.
- Provide a table of contents in outline form, with headings worded exactly as they appear in the body of the report.
- Include a list of illustrations if the report contains a large number of them.
- Include a synopsis (brief summary of the report) or executive summary (a condensed, "mini" version of the report) for longer reports.

B. Text of the report
- Draft an introduction that prepares the reader for the content that follows.
- Provide the information that supports your conclusions, recommendations, or proposals in the body of the report.
- Don't overload the body with unnecessary detail.
- Close with a summary of your main idea.

C. Supplementary parts
- Use appendixes to provide supplementary information or supporting evidence.
- List any secondary sources you used in a bibliography.
- Provide an index if your report contains a large number of terms or ideas and is likely to be consulted over time.

Adobe's portable document format (PDF) is a safe and common way to distribute reports electronically.

For electronic distribution, unless your audience specifically requests a word-processor file, provide documents as PDF files. Many people are reluctant to open word-processor files these days, particularly from outsiders, given the vulnerability of such files to macro viruses and other contaminations. Moreover, using PDF files lets you control how your document is displayed on your audience's computer, ensuring that your readers see your document as you intended. In addition, making documents available as downloadable PDF files is almost universally expected these days, if only for the sake of convenience.

If your company or client expects you to distribute your reports via a web-based content management system, intranet, or extranet, be sure to upload the correct file(s) to the correct online location. Verify the on-screen display of your report after you've posted it, too; make sure graphics, charts, links, and other elements are in place and operational.

Once you've completed your formal report or proposal and sent it off to your audience, your next task is to wait for a response. If you don't hear from your readers within a week or two, you might want to ask politely whether the report arrived. (Some RFPs specify a response timeframe. If so, *don't* pester the recipient ahead of schedule; you'll hurt your chances.) In hope of stimulating a response, you might ask a question about the report, such as "How do you think accounting will react to the proposed budget increase?" You might also offer to answer any questions or provide additional information. To review the ideas presented in this chapter, see "Checklist: Producing Formal Reports and Proposals."

WRITING REQUESTS FOR PROPOSALS

6 LEARNING OBJECTIVE

Identify the major components to include in a request for proposals (RFP)

At some point in your career, you might be the one receiving proposals, and learning how to request effective proposals will simplify the process considerably. Various organizations handle RFPs in different ways. For example, the Gates Foundation's education program does not accept unsolicited proposals, so grant proposals must be in written in response to a published RFP. The health program also emphasizes RFPs but does invite inquiries regarding projects that align with its funding priorities, even if a specific RFP hasn't been issued for a particular project area. In these cases, organizations are asked to submit a letter of inquiry (LOI) via an online form. If an LOI is accepted, the organization is then invited to submit a grant proposal.[10]

When writing an RFP, remember that it is more than just a request; it's an informational report that provides potential bidders with the information they need to craft effective proposals. Writing an RFP demands careful consideration because it starts a process that leads to a proposal, a contract, and eventually the delivery of a product or the performance of a service. In other words, mistakes at the RFP stage can ripple throughout the process and create costly headaches for everyone involved.

An RFP's specific content will vary widely from industry to industry, but all RFPs should include some combination of the following elements:[11]

- **Company background.** Give potential bidders some background information on your organization, your business priorities, and other information they might need in order to respond in an informed manner.
- **Project description.** Put your requirements in context; are you seeking bids for routine supplies or services, or do you need a major computer system?
- **Requirements.** The requirements section should spell out everything you expect from potential vendors; don't leave anything to unstated assumptions. Will potential vendors provide key equipment, or will you? Will you expect vendors to work under confidentiality restrictions, such as a nondisclosure agreement? Who will pay if costs run higher than expected? Will you require ongoing service or support? For instance, if you are requesting proposals for a corporate website project, you would specify everything, including how much experience your company has with websites, what type of design and technical requirements you have, who will develop the website content, and what type of service and maintenance will be provided after the site is set up.[12] As you can imagine, the details of your requirements can run to many pages and necessitate the input of numerous subject-area experts throughout your company. Providing this information can be a lot of work, but again, overlooking anything at this point is likely to create considerable problems once the project gets rolling.
- **Decision criteria.** Let bidders know how you'll be making the decision. Is quality more important than cost? Will you consider only certain types of vendors or only those that use certain processes or technologies? Will you entertain bids from companies that have never worked in your particular industry? The answers to such questions not only help bidders determine whether they're right for your project but also help them craft proposals that meet your needs.
- **Proposal requirements.** Explain exactly what you expect to see in the proposal itself—which sections, what media, how many copies, and so on.
- **Submission and contact information.** A well-written RFP answers most potential questions, and it also tells people when, where, and how to respond. In addition, effective RFPs always give bidders a contact name within the organization who can answer detailed questions.

When writing an RFP, be sure to give potential respondents all the information they need to craft a meaningful response to your request.

A smart approach to managing RFPs can minimize the work involved for everyone and maximize the effectiveness of the RFP. First identify your decision criteria, then brainstorm the information you need to measure against those criteria. Don't ask bidders to submit information about every aspect of their operations if such details aren't relevant to your decision. Making such unreasonable demands is unfair to bidders, will unnecessarily complicate your review process, and will discourage some potentially attractive bidders from responding.

Second, to get quality responses that match your unique business needs, give bidders plenty of time to respond. Good companies are usually busy responding to other RFPs and working on other projects. Therefore, you can't expect them to drop everything to focus solely on your RFP.

Third, if your company generates numerous RFPs, tracking proposals can become a full-time job. Consider establishing an online system for tracking responses automatically.[13]

COMMUNICATION CHALLENGES AT THE BILL AND MELINDA GATES FOUNDATION

Patty Stonesifer and her colleagues at the Bill and Melinda Gates Foundation not only read numerous reports and proposals every year, they also write and produce many reports, for both internal and external audiences. In fact, communication is one of the foundation's most important functions as it seeks to improve the health and education of children worldwide. In addition, the foundation is known as one of the most efficiently managed charities in the world, so cost-effectiveness is a vital concern in every phase of the communication process. Stonesifer recently hired you as an assistant director of communication, and your responsibilities include developing new ways for the foundation to produce effective reports as efficiently as possible.

Individual Challenge: Review several of the reports and other publications posted online (as PDF files) at www.gatesfoundation.org. Compare the design and layout of these documents. Do you see evidence of standardized design across documents? Write a brief e-mail to Stonesifer explaining the financial advantages of using a single design scheme for all external foundation documents.

Team Challenge: As a champion of new technologies, Bill Gates has a strong interest in applying information technology to the challenge of global communication. In a small team, research the opportunities for electronic delivery of health information to remote villages in India. Prepare a one-page report summarizing your findings.

SUMMARY OF LEARNING OBJECTIVES

1 Summarize the four tasks involved in completing business reports and proposals. To complete business reports and proposals, you first need to revise, produce, and proofread the document just as you would with any other business message. Revising reports and proposals involves evaluating content, style, organization, and tone; reviewing for readability; and editing for clarity and conciseness. After you've verified a report's quality, the fourth step is distributing the report and all supporting materials to the intended audience.

2 Explain how computers have both simplified and complicated the report-production process. Computers have simplified report preparation by giving all businesspeople production and distribution capabilities that only a few years ago either required specialized skills and expensive equipment or weren't possible at all. The downside is that so many audiences have seen these highly polished reports that they have come to expect a high level of production quality in nearly all business reports.

3 Identify the circumstances in which you should include letters of authorization and letters of acceptance in your reports. If you received a letter of authorization to begin work on a report and you wrote a letter of acceptance when you took on the assignment, it's a good idea to include both items in your report whenever there's a chance that your audience might not expect the material you're about to deliver. Either or both of these documents can help clarify what you did and why you did it.

4 Explain the difference between a synopsis and an executive summary. A synopsis is a brief overview of the entire report and may either highlight the main points as they appear in the text or simply tell the reader what the report is about. It is designed to entice the audience to read the report, but it is not intended to replace the report. By contrast, an executive summary is more comprehensive than a synopsis; it is essentially a "mini" version of the report. It may contain headings, visual aids, and enough information to help busy executives make quick decisions. Although executive summaries are not designed to replace the report, in some cases it may be the only thing that a busy executive reads carefully.

5 Describe the three supplementary parts of a formal report. Formal reports may include an appendix, a bibliography, and an index. The appendix contains a variety of additional information that is useful but not critical to the report. Some of this material may be too detailed or bulky to be included in the report body. A bibliography is a list of secondary sources consulted when preparing the report; these sources may or may not be mentioned in the report body. An index is an alphabetical list of names, places, and subjects mentioned in the report along with their corresponding pages.

6 **Identify the major components to include in a request for proposals (RFP).** The content of RFPs varies widely from industry to industry and project to project, but most will include background on your company, a description of the project, your solution requirements, the criteria you'll use to make your selection decisions, your expectations for submitted proposals, and any relevant submission and contact information.

Test Your Knowledge

1. What are the tasks involved in revising a report or proposal?
2. When should you start a report section on a new page?
3. What information is included on the title page of a report?
4. What is the difference between a letter of authorization and a letter of acceptance?
5. What is a letter of transmittal, and where is it positioned within a report?
6. When are executive summaries useful?
7. What are three supplementary parts often included in formal reports?
8. What types of material does an appendix contain?
9. Why do some writers cite references in the report text?
10. What is the equivalent of a letter of authorization for a proposal?

Apply Your Knowledge

1. Is an executive summary a persuasive message? Explain your answer.
2. Under what circumstances would you include more than one index in a lengthy report?
3. If you were submitting a solicited proposal to build a small shopping center, would you include as references the names and addresses of other clients for whom you recently built similar facilities? Where in the proposal would you include these references? Why?
4. If you included a bibliography in your report, would you also need to include in-text citations? Please explain.
5. **Ethical Choices** How would you report on a confidential survey in which employees rated their managers' capabilities? Both employees and managers expect to see the results. Would you give the same report to employees and managers? What components would you include or exclude for each audience? Explain your choices.

Practice Your Knowledge

Message for Analysis

Visit the website of the U.S. Citizenship and Immigration Services (a division of the U.S. Department of Homeland Security) at http://uscis.gov. Find a report titled "Triennial Comprehensive Report on Immigration" and follow the link to the executive summary. Using the information in this chapter, analyze the executive summary and offer specific suggestions for revising it.

Exercises

For active links to all websites discussed in this chapter, visit this text's website at www.prenhall.com/bovee. Locate your book and click on its Companion Website link. Then select Chapter 15, and click on "Featured Websites." Locate the name of the page or the URL related to the material in the text. Please note that links to sites that become inactive after publication of the book will be removed from the Featured Websites section.

15.1 **Revising for Clarity and Conciseness** The following sentence appears in your first draft of a report that analyzes perceived shortcomings in your company's employee health benefits: "Among the many criticisms and concerns expressed by the workforce, at least among the 376 who responded to our online survey (out of 655 active employees), the issues of elder care, health insurance during retirement, and the increased amount that employees are being forced to pay every month as the company's contribution to health insurance coverage has declined over the past two years were identified as the most important." Revise this 69-word sentence to make it shorter, more direct, and more powerful.

15.2 **Teamwork** You and a classmate are helping Linda Moreno prepare her report on Electrovision's travel and entertainment costs (see "Report Writer's Notebook"). This time, however, the report is to be informational rather than analytical, so it will not include recommendations. Review the existing report and determine what changes would be needed to make it an informational report. Be as specific as possible. For example, if your team decides the report needs a new title, what title would you use? Now draft a transmittal memo for Moreno to use in conveying this informational report to Dennis McWilliams, Electrovision's vice president of operations.

15.3 **Producing Reports: Letter of Transmittal** You are president of the Friends of the Library, a nonprofit group that raises funds and provides volunteers to support your local library. Every February, you send a report of the previous year's activities and accomplishments to the County Arts Council, which provides an annual grant of $1,000 toward your group's summer reading festival. Now it's February 6, and you've completed your formal report. Here are the highlights:
   - Back-to-school book sale raised $2,000.
   - Holiday craft fair raised $1,100.
   - Promotion and prizes for summer reading festival cost $1,450.
   - Materials for children's program featuring local author cost $125.
   - New reference databases for library's career center cost $850.
   - Bookmarks promoting library's website cost $200.

Write a letter of transmittal to Erica Maki, the council's director. Because she is expecting this report, you can use the direct approach. Be sure to express gratitude for the council's ongoing financial support.

15.4 **Internet** Government reports vary in purpose and structure. Read through the Department of Education's report, "Helping Your Child Become a Reader," available online at www.ed.gov. What is the purpose of this document? Does the title communicate this purpose? What type of report is this, and what is the report's structure? Which prefatory and supplementary parts are included? Now analyze the visuals. What types are included in this report? Are they all necessary? Are the titles and legends sufficiently informative? How does this report take advantage of the online medium to enhance readability?

15.5 **Ethical Choices: Team Challenge** You submitted what you thought was a masterful report to your boss over three weeks ago. The report analyzes current department productivity and recommends several steps that you think will improve employee output without increasing individual workloads. Brilliant, you thought. But you haven't heard a word from your boss. Did you overstep your boundaries by making recommendations that might imply that she has not been doing a good job? Did you overwhelm her with your ideas? You'd like some feedback. In your last e-mail to her, you asked if she had read your report. So far you've received no reply. Then yesterday, you overheard the company vice president talk about some productivity changes in your department. The changes were ones that you had recommended in your report. Now you're worried that your boss submitted your report to senior management and will take full credit for your terrific ideas. What, if anything, should you do? Should you confront your boss about this? Should you ask to meet with the company vice president? Discuss this situation among your teammates and develop a solution to this sticky situation. Present your solution to the class, explaining the rationale behind your decision.

Expand Your Knowledge

Exploring the Best of the Web

Preview Before You Produce
www.dogpile.com
A good way to get ideas for the best style, organization, and format of a report is by looking at copies of professional business reports. To find samples of various types of reports, you can use a metasearch engine such as Dogpile. Choose a metasearch engine (refer to Table 11.3 on page 341). Try several search terms, such as *status report, progress report, sales report, business plan,* or *marketing plan* until you uncover an interesting-looking report. Review the report, then answer the following questions:

1. What is the purpose of the report you read? Who is its target audience? Explain why the structure and style of the report make it easy or difficult to follow the main idea.
2. What type of report did you read? Briefly describe the main message. Is the information well organized? If you answer yes, explain how you can use the report as a guide for a report you might write. If you answer no, explain why the report is not helpful.
3. Drawing on what you know about the qualities of a good business report, review a report and describe what features contribute to its readability.

Surfing Your Way to Career Success

Bovée and Thill's Business Communication Resources offers links to hundreds of online resources that can help you with this course, your other college courses, and your career. Visit www.buscommresources.com, then click on "Business Communication Web Directory." The "Teaching" section offers access to a variety of resources that would be helpful to anyone considering a career in education, training, course development, and related fields. Identify three websites from this section that could be useful in your business career. For each site, write a two-sentence summary of what the site offers and how it could help you launch and build your career.

Learn Interactively

Interactive Study Guide

Visit www.prenhall.com/bovee, then locate your book and click on its "Companion Website" link. Select Chapter 15 to take advantage of the interactive "Chapter Quiz" to test your knowledge of chapter concepts. Receive instant feedback on whether you need additional studying. Also, visit the "Study Hall," where you'll find an abundance of valuable resources that will help you succeed in this course.

Peak Performance Grammar and Mechanics

If your instructor has required the use of "Peak Performance Grammar and Mechanics," either in your online course or on CD, you can continue to improve your skill with document mechanics by using the "Peak Performance Grammar and Mechanics" module. Click "Mechanics of Style." Take the Pretest to determine whether you have any weak areas. Then review those areas in the Refresher Course. Take the Follow-Up Test to check your grasp of mechanics. For an extra challenge or advanced practice, take the Advanced Test. Finally, for additional reinforcement, visit the Companion Website, click on any chapter, then click on "Improve Your Grammar, Mechanics, and Usage."

CASES

Applying the Three-Step Writing Process to Cases

Apply each step to the following cases, as assigned by your instructor.

SHORT FORMAL REPORTS REQUIRING NO ADDITIONAL RESEARCH

▌ **Portfolio**
▌ **BUILDER**

1. Giving it the online try: Report analyzing the advantages and disadvantages of corporate online learning As the newest member of the corporate training division of Paper Products, Inc., you have been asked to investigate and analyze the merits of creating online courses for the company's employees. The president of your company thinks so-called e-learning might be a good employee benefit as well as a terrific way for employees to learn new skills that they can use on the job. You've already done your research and here's a copy of your notes:

Online courses open up new horizons for working adults, who often find it difficult to juggle conventional classes with jobs and families.
Adults over 25 now represent nearly half of higher-ed students; most are employed and want more education to advance their careers.
Some experts believe that online learning will never be as good as face-to-face instruction.
Online learning requires no commute and is appealing for employees who travel regularly.
Enrollment in courses offered online by postsecondary institutions is expected to increase from 2 million students in 2001 to 5 million students in 2006.
E-learning is a cost-effective way to get better-educated employees.
More than one-third of the $50 billion spent on employee training every year is spent on e-learning.
At IBM, some 200,000 employees received education or training online last year, and 75 percent of the company's Basic Blue course for new managers is online. E-learning cut IBM's training bill by $350 million last year—mostly because online courses don't require travel.
There are no national statistics, but a recent report from the *Chronicle of Higher Education* found that institutions are seeing dropout rates that range from 20 to 50 percent for online learners. The research does not adequately explain why the dropout rates for e-learners are higher.
A recent study of corporate online learners reported that employees want the following things from their online courses: college credit or a certificate; active correspondence with an online facilitator who has frequent virtual office hours; access to 24-hour, seven-day-a-week technical support; and the ability to start a course anytime.

Corporate e-learners said that their top reason for dropping a course was lack of time. Many had trouble completing courses from their desktops because of frequent distractions caused by co-workers. Some said they could only access courses through the company's intranet, so they couldn't finish their assignments from home.
Besides lack of time, corporate e-learners cited the following as e-learning disadvantages: lack of management oversight, lack of motivation, problems with technology, lack of student support, individual learning preferences, poorly designed courses, substandard/inexperienced instructors.
A recent study by GE Capital found that finishing a corporate online course was dependent on whether managers gave reinforcement on attendance, how important employees were made to feel, and whether employee progress in the course was tracked.
Sun Microsystems found that interactivity can be a critical success factor for online courses. Company studies showed that only 25 percent of employees finish classes that are strictly self-paced. But 75 percent finish when given similar assignments and access to tutors through e-mail, phone, or online discussion groups.
Company managers must supervise e-learning just as they would any other important initiative.
For online learning to work, companies must develop a culture that takes online learning just as seriously as classroom training.
For many e-learners, studying at home is optimal. Whenever possible, companies should offer courses through the Internet or provide intranet access at home. Having employees studying on their own time will more than cover any added costs.
Corporate e-learning has flared into a $2.3 billion market, making it one of the fastest-growing segments of the education industry.
Rather than fly trainers to 7,000 dealerships, General Motors University now uses interactive satellite broadcasts to teach salespeople the best way to highlight features on the new Buick.
Fast and cheap, e-training can shave companies' training costs while it saves employees' travel time.
Pharmaceutical companies such as Merck are conducting live, interactive classes over the web, allowing sales reps to learn about the latest product information at home rather than fly them to a conference center.
McDonald's trainers can log into Hamburger University to learn such skills as how to assemble a made-to-order burger or properly place the drink on a tray.

One obstacle to the spread of online corporate training is the mismatch between what employees really need—customized courses that are tailored to a firm's products and its unique corporate culture—and what employers can afford.

Eighty percent of companies prefer developing their own online training courses in-house. But creating even one customized e-course can take months, involve armies of experts, and cost anywhere from $25,000 to $50,000. Thus, most companies either stick with classroom training or buy generic courses on such topics as how to give performance appraisals, understanding basic business ethics, and so on. Employers can choose from a wide selection of noncustomized electronic courses.

For online learning to be effective, content must be broken into short "chunks" with lots of pop quizzes, online discussion groups, and other interactive features that let students demonstrate what they've learned. For instance, Circuit City's tutorial on digital camcorders consists of three 20-minute segments. Each contains audio demonstrations of how to handle customer product queries, tests on terminology, and "try-its" that propel trainees back onto the floor to practice what they've learned.

Dell Computer expects 90 percent of its learning solutions to be totally or partially technology enabled.

The Home Depot has used e-training to cut a full day from the time required to train new cashiers.

Online training has freed up an average of 17 days every year for Black & Decker's sales representatives.

Your task: Write a short (three to five pages) memo report to the director of human resources, Kerry Simmons, presenting the advantages and disadvantages of e-learning and making a recommendation as to whether Paper Products, Inc., should invest time and money in training its employees this way. Be sure to organize your information so that it is clear, concise, and logically presented. Simmons likes to read the "bottom line" first, so be direct: Present your recommendation up-front and support your recommendation with your findings.[14]

Portfolio BUILDER

2. Grumbling in the ranks: When departments can't agree on the value of work You've been in your new job as human resources director for only a week, and already you have a major personnel crisis on your hands. Some employees in the marketing department got their hands on a confidential salary report, only to learn that, on average, marketing employees earn less than engineering employees. In addition, several top performers in the engineering group make significantly more than anybody in marketing. The report was passed around the company instantly by e-mail, and now everyone is discussing the situation. You'll deal with the data security issue later; for now, you need to address the dissatisfaction in the marketing group.

Table 15.1 lists the salary and employment data you were able to pull from the employee database. You also had the oppor-

TABLE 15.1 Selected Employment Data for Engineers and Marketing Staff

EMPLOYMENT STATISTIC	ENGINEERING DEPARTMENT	MARKETING DEPARTMENT
Average number of years of work experience	18.2	16.3
Average number of years of experience in current profession	17.8	8.6
Average number of years with company	12.4	7.9
Average number of years of college education	6.9	4.8
Average number of years between promotions	6.7	4.3
Salary range	$58k–$165k	$45k–$85k
Median salary	$77k	$62k

tunity to interview the engineering and marketing directors to get their opinions on the pay situation; their answers are listed in Table 15.2.

Your task: The CEO has asked for a short report summarizing whatever data and information you have on engineering and marketing salaries. Feel free to offer your own interpretation of the situation as well (make up any information you need), but keep in mind that as a new manager with almost no experience in the company, your opinion might not have a lot of influence.

Portfolio BUILDER

3. Building a new magazine: Finding opportunity in the remodeling craze Spurred on in part by the success of such hit shows as *Changing Rooms*, *Trading Spaces*, and *Designers' Challenge*, homeowners across the country are redecorating, remodeling, and rebuilding. Many people are content with superficial changes, such as new paint or new accessories, but some are more ambitious. These homeowners want to move walls, add rooms, redesign kitchens, convert garages to home theaters—the big stuff.

As with many consumer trends, publishers try to create magazines that appeal to carefully identified groups of potential readers and the advertisers who'd like to reach them. The do-it-yourself (DIY) market is already served by numerous magazines, but you see an opportunity in those homeowners who tackle the heavy-duty projects. Tables 15.3 through 15.5 summarize the results of some preliminary research you asked your company's research staff to conduct.

Your task: You think the data show a real opportunity for a "big projects" DIY magazine, although you'll need more extensive research to confirm the size of the market and refine the editorial di-

TABLE 15.2 Summary Statements from Department Director Interviews

QUESTION	ENGINEERING DIRECTOR	MARKETING DIRECTOR
1. Should engineering and marketing professionals receive roughly similar pay?	In general, yes, but we need to make allowances for the special nature of the engineering profession. In some cases, it's entirely appropriate for an engineer to earn more than a marketing person.	Yes.
2. Why or why not?	Several reasons: (1) top engineers are extremely hard to find and we need to offer competitive salaries; (2) the structure of the engineering department doesn't provide as many promotional opportunities, so we can't use promotions as a motivator the way marketing can; (3) many of our engineers have advanced degrees and nearly all pursue continuous education to stay on top of the technology.	Without marketing, the products the engineers create wouldn't reach customers and the company wouldn't have any revenue. The two teams make equal contributions to the company's success.
3. If we decide to balance pay between the two departments, how should we do it?	If we do anything to cap or reduce engineering salaries, we'll lose key people to the competition.	If we can't increase payroll immediately to raise marketing salaries, the only fair thing to do is freeze raises in engineering and gradually raise marketing salaries over the next few years.

TABLE 15.3 Rooms Most Frequently Remodeled by DIYers

ROOM	PERCENTAGE OF HOMEOWNERS SURVEYED WHO HAVE TACKLED OR PLAN TO TACKLE AT LEAST A PARTIAL REMODEL
Kitchen	60
Bathroom	48
Home office/study	44
Bedroom	38
Media room/home theater	31
Den/recreation room	28
Living room	27
Dining room	12
Sun room/solarium	8

TABLE 15.4 Average Amount Spent on Remodeling Projects

ESTIMATED AMOUNT	PERCENTAGE OF SURVEYED HOMEOWNERS
Under $5k	5
$5k–$10k	21
$10k–$20k	39
$20k–$50k	22
More than $50k	13

TABLE 15.5 Tasks Performed by Homeowner on a Typical Remodeling Project

TASK	PERCENTAGE OF SURVEYED HOMEOWNERS WHO PERFORM OR PLAN TO PERFORM MOST OR ALL OF THIS TASK THEMSELVES
Conceptual design	90
Technical design/ architecture	34
Demolition	98
Foundation work	62
Framing	88
Plumbing	91
Electrical	55
Heating/cooling	22
Finish carpentry	85
Tile work	90
Painting	100
Interior design	52

rection of the magazine. Prepare a brief analytical report that presents the data you have, identifies the opportunity or opportunities you've found (suggest your own ideas based on the tables), and requests funding from the editorial board to pursue further research.

SHORT FORMAL REPORTS REQUIRING ADDITIONAL RESEARCH

4. Picking the better path: Research report assisting a client in a career choice You are employed by Open Options, a career-counseling firm, where your main function is to help clients make career choices. Today a client with the same name as yours (a truly curious coincidence!) came to your office and asked for help deciding between two careers—careers that you yourself had been interested in (an even greater coincidence!).

Your task: Do some research on the two careers and then prepare a short report that your client can study. Your report should compare at least five major areas, such as salary, working conditions, and education required. Interview the client to understand her or his personal preferences regarding each of the five areas. For example, what is the minimum salary the client will accept? By comparing the client's preferences with the research material you collect, such as salary data, you will have a basis for concluding which of the two careers is best. The report should end with a career recommendation. (Note: One good place for career-related information is the Occupational Outlook Handbook, published by the U.S. Bureau of Labor Statistics, available in print and online at www.bls.gov/oco.)

▌Portfolio BUILDER

5. Selling overseas: Research report on the prospects for marketing a product in another country Select a fairly inexpensive product that you currently own and a country that you're not very familiar with. The product could be a moderately priced watch, radio, or other device. Now imagine that you are with the international sales department of the company that manufactures and sells the item and that you are proposing to make it available in the country you have selected.

The first step is to learn as much as possible about the country where you plan to market the product. Check almanacs, encyclopedias, the Internet, and library databases for the most recent information, paying particular attention to descriptions of the social life of the inhabitants, their economic conditions, and cultural traditions that would encourage or discourage use of the product.

Your task: Write a short report that describes the product you plan to market abroad, briefly describes the country you have selected, indicates the types of people in this country who would find the product attractive, explains how the product would be transported into the country (or possibly manufactured there if materials and labor are available), recommends a location for a regional sales center, and suggests how the product should be sold. Your report is to be submitted to the chief operating officer of the company, whose name you can either make up or find in a corporate directory. The report should include your conclusions (how the product will do in this new environment) and your recommendations for marketing (steps the company should take immediately and those it should develop later).

▌Portfolio BUILDER

6. A ready-made business: Finding the right franchise opportunity After 15 years in the corporate world, you're ready to

strike out on your own. Rather than building a business from the ground up, however, you think that buying a franchise is a better idea. Unfortunately, some of the most lucrative franchise opportunities, such as the major fast-food chains, require significant start-up costs—some more than a half-million dollars. Fortunately, you've met several potential investors who seem willing to help you get started in exchange for a share of ownership. Between your own savings and these investors, you estimate that you can raise from $350,000 to $600,000, depending on how much ownership share you want to concede to the investors.

You've worked in several functional areas already, including sales and manufacturing, so you have a fairly well-rounded business résumé. You're open to just about any type of business, too, as long as it provides the opportunity to grow; you don't want to be so tied down to the first operation that you can't turn it over to a hired manager and expand into another market.

Your task: To convene a formal meeting with the investor group, you need to first draft a report outlining the types of franchise opportunities you'd like to pursue. Write a brief report identifying five franchises that you would like to explore further (choose five based on your own personal interests and the criteria already identified). For each possibility, identify the nature of the business, the financial requirements, the level of support the company provides, and a brief statement of why you could run such a business successfully (make up any details you need). Be sure to carefully review the information you find about each franchise company to make sure you can qualify for it. For instance, McDonald's doesn't allow investment partnerships to buy franchises, so you won't be able to start up a McDonald's outlet until you have enough money to do it on your own.

For a quick introduction to franchising, see How Stuff Works (www.howstuffworks.com/franchising). You can learn more about the business of franchising at Franchising.com (www.franchising.com) and search for specific franchise opportunities at FranCorp Connect (www.francorpconnect.com). In addition, many companies that sell franchises, such as Subway, offer additional information on their websites.

LONG FORMAL REPORTS REQUIRING NO ADDITIONAL RESEARCH

▌Portfolio ▌BUILDER

7. You can get anything online these days: Shopping for automobiles on the Internet As a researcher in your state's consumer protection agency, you're frequently called on to investigate consumer topics and write reports for the agency's website. Thousands of consumers have arranged the purchase of cars online, and millions more do at least some of their research online before heading to the dealership. Some want to save time and money, some want to be armed with as much information as possible before talking to a dealer, while others want to completely avoid the often-uncomfortable experience of negotiating prices with car salespeople. In response, a variety of online services have emerged to meet these consumer needs. Some let you compare information on various car models, some connect you to local dealers to complete the transaction, and some complete nearly all of the transaction details for you, including negotiating the price. Some search the inventory of thousands of dealers, whereas others search only a single dealership or a network of affiliated dealers. In other words, a slew of new tools are available for car buyers, but it's not always easy to figure out where to go and what to expect. That's where your report will help.

By visiting a variety of car-related websites and reading magazine and newspaper articles on the car-buying process, you've compiled a variety of notes related to the subject:

- *Process overview.* The process is relatively straightforward and fairly similar to other online shopping experiences, with two key differences. In general, a consumer identifies the make and model of car he or she wants, then the online car-buying service searches the inventories of car dealers nationwide and presents the available choices. The consumer chooses a particular car from that list, then the service handles the communication and purchase details with the dealer. When the paperwork is finished, the consumer then visits the dealership and picks up the car. The two biggest differences with online auto buying are that (1) you can't actually complete the purchase over the Internet (in most cases, you must visit a local dealer to pick up the car and sign the papers, although in some cities, a dealer or a local car-buying service will deliver it to your home) and (2) in most states, it's illegal to purchase a new car from anyone other than a franchise dealer (i.e., you can't buy directly from the manufacturer, the way you can buy a Dell computer directly from Dell, for instance).
- *Information you can find online (not all information is available at all sites).* Makes, models, colors, options, option packages (often, specific options are available only as part of a package; you need to know these constraints before you select your options), photos, specifications (everything from engine size to interior space), mileage estimates, performance data, safety information, predicted resale value, reviews, comparable models, insurance costs, consumer ratings, repair and reliability histories, available buyer incentives and rebates, true ownership costs (which include fuel, maintenance, repair, etc.), warranty, loan and lease payments, and maintenance requirements.
- *Advantages of shopping online.* Shopping from the comfort and convenience of home, none of the dreaded negotiating at the dealership (in many cases), the ability to search far and wide for a specific car (even nationwide on many sites), the rapid access to considerable amounts of data and information, reviews from both professional automotive journalists and other consumers. In general, online auto shopping reduces a key advantage that auto dealers used to have, which was control of most of the information in the purchase transaction. Now consumers can find out how reliable each model is, how quickly it will depreciate, how often it is likely to need repairs, what other drivers think of it, how much the dealer paid the manufacturer for it, and so on.
- *Changing nature of the business.* The relationship between "third-party" websites (such as CarsDirect.com and Vehix.com) continues to evolve. At first, the relationship was more antagonistic, as some third-party sites and dealers frequently competed for the same customers, and both sides made bold proclamations about driving the other out of business. However, the relationship is more collaborative in many cases now, with dealers realizing that some third-party sites already have wide brand awareness and nationwide audiences. As the percentage of new car sales that originate via the Internet continues to increase, dealers are more receptive to working with third-party sites.
- *Compare information from multiple sources.* Consumers shouldn't rely solely on the information from a single website. Each site has its own way of organizing information and many have their own ways of evaluating car models and connecting buyers with sellers.
- *Understand what each site is doing.* For instance, some search thousands of dealers, regardless of ownership connections. Others, such as AutoNation, search only affiliated dealers. A search for a specific model might yield only a half-dozen cars on one site but dozens of cars on another site. Find out who owns the site and what their business objectives are, if you can; this will help you assess the information you receive.
- *Leading websites.* Consumers can check out a wide variety of websites, some of which are full-service operations, offering everything from research to negotiation; others provide more specific and limited services. For instance, CarsDirect (www.carsdirect.com) provides a full range of services, whereas Carfax (www.carfax.com) specializes in uncovering the repair histories of individual used cars. Table 15.6 lists some of the leading car-related websites.

Your task: Write an informational report based on your research notes. The purpose of the report is to introduce consumers to the basic concepts of integrating the Internet into their car-buying activities and to educate them about important issues.[15]

▌Portfolio ▌BUILDER

8. Moving the workforce: Understanding commute patterns Your company is the largest private employer in your metropolitan area, and the 43,500 employees in your workforce have a tremendous impact on local traffic. A group of city and county transportation

TABLE 15.6 Leading Automotive Websites

SITE	URL
AutoAdvice	www.autoadvice.com
Autobytel	www.autobytel.com
AutoDirectory.com	www.autodirectory.com
Autos.com	www.autos.com
AutoVantage	www.autovantage.com
Autoweb	www.autoweb.com
CarBargains	www.carbargains.com
Carfax	www.carfax.com
CarPrices.com	www.carprices.com
Cars.com	www.cars.com
CarsDirect	www.carsdirect.com
CarSmart	www.carsmart.com
Consumer Reports	www.consumerreports.com
eBay Motors	www.ebaymotors.com
Edmunds	www.edmunds.com
iMotors	www.imotors.com
IntelliChoice	www.intellichoice.com
InvoiceDealers	www.invoicedealers.com
J.D. Power	www.jdpower.com
Kelley Blue Book	www.kbb.com
MSN Autos	http://autos.msn.com
PickupTruck.com	www.pickuptruck.com
The Car Connection	www.thecarconnection.com
Vehix.com	www.vehix.com
Yahoo! Autos	www.autos.yahoo.com

TABLE 15.7 Employee Carpool Habits

FREQUENCY OF USE: CARPOOLING	PORTION OF WORKFORCE
Every day, every week	10,138 (23%)
Certain days, every week	4,361 (10%)
Randomly	983 (2%)
Never	28,018 (64%)

TABLE 15.8 Use of Public Transportation

FREQUENCY OF USE: PUBLIC TRANSPORTATION	PORTION OF WORKFORCE
Every day, every week	23,556 (54%)
Certain days, every week	2,029 (5%)
Randomly	5,862 (13%)
Never	12,053 (28%)

TABLE 15.9 Effect of Potential Improvements to Public Transportation

WHICH OF THE FOLLOWING WOULD ENCOURAGE YOU TO USE PUBLIC TRANSPORTATION MORE FREQUENTLY? (CHECK ALL THAT APPLY)	PORTION OF RESPONDENTS
Increased perceptions of safety	4,932 (28%)
Improved cleanliness	852 (5%)
Reduced commute times	7,285 (41%)
Greater convenience: fewer transfers	3,278 (18%)
Greater convenience: more stops	1,155 (6%)
Lower (or subsidized) fares	5,634 (31%)
Nothing could encourage me to take public transportation	8,294 (46%)

Note: This question was asked of those respondents who use public transportation randomly or never, a subgroup that represents 17,915 employees or 41 percent of the workforce

officials recently approached your CEO with a request to explore ways to reduce this impact. The CEO has assigned you the task of analyzing the workforce's transportation habits and attitudes as a first step toward identifying potential solutions. He's willing to consider anything from subsidized bus passes to company-owned shuttle buses to telecommuting, but the decision requires a thorough understanding of employee transportation needs. Tables 15.7 through 15.11 summarize data you collected in an employee survey.

Your task: Present the results of your survey in an informational report using the data provided in Tables 15.7 through 15.11.

LONG FORMAL REPORTS REQUIRING ADDITIONAL RESEARCH

Portfolio BUILDER

9. **Face-off: Informational report comparing and contrasting two companies in the same industry** Your boss, Dana Hansell, has been searching for some solid companies to personally invest

TABLE 15.10 Distance Traveled to/from Work

DISTANCE YOU TRAVEL TO WORK (ONE WAY)	PORTION OF WORKFORCE
Less than 1 mile	531 (1%)
1–3 miles	6,874 (16%)
4–10 miles	22,951 (53%)
11–20 miles	10,605 (24%)
More than 20 miles	2,539 (6%)

TABLE 15.11   Is Telecommuting an Option?

DOES THE NATURE OF YOUR WORK MAKE TELECOMMUTING A REALISTIC OPTION?	PORTION OF WORKFORCE
Yes, every day	3,460 (8%)
Yes, several days a week	8,521 (20%)
Yes, random days	12,918 (30%)
No	18,601 (43%)

in for the long term. After reviewing security analysts' reports and financial statements for several candidates, Hansell has narrowed the list to these leading industry competitors:

- Boeing; Airbus (aerospace and airline industry)
- HP; Dell (computers and software industry)
- Merrill Lynch; Schwab (finance, banking, and insurance industry)
- Barnes & Noble; Amazon.com (online retailing)
- UPS; FedEx (trucking and freight industry)

According to Hansell, all of these candidates have about the same financial outlook for the future, so she is not interested in obtaining more financial performance detail. Instead, your boss is looking for more qualitative information, such as

- Fundamental philosophical differences in management styles, launching and handling products and services, marketing products and services, and approach to e-commerce that sets one rival company apart from the other
- Future challenges that each competitor faces
- Important decisions made by the two competitors and how those decisions affected their company
- Fundamental differences in each company's vision of their industry's future (for instance, do they both agree on what consumers want, what products to deliver, and so on?)
- Specific competitive advantages held by each rival
- Past challenges each competitor has faced and how each met those challenges

- Strategic moves made by one rival that might affect the other
- Company success stories
- Brief company background information (Hansell already has some from the brokers' reports)
- Brief comparative statistics such as annual sales, market share, number of employees, number of stores, types of equipment, number of customers, sources of revenue, and so on

Hansell has heard that you are the department's most proficient researcher and an effective writer. You have been assigned the task of preparing a formal, long informational report for her. You need not make a recommendation or come to any conclusions; Hansell will do that based on the informational content of your report.

Your task: Select two industry competitors from the preceding list (or another list provided by your instructor) and write a long formal informational report comparing and contrasting how the two companies are addressing the topics outlined by Hansell. Of course, not every topic will apply to each company, and some will be more important than others—depending on the companies you select. Hansell will invest in only one of the two companies in your report. (Note: Because these topics require considerable research, your instructor may choose to make this a team project.)

10. Is there any justice? Report critiquing legislation Plenty of people complain about their state legislators, but few are specific about their complaints. Here's your chance.

Your task: Write a long formal report about a law that you believe should not have been enacted or should be enacted. Be objective. Write the report using specific facts to support your beliefs. Reach conclusions and offer your recommendation at the end of the report. As a final step, send a copy of the report to an appropriate state official or legislator.

11. Travel opportunities: Report comparing two destinations You are planning to take a two-week trip abroad sometime within the next year. Because there are a couple of destinations that appeal to you, you are going to have to do some research before you can make a decision.

Your task: Prepare a lengthy comparative study of two countries that you would like to visit. Begin by making a list of important questions you will need to answer. Do you want a relaxing vacation or an educational experience? What types of services will you require? What will your transportation needs be? Where will you have the least difficulty with the language? Using resources in your library, the Internet, and perhaps travel agencies, analyze the suitability of these two destinations with respect to your own travel criteria. At the end of the report, recommend the better country to visit this year.

Portfolio BUILDER

12. Secondary sources: Report based on library and online research As a college student and active consumer, you may have considered one or more of the following questions at some point in the past few years:

a. What criteria distinguish the top-rated MBA programs in the country? How well do these criteria correspond to the needs and expectations of business? Are the criteria fair for students, employers, business schools?

b. Which of three companies you might like to work for has the strongest corporate ethics policies?

c. What will the music industry look like in the future? What's next after online stores such as Apple iTunes and digital players such as the iPod?

d. Which industries and job categories are forecast to experience the greatest growth—and therefore the greatest demands for workers—in the next 10 years?

e. What has been the impact of Starbucks' aggressive growth on small, independent coffee shops? On midsized chains or franchises? In the United States or in another country?

f. How large is the "industry" of major college sports? How much do the major football or basketball programs contribute—directly or indirectly—to other parts of a typical university?

g. How much have minor league sports—baseball, hockey, arena football—grown in small- and medium-market cities? What is the local economic impact when these municipalities build stadiums and arenas?

Your task: Answer one of those questions using secondary research sources for information. Be sure to document your sources in the correct form. Give conclusions and offer recommendations where appropriate.

▌Portfolio ▌BUILDER

13. Doing business abroad: Report summarizing the social and business customs of a foreign country Your company would like to sell its products overseas. Before they begin negotiating on the international horizon, however, the management team members must have a clear understanding of the social and business customs of the countries where they intend to do business.

Your task: Choose a non-English-speaking country and write a long formal report summarizing the country's social and business customs. Review Chapter 3 and use Table 3.1 as a guide for the types of information you should include in your report.

FORMAL PROPOSALS

▌Portfolio ▌BUILDER

14. Polishing the presenters: Offering your services as a presentation trainer Presentations can make—or break—both careers and businesses. A good presentation can bring in millions of dollars in new sales or fresh investment capital. A bad presentation might cause any number of troubles, from turning away potential customers to upsetting fellow employees to derailing key projects. To help business professionals plan, create, and deliver more effective presentations, you offer a three-day workshop that covers the essentials of good presentations:

- Understanding your audience's needs and expectations
- Formulating your presentation objectives
- Choosing an organizational approach
- Writing openings that catch your audience's attention
- Creating effective graphics and slides

- Practicing and delivering your presentation
- Leaving a positive impression on your audience
- Avoiding common mistakes with Microsoft PowerPoint
- Making presentations online using webcasting tools
- Handling questions and arguments from the audience
- Overcoming the top 10 worries of public speaking (including *How can I overcome stage fright?* and *I'm not the performing type; can I still give an effective presentation?*)

Workshop benefits: Students will learn how to prepare better presentations in less time and deliver them more effectively.

Who should attend: Top executives, project managers, employment recruiters, sales professionals, and anyone else who gives important presentations to internal or external audiences.

Your qualifications: 18 years of business experience, including 14 years in sales and 12 years in public speaking. Experience speaking to audiences as large as 5,000 people. More than a dozen speech-related articles published in professional journals. Have conducted successful workshops for nearly 100 companies.

Workshop details: Three-day workshop (9 A.M. to 3:30 P.M.) that combines lectures, practice presentations, and both individual and group feedback. Minimum number of students: 6. Maximum number of students per workshop: 12

Pricing: The cost is $3,500, plus $100 per student. 10 percent discount for additional workshops.

Other information: Each attendee will have the opportunity to give three practice presentations that will last from three to five minutes. Everyone is encouraged to bring PowerPoint files containing slides from actual business presentations. Each attendee will also receive a workbook and a digital video recording of his or her final class presentation. You'll also be available for phone or e-mail coaching for six months after the workshop.

Your task: Identify a company in your local area that might be a good candidate for your services. Learn more about the company by visiting its website so you can personalize your proposal. Using the information listed earlier in this exercise, prepare a sales proposal that explains the benefits of your training and what students can expect during the workshop.

Portfolio BUILDER

15. Healthy alternatives: Proposal to sell snacks and beverages at local schools For years, a controversy has been brewing over the amount of junk food and soft drinks being sold through vending machines in local schools. Schools benefit from revenue-sharing arrangements, but many parents and health experts are concerned about the negative effects of these snacks and beverages. You and your brother have almost a decade of experience running espresso and juice stands in malls and on street corners, and you'd love to find some way to expand your business into schools. After a quick brainstorming session, the two of you craft a plan that makes good business sense while meeting the financial concerns of school administrators and the nutritional concerns of parents and dieticians. Here are the notes from your brainstorming session:

- Set up portable juice bars on school campuses, offering healthy fruit and vegetable drinks along with simple, healthy snacks.
- Offers schools 30 percent of profits in exchange for free space and long-term contracts.
- Provide job training opportunities for students (during athletic events, etc.).
- Provide detailed dietary analysis of all products sold.
- Establish a nutritional advisory board composed of parents, students, and at least one certified health professional.
- Assure schools and parents that all products are safe (e.g., no stimulant drinks, no dietary supplements, and so on).
- Support local farmers and specialty food preparers by buying locally and giving these vendors the opportunity to test market new products at your stands.

Your task: Based on the ideas listed, draft a formal proposal to the local school board, outlining your plan to offer healthier alternatives to soft drinks and prepackaged snack foods. Invent any details you need to complete your proposal.

Portfolio BUILDER

16. Career connections: Helping employees get the advice they need to move ahead Seems like everybody in the firm is frustrated. On the one hand, top executives complain about the number of lower-level employees who want promotions but just don't seem to "get it" when it comes to dealing with customers and the public, recognizing when to speak out and when to be quiet, knowing how to push new ideas through the appropriate channels, and performing other essential but difficult-to-teach tasks. On the other hand, ambitious employees who'd like to learn more feel that they have nowhere to turn for career advice from people who've been there. In between, a variety of managers and mid-level executives are overwhelmed by the growing number of mentoring requests they're getting, sometimes from employees they don't even know.

You've been assigned the challenge of proposing a formal mentoring program—and a considerable challenge it is:

- The number of employees who want mentoring relationships far exceeds the number of managers and executives willing and able to be mentoring; how will you select people for the program?
- The people most in demand for mentoring also tend to be some of the busiest people in the organization.
- After several years of belt tightening and staff reductions, the entire company feels overworked; few people can imagine adding another recurring task to their seemingly endless to-do lists.
- What's in it for the mentors? Why would they be motivated to help lower-level employees?
- How will you measure success or failure of the mentoring effort?

Your task: Identify potential solutions to the issues (make up any information you need), then draft a proposal to the executive committee for a formal, companywide mentoring program that would match selected employees with successful managers and executives.

PART 6

Designing and Delivering Oral and Online Presentations

CHAPTER 16
Creating and Delivering Oral and Online Presentations

CHAPTER 17
Enhancing Presentations with Slides and Other Visuals

CHAPTER 16

Creating and Delivering Oral and Online Presentations

LEARNING OBJECTIVES

After studying this chapter, you will be able to

1 Explain the importance of oral and online presentations in your career success

2 Explain how to adapt the three-step writing process to oral presentations

3 Identify the two primary reasons that limiting your scope is especially important for oral presentations

4 Distinguish a planning outline from a speaking outline and explain the purpose of each

5 Discuss the three functions of an effective introduction

6 Identify six ways to get your audience's attention and six ways to hold it

7 Describe the techniques you can use to feel more confident in front of an audience

COMMUNICATION CLOSE-UP AT FITCH

www.fitch.com

Figure out what the audience expects to get from a presentation—and then *don't* give it to them? A risky strategy, indeed, but it's working for Fitch, a global design consultancy with offices in North America, Europe, Asia, and the Middle East. Fitch designs everything from restaurant layouts and consumer products to corporate events and websites.

For most professional services firms, a sales presentation follows a predictable pattern: speak about the company's capabilities, introduce a small army of talented people to impress the potential client, present examples of work done for other clients, then ask the audience for a decision. Most presenters prefer this approach because they get to speak from a position of confidence (based on all the great work they've done for other clients) and their level of risk is low (they don't have to present any new ideas until they get a contract).

Even though potential clients expect a traditional "pitch" with all this information, Fitch doesn't offer it. Instead, the

Presenters at Fitch often take chances in their presentations by going against audience expectations. The strategy works if it stimulates new thinking and ultimately meets audience needs.

company's designers study the client's business, develop a strong point of view regarding the challenge at hand, then work on a design concept—all before making a presentation. When it comes time for a presentation, Fitch essentially says, "Here's the design we think is right for you. Love it or leave it." According to Eric Ashworth, a Fitch marketing executive, the goal is to inspire an "A-ha!" moment that makes the audience excited—and maybe just a little nervous.

Does this brash approach work? Ashworth says this style of presentation is 30 percent more effective in generating sales and has led to contracts with such clients as 3M, LEGO, Nissan, Nokia, and the BBC. However, he does offer a caution: the approach can work wonders—or "get you pushed out of the room."[1]

BUILDING YOUR CAREER WITH ORAL PRESENTATIONS

1 LEARNING OBJECTIVE

Explain the importance of oral and online presentations in your career success

No matter how expected or unexpected your next presentation might be, Fitch's Eric Ashworth (profiled in the chapter-opening "Communication Close-Up) can verify that oral presentations offer you important opportunities to put all your communication skills on display—not only in research, planning, writing, and visual design, but in interpersonal and nonverbal communication, too. Oral presentations can also give you a chance to demonstrate your abilities to think on your feet, grasp complex issues, and handle challenging situations—all attributes that executives look for when searching for talented employees to promote within the organization. Perhaps best of all, oral presentations let your personality shine through in ways that even the best-written reports can't provide.

The nature and frequency of the presentations you make will vary widely, depending on your career path. For instance, if you move into sales or professional services, you might give several presentations a week or even several a day. In other situations, you might give weekly or monthly status updates to your colleagues or quarterly and annual financial updates to investors and stock market analysts. If you work in the human resources department, you may give orientation briefings to new employees or explain company policies, procedures, and benefits at companywide meetings. If you're a technical expert, you might conduct training programs.

Feeling nervous is perfectly normal when you're faced with an oral presentation; the good news is there are positive steps you can take to reduce your anxiety.

If the thought of giving a speech or presentation makes you nervous, try to keep three points in mind. First, everybody gets nervous when speaking in front of a group. Even professional speakers and entertainers get nervous after years of experience. Second, being nervous is actually a good thing; it means you care about the topic, your audience, and your career success. With practice, you can convert those nervous feelings into positive energy. Third, you don't have to be a victim of your own emotions when it comes to oral presentations. You can take control of the situation by using the planning and development techniques that you'll learn in this chapter—starting with how to adapt the three-step writing process to the unique challenges of oral and online presentations.

While you don't usually write your oral presentations word for word, the three-step writing process is easily adaptable to oral presentations.

You will rarely write out a presentation word for word; nevertheless, nearly every task in the three-step writing process applies to oral presentations, with some modifications (see Figure 16.1). In addition, a few extra steps will help you prepare both your material and yourself for the actual presentation. As with written reports, people often judge the quality of the content by the quality of the presentation, so your delivery style and the packaging of any visual support materials can be as important as your message. This chapter walks you through the three-step development process, then Chapter 17 offers advice on creating visual materials to enhance your presentation.

PLANNING YOUR PRESENTATION

2 LEARNING OBJECTIVE

Explain how to adapt the three-step writing process to oral presentations

Planning presentations is much like planning any other business message: You (1) analyze the situation, (2) gather information, (3) select the right medium, and (4) organize the information. Gathering information for oral presentations is essentially the same as it is for written communication projects (see Chapter 11). The other three planning tasks have some special applications when it comes to oral presentations; they are covered in the following sections.

FIGURE 16.1   The Three-Step Process for Developing Oral and Online Presentations
Although you rarely "write" a presentation or speech in the sense of composing every word ahead of time, the tasks in the three-step writing process adapt quite well to the challenge of planning, creating, and delivering both oral and online presentations.

Plan

Analyze the Situation
Define your purpose and develop a profile of your audience, including their emotional states and language preferences.

Gather Information
Determine audience needs and obtain the information necessary to satisfy those needs.

Select the Right Medium
Choose the best medium or combination of media for delivering your presentation, including handouts and other support materials.

Organize the Information
Define your main idea, limit your scope and verify timing, select a direct or an indirect approach, and outline your content.

1

Write

Adapt to Your Audience
Be sensitive to audience needs and expectations with a "you" attitude, politeness, positive emphasis, and bias-free language. Build a strong relationship with your audience by establishing your credibility and projecting your company's image. Adjust your delivery style to fit the situation, from casual to formal.

Compose Your Presentation
Outline an effective introduction, body, and close. Prepare supporting visuals and speaking notes.

2

Complete

Revise the Message
Evaluate your content and speaking notes.

Master Your Delivery
Choose your delivery mode and practice your presentation.

Prepare to Speak
Verify facilities and equipment, including online connections and software setups. Hire an interpreter if necessary.

Overcome Anxiety
Take steps to feel more confident and appear more confident on stage.

3

Analyzing the Situation

As with written communications, analyzing the situation involves defining your purpose and developing an audience profile. The purpose of most of your presentations will be to inform or to persuade, although you may occasionally need to make a collaborative presentation, such as when you're leading a problem-solving or brainstorming session. Given the time limitations of most presentations and the "live" nature of the event, make sure your purpose is crystal clear. For instance, with Fitch's unusual presentation strategy, the company skips something audience members expect to hear (descriptions of work done in the past) in order to focus on something audience members really want to hear (how Fitch can help them in the future). Whether your message is expected or not, clarity of purpose is essential to communicating efficiently and effectively.

The purpose of most business presentations is to inform or persuade; you may also give presentations designed primarily to collaborate with others.

When you develop your audience profile, try to anticipate what sort of emotional state your audience members are likely to be in. Will they accept your message automatically, or will they fight you every step of the way? Even though such concerns apply to written messages as well, they become even more important in live-audience situations, because individual emotions can play off one another. In a worst-case scenario, a herd mentality can take over, and people who might accept your message in a calm, one-on-one setting wind up rejecting it under the influence of the crowd's emotions.

Knowing your audience's state of mind will help you adjust both your message and your delivery.

You also need to determine whether your audience is comfortable listening to the language you speak. Listening to an unfamiliar language is much harder than reading that language, so an audience that might be able to read a written report might not be able to understand an oral presentation covering the same material (see "Communicating Across Cultures: Five Tips for Making Presentations Around the World").

As you analyze the situation, also consider the specific circumstances in which you'll be making your presentation. Will you speak to five people in a conference room, where you can control everything from light to sound to temperature? Or will you be demonstrating a

Communicating Across Cultures

Five Tips for Making Presentations Around the World

When speaking to an international audience, keep in mind that members' language fluency might vary widely. So take special care to ensure clear communication:

1. **Speak slowly and distinctly.** The most common complaint of international audiences is that English speakers talk too fast. Articulate every word carefully, emphasize consonants for clarity, and pause frequently.
2. **Repeat key words and phrases.** When audiences are less familiar with your language, they need to hear important information more than once. Also, they may not be familiar with synonyms, so word key points in the same way throughout your presentation.
3. **Aim for clarity.** Keep your message simple. Eliminate complex sentence structure, abbreviations, and acronyms. Replace two-word verbs with one-word alternatives (such as *review* instead of *look over*). Such verbs are confusing because the definition of each separate word differs from the meaning of the two words combined. Similarly, avoid cultural idioms, such as *once in a blue moon*, which may be unfamiliar to an international audience.
4. **Communicate with body language.** Emphasize and clarify verbal information with gestures and facial expres-

sions. For instance, smile to emphasize positive points and use gestures to illustrate the meaning of words such as *up*, *down*, or *under*.
5. **Support your spoken message with visuals.** Simple, clear visuals, from flip charts to electronic slides, can help you describe your key points. If possible, prepare captions both in English and in your audience's native language.

CAREER APPLICATIONS

1. One of the most important changes speakers need to make when addressing audiences in other cultures is to avoid colloquial figures of speech. Replace each of these phrases with wording that is more likely to be understood by non-native English speakers or audiences in other countries: "hit one out of the park," "go for broke," and "get your ducks lined up."
2. Make a list of 10 two-word verbs. How does the meaning of each separate word differ from the definition of the combined words? Replace each two-word verb with a single, specific word that will be clearer to an international audience.

Try to learn as much as you can about the setting and circumstances of your presentation, from the size of the audience to potential interruptions.

product on the floor of a trade show, where you might have anywhere from 5 to 500 people and little control over the environment? Will everyone be in the same room, or will some or all of your audience participate from remote locations via the Internet? What equipment will you have at your disposal? All these variables can influence not only the style of your presentation but even the content itself. For instance, in a public environment full of distractions and uncertainties, you're probably better off keeping your content simple and short because chances are you won't be able to keep everyone's attention for the duration of your presentation.

Table 16.1 offers a summary of the key steps in analyzing an audience for oral presentations. For even more insight into audience evaluation (including emotional and cultural issues), consult a good public-speaking textbook.

Selecting the Right Medium

Expect to give many online presentations in your career.

The task of selecting the right medium might seem obvious—after all, you are speaking, so it's an oral medium. However, technology offers an array of choices these days, ranging from live, in-person presentations to podcasts to webcasts that people view on your website whenever doing so fits their individual schedules. Explore these options early on so that you can take full advantage of the ones at your disposal. For example, to reach an international audience, you might want to conduct a live presentation with a question-and-answer session for the on-site audience and post a video archive of this meeting on your website for audience members in other time zones.

Organizing Your Presentation

Organizing a presentation involves the same tasks as organizing a written message: Define your main idea, limit your scope, select a direct or an indirect approach, and outline your

TABLE 16.1 Analyzing an Audience for Oral Presentations

TASK	ACTIONS
To determine audience size and composition	• Estimate how many people will attend and whether they will all attend in person, online, or a mix of both. • Consider whether they share professional interests or other affiliations that can help you establish common ground with them. • Analyze the mix of men and women, age ranges, socioeconomic and ethnic groups, occupations, and geographic regions represented.
To predict the audience's probable reaction	• Analyze why audience members are attending the presentation. • Determine the audience's general attitude toward the topic: interested, moderately interested, unconcerned, open-minded, or hostile. • Analyze the mood that people will be in when you speak to them. • Find out what kind of backup information will most impress the audience: technical data, historical information, financial data, demonstrations, samples, and so on. • Consider whether the audience has any biases that might work against you. • Anticipate possible objections or questions.
To gauge the audience's level of understanding	• Analyze whether everybody has the same background and experience. • Determine what the audience already knows about the subject. • Decide what background information the audience will need to better understand the subject. • Consider whether the audience is familiar with your vocabulary. • Analyze what the audience expects from you. • Think about the mix of general concepts and specific details you will need to present.

content. As you work through these tasks, keep in mind that oral media have certain restraints. When reading written reports, audiences can skip back and forth, backing up if they miss a point or become confused and jumping ahead if they aren't interested in a particular part or are already familiar with the content. However, audiences for oral presentations are more or less trapped in your time frame and sequence. Other than interrupting you, they have no choice but to listen to your content in the exact order in which you present it. (Of course, if you've made your presentation available as a webcast or podcast, listeners do have the option of moving back and forth at their own pace.)

Define Your Main Idea

If you've ever heard a speaker struggle to get his or her point across ("What I really mean to say is . . ."), you know how frustrating such an experience can be for an audience. To avoid that struggle, figure out the one message you want audience members to walk away with. Know what you want them to do after listening to you. Then compose a one-sentence summary that links your subject and purpose to your audience's frame of reference, much as an advertising slogan points out how a product can benefit consumers. Here are some examples of how to word your main idea:

If you can't express your main idea in a single sentence, you probably haven't defined it clearly enough.

- Convince management that reorganizing the technical support department will improve customer service and reduce employee turnover.
- Convince the board of directors that we should build a new plant in Texas to eliminate manufacturing bottlenecks and improve production quality.
- Address employee concerns regarding a new health-care plan by showing how the plan will reduce costs and improve the quality of their care.

Each of these statements puts a particular slant on the subject, one that directly relates to the audience's interests. Make sure your purpose is based on a clear understanding of audience needs so that you can deliver information your audience truly cares about.[2] For example, a group of new employees will be much more responsive to your discussion of plant safety procedures if you focus on how the procedures can save lives and prevent injuries, rather than focusing on company rules, saving the company money, or conforming to Occupational Safety and Health Administration (OSHA) guidelines.

Limit Your Scope

3 LEARNING OBJECTIVE

Identify the two primary reasons that limiting your scope is especially important for oral presentations

Limiting your scope is important for two reasons: to ensure that your presentation fits the allotted time and to make sure your content meets audience needs and expectations.

Effective presentations not only focus on the audience's needs but also tailor the material to the time allowed, which is often strictly regulated. Moreover, in many situations, multiple presenters are scheduled to speak one right after the other, so time allotments are rigid, permitting little or no flexibility. If you overestimate the amount of material you can cover within your allotted time, you're left with only unpleasant alternatives: rushing through your presentation, skipping some of the information you've so carefully prepared, or trying to steal a few minutes from the next presenter. Or if don't have enough material prepared to fill your time slot, you might be left standing in front of the audience trying to ad lib information you haven't prepared.

Limiting your scope also involves matching your message with your audience's needs and expectations. Studies show that audience attention levels and retention rates drop sharply after 20 minutes, and venture capitalists (investors who fund many new companies) expect entrepreneurs to get to the point within 15 minutes.[3] In addition, if you try to cover too many details in a presentation, you can leave the audience feeling confused and frustrated. Often a better approach is to explain important concepts in your oral presentation and refer your audience to printed documents or websites for supporting details.

The only sure way to measure the length of your presentation is to complete a practice run.

Once you've decided on the right amount of information to cover, do your best to estimate the time required to present that material or to estimate the amount of material you can cover within a fixed amount of time. The only sure way to do so is to practice. As an alternative to a complete practice run, you can try several techniques for estimating time requirements. First, if you're in one of those rare situations in which you're reciting your material verbatim or reading from a prepared script (more on that later in the chapter), you can divide your word count by 125 (if you speak slower than average) or 150 (if you're faster than average) to get a rough idea of how many minutes you'll need. Most speakers can comfortably deliver between 125 and 150 words per minute. Second, you can measure how long it takes to talk through a small portion of your presentation, then extrapolate how long the entire presentation will take. This method isn't terribly accurate, but it can help identify major timing problems. Third, after you get some experience giving presentations with either overhead transparencies or electronic slides, you'll get a feel for the time you typically need to cover a single slide. As a general guideline, figure on 3 or even 4 minutes per slide.[4] For instance, if you have 20 minutes, plan on roughly five to seven slides. If you're whipping through slides faster than that, chances are you might be simply reading bullet points from your slides or not engaging the audience with enough discussion about each slide.

Of course, be sure to factor in time for introductions, coffee breaks, demonstrations, question-and-answer sessions, and anything else that takes away from your speaking time.

Choose Your Approach

Organize a short presentation the same way you would a brief written message; organize a longer presentation as you would a report.

If you have 10 minutes or less to deliver your message, organize your presentation much as you would a brief written message: Use a direct approach if the subject involves routine information or good news, and use an indirect approach if the subject involves negative news or persuasion. Plan your introduction to arouse interest and to give a preview of what's to come. For the body of the presentation, be prepared to explain the who, what, when, where, why, and how of your subject. In the final few moments, review the points you've made, and close with a statement that will help your audience remember the subject of your speech (see Figure 16.2).

Longer presentations are organized like reports. If the purpose is to inform, use a direct approach and a structure imposed naturally by the subject: importance, sequence, chronology, spatial orientation, geography, or category (as discussed in Chapter 13). If your purpose is to analyze, persuade, or collaborate, organize your material around conclusions and rec-

---

Progress Report: August 2008

Purpose: To update the Executive Committee on our product development schedule.

I.   Review goals and progress.
    A. Mechanical design:
       1. Goal: 100%
       2. Actual: 80%
       3. Reason for delay: Unanticipated problems with case durability
    B. Software development:
       1. Goal: 50%
       2. Actual: 60%
    C. Material sourcing:
       1. Goal: 100%
       2. Actual: 45% (and materials identified are at 140% of anticipated costs)
       3. Reason for delay: Purchasing is understaffed and hasn't been able to research sources adequately.
II. Discuss schedule options.
    A. Option 1: Reschedule product launch date.
    B. Option 2: Launch on schedule with more expensive materials.
III. Suggest goals for next month.
IV. Q&A

FIGURE 16.2 Effective Outline for a 10-Minute Progress Report
Here is an outline of a short presentation that updates management on the status of a key project; the presenter has some bad news to deliver, so she opted for an indirect approach to lay out the reasons for the delay before sharing the news of the schedule slip.

ommendations or around a logical argument. Use a direct approach if the audience is receptive and an indirect approach if you expect resistance.

As you develop your presentation, keep in mind that oral reports have one important advantage over written reports: you can adjust your outline on the fly if you need to. Identify the critical points in your presentation and ask yourself some "what if" questions to address possible audience reactions. For instance, if you're worried that the audience might not agree with the financial assumptions you've made, you might prepare a detailed analysis that you can include in your presentation if you sense that a negative reaction is building or if someone openly questions you about it. As you'll see in Chapter 17, presentation software such as Microsoft PowerPoint makes it easy to adjust your presentation as you move along, allowing you the chance to skip over any parts you decide not to use or to insert backup material at the last minute.

Regardless of the length of your presentation, remember that simplicity of organization is especially valuable in oral communication. If listeners lose the thread of your presentation, they'll have a hard time catching up and following your message in the remainder of your speech. Look for the most obvious and natural way to organize your ideas, using a direct approach whenever possible. Explain at the beginning how you've organized your material, and try to limit the number of main points to three or four—even when the speech or presentation is lengthy.

Simplicity is critical in the organization of oral and online presentations.

Finally, remind yourself that just like every good business message, effective presentations have a clear introduction, body, and close. In fact, one noted presentation expert even advises a three-act storytelling structure (the approach used in many novels, movies, and TV shows). Act I introduces the "story" you're about to tell and grabs the audience's attention. Act II explores the complications, evidence, support points, and other information needed to understand the story and its conclusion. Act III resolves all the complications and presents a solution that addresses the problem introduced in Act I and that is strongly supported by all the evidence introduced in Act II.[5]

Prepare Your Outline

A presentation outline helps you plan your speaking notes as well as your presentation.

A presentation outline (see Figure 16.3) performs the same function as an outline for a written document: helping you organize the message in a way that maximizes its impact on your audience. However, a presentation outline can also serve as the foundation of your speaking notes, so as you write your outline, start thinking about the words you'll want to use when you deliver your presentation. To ensure effective organization, prepare your outline in several stages:[6]

- **State your purpose and main idea.** As you develop your outline, check frequently to be sure that the points, organization, connections, and title relate to your purpose and main idea.
- **Organize your major points and subpoints.** Express each major point as a single, complete sentence to help you keep track of the one specific idea you want to convey in

FIGURE 16.3 Effective Outline for a 30-Minute Presentation
This outline clearly identifies the purpose and the distinct points to be made in the introduction, body, and close. Notice also how the speaker wrote her major transitions in full sentence form to be sure she can clearly phrase these critical passages when it's time to speak.

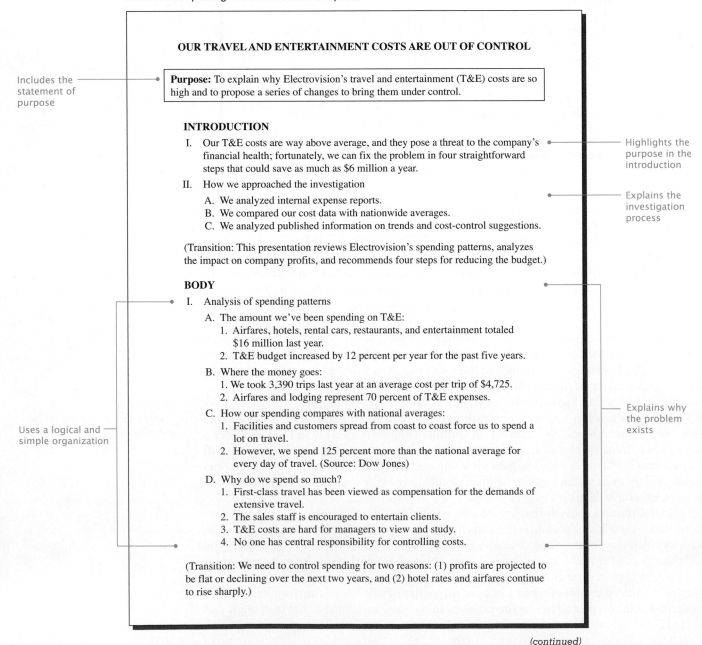

Includes the statement of purpose

OUR TRAVEL AND ENTERTAINMENT COSTS ARE OUT OF CONTROL

Purpose: To explain why Electrovision's travel and entertainment (T&E) costs are so high and to propose a series of changes to bring them under control.

INTRODUCTION

I. Our T&E costs are way above average, and they pose a threat to the company's financial health; fortunately, we can fix the problem in four straightforward steps that could save as much as $6 million a year. — Highlights the purpose in the introduction

II. How we approached the investigation
   A. We analyzed internal expense reports.
   B. We compared our cost data with nationwide averages.
   C. We analyzed published information on trends and cost-control suggestions. — Explains the investigation process

(Transition: This presentation reviews Electrovision's spending patterns, analyzes the impact on company profits, and recommends four steps for reducing the budget.)

BODY

I. Analysis of spending patterns
   A. The amount we've been spending on T&E:
      1. Airfares, hotels, rental cars, restaurants, and entertainment totaled $16 million last year.
      2. T&E budget increased by 12 percent per year for the past five years.
   B. Where the money goes:
      1. We took 3,390 trips last year at an average cost per trip of $4,725.
      2. Airfares and lodging represent 70 percent of T&E expenses.
   C. How our spending compares with national averages:
      1. Facilities and customers spread from coast to coast force us to spend a lot on travel.
      2. However, we spend 125 percent more than the national average for every day of travel. (Source: Dow Jones) — Explains why the problem exists
   D. Why do we spend so much?
      1. First-class travel has been viewed as compensation for the demands of extensive travel.
      2. The sales staff is encouraged to entertain clients.
      3. T&E costs are hard for managers to view and study.
      4. No one has central responsibility for controlling costs.

Uses a logical and simple organization

(Transition: We need to control spending for two reasons: (1) profits are projected to be flat or declining over the next two years, and (2) hotel rates and airfares continue to rise sharply.)

(continued)

that point. Then look at the order of points to make sure their arrangement is logical and effective.

- **Identify your introduction, body, and close.** Start with the body, numbering each major point and subpoint according to its level in your outline. Then lay out the points for your introduction and close.
- **Show your connections.** Write out in sentence form the transitions you plan to use to move from one part to the next. Remember to include additional transitions between major points in the body of your speech.
- **Show your sources.** Prepare your bibliography, making sure that it reads easily, follows a consistent format, and includes all the details needed to identify your various sources. As needed, be prepared to mention key sources during your talk.
- **Choose a title.** Not all presentations or speeches have a title. However, a title can be useful if your presentation will be publicized ahead of time or introduced by someone else. The title sets everyone's expectations, so make it compelling and audience-centered.

The outline in Figure 16.3 is for a 30-minute analytical presentation that uses a direct approach, organized around conclusions. This outline is based on Chapter 15's Electrovision report, written by Linda Moreno.

FIGURE 16.3 *Continued*

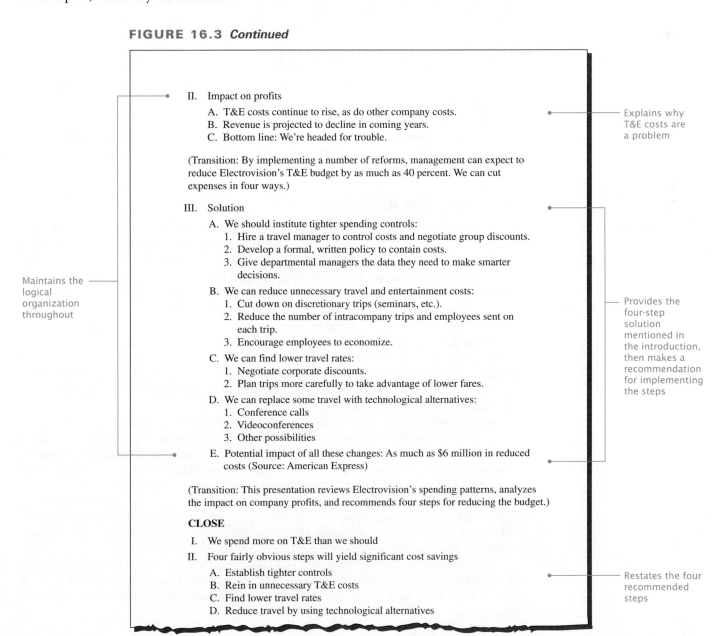

II. Impact on profits
    A. T&E costs continue to rise, as do other company costs.
    B. Revenue is projected to decline in coming years.
    C. Bottom line: We're headed for trouble.

Explains why T&E costs are a problem

(Transition: By implementing a number of reforms, management can expect to reduce Electrovision's T&E budget by as much as 40 percent. We can cut expenses in four ways.)

III. Solution
    A. We should institute tighter spending controls:
        1. Hire a travel manager to control costs and negotiate group discounts.
        2. Develop a formal, written policy to contain costs.
        3. Give departmental managers the data they need to make smarter decisions.
    B. We can reduce unnecessary travel and entertainment costs:
        1. Cut down on discretionary trips (seminars, etc.).
        2. Reduce the number of intracompany trips and employees sent on each trip.
        3. Encourage employees to economize.
    C. We can find lower travel rates:
        1. Negotiate corporate discounts.
        2. Plan trips more carefully to take advantage of lower fares.
    D. We can replace some travel with technological alternatives:
        1. Conference calls
        2. Videoconferences
        3. Other possibilities
    E. Potential impact of all these changes: As much as $6 million in reduced costs (Source: American Express)

Maintains the logical organization throughout

Provides the four-step solution mentioned in the introduction, then makes a recommendation for implementing the steps

(Transition: This presentation reviews Electrovision's spending patterns, analyzes the impact on company profits, and recommends four steps for reducing the budget.)

CLOSE

I. We spend more on T&E than we should
II. Four fairly obvious steps will yield significant cost savings
    A. Establish tighter controls
    B. Rein in unnecessary T&E costs
    C. Find lower travel rates
    D. Reduce travel by using technological alternatives

Restates the four recommended steps

*You may find it helpful to create a
simpler speaking outline from your
planning outline.*

Many speakers like to prepare both a detailed *planning outline* and a simpler *speaking
outline* that provides all the cues and reminders they need to present their material.[7] Here
are some guidelines for preparing an effective speaking outline:[8]

- **Follow the planning outline.** Follow the same format as you used for your planning
  outline so it will be familiar as you talk. However, strip away anything you don't plan to
  say to your audience (statements of general purpose, specific purpose, main idea, detailed bibliography, etc.).
- **Condense points and transitions to keywords.** Choose words that will prompt you to
  remember what each point is about so that you can speak fluently. Be sure to write out
  statistics, quotations, and other specifics so that you don't stumble over them. You may
  also want to write complete sentences for transitions that connect main points or for
  critical points in your introduction or your close.
- **Add delivery cues.** During rehearsals, note the places in your outline where you plan
  to pause for emphasis, speak more slowly, use a visual, and so on.
- **Arrange your notes.** Make sure your note cards are legible and numbered so that you
  can keep them in order before and during your presentation.

If you plan to use PowerPoint or other presentation software, you can also use the "notes"
field on each slide for speaking notes.

WRITING YOUR PRESENTATION

Although you may never actually write out a presentation word for word, you still engage
in the writing process—developing your ideas, structuring support points, phrasing your
transitions, and so on. Depending on the situation and your personal style, you might follow these initial words closely during your actual presentation, or you might express your
thoughts in fresh, spontaneous language. Before you get to the actual writing phase, consider how you should adapt your style to your audience.

Adapting to Your Audience

*Adapting to your audience
addresses a number of issues, from
speaking style to technology
choices.*

What does your audience expect from your presentation? Will you stage a formal presentation in an impressive setting with professionally produced visuals? Or will you lead a casual,
roll-up-your-sleeves working session? Adapt your approach to fit the occasion. Your audience's size, your subject, your purpose, your budget, and the time available for preparation
all influence the style of your presentation. Your style sends a message, and that message is
open to interpretation. For example, a glitzy, multimedia presentation might attract new
clients, but it might cause potential investors to question your fiscal prudence.

If you're speaking to a small group, particularly people you already know, you can use
a casual style that encourages audience participation. A small conference room, with your
audience seated around a table, may be appropriate. Use simple visuals, and invite your audience to interject comments. Deliver your remarks in a conversational tone, using notes to
jog your memory if necessary.

If you're addressing a large audience and the event is an important one, you'll want to
establish a more formal atmosphere. A formal style is well suited to announcements about
mergers or acquisitions, new products, financial results, and other business milestones.
During formal presentations, speakers often stand on a *podium* or stage, behind a *lectern*
that can hold their notes, a microphone, and controls for the presentation equipment.

Whether your presentation is informal or formal, always choose your words carefully.
If you try to impress your audience with obscure or unfamiliar vocabulary, your message
will be lost. Make sure you can define all the words you use. And keep things simple. If you
repeatedly stumble over a word as you rehearse, use a different one.[9]

Finally, when you're pondering how you'll adapt to your audience, take public speaking
etiquette into account. Show consideration for your audience members by making good use
of their time, addressing them respectfully, and maintaining a professional presence during
your speech.

Composing Your Presentation

Just like written documents, presentations are composed of distinct elements: the introduction, the body, and the close.

Introduction

A good introduction arouses the audience's interest in your topic, establishes your credibility, and prepares the audience for what will follow. That's a lot to pack into the first few minutes of your presentation, so give yourself plenty of time to develop the words and visuals you'll use to get your presentation off to a great start.

Arousing Audience Interest   Some subjects are naturally more interesting than others. If you will be discussing a matter of profound significance that will personally affect the members of your audience, chances are they'll listen regardless of how you begin. All you really have to do is announce your topic, and you'll have their attention.

Other subjects call for more imagination. How do you get people to listen if you're explaining your pension program to a group of new clerical employees, none of whom will be fully eligible for the program for another five years and many of whom might leave the company within two? The best approach to dealing with an uninterested audience is to appeal to human nature and encourage people to take the subject personally. Show them how they'll be affected as individuals. For example, you might begin by addressing the new clerical employees like this:

> If somebody offered to give you $200,000 in exchange for $5 per week, would you be interested? That's the amount you can expect to collect during your retirement years if you choose to contribute to the voluntary pension plan. During the next two weeks, you will have to decide whether you want to participate. Although retirement is many years away for most of you, it is an important financial decision. During the next 20 minutes, I hope to give you the information you need to make a decision that's best for you and your families.

Another way to arouse the audience's interest is to draw out ideas and encourage comments from the audience throughout your presentation. Of course, this technique works better with a small group of co-workers than it does when you're addressing a large audience—particularly if the members of that large audience are hostile or unknown to you. When addressing large audiences, responding to questions and comments can interrupt the flow of information, weaken your argument, and reduce your control of the situation. In such situations, it's often best to ask people to hold their questions until after you have concluded your remarks. Just be sure to allow ample time for audience questions at the end of your presentation.

Table 16.2 suggests six techniques you can use to arouse audience interest during your introduction, and "Holding Your Audience's Attention" on page 509 lists six ways to keep audience members' attention throughout your presentation. Regardless of which technique you choose, make sure you can give audience members a reason to care and to believe that the time they're about to spend listening to you will be worth their while.[10]

Building Your Credibility   In addition to grabbing the audience's attention, your introduction has to establish your credibility. If you're a well-known expert in the subject matter or have earned your audience's trust in other situations, you're already ahead of the game. However, if you have no working relationship with your audience or if you're speaking in an area outside your known expertise, you need to establish credibility and do so quickly; people tend to decide within a few minutes whether you're worth listening to.[11] For instance, in its presentations to potential clients, Fitch (see page 497) seeks to build credibility by showing how well its designers understand the audience's business needs.

Techniques for building credibility vary depending on whether you will be introducing yourself or having someone else introduce you. If a master of ceremonies, conference chair, or other person will introduce you, he or she can present your credentials so that you won't appear boastful. However, make sure that the person introducing you doesn't exaggerate your qualifications; your credibility will probably go down rather than up if this happens.

5 LEARNING OBJECTIVE

Discuss the three functions of an effective introduction

If your audience members aren't likely to be naturally interested in your topic, your introduction will need to build interest by relating the subject to their personal concerns.

6 LEARNING OBJECTIVE

Identify six ways to get your audience's attention and six ways to hold it

If someone else will be introducing you to the audience, you can ask this person to present your credentials.

TABLE 16.2 Six Ways to Get Attention During Your Introduction

TASK	ACTIONS
Unite the audience around common goal	Invite them to help solve a problem, capitalize on an opportunity, or otherwise engage in the a topic of your presentation.
Tell a story	Slice-of-life stories are naturally interesting and can be compelling. Be sure your story illustrates an important point.
Pass around a sample	Psychologists say that you can get people to remember your points by appealing to their senses. The best way to do so is to pass around a sample. If your company is in the textile business, let the audience handle some of your fabrics. If you sell chocolates, give everybody a taste.
Ask a question	Asking questions will get the audience actively involved in your presentation and, at the same time, will give you information about them and their needs.
State a startling statistic	People love details. If you can interject an interesting statistic, you can often wake up your audience.
Use humor	Even though the subject of most business presentations is serious, including a light comment now and then can perk up the audience. Just be sure the humor is relevant to the presentation and not offensive to the audience. In general, avoid humor when you and the audience don't share the same native language.

If you will be introducing yourself, keep your comments simple. At the same time, don't be afraid to mention your accomplishments. Your listeners will be curious about your qualifications, so tell them briefly who you are and why you're the right person to be giving this presentation. You might say something like this:

> I'm Karen Whitney, a market research analyst with Information Resources Corporation. For the past five years, I've specialized in studying high-technology markets. Your director of engineering, John LaBarre, has asked me to talk to you about recent trends in computer-aided design so that you'll have a better idea of how to direct your research efforts.

This speaker establishes credibility by tying her credentials to the purpose of her presentation, without boasting. By mentioning her company's name, her specialization and position, and the name of the audience's boss, she lets her listeners know immediately that she is qualified to tell them something they need to know. She connects her background to their concerns.

If you will be introduced by a master of ceremonies or another speaker, that person may be able to briefly itemize your qualifications as a way to build your credibility with the audience.

Previewing Your Message In addition to arousing audience interest and building your credibility, a good introduction gives your audience members a preview of what's ahead, helping them understand the structure and content of your message. A reader can learn these things by looking at the table of contents and scanning the headings, but in an oral presentation, you need to provide that framework with a preview.

Your preview should summarize the main idea of your presentation, identify major supporting points, and indicate the order in which you'll develop those points. Tell your listeners in so many words, "This is the subject, and these are the points I will cover." Once you've established the framework, you can be confident that the audience will understand how the individual facts and figures are related to your main idea as you move into the body of your presentation.

Body

The bulk of your speech or presentation is devoted to a discussion of the three or four main points in your outline. Use the same organizational patterns you'd use in a letter, memo, or report, but keep things simple. Your goals are to make sure that (1) the organization of your presentation is clear and (2) your presentation holds the audience's attention.

Connecting Your Ideas Making sure your audience doesn't get lost is always important, but clarity is doubly critical with spoken communication for the simple reason that your audience members can't back up and reread if they get confused. In written documents, you can show how ideas are related on the page or screen by employing a variety of design clues, such as headings, paragraph indentions, and lists. However, with oral communication—particularly when you aren't using visuals for support—you have to rely primarily on words to link various parts and ideas.

For the small links between sentences and paragraphs, use one or two transitional words: *therefore, because, in addition, in contrast, moreover, for example, consequently, nevertheless,* or *finally.* To link major sections of a presentation, use complete sentences or paragraphs, such as "Now that we've reviewed the problem, let's take a look at some solutions." Every time you shift topics, be sure to stress the connection between ideas. Summarize what's been said, then preview what's to come.

The longer your presentation, the more important your transitions become. If you will be presenting many ideas, audience members may have trouble absorbing them and seeing the relationships among them. Your listeners need clear transitions to guide them to the most important points. Furthermore, they'll appreciate brief, interim summaries to pick up any ideas they might have missed. So by repeating key ideas in your transitions, you can compensate for lapses in your audience's attention. You might also want to call attention to the transitions by using gestures, changing your tone of voice, or introducing a visual, as Chapter 17 points out.

Use transitions to repeat key ideas and help the audience follow along, particularly in longer presentations.

Holding Your Audience's Attention Once you've successfully captured your audience's attention in your introduction, you need to work to keep it throughout the body of your presentation. In addition to the general challenge of keeping readers interested, you have to compensate for another inescapable fact of oral presentations: your audience can think and read faster than you can speak. And with online presentations, where people in remote locations are sitting alone at their computers, the temptation to sneak in other work can be strong. If you don't keep their minds engaged, they'll start thinking of other pressing subjects, reading ahead through your handouts, checking e-mail on wireless handhelds, or doing a thousand other things besides paying attention to you. Here are a few helpful tips for keeping the audience tuned into your message:

The most important way to hold audience members' attention is to show how your message relates to their individual needs and concerns.

- **Relate your subject to your audience's needs.** People are interested in things that affect them personally. As much as possible, present every point in light of your audience's needs and values.
- **Anticipate your audience's questions.** Try to anticipate as many questions as you can, and address these questions in the body of your presentation. You'll also want to prepare and reserve additional material to use during the question-and-answer period should the audience ask for greater detail.
- **Use clear, vivid language.** People become bored quickly when they don't understand the speaker. If your presentation will involve abstract ideas, show how those abstractions connect with everyday life. Use familiar words, short sentences, and concrete examples. Be sure to throw in some variety as well; repeating the same words and phrases puts people to sleep.
- **Explain the relationship between your subject and familiar ideas.** Show how your subject is related to ideas that audience members already understand, and give people a way to categorize and remember your points.[12]

When attempting to hold an audience's attention, public speakers sometimes face distractions in the background. It takes a focused speaker to overcome such physical interruptions and get his or her message across.

- **Ask for opinions or pause occasionally for questions or comments.** Audience feedback helps you determine whether your listeners understand a key point before you launch into another section. Feedback also gives your audience members a chance to switch for a time from listening to participating, which helps them engage with your message and develop a sense of shared ownership.
- **Illustrate your ideas with visual aids.** As Chapter 17 discusses, you may wish to develop visuals for your presentation and coordinate them with your delivery. Visuals enliven your message, help you connect with audience members, and help them remember your message more effectively.

Close

Plan your close carefully so that your audience members leave with your main idea fresh in their minds.

The close of a speech or presentation is critical for two reasons: First, audience members' attention tends to peak at this point because they anticipate moving on to the next activity in their busy day; and second, audience members will leave with your final words ringing in their ears. Before closing your presentation, tell listeners that you're about to finish so that they'll make one final effort to listen intently. Don't be afraid to sound obvious. Consider saying something such as "In conclusion" or "To sum it all up." You want people to know that this is the final segment of your presentation.

Restating Your Main Points   Once you've decided how to announce your close, repeat your main idea. Emphasize what you want your audience to do or to think, and stress the key motivating factor that will encourage them to respond that way. Finally, reinforce your theme by restating your main supporting points. A few sentences are generally enough to refresh people's memories. One speaker ended a presentation on the company's executive compensation program by repeating his four specific recommendations and then concluding with a memorable statement that would motivate his audience to take action:

> We can all be proud of the way our company has grown. However, if we want to continue that growth, we need to adjust our executive compensation program to reflect competitive practices. If we don't, our best people will look for opportunities elsewhere. In summary, our survey has shown that we need to do four things to improve executive compensation:
>
> - Increase the overall level of compensation
> - Install a cash bonus program
> - Offer a variety of stock-based incentives
> - Improve our health insurance and pension benefits
>
> By making these improvements, we can help our company cross the threshold of growth to face our industry's largest competitors.

Such repetition of key ideas greatly improves the chance that your audience will hear your message in the way you intended.

If you need to have the audience make a decision or agree to take action, make sure the responsibilities for doing so are clear.

Describing Next Steps   Some presentations require the audience to reach a decision or agree to take specific action, in which case the close offers an opportunity to verify these steps. If audience members agree on an issue covered in the presentation, review the consensus in a sentence or two. If they don't agree, make the lack of consensus clear by saying something like "We seem to have some fundamental disagreement on this question." Then be ready to suggest a method of resolving the differences. If you're not sure in advance how your audience will respond, prepare alternative closes so that you don't have to scramble for an ending if things don't work as you had planned.

If you expect any action to occur as a result of your speech, be sure to explain who is responsible for doing what and by when. One effective technique is to list the action items, with an estimated completion date and the name of the person or team responsible. You can present this list in a visual and ask each person on the list to agree to accomplish his or her assigned task by the target date. This public commitment to action is good insurance that something will happen.

Ending on a Strong Note Make sure that your final remarks are encouraging and memorable. After summarizing the key points of your presentation, conclude with a quote, a call to action, or some encouraging words. For instance, you might stress the benefits of action or express confidence in the listeners' ability to accomplish the work ahead. An alternative is to end with a question or a statement that will leave your audience thinking.

Plan your final statement carefully so you can end on a strong, positive note.

At the completion of your presentation, your audience should feel satisfied. The close is not the place to introduce new ideas or to alter the mood of the presentation. Even if parts of your presentation are downbeat, close on a positive note. Also, avoid using a staged finale—keep it natural. As with everything else in your oral presentation, compose your closing remarks carefully. You don't want to wind up with nothing to say but "Well, I guess that's it."

COMPLETING YOUR PRESENTATION

With an outline and speaking notes in hand, you're ready to complete the development of your presentation. As with written communication, this third step starts with the all-important task of revising your message to ensure appropriate content. Edit your presentation for clarity and conciseness as you would any business message. For presentations, you'll go beyond these now familiar tasks and pay special attention to four special tasks: mastering the art of delivery, preparing to speak, overcoming anxiety, and handling questions responsively.

Mastering the Art of Delivery

Once you've written your presentation and created the visuals you will use, you're ready to begin practicing your delivery. You have a variety of delivery methods to choose from, some of which are easier to handle than others:

- **Memorizing.** Unless you're a trained actor, avoid memorizing your speech, especially a long one. In the best of circumstances, you'll probably sound stilted; in the worst, you might forget your lines. Besides, you'll often need to address audience questions during your speech, so you must be flexible enough to adjust your speech as you go. However, memorizing a quotation, an opening paragraph, or a few concluding remarks can bolster your confidence and strengthen your delivery.
- **Reading.** If you're delivering a technical or complex presentation, you may want to read it. For instance, policy statements are sometimes read in full because the wording can be critical. However, unless you're required or expected to read your presentation verbatim, reading is usually not your best option. If you read from a prepared script, chances are you won't speak as naturally as you would otherwise, and the result will be a monotonous, uninspiring presentation.[13] After all, if all you're doing is reading, why not just write a report and let your audience members read it themselves? If you do plan to read your speech for whatever reason, practice enough so that you can still maintain eye contact with your audience. Triple-spaced copy, wide margins, and large type will help. You might even want to include stage cues, such as *pause, raise hands*, or *lower voice*.

Speaking from carefully prepared notes is the easiest and most effective delivery mode for most presenters.

- **Speaking from notes.** Making a presentation with the help of an outline, note cards, or visuals is usually the easiest and most effective delivery mode. This approach gives you something to refer to and still allows for plenty of eye contact, interaction with the audience, and improvisation in response to audience feedback. When speaking from notes, be sure to use stiff note cards; nervousness is more easily exposed by shaking sheets of paper.

Practicing a presentation with a co-worker or a friend is a terrific way to polish your public-speaking skills in a relaxed setting.

- **Impromptu speaking.** From time to time, you may have to give an impromptu, or unrehearsed, speech: you may be called on to speak unexpectedly or circumstances may prevent you from preparing a planned speech. If you have the option, avoid speaking unprepared unless you're well versed in the topic or have lots of experience at improvising in front of a live audience. When you're asked to speak "off the cuff," take a moment to think through what you'll say and then focus on your key points. If you absolutely cannot say something intelligent and effective on the subject at hand, it's usually better to explain that you can't and ask for an opportunity to prepare some remarks for a later time or date.

Regardless of which delivery mode you use, be sure that you're thoroughly familiar with your subject. Knowing what you're speaking about is the best way to build your self-confidence. If you stumble, get interrupted, or suffer equipment failures, your expertise will help you restart and get back on track.

Practice is key to success as a presenter, no matter how much experience you have. Apple co-founder and CEO Steve Jobs, who is widely admired for his new-product presentations and has decades of experience speaking in front of massive crowds, still spends hours practicing his delivery.[14] If you rehearse in front of a mirror, try to visualize the room filled with listeners. Try to record your speech to check the sound of your voice, as well as your timing, phrasing, and emphasis. And if possible, rehearse on video to see yourself as your audience will.

Preparing to Speak

Schedule plenty of practice time whenever you're developing a high-profile presentation.

In addition to knowing your material thoroughly and practicing your delivery, make sure that (a) your location is ready and you have everything you'll need, and that (b) you're prepared to address audiences from other cultures.

If possible, visit the speaking venue ahead of time to familiarize yourself with the facilities and the equipment.

Whenever you can, check the location for your presentation in advance. Check the seating arrangements to make sure they're appropriate for both your needs and the audience's. Verify the availability and operation of all the equipment and supplies you're counting on, from a laptop and LCD projector to simple but vital necessities such as flip charts and marking pens. Many corporate conference rooms now have permanent projection systems that require you to e-mail your presentation file ahead of time or bring it on a disk. Just make sure that you know what to expect in advance.

If you're addressing audience members who speak a different native language, consider using an interpreter. Working with an interpreter does constrain your presentation somewhat. For one thing, you must speak slowly enough for the interpreter to keep up with you. Send your interpreter a copy of your speaking notes and your visuals as far in advance of your presentation as possible. If your audience is likely to include persons with hearing impairments, be sure to team up with a sign-language interpreter as well.

Any time you deliver an oral presentation to people from other cultures, you may need to adapt the content of your presentation. It is also important to take into account any cultural preferences for appearance, mannerisms, and other customs. Your interpreter or host will be able to suggest appropriate changes for a specific audience or particular occasion.

Overcoming Anxiety

Preparation is the best antidote for anxiety.

Even polished speakers with years of experience feel some anxiety about getting up in front of an audience. The difference is that they know how to use this *stage fright* to their advantage. Think of nervousness as a positive indication that you care about your audience, your topic, and the occasion. If your palms get wet or your mouth goes dry, don't think of it as nerves—think of it as excitement. Such stimulation can give you the extra energy you need to make your presentation sparkle. Here are some ways to harness your nervous energy to become a more confident speaker.[15]

- **Prepare more material than necessary.** Combined with a genuine interest in your topic, extra knowledge will reduce your anxiety.
- **Practice, practice, practice.** The more familiar you are with your material, the less panic you'll feel. Whenever you can, record your presentations (both practice sessions and actual presentations), then listen and watch yourself in action. This might not be a comforting experience at first, but it's a great way to assess your skills and identify areas that need improvement.[16]
- **Think positively.** See yourself as polished and professional, and your audience will too. If you're in a leadership position, remember that your employees take cues from your attitude; if you want them to think positively, you need to be seen as positive yourself.
- **Visualize your success.** Use the few minutes before you actually begin speaking to tell yourself you're on and you're ready. Visualize mental images of yourself in front of the audience, feeling confident, prepared, and able to handle any situation that might arise.[17]
- **Take a few deep breaths.** Before you begin to speak, remember that your audience wants you to succeed, too.
- **Be ready.** Have your first sentence memorized and on the tip of your tongue.
- **Be comfortable.** Dress appropriately for the situation but as comfortably as possible. Drink plenty of water before your scheduled presentation time to ensure that your voice is well hydrated (bring a bottle of water with you, too). If possible, adjust the temperature in the room to your personal preference.
- **Don't panic.** If you sense that you're starting to race—a natural response when you're nervous—stop for a second and arrange your notes or perform some other small task while taking several deep breaths. Then start again at your normal pace. If you feel that you're losing your audience members, try to pull them back by involving them in the action; ask for their opinions or pause for questions.
- **Concentrate on your message and your audience, not on yourself.** When you're busy thinking about your subject and observing your audience's response, you tend to forget your fears.
- **Maintain eye contact with friendly audience members.** Once your presentation is under way, be sure to maintain eye contact with your audience, shifting your gaze periodically around the room. However, be sure to connect with individual audience members, rather than just glancing back and forth at no one in particular.[18] Looking directly at your listeners will make you appear sincere, confident, and trustworthy. It also helps you judge the impression you're creating.
- **Keep going.** Things usually get better as you move along, with each successful minute giving you more and more confidence.

No one welcomes mistakes, equipment failures, and other troubles, but they are survivable. To learn how several experienced presenters have overcome some serious glitches, see "Communication Miscues: Recovering from Disasters."

Most of the steps you take to *feel* more confident will also make you *appear* more confident to your audience. In addition to the advice just listed, try to be aware of the nonverbal signals you're transmitting throughout your presentation. Regardless of how you feel inside, your effectiveness depends to a large degree on how you look and sound.

Effective delivery starts as soon as you become the focus of attention, before you even begin to speak, so don't rush. As you approach the front of the room, walk with confidence, breathe deeply, and stand up straight. Face your audience, adjust the microphone and other equipment as needed, count to three slowly, and then survey the audience. When you find a friendly face, make eye contact and smile. Count to three again and then begin your presentation.[19] If you are nervous, this slow, controlled beginning will help you establish rapport and appear more confident.

Your posture is also important in projecting more confidence. Stand tall, with your weight on both feet and your shoulders back. Avoid gripping the lectern or other physical structure. In fact, you might step out from behind the lectern to help your audience feel

7 LEARNING OBJECTIVE

Describe the techniques you can use to feel more confident in front of an audience

Nonverbal signals tell the audience how you're feeling, so pay attention to the signals you send.

Communication Miscues

Recovering from Disasters

You've researched your topic, analyzed your audience, prepared a compelling message, crafted eye-catching visuals, and practiced until you're running like a smooth machine. You're ready to go.

Then you wake up with a sore throat and half a voice. You grab a few lozenges, hope for the best, and drive to the conference facility in plenty of time to set up your equipment. Oops, somebody forgot to tell you that your presentation has been moved up by an hour, and your audience is already in the room waiting for you. You scramble to turn on your laptop and get it connected to the projector, only to discover that you forgot to pack the power cord for your laptop and your battery is low on juice. But that won't be a problem: your laptop is dead anyway. Feeling smart, you pull out a CD-ROM with a backup copy of your PowerPoint slides and ask to use one of the several laptops you see scattered around the room. Nice idea, but they're equipped only with USB flash drives, so your CD is useless. The audience is getting restless; a few people get up to leave. You keep hoping you'll wake up from this bad dream so that your great day can really start. Sorry—this *is* your day.

Ask any business speaker with a few years of experience, and you'll hear all these horror stories and a few more. People who've driven to the wrong conference center, hit themselves in the head with a microphone, tripped over wires, started with a sure-fire joke that generated nothing but cold stares, or been rendered speechless by tough questions. Hoping you'll be spared isn't an effective response. You must be prepared for when—not if—something goes wrong.

If you assume that something *will* go wrong at some point, you can make peace with the possibility and focus on backup planning. Experts suggest you make a list of every major problem you might encounter and imagine how you'll respond when these calamities strike you on the day of a big presentation. As much as possible, create a backup plan, such as calling ahead to reserve a second projector in the event yours gets lost in transit. You won't be able to put backup resources in place for every possible glitch, but by at least thinking through the possibilities, you can decide how you'll respond. When disaster does strike, you'll look like a polished pro instead of a befuddled novice.

CAREER APPLICATIONS

1. If you spy trouble ahead in your presentation, such as noticing that your laptop battery is about to go dead or that you somehow have an old copy of the presentation file, should you tell your audience what's wrong? Or should you try to "wing it"? Explain your answer.

2. What steps can you take to make absolutely sure that you have a usable backup copy of your electronic presentation slides outside your office? Why is this important?

---

more comfortable with you and to express your own comfort and confidence in what you're saying. Use your hands to emphasize your remarks with appropriate gestures. Meanwhile, vary your facial expressions to make the message more dynamic.

Finally, think about the sound of your voice. Studies indicate that people who speak with lower pitches at a slightly faster than average rate are perceived as being more credible.[20] Try to sound poised and confident, varying your pitch and speaking rate to add emphasis. For instance, slow down slightly when you're making an important point.[21] Speak clearly and crisply, articulating all the syllables, and sound enthusiastic about what you're saying. Use silence instead of meaningless filler words such as *um, you know, OK,* and *like.* Silence adds dramatic punch and gives the audience time to think about your message. That slight pause might feel like it lasts an hour when you're in the spotlight, but it'll seem natural to your audience.

Handling Questions Responsively

Don't leave the question-and-answer period to chance: anticipate likely questions and think through your answers.

The question-and-answer period is often one of the most important parts of an oral presentation. Questions give you a chance to obtain important information, to emphasize your main idea and supporting points, and to build enthusiasm for your point of view. In fact, if you don't take advantage of interaction with the audience, you're wasting the chief advantage of an oral format. In addition to giving you valuable feedback, this period gives you a chance to emphasize the points you made earlier, work in any material that didn't fit into the formal presentation, and try to identify and overcome audience resistance.

Many speakers do well delivering their oral presentation only to falter during the question-and-answer period. However, if you spend time anticipating the questions that audience members might ask, you will be ready with answers. Some experts even recommend that you hold back some dramatic statistics as ammunition for the question-and-answer session.[22] If your message is unpopular, you should also be prepared for hostile questions. Treat them as legitimate requests for information. Maintaining your professionalism will improve your credibility.

The following sections offer specific advice that will help you shine during the question-and-answer session.

Focus on the Questioner

When someone poses a question, focus your attention on that individual. Pay attention to the questioner's body language and facial expression to help determine what he or she really means. Nod your head to acknowledge the question; then repeat it aloud to confirm your understanding and to ensure that the entire audience has heard it. If the question is vague or confusing, ask for clarification; then give a simple, direct answer. If you're asked to choose between two alternatives, don't feel you must do so. Offer your own choice instead, if it makes more sense.[23]

For online presentations, you may not be able to use body language to help assess a questioner's real intent. Listen carefully to his or her voice if you have an audio connection. If you're not sure you've picked up the unspoken part of the question (such as sarcasm or a challenge to your authority), ask the questioner to clarify exactly what he or she would like to know.

The question-and-answer session is often the most valuable part of a presentation, so prepare for it by researching answers to likely questions.

Respond Appropriately

This might sound like obvious advice, but be sure to answer the question you're asked. Don't sidestep it, ignore it, laugh it off, or get so caught up in the situation that you forget to respond. Gauge the length of your response to the importance of the question, the status of the questioner, and the time you have left. If giving an adequate answer would take too long, simply say, "I'm sorry, we don't have time to get into that issue right now, but if you'll see me after the presentation, I'll be happy to discuss it with you." If you don't know the answer, don't pretend that you do. Instead, say something like "I don't have those figures. I'll get them for you as quickly as possible." In some cases, you won't have time to answer every question that is asked; if possible, arrange another means to give people the information they need.

Maintain Control

Unlike the delivery phase of your presentation, you have less control during the question-and-answer session. However, you can help maintain control during this crucial period by establishing some ground rules up front. Before you begin, announce a time limit or a question limit per person. Establishing limits will protect you from getting into a heated exchange with one member of the audience and from allowing one or two people to monopolize the question period. Give as many audience members as possible a chance to participate by calling on people from different parts of the room. If the same person keeps angling for attention, restate the question limit or say something like "Several other people have questions; I'll get back to you if time permits." Engaging as many people as possible is particularly important during online presentations, because it's easy to feel excluded as a remote member of the audience.

If audience members try to turn a question into an opportunity to make their own mini-presentations, remember that's it's up to you to stay in control. You might ask people to identify themselves before they ask questions. People are more likely to behave themselves

Maintaining control during the question-and-answer session can be a challenge, particularly if any audience members outrank you in the corporate hierarchy.

when everyone knows their name.[24] You might admit that you and the questioner have differing opinions and, before calling on someone else, offer to get back to the questioner once you've done more research. Or you might simply respond with a brief answer, avoiding a lengthy debate or additional questions.[25] Finally, you might thank the person for the comments and then remind everyone that you were looking for specific questions.

Survive the Hot Seat

If you ever face hostile questions, don't duck; respond honestly and directly while keeping your cool.

Whether it's an overdue project or quarterly financial results that didn't meet investor expectations, chances are you'll have to answer some tough questions during some of your presentations. When this happens, respond honestly, but remember to keep your cool. Look the person in the eye, answer the question as well as you can, and try not to show your feelings. Whatever the situation, avoid getting into a heated argument. Even if you win, you'll leave the audience feeling uncomfortable about both the situation and your ability to handle conflict. Recognize that questioners who challenge your ideas, logic, or facts may just be trying to push you into overreacting. Defuse hostility by paraphrasing the question and asking the questioner to confirm that you've understood it correctly. Break long, complicated questions into parts that you can answer simply. State your response accurately and factually, then move on to the next question. Avoid postures or gestures that might seem antagonistic. Maintain a businesslike tone of voice and a pleasant expression.[26] Don't resort to insults, either—they will most likely backfire and make the audience more sympathetic to the questioner.

Encourage Questions

Listeners who are deadly quiet can be just as uncomfortable as noisy, hostile audiences. If there's a chance your audience members will be too timid or too angry to ask questions, consider arranging a few questions ahead of time with a cooperative member of the audience. If a friend or the meeting organizer gets the ball rolling, other people in the audience will probably join in. You might ask a question yourself: "Would you like to know more about . . . ?" If someone in the audience answers, act as if the question came from that person in the first place. When all else fails, say something like "I know from experience that most questions are asked after the question-and-answer period. So I'll be around afterward to talk."[27]

Conclude Your Presentation

No matter how the presentation has gone, conclude in a strong, confident manner.

When the time allotted for your presentation is up, call a halt to the question-and-answer session, even if more people want to talk. Prepare the audience for the end by saying, "Our time is almost up. Let's have one more question." After you've made your reply, summarize

---

 CHECKLIST: Developing Oral and Online Presentations

A. Plan your presentation.
- Analyze the situation by defining your purpose and developing an audience profile.
- Select the right medium.
- Organize your presentation by defining the main idea, limiting the scope, choosing your approach, and preparing your outline.

B. Write your presentation.
- Adapt to your audience by tailoring your style and language.
- Compose your presentation by preparing an introduction, body, and close.
- Use your introduction to arouse audience interest, build your credibility, and preview your message.

- Use the body to connect your ideas and hold your audience's attention.
- Use the close to restate your main points and describe the next steps.

C. Complete your presentation.
- Master the art of delivery by choosing a delivery method, knowing your material, and practicing your delivery.
- Check the location and equipment, including online setups if needed, in advance.
- Determine whether you should use an interpreter.
- Overcome anxiety by preparing thoroughly.
- Handle questions responsively.

the main idea of the presentation and thank people for their attention. Conclude the way you opened: by looking around the room and making eye contact. Then gather your notes and leave the stage, maintaining the same confident demeanor you've had from the beginning.

For a reminder of the steps to take in developing an oral presentation, refer to "Checklist: Developing Oral and Online Presentations."

COMMUNICATION CHALLENGES AT FITCH

 Pacific Theaters, a Southern California movie-theater operator, is preparing to launch a new chain called ArcLight Cinemas (**www.arclightcinemas.com**). The company wants to present ArcLight as a more enjoyable, upscale movie-going experience, something clearly differentiated from the run-of-the mill theaters across the country. Yesterday, Fitch's Eric Ashworth met with Pacific Theaters' management to discuss the possibility of creating a compelling image for ArcLight. Today, he selected you and three others to form the account team and asked that the group start developing ideas. From his meeting notes, it's clear the client envisions a typical presentation about logos, marketing slogans, and color schemes—the usual stuff in a traditional agency pitch. Not the Fitch way, for sure.

Individual Challenge: Two weeks have passed and, true to the Fitch mentality, you and your teammates have developed a strong vision for ArcLight. Your concept centers on the notion of recapturing the old-time glamour and excitement of going to the movies—back when going to the movies was a special event. Now it's time to outline your sales presentation, from introduction to body to close. How will you grab and hold the audience's attention? How can you make audience members excited and inspire the big "A-ha!" that Fitch aims for? Prepare a one-page outline.

Team Challenge: In a small group, brainstorm ways to describe the glamour of old-time Hollywood to younger audiences who may have grown up on teen comedies and horror movies. Assume you're going to speak to a group of young managers at Pacific Theaters and outline a short presentation that would help them get a sense of what Hollywood was like in the days of Clark Gable, Vivien Leigh, Rita Hayworth, and Cary Grant. Provide your instructor with an outline and a brief description of the visuals you might use.

SUMMARY OF LEARNING OBJECTIVES

1 Explain the importance of oral and online presentations in your career success. Oral and online presentations give the opportunity to use all of your communication skills, from research to writing to speaking. Presentations also demonstrate your ability to think quickly, to adapt to challenging situations, and to handle touchy questions and complex issues. They also let your personality shine through in ways that aren't always possible in written media.

2 Explain how to adapt the three-step writing process to oral presentations. Although you rarely want to write out your presentation word for word, the three-step writing process is easy to adapt to oral presentations. The steps you take in planning oral presentations are generally the same as with any other business message: (1) analyzing the situation (be sure to gauge audience members' likely emotional state and their comfort level with your language), (2) gathering information, (3) selecting the right medium (expect to deliver many presentations online during your

career), and (4) organizing the information (you may want to create a speaking outline in addition to your planning outline). To write your presentation, you don't actually "write" your presentation in most cases but, rather, plan your word and phrase choices so you can speak in a way that delivers planned messages in a spontaneous way. This step also includes creating whatever visual support materials you plan to use. And, of course, adapting to your audience is every bit as important with oral messages as with written messages. Completing the third step in the three-step process is where oral and online presentations differ the most from written messages. You still want to revise carefully and proofread all handouts and visual materials to ensure clarity and accuracy. You also need to practice and perfect your delivery, prepare to speak by verifying facilities and equipment (and working with an interpreter if needed), take steps to manage anxiety, and plan your approach to handling questions. For online presentations, make sure your audience can access your presentation materials, including audio and video feeds.

3 **Identify the two primary reasons that limiting your scope is especially important for oral presentations.** Limiting the scope of presentations is crucial because (1) you generally have a fixed amount of time in which to speak, so you need to fit your material to the time allotted; and (2) if you don't align your content with your audience members' needs and expectations, they may not understand it or bother to listen to it.

4 **Distinguish a planning outline from a speaking outline, and explain the purpose of each.** A planning outline identifies and organizes the content of your presentation, whereas a speaking outline emphasizes the cues and reminders you'll use to present your material.

5 **Discuss the three functions of an effective introduction.** An effective introduction arouses audience interest in your topic, builds your credibility, and offers your audience a preview of your message. If your topic doesn't naturally interest the audience, you need to work extra hard in your introduction (and throughout the presentation) to relate the material to the audience in as personal a manner as possible. Speaker credibility is a crucial aspect of any presentation because audiences are more likely to pay attention to messages coming from someone they perceive to be an expert in the subject area. If you can't demonstrate credibility in your subject area, you "borrow" credibility from recognized experts by incorporating their insights and opinions into your presentation (giving proper credit, of course). Previewing your message in the introduction helps the audience recognize the importance of your material and gives them a chance to prepare for it by understanding how you plan to present it.

6 **Identify six ways to grab your audience's attention and six ways to hold it.** To grab your audience's attention during your introduction, you can unite the audience around a common goal, tell a story, pass around a sample, ask a question, state a startling statistic, or use humor (although humor must be approached with great care and avoided if there is any chance it will not go over well with your audience). To hold your audience's attention after you've captured it with a compelling introduction, continue to relate your subject to your audience's needs, anticipate audience questions and prepare effective responses, use clear and vivid language, relate your subject to ideas the audience is already familiar and comfortable with, ask for questions or comments, and illustrate your ideas with visuals.

7 **Describe the techniques you can use to feel more confident in front of an audience.** To overcome anxiety and feel more confident as a speaker, prepare more material than necessary so that the extra knowledge will reduce your nervousness. Rehearse your oral presentation to become as familiar as possible with your topic. Think positively and see yourself as a polished professional. Right before speaking, visualize your success and tell yourself you're ready. Take a few deep breaths and remember that your audience actually wants you to succeed. Be ready by memorizing your first sentence. Be comfortable by sipping some water. If you feel you're losing your audience members, don't panic; instead, pull them back by asking for their opinions or questions and involving them in the action. Keep going no matter what, because you'll get better as you go.

Test Your Knowledge

1. What issues do you need to consider when planning an oral presentation?
2. What are the two most common purposes for giving oral presentations?
3. Why do you have to limit your scope when planning a presentation?
4. Why is simplicity of organization important in oral communication?
5. How can outlines help you with the writing and delivery of an oral presentation?
6. What three goals should you accomplish during the introduction of an oral presentation?
7. How can you get and keep the audience's attention?
8. How does the delivery method of impromptu speaking differ from the delivery method of speaking from notes?
9. As a speaker, what nonverbal signals can you send to appear more confident?
10. What can speakers do to maintain control during the question-and-answer period of a presentation?

Apply Your Knowledge

1. Would you rather (a) deliver an oral presentation to an external audience, (b) be interviewed for a news story that involves a serious accident at your company, or (c) make a presentation to a departmental meeting? Why? How do the communication skills differ among those situations? Explain.

2. How might the audience's attitude affect the amount of audience interaction during or after a presentation? Explain your answer.

3. If you were giving an oral presentation on the performance of a company product, what three attention-getters might you use to enliven your speech?

4. From the speaker's perspective, what are the advantages and disadvantages of responding to questions from the audience throughout an oral presentation rather than just afterward? From the listener's perspective, which approach would you prefer? Why?

5. **Ethical Choices** Business speakers don't always have the luxury of complete confidence in the material they have to present. For instance, sales forecasts for new products are notoriously difficult to make because they depend on so many factors in the marketplace. If you were presenting a forecast that was the best available answer but not one that you had much confidence in, should you still follow this chapter's guidelines for appearing confident in front of your audience? Explain your answer.

Practice Your Knowledge

Messages for Analysis

Message 16.A: Analyzing the Structure of a Presentation

Find the transcript of a business-oriented speech or presentation by searching online for "speech transcription" or "presentation transcription." Examine both the introduction and the close and analyze how these two sections work together to emphasize the main idea. Does the speaker want the audience to take any specific actions? To change any particular beliefs or feelings?

Next, identify the transitional sentences or phrases that clarify the speech's structure for the listener, especially those that help the speaker shift between supporting points. Using these transitions as clues, list the main message and supporting points; then indicate how each transitional phrase links the current supporting point to the succeeding one. Finally, prepare a brief (two- to three-minute) oral presentation summarizing your analysis for your class.

Message 16.B: Did the Introduction Get Your Attention?

To access this recorded message, visit www.businesscommunic-ationheadlinenews. com and click on Textbook Resources. Locate *Business Communication Today*, 9th ed., click on Chapter 16, then select page 519, Message 16.B. Download and listen to this podcast, which is the introduction of a presentation to college seniors. Identify at least two techniques the speaker uses to try to grab your attention.

Exercises

For active links to all websites discussed in this chapter, visit this text's website at www.prenhall.com/bovee. Locate your book and click on its Companion Website link. Then select Chapter 16, and click on "Featured Websites." Locate the name of the page or the URL related to the material in the text. Please note that links to sites that become inactive after publication of the book will be removed from the Featured Websites section.

16.1 **Internet** For many years, Toastmasters has been dedicated to helping its members give speeches. Instruction, good speakers as models, and practice sessions aim to teach members to convey information in lively and informative ways. Visit the Toastmasters website at www.toastmasters.org, and review the organization's vision and mission statements. Evaluate the information and outline a three-minute presentation to your class, telling why Toastmasters would or would not help you and your classmates write and deliver an effective speech.

16.2 **Mastering Delivery: Analysis** Attend a presentation at your school or in your town, or watch a speech on television. Categorize the speech as one that motivates or entertains, one that informs or analyzes, or one that persuades or urges collaboration. Then compare the speaker's delivery with this chapter's "Checklist: Developing Oral and Online Presentations." Write a two-page report analyzing the speaker's performance and suggesting improvements.

16.3 **Mastering Delivery: Nonverbal Signals** Observe and analyze the delivery of a speaker in a school, work, or other setting. What type of delivery did the speaker use? Was this delivery appropriate for the occasion? What nonverbal signals did the speaker use to emphasize key points? Were these signals effective? Which nonverbal signals would you suggest to further enhance the delivery of this oral presentation—and why?

16.4 **Ethical Choices** Think again about the oral presentation you observed and analyzed in Exercise 16.3. How could the speaker have used nonverbal signals to unethically manipulate the audience's attitudes or actions?

16.5 **Teamwork** You've been asked to give an informative 10-minute presentation on vacation opportunities in your home state. Draft your introduction, which should last no more than two minutes. Then pair off with a classmate and analyze each other's introductions. How well do these two introductions arouse the audience's interest, build credibility, and preview the presentation? Suggest how these introductions might be improved.

16.6 **Completing Oral Presentations: Self-Assessment** How good are you at planning, writing, and delivering oral presentations? At the top of the next page, rate yourself on each of the elements of the oral presentation process. Then examine your ratings to identify where you are strongest and where you can improve, using the tips in this chapter.

Elements of the Presentation Process	Always	Frequently	Occasionally	Never
1. I start by defining my purpose.	___	___	___	___
2. I analyze my audience before writing an oral presentation.	___	___	___	___
3. I match my presentation length to the allotted time.	___	___	___	___
4. I begin my oral presentations with an attention-getting introduction.	___	___	___	___
5. I look for ways to build credibility as a speaker.	___	___	___	___
6. I cover only a few main points in the body of my presentation.	___	___	___	___
7. I use transitions to help listeners follow my ideas.	___	___	___	___
8. I review main points and describe next steps in the close.	___	___	___	___
9. I practice my presentation beforehand.	___	___	___	___
10. I prepare in advance for questions and objections.	___	___	___	___
11. I conclude oral presentations by summarizing my main idea.	___	___	___	___

16.7 Delivering Oral Presentations: Possible Topics Browse through the following topics to see which ones interest you:

a. What I expect to learn in this course
b. Past public speaking experiences: the good, the bad, and the ugly
c. I would be good at teaching _____.
d. I am afraid of _____.
e. It's easy for me to _____.
f. I get angry when _____.
g. I am happiest when I _____.
h. People would be surprised if they knew that I _____.
i. My favorite older person
j. My favorite charity
k. My favorite place
l. My favorite sport
m. My favorite store
n. My favorite television show
o. The town you live in suffers from a great deal of juvenile vandalism. Explain to a group of community members why juvenile recreational facilities should be built instead of a juvenile detention complex.
p. You are speaking to the Humane Society. Support or oppose the use of animals for medical research purposes.
q. You are talking to civic leaders of your community. Try to convince them to build an art gallery.
r. You are speaking to a first-grade class at an elementary school. Explain why they should brush their teeth after meals.
s. You are speaking to a group of traveling salespeople. Convince them that they should wear their seatbelts while driving.
t. You are speaking to a group of elderly people. Convince them to adopt an exercise program.
u. Energy issues (supply, conservation, alternative sources, national security, global warming, pollution, etc.)
v. Financial issues (banking, investing, family finances, etc.)
w. Government (domestic policy, foreign policy, social security taxes, welfare, etc.)
x. Interesting new technologies (virtual reality, geographic information systems, nanotechnology, bioengineering, etc.)
y. Politics (political parties, elections, legislative bodies and legislation, the presidency, etc.)
z. Sports (amateur and professional, baseball, football, golf, hang gliding, hockey, rock climbing, tennis, etc.)

Choose a topic and prepare a brief presentation (5–10 minutes) to be given to your class.

Expand Your Knowledge

Exploring the Best of the Web

Learn from the Presentation Pros
www.presentations.com
The online home of *Presentations* magazine offers a wealth of articles that offer practical advice on creating and delivering business presentations. Under the "Presentations" tab, browse the Creation, Delivery, Venue, Technology, and Products sections to find resources that will help you complete the following tasks.

1. Find several articles that discuss the unique challenges of making presentations at trade shows. Identify three to five tips that will help you succeed in these environments.
2. Find a recent article that discusses tips, techniques, or traps of using PowerPoint for business presentations. Summarize the article's advice in a brief message that could be posted on your company's internal blog.
3. Find one or more articles that discuss techniques for improving vocal delivery. Identify three points that speakers can use to make more effective use of their voice during presentations.

Surfing Your Way to Career Success

Bovée and Thill's Business Communication Resources offers links to hundreds of online resources that can help you with this course, your other college courses, and your career. Visit www.buscommresources.com, then click on "Business Communication Web Directory." The "Oral Communication" section connects you to a variety of websites and articles on speeches, stage fright, presentations, PowerPoint tips, podcasts, webcasts, and videoconferencing. Identify three websites from this section that could be useful in your business career. For each site, write a two-sentence summary of what the site offers and how it could help you launch and build your career.

Learn Interactively

Interactive Study Guide

Visit www.prenhall.com/bovee, then locate your book and click on its "Companion Website" link. Select Chapter 16 to take advantage of the interactive "Chapter Quiz" to test your knowledge of chapter concepts. Receive instant feedback on whether you need additional studying. Also, visit the "Study Hall," where you'll find an abundance of valuable resources that will help you succeed in this course.

Peak Performance Grammar and Mechanics

If your instructor has required the use of "Peak Performance Grammar and Mechanics," either in your online course or on CD, you can improve your skill with vocabulary by using the "Peak Performance Grammar and Mechanics" module. Click "Vocabulary," then click "Vocabulary I." Take the Pretest to determine whether you have any weak areas. Then review those areas in the Refresher Course. Take the Follow-Up Test to check your grasp of vocabulary. For an extra challenge or advanced practice, take the Advanced Test. Finally, for additional reinforcement, visit the Companion Website, click on any chapter, then click on "Improve Your Grammar, Mechanics, and Usage."

CHAPTER 17

Enhancing Presentations with Slides and Other Visuals

LEARNING OBJECTIVES

After studying this chapter, you will be able to

1 Explain how visuals enhance oral presentations, and list several popular types of visuals

2 Describe the steps needed to write readable content for slides

3 Explain the importance of design consistency in electronic slides and other visuals

4 Describe the effective use of transitions and builds in electronic presentations

5 Identify three types of noncontent slides you can use to support your presentation

6 List the seven questions you should ask yourself to determine whether you're ready to give your presentation

7 Highlight nine major issues to consider when you're preparing to give a presentation online

COMMUNICATION CLOSE-UP AT HEWLETT-PACKARD

www.hp.com

Presentations make everyone nervous, but imagine how nervous you might be if you were making a presentation with millions or billions of dollars on the line. That's business as usual for Dan Talbott of HP Managed Services, a unit of Hewlett-Packard that manages computer operations for other companies.

A great example was the pursuit of a huge contract with Procter & Gamble (P&G), the consumer-products giant that markets over 300 brands, including Charmin, Crest, and Tide. P&G was looking to lower its costs by hiring an outside organization to take over its global information system—a network of more than 80,000 computers. HP was facing two tough competitors for the contract, Electronic Data Systems and IBM, and had to be considered a distant third-place contender because it had never landed a contract the size of the P&G deal. And as if that wasn't enough, P&G had published a 10,000-page request for proposals (RFP) and limited the response time to just 56 days—9 to 12 months is typical on projects of this magnitude.

Dan Talbott (far right) led a team whose presentation skills helped land a multibillion-dollar contract for Hewlett-Packard.

As a seasoned industry veteran but a rookie at HP, Talbott was eager to show that he could bring his new employer this mammoth piece of business. He moved his team into an HP office near P&G's Cincinnati headquarters, tapped the brainpower of 80 colleagues from around the world, and began developing the series of presentations that were specified in the RFP. Talbott told the group, "Our job is to ensure that every conversation is a win." However, HP's initial presentation was shaky, so he asked the presenters to print their PowerPoint slides—over 200 in all—and post them on the walls of a conference room. He conducted a slide-by-slide critique, questioning every slide that lacked a clear message. The team revised and kept revising until the presentation was audience centered and crystal clear from beginning to end.

That rigorous review produced a string of successful presentations that ultimately helped Talbott and his team win a 10-year contract worth $3 billion—a stunning success that announced HP's arrival as a serious contender in computer services.[1]

PLANNING YOUR PRESENTATION VISUALS

You may never be on stage with $3 billion at stake (see the chapter-opening Communication Close-Up), but you can take Dan Talbott's rigorous approach to presentation quality and make every one of your presentations a success. By following the three-step development process in Chapter 16, you'll have a well-crafted, audience- focused message. The techniques in this chapter will help you enhance the delivery of that message with creative and effective visuals.

Visuals can improve the quality and impact of your oral presentation by creating interest, illustrating points that are difficult to explain in words alone, adding variety, and increasing the audience's ability to absorb and remember information. Behavioral research has shown that visuals can improve learning by up to 400 percent because humans can process visuals 60,000 times faster than text.[2]

As a speaker, you'll find that visuals can help you remember the details of the message (no small feat in a lengthy presentation) and improve your professional image: Speakers who use presentation visuals generally appear better prepared and more knowledgeable than speakers who do not.

For all their communication power, however, don't make the mistake of thinking that your visuals *are* your presentation. Particularly when using presentation software such as Microsoft PowerPoint or Apple Keynote, communicators sometimes fall into the trap of letting the slides take center stage. Remember that you and your message are the presentation, not your visuals; your visuals are there to help support and clarify what you have to say.[3]

Selecting the Type of Visuals to Use

You can select from a variety of visuals to enhance oral presentations, each with unique advantages and disadvantages:

- **Electronic presentations.** Electronic presentations created with Microsoft PowerPoint or similar programs are the visual of choice in most business situations today. An **electronic presentation** or *slide show* consists of a series of individual **electronic slides**. To display an electronic presentation, you simply connect your computer to a portable projector or a built-in unit that's part of a multimedia system in a conference room. Electronic presentations have numerous advantages: They are easy to edit and update (right up to the last second before your presentation starts, plus you can even modify the sequence of slides while you're presenting); you can add sound, photos, video, and animation; they can be incorporated into online meetings, webcasts, and *webinars* (a common term for web-based seminars); and you can record self-running presentations for trade shows, websites, and other uses. The primary disadvantages are the cost of equipment, the potential complexity involved in creating multimedia presentations, and the risk, however slight these days, that your hardware or software won't cooperate when it's show time. Plus, the extreme flexibility of electronic presentations makes it that much easier for inexperienced users to create poorly designed slides full of distracting special effects.
- **Overhead transparencies.** Overhead transparencies have been the workhorses of business presentations for decades (you've no doubt seen a few thousand during your

---

1 LEARNING OBJECTIVE

Explain how visuals enhance oral presentations, and list several popular types of visuals

Remember that the purpose of visuals is to support your presentation, not replace it.

In most businesses, electronic presentations are now the technology of choice, although they're certainly not the only option.

school years as well). Some business professionals still prefer them to electronic presentations. You can create overheads using software such as Microsoft PowerPoint, other graphics programs, your word processor, a typewriter, or even a pen. Moreover, simple transparencies don't require the latest computer or projection equipment. You can write on them during a presentation, and they never crash on you—as computers have been known to do. On the downside, they're limited to static displays, they're impossible to edit once you've printed them, and you or a partner are forced to stand next to the projector throughout your entire presentation.

- **Chalkboards and whiteboards.** Chalkboards and whiteboards are effective tools for recording points made during small-group sessions. Because these visuals are produced on the spot, they are great for the flexible, spontaneous nature of workshops and brainstorming sessions. New electronic whiteboards can overcome the biggest drawback of their mechanical counterparts: capturing the information written on them. After you and your team brainstorm a complex product design or a long list of marketing ideas, you simply hit a button to print a hardcopy or distribute an electronic version via e-mail.

- **Flip charts.** Large sheets of paper attached at the top like a tablet can be propped on an easel so that you can flip the pages as you speak, with each chart illustrating or clarifying a point. You might have a few lines from your outline on one, a graph or diagram on another, and so on. By using felt-tip markers of various colors, you can also record ideas generated during a discussion. Flip charts are also great for recording comments and questions during your presentation or for creating a "group memory" during brainstorming sessions, keeping track of all the ideas the team generates. Flip charts are about as low tech as you can get, but they're inexpensive and 100 percent dependable.

- **Other visuals.** Be creative when choosing visuals to support your presentation. A videotape of a focus group talking about your company can have a lot more impact than a series of slides that summarize what they said. In technical or scientific presentations, a sample of a product or type of material lets your audience experience your subject directly. Designers and architects use mock-ups and models to help people envision what a final creation will look like. You might also want to incorporate other software in your presentation, such as a spreadsheet to show financial data

Electronic whiteboards let you capture notes and feedback during presentations, then print them out or e-mail them to audience members.

or a computer-aided design program to show a new product's design. If you're demonstrating the use of particular software program, for instance, you can create a **screencast**, which records everything you do on screen—moving the mouse, opening windows, making menu selections, and so on. Most screencasting software also lets you add on-screen annotations and record an audio track to explain what is happening on screen.

Sometimes the best strategy is to use a combination of visuals, such as electronic slides to present your ideas to the audience and a flip chart to record any feedback you receive. This chapter focuses on electronic presentations, the mainstay of business presentations today, although most of these design tips apply to overhead transparencies as well.

Verifying Your Design Plans

Once you've decided on the form your visuals will take, think through your presentation plan carefully before you start creating anything. You don't want your audience to leave the room impressed with your multimedia show but confused about what you said. In addition, don't expect your visuals to rescue a weak message. Discerning audience members—the sort of people who can influence the direction of your career—are not easily fooled by visual razzle-dazzle. If your analysis is shaky or your conclusions suspect, an over-the-top visual production won't help your presentation succeed.

Think through your presentation outline carefully before designing your visuals.

Before you start to create visuals, review the plan for each visual and ask yourself how it will help your audience understand and appreciate your message. This simple test alone can eliminate the twin scourges of the modern conference room: PowerPoint presentations that are (a) festooned with flying objects, dancing text, swirling transitions, meaningless sound effects, and other electronic distractions; or (b) nothing but one dry list of bullet points after another. Think through the words you'll use while displaying each visual, making sure your words and visuals will work in harmony. Also take the time to double-check any cultural assumptions that might be inappropriate. Are you highlighting with a color that has negative emotional connotations in your audience's culture? Would your materials be too playful for a serious audience? Too serious for an audience that values creativity (see Figure 17.1)?

When it comes time to make design choices, from selecting fonts to deciding whether to include a photo, remember the advice from Chapter 16 and let accuracy and simplicity be your guides. Doing so has several advantages. First, it takes less time to create simple materials, and time is the most precious commodity in today's business environment. Second, simple visuals reduce the chances of distraction and misinterpretation. Third, the more

Accuracy and simplicity are keys to effective visuals.

FIGURE 17.1 Presentation Style
These two PowerPoint slides use the same words, but do they send the same message?

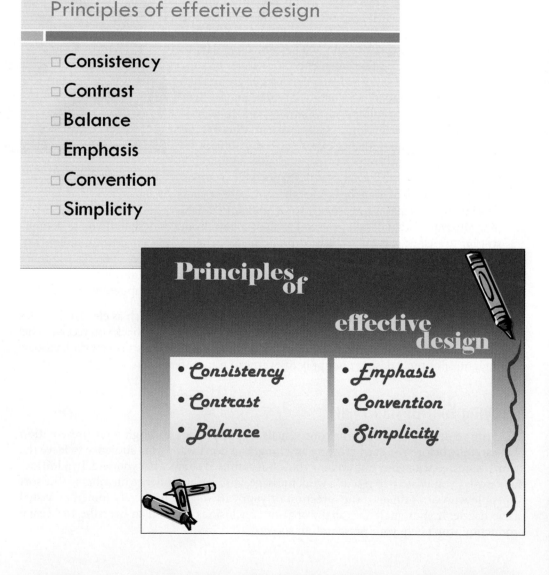

"bells and whistles" you have in your presentation, the more likely it is that something will go wrong.

Finally, use your time wisely. Presentation software in particular can eat up hours and hours of time you probably don't have. You can spend days trying to fine-tune and adjust a single presentation, whether you're trying to change a simple color block to a multicolor blend, add drop shadows behind all your photographs, or incorporate one of the other endless possibilities from today's software. Based on your audience and situation, decide upfront how much sophistication is good enough, then stop when you get there. Use the time you'll save to rehearse your presentation and get a good night's sleep before the big day.

CREATING EFFECTIVE SLIDES

Creating effective slides can be a challenge because you need both your rational and creative instincts. As you create each slide, start by verifying the message it needs to convey, write the text that will be displayed on the slide, then add graphics and other visual elements. If you start with special effects or eye-catching multimedia, these aspects are likely to become the focus of your slides rather than the message. So get your message and text in place first, then think about graphics. This approach can rescue you from schedule nightmares, too; if you run out of time, at least you'll have the message in place, even if you didn't have time to dress it up with as many graphic elements as you had planned.

Develop the message and text for each slide first, then move on to graphics and special effects.

Writing Readable Content

In a typical business presentation, many or even most of the slides are composed primarily of text. Even slides that are mostly graphical usually have at least a slide title and perhaps labels or a caption. When writing text for slides, you have two decisions: what to cover and how much detail to include. As you make these decisions, recognize that effective slide text (a) supports rather than replaces your spoken message and (b) is easy for the audience to read and comprehend. Perhaps the single most common mistake people make when writing text for slides is including too much text. Doing so not only puts more work on the audience but also forces you to use smaller type sizes, making the material difficult or impossible to read. Keep in mind that slide text is not supposed to display your entire speaking script or highlight every point you intend to make.[4]

Use slide text to emphasize key points, not to convey your entire message.

Choose words and short phrases that help your audience follow the flow of ideas, without forcing people to read in depth. You primarily want your audience to *listen*, not to *read*. Highlight key points, summarize and preview your message, signal major shifts in thought, illustrate concepts, or help create interest in your spoken message.

Slides with too much text, long sentences, or wordy bullets are difficult to read and difficult to understand. They confuse and distract the audience, and they diminish your credibility as a speaker.[5] Reducing the number of words can also help you focus each slide on a single, clear message, which is essential to keeping your audience's attention. When HP's first presentation to Proctor & Gamble (see page 523) was not as successful as he had hoped, Dan Talbott reviewed and edited every single one of more than 200 slides to make sure each carried a clear, audience-focused message.[6]

When writing content for text slides, keep your message short and simple (see Figure 17.2):

- Limit each slide to one thought, concept, or idea.
- Limit the content to about 40 words—roughly six lines of text containing about six or seven words per line. For larger rooms in which some audience members will be a long distance from the screen, use even fewer words in larger type.
- Write short bulleted phrases rather than long sentences.
- Use sentences only when you need to share a quotation or other text item verbatim.[7]
- Phrase list items in parallel grammatical form to facilitate quick reading.
- Use the active voice.
- Include short informative titles.

2 LEARNING OBJECTIVE

Describe the steps needed to write readable content for slides

FIGURE 17.2 **Writing Readable Content**

What Is Supply-Chain Management?

Developing long-term partnerships among channel members working together to create a distribution system that reduces inefficiencies, costs, and redundancies while creating a competitive advantage and satisfying customers

Figure 17.2a—Inefficient paragraph style

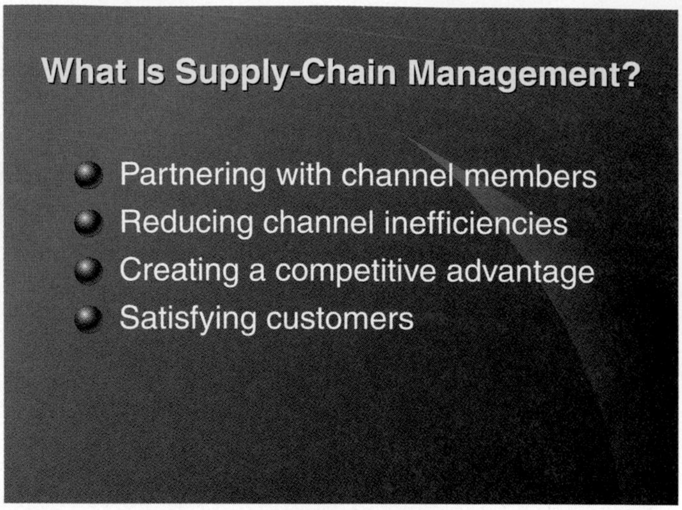

What Is Supply-Chain Management?

- Partnering with channel members
- Reducing channel inefficiencies
- Creating a competitive advantage
- Satisfying customers

Figure 17.2b—Efficient bulleted phrases

The paragraph style in Figure 17.2a is much more difficult to read, particularly from a distance, than the bulleted style in Figure 17.2b. The speaker will explain these bullet points while showing the slide.

Benefits of Integrated Supply Chain

- Companies can carry less inventory
- Companies can design, ramp up, and retire products rapidly
- Companies can outsource some or all of the manufacturing function
- Online order entry contributes to enhanced customer satisfaction
- Shorter engineering-to-production cycle times help increase market share

Figure 17.2c—Wordy bullets

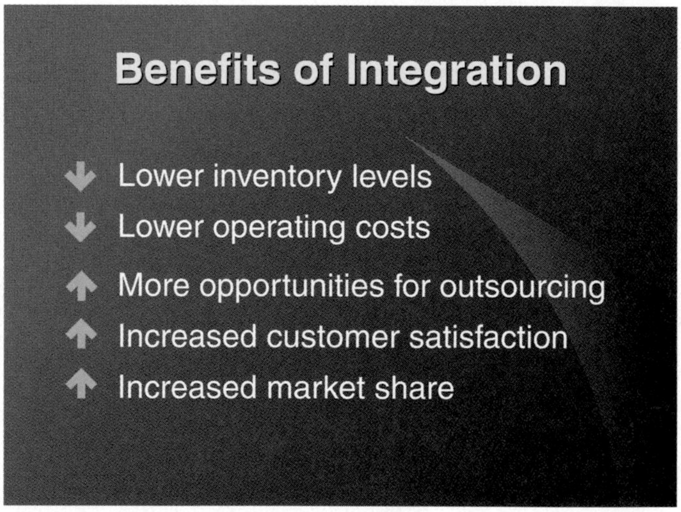

Benefits of Integration

- ⬇ Lower inventory levels
- ⬇ Lower operating costs
- ⬆ More opportunities for outsourcing
- ⬆ Increased customer satisfaction
- ⬆ Increased market share

Figure 17.2d—Concise bullets

Unnecessary words in Figure 17.2c make these bullets harder to read. With the concise bullets in Figure 17.2d, the audience can quickly grasp key message points as the speaker provides additional information. Note also how the phrases in Figure 17.2d are parallel and the font is larger, both of which make this slide easier to read.

Modifying Graphics for Slides

Many graphics that work well in printed form need to be simplified for use in presentations because they are too dense and too complicated to be easily viewed on screen.

Just as text needs to be simplified for projection, so too do many charts, graphs, tables, and other visual elements. Detailed visuals that might look fine on the printed page can be too dense and complicated for presentations. Just as with text slides, don't force the audience to study your charts and graphs in order to get the message. You can create effective presentation visuals by following these guidelines (see Figure 17.3):

- **Reduce the detail.** Eliminate anything that is not absolutely essential to the message. Show only key numbers on a chart. If people need to see only trends, then show only the trend line and not the numbers. If necessary, break information into more than one graphic illustration. If a deeper level of detail is helpful or necessary, hand out printed visuals that people can review during or after the presentation.

FIGURE 17.3 Modifying Graphs for Slides
By simplifying the graph from Figure 17.3a, Figure 17.3b not only reduces the amount of detail but increases the area available for the graphical content, making it easier to read.

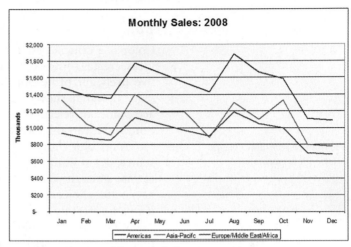

Figure 17.3a—Detailed graph from print report

Figure 17.3b—Simplified graph for presentation

- **Avoid repetition.** For example, if a bar chart is segmented by week, don't write "Week of 12/01," "Week of 12/08," and so on. Use the "Week of" label once, then just include the dates. Similarly, you might be able to remove the vertical scale from the left side of the chart and just show individual values above each bar.[8]
- **Shorten numbers.** For instance, use 08 for the year 2008 or round off numbers such as $12,500.72 to $12 or $12.5, and then label the axis to indicate thousands.
- **Limit data.** Line graphs look busy with more than two or three lines, bar charts look crowded with more than five or six bars, and tables are difficult to read with too many rows or columns.
- **Highlight key points.** Use arrows, boldface type, and color to direct your audience's eyes to the main point of a visual. Summarize the intent of the graphic in one clear title, such as "Earnings have increased by 15 percent."
- **Adjust the size and design.** Modify the size of the graphic to accommodate the size of a slide. Leave plenty of white space so that audience members can view and interpret content from a distance. Use colors that stand out from the slide's background, and choose a font that's clear and easy to read.

However, guard against oversimplifying text or graphic information to such an extent that your audience can't grasp the entire message. For instance, in recent years, a number of critics have begun to accuse bullet-point-heavy slides of encouraging the fracturing of, and the oversimplification of, complex ideas. On the other side of the argument, Microsoft and its supporters contend that PowerPoint is simply a tool and that it's up to users to employ the tool appropriately and intelligently.[9]

Simplicity is critical, but don't oversimplify to the extent that the audience doesn't get the important nuances or connections in your message.

Selecting Design Elements

Once you've composed the text and graphic elements of your slides, you're ready to focus on their design. Nothing detracts from good content as much as poorly designed slides. However, by paying attention to a few design basics, you can transform a dull presentation into one that is not only dynamic but also readable.

Chapter 12 highlighted six principles of effective design: consistency, contrast, balance, emphasis, convention, and simplicity. Pay close attention to these principles as you select the color, background design, artwork, fonts, and typestyles for your slides. Then

To design effective slides, you need to consider six principles of effective design: consistency, contrast, balance, emphasis, convention, and simplicity.

once you have selected the best design elements for your slides, stick with them throughout your presentation unless a compelling reason arises to change them based on your message.

Color

Color is a critical design element. It grabs the viewer's attention, emphasizes important ideas, creates contrast, and isolates slide elements. Color can make your slides more attractive, lively, and professional. It can also play a key role in the overall acceptance of your message. Research shows that color visuals can account for 60 percent of an audience's acceptance or rejection of an idea. Color can increase willingness to read by up to 80 percent, and it can enhance learning and improve retention by more than 75 percent.[10]

Use color to stimulate specific emotional responses.

Your color choices can also stimulate various emotions, as Table 17.1 suggests. For instance, if you want to excite your audience, add some warm colors such as red and orange to your slides. If you want to achieve a more relaxed and receptive environment, blue would be a better choice.[11] Remember, color may have a different meaning in certain cultures. So if you are creating slides for international audiences, research these cultural differences.

When selecting color, limit your choices to a few compatible ones, and keep in mind that some colors work better together than others. Contrasting colors, for example, increase readability. So when selecting color for backgrounds, titles, and text, avoid choosing colors that are close in hue: yellow text on a white background, brown on green, blue on black, blue on purple, and so on.[12] If you'll be presenting in a dark room, use dark colors such as blue for the background, a midrange of brightness for illustrations, and light colors for text. If you are showing overhead transparencies in well-lit rooms, reverse the colors: Use light colors for the background and dark colors for text. If you have some reason to change colors between slides, don't switch back and forth from very dark to very bright; the effect is jarring to the audience's eyes.[13]

Background Designs and Artwork

Electronic slides and other visuals have two layers or levels of graphic design: the background and foreground. The *background* is the equivalent of paper in a printed report and normally stays the same from slide to slide. The *foreground* contains the unique text and graphic elements that make up each individual slide.

A good background should stay in the background, not compete with the foreground.

Generally speaking, the less your background does, the better. Cluttered or flashy backgrounds tend to distract from your message. Look through the design templates next time you use PowerPoint; you'll find a selection of designs with backgrounds that range from the subtle and visually "quiet" to some that are quite colorful and too playful for business use. When in doubt, go for subtle and simple; no one will fault you for using a background that's "boring." (A boring foreground is another matter; more on that in a minute.) In fact, for routine presentations, a single color in the background might be all you really need in terms

TABLE 17.1 Color and Emotion

COLOR	EMOTIONAL ASSOCIATIONS	BEST USES
Blue	Peaceful, soothing, tranquil, cool, trusting	Background for electronic business presentations (usually dark blue); safe and conservative
White	Neutral, innocent, pure, wise	Font color of choice for most electronic business presentations with a dark background
Yellow	Warm, bright, cheerful, enthusiastic	Text bullets and subheadings with a dark background
Red	Passionate, dangerous, active, painful	Promote action or stimulate audience; seldom used as a background ("in the red" specifically refers to financial losses)
Green	Assertive, prosperous, envious, relaxed	Highlight and accent color (green symbolizes money in the United States but not in other countries)

of design. Just remember that the background needs to stay in the background; it shouldn't compete with the foreground elements.

You may also want to add your company logo, the date, the presentation title, and a running slide number to help both you and the audience follow along. Just be sure to keep all these elements small and unobtrusive. Also, be sure to check whether your company has a standard design; many companies now have custom-designed PowerPoint templates that ensure consistency for all their presentations.

In the foreground, artwork can be either functional or decorative. *Functional artwork* includes photos, technical drawings, charts, and other visual elements containing information that's part of your message. In contrast, *decorative artwork* is there simply to enhance the look of your slides. Decorative artwork is the least important element of any slide, but it tends to cause the most trouble for anyone inexperienced in designing slides (see Figure 17.4).

Artwork can be either decorative or functional; use decorative artwork sparingly.

Clip art is probably the biggest troublemaker in decorative art because it is so easy to use and therefore so easy to misuse. You can find thousands and thousands of pieces of clip art, but few of them add any information value. Use them judiciously, or they'll add a cartoony feel to your slides. In general, keep clip art small—treat it like jewelry, not clothing. For title slides and other instances in which you don't have a lot of information on a slide, you can sometimes get away with larger clip art. In any event, don't use clip art just because you see it in a lot of other presentations; use it only if it helps make your presentation more appealing to your audience.

Use clip art only if it makes your presentation more effective and compelling.

Avoid the temptation to find a piece of clip art for every slide in your presentation. Unless you have access to a comprehensive, high-quality collection of artwork, chances are you won't find a good image for every single slide. At the very least, you'll spend a lot of time trying to fit images to slide content, and that time is probably better spent on other tasks.

Fonts and Type Styles

The most important factor to consider when selecting fonts is how well a font will display through a projection system. Many fonts that are easy to read on paper are difficult to read on screen because computer displays and projectors have lower resolution than printers. When selecting fonts and type styles for slides, follow these guidelines:

Many of the fonts available on your computer are difficult to read on screen, so they aren't good choices for presentation slides.

- Avoid script or decorative fonts.
- Limit your fonts to one or two per slide (if two fonts are used, reserve one for headings and the other for slide text).

FIGURE 17.4
Distractions from Decorative Artwork
Clip art and other pieces of purely decorative artwork must be used with great care to avoid distracting your audience. The clip art in this slide doesn't add any information value, and it creates a cartoony, unprofessional look.

FIGURE 17.5 Selecting Readable Fonts and Type Styles

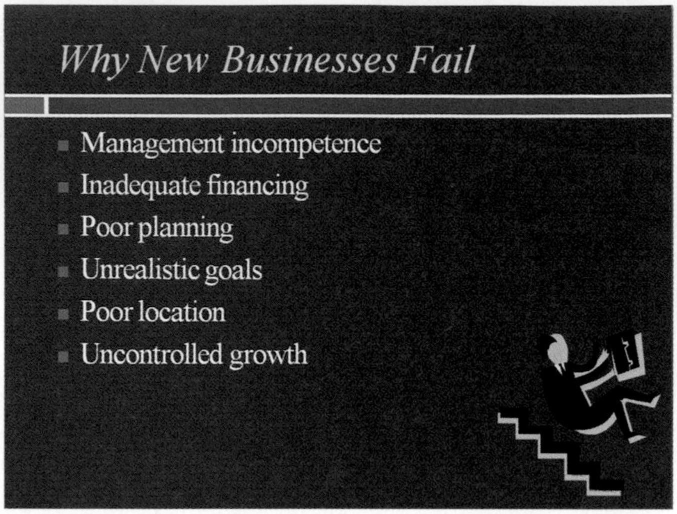

Figure 17.5a Times New Roman font

Figure 17.5b Arial font

Times New Roman is a standard font for many print documents; however, as Figure 17.5a demonstrates, the serifs at the end of each letter make this font difficult to read on screen, and so does the italicized type. As Figure 17.5b shows, san serif fonts such as Arial are a better choice for slides; they are clearer and easier to read from a distance.

- For thinner fonts, use boldface type so that letters won't look washed out.
- Avoid italicized type because it is difficult to read when projected.
- Avoid all-capitalized words and phrases.
- Allow extra white space between lines of text.
- Be consistent with fonts, type styles, colors, and sizes.

When selecting type sizes, consider the room(s) in which you'll be presenting. The farther the audience will be from the screen, the larger your type needs to be in order to be readable from everywhere in the room. Start with type between 24 and 36 points, reserving the larger size for titles and the smaller size for text items. Headings of the same level of importance should use the same font, type size, and color. Once you have selected your fonts and type styles, test them for readability by viewing sample slides from your audience's viewing location (see Figure 17.5).

Achieving Design Consistency

3 LEARNING OBJECTIVE

Explain the importance of design consistency in electronic slides and other visuals

Design inconsistencies confuse and annoy audiences; don't change colors and other design elements randomly in your presentation.

Audiences start to assign meaning to visual elements beginning with the first slide. For instance, if the first slide presents the most important information in bright yellow, 36-point Arial, your audience will expect the same font treatment for the most important information on the second and third slides as well; so when choosing fonts and point size, be consistent. Also be consistent in your layout. Make sure that items that repeat on every slide, such as the date and the company logo, are in the same location on every slide. Otherwise, you'll distract your readers as they try to figure out the arrangement of each new slide.

Fortunately, software designed specifically for presentations (as opposed to general graphics software) makes consistency easy to achieve. You simply adjust the slide master using the colors, fonts, and other design elements you've chosen; these choices will then automatically show up on every slide in the presentation (see Figure 17.6). In addition, you can maintain consistency by choosing a predefined layout from those available in your software—which helps ensure that bulleted lists, charts, graphics, and other elements show up in predictable places on each slide. Something as simple as switching from a single column of bullet points to two columns can throw readers off as they try to figure out the meaning of the new arrangement. The less that readers have to work to interpret your slide designs, the more attention they can pay to your message.

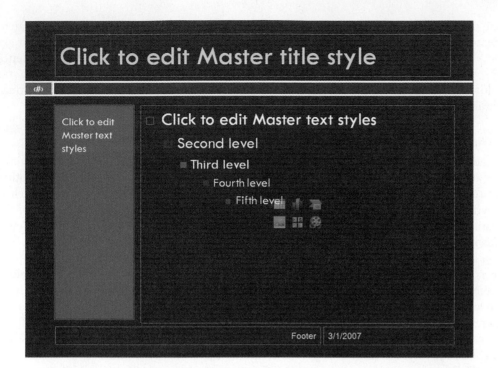

Click to edit Master title style

FIGURE 17.6
Presentation Slide Master
The slide master feature in PowerPoint and other presentation programs makes it easy to create consistent slides. Simply adjust the master as you need, and all the slides in your presentation will change accordingly.

Now, after all this advice about simplicity and consistency, a word of caution: Too much of a good thing can make your slides dull and lifeless. Particularly in a long presentation, one identical-looking slide after another can lull your audience to sleep. By adding some carefully planned animation and other special effects to your slides, you can keep your audience members involved without distracting them from your message.

With some practice (as both a presenter and an audience member), you'll get a feel for how much consistency is too much—when a design goes from being cohesive to being bland and uninteresting.

Adding Animation and Special Effects

Today's presentation software offers a wide array of options for livening up your slides, including sound, animation, video clips, transition effects from one slide to the next, and hyperlinks to websites and other resources. As with every other visual element, the key is to make sure that any effects you use support your message. Always consider the impact that all these effects will have on your audience and use only those special effects that support your message.[14]

Animation and special effects can be grouped into four categories: functional animation, transitions and builds, hyperlinks, and multimedia. These capabilities are briefly discussed in the following sections, but to learn more about them, consult the Help menu in your software or some of the many online resources that offer advice on using PowerPoint (see the Oral Communication section of the Business Communication Web Directory at www.buscommresources.com).

Functional Animation

PowerPoint and other presentation packages now offer a mind-boggling set of tools for moving and changing things on the screen. You can have a block of text cartwheel in from outer space, change colors, change font and font size, spin around in circles, blink on and off, wave back and forth, crawl around the screen following a predefined path, then disappear one letter at a time like some sort of erasing typewriter. You *can* do all this, but *should* you?

You can animate just about everything in an electronic presentation, but resist the temptation to do so—make sure the animation has a purpose.

Just as static graphic elements can be either functional or decorative, so too can animated elements. For instance, having each bullet point fly in from the left side of the screen doesn't add any functional value to your communication effort. In contrast, a highlight arrow or color bar that moves around the screen to emphasize specific points in a technical diagram can be an effective use of animation and a welcome alternative to a laser pointer. You can control every aspect of the animation, so it's easy to coordinate the movement with the points you're making in your presentation. Controlled animation is also a great way to demonstrate sequences and procedures. For a training session on machinery repair, for example, you can show a schematic diagram of the machinery and walk your audience through each step of the troubleshooting process, highlighting each step on screen as you address it verbally. Again, use animation in support of your message, not simply for animation's sake.

Transitions and Builds

In addition to animating specific elements on your slides, PowerPoint also provides options for adding motion between slides. These **transitions** control how one slide replaces another on screen. Subtle transitions can ease your viewers' gaze from one slide to the next—such as having the current slide gently fade out before the next slide fades in. However, most of the transitions currently available (such as checkerboards, pinwheels, and spinning "newsflashes") are like miniature animated shows themselves and therefore too distracting. You can even add sound effects, from drumrolls to explosions. These exaggerated transition effects not only disrupt the flow of your presentation, they can make your entire presentation seem amateurish. If you use a transition effect, use the same one throughout your entire presentation (so that audiences don't wonder if there is some significance to a new transition at some point during the presentation) and choose the effect carefully. Aim for a smooth, subtle, artful effect that is easy on the eye. And unless a sound effect is somehow integral to the message, there is no reason to add audio to the transition.

Carefully designed builds can be a great way to present information in easy-to-process pieces.

Builds are somewhat similar to transitions but much more useful. These effects control the release of text, graphics, and other elements on individual slides. For instance, with builds you can make your bullet points appear one at a time rather than having all of them appear on a slide at once, which makes it difficult to focus on a single point. This controlled release of information helps draw the audience's attention to the point being discussed and prevents the audience from reading ahead.

As with transitions, stick with the subtle, basic options for builds. The point of a build, after all, is to release information in a controlled fashion, not to distract or entertain the audience. Another useful option is to change the color of bullet points as you discuss each one. For instance, if your primary text color is a strong blue, you might have the text in each bullet change to a light gray after you've finished talking about it. This adds some subtle activity to the screen and keeps the audience's attention focused on the current bullet point.

Once you've assigned builds to your slides, you can control the build activity with a mouse or a remote control device. Experiment with the options in your software to find the most effective build scheme. In addition to building up text, you can build up graphical elements. For instance, to discuss monthly sales of three products over the past year, you can have a line graph of the first product appear by itself while you discuss it, then click the mouse to display the second product's sales line, then the third.

As with all design elements, you'll generally want to use the same build design throughout your presentation. Don't introduce text that builds from left to right on one slide and from top to bottom on the next. Unnecessary changes that don't add any information value only distract the audience.

Hyperlinks and Action Buttons

You can increase the flexibility of your presentation slides with hyperlinks that let you jump to slides, websites, or other software screens at the click of a mouse.

Hyperlinks and action buttons can be quite handy when you need flexibility in your presentations or want to share different kinds of files with the audience. A **hyperlink** instructs your computer to jump to another slide in your presentation, to a website, or to another program entirely. Hyperlinks either can be simple underlined text (like most of the links you see on a website) or can be assigned to **action buttons**, which are a variety of preprogrammed hyperlink icons available in PowerPoint.

Hyperlinks are also a great way to customize your presentations in advance. For instance, if you work in sales and call on a variety of customers, you can never be sure what

FIGURE 17.7 Building Slides with Hyperlinks
Both of these slides contain multiple hyperlinks embedded in the text of bullet points, making it easy for the speaker to navigate in and out of detail slides based on questions from the audience. By clicking on any of the bullets in Figure 17.7a, the speaker can advance to a new slide explaining the details of that particular program. For instance, if the speaker clicks on *Coupons*, the slide show will advance to Figure 17.7b, which outlines the coupon program. Each of the bullets in Figure 17.7b is also a hyperlink, so the speaker can advance further into the details of each type of coupon. For example, the *Website* bullet links to a live website that shows the audience how the online coupon program works. To return to Figure 17.7a, the speaker clicks on the *[Incentives]* link in the lower left corner.

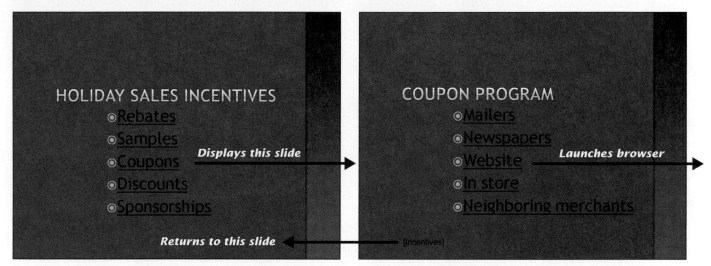

Figure 17.7a   Main slide for holiday sales incentives   Figure 17.7b   Detail slide on coupon program

sort of situation you'll encounter at each customer's site. You might be prepared to give an in-depth technical presentation to a group of engineers, only to have the company president walk in and request a five-minute overview. Or you might prepare a set of detailed technical slides but not show them unless the audience asks detailed questions. Another common situation is finding out at the last minute that you have only a fraction of the time you thought you had to make your presentation. With some foresight and planning, you won't need to rush through your entire presentation or scramble on the spot to find the most important slides. Instead, you can simply click an action button labeled "Five-minute overview" and jump right to the two or three most important slides in your presentation. With hyperlinks, you can even switch from an indirect approach to a direct approach or vice versa, based on the response you're getting from your audience. By building in links that accommodate these various scenarios, you can adjust your presentation at a moment's notice—and look polished and professional while you do it (see Figure 17.7).

Multimedia Elements

For some presentations, audio or video clips are an effective way to get your message across. For instance, if a few words from your company president would help bolster your argument but she's not available to speak during your presentation, you can capture her on video beforehand and include the video clip in your presentation file. As you'll see at the end of the chapter (under "Giving Presentations Online"), the combination of video and electronic slides offers a great way to give presentations over the Internet.

Video clips can add memorable, engaging content to your presentations—as long as they are relevant, interesting, and brief.

You can incorporate various media elements with PowerPoint using tools such as Microsoft Producer, an add-in to PowerPoint. In addition, dozens of software programs are now available to assist with video editing, from basic tools sometimes included with digital cameras or camcorders to professional packages such as Adobe Premiere Pro.

Connecting with Technology

Creating High-Octane Presentations

The board of directors wants to know how your division is doing: revenues, profits, employee satisfaction, customer satisfaction, and half a dozen other metrics. You have all the data—for all 10,000 of your customers in 38 countries, which are supported by 58 offices staffed by nearly 2,000 employees. Data isn't the problem. The problem is time: the board has given you 10 minutes on this month's agenda. How can you possibly summarize so many important issues in so little time? And what if the directors ask questions about any one of the thousands of pieces of underlying data; how can you access all your supporting information quickly?

Despair not, brave presenter: a new generation of software tools can help. As one of the many examples now available, Crystal Xcelsius from Business Objects lets you create eye-catching, interactive visuals based on data contained in

Excel spreadsheets. For instance, you can use it to create the "gas gauge" style graphs that are popular in executive dashboard displays or interactive bar and pie charts that let you click through reams of data in seconds. And because the charts and graphs are "live" (always connected to updated data in your spreadsheet), you can continue to update the data over time without having to recreate your presentation visuals.

For instance, the following screen shows key performance variables for the operation of a hotel chain. By clicking on each hotel location on the left, a manager can display up-to-the-minute data on customer satisfaction, bookings, new income, and other important measures. (Note that while such screens present much more data than a typical slide graph, they are designed for closer study by the audience.)

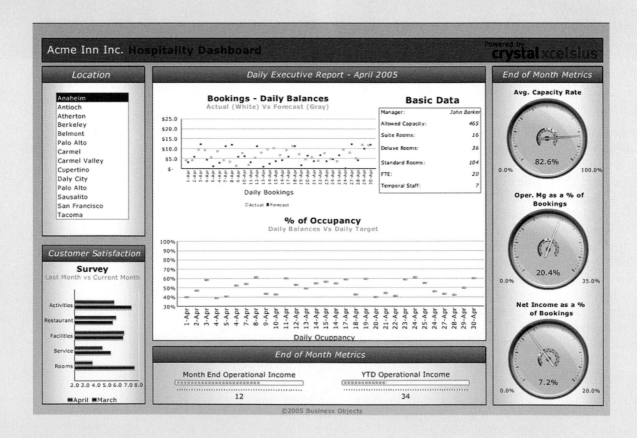

CAREER APPLICATIONS

1. Research one of the executive dashboard tools available for Excel or PowerPoint and explain how your college's placement office could use it to display information on the job market facing this year's graduates.

2. Discuss the potential risks of presenting complex data as simple graphic elements.

COMPLETING SLIDES AND SUPPORT MATERIALS

Just as you would review any message for content, style, tone, readability, clarity, and conciseness, you should apply the same quality control to your slides and other visuals. As you look over your presentation for the final time, make sure that all visuals are:

Review each slide carefully to make sure it is clear and readable.

- **Readable.** Are the font sizes large enough? Too large? Can they be seen from the back of the room? Does the text stand out from the background?
- **Consistent.** Are colors and design elements used consistently?
- **Simple.** Should some information be illustrated by a chart, diagram, or picture? Should some information be eliminated or moved to handouts or backup slides? Should some slides be eliminated altogether?
- **Audience centered.** Are design elements such as clip art and color appropriate for your audience?
- **Clear.** Is the main point of a slide obvious? Easy to understand? Can the audience grasp the main point in five to eight seconds?
- **Concise and grammatical.** Is text written in concise phrases? Are the phrases parallel?
- **Focused.** Does each slide cover only one thought, concept, or idea? Does the slide grab the viewer's attention in the right place and support the key points of the message? Are arrows, symbols, or other techniques used to draw the audience's attention to the key sections of a chart or diagram?
- **Fully operational.** Have you verified every slide in your presentation? Do all the animations and other special effects work as you intended?

Remember, you want the audience to listen to you, not study the slides, so make sure your slides are not distracting in any way.

Electronic presentation software can help you during the editing and revision process. As Figure 17.8 shows, the *slide sorter view* lets you see a file's batch of slides, either all at once or in significant portions (for lengthy presentations). Using the slide sorter makes it easy to add and delete slides, reposition slides, and check slides for design consistency. You can also use this view to preview animation and transition effects and experiment with design elements. For instance, if you want to experiment with a different background design or different font, select a new design element and preview it in your slides. If you choose to keep the new design, execute the "apply all" command to update all existing slides and to change the slide master, which applies the design changes to any new slides you create. Note that you can also use the slide sorter view as a *storyboard* to plan your presentation.[15]

Use the slide sorter view to verify and modify the organization of your slides.

With your slides working properly and in clear, logical order, you're just a few steps away from being ready. Now is a good time to think about a backup plan. What will you do if your laptop won't turn on or the projector dies? Can you get by without your slides? For important presentations, consider having backup equipment on standby, loaded with your presentation, and ready to go. At the very least, have enough printed handouts ready to give the audience so that, as a last resort, you can give your presentation "on paper."

With three additional tasks, you should be ready to go: create navigational and support slides, create handout material, and practice your delivery.

Creating Navigation and Support Slides

At this point, you've created the slides that will deliver the content of your presentation. You can enhance your presentation with a few additional slides that add "finish" to your presentation and provide additional information to benefit your audience:

5 LEARNING OBJECTIVE

Identify three types of noncontent slides you can use to support your presentation

- **Title slide(s).** Make a good first impression on your audience with one or two title slides, the equivalent of a report's cover and title page (see Figures 17.9a and 17.9b) A title slide should contain the title of your presentation (and subtitle if appropriate), your name, your department affiliation (for internal audiences), and your company affiliation (for external audiences). You may also include the presentation date and an appropriate graphic element. Depending on the amount of information you

FIGURE 17.8 Slide Sorter View
Examining thumbnails of slides on one screen is the best way to check the overall design of your final product. The slide sorter also makes it easy to review the order and organization of your presentation; you can even use this screen to storyboard your presentation before creating slides.

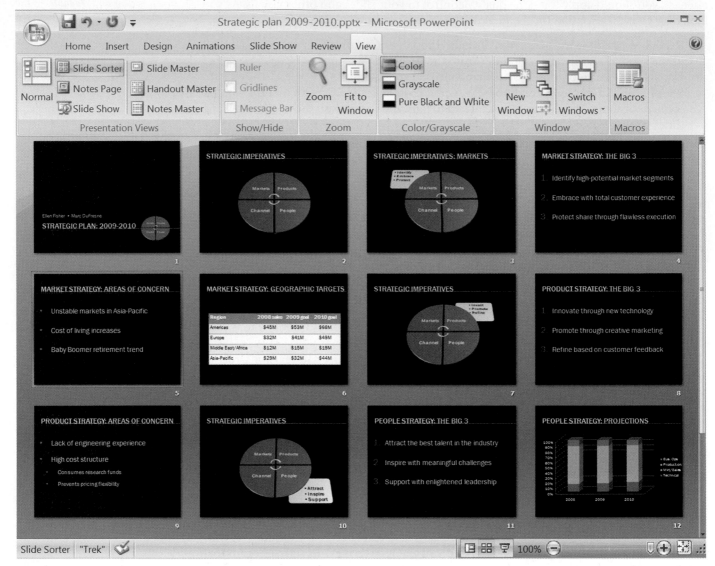

need to convey at this point, two title slides might be appropriate: one focusing on the topic of the presentation and a second slide with your affiliation and other information. This second slide can also be used to introduce the speaker and list his or her credentials.

- **Agenda and program details.** These slides communicate both the agenda for your presentation and any additional information that your audience might need. Because presentations pull your audience members away from their daily routines and work responsibilities, people can have questions about anything from break times or lunch plans to opportunities to plug into a network to check their e-mail (see Figures 17.9c and 17.9d). By answering these questions at the beginning of your presentation, you'll minimize disruptions later and help the audience stay focused on your message.

Navigation slides help your audience keep track of what you've covered already and what you plan to cover next.

- **Navigation slides.** To tell your audience where you're going and where you've been, you can use a series of **navigation slides** based on your outline or agenda. This technique is

FIGURE 17.9 Navigation and Support Slides
You can use a variety of navigation and support slides to introduce yourself and your presentation, to let the audience know what your presentation will cover, and to provide essential details.

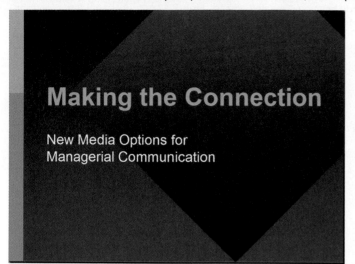

Figure 17.9a

Figure 17.9b

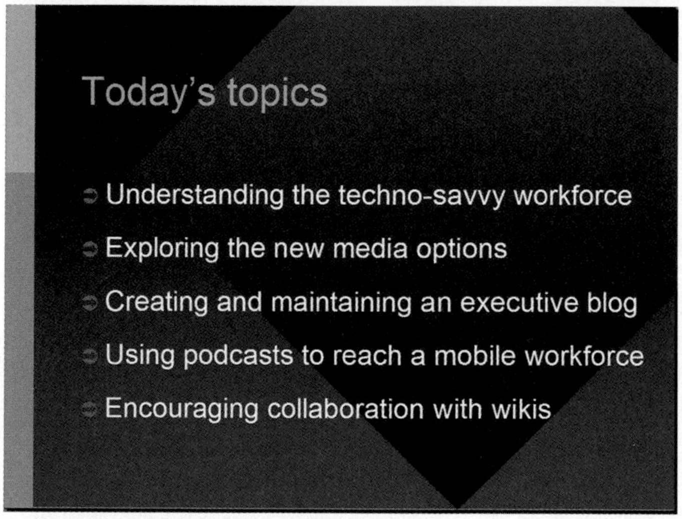

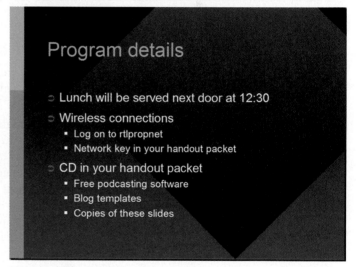

Figure 17.9c

Figure 17.9d

most useful in longer presentations with several major sections. As you complete each section, repeat the slide but indicate which material has been covered and which section you are about to begin (see Figure 17.10). This sort of slide is sometimes referred to as a *moving blueprint.* You can then use the original slide again in the close of your presentation to review the points you've covered. As an alternative to the repeating agenda slide, you can insert a simple *bumper slide* at each major section break, announcing the title of the section you're about to begin.[16]

In addition to navigation slides, you can use *running headers* to remind the audience where you are in the presentation, in much the same way that this book repeats the chapter title at the top of every right-hand page. Finally, if your presentation will include product demonstrations or other activities, include a simple slide that indicates the nature of the activity (such as "Product Demonstration" or "Group Discussion"). You can use this slide to introduce the activity to the audience, and the slide can remind you to stop at the appropriate point in the presentation to initiate it.

FIGURE 17.10 Moving Blueprint Slides
Here are two of the ways you can use a blueprint slide as a navigational aid to help your audience stay on track with the presentation. Figure 17.10a visually "mutes" and checks off the sections of the presentation that have already been covered. In contrast, Figure 17.10b uses a sliding highlight box to indicate the next section to be covered.

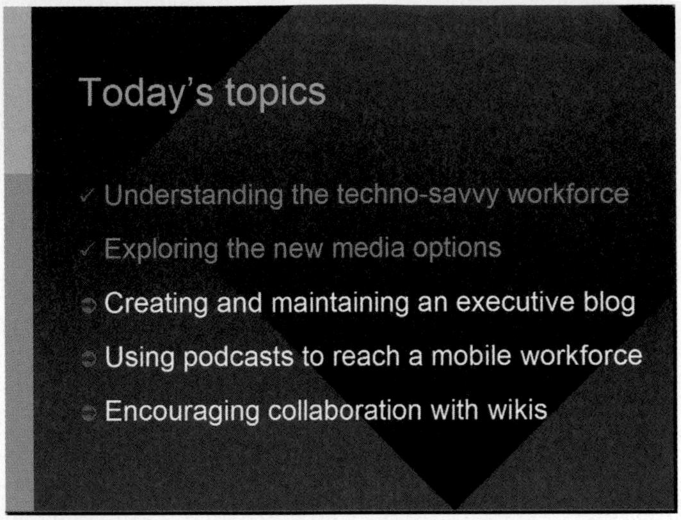

Figure 17.10a

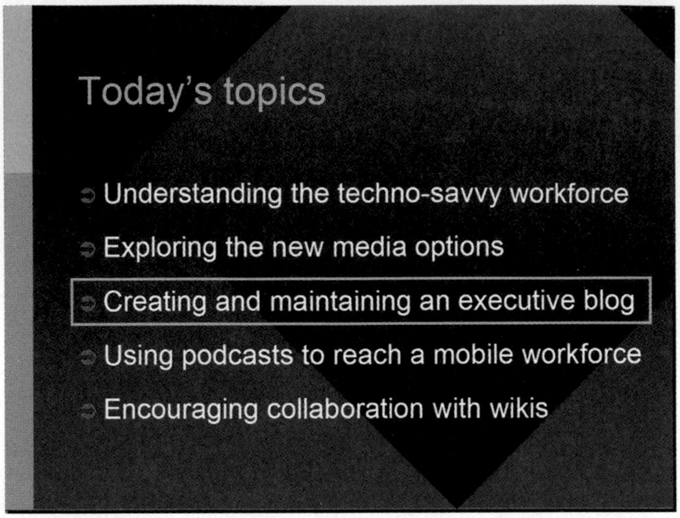

Figure 17.10b

Creating Effective Handouts

Use handout materials to support the points made in your presentation and to offer the audience additional information on your topic.

Providing handouts is a great way to offer your audience additional material without overloading your slides with information. Possibilities for good handout materials include the following:[17]

- **Complex charts and diagrams.** Charts and tables that are too unwieldy for the screen or that demand thorough analysis make good handouts. A common approach is to create a stripped-down version of a chart or graphic for the presentation slide and include a more detailed version in your handouts.
- **Articles and technical papers.** Magazine articles that supplement the information in your presentation make good handout materials, as do technical papers that provide in-depth coverage of the material you've highlighted in your presentation.
- **Case studies.** Summaries of case studies along with references and contact information make good supplemental reading material.
- **Websites.** Lists of websites related to your topic are useful; provide each site's URL and a one- or two-sentence summary of its content.
- **Copies of presentation slides.** In many cases, audiences like to have print versions of the slides used by a speaker, containing the speaker's comments about each slide and blank lines for note taking. PowerPoint gives you several options for printing handouts, from a single slide per page to as many as nine per page.

Other good handout materials include brochures, pictures, outlines, a copy of the presentation agenda, and other program details. Make sure the information is all useful and relevant.

Timing the distribution of handouts depends on the content of your handouts, the nature of your presentation, and your personal preference. Some speakers prefer to distribute handout copies of their slides before the presentation begins so that the audience can take notes. This can be risky, however, if you've organized your talk with an indirect approach, because the audience can read ahead and reach the conclusion and recommendations before you're able to build up to them yourself. Other speakers simply advise the audience of the types of information they are including in handouts but delay distributing anything until they have finished speaking.

DOCUMENT MAKEOVER

IMPROVE THESE SLIDES

To practice correcting drafts of actual documents, visit your online course or the access-code-protected portion of the Companion Website. Click "Document Makeovers," then click Chapter 17. You will find a series of slides containing problems and errors relating to what you've learned in this chapter about enhancing oral presentations with electronic slides. Use the Final Draft decision tool to create an improved version of these slides. Check the slides for wordiness, clarity, consistency, complexity, necessity, readability, active versus passive voice, appropriateness of ideas, spelling, and grammar.

Practicing Your Delivery

In addition to rehearsing your speaking material as Chapter 16 advises, you should practice all aspects of your presentation, from the way you plan to introduce important slides to handling product demonstrations and other activities. Many things can go wrong in a major presentation, including equipment glitches, confusing slides, and the unpleasant discovery that you're out of time but only halfway through your material. That's why experienced speakers always practice important presentations. If you can arrange an audience of several helpful colleagues, by all means do so. They can tell you if your slides are understandable and whether your delivery is effective. A day or two before you're ready to step on stage for an important talk, make sure you can give a positive response to the following questions:

The more you practice, the more confidence you'll have in yourself and your material.

- **Can you present your material naturally, without reading your slides word for word?** Reading your slides is one of the worst mistakes a presenter can make. If you need to refer to your speaking notes, either print a copy or take advantage of the "Presenter View" feature in Microsoft PowerPoint. With Presenter View (which requires a PC capable of displaying on two monitors at once), you can see your notes privately on your own PC screen while your audience sees your regular slides on the presentation screen.
- **Is the equipment working—and do you know how to work it?** Verify that your computer will work with the projector; sometimes you need to adjust the resolution of your computer screen to make it compatible with a particular projector. Also, many conference rooms are now equipped with sophisticated wireless remote controls and other high-tech devices. You don't want to find yourself struggling to turn on the projector in front of a restless audience. In addition, some presentation tools, such as wireless remote controls for your laptop computer, need to have software installed on your computer before they'll operate.
- **Is your timing on track?** Your practice runs, particularly if you can arrange to speak in front of a test audience, will give you a good idea of how much time you'll need. Now is the time to trim, not when you're live on stage.
- **Can you easily pronounce all the words you plan to use?** Everyone stumbles over certain words, and your tongue is more likely to get tied up when you're under pressure and your mouth is dry.
- **Have you decided how you're going to introduce your slides?** Effective speakers usually introduce the slide before they show it. Doing so allows you to set the stage before your audience starts reading the slide and jumping to their own conclusions.
- **Have you anticipated likely questions and objections?** Put yourself in the audience's shoes and try to imagine what issues the various audience members might have about your content, then think through your answers ahead of time. Don't assume you can handle whatever comes up.[18]
- **Does your message come through clearly?** When you think you're ready, step back and look at everything you plan to present. Are you presenting the right material in the right quantity to get your message across? Don't make the common mistake of worrying so much about the supporting evidence that your message gets lost in the all details.[19] If you're in danger of overloading the audience with data, now is the time to edit your slide set down to a more reasonable number.

With experience, you'll get a feel for how much practice is enough in any given situation. If you find yourself constantly stumbling with the software and hardware or referring to your slides to remind yourself of key points, you need more practice. For an important presentation, four or five practice runs is not excessive. Your credibility is dramatically enhanced when you move seamlessly through your presentation, matching effective words with each slide. Practicing helps keep you on track, helps you maintain a conversational tone with your audience, and boosts your confidence and composure.

6 LEARNING OBJECTIVE

List the seven questions you should ask yourself to determine whether you're ready to give your presentation

Learning to focus on audience members and interact with them while using electronic slides or other visuals takes practice.

CHECKLIST: Enhancing Presentations with Visuals

A. Planning Your Presentation Visuals
- Make sure you and your message remain the focus of your presentation, not your visuals.
- Select your visuals carefully to support your message; use a combination of visuals if needed.
- Review your plan for each visual to make sure it truly supports your message.
- Follow effective design principles, with an emphasis on accuracy and simplicity.
- Use your time wisely so that you have plenty of time to practice your presentation.

B. Creating Effective Slides
- Write content that will be readable from everywhere in the room.
- Write short, active, parallel phrases that support, not replace, your spoken message.
- Avoid complete sentences unless you need to quote verbatim.
- Limit the amount of text so that your audience can focus on listening, not reading.
- Simplify print graphics for use on slides but don't oversimplify.
- Use color to emphasize important ideas, create contrast, and isolate visual elements.
- Limit color to a few compatible choices and use them consistently.
- Make sure your slide background doesn't compete with the foreground.

- Use decorative artwork sparingly; focus on functional artwork that supports your message.
- Choose fonts that are easy to read on screen; limit the number of fonts and use them consistently.
- Use slide masters to maintain consistency throughout your presentation.
- Use functional animation when it can support your message.
- Make sure slide transitions are subtle.
- Use builds carefully to control the release of information.
- Use hyperlinks and action buttons to add flexibility to your presentation.
- Incorporate multimedia elements that can help engage your audience and deliver your message.

C. Completing Slides and Support Materials
- Review every slide carefully to ensure accuracy, consistency, and clarity.
- Make sure that all slides are fully operational.
- Use the slide sorter to verify and adjust the sequence of slides if needed.
- Have a backup plan in case your electronic presentation plan fails.
- Create navigation and support slides.
- Create handouts to back up your presentation message.
- Practice your delivery to ensure a smooth presentation.

For a quick review of the key steps in creating effective visuals, see "Checklist: Enhancing Presentations with Visuals."

GIVING PRESENTATIONS ONLINE

Online presentations give you a way to reach more people in less time, but they require special preparation and skills.

You can expect that at some point in your career, you'll be asked to deliver a presentation online. In some companies, online presentations have already become a routine matter, conducted via internal groupware, virtual meeting systems, or webcast systems designed specifically for online presentations. Capabilities vary from one system to another, so it's a good idea, well in advance of your presentation, to make sure you're familiar with the system you'll be using. In most cases, you'll communicate through some combination of audio, video, and data presentations (for instance, your electronic slides). Your audience will view your presentation either on individual computer screens or via a projector in a conference room.

The benefits of online presentations are considerable, including the opportunity to communicate with a geographically dispersed audience at a fraction of the cost of travel and the ability for a project team or an entire organization to meet at a moment's notice. Online presentations can also be less disruptive for the members of your audience, giving them the options of viewing your presentation from their desk and listening to only those parts that apply to them. However, the challenges for a presenter can be considerable, thanks to that layer of technology between you and your audience. Many of those "human moments" that guide and encourage you through an in-person presentation won't travel across the digital divide. However, online systems continue to improve, and presenters who master this new mode of communication will definitely have an advantage in tomorrow's business environment.

To ensure successful online presentations, keep the following advice in mind:

- **Consider sending preview study materials ahead of time.** If your presentation covers complicated or unfamiliar material, consider sending a brief message ahead of time so that your audience members can familiarize themselves with any important background information. Doing so can be particularly helpful if you're not sure whether everyone in the audience has the same level of understanding of the topic. In addition to preview materials, also consider sending technical "how-to" information to help inexperienced users connect to the system.[20]

- **Keep your content—and your presentation of it—as simple as possible.** Break complicated slides down into multiple slides if necessary and keep the direction of your discussion clear so that no one gets lost. Moreover, make sure any streaming video presentations are short; viewers don't like to sit through recorded speeches online.[21]

Online presentations let you reach a wider audience, but the lack of direct contact forces you to take a more active role in engaging your audience.

- **Ask for feedback frequently.** You won't have as much of the visual feedback that alerts you when audience members are confused (such as perplexed looks or blanks stares), and many online viewers will be reluctant to call attention to themselves by interrupting you to ask for clarification. So you'll have to draw out feedback as you go.

7 LEARNING OBJECTIVE

Highlight nine major issues to consider when you're preparing to give a presentation online

- **Consider the viewing experience from the audience's side.** Will participants be able to see what you think they can see? For instance, webcast video is typically displayed in a small window on screen, particularly with slower Internet connects. (Viewers can expand the size of the window, but then they lose visual resolution.) Consequently, if you try to use video to demonstrate the detailed operation of a piece of equipment, your audience might not even be able to see those details.

- **Improve any sections of your presentation that might be slow or difficult.** When people are viewing your presentation from their offices, potential distractions abound: e-mail, instant messaging, telephone calls, drop-in visitors, and so on. You need to work even harder than usual to make sure you keep everyone interested and involved in what you're presenting.

- **Make sure your audience can receive the sort of content you intend to use.** For instance, some corporate firewalls (electronic "safety gates" on corporate networks) don't allow streaming media, so your webcast video might not survive the trip.[22]

- **Allow plenty of time for everyone to get connected and familiar with the screens they're viewing.** Build extra time into your schedule to ensure that everyone is connected, particularly if some are connecting from remote locations.

- **Consider assigning a moderator to host the event and handle the software.** For anything beyond basic presentations to internal audiences, trying to play the triple roles of host, technical expert, and presenter can be overwhelming. By assigning a colleague to handle all the logistics, you can focus on delivering your message.

- **Engage the audience frequently.** With remote viewers and limited nonverbal feedback, online presentations present greater risk of losing the audience. To help avoid this situation, plan to engage the audience at regular intervals. For instance, many meeting systems let you conduct online polls, in which audience members are asked to vote on issues or respond to questions.[23]

Last but not least, don't get lost in the technology. With virtual white boards, real-time polling, collaborative editing, and other powerful features, electronic communication systems have lots of gadgets that can distract both you and your audience. Use these tools whenever they'll help, but remember that the most important aspect of any presentation is getting the audience to receive, understand, and embrace your message.

Once you master the technology, you can spend less time thinking about it and more time thinking about the most important elements of the presentation: your message and your audience.

COMMUNICATION CHALLENGES AT HEWLETT-PACKARD

HP continues to pursue major contracts with other global companies, and you've recently joined the company as a sales representative. Dan Talbott's group is pursuing a big project with Walt Disney Imagineering, the organization that unites the artistic, engineering, production, and installation teams responsible for creating Disney theme parks. As with the Procter & Gamble deal, Talbott has assembled a team—including you—in an HP sales office near Disney's headquarters in Burbank, California.

Individual Challenge: In his first meeting with the team, Talbott mentioned two significant links between the companies. First, in 1939 when HP was just starting out (as a maker of electronic instrumentation), Disney was one of its first customers, buying equipment that was used in the production of the movie *Fantasia*. Second, both companies value innovation, imagination, and creativity. To help prepare your part of the presentation—and get ready for Dan's rigorous review—create a list of the images and electronic presentation capabilities that can help convey HP's passion for innovation.

Team Challenge: In a small group, discuss the risks and rewards of using visual effects, sound effects, and animation in an electronic presentation when you'll be facing a visually sophisticated audience such as Walt Disney Imagineering. List the major pros and cons in a brief e-mail memo to your instructor.

SUMMARY OF LEARNING OBJECTIVES

1 Explain how visuals enhance oral presentations, and list several popular types of visuals. Visuals create interest, illustrate and clarify important points, add variety, and help the listener absorb the information you're presenting. In most businesses today, electronic presentations are the most common tool, but you might also use overhead transparencies, chalkboards and whiteboards (including electronic whiteboards), flip charts, product samples, models, video, and various software programs.

2 Describe the steps needed to write readable content for slides. The key point to keep in mind when drafting textual content slides is that you can't use as many words as you would in a printed message covering the same material. Follow these steps to make sure your text slides are easy for the audience to read: limit each slide to one thought or message point, limit content to 40 words or so (six lines of six words each is a good baseline), use short bulleted phrases rather than sentences or paragraphs, phrase list items in parallel grammatical form, use the active voice, and include short informative titles.

3 Explain the importance of design consistency in electronic slides and other visuals. Consistency is important because your audience looks for patterns in the way you use color, font size, and other design elements. If the first slide shows major points in blue text and minor points in green text, your audience will expect that pattern to continue throughout the presentation. If you change color assignments from slide to slide, you'll lose viewers' attention as they try to figure out what's important on each slide.

Anything that distracts audience members diminishes the concentration they can direct toward your presentation.

4 Describe the effective use of transitions and builds in electronic presentations. Transitions between slides can ease the viewer from one slide to the next, provided they are chosen artfully, with an emphasis on visual calm and subtlety. In contrast, hyperactive visuals with excessive motion and noise distract audiences and can disrupt the train of thought you're trying hard to keep them on as you move through your presentation. Whereas transitions are effects that occur between slides, builds are transitions within a single slide and affect the way that the various text and graphic elements are presented. A common build effect is displaying a bulleted list one item at a time, rather than all at once. Used judiciously, builds can be a good way to layer information as you work toward a conclusion.

5 Identify three types of noncontent slides you can use to support your presentation. In addition to the slides that convey your content, you can create one or more *title slides* to introduce your presentation (and yourself if necessary), *agenda and program detail slides* that tell viewers what to expect during the presentation and provide information to help them plan their time, and *navigation slides* that help you and your audience keep track of where you are in the presentation.

6 List the seven questions you should ask yourself to determine whether you're ready to give your presentation. A day or two before every major presentation, ask yourself these questions: (1) Can you present your material naturally, without reading your slides word for word? (2) Is the equipment working—and do you know how to work it? (3) Does the timing of your presentation match the time allotted to you? (4) Can you easily pronounce all the words you plan to use? (5) Have you decided how you're going to introduce your slides (whether you discuss the slide before you show it or show the slide first)? (6) Have you anticipated likely questions and objections, and have you prepared responses to these issues?

7 **Highlight nine major issues to consider when you're preparing to give a presentation online.** Review these points to help plan a successful online presentation:

(1) Consider sending preview materials ahead of time so your audience can familiarize themselves with the issues you plan to discuss. (2) Keep your content and presentation as simple as possible. (3) Plan to ask for feedback frequently because you might not get all the nonverbal signals that normally alert you to confusion or disagreement. (4) Consider the viewing experience from the audience's side to make sure your displayed content is easy to view. (5) Improve any sections of your presentation that might be slow or difficult because they'll be even harder to manage long-distance. (6) Make sure your audience can receive the sort of content you intend to use, such as video clips. (7) Allow plenty of time for everyone to get connected and familiar with the screen they're viewing.

Test Your Knowledge

1. When creating slides for presentations, which should you do first: select the background design for your slides or create your content? Explain your answer.
2. What is the recommended number of fonts you should use per slide?
3. How can hyperlinks be used in electronic slides?
4. How does slide sorter view facilitate the editing process for an electronic presentation?
5. How is a blueprint slide used in a presentation?
6. When should you distribute handouts? Why?
7. What is the difference between decorative and functional artwork and animation?
8. What is the advantage of practicing an oral presentation with visuals before a live audience?
9. When should you introduce slides?
10. On average, how many slides should you create for a 30-minute presentation?

Apply Your Knowledge

1. If a colleague needs to convert a 10-page report to a presentation, what advice would you give in terms of converting paragraphs of text to effective electronic slides?
2. How might you modify a graph appearing in a printed document to make it appropriate for a slide?
3. What should you strive for when selecting background designs, fonts, and type styles for your slides?
4. How can you use slide master to enhance the effectiveness of your slides?
5. **Ethical Choices** Is it ethical to use design elements and special effects to persuade an audience? Why or why not?

Practice Your Knowledge

Messages for Analysis

Message 17.A: Improving a Slide

Examine the slide in Figure 17.11 and point out any problems you notice. How would you correct these problems?

FIGURE 17.11 Piece of Cake Bakery Customer Survey

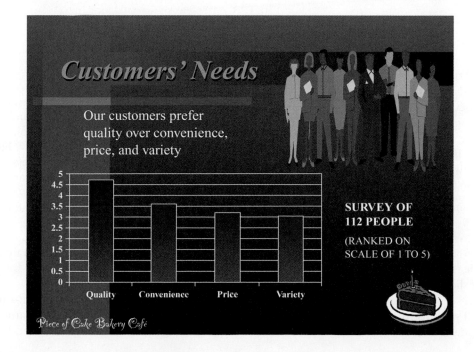

FIGURE 17.12
CommuniCo Employee
Training Costs

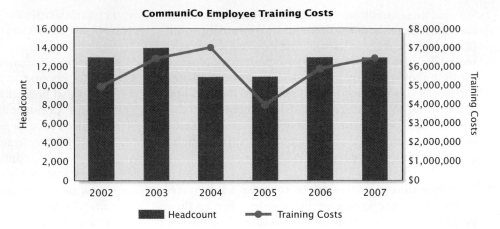

CommuniCo Employee Training Costs

Message 17.B: Modifying for Presentation

Examine the graph in Figure 17.12 and explain how to modify it for an electronic presentation using the guidelines discussed in this chapter.

Message 17.C: Analyzing the Animation

To access this PowerPoint presentation, visit www.businesscommunicationheadlinenes.com and click on Textbook Resources. Locate *Business Communication Today*, 9th ed., click on Chapter 17, then select page 546, Message 17.C. Download and watch the presentation in slide show mode (after you select Slide Show from the View menu, simply click your mouse to advance through the slides). After you've watched the presentation, identify at least three ways in which various animations, builds, and transitions either enhanced or impeded your understanding of the subject matter.

Exercises

For active links to all websites discussed in this chapter, visit this text's website at www.prenhall.com/bovee. Locate your book and click on its Companion Website link. Then select Chapter 17, and click on "Featured Websites." Locate the name of the page or the URL related to the material in the text. Please note that links to sites that become inactive after publication of the book will be removed from the Featured Websites section.

❚ Portfolio
❚ BUILDER

17.1 **Creating Effective Slides: Content** Look through recent issues (print or online) of *BusinessWeek*, *Fortune*, or other business publications for articles discussing issues a specific company or industry is facing. Using the articles and the guidelines discussed in this chapter, create three to five slides summarizing these issues. If you don't have access to computer presentation software or a word processor, you can draw the slides on plain paper.

17.2 **Creating Effective Slides: Content and Design** You've been asked to give an informative 10-minute talk to a group of convention attendees on great things to see and do while visiting your hometown. Write the content for three or four slides (including a title slide). Then think about the design elements for your slides. Describe design choices you would make, particularly in terms of colors, fonts, drawings, and photography. If your instructor directs, create the slides that you've described.

17.3 **Completing Electronic Presentations: Slide Sorter View** PowerPoint comes with a number of content templates for presentations. Use the software's AutoContent Wizard to create a short presentation by selecting a presentation type and supplying information for the slide templates (feel free to make up material). Then use the *slide sorter view* to critique the content, layout, and design elements of your presentation. Edit and revise the slides to improve their overall effectiveness.

17.4 **Creating Effective Slides: Design Elements** Most personal computers offer a large selection of fonts. Review the fonts available to you and select three to five fonts suitable for electronic slides or overhead transparencies. Explain the criteria you use for your selections.

17.5 **Internet** Creating hyperlinks to live websites can perk up an electronic presentation, but it also means being prepared for the unexpected. What are some of the obstacles you might encounter when creating live Internet links for use during a presentation? How can you prepare in advance to overcome such obstacles?

Expand Your Knowledge

Exploring the Best of the Web

Look Smart in Your Electronic Presentations
www.3m.com/meetingnetwork/presentations
Visit the presentation center at 3M, and follow the expert advice on creating and delivering effective oral presentations. Find out why a bad presentation can kill even the best idea. Did you pick the right colors? Is your presentation too long? Too wordy? Find out why a strong template is the key to positive first impressions. Review the five tips for better presentations. Log on and learn the secrets from the pros, then address these questions:

1. What three questions should you answer for a successful presentation?
2. What common PowerPoint pitfalls should you avoid?
3. What are the two common causes of presentation paralysis?

Surfing Your Way to Career Success

Bovée and Thill's Business Communication Resources offers links to hundreds of online resources that can help you with this course, your other college courses, and your career. Visit www.buscommresources.com, then click on "Business Communication Web Directory." The "Tutorials" section connects you to online tutorials on numerous communication topics, from writing business letters to mentoring to webcasting. Identify three websites from this section that could be useful in your business career. For each site, write a two-sentence summary of what the site offers and how it could help you launch and build your career.

Learn Interactively

Interactive Study Guide

Visit www.prenhall.com/bovee, then locate your book and click on its "Companion Website" link. Select Chapter 17 to take advantage of the interactive "Chapter Quiz" to test your knowledge of chapter concepts. Receive instant feedback on whether you need additional studying. Also, visit the "Study Hall," where you'll find an abundance of valuable resources that will help you succeed in this course.

Peak Performance Grammar and Mechanics

If your instructor has required the use of "Peak Performance Grammar and Mechanics," either in your online course or on CD, you can continue to improve your skill with vocabulary by using the "Peak Performance Grammar and Mechanics" module. Click "Vocabulary," then click "Vocabulary II." Take the Pretest to determine whether you have any weak areas. Then review those areas in the Refresher Course. Take the Follow-Up Test to check your grasp of vocabulary. For an extra challenge or advanced practice, take the Advanced Test. Finally, for additional reinforcement, visit the Companion Website, click on any chapter, then click on "Improve Your Grammar, Mechanics, and Usage."

CASES

Applying the Three-Step Writing Process to Cases

Apply each step to the following cases, as assigned by your instructor.

Portfolio BUILDER

1. Is anybody out there? Explaining Loopt's social mapping service How many times have you been out shopping or clubbing and wondered if any of your friends were in the neighborhood? A new *social mapping* service from Loopt can provide the answer. It lets you put yourself on a map that your friends can see on their mobile phones, and you can see their locations as well. You can even get automatic alerts whenever friends are near.

Your task: Create a brief presentation explaining the Loopt concept to someone who is comfortable using text messaging and other mobile phone features. Be sure to explain what type of phone is required, and include one slide that discusses safety issues. You can learn more about it at www.loopt.com.[24]

Portfolio BUILDER

2. I'll find my space somewhere else, thanks: Promoting alternatives to MySpace With a user base well on its way toward 200 million people, MySpace is the king of social networking sites. However, it doesn't appeal to everyone. Some people want to be able to customize their online presence more than MySpace allows, while others want more control over who sees what aspects of their online profiles.

Your task: Choose one of the lesser-known alternatives to MySpace, such as Ning (www.ning.com), Vox (www.vox.com), Esnips (www.esnips.com), or any other site that offers some degree of social networking. Compare its features and functions to MySpace, then prepare a brief presentation that highlights the similarities and differences of the two sites. In your presentation, identify the sort of people most likely to prefer the site you've chosen over MySpace.[25]

3. Face to face: Updating management on your monthly progress Imagine that you've just completed the impressive-looking online progress report shown in Figure 14.5 (page 434), when your boss decides he'd like to hear a presentation from you instead.

Your task: Adapt the information in Figure 14.5 to a brief electronic slide show. Your boss might want to see maps of the four locations listed, so have slides with maps ready (because you don't have the specific addresses, just capture an online map for each general area; Lakewood and Glendale are both suburbs of Denver, and Pepsi Center is a sports arena in Denver).

Portfolio BUILDER

4. Hot topics: Identifying key elements in an important business issue In your job as a business development researcher for a major corporation, you're asked to gather and process information on a wide variety of subjects. Management has gained confidence in your research and analysis skills and would now like you to begin making regular presentations at management retreats and other functions. Topics are likely to include the following:

- Offshoring of U.S. jobs
- Foreign ownership of U.S. firms
- Employment issues involving immigrants
- Tax breaks offered by local and state governments to attract new businesses
- Economic impact of environmental regulations

Your task: Choose one of the topics from the list and conduct enough research to familiarize yourself with the topic. Identify at least three important issues that anyone involved with this topic should know about. Prepare a 10-minute presentation that introduces the topic, comments on its importance to the U.S. economy, then discusses the issues you've identified. Assume your audience is a cross-section of business managers who don't have any particular experience in the topic you've chosen.

PART 7

Writing Employment Messages and Interviewing for Jobs

CHAPTER 18
Building Careers and Writing Résumés

CHAPTER 19
Interviewing for Employment and Following Up

Building Careers and Writing Résumés

LEARNING OBJECTIVES

After studying this chapter, you will be able to

1 Describe the approach most employers take to finding potential new employees

2 Explain the importance of networking in your career search

3 Discuss how to choose the appropriate résumé organization and list the advantages and disadvantages of the three common options

4 Describe the problem of résumé fraud

5 List the major sections of a traditional résumé

6 Identify six different formats in which you can produce a résumé

7 Describe what you should do to adapt your résumé to a scannable format

COMMUNICATION CLOSE-UP AT HERSHA HOSPITALITY MANAGEMENT

www.hershahotels.com

For applicants, the job search process might be long and grueling, but at least it has a definite beginning, middle, and end. For managers in charge of recruiting, though, such as Hersha Hospitality Management's vice president of human resources Jeffrey Wade, the process never ends. Hersha provides operational management services to a growing number of hotels in the eastern United States, and as the company grows, its need to add top-quality employees never ends.

Growth is not the only force that puts demands on Wade and his team. "Recruiting in the hospitality industry is always a challenge because many of the positions are lower-wage jobs, and front-office positions are often filled by college students who want to move on with their careers," he explains. In other words, even as the company expands and needs to bring in more new employees, many existing employees are looking to move up and out. The result is relentless pressure to select new people to join the Hersha family. Moreover, Wade isn't interested in hiring just

An applicant tracking system has helped Jeffrey Wade and his team at Hersha Hospitality Management efficiently recruit the customer-service-driven employees that Hersha relies on.

anybody; the company has extremely high customer-service standards for everyone from entry-level hotel workers to top management.

Many managers in Wade's position, particularly in small to midsize companies, *outsource* the recruiting function, paying an outside company to find and filter candidates. However, Wade believes that recruiting is too essential to Hersha's success to be left in the hands of an outsider.

His answer to the challenge of endless hiring is to use an *applicant tracking system* (ATS), a computer-based solu-

tion that integrates the entire recruiting and employee records management effort—from job seekers' submission of online résumés and applications through interviewing, hiring, orientation, promotions, and eventual leaving of the company. Although it is highly computerized, the process is far from impersonal. In fact, by managing all the details, the system frees up Wade and his staff to spend time talking with applicants, assessing their personalities and potential fit with Hersha's service-oriented culture.[1]

SECURING EMPLOYMENT IN TODAY'S JOB MARKET

Hersha's approach to managing the employee application process (profiled in the chapter-opening "Communication Close-Up") highlights the ever-evolving nature of the job market. To keep up with the demand for good employees—and the flood of résumés coming in from all over the Internet—many companies now use some form of automation to find the best candidates and shepherd them through the selection process.

Understanding how employers approach the hiring process is just one of many insights and skills you'll need to conduct a successful job search. After you've armed yourself with knowledge of today's workplace and your potential role in it, it's time to launch an efficient, productive process to find that ideal position. (Before you read this chapter, make sure you've read the Prologue, "Building a Career with Your Communication Skills," starting on page P-1.) Figure 18.1 shows the six most important tasks in the job search process. This chapter and the Prologue discuss the first two, and Chapter 19 explores the final four. The more you know about this process, the more successful you'll be in your job search. Plus, it's important to keep in mind that employers and job candidates approach the process differently.

1 LEARNING OBJECTIVE

Describe the approach most employers take to finding potential new employees

Understanding Employers' Approach to the Employment Process

You can save considerable time and effort by understanding how employers approach the recruiting process (see Figure 18.2). Generally, employers prefer to look for candidates within their own organization or through referrals from people they know and trust. Overall, personal contacts appear to be the prime source of jobs, regardless of whether a candi-

FIGURE 18.1 The Employment Search
Finding the ideal job opportunity is a six-step process, which you might repeat a number of times during your career.

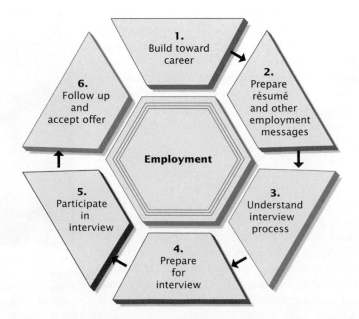

1. Build toward career
2. Prepare résumé and other employment messages
3. Understand interview process
4. Prepare for interview
5. Participate in interview
6. Follow up and accept offer

Employment

FIGURE 18.2 How Organizations Prefer to Find New Employees
Employers usually prefer to look at their existing workforce to find candidates for newly created jobs and promotional opportunities. If no suitable candidates can be found, they'll begin to look outside the firm, starting with people whom company insiders already know.

date has just graduated from college or has been out of school for several years.[2] Increasingly, these personal referrals can come through social networking websites, a fact that highlights the importance of networking (see page 553).

Many employers send representatives to college campuses to conduct student interviews, which are usually coordinated by the campus placement office. In addition, many employers accept unsolicited résumés, and most keep unsolicited résumés on file or in a database. **Applicant tracking systems**, such as the one used by Hersha, help employers sift through the hundreds or thousands of résumés they receive each year. Employers also recruit candidates through employment agencies, state employment services, temporary staffing services, and the employment bureaus operated by some trade associations. They also post jobs through advertisements in newspapers, trade magazines, campus publications, their own websites, and job sites such as Monster.com. In fact, major job boards such as Monster.com and CareerBuilder.com have grown so popular that some employers feel deluged with résumés, and some job seekers fear it's becoming impossible to stand out from the crowd when hundreds or thousands of people are applying for the same jobs. As a result, many specialized websites are now springing up, focusing on narrow parts of the job market or offering technology that promises to do a better job of matching employers and job searchers. For example, www.mkt10.com uses in-depth questionnaires to match employers and employees. The service also lets applicants know how their chances compare with those of other people applying for the same jobs and suggests alternative jobs that might be better fits.[3]

Look again at Figure 18.2, and you'll notice that the easiest way for you to find out about new opportunities—through the employer's outside advertising—is the employer's least-preferred way of finding new employees. As many as 80 percent of all job openings are never advertised, a phenomenon known as the *hidden job market*.[4] In other words, employers have looked in quite a few other places before they come looking for you. To find the best opportunities, it's up to you to take action to get yourself noticed. But fear not—throughout this course, you've developed the communication skills to present yourself to the world effectively.

It's important to understand that the easiest way for you to find jobs (through companies' help-wanted advertising) is the least-preferred channel for many companies to find new employees.

Organizing Your Approach to the Employment Process

The employment process can consume many hours of your time over weeks or months, so organize your efforts in a logical, careful manner to save time and maximize your chances. Begin by finding out where the job opportunities are, which industries are strong, which parts of the country are booming, and which specific job categories offer the best prospects for the future. From there you can investigate individual organizations, doing your best to learn as much about them as possible. If you plan to search in another country, heed the advice in "Communicating Across Cultures: Looking for Work Around the World."

Staying Abreast of Business and Financial News

Thanks to the Internet, staying on top of business news is easy today. In fact, your biggest challenge will be selecting new material from the many available sources. To help you get

Communicating Across Cultures

Looking for Work Around the World

With his eyes fixed on a career in international law, University of Michigan graduate Andrew Jaynes knew that overseas work experience would help his law school admission chances and expand his intercultural background.

Jaynes started with the Overseas Opportunities Office at UM's International Center, which offers UM students extensive information on its website and access to advisers and students who have international work experience. With that information as a starting point, he signed on with one of several companies that offer students assistance with foreign work permits and provide housing and job leads. He eventually found a job on his own, working at the American Library in Paris. "It took longer than I expected, but every day I learned more about the real lives of working Parisians—an awareness you can't get as a tourist."

To help ensure success in your own search for employment abroad, keep these points in mind:

- **Give yourself plenty of time.** Finding a job in another country is a complicated process that requires extensive and time-consuming research.
- **Research thoroughly, both online and off.** In addition to your school's resources, you can find numerous websites that offer advice, job listings, and other information. For a good look at the range of international opportunities, visit www.InternAbroad.com, www.VolunteerAbroad.com, www.TeachAbroad.com, and www.JobsAbroad.com. However, Jaynes and others with international experience will tell you that you can't limit your research to the web. Like any job search, networking is crucial, so join cul-

tural societies with international interests, volunteer with exchange student programs, or find other ways to connect with people who have international experience.

- **Consider all the possibilities.** Keep an open mind when you're exploring your options; you'll probably run across situations you hadn't considered at the beginning of your search. For instance, you might find that an unpaid internship in your future profession would help your career prospects more than a paying position in some other industry.
- **Be flexible.** If you have to settle for something less than that dream job, focus on the big picture, which for most students is the cultural opportunity.

Finding a job in another country can be a lot of work, but the rewards can be considerable. "I had studied abroad for a year and traveled through many countries around the world," Jaynes says, "but nothing gives you the same feel for a culture as working in it."

CAREER APPLICATIONS

1. How might international work experience help you in a career in the United States, even if you never work abroad again?
2. If your work history involves religious or political activities, either paid or volunteer, explain how you might present this information on a *curriculum vitae* (the version of a résumé used in many countries) intended for international readers?

With so many print and electronic resources available today, it's easy to stay in touch with what's happening in the business world.

started, here is a selection of periodical websites that offer business news (in some cases, you need to be a subscriber to access all of the material, including archives):

- *Wall Street Journal:* http://online.wsj.com/public/us
- *New York Times:* www.nyt.com
- *USA Today:* www.usatoday.com
- *BusinessWeek:* www.businessweek.com
- *Business 2.0:* www.business2.com
- *Fast Company:* www.fastcompany.com
- *Fortune:* www.fortune.com
- *Forbes:* www.forbes.com

In addition, thousands of bloggers and podcasters now offer news and commentary on the business world. To identify those you might find helpful, start with directories such as Technorati (www.technorati.com/blogs/business) for blogs or Podcast Alley (www.podcastalley.com; select the "business" genre) for podcasts. For all of these online resources, be sure to use a newsfeed aggregator to select the type of stories you're interested in and have them delivered to your screen automatically.

Of course, with all the business information available today, it's easy to get lost in the details. Try not to get too caught up in the daily particulars of business. Start by examining "big picture" topics—trends, issues, industrywide challenges, and careers—before delving into specific companies that look attractive.

Researching Specific Companies

Chapter 11 discusses how to find information on individual industries and companies, and it provides a list of helpful research resources. Review those sources, as well as professional journals and websites in the fields that interest you. Once you've identified a promising industry and career field, consult directories of employers at your college library, at your career center, or on the web and compile a list of specific organizations that appeal to you.

In addition to gaining detailed information about prospective employers, you can use the web to look for and respond to job openings. Most companies, even small firms, offer at least basic information about themselves on their websites. Look for the "About Us" or "Company" part of the site to find a company profile, executive biographies, press releases, financial information, and information on employment opportunities. You'll often find information about an organization's mission, products, annual reports, and employee benefits. Plus, you can often download annual reports, brochures, and other materials. Any company's website is going to present the firm in the most positive light possible, of course, so look for outside sources as well, including the business sections of local newspapers and trade publications that cover the company's industries and markets.

Table 18.1 lists some of the many websites where you can learn more about companies and find job openings. Start with The Riley Guide, **www.rileyguide.com**, which offers links to hundreds of specialized websites that post openings in specific industries and professions. Your college's career center placement office probably maintains an up-to-date list as well.

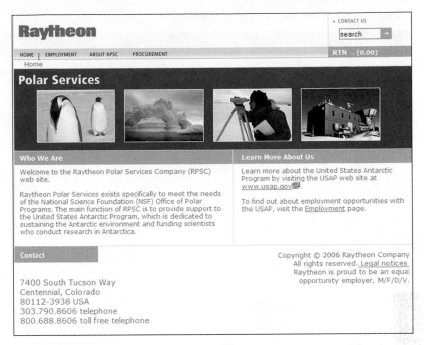

Are you willing to go to the ends of the earth to pursue your career? Raytheon Polar Services, which staffs U.S. research bases in Antarctica, might be the company for you. No matter what your interests, be creative in your job search and look for fascinating challenges such as this.

Go beyond every company's own communication materials; find out what others in their industries and communities think about them.

Networking

Networking is the process of making informal connections with a broad sphere of mutually beneficial business contacts. According to one recent survey, networking is the most common way that employees find jobs.[5] Networking takes place wherever and whenever people talk: at industry functions, at social gatherings, at sports events and recreational activities, in online newsgroups, at alumni reunions, and so on. Increasingly, business-oriented social networking sites such as LinkedIn (**www.linkedin.com**) and Ryze (**www.ryze.com**) have become important ways to get connected with job openings. Some of these sites are even linked to job posting websites, and when you apply for a job at a particular company, you can see a list of people in your network who work at that company.

To find helpful networks, both the in-person and online variety, read news sites, blogs, and other online sources. Participate in student business organizations, especially those with ties to professional organizations such as the American Marketing Association or the American Management Association. Visit trade shows that cater to an industry you're interested in. Not only will you learn plenty about that sector of the workplace, but you'll rub shoulders with people who actually work in the industry.[6] Hundreds of trade shows are held every year around the country, and many are open to the public for free or for a nominal fee. Don't overlook volunteering in social, civic, and religious organizations. As a volunteer, you not only meet people but also demonstrate your ability to solve problems, plan projects, and so on. You can do some good while creating a network for yourself.

2 LEARNING OBJECTIVE

Explain the importance of networking in your career search

Start thinking like a networker now; your classmates could turn out to be some of your most important business contacts.

TABLE 18.1 Netting a Job on the Web

WEBSITE*	URL	HIGHLIGHTS
Riley Guide	www.rileyguide.com	Vast collection of links to both general and specialized job sites for every career imaginable; don't miss this one—it'll save you hours and hours of searching
CollegeRecruiter.com	www.collegerecruiter.com	Focuses on opportunities for graduates with less than three years of work experience
Monster	www.monster.com	One of the most popular job sites, with hundreds of thousands of openings, many from hard-to-find smaller companies; extensive collection of advice on the job search process
MonsterTrak	www.monstertrak.com	Focused on job searches for new college grads; your school's career center site probably links here
Yahoo! HotJobs	http://hotjobs.yahoo.com	Another leading job board, formed by recent merger of HotJobs and Yahoo! Careers
CareerBuilder	www.careerbuilder.com	Fast-growing site affiliated with more than 100 local newspapers around the country
USA Jobs	www.usajobs.opm.gov	The official job search site for the U.S. government, featuring everything from economists to astronauts to border patrol agents
IMDiversity	www.imdiversity.com	Good resource on diversity in the workplace, with job postings from companies that have made a special commitment to promoting diversity in their workforces
Dice.com	www.dice.com	One of the best sites for high-technology jobs
Net-Temps	www.net-temps.com	Popular site for contractors and freelancers looking for short-term assignments
InternshipPrograms.com	www.internships.wetfeet.com	Posts listings from companies looking for interns in a wide variety of professions
SimplyHired.com Indeed.com	www.simplyhired.com www.indeed.com	Specialized search engines that look for job postings on hundreds of websites worldwide; find many postings that aren't listed on "job board" sites such as Monster.com

*Note: This list represents only a small fraction of the hundreds of job-posting sites and other resources available online; be sure to check with your college's career center for the latest information.

Novice job seekers sometimes misunderstand networking and unknowingly commit breaches of etiquette. Networking isn't a matter of walking up to strangers at social events, handing over your résumé, and asking them to find you a job. Rather, it involves the sharing of information between people who might be able to offer mutual help at some point in the future. Think of it as an organic process, in which you cultivate the possibility of finding that perfect opportunity. Networking can take time, and it can operate in unpredictable ways. You may not get results for months, so it's important to start early and make it part of your lifelong program of career management.

Remember that you need to contribute to the networking process, too.

To become a valued network member, you need to be able to help others in some way. You may not have any influential contacts yet, but because you're actively researching a number of industries and trends in your own job search, you probably have valuable information to share. Or you might simply be able to connect one person with another who can help. The more you network, the more valuable you become in your network—and the more valuable your network becomes to you.

Seeking Career Counseling

College placement offices offer individual counseling, credential services, job fairs, on-campus interviews, and job listings. They can give you advice on résumé-writing software and provide workshops in job search techniques, résumé preparation, interview techniques, and more.[7] You can also find job counseling online. You might begin your self-assessment, for example, with the Keirsey Temperament Sorter, an online personality test at **www.advisorteam.com**. For excellent job-seeking pointers and counseling, visit college- and university-run online career centers. Major online job boards such as Monster.com also offer a variety of career planning resources.

PREPARING RÉSUMÉS

Your job search process will involve many forms of communication, but the centerpiece of this effort is a well-written résumé. In fact, your success in finding a job may well depend on how carefully you plan, write, and complete your résumé. Some job searchers are intimidated by the prospect of writing a résumé, but your résumé is really just another specialized business message. Follow the three-step writing process, and it'll be easier than you thought (see Figure 18.3).

Career fairs give companies the chance to meet potential employees—and for you to learn more about career opportunities.

FIGURE 18.3 Three-Step Writing Process for Résumés
Writing your résumé doesn't need to be a long, painful experience if you follow the three-step writing process. Pay particular attention to the "you" attitude and presentation quality; your résumé will probably get tossed aside if it doesn't speak to audience needs or if it has mistakes.

Plan ➤	Write ➤	Complete ➤
Analyze the Situation Recognize that the purpose of your résumé is to get an interview, not to get a job.	**Adapt to Your Audience** Plan your wording carefully so that you can catch a recruiter's eye within seconds; translate your education and experience into attributes that target employers find valuable.	**Revise the Message** Evaluate content and review readability, then edit and rewrite for conciseness and clarity.
Gather Information Research target industries and companies so that you know what theyre looki ng for in new hires; learn about various jobs and what to expect; learn about the hiring manager, if possible.	**Compose the Message** Write clearly and succinctly, using active, powerful language that is appropriate to the industries and companies you're targeting; use a professional tone in all communications, even when using e-mail.	**Produce the Message** Use effective design elements and suitable layout for a clean, professional appearance; seamlessly combine text and graphical elements.
Select the Right Medium Start with a traditional paper résumé and develop scannable, electronic plain text, HTML, or PDF versions as needed.		**Proofread the Message** Review for errors in layout, spelling, and mechanics; mistakes can cost you interview opportunities.
Organize the Information Choose an organizational model that highlights your strengths and downplays your shortcomings; use the chronological approach unless you have a strong reason not to.		**Distribute the Message** Deliver your résumé following the specific instructions of each employer or job board website.
1	**2**	**3**

Planning Your Résumé

Your résumé must be more than a simple list of the jobs you've held. It needs to tell the "story of you"—who you are, what you've accomplished, and most important, what you can contribute to any organization that hires you. As with other business messages, planning a résumé means analyzing your purpose and your audience, gathering information, choosing the best medium, and organizing your content. Be prepared to craft several or perhaps many versions of your résumé. By making some simple changes in wording or organization, you'll probably be able to match your value more closely to the specific opportunities offered by particular employers.

Analyzing Your Purpose and Audience

Once you view your résumé as a persuasive business message, it's easier to decide what should and shouldn't be in it.

A **résumé** is a structured, written summary of a person's education, employment background, and job qualifications. Before you begin writing a résumé, make sure you understand its true function—it is a persuasive business message intended to stimulate an employer's interest in meeting you and learning more about you. (Table 18.2 lists some of the common misconceptions about résumés.) A successful résumé inspires a prospective employer to invite you to interview with the company. In other words, your purpose in writing your résumé is to create interest—*not* to tell readers every little detail.[8]

Because you've already completed a good deal of research on specific companies, you should know quite a bit about the organizations you'll be applying to. But take some time now to learn what you can about the individuals who may be reading your résumé. For example, if you learned of an opportunity through your networking efforts, chances are you'll have both a name and some personalized advice to help fine-tune your writing. Search online using the person's name; you might find him or her mentioned in a news release, magazine article, or blog. Any bit of information can help you craft a more effective message. Even if you can't identify a specific hiring manager's name, try to put yourself in that person's shoes so that you can tailor your résumé to satisfy your audience's needs. Why would that person be interested in learning more about you?

By the way, if employers ask to see your "CV," they're referring to your *curriculum vitae*, the term used instead of *résumé* in some professions and in many countries outside the United States. Résumés and CVs are essentially the same, although CVs can be more de-

TABLE 18.2 **Fallacies and Facts About Résumés**

FALLACIES	FACTS
• The purpose of a résumé is to list all your skills and abilities.	• The purpose of a résumé is to generate interest and an interview.
• A good résumé will get you the job you want.	• All a résumé can do is get you in the door.
• Your résumé will be read carefully and thoroughly.	• In most cases, your résumé needs to make a positive impression within 30 or 45 seconds; moreover, it may be screened by a computer looking for keywords first—and if it doesn't contain the right keywords, a human being may never see it.
• The more good information you present about yourself in your résumé, the better.	• Recruiters don't need that much information about you at the initial screening stage, and they probably won't read it.
• If you want a really good résumé, have it prepared by a résumé service.	• You have the skills needed to prepare an effective résumé, so prepare it yourself—unless the position is especially high-level or specialized. Even then, you should check carefully before using a service.

tailed. If you need to adapt a U.S.-style résumé to CV format, or vice versa, Monster.com has helpful guidelines on the subject.

Gathering Pertinent Information

If you haven't been building an employment portfolio thus far, you may need to do some research on yourself at this point. Gather all the pertinent personal history you can think of, including all the specific dates, duties, and accomplishments of any previous jobs you've held. Collect every piece of relevant educational experience that adds to your qualifications—formal degrees, skills certificates, academic awards, or scholarships. Also, gather any relevant information about personal endeavors: dates of your membership in an association, offices you may have held in a club or professional organization, any presentations you might have given to a community group. You probably won't use every piece of information you come up with, but you'll want to have it at your fingertips before you begin composing your résumé.

Selecting the Best Medium

Selecting the medium for your résumé used to be a simple matter: it was typed on paper. These days, though, your job search might involve various forms, including an uploaded Word document, a plain-text document that you paste into an online form, or a multimedia résumé that is part of your online e-portfolio. Explore all your options and choose those that (a) meet the requirements of target employers and (b) allow you to present yourself in a compelling fashion. For instance, if you're applying for a sales position, in which your personal communication skills would be a strong point, a vidcast showing you making a sales presentation (even a mock presentation) could be a strong persuader.

No matter how many different media you eventually use, it's always a good idea to prepare a basic paper résumé and keep copies on hand. You'll never know when someone might ask for it, and not all employers want to bother with electronic media when all they want to know is your basic profile. In addition, starting with a traditional paper résumé is a great way to organize your background information and identify your unique strengths.

Organizing Your Résumé Around Your Strengths

The most successful résumés convey seven qualities that employers seek: they demonstrate that you (1) think in terms of results, (2) know how to get things done, (3) are well rounded, (4) show signs of career progress and professional development, (5) have personal standards of excellence, (6) are flexible and willing to try new things, and (7) communicate effectively. Organizing your résumé is a question of portraying these seven attributes in the strongest possible light.

Although you may want to include some information in all categories, you'll naturally want to emphasize the information that does the best job of aligning your career objectives with the needs of your target employers—and that does so without distorting or misrepresenting the facts.[9] While you're pondering your strengths, you also need to consider any perceived weaknesses you may have. Do you have something in your history that might trigger an employer's red flag? Here are some common problems and quick suggestions for overcoming them:[10]

3 LEARNING OBJECTIVE

Discuss how to choose the appropriate résumé organization and list the advantages and disadvantages of the three common options

- **Frequent job changes.** If you've had a number of short-term jobs of a similar nature, such as independent contracting and temporary assignments, see if you can group them under a single heading. Also, if you were a victim of circumstances in positions that were eliminated as a result of mergers or other factors beyond your control, find a subtle way to convey that information (if not in your résumé, then in your cover letter). Reasonable employers understand that many otherwise stable employees have been forced to job hop in recent years.

- **Gaps in work history.** Mention relevant experience and education you gained during employment gaps, such as volunteer or community work. If gaps are due to personal problems such as drug or alcohol abuse or mental illness, you can use a cover letter to offer honest but general explanations about your absences ("I had serious health concerns and had to take time off to fully recover").

Frequent job changes and gaps in your work history are two of the more common issues that employers may perceive as weaknesses, so plan to address these if they pertain to you.

- **Inexperience.** Mention related volunteer work. List relevant course work and internships. If appropriate, offer hiring incentives such as "willing to work nights and weekends."
- **Overqualification.** Tone down your résumé, focusing exclusively on the experience and skills that relate to the position.
- **Long-term employment with one company.** Itemize each position held at the firm to show career progress with increasing responsibilities.
- **Job termination for cause.** Be honest with interviewers. Show that you're a hard-working employee and counter their concerns with proof, such as recommendations and examples of completed projects.
- **Criminal record.** If you have a criminal record, you obviously need to consider carefully when and how to disclose this information to potential employers. You don't necessarily need to disclose a criminal record or time spent incarcerated on your résumé, but you may be asked about it on a job application form. Laws regarding what employers may ask (and whether they can conduct a criminal background check) vary by state and profession, but if you are asked and the question applies to you, you must answer truthfully or you risk being terminated later if the employer finds out. Use the interview process to explain any mitigating circumstances and to emphasize your rehabilitation and commitment to being a law-abiding, trustworthy employee.[11]

To focus attention on your strongest points, adopt the appropriate organizational approach, based on your background and your goals.

The chronological résumé is the most common approach, but it might not be right for you at a particular stage in your career.

The Chronological Résumé　In a **chronological résumé**, the work experience section dominates and is placed in the most prominent slot, immediately after your name and address and optional objective. Develop this section by listing your jobs sequentially in reverse order, beginning with the most recent position. Under each listing, describe your responsibilities and accomplishments, giving the most space to the most recent and most relevant positions. If you're just graduating from college with limited professional experience, you can vary this chronological approach by putting your educational qualifications before your experience, thereby focusing attention on your academic credentials.

The chronological approach is the most common way to organize a résumé, and many employers prefer it. This approach has three key advantages: (1) Employers are familiar with it and can easily find information, (2) it highlights growth and career progression, and (3) it highlights employment continuity and stability.[12] As vice president with Korn/Ferry International, Robert Nesbit speaks for many hiring managers and recruiters: "Unless you have a really compelling reason, don't use any but the standard chronological format. Your résumé should not read like a treasure map, full of minute clues to the whereabouts of your jobs and experience. I want to be able to grasp quickly where a candidate has worked, how long, and in what capacities."[13]

The chronological approach is especially appropriate if you have a strong employment history and are aiming for a job that builds on your current career path (see Figures 18.4 and 18.5).

The functional résumé is often used by people with little employment history or gaps in their work history, but some employers suspect that people who use this approach are trying to hide weaknesses in their backgrounds.

The Functional Résumé　A **functional résumé**, sometimes called a *skills résumé*, emphasizes your skills and capabilities while identifying employers and academic experience in subordinate sections. This pattern stresses individual areas of competence, so it's useful for people who are just entering the job market, who want to redirect their careers, or who have little continuous career-related experience. The functional approach also has three advantages: (1) Without having to read through job descriptions, employers can see what you can do for them; (2) you can emphasize earlier job experience; and (3) you can de-emphasize any lack of career progress or lengthy unemployment. However, you should be aware that because the functional résumé can obscure your work history, many employment professionals are suspicious of it—and some assume that candidates who use it are trying to hide something. In fact, Monster.com lists the functional résumé as one of employers' "Top 10 Pet Peeves."[14] If you don't have a strong, uninterrupted history of relevant work, the combination résumé might be a better choice.

FIGURE 18.4 Ineffective Chronological Résumé
This chronological résumé exhibits a wide range of problems. The language is self-centered and unprofessional, and the organization forces the reader to dig out essential details—and today's recruiters don't have the time or the patience for that. Compare this with the improved version in Figure 18.5.

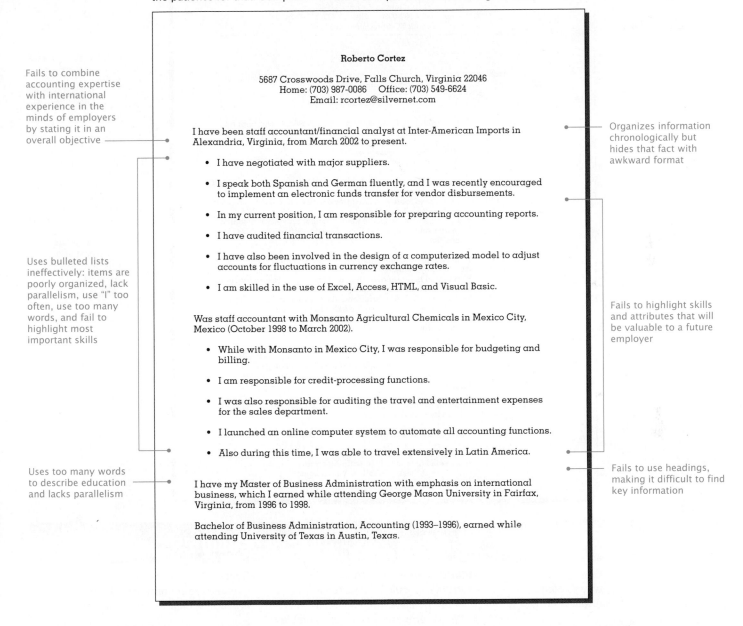

Fails to combine accounting expertise with international experience in the minds of employers by stating it in an overall objective

Uses bulleted lists ineffectively: items are poorly organized, lack parallelism, use "I" too often, use too many words, and fail to highlight most important skills

Uses too many words to describe education and lacks parallelism

Organizes information chronologically but hides that fact with awkward format

Fails to highlight skills and attributes that will be valuable to a future employer

Fails to use headings, making it difficult to find key information

---

Roberto Cortez

5687 Crosswoods Drive, Falls Church, Virginia 22046
Home: (703) 987-0086   Office: (703) 549-6624
Email: rcortez@silvernet.com

I have been staff accountant/financial analyst at Inter-American Imports in Alexandria, Virginia, from March 2002 to present.

- I have negotiated with major suppliers.
- I speak both Spanish and German fluently, and I was recently encouraged to implement an electronic funds transfer for vendor disbursements.
- In my current position, I am responsible for preparing accounting reports.
- I have audited financial transactions.
- I have also been involved in the design of a computerized model to adjust accounts for fluctuations in currency exchange rates.
- I am skilled in the use of Excel, Access, HTML, and Visual Basic.

Was staff accountant with Monsanto Agricultural Chemicals in Mexico City, Mexico (October 1998 to March 2002).

- While with Monsanto in Mexico City, I was responsible for budgeting and billing.
- I am responsible for credit-processing functions.
- I was also responsible for auditing the travel and entertainment expenses for the sales department.
- I launched an online computer system to automate all accounting functions.
- Also during this time, I was able to travel extensively in Latin America.

I have my Master of Business Administration with emphasis on international business, which I earned while attending George Mason University in Fairfax, Virginia, from 1996 to 1998.

Bachelor of Business Administration, Accounting (1993–1996), earned while attending University of Texas in Austin, Texas.

The Combination Résumé   A **combination résumé** includes the best features of the chronological and functional approaches (see Figure 18.6). Nevertheless, it is not commonly used, and it has two major disadvantages: (1) It tends to be longer, and (2) it can be repetitious if you have to list your accomplishments and skills in both the functional section and the chronological job descriptions.[15]

As you look at a number of sample résumés, you'll probably notice variations on the three basic formats presented here. Study these other options; if you find one that seems like the best fit for your unique situation, by all means use it—but always apply the principles of effective business communication you've learned in this course.

If you don't have a lot of work history, consider a combination résumé to highlight your skills while still providing a chronological history of your employment.

FIGURE 18.5 Effective Chronological Résumé

This version does a much better job of presenting the candidate's ability to contribute to a new employer. Notice in particular how easy it is to skim through this résumé to find sections of interest.

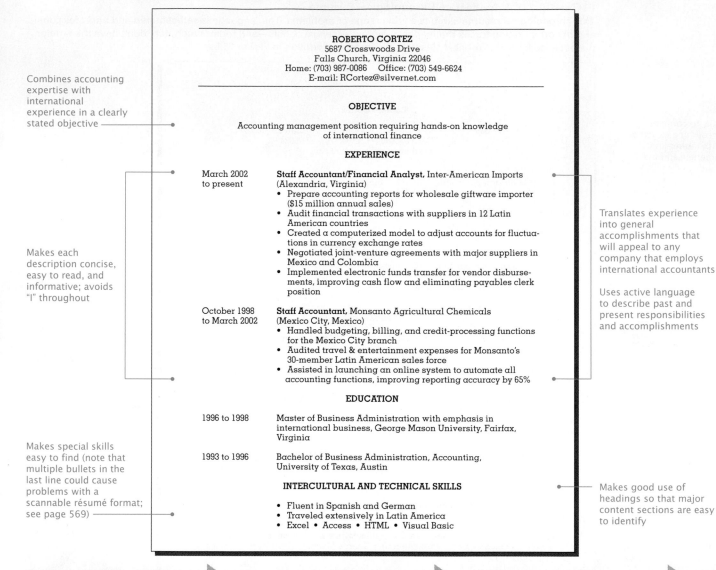

Combines accounting expertise with international experience in a clearly stated objective

Makes each description concise, easy to read, and informative; avoids "I" throughout

Makes special skills easy to find (note that multiple bullets in the last line could cause problems with a scannable résumé format; see page 569)

ROBERTO CORTEZ
5687 Crosswoods Drive
Falls Church, Virginia 22046
Home: (703) 987-0086   Office: (703) 549-6624
E-mail: RCortez@silvernet.com

OBJECTIVE

Accounting management position requiring hands-on knowledge of international finance

EXPERIENCE

March 2002 to present

Staff Accountant/Financial Analyst, Inter-American Imports (Alexandria, Virginia)
- Prepare accounting reports for wholesale giftware importer ($15 million annual sales)
- Audit financial transactions with suppliers in 12 Latin American countries
- Created a computerized model to adjust accounts for fluctuations in currency exchange rates
- Negotiated joint-venture agreements with major suppliers in Mexico and Colombia
- Implemented electronic funds transfer for vendor disbursements, improving cash flow and eliminating payables clerk position

October 1998 to March 2002

Staff Accountant, Monsanto Agricultural Chemicals (Mexico City, Mexico)
- Handled budgeting, billing, and credit-processing functions for the Mexico City branch
- Audited travel & entertainment expenses for Monsanto's 30-member Latin American sales force
- Assisted in launching an online system to automate all accounting functions, improving reporting accuracy by 65%

EDUCATION

1996 to 1998

Master of Business Administration with emphasis in international business, George Mason University, Fairfax, Virginia

1993 to 1996

Bachelor of Business Administration, Accounting, University of Texas, Austin

INTERCULTURAL AND TECHNICAL SKILLS

- Fluent in Spanish and German
- Traveled extensively in Latin America
- Excel • Access • HTML • Visual Basic

Translates experience into general accomplishments that will appeal to any company that employs international accountants

Uses active language to describe past and present responsibilities and accomplishments

Makes good use of headings so that major content sections are easy to identify

Plan → Write → Complete

1 Plan

Analyze the Situation
Decide on the best way to combine finance and international experience.

Gather Information
Research target positions to identify key employer needs.

Select the Right Medium
Start with a traditional paper résumé and develop scannable or plain text versions as needed.

Organize the Information
Choose the chronological format since it fits this strong employment history perfectly.

2 Write

Adapt to Your Audience
Translate specific experience into general qualifications that all international companies will find valuable.

Compose the Message
Write clearly and succinctly, using active, powerful language that is appropriate to the financial management profession.

3 Complete

Revise the Message
Evaluate your content and review readability, clarity, and accuracy.

Produce the Message
Use effective design elements and suitable layout for a clean, professional appearance.

Proofread the Message
Review for errors in layout, spelling, and mechanics.

Distribute the Message
Deliver your résumé and other employment messages following the specific instructions of each employer or job board website.

FIGURE 18.6 Combination Résumé

With limited work experience in her field of interest, Erica Vorkamp opted for a combination résumé to highlight her skills. Her employment history is complete and easy to find, but it isn't featured to the same degree as the other elements. Also, because she created an HTML version and posted it on her personal website, she is able to provide instant links to other information, such as samples of her work and testimonials from people who have worked with her in the past.

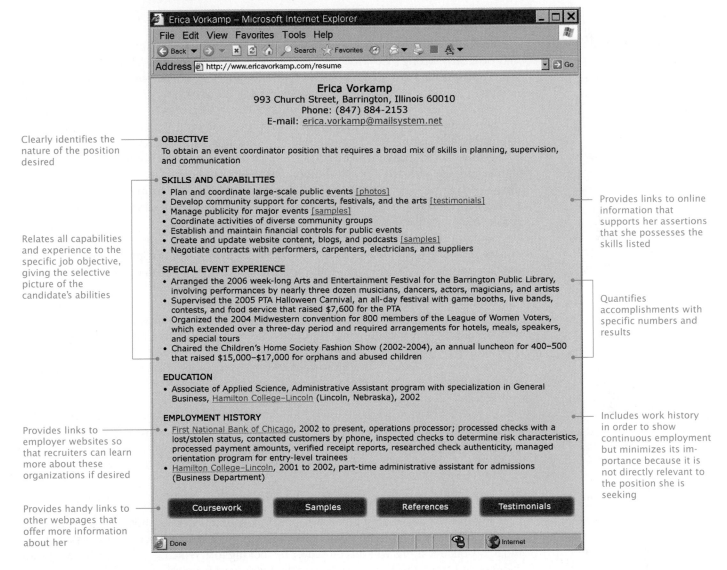

Clearly identifies the nature of the position desired

Relates all capabilities and experience to the specific job objective, giving the selective picture of the candidate's abilities

Provides links to employer websites so that recruiters can learn more about these organizations if desired

Provides handy links to other webpages that offer more information about her

Provides links to online information that supports her assertions that she possesses the skills listed

Quantifies accomplishments with specific numbers and results

Includes work history in order to show continuous employment but minimizes its importance because it is not directly relevant to the position she is seeking

---

Erica Vorkamp
993 Church Street, Barrington, Illinois 60010
Phone: (847) 884-2153
E-mail: erica.vorkamp@mailsystem.net

OBJECTIVE

To obtain an event coordinator position that requires a broad mix of skills in planning, supervision, and communication

SKILLS AND CAPABILITIES

- Plan and coordinate large-scale public events [photos]
- Develop community support for concerts, festivals, and the arts [testimonials]
- Manage publicity for major events [samples]
- Coordinate activities of diverse community groups
- Establish and maintain financial controls for public events
- Create and update website content, blogs, and podcasts [samples]
- Negotiate contracts with performers, carpenters, electricians, and suppliers

SPECIAL EVENT EXPERIENCE

- Arranged the 2006 week-long Arts and Entertainment Festival for the Barrington Public Library, involving performances by nearly three dozen musicians, dancers, actors, magicians, and artists
- Supervised the 2005 PTA Halloween Carnival, an all-day festival with game booths, live bands, contests, and food service that raised $7,600 for the PTA
- Organized the 2004 Midwestern convention for 800 members of the League of Women Voters, which extended over a three-day period and required arrangements for hotels, meals, speakers, and special tours
- Chaired the Children's Home Society Fashion Show (2002-2004), an annual luncheon for 400–500 that raised $15,000–$17,000 for orphans and abused children

EDUCATION

- Associate of Applied Science, Administrative Assistant program with specialization in General Business, Hamilton College–Lincoln (Lincoln, Nebraska), 2002

EMPLOYMENT HISTORY

- First National Bank of Chicago, 2002 to present, operations processor; processed checks with a lost/stolen status, contacted customers by phone, inspected checks to determine risk characteristics, processed payment amounts, verified receipt reports, researched check authenticity, managed orientation program for entry-level trainees
- Hamilton College–Lincoln, 2001 to 2002, part-time administrative assistant for admissions (Business Department)

| Coursework | Samples | References | Testimonials |

Writing Your Résumé

Your résumé is one of the most important documents you will ever write. Even so, you needn't work yourself into a panic—all the advice you'll need to write effective résumés is presented in this chapter. Follow the three-step process and help ensure success by remembering four key points: First, treat your résumé with the respect it deserves. Until you're able to meet with employers in person, you *are* your résumé, and a single mistake or oversight can cost you interview opportunities. Second, give yourself plenty of time. Don't put off preparing your résumé until the last second and then try to write it in one sitting. Third, learn from good models. You can find thousands of sample résumés online at college websites and job sites such as Monster.com. Fourth, don't get frustrated by the conflicting advice you'll read about résumés; they are more art than science. Consider the alternatives and choose the approach that makes the most sense to you, given everything you know about successful business communication.

You can take some comfort in the fact that many people, even accomplished writers, find it difficult to write their own résumés. Part of this problem stems from the challenge of

Until employers meet you in person, your résumé (and perhaps your cover letter) is usually the only information they have about you, so make sure that information is clear and compelling.

writing a compelling message in limited space, and part from the awkward feeling of talking about oneself to strangers. You might find it helpful to distance yourself emotionally from the task; you can even pretend you're writing about someone else. You might also find a classmate or friend who's also writing a résumé and swap projects for a while. By working on each other's résumés, you might be able to speed up the process for both of you.

Keeping Your Résumé Honest

4 LEARNING OBJECTIVE

Describe the problem of résumé fraud

At some point in the writing process, you're sure to run into the question of honesty. A claim may be clearly wrong ("So what if I didn't get those last two credits—I got the same education as people who did graduate, so it's OK to say that I graduated too"). Or a rationalization may be more subtle ("Organizing snacks for the company picnic—that qualifies as 'project management'"). Either way, the information is dishonest.

Somehow, the idea that "everybody lies on their résumés" has crept into popular consciousness, and résumé fraud has reached epidemic proportions. As many as half of the résumés now sent to employers contain false information. And we're not just talking about the simple fudging of a fact here and there. Dishonest applicants are getting bolder all the time—buying fake diplomas online, paying computer hackers to insert their names into prestigious universities' graduation records, and signing up for services that offer phony employment verification.[16]

Applicants with integrity know they don't need to lie on their résumés to catch the attention of potential employers.

Applicants with integrity know they don't need to stoop to lying to compete in the job market. If you are tempted to stretch the truth, bear in mind that professional recruiters have seen every trick in the book, and employers who are fed up with the dishonesty are getting more aggressive at uncovering the truth. Roughly 80 percent now contact references and conduct criminal background checks when allowed, and many do credit checks when the job involves financial responsibility.[17] In a recent survey in Great Britain, 25 percent of employers reported withdrawing job offers after discovering that applicants had lied on their résumés.[18] And even if you were to get past these filters, you'd probably be exposed on the job when you couldn't live up to your own résumé. From college coaches to CEOs, résumé fabrications have been known to catch up to people many years into their careers, with embarrassing consequences.[19]

If you're not sure whether to include something in your résumé, ask yourself this: Would you be willing to say the same thing to an interviewer in person? If you wouldn't be comfortable saying it in person, don't say it in your résumé. Keep your résumé honest so that it represents who you really are and leads you toward jobs that are truly right for you.

Adapting Your Résumé to Your Audience

One of the biggest challenges in writing a résumé is to make your unique qualities apparent to readers quickly; they won't search through details if you don't look like an appealing candidate.

Your résumé needs to make a positive impression in a matter of seconds, so be sure to adopt a "you" attitude and think about your résumé from the employer's perspective. Ask yourself: What key qualifications will this employer be looking for? Which of these qualifications are your greatest strengths? What quality would set you apart from other candidates in the eyes of a potential employer? What are three or four of your greatest accomplishments, and what resulted from these accomplishments? No matter which format you use or what information you include, the single most important concept to keep in mind as you write is to translate your past accomplishments into perceived future potential. In other words, employers are certainly interested in what you've done in the past, but they're more interested in what you can do for them in the future. If necessary, customize your résumé for individual companies, too.

You may also need to translate your skills and experiences into the terminology of the hiring organization. For instance, military experience can develop a number of skills that are valuable in business, but military terminology can sound like a foreign language to people who aren't familiar with it. Isolate the important general concepts and present them in common business language. Similarly, educational achievements in other countries might not align with U.S. definitions of high schools, community colleges, technical and trade schools, and universities. If necessary, include a brief statement explaining how your degree or certificate relates to U.S. expectations—or how your U.S. degree relates to expectations in other countries, if you're applying for work abroad.

Regardless of your background, it's up to you to combine your experiences into a straightforward message that communicates what you can do for your potential employer.[20] Think in terms of an image or a theme you'd like to project. Are you academically gifted? A strong leader? A well-rounded person? A creative genius? A technical wizard? By knowing yourself and your audience, you'll focus successfully on the strengths needed by potential employers.

Although your résumé is a highly factual document, it should still tell the "story of you," giving readers a clear picture of the sort of employee you are.

Composing Your Résumé

To save readers time and to state your information as forcefully as possible, write your résumé using a simple and direct style (you may need to modify your approach for other countries). Use short, crisp phrases instead of whole sentences, and focus on what your reader needs to know. Avoid using the word *I*, which can sound both self-involved and repetitious by the time you identify all your skills and accomplishments. Instead, start your phrases with strong action verbs such as these:[21]

Draft your résumé using short, crisp phrases built around strong verbs and nouns.

accomplished	coordinated	initiated	participated	set up
achieved	created	installed	performed	simplified
administered	demonstrated	introduced	planned	sparked
approved	developed	investigated	presented	streamlined
arranged	directed	joined	proposed	strengthened
assisted	established	launched	raised	succeeded
assumed	explored	maintained	recommended	supervised
budgeted	forecasted	managed	reduced	systematized
chaired	generated	motivated	reorganized	targeted
changed	identified	operated	resolved	trained
compiled	implemented	organized	saved	transformed
completed	improved	oversaw	served	upgraded

For instance, you might say, "Created a campus organization for students interested in entrepreneurship" or "Managed a fast-food restaurant and four employees." Whenever you can, quantify the results so that your claims don't come across as empty puffery. Don't just say you're a team player or detail oriented—show you are by offering concrete proof.[22] Here are some examples of phrasing accomplishments using active statements that show results:

AVOID WEAK STATEMENTS	USE ACTIVE STATEMENTS THAT SHOW RESULTS
Responsible for developing a new filing system	Developed a new filing system that reduced paperwork by 50 percent
I was in charge of customer complaints and all ordering problems	Handled all customer complaints and resolved all product order discrepancies
I won a trip to Europe for opening the most new customer accounts in my department	Generated the highest number of new customer accounts in my department
Member of special campus task force to resolve student problems with existing cafeteria assignments	Assisted in implementing new campus dining program that balances student wishes with cafeteria capacity

In addition to presenting your accomplishments effectively, think carefully about the way you will craft the major sections of a traditional résumé: your name and contact information, educational credentials, employment history, activities and achievements, and relevant personal data.

5 LEARNING OBJECTIVE

List the major sections of a traditional résumé

Be sure to provide complete and accurate contact information; mistakes in this section of the résumé are surprisingly common.

Name and Contact Information

The first thing an employer needs to know is who you are and where you can be reached. Your name and contact information constitute the heading of your résumé, so include the following:

- Your name
- Physical address (both permanent and temporary if you're likely to move during the job search process; however, if you're posting a résumé in an unsecured location online, leave off your physical address for security purposes)
- E-mail address
- Phone number(s)
- The URL of your personal webpage or e-portfolio (if you have one)

Be sure that everything in your résumé heading is well organized and clearly laid out on the page.

Get a professional-sounding e-mail address for business correspondence (such as firstname.lastname@ something.com), if you don't already have one.

If the only e-mail address you have is through your current employer, get a free personal e-mail address from one of the many services that offer them. It's not fair to your current employer to use company resources for a job search; moreover, it sends a bad signal to potential employers. Also, if your personal e-mail address is anything like *precious.princess@ something.com* or *PsychoDawg@something.com*, get a new e-mail address for your business correspondence.

Career Objective or Summary of Qualifications

Experts disagree about the need to state a career objective on your résumé. Some argue that your objective is obvious from your qualifications, so stating your objective seems redundant. Some also maintain that such a statement labels you as being interested in only one thing and thus limits your possibilities as a candidate (especially if you want to be considered for a variety of openings). Other experts argue that employers will try to categorize you anyway, so you might as well make sure they attach the right label. They maintain that stating your objective up-front gives employers an immediate idea of what you're all about.

Whether you choose to open with a career objective or a summary of qualifications, remember that the important point is to generate interest immediately.

Remember, your goal is to generate interest immediately. Consider the situation and the qualities the employer is looking for. If a stated objective will help you look like the perfect fit, then you should definitely consider adding it. Consider the following objectives:

A software sales position in a growing company requiring international experience

Advertising assistant with multimedia emphasis requiring strong customer-contact skills

With some careful writing, you can phrase your career objective in terms that highlight the reader's needs.

Both these objectives have an important aspect: even though they are stating "your" objective, they are really about the employer's needs. Avoid such self-absorbed (but all too common) statements such as "A fulfilling position that provides ample opportunity for career growth and personal satisfaction." Writers who include such statements have completely forgotten about audience focus and the "you" attitude.

A good alternative to a simple statement of career objectives is to highlight your strongest points in a brief *summary of qualifications*. A good summary of qualifications not only identifies the type of job you're interested in but also gives employers a compelling reason to consider you. Use short, direct phrases that highlight what you can bring to a new employer, such as in this example:

Summary of qualifications: Ten years of experience in commission selling, consistently meeting or exceeding sales goals through creative lead generation, effective closing techniques, and solid customer service.

If you include either a career objective or a summary of qualifications, make it strong, concise, and convincing.

Your education is likely to be one of your strongest selling points, so think carefully about how you will present it.

Education

If you're still in school, education is probably your strongest selling point. Present your educational background in depth, choosing facts that support your "theme." Give this section a heading such as "Education," "Technical Training," or "Academic Preparation," as appropriate. Then, starting with the most recent, list the name and location of each school you attended, along with the term of your enrollment (in months and years), your major and minor fields of study, significant skills and abilities you've developed in your course work, and the degrees or certificates you've earned. If you're still working toward a degree, include in parentheses the expected date of completion. Showcase your qualifications by listing courses that have directly equipped you for the job you are seeking, and indicate any scholarships, awards, or academic honors you've received.

The education section also includes off-campus training sponsored by business or government. Include any relevant seminars or workshops you've attended, as well as the certificates or other documents you've received. Mention high school or military training only if the associated achievements are pertinent to your career goals.

Whether you list your grade-point average depends on the job you want and the quality of your grades. If you choose to show a grade-point average, be sure to mention the scale, especially if a five-point scale is used instead of a four-point scale. If you don't show your GPA on your résumé—and there's no rule saying you have to—be prepared to answer questions about it during the interview process, because many employers will assume that your GPA is not spectacular if you didn't show it on your résumé. If your grades are better within your major than in other courses, you can also list your GPA as "Major GPA" and include only those courses within your major (that D you received in scuba diving or Sanskrit doesn't need to hurt your accounting career).

Education is usually given less emphasis in a résumé after you've worked in your chosen field for a year or more. If work experience is your strongest qualification, save the section on education for later in the résumé and provide less detail.

Work Experience, Skills, and Accomplishments   Like the education section, the work experience section should focus on your overall theme. Align your past with the employer's future. Call attention to the skills you've developed on the job and to your ability to handle increasing responsibility.

When you describe past job responsibilities, be sure to relate them to the needs of potential employers—identify the skills and knowledge from these previous jobs that you can apply to a future job.

List your jobs in reverse chronological order and include any part-time, summer, or intern positions, even if unrelated to your current career objective. Employers will see that you have the ability to get and hold a job—an important qualification in itself. If you have worked your way through school and contributed significantly to your education expenses, say so. Many employers interpret this accomplishment as a sign of both character and the ability to manage your time.

In each listing, include the name and location of the employer. If readers are unlikely to recognize the organization, briefly describe what it does. When you want to keep the name of your current employer confidential, you can identify the firm by industry only ("a large video-game developer"). Alternatively, you might use the firm's name and request confidentiality in your application letter or include an underlined note at the top or bottom of your résumé: "Résumé submitted in confidence." If an organization's name or location has changed since you worked there, state the current name and location, and then include the old information as "formerly. . . ."

Before or after each job listing, state your functional title, such as "records clerk" or "salesperson." If you were a dishwasher, say so. Don't try to make your role seem more important by glamorizing your job title, functions, or achievements. List the years you worked in the job, and use the phrase "to present" to denote current employment. If a job was part-time, say so.

Whenever you can, quantify your accomplishments in numerical terms: sales increases, customer satisfaction scores, measured productivity, and so on.

Devote the most space to the jobs that are related to your target position. If you were personally responsible for something significant, be sure to mention it ("Devised a new collection system that accelerated payment of overdue receivables"). Facts about your skills and accomplishments are the most important information you can give a prospective employer, so quantify them whenever possible:

> Designed a new ad that increased sales by 9 percent
>
> Raised $2,500 in 15 days for cancer research

One helpful exercise is to write a 30-second "commercial" for each major skill you want to highlight. The commercial should offer proof that you really do possess the skill. For your résumé, distill the commercials down to brief phrases such as those shown earlier, then you can use the more detailed proof statements in cover letters and as answers to interview questions.[23]

You may also include information describing other aspects of your background that pertain to your career objective, such as fluency in another language. If you have an array of special skills, group them together and include them near your education or work experience section. You might categorize such additional information as "Special Skills," "Work-Related Skills," "Other Experience," "Language Skills," or "Computer Skills."

If samples of your work might increase your chances of getting the job, insert a line at the end of your résumé offering to supply them on request, or indicate they're available in your e-portfolio. You may put "References available upon request" at the end of your résumé, but doing so is not necessary; the availability of references is usually assumed. Don't include actual names of references, but have them available.

Don't overlook personal accomplishments that indicate special skills or qualities, but make sure they are relevant to the jobs you're seeking.

Activities and Achievements   Your résumé should describe any volunteer activities that demonstrate your abilities. List projects that require leadership, organization, teamwork, and cooperation. Emphasize career-related activities such as "member of the Student Marketing Association." List skills you learned in these activities, and explain how these skills are related to the job you're applying for. Include speaking, writing, or tutoring experience; participation in athletics or creative projects; fund-raising or community-service activities; and offices held in academic or professional organizations. (However, mention of political or religious organizations may be a red flag to someone with differing views, so use your judgment.)

Note any relevant awards you've received. Again, quantify your achievements whenever possible. Instead of saying that you addressed various student groups, state how many and the approximate audience sizes. If your activities have been extensive, you may want to group them into divisions such as "College Activities," "Community Service," "Professional Associations," "Seminars and Workshops," and "Speaking Activities." An alternative is to divide them into two categories: "Service Activities" and "Achievements, Awards, and Honors."

Personal Data   Personal data is another common source of confusion with résumés. Most experts advise you to skip personal interests unless including them enhances the employer's understanding of why you would be the best candidate for the job.[24] Do personal interests and accomplishments relate to the employer's business, culture, or customers? However, your achievements as an amateur artist could appeal to an advertising agency, even if you're applying for a technical or business position, because its shows an appreciation for the creative process. Similarly, an interest in sports and outdoor activities could show that you'll fit in nicely at a company such as REI, Nike, or Patagonia, but not necessarily at other companies.

Some information is best excluded from your résumé. Civil rights laws prohibit employers from discriminating on the basis of gender, marital or family status, age (although only persons aged 40 to 70 are protected), race, religion, national origin, and physical or mental disability. So be sure to exclude any items that could encourage discrimination, even subconsciously. Experts also recommend excluding salary information, reasons for leaving jobs, names of previous supervisors, your Social Security number, and other identification codes. Save these items for the interview, and then offer them only if the employer specifically requests them.

If military service is relevant to the position, you may list it in this section (or under "Education" or "Work Experience"). List the date of induction, the branch of service, where you served, the highest rank you achieved, any accomplishments related to your career goals, and the date you were discharged.

Completing Your Résumé

The last step in the three-step writing process is no less important than the other two. As with any other business message, you need to revise your résumé, produce it in an appropriate form, and proofread it for any errors before distributing it to your target employers.

Try to keep your résumé to one page. If you have a great deal of experience and are applying for a higher-level position, you may need to prepare a somewhat longer résumé. The important thing is to have enough space to present a persuasive, accurate, and concise portrait of your skills and accomplishments.

Revising Your Résumé

Ask professional recruiters to list the most common mistakes they see on résumés, and you'll hear the same things over and over again. Keep your résumé out of the recycling bin by avoiding these flaws:

Avoid the common errors that will get your résumé excluded from consideration.

- **Too long.** The résumé is not concise, relevant, and to the point.
- **Too short or sketchy.** The résumé does not give enough information for a proper evaluation of the applicant.
- **Hard to read.** The résumé lacks enough white space and devices such as indentions and boldfacing to make the reader's job easier.
- **Wordy.** Descriptions are verbose, using numerous words describing simple concepts.
- **Too slick.** The résumé appears to have been written by someone other than the applicant, which raises the question of whether the qualifications have been exaggerated.
- **Amateurish.** The résumé includes the wrong information or presents it awkwardly, which indicates that the applicant has little understanding of the business world or of a particular industry.
- **Poorly produced.** The print is faint and difficult to read or the paper is cheap and inappropriate.
- **Misspelled and ungrammatical throughout.** The document contains spelling and grammar mistakes that indicate the candidate lacks both communication skills and attention to quality.
- **Boastful.** The overconfident tone makes the reader wonder whether the applicant's self-evaluation is realistic.
- **Generic.** Customize your résumé to fit specific industries, companies, and positions.
- **Gimmicky.** The words, structure, decoration, or material used in the résumé depart so far from the usual as to make the résumé ineffective.

Producing Your Résumé

Good design is a must, and it's not hard to achieve. As you can see in Figures 18.4, 18.5, and 18.6, good designs feature simplicity, order, plenty of white space, and straightforward typefaces such as Times Roman or Arial (keep in mind that many of the fonts on your computer are not appropriate for a résumé). Make your subheadings easy to find and easy to read, placing them either above each section or in the left margin. Use lists to itemize your most important qualifications, and leave plenty of white space. Color is not necessary by any means, but if you add color, make it subtle and sophisticated, such as in a thin horizontal line under your name and address. The most common way to get into trouble with résumé design is going overboard. If any part of the design "jumps out at you," tone it down. To see how jarring and unprofessional a truly poor design looks to an employer, compare Figures 18.4, 18.5, and 18.6 with the "creative" design in Figure 18.7. An amateurish design could end your chances of getting an interview. As one experienced recruiter put it recently, "At our office, these résumés are rejected without even being read."[25]

Effective résumé designs are simple, clean, and professional—not gaudy, clever, or cute.

Depending on the companies you apply to, you might want to produce your résumé in as many as six forms (all are explained in the following sections):

6 LEARNING OBJECTIVE

Identify six different formats in which you can produce a résumé

- Printed traditional résumé
- Printed scannable résumé
- Electronic plain-text file
- Microsoft Word file
- HTML format
- PDF file

Most of these versions are easy to create, as you'll see in the following sections.

In addition to these six common options, you might consider creating a résumé slide show in Microsoft PowerPoint. Two key advantages of a PowerPoint résumé are the

FIGURE 18.7 Ineffective Résumé Design
This truly jarring résumé exhibits numerous flaws: distracting lines, bad font choices, and unprofessional colors. The well-written information is completely lost in all the visual "noise."

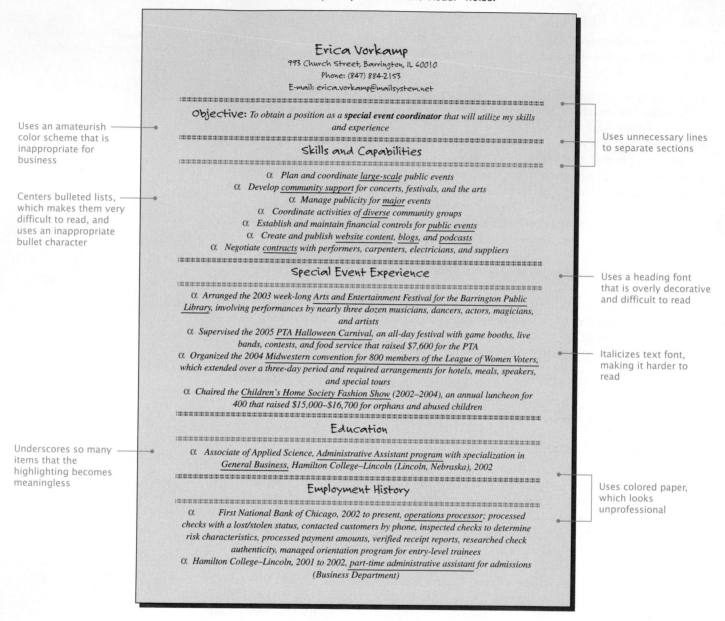

Uses an amateurish color scheme that is inappropriate for business

Centers bulleted lists, which makes them very difficult to read, and uses an inappropriate bullet character

Underscores so many items that the highlighting becomes meaningless

Uses unnecessary lines to separate sections

Uses a heading font that is overly decorative and difficult to read

Italicizes text font, making it harder to read

Uses colored paper, which looks unprofessional

flexibility and multimedia capabilities. For instance, you can present a menu of choices on the opening screen and allow viewers to click through to such items as a brief biography, photos that document important accomplishments (such as an event you planned or a project you created for a class), or screen shots of websites that you were involved in creating. Be creative—and make sure you don't simply re-create your résumé in PowerPoint; doing so would result in a rather dull presentation that is actually harder to read than a regular printed version.

Printing a Traditional Résumé The traditional paper résumé still has a place in this world of electronic job searches, if only to have a few copies ready whenever one of your networking contacts asks for one. Spend a few minutes in the paper aisle at an office supply store, and you'll notice that paper falls into three general categories: basic, low-cost white bond paper used for photocopying and printing (avoid this paper; it makes your résumé look cheap); predesigned papers with borders and backgrounds (avoid these; they make

Strive for a clean, classy look in your printed résumé, using professional-grade paper and a clean, high-quality printer.

your résumé look gimmicky); and heavier, higher-quality papers designed specifically for résumés and other important documents. Choose a white or slightly off-white paper from this third category; these papers are more expensive, but you don't need much, and it's a worthwhile investment.

When you're ready to print your résumé, use a well-maintained, quality printer. Don't tolerate any streaks, stray lines, or poor print quality. You wouldn't walk into an interview looking messy, so make sure your résumé doesn't look that way, either.

Printing a Scannable Résumé To cope with the flood of unsolicited paper résumés in recent years, many companies now optically scan incoming résumés into a database. When hiring managers want to interview candidates for job openings, they search the database for the most attractive candidates. In simpler systems, the search is based on keyword matching for a specific position. More advanced systems use sophisticated linguistic analysis to find good matches. With either approach, the system displays a list of possible candidates, each with a percentage score indicating how closely the résumé reflects the employer's requirements.[26] Nearly all large companies now use these systems, as do many mid-sized companies and even some smaller firms.[27]

The emergence of such scanning systems has important implications for your résumé. First, computers are interested only in matching information to search parameters, not in artistic attempts at résumé design. In fact, complex designs can cause errors in the scanning process. Second, *optical character recognition* (*OCR*) software doesn't technically "read" anything; it merely looks for shapes that match stored profiles of characters. If the OCR software can't make sense of your fancy fonts or creative page layout, it will enter gibberish into the database (for instance, your name might go in as "W<$..3r ?00!#" instead of "Walter Jones"). Third, even the most sophisticated databases cannot conduct a search with the nuance and intuition of an experienced human recruiter.

For job searchers, this situation creates two requirements for a successful scannable résumé: (1) use a plain font and simplified design, and (2) compile a **keyword summary** that lists all the terms that could help match your résumé to the right openings. Other than the keyword summary, a scannable résumé contains the same information as your traditional résumé but is formatted to be OCR-friendly (see Figure 18.8):[28]

- Use a clean, common sans serif font such as Optima or Arial, and size it between 10 and 14 points.
- Make sure that characters do not touch one another (whether numbers, letters, or symbols—including the slash [/]).
- Don't use side-by-side columns (the OCR software reads one line all the way across the page).
- Don't use ampersands (&), percent signs (%), foreign-language characters (such as é and ö), or bullet symbols (use a dash—not a lower-case 'o'—in place of a bullet symbol).
- Put each phone number and e-mail address on its own line.
- Print on white, plain paper (speckles and other background coloration can confuse the OCR software).

Your scannable résumé will probably be longer than your traditional résumé because you can't compress text into columns and because you need plenty of white space between headings and sections. If your scannable résumé runs more than one page, make sure your name appears on every subsequent page (in case the pages become separated). Before sending a scannable résumé, check the company's website or call the human resources department to see whether it has any specific requirements other than those discussed here.

When adding a keyword summary to your résumé, keep your audience in mind. Employers generally search for nouns (because verbs tend to be generic rather than specific to a particular position or skill), so make your keywords nouns as well. Use abbreviations sparingly and only when they are well-known and unambiguous, such as *MBA*. List 20 to 30 words and phrases that define your skills, experience, education, professional affiliations,

Converting your résumé to scannable format is easy and extremely important.

7 LEARNING OBJECTIVE

Describe what you should do to adapt your résumé to a scannable format

Think carefully about the keywords you include in your scannable résumé; they need to appeal to recruiters and reflect your qualities accurately.

FIGURE 18.8 Scannable Résumé
This version of the chronological résumé from Figure 18.5 shows the changes necessary for it to be successfully scanned. Notice that it doesn't have any special characters or design elements that are likely to confuse the scanning software.

Removes all boldfacing, nontext characters such as bullets, and two-column formatting

Includes carefully selected keyword list derived from descriptions of target jobs

Uses a dash instead of bullet point character in bulleted lists

Uses ample white space to help ensure accurate scanning

Roberto Cortez
5687 Crosswoods Drive
Falls Church, Virginia 22046
Home phone: (703) 987-0086
Office phone: (703) 549-6624
E-mail: RCortez@silvernet.com

KEYWORDS

Financial executive, accounting management, international finance, financial analyst, accounting reports, financial audit, computerized accounting model, exchange rates, joint-venture agreements, budgets, billing, credit processing, online systems, MBA, fluent Spanish, fluent German, Excel, Access, Visual Basic, team player, willing to travel

OBJECTIVE

Accounting management position requiring hands-on knowledge of international finance

EXPERIENCE

Staff Accountant/Financial Analyst, Inter-American Imports (Alexandria, Virginia), March 2002 to present
— Prepare accounting reports for wholesale giftware importer ($15 million annual sales)
— Audit financial transactions with suppliers in 12 Latin American countries
— Created a computerized model to adjust for fluctuations in currency exchange rates
— Negotiated joint-venture agreements with major suppliers in Mexico and Colombia
— Implemented electronic funds transfer for vendor disbursements, improving cash flow and eliminating payables clerk position

Staff Accountant, Monsanto Agricultural Chemicals (Mexico City, Mexico), October 1998 to March 2002
— Handled budgeting, billing, and credit-processing functions for the Mexico City branch
— Audited travel & entertainment expenses for Monsanto's 30-member Latin American sales force
— Assisted in launching an online system to automate all accounting functions, improving reporting accuracy by 65%

EDUCATION

Master of Business Administration with emphasis in international business, George Mason University (Fairfax, Virginia), 1996 to 1998

Bachelor of Business Administration, Accounting, University of Texas (Austin, Texas), 1993 to 1996

INTERCULTURAL AND TECHNICAL SKILLS

— Fluent in Spanish and German
— Traveled extensively in Latin America
— Excel, Access, HTML, Visual Basic

and so on. Place this list right after your name and address. Figure 18.8 offers an example of a keyword summary for an accountant.

One good way to identify which keywords to include in your summary is to note all the skills listed in ads for the types of jobs you're interested in. And another advantage of staying current by reading periodicals, networking, and so on is that you'll develop a good ear for current terminology. Be sure to include only those keywords that correspond with your skills and experience. Trying to get ahead of the competition by listing skills you don't have is unethical; moreover, your efforts will be quickly exposed when your keywords don't match your job experience or educational background.

Creating a Plain-Text File of Your Résumé An increasingly common way to get your information into an employer's database is by entering a **plain-text version** (sometimes referred to as an *ASCII text version*) of your résumé into an online form. This approach has the same goal as a scannable résumé, but it's faster, easier, and less prone to errors than the scanning process. If you have the option of mailing a scannable résumé or submitting plain text online, go with plain text.

In addition, when employers or networking contacts ask you to e-mail your résumé, they'll often want to receive it in plain-text format in the body of your e-mail message. Thanks to the prevalence of computer viruses these days, many employers will refuse to open an e-mail attachment. Plain text is also helpful when you're completing online application forms; simply copy and paste from your plain-text file into the appropriate fields.

Plain text is just what it sounds like: no font selections, no bullet symbols, no colors, no lines or boxes, and so on. A plain-text version is easy to create with your word processor. Start with the file you used to create your traditional printed résumé, use the *save as* choice to save it as "plain text" or whichever similarly labeled option your software has, then verify the result.

The verification step is crucial because you can never be quite sure what happens to your layout. Open the text file to view the layout, but don't use your word processor; instead, open the file with a basic text editor (such as Microsoft's Notepad) so that the text doesn't get reformatted in any way. If necessary, adjust the page manually, moving text and inserting spaces as needed. For simplicity's sake, left justify all your headings, rather than trying to center them manually. You can put headings in all caps or underline them with a row of dashes to separate them from blocks of text.

Creating a Word File of Your Traditional Résumé

In some cases, an employer or job-posting website will let you upload a Microsoft Word file directly. (Although there are certainly other word processors on the market, Microsoft Word is the de facto standard in business these days.) Read the instructions on each site carefully. For instance, you can upload a Word résumé to Monster.com, but the site asks you to follow some specific formatting instructions to make sure your file isn't garbled.[29]

Before you submit a Word file to anyone, make sure your system is free from computer viruses. Infecting a potential employer's PC is not the way to make a good first impression.

Creating an HTML Version of Your Résumé

You can probably find several uses for an HTML version of your résumé, including sending it as a fully formatted e-mail message and including it in your e-portfolio. A key advantage of an HTML version is that you can provide links to supporting details and other materials from within your résumé. Even if you don't have HTML experience, you can save your résumé as a webpage from within Word; this method won't necessarily create the most spectacularly beautiful webpage, but it should be functional at least.

As you design your HTML résumé, think of important keywords to use as hyperlinks—words that will grab an employer's attention and make the recruiter want to click on that hyperlink to learn more about you. You can link to papers you've written, recommendations you've received, and sound or video clips that directly support your résumé. However, be sure to have permission to publish or link to material created for a previous employer.

Creating a PDF Version of Your Résumé

Creating a PDF version of your résumé is a simple procedure, but you need the right software. Adobe Acrobat (not the free Acrobat Reader) is the best known program, but many others are available, including some free versions. You can also use Adobe's online service at **http://createpdf.adobe.com** to create PDFs without buying software.

Proofreading Your Résumé

Employers view your résumé as a concrete example of how you will prepare material on the job. It doesn't need to be good or pretty good; it needs to be *perfect*. Job seekers have

A plain-text version of your résumé is simply a computer file without any of the formatting that you typically apply using a word processor.

Make sure you verify the plain-text file that you create with your word processor and adjust it as needed.

You have many options for posting your résumé online, but remember that you could be displaying your personal information for all the world to see, so think carefully about privacy and security.

Your résumé can't be "pretty good" or "almost perfect"—it needs to be perfect, so proofread it thoroughly and ask several other people to verify it, too.

DOCUMENT MAKEOVER

committed every error from forgetting to put their own names on their résumés to misspelling "Education."[30] Even seemingly tiny errors signal that you don't pay attention to details.[31] Not only is your résumé one of the most important documents you'll ever write, it's also one of the shortest, so there's no reason not to make it perfect. Check all headings and lists for clarity and parallelism, and be sure that your grammar, spelling, and punctuation are correct. Ask at least three or four other people to read it, too. As the creator of the material, you could stare at a mistake for weeks and not see it.

You also need to make sure your résumé works in every format you create, so double- and triple-check your scannable and plain-text résumés closely. Many personal computer users now have low-cost scanners with OCR software, so you can even test the scannability of your résumé. These OCR tools aren't as accurate as commercial systems, but you'll get a rough idea of what your résumé will look like on the other end of the scanning process. And always test your plain-text version. Simply copy it into an e-mail message and send it to yourself and several friends on different e-mail systems. Doing so will tell you if previously hidden characters are suddenly showing up or if your formatting fell apart.

Once your résumé is complete, update it continuously. As flexible as employment has become these days, you'll probably want or need to change employers several times in your career. You may also need a current résumé to apply for membership to professional organizations and to apply for a promotion. Moreover, regularly updating your résumé helps you see how your career is progressing. To help focus your career growth efforts, you can even create a "future résumé" that identifies the skills and accomplishments you'd like to have at some point.

Distributing Your Résumé

When distributing your résumé, pay close attention to the specific wishes of every employer.

What you do to distribute your résumé depends on the number of employers you target and their preferences for receiving résumés. Employers usually list their preferences on their websites, so verify this information to make sure that your résumé ends up in the right format and in the right channel. Beyond that, here are some general delivery tips:

- **Mailing your traditional and scannable résumés.** Take some care with the packaging. Spend a few extra cents to mail these documents in a flat 9 by 12 envelope, or better yet, use Priority Mail, which gives you a sturdy cardboard mailer and faster delivery for just a few more dollars. Consider sending both versions to each employer. In your cover letter, explain that for the employer's convenience, you're sending both standard and scannable versions.

- **Faxing your traditional and scannable résumés.** If you know that an employer prefers résumés via fax, be sure to include a standard fax cover sheet, along with your cover letter, followed by your résumé. Set the fax machine to "fine" mode to help ensure a high-quality printout on the receiving end.

- **E-mailing your résumé.** Unless someone specifically asks for a Word document as an attachment, don't send it—it probably won't be opened. Instead, insert plain text into the body of the e-mail message, attach a PDF file, or include a hyperlink in the e-mail that links back to your webpage résumé. If you know a reference number or a job ad number, include it in your e-mail subject line.

- **Submitting your résumé online.** The details of submitting résumés online vary from site to site, so be sure to read the instructions thoroughly. Some sites let you upload files directly from your computer; others instruct you to copy and paste blocks of plain text into specific fields in an online form. Whenever you do this, be sure to copy and paste rather than re-typing information; you've already proofed this material, and you don't want to create any new mistakes while re-keying it.

CHECKLIST: Writing an Effective Résumé

A. Plan your résumé.
- Analyze your purpose and audience carefully to make sure your message meets employers' needs.
- Gather pertinent information about your target companies.
- Select the best medium by researching the preferences of each employer.
- Organize your résumé around your strengths, choosing the chronological, functional, or combination structure (be careful about using the functional structure).

B. Write your résumé.
- Keep your résumé honest.
- Adapt your résumé to your audience to highlight the qualifications each employer is looking for.

- Use powerful language to convey your name and contact information, career objective or summary of qualifications, education, work experience, skills, work or school accomplishments, and personal activities and achievements.

C. Complete your résumé.
- Revise your résumé until it is clear, concise, and compelling.
- Produce your résumé in all the formats you might need: traditional printed résumé, scannable, plain-text file, Microsoft Word file, HTML, or PDF file.
- Proofread your résumé to make sure it is letter perfect.
- Distribute your résumé using the means that each employer prefers.

- **Posting a résumé on your website.** If you want to post your résumé on your website, you'll need to find some way of providing potential employers with your URL; recruiters won't take the time to use search engines to find your site.[32]
- **Posting your résumé with an index service or job site.** Make sure you explore all your online options. Websites such as Monster.com, CareerBuilder.com, and Yahoo HotJobs have rapidly become a major force in recruiting. Don't forget to check specialty sites as well, such as those maintained by professional societies in your fields of interest. However, before you upload your résumé to any site, learn about its confidentiality protection. Some sites allow you to specify levels of confidentiality, such as letting employers search your qualifications without seeing your personal contact information or preventing your current employer from seeing your résumé. In any case, carefully limit the amount of personal information you provide online. Never put your home address, Social Security number, student ID number, or driver's license number online.

For a quick summary of the steps to take when planning, writing, and completing your résumé, refer to "Checklist: Writing an Effective Résumé."

COMMUNICATION CHALLENGES AT HERSHA HOSPITALITY MANAGEMENT

You recently joined Jeffrey Wade's recruiting team at Hersha, and your responsibilities include analyzing résumés and applications to help the company identify the most promising candidates to be interviewed. Study the two scenarios that follow and apply what you learned about recruiting and résumés in this chapter.

Individual Challenge: One of today's tasks is selecting candidates to be interviewed for a management trainee position. This position involves significant interaction with other departments, so communication skills are vital. The applicant tracking system has turned up two candidates with almost identical qualifications. You have time to interview only one of them, however. Based on the way the two candidates described their education, which one would you invite in for an interview—and why?

   a. Morehouse College, Atlanta, GA, 2003–2007. Received BA degree with a major in Business Administration and a minor in Finance. Graduated with a 3.65 grade-point average. Played varsity football and basketball. Worked 15 hours per week in the library. Coordinated the local student chapter of the American Management Association. Member of Alpha Phi Alpha social fraternity.

   b. I attended Wayne State University in Detroit, Michigan, for two years and then transferred to the University of Michigan at Ann Arbor, where I completed my studies. My major was economics, but I also took many business management courses, including employee motivation, small business administration, history of business start-ups, and organizational behavior. I selected courses based on the professors' reputation for excellence, and I received mostly As and Bs. Unlike many college students, I viewed the acquisition of knowledge—rather than career preparation—as my primary goal. I believe I have received a well-rounded education that has prepared me to approach management situations as problem-solving exercises.

Team Challenge: To find candidates for an accounting associate position (a job typically filled by college graduates, rather than more experienced professionals), you searched the application tracking system and found the following rather unconventional résumé. With one or two other students, study the résumé in light of what you know about both the recruiting process at Hersha and effective résumés, then decide whether you should (a) invite this candidate for an interview; (b) reject the application without further analysis; (c) review the candidate's web-based e-portfolio, then make a decision about inviting him in for an interview; or (d) compare the candidate's qualifications relative to those of other applicants and invite him in for an interview only if you cannot find several qualified applicants. Explain your choice.

Darius Jaidee
809 N. Perkins Rd, Stillwater, OK 74075
Phone: (405) 369-0098
E-mail: dariusj@okstate.edu

Career Objective: To build a successful career in financial management

Summary of Qualifications: As a student at the University of Oklahoma, Stillwater, completed a wide variety of assignments that demonstrate skills related to accounting and management. For example:

Planning skills: As president of the university's foreign affairs forum, organized six lectures and workshops featuring 36 speakers from 16 foreign countries within a nine-month period. Identified and recruited the speakers, handled their travel arrangements, and scheduled the facilities.

Communication skills: Wrote more than 25 essays and term papers on various academic topics, including at least 10 dealing with business and finance. As a senior, wrote a 20-page analysis of financial trends in the petroleum industry, interviewing five high-ranking executives in accounting and finance positions at ConocoPhillip's refinery in Ponca City, Oklahoma, and company headquarters in Houston, Texas.

Accounting and computer skills: Competent in all areas of Microsoft Office, including Excel spreadsheets and Access databases. Assisted with bookkeeping activities in parents' small business, including the conversion from paper-based to computer-based accounting (Peachtree software). Have taken courses in accounting, financial planning, database design, web design, and computer networking.

For more information, including employment history, please access my e-portfolio at **http://dariusjaidee. tripod.com**

SUMMARY OF LEARNING OBJECTIVES

1 **Describe the approach most employers take to finding potential new employees.** Employers look for new employees in as many as five different sources, and most have definite preferences from among these five. The preferred source is the employer's current workforce (most employers try to promote and hire from within before looking anywhere else), followed by the hiring manager's own personal contacts and personal recommendations from other trusted professionals. If these sources don't yield the right candidates or enough of them, employers will consider hiring an employment agency or search firm (sometimes called a "headhunter") and begin to review unsolicited résumés (often with the computerized assistance of a résumé database). Finally, employers will solicit applications from the general public, through their own websites, job boards such as Monster.com, and a variety of advertising efforts.

2 **Explain the importance of networking in your career search.** Networking is vital in today's job market because many job opportunities are never advertised to the public, or at least not until an employer has exhausted other opportunities. As an active networker, you might hear about opportunities that you would never know about otherwise. In addition, networking often allows you to learn information about employers and hiring managers that isn't available to the general public. Finally, your network contacts can often endorse your qualifications to a potential employer, giving you an advantage over other applicants.

3 **Discuss how to choose the appropriate résumé organization, and list the advantages or disadvantages of the three common options.** Each organizational approach emphasizes different strengths. If you have a lot of employment experience, you would choose the chronological approach because it focuses on your work history. The advantages of the chronological résumé are that (1) it helps employers easily locate necessary information, (2) it highlights your professional growth and career progress, and (3) it emphasizes continuity and stability in your employment background. The functional approach focuses on particular skills and competencies you've developed. The advantages of the functional résumé are that (1) it helps employers easily see what you can do for them, (2) it allows you to emphasize earlier job experience, and (3) it lets you downplay any lengthy periods of unemployment or a lack of career progress.

However, many employers are suspicious of the functional résumé for this very reason. The combination approach uses the best features of the other two, but it has two disadvantages: (1) It tends to be longer, and (2) it can be repetitious if you must list accomplishments and skills in the functional section as well as in the individual job descriptions.

4 **Describe the problem of résumé fraud.** Surveys continue to show that résumé fraud has reached epidemic proportions. Perhaps half of all résumés now contain inaccurate information, and some desperate job seekers even go so far as inventing college degrees they never earned or job experiences they never had. However, employers are fighting back with increasingly detailed background checks, so the chances of getting caught could be increasing as well.

5 **List the major sections of a traditional résumé.** Your résumé must include three sections: (1) your contact information (including name, address, telephone, and e-mail), (2) your education background (with related skills and accomplishments), and (3) your work experience (with related skills and accomplishments). Options include listing your career objective or a summary of qualifications, describing related activities and achievements, and perhaps (although not necessarily recommended) providing relevant personal data.

6 **Identify six different formats in which you can produce a résumé.** The six formats are traditional printed résumé, scannable, electronic plain text, Word file, HTML, and PDF.

7 **Describe what you should do to adapt your résumé to a scannable format.** A scannable résumé requires two significant changes to the traditional printed format: removing all formatting (including multiple columns of bullet points) and adding a list of keywords. You can remove all the formatting manually, but it's easier to just save a plain text version of your traditional résumé file, then verify its appearance using a simple text editor such as NotePad. You may need to move a few items around and insert or remove blank lines and spaces to make sure all the items line up appropriately. Then add a list of keywords (nouns) that define your skills, experience, and education. Make sure it also includes important jargon that is characteristic of the language in your field.

Test Your Knowledge

1. What is the most-preferred source of new employee leads for most employers?
2. Why is it important to have an organized approach to finding a new job?
3. Why is it important to contribute to any networks you belong to, in addition to looking for assistance for your own career?
4. What is a résumé, and why is it important to adopt a "you" attitude when preparing one?
5. How does a chronological résumé differ from a functional résumé, and when is each appropriate?
6. Why are some employers suspicious of the functional résumé?
7. What elements are commonly included in a résumé?
8. What are some of the most common problems with résumés?
9. Why is it important to provide a keyword summary in a scannable or electronic résumé?
10. Should you include personal data on a résumé? Explain your answer.

Apply Your Knowledge

1. If you're still a year or two away from graduation, should you worry about your job search? Explain your answer.
2. One of the disadvantages of computerized résumé scanning is that some qualified applicants will be missed because the technology isn't perfect. However, more companies are using this approach to deal with the flood of résumés they receive. Do you think that scanning is a good idea? Please explain.
3. Stating your career objective on a résumé or application might limit your opportunities by labeling you too narrowly. Not stating your objective, however, might lead an employer to categorize you incorrectly. Which outcome is riskier? Do summaries of qualifications overcome such drawbacks? If so, how? Explain briefly.
4. Some people don't have a clear career path when they enter the job market. If you're in that situation, how would your uncertainty affect the way your write your résumé?
5. **Ethical Choices** Between your sophomore and junior years, you quit school for a year to earn the money to finish college. You worked as a loan processing assistant in a finance company, checking references on loan applications, typing, and filing. Your manager made a lot of the fact that he had never attended college. He seemed to resent you for pursuing your education, but he never criticized your work, so you thought you were doing okay. After you'd been working there for six months, he fired you, saying that you failed to be thorough enough in your credit checks. You were actually glad to leave, and you found another job right away at a bank doing similar duties. Now that you've graduated from college, you're writing your résumé. Will you include the finance company job in your work history? Please explain.

Practice Your Knowledge

Message for Analysis

Read the following résumé information, then (1) analyze the strengths or weaknesses of the information, and (2) create a résumé that follows the guidelines presented in this chapter.

Message 18.A: Writing a Résumé

Sylvia Manchester
765 Belle Fleur Blvd.
New Orleans, LA 70113
(504) 312-9504
smanchester@rcnmail.com

PERSONAL: Single, excellent health, 5'8", 116 lbs.; hobbies include cooking, dancing, and reading.

JOB OBJECTIVE: To obtain a responsible position in marketing or sales with a good company.

EDUCATION: BA degree in biology, University of Louisiana, 1998. Graduated with a 3.0 average. Member of the varsity cheerleading squad. President of Panhellenic League. Homecoming queen.

WORK EXPERIENCE

Fisher Scientific Instruments, 2004 to now, field sales representative. Responsible for calling on customers and explaining the features of Fisher's line of laboratory instruments. Also responsible for writing sales letters, attending trade shows, and preparing weekly sales reports.

Fisher Scientific Instruments, 2001–2003, customer service representative. Was responsible for handling incoming phone calls from customers who had questions about delivery, quality, or operation of Fisher's line of laboratory instruments. Also handled miscellaneous correspondence with customers.

Medical Electronics, Inc., 1998–2001, administrative assistant to the vice president of marketing. In addition to handling typical secretarial chores for the vice president of marketing, I was in charge of compiling the monthly sales reports, using figures provided by members of the field sales force. I also was given responsibility for doing various market research activities.

New Orleans Convention and Visitors Bureau, 1995–1998, summers, tour guide. During the summers of my college years, I led tours of New Orleans for tourists visiting the city. My duties included greeting conventioneers and their spouses at hotels, explaining the history and features of the city during an all-day sightseeing tour, and answering questions about New Orleans and its attractions. During my fourth summer with the bureau, I was asked to help train the new tour guides. I prepared a handbook that provided interesting facts about the various tourist attractions, as well as answers to the most commonly asked tourist questions. The Bureau was so impressed with the handbook they had it printed up so that it could be given as a gift to visitors.

University of Louisiana, 1995–1998, part-time clerk in admissions office. While I was a student in college, I worked 15 hours a week in the admissions office. My duties included filing, processing applications, and handling correspondence with high school students and administrators.

Exercises

For active links to all websites discussed in this chapter, visit this text's website at www.prenhall.com/bovee. Locate your book and click on its Companion Website link. Then select Chapter 18, and click on "Featured Websites." Locate the name of the page or the URL related to the material in the text. Please note that links to sites that become inactive after publication of the book will be removed from the Featured Websites section.

18.1 Internet Based on the preferences you identified in your career self-assessment (see page P-4) and the academic, professional, and personal qualities you have to offer, perform an online search for a career that matches your interests (start with the websites listed in Table 18.1). Draft a brief report for your instructor indicating how the career you select and the job openings you find match your strengths and preferences.

18.2 Teamwork Working with another student, change the following statements to make them more effective for a résumé by using action verbs.
  a. Have some experience with database design.
  b. Assigned to a project to analyze the cost accounting methods for a large manufacturer.
  c. I was part of a team that developed a new inventory control system.
  d. Am responsible for preparing the quarterly department budget.
  e. Was a manager of a department with seven employees working for me.
  f. Was responsible for developing a spreadsheet to analyze monthly sales by department.
  g. Put in place a new program for ordering supplies.

18.3 Résumé Preparation: Work Accomplishments Using your team's answers to Exercise 18.2, make the statements stronger by quantifying them (make up any numbers you need).

18.4 Ethical Choices Assume that you achieved all the tasks shown in Exercise 18.2, not as an individual employee but as part of a work team. In your résumé, must you mention other team members? Explain your answer.

18.5 Résumé Preparation: Electronic Plain-Text Version Using your revised version of Message for Analysis 18.A, prepare a fully formatted print résumé. What formatting changes would Sylvia Manchester need to make if she were uploading her résumé to a website as a plain-text file? Develop a keyword summary and make all the changes needed to complete this plain-text résumé.

18.6 Résumé Preparation: HTML Version Using your revised version of the résumé in Message for Analysis 18.A, prepare an HTML version. Your instructor may direct you to a particular HTML editing tool, or you can use the "Save as Web Page" function in Microsoft Word. Word also lets you insert hyperlinks: Somewhere in the Work Experience section, create a hyperlink that takes the reader to a secondary page in order to show a work sample. For this new page, you can either use one of your own

assignments from this course or simply create a blank page titled "Work Sample for Sylvia Manchester." On this page, create a hyperlink that takes the reader back to the main résumé page.

Be sure to test your finished files using a web browser. Adjust your formatting as necessary to ensure a clean, professional design. When your files are complete, submit as your instructor indicates.

18.7 It's Show Time: Creating a Vidcast to Supplement Your Application Imagine you are applying for work in a field that involves speaking in front of an audience, such as sales, consulting, management, or training. Using material you created for any of the exercises or cases in Chapters 16 or 17, plan a two- to three-minute video demonstration of your speaking and presentation skills. Using a digital camcorder, a digital camera with video capability, or a webcam, record yourself speaking to an imaginary audience. If possible, use PowerPoint slides or other visuals. As your instructor directs, either submit this movie clip or use it to create a video podcast. For a good tutorial on creating vidcasts on Apple computers running Mac OS X, visit www.apple.com/quicktime/tutorials/videopodcasts.html; for Windows computers, visit www.apple.com/quicktime/tutorials/videopodcasts_win.html.

Expand Your Knowledge

Exploring the Best of the Web

Post an Online Résumé
www.careerbuilder.com
At CareerBuilder, you'll find sample résumés, tips on preparing different types of résumés (including scannable ones), links to additional articles, and expert advice on creating résumés that bring positive results. After you've polished your résumé-writing skills, you can search for jobs online using the site's numerous links to national and international industry-specific websites. You can access the information at CareerBuilder to develop your résumé and then post it with prospective employers—all free of charge. Use the site's advice to complete these tasks:
  1. Before writing a new résumé, make a list of action verbs that describe your skills and experience.
  2. Describe the advantages and disadvantages of chronological and functional résumé formats. Do you think a combination résumé would be an appropriate format for your new résumé? Explain why or why not.
  3. List some of the tips you learned for preparing an electronic résumé.

Surfing Your Way to Career Success

Bovée and Thill's Business Communication Resources offers links to hundreds of online resources that can help you with this course, your other college courses, and your career. Visit www.buscommresources.com, then click on "Business Communication Web Directory." The "Employment" section connects you to a variety of articles and websites covering such key topics as career planning, résumé writing, employment portfolios, background checks, and salary information. Identify three websites from this section that could be useful in your business career. For each site, write a two-sentence summary of what the site offers and how it could help you launch and build your career.

Learn Interactively

Interactive Study Guide

Visit www.prenhall.com/bovee, then locate your book and click on its "Companion Website" link. Select Chapter 18 to take advantage of the interactive "Chapter Quiz" to test your knowledge of chapter concepts. Receive instant feedback on whether you need additional studying. Also, visit the "Study Hall," where you'll find an abundance of valuable resources that will help you succeed in this course.

Peak Performance Grammar and Mechanics

If your instructor has required the use of "Peak Performance Grammar and Mechanics," either in your online course or on CD, you can improve your skill with frequently confused, misused, and misspelled words by using the "Peak Performance Grammar and Mechanics" module. Click "Spelling." Take the Pretest to determine whether you have any weak areas. Then review those areas in the Refresher Course. Take the Follow-Up Test to check your grasp of handling these tricky words. For an extra challenge or advanced practice, take the Advanced Test. Finally, for additional reinforcement, go to the "Improve Your Grammar, Mechanics, and Usage" section that follows, and complete those exercises.

CASES

Applying the Three-Step Writing Process to Cases
Apply each step to the following cases, as assigned by your instructor.

1. Taking stock and taking aim: Résumé tailored for the right job Think about yourself. What are some things that come easily to you? What do you enjoy doing? In what part of the country would you like to live? Do you like to work indoors? Outdoors? A combination of the two? How much do you like to travel? Would you like to spend considerable time on the road? Do you like to work closely with others or more independently? What conditions make a job unpleasant? Do you delegate responsibility easily, or do you like to do things yourself? Are you better with words or numbers? Better at speaking or writing? Do you like to work under fixed deadlines? How important is job security to you? Do you want your supervisor to state clearly what is expected of you, or do you like the freedom to make many of your own decisions?

Your task: After answering these questions, gather information about possible jobs that suit your profile by consulting reference materials (from your college library or placement center) and by searching the Internet (using some of the search strategies discussed in Chapter 10). Next, choose a location, a company, and a job that interests you. With guidance from your instructor, decide whether to apply for a job you're qualified for now or one you'll be qualified for with additional education. Then, as directed by your instructor, write a résumé.

2. Scanning the possibilities: Résumé for the Internet In your search for a position, you discover Career Magazine, a website that lists hundreds of companies advertising on the Internet. Your chances of getting an interview with a leading company will be enhanced if you submit your résumé and cover letter electronically. On the web, explore www.careermag.com.

Your task: Prepare a scannable résumé that could be submitted to one of the companies advertising at the Career Magazine website. Print out the résumé for your instructor.

3. "Help wanted": Application for a job listed in the classified section Among the jobs listed in today's *Chicago Tribune* (435 N. Michigan Avenue, Chicago, IL 60641) are the following:

Accounting Assistant

Established leader in the vacation ownership industry has immediate opening in its Northbrook corp. accounting dept. for an Accounting Assistant. Responsibilities include: bank reconciliation, preparation of deposits, AP, and cash receipt posting. Join our fast-growing company and enjoy our great benefits package. Flex work hours, medical, dental insurance. Fax résumé to Lisa: 847-564-3876.

Administrative Assistant

Fast-paced Wood Dale office seeks professional with strong computer skills. Proficient in MS Word & Excel, PowerPoint a plus. Must be detail oriented, able to handle multiple tasks, and possess strong communication skills. Excellent benefits, salary, and work environment. Fax résumé to 630-350-8649.

Customer Service

A nationally known computer software developer has an exciting opportunity in customer service and inside sales support in its fast-paced downtown Chicago office. You'll help resolve customer problems over the phone, provide information, assist in account management, and administer orders. If you're friendly, self-motivated, energetic, and have two years of experience, excellent problem-solving skills, organizational, communication, and PC skills, and communicate well over the phone, send résumé to J. Haber, 233 North Lake Shore Drive, Chicago, IL 60641.

Sales-Account Manager

MidCity Baking Company is seeking an Account Manager to sell and coordinate our programs to major accounts in the Chicago market. The candidate should possess strong analytical and selling skills and demonstrate computer proficiency. Previous sales experience with major account level assignment desired. A degree in business or equivalent experience preferred. For confidential consideration please mail résumé to Steven Crane, Director of Sales, MidCity Baking Company, 133 N. Railroad Avenue, Northlake, IL 60614.

Your task: Write a résumé for one of these potential employers (make up any information you need or adapt your résumé).

CHAPTER 19

Interviewing for Employment and Following Up

LEARNING OBJECTIVES

After studying this chapter, you will be able to

1 Define the purpose of application letters and explain how to apply the AIDA organizational approach to them

2 Describe the typical sequence of job interviews

3 Describe briefly what employers look for during an employment interview and preemployment testing

4 List six tasks you need to complete to prepare for a successful job interview

5 Explain the three stages of a successful employment interview

6 Identify the most common employment messages that follow an interview and explain when you would use each one

COMMUNICATION CLOSE-UP AT GOOGLE

www.google.com

As you prepare for your job interviews, knowing just the basic facts and figures about a company isn't always enough to impress top recruiters. For instance, most web surfers know Google as the leading online search engine, but the company is also helping to revolutionize advertising, publishing, geographic information systems, shopping—if it involves digital information, chances are Google has looked into opportunities to build a business out of it.

Learning how a company recruits not only helps you succeed in your job search but can also give you important insights into its culture. As Google continues its rapid growth, recruiting manager Arnnon Geshuri and his staff dedicate considerable time, energy, and resources to employee recruiting. However, finding the right people is so important to the company that helping the recruiting effort is considered the responsibility of virtually every manager and employee. In fact, John Sullivan of San Francisco State University, who has studied the company's recruiting efforts closely, says that recruiting permeates the company so thoroughly that Google has created what he terms the world's first "recruiting culture."

Arnnon Geshuri heads Google's recruiting effort as the company looks to hire several thousand of the most innovative online business and technical specialists in the world.

Moreover, as befits a company focused on innovation, the people Google pursues don't fit the traditional corporate mold. Most are either risk takers with adventurous outside interests or experienced superstars from top research labs or respected technology firms. Googlers, as employees are informally known, hail from every corner of the business world—and beyond. As the company puts it, "Googlers have been Olympic athletes and Jeopardy champions; professional chefs and independent filmmakers."

You may never apply to Google, but gaining similar insights about the companies you are interested in will give you a competitive edge. Google provides quite a bit of information on its website about work life at the company, but you can't always hop on a company website to find these insights. However, some extra digging through magazines, reading employment-related blogs, networking with others in your chosen field, and taking every other opportunity to unearth insights will help you prepare for every stage of the employment search process.[1]

WRITING APPLICATION LETTERS AND OTHER EMPLOYMENT MESSAGES

Whether you plan to apply to Google (as profiled in the chapter-opening "Communication Close-Up") or any other company, your résumé will usually be the centerpiece of your job search package. However, it needs support from several other employment messages, including application letters, job-inquiry letters, application forms, and follow-up notes.

Application Letters

1 LEARNING OBJECTIVE

Define the purpose of application letters and explain how to apply the AIDA organizational approach to them

Whenever you submit your résumé, accompany it with a cover, or application, letter to let readers know what you're sending, why you're sending it, and how they can benefit from reading it. Always send your résumé and application letter together, because each has a unique job to perform. The purpose of your résumé is to get employers interested enough to contact you for an interview. The purpose of your application letter is to get employers interested enough to read your résumé.

The three-step process of planning, writing, and completing an application letter involves the same tasks you've been using for other communication efforts throughout this course. Start by researching the organization you're applying to, then focus on your audience so that you can show you've done your homework. During your research, try to find out the name, title, and department of the person you're writing to. Although you won't always be able to find a specific individual to address your letter to, doing so is a major advantage whenever you can. If you can't find a specific name, avoid canned phrases such as "To Whom It May Concern" or gender-limited phrases such as "Dear Sir." Instead, use something like "Dear Hiring Manager."[2] If you're applying for work in another country, be sure to research the hiring practices prevalent in that culture and adjust your letter format as needed.

Use the three-step process to create attention-getting application letters.

Impress your reader with knowledge and professionalism— not gimmicks.

When putting yourself in your reader's shoes, remember that this person's inbox is probably overflowing with résumés and cover letters. So respect your reader's time. Steer clear of gimmicks, which almost never work, and don't waste time covering information that already appears in your résumé. Keep your letter straightforward, fact-based, short, upbeat, and professional. Here are some quick tips to help you write effective cover letters:[3]

- **Be specific.** Avoid general objectives. Be as clear as possible about the kind of opportunity and industry you're looking for. Show that you understand the company and the position by echoing the key messages you picked up from the job ad, company brochure, or other information source.
- **Never volunteer salary information unless an employer asks for it.** And even if you are asked, you probably don't want to pin down a specific number at this point in the process. See "Discussing Salary" on page 602 for more information.
- **Keep it short—and keep e-mail cover letters even shorter.** In just two or three paragraphs, convey how your strengths and character would fit the position. If you find you need more space, you probably haven't thought through the opportunity sufficiently.

When sending a cover letter by e-mail, make it even shorter than traditional application letters. Remember, e-mail readers want the gist as quickly as possible.

- **Show some personality.** Because your application letter is in your own style (rather than the choppy, shorthand style of your résumé), make the most of your chance to reveal not only your excellent communication skills but also some of your personality. Keep it professional, of course.

- **Aim for high quality.** Meticulously check your spelling, mechanics, and grammar. Recruiters are complaining about the declining quality of written communication, including cover letters. Since spellcheckers are only a mouse click away, there's really no excuse for misspelled words. Don't think that typos don't matter, either; readers equate typos with writing ability. Second, don't let the ease and speed of e-mail lull you into thinking it's a casual medium. Recruiters who complain about writing quality specifically mention sloppy e-mail cover letters from younger applicants who are accustomed to casual online communication with their friends—but who don't seem to recognize that expectations in the business world are much different. At least until potential employers get to know you, they will treat your e-mail messages every bit as seriously as formal, printed letters.[4]

The casual e-mail style you may be accustomed to with your friends is unacceptable for employment messages.

If you're sending a **solicited application letter** in response to an announced job opening, you'll usually know what qualifications the organization is seeking (see Figure 19.1). You'll also face more competition for the position because hundreds of other job seekers will have seen the listing and may be sending applications too. The letter in Figure 19.1 was written in response to a help-wanted ad.

If you're sending an **unsolicited letter** to an organization that has not announced an opening, it may actually have a better chance of being read and receiving individualized attention (see Figure 19.2).

Both solicited and unsolicited application letters present your qualifications similarly. The main difference is in the opening paragraph. In a solicited letter, you need no special attention-getter because you have been invited to apply. In an unsolicited letter, you need to start by capturing the reader's attention and interest.

Getting Attention

Like your résumé, your application letter is a form of advertising, so organize it as you would a sales letter: Use the AIDA approach, focus on your audience, and emphasize reader benefits (as discussed in Chapter 10). Make sure your style projects confidence, without being arrogant. To sell a potential employer on your merits, you must believe in yourself and sound as though you do.

The opening paragraph of your application letter has two important tasks to accomplish: (1) clearly stating your reason for writing and (2) giving the recipient a reason to keep reading. Why would a recruiter want to keep reading your letter instead of the hundred others piling up on his or her desk? Because you show some immediate potential for meeting the company's needs. You've researched the company and the position, and you know something about the industry and its current challenges. Consider this opening:

The opening paragraph of your application letter needs to clearly convey the reason you're writing and give the recipient a compelling reason to keep reading.

> With the recent slowdown in corporate purchasing, I can certainly appreciate the challenge of new fleet sales in this business environment. With my high energy level and 16 months of new-car sales experience, I believe I can produce the results you listed as vital in your September 23 ad in the *Baltimore Sun*.

This applicant does a smooth job of mirroring the company's stated needs while highlighting his personal qualifications along with evidence that he understands the broader market. Although 16 months may not be considered a lot of experience, the letter balances that shortfall with enthusiasm and genuine interest in the position.

Use the subject line in your e-mail message or cover letter to get the employer's attention: simply identify the job you are applying for. Table 19.1 on page 586 highlights some other ways that you can spark interest and grab attention in your opening paragraph. All these openings demonstrate the "you" attitude, and many indicate how the applicant can serve the employer.

FIGURE 19.1 Effective Solicited Application Letter
In this letter written in response to a help-wanted ad, notice how Kenneth Sawyer highlights his qualifications and mirrors the requirements specified in the ad. He grabs attention by focusing on the phrase "proven skills," which was used in the ad: He not only elaborates on his own proven skills throughout the letter but even mentions the term in his closing paragraph.

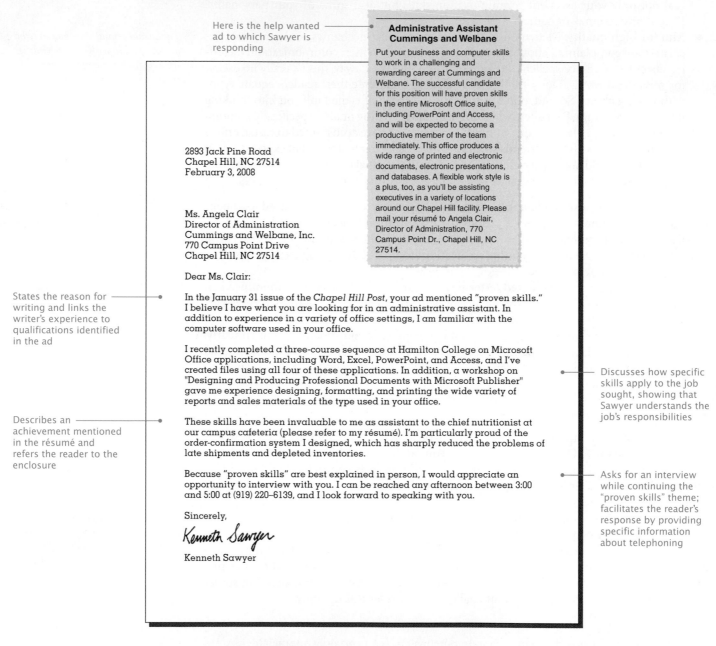

Here is the help wanted ad to which Sawyer is responding

Administrative Assistant
Cummings and Welbane

Put your business and computer skills to work in a challenging and rewarding career at Cummings and Welbane. The successful candidate for this position will have proven skills in the entire Microsoft Office suite, including PowerPoint and Access, and will be expected to become a productive member of the team immediately. This office produces a wide range of printed and electronic documents, electronic presentations, and databases. A flexible work style is a plus, too, as you'll be assisting executives in a variety of locations around our Chapel Hill facility. Please mail your résumé to Angela Clair, Director of Administration, 770 Campus Point Dr., Chapel Hill, NC 27514.

2893 Jack Pine Road
Chapel Hill, NC 27514
February 3, 2008

Ms. Angela Clair
Director of Administration
Cummings and Welbane, Inc.
770 Campus Point Drive
Chapel Hill, NC 27514

Dear Ms. Clair:

States the reason for writing and links the writer's experience to qualifications identified in the ad

In the January 31 issue of the *Chapel Hill Post*, your ad mentioned "proven skills." I believe I have what you are looking for in an administrative assistant. In addition to experience in a variety of office settings, I am familiar with the computer software used in your office.

I recently completed a three-course sequence at Hamilton College on Microsoft Office applications, including Word, Excel, PowerPoint, and Access, and I've created files using all four of these applications. In addition, a workshop on "Designing and Producing Professional Documents with Microsoft Publisher" gave me experience designing, formatting, and printing the wide variety of reports and sales materials of the type used in your office.

Discusses how specific skills apply to the job sought, showing that Sawyer understands the job's responsibilities

Describes an achievement mentioned in the résumé and refers the reader to the enclosure

These skills have been invaluable to me as assistant to the chief nutritionist at our campus cafeteria (please refer to my résumé). I'm particularly proud of the order-confirmation system I designed, which has sharply reduced the problems of late shipments and depleted inventories.

Because "proven skills" are best explained in person, I would appreciate an opportunity to interview with you. I can be reached any afternoon between 3:00 and 5:00 at (919) 220–6139, and I look forward to speaking with you.

Asks for an interview while continuing the "proven skills" theme; facilitates the reader's response by providing specific information about telephoning

Sincerely,

Kenneth Sawyer

Kenneth Sawyer

Building Interest and Increasing Desire

Use the middle section of your letter to expand on your opening, presenting a more complete picture of your strengths.

The middle section of your application letter presents your strongest selling points in terms of their potential benefit to the organization, thereby building interest in you and creating a desire to interview you. Don't repeat whatever selling points you may have used in your opening; instead, use this section to create a more rounded picture of your potential to contribute to the organization. As with the opening, the more specific you can be, the better. And back up your assertions with some convincing evidence of your ability to perform:

> **Poor:** I completed three college courses in business communication, earning an A in each course, and have worked for the past year at Imperial Construction.

FIGURE 19.2 Effective Unsolicited Application Letter
Glenda Johns's experience as a clerk and an assistant manager gives her a good idea of the qualities that Wal-Mart is likely to be looking for in future managers. She uses these insights to craft the opening of her letter.

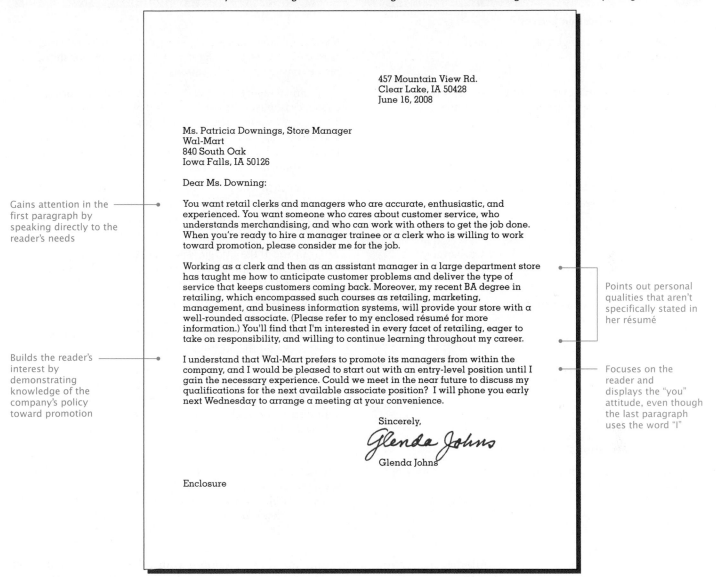

Gains attention in the first paragraph by speaking directly to the reader's needs

Builds the reader's interest by demonstrating knowledge of the company's policy toward promotion

Points out personal qualities that aren't specifically stated in her résumé

Focuses on the reader and displays the "you" attitude, even though the last paragraph uses the word "I"

Improved: Using the skills gained from three semesters of college training in business communication, I developed a collection system for Imperial Construction that reduced annual bad-debt losses by 25 percent. By emphasizing a win-win scenario for the company and its clients with incentives for on-time payment, the system was also credited with improving customer satisfaction.

When writing a solicited letter in response to an advertisement, be sure to discuss each requirement specified in the ad. If you are deficient in any of these requirements, stress other solid selling points to help strengthen your overall presentation.

Don't restrict your message to just core job duties, either. Also highlight personal characteristics, as long as they apply to the targeted position, such as your diligence or your ability to work hard, learn quickly, handle responsibility, or get along with people:

While attending college full-time, I trained 3 hours a day with the varsity track team. In addition, I worked part-time during the school year and up to 60 hours a week each summer in order to be totally self-supporting while in college. I can offer your organization the same level of effort and perseverance.

TABLE 19.1 Tips for Getting Attention in Application Letters

TIP	EXAMPLE
Unsolicited Application Letters	
• Show how your strongest skills will benefit the organization	If you need a regional sales specialist who consistently meets sales targets while fostering strong customer relationships, please consider my qualifications.
• Describe your understanding of the job's requirements and then show how well your qualifications fit them	Your annual report stated that improving manufacturing efficiency is one of the company's top priorities for next year. Through my postgraduate research in systems engineering and consulting work for several companies in the industry, I've developed reliable methods for quickly identifying ways to cut production time while reducing resource usage.
• Mention the name of a person known to and highly regarded by the reader	When Janice McHugh of your franchise sales division spoke to our business communication class last week, she said you often need promising new marketing graduates at this time of year.
• Refer to publicized company activities, achievements, changes, or new procedures	Today's issue of the *Detroit News* reports that you may need the expertise of computer programmers versed in robotics when your Lansing tire plant automates this spring.
• Use a question to demonstrate your understanding of the organization's needs	Can your fast-growing market research division use an interviewer with two years of field survey experience, a B.A. in pubic relations, and a real desire to succeed? If so, please consider me for the position.
• Use a catchphrase opening if the job requires ingenuity and imagination	*Haut monde*—whether said in French, Italian, or Arabic, it still means "high society." As an interior designer for your Beverly Hills showroom, not only could I serve and sell to your distinguished clientele, but I could do it in all these languages. I speak, read, and write them fluently.
Solicited Application Letters	
• Identify where you discovered the job opening; describe what you have to offer	Your ad in the April issue of *Travel & Leisure* for a cruise-line social director caught my eye. My eight years of experience as a social director in the travel industry would allow me to serve your new Caribbean cruise division well.

Don't bring up salary in your application letter unless the recipient has previously asked you to include your salary requirements.

Another matter you might bring up in this section is your salary requirements—but *only* if the organization has asked you to state them. If you don't know the salary that's appropriate for the position and someone with your qualifications, you can find salary ranges for hundreds of jobs at the Bureau of Labor Statistics website, **www.bls.gov** or a number of commercial sites, including Monster.com. If you do state a target salary, tie it to the benefits you would bring to the organization (much as you would handle price in a sales letter):

> For the past two years, I have been helping a company similar to yours organize its database marketing efforts. I would therefore like to receive a salary in the same range (the mid-60s) for helping your company set up a more efficient customer database.

Toward the end of this section, refer the reader to your résumé by citing a specific fact or general point covered there:

> As you can see in the enclosed résumé, I've been working part-time with a local publisher since my sophomore year. During that time, I've used client interactions as an opportunity to build strong customer service skills.

Motivating Action

The final paragraph of your application letter has two important functions: to ask the reader for a specific action and to facilitate a reply. In almost all cases, the action you request is an interview. Don't demand it, however; try to sound natural and appreciative. Offer to come to the employer's office at a convenient time or, if the firm is some distance away, to meet with its nearest representative or arrange a telephone interview. Make the request easy to fulfill by stating your phone number and the best time to reach you—or, if you want to be in control, by mentioning that you will follow up with a phone call in a few days. Refer again to your strongest selling point and, if desired, your date of availability:

> *In the final paragraph of your application letter, respectfully ask for specific action and make it easy for the reader to respond.*

> After you have reviewed my qualifications, could we discuss the possibility of putting my marketing skills to work for your company? Because I will be on spring break the week of March 8, I would like to arrange a time to talk then. I will call in late February to schedule a convenient time when we could discuss employment opportunities at your company.

Once you have edited and proofread your application letter, give it a final quality check by referring to "Checklist: Writing Application Letters." Then print it and send it (or e-mail it) along with your résumé promptly, especially if you are responding to an ad or online job posting.

Be aware that at some point in the application or interviewing process, some organizations will require you to complete a paper or online application form, a standardized data sheet that simplifies the comparison of applicants' qualifications. For instance, you might encounter one of these forms when submitting a résumé online or when you show up for a job interview. Even though the form may ask for information that is already on your résumé, be sure to fill it out accurately and completely. Enter "Not applicable" or "N/A" if a question doesn't apply to you. If you can't remember something and have no record of it, provide the closest estimate possible.

Application Follow-Ups

If your application letter and résumé fail to bring a response within a month or so, follow up with a second letter to keep your file active. This follow-up letter also gives you a chance to update your original application with any recent job-related information:

> Since applying to you on May 3 for a position in your management training program, I have completed three courses in business and management at South River Community College and received straight A's.
>
> Please keep my application in your active file; I would welcome another opportunity to apply for the program.

 CHECKLIST: Writing Application Letters

- Open the letter by capturing the reader's attention in a businesslike way.
- Use specific language to clearly state your interests and objectives.
- Build interest and desire in your potential contribution by presenting your key qualifications for the job.
- Link your education, experience, and personal qualities to the job requirements.

- Outline salary requirements only if the organization has requested that you provide them.
- Request an interview at a time and place that is convenient for the reader.
- Make it easy to comply with your request by providing your complete contact information and good times to reach you.
- Adapt your style for cultural variations if required.

Even if you've received a letter acknowledging your application and saying that it will be kept on file, don't hesitate to send a follow-up letter three months later to show that you are still interested:

> Three months have elapsed since I applied to you for an underwriting position, but I want to let you know that I am still very interested in joining your company.
>
> I recently completed a four-week temporary work assignment at a large local insurance agency. I learned several new verification techniques and gained experience in using the online computer system. This experience could increase my value to your underwriting department.
>
> Please keep my application in your active file, and let me know when a position opens for a capable underwriter.

Think creatively about a follow-up message; show that you've continued to add to your skills or that you've learned more about the company or the industry.

You can still write this sort of follow-up message even if you have no new accomplishments to share. Do some quick research on the company and its industry to find something that you can feature in your message ("I've been reading about the new technical challenges facing your industry . . ."). Your initiative and knowledge will impress recruiters. Without a follow-up communication from you, the human resources office is likely to assume that you've already found a job and are no longer interested in the organization. Moreover, a company's requirements change. A follow-up letter can demonstrate that you're sincerely interested in working for the organization, persistent in pursuing your goals, and committed to upgrading your skills. And it might just get you an interview.

UNDERSTANDING THE INTERVIEWING PROCESS

Like Google's Arnnon Geshuri, all recruiters have a list of qualities and accomplishments they are looking for in job candidates. An **employment interview** is a formal meeting during which both you and the prospective employer ask questions and exchange information. These meetings have a dual purpose: (1) The organization's main objective is to find the best person available for the job by determining whether you and the organization are a good match, and (2) your main objective is to find the job best suited to your goals and capabilities. While recruiters such as those at Google are trying to decide whether you are right for them, you must decide whether Google or any other company is right for you.

Large organizations that hire hundreds of new employees every year typically take a more systematic approach to the recruiting and interviewing process than small local businesses that hire only a few new people each year. You'll need to adjust your job search according to the company's size and hiring practices. In general, the easiest way to connect with a big company is through your campus placement office; the most efficient way to approach a smaller business is often contacting the company directly.

Regardless of which path you choose, interviewing takes time, so start seeking jobs well in advance of the date you want to start work. Some students begin their job search as much as nine months before graduation. During downturns in the economy, early planning is even more crucial. Many employers become more selective and many corporations reduce their campus visits and campus hiring programs, so more of the job-search burden falls on you. Whatever shape the economy is in, try to secure as many interviews as you can, both to improve the chances of receiving a job offer and to give yourself more options when you do get offers.

Asking questions of your own is as important as answering the interviewer's questions. Not only do you get vital information, but you show initiative and curiosity.

The Typical Sequence of Interviews

Not all organizations interview potential candidates the same way. At Southwest Airlines, for example, a candidate undergoes a rigorous interview process that can take as long as six weeks.[5] However, most employers interview an applicant two or three times before deciding to make a job offer. Applicants often face a sequence of interviews, each with a different purpose.

First is the preliminary *screening stage*, which is generally held on campus for new college hires and which helps employers screen out unqualified applicants. Those candidates who best meet the organization's requirements are invited to visit company offices for further evaluation. Interviews at the screening stage are fairly structured, so applicants are often asked roughly the same questions. Many companies use standardized evaluation sheets to "grade" the applicants so that all the candidates will be measured against the same criteria. In some cases, technology has transformed the initial, get-to-know-you interview, allowing employers to screen candidates by phone, video interview, or computer.[6]

Your best approach to an interview at the screening stage is to follow the interviewer's lead. Keep your responses short and to the point. Time is limited, so talking too much can be a big mistake. However, to give the interviewer a way to differentiate you from other candidates and to demonstrate your strengths and qualifications, try to emphasize the "theme" you used in developing your résumé.

The next stage of interviews helps the organization narrow the field a little further. Typically, if you're invited to visit a company, you will talk with several people in succession, such as a member of the human resources department, one or two potential colleagues, and one or more managers, including your potential supervisor. You might face a **panel interview**, during which several interviewers ask questions during a single session. Your best approach during this *selection stage* of interviews is to show interest in the job, relate your skills and experience to the organization's needs, listen attentively, ask insightful questions, and display enthusiasm.

If the interviewers agree that you're a good candidate, you may receive a job offer, either on the spot or a few days later by phone or mail. In other cases, you may be invited back for a final evaluation by a higher-ranking executive who has the authority to make the hiring decision and to decide on your compensation. An underlying objective of the *final stage* is often to sell you on the advantages of joining the organization.

Common Types of Interviews

Organizations use various types of interviews to discover as much as possible about you and other applicants. A **structured interview** is generally used in the screening stage. The employer controls the interview by asking a series of prepared questions in a set order. Working from a checklist, the interviewer asks you each question, staying within an allotted time period. All answers are noted. Although useful for gathering facts, the structured interview is generally regarded as a poor measure of an applicant's personal qualities. Nevertheless, some companies use structured interviews to create uniformity in their hiring process.[7]

By contrast, the **open-ended interview** is less formal and unstructured. The interviewer poses broad, open-ended questions and encourages you to talk freely. This type of interview is good for bringing out your personality and for testing professional judgment. However, some candidates reveal too much, rambling on about personal or family problems that have nothing to do with their qualifications for employment, their ability to get along with coworkers, or any personal interests that could benefit their performance on the job. So be careful. You need to strike a balance between being friendly and remembering that you're in a business situation.

Some organizations perform **group interviews**, meeting with several candidates simultaneously to see how they interact. This type of interview isn't nearly as common as the other types, but some companies use it to assess interpersonal skills and the ability to work with a team.[8]

The most unnerving type of interview is the **stress interview**, during which you might be asked pointed questions designed to irk or unsettle you, or you might be subjected to long periods of silence, criticisms of your appearance, deliberate interruptions, and abrupt or even hostile reactions by the interviewer. The theory behind this approach is that you'll reveal how well you handle stressful situations, although some experts find the technique of dubious value—particularly if the stress induced during the interview has no relationship to the job in question.[9] If you find yourself in a stress interview, pause for a few seconds to collect your thoughts, then continue knowing what the interviewer is up to.

---

2 LEARNING OBJECTIVE

Describe the typical sequence of job interviews

During the screening stage, try to differentiate yourself from other candidates.

During the selection stage, you may interview with several people, perhaps at the same time.

During the final stage, the interviewer may try to sell you on working for the firm.

A structured interview is controlled by the interviewer to gather facts.

In an open-ended interview, the recruiter encourages you to speak freely.

Group interviews help recruiters see how several candidates interact with one another.

Stress interviews help recruiters see how you handle yourself under pressure.

In situational interviews, you're asked to explain how you would handle a specific set of circumstances.

Many companies have learned that no strong correlation exists between how well people answer interview questions in a traditional interview and how well they perform on the job. In response, these firms have adopted a variety of new interviewing strategies. In the **situational interview**, various on-the-job scenarios are described, and candidates are asked how they would respond. Similarly, a **behavioral interview** asks candidates to describe real situations in the past and explain how they responded.[10] The most realistic approach is the **working interview**, in which the candidate is asked to perform the actual work that he or she would be doing on the job. For instance, a copywriting candidate in an advertising agency could be asked to write text for a webpage or an executive assistant could be asked to answer phones, demonstrate computer skills, and so on.[11]

Interview Media

In addition to a variety of interview formats, expect to be interviewed through a variety of media. Employers trying to cut travel costs and the demands on staff time now interview candidates via telephone, e-mail, instant messaging, virtual online systems, and videoconferencing. These alternative media options are used most frequently in the screening stage but can be used into the selection stage as well.

Treat a telephone interview as seriously as you would an in-person interview.

To succeed at a telephone interview, make sure you treat it as seriously as an in-person interview. Be prepared with a copy of all the materials you have sent the employer, including your résumé and any correspondence. In addition, prepare some note cards with key message points you'd like to make and your supporting evidence (such as an impressive success story from your current job). If possible, arrange to speak on a landline so you don't have to worry about cell phone reception problems. And remember that you won't be able to use a pleasant smile, a firm handshake, and other nonverbal signals to create a good impression. A positive, alert tone of voice is vital.[12]

When interviewing via e-mail or IM, be sure to take a second to review your responses before sending them.

E-mail and IM are also sometimes used in the screening stage. While you have even less opportunity to send and receive nonverbal signals, you do have the major advantage of being able to review and edit each response before you send it. Maintain a professional style in your responses and be sure to ask questions that demonstrate your knowledge of the company and the position.[13]

Computer-based virtual interviews range from simple structured interviews to realistic job simulations.

Virtual online interviews can range from simple structured interviews to sophisticated job simulations that are similar to working interviews. People applying for teller positions at SunTrust, a regional bank based in Atlanta, interact with video-game-like characters while performing job-related tasks. These job simulations not only identify better candidates but also reduce the risk of employment discrimination lawsuits because they closely mimic actual job skills.[14] The latest innovation in simulators uses prerecorded video of real people asking questions and records the candidate's answers on video as well.[15]

In a video interview, speak to the camera as though you are addressing the interviewer in person.

Many large companies use videoconferencing systems to screen middle-management candidates or to interview new recruits at universities. Experts recommend that candidates prepare a bit differently for a video interview than for an in-person meeting:[16]

- Ask for a preliminary phone conversation to establish rapport with the interviewer.
- Dress conservatively, in solid colors with minimal jewelry.
- Arrive early enough to get used to the equipment and setting.
- During the interview, speak clearly but not more slowly than normal.
- Sit straight.
- Talk to the camera.
- Keep your mannerisms lively without looking forced or fake.

3 LEARNING OBJECTIVE

Describe briefly what employers look for during an employment interview and preemployment testing

What Employers Look For in an Interview

Chapter 18 points out the attributes employers look for when reviewing résumés. The interview gives them a chance to go beyond this basic data to answer two essential questions during the interview process: Will the candidate be a good fit with the organization, and can he or she handle the responsibilities of the position? For instance, TechTarget, an interactive media company, gives employees an unusual amount of freedom, including the freedom to set their own hours and take as many days off for illness, personal matters, and vacation as they want or need—provided they meet their work objectives. It may sound like a wonderful arrangement, but CEO Greg Strakosch recognizes that some people can't handle the responsibility that comes with such independence. As a result, TechTarget's hiring process is focused on filtering out candidates who need a more structured environment.[17]

Some interviewers believe that personal background indicates how well the candidate will fit in, so they might ask about your interests, hobbies, awareness of world events, and so forth. You can expand your potential along these lines by reading widely, making an effort to meet new people, and participating in discussion groups, seminars, and workshops. For instance, Google (see page 581) values diverse interests and experiences, and rampant curiosity about virtually any subject is always welcome.

Beyond your organizational fit, interviewers are likely to consider your personal style as well. You're likely to impress an employer by being open, enthusiastic, and interested. Some interviewers also look for courtesy, sincerity, willingness to learn, and a style that is positive and self-confident. All of these qualities help a new employee adapt to a new workplace and new responsibilities.

Preemployment Testing

In an effort to improve the predictability of the selection process and reduce the reliance on the brief interaction that an interview allows, many employers now conduct a variety of preemployment tests.[18] These tests attempt to assess such factors as integrity, personality, job skills, and substance use. Google uses testing in creative ways not only to measure skills of potential hires but also to build interest in the company as a fun place to work. Thousands of computer programmers compete in the annual Google Code Jam, vying for not only valuable prizes but the chance to visit Google and explore job opportunities.[19]

TechTarget CEO Greg Strakosch offers his employees extraordinary amounts of freedom, so he works hard to find employees who can handle the responsibility of setting their own schedules.

Preemployment tests attempt to provide objective, quantitative information about a candidate's skills, attitudes, and habits.

Testing is a complex topic that varies widely by industry and position, and it also involves a wide range of legal and ethical issues, including discrimination and privacy. For instance, any testing that can be construed as a preemployment medical examination is prohibited by the Americans with Disabilities Act. One national retailer was successfully sued by applicants for a preemployment test that included questions designed to uncover applicants' sexual orientation.[20] Here is an overview of the most common types of tests:

- **Integrity tests.** You might not think that a test could identify job candidates who are more likely to steal from their employers or commit other ethical or legal infractions, but employers have had some success in using integrity tests. For example, one nationwide retailer found that preemployment integrity screening reduced its inventory shrinkage by 35 percent (*shrinkage* is an umbrella term for all inventory items that disappear before they can be sold).[21]
- **Personality tests.** Personality tests are used to assess either general character or suitability for the demands of a specific profession. General tests attempt to profile overall intellectual ability, attitudes toward work, interests, and managerial potential, as well as such characteristics as dependability, commitment, honesty, and motivation. The specific tests evaluate whether a candidate is suited to the emotional rigors of demanding positions, such as flight crews, air marshals, police and fire services, and nuclear power plant operators (in fact, federal law requires such tests for certain positions).[22]
- **Job skills tests.** The most common type of preemployment tests are those designed to assess the competency or specific abilities needed to perform a job. The skills you might be tested on vary according to the position, naturally, but the most frequently tested include basic computer skills, clerical tasks, basic business financial tasks, and legal and medical terminology.[23]
- **Substance tests.** Drug and alcohol testing is one of the most controversial issues in business today. Some employers believe such testing is absolutely necessary to maintain workplace safety, whereas others view it as an invasion of employee privacy and a sign of disrespect. Some companies test only applicants, but not employees.[24] Companies

test for three reasons: (1) to cut the costs (approximately $100 billion a year) and the reduced productivity associated with drug abuse, (2) to reduce the number of accidents (substance abusers have two to four times as many accidents as other employees, and drug use is linked to 40 percent of industrial fatalities), and (3) to reduce legal liability for negligent hiring practices if an employee harms an innocent party on the job.[25] In recent years, as many as 80 percent of U.S. employers conducted drug testing, but that percentage appears to be declining.[26]

- **Background checks.** Although not a test in the usual sense, a background check also helps employers learn more about you. And while drug testing may be waning slightly, the use of background checks has been growing rapidly; 80 percent of U.S. employers now conduct criminal background checks, for instance. Other types of background checks try to verify the credentials on your résumé, see how well you manage credit, or determine whether you might be on a terrorist watch list.[27] Such investigations can generate considerable controversy, because some people consider them an invasion of privacy. However, many employers believe they have no choice, given the magnitude of the risks they now face. Employers can be held liable for the actions of employees who obtained jobs under false pretenses—and lying by job candidates is depressingly common these days. In one recent survey of more than 2 million job applicants, 44 percent lied about their employment history, 41 percent lied about their education, and 23 percent claimed to have professional credentials or licenses they didn't have.[28]

If you're concerned about any preemployment test, ask the employer for more information or ask your college placement office for advice. You can also get more information from the Equal Employment Opportunity Commission at www.eeoc.gov. Moreover, with so many employers performing background checks these days, you might want to check up on yourself before applying for work. For instance, make sure your college transcript and credit record are correct and up to date so that any errors don't cause problems when a potential employer looks into your background.[29]

4 LEARNING OBJECTIVE

List six tasks you need to complete to prepare for a successful job interview

PREPARING FOR A JOB INTERVIEW

The more prepared you are, the less nervous you'll be about the interviewing process. Be sure to consider any cultural differences when preparing for interviews, and base your approach on what your audience expects (see "Communicating Across Cultures: Successfully Interviewing Across Borders"). To prepare for a successful interview, learn about the organization, think ahead about questions, bolster your confidence, polish your interview style, plan to look good, and be ready when you arrive.

Your college's career center has numerous resources to help you prepare for interviews.

Learn About the Organization

Today's companies expect serious candidates to demonstrate an understanding of the company's operations, its markets, and its strategic and tactical challenges.[30] When you were planning your employment search, you probably already researched the companies you sent your résumé to. But now that you've been invited for an interview, you'll want to fine-tune your research and brush up on the facts you've collected. Table 19.2 offers tips on researching both companies and jobs.

Think Ahead About Questions

Planning ahead for the interviewer's questions will help you handle them more confidently and successfully. As you consider answers to questions you might encounter, think about how you can relate your qualifications to the organization's needs. In addition, you will want to prepare insightful questions of your own.

Communicating Across Cultures

Successfully Interviewing Across Borders

Interviewing for a job in another country can be one of the most exciting steps in your career. To succeed, you need to pay even closer attention to the important elements of the interviewing process, including personal appearance, an awareness of what interviewers are really trying to learn about you, and what you should learn about the organization you're hoping to join.

Some countries and cultures place a much higher importance on dress and personal grooming than many employees in the United States are accustomed to; moreover, expectations of personal appearance can vary dramatically from country to country. Ask people who've been to the country before and observe local businesspeople when you arrive. Many people interpret inappropriate dress as more than a simple fashion mistake; they view it as an inability or unwillingness to understand another culture.

Whether or not these things should matter isn't the question; they do matter, and successful job candidates learn how to respond to differing expectations. For instance, business image consultant Ashley Rothschild points out that you could get away with wearing a boldly colored suit in Italy but probably not in Japan. Business professionals do tend to dress formally in Italy, but as a worldwide fashion leader, the country has a broad definition of what is appropriate businesswear.

Smart U.S. recruiters always analyze both nonverbal signals and verbal messages to judge whether an applicant truly has the qualities necessary for a job. In international employment situations, you'll probably be under even closer scrutiny. Recruiters abroad will want to know if you really have what it takes to succeed in unfamiliar social settings, how your family will handle the transition, and whether you can adapt your personal work style and habits enough to blend in with the hiring organization.

Remember to ask plenty of questions and do your research, both before and after the interview. Some employees view overseas postings as grand adventures, only to collide headfirst with the reality of what it's like to live and work in a completely different culture. For instance, if you've grown accustomed to the independent work style you enjoy in your current job or in school, could you handle a more structured work environment with a hierarchical chain of command? Make sure to get a sense of the culture both within the company and within its social community before you commit to a job in another country.

CAREER APPLICATIONS

1. Explain how you could find out what is appropriate dress for a job interview in South Africa.
2. Would it be appropriate to ask an interviewer to describe the culture in his or her country? Explain your answer.

Planning for the Employer's Questions

Employers usually gear their interview questions to specific organizational needs. You can expect to be asked about your skills, achievements, and goals, as well as about your attitude toward work and school, your relationships with others (work supervisors, colleagues, and fellow students), and occasionally your hobbies and interests. You'll also need to anticipate and give a little extra thought to a few particularly tough questions, such as these:

As you plan your responses to potential interview questions, be prepared to relate your qualifications to the organization's needs.

- **What was the hardest decision you ever had to make?** Be prepared with a good example, explaining why the decision was difficult and how you finally made it.
- **What are your greatest weaknesses?** This question seems to be a stock favorite of some interviewers, although it probably rarely yields useful information. The standard way to reply is to describe a weakness so that it sounds like a virtue—revealing something about yourself while showing how it works to an employer's advantage. For instance, if you sometimes drive yourself too hard, explain that it has helped when you've had to meet deadlines. Of course, interviewers who have asked this question many times have heard similar responses many times as well. An alternative is to describe a relatively minor shortcoming and explain how you're working to improve.
- **What didn't you like about previous jobs you've held?** State what you didn't like and discuss what the experience taught you. Avoid making negative references to former employers or colleagues. Be aware that when employers ask this question, they're trying to predict if you'll be an unhappy or difficult employee in the event they hire you, so plan your answer with care.[31]

TABLE 19.2 Finding Out About an Organization and a Job Opportunity

WHERE TO LOOK AND WHAT YOU CAN LEARN

- **Company website:** Overall information about the company, including key executives, products and services, locations and divisions, employee benefits, job descriptions
- **Competitors' websites:** Similar information from competitors, including the strengths these companies claim to have
- **Industry-related websites:** Objective analysis and criticism of the company, its products, its reputation, and its management
- **Marketing materials (brochures, catalogs, etc.):** The company's marketing strategy and customer communication style
- **Company publications (both print and electronic):** Key events, stories about employees, new products
- **Blogs:** Analysis and criticism (not always fair or unbiased) of the company, its products and services, its reputation, and its management
- **Periodicals (newspapers and trade journals, both print and online):** In-depth stories about the company and its strategies, products, successes, and failures; you may find profiles of top executives
- **Career center at your college:** Often provide wide array of information about companies that hire graduates
- **Current and former employees:** Insights into the work environment

POINTS TO LEARN ABOUT THE ORGANIZATION

- Full name
- Location (headquarters and divisions, branches, subsidiaries, or other units)
- Age and brief history
- Products and services
- Industry position (is the company a leader or a minor player; is it an innovator or more of a follower)
- Key financial points (such as stock price and trend, if a public company)
- Growth prospects (is the company investing in its future through research and development; is it in a thriving industry)

POINTS TO LEARN ABOUT THE POSITION

- Title
- Functions and responsibilities
- Qualifications and expectations
- Career path
- Salary range
- Travel expectations and opportunities
- Relocation expectations and opportunities

- **Where do you want to be five years from now?** This questions tests (1) whether you're merely using this job as a stopover until something better comes along and (2) whether you've given thought to your long-term goals. Saying that you'd like to be company president is unrealistic, and yet few employers want people who are content to sit still. Whatever you plan to say, your answer should reflect your desire to contribute to the employer's long-term goals, not just your own goals.
- **Tell me something about yourself.** Answer that you'll be happy to talk about yourself, and ask what the interviewer wants to know. If this point is clarified, respond. If it isn't, explain how your skills can contribute to the job and the organization. This is a great chance to sell yourself.

Practice answering typical interview questions so that you can respond with confidence and complete answers.

For a look at the types of questions often asked, see Table 19.3. Jot down a brief answer to each one. Then read over the answers until you feel comfortable with each of them. You might also give a list of interview questions to a friend or relative and have that person ask you various questions at random. This method helps you learn to articulate answers and to look at the person as you answer.

Planning Questions of Your Own

Remember that the interview is a two-way street: the questions you ask are just as important as the answers you provide. By asking insightful questions, you can demonstrate your understanding of the organization, you can steer the discussion into those areas that allow you to present your qualifications to the best advantage, and you can verify for yourself whether this is the right opportunity for you. Before the interview, prepare a list

TABLE 19.3 **Twenty-Five Common Interview Questions**

QUESTIONS ABOUT COLLEGE

1. What courses in college did you like most? Least? Why?

2. Do you think your extracurricular activities in college were worth the time you spent on them? Why or why not?

3. When did you choose your college major? Did you ever change your major? If so, why?

4. Do you feel you did the best scholastic work you are capable of?

5. Which of your college years was the toughest? Why?

QUESTIONS ABOUT EMPLOYERS AND JOBS

6. What jobs have you held? Why did you leave?

7. What percentage of your college expenses did you earn? How?

8. Why did you choose your particular field of work?

9. What are the disadvantages of your chosen field?

10. Have you served in the military? What rank did you achieve? What jobs did you perform?

11. What do you think about how this industry operates today?

12. Why do you think you would like this particular type of job?

QUESTIONS ABOUT PERSONAL ATTITUDES AND PREFERENCES

13. Do you prefer to work in any specific geographic location? If so, why?

14. How much money do you hope to be earning in 5 years? In 10 years?

15. What do you think determines a person's progress in a good organization?

16. What personal characteristics do you feel are necessary for success in your chosen field?

17. Tell me a story.

18. Do you like to travel?

19. Do you think grades should be considered by employers? Why or why not?

QUESTIONS ABOUT WORK HABITS

20. Do you prefer working with others or by yourself?

21. What type of boss do you prefer?

22. Have you ever had any difficulty getting along with colleagues or supervisors? With instructors? With other students?

23. Would you prefer to work in a large or a small organization? Why?

24. How do you feel about overtime work?

25. What have you done that shows initiative and willingness to work?

of about a dozen questions you need answered in order to evaluate the organization and the job.

Don't limit your questions to those you think will impress the interviewer, or you won't get the information you'll need to make a wise decision if you're offered the job. Here's a list of some things you might want to find out:

Plan questions that will help you decide whether the work and the organization are compatible with your goals and values.

- **Are these my kind of people?** Observe the interviewer, and if you can, arrange to talk with other employees.
- **Can I do this work?** Compare your qualifications with the requirements described by the interviewer.
- **Will I enjoy the work?** Know yourself and what's important to you. Will you find the work challenging? Will it give you feelings of accomplishment, of satisfaction, and of making a real contribution?

TABLE 19.4   Ten Questions to Ask the Interviewer

1. What are the job's major responsibilities?
2. What qualities do you want in the person who fills this position?
3. How do you measure success for someone in this position?
4. What is the first problem that needs the attention of the person you hire?
5. Would relocation be required now or in the future?
6. Why is this job now vacant?
7. What makes your organization different from others in the industry?
8. How would you define your organization's managerial philosophy?
9. What additional training does you organization provide?
10. Do employees have an opportunity to continue their education with help from the organization?

- **Is the job what I want?** You may never find a job that fulfills all your wants, but the position you accept should satisfy at least your primary ones. Will it make use of your best capabilities? Does it offer a career path to the long-term goals you've set?
- **Does the job pay what I'm worth?** By comparing jobs and salaries before you're interviewed, you'll know what's reasonable for someone with your skills in your industry.
- **What kind of person would I be working for?** If the interviewer is your prospective boss, watch how others interact with that person, tactfully query other employees, or pose a careful question or two during the interview. If your prospective boss is someone else, ask for that person's name, job title, and responsibilities. Try to learn all you can.
- **What sort of future can I expect with this organization?** How healthy is the organization? Can you look forward to advancement? Does the organization offer insurance, pension, vacation, or other benefits?

You don't necessarily have to wait until the interviewer asks if you have any questions of your own; look for smooth ways to work prepared questions into the conversation.

Impress the interviewer with your ability to organize and be thorough by bringing a list of questions to the job interview.

Rather than bombarding the interviewer with questions the minute you walk in the room, work them into the conversation naturally, without trying to take control of the interview. For a list of good questions you might as use as a starting point, see Table 19.4.

Write your list of questions on a notepad and take it to the interview. If you need to, jot down brief notes during the meeting, and be sure to record answers in more detail afterward. Having a list of questions should impress the interviewer with your organization and thoroughness. It will also show that you're there to evaluate the organization and the job as well as to promote yourself.

Bolster Your Confidence

By building your confidence, you'll make a better impression and make the whole process less stressful. The best way to counteract any apprehension is to remove its source. You may feel shy or self-conscious because you think you have some flaw that will prompt others to reject you. Bear in mind, however, that you're often much more conscious of your limitations than other people are.

If some aspect of your appearance or background makes you uneasy, correct it or offset it by emphasizing positive traits such as warmth, wit, intelligence, or charm. Instead of dwelling on your weaknesses, focus on your strengths. Instead of worrying about how you will perform in the interview, focus on how you can help the organization succeed. Remember that all the other candidates for the job are just as nervous as you are. The interviewers may be nervous, too; after all, they're judged on how well they assess candidates, so help them see your positive qualities clearly.

Polish Your Interview Style

Competence and confidence are the foundation of your interviewing style, and you can enhance those by giving the interviewer an impression of poise, good manners, and good judgment. Some job seekers hire professional coaches and image consultants to create just the right impression. These experts teach clients how to adopt appropriate communication styles, using role-playing, videotaping, and audiotaping.[32] You can use these techniques too.

For example, you can develop an adept style by staging mock interviews with a friend. You can record these practice sessions and then evaluate them yourself. The taping process can be intimidating, but it helps you work out any problems before you begin actual job interviews. Also, see if your career center has one of the computer-based interview simulators that are now available (see Figure 19.3). You can search online for "practice interviews" or "interview simulators."

Staging mock interviews with a friend is a good way to hone your style.

After each practice session, try to identify opportunities for improvement. Have your mock interview partner critique your performance, or critique yourself if you're able to record your practice interviews, using the list of warning signs shown in Table 19.5.

As you stage your mock interviews, pay particular attention to your nonverbal behavior. In the United States, you are more likely to have a successful interview if you maintain eye contact, smile frequently, sit in an attentive position, and use frequent hand gestures. These nonverbal signals convince the interviewer that you're alert, assertive, dependable, confident, responsible, and energetic.[33] Some companies based in the United States are owned and managed by people from other cultures, so during your research, find out about the company's cultural background and preferences regarding nonverbal behavior.

Nonverbal behavior has a significant effect on the interviewer's opinion of you.

The sound of your voice can also have a major impact on your success in a job interview.[34] You can work with a tape recorder to overcome voice problems. If you tend to speak too rapidly, practice speaking more slowly. If your voice sounds too loud or too soft, practice adjusting it. Work on eliminating speech mannerisms such as *you know*, *like*, and *um*, which might make you sound inarticulate.

The way you speak is almost as important as what you say.

Plan to Look Good

Physical appearance is important because clothing and grooming reveal something about a candidate's personality, professionalism, and ability to sense the unspoken "rules" of a situation. When it comes to clothing, the best policy is to dress conservatively. Wear the

FIGURE 19.3 Interview Simulators
Experts advise you to practice your interview skills as much as possible. You can use a friend or classmate as a practice partner, or you might be able to use one of the interview simulators now available, such as this system from Perfect Interview. Ask at your career center for more information.

TABLE 19.5 Warning Signs: 25 Attributes That Interviewers Don't Like to See

• Poor personal appearance	• Poor scholastic record; just got by
• Overbearing, overaggressive, conceited demeanor; a "superiority complex" know-it-all attitude	• Unwillingness to start at the bottom; expecting too much too soon
• Inability to express ideas clearly; poor voice, diction, grammar	• Tendency to make excuses
• Lack of knowledge or experience	• Evasive answers; hedges on unfavorable factors in record
• Poor preparation for the interview	• Lack of fact
• Lack of interest in the job	• Lack of maturity
• Lack of planning for career; lack of purpose, goals	• Lack of courtesy; ill-mannered
• Lack of enthusiasm; passive and indifferent demeanor	• Condemnation of past employers
• Lack of confidence and pose; appearance of being nervous and ill at ease	• Lack of social skills
• Insufficient evidence of achievement	• Marked dislike for schoolwork
• Failure to participate in extracurricular activities	• Lack of vitality
• Overemphasis on money; interest only in the best dollar offer	• Failure to look interviewer in the eye
	• Limp, weak handshake

Make a positive first impression with careful grooming and attire. You don't need to spend a fortune on new clothes, but you do need to look clean, prepared, and professional.

Be ready to go the minute you arrive at the interviewing site; don't fumble around for your résumé or your list of questions.

best-quality businesslike clothing you can, preferably in a dark, solid color. Wearing clothes that are appropriate and clean is far more important than wearing clothes that are expensive. Avoid flamboyant styles, colors, and prints. Even in companies in which interviewers may dress casually, it's important to show good judgment by dressing—and acting—in a professional manner. Even minor points of etiquette can make a lasting impression on recruiters.

Some candidates ask interviewers ahead of time what they should wear. One human resources executive tells job seekers to dress business casual because dressing in a suit, for example, looks awkward at his company.[35] However, in other companies, business casual would be completely out of place in a job interview. Your research into various industries and professions should give you insight into expectations for business attire, too. If you're not sure, being a little too formal is a better guess than being too casual.

Good grooming makes any style of clothing look better. Make sure your clothes are clean and unwrinkled, your shoes unscuffed and well shined, your hair neatly styled and combed, your fingernails clean, and your breath fresh. If possible, check your appearance in a mirror before entering the room for the interview. Finally, remember that one of the best ways to look good is to smile at appropriate moments.

Make professional appearance and habits a routine part of your day after you land that first job, too. Some students fail to recognize the need to adjust their dress and personal habits when they make the transition to professional life. Behaviors you may not think about, such as showing up five minutes late to every meeting or wearing a T-shirt to a client's office, could limit your career potential. Again, these may seem like minor issues, but many people are sensitive to these points of business etiquette and consider them a sign of mutual respect.

Be Ready When You Arrive

When you go to your interview, take a small notebook, a pen, a list of the questions you want to ask, two copies of your résumé (protected in a folder), an outline of what you have learned about the organization, and any past correspondence about the position. You may also want to take a small calendar, a transcript of your college grades, a list of references, and a portfolio containing samples of your work, performance reviews, and certificates of achievement.[36]

CHECKLIST: Planning for a Successful Job Interview

- Learn about the organization, including its operations, markets, and challenges.
- Plan for the employer's questions, including questions about tough decisions you've made, your weaknesses, what you didn't like about previous jobs, and your career plans.
- Plan questions of your own to find out whether this is really the job and the organization for you, and to show that you've done your research.
- Bolster your confidence by removing as many sources of apprehension as you can.

- Polish your interview style by staging mock interviews.
- Plan to look good with appropriate dress and grooming.
- Be ready when you arrive, and bring along a pen, paper, list of questions, two résumés, an outline of your research on the company, and any correspondence you've had regarding the position.
- Double-check the location and time of the interview and map out the route beforehand.
- Relax and be flexible; the schedule and interview arrangements may change when you arrive.

Be sure you know when and where the interview will be held. The worst way to start any interview is to be late. Check the route you will take, even if it means phoning ahead to ask. Find out how much time it takes to get there; then plan to arrive early. Allow a little extra time in case you run into a problem on the way.

Once you arrive, remind yourself that you are fully prepared and confident, then try to relax. You may have to wait, so bring along something business-oriented to read. If company literature is available in the lobby, read it while you wait. At every step, show respect for everyone you encounter. If the opportunity presents itself, ask a few questions about the organization or express enthusiasm for the job. Refrain from smoking before the interview (nonsmokers can smell smoke on the clothing of interviewees), and avoid chewing gum or otherwise eating or drinking in the waiting room. Anything you do or say while you wait may well get back to the interviewer, so make sure your best qualities show from the moment you enter the premises. That way you'll be ready for the interview itself once it actually begins. To review the steps for planning a successful interview, see "Checklist: Planning for a Successful Job Interview."

INTERVIEWING FOR SUCCESS

Your approach to interviews evolves as you move through each stage of the process. The techniques for success are similar throughout, even though the focus and purpose of the interviews do change—both for you and for the employer. To increase your chances of success, follow the tips from successful interviewers about how to make a positive impression by avoiding mistakes (see "Communication Miscues: Make Sure You Don't Talk Yourself Right out of a Job").

If you're being interviewed for the first time, your main objective is to differentiate yourself from the many other candidates who are also being screened. Without resorting to gimmicks, call attention to one key aspect of your personal or professional background so that the recruiter can say, "Oh yes, I remember Brenda Jones—the one who built a computerized home weather station to wake her up a few minutes early whenever it snowed overnight." Just be sure the trait you accentuate is relevant to the job in question. In addition, you'll want to be prepared in case an employer expects you to demonstrate a particular skill (perhaps problem solving) during the screening interview.

Present a memorable "headline" during an interview at the screening stage.

If you progress to the initial selection interview, broaden your promotional message. Instead of telegraphing the "headline," give the interviewer the whole story. Touch briefly on all your strengths, but explain three or four of your best qualifications in depth. At the same time, probe for information that will help you evaluate the position objectively.

Cover all your strengths during an interview at the selection stage.

If you're asked back for a final visit, your chances of being offered a position have improved considerably. At this point, you'll probably talk to a person who has the authority to make an offer and negotiate terms. This individual may have already concluded that your

Emphasize your personality, motivations, and values during a final interview.

Communication Miscues

Make Sure You Don't Talk Yourself Right out of a Job

Even well-qualified applicants sometimes talk themselves right out of an opportunity by making avoidable blunders during the job interview. Take care to avoid these all-too-common mistakes:

- **Being defensive.** An interview isn't an interrogation, and the interviewer isn't out to get you. Treat interviews as business conversations, an exchange of information in which both sides have something of value to share. You'll give (and get) better information that way.
- **Failing to ask questions.** Interviewers expect you to ask questions, both during the interview and at its conclusion when they ask if you have any questions. If you have nothing to ask, you come across as someone who isn't really interested in the job or the company. Prepare a list of questions before every interview.
- **Failing to answer questions—or trying to bluff your way through difficult questions.** If you simply can't answer a question, don't try to talk your way around it or fake your way through it. Remember that sometimes interviewers ask strange questions just to see how you'll respond. What kind of fish would you like to be? How would you go about nailing jelly to the ceiling? Why are manhole covers round? Some of these questions are designed to test your grace under pressure, whereas others actually expect you to think through a logical answer (manhole covers are round because that's the only shape that can't fall through an open hole of slightly smaller size, by the way). Don't act like the question is stupid or refuse to answer it. Sit quietly for a few seconds, try to imagine why the interviewer has

asked the question, then frame an answer that links your strengths to the company's needs.

- **Freezing up.** The human brain seems to have the capacity to just freeze up under stressful situations. An interviewer might have asked you a simple question, or perhaps you were halfway through an intelligent answer, and poof—all your thoughts disappear and you can't organize words in any logical order. Try to quickly replay the last few seconds of the conversation in your mind to see if you can recapture the conversational thread. If that fails, you're probably better off explaining to the reviewer that your mind has gone blank and asking him or her to repeat the question. Doing so is embarrassing, but not as embarrassing as chattering on and on with no idea of what you're saying, hoping you'll stumble back onto the topic.
- **Failing to understand your potential to contribute to the organization.** Interviewers care less about your history than about how you can help their organization in the future. Unless you've inventoried your own skills, researched their needs, and found a match between the two, you won't be able to answer these questions quickly and intelligently.

CAREER APPLICATIONS

1. What should you do if you if you suddenly realize that something you said earlier in the interview is incorrect or incomplete? Explain your answer.
2. How would you answer the following question: "How do you respond to colleagues who make you angry?" Explain your answer.

---

5 LEARNING OBJECTIVE

Explain the three stages of a successful employment interview

background is right for the job and may be more concerned with sizing up your personality. Both you and the employer need to find out whether there is a good psychological fit. Be honest about your motivations and values. If the interview goes well, your objective should be to clinch the deal on the best possible terms.

Regardless of where you are in the interview process, every interview will proceed through three stages: the warm-up, the question-and-answer session, and the close.

The Warm-Up

The first minute of the interview is crucial, so be ready and stay on your toes.

Of the three stages, the warm-up is the most important, even though it may account for only a small fraction of the time you spend in the interview. Studies suggest that many interviewers, particularly those who are poorly trained in interviewing techniques, make up their minds within the first 20 seconds of contact with a candidate.[37] Don't let your guard down if the interviewer wants to engage in what feels like small talk; these exchanges are every bit as important as structured questions.

Body language is important at this point. Because you won't have time to say much in the first minute or two, you must sell yourself nonverbally. Begin by using the interviewer's name if you're sure you can pronounce it correctly. If the interviewer extends a hand, respond with a firm but not overpowering handshake, and wait until you're asked to be seated. Let the interviewer start the discussion, and listen for cues that tell you what he or she is interested in knowing about you as a potential employee.

The Question-and-Answer Stage

Questions and answers will consume the greatest part of the interview. The interviewer will ask you about your qualifications and discuss many of the points mentioned in your résumé. You'll also be asking questions of your own.

Dealing with Questions

Let the interviewer lead the conversation, and never answer a question before he or she has finished asking it—the last few words of the question might alter how you respond. As questions are asked, tailor your answers to make a favorable impression. Don't limit yourself to yes or no answers. If you're asked a difficult question, be sure you pause to think before responding. The recruiter may know that you can't answer a question and only wants to know how you'll respond.

Tailor your answers to emphasize your strengths.

If you periodically ask a question or two from the list you've prepared, you'll not only learn something but also demonstrate your interest. Probe for what the company is looking for in its new employees so that you can show how you meet the firm's needs. Also try to zero in on any reservations the interviewer might have about you so that you can dispel them.

Listening to the Interviewer

Paying attention when the interviewer speaks can be as important as giving good answers or asking good questions. Review the tips on listening offered in Chapter 2.

The interviewer's facial expressions, eye movements, gestures, and posture may tell you the real meaning of what is being said. Be especially aware of how your comments are received. Does the interviewer nod in agreement or smile to show approval? If so, you're making progress. If not, you might want to introduce another topic or modify your approach.

Paying attention to both verbal and nonverbal messages can help you turn the question-and-answer stage to your advantage.

Fielding Discriminatory Questions

Employers cannot legally discriminate against a job candidate on the basis of race, color, gender, age (at least if you're between 40 and 70), marital status, religion, national origin, or disability. Accordingly, federal regulations are in place to prevent interviewers from asking questions in ways that would allow them to discriminate according to any of these factors. Individual states and cities have enacted a variety of laws concerning interview questions, so you may have additional protections beyond the federal standards.[38] Table 19.6 compares specific questions that may and may not be asked during an employment interview.

Well-trained interviewers are aware of questions they shouldn't ask.

If your interviewer asks these personal questions, how you respond depends on how badly you want the job, how you feel about revealing the information asked for, what you think the interviewer will do with the information, and whether you want to work for a company that asks such questions. Remember that you always have the option of simply refusing to answer or of telling the interviewer that you think a particular question is unethical—although either of these responses is likely to leave an unfavorable impression.[39] If you do want the job, you might (1) ask how the question is related to your qualifications, (2) explain that the information is personal, (3) respond to what you think is the interviewer's real concern, or (4) answer both the question and the concern.

Think about how you might respond if you are asked a potentially unlawful question.

If you do answer an unethical or unlawful question, you run the risk that your answer may hurt your chances, so think carefully before answering.[40] In any event, don't forget the two-way nature of the interview process: The organization is learning about you and you're learning about the organization. Would you want to work for an organization that condones illegal or discriminatory questions or that doesn't train its employees enough to avoid them?

If you believe an interviewer's questions are unreasonable, unrelated to the job, or an attempt to discriminate, you may complain to the nearest field office of the EEOC (find offices online at www.eeoc.gov) or to the state agency that regulates fair employment practices. To report discrimination on the basis of age or physical disability, contact the

TABLE 19.6 Interview Questions That May and May Not Be Asked

INTERVIEWERS MAY ASK THIS . . .	BUT NOT THIS . . .
What is your name?	What was your maiden name?
Are you over 18?	When were you born?
Did you graduate from high school?	When did you graduate from high school?
[No questions about race are allowed.]	What is your race?
Can you perform [specific tasks]?	Do you have physical or mental disabilities?
	Do you have a drug or alcohol problem?
	Are you taking any prescription drugs?
Would you be able to meet the job's requirements to frequently work weekends?	Would working on weekends conflict with your religion?
Do you have the legal right to work in the United States?	What country are you a citizen of?
Have you ever been convicted of a felony?	Have you ever been arrested?
This job requires that you speak Spanish. Do you?	What language did you speak in your home when you were growing up?

employer's equal opportunity officer or the U.S. Department of Labor. If you file a complaint, be prepared to spend a lot of time and effort on it—and keep in mind that you may not win.[41]

The Close

Like the warm-up, the end of the interview is more important than its brief duration would indicate. In the last few minutes, you need to evaluate how well you've done. You also need to correct any misconceptions the interviewer might have.

Concluding Gracefully

Conclude the interview with courtesy and enthusiasm.

You can generally tell when the interviewer is trying to conclude the session. He or she may ask whether you have any more questions, sum up the discussion, change position, or indicate with a gesture that the interview is over. When you get the signal, respond promptly, but don't rush. Be sure to thank the interviewer for the opportunity and express an interest in the organization. If you can do so comfortably, try to pin down what will happen next, but don't press for an immediate decision.

If this is your second or third visit to the organization, the interview may culminate with an offer of employment. You have two options: Accept it or request time to think it over. The best course is usually to wait. If no job offer is made, the interviewer may not have reached a decision yet, but you may tactfully ask when you can expect to know the decision.

Discussing Salary

Research salary ranges in your job, industry, and geographic region before you try to negotiate salary.

If you do receive an offer during the interview, you'll naturally want to discuss salary. However, let the interviewer raise the subject. If asked your salary requirements during the interview or on a job application, you can say that your salary requirements are open or negotiable or that you would expect a competitive compensation package.[42] If you have added qualifications, point them out: "With my 18 months of experience in the field, I would expect to start in the middle of the normal salary range." You can find industry salary ranges at the Bureau of Labor Statistics website, www.bls.gov, or at several of the popular job websites.

If you don't like the offer, you might try to negotiate, provided you're in a good bargaining position and the organization has the flexibility to accommodate you. You'll be in a fairly strong position if your skills are in short supply and you have several other offers. It also helps if you're the favorite candidate and the organization is booming. However, many or-

CHECKLIST: Making a Positive Impression in Job Interviews

A. The Warm-Up
- Stay on your toes; even initial small talk is part of the interviewing process.
- Greet the interviewer by name, with a smile and direct eye contact.
- Offer a firm (not crushing) handshake if the interviewer extends a hand.
- Take a seat only after the interviewer invites you to sit or has taken his or her own seat.
- Listen for cues about what the questions are trying to reveal about you and your qualifications.

B. The Question-and-Answer Stage
- Let the interviewer lead the conversation.
- Never answer a question before the interviewer finishes asking it.
- Listen carefully to the interviewer and watch for nonverbal signals.
- Don't limit yourself to simple yes or no answers; expand on the answer to show your knowledge of the company (but don't ramble on).

- If you encounter a potentially discriminatory question, decide how you want to respond before you say anything.
- When you have the opportunity, ask questions from the list you've prepared; remember that interviewers expect you to ask questions.

C. The Close
- Watch and listen for signs that the interview is about to end.
- Quickly evaluate how well you've done and correct any misperceptions the interviewer might have.
- If you receive an offer and aren't ready to decide, it's entirely appropriate to ask for time to think about it.
- Don't bring up salary, but be prepared to discuss it if the interviewer raises the subject.
- End with a warm smile and a handshake, and thank the interviewer for meeting with you.

ganizations are relatively rigid in their salary practices, particularly at the entry level. In the United States and some European countries, it is perfectly acceptable to ask, "Is there any room for negotiation?"

Salary will probably be the most important component of your compensation and benefits package, but it's not the only factor by any means. And even if salary isn't negotiable, you may find flexibility in a signing bonus, profit sharing, pension and other retirement benefits, health coverage, vacation time, stock options, and other valuable elements in the overall compensation and benefits package.[43]

Negotiating benefits may be one way to get more value from an employment package.

To review the important tips for successful interviews, see "Checklist: Making a Positive Impression in Job Interviews."

Interview Notes

If yours is a typical job search, you'll have many interviews before you accept an offer. For that reason, keeping a notebook or simple database of interview notes can help you refresh your memory of each conversation. As soon as you leave the interview facility, jot down the names and titles of the people you met. Briefly summarize the interviewer's answers to your questions. Then quickly evaluate your performance during the interview, listing what you handled well and what you didn't. Going over these notes can help you improve your performance in the future.[44] In addition to improving your performance during interviews, interview notes will help you keep track of any follow-up messages you'll need to send.

Keep a written record of your job interviews, and keep them organized so that you can compare companies and opportunities.

FOLLOWING UP AFTER THE INTERVIEW

Touching base with the prospective employer after the interview, either by phone or in writing, shows that you really want the job and are determined to get it. This also gives you another chance to demonstrate your communication skills and sense of business etiquette. Following up brings your name to the interviewer's attention once again and reminds him or her that you're actively looking and waiting for the decision.

6 LEARNING OBJECTIVE

Identify the most common employment messages that follow an interview and explain when you would use each one

Six types of follow-up messages:
- *Thank-you message*
- *Message of inquiry*
- *Request for a time extension*
- *Letter of acceptance*
- *Letter declining a job offer*
- *Letter of resignation*

The two most common forms of follow-up are the thank-you message and the inquiry. These messages are often handled by letter, but an e-mail or a phone call can be just as effective, particularly if the employer seems to favor a casual, personal style. Other types of follow-up messages—letters requesting a time extension, letters of acceptance, letters declining a job offer, and letters of resignation—are best handled in writing to document any official actions relating to your employment.

Thank-You Message

Express your thanks within two days after the interview, even if you feel you have little chance for the job. Not only is this good etiquette, but it leaves a positive impression. Acknowledge the interviewer's time and courtesy, and convey your continued interest, then ask politely for a decision (see Figure 19.4).

Keep your thank-you message brief (less than five minutes for a phone call or just two or three paragraphs for a letter or e-mail message), and organize it like a routine message. Demonstrate the "you" attitude, and sound positive without sounding overconfident. Even if the interviewer has said that you are unqualified for the job, a thank-you message may keep the door open to future opportunities.

Message of Inquiry

To inquire about a hiring decision, follow the model for a direct request.

If you're not advised of the interviewer's decision by the promised date or within two weeks, you might make an inquiry. A message of inquiry is particularly appropriate if you've received a job offer from a second firm and don't want to accept it before you have an answer from the first. The following message illustrates the general plan for a direct request; the

FIGURE 19.4 Thank-You Message
In three brief paragraphs, Michael Espinosa acknowledges the interviewer's time and consideration, expresses his continued interest in the position, explains a crucial discussion point that he has reconsidered, and asks for a decision.

Reminds the interviewer of the reasons for meeting and graciously acknowledges the consideration shown to the applicant

Reminds the recruiter of special qualifications

Indicates the writer's flexibility and commitment to the job if hired

Closes on a confident, you-oriented note with a request for a decision

writer assumes that a simple oversight or routine delay, and not outright rejection, is the reason for the delay:

> When we talked on April 7 about the fashion coordinator position in your Park Avenue showroom, you indicated that a decision would be made by May 1. I am still enthusiastic about the position and eager to know what conclusion you've reached.
>
> To complicate matters, another firm has now offered me a position and has asked that I reply within the next two weeks.
>
> Because your company seems to offer a greater challenge, I would appreciate knowing about your decision by Thursday, May 12. If you need more information before then, please let me know.

— Identifies the position and introduces the main idea

— Places the reason for the request second

— Makes a courteous request for specific action last, while clearly stating a preference for this organization

Request for a Time Extension

If you receive a job offer while other interviews are still pending, you'll probably want more time to decide, so write to the offering organization and ask for a time extension. Employers understand that candidates often interview with several companies. They want you to be sure you're making the right decision, so most are happy to accommodate you with a reasonable extension.

Preface your request with a friendly opening. Ask for more time, stressing your enthusiasm for the organization. Conclude by allowing for a quick decision if your request for additional time is denied. Ask for a prompt reply confirming the time extension if the organization grants it. This type of message is, in essence, a direct request. However, because the recipient may be disappointed, be sure to temper your request for an extension with statements indicating your continued interest (see Figure 19.5).

DOCUMENT MAKEOVER

IMPROVE THIS LETTER

To practice correcting drafts of actual documents, visit your online course or the access-code-protected portion of the Companion Website. Click "Document Makeovers," then click Chapter 19. You will find a letter that contains problems and errors relating to what you've learned in this chapter about applying and interviewing for employment. Use the "Final Draft" decision tool to create an improved version of this request for a time extension. Check the letter for all the elements necessary to reassure the potential employer, ask for the extension, explain the reasons for the request, offer to compromise, and facilitate a quick reply.

Letter of Acceptance

When you receive a job offer that you want to accept, reply within five days. Begin by accepting the position and expressing thanks. Identify the job that you're accepting. In the next paragraph, cover any necessary details. Conclude by saying that you look forward to reporting for work. As always, a positive message such as this should convey your enthusiasm and eagerness to cooperate:

Use the model for positive messages when you write a letter of acceptance.

> I'm delighted to accept the graphic design position in your advertising department at the salary of $2,975 a month.
>
> Enclosed are the health insurance forms you asked me to complete and sign. I've already given notice to my current employer and will be able to start work on Monday, January 18.
>
> The prospect of joining your firm is exciting. Thank you for giving me this opportunity for what I'm sure will be a challenging future.

— Confirms the specific terms of the offer with a good-news statement at the beginning

— Covers miscellaneous details in the middle

— Closes with another reference to the good news and a look toward the future

Be aware that a job offer and a written acceptance of that offer can constitute a legally binding contract, for both you and the employer. Before you write an acceptance letter, be sure you want the job.

FIGURE 19.5 Effective Request for a Time Extension
If you need to request more time to make a decision about a job offer, be sure to explain why you need the extension and reaffirm that you are still interested in the job.

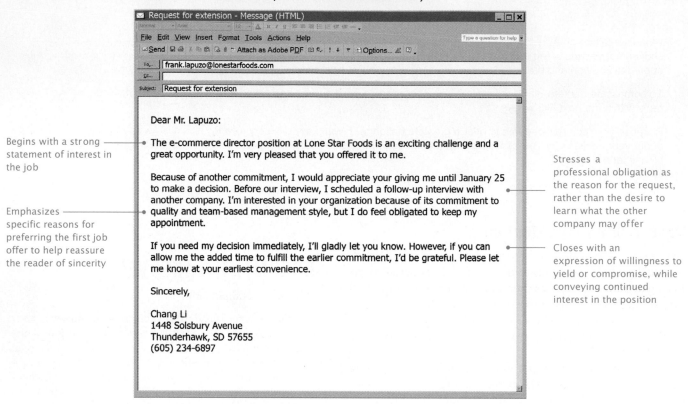

Begins with a strong statement of interest in the job

Emphasizes specific reasons for preferring the first job offer to help reassure the reader of sincerity

Stresses a professional obligation as the reason for the request, rather than the desire to learn what the other company may offer

Closes with an expression of willingness to yield or compromise, while conveying continued interest in the position

Letter Declining a Job Offer

A letter declining a job offer follows the model for negative messages.

After all your interviews, you may find that you need to write a letter declining a job offer. Use the techniques for negative messages (see Chapter 9): Open warmly; state the reasons for refusing the offer; decline the offer explicitly; and close on a pleasant note, expressing gratitude. By taking the time to write a sincere, tactful letter, you leave the door open for future contact:

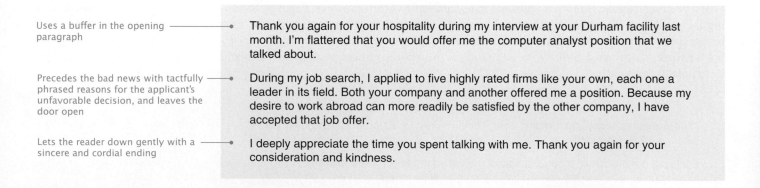

Uses a buffer in the opening paragraph

Precedes the bad news with tactfully phrased reasons for the applicant's unfavorable decision, and leaves the door open

Lets the reader down gently with a sincere and cordial ending

Letter of Resignation

Letters of resignation should always be written in a gracious and professional style that avoids criticism of your employer or your colleagues.

If you get a job offer and are currently employed, you can maintain good relations with your current employer by writing a letter of resignation to your immediate supervisor. Follow the approach for negative messages, and make the letter sound as positive as possible, regardless of how you feel. Don't take this letter as an opportunity to vent any frustrations you may have. Say something favorable about the organization, the people you work with, or what you've learned on the job. Then state your intention to leave and give the date of your last day on the job. Be sure you give your current employer at least two weeks' notice:

My sincere thanks to you and to all the other Emblem Corporation employees for helping me learn so much about serving the public these past two years. You have given me untold help and encouragement.	Uses an appreciative opening to serve as a buffer
You may recall that when you first interviewed me, my goal was to become a customer relations supervisor. Because that opportunity has been offered to me by another organization, I am submitting my resignation. I will miss all of you, but I want to take advantage of this opportunity.	States reasons before the bad news itself, using tactful phrasing to help keep the relationship friendly, should the writer later want letters of recommendation
I would like to terminate my work here two weeks from today but can arrange to work an additional week if you want me to train a replacement.	Discusses necessary details in an extra paragraph
Best wishes to all of you.	Tempers any disappointment with a cordial close

To verify the content and style of your follow-up messages, consult the tips in "Checklist: Writing Follow-Up Messages."

 CHECKLIST: Writing Follow-Up Messages

A. Thank-You Messages
- Write a brief thank-you letter within two days of the interview.
- Acknowledge the interviewer's time and courtesy.
- Restate the specific job you're applying for.
- Express your enthusiasm about the organization and the job.
- Add any new facts that may help your chances.
- Politely ask for a decision.

B. Messages of Inquiry
- If you haven't heard from the interviewer by the promised date, write a brief message of inquiry.
- Use a direct approach: main idea, necessary details, specific request.

C. Requests for a Time Extension
- Request an extension if you have pending interviews and need time to decide about an offer.
- Open on a friendly note.
- Explain why you need more time and express continued interest in the company.
- In the close, promise a quick decision if your request is denied, and ask for a confirmation if your request is granted.

D. Letters of Acceptance
- Send this message within five days of receiving the offer.
- State clearly that you accept the offer, identify the job you're accepting, and confirm vital details such as salary and start date.
- Make sure you want the job; an acceptance letter can be treated as a legally binding contract.

E. Letters Declining a Job Offer
- Use the model for negative messages.
- Open on a warm and appreciative note, then explain why you are refusing the offer.
- End on a sincere, positive note.

F. Letters of Resignation
- Send a letter of resignation to your current employer as soon as possible.
- Begin with an appreciative buffer.
- In the middle section, state your reasons for leaving, and actually state that you are resigning.
- Close cordially.

COMMUNICATION CHALLENGES AT GOOGLE

After a few years of experience in the human resources department of a publishing company, you recently joined Google's recruiting team under Arnnon Geshuri. Today, Geshuri asked you to help with the recruiting and hiring of the project coordinators. These people will provide administrative help to the various engineering teams in the company and also serve as liaisons to other departments.

Individual Challenge: Geshuri is looking for experienced administrative support people who remain calm when things get chaotic and are flexible enough to interact successfully not only with engineers but also with accountants, marketing managers, salespeople, facilities staff, and others. With those requirements in mind, create a list of three or four questions to use during the screening interviews for project coordinators.

Team Challenge: Seven candidates survived the screening process and now you're planning the onsite interviews. In a small group, discuss the types of people to include on the interview team (consult a management textbook if you're unfamiliar with positions in a typical corporation): Who should serve as host and handle the warm-up stage? Who should be involved in the question-and-answer stage? Who should handle the close? In all cases, explain why.

SUMMARY OF LEARNING OBJECTIVES

1 Define the purpose of application letters, and explain how to apply the AIDA organizational approach to them. In addition to explaining why you're sending a résumé, the purpose of an application letter is to convince readers to look at your résumé. This makes application letters a type of sales letter, so you'll want to use the AIDA organizational approach. Get attention in the opening paragraph by showing how your work skills could benefit the organization, by explaining how your qualifications fit the job, or by demonstrating an understanding of the organization's needs. Build interest and desire by showing how you can meet the job requirements, and be sure to refer your reader to your résumé near the end of this section. Finally, motivate action by making your request easy to fulfill and by including all necessary contact information.

2 Describe the typical sequence of job interviews. The typical sequence of interviews involves three stages. During the first or *screening stage*, employers administer fairly structured interviews to eliminate unqualified applicants. During the second or *selection stage*, the pool of applicants is narrowed considerably. The employer administers a series of structured and unstructured interviews to find the best candidates for the job. Those candidates who advance to the third or *final stage* of the sequence have a good chance of receiving a job offer. During this stage, candidates meet with executives who have the authority to offer the job and set compensation. The underlying objective of this final stage is to select the final candidate(s) and convince the candidate(s) to accept a job offer.

3 Describe briefly what employers look for during an employment interview and preemployment testing. Employers look for two things during an employment interview. First, they seek evidence that an applicant will be compatible with the other people in the organization. Whether interviewers focus on personal background or personal style, they are interested in finding someone who will easily adapt to a new workplace and new responsibilities. Second, employers seek evidence that an applicant is qualified for the position. Even though interviewers have already reviewed your résumé, they want to see how well your skills match their requirements and perhaps even get a sense of your ability to be flexible and apply diverse skills in more than one area. Sometimes, interviewers will use preemployment tests to help them gather the evidence they need to make a decision.

4 List six tasks you need to complete to prepare for a successful job interview. To prepare for a successful job interview, begin by (1) refining the research you did when planning your résumé. Knowing as much as you can about the company and its needs helps you highlight the aspects of your background and qualifications that will appeal to the organization. (2) Next, think ahead about questions—both those you'll need to answer and those you'll want to ask. (3) Bolster your confidence by focusing on your strengths to overcome any apprehension. (4) Polish your style by staging mock interviews and paying close attention to nonverbal behaviors, including voice problems. (5) Plan to look your best with businesslike clothing and good grooming. And (6) arrive on time and ready to begin.

5 **Explain the three stages of a successful employment interview.** All employment interviews have three stages. The warm-up stage is the most important, because first impressions greatly influence an interviewer's decision. The question-and-answer stage is the longest, during which you will answer and ask questions. Listening carefully and watching the interviewer's nonverbal clues help you determine how the interview is going. The close is also important because you need to evaluate your performance to see whether the interviewer has any misconceptions that you must correct.

6 **Identify the most common employment messages that follow an interview, and explain when you would use each one.** The two most common types of follow-up messages are usually in letter form but can also be effective by phone or e-mail. You send the *thank-you* message within two days after your interview to show appreciation, express your continued interest in the job, and politely ask for a decision. You send an *inquiry* if you haven't received the interviewer's decision by the date promised or within two weeks of the interview—especially if you've received a job offer from another firm. The remaining four employment messages are best sent in letter form, to document any official action. You request a *time extension* if you receive a job offer while other interviews are pending and you want more time to complete those interviews before making a decision. You send a *letter of acceptance* within five days of receiving a job offer that you want to take. You send a *letter declining a job offer* when you want to refuse an offer tactfully and leave the door open for future contact. You send a *letter of resignation* when you receive a job offer that you want to accept while you are currently employed.

Test Your Knowledge

1. How does the AIDA model apply to an application letter?
2. How does a structured interview differ from an open-ended interview and a situational interview?
3. What is the purpose of a working interview?
4. Why do employers conduct preemployment testing?
5. Why are the questions you ask during an interview as important as the answers you give to the interviewer's questions?
6. What are the three stages of every interview, and which is the most important?
7. How should you respond if an interviewer at a company where you want to work asks you a question that seems too personal or unethical?
8. What should you say in a thank-you message after an interview?
9. What is the purpose of sending a letter of inquiry after an interview?
10. What is the legal significance of a letter of acceptance?

Apply Your Knowledge

1. How can you distinguish yourself from other candidates in a screening interview and still keep your responses short and to the point? Explain.
2. What can you do to make a favorable impression when you discover that an open-ended interview has turned into a stress interview? Briefly explain your answer.
3. If you want to switch jobs because you can't work with your supervisor, how can you explain this situation to a prospective employer? Give an example.
4. If you lack one important qualification for a job but have made it past the initial screening stage, how should you prepare to handle this issue during the next round of interviews? Explain your answer.
5. **Ethical Choices** Why is it important to distinguish unethical or illegal interview questions from acceptable questions? Explain.

Practice Your Knowledge

Messages for Analysis

Read the following documents, then (1) analyze the strengths or weaknesses of each document and (2) revise each document so that it follows this chapter's guidelines.

Message 19.A: Writing an Application Letter

I'm writing to let you know about my availability for the brand manager job you advertised. As you can see from my enclosed résumé, my background is perfect for the position. Even though I don't have any real job experience, my grades have been outstanding considering that I went to a top-ranked business school.

I did many things during my undergraduate years to prepare me for this job:

- Earned a 3.4 out of a 4.0 with a 3.8 in my business courses
- Elected representative to the student governing association
- Selected to receive the Lamar Franklin Award
- Worked to earn a portion of my tuition

I am sending my résumé to all the top firms, but I like yours better than any of the rest. Your reputation is tops in the industry, and I want to be associated with a business that can pridefully say it's the best.

If you wish for me to come in for an interview, I can come on a Friday afternoon or anytime on weekends when I don't have classes. Again, thanks for considering me for your brand manager position.

Message 19.B: Writing Application Follow-Up Messages

Did you receive my résumé? I sent it to you at least two months ago and haven't heard anything. I know you keep résumés on file, but I just want to be sure that you keep me in mind. I heard you are hiring health-care managers and certainly would like to be considered for one of those positions.

Since I last wrote you, I've worked in a variety of positions that have helped prepare me for management. To wit, I've become lunch manager at the restaurant where I work, which involved a raise in pay. I now manage a waitstaff of 12 girls and take the lunch receipts to the bank every day.

Of course, I'd much rather be working at a real job, and that's why I'm writing again. Is there anything else you would like to know about me or my background? I would really like to know more about your company. Is there any literature you could send me? If so, I would really appreciate it.

I think one reason I haven't been hired yet is that I don't want to leave Atlanta. So I hope when you think of me, it's for a position that wouldn't require moving. Thanks again for considering my application.

Message 19.C: Thank-You Message

Thank you for the really marvelous opportunity to meet you and your colleagues at Starret Engine Company. I really enjoyed touring your facilities and talking with all the people there. You have quite a crew! Some of the other companies I have visited have been so rigid and uptight that I can't imagine how I would fit in. It's a relief to run into a group of people who seem to enjoy their work as much as all of you do.

I know that you must be looking at many other candidates for this job, and I know that some of them will probably be more experienced than I am. But I do want to emphasize that my two-year hitch in the Navy involved a good deal of engineering work. I don't think I mentioned all my shipboard responsibilities during the interview.

Please give me a call within the next week to let me know your decision. You can usually find me at my dormitory in the evening after dinner (phone: 877-9080).

Message 19.D: Letter of Inquiry

I have recently received a very attractive job offer from the Warrington Company. But before I let them know one way or another, I would like to consider any offer that your firm may extend. I was quite impressed with your company during my recent interview, and I am still very interested in a career there.

I don't mean to pressure you, but Warrington has asked for my decision within 10 days. Could you let me know by Tuesday whether you plan to offer me a position? That would give me enough time to compare the two offers.

Message 19.E: Letter Declining a Job Offer

I'm writing to say that I must decline your job offer. Another company has made me a more generous offer, and I have decided to accept. However, if things don't work out for me there, I will let you know. I sincerely appreciate your interest in me.

Exercises

For active links to all websites discussed in this chapter, visit this text's website at www.prenhall.com/bovee. Locate your book and click on its Companion Website link. Then select Chapter 19, and click on "Featured Websites." Locate the name of the page or the URL related to the material in the text. Please note that links to sites that become inactive after publication of the book will be removed from the Featured Websites section.

19.1 **Internet** Select a large company (one that you can easily find information on) where you might like to work. Use online sources to gather some preliminary research on the company; don't limit your search to the company's own website.

    a. What did you learn about this organization that would help you during an interview there?

    b. What online sources did you use to obtain this information?

    c. Armed with this information, what aspects of your background do you think might appeal to this company's recruiters?

    d. Based on what you've learned about this company's culture, what aspects of your personality should you try to highlight during an interview?

19.2 **Teamwork** Divide the class into two groups. Half the class will be recruiters for a large chain of national department stores looking to fill manager trainee positions (there are 15 openings). The other half of the class will be candidates for the job. The company is specifically looking for candidates who demonstrate these three qualities: initiative, dependability, and willingness to assume responsibility.

    a. Have each recruiter select and interview an applicant for 10 minutes.

    b. Have all the recruiters discuss how they assessed the applicant in each of the three desired qualities. What questions did they ask or what did they use as an indicator to determine whether the candidate possessed the quality?

    c. Have all the applicants discuss what they said to convince the recruiters that they possessed each of these qualities.

19.3 **Interviews: Understanding Qualifications** Write a short e-mail to your instructor, discussing what you believe are your greatest strengths and weaknesses from an employment perspective. Next, explain how these strengths and weaknesses would be viewed by interviewers evaluating your qualifications.

19.4 **Interviews: Being Prepared** Prepare written answers to 10 of the questions listed in Table 19.3, "Twenty-Five Common Interview Questions."

19.5 **Ethical Choices** You have decided to accept a new position with a competitor of your company. Write a letter of resignation to your supervisor, announcing your decision.

    1. Will you notify your employer that you are joining a competing firm? Please explain.

    2. Will you use the direct or the indirect approach? Please explain.

    3. Will you send your letter by e-mail, send it by regular mail, or place it on your supervisor's desk?

Expand Your Knowledge

Exploring the Best of the Web

Prepare and Practice Before That First Interview
www.job-interview.net
How can you practice for a job interview? What are some questions that you might be asked, and how should you respond?

What questions are you not obligated to answer? Job-interview.net provides mock interviews based on actual job openings. It provides job descriptions, questions and answers for specific careers and jobs, and links to company guides and annual reports. You'll find a step-by-step plan that outlines key job requirements, lists practice interview questions, and helps you put together practice interviews. The site offers tips on the keywords to look for in a job description, which will help you narrow your search and anticipate the questions you might be asked on your first or next job interview. Explore the site, then answer these questions:

1. What are some problem questions you might be asked during a job interview? How would you handle these questions?

2. Choose a job title from the list, and read more about it. What did you learn that could help during an actual interview for the job you selected?

3. Developing an "interview game plan" ahead of time helps you make a strong, positive impression during an interview. What are some of the things you can practice to help make everything you do during an interview seem to come naturally?

Surfing Your Way to Career Success

Bovée and Thill's Business Communication Resources offers links to hundreds of online resources that can help you with this course, your other college courses, and your career. Visit www.buscommresources.com, then click on "Business Communication Web Directory." The "Reference" section connects you to a variety of websites that can help in all aspects of business communication, writing centers and online libraries to dictionaries and encyclopedias and more. Identify three websites from this section that could be useful in your business career. For each site, write a two-sentence summary of what the site offers and how it could help you launch and build your career.

Learn Interactively

Interactive Study Guide

Visit www.prenhall.com/bovee, then locate your book and click on its "Companion Website" link. Select Chapter 19 to take advantage of the interactive "Chapter Quiz" to test your knowledge of chapter concepts. Receive instant feedback on whether you need additional studying. Also, visit the "Study Hall," where you'll find an abundance of valuable resources that will help you succeed in this course.

Peak Performance Grammar and Mechanics

If your instructor has required the use of "Peak Performance Grammar and Mechanics," either in your online course or on CD, you can review the grammar and mechanics skills that you've learned throughout this course. Retake the Pretests, Follow-Up Tests, and even the Advanced Tests to measure your progress, and review weak areas in the Refresher Courses.

CASES

Applying the Three-Step Writing Process to Cases
Apply each step to the following cases, as assigned by your instructor.

PREPARING OTHER TYPES OF EMPLOYMENT MESSAGES

1. Online application: Electronic cover letter introducing a résumé While researching a digital camera purchase, you stumble on the webzine *Megapixel* (www.megapixel.net), which offers product reviews on a wide array of camera models. The quality of the reviews and the stunning examples of photography on the site inspire you to a new part-time business idea—you'd like to write a regular column for *Megapixel*. The webzine does a great job addressing the information needs of experienced camera users, but you see an opportunity to write for "newbies," people who are new to digital photography and need a more basic level of information.

Your task: Write an e-mail message that will serve as your cover letter and address your message to Denys Bouton, who edits the English edition of *Megapixel* (it is also published in French). Try to limit your message to one screen (roughly 20 to 25 lines). You'll need a creative "hook" and a reassuring approach that identifies you as the right person to launch this new feature in the webzine (make up any details about your background that you may need to complete the letter).

2. All over the map: Application letter to Google Earth You've applied yourself with vigor and resolve for four years, and you're just about to graduate with your business degree. While cruising the web to relax one night, you stumble on something called Google Earth. You're hooked instantly by the ability to zoom all around the globe and look at detailed satellite photos of places you've been to or dreamed of visiting. You can even type in the address of your apartment and get an aerial view of your neighborhood. You're amazed at the three-dimensional renderings of major U.S. cities. Plus, the photographs and maps are linked to Google's other search technologies, allowing you to locate everything from ATMs to coffee shops in your neighborhood.

You've loved maps since you were a kid, and discovering Google Earth is making you wish you would have majored in geography instead. Knowing how important it is to follow your heart, you decide to apply to Google anyway, even though you don't have a strong background in geographic information systems. What you do have is a ton of passion for maps and a good head for business.

Your task: Visit http://earth.google.com and explore the system's capabilities (you can download a free copy of the software). In particular, look at the business and government applications of the technology, such as customized aerial photos and maps for real estate sales, land use and environmental impact analysis, and emergency planning for homeland security agencies. Be sure to visit the Community pages as well, where you can learn more about the many interesting applications of this technology. Now draft an e-mail application to Google (address it to jobs@google.com), asking to be considered for the Google Earth team. Think about how you could help the company develop the commercial potential of this product line, and make sure your enthusiasm shines through in the message.

INTERVIEWING WITH POTENTIAL EMPLOYERS

3. Interviewers and interviewees: Classroom exercise in interviewing Interviewing is clearly an interactive process involving at least two people. The best way to practice for interviews is to work with others.

Your task: You and all other members of your class are to write letters of application for an entry-level or management-trainee position requiring a pleasant personality and intelligence but a minimum of specialized education or experience. Sign your letter with a fictitious name that conceals your identity. Next, polish (or create) a résumé that accurately identifies you and your educational and professional accomplishments.

Now, three members of the class who volunteer as interviewers divide up all the anonymously written application letters. Then each interviewer selects a candidate who seems the most pleasant and convincing in his or her letter. At this time the selected candidates identify themselves and give the interviewers their résumés.

Each interviewer then interviews his or her chosen candidate in front of the class, seeking to understand how the items on the résumé qualify the candidate for the job. At the end of the interviews, the class may decide who gets the job and discuss why this candidate was successful. Afterward, retrieve your letter, sign it with the right name, and submit it to the instructor for credit.

4. Internet interview: Exercise in interviewing Locate the website of a company in an industry in which you might like to work, then identify an interesting position within the company. Study the company, using any of the online business resources discussed in Chapter 11, and prepare for an interview with that company.

Your task: Working with a classmate, take turns interviewing each other for your chosen positions. Interviewers should take notes during the interview. Once the interview is complete, critique each other's performance (interviewers should critique how well candidates prepared for the interview and answered the questions; interviewees should critique the quality of the questions asked). Write a follow-up letter thanking your interviewer and submit the letter to your instructor.

FOLLOWING UP AFTER THE INTERVIEW

5. A slight error in timing: Letter asking for delay of an employment decision Thanks to a mix-up in your job application scheduling, you accidentally applied for your third-choice job before going after what you really wanted. What you want to do is work in retail marketing with the upscale department store Neiman Marcus in Dallas; what you have been offered is a similar job with Longhorn Leather and Lumber, 55 dry and dusty miles away in Commerce, just south of the Oklahoma panhandle.

You review your notes. Your Longhorn interview was three weeks ago with the human resources manager, R. P. Bronson, a congenial person who has just written to offer you the position. The store's address is 27 Sam Rayburn Drive, Commerce, TX 75428. Mr. Bronson notes that he can hold the position open for 10 days. You have an interview scheduled with Neiman Marcus next week, but it is unlikely that you will know the store's decision within this 10-day period.

Your task: Write to R. P. Bronson, requesting a reasonable delay in your consideration of his job offer.

6. Job hunt: Set of employment-related letters to a single company Where would you like to work? Choose one of your favorite products, find out which company either manufactures it or sells it in the United States (if it's manufactured in another country). Assume that a month ago you sent your résumé and application letter. Not long afterward, you were invited to come for an interview, which seemed to go very well.

Your task: Use your imagination to write the following: (a) a thank-you letter for the interview, (b) a note of inquiry, (c) a request for more time to decide, (d) a letter of acceptance, and (e) a letter declining the job offer.

The format and layout of business documents vary from country to country; they even vary within regions of the United States. In addition, many organizations develop their own variations of standard styles, adapting documents to the types of messages they send and the kinds of audiences they communicate with. The formats described here are more common than others.

FIRST IMPRESSIONS

Your documents tell readers a lot about you and about your company's professionalism. So all your documents must look neat, present a professional image, and be easy to read. Your audience's first impression of a document comes from the quality of its paper, the way it is customized, and its general appearance.

Paper

To give a quality impression, businesspeople consider carefully the paper they use. Several aspects of paper contribute to the overall impression:

- **Weight.** Paper quality is judged by the weight of four reams (each a 500-sheet package) of letter-size paper. The weight most commonly used by U.S. business organizations is 20-pound paper, but 16- and 24-pound versions are also used.
- **Cotton content.** Paper quality is also judged by the percentage of cotton in the paper. Cotton doesn't yellow over time the way wood pulp does, plus it's both strong and soft. For letters and outside reports, use paper with a 25 percent cotton content. For memos and other internal documents, you can use a lighter-weight paper with lower cotton content. Airmail-weight paper may save money for international correspondence, but make sure it isn't too flimsy.[1]
- **Size.** In the United States, the standard paper size for business documents is 8 1/2 by 11 inches. Standard legal documents are 8 1/2 by 14 inches. Executives sometimes have heavier 7-by-10-inch paper on hand (with matching envelopes) for personal messages such as congratulations and recommendations.[2] They may also have a box of note cards imprinted with their initials and a box of plain folded notes for condolences or for acknowledging formal invitations.
- **Color.** White is the standard color for business purposes, although neutral colors such as gray and ivory are sometimes used. Memos can be produced on pastel-colored paper to distinguish them from external correspondence. In addition, memos are sometimes produced on various colors of paper for routing to separate departments. Light-colored papers are appropriate, but bright or dark colors make reading difficult and may appear too frivolous.

Customization

For letters to outsiders, U.S. businesses commonly use letterhead stationery, which may be either professionally printed or designed in-house using word-processing templates and graphics. The letterhead includes the company's name and address, usually at the top of the page but sometimes along the left side or even at the bottom. Other information may be included in the letterhead as well: the company's telephone number, fax number, cable address, website address, product lines, date of establishment, officers and directors, slogan, and symbol (logo). Well-designed letterhead gives readers[3]

- Pertinent reference data
- A favorable image of the company
- A good idea of what the company does

For as much as it's meant to accomplish, the letterhead should be as simple as possible. Too much information makes the page look cluttered, occupies space needed for the message, and might become outdated before all the stationery can be used. If you correspond frequently with people abroad, your letterhead must be intelligible to foreigners. It must include the name of your country in addition to your cable, telex, e-mail, or fax information.

In the United States, businesses always use letterhead for the first page of a letter. Successive pages are usually plain sheets of paper that match the letterhead in color and quality. Some companies use a specially printed second-page letterhead that bears only the company's name. Other countries have other conventions.

Many companies also design and print standardized forms for memos and frequently written reports that always require the same sort of information (such as sales reports and expense reports). These forms may be printed in sets for use with carbon paper or in carbonless-copy sets that produce multiple copies automatically. More and more organizations use computers to generate their standardized forms, which can save them both money and time.[4]

Appearance

Produce almost all of your business documents using either a printer (letter-quality, not a dot matrix) or a typewriter. Certain documents, however, should be handwritten (such as a short informal memo or a note of condolence). Be sure to handwrite, print, or type the envelope to match the document. However, even a letter on the best-quality paper with the best-designed letterhead may look unprofessional if it's poorly produced. So pay close attention to all the factors affecting appearance, including the following:

- **Margins.** Companies in the United States make sure that documents (especially external ones) are centered on the page, with margins of at least an inch all around. Using word-processing software, you can achieve this balance simply by defining the format parameters.
- **Line length.** Lines are rarely justified, because the resulting text looks too much like a form letter and can be hard to read (even with proportional spacing). Varying line length makes the document look more personal and interesting.
- **Line spacing.** You can adjust the number of blank lines between elements (such as between the date and the inside address) to ensure that a short document fills the page vertically or that a longer document extends at least two lines of the body onto the last page.
- **Character spacing.** Use proper spacing between characters and after punctuation. For example, U.S. conventions include leaving one space after commas, semicolons, colons, and sentence-ending periods. Each letter in a person's initials is followed by a period and a single space. However, abbreviations such as U.S.A. or MBA may or may not have periods, but they never have internal spaces.
- **Special symbols.** Take advantage of the many special symbols available with your computer's selection of fonts. (In Microsoft Word, click on the Insert menu, then select Symbol.) Table A.1 shows some of the more common symbols used in business documents. In addition, see if your company has a style guide for documents, which may include other symbols you are expected to use.

TABLE A.1 Special Symbols on Computer

	COMPUTER SYMBOL
Case fractions	1/2
Copyright	©
Registered trademark	®
Cents	¢
British pound	£
Paragraph	¶
Bullets	●, ♦, ■, □, ✓, ☑, ⊗
Em dash	—
En dash	–

- **Corrections.** Messy corrections are unacceptable in business documents. If you notice an error after printing a document with your word processor, correct the mistake and reprint. (With informal memos to members of your own team or department, the occasional small correction in pen or pencil is acceptable, but never in formal documents.)

LETTERS

All business letters have certain elements in common. Several of these elements appear in every letter; others appear only when desirable or appropriate. In addition, these letter parts are usually arranged in one of three basic formats.

Standard Letter Parts

The letter in Figure A.1 shows the placement of standard letter parts. The writer of this business letter had no letterhead available but correctly included a heading. All business letters typically include these seven elements.

Heading

Letterhead (the usual heading) shows the organization's name, full address, telephone number (almost always), and e-mail address (often). Executive letterhead also bears the name of an individual within the organization. Computers allow you to design your own letterhead (either one to use for all correspondence or a new one for each piece of correspondence). If letterhead stationery is not available, the heading includes a return address (but no name) and starts 13 lines from the top of the page, which leaves a two-inch top margin.

Date

If you're using letterhead, place the date at least one blank line beneath the lowest part of the letterhead. Without letterhead, place the date immediately below the return address. The standard method of writing the date in the United States uses the full name of the month (no abbreviations), followed by the day (in numerals, without *st, nd, rd*, or *th*), a comma, and then the year: July 14, 2008 (7/14/08). Some organizations follow other conventions (see Table A.2). To maintain the utmost clarity in international correspondence, always spell out the name of the month in dates.[5]

When communicating internationally, you may also experience some confusion over time. Some companies in the United States refer to morning (A.M.) and afternoon (P.M.), dividing a 24-hour day into 12-hour blocks so that they refer to four o'clock in the morning (4:00 A.M.) or four o'clock in the afternoon (4:00 P.M.). The U.S. military and European companies refer to one 24-hour period so that 0400 hours (4:00 A.M.) is always in the morning and 1600 hours (4:00 P.M.) is always in the afternoon.[6] Make sure your references to time are as clear as possible, and be sure you clearly understand your audience's time references.

FIGURE A.1 Standard Letter Parts

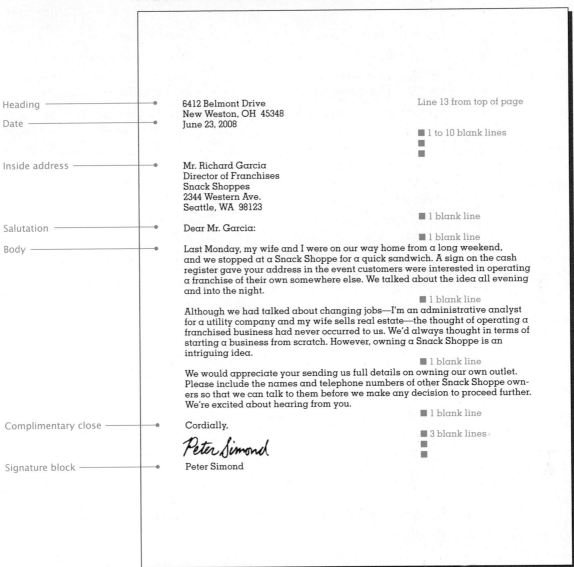

Inside Address

The inside address identifies the recipient of the letter. For U.S. correspondence, begin the inside address at least one line below the date. Precede the addressee's name with a courtesy title, such as *Dr.*, *Mr.*, or *Ms.* The accepted courtesy title for women in business is *Ms.*, although a woman known to prefer the title *Miss* or *Mrs.* is always accommodated. If you don't know whether a person is a man or a woman (and you have no way of finding out), omit the courtesy title. For example, *Terry Smith* could be either a man or a woman. The first line of the inside address would be just *Terry Smith*, and the salutation

TABLE A.2 Common Date Forms

CONVENTION	DESCRIPTION	DATE—MIXED	DATE—ALL NUMERALS
U.S. standard	Month (spelled out) day, year	July 14, 2008	7/14/08
U.S. government and some U.S. industries	Day (in numerals) month (spelled out) year	14 July 2008	14/7/08
European	Replace U.S. solidus (diagonal line) with periods	14 July 2008	14.7.2008
International standard	Year month day	2008 July 14	2008,7,14

TABLE A.3 Forms of Address

PERSON	IN ADDRESS	IN SALUTATION
PERSONAL TITLES		
Man	Mr. [first & last name]	Dear Mr. [last name]:
Woman[1]	Ms. [first & last name]	Dear Ms. [last name]:
Two men (or more)	Mr. [first & last name] and Mr. [first & last name]	Dear Mr. [last name] and Mr. [last name] *or* Messrs. [last name] and [last name]:
Two women (or more)	Ms. [first & last name] and Ms. [first & last name]	Dear Ms. [last name] and Ms. [last name] *or* Mses. [last name] and [last name]:
One woman and one man	Ms. [first & last name] and Mr. [first & last name]	Dear Ms. [last name] and Mr. [last name]:
Couple (married)	Mr. [husband's first name] and Ms. [wife's first name] [couple's last name]	Dear Mr. and Mrs. [last name]:
Couple (married with different last names)	Mr. [first & last name of husband] Ms. [first & last name of wife]	Dear Mr. [husband's last name] and Ms. [wife's last name]:
Couple (married professionals with same title and same last name)	[title in plural form] [husband's first name] and [wife's first name] [couple's last name]	Dear [title in plural form] [last name]:
Couple (married professionals with different titles and same last name)	[title] [first & last name of husband] and [title] [first & last name of wife]	Dear [title] and [title] [last name]:
PROFESSIONAL TITLES		
President of a college or university	[title] [first & last name], President	Dear [title] [last name]:
Dean of a school of college	Dean [first & last name] *or* Dr., Mr., *or* Ms. [first & last name], Dean of (title)	Dear Dean [last name]: *or* Dear Dr., Mr., *or* Ms., [last name]:
Professor	Professor *or* Dr. [first & last name]	Dear Professor *or* Dr. [last name]:
Physician	[first & last name], M.D.	Dear Dr. [last name]:
Lawyer	Mr., *or* Ms. [first & last name] Attorney at Law	Dear Mr. *or* Ms. [last name]:
Service personnel	[full rank, first & last name, abbreviation of service designation] (add *Retired* if applicable)	Dear [rank] [last name]:
Company or corporation	[name of organization]	Ladies and Gentlemen *or* Gentlemen and Ladies
GOVERNMENTAL TITLES		
President of the United States	The President	Dear Mr. *or* Madam President:
Senator of the United States	Honorable [first & last name]	Dear Senator [last name]:
Cabinet member Postmaster General Attorney General	Honorable [first & last name]	Dear Mr. *or* Madam Secretary: Dear Mr. *or* Madam Postmaster General: Dear Mr. *or* Madam Attorney General:
Mayor	Honorable [first & last name], Mayor of [name of city]	Dear Mayor [last name]:
Judge	The Honorable [first & last name]	Dear Judge [last name]:

[1]Use *Mrs.* or *Miss* only if the recipient has specifically requested that you use one of these titles; otherwise *always* use *Ms.* in business correspondence. Also, never refer to a woman by her husband's name (e.g., Mrs. Robert Washington) unless she specifically requests that you do so.

would be *Dear Terry Smith*. The same is true if you know only a person's initials, as in *S. J. Adams*.

Spell out and capitalize titles that precede a person's name, such as *Professor* or *General* (see Table A.3 for the proper forms of address). The person's organizational title, such as *Director,* may be included on this first line (if it is short) or on the line below; the name of a department may follow. In addresses and signature lines, don't forget to capitalize any professional title that follows a person's name:

Mr. Ray Johnson, Dean

Ms. Patricia T. Higgins

Assistant Vice President

However, professional titles not appearing in an address or signature line are capitalized only when they directly precede the name.

President Kenneth Johanson will deliver the speech.

Maria Morales, president of ABC Enterprises, will deliver the speech.

The Honorable Helen Masters, senator from Arizona, will deliver the speech.

If the name of a specific person is unavailable, you may address the letter to the department or to a specific position within the department. Also, be sure to spell out company names in full, unless the company itself uses abbreviations in its official name.

Other address information includes the treatment of buildings, house numbers, and compass directions (see Table A.4). The following example shows all the information that may be included in the inside address and its proper order for U.S. correspondence:

Ms. Linda Coolidge, Vice President
Corporate Planning Department
Midwest Airlines
Kowalski Building, Suite 21-A
7279 Bristol Ave.
Toledo, OH 43617

Canadian addresses are similar, except that the name of the province is usually spelled out:

Dr. H. C. Armstrong
Research and Development
Commonwealth Mining Consortium
The Chelton Building, Suite 301
585 Second St. SW
Calgary, Alberta T2P 2P5

The order and layout of address information vary from country to country. So when addressing correspondence for other countries, carefully follow the format and information that appear in the company's letterhead. However, when you're sending mail from the United States, be sure that the name of the destination country appears on the last line of the address in capital letters. Use the English version of the country name so that your mail is routed from the United States to the right country. Then, to be sure your mail is routed correctly within the destination country, use the foreign spelling of the city name (using the characters and diacritical marks that would be commonly used in the region). For example, the following address uses *Köln* instead of *Cologne:*

H. R. Veith, Director	Addressee
Eisfieren Glaswerk	Company Name
Blaubachstrasse 13	Street address
Postfach 10 80 07	Post office box
D-5000 Köln I	District, city
GERMANY	Country

For additional examples of international addresses, see Table A.5.

Be sure to use organizational titles correctly when addressing international correspondence. Job designations vary around the world. In England, for example, a managing director is often what a U.S. company would call its chief executive officer or president, and a British deputy is the equivalent of a vice president. In France, responsibilities are assigned to individuals without regard to title or organizational structure, and in China the title *project manager* has meaning, but the title *sales manager* may not.

To make matters worse, businesspeople in some countries sign correspondence without their names typed below. In Germany, for example, the belief is that employees represent the company, so it's inappropriate to emphasize personal names.[7] Use the examples in Table A.5 as guidelines when addressing correspondence to countries outside the United States.

TABLE A.4 Inside Address Information

DESCRIPTION	EXAMPLE
Capitalize building names.	Empire State Building
Capitalize locations within buildings (apartments, suites, rooms).	Suite 1073
Use numerals for all house or building numbers, except the number *one*.	One Trinity Lane 637 Adams Ave., Apt. 7
Spell out compass directions that fall within a street address	1074 West Connover St.
Abbreviate compass directions that follow the street address	783 Main St. N.E., Apt. 27

TABLE A.5 International Addresses and Salutations

COUNTRY	POSTAL ADDRESS	ADDRESS ELEMENTS	SALUTATIONS
Argentina	Sr. Juan Pérez Editorial Internacional S.A. Av. Sarmiento 1337, 8° P. C. C1035AAB BUENOS AIRES – CF ARGENTINA	S.A. = Sociedad Anónima (corporation) Av. Sarmiento (name of street) 1337 (building number) 8°= 8th. P = Piso (floor) C (room or suite) C1035AAB (postcode + city) CF = Capital Federal (federal capital)	Sr. = Señor (Mr.) Sra. = Señora (Mrs.) Srta. = Señorita (Miss) Don't use given names except with people you know well.
Australia	Mr. Roger Lewis International Publishing Pty. Ltd. 166 Kent Street, Level 9 GPO Box 3542 SYDNEY NSW 2001 AUSTRALIA	Pty. Ltd. = Proprietory Limited (corp.) 166 (building number) Kent Street (name of street) Level (floor) GPO Box (post office box) city + state (abbrev.) + postcode	Mr. and Mrs. used on first contact. Ms. not common (avoid use). Business is informal—use given name freely.
Austria	Herrn Dipl.-Ing. J. Gerdenitsch International Verlag Ges.m.b.H. Glockengasse 159 1010 WIEN AUSTRIA	Herrn = To Mr. (separate line) Dipl.-Ing. (engineering degree) Ges.m.b.H. (a corporation) Glockengasse (street name) 159 (building number) 1010 (postcode + city) WIEN (Vienna)	Herr (Mr.) Frau (Mrs.) Fräulein (Miss) obsolete in business, so do not use. Given names are almost never used in business.
Brazil	Ilmo. Sr. Gilberto Rabello Ribeiro Editores Internacionais S.A. Rua da Ajuda, 228–6° Andar Caixa Postal 2574 20040–000 RIO DE JANEIRO – RJ BRAZIL	Ilmo. = Ilustrissimo (honorific) Ilma. = Ilustrissima (hon. female) S.A. = Sociedade Anônima (corporation) Rua = street, da Ajuda (street name) 228 (building number) 6° = 6th. Andar (floor) Caixa Postal (P.O. box) 20040–000 (postcode + city) - RJ (state abbrev.)	Sr. = Senhor (Mr.) Sra. = Senhora (Mrs.) Srta. = Senhorita (Miss) Family name at end, e.g., Senhor Ribeiro (Rabello is mother's family—as in Portugal) Given names readily used in business.
China	Xia Zhiyi International Publishing Ltd. 14 Jianguolu Chaoyangqu BEIJING 100025 CHINA	Ltd. (limited liability corporation) 14 (building number) Jianguolu (street name), lu (street) Chaoyangqu (district name) (city + postcode)	Family name (single syllable) first. Given name (2 syllables) second, sometimes reversed. Use Mr. or Ms. at all times (Mr. Xia).
France	Monsieur LEFÈVRE Alain Éditions Internationales S.A. Siège Social Immeuble Le Bonaparte 64–68, av. Galliéni B.P. 154 75942 PARIS CEDEX 19 FRANCE	S.A. = Société Anonyme Siège Social (head office) Immeuble (building + name) 64–68 (building occupies 64, 66, 68) av. = avenue (no initial capital) B.P. = Boîte Postale (P.O. box) 75942 (postcode) CEDEX (postcode for P.O. box)	Monsieur (Mr.) Madame (Mrs.) Mademoiselle (Miss) Best not to abbreviate. Family name is sometimes in all caps with given name following.
Germany	Herrn Gerhardt Schneider International Verlag GmbH Schillerstraße 159 44147 DORTMUND GERMANY	Herrn = To Herr (on a separate line) GmbH (inc.—incorporated) -straße (street—'ß' often written 'ss') 159 (building number) 44147 (postcode + city)	Herr (Mr.) Frau (Mrs.) Fräulein (Miss) obsolete in business. Business is formal: (1) do not use given names unless invited, and (2) use academic titles precisely.

(continued)

TABLE A.5 *Continued*

COUNTRY	POSTAL ADDRESS	ADDRESS ELEMENTS	SALUTATIONS
India	Sr. Shyam Lal Gupta International Publishing (Pvt.) Ltd. 1820 Rehaja Centre 214, Darussalam Road Andheri East BOMBAY – 400049 INDIA	(Pvt.) (privately owned) Ltd. (limited liability corporation) 1820 (possibly office #20 on 18th floor) Rehaja Centre (building name) 214 (building number) Andheri East (suburb name) (city + hyphen + postcode)	Shri (Mr.), Shrimati (Mrs.) but English is common business language, so use Mr., Mrs., Miss. Given names are used only by family and close friends.
Italy	Egr. Sig. Giacomo Mariotti Edizioni Internazionali S.p.A. Via Terenzio, 21 20138 MILANO ITALY	Egr. = Egregio (honorific) Sig. = Signor (not nec. a separate line) S.p.A. = Societá per Azioni (corp.) Via (street) 21 (building number) 20138 (postcode + city)	Sig. = Signore (Mr.) Sig.ra = Signora (Mrs.) Sig.a (Ms.) Women in business are addressed as Signora. Use given name only when invited.
Japan	Mr. Taro Tanaka Kokusai Shuppan K.K. 10–23, 5-chome, Minamiazabu Minato-ku TOKYO 106 JAPAN	K.K. = Kabushiki Kaisha (corporation) 10 (lot number) 23 (building number) 5-chome (area #5) Minamiazabu (neighborhood name) Minato-ku (city district) (city + postcode)	Given names not used in business. Use family name + job title. Or use family name + "-san" (Tanaka-san) or more respectfully, add "-sama" or "-dono."
Korea	Mr. Kim Chang-ik International Publishers Ltd. Room 206, Korea Building 33–4 Nonhyon-dong Kangnam-ku SEOUL 135–010 KOREA	English company names common Ltd. (a corporation) 206 (office number inside the building) 33–4 (area 4 of subdivision 33) -dong (city neighborhood name) -ku (subdivision of city) (city + postcode)	Family name is normally first but sometimes placed after given name. A two-part name is the given name. Use Mr. or Mrs. in letters, but use job title in speech.
Mexico	Sr. Francisco Pérez Martínez Editores Internacionales S.A. Independencia No.322 Col. Juárez 06050 MEXICO D.F.	S.A. = Sociedad Anónima (corporation) Independencia (street name) No. = Número (number) 322 (building number) Col. = Colonia (city district) Juárez (locality name) 06050 (postcode + city) D.F. = Distrito Federal (federal capital)	Sr. = Señor (Mr.) Sra. = Señora (Mrs.) Srta. = Señorita (Miss) Family name in middle: e.g., Sr. Pérez (Martínez is mother's family). Given names are used in business.
South Africa	Mr. Mandla Ntuli International Publishing (Pty.) Ltd. Private Bag X2581 JOHANNESBURG 2000 SOUTH AFRICA	Pty. = Proprietory (privately owned) Ltd. (a corporation) Private Bag (P.O. Box) (city + postcode) or (postcode + city)	Mnr. = Meneer (Mr.) Mev. = Mevrou (Mrs.) Mejuffrou (Miss) is not used in business. Business is becoming less formal, so the use of given names is possible.
United Kingdom	Mr. N. J. Lancaster International Publishing Ltd. Kingsbury House 12 Kingsbury Road EDGEWARE Middlesex HA8 9XG ENGLAND	N. J. (initials of given names) Ltd. (limited liability corporation) Kingsbury House (building name) 12 (building number) Kingsbury Road (name of street/road) EDGEWARE (city—all caps) Middlesex (county—not all caps) HA8 9XG	Mr. and Ms. used mostly. Mrs. and Miss sometimes used in North and by older women. Given names—called Christian names—are used in business after some time. Wait to be invited.

Salutation

In the salutation of your letter, follow the style of the first line of the inside address. If the first line is a person's name, the salutation is *Dear Mr.* or *Ms. Name.* The formality of the salutation depends on your relationship with the addressee. If in conversation you would say "Mary," your letter's salutation should be *Dear Mary,* followed by a colon. Otherwise, include the courtesy title and last name, followed by a colon. Presuming to write *Dear Lewis* instead of *Dear Professor Chang* demonstrates a disrespectful familiarity that the recipient will probably resent.

If the first line of the inside address is a position title such as *Director of Personnel,* then use *Dear Director.* If the addressee is unknown, use a polite description, such as *Dear Alumnus, Dear SPCA Supporter,* or *Dear Voter.* If the first line is plural (a department or company), then use *Ladies and Gentlemen* (look again at Table A.3). When you do not know whether you're writing to an individual or a group (for example, when writing a reference or a letter of recommendation), use *To whom it may concern.*

In the United States some letter writers use a "salutopening" on the salutation line. A salutopening omits *Dear* but includes the first few words of the opening paragraph along with the recipient's name. After this line, the sentence continues a double space below as part of the body of the letter, as in these examples:

Thank you, Mr. Brown,	Salutopening
for your prompt payment of your bill.	Body
Congratulations, Ms. Lake!	Salutopening
Your promotion is well deserved.	Body

Whether your salutation is informal or formal, be especially careful that names are spelled right. A misspelled name is glaring evidence of carelessness, and it belies the personal interest you're trying to express.

Body

The body of the letter is your message. Almost all letters are single-spaced, with one blank line before and after the salutation or salutopening, between paragraphs, and before the complimentary close. The body may include indented lists, entire paragraphs indented for emphasis, and even subheadings. If it does, all similar elements should be treated in the same way. Your department or company may select a format to use for all letters.

Complimentary Close

The complimentary close begins on the second line below the body of the letter. Alternatives for wording are available, but currently the trend seems to be toward using one-word closes, such as *Sincerely* and *Cordially.* In any case, the complimentary close reflects the relationship between you and the person you're writing to. Avoid cute closes, such as *Yours for bigger profits.* If your audience doesn't know you well, your sense of humor may be misunderstood.

Signature Block

Leave three blank lines for a written signature below the complimentary close, and then include the sender's name (unless it appears in the letterhead). The person's title may appear on the same line as the name or on the line below:

Cordially,

Raymond Dunnigan
Director of Personnel

Your letterhead indicates that you're representing your company. However, if your letter is on plain paper or runs to a second page, you may want to emphasize that you're speaking legally for the company. The accepted way of doing that is to place the company's name in capital letters a double space below the complimentary close and then include the sender's name and title four lines below that:

Sincerely,
WENTWORTH INDUSTRIES

(Mrs.) Helen B. Taylor
President

If your name could be taken for either a man's or a woman's, a courtesy title indicating gender should be included, with or without parentheses. Also, women who prefer a particular courtesy title should include it:

Mrs. Nancy Winters

(Miss) Juana Flores

Ms. Pat Li

(Mr.) Jamie Saunders

Additional Letter Parts

Letters vary greatly in subject matter and thus in the identifying information they need and the format they adopt. The letter in Figure A.2 shows how these additional parts should be arranged. The following elements may be used in any combination, depending on the requirements of the particular letter:

- **Addressee notation.** Letters that have a restricted readership or that must be handled in a special way should include such addressee notations as *Personal, Confidential,* or *Please Forward.* This sort of notation appears a double space above the inside address, in all-capital letters.
- **Attention line.** Although not commonly used today, an attention line can be used if you know only the last name of the person you're writing to. It can also direct a letter to a position title or department. Place the attention line on the first line of the inside address and put the company name on the second.[8] Match the address on the envelope with the style of the inside address. An attention line may take any of the following forms or variants of them:

Attention: Dr. McHenry

Attention Director of Marketing

Attention Marketing Department

FIGURE A.2 Additional Letter Parts

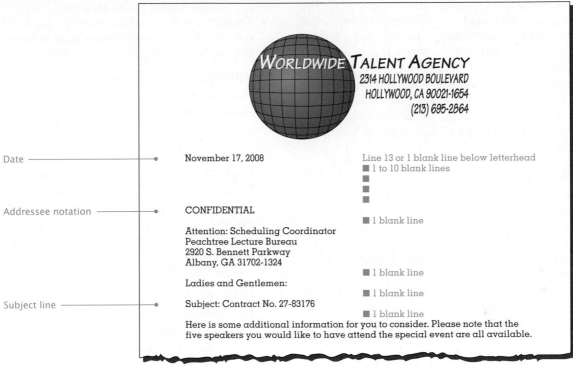

Date

November 17, 2008

Line 13 or 1 blank line below letterhead
■ 1 to 10 blank lines
■
■
■

Addressee notation

CONFIDENTIAL

■ 1 blank line

Attention: Scheduling Coordinator
Peachtree Lecture Bureau
2920 S. Bennett Parkway
Albany, GA 31702-1324

■ 1 blank line

Ladies and Gentlemen:

■ 1 blank line

Subject line

Subject: Contract No. 27-83176

■ 1 blank line

Here is some additional information for you to consider. Please note that the five speakers you would like to have attend the special event are all available.

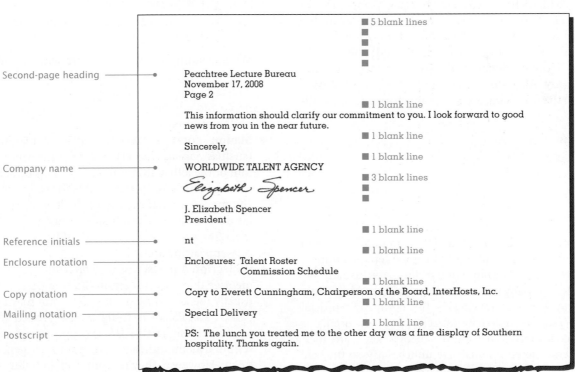

■ 5 blank lines
■
■
■
■

Second-page heading

Peachtree Lecture Bureau
November 17, 2008
Page 2

■ 1 blank line

This information should clarify our commitment to you. I look forward to good news from you in the near future.

■ 1 blank line

Sincerely,

■ 1 blank line

Company name

WORLDWIDE TALENT AGENCY

■ 3 blank lines
■
■

J. Elizabeth Spencer
President

■ 1 blank line

Reference initials

nt

■ 1 blank line

Enclosure notation

Enclosures: Talent Roster
                   Commission Schedule

■ 1 blank line

Copy notation

Copy to Everett Cunningham, Chairperson of the Board, InterHosts, Inc.

■ 1 blank line

Mailing notation

Special Delivery

■ 1 blank line

Postscript

PS: The lunch you treated me to the other day was a fine display of Southern hospitality. Thanks again.

- **Subject line.** The subject line tells recipients at a glance what the letter is about (and indicates where to file the letter for future reference). It usually appears below the salutation, either against the left margin, indented (as a paragraph in the body), or centered. It can be placed above the salutation or at the very top of the page, and it can be underscored. Some businesses omit the word *Subject,* and some organizations replace it with *Re:* or *In re:* (meaning "concerning" or "in the matter of"). The subject line may take a variety of forms, including the following:

Subject: RainMaster Sprinklers

About your February 2, 2008, order

FALL 2008 SALES MEETING

Reference Order No. 27920

- **Second-page heading.** Use a second-page heading whenever an additional page is required. Some companies have second-page letterhead (with the company name and address on one line and in a smaller typeface). The heading bears the name (person or organization) from the first line of the inside address, the page number, the date, and perhaps a reference number. Leave two blank lines before the body. Make sure that at least two lines of a continued paragraph appear on the first and second pages. Never allow the closing lines to appear alone on a continued page. Precede the complimentary close or signature lines with at least two lines of the body. Also, don't hyphenate the last word on a page. All the following are acceptable forms for second-page headings:

Ms. Melissa Baker

May 10, 2008

Page 2

Ms. Melissa Baker, May 10, 2008, Page 2

Ms. Melissa Baker   -2-   May 10, 2008

- **Company name.** If you include the company's name in the signature block, put it all in capital letters a double space below the complimentary close. You usually include the company's name in the signature block only when the writer is serving as the company's official spokesperson or when letterhead has not been used.
- **Reference initials.** When businesspeople keyboard their own letters, reference initials are unnecessary, so they are becoming rare. When one person dictates a letter and another person produces it, reference initials show who helped prepare it. Place initials at the left margin, a double space below the signature block. When the signature block includes the writer's name, use only the preparer's initials. If the signature block includes only the department, use both sets of initials, usually in one of the following forms: *RSR/sm, RSR:sm,* or *RSR:SM* (writer/preparer). When the writer and the signer are different people, at least the file

copy should bear both their initials as well as the typist's: *JFS/RSR/sm* (signer/writer/preparer).

- **Enclosure notation.** Enclosure notations appear at the bottom of a letter, one or two lines below the reference initials. Some common forms include the following:

Enclosure

Enclosures (2)

Enclosures: Résumé

       Photograph

       Attachment

- **Copy notation.** Copy notations may follow reference initials or enclosure notations. They indicate who's receiving a *courtesy copy* (*cc*). Some companies indicate copies made on a photocopier (*pc*), or they simply use *copy* (*c*). Recipients are listed in order of rank or (rank being equal) in alphabetical order. Among the forms used are the following:

cc: David Wentworth, Vice President

pc: Dr. Martha Littlefield

Copy to Hans Vogel

       748 Chesterton Rd.

       Snowhomish, WA 98290

       c: Joseph Martinez with brochure and technical sheet

When sending copies to readers without other recipients knowing place *bc, bcc,* or *bpc* ("blind copy," "blind courtesy copy," or "blind photocopy") along with the name and any other information only on the copy, not on the original.

- **Mailing notation.** You may place a mailing notation (such as *Special Delivery* or *Registered Mail*) at the bottom of the letter, after reference initials or enclosure notations (whichever is last) and before copy notations. Or you may place it at the top of the letter, either above the inside address on the left side or just below the date on the right side. For greater visibility, mailing notations may appear in capital letters.
- **Postscript.** A postscript is an afterthought to the letter, a message that requires emphasis, or a personal note. It is usually the last thing on any letter and may be preceded by *P.S., PS., PS:,* or nothing at all. A second afterthought would be designated *P.P.S.* (post postscript). Since postscripts usually indicate poor planning, generally avoid them. However, they're common in sales letters as a punch line to remind readers of a benefit for taking advantage of the offer.

Letter Formats

A letter format is the way of arranging all the basic letter parts. Sometimes a company adopts a certain format as its policy; sometimes the individual letter writer or preparer is allowed to choose the most appropriate format. In the United States, three major letter formats are commonly used:

- **Block format.** Each letter part begins at the left margin. The main advantage is quick and efficient preparation (see Figure A.3).
- **Modified block format.** Same as block format, except that the date, complimentary close, and signature block start near the center of the page (see Figure A.4). The modified block format does permit indentions as an option. This format mixes preparation speed with traditional placement of some letter parts. It also looks more balanced on the page than the block format does.
- **Simplified format.** Instead of using a salutation, this format often weaves the reader's name into the first line or

two of the body and often includes a subject line in capital letters (see Figure A.5). With no complimentary close, your signature appears after the body, followed by your printed (or typewritten) name (usually in all capital letters). This format is convenient when you don't know the reader's name; however, some people object to it as mechanical and impersonal (a drawback you can overcome with a warm writing style). Because certain letter parts are eliminated, some line spacing is changed.

These three formats differ in the way paragraphs are indented, in the way letter parts are placed, and in some punctuation. However, the elements are always separated by at least one blank line, and the printed (or typewritten) name is always separated from the line above by at least three blank lines

FIGURE A.3 Block Letter Format

NATIONAL GEOGRAPHIC SOCIETY

September 5, 2008

Line 13 or one line below letterhead
■ 1 to 10 blank lines
■

Mr. Stanley Comiskey, General Manager
The Map Store
475 Kenwood Dr.
Duluth, MN 55811

■ 1 blank line

Dear Mr. Comiskey:

■ 1 blank line

You should receive your shipment of wall maps and topographical maps within two weeks, just in time for the holiday shopping season. The merchandise is being shipped by UPS. As the enclosed invoice indicates, the amount due is $352.32.

■ 1 blank line

When preparing to ship your order, I noticed that this is your fifteenth year as a National Geographic Society customer. During that period, you have sold over 3,750 maps! Thanks for your hard work marketing our maps to the public.

■ 1 blank line

Your customers should be particularly excited about the new CD-ROM Topo maps with GPS upgrade. The Topo GPS USA is the ultimate planning software for outdoor recreation. GPS enthusiasts will love using this CD-ROM to plan treks, interact with maps, and live track with a GPS receiver.

■ 1 blank line

Next month, you'll receive our spring catalog. Notice the new series of wall maps that offer a mural-sized panorama. They come in three sections that hang like wallpaper. As a special introductory incentive, you'll receive 15 percent off on all items in this line until the end of January. Please order soon.

■ 1 blank line

Sincerely,

■ 3 blank lines
■
■

Ms. Zeneesia Johnson
Commercial Service Representative

■ 1 blank line

kjc

■ 1 blank line

Enclosure

1145 17th Street N.W., Washington, D.C. 20036-4688

FIGURE A.4 Modified Block Letter Format

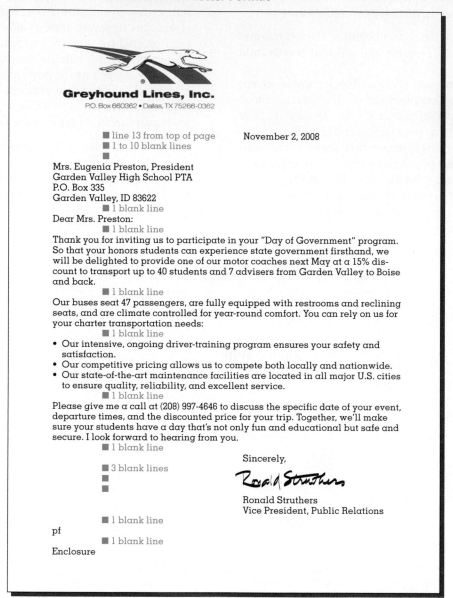

to allow space for a signature. If paragraphs are indented, the indention is normally five spaces. The most common formats for intercultural business letters are the block style and the modified block style.

In addition to these three letter formats, letters may also be classified according to their style of punctuation. *Standard,* or *mixed, punctuation* uses a colon after the salutation (a comma if the letter is social or personal) and a comma after the complimentary close. *Open punctuation* uses no colon or comma after the salutation or the complimentary close. Although the most popular style in business communication is mixed punctuation, either style of punctuation may be used with block or modified block letter formats. Because the simplified letter format has no salutation or complimentary close, the style of punctuation is irrelevant.

ENVELOPES

For a first impression, the quality of the envelope is just as important as the quality of the stationery. Letterhead and envelopes should be of the same paper stock, have the same color ink, and be imprinted with the same address and logo. Most envelopes used by U.S. businesses are No. 10 envelopes (9 1/2 inches long), which are sized for an 8 1/2-by-11-inch piece of paper folded in thirds. Some occasions call for a smaller, No. 6 3/4, envelope or for envelopes proportioned to fit special stationery. Figure A.6 shows the two most common sizes.

Addressing the Envelope

No matter what size the envelope, the address is always single-spaced with all lines aligned on the left. The address on the en-

FIGURE A.5 Simplified Letter Format

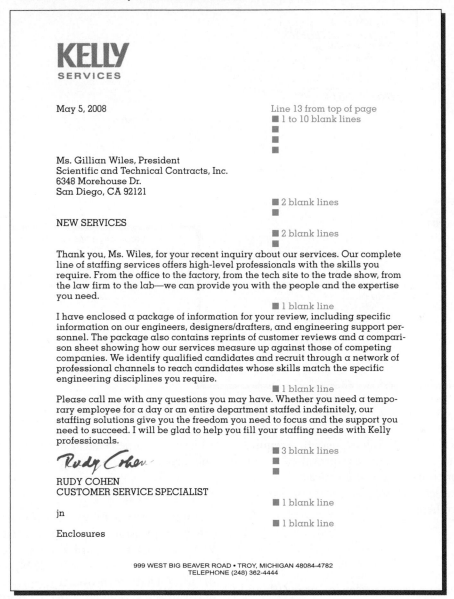

velope is in the same style as the inside address and presents the same information. The order to follow is from the smallest division to the largest:

1. Name and title of recipient
2. Name of department or subgroup
3. Name of organization
4. Name of building
5. Street address and suite number, or post office box number
6. City, state or province, and ZIP code or postal code
7. Name of country (if the letter is being sent abroad)

Because the U.S. Postal Service uses optical scanners to sort mail, envelopes for quantity mailings, in particular, should be addressed in the prescribed format. Everything is in capital letters, no punctuation is included, and all mailing instructions of interest to the post office are placed

above the address area (see Figure A.6). Canada Post requires a similar format, except that only the city is all in capitals, and the postal code is placed on the line below the name of the city. The post office scanners read addresses from the bottom up, so if a letter is to be sent to a post office box rather than to a street address, the street address should appear on the line above the box number. Figure A.6 also shows the proper spacing for addresses and return addresses.

The U.S. Postal Service and the Canada Post Corporation have published lists of two-letter mailing abbreviations for states, provinces, and territories (see Table A.6 on page A-15). Postal authorities prefer no punctuation with these abbreviations, but some executives prefer to have state and province names spelled out in full and set off from city names by a comma. The issue is unresolved, although the comma is most

FIGURE A.6 Prescribed Envelope Format

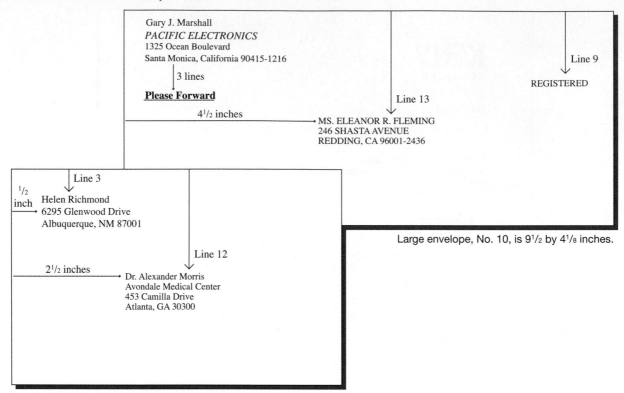

Small envelope, No. 6³/₄, is 6¹/₂ by 3⁵/₈ inches.

often included. Quantity mailings follow post office requirements. For other letters, a reasonable compromise is to use traditional punctuation, uppercase and lowercase letters for names and street addresses, but two-letter state or province abbreviations, as shown here:

Mr. Kevin Kennedy
2107 E. Packer Dr.
Amarillo, TX 79108

For all out-of-office correspondence, use ZIP and postal codes that have been assigned to speed mail delivery. The U.S. Postal Service has divided the United States and its territories into 10 zones (0 to 9); this digit comes first in the ZIP code. The second and third digits represent smaller geographical areas within a state, and the last two digits identify a "local delivery area." Canadian postal codes are alphanumeric, with a three-character "area code" and a three-character "local code" separated by a single space (K2P 5A5). ZIP codes should be separated from state and province names by one space. Canadian postal codes may be treated the same or may be put in the bottom line of the address all by itself.

The U.S. Postal Service has added ZIP + 4 codes, which add a hyphen and four more numbers to the standard ZIP codes. The first two of the new numbers may identify an area as small as a single large building, and the last two digits may identify one floor in a large building or even a specific department of an organization. The ZIP + 4 codes are especially useful for business correspondence. The Canada Post Corporation achieves the same result with special postal codes assigned to buildings and organizations that receive a large volume of mail.

Folding to Fit

The way a letter is folded also contributes to the recipient's overall impression of your organization's professionalism. When sending a standard-size piece of paper in a No. 10 envelope, fold it in thirds, with the bottom folded up first and the top folded down over it (see Figure A.7 on page A-16); the open end should be at the top of the envelope and facing out. Fit smaller stationery neatly into the appropriate envelope simply by folding it in half or in thirds. When sending a standard-size letterhead in a No. 6 3/4 envelope, fold it in half from top to bottom and then in thirds from side to side.

International Mail

Postal service differs from country to country. For example, street addresses are uncommon in India, and the mail there is unreliable.[9] It's usually a good idea to send international correspondence by airmail and to ask that responses be sent that way as well. Also, remember to check the postage; rates for sending mail to most other countries differ from the rates for sending mail within your own country.

International mail falls into three main categories:

- **LC mail.** An abbreviation of the French *Lettres et Cartes* ("letters and cards"), this category consists of letters, letter packages, aerograms, and postcards.

TABLE A.6 Two-Letter Mailing Abbreviations for the United States and Canada

STATE/ TERRITORY/ PROVINCE	ABBREVIATION	STATE/ TERRITORY/ PROVINCE	ABBREVIATION	STATE/ TERRITORY/ PROVINCE	ABBREVIATION
United States		Massachusetts	MA	Texas	TX
Alabama	AL	Michigan	MI	Utah	UT
Alaska	AK	Minnesota	MN	Vermont	VT
American Samoa	AS	Mississippi	MS	Virginia	VA
Arizona	AZ	Missouri	MO	Virgin Islands	VI
Arkansas	AR	Montana	MT	Washington	WA
California	CA	Nebraska	NE	West Virginia	WV
Canal Zone	CZ	Nevada	NV	Wisconsin	WI
Colorado	CO	New Hampshire	NH	Wyoming	WY
Connecticut	CT	New Jersey	NJ	**Canada**	
Delaware	DE	New Mexico	NM	Alberta	AB
District of Columbia	DC	New York	NY	British Columbia	BC
Florida	FL	North Carolina	NC	Labrador	NL
Georgia	GA	North Dakota	ND	Manitoba	MB
Guam	GU	Northern Mariana	MP	New Brunswick	NB
Hawaii	HI	Ohio	OH	Newfoundland	NL
Idaho	ID	Oklahoma	OK	Northwest Territories	NT
Illinois	IL	Oregon	OR	Nova Scotia	NS
Indiana	IN	Pennsylvania	PA	Nunavut	NU
Iowa	IA	Puerto Rico	PR	Ontario	ON
Kansas	KS	Rhode Island	RI	Prince Edward Island	PE
Kentucky	KY	South Carolina	SC	Quebec	QC
Louisiana	LA	South Dakota	SD	Saskatchewan	SK
Maine	ME	Tennessee	TN	Yukon Territory	YT
Maryland	MD	Trust Territories	TT		

- **AO mail.** An abbreviation of the French *Autres Objets* ("other articles"), this category includes regular printed matter, books and sheet music, matter for the blind, small packets, and publishers' periodicals (second class).
- **CP mail.** An abbreviation of the French *Colis Postaux* ("parcel post"), this category resembles fourth-class mail, including packages of merchandise or any other articles not required to be mailed at letter rates.

Along with several optional special services, the U.S. Postal Service also offers the following:

- **Express Mail International Service (EMS).** A high-speed mail service to many countries
- **International Priority Airmail (IPA).** An international service that's as fast as or faster than regular airmail service

- **International Surface Air Lift (ISAL).** A service providing quicker delivery and lower cost for all kinds of printed matter
- **Bulk Letter Service to Canada.** An economical airmail service for letters weighing 1 ounce or less
- **VALUEPOST/CANADA.** A reduced postage rate for bulk mailings
- **International Electronic Post (INTELPOST).** A service offering same- or next-day delivery of fax documents
- **International Postal Money Orders.** A service for transferring funds to other countries

To prepare your mail for international delivery, follow the instructions in the U.S. Postal Service Publication 51, *International Postal Rates and Fees.* Be sure to note instructions

FIGURE A.7 Folding Standard-Size Letterhead

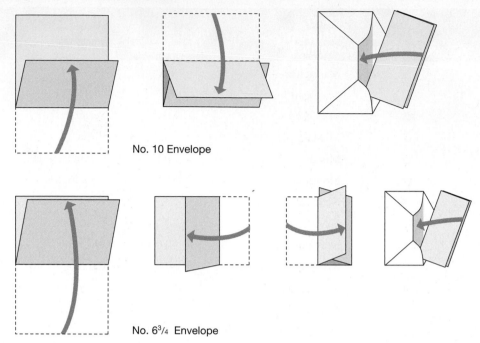

No. 10 Envelope

No. 6³/₄ Envelope

for the address, return address, and size limits. Envelopes and wrappers must be clearly marked to show their classification (letter, small packet, printed matter, airmail). All registered letters, letter packages, and parcel post packages must be securely sealed. Printed matter may be sealed only if postage is paid by permit imprint, postage meter, precanceled stamps, or second-class imprint. Otherwise, prepare contents so that they're protected without hindering inspection. Finally, because international mail is subject to customs examination in the country of destination, the contents and value must be declared on special forms.

MEMOS

Many organizations have memo forms preprinted, with labeled spaces for the recipient's name (or sometimes a checklist of all departments in an organization or all persons in a department), the sender's name, the date, and the subject (see Figure A.8). If such forms don't exist, you can use a memo template (which comes with word-processing software and provides margin settings, headings, and special formats), or you can use plain paper.

On your document, include a title such as *MEMO* or *INTEROFFICE CORRESPONDENCE* (all in capitals) centered at the top of the page or aligned with the left margin. Also at the top, include the words *To, From, Date,* and *Subject*—followed by the appropriate information—with a blank line between, as shown here:

MEMO

TO:

FROM:

DATE:

SUBJECT:

Sometimes the heading is organized like this:

MEMO

TO: DATE:

FROM: SUBJECT:

FIGURE A.8 Preprinted Memo Form

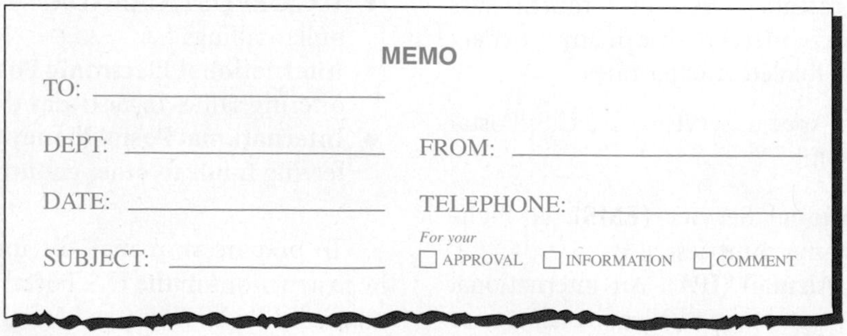

MEMO

TO: _____

DEPT: _____   FROM: _____

DATE: _____   TELEPHONE: _____

                               For your
SUBJECT: _____   ☐ APPROVAL ☐ INFORMATION ☐ COMMENT

You can arrange these four pieces of information in almost any order. The date sometimes appears without the heading *Date*. The subject may be presented with the letters *Re:* (in place of *SUBJECT:*) or may even be presented without any heading (but in capital letters so that it stands out clearly). You may want to include a file or reference number, introduced by the word *File*.

The following guidelines will help you effectively format specific memo elements:

- **Addressees.** When sending a memo to a long list of people, include the notation *See distribution list* or *See below* in the *To* position at the top; then list the names at the end of the memo. Arrange this list alphabetically, except when high-ranking officials deserve more prominent placement. You can also address memos to groups of people—*All Sales Representatives, Production Group, New Product Team*.
- **Courtesy titles.** You need not use courtesy titles anywhere in a memo; first initials and last names, first names, or even initials alone are often sufficient. However, use a courtesy title if you would use one in a face-to-face encounter with the person.
- **Subject line.** The subject line of a memo helps busy colleagues quickly find out what your memo is about. Although the subject "line" may overflow onto a second line, it's most helpful when it's short (but still informative).
- **Body.** Start the body of the memo on the second or third line below the heading. Like the body of a letter, it's usually single-spaced with blank lines between paragraphs. Indenting paragraphs is optional. Handle lists, important passages, and subheadings as you do in letters. If the memo is very short, you may double-space it.
- **Second page.** If the memo carries over to a second page, head the second page just as you head the second page of a letter.
- **Writer's initials.** Unlike a letter, a memo doesn't require a complimentary close or a signature, because your name is already prominent at the top. However, you may initial the memo—either beside the name appearing at the top of the memo or at the bottom of the memo—or you may even sign your name at the bottom, particularly if the memo deals with money or confidential matters.
- **Other elements.** Treat elements such as reference initials, enclosure notations, and copy notations just as you would in a letter.

Memos may be delivered by hand, by the post office (when the recipient works at a different location), or through interoffice mail. Interoffice mail may require the use of special reusable envelopes that have spaces for the recipient's name and department or room number; the name of the previous recipient is simply crossed out. If a regular envelope is used, the words *Interoffice Mail* appear where the stamp normally goes, so that it won't accidentally be stamped and mailed with the rest of the office correspondence.

Informal, routine, or brief reports for distribution within a company are often presented in memo form. Don't include report parts such as a table of contents and appendixes, but write the body of the memo report just as carefully as you'd write a formal report.

E-MAIL

Because e-mail messages can act both as memos (carrying information within your company) and as letters (carrying information outside your company and around the world), their format depends on your audience and purpose. You may choose to have your e-mail resemble a formal letter or a detailed report, or you may decide to keep things as simple as an interoffice memo. A modified memo format is appropriate for most e-mail messages.[10] All e-mail programs include two major elements: the header and the body (see Figure A.9).

Header

The e-mail header depends on the particular program you use. Some programs even allow you to choose between a shorter and a longer version. However, most headers contain similar information.

- **To:** Contains the audience's e-mail address (see Figure A.10). Most e-mail programs also allow you to send mail to an entire group of people all at once. First, you create a distribution list. Then you type the name of the list in the *To:* line instead of typing the addresses of every person in the group.[11] The most common e-mail addresses are addresses such as

  nmaa.betsy@c.si.edu (Smithsonian Institution's National Museum of American Art)

  webwsj@dowjones.com (*Wall Street Journal* homepage)

  relpubli@mairie-toulouse.mipnet.fr (Municipal Services, Toulouse, France)

- **From:** Contains your e-mail address.
- **Date:** Contains the day of the week, date (day, month, year), time, and time zone.
- **Subject:** Describes the content of the message and presents an opportunity for you to build interest in your message.
- **Cc:** Allows you to send copies of a message to more than one person at a time. It also allows everyone on the list to see who else received the same message.
- **Bcc:** Lets you send copies to people without the other recipients knowing—a practice considered unethical by some.[12]
- **Attachments:** Contains the name(s) of the file(s) you attach to your e-mail message. The file can be a word-processing document, a digital image, an audio or video message, a spreadsheet, or a software program.[13]

Most e-mail programs now allow you the choice of hiding or revealing other lines that contain more detailed information, including

FIGURE A.9 A Typical E-Mail Message

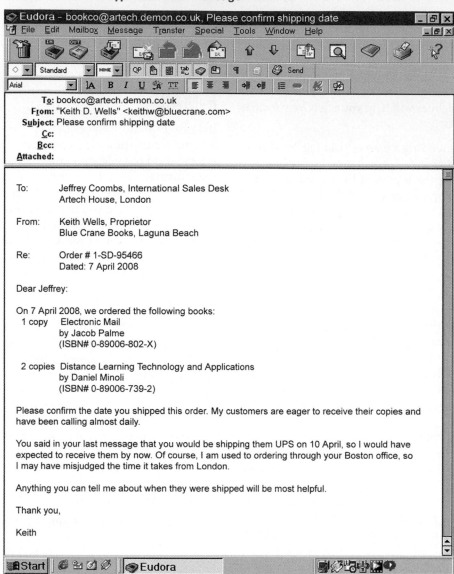

- **Message-Id:** The exact location of this e-mail message on the sender's system
- **X-mailer:** The version of the e-mail program being used
- **Content type:** A description of the text and character set that is contained in the message
- **Received:** Information about each of the systems your e-mail passed through en route to your mailbox.[14]

Body

The rest of the space below the header is for the body of your message. In the *To:* and *From:* lines, some headers actually print out the names of the sender and receiver (in addition to their e-mail addresses). Other headers do not. If your mail program includes only the e-mail addresses, you might consider including your own memo-type header in the body of your message, as in Figure A.9. The writer even included a second, more specific subject line in his memo-type header.

Some recipients may applaud the clarity of such second headers; however, others will criticize the space it takes. Your decision depends on how formal you want to be.

Do include a greeting in your e-mail. As pointed out in Chapter 7, greetings personalize your message. Leave one line space above and below your greeting to set it off from the rest of your message. You may end your greeting with a colon (formal), a comma (conversational), or even two hyphens (informal)—depending on the level of formality you want.

Your message begins one blank line space below your greeting. Just as in memos and letters, skip one line space between paragraphs and include headings, numbered lists, bulleted lists, and embedded lists when appropriate. Limit your line lengths to a maximum of 80 characters by inserting a hard return at the end of each line.

One blank line space below your message, include a simple closing, often just one word. A blank line space below

FIGURE A.10 Anatomy of an E-Mail Address

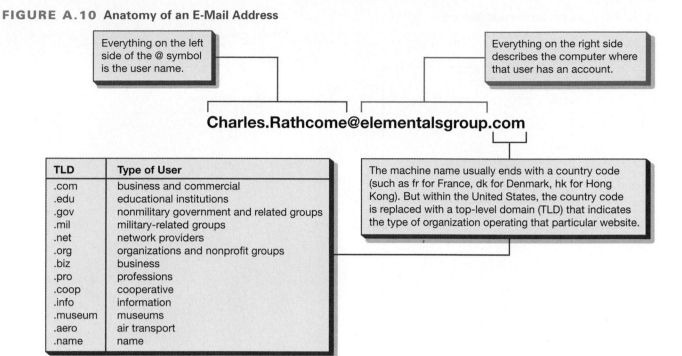

Everything on the left side of the @ symbol is the user name.

Everything on the right side describes the computer where that user has an account.

Charles.Rathcome@elementalsgroup.com

The machine name usually ends with a country code (such as fr for France, dk for Denmark, hk for Hong Kong). But within the United States, the country code is replaced with a top-level domain (TLD) that indicates the type of organization operating that particular website.

TLD	Type of User
.com	business and commercial
.edu	educational institutions
.gov	nonmilitary government and related groups
.mil	military-related groups
.net	network providers
.org	organizations and nonprofit groups
.biz	business
.pro	professions
.coop	cooperative
.info	information
.museum	museums
.aero	air transport
.name	name

that, include your signature. Whether you type your name or use a signature file, including your signature personalizes your message.

REPORTS

Enhance your report's effectiveness by paying careful attention to its appearance and layout. Follow whatever guidelines your organization prefers, always being neat and consistent throughout. If it's up to you to decide formatting questions, the following conventions may help you decide how to handle margins, headings, spacing and indention, and page numbers.

Margins

All margins on a report page are at least 1 inch wide. For double-spaced pages, use 1-inch margins; for single-spaced pages, set margins between 1 1/4 and 1 1/2 inches. The top, left, and right margins are usually the same, but the bottom margins can be 1 1/2 times deeper. Some special pages also have deeper top margins. Set top margins as deep as 2 inches for pages that contain major titles: prefatory parts (such as the table of contents or the executive summary), supplementary parts (such as the reference notes or bibliography), and textual parts (such as the first page of the text or the first page of each chapter).

If you're going to bind your report at the left or at the top, add half an inch to the margin on the bound edge (see Figure A.11). The space taken by the binding on left-bound reports makes the center point of the text a quarter inch to the right

of the center of the paper. Be sure to center headings between the margins, not between the edges of the paper. Computers can do this for you automatically. Other guidelines for report formats are in the Chapter 14 samples.

Headings

Headings of various levels provide visual clues to a report's organization. Figure 11.16, on page 378, illustrates one good system for showing these levels, but many variations exist. No matter which system you use, be sure to be consistent.

Spacing and Indentions

If your report is double-spaced (perhaps to ease comprehension of technical material), indent all paragraphs five character spaces (or about 1/2 inch). In single-spaced reports, block the paragraphs (no indentions) and leave one blank line between them.

Make sure the material on the title page is centered and well balanced, as on the title page of the sample report in Chapter 15. When using a typewriter, proper spacing takes some calculation. To center text in left-bound reports, start a quarter inch to the right of the paper's center. From that point, backspace once for each two letters in the line. The line will appear centered once the report is bound.

To place lines of type vertically on the title page, follow these steps:

1. Count the number of lines in each block of copy, including blank lines.
2. Subtract that total from 66 (the number of lines on an 11-inch page); the result is the number of unused lines.

FIGURE A.11 Margins for Formal Reports

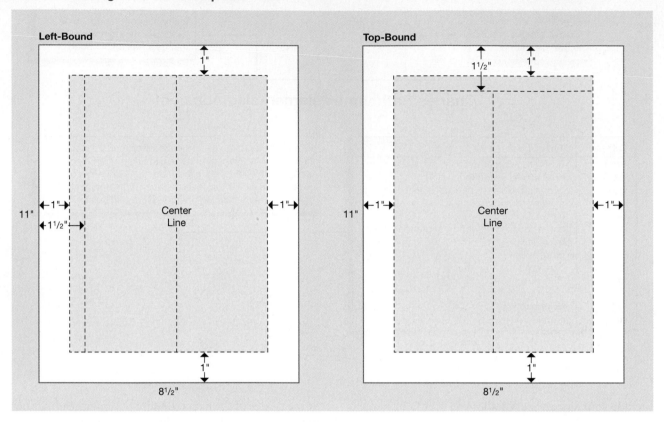

3. Divide the number of unused lines by the number of blank areas (always one more than the number of blocks of copy). The result is the number of blank lines to allocate above, between, and below the blocks of copy.

A computer with a good word-processing program will do these calculations for you at the click of a mouse.

Page Numbers

Remember that every page in the report is counted; however, not all pages show numbers. The first page of the report, normally the title page, is unnumbered. All other pages in the prefatory section are numbered with a lowercase roman numeral, beginning with *ii* and continuing with *iii, iv, v,* and so on. The unadorned (no dashes, no period) page number is centered at the bottom margin.

Number the first page of the text of the report with the unadorned arabic numeral 1, centered at the bottom margin (double- or triple-spaced below the text). In left-bound reports, number the following pages (including the supplementary parts) consecutively with unadorned arabic numerals (2, 3, and so on), placed at the top right-hand margin (double- or triple-spaced above the text). For top-bound reports and for special pages having 2-inch top margins, center the page numbers at the bottom margin.

Appendix B
Documentation of Report Sources

Documenting a report is too important a task to undertake haphazardly. By providing information about your sources, you improve your own credibility as well as the credibility of the facts and opinions you present. Documentation gives readers the means for checking your findings and pursuing the subject further. Also, documenting your report is the accepted way to give credit to the people whose work you have drawn from.

What style should you use to document your report? Experts recommend various forms, depending on your field or discipline. Moreover, your employer or client may use a form different from those the experts suggest. Don't let this discrepancy confuse you. If your employer specifies a form, use it; the standardized form is easier for colleagues to understand. However, if the choice of form is left to you, adopt one of the styles described here. Whatever style you choose, be consistent within any given report, using the same order, punctuation, and format from one reference citation or bibliography entry to the next.

A wide variety of style manuals provide detailed information on documentation. Here is a brief annotated list:

- American Psychological Association, *Publication Manual of the American Psychological Association,* 5th ed. (Washington, DC: American Psychological Association, 2001). Details the author-date system, which is preferred in the social sciences and often in the natural sciences as well.
- *The Chicago Manual of Style,* 15th ed. (Chicago: University of Chicago Press, 2003). Often referred to only as *"Chicago"* and widely used in the publishing industry; provides detailed treatment of source documentation and many other aspects of document preparation.
- Joseph Gibaldi, *MLA Style Manual and Guide to Scholarly Publishing,* 2d ed. (New York: Modern Language Association, 1998). Serves as the basis for the note and bibliography style used in much academic writing and is recommended in many college textbooks on writing term papers; provides a lot of examples in the humanities.
- Andrew Harnack and Eugene Kleppinger, *Online! A Reference Guide to Using Internet Sources with 2003 Update* (New York: St. Martin's Press, 2003). Offers an approach to style for citing online references.

Although many schemes have been proposed for organizing the information in source notes, all of them break the information into parts: (1) information about the author (name), (2) information about the work (title, edition, volume number), (3) information about the publication (place, publisher), (4) information about the date, and (5) information on relevant page ranges.

In the following sections, we summarize the major conventions for documenting sources in three styles: *The Chicago Manual of Style* (Chicago), the *Publication Manual of the American Psychological Association* (APA), and the *MLA Style Manual* (MLA).

CHICAGO HUMANITIES STYLE

The Chicago Manual of Style recommends two types of documentation systems. The *documentary-note,* or *humanities,* style gives bibliographic citations in notes—either footnotes (when printed at the bottom of a page) or endnotes (when printed at the end of the report). The humanities system is often used in literature, history, and the arts. The other system strongly recommended by Chicago is the *author-date* system, which cites the author's last name and the date of publication in the text, usually in parentheses, reserving full documentation for the reference list (or bibliography). For the purpose of comparing styles, we will concentrate on the humanities system, which is described in detail in Chicago.

In-Text Citation—Chicago Humanities Style

To document report sources in text, the humanities system relies on superscripts—arabic numerals placed just above the line of type at the end of the reference:

> Toward the end of his speech, Myers sounded a note of caution, saying that even though the economy is expected to grow, it could easily slow a bit.[10]

The superscript lets the reader know how to look for source information in either a footnote or an endnote (see Figure B.1 on the following page). Some readers prefer footnotes so that they can simply glance at the bottom of the page for information. Others prefer endnotes so that they can read the text without a clutter of notes on the page. Also, endnotes relieve the writer from worrying about how long each note will be and how much space it will take away from the page. Both footnotes and endnotes are handled automatically by today's word-processing software.

For the reader's convenience, you can use footnotes for **content notes** (which may supplement your main text with asides about a particular issue or event, provide a cross-reference to another section of your report, or direct the reader to a related source). Then you can use endnotes for **source notes** (which document direct quotations, paraphrased passages, and visual aids). Consider which type of note is most common in your report, and then choose whether to present these notes all as endnotes or all as footnotes. Regardless of the

FIGURE B.1 Sample Endnotes—Chicago Humanities Style

NOTES

Journal article with volume and issue numbers

1. James Assira, "Are They Speaking English in Japan?" *Journal of Business Communication* 36, no. 4 (Fall 2002): 72.

Brochure

2. BestTemp Staffing Services, *An Employer's Guide to Staffing Services,* 2d ed. (Denver: BestTemp Information Center, 2000), 31.

Newspaper article, no author

3. "Buying Asian Supplies on the Net," *Los Angeles Times,* 12 February 2000, sec. D, p. 3.

Annual report

4. Eurotec, *2001 Annual Report* (New York: Eurotec, Inc., 2001), 48.

Magazine article

5. Holly Graves, "Prospecting Online," *Business Week,* 17 November 2002, 43–5.

Television broadcast

6. Daniel Han, "Trade Wars Heating Up Around the Globe," *CNN Headline News* (Atlanta: CNN, 5 March 2002).

Internet, World Wide Web

7. "Intel—Company Capsule," Hoover's Online [cited 8 March 2003], 3 screens; available from www.hoovers.com/capsules/13787.html.

Book, component parts

8. Sonja Kuntz, "Moving Beyond Benefits," in *Our Changing Workforce,* ed. Randolf Jacobson (New York: Citadel Press, 2001), 213–27.

Unpublished dissertation or thesis

9. George H. Morales, "The Economic Pressures on Industrialized Nations in a Global Economy" (Ph.D. diss., University of San Diego, 2001), 32–47.

Paper presented at a meeting

10. Charles Myers, "HMOs in Today's Environment" (paper presented at the Conference on Medical Insurance Solution, Chicago, Ill., August 2001), 16–17.

Online magazine article

11. Preston Norwalk, "Training Managers to Help Employees Accept Change," in *Business Line* [online] (San Francisco, 2002 [updated 17 September 2002; cited 3 October 2002]); available from www.busline.com/news.

CD-ROM encyclopedia article, one author

12. Robert Parkings, "George Eastman," *The Concise Columbia Encyclopedia* (New York: Columbia University Press, 1998) [CD-ROM].

Interview

13. Georgia Stainer, general manager, Day Cable and Communications, interview by author, Topeka, Kan., 2 March 2000.

Newspaper article, one author

14. Evelyn Standish, "Global Market Crushes OPEC's Delicate Balance of Interests," *Wall Street Journal,* 19 January 2002, sec. A, p. 1.

Book, two authors

15. Miriam Toller and Jay Fielding, *Global Business for Smaller Companies* (Rocklin, Calif.: Prima Publishing, 2001), 102–3.

Government publication

16. U.S. Department of Defense, *Stretching Research Dollars: Survival Advice for Universities and Government Labs* (Washington, D.C.: GPO, 2002), 126.

---

method you choose for referencing textual information in your report, notes for visual aids (both content notes and source notes) are placed on the same page as the visual.

Bibliography—Chicago Humanities Style

The humanities system may or may not be accompanied by a bibliography (because the notes give all the necessary bibliographic information). However, endnotes are arranged in order of appearance in the text, so an alphabetical bibliography can be valuable to your readers. The bibliography may be titled *Bibliography, Reference List, Sources, Works Cited* (if you include only those sources you actually cited in your report), or *Works Consulted* (if you include uncited sources as

well). This list of sources may also serve as a reading list for those who want to pursue the subject of your report further, so you may want to annotate each entry—that is, comment on the subject matter and viewpoint of the source, as well as on its usefulness to readers. Annotations may be written in either complete or incomplete sentences. (See the annotated list of style manuals early in this appendix.) A bibliography may also be more manageable if you subdivide it into categories (a classified bibliography), either by type of reference (such as books, articles, and unpublished material) or by subject matter (such as government regulation, market forces, and so on). Following are the major conventions for developing a bibliography according to Chicago style (see Figure B.2):

FIGURE B.2 Sample Bibliography—Chicago Humanities Style

BIBLIOGRAPHY

Journal article with volume and issue numbers

Assira, James. "Are They Speaking English in Japan?" *Journal of Business Communication* 36, no. 4 (Fall 2002): 72.

Brochure

BestTemp Staffing Services. *An Employer's Guide to Staffing Services*. 2d ed. Denver: BestTemp Information Center, 2000.

Newspaper article, no author

"Buying Asian Supplies on the Net." *Los Angeles Times,* 12 February 2000, sec. D, p. 3.

Annual report

Eurotec. 2001 *Annual Report*. New York: Eurotec, Inc., 2001.

Magazine article

Graves, Holly. "Prospecting Online." *Business Week,* 17 November 2002, 43–5.

Television broadcast

Han, Daniel. "Trade Wars Heating Up Around the Globe." *CNN Headline News*. Atlanta: CNN, 5 March 2002.

Internet, World Wide Web

"Intel—Company Capsule." *Hoover's Online* [cited 8 March 2003]. 3 screens; Available from www.hoovers.com/capsules/13787.html.

Book, component parts

Kuntz, Sonja. "Moving Beyond Benefits." In *Our Changing Workforce*, edited by Randolf Jacobson. New York: Citadel Press, 2001.

Unpublished dissertation or thesis

Morales, George H. "The Economic Pressures on Industrialized Nations in a Global Economy." Ph.D. diss., University of San Diego, 2001.

Paper presented at a meeting

Myers, Charles. "HMOs in Today's Environment." Paper presented at the Conference on Medical Insurance Solutions, Chicago, Ill., August 2001.

Online magazine article

Norwalk, Preston. "Training Managers to Help Employees Accept Change." In *Business Line* [online]. San Francisco, 2002 [updated 17 September 2002; cited 3 October 2002]. Available from www.busline.com/news.

CD-ROM encyclopedia article, one author

Parkings, Robert. "George Eastman." *The Concise Columbia Encyclopedia*. New York: Columbia University Press, 1998. [CD-ROM].

Interview

Stainer, Georgia, general manager, Day Cable and Communications. Interview by author. Topeka, Kan., 2 March 2000.

Newspaper article, one author

Standish, Evelyn. "Global Market Crushes OPEC's Delicate Balance of Interests." *Wall Street Journal,* 19 January 2002, sec. A, p. 1.

Book, two authors

Toller, Miriam, and Jay Fielding. *Global Business for Smaller Companies*. Rocklin, Calif.: Prima Publishing, 2001.

Government publication

U.S. Department of Defense. *Stretching Research Dollars: Survival Advice for Universities and Government Labs*. Washington, D.C.: GPO, 2002.

- Exclude any page numbers that may be cited in source notes, except for journals, periodicals, and newspapers.
- Alphabetize entries by the last name of the lead author (listing last name first). The names of second and succeeding authors are listed in normal order. Entries without an author name are alphabetized by the first important word in the title.
- Format entries as hanging indents (indent second and succeeding lines three to five spaces).
- Arrange entries in the following general order: (1) author name, (2) title information, (3) publication information, (4) date, (5) periodical page range.
- Use quotation marks around the titles of articles from magazines, newspapers, and journals—capitalizing the first and

last words, as well as all other important words (except prepositions, articles, and coordinating conjunctions).
- Use italics to set off the names of books, newspapers, journals, and other complete publications—capitalizing the first and last words, as well as all other important words.
- For journal articles, include the volume number and the issue number (if necessary). Include the year of publication inside parentheses and follow with a colon and the page range of the article: *Journal of Business Communication* 36, no. 4 (2001): 72. (In this source, the volume is 36, the number is 4, and the page is 72.)
- Use brackets to identify all electronic references: [Online database] or [CD-ROM].

- Explain how electronic references can be reached: Available from www.spaceless.com/WWWVL.
- Give the citation date for online references: Cited 23 August 2008.

APA STYLE

The American Psychological Association (APA) recommends the author-date system of documentation, which is popular in the physical, natural, and social sciences. When using this system, you simply insert the author's last name and the year of publication within parentheses following the text discussion of the material cited. Include a page number if you use a direct quote. This approach briefly identifies the source so that readers can locate complete information in the alphabetical reference list at the end of the report. The author-date system is both brief and clear, saving readers time and effort.

In-Text Citation—APA Style

To document report sources in text using APA style, insert the author's surname and the date of publication at the end of a statement. Enclose this information in parentheses. If the author's name is referred to in the text itself, then the number can be omitted from parenthetical material.

> Some experts recommend both translation and back-translation when dealing with any non-English-speaking culture (Assira, 2001).

> Toller and Fielding (2000) make a strong case for small companies succeeding in global business.

Personal communications and interviews conducted by the author would not be listed in the reference list at all. Such citations would appear in the text only.

> Increasing the role of cable companies is high on the list of Georgia Stainer, general manager at Day Cable and Communications (personal communication, March 2, 2008).

List of References—APA Style

For APA style, list only those works actually cited in the text (so you would not include works for background or for further reading). Report writers must choose their references judiciously. Following are the major conventions for developing a reference list according to APA style (see Figure B.3):

- Format entries as hanging indents.
- List all author names in reversed order (last name first), and use only initials for the first and middle names.
- Arrange entries in the following general order: (1) author name, (2) date, (3) title information, (4) publication information, (5) periodical page range.
- Follow the author name with the date of publication in parentheses.
- List titles of articles from magazines, newspapers, and journals without underlines or quotation marks. Capi-

talize only the first word of the title, any proper nouns, and the first word to follow an internal colon.
- Italicize titles of books, capitalizing only the first word, any proper nouns, and the first word to follow a colon.
- Italicize names of magazines, newspapers, journals, and other complete publications—capitalizing all the important words.
- For journal articles, include the volume number (in italics) and, if necessary, the issue number (in parentheses). Finally, include the page range of the article: *Journal of Business Communication, 36*(4), 72. (In this example, the volume is 36, the number is 4, and the page number is 72.)
- Include personal communications (such as letters, memos, e-mail, and conversations) only in text, not in reference lists.
- Electronic references include author, date of publication, title of article, name of publication (if one), volume, date of retrieval (month, day, year), and the source.
- For electronic references, indicate the actual year of publication, and the exact date of retrieval.
- For electronic references, specify the URL, leave periods off the ends of URLs.

MLA STYLE

The style recommended by the Modern Language Association of America is used widely in the humanities, especially in the study of language and literature. Like APA style, MLA style uses brief parenthetical citations in the text. However, instead of including author name and year, MLA citations include author name and page reference.

In-Text Citation—MLA Style

To document report sources in text using MLA style, insert the author's last name and a page reference inside parentheses following the cited material: (Matthews 63). If the author's name is mentioned in the text reference, the name can be omitted from the parenthetical citation: (63). The citation indicates that the reference came from page 63 of a work by Matthews. With the author's name, readers can find complete publication information in the alphabetically arranged list of works cited that comes at the end of the report.

> Some experts recommend both translation and back-translation when dealing with any non-English-speaking culture (Assira 72).

> Toller and Fielding make a strong case for small companies succeeding in global business (102–03).

List of Works Cited—MLA Style

The *MLA Style Manual* recommends preparing the list of works cited first so that you will know what information to give in the parenthetical citation (for example, whether to add a short title if you're citing more than one work by the same au-

FIGURE B.3 Sample References—APA Style

REFERENCES

Journal article with volume and issue numbers

Assira, J. (2002). Are they speaking English in Japan? *Journal of Business Communication, 36*(4), 72.

Brochure

BestTemp Staffing Services. (2000). *An employer's guide to staffing services* (2d ed.) [Brochure]. Denver: BestTemp Information Center.

Newspaper article, no author

Buying Asian supplies on the net. (2000, February 12). *Los Angeles Times*, p. D3.

Annual report

Eurotec. (2001). 2001 *annual report*. New York: Eurotec.

Magazine article

Graves, H. (2002, November 17). Prospecting online. *Business Week*, 43–45.

Television broadcast

Han, D. (2002, March 5). Trade wars heating up around the globe. *CNN Headline News*. [Television broadcast]. Atlanta, GA: CNN.

Internet, World Wide Web

Hoover's Online. (2003). *Intel—Company Capsule*. Retrieved March 8, 2002, from http://www.hoovers.com/capsules/13787.html

Book, component parts

Kuntz, S. (2001). Moving beyond benefits. In Randolph Jacobson (Ed.), *Our changing workforce* (pp. 213–227). New York: Citadel Press.

Unpublished dissertation or thesis

Morales, G. H. (2001). *The economic pressures on industrialized nations in a global economy*. Unpublished doctoral dissertation, University of San Diego.

Paper presented at a meeting

Myers, C. (2001, August). *HMOs in today's environment*. Paper presented at the Conference on Medical Insurance Solutions, Chicago, IL.

Online magazine article

Norwalk, P. (2002, July 17). Training managers to help employees accept change. *Business Line*. Retrieved March 8, 2002, from http://www.busline.com/news

CD-ROM encyclopedia article, one author

Parkings, R. (1998). George Eastman. On *The concise Columbia encyclopedia*. [CD-ROM]. New York: Columbia University Press.

Interview

Cited in text only, not in the list of references.

Newspaper article, one author

Standish, E. (2002, January 19). Global market crushes OPEC's delicate balance of interests. *Wall Street Journal*, p. A1.

Book, two authors

Toller, M., & Fielding, J. (2001). *Global business for smaller companies*. Rocklin, CA: Prima Publishing.

Government publication

U.S. Department of Defense. (2002). *Stretching research dollars: Survival advice for universities and government labs*. Washington, DC: U.S. Government Printing Office.

---

thor, or whether to give an initial or first name if you're citing two authors who have the same last name). The list of works cited appears at the end of your report, contains all the works that you cite in your text, and lists them in alphabetical order. Following are the major conventions for developing a reference list according to MLA style (see Figure B.4):

- Format entries as hanging indents.
- Arrange entries in the following general order: (1) author name, (2) title information, (3) publication information, (4) date, (5) periodical page range.
- List the lead author's name in reverse order (last name first), using either full first names or initials. List second and succeeding author names in normal order.

- Use quotation marks around the titles of articles from magazines, newspapers, and journals—capitalize all important words.
- Italicize the names of books, newspapers, journals and other complete publications, capitalizing all main words in the title.
- For journal articles, include the volume number and the issue number (if necessary). Include the year of publication inside parentheses and follow with a colon and the page range of the article: *Journal of Business Communication* 36.4 (2001): 72. (In this source, the volume is 36, the number is 4, and the page is 72.)
- Electronic sources are less fixed than print sources, and they may not be readily accessible to readers. So citations

FIGURE B.4 Sample Works Cited—MLA Style

WORKS CITED

Journal article with volume and issue numbers	Assira, James. "Are They Speaking English in Japan?" *Journal of Business Communication* 36.4 (2002): 72.
Brochure	BestTemp Staffing Services. *An Employer's Guide to Staffing Services.* 2d ed. Denver: BestTemp Information Center, 2000.
Newspaper article, no author	"Buying Asian Supplies on the Net." *Los Angeles Times* 12 Feb. 2000: D3.
Annual report	Eurotec. *2000 Annual Report.* New York: Eurotec, Inc., 2001.
Magazine article	Graves, Holly. "Prospecting Online." *Business Week* 17 Nov. 2002: 43–45.
Television broadcast	Han, Daniel. "Trade Wars Heating Up Around the Globe." *CNN Headline News.* CNN, Atlanta. 5 Mar. 2002.
Internet, World Wide Web	"Intel—Company Capsule." *Hoover's Online.* 2003. Hoover's Company Information. 8 Mar. 2002 <http://www.hoovers.com/capsules/13787.html>.
Book, component parts	Kuntz, Sonja. "Moving Beyond Benefits." *Our Changing Workforce.* Ed. Randolf Jacobson. New York: Citadel Press, 2001. 213–27.
Unpublished dissertation or thesis	Morales, George H. "The Economic Pressures on Industrialized Nations in a Global Economy." Diss. U of San Diego, 2001.
Paper presented at a meeting	Myers, Charles. "HMOs in Today's Environment." Conference on Medical Insurance Solutions. Chicago. 13 Aug. 2001.
Online magazine article	Norwalk, Preston. "Training Managers to Help Employees Accept Change." *Business Line* 17 July 2002. 8 Mar. 2002 <http://www.busline.com/news>.
CD-ROM encyclopedia article, one author	Parkings, Robert. "George Eastman." *The Concise Columbia Encyclopedia.* CD-ROM. New York: Columbia UP, 1998.
Interview	Stainer, Georgia, general manager, Day Cable and Communications. Telephone interview. 2 Mar. 2000.
Newspaper article, one author	Standish, Evelyn. "Global Market Crushes OPEC's Delicate Balance of Interests." *Wall Street Journal* 19 Jan. 2002: A1.
Book, two authors	Toller, Miriam, and Jay Fielding. *Global Business for Smaller Companies.* Rocklin, CA: Prima Publishing, 2001.
Government publication	United States. Department of Defense. *Stretching Research Dollars: Survival Advice for Universities and Government Labs.* Washington: GPO, 2002.

for electronic sources must provide more information. Always try to be as comprehensive as possible, citing whatever information is available.

- The date for electronic sources should contain both the date assigned in the source and the date accessed by the researcher.

- The URL for electronic sources must be as accurate and complete as possible, from access-mode identifier (http, ftp, gopher, telnet) to all relevant directory and file names. Be sure to enclose this path inside angle brackets: <http://www.hoovers.com/capsules/13787.html>.

Appendix C
Correction Symbols

Instructors often use these short, easy-to-remember correction symbols and abbreviations when evaluating students' writing. You can use them too, to understand your instructor's suggestions and to revise and proofread your own letters, memos, and reports. Refer to the Handbook of Grammar, Mechanics, and Usage (pages H-1– H-20) for further information.

CONTENT AND STYLE

Acc	Accuracy. Check to be sure information is correct.
ACE	Avoid copying examples.
ACP	Avoid copying problems.
Adp	Adapt. Tailor message to reader.
App	Follow proper organization approach. (Refer to Chapter 4.)
Assign	Assignment. Review instructions for assignment.
AV	Active verb. Substitute active for passive.
Awk	Awkward phrasing. Rewrite.
BC	Be consistent.
BMS	Be more sincere.
Chop	Choppy sentences. Use longer sentences and more transitional phrases.
Con	Condense. Use fewer words.
CT	Conversational tone. Avoid using overly formal language.
Depers	Depersonalize. Avoid attributing credit or blame to any individual or group.
Dev	Develop. Provide greater detail.
Dir	Direct. Use direct approach; get to the point.
Emph	Emphasize. Develop this point more fully.
EW	Explanation weak. Check logic; provide more proof.
Fl	Flattery. Avoid compliments that are insincere.
FS	Figure of speech. Find a more accurate expression.
GNF	Good news first. Use direct order.
GRF	Give reasons first. Use indirect order.
GW	Goodwill. Put more emphasis on expressions of goodwill.
H/E	Honesty/ethics. Revise statement to reflect good business practices.
Imp	Imply. Avoid being direct.
Inc	Incomplete. Develop further.
Jar	Jargon. Use less specialized language.

Log	Logic. Check development of argument.
Neg	Negative. Use more positive approach or expression.
Obv	Obvious. Do not state point in such detail.
OC	Overconfident. Adopt humbler language.
OM	Omission.
Org	Organization. Strengthen outline.
OS	Off the subject. Close with point on main subject.
Par	Parallel. Use same structure.
Pom	Pompous. Rephrase in down-to-earth terms.
PV	Point of view. Make statement from reader's perspective rather than your own.
RB	Reader benefit. Explain what reader stands to gain.
Red	Redundant. Reduce number of times this point is made.
Ref	Reference. Cite source of information.
Rep	Repetitive. Provide different expression.
RS	Resale. Reassure reader that he or she has made a good choice.
SA	Service attitude. Put more emphasis on helping reader.
Sin	Sincerity. Avoid sounding glib or uncaring.
SL	Stereotyped language. Focus on individual's characteristics instead of on false generalizations.
Spec	Specific. Provide more specific statement.
SPM	Sales promotion material. Tell reader about related goods or services.
Stet	Let stand in original form.
Sub	Subordinate. Make this point less important.
SX	Sexist. Avoid language that contributes to gender stereotypes.
Tone	Tone needs improvement.
Trans	Transition. Show connection between points.
UAE	Use action ending. Close by stating what reader should do next.
UAS	Use appropriate salutation.
UAV	Use active voice.
Unc	Unclear. Rewrite to clarify meaning.
UPV	Use passive voice.
USS	Use shorter sentences.
V	Variety. Use different expression or sentence pattern.
W	Wordy. Eliminate unnecessary words.
WC	Word choice. Find a more appropriate word.
YA	"You" attitude. Rewrite to emphasize reader's needs.

GRAMMAR, MECHANICS, AND USAGE

Ab	Abbreviation. Avoid abbreviations in most cases; use correct abbreviation.
Adj	Adjective. Use adjective instead.
Adv	Adverb. Use adverb instead.
Agr	Agreement. Make subject and verb or noun and pronoun agree.
Ap	Appearance. Improve appearance.
Apos	Apostrophe. Check use of apostrophe.
Art	Article. Use correct article.
BC	Be consistent.
Cap	Capitalize.
Case	Use cases correctly.
CoAdj	Coordinate adjective. Insert comma between coordinate adjectives; delete comma between adjective and compound noun.
CS	Comma splice. Use period or semicolon to separate clauses.
DM	Dangling modifier. Rewrite so that modifier clearly relates to subject of sentence.
Exp	Expletive. Avoid expletive beginnings, such as it is, there are, there is, this is, and these are.
F	Format. Improve layout of document.
Frag	Fragment. Rewrite as complete sentence.
Gram	Grammar. Correct grammatical error.
HCA	Hyphenate compound adjective.
lc	Lowercase. Do not use capital letter.
M	Margins. Improve frame around document.
MM	Misplaced modifier. Place modifier close to word it modifies.
NRC	Nonrestrictive clause (or phrase). Separate from rest of sentence with commas.
P	Punctuation. Use correct punctuation.
Par	Parallel. Use same structure.
PH	Place higher. Move document up on page.
PL	Place lower. Move document down on page.
Prep	Preposition. Use correct preposition.
RC	Restrictive clause (or phrase). Remove commas that separate clause from rest of sentence.
RO	Run-on sentence. Separate two sentences with comma and coordinating conjunction or with semicolon.
SC	Series comma. Add comma before *and*.
SI	Split infinitive. Do not separate *to* from rest of verb.
Sp	Spelling error. Consult dictionary.
S-V	Subject-verb pair. Do not separate with comma.
Syl	Syllabification. Divide word between syllables.
WD	Word division. Check dictionary for proper end-of-line hyphenation.
WW	Wrong word. Replace with another word.

PROOFREADING MARKS

Symbol	Meaning	Symbol Used in Context	Corrected Copy
═══	Align horizontally	meaningful ᴿᵉsult	meaningful result
‖	Align vertically	1. Power cable 2. Keyboard	1. Power cable 2. Keyboard
≡	Capitalize	Pepsico, Inc.	PepsiCo, Inc.
⊐⊏	Center	⊐Awards Banquet⊏	Awards Banquet
◡	Close up space	self- confidence	self-confidence
ℓ	Delete	harassment and abuse ℓ	harassment
(ds)	Double-space	text in first line text in second line (ds)	text in first line text in second line
∧	Insert	turquoise shirts (and white)	turquoise and white shirts
∨	Insert apostrophe	our teams goals	our team's goals
∧	Insert comma	a, b and c	a, b, and c
=	Insert hyphen	third quarter sales	third-quarter sales
⊙	Insert period	Harrigan et al⊙	Harrigan et al.
∨ ∨	Insert quotation marks	This team isn't cooperating.	This "team" isn't cooperating.
#	Insert space	real estate testcase	real estate test case
/	Lowercase	TULSA, South of here	Tulsa, south of here
⌞ ⌟	Move down	Sincerely,	Sincerely,
⊏	Move left	Attention: ⊏Security	Attention: Security
⊐	Move right	February 2, 2003 ⊐	February 2, 2003
⌐⌐	Move up	THIRD-QUARTER SALES	THIRD-QUARTER SALES
(STET)	Restore	staff talked openly and frankly ℓ (STET)	staff talked openly
⌇	Run lines together	Manager, Distribution	Manager, Distribution
(ss)	Single space	text in first line text in second line	text in first line text in second line
⬯	Spell out	(COD)	cash on delivery
(sp)	Spell out	(sp) (Assn. of Biochem. Engrs.)	Association of Biochemical Engineers
⌐	Start new line	Marla Fenton, Manager, Distri-bution	Marla Fenton, Manager, Distribution
¶	Start new paragraph	¶The solution is easy to determine but difficult to implement in a competitive environment like the one we now face.	The solution is easy to determine but difficult to implement in a competitive environment like the one we now face.
∼	Transpose	airy, light, casual tone	light, airy, casual tone
(bf)	Use boldface	Recommendations (bf)	**Recommendations**
(ital)	Use italics	Quarterly Report (ital)	*Quarterly Report*

Your instructor may elect to show you one or more of the videos described on the following pages. These programs supplement course concepts with real-life examples of businesspeople meeting important communication challenges. This video guide includes several review and analysis questions as well as exercises for each video. Be sure to review the appropriate page ahead of time so that you'll know what to look for when you watch the video.

ETHICAL COMMUNICATION

Learning Objectives

After viewing this video, you will be able to

1. Describe a process for deciding what is ethical or unethical
2. Explain the importance of meeting your personal and professional responsibilities in an ethical manner
3. Discuss the possible consequences of ethical and unethical choices and talk about the impact of these choices on direct and related audiences

Background Information

Communication is ethical when it includes all relevant information, when it's true in every sense, and when it isn't deceptive in any way. In contrast, communication is unethical when it includes false information, fails to include important information, or otherwise misleads an audience. To avoid unethical choices in your communication efforts, you must consider not only legal issues but also the needs of your audience and the expectations of society and your employer. In turn, companies that demonstrate high standards of ethics maintain credibility with employees, customers, and other stakeholders.

The Video

This video identifies two important tools in a communicator's toolbox: honesty and objectivity. These tools help businesspeople resolve ethical dilemmas and avoid ethical lapses, both within the company and during interactions with outside audiences. Poor ethical choices can damage a company's credibility and put employees, customers, and the surrounding community at risk. Unfortunately, some ethical choices are neither clear nor simple, and you may face situations in which the needs of one group or individual must be weighed against the needs of another.

Discussion Questions

1. Would you ever consider compromising your ethics for self-gain? If so, under what circumstances? If not, why?

2. The video mentions the role of misrepresentations in the collapse of Enron. If you were the head of communications at Enron and had some knowledge of the true nature of the company's financial condition, what would you have done?
3. Identify risks involved when you choose to act in an unethical manner.
4. How can you be an effective business communicator without credibility?
5. Is it ethical to call in sick to work, even though you are not ill? What happens to your credibility if someone finds out you were not sick?

Follow-Up Assignment

Many businesses, from small companies to large corporations, formulate codes of ethics that outline ethical standards for employees. Review IBM's guidelines, which are posted on its website at www.ibm.com/investor/corpgovernance/cgbcg.phtml. Now answer the following questions:

1. What does IBM want employees to do if they are aware of unethical situations within the organization?
2. How does IBM view misleading statements or innuendos about competitors?
3. What advice does IBM give employees on the subject of receiving gifts from people outside the company?

For Further Research

Advertising communications, particularly advertising aimed at children, can present a variety of ethical concerns. Retrieve the report "Childhood for Sale" at www.ppionline.org/documents/MARKETING_0804.pdf, which lists the many ways advertisers try to deliver their messages to children. Which of these marketing techniques are unethical in your opinion? Do you agree with the report writer's recommendations for shiedling children from pervasive advertising? Why or why not?

LEARNING TO LISTEN: SECOND CITY COMMUNICATIONS

Learning Objectives

After viewing this video, you will be able to

1. Understand the functions of interpersonal communication in the workplace
2. Identify the ways to overcome barriers to effective communication
3. Discuss the importance of active listening both socially and professionally

Background Information

Chicago's Second City Improv is more than the world's best-known comedy theater. Second City now brings its famous brand of humor to corporate giants such as Coca-Cola, Motorola, and Microsoft. With over 40 years of experience in corporate services, Second City's teachers help business professionals develop communication skills through lessons in improvisational theater. Business Communications Training is Second City's fastest-growing practice, fueled by the demands of more than two hundred Fortune 500 companies. Workshops are tailored to client's needs in such areas as listening and giving presentations, collaborative leadership and team skills, interviewing, breaking down barriers to successful communication, and using humor to convey important messages. The next time you watch improvisational sketch comedy, ask yourself how a lesson in the art of "improv" might give your career a boost.

The Video

In these two video segments, you'll see Second City's training techniques in action. The first segment addresses the need to listen actively, and the second explores techniques for encouraging innovation. The second clip is less focused on communication, but you can see how the techniques for stimulating innovation work equally well for fostering meaningful, two-way conversation that encourages people to open up rather than shut down.

Discussion Questions

1. How do the exercises featured in this video address the contrasting needs of the trial lawyer, the divorce lawyer, and the media buyer?
2. Would ABC's talkative guest Kay Jarman, the 47-year-old award-winning salesperson, be a good candidate for Second City's training workshop?
3. What other workshops might Tom Yorton want to offer companies in response to the current economic and political climate?
4. How might the "yes and" rule of improvisation be used to train customer service representatives at an L.L.-Bean or a Dell computer call center? Without physical cues, such as facial expression and body language, is the "yes and" rule still effective?
5. As President and Managing Director of Second City Communications, Tom Yorton says the following: "You have to be willing to fail to be able to get the results you want...to connect with an audience." Do you agree that this statement is as true in business as it is in comedy? Support your chosen position.

Follow-Up Assignment

Enjoy Second City Communication's website at www.secondcity.com. If you are a loyal fan, you might want to check out the book titles offered and read more about the group's history. Now explore Second City's Corporate Ser-vices: Scan the client roster, read the testimonials, and then select a case study that you find compelling. If you are currently employed, which workshop would be most beneficial to you and to your work team? Explain your choice. If you are not currently employed, how might you and your fellow business students benefit from a Second City workshop? Which workshop would you most like to participate in? Explain how you think it might help you in terms of your social life, your career planning, and your interviewing skills.

For Further Research

The importance of active listening is at the core of *consultative selling*, an approach that emphasizes posing questions to the potential buyer in order to identify needs and expectations—rather than rattling off a prepared sales speech. PublicSpeakingSkills.com (www.publicspeakingskills.com) is one of many companies that offer training in consultative selling. Review the description of the company's Consultative Selling and Negotiating Skills course. Do the principles espoused match the concept of the "you" attitude and the elements of ethical communication that you've learned so far?

COMMUNICATING IN THE GLOBAL WORKPLACE

Learning Objectives

After viewing this video, you will be able to

1. Discuss the challenges of communicating in the global workplace
2. Identify barriers to effective communication across borders
3. Explain the critical role of time in global communication efforts

Background Information

Many businesses are crossing national boundaries to engage in international business. However, operating in a global environment presents a variety of challenges related to culture and communication. Understanding and respecting these challenges can mean the difference between success and failure, so executives must make sure that employees are educated on cultural issues before attempting to do business in other countries.

The Video

This video identifies the challenges to effective communication in the global marketplace, including the barriers posed by language, culture, time, and technology. You will see that a significant amount of research needs to be conducted before a company can engage in successful global business ventures. For instance, if communicators are unaware of differences in gestures, expressions, and dialect, they can inadvertently offend or confuse their audiences. In addition, time zone differences require organizations to plan carefully in advance so that they can develop, translate, and deliver information in a timely manner.

Discussion Questions

1. Language can be a barrier to effective communication. What steps can a company take to minimize language barriers across borders?
2. What characteristics of a country's culture need to be researched to ensure business success across borders?
3. How does a company ensure that a message is properly translated into the local language and dialect of the people it conducts business with?
4. What challenges does a company face when trying to hold a conference call or video meeting with affiliates and employees around the world?
5. The video mentions that some companies have trusted contacts in a country they want to do business with, while other companies rely on a significant amount of research to learn more about culture and other local characteristics. What method do you feel is most effective for gathering useful, accurate, and up-to-date information regarding cultural issues?

Follow-Up Assignment

The Coca-Cola Company has local operations in more than 200 countries throughout the world. Visit www.coca-cola.com to learn more about the company's business activities in a variety of countries. What steps does Coke take to communicate through its website with customers around the world? Does the company strive to develop products that meet local tastes and needs? If so, how and why?

For Further Research

Choose a country other than the United States, and research your selection using both online and library resources to identify important cultural characteristics specific to that country. For example, you may want to gather information about gestures and other nonverbal communication that would be considered offensive, about work habits, or about laws related to conducting business in that country. The characteristics you identify should be useful and accurate.

Based on what you've learned about this country and your personal beliefs, values, and life experiences, is there any risk that you might have a prejudiced or ethnocentric viewpoint regarding people from this country? Why or why not?

IMPACT OF CULTURE ON BUSINESS: SPOTLIGHT ON LATIN AMERICA

Learning Objectives

After viewing this video, you will be able to

1. List key aspects of Latin American culture and indicate the influences on their development

2. Identify factors that might lead to cultural change in Latin America
3. Explain some of the major cultural contrasts within Latin America and their impact on international business operations

Background Information

To a large degree, culture defines the way all human beings interpret and respond to life's changing circumstances. When you interact with people from your own culture, your shared experiences and expectations usually enhance the communication process by providing a common language and frame of reference. However, when you communicate across cultural boundaries, a lack of awareness of your audience's culture—and the subconscious ways that your own culture shapes your perceptions—can result in partial or even total failure of the communication process. Moreover, culture is rarely static, so impressions you may have gathered at one point in your life may need to be revisited and revised over time.

The Video

This video takes a broad look at Latin America's various countries and cultures and explores the business implications of cultural similarities and differences. You'll learn how cultural groups that may appear identical on the surface can in fact have subtle but profound differences. Although communication is just one of many topics discussed in the video, you will get a sense of just how important—and challenging—communication can be when conducting business across cultural boundaries.

Discussion Questions

1. Explain what the video means when it says that your own culture can "sneak up on you."
2. How is business influencing the economic gulf between urban and rural populations in Latin America?
3. How have imperial conquests and slavery affected the populations and cultures of Latin America?
4. How do many outsiders view the issue of business and government corruption in Latin America?
5. Is business etiquette in most of Latin America considered relatively formal or relatively informal?

Follow-Up Assignment

The World Bank plays an important role in today's fast-changing, closely meshed global economy. Visit the bank's website at www.worldbank.org and explore the initiatives programs under way in the Latin American region. How is the bank using this website to foster better communication between Latin America and the rest of the world?

For Further Research

In today's global marketplace, knowing as much as possible about your international customers' business practices and customs could give you a strategic advantage. To help you successfully conduct business around the globe, navigate the resources at the U.S. Government Export Portal. Start at www.export.gov, then click on "Find Country Information" and follow the links to learn more about any country.

How can resources such as this website help U.S. businesses communicate more successfully with customers, employees, and other groups in Latin America?

TECHNOLOGY AND THE TOOLS OF COMMUNICATION

Learning Objectives

After viewing this video, you will be able to

1. Identify technology-related issues to consider when developing communication strategies
2. Identify advantages of using technology as a tool for effective communication
3. Differentiate between "push" and "pull" communication

Background Information

From instant messaging to online meetings, technology has become an integral element of business communication. When used with care, technological tools can help you reach more people in less time with more effective messages. However, when technology is misused or misunderstood, it can cause more problems than it solves. Knowing which technologies to use in every situation—and knowing how to use each one—are vital to your success.

The Video

This video discusses how the Internet, e-mail, voicemail, and other devices have revolutionized the way people communicate. These technological tools increase the speed, frequency, and range of business communication. The video also discusses factors to consider when choosing the most appropriate vehicle for your communication, including the all-important challenge of getting and keeping your audience's attention. The advantages of using technological communication tools are presented throughout the video.

Discussion Questions

1. Identify six questions you need to consider when choosing a technology vehicle for your messages.
2. List the advantages of communicating via e-mail within an organization.
3. What role does technology play in ensuring effective communication within an organization?
4. What are some of the more common challenges that business communicators can encounter when they use technology for communication purposes?
5. Identify the difference between "push" and "pull" communications, and provide an example of each method.

Follow-Up Assignment

VolResource (at www.volresource.org.uk/samples/olcomms.htm) provides practical and informative resources for volunteer organizations that are trying to develop online communication strategies. The VolResource website further details questions that need to be addressed in the process of developing an effective communication strategy for any organization. What issues do you think are the most important to consider? Why?

For Further Exploration

Visit the Yellow Freight website at www.yellowfreight.com and explore the various e-commerce tools this company utilizes to communicate effectively with its customers. Examine these tools and consider their effectiveness. What are some of the advantages of these online communication tools? How do they benefit the client? How do they benefit Yellow Freight?

EFFECTIVE ORAL PRESENTATIONS

Learning Objectives

After viewing this video, you will be able to

1. Reiterate the importance of knowing your audience before creating and delivering oral presentations
2. Discuss the role of teamwork in preparing and delivering complex presentations
3. Explain the importance of anticipating objections likely to be raised during a presentation

Background Information

Oral presentations are a vital communication medium in most companies. In particular, important decisions often involve one or more presentations, either in person or online, in which people advocating a specific choice present their case to the people responsible for making the decision. Such presentations usually combine informational and analytical reporting, along with the persuasive aspects of a proposal. Beyond the mere delivery of information, however, presentations also involve an element of performance. Audiences search for both verbal and nonverbal clues to help them assess presenters' knowledge, confidence, and credibility.

The Video

This video follows three colleagues as they create and deliver a presentation that seeks to convince the audience to approve the purchase of a particular software system that will be used to manage the company's sales force. The presenters explain the importance of understanding the expectations of their audience, from the types of visuals they prefer to the objections they are likely to raise. The team also explains how they took advantage of each member's individual strengths to create a more effective presentation.

Discussion Questions

1. How did the presenters demonstrate their knowledge of the audience?
2. Why did one presenter use a $100 bill as a prop?
3. What are the risks of using props such as the $100 bill?
4. How did the presenters prepare for objections raised by the audience?
5. How would the team need to modify its presentation for an online webcast instead of an in-person oral presentation?

Follow-Up Assignment

Podcasts (audio only) and vidcasts (podcasts with video) are quickly catching on as a medium for business presentations. Visit http://podcasts.yahoo.com/ and click on the Business category. Select any three podcasts. Listen to them while taking careful notes so that you can compare the three selections in terms of grabbing your attention, keeping your attention, and effectively communicating the podcast's information. Which of the three podcasts is the most effective? Why?

For Further Research

Musicians, actors, jugglers—virtually everyone who performs in public experiences *performance anxiety* or *stage fright*, as it is commonly known. This anxiety is simply the natural outcome of caring about how well you do. After all, if you didn't care, you wouldn't feel anxious. Seasoned performers not only recognize that anxiety is natural but they also have learned how to use this emotion to their advantage by giving them extra energy. Visit www.petethomas.co.uk/performance-nerves.html and www.jugglingdb.com (search for "stage fright," then click on the "Collective wisdom on stage fright") and read how these accomplished performers handle the anxiety of performing in public. How can you adapt their techniques to business presentations?

INTERVIEWING SKILLS

Learning Objectives

After viewing this video, you will be able to

1. Explain how the AIDA approach helps create effective application letters
2. Identify mistakes that can cause an otherwise qualified candidate to lose out on a job opportunity
3. Explain why planning for tough questions is such an important part of your interviewing strategy

Background Information

Most companies would admit that the employment interview is an imperfect test of a candidate's skills and personally fit with the organization. In response, some are beginning to add testing, job simulations, and other evaluation tools to the selection process. However, the classic face-to-face interview remains the dominant decision-making tool in the hiring process, so developing your interviewing skills will be vital to your success at every stage in your career.

The Video

This video follows the progress of two candidates applying and interviewing for a technical writing position. One candidate has more experience in this area, but his approach to the interview process ends up costing him the job opportunity. In contrast, a candidate with less experience takes a confident and creative approach that nets her the job.

Discussion Questions

1. Why are multiple StayCom managers involved in this interviewing process? Couldn't one manager handle it?
2. Why does one of the managers compare an application letter to a news story?
3. What steps did Cheryl Yung take to overcome a potential shortcoming in her qualifications?
4. What mistakes did candidate Buddy McCoy make in his interview?
5. Why would the interviewers care about the interpersonal skills of someone who will be writing for a living?

Follow-Up Assignment

Nonverbal cues are important in every communication scenario, but perhaps never more important than in job interviews. Not only are interviewers looking for any clues they can find that will guide their decisions but they also tend to make up their minds quickly—perhaps even before the candidate has said anything at all. Read the advice on nonverbal communication in interviews at www.careerjournal.com/jobhunting/ interviewing/20021205-raudsepp.html. Distill this information down to a half-dozen or so key points that you can write on a note card to study before you step into your next job interview.

For Further Research

You look great in your new interview outfit, your hair is perfect but not too perfect, your smile radiates positive energy, and you're ready to dazzle the interviewer. Then, oops—you discover that your first interview will be held over the telephone, so none of your visual cues will help you at this stage. Don't fret; read the telephone interviewing advice at http://interview.monster.com/articles/phone, and you'll be ready to dazzle the interviewer long-distance.

Handbook of Grammar, Mechanics, and Usage

Grammar and mechanics are nothing more than the way words are combined into sentences. Usage is the way words are used by a network of people—in this case, the community of businesspeople who use English. You'll find it easier to get along in this community if you know the accepted standards of grammar, mechanics, and usage. This handbook offers you valuable opportunities in three sections:

- **Diagnostic Test of English Skills.** Testing your current knowledge of grammar, mechanics, and usage helps you find out where your strengths and weaknesses lie. This test offers 50 items taken from the topics included in this Handbook.
- **Assessment of English Skills.** After completing the diagnostic test, use the assessment form to highlight those areas you most need to review. (To check your answers, you will need to get an answer sheet from your instructor.)
- **Essentials of Grammar, Mechanics, and Usage.** This section helps you brush up on the basics. You can study issues that you've probably already learned but may have forgotten related to the parts of speech, sentence construction, punctuation, capitalization, abbreviations, number style, spelling, proper word usage, and so on. Use this essential review not only to study and improve your English skills but also as a reference for any questions you may have during this course.

Without a firm grasp of the basics of grammar, mechanics, and vocabulary, you risk being misunderstood, damaging your company's image, losing money for your company, and possibly even losing your job. However, once you develop strong English skills, you should be able to create clear and concise messages, to enhance your company's image as well as your own, and to expand your chances of success.

DIAGNOSTIC TEST OF ENGLISH SKILLS

Use this test to help you determine whether you need more practice with grammar, punctuation, mechanics, or vocabulary. When you've answered all the questions, ask your instructor for an answer sheet so that you can score the test. On the Assessment of English Skills form (page H-2), record the number of questions you answered correctly in each section.

The following choices apply to items 1–10. In each blank, write the letter of the choice that best describes the problem with each sentence.

A. sentence incomplete
B. too many phrases/clauses strung together
C. modifying elements misplaced (dangling)
D. structure not parallel
E. nothing wrong

_____ 1. Stop here.
_____ 2. Your duties are interviewing, hiring, and also to fire employees.
_____ 3. After their presentation, I was still undecided.
_____ 4. Speaking freely, the stock was considered a bargain.
_____ 5. Margaret, pressed for time, turned in unusually sloppy work.
_____ 6. Typing and filing, routine office chores.
_____ 7. What do you think he is up to?
_____ 8. When Paul came to work here, he brought some outmoded ideas that were not useful, now he has accepted our modern methods.
_____ 9. To plan is better than improvising.
_____ 10. Hoping to improve performance, practice is advisable.

The following choices apply to items 11–20. In each blank, write the letter of the choice that identifies the underlined word(s) in each sentence.

A. subject
B. predicate (verb)
C. object
D. modifier
E. conjunction/preposition

_____ 11. Take his <u>memo</u> upstairs.
_____ 12. Before leaving, he <u>repaired</u> the photocopier.
_____ 13. <u>Velnor, Inc.</u>, will soon introduce a new product line.
_____ 14. We must hire only <u>qualified</u>, ambitious graduates.
_____ 15. They <u>are having</u> trouble with their quality control systems.
_____ 16. <u>After</u> she wrote the report, Jill waited eagerly for a response.
_____ 17. The route to the plant isn't paved <u>yet</u>.
_____ 18. See <u>me</u> after the meeting.
_____ 19. Your new <u>home</u> is ready and waiting.
_____ 20. BFL is large <u>but</u> caring.

In the blanks for items 21–30, write the letter of the word that best completes each sentence.

_____ 21. Starbucks (A. is, B. are) opening five new stores in San Diego in the next year.
_____ 22. There (A. is, B. are) 50 applicants for the job opening.
_____ 23. Anyone who wants to be (A. their, B. his or her) own boss should think about owning a franchise.

_____ **24.** Neither of us (A. was, B. were) prepared for the meeting.

_____ **25.** Another characteristic of a small business is that (A. they tend, B. it tends) to be more innovative than larger firms.

_____ **26.** After he had (A. saw, B. seen) the revised budget, Raymond knew he wouldn't be getting a new desk.

_____ **27.** The number of women-owned small businesses (A. has, B. have) increased sharply in the past two decades.

_____ **28.** If I (A. was, B. were) you, I'd stop sending personal e-mails at work.

_____ **29.** Eugene (A. lay, B. laid) the files on the desk.

_____ **30.** Either FedEx or UPS (A. has, B. have) been chosen as our preferred shipping service.

The following choices apply to items 31–40. In each blank, write the letter of the choice that best describes the problem with each sentence.

A. error in punctuation
B. error in use of abbreviations or symbols
C. error in use of numbers
D. error in capitalization
E. no errors

_____ **31.** Most of last year's sales came from the midwest.

_____ **32.** We can provide the items you are looking for @ $2 each.

_____ **33.** Alex noted: "few of our competitors have tried this approach."

_____ **34.** Address the letter to professor Elliott Barker, Psychology Department, North Dakota State University.

_____ **35.** They've recorded 22 complaints since yesterday, all of them from long-time employees.

_____ **36.** Leslies' presentation—'New Markets for 2010'—was well-organized.

_____ **37.** We're having a sale in the childrens' department, beginning Wednesday, August 15.

_____ **38.** About 50 of the newly inducted members will be present.

_____ **39.** Mister Spencer has asked me to find eleven volunteers.

_____ **40.** Let's meet in Beth and Larry's office at one o'clock.

In the blanks for items 41–50, write the letter of the word that best completes each sentence.

_____ **41.** Will having a degree (A. affect, B. effect) my chances for promotion?

_____ **42.** Place the latest drawings (A. beside, B. besides) the others.

_____ **43.** Try not to (A. loose, B. lose) this key; we will charge you a fee to replace it.

_____ **44.** Let us help you choose the right tie to (A. complement, B. compliment) your look.

_____ **45.** The five interviewers should discuss the candidates' qualifications (A. among, B. between) themselves.

_____ **46.** New employees spend their time looking for (A. perspective, B. prospective) clients.

_____ **47.** Are the goods you received different (A. from, B. than) the goods you ordered?

_____ **48.** He took those courses to (A. farther, B. further) his career.

_____ **49.** We are (A. anxious, B. eager) to see you next Thursday.

_____ **50.** All commissions will be (A. disbursed, B. dispensed, C. dispersed) on the second Friday of every month.

ASSESSMENT OF ENGLISH SKILLS

In the space provided, record the number of questions you answered correctly.

QUESTIONS	NUMBER YOU GOT CORRECT	SKILL AREA
1–10	_____	Sentence structure
11–20	_____	Grammar: Parts of speech
21–30	_____	Grammar: Verbs and agreement
31–40	_____	Punctuation and mechanics
41–50	_____	Vocabulary

If you scored 8 or lower in any of the skills areas, focus on those areas in the appropriate sections of this Handbook.

ESSENTIALS OF GRAMMAR, MECHANICS, AND USAGE

The following sentence looks innocent, but is it really?

We sell tuxedos as well as rent.

You sell tuxedos, but it's highly unlikely that you sell rent—which is what this sentence says. Whatever you're selling, some people will ignore your message because of a blunder like this. The following sentence has a similar problem:

Vice President Eldon Neale told his chief engineer that he would no longer be with Avix, Inc., as of June 30.

Is Eldon or the engineer leaving? No matter which side the facts are on, the sentence can be read the other way. Now look at this sentence:

The year before we budgeted more for advertising sales were up.

Confused? Perhaps this is what the writer meant:

The year before, we budgeted more for advertising. Sales were up.

Or maybe the writer meant this:

The year before we budgeted more for advertising, sales were up.

These examples show that even short, simple sentences can be misunderstood because of errors on the part of the writer. As you've learned in numerous courses over your schooling, an English sentence consists of the parts of speech being combined with punctuation, mechanics, and vocabulary to convey meaning. Making a point of brushing up on your grammar, punctuation, mechanics, and vocabulary skills will help ensure that you create clear, effective business messages.

1.0 GRAMMAR

Grammar is the study of how words come together to form sentences. Categorized by meaning, form, and function, English words fall into various parts of speech: nouns, pronouns, verbs, adjectives, adverbs, prepositions, conjunctions, articles, and interjections. You will communicate more clearly if you understand how each of these parts of speech operates in a sentence.

1.1 Nouns

A **noun** names a person, place, thing, or idea. Anything you can see or detect with one of your senses has a noun to name it. Some things you can't see or sense are also nouns—ions, for example, or space. So are things that exist as ideas, such as accuracy and height. (You can see that something is accurate or that a building is tall, but you can't see the idea of accuracy or the idea of height.) These names for ideas are known as **abstract nouns**. The simplest nouns are the names of things you can see or touch: *car, building, cloud, brick*; these are termed **concrete nouns**. A few nouns, such as *algorithm, software,* and *code,* are difficult to categorize as either abstract or concrete but can reasonably be considered concrete even though they don't have a physical presence.

1.1.1 Proper Nouns and Common Nouns

So far, all the examples of nouns have been **common nouns**, referring to general classes of things. The word *building* refers to a whole class of structures. Common nouns such as *building* are not capitalized.

If you want to talk about one particular building, however, you might refer to the Glazier Building. The name is capitalized, indicating that Glazier Building is a **proper noun**.

Here are three sets of common and proper nouns for comparison:

COMMON	PROPER
city	Kansas City
company	Blaisden Company
store	Books Galore

1.1.2 Nouns as Subject and Object

Nouns may be used in sentences as subjects or objects. That is, the person, place, thing, or idea that is being or doing (subject) is represented by a noun. So is the person, place, idea, or thing that is being acted on (object). In the following sentence, the nouns are underlined:

The <u>web designer</u> created the <u>home page</u>.

The web designer (subject) is acting in a way that affects the home page (object). The following sentence is more complicated:

The <u>installer</u> delivered the <u>carpeting</u> to the <u>customer</u>.

Installer is the subject. *Carpeting* is the object of the main part of the sentence (acted on by the installer), whereas *customer* is the object of the phrase to the customer. Nevertheless, both *carpeting* and *customer* are objects.

1.1.3 Plural Nouns

Nouns can be either singular or plural. The usual way to make a plural noun is to add *s* or *es* to the singular form of the word:

SINGULAR	PLURAL
file	files
tax	taxes
cargo	cargoes

Many nouns have other ways of forming the plural. Some plurals involve a change in a vowel (*mouse/mice, goose/geese, woman/women*), the addition of *en* or *ren* (*ox/oxen, child/children*), the change from a *y* to an *ie* (*city/cities, specialty/specialties*), or the change of an *f* to *v* (*knife/knives, half/halves*; some exceptions: *fifes, roofs*). Some words of Latin origin offer a choice of plurals (*phenomena/phenomenons, indexes/indices, appendixes/appendices*). It's always a good idea to consult a dictionary if you are unsure of the correct or preferred plural spelling of a word.

The plurals of compound nouns are usually formed by adding *s* or *es* to the main word of the compound (*fathers-in-law, editors-in-chief, attorneys-at-law*).

Some nouns are the same whether singular or plural (*sheep, deer, moose*). Some nouns are plural in form but singular in use (*ethics, measles*). Some nouns are used in the plural only (*scissors, trousers*).

Letters, numbers, and words used as words are sometimes made plural by adding an apostrophe and an *s* (*A's, Ph.D.'s, 1's*). However, if no confusion would be created by leaving off the apostrophe, it is common practice to just add the *s* (*1990s, RFPs, DVDs*).

1.1.4 Possessive Nouns

A noun becomes possessive when it's used to show the ownership of something. Then you add *'s* to the word:

the man's car   the woman's apartment

However, ownership does not need to be legal:

the secretary's desk   the company's assets

Also, ownership may be nothing more than an automatic association:

a day's work   the job's prestige

An exception to the rule about adding *'s* to make a noun possessive occurs when the word is singular and already has two "s" sounds at the end. In cases like the following, an apostrophe is all that's needed:

crisis' dimensions   Mr. Moses' application

When the noun has only one "s" sound at the end, however, retain the *'s*:

Chris's book   Carolyn Nuss's office

With compound (hyphenated) nouns, add *'s* to the last word:

COMPOUND NOUN	POSSESSIVE NOUN
mother-in-law	mother-in-law's
mayor-elect	mayor-elect's

To form the possessive of plural nouns, just begin by following the same rule as with singular nouns: add *'s*. However, if the plural noun already ends in an *s* (as most do), drop the one you've added, leaving only the apostrophe:

the clients' complaints   employees' benefits

To denote joint possession by two or more proper nouns, add the *'s* to the last name only (*Moody, Nation, and Smith's* ad agency). To denote individual possession by two or more persons, add an *'s* to each proper noun (*Moody's, Nation's, and Smith's* ad agencies).

1.1.5 Collective Nouns

Collective nouns encompass a group of people or objects: *crowd, jury, committee, team, audience, family, couple, herd, class*. They are often treated as singular nouns. (For more on collective nouns, see Section 1.3.4, Subject-Verb Agreement.)

1.2 Pronouns

A **pronoun** is a word that stands for a noun; it saves repeating the noun:

Employees have some choice of weeks for vacation, but *they* must notify the HR office of *their* preference by March 1.

The pronouns *they* and *their* stand in for the noun *employees*. The noun that a pronoun stands for is called the **antecedent** of the pronoun; *employees* is the antecedent of *they* and *their*.

When the antecedent is plural, the pronoun that stands in for it has to be plural; *they* and *their* are plural pronouns because *employees* is plural. Likewise, when the antecedent is singular, the pronoun has to be singular:

We thought the contract had expired, but we soon learned that *it* had not.

1.2.1 Multiple Antecedents

Sometimes a pronoun has a double (or even a triple) antecedent:

Kathryn Boettcher and Luis Gutierrez went beyond *their* sales quotas for January.

If taken alone, *Kathryn Boettcher* is a singular antecedent. So is *Luis Gutierrez*. However, when together they are the plural antecedent of a pronoun, so the pronoun has to be plural. Thus the pronoun is *their* instead of *her* or *his*.

1.2.2 Unclear Antecedents

In some sentences the pronoun's antecedent is unclear:

Sandy Wright sent Jane Brougham *her* production figures for the previous year. *She* thought they were too low.

To which person does the pronoun *her* refer? Someone who knew Sandy and Jane and knew their business relationship might be able to figure out the antecedent for *her*. Even with such an advantage, however, a reader might receive the wrong meaning. Also, it would be nearly impossible for any reader to know which name is the antecedent of *she*.

The best way to clarify an ambiguous pronoun is usually to rewrite the sentence, repeating nouns when needed for clarity:

Sandy Wright sent her production figures for the previous year to Jane Brougham. Jane thought they were too low.

The noun needs to be repeated only when the antecedent is unclear.

1.2.3 Pronoun Classes

Personal pronouns consist of *I, you, we/us, he/him, she/her, it*, and *they/them*.

Compound personal pronouns are created by adding *self* or *selves* to simple personal pronouns: *myself, ourselves, yourself, yourselves, himself, herself, itself, themselves*. Compound personal pronouns are used either *intensively*, to emphasize the identity of the noun or pronoun (I *myself* have seen the demonstration), or *reflexively*, to indicate that the subject is the receiver of his or her own action (I promised *myself* I'd finish by noon). Compound personal pronouns are used incorrectly if they appear in a sentence without their antecedent:

Walter, Virginia, and *me* (not *myself*) are the top salespeople.

You need to tell *her* (not *herself*) about the mixup.

Relative pronouns refer to nouns (or groups of words used as nouns) in the main clause and are used to introduce clauses:

Purina is the brand *that* most dog owners purchase.

The relative pronouns are *which, who, whom, whose,* and *what*. Other words used as relative pronouns include *that, whoever, whomever, whatever,* and *whichever*.

Interrogative pronouns are those used for asking questions: *who, whom, whose, which, what*.

Demonstrative pronouns point out particular persons, places, or things:

That is my desk.   *This* can't be correct.

The demonstrative pronouns are *this, these, that,* and *those.*

Indefinite pronouns refer to persons or things not specifically identified. They include *anyone, someone, everyone, everybody, somebody, either, neither, one, none, all, both, each, another, any, many,* and similar words.

1.2.4 Case of Pronouns

The case of a pronoun tells whether it's acting or acted upon:

She sells an average of five packages each week.

In this sentence, *she* is doing the selling. Because *she* is acting, *she* is said to be in the **nominative case**. Now consider what happens when the pronoun is acted upon:

After six months, Ms. Browning promoted *her.*

In this sentence, the pronoun *her* is acted upon and is thus said to be in the **objective case**.

Contrast the nominative and objective pronouns in this list:

NOMINATIVE	OBJECTIVE
I	me
we	us
he	him
she	her
they	them
who	whom
whoever	whomever

Objective pronouns may be used as either the object of a verb (such as *promoted*) or the object of a preposition (such as *with*):

Rob worked with *them* until the order was filled.

In this example, *them* is the object of the preposition *with* because Rob acted upon—worked with—them. Here's a sentence with three pronouns, the first one nominative, the second the object of a verb, and the third the object of a preposition:

He paid *us* as soon as the check came from *them.*

He is nominative; *us* is objective because it's the object of the verb *paid*; *them* is objective because it's the object of the preposition *from.*

Every writer sometimes wonders whether to use *who* or *whom:*

(Who, Whom) will you hire?

Because this sentence is a question, it's difficult to see that *whom* is the object of the verb *hire.* You can figure out which pronoun to use if you rearrange the question and temporar-

ily try *she* and *her* in place of *who* and *whom:* "Will you hire *she*?" or "Will you hire *her*?" *Her* and *whom* are both objective, so the correct choice is "Whom will you hire?" Here's a different example:

(Who, Whom) logged so much travel time?

Turning the question into a statement, you get:

He logged so much travel time.

Therefore, the correct statement is:

Who logged so much travel time?

1.2.5 Possessive Pronouns

Possessive pronouns work like possessive nouns: They show ownership or automatic association:

her job	their preferences
his account	its equipment

However, possessive pronouns are different from possessive nouns in the way they are written. That is, possessive pronouns never have an apostrophe:

POSSESSIVE NOUN	POSSESSIVE PRONOUN
the woman's estate	her estate
Roger Franklin's plans	his plans
the shareholders' feelings	their feelings
the vacuum cleaner's attachments	its attachments

The word *its* is the possessive of *it.* Like all other possessive pronouns, *its* has no apostrophe. Some people confuse *its* with *it's,* the contraction of *it is.* (Contractions are discussed in Section 2.9, Apostrophes.)

1.2.6 Pronoun-Antecedent Agreement

Like nouns, pronouns can be singular or plural. Pronouns must agree in number with their antecedents: a singular antecedent requires a singular pronoun:

The president of the board tendered *his* resignation.

Multiple antecedents require a plural pronoun:

The members of the board tendered *their* resignations.

A pronoun referring to singular antecedents connected by *or* or *nor* should be singular:

Neither Sean nor Terry made *his* quota.

But a pronoun referring to a plural and a singular antecedent connected by *or* or *nor* should be plural:

Neither Sean nor the twins made *their* quotas.

Formal English prefers the nominative case after the linking verb *to be:*

It is *I.*   That is *he.*

However, for general usage it's perfectly acceptable to use the more natural "It's me" and "That's him."

1.3 Verbs

A **verb** describes an action or acts as a link between a subject and words that define or describe that subject:

> They all *quit* in disgust.

> Working conditions *were* substandard.

The English language is full of **action verbs**. Here are a few you'll often run across in the business world:

verify	perform	fulfill
hire	succeed	send
leave	improve	receive
accept	develop	pay

You could undoubtedly list many more. The most common linking verbs are all the forms of *to be*: I *am*, *was*, or *will be*; you *are*, *were*, or *will be*. Other words that can serve as linking verbs include *seem, become, appear, prove, look, remain, feel, taste, smell, sound, resemble, turn,* and *grow*:

> It *seemed* a good plan at the time.

> She *sounds* impressive at a meeting.

> The time *grows* near for us to make a decision.

These verbs link what comes before them in the sentence with what comes after; no action is involved. (See Section 1.7.5 for a fuller discussion of linking verbs.)

An **auxiliary verb** is one that helps another verb and is used for showing tense, voice, and so on. A verb with its helpers is called a **verb phrase**. Verbs used as auxiliaries include *do, did, be, have, may, can, must, will, shall, might, could, would,* and *should*.

1.3.1 Verb Tenses

English has three simple verb tenses: present, past, and future:

Present: Our branches in Hawaii *stock* other items.

Past: We *stocked* Purquil pens for a short time.

Future: Rotex Tire Stores *will stock* your line of tires when you begin a program of effective national advertising.

With most verbs (the regular ones), the past tense ends in *ed*, and the future tense always has *will* or *shall* in front of it. But the present tense is more complex, depending on the subject:

	FIRST PERSON	SECOND PERSON	THIRD PERSON
Singular	I stock	you stock	he/she/it stocks
Plural	we stock	you stock	they stock

The basic form, *stock*, takes an additional *s* when *he, she, or it* precedes it. (See Section 1.3.4 for more on subject-verb agreement.)

In addition to the three simple tenses, the three **perfect tenses** are created by adding forms of the auxiliary verb *have*. The present perfect tense uses the past participle (regularly the past tense) of the main verb, *stocked*, and adds the present-tense *have* or *has* to the front of it:

> (I, we, you, they) *have stocked*.

> (He, she, it) *has stocked*.

The past perfect tense uses the past participle of the main verb, *stocked*, and adds the past-tense *had* to the front of it:

> (I, you, he, she, it, we, they) *had stocked*.

The future perfect tense also uses the past participle of the main verb, *stocked*, but adds the future-tense *will have*:

> (I, you, he, she, it, we, they) *will have stocked*.

Verbs should be kept in the same tense when the actions occur at the same time:

> When the payroll checks *came in*, everyone *showed up* for work.

> We *have found* that everyone *has pitched in* to help.

When the actions occur at different times, you may change tense accordingly:

> The shipment *came* last Wednesday, so if another one *comes* in today, please return it.

> The new employee *had been* ill at ease, but now she *has become* a full-fledged member of the team.

1.3.2 Irregular Verbs

Many verbs don't follow some of the standard patterns for verb tenses. The most irregular of these verbs is *to be*:

TENSE	SINGULAR	PLURAL
Present:	I *am*	we *are*
	you *are*	you *are*
	he, she, it *is*	they *are*
Past:	I *was*	we *were*
	you *were*	you *were*
	he, she, it *was*	they *were*

The future tense of *to be* is formed in the same way that the future tense of a regular verb is formed.

The perfect tenses of *to be* are also formed as they would be for a regular verb, except that the past participle is a special form, *been*, instead of just the past tense:

Present perfect:	you have been
Past perfect:	you had been
Future perfect:	you will have been

Here's a sampling of other irregular verbs:

PRESENT	PAST	PAST PARTICIPLE
begin	began	begun
shrink	shrank	shrunk
know	knew	known
rise	rose	risen
become	became	become
go	went	gone
do	did	done

Dictionaries list the various forms of other irregular verbs.

1.3.3 Transitive and Intransitive Verbs

Many people are confused by three particular sets of verbs:

lie/lay   sit/set   rise/raise

Using these verbs correctly is much easier when you learn the difference between transitive and intransitive verbs.

Transitive verbs require a receiver; they "transfer" their action to an object. Intransitive verbs do not have a receiver for their action. Some intransitive verbs are complete in themselves and need no help from other words (prices *dropped*; we *won*). Other intransitive words must be "completed" by a noun or adjective called a **complement**. Complements occur with linking verbs.

Here are some sample uses of transitive and intransitive verbs:

INTRANSITIVE	TRANSITIVE
We should include in our new offices a place to *lie* down for a nap.	The workers will be here on Monday to *lay* new carpeting.
Even the way an interviewee *sits* is important.	That crate is full of stemware, so *set* it down carefully.
Salaries at Compu-Link, Inc., *rise* swiftly.	They *raise* their level of production every year.

The workers *lay* carpeting, you *set down* the crate, they *raise* production; each action is transferred to something. In the intransitive sentences, a person *lies down*, an interviewee *sits*, and salaries *rise* without affecting anything else. Intransitive sentences are complete with only a subject and a verb; transitive sentences are not complete unless they also include an object, or something to transfer the action to.

Tenses are a confusing element of the lie/lay problem:

PRESENT	PAST	PAST PARTICIPLE
I *lie*	I *lay*	I *have lain*
I *lay* (something down)	I *laid* (something down)	I *have laid* (something down)

The past tense of *lie* and the present tense of *lay* look and sound alike, even though they're different verbs.

1.3.4 Subject-Verb Agreement

Whether regular or irregular, every verb must agree with its subject, both in person (first, second, or third) and in number (singular or plural):

	FIRST PERSON	SECOND PERSON	THIRD PERSON
Singular	I *am*; I *write*	you *are*; you *write*	he/she/it *is*; he/she/it *writes*
Plural	we *are*; we *write*	you *are*; you *write*	they *are*; they *write*

In a simple sentence, making a verb agree with its subject is a straightforward task:

Hector Ruiz *is* a strong competitor. (third-person singular)

We *write* to you every month. (first-person plural)

Confusion sometimes arises when sentences are a bit more complicated. For example, be sure to avoid agreement problems when words come between the subject and verb. In the following examples, the verb appears in italics, and its subject is underlined:

The <u>analysis</u> of existing documents *takes* a full week.

Even though *documents* is a plural, the verb is in the singular form. That's because the subject of the sentence is *analysis*, a singular noun. The phrase *of existing documents* can be disregarded. Here is another example:

The <u>answers</u> for this exercise *are* in the study guide.

Take away the phrase *for this exercise* and you are left with the plural subject *answers*. Therefore, the verb takes the plural form.

Verb agreement is also complicated when the subject is a collective noun or pronoun or when the subject may be considered either singular or plural. In such cases, you often have to analyze the surrounding sentence to determine which verb form to use:

The <u>staff</u> *is* quartered in the warehouse.

The <u>staff</u> *are* at their desks in the warehouse.

The <u>computers</u> and the <u>staff</u> *are* in the warehouse.

Neither the staff nor the <u>computers</u> *are* in the warehouse.

<u>Every</u> computer *is* in the warehouse.

Many a <u>computer</u> *is* in the warehouse.

Did you notice that words such as *every* use the singular verb form? In addition, when an *either/or* or a *neither/nor* phrase combines singular and plural nouns, the verb takes the form that matches the noun closest to it.

In the business world, some subjects require extra attention. Company names, for example, are considered singular and therefore take a singular verb in most cases—even if they contain plural words:

Stater Brothers *offers* convenient grocery shopping.

In addition, quantities are sometimes considered singular and sometimes plural. If a quantity refers to a total amount, it takes a singular verb; if a quantity refers to individual, countable units, it takes a plural verb:

> Three hours *is* a long time.

> The eight dollars we collected for the fund *are* tacked on the bulletin board.

Fractions may also be singular or plural, depending on the noun that accompanies them:

> One-third of the warehouse *is* devoted to this product line.

> One-third of the products *are* defective.

To decide whether to use a singular or plural verb with subjects such as *number* and *variety*, follow this simple rule: If the subject is preceded by *a*, use a plural verb:

> *A* number of products *are* being displayed at the trade show.

If the subject is preceded by *the*, use a singular verb:

> *The* variety of products on display *is* mind-boggling.

For a related discussion, see Section 1.7.1, Longer Sentences.

1.3.5 Voice of Verbs

Verbs have two voices, active and passive. When the subject comes first, the verb is in **active voice**; when the object comes first, the verb is in **passive voice**:

> Active: The buyer *paid* a large amount.

> Passive: A large amount *was paid* by the buyer.

The passive voice uses a form of the verb *to be*, which adds words to a sentence. In the example, the passive-voice sentence uses eight words, whereas the active-voice sentence uses only six to say the same thing. The words *was* and *by* are unnecessary to convey the meaning of the sentence. In fact, extra words usually clog meaning, so be sure to opt for the active voice when you have a choice.

At times, however, you have no choice:

> Several items *have been taken*, but so far we don't know who took them.

The passive voice becomes necessary when you don't know (or don't want to say) who performed the action; the active voice is bolder and more direct.

1.3.6 Mood of Verbs

Verbs can express one of three moods: indicative, imperative, or subjunctive. The **indicative mood** is used to make a statement or to ask a question:

> The secretary mailed a letter to each supplier.

> Did the secretary mail a letter to each supplier?

Use the **imperative mood** when you wish to command or request:

> Please mail a letter to each supplier.

With the imperative mood, the subject is the understood *you*.

The **subjunctive mood** is used to express doubt or a wish or a condition contrary to fact:

> If I *were* you, I wouldn't send that e-mail.

The subjunctive is also used to express a suggestion or a request:

> I asked that Rosario *be* [not *is*] present at the meeting.

1.3.7 Verbals

Verbals are verbs that are modified to function as other parts of speech. They include infinitives, gerunds, and participles.

Infinitives are formed by placing a *to* in front of the verb (*to go, to purchase, to work*). They function as nouns. Although many of us were taught that it is "incorrect" to split an infinitive—that is, to place an adverb between the *to* and the verb—that rule is not a hard and fast one. In some cases, the adverb is best placed in the middle of the infinitive to avoid awkward constructions or ambiguous meaning:

> Production of steel is expected *to moderately exceed* domestic use.

Gerunds are verbals formed by adding *ing* to a verb (*going, having, working*). Like infinitives, they function as nouns. Gerunds and gerund phrases take a singular verb:

> *Borrowing* from banks *is* preferable to getting venture capital.

Participles are verb forms used as adjectives. The present participle ends in *ing* and generally describes action going on at the same time as other action:

> *Checking* the schedule, the contractor was pleased with progress on the project.

The past participle is usually the same form as the past tense and generally indicates completed action:

> When *completed*, the project will occupy six city blocks.

The **perfect participle** is formed by adding *having* to the past participle:

> *Having completed* the project, the contractor submitted his last invoice.

1.4 Adjectives

An **adjective** modifies (tells something about) a noun or pronoun. Each of the following phrases says more about the noun or pronoun than the noun or pronoun would say alone:

> an *efficient* staff   a *heavy* price

> *brisk* trade   *light* web traffic

Adjectives modify nouns more often than they modify pronouns. When adjectives do modify pronouns, however, the sentence usually has a linking verb:

> They were *attentive*.   It looked *appropriate*.

> He seems *interested*.   You are *skillful*.

1.4.1 Types of Adjectives

Adjectives serve a variety of purposes. **Descriptive adjectives** express some quality belonging to the modified item (*tall, successful, green*). **Limiting or definitive adjectives**, on the other hand, point out the modified item or limit its meaning without expressing a quality. Types include:

- Numeral adjectives (*one, fifty, second*)
- Articles (*a, an, the*)
- Pronominal adjectives: pronouns used as adjectives (*his* desk, *each* employee)
- Demonstrative adjectives: *this, these, that, those* (*these* tires, *that* invoice)

Proper adjectives are derived from proper nouns:

  Chinese customs   *Orwellian* overtones

Predicate adjectives complete the meaning of the predicate and are introduced by linking verbs:

  The location is *perfect.*   Prices are *high.*

1.4.2 Comparative Degree

Most adjectives can take three forms: simple, comparative, and superlative. The simple form modifies a single noun or pronoun. Use the comparative form when comparing two items. When comparing three or more items, use the superlative form:

SIMPLE	COMPARATIVE	SUPERLATIVE
hard	harder	hardest
safe	safer	safest
dry	drier	driest

The comparative form adds *er* to the simple form, and the superlative form adds *est.* (The *y* at the end of a word changes to *i* before the *er* or *est* is added.)

A small number of adjectives are irregular, including these:

SIMPLE	COMPARATIVE	SUPERLATIVE
good	better	best
bad	worse	worst
little	less	least

When the simple form of an adjective is two or more syllables, you usually add *more* to form the comparative and *most* to form the superlative:

SIMPLE	COMPARATIVE	SUPERLATIVE
useful	more useful	most useful
exhausting	more exhausting	most exhausting
expensive	more expensive	most expensive

The most common exceptions are two-syllable adjectives that end in *y*:

SIMPLE	COMPARATIVE	SUPERLATIVE
happy	happier	happiest
costly	costlier	costliest

If you choose this option, change the *y* to *i*, and tack *er* or *est* onto the end.

Some adjectives cannot be used to make comparisons because they themselves indicate the extreme. For example, if something is perfect, nothing can be more perfect. If something is unique or ultimate, nothing can be more unique or more ultimate.

1.4.3 Hyphenated Adjectives

Many adjectives used in the business world are actually combinations of words: *up-to-date* report, *last-minute* effort, *fifth-floor* suite, *well-built* engine. As you can see, they are hyphenated when they come before the noun they modify. However, when such word combinations come after the noun they modify, they are not hyphenated. In the following example, the adjectives appear in italics, and the nouns they modify are underlined:

  The <u>report</u> is *up to date* because of our team's *last-minute* <u>efforts.</u>

Hyphens are not used when part of the combination is a word ending in *ly* (because that word is usually not an adjective). Hyphens are also omitted from word combinations that are used so frequently that readers are used to seeing the words together:

  We live in a *rapidly shrinking* world.

  Our *highly motivated* employees will be well paid.

  Please consider renewing your *credit card* account.

  Send those figures to our *data processing* department.

  Our new intern is a *high school* student.

1.5 Adverbs

An **adverb** modifies a verb, an adjective, or another adverb:

Modifying a verb:	Our marketing department works *efficiently.*
Modifying an adjective:	She was not dependable, although she was *highly* intelligent.
Modifying another adverb:	When signing new clients, he moved *extremely* cautiously.

An adverb can be a single word (*clearly*), a phrase (*very clearly*), or a clause (*because it was clear*).

1.5.1 Types of Adverbs

Simple adverbs are simple modifiers:

  The door opened *automatically.*

  The order arrived *yesterday.*

  Top companies were *there.*

Interrogative adverbs ask a question:

> *Where* have you been?

Conjunctive adverbs connect clauses:

> We can't start *until* Maria gets here.

> Jorge tried to explain *how* the new software works.

Words frequently used as conjunctive adverbs include *where, wherever, when, whenever, while, as, how, why, before, after, until,* and *since.*

Negative adverbs include *not, never, seldom, rarely, scarcely, hardly,* and similar words. Negative adverbs are powerful words and therefore do not need any help in conveying a negative thought. In fact, using double negatives gives a strong impression of illiteracy, so avoid sentences like these:

> I don't want no mistakes.

(Correct: "I don't want any mistakes," or "I want no mistakes.")

> They couldn't hardly read the report.

(Correct: "They could hardly read the report," or "They couldn't read the report.")

> They scarcely noticed neither one.

(Correct: "They scarcely noticed either one," or "They noticed neither one.")

1.5.2 Adverb-Adjective Confusion

Many adverbs are adjectives turned into adverbs by adding *ly: highly, extremely, officially, closely, really.* In addition, many words can be adjectives or adverbs, depending on their usage in a particular sentence:

The *early* bird gets the worm (adjective).	We arrived *early* (adverb).
It was a *hard* decision (adjective).	He hit the wall *hard* (adverb).

Because of this situation, some adverbs are difficult to distinguish from adjectives. For example, in the following sentences, is the underlined word an adverb or an adjective?

> They worked <u>well</u>.

> The baby is <u>well</u>.

In the first sentence, *well* is an adverb modifying the verb *worked.* In the second sentence, *well* is an adjective modifying the noun *baby.* To choose correctly between adverbs and adjectives, remember that linking verbs are used to connect an adjective to describe a noun. In contrast, you would use an adverb to describe an action verb:

ADJECTIVE	ADVERB
He is a *good* worker.	He works *well.*
(What kind of worker is he?)	(How does he work?)
It is a *real* computer.	It *really* is a computer.

(What kind of computer is it?)	(To what extent is it a computer?)
The traffic is *slow.* (What quality does the traffic have?)	The traffic moves *slowly.* (How does the traffic move?)
This food tastes *bad* without salt. (What quality does the food have?)	This food *badly* needs salt. (How much is it needed?)

1.5.3 Comparative Degree

Like adjectives, adverbs can be used to compare items. Generally, the basic adverb is combined with *more* or *most,* just as long adjectives are. However, some adverbs have one-word comparative forms:

ONE ITEM	TWO ITEMS	THREE ITEMS
quickly	more quickly	most quickly
sincerely	less sincerely	least sincerely
fast	faster	fastest
well	better	best

1.6   Other Parts of Speech

Nouns, pronouns, verbs, adjectives, and adverbs carry most of the meaning in a sentence. Four other parts of speech link them together in sentences: prepositions, conjunctions, articles, and interjections.

1.6.1 Prepositions

Nouns, pronouns, verbs, adjectives, and adverbs carry most of the meaning in a sentence. Four other parts of speech link them together in sentences: prepositions, conjunctions, articles, and interjections. A **preposition** is a word or group of words that describes a relationship between other words in a sentence. A simple preposition is made up of one word: *of, in, by, above, below.* A *compound preposition* is made up of two prepositions: *out of, from among, except for, because of.*

A **prepositional phrase** is a group of words introduced by a preposition that functions as an adjective (an adjectival phrase) or as an adverb (adverbial phrase) by telling more about a pronoun, noun, or verb:

> The shipment will be here *by next Friday.*

> Put the mail *in the out-bin.*

Prepositional phrases should be placed as close as possible to the element they are modifying:

> Shopping *on the Internet* can be confusing for the uninitiated. (*not* Shopping can be confusing for the uninitiated *on the Internet.*)

Some prepositions are closely linked with a verb. When using phrases such as *look up* and *wipe out,* keep them intact and do not insert anything between the verb and the preposition.

You may have been told that it is unacceptable to put a preposition at the end of a sentence. However, that is not a hard-and-fast-rule and trying to follow it can sometimes be a challenge. You can end a sentence with a preposition as along as the sentence sounds natural and as long as rewording the sentence would create awkward wording:

> I couldn't tell what they were interested in.

> What did she attribute it to?

> What are you looking for?

Avoid using unnecessary prepositions. In the following examples, the prepositions in parentheses should be omitted:

> All (of) the staff members were present.

> I almost fell off (of) my chair with surprise.

> Where was Mr. Steuben going (to)?

> They couldn't help (from) wondering.

The opposite problem is failing to include a preposition when you should. Consider these two sentences:

> Sales were over $100,000 for Linda and Bill.

> Sales were over $100,000 for Linda and for Bill.

The first sentence indicates that Linda and Bill had combined sales over $100,000; the second, that Linda and Bill each had sales over $100,000, for a combined total in excess of $200,000. The preposition *for* is critical here.

When the same preposition can be used for two or more words in a sentence without affecting the meaning, only the last preposition is required:

> We are familiar (with) and satisfied with your company's products.

But when different prepositions are normally used with the words, all the prepositions must be included:

> We are familiar with and interested in your company's products.

Some prepositions have come to be used in a particular way with certain other parts of speech. Here is a partial list of some prepositions that have come to be used with certain words:

according to	independent of
agree to (a proposal)	inferior to
agree with (a person)	plan to
buy from	prefer to
capable of	prior to
comply with	reason with
conform to	responsible for
differ from (things)	similar to
differ with (person)	talk to (without interaction)
different from	talk with (with interaction)
get from (receive)	wait for (person or thing)
get off (dismount)	wait on (like a waiter)

If you are unsure of the correct idiomatic expression, check a dictionary.

Some verb-preposition idioms vary depending on the situation: You agree *to* a proposal but *with* a person, *on* a price, or *in* principle. You argue *about* something, *with* a person, and *for* or *against* a proposition. You compare one item *to* another to show their similarities; you compare one item *with* another to show differences.

Here are some other examples of preposition usage that have given writers trouble:

among/between: *Among* is used to refer to three or more (Circulate the memo *among* the staff); *between* is used to refer to two (Put the copy machine *between* Judy and Dan).

as if/like: *As if* is used before a clause (It seems *as if* we should be doing something); *like* is used before a noun or pronoun (He seems *like* a nice guy).

have/of: *Have* is a verb used in verb phrases (They should *have* checked first); *of* is a preposition and is never used in such cases.

in/into: *In* is used to refer to a static position (The file is *in* the cabinet); *into* is used to refer to movement toward a position (Put the file *into* the cabinet).

1.6.2 Conjunctions

Conjunctions connect the parts of a sentence: words, phrases, and clauses. A **coordinating conjunction** connects two words, phrases, or clauses of equal rank. The simple coordinating conjunctions include *and, but, or, nor, for, yet,* and *so.* **Correlative conjunctions** are coordinating conjunctions used in pairs: *both/and, either/or, neither/nor, not only/but also.* Constructions with correlative conjunctions should be parallel, with the same part of speech following each element of the conjunction:

> The purchase was *not only* expensive *but* unnecessary.

> The purchase *not only was* expensive *but was* unnecessary.

Conjunctive adverbs are adverbs used to connect or show relationships between clauses. They include *however, nevertheless, consequently, moreover,* and *as a result.*

A **subordinate conjunction** connects two clauses of unequal rank; it joins a dependent (subordinate) clause to the independent clause on which it depends (for more on dependent and independent clauses, see Section 1.7.1). Subordinate conjunctions include *as, if, because, although, while, before, since, that, until, unless, when, where,* and *whether.*

1.6.3 Articles and Interjections

Only three **articles** exist in English: *the, a,* and *an.* These words are used, like adjectives, to specify which item you are talking about. *The* is called the *definite article* because it indicates a specific noun; *a* and *an* are called the *indefinite articles* because they are less specific about what they are referring to.

If a word begins with a vowel (soft) sound, use *an*; otherwise use *a.* It's *a history,* not *an history; a hypothesis,* not *an hypothesis.* Use *an* with an "h" word only if it is a soft "h," as in *honor* and *hour.* Use *an* with words that are pronounced with a soft vowel sound even if they are spelled beginning with a consonant (usually in the case of abbreviations): *an SEC application, an MP3 file.* Use *a* with words that begin with vowels if they are pronounced with a hard sound: *a university, a Usenet account.*

Repeat an article if adjectives modify different nouns: *The red house and the white house are mine.* Do not repeat an article if all adjectives modify the same noun: *The red and white house is mine.*

Interjections are words that express no solid information, only emotion:

Wow!	Well, well!
Oh, no!	Good!

Such purely emotional language has its place in private life and advertising copy, but it only weakens the effect of most business writing.

1.7 Sentences

Sentences are constructed with the major building blocks, the parts of speech. Take, for example, this simple two-word sentence:

Money talks.

It consists of a noun (*money*) and a verb (*talks*). When used in this way, the noun works as the first requirement for a sentence, the **subject**, and the verb works as the second requirement, the **predicate**. Without a subject (who or what does something) and a predicate (the doing of it), you have merely a collection of words, not a sentence.

1.7.1 Longer Sentences

More complicated sentences have more complicated subjects and predicates, but they still have a simple subject and a predicate verb. In the following examples, the subject is underlined once, the predicate verb twice:

Marex and Contron enjoy higher earnings each quarter.

Marex [and] *Contron* do something; *enjoy* is what they do.

My interview, coming minutes after my freeway accident, did not impress or move anyone.

Interview is what did something. What did it do? It *did* [not] *impress* [or] *move.*

In terms of usable space, a steel warehouse, with its extremely long span of roof unsupported by pillars, makes more sense.

Warehouse is what *makes.*

These three sentences demonstrate several things. First, in all three sentences, the simple subject and predicate verb are the "bare bones" of the sentence, the parts that carry the core idea of the sentence. When trying to find the subject and predicate verb, disregard all prepositional phrases, modifiers, conjunctions, and articles.

Second, in the third sentence, the verb is singular (*makes*) because the subject is singular (*warehouse*). Even though the plural noun *pillars* is closer to the verb, *warehouse* is the subject. So *warehouse* determines whether the verb is singular or plural. Subject and predicate must agree.

Third, the subject in the first sentence is compound (*Marex* [and] *Contron*). A compound subject, when connected by *and,* requires a plural verb (*enjoy*). Also, the second sentence shows how compound predicates can occur (*did* [not] *impress* [or] *move*).

Fourth, the second sentence incorporates a group of words—*coming minutes after my freeway accident*—containing a form of a verb (*coming*) and a noun (*accident*). Yet, this group of words is not a complete sentence for two reasons:

- Not all nouns are subjects: *Accident* is not the subject of *coming.*
- Not all verbs are predicates: A verb that ends in *ing* can never be the predicate of a sentence (unless preceded by a form of *to be,* as in *was coming*).

Because they don't contain a subject and a predicate, the words *coming minutes after my freeway accident* (called a **phrase**) can't be written as a sentence. That is, the phrase cannot stand alone; it cannot begin with a capital letter and end with a period. So a phrase must always be just one part of a sentence.

Sometimes a sentence incorporates two or more groups of words that do contain a subject and a predicate; these word groups are called **clauses**:

My interview, because it came minutes after my freeway accident, did not impress or move anyone.

The **independent clause** is the portion of the sentence that could stand alone without revision:

My interview did not impress or move anyone.

The other part of the sentence could stand alone only by removing *because*:

(because) It came minutes after my freeway accident.

This part of the sentence is known as a **dependent clause**; although it has a subject and a predicate (just as an independent clause does), it's linked to the main part of the sentence by a word (*because*) showing its dependence.

In summary, the two types of clauses—dependent and independent—both have a subject and a predicate. Dependent clauses, however, do not bear the main meaning of the sentence and are therefore linked to an independent clause. Nor can phrases stand alone, because they lack both a subject and a predicate. Only independent clauses can be written as sentences without revision.

1.7.2 Types of Sentences

Sentences come in four main types, depending on the extent to which they contain clauses. A **simple sentence** has one subject and one predicate; in short, it has one main independent clause:

Boeing is the world's largest aerospace company.

A **compound sentence** consists of two independent clauses connected by a coordinating conjunction (*and, or, but,* etc.) or a semicolon:

> Airbus outsold Boeing for several years, but Boeing has recently regained the lead.

A **complex sentence** consists of an independent clause and one or more dependent clauses:

> Boeing is betting [independent clause] that airlines will begin using moderately smaller planes to fly passengers between smaller cities [dependent clause introduced by *that*].

A **compound-complex sentence** has two main clauses, at least one of which contains a subordinate (dependent) clause:

> Boeing is betting [independent clause] that airlines will begin using moderately smaller planes to fly passengers between smaller cities [dependent clause], and it anticipates that new airports will be developed to meet passenger needs [independent clause].

1.7.3 Sentence Fragments

An incomplete sentence (a phrase or a dependent clause) that is written as though it were a complete sentence is called a **fragment**. Consider the following sentence fragments:

> Marilyn Sanders, having had pilferage problems in her store for the past year. Refuses to accept the results of our investigation.

This serious error can easily be corrected by putting the two fragments together:

> Marilyn Sanders, having had pilferage problems in her store for the past year, refuses to accept the results of our investigation.

The actual details of a situation will determine the best way for you to remedy a fragment problem.

The ban on fragments has one exception. Some advertising copy contains sentence fragments, written knowingly to convey a certain rhythm. However, advertising is the only area of business in which fragments are acceptable.

1.7.4 Fused Sentences and Comma Splices

Just as there can be too little in a group of words to make it a sentence, there can also be too much:

> All our mail is run through a postage meter every afternoon someone picks it up.

This example contains two sentences, not one, but the two have been blended so that it's hard to tell where one ends and the next begins. Is the mail run through a meter every afternoon? If so, the sentences should read:

> All our mail is run through a postage meter every afternoon. Someone picks it up.

Perhaps the mail is run through a meter at some other time (morning, for example) and is picked up every afternoon:

> All our mail is run through a postage meter. Every afternoon someone picks it up.

The order of words is the same in all three cases; sentence division makes all the difference. Either of the last two cases is grammatically correct. The choice depends on the facts of the situation.

Sometimes these so-called **fused sentences** have a more obvious point of separation:

> Several large orders arrived within a few days of one another, too many came in for us to process by the end of the month.

Here, the comma has been put between two independent clauses in an attempt to link them. When a lowly comma separates two complete sentences, the result is called a **comma splice**. A comma splice can be remedied in one of three ways:

- Replace the comma with a period and capitalize the next word: "... one another. Too many ..."
- Replace the comma with a semicolon and do not capitalize the next word: "... one another; too many ..." This remedy works only when the two sentences have closely related meanings.
- Change one of the sentences so that it becomes a phrase or a dependent clause. This remedy often produces the best writing, but it takes more work.

The third alternative can be carried out in several ways. One is to begin the sentence with a subordinating conjunction:

> Whenever several large orders arrived within a few days of one another, too many came in for us to process by the end of the month.

Another way is to remove part of the subject or the predicate verb from one of the independent clauses, thereby creating a phrase:

> Several large orders arrived within a few days of one another, too many for us to process by the end of the month.

Finally, you can change one of the predicate verbs to its *ing* form:

> Several large orders arrived within a few days of one another, too many coming in for us to process by the end of the month.

In many cases, simply adding a coordinating conjunction can separate fused sentences or remedy a comma splice:

> You can fire them, or you can make better use of their abilities.

> Margaret drew up the designs, and Matt carried them out.

> We will have three strong months, but after that sales will taper off.

Be careful with coordinating conjunctions: Use them only to join simple sentences that express similar ideas.

Also, because they say relatively little about the relationship between the two clauses they join, avoid using coordinating conjunctions too often: *and* is merely an addition sign; *but* is just a turn signal; *or* only points to an alternative. Subordinating conjunctions such as *because* and *whenever* tell the reader a lot more.

1.7.5 Sentences with Linking Verbs

Linking verbs were discussed briefly in the section on verbs (Section 1.3). Here, you can see more fully the way they function in a sentence. The following is a model of any sentence with a linking verb:

A (*verb*) B.

Although words such as *seems* and *feels* can also be linking verbs, let's assume that the verb is a form of *to be*:

A *is* B.

In such a sentence, A and B are always nouns, pronouns, or adjectives. When one is a noun and the other is a pronoun, or when both are nouns, the sentence says that one is the same as the other:

She is president.

Rachel is president.

She is forceful.

Recall from Section 1.3.3 that the noun or adjective that follows the linking verb is called a *complement*. When it is a noun or noun phrase, the complement is called a *predicate nominative*; when the complement is an adjective, it is referred to as a *predicate adjective*.

1.7.6 Misplaced Modifiers

The position of a modifier in a sentence is important. The movement of *only* changes the meaning in the following sentences:

Only we are obliged to supply those items specified in your contract.

We are obliged only to supply those items specified in your contract.

We are obliged to supply only those items specified in your contract.

We are obliged to supply those items specified only in your contract.

In any particular set of circumstances, only one of those sentences would be accurate. The others would very likely cause problems. To prevent misunderstanding, place such modifiers as close as possible to the noun or verb they modify.

For similar reasons, whole phrases that are modifiers must be placed near the right noun or verb. Mistakes in placement create ludicrous meanings:

Antia Information Systems has bought new computer chairs for the programmers with more comfortable seats.

The anatomy of programmers is not normally a concern of business writers. Obviously, the comfort of the chairs was the issue:

Antia Information Systems has bought new computer chairs with more comfortable seats for the programmers.

Here is another example:

I asked him to file all the letters in the cabinet that had been answered.

In this ridiculous sentence, the cabinet has been answered, even though no cabinet in history is known to have asked a question. *That had been answered* is too far from *letters* and too close to *cabinet*. Here's an improvement:

I asked him to file in the cabinet all the letters that had been answered.

The term **dangling modifier** is often used to refer to a clause or phrase that because of its position in the sentence seems to modify a word that it is not meant to modify. For instance:

Lying motionless, co-workers rushed to Barry's aid.

Readers expect an introductory phrase to modify the subject of the main clause. But in this case it wasn't the *co-workers* who were lying motionless but rather *Barry* who was in this situation. Like this example, most instances of dangling modifiers occur at the beginning of sentences. The source of some danglers is a passive construction:

To find the needed information, the whole book had to be read.

In such cases, switching to the active voice can usually remedy the problem:

To find the needed information, you will need to read the whole book.

1.7.7 Parallelism

Two or more sentence elements that have the same relation to another element should be in the same form. Otherwise, the reader is forced to work harder to understand the meaning of the sentence. When a series consists of phrases or clauses, the same part of speech (preposition, gerund, etc.) should introduce them. Do not mix infinitives with participles or adjectives with nouns. Here are some examples of nonparallel elements:

Andersen is hiring managers, programmers, and people who work in accounting. [nouns not parallel]

Andersen earns income by auditing, consulting, and by bookkeeping. [prepositional phrases not parallel]

Andersen's goals are to win new clients, keeping old clients happy, and finding new enterprises. [infinitive mixed with gerunds]

2.0 PUNCTUATION

On the highway, signs tell you when to slow down or stop, where to turn, and when to merge. In similar fashion, punctuation helps readers negotiate your prose. The proper use of punctuation keeps readers from losing track of your meaning.

2.1 Periods

Use a period (1) to end any sentence that is not a question, (2) with certain abbreviations, and (3) between dollars and cents in an amount of money.

2.2 Question Marks

Use a question mark after any direct question that requests an answer:

> Are you planning to enclose a check, or shall we bill you?

Don't use a question mark with commands phrased as questions for the sake of politeness:

> Will you send us a check today.

A question mark should precede quotation marks, parentheses, and brackets if it is part of the quoted or parenthetical material; otherwise, it should follow:

> This issue of *Inc.* has an article titled "What's Your Entrepreneurial IQ?"

> Have you read the article "Five Principles of Guerrilla Marketing"?

Do not use the question mark with indirect questions or with requests:

> Mr. Antonelli asked whether anyone had seen Nathalia lately.

Do not use a comma or a period with a question mark; the question mark takes the place of these punctuation marks.

2.3 Exclamation Points

Use exclamation points after highly emotional language. Because business writing almost never calls for emotional language, you will seldom use exclamation points.

2.4 Semicolons

Semicolons have three main uses. One is to separate two closely related independent clauses:

> The outline for the report is due within a week; the report itself is due at the end of the month.

A semicolon should also be used instead of a comma when the items in a series have commas within them:

> Our previous meetings were on November 11, 2004; February 20, 2005; and April 28, 2006.

Finally, a semicolon should be used to separate independent clauses when the second one begins with a conjunctive adverb such as *however*, *therefore*, or *nevertheless* or a phrase such as *for example* or *in that case*:

> Our supplier has been out of part D712 for 10 weeks; however, we have found another source that can ship the part right away.

> His test scores were quite low; on the other hand, he has a lot of relevant experience.

Section 4.4 has more information on using transitional words and phrases.

Semicolons should always be placed outside of question marks or parenthesis.

2.5 Colons

Use a colon after the salutation in a business letter. You should also use a colon at the end of a sentence or phrase introducing a list or (sometimes) a quotation:

> Our study included the three most critical problems: insufficient capital, incompetent management, and inappropriate location.

A colon should not be used when the list, quotation, or idea is a direct object of the verb or preposition. This rule applies whether the list is set off or run in:

> We are able to supply
> staples
> wood screws
> nails
> toggle bolts

> This shipment includes 9 DVDs, 12 CDs, and 4 USB flash drives.

Another way you can use a colon is to separate the main clause and another sentence element when the second explains, illustrates, or amplifies the first:

> Management was unprepared for the union representatives' demands: this fact alone accounts for their arguing well into the night.

However, in contemporary usage, such clauses are frequently separated by a semicolon.

Colons should always be placed outside of question marks or parenthesis.

2.6 Commas

Commas have many uses; the most common is to separate items in a series:

> He took the job, learned it well, worked hard, and succeeded.

> Put paper, pencils, and paper clips on the requisition list.

Company style may dictate omitting the final comma in a series. However, if you have a choice, use the final comma; it's often necessary to prevent misunderstanding.

A second place to use a comma is between independent clauses that are joined by a coordinating conjunction (*and*, *but*, or *or*) unless one or both are very short:

> She spoke to the sales staff, and he spoke to the production staff.

> I was advised to proceed and I did.

A third use for the comma is to separate a dependent clause at the beginning of a sentence from an independent clause:

> Because of our lead in the market, we may be able to risk introducing a new product.

However, a dependent clause at the end of a sentence is separated from the independent clause by a comma only when the dependent clause is unnecessary to the main meaning of the sentence:

> We may be able to introduce a new product, although it may involve some risk.

A fourth use for the comma is after an introductory phrase or word:

> Starting with this amount of capital, we can survive in the red for one year.

> Through more careful planning, we may be able to serve more people.

> Yes, you may proceed as originally planned.

However, with short introductory prepositional phrases and some one-syllable words (such as hence and thus), the comma is often omitted:

> Before January 1 we must complete the inventory.

> Thus we may not need to hire anyone.

> In July we will complete the move to Tulsa.

Fifth, paired commas are used to set off nonrestrictive clauses and phrases. A **restrictive clause** is one that cannot be omitted without altering the meaning of the main clause, whereas a **nonrestrictive clause** can be:

> The *Time Magazine* website, which is produced by Steve Conley, has won several design awards. [nonrestrictive: the material in parentheses could be omitted]

> The website that is produced by Steve Conley has won several design awards. [restrictive: no commas are used before and after *that is produced by Steve Conley* because this information is necessary to the meaning of the sentence— it specifies which website]

A sixth use for paired commas is to set off appositive words and phrases (an **appositive** has the same meaning as the word it is in apposition to). Like nonrestrictive clauses, appositives can be dropped without changing or obscuring the meaning of the sentence:

> Conley, a freelance designer, also produces the websites for several nonprofit corporations.

Seventh, commas are used between adjectives modifying the same noun (coordinate adjectives):

> She left Monday for a long, difficult recruiting trip.

To test the appropriateness of such a comma, try reversing the order of the adjectives: *a difficult, long recruiting trip*. If the order cannot be reversed, leave out the comma (a *good old friend* isn't the same as an *old good friend*). A comma should not be used when one of the adjectives is part of the noun. Compare these two phrases:

> a distinguished, well-known figure

> a distinguished public figure

The adjective-noun combination of *public* and *figure* has been used together so often that it has come to be considered a single thing: *public figure*. So no comma is required.

Eighth, commas are used both before and after the year in sentences that include month, day, and year:

> It will be sent by December 15, 2007, from our Cincinnati plant.

Some companies write dates in another form: 15 December 2007. No commas should be used in that case. Nor is a comma needed when only the month and year are present (December 2007).

Ninth, commas are used to set off a variety of parenthetical words and phrases within sentences, including state names, dates, abbreviations, transitional expressions, and contrasted elements:

> They were, in fact, prepared to submit a bid.

> Habermacher, Inc., went public in 1999.

> Our goal was increased profits, not increased market share.

> Service, then, is our main concern.

> The factory was completed in Chattanooga, Tennessee, just three weeks ago.

> Joanne Dubiik, M.D., has applied for a loan from First Savings.

> I started work here on March 1, 2003, and soon received my first promotion.

Tenth, a comma is used to separate a quotation from the rest of the sentence:

> Your warranty reads, "These conditions remain in effect for one year from date of purchase."

However, the comma is left out when the quotation as a whole is built into the structure of the sentence:

> He hurried off with an angry "Look where you're going."

Finally, a comma should be used whenever it's needed to avoid confusion or an unintended meaning. Compare the following:

> Ever since they have planned new ventures more carefully.

> Ever since, they have planned new ventures more carefully.

2.7 Dashes

Use a dash to surround a comment that is a sudden turn in thought:

> Membership in the IBSA—it's expensive but worth it— may be obtained by applying to our New York office.

A dash can also be used to emphasize a parenthetical word or phrase:

> Third-quarter profits—in excess of $2 million—are up sharply.

Finally, use dashes to set off a phrase that contains commas:

> All our offices—Milwaukee, New Orleans, and Phoenix—have sent representatives.

Don't confuse a dash with a hyphen. A dash separates and emphasizes words, phrases, and clauses more strongly than a comma or parentheses can; a hyphen ties two words so tightly that they almost become one word.

When using a computer, use the em-dash symbol. When typing a dash in e-mail or on a typewriter, type two hyphens with no space before, between, or after.

A second type of dash, the en-dash, can be produced with computer word-processing and page-layout programs. This kind of dash is shorter than the regular dash and longer than a hyphen. It is reserved almost exclusively for indicating "to" or "through" with numbers such as dates and pages: *2001–2002*; *pages 30–44*.

2.8   Hyphens

Hyphens are mainly used in three ways. The first is to separate the parts of compound words beginning with such prefixes as *self-*, *ex-*, *quasi-*, and *all-*:

> self-assured   quasi-official
>
> ex-wife   all-important

However, do not use hyphens in words that have prefixes such as *pro, anti, non, re, pre, un, inter,* and *extra*:

> prolabor   nonunion
>
> antifascist   interdepartmental

Exceptions occur when (1) the prefix occurs before a proper noun or (2) the vowel at the end of the prefix is the same as the first letter of the root word:

> pro-Republican   anti-American
>
> anti-inflammatory   extra-atmospheric

When in doubt, consult your dictionary.

Hyphens are used in some types of spelled-out numbers. For instance, they are used to separate the parts of a spelled-out number from *twenty-one* to *ninety-nine* and for spelled-out fractions: *two-thirds, one-sixth* (although some style guides say not to hyphenate fractions used as nouns).

Certain compound nouns are formed by using hyphens: *secretary-treasurer, city-state*. Check your dictionary for compounds you're unsure about.

Hyphens are also used in some compound adjectives, which are adjectives made up of two or more words. Specifically, you should use hyphens in compound adjectives that come before the noun:

> an interest-bearing account   well-informed executives

However, you need not hyphenate when the adjective follows a linking verb:

> This account is interest bearing.

> Their executives are well informed.

You can shorten sentences that list similar hyphenated words by dropping the common part from all but the last word:

> Check the costs of first-, second-, and third-class postage.

Finally, hyphens may be used to divide words at the end of a typed line. Such hyphenation is best avoided, but when you have to divide words at the end of a line, do so correctly (see Section 3.5). A dictionary will show how words are divided into syllables.

2.9   Apostrophes

Use an apostrophe in the possessive form of a noun (but not in a pronoun):

> On his desk was a reply to Bette *Ainsley's* application for the manager's position.

Apostrophes are also used in place of the missing letter(s) of a contraction:

WHOLE WORDS	CONTRACTION
we will	we'll
do not	don't
they are	they're

2.10   Quotation Marks

Use quotation marks to surround words that are repeated exactly as they were said or written:

> The collection letter ended by saying, "This is your third and final notice."

Remember: (1) When the quoted material is a complete sentence, the first word is capitalized. (2) The final comma or period goes inside the closing quotation marks.

Quotation marks are also used to set off the title of a newspaper story, magazine article, or book chapter:

> You should read "Legal Aspects of the Collection Letter" in *Today's Credit*.

Quotation marks may also be used to indicate special treatment for words or phrases, such as terms that you're using in an unusual or ironic way:

> Our management "team" spends more time squabbling than working to solve company problems.

When you are defining a word, put the definition in quotation marks:

> The abbreviation *etc.* means "and so forth."

When using quotation marks, take care to insert the closing marks as well as the opening ones.

Although periods and commas go inside any quotation marks, colons and semicolons go outside them. A question mark goes inside the quotation marks only if the quotation is a question:

> All that day we wondered, "Is he with us?"

If the quotation is not a question but the entire sentence is, the question mark goes outside:

> What did she mean by "You will hear from me"?

For quotes within quotes, use single quotation marks within double:

> As David Pottruck, former co-CEO of Charles Schwab, told it, "I assembled about 100 managers at the base of the Golden Gate Bridge and gave them jackets emblazoned with the phrase 'Crossing the Chasm' and then led them across the bridge."

Otherwise, do not use single quotation marks for anything, including titles of works—that's British style.

2.11 Parentheses and Brackets

Use parentheses to surround comments that are entirely incidental or to supply additional information:

> Our figures do not match yours, although (if my calculations are correct) they are closer than we thought.

> These kinds of supplements do not require FDA (Food and Drug Administration) approval.

Parentheses are used in legal documents to surround figures in arabic numerals that follow the same amount in words:

> Remittance will be One Thousand Two Hundred Dollars ($1,200).

Be careful to put punctuation marks (period, comma, and so on) outside the parentheses unless they are part of the statement in parentheses. And keep in mind that parentheses have both an opening and a closing mark; both should always be used, even when setting off listed items within text: *(1)*, not *1)*.

Brackets are used for notation, comment, explanation, or correction within quoted material:

> In the interview, multimillionaire Bob Buford, said, "One of my major influences was Peter [Drucker], who encourages people and helps them believe in themselves."

Brackets are also used for parenthetical material that falls within parentheses:

> Drucker's magnum opus (*Management: Tasks, Responsibilities, and Practices* [Harper & Row, 1979]) has influenced generations of entrepreneurs.

2.12 Ellipses

Use ellipsis points, or three evenly spaced periods, to indicate that material has been left out of a direct quotation. Use them only in direct quotations and only at the point where material was left out. In the following example, the first sentence is quoted in the second:

> The Dow Jones Industrial Average fell 276.39 points, or 2.6%, during the week to 10292.31.

> According to the *Wall Street Journal*, "The Dow Jones Industrial Average fell 276.39 points . . . to 10,292.31."

The number of dots in ellipses is not optional; always use three. Occasionally, the points of ellipsis come at the end of a sentence, where they seem to grow a fourth dot. Don't be fooled: One of the dots is a period. Ellipsis points should always be preceded and followed by a space.

Avoid using ellipses to represent a pause in your writing; use a dash for that purpose:

> At first we had planned to leave for the conference on Wednesday—but then we changed our minds. [not *on Wednesday . . . but then*]

3.0 MECHANICS

The most obvious and least tolerable mistakes that a business writer makes are probably those related to grammar and punctuation. However, a number of small details, known as writing mechanics, demonstrate the writer's polish and reflect on the company's professionalism.

When it comes to mechanics, also called *style*, many of the "rules" are not hard and fast. Publications and organizations vary in their preferred styles for capitalization, abbreviations, numbers, italics, and so on. Here, we'll try to differentiate between practices that are generally accepted and those that can vary. When you are writing materials for a specific company or organization, find out the preferred style (such as *The Chicago Manual of Style* or *Webster's Style Manual*). Otherwise, choose a respected style guide. The key to style is consistency: If you spell out the word *percent* in one part of a document, don't use the percent sign in a similar context elsewhere in the same document.

3.1 Capitalization

With capitalization, you can follow either an "up" style (when in doubt, capitalize: *Federal Government, Board of Directors*) or a "down" style (when in doubt, use lowercase: *federal government, board of directors*). The trend over the last few decades has been toward the down style. Your best bet is to get a good style manual and consult it when you have a capitalization question. Following are some rules that most style guides agree on. Capital letters are used at the beginning of certain word groups:

- **Complete sentence:** Before hanging up, he said, "We'll meet here on Wednesday at noon."
- **Formal statement following a colon:** She has a favorite motto: Where there's a will, there's a way.
- **Phrase used as sentence:** Absolutely not!
- **Quoted sentence embedded in another sentence:** Scott said, "Nobody was here during lunch hour except me."
- **List of items set off from text:** Three preliminary steps are involved:

> Design review
> Budgeting
> Scheduling

Capitalize proper adjectives and proper nouns (the names of particular persons, places, and things):

> Darrell Greene lived in a Victorian mansion.

> We sent Ms. Larson an application form, informing her that not all applicants are interviewed.

> Let's consider opening a branch in the West, perhaps at the west end of Tucson, Arizona.

> As office buildings go, the Kinney Building is a pleasant setting for TDG Office Equipment.

> We are going to have to cancel our plans for hiring French and German sales reps.

Larson's name is capitalized because she is a particular applicant, whereas the general term *applicant* is left uncapitalized. Likewise, *West* is capitalized when it refers to a particular place but not when it means a direction. In the same way, *office* and *building* are not capitalized when they are general terms (common nouns), but they are capitalized when they are part of the title of a particular office or building (proper nouns). Some proper adjectives are lowercased when they are part of terms that have come into common use, such as *french fries* and *roman numerals*.

Titles within families or companies as well as professional titles may also be capitalized:

> I turned down Uncle David when he offered me a job, since I wouldn't be comfortable working for one of my relatives.

> We've never had a president quite like President Sweeney.

People's titles are capitalized when they are used in addressing a person, especially in a formal context. They are not usually capitalized, however, when they are used merely to identify the person:

> Address the letter to Chairperson Anna Palmer.

> I wish to thank Chairperson Anna Palmer for her assistance.

> Anna Palmer, chairperson of the board, took the podium.

Also capitalize titles if they are used by themselves in addressing a person:

> Thank you, Doctor, for your donation.

Always capitalize the first word of the salutation and complimentary close of a letter:

> *Dear* Mr. Andrews: *Yours* very truly,

The names of organizations are capitalized, of course; so are the official names of their departments and divisions. However, do not use capitals when referring in general terms to a department or division, especially one in another organization:

> Route this memo to Personnel.

> Larry Tien was transferred to the Microchip Division.

> Will you be enrolled in the Psychology Department?

> Someone from the personnel department at EnerTech stopped by the booth.

Capitalization is unnecessary when using a word like *company*, *corporation*, or *university* alone:

> The corporation plans to issue 50,000 shares of common stock.

Likewise, the names of specific products are capitalized, although the names of general product types are not:

Apple computer   Tide laundry detergent   Xerox machine

When it comes to government terminology, here are some guides to capitalization: (1) Lowercase *federal* unless it is part of an agency name; (2) capitalize names of courts, departments, bureaus, offices, and agencies, but lowercase such references as *the bureau* and *the department* when the full name is not used; (3) lowercase the titles of government officers unless they precede a specific person's name: *the secretary of state, the senator, the ambassador, the governor, the mayor,* but *Mayor Gonzalez* (note: style guides vary on whether to capitalize *president* when referring to the president of the United States without including the person's name); capitalize the names of laws and acts: *the Sherman Antitrust Act, the Civil Rights Act;* (5) capitalize the names of political parties, but lowercase the word *party: Democratic party, Libertarian party.*

One problem that often arises in writing about places is the treatment of two or more proper nouns of the same type. When the common word comes before the specific names, it is capitalized; when it comes after the specific names, it is not:

> Lakes Ontario and Huron

> Allegheny and Monongahela rivers

The names of languages, races, and ethnic groups are capitalized: Japanese, Caucasian, Hispanic. But racial terms that denote only skin color are not capitalized: black, white.

When referring to the titles of books, articles, magazines, newspapers, reports, movies, and so on, you should capitalize the first and last words and all nouns, pronouns, adjectives, verbs, and adverbs, and capitalize prepositions and conjunctions with five letters or more. Except for the first and last words, do not capitalize articles:

> *Economics During the Great War*

> "An Investigation into the Market for Long-Distance Services"

> "What Successes Are Made Of"

When *the* is part of the official name of a newspaper or magazine, it should be treated this way too:

> *The Wall Street Journal*

Style guides vary in their recommendations regarding capitalization of hyphenated words in titles. A general guide is to capitalize the second word in a temporary compound (a compound that is hyphenated for grammatical reasons and not spelling reasons), such as *Law-Abiding Citizen,* but to lowercase the word if the term is always hyphenated, such as *Son-in-law*).

References to specific pages, paragraphs, lines, and the like are not capitalized: *page 73, line 3*. However, in most other numbered or lettered references, the identifying term is capitalized:

Chapter 4, Serial No. 382–2203, Item B-11

Finally, the names of academic degrees are capitalized when they follow a person's name but are not capitalized when used in a general sense:

I received a bachelor of science degree.

Thomas Whitelaw, Doctor of Philosophy, will attend.

Similarly, general courses of study are not capitalized, but the names of specific classes are:

She studied accounting as an undergraduate.

She is enrolled in Accounting 201.

3.2 Underscores and Italics

Usually a line typed underneath a word or phrase either provides emphasis or indicates the title of a book, magazine, or newspaper. If possible, use italics instead of an underscore. Italics (or underlining) should also be used for defining terms and for discussing words as words:

In this report *net sales* refers to after-tax sales dollars.

The word *building* is a common noun and should not be capitalized.

Also use italics to set off foreign words, unless the words have become a common part of English:

Top Shelf is considered the *sine qua non* of comic book publishers.

Chris uses a laissez-faire [no italic] management style.

3.3 Abbreviations

Abbreviations are used heavily in tables, charts, lists, and forms. They're used sparingly in prose. Here are some abbreviation situations to watch for:

- In most cases do not use periods with acronyms (words formed from the initial letter or letters of parts of a term): *CEO, CD-ROM, DOS, YWCA, FDA*; but: *Ph.D., M.A., M.D.*
- Use periods with abbreviations such as *Mr., Ms., Sr., Jr., a.m., p.m., B.C.,* and *A.D.*
- The trend is away from using periods with such units of measure as *mph, mm,* and *lb.*
- Use periods with such Latin abbreviations as *e.g., i.e., et al.,* and *etc.* However, style guides recommend that you avoid using these Latin forms and instead use their English equivalents (*for example, that is, and others, and,* respectively). If you must use these abbreviations, such as in parenthetical expressions or footnotes, do not put them in italics.
- Some companies have abbreviations as part of their names (*&, Co., Inc., Ltd.*). When you refer to such firms by name, be sure to double-check the preferred spelling, including spacing: *AT&T; Barnes & Noble; Carson Pirie Scott & Company; PepsiCo; Kate Spade, Inc.; National Data Corporation; Siemens Corp.; Glaxo Wellcome PLC; US Airways; U.S. Business Reporter.*
- Most style guides recommend that you spell out *United States* as a noun and reserve *U.S.* as an adjective.

One way to handle an abbreviation that you want to use throughout a document is to spell it out the first time you use it, follow it with the abbreviation in parentheses, and then use the abbreviation in the remainder of the document.

3.4 Numbers

Numbers may be correctly handled many ways in business writing, so follow company style. In the absence of a set style, however, generally spell out all numbers from one to nine and use arabic numerals for the rest.

There are some exceptions to this general rule. For example, never begin a sentence with a numeral:

Twenty of us produced 641 units per week in the first 12 weeks of the year.

Use numerals for the numbers one through nine if they're in the same list as larger numbers:

Our weekly quota rose from 9 to 15 to 27.

Use numerals for percentages, time of day (except with o'clock), dates, and (in general) dollar amounts:

Our division is responsible for 7 percent of total sales.

The meeting is scheduled for 8:30 a.m. on August 2.

Add $3 for postage and handling.

When using numerals for time, be consistent: It should be *between 10:00 a.m. and 4:30 p.m.*, not *between 10 a.m. and 4:30 p.m.* Expressions such as *4:00 o'clock* and *7 a.m. in the morning* are redundant.

Use a comma in numbers expressing thousands (1,257), unless your company specifies another style. When dealing with numbers in the millions and billions, combine words and figures: 7.3 million, 2 billion.

When writing dollar amounts, use a decimal point only if cents are included. In lists of two or more dollar amounts, use the decimal point either for all or for none:

He sent two checks, one for $67.92 and one for $90.00.

When two numbers fall next to each other in a sentence, use figures for the number that is largest, most difficult to spell, or part of a physical measurement; use words for the other:

I have learned to manage a classroom of 30 twelve-year-olds.

She's won a bonus for selling 24 thirty-volume sets.

You'll need twenty 3-inch bolts.

In addresses, all street numbers except One are in figures. So are suite and room numbers and ZIP Codes. For street names that are numbered, practice varies so widely that you should use the form specified on an organization's letterhead or in a reliable directory. All of the following examples are correct:

One Fifth Avenue   297 Ninth Street
1839 44th Street   11026 West 78 Place

Telephone numbers are always expressed in figures. Parentheses may separate the area code from the rest of the number, but a slash or a dash may be used instead, especially if the entire phone number is enclosed in parentheses:

382–8329   (602/382–8329) 602–382–8329

Percentages are always expressed in figures. The word *percent* is used in most cases, but *%* may be used in tables, forms, and statistical writing.

Physical measurements such as distance, weight, and volume are also often expressed in figures: *9 kilometers, 5 feet 3 inches, 7 pounds 10 ounces.*

Decimal numbers are always written in figures. In most cases, add a zero to the left of the decimal point if the number is less than one and does not already start with a zero:

1.38   .07   0.2

In a series of related decimal numbers with at least one number greater than one, make sure that all numbers smaller than one have a zero to the left of the decimal point: 1.20, 0.21, 0.09.

Simple fractions are written in words, but more complicated fractions are expressed in figures or, if easier to read, in figures and words:

two-thirds   9/32   2 hundredths

Most style guides recommend that you use a comma with numbers consisting of four digits: *2,345,* not *2345.*

When typing ordinal numbers, as *3rd edition* or *21st century,* your word-processing program may automatically make the letters *rd* (or *st, th,* or *nd*) into a superscript. Do yourself a favor and turn that formatting function off in your "Preferences," as superscripts should not be used in regular prose or even in bibliographies.

3.5 Word Division

In general, avoid dividing words at the ends of lines. When you must do so, follow these rules:

- Don't divide one-syllable words (such as *since, walked,* and *thought*), abbreviations (*mgr.*), contractions (*isn't*), or numbers expressed in numerals (*117,500*).
- Divide words between syllables, as specified in a dictionary or word-division manual.
- Make sure that at least three letters of the divided word are moved to the second line: *sin-cerely* instead of *sincere-ly.*
- Do not end a page or more than three consecutive lines with hyphens.
- Leave syllables consisting of a single vowel at the end of the first line (*impedi-ment* instead of *imped-iment*), except

when the single vowel is part of a suffix such as *-able, -ible, -ical,* or *-ity* (*re-spons-ible* instead of *re-sponsi-ble*).
- Divide between double letters (*tomor-row*), except when the root word ends in double letters (*call-ing* instead of *cal-ling*).
- Wherever possible, divide hyphenated words at the hyphen only: instead of *anti-inde-pendence,* use *anti-in-dependence.*

4.0 VOCABULARY

Using the right word in the right place is a crucial skill in business communication. However, many pitfalls await the unwary.

4.1 Frequently Confused Words

Because the following sets of words sound similar, be careful not to use one when you mean to use the other:

WORD	MEANING
accede	to comply with
exceed	to go beyond
accept	to take
except	to exclude
access	admittance
excess	too much
advice	suggestion
advise	to suggest
affect	to influence
effect	the result
allot	to distribute
a lot	much or many
all ready	completely prepared
already	completed earlier
born	given birth to
borne	carried
capital	money; chief city
capitol	a government building
cite	to quote
sight	a view
site	a location
complement	complete amount; to go well with
compliment	expression of esteem; to flatter
corespondent	party in a divorce suit
correspondent	letter writer
council	a panel of people
counsel	advice; a lawyer
defer	to put off until later
differ	to be different
device	a mechanism
devise	to plan
die	to stop living; a tool
dye	to color

WORD	MEANING
discreet	careful
discrete	separate
envelop	to surround
envelope	a covering for a letter
forth	forward
fourth	number four
holey	full of holes
holy	sacred
wholly	completely
human	of people
humane	kindly
incidence	frequency
incidents	events
instance	example
instants	moments
interstate	between states
intrastate	within a state
later	afterward
latter	the second of two
lead	a metal; to guide
led	guided
lean	to rest at an angle
lien	a claim
levee	embankment
levy	tax
loath	reluctant
loathe	to hate
loose	free; not tight
lose	to mislay
material	substance
materiel	equipment
miner	mineworker
minor	underage person
moral	virtuous; a lesson
morale	sense of well-being
ordinance	law
ordnance	weapons
overdo	to do in excess
overdue	past due
peace	lack of conflict
piece	a fragment
pedal	a foot lever
peddle	to sell
persecute	to torment
prosecute	to sue
personal	private
personnel	employees
precedence	priority
precedents	previous events

principal	sum of money; chief; main
principle	general rule
rap	to knock
wrap	to cover
residence	home
residents	inhabitants
right	correct
rite	ceremony
write	to form words on a surface
role	a part to play
roll	to tumble; a list
root	part of a plant
rout	to defeat
route	a traveler's way
shear	to cut
sheer	thin, steep
stationary	immovable
stationery	paper
than	as compared with
then	at that time
their	belonging to them
there	in that place
they're	they are
to	a preposition
too	excessively; also
two	the number
waive	to set aside
wave	a swell of water; a gesture
weather	atmospheric conditions
whether	if
who's	contraction of "who is" or "who has"
whose	possessive form of who

In the preceding list, only enough of each word's meaning is given to help you distinguish between the words in each group. Several meanings are left out entirely. For more complete definitions, consult a dictionary.

4.2 Frequently Misused Words

The following words tend to be misused for reasons other than their sound. Reference books (including the *Random House College Dictionary*, revised edition; Follett's *Modern American Usage*; and Fowler's *Modern English Usage*) can help you with similar questions of usage:

a lot: When the writer means "many," *a lot* is always two separate words, never one.

aggravate/irritate: *Aggravate* means "to make things worse: Sitting in the smoke-filled room *aggravated* his sinus condition. *Irritate* means "to annoy": Her constant questions *irritated* [not *aggravated*] me.

anticipate/expect: *Anticipate* means "to prepare for": Macy's *anticipated* increased demand for athletic shoes in spring by ordering in November. In formal usage, it is incorrect to use *anticipate* for *expect*: I *expected* (not *anticipated*) a better response to our presentation than we actually got.

compose/comprise: The whole comprises the parts:

> The company's distribution division *comprises* four departments.

It would be incorrect usage to say

> The company's distribution division *is comprised of* four departments.

In that construction, *is composed of* or *consists of* would be preferable. It might be helpful to think of *comprise* as meaning "encompasses" or "contains."

continual/continuous: *Continual* refers to ongoing actions that have breaks:

> Her *continual* complaining will accomplish little in the long run.

Continuous refers to ongoing actions without interruptions or breaks:

> A *continuous* stream of paper came out of the fax machine.

convince/persuade: One is *convinced* of a fact or that something is true; one is *persuaded* by someone else to do something. The use of *to* with *convince* is unidiomatic—you don't convince someone to do something, you persuade them to do it.

correspond with: Use this phrase when you are talking about exchanging letters. Use *correspond to* when you mean "similar to." Use either *correspond with* or *correspond to* when you mean "relate to."

dilemma/problem: Technically, a *dilemma* is a situation in which one must choose between two undesirable alternatives. It shouldn't be used when no choice is actually involved.

disinterested: This word means "fair, unbiased, having no favorites, impartial." If you mean "bored" or "not interested," use *uninterested*.

etc.: This abbreviated form of the Latin phrase *et cetera* means "and so on" or "and so forth," so it is never correct to write *and etc.* The current tendency among business writers is to use English rather than Latin.

flaunt/flout: To *flaunt* is to be ostentatious or boastful; to *flout* is to mock or scoff at.

impact: Avoid using *impact* as a verb when *influence* or *affect* is meant.

imply/infer: Both refer to hints. Their great difference lies in who is acting. The writer *implies*; the reader *infers*, sees between the lines.

lay: This word is a transitive verb. Never use it for the intransitive lie. (See Section 1.3.3.)

lend/loan: *Lend* is a verb; *loan* is a noun. Usage such as "Can you loan me $5?" is therefore incorrect.

less/fewer: Use *less* for uncountable quantities (such as amounts of water, air, sugar, and oil). Use *fewer* for countable quantities (such as numbers of jars, saws, words, pages, and humans). The same distinction applies to *much* and *little* (uncountable) versus *many* and *few* (countable).

liable/likely: *Liable* means "responsible for": I will hold you *liable* if this deal doesn't go through. It is incorrect to use *liable* for "possible": Anything is *likely* (not *liable*) to happen.

literally: *Literally* means "actually" or "precisely"; it is often misused to mean "almost" or "virtually." It is usually best left out entirely or replaced with *figuratively*.

many/much: See *less.*

regardless: The *less* suffix is the negative part. No word needs two negative parts, so don't add *ir* (a negative prefix) to the beginning. There is no such word as *irregardless*.

try: Always follow with *to*, never *and*.

4.3 Frequently Misspelled Words

All of us, even the world's best spellers, sometimes have to check a dictionary for the spelling of some words. People who have never memorized the spelling of commonly used words must look up so many that they grow exasperated and give up on spelling words correctly.

Don't expect perfection, and don't surrender. If you can memorize the spelling of just the words listed here, you'll need the dictionary far less often and you'll write with more confidence:

absence	assistant
absorption	asterisk
accessible	auditor
accommodate	bankruptcy
accumulate	believable
achieve	brilliant
advantageous	bulletin
affiliated	calendar
aggressive	campaign
alignment	category
aluminum	ceiling
ambience	changeable
analyze	clientele
apparent	collateral
appropriate	committee
argument	comparative
asphalt	competitor

concede	irresistible	ridiculous	tangible
congratulations	jewelry	salable	tariff
connoisseur	judgment	secretary	technique
consensus	judicial	seize	tenant
convenient	labeling	separate	truly
convertible	legitimate	sincerely	unanimous
corroborate	leisure	succeed	until
criticism	license	suddenness	vacillate
definitely	litigation	superintendent	vacuum
description	maintenance	supersede	vicious
desirable	mathematics	surprise	
dilemma	mediocre		
disappear	minimum		
disappoint	necessary		
disbursement	negligence		
discrepancy	negotiable		
dissatisfied	newsstand		
dissipate	noticeable		
eligible	occurrence		
embarrassing	omission		
endorsement	parallel		
exaggerate	pastime		
exceed	peaceable		
exhaust	permanent		
existence	perseverance		
extraordinary	persistent		
fallacy	personnel		
familiar	persuade		
flexible	possesses		
fluctuation	precede		
forty	predictable		
gesture	preferred		
grievous	privilege		
haphazard	procedure		
harassment	proceed		
holiday	pronunciation		
illegible	psychology		
immigrant	pursue		
incidentally	questionnaire		
indelible	receive		
independent	recommend		
indispensable	repetition		
insistent	rescind		
intermediary	rhythmical		

4.4 Transitional Words and Phrases

The following sentences don't communicate as well as they could because they lack a transitional word or phrase:

> Production delays are inevitable. Our current lag time in filling orders is one month.

A semicolon between the two sentences would signal a close relationship between their meanings, but it wouldn't even hint at what that relationship is. Here are the sentences again, now linked by means of a semicolon, with a space for a transitional word or phrase:

> Production delays are inevitable; _____ our current lag time in filling orders is one month.

Now read the sentence with *nevertheless* in the blank space. Then try *therefore, incidentally, in fact,* and *at any rate* in the blank. Each substitution changes the meaning of the sentence.

Here are some transitional words (conjunctive adverbs) that will help you write more clearly:

accordingly	furthermore	moreover
anyway	however	otherwise
besides	incidentally	still
consequently	likewise	therefore
finally	meanwhile	

The following transitional phrases are used in the same way:

as a result	in other words
at any rate	in the second place
for example	on the other hand
in fact	to the contrary

When one of these words or phrases joins two independent clauses, it should be preceded by a semicolon and followed by a comma:

> The consultant recommended a complete reorganization; moreover, she suggested that we drop several products.

References

PROLOGUE

1. Maureen Jenkins, "Yours for the Taking," *Boeing Frontiers Online*, June 2004 [accessed 25 September 2005] www.boeing.com; "Firm Predicts Top 10 Workforce/Workplace Trends for 2004," *Enterprise*, 8–14 December 2003, 1–2; Scott Hudson, "Keeping Employees Happy," *Community Banker*, September 2003, 34+; Marvin J. Cetron and Owen Davies, "Trends Now Changing the World: Technology, the Workplace, Management, and Institutions," *Futurist* 35, no. 2 (March/April 2001): 27–42.
2. Steve Crabtree, "Beyond the Dot-Com Bust; How Managers Can Help Younger Workers Regain Their Lost Momentum," *Gallup Management Journal*, 11 December 2003, 1+.
3. Jim Puzzanghera, "Coalition of High-Tech Firms to Urge Officials to Help Keep U.S. Competitive," *San Jose Mercury News*, 8 January 2004 [accessed 14 February 2004] www.ebscohost.com.
4. Amanda Bennett, "GE Redesigns Rungs of Career Ladder," *Wall Street Journal*, 15 March 1993, B1, B3.
5. Robin White Goode, "International and Foreign Language Skills Have an Edge," *Black Enterprise*, May 1995, 53.
6. Nancy M. Somerick, "Managing a Communication Internship Program," *Bulletin of the Association for Business Communication* 56, no. 3 (1993): 10–20.
7. Joan Lloyd, "Changing Workplace Requires You to Alter Your Career Outlook," *Milwaukee Journal Sentinel*, 4 July 1999, 1; Camille DeBell, "Ninety Years in the World of Work in America," *Career Development Quarterly* 50, no. 1 (September 2001): 77–88.
8. Jeffrey R. Young, "'E-Portfolios' Could Give Students a New Sense of Their Accomplishments," *Chronicle of Higher Education*, 8 March 2002, A31.
9. Brian Carcione, e-portfolio [accessed 20 December 2006] http://eportfolio.psu.edu.

CHAPTER 1

1. Six Apart website [accessed 4 August 2006] www.sixapart.com; David Kirkpatrick and Daniel Roth, "Why There's No Escaping the Blog," *Fortune*, 10 January 2005, 44–50; "People of the Year," *PC Magazine*, 12 December 2004 [accessed 21 June 2005] www.pcmag.com; Thomas Mucha, "A Motor City Marketing Lesson," *Business 2.0*, 10 March 2005 [accessed 13 March 2005] www.business2.com; Lee Gomes, "How the Next Big Thing in Technology Morphed into a Really Big Thing," *Wall Street Journal*, 4 October 2004, B1; David Kirkpatrick, "It's Hard to Manage If You Don't Blog," *Fortune*, 4 October 2004, 46.
2. Julie Connelly, "Youthful Attitudes, Sobering Realities," *New York Times*, 28 October 2003, E1, E6; Nigel Andrews and Laura D'Andrea Tyson, "The Upwardly Global MBA," *Strategy + Business*, Issue 36, 6069; Jim McKay, "Communication Skills Found Lacking," *Pittsburgh Post-Gazette*, 28 February 2005 [accessed 28 February 2005] www.delawareonline.com.
3. Richard L. Daft, *Management*, 6th ed. (Cincinnati: Thomson South-Western, 2003), 580.
4. Based in part on Nicholas Carr, "Lessons in Corporate Blogging," *BusinessWeek*, 18 July 2006, 9; Susan Meisinger, "To Keep Employees, Talk—and Listen—to Them!" *HR Magazine*, August 2006, 10.
5. Daft, *Management*, 147.
6. Gareth R. Jones and Jennifer M. George, *Contemporary Management*, 3rd ed. (New York: McGraw-Hill Irwin, 2003), 512, 517.
7. Philip C. Kolin, *Successful Writing at Work*, 6th ed. (Boston: Houghton Mifflin, 2001), 17–23.

8. Donald O. Wilson, "Diagonal Communication Links with Organizations," *Journal of Business Communication* 29, no. 2 (Spring 1992): 129–143.
9. J. David Johnson, William A. Donohoe, Charles K. Atkin, and Sally Johnson, "Differences Between Formal and Informal Communication Channels," *Journal of Business Communication* 31, no. 2 (1994): 111–122.
10. David Pescovitz, "Technology of the Year: Social Network Applications," *Business 2.0*, November 2003, 113–114.
11. Tim Laseter and Rob Cross, "The Craft of Connection," *Strategy + Business*, Autumn 2006, 26–32.
12. "Do-It-Yourself Skills Enhancement: CFOs Value Communication Skills, But Few Firms Provide Training, Survey Shows," Press release, Accountemps, 28 July 2006 [accessed 8 August 2006] www.accountemps.com.
13. Don Hellriegel, Susan E. Jackson, and John W. Slocum, Jr., *Management: A Competency-Based Approach* (Cincinnati: Thomson South-Western, 2002), 447.
14. Jonathan Baldwin and Lucienne Roberts, *Visual Communication: From Theory to Practice* (Lausanne, Switzerland: AVA, 2006), 5.
15. Jeff Davidson, "Fighting Information Overload," *Canadian Manager*, Spring 2005, 16+.
16. Scott Ginsberg, "How to Give Your Staff Permission to Talk to You," Hello My Name Is Scott (website) [accessed 11 August 2006] www.hellomynameisscott.com.
17. Paul Martin Lester, *Visual Communication: Images with Messages* (Belmont, Calif.: Thomson South-Western, 2006), 6–8.
18. Michael R. Solomon, *Consumer Behavior: Buying, Having, and Being*, 6th ed. (Upper Saddle River, N.J.: Pearson Prentice Hall, 2004), 65.
19. Anne Field, "What You Say, What They Hear," *Harvard Management Communication Letter*, Winter 2005, 3–5.
20. Chuck Williams, *Management*, 2nd ed. (Cincinnati: Thomson South-Western, 2002), 690.
21. Charles G. Morris and Albert A. Maisto, *Psychology: An Introduction*, 12th ed. (Upper Saddle River, N.J.: Pearson Prentice Hall, 2005), 226–239; Saundra K. Ciccarelli and Glenn E. Meyer, *Psychology* (Upper Saddle River, N.J.: Prentice Hall, 2006), 210–229; Mark H. Ashcraft, *Cognition*, 4th ed. (Upper Saddle River, N.J.: Prentice Hall, 2006), 44–54.
22. Stephanie Armour, "Music Hath Charms for Some Workers—Others It Really Annoys," *USA Today*, 24 March 2006, B1–B2.
23. Debbie Weil, *The Corporate Blogging Book* (New York: Portfolio, 2006), 60.
24. Hellriegel et al., *Management: A Competency-Based Approach*, 451.
25. Laura L. Myers and Mary L. Tucker, "Increasing Awareness of Emotional Intelligence in a Business Curriculum," *Business Communication Quarterly*, March 2005, 44–51.
26. John Owens, "Good Communication in Workplace Is Basic to Getting Any Job Done," *Knight Ridder/Tribune Business News*, 9 July 2003, 1.
27. Tamar Lewin, "Study Finds Widespread Neglect of Writing Skills," *Desert Sun*, 26 April 2003, A12.
28. Williams, *Management*, 706–707.
29. Del Jones, "Watch Your Language, Ladies," *USA Today*, 24 November 2004, 3B.
30. "Employers, Beware: 'Techno Addicts' May Be More Liability Than Boon," Lockergnome.com, 18 August 2006 [accessed 23 August 2006] www.lockergnome.com.

31. Eric J. Sinrod, "Perspective: It's My Internet—I Can Do What I Want," News.com, 29 March 2006 [accessed 12 August 2006] www.news.com.

32. "The Hidden Dangers of Instant Messaging," Newsfactor.com, 5 July 2006 [accessed 12 August 2006] www.newsfactor.com.

33. Eric J. Sinrod, "Time to Crack Down on Tech at Work?" News.com, 14 June 2006 [accessed 12 August 2006] www.news.com.

34. A. Thomas Young, "Ethics in Business: Business of Ethics," *Vital Speeches*, 15 September 1992, 725–730.

35. "Undercover Marketing Uncovered," CBSnews.com, 25 July 2004 [accessed 11 April 2005] www.cbsnews.com; Stephanie Dunnewind, "Teen Recruits Create Word-of-Mouth 'Buzz' to Hook Peers on Products," *Seattle Times*, 20 November 2004 [accessed 11 April 2005] www.seattletimes.com.

36. Kolin, *Successful Writing at Work*, 24–30.

37. Nancy K. Kubasek, Bartley A. Brennan, and M. Neil Browne, *The Legal Environment of Business*, 3d ed. (Upper Saddle River, N.J.: Prentice-Hall, 2003), 172.

38. Kelli Esters, "Insurance Company to Repay $1.1 Million to Georgia Soldiers," *Ledger-Enquirer* (Columbus, Ga.), 26 May 2005 [accessed 28 June 2005] www.ebsco.com; Diana B. Henriques, "Insurer to Refund Money to Soldiers Who Bought High-Cost Life Policies," *New York Times*, 23 September 2004, C1, C4; Diana B. Henriques, "Going Off to War, and Vulnerable to the Pitches of Salesmen," *New York Times*, 20 July 2004, C1, C6.

39. Daft, *Management*, 155.

40. "Less Than Half of Companies Encourage Discussion of Ethical Issues at the Workplace," press release, International Association of Business Communicators Research Foundation, 23 May 2006 [accessed 12 August 2006] www.iabc.com.

41. Joanne Sammer, "United Technologies Offers a Model for Reporting Ethical Issues," *Workforce Management*, August 2004, 64–66.

42. Based in part on Robert Kreitner, *Management*, 9th ed. (Boston: Houghton Mifflin, 2004), 163.

43. Henry R. Cheeseman, *Contemporary Business and E-Commerce Law*, 4th ed. (Upper Saddle River, N.J.: Prentice Hall, 2003), 841–843.

44. Cheeseman, *Contemporary Business and E-Commerce Law*, 201.

45. John Jude Moran, *Employment Law: New Challenges in the Business Environment*, 2nd ed. (Upper Saddle River, N.J.: Prentice Hall, 2002), 186–187; Kubasek, et al, *The Legal Environment of Business*, 562.

46. Cheeseman, *Contemporary Business and E-Commerce Law*, 325.

47. Kubasek et al., *The Legal Environment of Business*, 306.

CHAPTER 2

1. The Container Store website [accessed 19 January 2006] www.containerstore.com; "2005: Best Companies to Work For," *Fortune*, 24 January 2005 [accessed 11 March 2005] www.fortune.com; Bob Nelson, "Can't Contain Excitement at The Container Store," BizJournals.com [accessed 11 March 2005] www.bizjournals.com; Mike Duff, "Top-Shelf Employees Keep Container Store on Track," *DSN Retailing Today*, 8 March 2004, 7, 49; Bob Nelson, "The Buzz at The Container Store," *Corporate Meetings & Incentives*, June 2003, 32; Jennifer Saba, "Balancing Act," *Potentials*, 1 October 2003 [accessed 15 April 2004] www.highbeam.com; Peter S. Cohan, "Corporate Heroes," *Financial Executive*, 1 March 2003 [accessed 15 April 2004] www.highbeam.com; Margaret Steen, "Container Store's Focus on Training a Strong Appeal to Employees," *Mercury News* (San Jose, Calif.), 6 November 2003 [accessed 15 April 2004] www.highbeam.com; Holly Hayes, "Container Store Brings Clutter Control to San Jose, Calif.," 17 October 2003, *Mercury News* (San Jose, Calif.), 1F; "Performance Through People Award," press release, 10 September 2003; David Lipke, "Container Store's CEO: People Are Most Valued Asset," 13 January 2003, *HFN* [accessed 9 March 2003] www.highbeam.com; Lorrie Grant, "Container Store's Workers Huddle Up to Help You Out," 30 April 2002, *USA Today*, B1.

2. Courtland L. Bovée and John V. Thill, *Business in Action*, 3rd ed. (Upper Saddle River, N.J.: Pearson Prentice Hall, 2005), 175.

3. "Five Case Studies on Successful Teams," *HR Focus*, April 2002, 18+.

4. Stephen R. Robbins, *Essentials of Organizational Behavior*, 6th ed. (Upper Saddle River, N.J.: Prentice Hall, 2000), 98.

5. Max Landsberg and Madeline Pfau, "Developing Diversity: Lessons from Top Teams," *Strategy + Business*, Winter 2005, 10–12.

6. "Groups Best at Complex Problems," *Industrial Engineer*, June 2006, 14.

7. Lynda McDermott, Bill Waite, and Nolan Brawley, "Executive Teamwork," *Executive Excellence*, May 1999, 15.

8. Nicola A. Nelson, "Leading Teams," *Defense AT&L*, July–August 2006, 26–29; Larry Cole and Michael Cole, "Why Is the Teamwork Buzz Word Not Working?" *Communication World*, February– March 1999, 29; Patricia Buhler, "Managing in the 90s: Creating Flexibility in Today's Workplace," *Supervision*, January 1997, 241; Allison W. Amason, Allen C. Hochwarter, Wayne A. Thompson, and Kenneth R. Harrison, "Conflict: An Important Dimension in Successful Management Teams," *Organizational Dynamics*, Autumn 1995, 201.

9. Richard L. Daft, *Management*, 6th ed. (Cincinnati: Thomson South-Western, 2003), 614.

10. Geoffrey Colvin, "Why Dream Teams Fail," *Fortune*, 12 June 2006, 87–92.

11. Vijay Govindarajan and Anil K. Gupta, "Building an Effective Global Business Team," *MIT Sloan Management Review*, Summer 2001, 631.

12. Louise Rehling, "Improving Teamwork Through Awareness of Conversational Styles," *Business Communication Quarterly*, December 2004, 475–482.

13. Jon Hanke, "Presenting as a Team," *Presentations*, January 1998, 74–82.

14. William P. Galle, Jr., Beverly H. Nelson, Donna W. Luse, and Maurice F. Villere, *Business Communication: A Technology-Based Approach* (Chicago: Irwin, 1996), 260.

15. Mary Beth Debs, "Recent Research on Collaborative Writing in Industry," *Technical Communication*, November 1991, 476–484.

16. "Twiki Success Stories," Twiki website [accessed 18 August 2006] www.twiki.org.

17. Mark Choate, "What Makes an Enterprise Wiki?" CMS Watch website, 28 April 2006 [accessed 18 August 2006] www.cmswatch.com.

18. Choate, "What Makes an Enterprise Wiki?"

19. "Codex: Guidelines," WordPress website [accessed 18 August 2006] www.wordpress.org; Michael Shanks, "Wiki Guidelines," Traumwerk website [accessed 18 August 2006] http://metamedia.stanford.edu/projects/traumwerk/home; Joe Moxley, MC Morgan, Matt Barton, and Donna Hanak, "For Teachers New to Wikis," Writing Wiki [accessed 18 August 2006] http://writingwiki.org; "Wiki Guidelines," PsiWiki [accessed 18 August 2006] http://psi-im.org.

20. Colvin, "Why Dream Teams Fail," 87–92.

21. Tiziana Casciaro and Miguel Sousa Lobo, "Competent Jerks, Lovable Fools, and the Formation of Social Networks," *Harvard Business Review*, June 2005, 92–99.

22. Stephen P. Robbins and David A. DeCenzo, *Fundamentals of Management*, 4th ed. (Upper Saddle River, N.J.: Prentice Hall, 2004), 266–267; Jerald Greenberg and Robert A. Baron, *Behavior in Organizations*, 8th ed. (Upper Saddle River, N.J.: Prentice Hall, 2003), 279–280.

23. "Team Building: Managing the Norms of Informal Groups in the Workplace," Accel-Team.com [accessed 16 August 2006] www.accel-team.com.

24. B. Aubrey Fisher, *Small Group Decision Making: Communication and the Group Process*, 2nd ed. (New York: McGraw-Hill, 1980), 145–149; Robbins and De Cenzo, *Fundamentals of Management*, 334–335; Daft, *Management*, 602–603.

25. Michael Laff, "Effective Team Building: More Than Just Fun at Work," *Training + Development*, August 2006, 24–35.

26. Claire Sookman, "Building Your Virtual Team," *Network World*, 21 June 2004, 91.

27. Jared Sandberg, "Brainstorming Works Best If People Scramble for Ideas on Their Own," *Wall Street Journal*, 13 June 2006, B1.

28. Mark K. Smith, "Bruce W. Tuckman—Forming, Storming, Norming, and Performing in Groups," Infed.org [accessed 5 July 2005] www.infed.org.

29. Robbins and DeCenzo, *Fundamentals of Management*, 258–259.

30. Daft, *Management*, 609–612.

31. Andy Boynton and Bill Fischer, *Virtuoso Teams: Lessons from Teams That Changed Their Worlds* (Harrow, England: FT Prentice Hall, 2005), 10.

32. Thomas K. Capozzoli, "Conflict Resolution—A Key Ingredient in Successful Teams," *Supervision*, November 1999, 14–16.

33. Janis Graham, "Sharpen Your Negotiating Skills," *Sylvia Porter's Personal Finance*, December 1985, 54–58.

34. Amason, Hochwarter, Thompson, and Harrison, "Conflict."

35. Jesse S. Nirenberg, *Getting Through to People* (Paramus, N.J.: Prentice Hall, 1973), 134–142.

36. Nirenberg, *Getting Through to People*.

37. Nirenberg, *Getting Through to People*.

38. Dana May Casperson, *Power Etiquette: What You Don't Know Can Kill Your Career* (New York: AMACOM, 1999), 9.

39. Marilyn Pincus, *Everyday Business Etiquette* (Hauppauge, N.Y.: Barron's Educational Series, 1996), 7, 133.

40. Pincus, *Everyday Business Etiquette*, 136.

41. Casperson, *Power Etiquette: What You Don't Know Can Kill Your Career*, 23.

42. Gerald H. Graham, Jeanne Unrue, and Paul Jennings, "The Impact of Nonverbal Communication in Organizations: A Survey of Perceptions," *Journal of Business Communication* 28, no. 1 (Winter 1991): 45–62.

43. Pincus, *Everyday Business Etiquette*, 100–101.

44. Maggie Jackson, "Turn Off That Cellphone. It's Meeting Time," *New York Times*, 2 March 2003, sec. 3, 12.

45. Casperson, *Power Etiquette: What You Don't Know Can Kill Your Career*, 10–14; Ellyn Spragins, "Introducing Politeness," *Fortune Small Business*, November 2001, 30.

46. Tanya Mohn, "The Social Graces as a Business Tool," *New York Times*, 10 November 2002, sec. 3, 12.

47. Casperson, *Power Etiquette: What You Don't Know Can Kill Your Career*, 19; Pincus, *Everyday Business Etiquette*, 7–8.

48. Casperson, *Power Etiquette: What You Don't Know Can Kill Your Career*, 44–46.

49. Casperson, *Power Etiquette: What You Don't Know Can Kill Your Career*, 109–110.

50. "Better Meetings Benefit Everyone: How to Make Yours More Productive," *Working Communicator Bonus Report*, July 1998, 1.

51. Ken Blanchard, "Meetings Can Be Effective," *Supervisory Management*, October 1992, 5.

52. "Better Meetings Benefit Everyone."

53. IBM InnovationJam website [accessed 15 August 2006] www.globalinnovationjam.com; "Big Blue Brainstorm," *BusinessWeek*, 7 August 2006 [accessed 15 August 2006] www.businessweek.com.

54. Tony Kontzer, "Learning to Share," *InformationWeek*, 5 May 2003, 28; Jon Udell, "Uniting Under Groove," *InfoWorld*, 17 February 2003 [accessed 9 September 2003] www.elibrary.com; Alison Overholt, "Virtually There?" *Fast Company*, 14 February 2002, 108.

55. Nicole Ridgway, "A Safer Place to Meet," *Forbes*, 28 April 2003, 97.

56. Judi Brownell, *Listening*, 2nd ed. (Boston: Allyn & Bacon, 2002), 9, 10.

57. Augusta M. Simon, "Effective Listening: Barriers to Listening in a Diverse Business Environment," *Bulletin of the Association for Business Communication* 54, no. 3 (September 1991): 73–74.

58. Robyn D. Clarke, "Do You Hear What I Hear?" *Black Enterprise*, May 1998, 129.

59. Eric Engleman, "Financial Finesse," *Puget Sound Business Journal*, 5–11 November 2004, 8A.

60. Larry Barker and Kittie Watson, *Listen Up* (New York: St. Martin's, 2000), 24–27.

61. Terri Somers, "Gen-Probe's Nordhoff Listens Well, Then Acts," *San Diego Union-Tribune*, 2 November 2004, C1, C6.

62. Dennis M. Kratz and Abby Robinson Kratz, *Effective Listening Skills* (New York: McGraw-Hill, 1995), 45–53; J. Michael Sproule, *Communication Today* (Glenview, Ill.: Scott Foresman, 1981), 69.

63. Brownell, *Listening*, 230–231.

64. Kratz and Kratz, *Effective Listening Skills*, 78–79; Sproule, *Communication Today*.

65. Bill Brooks, "The Power of Active Listening," *American Salesman*, June 2003, 12; "Active Listening," Study Guides and Strategies [accessed 5 February 2005] www.studygs.net.

66. Bob Lamons, "Good Listeners Are Better Communicators," *Marketing News*, 11 September 1995, 13+; Phillip Morgan and H. Kent Baker, "Building a Professional Image: Improving Listening Behavior," *Supervisory Management*, November 1985, 35–36.

67. Clarke, "Do You Hear What I Hear?"; Dot Yandle, "Listening to Understand," *Pryor Report Management Newsletter Supplement* 15, no. 8 (August 1998): 13.

68. Brownell, *Listening*, 14; Kratz and Kratz, *Effective Listening Skills*, 8–9; Sherwyn P. Morreale and Courtland L. Bovée, *Excellence in Public Speaking* (Orlando, Fla.: Harcourt Brace, 1998), 72–76; Lyman K. Steil, Larry L. Barker, and Kittie W. Watson, *Effective Listening: Key to Your Success* (Reading, Mass.: Addison Wesley, 1983), 21–22.

69. Patrick J. Collins, *Say It with Power and Confidence* (Upper Saddle River, N.J.: Prentice Hall, 1997), 40–45.

70. Morreale and Bovée, *Excellence in Public Speaking*, 296.

71. Judee K. Burgoon, David B. Butler, and W. Gill Woodall, *Nonverbal Communication: The Unspoken Dialog* (New York: McGraw-Hill, 1996), 137.

72. "Study: Human Lie Detectors Rarely Wrong," CNN.com, 14 October 2004 [accessed 14 October 2004] www.cnn.com.

73. Dale G. Leathers, *Successful Nonverbal Communication: Principles and Applications* (New York: Macmillan, 1986), 19.

74. Gerald H. Graham, Jeanne Unrue, and Paul Jennings, "The Impact of Nonverbal Communication in Organizations: A Survey of Perceptions," *Journal of Business Communication* 28, no. 1 (Winter 1991): 45–62.

75. Virginia P. Richmond and James C. McCroskey, *Nonverbal Behavior in Interpersonal Relations* (Boston: Allyn & Bacon, 2000), 153–157.

76. Richmond and McCroskey, *Nonverbal Behavior in Interpersonal Relations*, 2–3.

CHAPTER 3

1. IBM website [accessed 20 August 2006] www.ibm.com; "Executive Corner: Letter from IBM's Vice President, Global Workforce Diversity," IBM website [accessed 5 July 2005] www.ibm.com; "IBM—Diversity as a Strategic Imperative," *Global Diversity @ Work* [accessed 6 July 2005] www.diversityatwork.com; Cliff Edwards, "The Rewards of Tolerance," *BusinessWeek*, 15 December 2003 [accessed 6 July 2005] www.businessweek.com; David A. Thomas, "IBM Finds Profit in Diversity," *HBS Working Knowledge*, 27 September 2004 [accessed 5 July 2005] http://hbswk.hbs.edu; "IBM Diversity Executive to Speak at the University of Virginia," *University of Virginia News*, 7 November 2003 [accessed 5 July 2005] www.virginia.edu.

2. Michael R. Carrell, Everett E. Mann, and Tracey Honeycutt Sigler, "Defining Workforce Diversity Programs and Practices in Organizations: A Longitudinal Study," *Labor Law Journal*, Spring 2006, 5–12.

3. "Top Trading Partners—Total Trade, Exports, Imports June 2006," U.S. Census Bureau [accessed 23 August 2006] www.census.gov.

4. Ford Motor Co. website [accessed 12 July 2005] www.ford.com.

5. Nancy R. Lockwood, "Workplace Diversity: Leveraging the Power of Difference for Competitive Advantage," *HR Magazine*, June 2005, special section 1–10.

6. Carol Hymowitz, "Managers Err If They Limit Their Hiring to People Like Them," *Wall Street Journal*, 12 October 2004, B1.

7. Rona Gindin, "Dealing with a Multicultural Workforce," *Nation's Restaurant News,* September–October 1998, 31, 83; Howard Gleckman, "A Rich Stew in the Melting Pot," *Business Week,* 31 August 1998, 76+; Toby B. Gooley, "A World of Difference," *Logistics Management and Distribution Report,* June 2000, 51–55; William H. Miller, "Beneath the Surface," *Industry Week,* 20 September 1999, 13–16.

8. Robert Kreitner, *Management,* 9th ed. (Boston: Houghton Mifflin, 2004), 84.

9. Linda Beamer and Iris Varner, *Intercultural Communication in the Workplace,* 2nd ed. (New York: McGraw-Hill Irwin, 2001), xiii.

10. Tracy Novinger, *Intercultural Communication, A Practical Guide* (Austin, Tex.: University of Texas Press, 2001), 15.

11. Beamer and Varner, *Intercultural Communication in the Workplace,* 3.

12. Randolph E. Schmid, "Asians, Americans See World Differently," *SF Gate,* 22 August 2005 [accessed 23 August 2006] http://chineseculture.about.com.

13. "Languages of the USA," Ethnologue.com [accessed 22 August 2006] www.ethnologue.com.

14. Philip R. Harris and Robert T. Moran, *Managing Cultural Differences,* 3rd ed. (Houston: Gulf, 1991), 394–397, 429–430.

15. Lillian H. Chaney and Jeanette S. Martin, *Intercultural Business Communication,* 2nd ed. (Upper Saddle River, N.J.: Prentice Hall, 2000), 6.

16. Beamer and Varner, *Intercultural Communication in the Workplace,* 4.

17. Chaney and Martin, *Intercultural Business Communication,* 2nd ed., 9.

18. Richard L. Daft, *Management,* 6th ed. (Cincinnati: Thomson South-Western, 2003), 455.

19. Lillian H. Chaney and Jeanette S. Martin, *Intercultural Business Communication,* 4th ed. (Upper Saddle River, N.J.: Pearson Prentice Hall, 2007), 53.

20. Project Implicit website [accessed 12 July 2005] http://implicit.harvard.edu/implicit.

21. Larry A. Samovar and Richard E. Porter, "Basic Principles of Intercultural Communication," in *Intercultural Communication: A Reader,* 6th ed., edited by Larry A. Samovar and Richard E. Porter (Belmont, Calif.: Wadsworth, 1991), 12.

22. Chaney and Martin, *Intercultural Business Communication,* 2nd ed., 159.

23. Linda Beamer, "Teaching English Business Writing to Chinese-Speaking Business Students," *Bulletin of the Association for Business Communication* 57, no. 1 (1994): 12–18.

24. Edward T. Hall, "Context and Meaning," in *Intercultural Communication,* edited by Samovar and Porter, 46–55.

25. Daft, *Management,* 459.

26. Beamer, "Teaching English Business Writing to Chinese-Speaking Business Students."

27. Charley H. Dodd, *Dynamics of Intercultural Communication,* 3rd ed. (Dubuque, Iowa: Brown, 1991), 69–70.

28. Daft, *Management,* 459.

29. Beamer and Varner, *Intercultural Communication in the Workplace,* 230–233.

30. James Wilfong and Toni Seger, *Taking Your Business Global* (Franklin Lakes, N.J.: Career Press, 1997), 277–278.

31. Harris and Moran, *Managing Cultural Differences,* 260.

32. Ishbel Matheson, "Kenyans Dance Against Graft," *BBC News,* 18 September 2001 [accessed 23 August 2006] http://news.bbc.co.uk.

33. Skip Kaltenheuser, "Bribery Is Being Outlawed Virtually Worldwide," *Business Ethics,* May–June 1998, 11; Thomas Omestad, "Bye-Bye to Bribes," *U.S. News & World Report,* 22 December 1997, 39, 42–44.

34. "Big Oil's Dirty Secrets," *The Economist,* 10 May 2003, 62; Skip Kaltenheuser, "A Little Dab Will Do You?" *World Trade,* January 1999, 58–63; James Walsh, "A World War on Bribery," *Time,* 22 June 1998, 16.

35. Guo-Ming Chen and William J. Starosta, *Foundations of Intercultural Communication* (Boston: Allyn & Bacon, 1998), 288–289.

36. Mark Landler and Michael Barbaro, "Wal-Mart Finds That Its Formula Doesn't Fit Every Culture," *New York Times,* 2 August 2006 [accessed 23 August 2006] www.nytimes.com.

37. Mary A. DeVries, *Internationally Yours* (New York: Houghton Mifflin, 1994), 194.

38. Robert O. Joy, "Cultural and Procedural Differences That Influence Business Strategies and Operations in the People's Republic of China," *SAM Advanced Management Journal,* Summer 1989, 29–33.

39. Chaney and Martin, *Intercultural Business Communication,* 2nd ed., 122–123.

40. Novinger, *Intercultural Communication: A Practical Guide,* 54.

41. Peter Coy, "Old. Smart. Productive." *BusinessWeek,* 27 June 2005 [accessed 24 August 2006] www.businessweek.com; Beamer and Varner, *Intercultural Communication in the Workplace,* 107–108.

42. Beamer and Varner, *Intercultural Communication in the Workplace,* 107–108.

43. Michael Kinsman, "Respect Helps Mix of Generations Work Well Together," *San Diego Union-Tribune,* 19 September 2004, H2.

44. Archer Daniels Midland website [accessed 23 August 2006] www.admworld.com; Ann Harrington and Petra Bartosiewicz, "50 Most Powerful Women," *Fortune,* 18 October 2004, 181–190.

45. Tonya Vinas, "A Place at the Table," *Industry Week,* 1 July 2003, 22.

46. Daft, *Management,* 445.

47. John Gray, *Mars and Venus in the Workplace* (New York: Harper-Collins, 2002), 10, 25–27, 61–63.

48. Chaney and Martin, *Intercultural Business Communication,* 4th ed., 62.

49. Todd Henneman, "A New Approach to Faith at Work," *Workforce Management,* October 2004, 76–77.

50. IBM Accessibility Center [accessed 24 August 2006] www.3.ibm.com/able; AssistiveTech.net [accessed 24 August 2006] www.assistivetech.net; Business Leadership Network website [accessed 24 August 2006] www.usbln.com; National Institute on Disability and Rehabilitation Research website [accessed 24 August 2006] www.ed.gov/about/offices/list/osers/nidrr; Rehabilitation Engineering & Assistive Technology Society of North America website [accessed 24 August 2006] www.resna.org.

51. Sana Reynolds and Deborah Valentine, *Guide for Internationals: Culture, Communication, and ESL* (Upper Saddle River, N.J.: Pearson Prentice Hall, 2006), 3-11, 14-19, 25.

52. P. Christopher Earley and Elaine Mosakowsi, "Cultural Intelligence," *Harvard Business Review,* October 2004, 139–146.

53. Wendy A. Conklin, "An Inside Look at Two Diversity Intranet Sites: IBM and Merck," *The Diversity Factor,* Summer 2005.

54. Craig S. Smith, "Beware of Green Hats in China and Other Cross-Cultural Faux Pas," *New York Times,* 30 April 2002, C11.

55. Francesca Bargiela-Chiappini, Anne Marie Bülow-Møller, Catherine Nickerson, Gina Poncini, and Yunxia Zhu, "Five Perspectives on Intercultural Business Communication," *Business Communication Quarterly,* September 2003, 73–96.

56. Paul Johnson, "Must the Whole World Speak English?" *Forbes,* 29 November 2004, 39; Randolph E. Schmid, "Study Says English Language Is Losing Cultural Dominance," *Desert Sun,* 29 February 2004, A25.

57. Miki Fujii, "English: Bane or Blessing? English Transforms Nissan, Mazda Culture," *Yomiuri Shimbun,* 1 April 2000, 1.

58. Mary Beth Sheridan, "Learning the New Language of Labor," *Washington Post,* 20 August 2002, A1.

59. Bob Nelson, "Motivating Workers Worldwide," *Global Workforce,* November 1998, 25–27.

60. Mona Casady and Lynn Wasson, "Written Communication Skills of International Business Persons," *Bulletin of the Association for Business Communication* 57, no. 4 (1994): 36–40.

61. "From Plain English to Global English," Quickit Limited website [accessed 24 August 2006] www.webpagecontent.com.

62. Myron W. Lustig and Jolene Koester, *Intercultural Competence,* 4th ed., (Boston: Allyn & Bacon, 2003), 196.
63. Daren Fonda, "Selling in Tongues," *Time,* 26 November 2001, B12+.
64. Wilfong and Seger, *Taking Your Business Global,* 232.
65. Mark Lasswell, "Lost in Translation," *Business 2.0,* August 2004, 68–70.
66. Sheridan Prasso, ed., "It's All Greek to These Sites," *Business Week,* 22 July 2002, 18.

CHAPTER 4

1. Complete Idiot's Guide website [accessed 28 August 2006] www.idiotsguides.com; Chris Taylor, "One-Minute Photo Smile!," *Time,* 23 December 2002, 80; "Writers Seek Simple Ways to Describe New Products," *Washington Times,* 7 November 2002 [accessed 28 October 2003] www.elibrary.com; Caroline E. Mayer, "Why Won't We Read the Manual?," *Washington Post,* 26 May 2002, H01.
2. Sanford Kaye, "Writing Under Pressure," *Soundview Executive Book Summaries* 10, no. 12, part 2 (December 1988): 1–8.
3. Peter Bracher, "Process, Pedagogy, and Business Writing," *Journal of Business Communication* 24, no. 1 (Winter 1987): 43–50.
4. Laurey Berk and Phillip G. Clampitt, "Finding the Right Path in the Communication Maze," *IABC Communication World,* October 1991, 28–32.
5. Linda Duyle, "Get Out of Your Office," *HR Magazine,* July 2006, 99–101.
6. Skype website [accessed 30 August 2006] www.skype.com.
7. Kris Maher, "The Jungle," *Wall Street Journal,* 5 October 2004, B10.
8. Kevin Maney, "Surge in Text Messaging Makes Cell Operators :-)," *USA Today,* 28 July 2005, B1–B2.
9. David Kirkpatrick, "It's Hard to Manage If You Don't Blog," *Fortune,* 4 October 2004, 46; Lee Gomes, "How the Next Big Thing in Technology Morphed into a Really Big Thing," *Wall Street Journal,* 4 October 2004, B1; Jeff Meisner, "Cutting Through the Blah, Blah, Blah," *Puget Sound Business Journal,* 19–25 November 2004, 27–28; Lauren Gard, "The Business of Blogging," *BusinessWeek,* 13 December 2004, 117–119; Heather Green, "Online Video: The Sequel," *BusinessWeek,* 10 January 2005, 40; Michelle Conlin and Andrew Park, "Blogging with the Boss's Blessing," *BusinessWeek,* 28 June 2004, 100–102.
10. Berk and Clampitt, "Finding the Right Path in the Communication Maze."
11. Berk and Clampitt, "Finding the Right Path in the Communication Maze."
12. Berk and Clampitt, "Finding the Right Path in the Communication Maze."
13. Raymond M. Olderman, *10 Minute Guide to Business Communication* (New York: Alpha Books, 1997), 19–20.
14. Mohan R. Limaye and David A. Victor, "Cross-Cultural Business Communication Research: State of the Art and Hypotheses for the 1990s," *Journal of Business Communication* 28, no. 3 (Summer 1991): 277–299.
15. Holly Weeks, "The Best Memo You'll Ever Write," *Harvard Management Communication Letter,* Spring 2005, 3–5.

CHAPTER 5

1. Creative Commons website [accessed 19 September 2006] www.creativecommons.org; Ariana Eunjung Cha, "Creative Commons Is Rewriting Rules of Copyright," *Washington Post,* 15 March 2005 [accessed 3 August 2005] www.washingtonpost.com; Steven Levy, "Lawrence Lessig's Supreme Showdown," *Wired,* October 2002 [accessed 3 August 2005] www.wired.com; "Happy Birthday: We'll Sue," Snopes.com [accessed 3 August 2005] www.snopes.com.
2. Elizabeth Blackburn and Kelly Belanger, "You-Attitude and Positive Emphasis: Testing Received Wisdom in Business Communication," *Bulletin of the Association for Business Communication* 56, no. 2 (June 1993): 1–9.
3. Placard at Alaska Airlines ticket counters, Seattle-Tacoma International Airport, 3 October 2003.
4. Annette N. Shelby and N. Lamar Reinsch, Jr., "Positive Emphasis and You Attitude: An Empirical Study," *Journal of Business Communication* 32, no. 4 (1995): 303–322.
5. Sherryl Kleinman, "Why Sexist Language Matters," *Qualitative Sociology* 25, no. 2 (Summer 2002): 299–304.
6. Judy E. Pickens, "Terms of Equality: A Guide to Bias-Free Language," *Personnel Journal,* August 1985, 24.
7. Lisa Taylor, "Communicating About People with Disabilities: Does the Language We Use Make a Difference?" *Bulletin of the Association for Business Communication* 53, no. 3 (September 1990): 65–67.
8. Susan Benjamin, *Words at Work* (Reading, Mass.: Addison Wesley, 1997), 136–137.
9. Stuart Crainer and Des Dearlove, "Making Yourself Understood," *Across the Board,* May/June 2004, 23–27.
10. Plain English Campaign website [accessed 3 October 2003] www.plainenglish.co.uk.
11. Creative Commons website [accessed 20 September 2006] www.creativecommons.org.
12. Joseph Kimble, "Answering the Critics of Plain Language," The Plain Language Network website, 12 April 2003 [accessed 22 September 2006] www.plainlanguagenetwork.org.
13. Peter Crow, "Plain English: What Counts Besides Readability?" *Journal of Business Communication* 25, no. 1 (Winter 1988): 87–95.
14. Susan Jaderstrom and Joanne Miller, "Active Writing," *Office Pro,* November/December 2003, 29.
15. Gap website [accessed 20 September 2006] www.gap.com.
16. Mary Munter, *Guide to Managerial Communication,* 7th ed. (Upper Saddle River, N.J.: Pearson Prentice Hall, 2006), 41.
17. Portions of this section are adapted from Courtland L. Bovée, *Techniques of Writing Business Letters, Memos, and Reports* (Sherman Oaks, Calif.: Banner Books International, 1978), 13–90.
18. Janice Obuchowski, "Communicate to Inform, Not Impress," *Harvard Management Communication Letter,* Winter 2006, 3–4; Robert Hartwell Fiske, *The Dimwit's Dictionary* (Oak Park, Ill.: Marion Street Press, 2002), 1620.
19. Beverly Ballaro and Christina Bielaszka-DuVernay, "Building a Bridge over the River Boredom," *Harvard Management Communication Letter,* Winter 2005, 3–5.
20. David A. Fryxell, "Lost in Transition?" *Writers Digest,* January 2005, 24–26.
21. Food Allergy Initiative website [accessed 23 September 2006] www.foodallergyinitiative.org; Diana Keough, "Snacks That Can Kill; Schools Take Steps To Protect Kids Who Have Severe Allergies to Nuts," *Plain Dealer,* 15 July 2003, E1; "Dawdling Over Food Labels," *New York Times,* 2 June 2003, A16; Sheila McNulty, "A Matter of Life and Death," *Financial Times,* 10 September 2003, 14.
22. Apple iTunes website [accessed 23 September 2006] www.apple.com/itunes.

CHAPTER 6

1. Mercedes-AMG website [accessed 25 September 2006] www.mercedes-amg.com; Avenue A | Razorfish website [accessed 25 September 2006] www.avenuea-razorfish.com; "Mercedes-AMG Website Wins Webby Award," 12 June 2006, eMercedesBenz website [accessed 25 September 2006] www.emercedesbenz.com.
2. William Zinsser, *On Writing Well,* 5th ed. (New York: HarperCollins, 1994), 9.
3. Zinsser, *On Writing Well,* 7, 17.
4. Mary A. DeVries, *Internationally Yours* (Boston: Houghton Mifflin, 1994), 160.
5. Zinsser, *On Writing Well,* 126.
6. Deborah Gunn, "Looking Good on Paper," *Office Pro,* March 2004, 10–11.
7. Jennifer Saranow, "Memo to Web Sites: Grow Up!" *Wall Street Journal,* 15 November 2004, R14–R15.

8. Jacci Howard Bear, "Desktop Publishing Rules of Page Layout," About.com [accessed 22 August 2005] www.about.com.

9. Jacci Howard Bear, "Desktop Publishing Rules for How Many Fonts to Use," About.com [accessed 22 August 2005] www.about.com.

10. The writing samples in this exercise were adapted from material on the Mercedes-AMG website [accessed 2 October 2006] www.mercedes-amg.com.

11. The writing sample in this exercise was adapted from material on the Marsh Risk Consulting website [accessed 2 October 2006] www.marshriskconsulting.com.

CHAPTER 7

1. Josh Hallett, "Boeing Updates Randy's Blog to Be More Bloggy," Hyku blog, 11 April 2005 [accessed 5 October 2006] www.hyku.com; "Into the Wild Blog Yonder," *BusinessWeek Online*, 22 May 2006 [accessed 5 October 2006] www.businessweek.com; Randy Baseler, Randy's Journal blog [accessed 5 October 2006] www.boeing.com/randy; Anil Dash, "Boeing Blog Relaunches," Six Apart Professional Network blog, 12 April 2005 [accessed 5 October 2006] www.sixapart.com.

2. Dave Carpenter, "Companies Discover Marketing Power of Text Messaging," *Seattle Times*, 25 September 2006 [accessed 25 September 2006] www.seattletimes.com.

3. Hilary Potkewitz and Rachel Brown, "Spread of E-Mail Has Altered Communication Habits at Work," *Los Angeles Business Journal*, 18 April 2005 [accessed 30 April 2006] www.findarticles.com; Nancy Flynn, *Instant Messaging Rules* (New York: AMACOM, 2004), 47–54.

4. "Employee Communication Is Cause for Concern," Duane Morris LLP website, 23 August 2006 [accessed 4 October 2006] www.duanemorris.com.

5. Greg Burns, "For Some, Benefits of E-Mail Not Worth Risk," *San Diego Union-Tribune*, 16 August 2005, A1, A8; Pui-Wing Tam, Erin White, Nick Wingfield, and Kris Maher, "Snooping E-Mail by Software Is Now a Workplace Norm," *Wall Street Journal*, 9 March 2005, B1+.

6. Matt Cain, "Managing E-Mail Hygiene," ZD Net Tech Update, 5 February 2004 [accessed 19 March 2004] www.techupdate.zdnet.com.

7. Lizette Alvarez, "Got 2 Extra Hours for Your E-Mail?" *New York Times*, 10 November 2005 [accessed 10 November 2005] www.nytimes.com.

8. Jack Trout, "Beware of 'Infomania,'" *Forbes*, 11 August 2006 [accessed 5 October 2006] www.forbes.com.

9. Reid Goldsborough, "'Creeping Informality' Can Be Big Mistake in Business E-Mails," *New Orleans City Business*, 14 March 2005, 18; Jack E. Appleman, "Bad Writing Can Cost Insurers Time & Money," *National Underwriter*, 27 September 2004, 34; Adina Genn, "RE: This Is an Important Message, Really," *Long Island Business News*, 5–11 December 2003, 21A; Lynn Lofton, "Regardless of What You Thought, Grammar Rules *Do* Apply to E-Mail," *Mississippi Business Journal*, 23–29 May 2005, 1.

10. Mary Munter, Priscilla S. Rogers, and Jone Rymer, "Business E-Mail: Guidelines for Users," *Business Communication Quarterly*, March 2003, 26+; Renee B. Horowitz and Marian G. Barchilon, "Stylistic Guidelines for E-Mail," *IEEE Transactions on Professional Communication* 37, no. 4 (December 1994): 207–212.

11. "E-Mail Is So Five Minutes Ago," *BusinessWeek Online*, 28 November 2005 [accessed 3 May 2006] www.businessweek.com.

12. Robert J. Holland, "Connected—More or Less," Richmond.com, 8 August 2006 [accessed 5 October 2006] www.richmond.com.

13. Vayusphere website [accessed 22 January 2006] www.vayusphere.com; Christa C. Ayer, "Presence Awareness: Instant Messaging's Killer App," *Mobile Business Advisor*, 1 July 2004 [accessed 22 January 2006] www.highbeam.com; Jefferson Graham, "Instant Messaging Programs Are No Longer Just for Messages," *USA Today*, 20 October 2003, 5D; Todd R. Weiss, "Microsoft Targets Corporate Instant Messaging Customers," *Computerworld*, 18 November 2002, 12; "Banks Adopt Instant Messaging to Create a Global Business Network," *Computer Weekly*, 25 April 2002, 40; Michael D. Osterman, "Instant Messaging in the Enterprise," *Business Communications Review*, January 2003, 59–62; John Pallato, "Instant Messaging Unites Work Groups and Inspires Collaboration," *Internet World*, December 2002, 14+.

14. Paul Kedrosky, "Why We Don't Get the (Text) Message," *Business 2.0*, 2 October 2006 [accessed 4 October 2006] www.business2.com; Carpenter, "Companies Discover Marketing Power of Text Messaging."

15. Mark Gibbs, "Racing to Instant Messaging," *NetworkWorld*, 17 February 2003, 74.

16. "E-Mail Is So Five Minutes Ago."

17. Elizabeth Millard, "Instant Messaging Threats Still Rising," Newsfactor.com, 6 July 2005 [accessed 5 October 2006] www.newsfactor.com.

18. Walaika K. Haskins, "New Virus Spreads By Chatting with You," Newsfactor.com, 9 December 2005 [accessed 5 October 2006] www.newsfactor.com.

19. Clint Boulton, "IDC: IM Use Is Booming in Business," InstantMessagingPlanet.com, 5 October 2005 [accessed 22 January 2006] www.instantmessagingplanet.com; Jenny Goodbody, "Critical Success Factors for Global Virtual Teams," *Strategic Communication Management*, February/March 2005, 18–21; Ann Majchrzak, Arvind Malhotra, Jeffrey Stamps, and Jessica Lipnack, "Can Absence Make a Team Grow Stronger?" *Harvard Business Review*, May 2004, 131–137; Christine Y. Chen, "The IM Invasion," *Fortune*, 26 May 2003, 135–138; Yudhijit Bhattacharjee, "A Swarm of Little Notes," *Time*, September 2002, A3–A8; Mark Bruno, "Taming the Wild Frontiers of Instant Messaging," *Bank Technology News*, December 2002, 30–31; Richard Grigonis, "Enterprise-Strength Instant Messaging," Convergence.com, 10–15 [accessed March 2003] www.convergence.com.

20. Pallato, "Instant Messaging Unites Work Groups and Inspires Collaboration," 14+.

21. Anita Hamilton, "You've Got Spim!" *Time*, 2 February 2004 [accessed 1 March 2004] www.time.com.

22. Scoble and Israel, *Naked Conversations*, 15–18.

23. GM FastLane blog [accessed 4 May 2006] http://fastlane.gmblogs.com.

24. Paul Chaney, "Thinking Out Loud About a New Branding Strategy and Blog," 31 March 2006 [accessed 4 May 2006] http://radiantmarketinggroup.com.

25. Fredrik Wackå, "Six Types of Blogs—A Classification," CorporateBloggingInfo website, 10 August 2004 [accessed 5 October 2006] www.corporateblogginginfo.com.

26. Stephen Baker, "The Inside Story on Company Blogs," *BusinessWeek Online*, 14 February 2006 [accessed 15 February 2006] www.businessweek.com; Jeremy Wright, *Blog Marketing* (New York: McGraw-Hill, 2006), 45–56; Paul Chaney, "Blogs: Beyond the Hype!" 26 May 2005 [accessed 4 May 2006] http://radiantmarketinggroup.com.

27. Evolve24 website [accessed 5 October 2006] www.evolve24.com.

28. Stephen Baker and Heather Green, "Blogs Will Change Your Business," *BusinessWeek*, 2 May 2005, 57–67.

29. Julie Moran Alterio, "Podcasts a Hit Inside and Outside IBM," *The Journal News* (White Plains, N.Y.), 9 January 2006 [accessed 5 May 2006] www.thejournalnews.com.

30. "Turn Your Feed into a Podcast," Lifehacker blog, 12 January 2006 [accessed 6 May 2006] www.lifehacker.com.

31. "Set Up Your Podcast for Success," FeedForAll website [accessed 4 October 2006] www.feedforall.com.

32. Shel Holtz, "Ten Guidelines for B2B Podcasts," Webpronews.com, 12 October 2005 [accessed 9 March 2006] www.webpronews.com

33. Todd Cochrane, *Podcasting: The Do-It-Yourself Guide* (Indianapolis, Ind.: Wiley, 2005), 107–109.

34. Michael W. Goeghegan and Dan Klass, *Podcast Solutions: The Complete Guide to Podcasting* (Berkeley, Calif.: Friends of Ed, 2005), 57–86; Cochrane, *Podcasting: The Do-It-Yourself Guide*, 87–136.

35. "Syndication Format," Answers.com [accessed 5 October 2006] www.answers.com.
36. FeedBurner website [accessed 5 October 2006] www.feedburner.com.
37. Adapted from "Comic-Con International," Wikipedia [accessed 16 January 2007] www.wikipedia.com; Comic-Con website [accessed 16 January 2007] www.comic-con.org; Tom Spurgeon, "Welcome to Nerd Vegas: A Guide to Visiting and Enjoying Comic-Con International in San Diego, 2006!" The Comics Reporter.com, 11 July 2006 [accessed 16 January 2007] www.comicsreporter.com.
38. Adapted from Tom Lowry, "ESPN.COM: Guys and Dollars," *BusinessWeek*, 17 October 2005 [accessed 16 January 2007] www.businessweek.com.
39. Adapted from Michael Mandel, "What's Really Propping Up the Economy," *BusinessWeek*, 25 September 2006 [accessed 16 January 2007] www.businessweek.com.
40. Adapted from Seymour Powell website [accessed 16 January 2007] www.seymourpowell.com; Sam Roberts, "51% of Women Now Living Without a Spouse," *New York Times*, 16 January 2007 [accessed 16 January 2007] www.nytimes.com.
41. Adapted from Sharon Terlep, "UAW: Expect Sacrifice," *Detroit News*, 16 January 2007 [accessed 17 January 2007] www.detnews.com; Ford Motor Company website [accessed 17 January 2007] www.ford.com.
42. Adapted from Bruce Einhorn and Ben Elgin, "Helping Big Brother Go High Tech," *BusinessWeek*, 18 September 2006, 47–52.
43. Adapted from Crutchfield website [accessed 17 January 2007] www.crutchfield.com.
44. Adapted from *Logan* website [accessed 16 January 2007] www.loganmagazine.com.
45. Adapted from job description for Global Marketing Manager–Apparel, New Balance website [accessed 24 August 2005] www.newbalance.com.
46. Adapted from "How Microsoft Reviews Suppliers," *Fast Company*, Issue 17 [accessed 3 September 2003] http://fastcompany.com.
47. Adapted from David Dukcevich, "Instant Business: Retailer Lands' End Profits from Online Chat," Forbes.com, Special to ABCNEWS.com, 29 July 2002 [accessed 21 July 2003] abcnews.go.com; Lands' End website [accessed 5 December 2003] www.landsend.com; Forbes.com staff, "Instant Messaging at Work," Forbes.com, 26 July 2002 [accessed 21 July 2003] www.forbes.com; Tischelle George and Sandra Swanson with Christopher T. Heun, "Not Just Kid Stuff," *InformationWeek*, 3 September 2001 [accessed 21 July 2003] www.informationweek.com.
48. Adapted from Liz Moyer, "California Dreaming," *Forbes*, 8 May 2006 [accessed 8 May 2006] www.forbes.com; "Wachovia to Acquire Golden West Financial, Nation's Most Admired and 2nd Largest Savings Institution," 7 May 2006, Wachovia website [accessed 8 May 2006] www.wachovia.com.

CHAPTER 8
1. Feeding Children Better website [accessed 12 October 2006] www.feedingchildrenbetter.org; "Awards & Accolades," Cone Inc. website [accessed 12 October 2006] www.coneinc.com; "Platinum PR Award Winner: Cause-Related Marketing; ConAgra Program Combats Child Hunger," *PR News*, 13 October 2003, 1; Jennifer Comiteau, "Do Do-Gooders Do Better?" *AdWeek*, 29 September 2003, 24; "ConAgra Foods Donates Refrigerated Trucks from Former Dot-Com Webvan to Help Feed Hungry Americans," *PR Newswire*, 2 May 2002, 1.
2. "Review Offer Letters Carefully to Avoid Binding Promises," *Fair Employment Practices Guidelines*, 15 May 2001, 5–6.
3. Fraser P. Seitel, *The Practice of Public Relations*, 9th ed. (Upper Saddle River, N.J.: Pearson Prentice Hall, 2004), 402–411; *Techniques for Communicators* (Chicago: Lawrence Ragan Communication, 1995), 34, 36.
4. Mary Mitchell, "The Circle of Life—Condolence Letters," Liveand Learn.com [accessed 18 July 2005] www.liveandlearn.com; Donna Larcen, "Authors Share the Words of Condolence," *Los Angeles Times*, 20 December 1991, E11.
5. Adapted from Tom Abate, "Need to Preserve Cash Generates Wave of Layoffs in Biotech Industry," *San Francisco Chronicle*, 10 February 2003 [accessed 18 July 2005] www.sfgate.com.
6. Adapted from Lisa DiCarlo, "IBM Gets the Message—Instantly," Forbes.com, 7 July 2002 [accessed 22 July 2003] www.forbes.com; "IBM Introduces Breakthrough Messaging Technology for Customers and Business Partners," *M2 Presswire*, 19 February 2003 [accessed 24 July 2003] www.proquest.com; "IBM and America Online Team for Instant Messaging Pilot," *M2 Presswire*, 4 February 2003 [accessed 24 July 2003] www.proquest.com.
7. Adapted from CES website [accessed 18 July 2005] www.cesweb.org.
8. Adapted from Floorgraphics website [accessed 25 October 2006] www.floorgraphics.com; John Grossman, "It's an Ad, Ad, Ad, Ad World," *Inc.*, March 2000, 23–26; David Wellman, "Floor Toons," *Supermarket Business*, 15 November 1999, 47; "Floorshow," *Dallas Morning News*, 4 September 1998, 11D.
9. Adapted from Bruce Frankel and Alex Tresniowski, "Stormy Skies," *People Weekly*, 31 July 2000, 112–115.
10. Adapted from Jamba Juice website [accessed 26 October 2006] jambacareers.com; Brenda Paik Sunoo, "Blending a Successful Workforce," *Workforce*, March 2000, 44–48; Michael Adams, "Kirk Perron: Jamba Juice," *Restaurant Business*, 15 March 1999, 38; "Live in a Blender," *Restaurant Business*, 1 December 2000, 48–50; David Goll, "Jamba Juices Up 24-Hour Fitness Clubs," *East Bay Business Times*, 30 June 2000, 6.
11. Eben Shapiro, "Blockbuster Rescue Bid Stars Viacom Top Guns," *Wall Street Journal*, 7 May 1997, B1, B10.
12. Adapted from Burt Helm, "Wal-Mart, Please Don't Leave Me," *BusinessWeek*, 9 October 2006, 84–89.
13. Adapted from Jane Costello, "Check Your Insurance Before Renting an SUV," *Wall Street Journal*, 13 June 2001 [accessed 14 June 2001] http://online.wsj.com/public/us.
14. Adapted from Calvin Sims, "Reporter Disciplined for Reading His Co-Workers' Electronic Mail," *New York Times*, 6 December 1993, A8.
15. Adapted from Michael Mescon, Courtland Bovée, and John Thill, *Business Today*, 10th ed. (Upper Saddle River, N.J.: Prentice Hall, 2002), 220.
16. "Entrepreneurs Across America," *Entrepreneur Magazine Online* [accessed 12 June 1997] www.entrepreneurmag.com.
17. Adapted from SitePoint website [accessed 12 May 2006] www.sitepoint.com; Dylan Tweney, "The Defogger: Slim Down That Homepage," *Business 2.0*, 13 July 2001 [accessed 1 August 2001] www.business2.com.
18. Adapted from Barbara Carton, "Farmers Begin Harvesting Satellite Data to Boost Yields," *Wall Street Journal*, 11 July 1996, B4.
19. Adapted from Public Relations Society of America website [accessed 18 June 2005] www.prsa.org.
20. Adapted from Keith H. Hammonds, "Difference Is Power," *Fast Company*, 36, 258 [accessed 11 July 2000] www.fastcompany.com; Terri Morrison, Wayne A. Conaway, and George A. Borden, Ph.D., *Kiss, Bow, or Shake Hands* (Holbrook, Mass.: Adams Media Corporation, April 1995).
21. Adapted from Jeff Nachtigal, "It's Easy and Cheap Being Green," *Fortune*, 16 October 2006, 53; "Adobe Wins Platinum Certification Awarded by U.S. Green Building Council," press release, 3 July 2006 [accessed 15 October 2006] www.adobe.com.
22. Adapted from Mitchell, "The Circle of Life—Condolence Letters"; Larcen, "Authors Share the Words of Condolence."

CHAPTER 9
1. "Revised KPMG Tax-Shelter Settlement Gets Final Approval," *Public Accounting Report*, 15 June 2006, 6–7; "Inside the KPMG Mess," *BusinessWeek*, 1 September 2005 [accessed 1 September 2005] www.businessweek.com; KPMG Careers website [accessed 19 August 2005] www.kpmgcareers.com; "KPMG LLP Statement

Regarding Department of Justice Matter," press release, 16 June 2005 [accessed 19 August 2005] www.us.kpmg.com; "KPMG May Avoid Indictment as U.S. Pushes Settlement, People Say," Bloomberg.com, 4 August 2005 [accessed 19 August 2005] www.bloomberg.com; "KPMG Offers Apology Over Illegal Tax Shelters," *Boston Globe*, 17 June 2005 [accessed 19 August 2005] www.boston.com; Jeff Bailey and Lynnley Browning, "KPMG May Dodge One Bullet, Only to Face Another," *New York Times*, 21 June 2005 [accessed 19 August 2005] www.nytimes.com.

2. Katie Grasso, "Deliver Bad News to Workers Face-to-Face, with Empathy," *Courier-Post* (Camden, N.J.), 8 February 2006 [accessed 14 May 2006] www.courierpostonline.com.

3. Carol David and Margaret Ann Baker, "Rereading Bad News: Compliance-Gaining Features in Management Memos," *Journal of Business Communication*, October 1994 [accessed 1 December 2003] www.elibrary.com.

4. Chad Terhune, "CEO Says Things Aren't Going Better with Coke," *Wall Street Journal*, 16 September 2004, A1, A10.

5. Ian McDonald, "Marsh Can Do $600 Million, But Apologize?" *Wall Street Journal*, 14 January 2005, C1, C3; Adrienne Carter and Amy Borrus, "What If Companies Fessed Up?" *BusinessWeek*, 24 January 2005, 59–60; Patrick J. Kiger, "The Art of the Apology," *Workforce Management*, October 2004, 57–62.

6. Ameeta Patel and Lamar Reinsch, "Companies Can Apologize: Corporate Apologies and Legal Liability," *Business Communication Quarterly*, March 2003 [accessed 1 December 2003] www.elibrary.com.

7. Iris I. Varner, "A Comparison of American and French Business Correspondence," *Journal of Business Communication* 24, no. 4 (Fall 1988): 55–65.

8. Susan Jenkins and John Hinds, "Business Letter Writing: English, French, and Japanese," *TESOL Quarterly* 21, no. 2 (June 1987): 327–349; Saburo Haneda and Hiosuke Shima, "Japanese Communication Behavior as Reflected in Letter Writing," *Journal of Business Communication* 19, no. 1 (1982): 19–32.

9. James Calvert Scott and Diana J. Green, "British Perspectives on Organizing Bad-News Letters: Organizational Patterns Used by Major U.K. Companies," *Bulletin of the Association for Business Communication* 55, no. 1 (March 1992): 17–19.

10. "Need to Deliver Bad News? How and Why to Tell It Like It Is," *HR Focus*, November 2003 [accessed 1 December 2003] www.elibrary.com.

11. "Advice from the Pros on the Best Way to Deliver Bad News," *Report on Customer Relationship Management*, 1 February 2003 [accessed 1 December 2003] www.elibrary.com.

12. Nelson D. Schwartz, "Can BP Recover?" *Fortune*, 16 October 2006, 90–96.

13. Jeffrey Pfeffer, "The Whole Truth and Nothing But," *Business 2.0*, October 2004, 78.

14. Walter Kiechel III, "Breaking Bad News to the Boss," *Fortune*, 9 April 1990 [accessed 2 December 2003] www.elibrary.com.

15. Michael Gannaway, "A Letter to Pillowtex Employees and Their Families," *Workforce Online*, August 2003 [accessed 16 October 2006] www.workforce.com.

16. Courtland L. Bovée, John V. Thill, George P. Dovel, and Marian Burk Wood, *Advertising Excellence* (New York: McGraw-Hill, 1995), 508–509; John Holusha, "Exxon's Public-Relations Problem," *New York Times*, 12 April 1989, D1.

17. Ken Ward Jr., "Report Criticizes Gap in Sago Rescue Info," *Charleston Gazette*, 25 July 2006 [accessed 16 October 2006] www.ebscohost.com.

18. "Throw Out the Old Handbook in Favor of Today's Crisis Drills," *PR News*, 27 January 2003, 1.

19. Thomas S. Brice and Marie Waung, "Applicant Rejection Letters: Are Businesses Sending the Wrong Message?" *Business Horizons*, March–April 1995, 59–62.

20. Gwendolyn N. Smith, Rebecca F. Nolan, and Yong Dai, "Job-Refusal Letters: Readers' Affective Responses to Direct and Indirect Organizational Plans," *Business Communication Quarterly* 59, no. 1 (1996): 67–73; Brice and Waung, "Applicant Rejection Letters."

21. John Zappe, "Building on Brand to Attract Top Employees," *Workforce Management*, 27 February 2006, 31.

22. Judi Brownell, "The Performance Appraisal Interviews: A Multipurpose Communication Assignment," *Bulletin of the Association for Business Communication* 57, no. 2 (1994): 11–21.

23. Brownell, "The Performance Appraisal Interviews."

24. Stephanie Gruner, "Feedback from Everyone," *Inc.*, February 1997, 102–103.

25. Howard M. Bloom, "Performance Evaluations," *New England Business*, December 1991, 14.

26. Patricia A. McLagan, "Advice for Bad-News Bearers: How to Tell Employees They're Not Hacking It and Get Results," *Industry Week*, 15 February 1993, 42; Michael Lee Smith, "Give Feedback, Not Criticism," *Supervisory Management*, 1993, 4; "A Checklist for Conducting Problem Performer Appraisals," *Supervisory Management*, December 1993, 7–9.

27. Carrie Brodzinski, "Avoiding Wrongful Termination Suits," *National Underwriter Property & Casualty—Risk & Benefits Management*, 13 October 2003 [accessed 2 December 2003] www.elibrary.com.

28. Jane R. Goodson, Gail W. McGee, and Anson Seers, "Giving Appropriate Performance Feedback to Managers: An Empirical Test of Content and Outcomes," *Journal of Business Communication* 29, no. 4 (1992): 329–342.

29. Craig Cox, "On the Firing Line," *Business Ethics*, May–June 1992, 33–34.

30. Cox, "On the Firing Line."

31. See Note 1.

32. Adapted from "FDA Notifies Public That Vail Products, Inc., Issues Nationwide Recall of Enclosed Bed Systems," FDA press release, 30 June 2005 [accessed 18 August 2005] www.fda.gov.

33. Adapted from "Bathtub Curve," *Engineering Statistics Handbook*, National Institute of Standards and Technology website [accessed 16 April 2005] www.nist.gov; Robert Berner, "The Warranty Windfall," *BusinessWeek*, 20 December 2004, 84–86; Larry Armstrong, "When Service Contracts Make Sense," *BusinessWeek*, 20 December 2004, 86.

34. Adapted from Union Bank of California teleservices, personal communication, 16 August 2001.

35. Adapted from United Airlines website [accessed 31 December 2003] www.united.com; "United Airlines First to Offer Inflight Email on Domestic Flights: Verizon Airfone® Outfits UAL's Fleet with JetConnect℠," United Airlines press release [accessed 21 July 2003] www.ual.com/press/detail/o,1442,51106,00.html; "Laptops Sprout Wings with Verizon Airfone JetConnect Service," *PR Newswire*, 24 September 2002 [accessed 21 July 2003] www.proquest.com; "Verizon Hopes Data Flies with Airfone JetConnect," *Wireless Data News*, 7 May 2003 [accessed 24 July 2003] www.proquest.com.

36. Adapted from Sean Doherty, "Dynamic Communications," *Network Computing*, 3 April 2003, 26 [accessed 24 July 2003] http://search.epnet.com; Todd Wasserman, "Post-Merger HP Invents New Image to Challenge Tech Foes IBM and Dell," *Brandweek*, 18 November 2002, 9 [accessed 24 July 2003] http://search.epnet.com; R. P. Srikanth, "IM Tools Are Latest Tech Toys for Corporate Users," *Express Computer*, 1 July 2002 [accessed 21 July 2003] www.expresscomputeronline.com.

37. "Viral Effect of Email Promotion," Alka Dwivedi blog [accessed 19 October 2006] www.alkadwivedi.com; Teresa Valdez Klein, "Starbucks Makes a Viral Marketing Misstep," Blog Business Summit website [accessed 19 October 2006] www.blogbusinesssummit.com.

38. Adapted from Michael H. Mescon, Courtland L. Bovée, and John V. Thill, *Business Today*, 10th ed. (Upper Saddle River, N.J.: Prentice Hall, 2002), 369; Bruce Upbin, "Profit in a Big Orange Box," *Forbes* 165, no. 2, 24 January 2000 (accessed 2 August 2001) www.forbes.com.

39. Michelle Higgins, "The Ballet Shoe Gets a Makeover, But Few Yet See the Pointe," *Wall Street Journal*, 8 August 1998, A1, A6; Gaynor Minden website [accessed 17 December 2003] www.dancer.com; American Ballet Theatre website [accessed 17 December 2003] www.abt.org.

40. Adapted from Wolf Blitzer, "More Employers Taking Advantage of New Cyber-Surveillance Software," CNN.com, 10 July 2000 [accessed 11 July 2000] www.cnn.com.

41. Adapted from Associated Press, "Employers Restricting Use of Cell Phones in Cars," CNN.com/Sci-Tech, 27 August 2001 [accessed 27 August 2001] www.cnn.com; Julie Vallese, "Study: All Cell Phones Distract Drivers," CNN.com/U.S., 16 August 2001 [accessed 7 September 2001] www.cnn.com.

42. Adapted from EQ Industry Services press releases [accessed 27 October 2006] www.eqonline.com; "N.C. Residents to Return After Fire," *Science Daily*, 6 October 2006 [accessed 27 October 2006] www.sciencedaily.com; "Hazardous Waste Plant Fire in N.C. Forces 17,000 to Evacuate," FOXNews.com, 6 October 2006 [accessed 27 October 2006] www.foxnews.com.

43. Adapted from Monterey Pasta Company website [accessed 27 October 2006] www.montereygourmetfoods.com; Alyce Lomax, "Monterey's High-Carb Woes," *The Motley Fool*, 23 December 2003 [accessed 23 December 2003] www.fool.com; "Monterey Pasta Announces Quarterly Sales Decline of 3%–5% Expected When Compared to Fourth Quarter, 2002" Monterey Pasta corporate press release, 23 December 2003 [accessed 23 December 2003] www.montereypasta.com; "Monterey Pasta Company Introduces Reduced Carbohydrate Product Line," Monterey Pasta corporate press release, 23 December 2003 [accessed 23 December 2003] www.montereypasta.com.

44. Adapted from Associated Press, "Children's Painkiller Recalled," CNN.com/Health website, 16 August 2001 [accessed 22 August 2001] www.cnn.com; Perrigo Company website [accessed 29 August 2001] www.perrigo.com.

45. Adapted from Pui-Wing Tam, Erin White, Nick Wingfield, and Kris Maher, "Snooping E-Mail by Software Is Now a Workplace Norm," *Wall Street Journal*, 9 March 2005, B1+.

46. Adapted from Sylvia Ann Hewlett and Carolyn Buck Luce, "Off-Ramps and On-Ramps," *Harvard Business Review*, March 2005, 43–54.

47. Adapted from Stanton website [accessed 18 August 2005] www.stanton.com.

48. Adapted from Capital One Auto Finance (formerly People First.com) website [accessed 23 December 2003] www.capitaloneautofinance.com.

49. Adapted from Julie Vallese, "Motorized Scooter Injuries on the Rise," CNN.com/U.S., 22 August 2001 [accessed 22 August 2001] www.cnn.com; The Sports Authority website [accessed 28 August 2001] www.sportsauthority.com.

50. Adapted from Alion website [accessed 19 August 2005] www.alionscience.com.

51. Ina Fried, "Hurd: HP's Founders Would Be Appalled," CNET News.com, 28 September 2006 [accessed 16 October 2006] www.cnet.com.

CHAPTER 10

1. ClubMom website [accessed 20 October 2006] www.clubmom.com; "ClubMom Introduces the MomNetwork—The Web's First Social Network for Moms," press release, 8 May 2006 [accessed 22 October 2006] www.hcp.com; "Laura Fortner Named Senior Vice President, Business Development at ClubMom," press release, 20 September 2006 [accessed 22 October 2006] http://newyork.dbusinessnews.com.

2. Jay A. Conger, "The Necessary Art of Persuasion," *Harvard Business Review*, May–June 1998, 84–95; Jeanette W. Gilsdorf, "Write Me Your Best Case for . . . ," *Bulletin of the Association for Business Communication* 54, no. 1 (March 1991): 7–12.

3. "Vital Skill for Today's Managers: Persuading, Not Ordering Others," *Soundview Executive Book Summaries*, September 1998, 1.

4. Mary Cross, "Aristotle and Business Writing: Why We Need to Teach Persuasion," *Bulletin of the Association for Business Communication* 54, no. 1 (March 1991): 3–6.

5. Abraham H. Maslow, *Motivation and Personality* (New York: Harper & Row, 1954), 12, 19.

6. Robert T. Moran, "Tips on Making Speeches to International Audiences," *International Management*, April 1980, 58–59.

7. Conger, "The Necessary Art of Persuasion."

8. Raymond M. Olderman, *10-Minute Guide to Business Communication* (New York: Macmillan Spectrum/Alpha Books, 1997), 57–61.

9. Gilsdorf, "Write Me Your Best Case for. . ."

10. John D. Ramage and John C. Bean, *Writing Arguments: A Rhetoric with Readings*, 3rd ed. (Boston: Allyn & Bacon, 1995), 430–442.

11. Philip Vassallo, "Persuading Powerfully: Tips for Writing Persuasive Documents," *Et Cetera*, Spring 2002, 65–71.

12. Dianna Booher, *Communicate with Confidence* (New York: McGraw-Hill, 1994), 102.

13. *Overview of the Web Accessibility Initiative*, W3C website [accessed 20 October 2006] www.w3.org.

14. iPod nano product page, Apple website [accessed 21 October 2006] www.apple.com/ipod.

15. Verizon Wireless website [accessed 23 August 2005] www.verizonwireless.com.

16. Saturn VUE product page, Saturn website [accessed 8 December 2003] www.saturn.com.

17. *Working and Living in France: The Ins and Outs* product page, Insider Paris Guides website [accessed 8 December 2003] www.insiderparisguides.com.

18. Verizon Wireless sales letter, received 1 December 2003.

19. Fast Break Backpack product page, Lands' End website [accessed 8 December 2003] www.landsend.com.

20. ClubMom website [accessed 21 October 2006] www.clubmom.com.

21. iPod nano product page.

22. Gilsdorf, "Write Me Your Best Case for. . ."

23. *Frequently Asked Advertising Questions: A Guide for Small Business*, U.S. Federal Trade Commission website [accessed 9 December 2003] www.ftc.gov.

24. Adapted from Samsung website [accessed 22 October 2006] www.samsung.com.

25. Adapted from GM Fastlane Blog [accessed 23 August 2005] http://fastlane.gmblogs.com.

26. Adapted from Starbucks website [accessed 23 August 2005] www.starbucks.com.

27. Adapted from John Case and Jerry Useem, "Six Characters in Search of a Strategy," *Inc.*, March 1996, 46–49.

28. Adapted from "'Power Nap' Prevents Burnout; Morning Sleep Perfects a Skill," National Institutes of Health press release, 2 July 2002 [accessed 31 October 2006] www.nih.gov; Albert R. Karr, "Work Week: Wake Up and Read This," *Wall Street Journal*, 6 May 1997, A1.

29. Adapted from IBM website [accessed 15 January 2004] www.ibm.com/ibm/ibmgives; "DAS Faces an Assured Future with IBM," IBM website [accessed 16 January 2004] www.306.ibm.com/software/success/cssdb.nsf/CS/DNSD-5S6KTF; "Sametime," IBM website [accessed 16 January 2004] www.lotus.com/products/lotussametime.nsf/wdocs/homepage.

30. Adapted from CNET Shopper.com [accessed 1 October 2001] http://shopper.cnet.com.

31. Adapted from Andrew Ferguson, "Supermarket of the Vanities," *Fortune*, 10 June 1996, 30, 32; Whole Foods Market website [accessed 9 January 2004] www.wholefoodsmarket.com.

32. Adapted from Courtland L. Bovée and John V. Thill, *Business in Action*, 3rd ed. (Upper Saddle River, N.J.: Pearson Prentice Hall, 2005), 236–237; International Telework Association & Council website [accessed 24 August 2005] www.telecommute.org; Jason Roberson, "Rush-Hour Rebellion," *Dallas Business Journal*, 22 June 2001, 31; Carole Hawkins, "Ready, Set, Go Home," *Black Enterprise*,

August 2001, 118–124; Wayne Tompkins, "Telecommuting in Transition," *Courier-Journal*, Louisville, Ky., 9 July 2001, 01C.

33. Adapted from Give Life website [accessed 23 August 2005] www.givelife.org; American Red Cross website [accessed 3 October 2001] www.redcross.org; American Red Cross San Diego Chapter website [accessed 3 October 2001] www.sdarc.org/blood.htm.

34. Adapted from Joe Sharkey, "Luggage Lock Plan Revisited, Again," *New York Times*, 6 January 2004 [accessed 6 January 2004] www.nytimes.com; Brookstone website [accessed 13 January 2004] www.brookstone.com.

35. Adapted from Norimitsu Onishi, "Making Liberty His Business: Ex-Political Prisoner Turns Freedom's Icon into a Career," *New York Times*, 18 April 1996, B1; Colbar Art website [accessed 9 January 2004] www.colbarart.com.

36. Adapted from American Beefalo International website [accessed 31 October 2006] www.ababeefalo.org.

37. Adapted from Sarah Plaskitt, "Case Study: Hilton Uses SMS with Success," *B&T Marketing & Media*, 27 June 2002 [accessed 22 July 2003] www.bandt.com.au/articles/ce/0c00eace.asp; "Wireless Messaging Briefs," *Instant Messaging Planet*, 4 October 2002 [accessed 22 July 2003] www.instantmessagingplanet.com/wireless/print.php/ 10766_1476111; Hilton Hotels Corporation, *Hoover's Company Capsules*, 1 July 2003 [accessed 24 July 2003] www.proquest.com; Matthew G. Nelson, "Hilton Takes Reservations Wireless," *InformationWeek*, 25 June 2001, 99 [accessed 24 July 2003] www.web22.epnet.com; Hilton Hotels website [accessed 15 January 2004] www.hilton.com.

38. Adapted from The Podcast Bunker website [accessed 25 August 2005] www.podcastbunker.com.

39. Adapted from Time Inc. website [accessed 25 August 2005] www.timewarner.com.

40. Adapted from Insure.com website [accessed 24 August 2005] www.insure.com.

41. Adapted from Kelly Services website [accessed 9 January 2004] www.kellyservices.com.

42. Adapted from Hangers Cleaners website [accessed 9 January 2004] www.hangersdrycleaners.com; Charles Fishman, "The Greener Cleaners," *Fast Company* website [accessed 11 July 2000] http://fastcompany.com; Micell Technologies website [accessed 1 September 2000] www.micell.com; Cool Clean Technologies, Inc., website [accessed 9 January 2004] www.co2olclean.com.

CHAPTER 11

1. "Competition and Profit," Food Marketing Institute website [accessed 5 November 2006] www.fmi.org; John E. Forsyth, Nicolo Galante, and Todd Guild, "Capitalizing on Customer Insights," *McKinsey Quarterly*, 2006 Issue 3, 42–53; "Company Spotlight: Tesco PLC," *MarketWatch: Global Round-Up*, July 2006, 76–81; Tesco website [accessed 5 November 2006] www.tesco.com; James Quilter, "Tesco Hands Senior Role to Brand Planning Chief," *Marketing*, 2 August 2006, 4; Don Longo, "The British Are Coming," *Progressive Grocer*, 15 April 2006, 66–75.

2. Courtland L. Bovée, Michael J. Houston, and John V. Thill, *Marketing*, 2nd ed. (New York: McGraw-Hill, 1995), 194–196.

3. Legal-Definitions.com [accessed 17 December 2003] www.legaldefinitions.com.

4. Tom Krazit, "FAQ: The HP 'Pretexting' Scandal," ZDNet.com, 6 September 2006 [accessed 26 October 2006] www.zdnet.com.

5. Information for this section was obtained from "Finding Industry Information" [accessed 3 November 1998] www.pitt.edu/~buslibry/industries.htm; Thomas P. Bergman, Stephen M. Garrison, and Gregory M. Scott, *The Business Student Writer's Manual and Guide to the Internet* (Upper Saddle River, N.J.: Prentice Hall, 1998), 67–80; Ernest L. Maier, Anthony J. Faria, Peter Kaatrude, and Elizabeth Wood, *The Business Library and How to Use It* (Detroit: Omnigraphics, 1996), 53–76; Sherwyn P. Morreale and Courtland L. Bovée, *Excellence in Public Speaking* (Fort Worth: Harcourt Brace College Publishers, 1998), 166–171.

6. "Deep Web," Wikipedia [accessed 25 October 2006] www.wikipedia.org; Joe Barker, "Invisible or Deep Web: What It Is, Why It Exists, How to Find It, and Its Inherent Ambiguity," 1 August 2006, UC Berkeley–Teaching Library Internet Workshops [accessed 25 October 2006] www.lib.berkeley.edu.

7. Open Directory [accessed 25 October 2006] http://dmoz.com.

8. AllTheWeb.com advanced search page [accessed 13 December 2003] www.alltheweb.com; Google advanced search page [accessed 13 December 2003] www.google.com; Yahoo! advanced search page [accessed 13 December 2003] www.yahoo.com.

9. Google Help Center [accessed 25 October 2006] www.google.com.

10. "About Google Desktop," Google website [accessed 3 November 2006] www.google.com; "Desktop Search Tools Matrix," Goebel Group website [accessed 3 November 2006] www.goebelgroup.com.

11. Net Snippets website [accessed 3 November 2006] www.netsnippets.com.

12. Antone Gonsalves, "Digg Dogged by Allegations of Manipulation," TechWeb, 7 September 2006 [accessed 3 November 2006] www.techweb.com; "Social Bookmarking," Wikipedia [accessed 3 November 2006] www.wikipedia.com.

13. "Top 10 Benefits of Microsoft Office OneNote 2007," Microsoft website [accessed 26 October 2006], www.microsoft.com.

14. "Copyright Office Basics," U.S. Copyright Office website [accessed 2 November 2006] www.copyright.gov.

15. Ellen Neuborne, "Survey Says," *Inc.*, October 2005, 44, 46.

16. A. B. Blankenship and George Edward Breen, *State of the Art Marketing Research* (Chicago: NTC Business Books, 1993), 136.

17. "How to Design and Conduct a Study," *Credit Union Magazine*, October 1983, 36–46.

18. Product features page, Survey Monkey website [accessed 29 October 2006] www.surveymonkey.com.

19. American Marketing Association [accessed 14 December 2003] www.marketingpower.com.

20. Karen J. Bannan, "Companies Save Time, Money with Online Surveys," *B to B*, 9 June 2003, 1+; Allen Hogg, "Online Research Overview," American Marketing Association website [accessed 15 December 2003] www.marketingpower.com.

21. Tesco website [accessed 5 November 2006] www.tesco.com.

22. Morreale and Bovée, *Excellence in Public Speaking*, 177.

23. Morreale and Bovée, *Excellence in Public Speaking*, 178–180.

24. Morreale and Bovée, *Excellence in Public Speaking*, 182.

25. A. B. Blankenship and George Edward Breen, *State of the Art Marketing Research* (Lincolnwood, Ill.: NTC Business Books, 1992), 225.

26. Lynn Quitman Troyka, *Simon & Schuster Handbook for Writers*, 6th ed. (Upper Saddle River, N.J.: Simon & Schuster, 2002), 481.

27. "How to Paraphrase Effectively: 6 Steps to Follow," Researchpaper.com [accessed 26 October 1998] www.researchpaper.com/writing_center/30.html.

28. Samuel Greengard, "What's in Store for 2004," *Workforce Management*, December 2003, 34+.

29. Kenneth C. Laudon and Jane P. Laudon, *Management Information Systems*, 8th ed. (Upper Saddle River, N.J.: Pearson Education, 2004), 325.

CHAPTER 12

1. Tim Horton's website [accessed 24 November 2006] www.timhortons.com; SYP website [accessed 24 November 2006] www.stoneyamashita.com; Christine Dyrness, "Expert Talks to Raleigh, N.C., Businesses About Fusion of Work, Creativity," *News & Observer*, 20 March 2003 [accessed 3 December 2003] www.elibrary.com; Polly LaBere, "Keith Yamashita Wants to Reinvent Your Company," *Fast Company*, November 2002, 88; James Aley, "Big Ideas for Hire," *Fortune*, 28 October 2002, 178; Pui-Wing Tam, "The Corporate Strategist," *Wall Street Journal*, 13 May 2002, R8.

2. Alexis Gerard and Bob Goldstein, *Going Visual* (Hoboken, N.J.: Wiley, 2005), 18.

3. Charles Kostelnick and Michael Hassett, *Shaping Information: The Rhetoric of Visual Conventions* (Carbondale, Ill.: Southern Illinois University Press, 2003), 177.

4. Gerard and Goldstein, *Going Visual*, 25–27.

5. "Fact Sheet Overview," *2003 National Assessment of Adult Literacy*, National Institute for Literacy [accessed 22 November 2006] www.nifl.gov.

6. Gerard and Goldstein, *Going Visual*, 103–106.

7. Edward R. Tufte, *Visual Explanations: Images and Quantities, Evidence and Narrative* (Cheshire, Conn.: Graphics Press, 1997), 82.

8. Joshua David McClurg-Genevese, "The Principles of Design," *Digital Web Magazine*, 13 June 2005 [accessed 23 November 2006] www.digital-web.com.

9. Kostelnick and Hassett, *Shaping Information: The Rhetoric of Visual Conventions*, 17.

10. Kostelnick and Hassett, *Shaping Information: The Rhetoric of Visual Conventions*, 216.

11. Edward R. Tufte, *The Visual Display of Quantitative Information* (Cheshire, Conn.: Graphic Press, 1983), 113.

12. Tufte, *Visual Explanations: Images and Quantities, Evidence and Narrative*, 73.

13. Based in part on Tufte, *Visual Explanations: Images and Quantities, Evidence and Narrative*, 29–37, 53; Paul Martin Lester, *Visual Communication: Images with Messages*, 4th ed. (Belmont, Calif.: Thomson Wadsworth, 2006), 95–105, 194–196.

14. Data from Hoover's Online [accessed 17 November 2006] www.hoovers.com.

15. Robert L. Harris, *Information Graphics: A Comprehensive Illustrated Reference* (New York: Oxford University Press, 1999), 14.

16. Gerard and Goldstein, *Going Visual*, 49.

17. Sheri Rosen, "What Is Truth?" *IABC Communication World*, March 1995, 40.

CHAPTER 13

1. Doug Walmisley, Kenwood USA, personal communication, 8 February 2007; Kenwood USA website [accessed 7 November 2006] www.kenwoodusa.com; "Kenwood Announces Strategic Organization Changes," Kenwood Corporation press release, 2 October 2006 [accessed 7 November 2006] http://biz.yahoo.com; Amy Gilroy, "Vendors Retool Lines to Combat Sales Slump," *TWICE*, 13 October 2003, 28; Amy Gilroy, "Car Audio in Double-Digit Slump," *TWICE*, 7 July 2003, 8; Martin Fackler, "Japan Profiles: Haruo Kawahara, Kenwood Chief," Dow Jones Newswires, *Far Eastern Economic Review*, 24 September 2003 [accessed 9 December 2003] http://online.wsj.com; Corey Goldman, "Satellite Radio's Future Still Up in the Air," *Toronto Star*, 11 August 2003 [accessed 9 December 2003] www.elibrary.com; Denis Storey, "Kenwood Chief Touts Turnaround," Mobile Radio Technology website, 1 February 2003 [accessed 9 December 2003] www.iwce-mrt.com; Erin Strout, "Ask SMM," *Sales and Marketing Management*, October 2002, 59.

2. See Note 1.

3. Adapted from Michael Gerber, "The Business Plan That Always Works," *Her Business*, May/June 2004, 23–25; J. Tol Broome, Jr., "How to Write a Business Plan," *Nation's Business*, February 1993, 29–30; Albert Richards, "The Ernst & Young Business Plan Guide," *R & D Management*, April 1995, 253; David Lanchner, "How Chitchat Became a Valuable Business Plan," *Global Finance*, February 1995, 54–56; Marguerita Ashby-Berger, "My Business Plan—And What Really Happened," *Small Business Forum*, Winter 1994–1995, 24–35; Stanley R. Rich and David E. Gumpert, *Business Plans That Win $$$* (New York: Harper Row, 1985).

4. Jakob Nielsen, "Reading on the Web" [accessed 11 November 2004] www.useit.com/alertbox/9710a.html.

5. Reid Goldsborough, "Words for the Wise," *Link-Up*, September–October 1999, 25–26.

6. Julie Rohovit, "Computer Eye Strain: The Dilbert Syndrome," Virtual Hospital website [accessed 9 November 2004] www.vh.org.

7. Nick Usborne, "Two Pillars of a Successful Site," *Excess Voice*, May 2004 [accessed 8 November 2004] www.excessvoice.com.

8. Shel Holtz, "Writing for the Wired World," *International Association of Business Communicators*, 1999, 6–9.

9. Holtz, "Writing for the Wired World," 28–29.

10. Iris Varner, *Contemporary Business Report Writing*, 2nd ed. (Chicago: Dryden Press, 1991), 170.

11. Curt Kampmeier, "How To Write a Proposal That's Accepted Every Time," *Consulting to Management*, September 2000, 62.

12. Varner, *Contemporary Business Report Writing*, 178.

13. See Note 1.

CHAPTER 14

1. Adapted from Tellabs website [accessed 11 November 2006] www.tellabs.com; Sid Cato, "World's Best 2005 Reports," Sid Cato's Office Annual Report Website [accessed 11 November 2006] www.sidcato.com; George Stenitzer, "New Challenges for Annual Reports," Presentation to National Investor Relations Institute, November 2005 [accessed 11 November 2006] www.niri-chicago.org.

2. A. S. C. Ehrenberg, "Report Writing—Six Simple Rules for Better Business Documents," *Admap*, June 1992, 39–42.

3. Michael Netzley and Craig Snow, *Guide to Report Writing* (Upper Saddle River, N.J.: Prentice Hall, 2001), 15.

4. "Tellabs Solutions and Applications," Tellabs 2005 Annual Report [accessed 11 November 2006] www.tellabs.com.

5. Claudia Mon Pere McIsaac, "Improving Student Summaries Through Sequencing," *Bulletin of the Association for Business Communication* (September 1987): 17–20.

6. David A. Hayes, "Helping Students GRASP the Knack of Writing Summaries," *Journal of Reading* (November 1989): 96–101.

7. Philip C. Kolin, *Successful Writing at Work*, 6th ed. (Boston: Houghton Mifflin, 2001), 552–555.

8. "Web Writing: How to Avoid Pitfalls," *Investor Relations Business*, 1 November 1999, 15.

9. Shel Holtz, "Writing for the Wired World," *International Association of Business Communicators*, 1999, 6–9.

10. Adapted from Air-Trak website [accessed 12 September 2005] www.air-trak.com.

CHAPTER 15

1. Gates Foundation website [accessed 13 November 2006] www.gatesfoundation.org; Richard Klausner and Pedro Alonso, "An Attack on All Fronts," *Nature*, 19 August 2004, 930–931; "Richard Klausner Spends to Save Lives," *Fast Company*, November 2002, 128; Kent Allen, "The Gatekeeper," *U.S. News & World Report*, 8 December 2003, 64–66.

2. John Morkes and Jakob Nielsen, "Concise, Scannable, and Objective: How to Write for the Web," UseIt.com [accessed 13 November 2006] www.useit.com.

3. Dean Allen, "Reading Design," *A List Apart*, 23 November 2001 [accessed 9 November 2004] www.alistapart.com.

4. Michael Netzley and Craig Snow, *Guide to Report Writing* (Upper Saddle River, N.J.: Prentice Hall, 2001), 57.

5. Patty Stonesifer, "Partners and Progress: A Message from Patty Stonesifer," Gates Foundation website [accessed 15 September 2005] www.gatesfoundation.org.

6. Oswald M. T. Ratteray, "Hit the Mark with Better Summaries," *Supervisory Management*, September 1989, 43–45.

7. Netzley and Snow, *Guide to Report Writing*, 43.

8. Alice Reid, "A Practical Guide for Writing Proposals" [accessed 31 May 2001] http://members.dca.net/areid/proposal.htm.

9. Toby B. Gooley, "Ocean Shipping: RFPs That Get Results," *Logistics Management*, July 2003, 47–52.

10. See Note 1.

11. Andrea Obana, "How to Write a Request for Proposals (RFP)," Fine Brand Media website [accessed 22 January 2004] www.finebrand.com; Gooley, "Ocean Shipping: RFPs That Get Results," 47–52.

12. Obana, "How to Write a Request for Proposals (RFP)."

13. Obana, "How to Write a Request for Proposals (RFP)"; Gooley, "Ocean Shipping: RFPs That Get Results," 47–52; "Writing a Good RFP," *Infrastructure Issues*, September 1998, Mead & Hunt website [accessed 23 January 2004] www.meadhunt.com.

14. Adapted from "Home Depot Says E-Learning Is Paying for Itself," *Workforce Management*, 25 February 2004 [accessed 28 February 2004] www.workforce.com; Robert Celaschi, "The Insider: Training," *Workforce Management*, August 2004, 67–69; Joe Mullich, "A Second Act for E-Learning," *Workforce Management*, February 2004, 51–55; Gail Johnson, "Brewing the Perfect Blend," *Training*, December 2003, 30+; Tammy Galvin, "2003 Industry Report," *Training*, October 2003, 21+; William C. Symonds, "Giving It the Old Online Try," *BusinessWeek*, 3 December 2001, 76–80; Karen Frankola, "Why Online Learners Drop Out," *Workforce*, October 2001, 52–60; Mary Lord, "They're Online and on the Job; Managers and Hamburger Flippers Are Being E-Trained at Work," *U.S. News & World Report*, 15 October 2001, 72–77.

15. Adapted from Ieva M. Augstumes, "Buyers Take the Driver's Seat," *Dallas Morning News*, 20 February 2004 [accessed 30 June 2004] www.highbeam.com; Jill Amadio, "A Click Away: Automotive Web Sites Are Revved Up and Ready to Help You Buy," *Entrepreneur*, 1 August 2003 [accessed 30 June 2004] www.highbeam.com; Dawn C. Chmielewski, "Car Sites Lend Feel-Good Info for Haggling," *San Jose Mercury News*, 1 August 2003 [accessed 30 June 2004] www.highbeam.com; Cromwell Schubarth, "Autoheroes Handle Hassle of Haggling," *Boston Herald*, 24 July 2003 [accessed 30 June 2004] www.highbeam.com; Rick Popely, "Internet Doesn't Change Basic Shopping Rules," *Chicago Tribune*, 28 February 2004 [accessed 30 June 2004] www.highbeam.com; Matt Nauman, "Walnut Creek, Calif., Firm Prospers as Online Car Buying Becomes More Popular," *San Jose Mercury News*, 21 June 2004 [accessed 30 June 2004] www.highbeam.com; Cliff Banks, "e-Dealer 100," *Ward's Dealer Business*, 1 April 2004 [accessed 30 June 2004] www.highbeam.com; Cars.com website [accessed 30 June 2004] www.cars.com; Cars Direct. com website [accessed 30 June 2004] www.carsdirect.com.

CHAPTER 16

1. "Fitch Fact Sheet," Fitch website [accessed 26 November 2006] www.fitchworldwide.com; "Fitch: Worldwide—A Different View," Fitch website [accessed 15 December 2003] www.fitchworldwide.com; "About Fitch: Worldwide," Fitch website [accessed 10 October 2003] www.fitchworldwide.com; Fara Warner, "How Fitch Makes Its (Fast) Pitch," *Fast Company*, March 2002, 126.

2. Irwin Pollack, "Don't Just Give Presentations, Impact Your Audience," *Fort Worth Business Press*, 1 May 2006, 10.

3. Carmine Gallo, "Loaded for Bore," *BusinessWeek Online*, 5 August 2005 [accessed 19 September 2005] www.businessweek.com.

4. Sarah Lary and Karen Pruente, "Powerless Point: Common PowerPoint Mistakes to Avoid," *Public Relations Tactics*, February 2004, 28.

5. Cliff Atkinson, *Beyond Bullet Points: Using Microsoft PowerPoint to Create Presentations That Inform, Motivate, and Inspire* (Redmond, Wash.: Microsoft Press, 2005), 29, 55, 65.

6. Sherwyn P. Morreale and Courtland L. Bovée, *Excellence in Public Speaking* (Fort Worth: Harcourt Brace, 1998), 234–237.

7. Morreale and Bovée, *Excellence in Public Speaking*, 230.

8. Morreale and Bovée, *Excellence in Public Speaking*, 241–243.

9. "Choose and Use Your Words Deliberately," *Soundview Executive Book Summaries* 20, no. 6, pt. 2 (June 1998): 3.

10. Carmine Gallo, "Grab Your Audience Fast," *BusinessWeek*, 13 September 2006, 19.

11. Walter Kiechel III, "How to Give a Speech," *Fortune*, 8 June 1987, 180.

12. *Communication and Leadership Program* (Santa Ana, Calif.: Toastmasters International, 1980), 44, 45.

13. Steve Adubato, "Throw Away That Script, Use an Outline Instead," *NJBiz*, 23 October 2006, 17.

14. Peter Burrows and Ronald Grover, "Steve Jobs' Magic Kingdom," *BusinessWeek*, 6 February 2006 [accessed 25 November 2006] www.businessweek.com.

15. Morreale and Bovée, *Excellence in Public Speaking*, 24–25.

16. Jeffrey Gitomer, "Develop Better Presentation (and Persuasion) Skills," *Central New York Business Journal*, 8 July 2005, 14, 17.

17. Jennifer Rotondo and Mike Rotondo, Jr., *Presentation Skills for Managers* (New York: McGraw-Hill, 2002), 9.

18. Lillian H. Chaney and Catherine G. Green, "Presenter Behaviors: Actions Often Speak Louder Than Words," *American Salesman*, April 2006, 22–27.

19. Judy Linscott, "Getting On and Off the Podium," *Savvy*, October 1985, 44.

20. Iris R. Johnson, "Before You Approach the Podium," *MW*, January–February 1989, 7.

21. "Advice from a Voice Coach: Say It and Sell It," *Presentations*, 6 November 2006 [accessed 27 November 2006] www.presentations.com.

22. Sandra Moyer, "Braving No Woman's Land," *The Toastmaster*, August 1986, 13.

23. "Control the Question-and-Answer Session," *Soundview Executive Book Summaries* 20, no. 6, pt. 2 (June 1998): 4.

24. "Control the Question-and-Answer Session."

25. Teresa Brady, "Fielding Abrasive Questions During Presentations," *Supervisory Management*, February 1993, 6.

26. Robert L. Montgomery, "Listening on Your Feet," *The Toastmaster*, July 1987, 14–15.

27. Adapted from Ronald L. Applebaum and Karl W. E. Anatol, *Effective Oral Communication: For Business and the Professions* (Chicago: Science Research Associates, 1982), 240–244.

CHAPTER 17

1. "Culture and Philosophy" and "Procter & Gamble Case Study," HP website [accessed 20 September 2005] www.hp.com; Paul McDougall, "Procter & Gamble's Deal with HP Grows," *InformationWeek*, 16 August 2004 [accessed 20 September 2005] www.outsourcingpipeline.com; Bill Breen, "The Big Score," *Fast Company*, September 2003, 64; "HP Finalizes $3 Billion Outsourcing Agreement to Manage Procter & Gamble's IT Infrastructure," press release, HP website, 6 May 2003 [accessed 10 October 2003] www.hp.com; "HP Selected by P&G for $3 Billion, 10-Year Services Contract," press release, HP website, 11 April 2003 [accessed 10 October 2003] www.hp.com.

2. "Polishing Your Presentation," 3M Meeting Network [accessed 8 June 2001] www.mmm.com/meetingnetwork/readingroom/meetingguide_pres.html.

3. Michael Hyatt, "Five Rules to Better PowerPoint Presentations," 21 June 2005, Working Smart blog [accessed 2 December 2006] www.michaelhyatt.com.

4. Claudyne Wilder and David Fine, *Point, Click & Wow* (San Francisco: Jossey-Bass Pfeiffer, 1996), 50.

5. Allbee, personal communication.

6. See Note 1.

7. Jerry Weissman, *Presenting to Win: The Art of Telling Your Story* (Upper Saddle River, N.J.: Pearson Prentice Hall, 2006), 124.

8. Weissman, *Presenting to Win*, 144–147.

9. Edward Tufte, "ET on Columbia Evidence—Analysis of Key Slide" [accessed 15 February 2004] www.edwardtufte.com; Edward Tufte, [introduction to] "Essay: The Cognitive Style of PowerPoint" [accessed 15 February 2004] www.edwardtufte.com; Clive Thompson, "PowerPoint Makes You Dumb," *New York Times Magazine*, 14 December 2003, 88; Mark Gibbs, "Blame the Workman," Network World, 2 February 2004, 50.

10. Margo Halverson, "Choosing the Right Colors for Your Next Presentation," 3M Meeting Network [accessed 8 June 2001] www.mmm.com/meetingnetwork/readingroom/meetingguide_right_color.html.

11. Carol Klinger and Joel G. Siegel, "Computer Multimedia Presentations," *CPA Journal*, June 1996, 46.

12. Jon Hanke, "Five Tips for Better Visuals," 3M Meeting Network [accessed 8 June 2001] www.mmm.com/meetingnetwork/presentations/pmag_better_visuals.html.

13. Hanke, "Five Tips for Better Visuals."

14. Sarah Lary and Karen Pruente, "Powerless Point: Common Power-Point Mistakes to Avoid," *Public Relations Tactics*, February 2004, 28.

15. Cliff Atkinson, *Beyond Bullet Points: Using Microsoft PowerPoint to Create Presentations That Inform, Motivate, and Inspire* (Redmond, Wash.: Microsoft Press, 2005), 16.

16. Weissman, *Presenting to Win*, 162.

17. Ted Simons, "Handouts That Won't Get Trashed," *Presentations*, February 1999, 47–50.

18. Jennifer Rotondo and Mike Rotondo, Jr., *Presentation Skills for Managers*, (New York: McGraw-Hill, 2002), 151.

19. Roly Grimshaw, "Communication by the Numbers," *Harvard Management Communication Letter*, Summer 2005, 3–4.

20. Julia Chang, "Best Practices for Web Presentations," *Sales & Marketing Management*, November 2005, 52.

21. Jeff Yocom, "TechRepublic Survey Yields Advice on Streaming Video," TechRepublic website [accessed 16 February 2004] www.techrepublic.com.

22. "Webcasting Tips & Advice," Spider Eye Solutions [accessed 13 February 2004] www.spidereye.com.

23. "Best Practices for Online Marketing Events with WebEx Event Center," WebEx Communications [accessed 3 December 2006] www.webex.com.

24. Adapted from Loopt website [accessed 9 December 2006] www.loopt.com; Boost Mobile website [accessed 9 December 2006] www.boostmobile.com.

25. Adapted from Robert D. Hof, "There's Not Enough 'Me' in MySpace," *BusinessWeek*, 4 December 2006, 40.

CHAPTER 18

1. Charles Handler, "What You Need to Know About What's Happening in the Pre-Employment Assessment Market," Ere.net, 20 July 2006 [accessed 12 December 2006] www.ere.net; Fay Hansen, "Growing Into Applicant Tracking Systems," *Workforce Management*, 10 October 2006 [accessed 12 December 2006] www.workforce.com; Connie Winkler, "Job Tryouts Go Virtual," *HR Magazine*, September 2006, 131–134; "Hersha Hospitality Management Selects ERC's Selectech Workforce Management Recruiting Solution," 7 December 2006, ERC website [accessed 12 December 2006] www.ercdataplus.com.

2. Robert J. Gerberg, *Robert Gerberg's Job Changing System*, summarized by Macmillan Book Clubs, Inc., in the "Macmillan Executive Summary Program," April 1987, 4.

3. Mkt10.com website [accessed 25 September 2005] www.mkt10.com; Olga Kharif, "The Job of Challenging Monster," *BusinessWeek Online*, 6 September 2005 [accessed 25 September 2005] www.businessweek.com; "Job Sites: The 'Second Generation,'" *BusinessWeek Online*, 7 September 2005 [accessed 25 September 2005] www.businessweek.com.

4. Caroline A. Drakeley, "Viral Networking: Tactics in Today's Job Market," *Intercom*, September–October 2003, 4–7.

5. Drakeley, "Viral Networking: Tactics in Today's Job Market," 5.

6. Anne Fisher, "Greener Pastures in a New Field," *Fortune*, 26 January 2004, 48.

7. Cheryl L. Noll, "Collaborating with the Career Planning and Placement Center in the Job-Search Project," *Business Communication Quarterly* 58, no. 3 (1995): 53–55.

8. Rockport Institute, "How to Write a Masterpiece of a Résumé" [accessed 25 September 2005] www.rockportinstitute.com.

9. Pam Stanley-Weigand, "Organizing the Writing of Your Résumé," *Bulletin of the Association for Business Communication* 54, no. 3 (September 1991): 11–12.

10. Susan Vaughn, "Answer the Hard Questions Before Asked," *Los Angeles Times*, 29 July 2001, W1–W2.

11. John Steven Niznik, "Landing a Job with a Criminal Record," About.com [accessed 12 December 2006] http://jobsearchtech.about.com.

12. Richard H. Beatty and Nicholas C. Burkholder, *The Executive Career Guide for MBAs* (New York: Wiley, 1996), 133.

13. Adapted from Burdette E. Bostwick, *How to Find the Job You've Always Wanted* (New York: Wiley, 1982), 69–70.

14. Norma Mushkat Gaffin, "Recruiters' Top 10 Résumé Pet Peeves," Monster.com [accessed 19 February 2004] www.monster.com; Beatty and Burkholder, *The Executive Career Guide for MBAs*, 151.

15. Rockport Institute, "How to Write a Masterpiece of a Résumé."

16. "Résumé Fraud Gets Slicker and Easier," CNN.com [accessed 11 March 2004] www.cnn.com.

17. "Résumé Fraud Gets Slicker and Easier"; Employment Screening Resources website [accessed 18 March 2004] www.erscheck.com.

18. "Employers Turn Their Fire on Untruthful CVs," *Supply Management*, 23 June 2005, 13.

19. Lore Croghan, "Candidates Unafraid to Fudge Résumés, Study Finds," *Seattle Times*, 12 March 2006 [accessed 12 March 2006] www.seattletimes.com.

20. Sal Divita, "If You're Thinking Résumé, Think Creatively," *Marketing News*, 14 September 1992, 29.

21. Rockport Institute, "How to Write a Masterpiece of a Résumé."

22. Lora Morsch, "25 Words That Hurt Your Résumé," CNN.com, 20 January 2006 [accessed 20 January 2006] www.cnn.com.

23. Karl L. Smart, "Articulating Skills in the Job Search," *Business Communication Quarterly* 67, no. 2 (June 2004): 198–205.

24. Rockport Institute, "How to Write a Masterpiece of a Résumé."

25. Ed Tazzia, "Wanted: A Résumé That Really Works," *Brandweek*, 15 May 2006, 26.

26. Ellen Joe Pollock, "Sir: Your Application for a Job Is Rejected; Sincerely, Hal 9000," *Wall Street Journal*, 30 July 1998, A1, A12.

27. "Scannable Résumé Design," ResumeEdge.com [accessed 19 February 2004] www.resumeedge.com.

28. Kim Isaacs, "Tips for Creating a Scannable Résumé," Monster.com [accessed 19 February 2004] www.monster.com.

29. Kim Isaacs, "Enhance Your Résumé for Monster Upload," Monster.com [accessed 19 February 2004] www.monster.com.

30. "The Rogue's Gallery of 25 Awful Résumé Mistakes," Career Explorer.net [accessed 19 February 2004] www.careerexplorer.net.

31. Lore Croghan, "Recruiters Cite Litany of Mistakes They've Seen on Résumés," *Seattle Times*, 20 November 2005 [accessed 20 November 2005] www.seattletimes.com.

32. Regina Pontow, "Electronic Résumé Writing Tips," Proven Résumés.com [accessed 18 October 1998] www.provenresumes.com/reswkshps/electronic/scnres.html.

CHAPTER 19

1. John Sullivan, "A Case Study of Google Recruiting," 5 December 2005, Electronic Recruiting Exchange [accessed 16 December 2006] www.ere.net; "What's It Like to Work At Google?" Google website [accessed 26 September 2005] www.google.com; Fred Vogelstein, "Can Google Grow Up?" *Fortune*, 8 December 2003, 102; Quentin Hardy, "All Eyes on Google," *Forbes*, 26 May 2003, 100; Keith H. Hammonds, "Growth Search," *Fast Company*, April 2003, 74–81; Stanley Bing, "How Not to Success (*sic*) in Business," *Fortune*, 30 December 2002, 210; Pierre Mornell, "Zero Defect Hiring," *Inc.*, March 1998, 74.

2. "The Writer Approach," *Los Angeles Times*, 17 November 2002, W1.

3. Toni Logan, "The Perfect Cover Story," *Kinko's Impress* 2 (2000): 32, 34.

4. James Gonyea, "Money Talks: Salary History Versus Salary Requirements," Monster.com [accessed 19 October 2004] www.monster.com; Marguerite Higgins, "Tech-Savvy Job Hunters Not So Suave in Writing; E-Mail Résumés Appall Employers," *Washington Times*, 17 December 2002 [accessed 22 February 2004] www.highbeam.com; "Keep Goal in Mind When Crafting a Résumé," Register-Guard (Eugene, Ore.), 3 August 2003 [accessed 22 February 2004] www.highbeam.com; Anis F. McClin, "Effects of Spelling Errors on the Perception of Writers," Journal of General Psychology, January 2002 [accessed 22 February 2004] www.highbeam.com.

5. George Donnelly, "Recruiting, Retention & Returns," *cfonet*, March 2000 [accessed 10 April 2000] www.cfonet.com/html/Articles/CFO/2000/00Marecr.html.

6. Stephanie Armour, "The New Interview Etiquette," *USA Today*, 23 November 1999, B1, B2.

7. Samuel Greengard, "Are You Well Armed to Screen Applicants?" *Personnel Journal*, December 1995, 84–95.

8. Caroline Levchuck, "Survival Tips for Group Interviews," Yahoo! HotJobs [accessed 16 December 2006] http://hotjobs.yahoo.com.

9. William Poundstone, "Beware the Interview Inquisition," *Harvard Business Review*, May 2003, 18+.

10. "Interview Preparation," Madison MacArthur website [accessed 13 December 2006] www.mmsearch.com.

11. Lynda M. Bassett, "Work the Working Interview," Monster.com [accessed 13 December 2006] www.monster.com.

12. Peter Vogt, "Mastering the Phone Interview," Monster.com [accessed 13 December 2006] www.monster.com; Nina Segal, "The Global Interview: Tips for Successful, Unconventional Interview Techniques," Monster.com [accessed 13 December 2006] www.monster.com.

13. Segal, "The Global Interview: Tips for Successful, Unconventional Interview Techniques."

14. Connie Winkler, "Job Tryouts Go Virtual," *HR Magazine*, September 2006, 131–134.

15. Steven Isbitts, "Virtual Interview," *Tampa Tribune*, 20 March 2006 [accessed 13 December 2006] www.ebscohost.com.

16. Carole Martin, "Smile, You're on Camera: Videoconference Interviews," Monster.com [accessed 13 December 2006] www.monster.com; Marcia Vickers, "Don't Touch That Dial: Why Should I Hire You?" *New York Times*, 13 April 1997, F11.

17. Patrick J. Sauer, "Open-Door Management," *Inc.*, June 2003, 44.

18. Dino di Mattia, "Testing Methods and Effectiveness of Tests," *Supervision*, August 2005, 4–5.

19. Sullivan, "A Case Study of Google Recruiting."

20. Steven Mitchell Sack, "The Working Woman's Legal Survival Guide: Testing," FindLaw.com [accessed 22 February 2004] www.findlaw.com; David W. Arnold and John W. Jones, "Who the Devil's Applying Now?" *Security Management*, March 2002, 85–88.

21. Arnold and Jones, "Who the Devil's Applying Now?" 86.

22. Arnold and Jones, "Who the Devil's Applying Now?" 86.

23. Adam Agard, "Preemployment Skills Testing: An Important Step in the Hiring Process," *Supervision*, June 2003, 7+.

24. Andy Meisler, "Negative Results," *Workforce Management*, October 2003, 35+.

25. Tyler D. Hartwell, Paul D. Steele, and Nathaniel F. Rodman, "Workplace Alcohol-Testing Programs: Prevalence and Trends," *Monthly Labor Review*, June 1998, 27–34; "Substance Abuse in the Workplace," HR Focus, February 1997, 1, 4+.

26. "Drug Test Company Official Disputes Report Pre-Employment Tests Falling," *Drug Detection Report*, 23 March 2006, 43.

27. Hope A. Comisky and Christopher P. Zubowicz, "The Law of Criminal Background Checks," *Employee Relations Law Journal* 32, no. 3 (Winter 2006): 66–85.

28. Thomas A. Buckhoff, "Preventing Fraud by Conducting Background Checks," *CPA Journal*, November 2003, 52.

29. "Check Yourself Before Employer Does," *CA Magazine*, June/July 2005, 12.

30. Austin, "Goodbye Gimmicks."

31. Katherine Spencer Lee, "Tackling Tough Interview Questions," *Certification Magazine*, May 2005, 35.

32. Leigh Dyer, "Job Hunters Should Think Carefully Before Using Job Counselor," *Charlotte Observer*, 30 July 2001 [accessed 29 September 2005] www.ebsco.com; Anne Field, "Coach, Help Me Out with This Interview," *Business Week*, 22 October 2001, 134E2, 134E4.

33. Robert Gifford, Cheuk Fan Ng, and Margaret Wilkinson, "Nonverbal Cues in the Employment Interview: Links Between Applicant Qualities and Interviewer Judgments," *Journal of Applied Psychology* 70, no. 4 (1985): 729.

34. Dale G. Leathers, *Successful Nonverbal Communication* (New York: Macmillan, 1986), 225.

35. Armour, "The New Interview Etiquette."

36. William S. Frank, "Job Interview: Pre-Flight Checklist," *The Career Advisor* [accessed 28 September 2005] http://careerplanning. about.com.

37. T. Shawn Taylor, "Most Managers Have No Idea How to Hire the Right Person for the Job," *Chicago Tribune*, 23 July 2002 [accessed 29 September 2005] www.ebsco.com.

38. Sack, "The Working Woman's Legal Survival Guide."

39. Gerald L. Wilson, "Preparing Students for Responding to Illegal Selection Interview Questions," *Bulletin of the Association for Business Communication* 54, no. 2 (1991): 44–49.

40. Jeff Springston and Joann Keyton, "Interview Response Training," *Bulletin of the Association for Business Communication* 54, no. 3 (1991): 28–30; Gerald L. Wilson, "An Analysis of Instructional Strategies for Responding to Illegal Selection Interview Questions," *Bulletin of the Association for Business Communication* 54, no. 3 (1991): 31–35.

41. Stephen J. Pullum, "Illegal Questions in the Selection Process: Going Beyond Contemporary Business and Professional Communication Textbooks," *Bulletin of the Association for Business Communication* 54, no. 3 (1991): 36–43; Alicia Kitsuse, "Have You Ever Been Arrested?" *Across the Board*, November 1992, 46–49; Christina L. Greathouse, "Ten Common Hiring Mistakes," *Industry Week*, 20 January 1992, 22–23, 26.

42. "Negotiating Salary: An Introduction," *InformationWeek* online [accessed 22 February 2004] www.infoweek.com

43. "Negotiating Salary: An Introduction."

44. Harold H. Hellwig, "Job Interviewing: Process and Practice," *Bulletin of the Association for Business Communication* 55, no. 2 (1992): 8–14.

APPENDIX A

1. Mary A. De Vries, *Internationally Yours* (Boston: Houghton Mifflin, 1994), 9.

2. Patricia A. Dreyfus, "Paper That's Letter Perfect," *Money*, May 1985, 184.

3. "When Image Counts, Letterhead Says It All," *Stamford (Conn.) Advocate and Greenwich Times*, 10 January 1993, F4.

4. Mel Mandell, "Electronic Forms Are Cheap and Speedy," *D&B Reports*, July–August 1993, 44–45.

5. Linda Driskill, *Business and Managerial Communication: New Perspectives* (Orlando, Fla.: Harcourt Brace Jovanovich, 1992), 470.

6. Driskill, *Business and Managerial Communication*, 470.

7. Lennie Copeland and Lewis Griggs, *Going International: How to Make Friends and Deal Effectively in the Global Marketplace*, 2d ed. (New York: Random House, 1985), 24–27.

8. De Vries, *Internationally Yours*, 8.

9. Copeland and Griggs, *Going International*, 24–27.

10. U.S. Postal Service, *Postal Addressing Standards* (Washington, D.C.: GPO, 1992).

11. Copeland and Griggs, *Going International*, 24–27.

12. Renee B. Horowitz and Marian G. Barchilon, "Stylistic Guidelines for E-Mail," *IEEE Transactions on Professional Communications*, 37, no. 4 (1994): 207–212.

13. Jill H. Ellsworth and Matthew V. Ellsworth, *The Internet Business Book* (New York: Wiley, 1994), 93.

14. William Eager, *Using the Internet* (Indianapolis: Que Corporation, 1994), 11.

15. Eager, *Using the Internet*, 10.

16. William Eager, Larry Donahue, David Forsyth, Kenneth Mitton, and Martin Waterhouse, *Net.Search* (Indianapolis: Que Corporation, 1995), 221.

17. Rosalind Resnick and Dave Taylor, *Internet Business Guide* (Indianapolis: Sams.net Publishing, 1995), 117.

18. James L. Clark and Lyn R. Clark, *How 7: A Handbook for Office Workers*, 7th ed. (Cincinnati: South-Western, 1995), 431–432.

Acknowledgments

TEXT

10 (Connecting with Technology: Is Web 2.0 the Future or the Past Revisited?) Adapted from Russell Shaw, "Web 2.0? It Doesn't Exist," ZDNet blogs, 17 December 2005 [accessed 13 August 2006] http://blogs.zdnet.com; Tim O'Reilly, "What Is Web 2.0? Design Patterns and Business Models for the Next Generation of Software," O'Reilly, 30 September 2005 [accessed 13 August 2006] www.oreillynet.com; "Web 2.0," Wikipedia.com [accessed 13 August 2006] www.wikipedia.org; John Dvorak, "Web 2.0 Baloney," PC Magazine online, 1 March 2006 [accessed 13 August 2006] www.pcmag.com; Nicholas Carr, "The Amorality of Web 2.0," (blog entry), 3 October 2005 [accessed 13 August 2006] http://roughtype.com. **55 (Communicating Across Cultures: Actions Speak Louder Than Words All Around the World)** Adapted from Lillian H. Chaney and Jeanette S. Martin, *Intercultural Business Communication*, 4th ed. (Upper Saddle River, N.J.: Pearson Prentice Hall, 2007), 126; David A. Victor, *International Business Communication* (New York: HarperCollins, 1992); David Wallace, "Mind Your Manners," *World Trade*, October 1992, 52, 54–55; Hannele Duvfa, "Innocents Abroad: The Politics of Cross-Cultural Communication," *Communication and Discourse Across Cultures and Languages*, 1991, 73–89; M. Katherine Glover, "Do's and Taboos: Cultural Aspects of International Business," *Business America*, 13 August 1990, 2–6; C. Barnum and N. Woniansky, "Taking Cues from Body Language," *Management Review*, June 1989, 59–60. **54 (Checklist: Improving Your Listening Skills)** Source: Robert A. Luke, Jr., "Improving Your Listening Ability," *Supervisory Management*, June 1992, 7; Madelyn Burley-Allen, "Listening for Excellence in Communication," *The Dynamics of Behavior Newsletter* 2, no. 2 (Summer 1992): 1; Bob Lamons, "Good Listeners Are Better Communicators," *Marketing News*, 11 September 1995, 13+. **56 (Checklist: Improving Nonverbal Communication Skills)** Source: Gerald H. Graham, Jeanne Unrue, and Paul Jennings, "The Impact of Nonverbal Communication in Organizations: A Survey of Perceptions," *Journal of Business Communication* 28, no. 1 (Winter 1991): 45–62; Dianna Booher, *Communicate with Confidence* (New York: McGraw-Hill, 1994), 363–370. **68 (Communicating Across Cultures: Test Your Intercultural Knowledge)** Adapted from David A. Ricks, "International Business Blunders: An Update," *Business & Economic Review*, January–March 1988, 25; Valerie Frazee, "Keeping Up on Chinese Culture," *Global Workforce*, October 1996, 16–17; Valerie Frazee, "Establishing Relations in Germany," *Global Workforce*, April 1997, 16–17; James Wilfong and Toni Seger, *Taking Your Business Global* (Franklin Lakes, N.J.: Career Press, 1997), 282. **82 (Connecting with Technology: The Gist of Machine Translation)** Adapted from Sheridan Prasso, ed., "It's All Greek to These Sites," *Business Week*, 22 July 2002, 18; Alis Technologies website [accessed 4 November 2003] www.alis.com; WorldLingo website [accessed 4 November 2003] www.worldlingo.com. **96 (Ethics Detective: Am I Getting the Whole Story?)** Adapted in part from product warning message at the Minwax website [accessed 1 November 2003] www.minwax.com. Note that the account depicted in this box is fictional; the Minwax website was referenced only for the product warning message included within the overall story. **109 (Connecting with Technology: Create and Collaborate with Powerful Outlining Tools)** Adapted from Microsoft Word Help text; Microsoft website [accessed 2 December 2003] www.microsoft.com/office; "What Electronic Outlining Tools Can Do for You," Web Writing That Works website [accessed 7 March 2004] www.webwritingthatworks.com. **130 (Communicating Across Cultures: Communicating with a Global Audience on the Web)** Adapted from Laura Morelli, "Writing for a Global Audience on the Web," *Marketing News*, 17 August 1998, 16; Yuri and Anna Radzievsky, "Successful Global Web Sites Look Through Eyes of the Audience," *Advertising Age's Business Marketing*, January 1998, 17; Sari Kalin, "The Importance of Being Multiculturally Correct," *Computerworld*, 6 October 1997, G16–G17; B. G. Yovovich, "Making Sense of All the Web's Numbers," *Editor & Publisher*, November 1998, 30–31; David Wilford, "Are We All Speaking the Same Language?" *The Times* (London), 20 April 2000, 4. **157 (Communication Miscues: Missing the Message with Prescription Medications)** "Medications—The Importance of Reading the Label," American Academy of Pediatrics [accessed 30 September 2006] www.medem.com; Sarah Bernard, "The Perfect Prescription," *New York Magazine*, 18 April 2005 [accessed 30 September 2006] www.newyorkmetro.com; "ClearRX at Target Pharmacy," Target website [accessed 30 September 2006] www.target.com. **183 (Connecting with Technology: More Ways to Spread the Message)** *Makezine* website [accessed 22 January 2006] www.makezine.com; Jane Spencer, "The Annoying New Face of Customer Service—Virtual Phone Reps Replace the Old Touch-Tone Menus; Making Claire Less Irritating," *Wall Street Journal*, 21 January 2003, D1; Allison Fass, "Speak Easy," *Forbes*, 6 January 2003, 135. **230 (Communication Miscues: When Recommendation Letters Lead to Lawsuits)** Adapted from Diane Cadrain, "HR Professionals Stymied by Vanishing Job References," *HR Magazine*, November 2004, 31–40; "Five (or More) Ways You Can Be Sued for Writing (or Not Writing) Recommendation Letters," *Fair Employment Practice Guidelines*, July 2006, 1, 3–4; Rochelle Kaplan, "Writing a Recommendation Letter," National Association of Colleges and Employers website [accessed 12 October 2006] www.naceweb.org; Maura Dolan and Stuart Silverstein, "Court Broadens Liability for Job References," *Los Angeles Times*, 28 January 1997, A1, A11; David A. Price, "Good References Pave Road to Court," *USA Today*, 13 February 1997, 11A; Frances A. McMorris, "Ex-Bosses Face Less Peril Giving Honest Job References," *Wall Street Journal*, 8 July 1996, B1, B8; Dawn Gunsch, "Gray Matters: Centralize Control of Giving References," *Personnel Journal*, September 1992, 114, 116–117; Betty Southard Murphy, Wayne E. Barlow, and D. Diane Hatch, "Manager's Newsfront: Job Reference Liability of Employees," *Personnel Journal*, September 1991, 22, 26; Ross H. Fishman, "When Silence is Golden," *Nation's Business*, July 1991, 48–49. **273 (Connecting with Technology: Controlling Rumors Online)** Adapted from Charles Wolrich, "Top Corporate Hate Web Sites," Forbes.com, 8 March 2005 [accessed 16 August 2005] www.forbes.com; PlanetFeedback.com [accessed 3 December 2003] www.planetfeedback.com/consumer; "Health Related Hoaxes and Rumors," Centers for Disease Control and Prevention website [accessed 16 August 2005] www.cdc.gov; Snopes.com [accessed 16 August 2005] www.snopes.com; "Pranksters, Activists and Rogues: Know Your Adversaries and Where They Surf," *PR News*, 26 June 2000 [accessed 3 December 2003] www.elibrary.com. **369 (Ethics Detective: Is Something Hiding Behind These Numbers?)** Adapted from A. S. C. Ehrenberg, "The Problem of Numeracy," *Admap*, February 1992, 37–40; Mary S. Auvil and Kenneth W. Auvil, *Introduction to Business Graphics: Concepts and Applications* (Cincinnati: South-Western, 1992), 40, 192–193; Peter H. Selby, *Using Graphs and Tables: A Self-Teaching Guide* (New York: Wiley, 1979), 8–9. **416 (Connecting with Technology: Proposals Get a Software Assist)** Adapted from Dan MacDougall, "Orchestrating Your Proposal," *Canadian Consulting Engineer*, March–April 2003, 51–56; Sant Corporation website [accessed 23 January 2004] www.santcorp.com; Pragmatech

Software website [accessed 23 January 2004] www.pragmattech.com. **500 (Communicating Across Cultures: Five Tips for Making Presentations Around the World)** Adapted from Patricia L. Kurtz, *The Global Speaker* (New York: AMACOM, 1995), 35–47, 56–68, 75–82, 87–100; David A. Victor, *International Business Communication* (New York: HarperCollins, 1992), 39–45; Lalita Khosla, "You Say Tomato," *Forbes*, 21 May 2001, 36; Stephen Dolainski, "Are Expats Getting Lost in the Translation?" *Workforce*, February 1997, 32–39. **514 (Communicating Miscues: Recovering from Disasters)** Adapted from C. Peter Guiliano and Frank J. Currilo, "Going Blank in the Boardroom," *Public Relations Quarterly*, Winter 2003, 35+; Jennifer Rotondo and Mike Rotondo, Jr., *Presentation Skills for Managers* (New York: McGraw-Hill, 2002), 160–162; Mark Merritt, "No More Nightmares," *Presentations*, April 2001, 44+. **522 (Communicating Across Cultures: Looking for Work Around the World)** Adapted from University of Michigan International Center Website [accessed 18 February 2004] www.umich.edu; Allan Hoffman, "Five Strategies for Finding Work Abroad," Monster.com [accessed 18 February 2004] www.monster.com; Personal communication, Andrew Jaynes, 18 February 2004. **593 (Communicating Across Cultures: Successfully Interviewing Across Borders)** Adapted from Jean-Marc Hachey, "Interviewing for an International Job," excerpt from *The Canadian Guide to Working and Living Overseas*, 3rd ed. [accessed 23 February 2004] www.workingoverseas.com; Rebecca Falkoff, "Dress to Impress the World: International Business Fashion," Monster.com [accessed 23 February 2004] www.monster.com; Mary Ellen Slater, "Navigating the Details of Landing an Overseas Job," *Washington Post*, 11 November 2002, E4. **600 (Communication Miscues: Talking Yourself Right Out of a Job)** Adapted from Thomas Pack, "Good Answers to Job Interview Questions," *Information Today*, January 2004, 35+; John Lees, "Make Them Believe You Are the Best," *The Times* (United Kingdom), 21 January 2004, 3; "Six Interview Mistakes," Monster.com [accessed 23 February 2004] www.monster.com.

FIGURES AND TABLES

16 (Figure 1-7) From Six Apart website [accessed 17 December 2005] www.sixapart. com. **69 (Figure 3-2)** Source: Mary O'Hara-Devereaux and Robert Johansen, *Global Work: Bridging Distance, Culture, and Time* (San Francisco: Jossey-Bass, 1994), 55, 59. **71 (Figure 3-3)** Source: "New ILO Study Highlights Labour Trends Worldwide," International Labour Organization [accessed 15 September 2003] www.ilo.org. **72 (Figure 3-4)** Source: Roger Axtell, *Gestures: The Do's and Taboos of Body Language Around the World* (New York: Wiley, 1991), 117–119. **191 (Table 7.2):** Robert Scoble and Shel Israel, *Naked Conversations* (Hoboken, N.J.: John Wiley & Sons, 2006), 78–81, 190–194; Paul McFedries, *The Complete Idiot's Guide to Creating a Web Page & Blog*, 6th ed. (New York: Alpha, 2004), 206–208, 272–276; Shel Holtz and Ted Demopoulos, *Blogging for Business* (Chicago: Kaplan, 2006), 54–59, 113–114; Denise Wakeman, "Top 10 Blog Writing Tips," Blogarooni.com [accessed 1 February 2006] www.blogarooni.com; Dennis A. Mahoney, "How to Write a Better Weblog," 22 February 2002, A List Apart [accessed 1 February 2006] www.alistapart.com. **225** Courtesy Herman Miller. **231** Courtesy Discover Communications. **337 (Table 11.2)** Adapted from "Industry Information," Thomas J. Long Business and Economics Library website, University of California, Berkeley [accessed 6 November 2006] www.lib.berkeley.edu; Hoovers website [accessed 6 November 2006] www.hoovers.com; MarketResearch.com [accessed 6 November 2006] www.marketresearch.com; Risk Management Association website [accessed 6 November 2006] www.rmahq.org; "Subscribed Sites," Sno-Isle Regional Library System [accessed 18 December 2003] www.sno-isle.org; "Business Directories: A Research Guide," University of Delaware Library website [accessed 6 November 2006] www.lib.udel.edu; Thomas P. Bergman, Stephen M. Garrison, and Gregory M. Scott, *The Business Student Writer's Manual and Guide to the Internet* (Paramus, N.J.: Prentice Hall, 1998), 67–80; Ernest L. Maier, Anthony J. Faria, Peter Kaatrude, and Elizabeth Wood, *The Business Library and How to Use It* (Detroit: Om-

nigraphics, 1996), 53–76. **380 (Figure 12.13a)** "Ranking of Census 2000 and Projected 2030 State Population and Change," U.S. Census Bureau [accessed 5 September 2005] www.census.gov. **554 (Table 18.1)** The Riley Guide [accessed 12 December 2006] www.rileyguide.com; Bethany McLean, "A Scary Monster," *Fortune*, 22 December 2003, 19+; Alan Cohen, "Best Job Hunting Sites," *Yahoo! Internet Life*, May 2002, 90–92; Richard N. Bolles, "Career Strategizing or, What Color Is Your Web Parachute?" *Yahoo! Internet Life*, May 1998, 116, 121; Tara Weingarten, "The All-Day, All-Night, Global, No-Trouble Job Search," *Newsweek*, 6 April 1998, 14; Michele Himmelberg, "Internet an Important Tool in Employment Search," *San Diego Union-Tribune*, 7 September 1998, D2; Gina Imperato, "35 Ways to Land a Job Online," *Fast Company*, August 1998, 192–197; Roberta Maynard, "Casting the Net for Job Seekers," *Nation's Business*, March 1997, 28–29. **551 (Figure 18.2)** Adapted from Richard Nelson Bolles, *What Color Is Your Parachute?* (Berkeley, Calif.: Ten Speed Press, 1997), 67. **596 (Table 19.4)** Adapted from Marilyn Sherman, "Questions R Us: What to Ask at a Job Interview," *Career World*, January 2004, 20; H. Lee Rust, *Job Search: The Completion Manual for Jobseekers* (New York: American Management Association, 1979), 56.

PHOTO CREDITS

16 Reprinted by permission of Six Apart. **20** Reprinted by permission of WebEx Communications, Inc. **21** Reprinted by permission of Web Ex Communications, Inc. **21** Groove Neworks screen shot reprinted with permission from Microsoft Corporation. **23** Reprinted by permission of CustomerReach. **23** Reprinted by permission of UserLand Software. Reprinted by permission of Portfolios.com. Reprinted by permission of Portfolios.com. Reprinted by permission of Portfolios.com. **39** Standard credit. **50** Microsoft product screen shot(s) reprinted with permission from Microsoft Corporation. **50** Reprinted by permission of WebEx Communications, Inc. **65** Copyright © 2005, SIL International, from the database of Ethnologue: Languages of the World, 15th ed., www.ethnologue.com. **71** From *New ILO Study Highlights Labour Trends Worldwide'*, www.ilo.org. The ILO shall accept no responsibility for any inaccuracy, errors or ommissions arising from the use of data in electronic format. **72** Roger Axtell, Gestures: The Do's and Taboos of Body Language Around the World, (New York: Wiley, 1991), 117–119. "This material is used by permission of John Wiley & Sons, Inc." **99** Reprinted by permission of XPLANE. **133** Reprinted by permission of The Moorings. **138** Reprinted by permission of Whirlpool Corporation. **149** Courtesy of Mercedes-Benz. **190** Reprinted by permission of Ford Motor Company. **198** © 2006 Yahoo! Inc. YAHOO! And the YAHOO! Logo are trademarks of Yahoo! Inc. **199** © 2006 Yahoo@ Inc. DEL.ICIO.US and the DEL.ICIO.US logo are trademarks of Yahoo! Inc. **215** Google blog screenshot © Google Inc. and is used with permission. **235** Reprinted by permission of Business Objects. **293** Reprinted by permission of CMI Marketing, Inc. **295** MASLOW, ABRAHAM H.; FRAGER, ROBERT D. (EDITOR); FADMAN, JAMES (EDITOR), MOTIVATION & PERSONALITY, 3rd Edition, © 1987. Electronically reproduced by permission of Pearson Education, Inc., Upper Saddle River, NJ **306** Reprinted by permission of Qantas. **307** Reprinted by permission of Home Depot. **312** Reprinted by permission of Premier Building Systems. **312** Reprinted by permission of The Diamond Trading Company. **313** General Motors Corp. Used with permission, GM Media Archives. **315** Reprinted by permission of Zazu Salon & Day Spa. **348** Ryan Finley, www.surveymonkey.com, Portland, Oregon USA. Reprinted with permission. **348** Reprinted by permission of ObjectPlanet. **406** Reprinted by permission of Bolthouse Farms. **428** © 2006 Yahoo! Inc. YAHOO! and the YAHOO! Logo are trademarks of Yahoo! Inc. **441** Copyright © Cancer Research UK 2004. cancer. info@cancer.org.uk. All Rights Reserved. **474** Reprinted by permission of Sprint Nextel. **533** Microsoft product screen shot(s) reprinted with permission from Microsoft Corporation. **536** Xcelscious screenshot reprinted by permission form Business Objects. **553** Reprinted by permission of Raytheon. **597** Courtesy of Perfect Interview.

Brand, Company, Name, Organization, and Website Index

Subject Index

A

a/an, H-11–H-12
a lot, H-23
abbreviations, H-20
  punctuation with, A-2
  for states, A-13, A-15
abstract words, 133–134, H-3
abstracts, in reports, 473
abusive language, 270
acceptance letters, 605
access control, 40
accidents, drug abuse and, 592
accuracy
  of information, 95, 430
  of visuals, 385–386
achievement, congratulating people
  on, 234
achievements section, on résumés, 566
acronyms, H-20
  in e-mail, 184
  in instant messaging, 188
action
  persuasive requests for, 304–305, 306
  routine requests for, 216, 217–219
action buttons, in PowerPoint, 534–535
action items, in oral presentations, 510
action phase, of AIDA model, 300, 301, 305,
  306, 313–314, 587
action plan, in reports, 433, 434
action verbs, 466, H-6
  on résumés, 563
active listening, 52
active voice, 130–131, H-8
address, proper forms of, A-3–A-4
addressee notation, A-8
addresses
  for envelopes, A-12–A-14
  for international correspondence, 78
  style for, H-20–H-21
adjectives, 134, 158, 159, 313, H-8–H-9,
  H-10
adjustments
  granting, 226–229
  persuasive requests for, 306–307
  refusing, 268–270
  requesting, 219, 221, 222
adverbs, 134, 158, 159, H-24, H-9–H-10
advertising, 308
  deceptive, 28, 314
  of job openings, 551
aerial photography, 380
age bias, 125, 126, 566, 601

age differences, culture and, 72–73
agenda
  for meetings, 47
  hidden, 37
  in oral presentations, 538
aggravate/irritate, H-23
aggregators, 192, 197, 198
aging, vision and, 164
agreement
  pronoun-antecedent, H-5
  subject-verb, H-7–H-8, H-12
AIDA model, 300–302
  for job application letters, 583–587
  for persuasive requests, 305, 306
  for proposals, 434–435
  for sales messages, 310–314
alcohol testing, 591–592
almanacs, 339
alphanumeric outline, 109
American Psychological Association (APA),
  476, A-21, A-25
Americans with Disabilities Act, 591
among/between, H-11
analogies, faulty, 303
analogy, arguing by, 302
analytical reports, 394, 396
  direct approach for, 410, 411, 433
  examples of, 413, 414–415, 458–471
  indirect approach for, 411–413, 433
  memo format for, 429–430
  organization of, 410–413
  planning, 407–413
  purpose of, 407
  statement of purpose for, 396
  2 + 2 approach to, 412, 414–415
  types of, 403, 407
  yardstick approach to, 412–413
  see also reports
animation, 372, 382, 533–534
announcements, company, 270–271
annual reports, 421, 422, 425
antecedents, H-4, H-5
anticipate/expect, H-23
anxiety
  in job interviews, 596
  in oral presentations, 512–513
AO mail, A-15
APA style, 471, 476, A-24, A-25
apologies
  controversy over, 253
  exaggerated, 227
  to customers, 266

apostrophes, H-17
  for plurals, H-3
  for possessives, H-3–H-4, H-5, H-17
appeals, emotional vs. logical, 302–303, 311,
  312
appearance, 44
  as nonverbal communication, 55
  for job interviews, 596, 597–598
appendixes, in reports, 475
applicant tracking system (ATS), 550, 551
application forms, 587
application letters, 582–587
appositives, H-16
appreciation, messages of, 234
Arabic, 81
area charts, 374
Argentina, A-6
arguments, logical, 302–304
Arial, 167, 532
articles (grammar), H-11
as if/like, H-11
assistive technologies, 74
attachments, file, 171, A-17
attacking, of opponents, 303
attention
  audience's, 502
  in job interviews, 601
  listening and, 53
  to nonverbal cues, 56
attention-getters, 310–311
  for job application letters, 583, 586
attention line, A-8
attention phase, of AIDA model, 300, 301,
  305, 306, 310–311, 507, 508, 583
attitudes, changing, 305–306
audience
  adapting to, 120–131
  amount of participation by, 92
  arousing interest of, 507
  attention span of, 502
  behavior, 12-15
  for blogs, 193, 198–199
  building relationship with, 126–127
  composition of, 93
  connecting with, 11–15
  emotional vs. logical appeals to, 302–303,
  311, 312
  expectations of, 13, 93, 363, 398, 401
  feedback from, 100
  geographic distribution of, 93
  global, 130
  holding attention of, 509–510

Photo Credits

CHAPTER 1
Chapter Opener, Mena & Ben Trott, Co-founders of Six Apart, Ltd; Page 3, Jose L. Pelaez, Corbis/Stock Market; Page 9, Ryan McVay, Getty Images, Inc.–Photodisc; Page 13, © Corbis All Rights Reserved; Page 20, (a) Spencer Grant, PhotoEdit Inc., (b) Dell, Inc. (c) Belkin Corp., (d) Getty Images–Digital Vision, (f) Ethan Hill; Page 21, (g) © Stuart Pearce, AGE Fotostock, (h) 3M, (k) Ethan Hill; Page 22, (m) Keith Dannemiller, Corbis/SABA Press Photos, Inc., (n) © J.D. Dallet, AGE Fotostock, (p) FedEx Corp., (q) © Peter Christopher, Masterfile, (r) United Parcel Service; Page 23, (s) Photomondo/Getty Images, Inc.–Taxi, (u) Photolibrary.com, (w) Staples, Inc., Marcio Jose Sanchez, AP Wide World Photos.

CHAPTER 2
Chapter Opener, Joe McDonald, The Westchester Journal News; Page 34 and 35, Jose L. Pelaez, Corbis/Stock Market; Page 37, Masterfile Corp.; Page 42, Christopher Bissell, Getty Images Inc.–Stone Allstock; Page 51, Image Source/Getty Images–Photodisc; Page 56, Getty Images–Photodisc.

CHAPTER 3
Chapter Opener, Charla Jones, NewsCom; Page 62 and 63, Jose L. Pelaez, Corbis/Stock Market; Page 65, Mark Richards; Page 67, Mark Gibson, Mark and Audra Gibson Photography; Page 73, Steve Cole, Getty Images–Photodisc; Page 81, © Corbis All Rights Reserved.

CHAPTER 4
Chapter Opener, Alpha Books/Penguin Group, USA; Page 89 © Paul Barton, Corbis; Page 91, Michael Newman, PhotoEdit Inc.; Page 98, Getty Images, Inc.

CHAPTER 5
Chapter Opener, Stanford Law School; Page 118, © Paul Barton, Corbis; Page 119, (a) © Paul Barton, (b) Corbis RF.

CHAPTER 6
Page 148 and 149, © Paul Barton, Corbis; Page 164, Frederic Neema, Corbis/Sygma.

CHAPTER 7
Chapter Opener, Courtesy of Boing Corporation; Page 180, Getty Images, Inc.; Page 181, Chris Strangemore, Craig Strangemore; Page 192, Ric Field, AP Wide World Photos; Page 196, Promethius Consulting, LLC; Page 205, Bill Stevenson, The Stock Connection; Page 211, SuperStock, Inc.

CHAPTER 8
Chapter Opener, Cone, Inc.; Page 212 and 213, Bachmann, PhotoEdit, Inc.; Page 229, David Deal; Page 242, © Corbis All Rights Reserved; 243, Amy C. Etra, PhotoEdit, Inc.; Page 245, © Mark Jenkinson, Corbis All Rights Reserved; Page 246, Dennis MacDonald, PhotoEdit, Inc.; Page 248, © Ed Kashi, Corbis; Page 250, Paul Sakuma, AP Wide World Photos.

CHAPTER 9
Chapter Opener, Landov LLC; Page 252 and 253, Bachmann, PhotoEdit Inc.; Page 255, Jeffrey Sauger, Bloomberg News/Landov LLC; Page 258, Lawrence Jackson, AP Wide World Photos; Page 284, © Corbis All Rights Reserved; Page 285, Tom Raymond Getty Images Inc.–Stone Allstock; Page 287, Thomas Babb, AP Wide World Photos; Page 289, Getty Images Inc.

CHAPTER 10
Page 292 and 293, Bachmann, PhotoEdit Inc.; Page 296, Paul Sakuma, AP Wide World Photos; Page 309, Courtesy of Wachovia Corp.; Page 321, Todd Bigelow, Aurorar & Quanta Productions, Inc.; Page 323, AP Wide World Photos; Page 324, Getty Images, Inc.; Page 325, Masterfile Corporation; Page 328, AP Wide World Photos.

CHAPTER 11
Chapter Opener, Getty Images, Inc.; Page 331, Jon Riley, Getty Images, Inc–Stone Allstock; Page 342, The Internet Public Library is one of the most important web directories for business researchers; Page 344, Reproduced with permission of Net Snippets.

CHAPTER 12
Chapter Opener, Stone Yamashita Partners; Page 360 and 361, Jon Riley, Getty Images Inc.–Stone Allstock; Page 363, Britt Erlandson, Image Bank/Getty Images; Page 383, (a & b) Alan Gough, Alan Gough Photography; Page 384, Getty Images, Inc.

CHAPTER 13
Chapter Opener, Courtesy Kenwood USA; Page 393, Jose Pelaez Photography, Corbis/Stock Market.

CHAPTER 14
Chapter Opener, Courtesy Tellabs, photo by Robert Seale; Page 424 and 425, Jose Pelaez Photography, Corbis/Stock Market; Page 449, Corbis/Bettmann; Page 450, John Decker, Landov LLC.

CHAPTER 15
Chapter Opener, Gilbert Liz, Corbis/Sygma; Page 452 and 453, Jose L. Pelaez, Corbis/Stock Market; Page 457, Masterfile Royalty Free Division; Page 490, Myrleen Ferguson Cate, PhotoEdit Inc.; Page 493, B. Roland, The Image Works; Page 494 and 495, SuperStock, Inc.

CHAPTER 16
Chapter Opener, Courtesy Fitch Columbus Studio; Page 497, Steve Niedorf, Getty Images Inc.–Image Bank; Page 508, Comstock/SuperStock, Inc.; Page 509, AP Wide World Photos; Page 512 and 515, Getty Images, Inc.

CHAPTER 17
Chapter Opener, Hewlett Packard; Page 522 and 523, Steve Niedorf, Getty Images Inc.–Image Bank; Page 525, Lance Davies Photography for Polyvision; Page 541, Dennis MacDonald, PhotoEdit Inc.; Page 543, © Corbis All Rights Reserved.

CHAPTER 18
Chapter Opener, Courtesy Hersha Hospitality Management, Jeffrey Wade, VP of Human Resources; Page 555, Mark Richards, PhotoEdit Inc.

CHAPTER 19
Chapter Opener, Reprinted with permission © Google Inc.; Page 580 and 581, Doug Menuez, Getty Images, Inc.–Photodisc; Page 588, AGE Fotostock America, Inc.–Royalty-free; Page 591, David Carmack Photography; Page 592, SuperStock, Inc.; Page 598, © Corbis All Rights Reserved.

PART OPENERS
Part One, Page 2, Jose L. Pelaez, Corbis/Stockmarket; Part Two, Page 88, © Paul Barton, Corbis; Part 3, Page 178k Bachmann/PhotoEdit Inc.; Part 4, Page 330, Jon Riley, Getty Images Inc.–Stone Allstock; Part 5, Page 392, Jose Pelaez Photographer, Corbis/Stock Market; Part 6, Page 496, Steve Niedorf, Getty Images Inc.–Image Bank; Part 7, Page 548, Doug Menuez, Getty Images, Inc.–Photodisc.